EXPERIENCING
Race, Class, and Gender in the United States

Fourth Edition

ROBERTA FISKE-RUSCIANO
Rider University

VIRGINIA CYRUS
Rider University

McGraw Hill

Boston   Burr Ridge, IL   Dubuque, IA   Madison, WI   New York   San Francisco   St. Louis
Bangkok   Bogotá   Caracas   Kuala Lumpur   Lisbon   London   Madrid   Mexico City
Milan   Montreal   New Delhi   Santiago   Seoul   Singapore   Sydney   Taipei   Toronto

3/05

#54685415

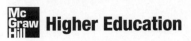

Higher Education

EXPERIENCING RACE, CLASS, AND GENDER IN THE UNITED STATES

Published by McGraw-Hill, a business unit of The McGraw-Hill Companies, Inc., 1221 Avenue of the Americas, New York, NY, 10020. Copyright © 2005, 2000, 1997, 1993, by The McGraw-Hill Companies, Inc. All rights reserved. No part of this publication may be reproduced or distributed in any form or by any means, or stored in a database or retrieval system, without the prior written consent of The McGraw-Hill Companies, Inc., including, but not limited to, in any network or other electronic storage or transmission, or broadcast for distance learning. Some ancillaries, including electronic and print components, may not be available to customers outside the United States.

This book is printed on acid-free paper.

1 2 3 4 5 6 7 8 9 0 FGR/FGR 0 9 8 7 6 5 4

ISBN 0 07 288614 5

Publisher: *Phillip A. Butcher*
Sponsoring editor: *Sherith H. Pankratz*
Editorial coordinator: *Amy M. Shaffer*
Senior marketing manager: *Daniel M. Loch*
Media coordinator: *Christie Ling*
Project manager: *Jean R. Starr*
Associate production supervisor: *Jason I. Huls*
Designer: *George Kokkonas*
Lead media project manager: *Marc Mattson*
Manager, Photo research: *Brian Pecko*
Permissions editor: *Marty Granahan*
Cover image: *Diana Ong/Superstock*
Typeface: *10/11 Garamond Light*
Compositor: *G&S Typesetters.*
Printer: *Quebecor World Fairfield Inc.*

Library of Congress Cataloging-in-Publication Data

Experiencing race, class, and gender in the United States / [edited by] Roberta
    Fiske-Rusciano, Virginia Cyrus.— 4th ed.
        p. cm.
    Includes index.
    ISBN 0-07-288614-5 (pbk. : alk. paper)
    1. United States—Social conditions—1980– 2. United States—Race
relations.   3. United States—Ethnic relations.   4. Social classes—United
States.   5. Pluralism (Social sciences)—United States.   6. Women—United
States—Social conditions.   7. Gays—United States—Social conditions.
8. Discrimination—United States.   I. Fiske-Rusciano, Roberta.   II. Cyrus,
Virginia.
HN59.2.E96 2005

2004042622

www.mhhe.com

In Loving Memory of My Parents,
Louise Hadley Fiske and Robert Fiske

CONTENTS

iv

CHANGE

PREFACE

The first few years of the new millennium have been saturated with debate concerning the fundamental ideals and principles by which people live worldwide. Large migrations of populations, due to shifts in economic opportunities, natural disasters, and especially war, have put into sharp relief the need for reassessing who we are and where we are headed as a society. Each nation, each identity group, does this in its own way, focusing on what seems most urgent and most potentially divisive or on a shared opinion that a group wants to voice. *Experiencing Race, Class, and Gender in the United States,* fourth edition, offers an opportunity to look at many of these issues as experienced by the diverse population of this country. Collecting details of the "American experience" is an ongoing effort that requires each of us to keep our eye on the shifts and different reflections of this richly varied and complex society. Learning more about the past and present through many voices will help us all problem solve with balance and wisdom, as valuable, participating members of this country and of the world.

Experiencing Race, Class, and Gender in the United States, fourth edition, introduces students to basic concepts of multiculturalism and to seminal debates taken up by social scientists, physical scientists, and political commentators. Some points, however, can be made only by the poets and literary writers included herein. This text encourages readers to examine their own lives, by challenging notions of hierarchy and stereotypes that often seem so natural and largely go unchallenged. Such a journey is transforming and lengthy and is part of an ongoing American experience. *Experiencing Race, Class, and Gender in the United States,* fourth edition, is a guide for students in the thoughtful exploration of the issues that surround personal and institutionalized bigotry. It encourages informed debate and avoids being doctrinaire, for learning to think through these issues is a far greater commitment than carefully agreeing with the professor.

Organization of the Book

This book is divided into three main divisions: "Identity" (Parts I–IV), "Power" (Parts V–VII), and "Change" (Parts VIII–X). The first division, "Identity," requires students to examine their own lives and those of others in order to understand how everyone's identity is shaped by the experience of race, ethnicity, gender, and socioeconomic class.

The book then moves to an exploration of the institutional forces that exert power over everyone. The second division, "Power," examines the important connections between social forces and individuals and groups to promote an understanding of the kinds of challenges and structural obstacles that prejudice and discrimination create. The readings probe the issues of structural discrimination and power—specifically, the dynamics of racism, sexism, and classism. The selections provide personal testimony, historical background, data from law and the social sciences, and analytical discussions of how power and discrimination operate in American life.

People who have not critically examined the inequities of American society may feel a combination of anger, frustration, and even despair when they first confront such knowledge. Thus, the third division, "Change," shows students how they can direct this emotional energy to improving the social order by acting positively on their own newfound awareness. Part VIII, "Taking Action," outlines concrete, step-by-step strategies for effecting personal change and initiating collective social action. Finally, the book closes as it begins—with individual experiences; Part IX, "Change Makers," introduces ordinary people who have succeeded, often at some substantial personal cost, to negotiate the issues involved in race, class, gender, and ethnicity and to effect real social change. Part X, "Race, Class, and Gender After 9/11," presents the challenges that now face us since the terrorist attacks on September 11, 2001. There are as many challenges to meet within our country's borders as there are abroad, and many of the questions are intertwined.

The introductions to the three main divisions and the ten parts provide a context for the readings, identifying the major concerns and issues and defining important theoretical terms (which are highlighted by boldface type). Definitions follow some of the readings to explain references that may be unfamiliar to students. Every selection is followed by a set of questions, "Understanding the Reading," to aid comprehension and to stimulate critical thinking about the issues the selection raises and by "Suggestions for Responding," writing topics and activities to encourage personal exploration of the issues. Finally, each of the three main divisions and the ten parts end with suggestions for additional activities, such as field or library research, individual and group projects, and life-experience exercises.

New to the Fourth Edition

The fourth edition has thirty-four new reading selections and an original sketch by Comanche artist and poet Lonnie Poco. It is a mixture of social science and the humanities, with two added sections: "Sexual Identity" and "Race, Class, and Gender

After 9/11." "Sexual Identity" features a previously unpublished autobiographical essay by Jessica Stearns: "A Transsexual's Story." "Race, Class, and Gender After 9/11" is a section that challenges students to become active in a rapidly changing society, with readings on domestic security and civil liberties, racial targeting of immigrant families, feminist perspectives on 9/11, the perception of Islam as evil, the plight of refugees, and working-class women as war heroes. Other new readings introduce the reader to anthropologists' statements on race, the ethics or practicality of racial profiling in a doctor's office, cosmetic surgery on racial features, racism in cyberspace, urban Indians, gay marriage, poems and short stories by American Indian artists, the Bush administration's denial of many research grants to scientists dealing with HIV/AIDS or teenage sexuality, and an updated discussion of affirmative action.

Background

Experiencing Race, Class, and Gender in the United States grew out of a five-year effort at Rider University to respond to the demographic realities of this nation as we move through the twenty-first century. Starting in 1987, we evaluated our curriculum to determine its inclusiveness. Although we found that it addressed diversity more fully than we had anticipated, we also felt that much more work needed to be done. Thus, with funding from the New Jersey Department of Higher Education, we implemented a comprehensive faculty development program. In addition to the more conventional tactic of revising traditional courses, we formed an interdisciplinary faculty team to create a course on the diversity of American cultures for first-year and second-year students. The first edition of this book was a direct outgrowth of that effort and was tested in multiple sections of our course as well as courses at other educational institutions.

From the beginning, the faculty team decided that understanding such complex concepts as power, racism, and sexual harassment required the insights of many disciplines. Accordingly, the interdisciplinary approach of this book provides a broad, integrative perspective on these issues. *Experiencing Race, Class, and Gender in the United States,* fourth edition, incorporates several kinds of sources: poems; individual stories, both literary and biographical; compilations of information and data from many fields, including anthropology, sociology, psychology, history, economics, and communications; and analytical pieces from a number of disciplines. The readings range from straightforward journalistic articles to literary works to complex analyses of data. The authors represent both genders as well as the broad spectrum of ethnicities, cultures, classes, and worldviews that make up the population of the United States.

Acknowledgments

I acknowledge the admirable scholarship and activism of my late colleague, Virginia Cyrus, who created the first three editions of *Experiencing Race, Class, and Gender in the United States.* In the spirit of her work, I continue to offer students material from many disciplines, in scholarly pursuit and understanding of the major debates of our society, surrounding racism, sexism, classism, and bigotry in its many forms. I am deeply grateful to colleagues at Rider University, who have either directly guided me to selections or have helped me think through ideas that have somehow found their way into this book: Frank Rusciano, Marc Wallace, Pearlie Peters, Bosah Ebo, Nancy Schluter, Judith Johnston, Millie Rice Jordan, Marv Goldstein, Joe Gowaskie, Lise Vogel, Jonathan Mendilow, and Minmin Wang. My special thanks to two former students, Clarethia Ellerbee and Derek Schork, who allowed me to publish their essays, and to the scores of students from whom I have learned so much. Special thanks to Rebecca Fiske and Jessica Stearns, who both trusted me with their splendid, previously unpublished essays; to Lonnie Poco, poet, artist, and long-lost friend; and to Carlos Cumpián, poet who helped me find Lonnie. My gratitude also goes to all the kind permissions coordinators and others who enabled me to include these specific works, as well as to Linda Tulli, who secured many of those precious permissions.

My heartfelt thanks go also to everyone at McGraw-Hill Publishing Company, who helped in innumerable ways, and who patiently waited as I crafted the book: Amy Shaffer, Editorial Coordinator for Sociology; Sherith Pankratz, Sociology/Women's Studies Editor; Maria Romano, Marketing Assistant; and Daniel Loch, Senior Marketing Manager, and Jean Starr, Project Manager.

Finally, I thank my family for their direct and indirect involvement in this manuscript: my husband, Frank, who has been an active partner in the entire process, hardly ever grumbled, and reminded me that writing is an act of faith; my son, Francesco, who debated and discussed; and my brother and sisters, Peter, Rebecca, Melissa, and Agnes, all of whom keep me anchored in this world.

Roberta Fiske-Rusciano

EXPERIENCING RACE, CLASS, AND GENDER IN THE UNITED STATES

The image of America* that existed in the 1950s and 1960s is a far cry from the American image of the twenty-first century. Two generations ago, most people thought of the "typical" American as being White and middle-class, speaking English, and living in a nuclear family where Father, the "head of the household" went off to his job every day, while Mother shopped, cleaned, and made brownies. While this image reflects some of the postwar ideals of our country, it definitely was not descriptive of most American families. Most important, this media-driven portrait denies the country's diversity of that time: one quarter of Americans were poor in the 1950s, and one third of native-born, White families could not get by with two incomes (Coontz, S., *The Way We Never Were*, c. 1992, pp. 27–28). Contrary to television depictions of the 1950s and 1960s, Blacks, Puerto Ricans, Mexicans, and other immigrant groups were flocking into American cities, looking for work.

Although today we are much more aware of the vast differences among us, this recognition presents us with many challenges. One quarter of the U.S. population is either Hispanic or Black, and the majority of Californians are no longer Caucasian. The nuclear family as the predominant social unit has given way to a varied list of family constellations, such as single, female-headed household with children; divorced parents with half-siblings and stepchildren in the household; and a gay or lesbian couple with or without children. Whatever arrangement, whoever is included as family, married couples comprise only about one half of all American households.

Gender roles, especially women's, have also changed as women have streamed into the workplace. In the years following World War II, fewer than one third of all women were in the labor force, but today more than half of all women and more than two thirds of women between ages twenty-five and fifty-four work outside the home. In 1950, only 12 percent of women with children under age six were employed, but by 1997 almost 63.6 percent were.

---

* *America* is used in this book in the vernacular sense, referring to the United States; it is not intended to detract from or dismiss the many other cultures and citizens of the Western Hemisphere.

As dramatic as these shifts seem, the future is likely to reflect even greater change. It is projected that White males will soon account for fewer than 10 percent of new entrants into the workforce. Women starting or returning to work will account for two thirds of the growth in employment, with minority and immigrant males accounting for most of the rest. Finally, by 2050, the majority of Americans will no longer be non-Hispanic White.

This book is designed to explore the challenges that arise from these shifts in our society, by enhancing our understanding of rapidly changing times, and help us prepare for life. The book rests on several assumptions. First, an awareness of the diversity of our society is essential for all of us as we face the future; we can adapt better to what we know and understand than to the unfamiliar or unknown.

The second assumption is that there is no single American experience; America is composed of many subgroups. This is why we begin by examining our individual and shared identities. In the first division, "Identity," we look at racial and ethnic heritages, gender, and socioeconomic class, which all directly affect identity.

Each of us has an individual identity, but we are also part of the larger community and are affected by the social attitudes and beliefs of that community, especially those relating to the various subgroups to which we belong. Because these various groups are thought of and treated differently, not everyone benefits equally from the privileges and advantages of society. In the second division, "Power," we examine how racist, sexist, heterosexist, and classist social convictions serve the interests of the powerful and how they disadvantage and oppress the powerless.

Finally, we assume that an awareness of the social forces that influence all of us makes it possible to shape and control their effects. Anyone, acting individually or in a group, can bring about social change, even in the face of individual or societal resistance, as we see in the third division, "Change." Before we get to these major themes, let's consider several general issues.

Names and Labels

In order to talk about social subgroups, we need to be able to name them appropriately. For instance, at what age does a male become a "man" instead of a "boy," and when does a "woman" stop being a "girl"? When, if ever, is it appropriate to call her a "lady"? What is the correct title for the person who runs a meeting—chairman, chairwoman, chairperson, or just plain chair? Some people consider the issue of names and language trivial, but what we are called and what we call ourselves powerfully influence our sense of self and the way others view us.

"What's in a name?" Shakespeare asked, going on to assert that "a rose by any other name would smell as sweet." In the context of this book, however, one can scarcely underestimate the significance of group labels. For instance, how do we identify non-White people? The word *non-White* itself is problematic in its implication that White is the standard one either meets or fails to meet. Similarly, the term *minority* gives *majority* status to Whites, who, while making up the greater proportion of American society, actually are in the minority globally. The label *third-world people* assumes that Whites populate a *first world,* which implies hierarchical superiority. However, the term *third-world people* does have the advantage of expressing a commonality of American minorities with the majority of all people in the world and suggests the oppression that they all have suffered at White people's hands. *People of color* seems to be the current preference, but it does imply that white is not a color. Moreover, it is a peculiarly western European and American term, since an Asian Indian and an African would not think of distinguishing themselves as *persons of color.*

Specific names for people from Africa, Asia, and South and Central America are equally problematic. A century ago, Americans of African descent were casually referred to by an offensive, derogatory term; in more polite company, they were called *colored people* (as in the National Association for the Advancement of Colored People, founded in 1909) or *Negroes* (as in the National Negro Business League, founded in 1900). During the civil rights movement, they declared themselves to be *Blacks* and asserted that "Black is beautiful." Since then, they have called themselves first *Afro-American* and most recently *African American,* while others object to any African designation. Each name represents a shift in the way the group sees itself and is seen by others.

The same holds true for other American minority groups. The U.S. Census Bureau lumps together as *Hispanic* people from different backgrounds solely on the basis of the language they speak: Spanish. This label excludes many immigrants from Central and South America simply because they speak Portuguese, French, or indigenous or other languages; and it conceals the reality that one can be both Hispanic and African American. *Hispanic peoples,* the label that is favored by most people of Spanish descent in the eastern United States, may prefer to be known as Latins, Latinas, or Latinos, as they do in the Southwest, or as Spanish Americans, Latin Americans, or *La Raza.* Some identify themselves by more specific labels, such as Mexican American, MexAmerican, or Chicana or Chicano (an identity that grew out of the civil rights movement). Others consider themselves to be Cuban or Cuban American; Puerto Rican, Puerto Rican American, or Newyorican; or Caribbean American, Dominican American, Haitian American, and so on.

Similarly, the label *Asian American,* formerly *Oriental,* includes peoples from at least nineteen distinct groups who actually represent very different cultures and social arrangements. Think about how much a Bengali has in common with a Mongolian, for example, or a Sri Lankan with a Japanese. The same is true of Native Americans (or are they American Indians?). They see themselves as members of distinct nations who usually prefer to be called by those names, such as Shoshone, Kiowa, Apache, Chickasaw, Seminole, Navajo, and so forth.

How, then, do we know what to call one another? Probably the best rule is to call people what they want to be called, recognizing that preferences change, and even within a group there is often disagreement rather than consensus about the implications of the alternative labels. In this book, we use the terms *African American* and *Black* interchangeably. In discussing the individual reading selections, we try to use the ethnic terminology that the author uses. Not everyone will agree with these language choices, however, and we acknowledge that they are debatable.

Theories About Diversity and Group Interaction

In addition to considering appropriate labels for the various American subgroups, we need to explore how the groups interact with one another and how they fit into the totality of American culture. Whether our ancestors came across a land bridge 10,000 years ago, were on the *Mayflower*, survived the Middle Passage on a slave ship, or endured steerage or whether we have just arrived, all Americans originated somewhere else. Where each of us or our ancestors came from affects not just who we are individually but what America is.

Three **theories,** systematic ways of organizing knowledge to explain a variety of occurrences, have been proposed to explain the impact that heterogeneous immigrant cultures have had on one another and on the American way of life. The **assimilation theory** argues that American culture demands that new arrivals become absorbed into the dominant culture, that they assimilate. According to this theory, early European immigrants—in particular, Protestants from England—created a society that reflected their roots. As new immigrants arrived or were transported here, as in the case of Africans, and as the native populations lost power and autonomy, all were forced to discard the unique features of their former cultures and adopt the values and norms of the European American culture. Even today, many people believe that current immigrants must assimilate in order to survive here.

Another theory rejects the idea of British or even European supremacy and describes America as an **amalgamation** or a **melting pot.** According to this theory, all the various heritages have influenced one another, blending together to create a unique American culture in which no group or single set of values is dominant. Everyone is equally American.

Today, many people consider America to be multicultural. The **pluralistic** or **multicultural theory** views American culture as a combination of many subsocieties. It claims that each group retains some of its customs and traditions, that these are accepted as valid and valuable, and that all groups coexist and interact with the larger system. This is obviously an overly optimistic picture of our society, but like the other two theories it does contain elements of truth. We are not all alike or assimilated, and it is obvious that some groups and values dominate American culture, whereas others are marginalized, devalued, or repressed. There are also some groups within the United States who wish to remain, as much as possible, apart from the dominant American culture. Nonetheless, we must learn to live with our differences.

Any theory is, of necessity, an abstraction. Thus, no single theory can adequately account for all specific, real experiences. In general, a combination of the three theories is needed to describe American society realistically. Clearly, European Americans played a central role in establishing American social institutions that served their interests. Although other groups have been shaped and controlled by these institutions, we cannot ignore the ways in which these "others" have helped shape social policies and practices as well. We all influence and are influenced by the larger society, yet we cannot fully escape our distinctive heritages, either.

Sociopolitical Positions

Recently, some people have expressed the worry that recognition of the multicultural dimension of society results in a devaluation or destruction of traditional values. According to these people, ethnic, racial, and gender perspectives distort and may even corrupt America's cultural and intellectual traditions. They are worried that advocates of the inclusion of these nontraditional perspectives are intolerant, extremist advocates of a radical program. They claim that supporters of diversity demand that everyone comply with their "politically correct" program. What is ironic about this position is that these people are the very ones who themselves advocate a single perspective, the traditional White, male, middle-class one, whereas multiculturalists value diversity and feel that examining society and ideas from multiple perspectives, including the traditional one, enhances and enriches our lives, our society, and our understanding of the world. All healthy cultures grow and adapt without losing their essential core. Following the wisdom of the Micmac Indians of Canada, the degree of flexibility of a society is a good index of its strength.

There are words less emotionally charged than political correctness or incorrectness to describe the various positions people take on social issues. In the United States, it is often claimed that conservatives favor less government involvement in people's lives, whereas liberals favor more government involvement. However, the social reality is more complex. Generally speaking, conservatives in the United States believe in government intervention to regulate social behavior (pornography, abortion, gay relations, gender roles), but they do not favor government intervention in economic relations (welfare, minimum wage, environmental regulations on businesses or consumers, etc.). Liberals tend to believe in government intervention in economic relations, but not to regulate social behavior. For example, conservatives may oppose a minimum wage law because they believe the market should set wages, whereas liberals support a minimum wage law. Conservatives advocate the banning of abortion, whereas liberals believe it should be a matter of personal choice. It is not uncommon to see a mixture of liberalism (or left wing) and conservatism (or right wing) within one person. Regardless of where we position ourselves on the political spectrum, this book raises issues that we need to consider and debate with open minds.

Ideological Principles

Each position reflects a different response to the traditional ideology of our culture. An **ideology** is a system of assumptions, theories, and beliefs characterizing a particular group or culture; the system supports and reinforces or questions political, social, and economic arrangements. Three ideological tenets of traditional American culture are relevant to our interests here, and all three have at one time or another been challenged by those who are disadvantaged by their consequent prejudices.

The first ideological principle is **Eurocentricity,** the assumption of the supremacy of European Americans and their values and traditions. For example, like most Europeans, most Americans are Judeo-Christian monotheists (believers in one god). These people tend to belittle Asian religions, such as Hinduism and Shinto, that worship multiple gods or gods in many forms. Most Americans also value the European principles of objectivity and scientific methodology and believe that verifiable truth can be established by measurement of physical phenomena and confirmed by repeatable experiments. Many European Americans also tend to devalue mysticism, the belief of many Native Americans and several Asian cultures that unseen, intangible spiritual forces animate and influence the natural world and human interactions with it.

The second ideological principle is that traditional American culture is a **patriarchy,** a hierarchical system of social organization in which structures of power, value, and culture are male-dominated. Under patriarchy, men are seen as "natural" heads of households, presidential candidates, corporate executives, college presidents, and so on. Women, on the other hand, are men's subordinates, playing such supportive roles as homemaker, mother, nurse, and secretary. As we know, patriarchy has been under serious attack during the past quarter century.

The third important principle of American ideology is the belief in our economic system, capitalism. Any economic system defines the production and distribution of goods in a society and beyond. Capitalism advocates individual ownership of production and distribution according to whoever can pay for the goods and services. One of the problems with unregulated capitalism is that it tends to concentrate wealth at the top. One of its virtues is that it has enormous productive capacity to create goods and services. An important feature of this system, in the context of this book, is that, in times of economic downturn, it can lead to poverty in the midst of wealth. Our culture, which holds each individual responsible for his or her own welfare, contrasts with cultures that make priorities of cooperation and mutual responsibility, as some Native American communities do.

The unique multiple-dimensionality of America that gives our country its rich texture also lends itself to divisiveness and inequity. All three ideological principles have been used to rationalize **prejudice,** negative attitudes about certain groups of people, and to justify **discrimination,** actions that flow from those prejudices and disadvantage members of "other" groups. In our country's history, Eurocentric prejudice and discrimination have resulted in **racism,** the subordination of certain groups of people based on their origins and physical characteristics. Patriarchal values have led to **sexism,** the subordination of women and the assumption of the superiority of men solely on the basis of sex. The **classism** that our capitalist society fosters has stigmatized poor and working-class people and their cultures and has assigned high status to the affluent and their culture solely because of their relative wealth.

As mentioned before, each of these ideological beliefs has been challenged by individuals who either act alone or organize united action. Racism has been under siege throughout much of our history, from the abolitionist crusade in the nineteenth century through the civil rights movement of the 1950s and 1960s to current activism by such groups as the National Association for the Advancement of Colored People and the Southern Poverty Law Center. From suffragists to modern **feminists,** advocates of equality between the sexes and of the value of females, women and men have struggled to combat the sexism in our society. Likewise, classism has been challenged by social reformers, labor unions, and Marxist socialists. Efforts by all these activists teach us that we do not have to resign ourselves to life in a society we think could be improved.

This book is intended to increase our awareness and understanding of the complexities of American society and culture. The readings have been selected to help us get inside the lives, minds, and hearts of the many peoples of America, so we can appreciate one another's interests, values, and concerns. The various authors speak in many distinctive voices, but despite their diversity they reveal common themes that connect us as members of American society. Some voices will sound familiar and speak to our background, values, and experiences. Others may seem alien and will challenge us, as the saying goes, to walk a mile in another's moccasins. Collectively, they will help us gain insight into who we are and what has shaped our identity. The readings will also enhance both our understanding of some of our social problems and our appreciation of the rich diversity of American life.

Who are you? The way you answer this question depends on many factors, not the least of which is the context in which it is asked. Most frequently—meeting a professor, for instance—you give your full name, but when you arrive at your dorm, you might instead respond that you are the new roommate. At a big family reunion with lots of relatives you've never met, you might identify yourself as Stan and Ruth's daughter. Think about the many other ways you could respond. "I'm a college student." "I'm an economics major." "I'm a big fan of yours." "I'm your new neighbor." "I'm Tony's spouse." "I'm Puerto Rican." "I'm the place kicker." "I'm the babysitter." "I'm a New Yorker." "I'm an American." The list is almost endless.

In fact, you are all these things. Your individual identity is a unique blend of the many aspects of your life. These elements include your gender, your age, your placement in your family, your religion and your devotion to it, your race, your ethnic heritage and how (or even whether) your family has preserved it, your sexual orientation and experience, your education, your employment history, your socioeconomic background. What else would you add?

Identity incorporates both those personal characteristics by which we recognize an individual and those that define one's affiliation with a group. American culture puts considerable emphasis on the former. From Daniel Boone to Rambo, we make heroes of the nonconforming loner who acts independently, often in opposition to or in defiance of society. Advertisers promote their products as having what it takes to set us apart from the crowd and demonstrate our unique individuality.

This view of identity seems to make some sense, in that some psychologists suggest that a personal sense of identity begins when a child first recognizes his or her mother as a separate being, who in turn recognizes the child as an individual. From there, however, we go through innumerable developmental stages, as we perceive and accept or reject the values and distinctions established by our particular lifestyle.

Despite the myth of American individualism, our **identity**—our self-definition or sense of selfhood—actually is shaped not by separation but by affiliation, by bonding and identifying with others. As children, we observe the people around us and learn the qualities associated with those who seem like us, especially in terms of such characteristics as gender, race, age, and religion. For example, we learn what it means to be female or male by our interactions with the women or men around us. Then we **internalize,** accept as part of our own thinking, the characteristics that we recognize as appropriate to various facets of our identities.

Psychologists have differing theories about how this internalization takes place. Some see it as a cognitive process by which we learn how people are labeled and accept those labels for ourselves. Others think it is behavioral, that we learn how to act in response to rewards and punishments. Still others believe internalization to be the emotional desire to feel connected with others like us.

Whatever the process may be, all agree that what we learn about who we are in childhood is central to how we perceive ourselves and act as adults. Even though most of us continue throughout our lives to develop new and more inclusive identities, the "new me" is most accurately understood as an integration of some new or newly discovered facet of ourselves with our previous identifications and self-images. Our individuality, our identity, is actually a constellation of the various affiliations we accept and that are attributed to us.

In this division, "Identity," we look at how race and ethnicity, gender, and socioeconomic status influence identity formation in American culture. Part I, "Racial and Ethnic Identity," explores the nature of race and ethnicity by considering them from both theoretical and personal perspectives and in both historical and contemporary contexts. Part II, "Gender Identity," examines how we learn to be male or female in our society and how gender roles affect the way we relate to and interact with one another. Part III, "Sexual Identity," helps us focus on the physicality and the accompanying social forces of sexual experiences, through several case studies. Part IV, "Economics and the American Dream," shows that, despite the belief that America is a classless society or that everyone is middle-class, sharp disparities in the distribution of wealth determine individual and group values and access to opportunity.

The purpose of the "Identity" division is to help us consider our own identity in the context of race, ethnicity, class, and gender. Even though any single reading selection may not speak specifically to your personal experience, the themes the readings explore will help you recognize and evaluate your place in the overall mosaic. As we come to realize that we actually have a great deal in common with some people who initially seemed different from us, when we discover that they and their experiences are more like our own than we had thought, we are more capable of understanding and sympathizing with the discrimination to which some people are subjected.

I

Racial and Ethnic Identity

YOU MAY BE SURPRISED TO LEARN IN PART I, "RACIAL and Ethnic Identity," that race and ethnicity are not as easily distinguished from each other as is commonly assumed. Even though we use these terms in everyday conversations, most of us don't have an accurate understanding of what they really mean and how imprecise they actually are.

When we identify someone as a member of an **ethnic** group, we mean that he or she belongs to some identifiable group within American society. This is the most important component of **ethnicity:** membership in a subgroup within an environment dominated by another culture.

Ethnic subgroups are defined by many complex, often variable traits, such as religion, language, culture, customs, traditions, physical characteristics, and, probably most important in this country, ancestral origin. Ancestral origin is the reason we often label ethnic groups as "compound Americans": African Americans, German Americans, Filipino Americans, Chinese Americans, and so on.

"Wait a minute," you are probably saying, "some of those groups are racial, not ethnic." Do not be so sure.

One definition of **race** in *The American Heritage Dictionary* is "any group of people united or classified together on the basis of common history, nationality, or geographical distribution."

In this sense, race does not differ substantially from ethnicity. Scientists identify race solely in terms of physical characteristics, such as skin color, texture and color of hair, and other attributes, especially facial features. However, these attributes are not as discrete or self-evident as it might seem at first. From earliest times, human populations have migrated and intermingled, mixing and blending their biological makeup. Precise lines of racial demarcation are blurred, so that, at best, systematic classifications of race are complex and must be carefully qualified.

For this reason, many people have come to believe that race is less a scientific actuality than it is a **social construct**—a classification based on social values. Consider, for example, a child whose mother is Black and father is White or one whose mother is White and father Japanese. Even though both are half White, in America the first would be categorized as Black and the other as Asian. This racial assignment reflects social assumptions rather than either child's genetic composition. In other words, each child's race is socially constructed.

Today, many of us tend to think of African Americans, Asian Americans, and Native Americans as racial groups and Jewish Americans, Italian Americans, and Irish Americans as ethnic groups. In the early part of the twentieth century, however, each of the latter three was called a race and was said to have distinctive physical features that marked group identity, a belief that now strikes us as quaintly absurd.

Although we tend to consider both ethnic and racial identity to be fixed and unalterable, in fact, they are fluid and quite subjective. You may call yourself German American because your forebears came from what is now Germany, but they may have seen themselves instead as Prussian or Bavarian, or members of one of the many other nation-states that only later were united to form the Germany we know today.

Our current racial and ethnic groupings reflect another blind spot in social thought: our insensitivity to the realities of cultural heritage. The label *European American,* for example, camouflages the differences between Scandinavians and the French and between those two groups and the Poles, the British, and the many other distinct European cultures. Most Native American Indians identify themselves as Sioux or even Lakota Sioux, Arapaho, Laguna, and so on, not as a categorical Indian or Native American.

Similarly, when we classify all African Americans as one homogeneous group, we ignore the extreme divergence of African cultures. The Ethiopian Plains culture differs tremendously from that which developed in Morocco or West Africa; moreover, like Native Americans, Africans are more likely to consider themselves Zulu, Ibo, Hausa, or Yoruba than South African or Nigerian—or even African. Finally, today there are at least nineteen Asian and Pacific Island populations lumped together under the *Asian American* label. These include the Hmong, Cambodians, Laotians, Sikh, and Burmese in addition to the more widely recognized groups representing Japan, China, Korea, India, and the Philippines.

Finally, it is important to note that all these subgroups exist within the American context, and every subgroup has been transformed by the influences of this larger society. Nevertheless, even when many historical features of the subgroup have been lost or altered, members may continue to identify with the re-created group. These are the compound Americans.

The readings in Part I present a sampling of the innumerable accounts that are part of this evolutionary process. Some of them and some of the themes they present may reflect your heritage; others may not. However, each of them is part of the American experience, and we need to understand them if we are to understand what it means to be American. This is where we are now, learning about and becoming sensitive to the multiplicity and complexity of the ethnic and racial cultures that have shaped the America we know today and that will mold our nation in the future.

The first reading selection is by Comanche artist and poet Lonnie Poco, who spent his first six school years in Ft. Sill Indian School, Lawton, Oklahoma. Indian boarding schools' purpose was to socialize Indians away from their culture and language, or "assimilation through total immersion," as their founder, Captain Richard Henry Pratt, described it. Pratt believed that differences seen in Indians were not innate or genetic but, rather, a matter of socialization. In the 1870s, he reasoned that slavery had socialized African Americans, so off-reservation Indian schools would accomplish the same. Much of this was done through physical and emotional abuse, beating children if they were heard speaking their native languages. Lonnie Poco spent much of his childhood running away from Ft. Sill, and getting sent back. Children were taught reading, writing, and arithmetic and were given domestic and manual training. The children were also used as cheap labor, making items for use in the school or for sale. Today, there are still six off-reservation Indian schools supported by the U.S. government's Bureau of Indian Affairs.

The second reading selection provides a general perspective on ethnic identity and explores several related issues. John Hope Franklin discusses historical changes in Americans' attitudes about and treatment of immigrants and ethnic groups, illuminating the distance between the American ideal that "all men are created equal" and the reality of exclusion.

The American Anthropological Association Statement on "Race" introduces some social scientists' recent position on the theoretical and practical questions surrounding our understanding and use of race as a category.

The next two readings describe the effects of **assimilation,** the process by which minority groups—under overt or subtle pressure from the majority group—abandoned the unique features of their former cultures and adapted to the values and norms of European American culture, which was dominated by the Anglo-Protestant ethic. In Grace Paley's story, Jewish immigrant parents see that their daughter's selection as the narrator of her public school's Christmas play is a difficult but necessary part of assimilation into American society. Polingaysi Qoyawayma, renamed Elizabeth Q. White by White missionaries, tells of a similar conflict when she returns for a visit to her traditional Hopi parents after her conversion at the Christian mission; her rejection of her parents' beliefs about the spiritual power of nature is painful to all three members of her family.

"People of Color Who Never Felt They Were Black" describes the experience of many immigrants from Latin America and Brazil who were never considered Black until they entered the United States. Similarly, in her interview with John Langston Gwaltney, Rosa Wakefield describes what being Black means to her, but her contemplation of the differences between Blacks and Whites and among Blacks exposes how complex and subjective ethnic identification is.

The following two readings reflect both sides of a debate concerning racial profiling in a doctor's office: essential or dangerous to the patient's health?

Many second-generation Americans struggle to understand their distinctive identity, achieving self-acceptance in different ways. For Celia Alvarez, work on an oral history project clarified her connections with working-class Puerto Rican women in the United States and taught her that she can be part of the larger American society and still retain her connections to her community of birth. Shanlon Wu tells of his lifelong search for positive Asian American role models, none of which really fit him until he realizes he must mold his own life.

On the other hand, ethnic identity is not necessarily problematic. Therese Saliba remembers her Lebanese grandmother and revels in the Arab heritage they shared when she was a child.

The next two readings explore the impact of recent population changes on American culture and society. As a Hindu, Bharati Mukherjee discusses the values she has developed as a naturalized American and how they differ from those held by many Indians and Indian Americans. Elizabeth Gordon addresses the issue of racial intermarriage. She remembers growing up in the hills of West Virginia with a White father and a Vietnamese mother.

The final selections directly address the complexities of living in our diverse nation. Eugenia Kaw writes of Asian American women and cosmetic surgery—choosing to erase racial markers, such as distinctively Asian eyes and nose. Then Chicano poet Carlos Cumpián reflects on Thanksgivings past and present. Finally, William A. Henry III reports on how contemporary changes in demography influence social, political, and economic realities in America.

By the time you have finished the readings in Part I, you will have some sense of the elements most central to ethnic identity and may have thought about your family and your life in light of those factors.

1

I Walk Alone

LONNIE POCO

As a small native child
I walk alone
along a dusty dirt road
near the Wichita.

My dark brown skin and black hair
make me who I am
brother to the sun
and all the world.

Those who laugh at me
laugh at their own
inanition.

Those who scourge me
tell me that the great spirit
is dead
and that the creator to all the
world is white.

They try to convince me
that color makes no difference
yet they feel deep down
that they are right.
that white is right.

These things I see
as a small child
as I walk alone
along a dusty dirt road
near the Wichita.   [1981]

Understanding the Reading

1. Why does the color of the poet's hair and skin make him brother to the sun?
2. Why are people trying to change his religion?
3. What does he think of these people?
4. Does he believe that "color makes no difference"?

Suggestions for Responding

1. Research Indian boarding schools like Ft. Sill, which the poet attended.

First published in "Beside the Wichita," by Lonnie Poco, Abrazo Press; ed. Carlos Cumpián.

Self-portrait from the Ft. Sill Indian School Yearbook.

2. Find historical or contemporary videos on American Indians; choose one nation and report on it.
3. Visit an Indian reservation; attend a pow-wow or another cultural event.
4. Listen to or read American Indian creation myths on tape or in books. ✦

2

Ethnicity in American Life: The Historical Perspective

JOHN HOPE FRANKLIN

The United States is unique in the ethnic composition of its population. No other country in the world can point to such a variety of cultural, racial, religious, and national backgrounds in its population. It was one of the salient features in the early history of this country; and it would continue to be so down into the twentieth century. From virtually every corner of the globe they came—some enthusiastically and some quite reluctantly. Britain and every part of the continent of Europe provided prospective Americans by the millions. Africa and Asia gave up great throngs. Other areas of the New World saw inhabitants desert their own lands to seek their fortunes in the colossus to the North. Those who came voluntarily were attracted by the prospect of freedom of religion, freedom from want, and freedom from various forms of oppression. Those who were forced to come were offered the consolation that if they were white they would some day inherit the earth, and if they were black they would some day gather their reward in the Christian heaven.

One of the interesting and significant features of this coming together of peoples of many tongues and races and cultures was that the backgrounds out of which they came would soon be minimized and that the process by which they evolved into Americans would be of paramount importance. Hector St. Jean de Crevecoeur sought to describe this process in 1782 when he answered his own question, "What, then, is the American, this new man?" He said, "He is either an European, or the descendant of an European, hence that strange mixture of blood, which you will find in no other country. . . . He is an American, who, leaving behind him all his ancient prejudices and manners, receives new ones from the new mode of the life he has embraced, the new government he obeys, and the new rank he holds. He becomes an American by being received in the broad lap of our great *Alma Mater*. Here individuals of all nations are melted into a new race of men, whose labours and posterity will one day cause great changes in the world."

This was one of the earliest expressions of the notion that the process of Americanization involved the creation of an entirely new mode of life that would replace the ethnic backgrounds of those who were a part of the process. It contained some imprecisions and inaccuracies that would, in time, become a part of the lore or myth of the vaunted melting pot and would

grossly misrepresent the crucial factor of ethnicity in American life. It ignored the tenacity with which the Pennsylvania Dutch held onto their language, religion, and way of life. It overlooked the way in which the Swedes of New Jersey remained Swedes and the manner in which the French Huguenots of New York and Charleston held onto their own past as though it was the source of all light and life. It described a process that in a distant day would gag at the notion that Irish Catholics could be assimilated on the broad lap of Alma Mater or that Asians could be seated on the basis of equality at the table of the Great American Feast.

By suggesting that only Europeans were involved in the process of becoming Americans, Crevecoeur pointedly ruled out three quarters of a million blacks already in the country who, along with their progeny, would be regarded as ineligible to become Americans for at least another two centuries. To be sure, the number of persons of African descent would increase enormously, but the view of their ineligibility for Americanization would be very slow to change. And when such a change occurred, even if it merely granted freedom from bondage, the change would be made most reluctantly and without any suggestion that freedom qualified one for equality on the broad lap of Alma Mater. It was beyond the conception of Crevecoeur, as it was indeed beyond the conception of the founding fathers, that Negroes, slave or free, could become true Americans, enjoying that fellowship in a common enterprise about which Crevecoeur spoke so warmly. It was as though Crevecoeur was arguing that ethnicity, where persons of African descent were concerned, was either so powerful or so unattractive as to make their assimilation entirely impossible or so insignificant as to make it entirely undesirable. In any case Americanization in the late eighteenth century was a precious commodity to be cherished and enjoyed only by a select group of persons of European descent.

One must admit, therefore, that at the time of the birth of the new nation there was no clear-cut disposition to welcome into the American family persons of any and all ethnic backgrounds. Only Europeans were invited to fight for independence. And when the patriots at long last relented and gave persons of African descent a chance to fight, the concession was made with great reluctance and after much equivocation and soul-searching. Only Europeans were regarded as full citizens in the new states and in the new nation. And when the founding fathers wrote the Constitution of the United States, they did not seem troubled by the distinctions on the basis of ethnic differences that the Constitution implied.

If the principle of ethnic exclusiveness was propounded so early and so successfully in the history of the United States, it is not surprising that it would, in time, become the basis for questioning the ethnic backgrounds of large numbers of prospective Americans, even Europeans. Thus, in 1819, a Jewish immigrant was chilled to hear a bystander refer to him and his companion as "more damned emigrants." A decade later there began a most scathing and multifaceted attack on the Catholic church. On two counts the church was a bad influence. First, its principal recruits were the Irish, the "very dregs" of the Old World social order; and secondly, its doctrine of papal supremacy ran counter to the idea of the political and religious independence of the United States. Roman Catholics, Protestant Americans warned, were engaged in a widespread conspiracy to subvert American institutions, through parochial schools, the Catholic press, immoral convents, and a sinister design to control the West by flooding it with Catholic settlers. The burning of convents and churches and the killing of Catholics themselves were indications of how deeply many Americans felt about religious and cultural differences for which they had a distaste and suspicion that bordered on paranoia.

Soon the distaste for the foreign-born became almost universal, with Roman Catholics themselves sharing in the hostility to those who followed them to the new Republic. Some expressed fear of the poverty and criminality that accompanied each wave of immigrants. Some felt that those newly arrived from abroad were a threat to republican freedom. Some saw in the ethnic differences of the newcomers an immediate danger to the moral standards of Puritan America. Some feared the competition that newcomers posed in the labor market. Some became convinced that the ideal of a national homogeneity would disappear with the influx of so

many unassimilable elements. Soon, nativist societies sprang up all across the land, and they found national expression in 1850 in a new organization called the Order of the Star Spangled Banner. With its slogan, "America for Americans," the order, which became the organizational basis for the Know-Nothing party, engendered a fear through its preachments that caused many an American to conclude that his country was being hopelessly subverted by the radical un-Americanism of the great variety of ethnic strains that were present in the United States.

If there was some ambivalence regarding the ethnic diversity of white immigrants before the Civil War, it was dispelled by the view that prevailed regarding immigrants in the post–Civil War years. The "old" immigrants, so the argument went, were at least assimilable and had "entered practically every line of activity in nearly every part of the country." Even those who had been non-English speaking had mingled freely with native Americans and had therefore been quickly assimilated. Not so with the "new" immigrants who came after 1880. They "congregated together in sections apart from native Americans and the older immigrants to such an extent that assimilation had been slow." Small wonder that they were different. Small wonder that they were barely assimilable. They came from Austro-Hungary, Italy, Russia, Greece, Rumania, and Turkey. They dressed differently, spoke in unfamiliar tongues, and clung to strange, if not exotic customs. It did not matter that Bohemians, Moravians, and Finns had lower percentages of illiteracy than had the Irish and Germans or that Jews had a higher percentage of skilled laborers than any group except the Scots. Nor did it matter that, in fact, the process of assimilation for the so-called "new" group was about as rapid as that of the so-called "old" group.

What did matter was that the new nativism was stronger and more virulent than any anti-immigration forces or groups of the early nineteenth century and that these groups were determined either to drive from the shores those who were different or to isolate them so that they could not contaminate American society. Old-stock Americans began to organize to preserve American institutions and the American way of life. Those who had been here for five years or a decade designated themselves as old-stock Americans and joined in the attack on those recently arrived. If the cult of Anglo-Saxon superiority was all but pervasive, those who were not born into the cult regarded themselves as honorary members. Thus, they could celebrate with as much feeling as any the virtues of Anglo-Saxon institutions and could condemn as vehemently as any those ideas and practices that were not strictly Anglo-Saxon. Whenever possible they joined the American Protective Association and the Immigrant Restriction League; and in so doing they sold their own ethnicity for the obscurity that a pseudoassimilation brought. But in the end, they would be less than successful. The arrogance and presumption of the Anglo-Saxon complex was not broad enough to embrace the Jews of eastern Europe or the Bohemians of central Europe or the Turks of the Middle East. The power and drive of the Anglo-Saxon forces would prevail; and those who did not belong would be compelled to console themselves by extolling the virtues of cultural pluralism.

By that time—near the end of the nineteenth century—the United States had articulated quite clearly its exalted standards of ethnicity. They were standards that accepted Anglo-Saxons as the norm, placed other whites on what may be called "ethnic probation," and excluded from serious consideration the Japanese, Chinese, and Negroes. It was not difficult to deal harshly with the Chinese and Japanese when they began to enter the United States in considerable numbers in the post–Civil War years. They simply did not meet the standards that the arbiters of American ethnicity had promulgated. They were different in race, religion, language, and public and private morality. They had to be excluded; and eventually they were.

The presence of persons of African descent, almost from the beginning, had helped whites to define ethnicity and to establish and maintain the conditions by which it could be controlled. If their color and race, their condition of servitude, and their generally degraded position did not set them apart, the laws and customs surrounding them more than accomplished that feat. Whether in Puritan Massachusetts or cosmopolitan New York or Anglican South Carolina, the colonists declared that Negroes, slave or free, did not and could not belong to the society of equal human beings. Thus, the newly arrived Crevecoeur could be as blind to the essential humanity of Negroes as the patriots who tried to keep them out of the Continental Army. They were not a part of America, these new men. And in succeeding years their presence would do more to define ethnicity than the advent of several scores of millions of Europeans.

It was not enough for Americans, already somewhat guilt-ridden for maintaining slavery in a free society, to exclude blacks from American society on the basis of race and condition of servitude. They proceeded from that point to argue that Negroes were inferior morally, intellectually, and physically. Even as he reviewed the remarkable accomplishments of Benjamin Banneker, surveyor, almanacker, mathematician, and clockmaker, Thomas Jefferson had serious doubts about the mental capabilities of Africans, and he expressed these doubts to his European friends. What Jefferson speculated about at the end of the eighteenth century became indisputable dogma within a decade after his death.

In the South every intellectual, legal, and religious resource was employed in the task of describing the condition of Negroes in such a way as to make them the least attractive human beings on the face of the earth. Slavery was not only the natural lot of blacks, the slaveowners argued, but it was in accordance with God's will that they should be kept in slavery. As one sanctimonious divine put it, "We feel that the souls of our slaves are a solemn trust and we shall strive to present them faultless and complete before the presence of God. . . . However the world may judge us in connection with our institution of slavery, we conscientiously believe it to be a great missionary institution—one arranged by God, as He arranges all moral and religious influences of the world so that the good may be brought out of seeming evil, and a blessing wrung out of every form of the curse." It was a difficult task that the owners of slaves set for themselves. Slaves had brought with them only heathenism, immorality, profligacy, and irresponsibility. They possessed neither the mental capacity nor the moral impulse to improve themselves. Only if their sponsors—those to whom were entrusted not only their souls but their bodies—were fully committed to their improvement could they take even the slightest, halting steps toward civilization.

What began as a relatively moderate justification for slavery soon became a vigorous, aggressive defense of the institution. Slavery, to the latter-day defenders, was the cornerstone of the republican edifice. To a governor of South Carolina, it was the greatest of all the great blessings which a kind Providence had bestowed upon the glorious region of the South. It was, indeed, one of the remarkable coincidences of history that such a favored institution had found such a favored creature as the African to give slavery the high value that was placed on it. A childlike race, prone to docility and manageable in every respect, the African was the ideal subject for the slave role. Slaveholders had to work hard to be worthy of this great Providential blessing.

Nothing that Negroes could do or say could change or seriously affect this view. They might graduate from college, as John Russwurm did in 1826, or they might write a most scathing attack against slavery, as David Walker did in 1829. It made no difference. They might teach in an all-white college, as Charles B. Reason did in New York in the 1850s, or publish a newspaper, as Frederick Douglass did during that same decade. Their racial and cultural backgrounds disqualified them from becoming American citizens. They could even argue in favor of their capacities and potentialities, as Henry Highland Garnet did, or they might argue their right to fight for union and freedom, as 186,000 did in the Civil War. Still, it made no sense for white Americans to give serious consideration to their arguments and their actions. They were beyond the veil, as the Jews had been beyond the veil in the barbaric and bigoted communities of eastern Europe.

The views regarding Negroes that had been so carefully developed to justify and defend slavery would not disappear with emancipation. To those who had developed such views and to the vast numbers who subscribed to them, they were much too valid to be discarded simply because the institution of slavery had collapsed. In fact, if Negroes were heathens and barbarians and intellectual imbeciles in slavery, they were hardly qualified to function as equals in a free society. And any effort to impose them on a free society should be vigorously and relentlessly resisted, even if it meant that a new and subordinate place for them had to be created.

When Americans set out to create such a place for the four million freedmen after the Civil War, they found that it was convenient to put their formulation in the context of the ethnic factors that militated against complete assimilation. To do it this way seemed more fitting, perhaps even more palatable, for the white members of a so-called free society. And they had some experience on which to rely. In an earlier day it had been the Irish or the Germans or the free Negroes who presented problems of assimilation. They were different in various ways and did not seem to make desirable citizens. In time the Irish, Germans, and other Europeans made it and were accepted on the broad lap of Alma Mater. But not the free Negroes, who continued to suffer disabilities even in the North in the years just before the Civil War. Was this the key to the solution of the postwar problems? Perhaps it was. After all, Negroes had always been a group apart in Boston, New York, Philadelphia, and other northern cities. They all lived together in one part of the city—especially if they could find no other place to live. They had their own churches—after the whites drove them out of theirs. They had their own schools—after they were excluded from the schools attended by whites. They had their own social organizations—after the whites barred them from theirs.

If Negroes possessed so many ethnic characteristics such as living in the same community, having their own churches, schools, and social clubs, and perhaps other agencies of cohesion, that was all very well. They even seemed "happier with their own kind," some patronizing observers remarked. They were like the Germans or the Irish or the Italians or the Jews. They had so much in common and so much to preserve. There was one significant difference, however. For Europeans, the ethnic factors that brought a particular group together actually eased the task of assimilation and, in many ways, facilitated the process of assimilation, particularly as hostile elements sought to disorient them in their drive toward full citizenship. And, in time, they achieved it.

For Negroes, however, such was not the case. They had been huddled together in northern ghettoes since the eighteenth century. They had had their own churches since 1792 and their own schools since 1800. And this separateness, this ostracism, was supported and enforced by the full majesty of the law, state and federal, just to make certain that Negroes did, indeed, preserve their ethnicity! And as they preserved their ethnicity—all too frequently as they looked down the barrel of a policeman's pistol or a militiaman's shotgun—full citizenship seemed many light years away. They saw other ethnic groups pass them by, one by one, and take their places in the sacred Order of the Star Spangled Banner, the American Protective Association, the Knights of the Ku Klux Klan—not always fully assimilated but vehemently opposed to the assimilation of Negroes. The ethnic grouping that was a way station, a temporary resting place for Europeans as they became Americans, proved to be a terminal point for blacks who found it virtually impossible to become Americans in any real sense.

There was an explanation or at least a justification for this. The federal government and the state governments had tried to force Negroes into full citizenship and had tried to legislate them into equality with the whites. This was not natural and could not possibly succeed. Negroes had not made it because they were not fit, the social Darwinists[1] said. Negroes were beasts, Charles Carroll declared somewhat inelegantly. "Stateways cannot change folkways," William Graham Sumner, the distinguished scholar, philosophized. The first forty years of Negro freedom had been a failure, said John R. Commons, one of the nation's leading economists. This so-called failure was widely acknowledged in the country as northerners of every rank and description acquiesced, virtually without a murmur of objection, to the southern settlement of the race problem characterized by disfranchisement, segregation, and discrimination.

Here was a new and exotic form of ethnicity. It was to be seen in the badges of inferiority and the symbols of racial degradation that sprang up in every sector of American life—in the exclusion from the polling places with its specious justification that Negroes were unfit to participate in the sacred rite of voting; the back stairway or the freight elevator to public places; the separate, miserable railway car; the separate and hopelessly inferior school; and even the Jim Crow[2] cemetery. Ethnic considerations had never been so important in the shaping of public policy. They had never before been used by the American government to define the role and place of other groups in American society. The United States had labored hard to create order out of its chaotic and diverse ethnic backgrounds. Having begun by meekly suggesting the difficulty in assimilating all groups into one great society, it had acknowledged failure by ruling out one group altogether, quite categorically, and frequently by law, solely on the basis of race.

It could not achieve this without doing irreparable harm to the early notions of the essential unity of America and Americans. The sentiments that promoted the disfranchisement and segregation of Negroes also encouraged the infinite varieties of discrimination against Jews, Armenians, Turks, Japanese, and Chinese. The conscious effort to degrade a particular ethnic group reflects a corrosive quality that dulls the sensitivities of both the perpetrators and the victims. It calls forth venomous hatreds and crude distinctions in high places as well as low places. It can affect the quality of mind of even the most cultivated scholar and place him in a position scarcely distinguishable from the Klansman or worse. It was nothing out of the ordinary, therefore, that at a dinner in honor of the winner of one of Harvard's most coveted prizes, Professor Barrett Wendell warned that if a Negro or a Jew ever won the prize the dinner would have to be canceled.

By the time that the Statue of Liberty was dedicated in 1886 the words of Emma Lazarus on the base of it had a somewhat hollow ring. Could anyone seriously believe that the poor, tired, huddled masses "yearning to breathe free," were really welcome here? This was a land where millions of black human beings whose ancestors had been here for centuries were consistently treated as pariahs and untouchables! What interpretation could anyone place on the sentiments expressed on the statue except that the country had no real interest in or sympathy for the down-trodden unless they were white and preferably Anglo-Saxon? It was a disillusioning experience for some newcomers to discover that their own ethnic background was a barrier to success in their adopted land. It was a searing and shattering experience for Negroes to discover over and over again that three centuries of toil and loyalty were nullified by the misfortune of their own degraded ethnic background.

In the fullness of time—in the twentieth century—the nation would confront the moment of truth regarding ethnicity as a factor in its own historical development. Crevecoeur's words would have no real significance. The words of the Declaration of Independence would have no real meaning. The words of Emma Lazarus would not ring true. All such sentiments would be put to the severe test of public policy and private deeds and would be found wanting. The Ku Klux Klan would challenge the moral and human dignity of Jews, Catholics, and Negroes. The quotas of the new immigration laws would define ethnic values in terms of race and national origin. The restrictive covenants[3] would arrogate to a select group of bigots the power of determining what races or ethnic groups should live in certain houses or whether, indeed, they should have any houses at all in which to live. If some groups finally made it through the escape hatch and arrived at the point of acceptance, it was on the basis of race, now defined with sufficient breadth to include all or most peoples who were not of African descent.

By that time ethnicity in American life would come to have a special, clearly definable meaning. Its meaning would be descriptive of that group of people vaguely defined in the federal census returns as "others" or "non-whites." It would have something in common with that magnificent term "cultural pluralism," the consolation prize for those who were not and could not be assimilated. It would signify the same groping for respectability that describes that group of people who live in what is euphemistically called "the inner city." It would represent a rather earnest search for a hidden meaning that would make it seem a bit more palatable and surely more sophisticated than something merely racial. But in 1969 even a little child would know what ethnicity had come to mean.

In its history, ethnicity, in its true sense, has extended and continues to extend beyond race. At times it has meant language, customs, religion, national origin. It has also meant race; and, to some, it has always meant only race. It had already begun to have a racial connotation in the eighteenth century. In the nineteenth century, it had a larger racial component, even as other factors continued to loom large. In the present century, as these other factors have receded in importance, racial considerations have come to have even greater significance. If the history of ethnicity has meant anything at all during the last three centuries, it has meant the gradual but steady retreat from the broad and healthy regard for cultural and racial differences to a narrow, counter-productive concept of differences in terms of whim, intolerance, and racial prejudice. We have come full circle. The really acceptable American is still that person whom Crevecoeur described almost two hundred years ago. But the true American, acceptable or not, is that person who seeks to act out his role in terms of his regard for human qualities irrespective of race. One of the great tragedies of American life at the beginning was that ethnicity was defined too narrowly. One of the great tragedies of today is that this continues to be the case. One can only hope that the nation and its people will all some day soon come to reassess ethnicity in terms of the integrity of the man rather than in terms of the integrity of the race.   [1989]

Terms

1. SOCIAL DARWINISM: The theory that applied Darwin's theory of evolution, "survival of the fittest," to society; it assumed that upper classes were naturally superior, and the failure of the lower classes was the result of their natural inferiority, not of social policies and practices.
2. JIM CROW: Laws and practices, especially in the South, that separated Blacks and Whites and enforced the subordination of Blacks.
3. RESTRICTIVE COVENANTS: Codes prohibiting members of some groups—often, Blacks, Jews, and Asians—from buying real estate in certain areas.

Understanding the Reading

1. Today, why do we find de Crevecoeur's 1782 definition of "the American, this new man" inadequate or inappropriate?
2. How did the principle of ethnic exclusion that omitted people of African descent affect later immigrant groups in the nineteenth century?

3. What does nativism mean?
4. How was the exclusion of African Americans from American society justified?
5. How was it maintained?
6. How did the treatment of African Americans affect other groups in the twentieth century?

Suggestions for Responding

1. According to Franklin, America has not lived up to its ideals. Do you think his pessimistic views are justified? What arguments would you offer to support or refute his analysis?
2. Is the "really acceptable American" today still that person whom de Crevecoeur described, as Franklin claims? Why or why not? ✦

3

American Anthropological Association Statement on "Race"

The following statement was adopted by the Executive Board of the American Anthropological Association, acting on a draft prepared by a committee of representative American anthropologists. It does not reflect a consensus of all members of the AAA, as individuals vary in their approaches to the study of "race." We believe that it represents generally the contemporary thinking and scholarly positions of a majority of anthropologists.

In the United States both scholars and the general public have been conditioned to viewing human races as natural and separate divisions within the human species based on visible physical differences. With the vast expansion of scientific knowledge in this century, however, it has become clear that human populations are not unambiguous, clearly demarcated, biologically distinct groups. Evidence from the analysis of genetics (e.g., DNA) indicates that most physical variation, about 94%, lies *within* so-called racial groups. Conventional geographic "racial" groupings differ from one another only in about 6% of their genes. This means that there is greater variation within "racial" groups than between them. In neighboring populations there is much overlapping of genes and their pheno-

typic (physical) expressions. Throughout history whenever different groups have come into contact, they have interbred. The continued sharing of genetic materials has maintained all of humankind as a single species.

Physical variations in any given trait tend to occur gradually rather than abruptly over geographic areas. And because physical traits are inherited independently of one another, knowing the range of one trait does not predict the presence of others. For example, skin color varies largely from light in the temperate areas in the north to dark in the tropical areas in the south; its intensity is not related to nose shape or hair texture. Dark skin may be associated with frizzy or kinky hair or curly or wavy or straight hair, all of which are found among different indigenous peoples in tropical regions. These facts render any attempt to establish lines of division among biological populations both arbitrary and subjective.

Historical research has shown that the idea of "race" has always carried more meanings than mere physical differences; indeed, physical variations in the human species have no meaning except the social ones that humans put on them. Today scholars in many fields argue that "race" as it is understood in the United States of America was a social mechanism invented during the 18th century to refer to those populations brought together in colonial America: the English and other European settlers, the conquered Indian peoples, and those peoples of Africa brought in to provide slave labor.

From its inception, this modern concept of "race" was modeled after an ancient theorem of the Great Chain of Being, which posited natural categories on a hierarchy established by God or nature. Thus "race" was a mode of classification linked specifically to peoples in the colonial situation. It subsumed a growing ideology of inequality devised to rationalize European attitudes and treatment of the conquered and enslaved peoples. Proponents of slavery in particular during the 19th century used "race" to justify the retention of slavery. The ideology magnified the differences among Europeans, Africans, and Indians, established a rigid hierarchy of socially exclusive categories, underscored and bolstered unequal rank and status differences, and provided the rationalization that the inequality was natural or God-given. The different physical traits of African-Americans and Indians became markers or symbols of their status differences.

As they were constructing U.S. society, leaders among European-Americans fabricated the cultural/behavioral characteristics associated with each "race," linking superior traits with Europeans and negative and inferior ones to blacks and Indians. Numerous arbitrary and fictitious beliefs about the different peoples were institutionalized and deeply embedded in American thought.

Early in the 19th century the growing fields of science began to reflect the public consciousness about human differences. Differences among the "racial" categories were projected to their greatest extreme when the argument was posed that Africans, Indians, and Europeans were separate species, with Africans the least human and closer taxonomically to apes.

Ultimately "race" as an ideology about human differences was subsequently spread to other areas of the world. It became a strategy for dividing, ranking, and controlling colonized people used by colonial powers everywhere. But it was not limited to the colonial situation. In the latter part of the 19th century it was employed by Europeans to rank one another and to justify social, economic, and political inequalities among their peoples. During World War II, the Nazis under Adolf Hitler enjoined the expanded ideology of "race" and "racial" differences and took them to a logical end: the extermination of 11 million people of "inferior races" (e.g., Jews, Gypsies, Africans, homosexuals, and so forth) and other unspeakable brutalities of the Holocaust.

"Race" thus evolved as a worldview, a body of prejudgments that distorts our ideas about human differences and group behavior. Racial beliefs constitute myths about the diversity in the human species and about the abilities and behavior of people homogenized into "racial" categories. The myths fused behavior and physical features together in the public mind, impeding our comprehension of both biological variations and cultural behavior, implying that both are genetically determined. Racial myths bear no relationship to the reality of human capabilities or behavior. Scientists today find that reliance on such folk beliefs about human differences in research has led to countless errors.

At the end of the 20th century, we now understand that human cultural behavior is learned, conditioned into infants beginning at birth, and always subject to modification. No human is born with a built-in culture or language. Our temperaments, dispositions, and personalities, regardless of genetic propensities, are developed within sets of meanings and values that we call "culture." Studies of infant and early childhood learning and behavior attest to the reality of our cultures in forming who we are.

It is a basic tenet of anthropological knowledge that all normal human beings have the capacity to learn any cultural behavior. The American experience with immigrants from hundreds of different language and cultural backgrounds who have acquired some version of American culture traits and behavior is the clearest evidence of this fact. Moreover, people of all physical variations have learned different cultural behaviors and continue to do so as modern transportation moves millions of immigrants around the world.

How people have been accepted and treated within the context of a given society or culture has a direct impact on how they perform in that society. The "racial" worldview was invented to assign some groups to perpetual low status, while others were permitted access to privilege, power, and wealth. The tragedy in the United States has been that the policies and practices stemming from this worldview succeeded all too well in constructing unequal populations among Europeans, Native Americans, and peoples of African descent. Given what we know about the capacity of normal humans to achieve and function within any culture, we conclude that present-day inequalities between so-called "racial" groups are not consequences of their biological inheritance but products of historical and contemporary social, economic, educational, and political circumstances.   [1998]

Understanding the Reading

1. How do anthropologists argue that human populations are never biologically distinct groups?

2. What was the Great Chain of Being?
3. How did we ever come to believe in the superiority and inferiority of races?

Suggestions for Responding

1. Have a debate on whether U.S. society should collect data on "racial" and ethnic groups. ◆

4

The Loudest Voice

GRACE PALEY

There is a certain place where dumb-waiters boom, doors slam, dishes crash; every window is a mother's mouth bidding the street shut up, go skate somewhere else, come home. My voice is the loudest.

There, my own mother is still as full of breathing as me and the grocer stands up to speak to her. "Mrs. Abramowitz," he says, "people should not be afraid of their children."

"Ah, Mr. Bialik," my mother replies, "if you say to her or her father 'Ssh,' they say, 'In the grave it will be quiet.'"

"From Coney Island to the cemetery," says my papa. "It's the same subway; it's the same fare."

I am right next to the pickle barrel. My pinky is making tiny whirlpools in the brine. I stop a moment to announce: "Campbell's Tomato Soup. Campbell's Vegetable Beef Soup. Campbell's S-c-otch Broth . . ."

"Be quiet," the grocer says, "the labels are coming off."

"Please, Shirley, be a little quiet," my mother begs me.

In that place the whole street groans: Be quiet! Be quiet! but steals from the happy chorus of my inside self not a tittle or a jot.

There, too, but just around the corner, is a red brick building that has been old for many years. Every morning the children stand before it in double lines which must be straight. They are not insulted. They are waiting anyway.

I am usually among them. I am, in fact, the first, since I begin with "A."

One cold morning the monitor tapped me on the shoulder. "Go to Room 409, Shirley Abramowitz," he said. I did as I was told. I went in a hurry up a down staircase to Room 409, which contained sixth-graders. I had to wait at the desk without wiggling until Mr. Hilton, their teacher, had time to speak.

After five minutes he said, "Shirley?"

"What?" I whispered.

He said, "My! My! Shirley Abramowitz! They told me you had a particularly loud, clear voice and read with lots of expression. Could that be true?"

"Oh yes," I whispered.

"In that case, don't be silly; I might very well be your teacher someday. Speak up, speak up."

"Yes," I shouted.

"More like it," he said. "Now, Shirley, can you put a ribbon in your hair or a bobby pin? It's too messy."

"Yes!" I bawled.

"Now, now, calm down." He turned to the class. "Children, not a sound. Open at page 39. Read till 52. When you finish, start again." He looked me over once more. "Now, Shirley, you know, I suppose, that Christmas is coming. We are preparing a beautiful play. Most of the parts have been given out. But I still need a child with a strong voice, lots of stamina. Do you know what stamina is? You do? Smart kid. You know, I heard you read 'The Lord is my shepherd' in Assembly yesterday. I was very impressed. Wonderful delivery. Mrs. Jordan, your teacher, speaks highly of you. Now listen to me, Shirley Abramowitz, if you want to take the part and be in the play, repeat after me, 'I swear to work harder than I ever did before.'"

I looked to heaven and said at once, "Oh, I swear." I kissed my pinky and looked at God.

"That is an actor's life, my dear," he explained. "Like a soldier's, never tardy or disobedient to his general, the director. Everything," he said, "absolutely everything will depend on you."

That afternoon, all over the building, children scraped and scrubbed the turkeys and the sheaves of corn off the schoolroom windows. Goodbye Thanksgiving. The next morning a monitor brought red paper and green paper from the office. We made new shapes and hung them on the walls and glued them to the doors.

The teachers became happier and happier. Their heads were ringing like the bells of childhood. My best friend Evie was prone to evil, but she did not get a single demerit for whispering. We learned "Holy Night" without an error. "How wonderful!" said Miss Glacé, the student teacher. "To think that some of you don't even speak the language!" We learned "Deck the Halls" and "Hark! The Herald Angels." . . . They weren't ashamed and we weren't embarrassed.

Oh, but when my mother heard about it all, she said to my father: "Misha, you don't know what's going on there. Cramer is the head of the Tickets Committee."

"Who?" asked my father. "Cramer? Oh yes, an active woman."

"Active? Active has to have a reason. Listen," she said sadly, "I'm surprised to see my neighbors making tra-la-la for Christmas."

My father couldn't think of what to say to that. Then he decided: "You're in America! Clara, you wanted to come here. In Palestine the Arabs would be eating you alive. Europe you had pogroms.[1] Argentina is full of Indians. Here you got Christmas. . . . Some joke, ha?"

"Very funny, Misha. What is becoming of you? If we came to a new country a long time ago to run away from tyrants, and instead we fall into a creeping pogrom, that our children learn a lot of lies, so what's the joke? Ach, Misha, your idealism is going away."

"So is your sense of humor."

"That I never had, but idealism you had a lot of."

"I'm the same Misha Abramovitch, I didn't change an iota. Ask anyone."

"Only ask me," says my mama, may she rest in peace. "I got the answer."

Meanwhile the neighbors had to think of what to say too.

Marty's father said: "You know, he has a very important part, my boy."

"Mine also," said Mr. Sauerfeld.

"Not my boy!" said Mrs. Klieg. "I said to him no. The answer is no. When I say no! I mean no!"

The rabbi's wife said, "It's disgusting!" But no one listened to her. Under the narrow sky of God's great wisdom she wore a strawberry-blond wig.

Every day was noisy and full of experience. I was Right-hand Man. Mr. Hilton said: "How could I get along without you, Shirley?"

He said: "Your mother and father ought to get down on their knees every night and thank God for giving them a child like you."

He also said: "You're absolutely a pleasure to work with, my dear, dear child."

Sometimes he said: "For God's sakes, what did I do with the script? Shirley! Shirley! Find it."

Then I answered quietly: "Here it is, Mr. Hilton."

Once in a while, when he was very tired, he would cry out: "Shirley, I'm just tired of screaming at those kids. Will you tell Ira Pushkov not to come in till Lester points to that star the second time?"

Then I roared: "Ira Pushkov, what's the matter with you? Dope! Mr. Hilton told you five times already, don't come in till Lester points to that star the second time."

"Ach, Clara," my father asked, "what does she do there till six o'clock she can't even put the plates on the table?"

"Christmas," said my mother coldly.

"Ho! Ho!" my father said. "Christmas. What's the harm? After all, history teaches everyone. We learn from reading this is a holiday from pagan times also, candles, lights, even Chanukah. So we learn it's not altogether Christian. So if they think it's a private holiday, they're only ignorant, not patriotic. What belongs to history, belongs to all men. You want to go back to the Middle Ages? Is it better to shave your head with a secondhand razor? Does it hurt Shirley to learn to speak up? It does not. So maybe someday she won't live between the kitchen and the shop. She's not a fool."

I thank you, Papa, for your kindness. It is true about me to this day. I am foolish but I am not a fool.

That night my father kissed me and said with great interest in my career, "Shirley, tomorrow's your big day. Congrats."

"Save it," my mother said. Then she shut all the windows in order to prevent tonsillitis.

In the morning it snowed. On the street corner a tree had been decorated for us by a kind city administration. In order to miss its chilly shadow our neighbors walked three blocks east to buy a loaf of bread. The butcher pulled down black window shades to keep the colored lights from shining on his chickens. Oh, not me. On the way to school, with both my hands I tossed it a kiss of tolerance. Poor thing, it was a stranger in Egypt.

I walked straight into the auditorium past the staring children. "Go ahead, Shirley!" said the monitors. Four boys, big for their age, had already started work as propmen and stagehands.

Mr. Hilton was very nervous. He was not even happy. Whatever he started to say ended in a sideward look of sadness. He sat slumped in the middle of the first row and asked me to help Miss Glacé. I did this, although she thought my voice too resonant and said, "Show-off!"

Parents began to arrive long before we were ready. They wanted to make a good impression. From among the yards of drapes I peeked out at the audience. I saw my embarrassed mother.

Ira, Lester, and Meyer were pasted to their beards by Miss Glacé. She almost forgot to thread the star on its wire, but I reminded her. I coughed a few times to clear my throat. Miss Glacé looked around and saw that everyone was in costume and in line waiting to play his part. She whispered, "All right. . . ." Then:

Jackie Sauerfeld, the prettiest boy in first grade, parted the curtains with his skinny elbow and in a high voice sang out:

"Parents dear
We are here
To make a Christmas play in time.
It we give
In narrative
And illustrate with pantomime."

He disappeared.

My voice burst immediately from the wings to the great shock of Ira, Lester, and Meyer, who were waiting for it but were surprised all the same.

"I remember, I remember, the house where I was born. . . ."

Miss Glacé yanked the curtain open and there it was, the house—an old hayloft, where Celia Kornbluh lay in the straw with Cindy Lou, her favorite doll. Ira, Lester, and Meyer moved slowly from the wings toward her, sometimes pointing to a moving star and sometimes ahead to Cindy Lou.

It was a long story and it was a sad story. I carefully pronounced all the words about my lonesome childhood, while little Eddie Braunstein wandered upstage and down with his shepherd's stick, looking for sheep. I brought up lonesomeness again, and not being understood at all except by some women everybody hated. Eddie was too small for that and Marty Groff took his place, wearing his father's prayer shawl. I announced twelve friends, and half the boys in the fourth grade gathered round Marty, who stood on an orange crate while my voice harangued. Sorrowful and loud, I declaimed about love and God and Man, but because of the terrible deceit of Abie Stock we came suddenly to a famous moment. Marty, whose remembering tongue I was, waited at the foot of the cross. He stared desperately at the audience. I groaned, "My God, my God, why hast thou forsaken me?" The soldiers who were sheiks grabbed poor Marty to pin him up to die, but he wrenched free, turned again to the audience, and spread his arms aloft to show despair and the end. I murmured at the top of my voice, "The rest is silence, but as everyone in this room, in this city—in this world—now knows, I shall have life eternal."

That night Mrs. Kornbluh visited our kitchen for a glass of tea.

"How's the virgin?" asked my father with a look of concern.

"For a man with a daughter, you got a fresh mouth, Abramovitch."

"Here," said my father kindly, "have some lemon, it'll sweeten your disposition."

They debated a little in Yiddish, then fell in a puddle of Russian and Polish. What I understood next was my father, who said, "Still and all, it was certainly a beautiful affair, you have to admit, introducing us to the beliefs of a different culture."

"Well, yes," said Mrs. Kornbluh. "The only thing . . . you know, Charlie Turner—that cute boy in Celia's class—a couple others? They got very small parts or no part at all. In very bad taste, it seemed to me. After all, it's their religion."

"Ach," explained my mother, "what could Mr. Hilton do? They got very small voices; after all, why should they holler? The English language they know from the beginning by heart. They're blond like angels. You think it's so important they should get in the play? Christmas . . . the whole piece of goods . . . they own it."

I listened and listened until I couldn't listen any more. Too sleepy, I climbed out of bed and kneeled. I made a little church of my hands and said, "Hear, O Israel . . . " Then I called out in Yiddish, "Please, good night, good night. Ssh."

My father said, "Ssh yourself," and slammed the kitchen door.

I was happy. I fell asleep at once. I had prayed for everybody: my talking family, cousins far away, passersby, and all the lonesome Christians. I expected to be heard. My voice was certainly the loudest.   [1956]

Terms

1. POGROM: An organized and often politically encouraged massacre or persecution of a minority group—in particular, one conducted against Jews.

Understanding the Reading

1. Characterize Shirley's family and neighbors.
2. What objections do the adults have to her part in the Christmas play?
3. Why do her parents allow her to participate?
4. What does she learn from this experience, and how does it change her?

Suggestions for Responding

1. Describe a situation in which you had to participate or at least confront a cultural activity that conflicted with or was alien to your own beliefs or values.
2. What does this story reveal about the lives and values of Jewish immigrants? ✦

5

To Be Hopi or American

POLINGAYSI QOYAWAYMA
(ELIZABETH Q. WHITE)

Like many converts to a new religion, Polingaysi was overly zealous. She was young, she was courageous, she was brash—brash enough to challenge her Hopi elders and the whole beautifully interwoven cultural pattern of Hopi life. Had she at that time been able to do so, she would have abolished all the age-old rites, the kiva[1] rituals, the sprinkling of sacred cornmeal, and especially the making of *pahos*, or prayer sticks.

At the same time, tempering her radical approach, she had a deep and unsatisfied curiosity concerning the very things that aroused in her the strongest resentment. As she walked across the field one day after visiting her family at New Oraibi, she saw a *paho* thrust into the sand on a little hillock, its single eagle feather fluttering at the end of a short length of white cotton string.

Prayer sticks, either the long, wandlike ones with many feathers tied to them, or the short, sharpened sticks called *pahos*, are held in reverence by the Hopi people. For four days after the "planting" of a prayer, these sticks are thought to possess the essence of the offered prayer and to be very powerful and sacred. To disturb one before it has lost its power is to court disaster. Accident, even death, Polingaysi had been taught, might result.

Well known to her was the story of the white woman who took prayer sticks from a shrine, then fell and broke her leg. Behind this accident the Hopi people saw the work of the invisible forces. The spirits had resented her action and had tripped her, they were convinced.

As she bent to pull the *paho* from the sand, Polingaysi felt a wave of superstitious fear sweep over her. But she was a Christian now, she reminded herself, and need not fear the magic in a stick with a feather on it. Defiantly, she carried it home and challenged her father with it.

"What does this stick mean to you and to the Hopi people?" she asked with more arrogance than she realized. "To me, pah! It means nothing. It has no power. It's just a stick with a bit of cornhusk and a feather attached to it. Why do you, in this day and age, when you can have the message of the Bible, still have faith in sticks and feathers?"

Her father, true Hopi that he was, recoiled from the proffered *paho,* refusing to touch it. There was a worried look in his eyes.

"Must you know?" he asked.

"Of course, I must know," Polingaysi declared. "Why shouldn't I know?"

"Lay it on the table," her father said, "and I will tell you."

She placed the stick on the rough board table which she had goaded the little man into making, and the two of them bent over it.

"Do you see that blue-green, chipped-off place here at the top?" her father asked, pointing. "That is the face of the prayer stick. It represents mossy places, moisture. Now this below is the body of the prayer stick. A red color, as you can see, like our colored sand. That represents the earth. Moisture to the earth, then, is what the *paho* is for."

"A prayer for rain?"

"That, yes, and more. The stick carries a bundle on its back."

"The bit of cornhusk, bound with string? What is it for? What does it mean?"

"I don't know what is bound up in the cornhusk," her father said, "and I won't open it to find out. However, I think you might find there some grass seeds, a pinch of cornmeal, a pinch of pollen, and a drop of honey."

"But, why, why?" Polingaysi demanded impatiently. "What good does it do?"

The little Hopi man had been carving a Kachina doll[2] from the dried root of a cottonwood. He turned away and went back to his work, sitting down crosslegged on the floor and picking up his knife and the unfinished doll. Polingaysi stood looking down at him, waiting for his answer. He thought before he began to speak.

"The good it does depends on many things, my daughter. It depends most of all on the faith of the one who made the *paho*. If all those things I mentioned are inside the little bundle that it carries on its back, it would mean that the one making the *paho* planted it in Mother Earth as a prayer for a plentiful harvest, with moisture enough to help Earth produce full ears of corn, plump beans, sweet melons." He looked up at her and his small face was worried. "Surely you have not forgotten the meaning of the feather? Feathers represent the spirits that are in all things. This one represents the spirit that is in the prayer the *paho* offers up."

Polingaysi turned away and took the *paho* in her hands. About to tear open the cornhusk, she looked down to see her father's hands stilled and horror in his expression. Suddenly she could not open the *paho*'s treasure without his permission. She could not fly in the face of tradition to that extent, knowing it would offend his spirit, however silent he remained, however little he reproached her openly.

"May I open it?"

Her father bent his head, possibly questioning the propriety of such an action and fearing the harm it might do him and his daughter. After a moment of hesitation, he sighed, saying, "It seems well weathered. I think it is more than four days old. If so, its purpose has been served and the power has left it. Use your left hand."

Gently, in spite of her pretended scorn, Polingaysi opened the bit of wrapped cornhusk. It had been folded while still green into a tiny triangle. In this little pouch there was a bit of material about the size of a pea. Seeds, cornmeal, pollen, held together with honey, as her father had predicted.

"Can't you see there's nothing of value in here?" Polingaysi cried.

"Not to you," her father agreed. "Not to me. But to the one who made it in prayer."

She would have questioned him further, but he took his work and went outside, his face enigmatic.

"For pity's sake, Mother," Polingaysi burst out, turning to Sevenka who had been working quietly on a basket during the discussion, "does everything in the life of a Hopi have a hidden meaning? Why, for instance, should I use my left hand to open that thing?"

"It seems foolish to you because you are young and do not understand everything," her mother said patiently. "Perhaps you are foolish because you do not understand Hopi ways, though you are a Hopi. I will tell you about the left hand.

"The left hand is on the heart side of the body. It is the hand that moves most slowly. It selects, instead of grabbing as the right hand does. It is cleaner. It does not touch the mouth during the eating of food, nor does it clean the body after release of waste materials.

"Do you remember watching our medicine man—the Man With Eyes—at his work? In his healing rites and also in his religious ceremonies he uses the left hand, for those reasons I have just given you. The left hand, then, is the hand that is of the heart and the spirit, not of nature and the earth."

Polingaysi struggled to deny the beauty of the words her mother had spoken. She sought a scoffing answer, but found none. After a moment the older woman continued.

"One more thing I will tell you about the *pa-hos*. They must be kept free of the white man's ways if they are to have the full power of old times. That is why Hopi people do not sharpen them to a point with white man's steel blades, but grind them to sharpness on sandstone."

At that moment Polingaysi saw one of her mother's brothers passing the window. He knew nothing of the discussion and she had no desire to reopen it. With her left hand she placed the *paho* on the window sill.

"Polingaysi!" the old man cried, his face crinkling into a big smile of welcome. "It is a great treat to my spirit to see you after so long a time. We are always happy to see our child come home, even if she does make us sit at a wooden platform when we eat."

Polingaysi lost some of her contentiousness and laughed. He had always complained about sitting at the table, insisting that he could not keep his feet warm while he was eating unless he sat on them, Hopi-fashion. Her little grandmother had been completely mystified by the table, and though Polingaysi had patiently explained its use, the old lady had laboriously climbed up onto it, instead of seating herself on the wooden bench that served as a chair.

She looked at her uncle and thought of all the new ideas she had gleaned during her life among white people. The old man had no desire to share her knowledge. To him the old way was best. He asked little of life: enough food to keep the breath in his thin, worn old body, a little heat in the fireplace, a drink of water when he was dry.

It was she who was forever holding out her cup to be filled with knowledge.   [1964]

Terms

1. KIVA: An underground room used by Hopi men for ceremonies or councils.
2. KACHINA DOLL: A doll made of wood and decorated with paint, feathers, and other materials that represents various spirits to Native Americans in the Southwest.

Understanding the Reading

1. Why does Polingaysi respond to the *paho* with both fear and arrogance?

2. Explain what Polingaysi means when she complains that "everything in the life of a Hopi has hidden meaning."
3. What does this selection tell you about "Hopi ways"?
4. Why would it be important that *pahos* "be kept free from white man's ways"?
5. What does the closing sentence mean?

Suggestions for Responding

1. Describe a generational conflict, especially one based on an ethnic tradition, between you and an older family member. What were the immediate and the long-term outcomes?
2. Both Paley and Qoyawayma describe the experience of assimilation. Some people feel this process was essential to creating a unified American society, whereas others believe that the costs, both the loss of cultural variety and the pain to individuals and families, were too high. Which position do you support? Why? ✦

6

People of Color Who Never Felt They Were Black

DARRYL FEARS

At her small apartment near the National Cathedral in Northwest Washington, Maria Martins quietly watched as an African American friend studied a picture of her mother. "Oh," the friend said, surprise in her voice. "Your mother is white."

She turned to Martins. "But you are black."

That came as news to Martins, a Brazilian who, for 30 years before immigrating to the United States, looked in the mirror and saw a *morena*—a woman with caramel-colored skin that is nearly equated with whiteness in Brazil and some other Latin American countries. "I didn't realize I was black until I came here," she said.

That realization has come to hundreds of thousands of dark-complexioned immigrants to the United States from Brazil, Colombia, Panama and other Latin nations with sizable populations

of African descent. Although most do not identify themselves as black, they are seen that way
as soon as they set foot in North America.

Their reluctance to embrace this definition
has left them feeling particularly isolated—
shunned by African Americans who believe they
are denying their blackness; by white Americans
who profile them in stores or on highways; and
by lighter-skinned Latinos whose images dominate Spanish-language television all over the
world, even though a majority of Latin people
have some African or Indian ancestry.

The pressure to accept not only a new language and culture, but also a new racial identity,
is a burden some darker-skinned Latinos say
they face every day.

"It's overwhelming," said Yvette Modestin, a
dark-skinned native of Panama who works as an
outreach coordinator in Boston. "There's not a
day that I don't have to explain myself."

E. Francisco Lopez, a Venezuelan-born attorney in Washington, said he had not heard the
term "minority" before coming to America.

"I didn't know what it meant. I didn't accept
it because I thought it meant 'less than,'" said
Martins, whose father is black. "'Where are you
from?' they ask me. I say I'm from Brazil. They
say, 'No, you are from Africa.' They make me
feel like I am denying who I am."

Exactly who these immigrants are is almost
impossible to divine from the 2000 Census. Latinos of African, mestizo and European descent—
or any mixture of the three—found it hard to answer the question "What is your racial origin?"

Some of the nation's 35 million Latinos scrib
bled in the margins that they were Aztec or
Mayan. A fraction said they were Indian. Nearly
forty-eight percent described themselves as
white, and only 2 percent as black. Fully 42 percent said they were "some other race."

BETWEEN BLACK AND WHITE

Race matters in Latin America, but it matters
differently.

Most South American nations barely have a
black presence. In Argentina, Chile, Peru and
Bolivia, there are racial tensions, but mostly between indigenous Indians and white descendants of Europeans.

The black presence is stronger along the
coasts of two nations that border the Caribbean
Sea, Venezuela and Colombia—which included
Panama in the 19th century—along with Brazil,
which snakes along the Atlantic coast. In many
ways, those nations have more in common
racially with Puerto Rico, Cuba and the Dominican Republic than they do with the rest of South
America.

This black presence is a legacy of slavery,
just as it is in the United States. But the experience of race in the United States and in these
Latin countries is separated by how slaves and
their descendants were treated after slavery was
abolished.

In the United States, custom drew a hard line
between black and white, and Jim Crow rules
kept the races separate. The color line hardened
to the point that it was sanctioned in 1896 by the
Supreme Court in its decision in *Plessy v. Ferguson,* which held that Homer Plessy, a white-
complexioned Louisiana shoemaker, could not
ride in the white section of a train because a
single ancestor of his was black.

Thus Americans with any discernible African
ancestry—whether they identified themselves as
black or not—were thrust into one category.
One consequence is that dark-complexioned
and light-complexioned black people combined
to campaign for equal rights, leading to the civil
rights movement of the 1960s.

By contrast, the Latin countries with a sizable
black presence had more various, and more
fluid, experiences of race after slavery.

African slavery is as much a part of Brazil's
history as it is of the United States's, said Sheila
Walker, a visiting professor of anthropology at
Spelman College in Atlanta and editor of the
book "African Roots/American Cultures." Citing
the census in Brazil, she said that nation has
more people of African descent than any other
in the world besides Nigeria, Africa's most populous country.

Brazil stands out in South America for that
and other reasons. Unlike most nations there, its
people speak Portuguese rather than Spanish,
prompting a debate over whether Brazil is part
of the Latino diaspora.

Brazilian slavery ended in 1889 by decree,
with no civil war and no Jim Crow—and mixing
between light- and dark-complexioned Indians,

Europeans, Africans and mulattoes was common and, in many areas, encouraged. Although discrimination against dark-complexioned Brazilians was clear, class played almost as important a role as race.

In Colombia, said Luis Murillo, a black politician in exile from that country, light-complexioned descendants of Spanish conquistadors and Indians created the "mestizo" race, an ideology that held that all mixed-race people were the same. But it was an illusion, Murillo said: A pecking order "where white people were considered superior and darker people were considered inferior" pervaded Colombia.

Murillo said the problem exists throughout Latin American and Spanish-speaking Caribbean countries with noticeable black populations. White Latinos control the governments even in nations with dark-complexioned majorities, he said. And in nations ruled by military juntas and dictators, there are few protests, Murillo said.

In Cuba, a protest by Afro-Cubans led to the arming of the island's white citizens and, ultimately, the massacre of 3,000 to 6,000 black men, women and children in 1912, according to University of Michigan historian Frank Guridy, author of "Race and Politics in Cuba, 1933–34."

American-influenced Cuba was also home to the Ku Klux Klan Kubano and other anti-black groups before Fidel Castro's revolution. Now, Cuban racism still exists, some say, but black, mulatto and white people mix much more freely. Lopez, the Afro-Venezuelan lawyer, said, "Race doesn't affect us there the way it does here," he said. "It's more of a class thing."

Jose Neinstein, a native white Brazilian and executive director of the Brazilian-American Cultural Institute in Washington, boiled down to the simplest terms how his people are viewed. "In this country," he said, "if you are not quite white, then you are black." But in Brazil, he said, "If you are not quite black, then you are white."

The elite in Brazil, as in most Latin American nations, are educated and white. But many brown and black people also belong in that class. Generally, brown Brazilians, such as Martins, enjoy many privileges of the elite, but are disproportionately represented in Brazilian slums.

Someone with Sidney Poitier's deep chocolate complexion would be considered white if his hair were straight and he made a living in a profession. That might not seem so odd, Brazilians say, when you consider that the fair-complexioned actresses Rashida Jones of the television show "Boston Public" and Lena Horne are identified as black in the United States.

Neinstein remembered talking with a man of Poitier's complexion during a visit to Brazil. "We were discussing ethnicity," Neinstein said, "and I asked him, 'What do you think about this from your perspective as a black man?' He turned his head to me and said, 'I'm not black,' "Neinstein recalled." . . . It simply paralyzed me. I couldn't ask another question."

By the same token, Neinstein said, he never perceived brown-complexioned people such as Maria Martins, who works at the cultural institute, as black. One day, when an African American custodian in his building referred to one of his brown-skinned secretaries as "the black lady," Neinstein was confused. "I never looked at that woman as black," he said. "It was quite a revelation to me."

Those perceptions come to the United States with the light- and dark-complexioned Latinos who carry them. But here, they collide with two contradictory forces: North American prejudice and African American pride. . . .   [2002]

Understanding the Reading

1. Why are some Latin Americans and Brazilians pressured to accept a different racial identity in the United States?
2. What is the reaction of many African Americans when Latin Americans are reluctant to identify as Black?
3. Why is the United States' view on race different from that of Brazil and many other Latin American countries?

Suggestions for Responding

1. Research the history of slavery in Brazil.
2. Research the Ku Klux Klan Kubano.
3. Listen to Brazilian music from Salvador, Bahia. ✦

7

Rosa Wakefield

John Langston Gwaltney

Florida-born, Miss Rosa Wakefield has known me practically all my life, and I have always thought of her as a worthy senior with so much dignity that the last thing she needs to think about is standing upon it. She is seventy-eight and hale and preeminently sound-minded. Her buttermilk pies and watermelon pork are as fine as they were when I was a fifth-grader puzzling with her over a text which asserted confidently that the Nigerian Hausa[1] were not black. I do not know anyone who has done more people more good with less noise than Miz Wakefield.

You understand that I am not an educated person. I was born with good sense and I read everything I can get to read. At least I know that I don't know very much. Now, if you still think I can help you, I'll be very glad to answer any question I can for you. I can't answer for nobody but myself. I will tell you what I think and why I happen to think that way. I was never the first person you heard when you came to my father's house or a party, but that never meant that I wasn't thinking as fast as some of these loud folks was talking.

Now, this first question is something I have thought about a great deal ever since I was a little girl. I think that I think more about anything I might think about than most people. That's because I was my father's oldest daughter and my mother died early, so I always had to think for more than one person. And that is a responsibility. It's bad enough when you make a mistake for one person, but when you make a mistake for more than one person—you know, when you make a mistake that's going to hurt somebody who can't think for herself or hisself—then you really feel that more than you would if you had just hurt yourself. I always thought about

This interview is one of the oral histories Black anthropologist Gwaltney recorded in an effort to preserve the values and diversity of Black culture in the South.

that. My father and I sort of brought the others up. Now, I don't want to brag on myself, but I guess we didn't do but so bad. Now, the truth is that I think we did a good job.

But now, right there you have one of the big differences between blackfolks, or colored folks, or whatsoever you might call us, and whitefolks. We don't like to spell things out but so much. We know what we mean, like you knew what I meant. You know that I don't really mean that I think we did a pretty good job in raising all those children. You know that I mean that it was very hard to do so and we did it right.

White people are some writing folks! They will write! They write everything. Now, they do that because they don't trust each other. Also, they are the kind of people who think that you can think about everything, about whatever you are going to do, before you do that thing. Now, that's bad for them because you cannot do that without wings. I think that maybe you can't even do that *with* wings. They say that God's brightest angel fell. Now, ask yourself! Do you think God would have made this brightest angel if He knew that this angel was going to turn against Him? Now, it don't make one bit of sense to think that He would have done that. If He knew this brightest angel was going to ape up, what would He want to go and make this angel for? Now, if the Lord can be surprised, who are we to think that we can think about everything before it happens? All you can do is do what you know has got to be done as right as you know how to do that thing. Now, white people don't seem to know that.

I worked hard to put the others through school, and now they help me so the old lady can stir up a little sweet bread and talk to nice people like you. But, you see, there is hard work behind everything we do. You know that this sweet bread didn't make itself. I was telling you about my trips. You know that trip to Africa and that trip to Norway didn't pay for themselves! But, you see, if you eats these dinners and don't cook 'em, if you wears these clothes and don't buy or iron them, then you might start thinking that the good fairy or some spirit did all that. They asked a little white girl in this family I used to work for who made her cake at one of her little tea parties. She said she made it and then she hid her face and said the good fairies made it. Well, you are looking at that good fairy.

Blackfolks don't have no time to be thinking like that. If I thought like that, I'd burn cakes and scorch skirts. But when you don't have anything else to do, you can think like that. It's bad for your mind, though. See, if you think about what is really happening, you will know why these things are happening. When I get these cards on my birthday or Easter, I know that's because I sent my younger brother to school as clean as I could send him and made him get some sense into his head by seeing that he did what that teacher told him to do. They all send me a card on Mother's Day because they say that I was a mother to them. Now, they know that I am living all these other days, too, and they see to it that I don't want for anything I really need and a lot of things the old lady might just want. Rosa has washed her dishes and a lot of other folks' dishes for a long time, so she doesn't really need any machine to wash dishes, but she got one sitting right there in that kitchen! Now, Rosa didn't buy it and she didn't tell anybody to buy it, but it was bought. Now, my youngest brother is a professor too, but if he comes in here and sees something that has to be done, from washing dishes to scrubbing that floor, the next thing you know he just goes on and does it like anybody else. I never married, but any niece or nephew I got will come here if they *think* I need something and go wherever I want to send them.

Now, our children are more mannerable, but now so many of our children are trying to act like white children that it's hard to tell the difference just by the way they act these days. Some of these sorry things passing for young men and ladies that you see in the streets these days are enough to make you hang your head in shame! But so far, praise God, all our children have kept level heads and are doing just fine. In the summer we get together more and they tell me some things that are really hard to believe. I tell them to be nice to everybody that is nice to them and not to do every fool thing that they see being done. Little Rosa, my niece, brought a girl from Nigeria and a girl from Sweden. Now, that pleased me because I have read about those places and I have seen those countries and people there were

nice to me, so I was glad to be nice to one of their girls.

We are revern' colored folks! We don't all have the same color skin, but we all have a strong family resemblance. My niece's mother is a German woman, and a finer lady you will never meet. But all you have to do is take one look at my niece and you will know that she is my niece. We all have a very strong family resemblance and we are a family that helps each other. If you know one of us, you know us all. We try to look out for each other. I told my brother about you and those mules and he said you looked just like a Wakefield. All you got to do to look just like a Wakefield is be black and do something good. But he's right this time—you do look a lot like us. You're quiet like we are, too. I guess in your work you have to be quiet because once you get us blackfolks talking, you won't get much of a chance to make much noise! But once a lady was out here, and she couldn't pay for her taxi because that driver had charged her way too much. We helped her and she swore that I looked just like her. Now, I'm a brown woman and this lady I'm telling you about looked as white as any white woman you will ever see. People like to claim kin with people they like. White people do that much more than we do, though. They can' stand the idea of anything good being black. If a black person does something good, they say he did that because of the white in him.

My father was sickly, but he worked hard all his life. He taught me and I tried to help teach the others. People have to go to school now, but they wouldn't have to do that if they would take up time with one another. I went to one college course to learn about the Negro. I'm sorry I did that now because all they did was to sit there and tell each other how they felt—I mean, how it felt to be black. Shoot! I have been feeling black all my life because I am not white! Now, what I wanted to know was not how they felt, because I already knew that; I wanted to know something about our great people and where we came from and how we kept on being folks all through slavery time.

My church and my folks got together and sent the old lady to Spain and Morocco. Everywhere I went I saw some of us. There was colored everywhere I set my foot. Now, I couldn't understand them, but I was looking at them and if I'm black, and we both know I am, there is nothing else in God's world for them to be but black too. There was all kinds of colors! Some of them were white like the people that call themselves white over here. Some of them looked mighty Wakefield. Now, I saw that in Spain and I saw that in Africa. In Morocco some of those people could have been your brother or mine. Some of them had kinky hair and some of them had straight hair and some had wavy hair. Some of them looked like Jews and Italians, but there was all kinds of folks. Most of those people looked like what we used to call munglas. I have read that the Moroccans are white and I know that Americans are supposed to be white, but it looks to me like they are just as mixed up as we are over here. Half of these whitefolks I see out here look like they are passing[2] to me. That's the same way it is in Cuba and Puerto Rico. I have seen those countries and I know that most of those people are colored, just like most of those people in Morocco. I'm telling you what I saw, not what somebody told me. A lot of these people from those foreign countries may not speak English, but you can look at them and see that they are Aun' Hagi's[3] children. A lot of them don't want to admit their color because they are afraid that these whitefolks over here would give them a hard time. Now, they are right about that.

I have been a cook and a maid and a housekeeper, and I have worked in hospitals. I still do every now and then, but I was in the hospital not long ago and I met this doctor that they said was an Arab. Well, he was darker than many people in my own family. I was proud to see one of the race better hisself. But, you know, that devil didn't want to hear a thing about his color! They had a lot of doctors from India and Jordan working there too. Now, a lot of the colored people didn't want to have anything to do with them because they said if they will pass like that, maybe they are not really doctors, either. I know folks that pass, but these doctors were just plain fools about it! I know people who pass to get a job that they should be able to get anyway, but they don't try to act like them all the time. There was this young Iraqian doctor there and he was darker than me, but he sure did everything he

could think of and then some to show how white he was supposed to be. I don't trust anybody who would deny their color like that. And if Rosa Wakefield can't put her trust in you, you will never get your hands on her blood pressure or her diabetes or anything else!   [1980]

Terms

1. NIGERIAN HAUSA: Black people of Niger and northern Nigeria.
2. PASSING: A reference to light-skinned Blacks trying to "pass" as Whites.
3. AUNT HAGI: A reference to the biblical figure Hagar, the servant of Sarah and Abraham and mother of Abraham's son, Ishmael.

Understanding the Reading

1. What values does Rosa Wakefield hold?
2. What characteristics does she think differentiate "blackfolks" from "whitefolks"?
3. Explain her beliefs about racial identity.
4. What questions do you think Gwaltney posed to elicit Wakefield's responses?

Suggestions for Responding

1. What advice do you think Rosa Wakefield might give to any one of the preceding writers?
2. If you were collecting oral histories from your family or your community, what kinds of information would you want to focus on? In other words, what characteristics and values do you expect to identify? What questions would you ask to obtain that information? ◆

8

I Am a Racially Profiling Doctor

SALLY SATEL

In practicing medicine, I am not colorblind. I always take note of my patient's race. So do many of my colleagues. We do it because certain diseases and treatment responses cluster by ethnicity. Recognizing these patterns can help us diagnose disease more efficiently and prescribe medications more effectively. When it comes to practicing medicine, stereotyping often works.

But to a growing number of critics, this statement is viewed as a shocking admission of prejudice. After all, shouldn't all patients be treated equally, regardless of the color of their skin? The controversy came to a boil last May in The New England Journal of Medicine. The journal published a study revealing that enalapril, a standard treatment for chronic heart failure, was less helpful to blacks than to whites. Researchers found that significantly more black patients treated with enalapril ended up hospitalized. A companion study examined carvedilol, a beta blocker; the results indicated that the drug was equally beneficial to both races.

These clinically important studies were accompanied, however, by an essay titled "Racial Profiling in Medical Research." Robert S. Schwartz, a deputy editor at the journal, wrote that prescribing medication by taking race into account was a form of "race-based medicine" that was both morally and scientifically wrong. "Race is not only imprecise but also of no proven value in treating an individual patient," Schwartz wrote. "Tax-supported trolling . . . to find racial distinctions in human biology must end."

Responding to Schwartz's essay in The Chronicle of Higher Education, other doctors voiced their support. "It's not valid science," charged Richard S. Cooper, a hypertension expert at Loyola Medical School. "I challenge any member of our species to show where this kind of analysis has come up with something useful."

But the enalapril researchers were doing something useful. Their study informed thousands of doctors that, when it came to their black patients, one drug was more likely to be effective than another. The study may have saved some lives. What's more useful than that?

Almost every day at the Washington drug clinic where I work as a psychiatrist, race plays a useful diagnostic role. When I prescribe Prozac to a patient who is African-American, I start at a lower dose, 5 or 10 milligrams instead of the usual 10-to-20 milligram dose. I do this in part because clinical experience and pharmacological research show that blacks metabolize antidepressants more slowly than Caucasians and Asians. As a result, levels of the medication can build up and make side effects more likely. To be sure, not every African-American is a slow metabolizer of antidepressants; only 40 percent are. But the risk of provoking side effects like nausea, insomnia or fuzzy-headedness in a depressed person—someone already terribly demoralized who may have been reluctant to take medication in the first place—is to worsen the patient's distress and increase the chances that he will flush the pills down the toilet. So I start all black patients with a lower dose, then take it from there.

In my drug-treatment clinic, where almost all of the patients use heroin by injection, a substantial number of them have hepatitis C, an infectious blood-borne virus that now accounts for 40 percent of all chronic liver disease. The standard treatment for active hepatitis C is an antiviral-drug combination of alpha interferon and ribavirin. But for some as yet undiscovered reason, African-Americans do not respond as well as whites to this regimen. In white patients, the double therapy reduces the amount of virus in the blood by over 90 percent after six months of treatment. In blacks, the reduction is only 50 percent. As a result, my black patients with hepatitis C must be given a considerably less reassuring prognosis than my white patients.

Without a doubt, there are many medical situations in which race is irrelevant. In an operation to repair a broken leg, for example, a patient's race doesn't matter. But there are countless situations in which the race factor should be considered. My colleague Ronald W. Dworkin, an anesthesiologist in a Baltimore-area hospital, takes race into account when performing one of his most important activities: intubation, the placement of a breathing tube down a patient's windpipe. During intubation, he says, black patients tend to salivate heavily, which can cause airway complications. As a precautionary measure, Dworkin gives many of his black patients a drying agent. "Not every black person fits this observation," he concedes, "but there is sufficient empirical evidence to make every anesthesiologist keep this danger in the back of his or her mind." The day I spoke with him, Dworkin attended a hysterectomy in a middle-aged Asian woman. "Asians tend to have a greater sensitivity to narcotics," he says, "so we always start with lower doses. They run the risk of apnea"—the cessation of breathing—"if we do not."

Could doctors make a diagnosis for and treat a patient properly if they did not know his race? "Most of the time," says Jerome P. Kassirer, a professor of medicine at Yale and Tufts. "But knowing that detail early on helps me make educated guesses more efficiently."

Kassirer, the former editor of The New England Journal of Medicine, is a renowned diagnostician. He is legendary among trainees for what he can tell about a case from just a few facts. He gave an example from a recent morning report, the daily session in which young doctors describe to senior physicians the most vexing cases admitted to the hospital the previous night. During one report, the resident began: "The patient is a 45-year-old Asian male who came to the emergency room complaining of 'feeling weak and wobbly in my legs' after drinking two bottles of beer." Kassirer stopped her right there. "Here's what I infer from that information," he said. "First, we know that sudden weakness can be caused by a low concentration of potassium in the blood, and we know that Asian males have an unusual propensity for a rare condition in which low potassium causes temporary paralysis. We know that these paralytic attacks are sometimes brought on by alcohol."

Of course, the patient could have been suffering from some other muscular or neurological disease, and Kassirer instructed the trainees to consider those as well. But in this case the patient's potassium was low, and the diagnosis was correct—and confirmed within 24 hours by simply observing the patient. Thanks to racial profiling, the Asian patient was spared an uncomfortable and costly work-up—not to mention the worry that he might have something like Lou Gehrig's disease.

"Rather than casting our net broadly, doctors quickly focus on a problem by recognizing patterns that have clinical significance," Kassirer says. "Typically, the clinician generates an initial hypothesis merely from a patient's age, sex, appearance, presenting complaints—and race."

All of these examples fly in the face of what we are increasingly told about race and biology:

namely, that the two have nothing to do with each other. When the preliminary sequence of the human genome was announced in June 2000, many felt the verdict was conclusive. Race, it was said, was an arbitrary, nefarious biological fiction. Scholars heralded the finding of the Human Genome Project that 99.9 percent of the human genetic complement is the same in everyone, regardless of race, as proof that race is biologically meaningless. Some prominent scientists said the same. J. Craig Venter, the geneticist whose company played a key role in mapping the human genome, proclaimed, "There is no basis in the genetic code for race."

What does it really mean, though, to say that 99.9 percent of our content is the same? In practical terms it means that the DNA of any two people will differ in one out of every 1,000 nucleotides, the building blocks of individual genes. With more than three billion nucleotides in the human genome, about three million nucleotides will differ among individuals. This is hardly a small change; after all, mutation of a single one can cause the gene within which it is embedded to produce an altered protein or enzyme. It may seem counterintuitive, but the 0.1 percent of human genetic variation is a medically meaningful fact.

Not surprisingly, many human genetic variations tend to cluster by racial groups—that is, by people whose ancestors came from a particular geographic region. Skin color itself is not what is at issue—it's the evolutionary history indicated by skin color. In Africa, for example, the genetic variant for sickle cell anemia cropped up at some point in the gene pool and was passed on to descendants; as a result, the disease is more common among blacks than whites. Similarly, Caucasians are far more likely to carry the gene mutations that cause multiple sclerosis and cystic fibrosis.

Admittedly, race is a rough marker. A black American may have dark skin—but her genes may well be a complex mix of ancestors from West Africa, Europe and Asia. No serious scientist, in fact, believes that genetically pure populations exist. Yet an imprecise clue is better than no clue at all.

Jay N. Cohn, a professor of medicine at the University of Minnesota, explains that skin color and other physical features can be a diagnostic surrogate for the genetic differences that influence disease and response to treatment. "Physical appearance, including skin color, is now the only way to distinguish populations for study," he says. "You'd have to use a blind-fold to keep a physician from paying attention to obvious differences that may and should influence diagnosis and treatment!" Lonnie Fuller, a professor emeritus at Morehouse School of Medicine, says: "Drugs can stay in the body longer when their metabolism in the liver is slower. We know this can vary by race, and doctors should keep it in mind."

Recognizing that our one-size-fits-all approach to medicine has serious flaws, some doctors are urging research into the development of racially targeted drugs. In March 2001, the Food and Drug Administration allowed the testing of a drug called BiDil in about 600 black subjects who will participate in the African-American Heart Failure Trial, the largest clinical trial ever to focus exclusively on African-Americans.

In previous studies including both white and black patients, BiDil provided a selective benefit for the black subjects. White subjects did no better on average than those given a placebo. The leading explanation for this disparity revolves around the molecule nitric oxide, a chemical messenger that helps regulate the constriction of blood vessels, an important mechanical dynamic in the control of blood pressure. High blood pressure contributes to and worsens heart failure because it makes the heart pump harder to overcome peripheral resistance in the arteries. BiDil acts by dilating blood vessels and replenishing local stores of nitric oxide. For unexplained reasons, blacks are more likely than whites to have nitric oxide insufficiency.

To be sure, a small percentage of blacks with high blood pressure do not have low nitric oxide activity. And the fact that BiDil's intended use relies on a crude predictor of drug response—"a poor man's clue" is how one scientist described race—is something its developers at the University of Minnesota School of Medicine readily acknowledge. Nevertheless, in the sometimes cloudy world of medicine, a poor man's clue is all you've got. Perhaps that's why members of the Congressional Black Caucus voiced support for the clinical trial. So did the Association of Black Cardiologists, which is helping recruit patients for the trial. B. Waine Kong, the organiza-

tion's head officer, put it simply: "It is in the name of science that we participate."

Doctors look forward to the day when they can, in good conscience, be colorblind. Researchers predict that it will eventually be common practice for doctors to generate a "genomic profile" of every patient—a precise analysis of a person's genetic makeup—so that decisions about therapies can be based on subtle characteristics of the patient's enzyme and receptor biology. At that point, racial profiling by doctors won't be necessary. Until then, however, group identity at least offers a starting point.

A high level of sensitivity about race is understandable in view of eugenics programs in early 20th-century America and ethnic cleansing abroad. The memory of the Tuskegee syphilis study, in which hundreds of rural blacks were never told they had the disease nor offered penicillin for it, still haunts the U.S. Public Health Service, the agency that conducted the study. Other scholars have expressed the worry that genetic differences among races could become the only explanation for the health disparities among them—allowing interest in examining social and economic factors to dwindle.

Indeed, the public seems to have embraced the idea of colorblind medicine. "In the last decade, many Americans have urged that the concept of race be abandoned, purged from our public discourse, rooted out of medicine and exiled from science," writes Troy Duster, a sociologist at N.Y.U.

But in this case, the public is wrong. As rough a biological classification as race may be, doctors must not be—blind to its clinical implications. So much of medicine is a guessing game—and race sometimes provides an invaluable clue. As citizens, we can celebrate our genetic similarity as evidence of our spiritual kinship. As doctors and patients, though, we must realize that it is not in patients' best interests to deny the reality of differences.   [2002]

Understanding the Reading

1. Why does the author racially profile her patients?
2. What do doctors say who criticize this practice?

3. Are there racial distinctions in human biology that a doctor should take into account?
4. When could racial profiling in medicine create a problem?

Suggestions for Responding

1. Research the Tuskegee Project and report on it.
2. Interview someone who says he or she has been racially profiled at the doctor's office or wishes he or she had been.
3. Research sickle cell anemia; find out if it is found only in Blacks.
4. Speak to a doctor about racial profiling; find out how or if this doctor uses race as an indicator for treatment. ✦

9

Are Doctors' Offices Places for Racial Profiling?

ARE RACE-BASED TREATMENTS UNETHICAL?

Sally Satel, MD, is proud to be a racially profiling doctor.

The practicing psychiatrist and fellow at the Washington, DC-based conservative think tank The American Enterprise Institute says it's important for clinicians to consider racial and ethnic factors when making diagnostic and treatment decisions for patients.

"Certain diseases and treatment responses cluster by ethnicity," she wrote in the May 5 issue of *The New York Times Magazine*.[1] "Recognizing these patterns can help us diagnose disease more efficiently and prescribe medications more effectively. When it comes to practicing medicine, stereotyping often works."

For example, clinical research and her own personal experience have shown her that African-American patients metabolize antidepressants more slowly than Caucasian and Asian patients do. If this happens, levels of the medication in the body can build over time and lead to side effects, such as insomnia, nausea, and confusion. Therefore, Satel frequently starts her black patients at a lower dose of antidepressants.

Admittedly, not all black people metabolize these medications slowly—only an estimated 40% do. But the likelihood is significant enough that she feels she should take this into consideration, she tells *Medical Ethics Advisor.* "If you were wrong to start the patient at a lower dose, you can simply raise the dose later."

This is preferable to initiating drug therapy that might cause side effects that may lead an already vulnerable patient to stop taking the medication altogether.

Satel is not alone in her approach. Other doctors agree that they have long considered racial and ethnic background as factors in making decisions based on their experience with certain groups of patients.

Now, clinical studies are beginning to examine how members of different ethnic groups respond to standard treatment regimens and whether these groups may be at higher risk for certain types of diseases.

A report in the May issue of the journal *Clinical Infectious Diseases* indicates Hispanic immigrants are at higher risk for infections that do not usually occur in the U.S.-born population. A recent study in the journal *Hepatology* reported on the higher prevalence of gall-bladder disease among American Indians, and a study in the June issue of *The American Journal of Clinical Nutrition* proposed a need for different body-mass index cutoffs in different racial and ethnic groups.

A pair of particularly controversial studies published in the May 2001 issue of the *New England Journal of Medicine* highlighted differences in response to certain heart medications observed between African-American and Caucasian men.

The first study, by Exner and colleagues, found that the drug enalapril was more effective in treating left-ventricular dysfunction in white patients than in black patients.[2] Another study in the same issue concluded that the drug carvedilol was equally effective in treating chronic heart disease in both white and black patients.[3]

But some doctors and researchers are criticizing such studies, claiming that their focus on linking treatment responses and risk factors to specific racial and ethnic groups is misleading and scientifically dangerous.

GENETICS, NOT RACE, IS THE KEY

"You have to bear in mind that, from a biological point of view, the definition of any race is arbitrary," says **Robert Schwartz,** MD, a deputy editor at the *New England Journal of Medicine,* who wrote an editorial commenting on the studies of racial differences in response to the heart medicines.

Genetic studies are showing what scientists have long believed—that there are no biologically distinct races of people, he says. Differences in response to treatment or risks for disease differ because of a person's genetic makeup.

People who are from one area of the world will tend to have similar genes and genetic mutations, he says. But, as world populations have intermingled it has become less likely that specific genetic mutations can be attributed to people of certain geographic origins.

"If you have an individual patient in your office, how do you know that patient has the gene that affects the metabolism of that drug?" Schwartz asks. "You can only guess. Just saying, 'Well, the patient is black and, therefore, I am not going to give him a beta-blocker' is, to me, not the way to practice medicine."

A recent study of the occurrence of genetic polymorphisms (gene mutations linked to specific traits) have found that of the five genes involved in metabolism, race was not an accurate predictor of the occurrence of the polymorphisms that made metabolism slower, he points out.

"The frequency of a polymorphism involving drug metabolism had the same frequency in Ethiopians as it did in Norwegians," he notes. "So that is why, from a biological point of view, we have to be very, very cautious."

The impetus behind many of these new studies is that for very many years, black people and members of other minority populations were not included in clinical research trials. So, information about effective treatments was largely determined by only studying one group of people, Schwartz admits.

But studies that now hope to remedy that situation risk making it worse by focusing on distinctions by racial groups or ethnic factors, which can lead to further stereotyping and stigmatization, he says.

The studies' real goal is to determine the environmental, cultural, and genetic factors that influence disease and response to treatment, so it would be better if researchers deliberately focused on these areas.

"Right now, we are on the edge of what many people are beginning to refer to as personalized therapy," he says. "You will be able to obtain accurate information on the likelihood of a response or no response from a single drop of blood, through DNA."

It's true that geographic ancestry and the currently identified racial groups are only rough markers for the genetic traits that may affect a person's response to treatment, but right now it is the best information available, and physicians would be remiss in ignoring it, argues Satel.

She does not advocate making a decision about a diagnosis or treatment based solely on a person's race or ethnicity, but says these factors, like so many others considered during a workup, must be considered.

"Diagnosing is a process of elimination," she explains. "You have to think of the likelihood of what is wrong, and you rule out with tests, typically. If that does not explain the pathology, you go on to the next potential diagnosis. The point is, you will get there eventually even if you do not know the person's race, but it is just a bit of information that might help you get there quicker."   [2002]

References

1. Satel S. I am a racially profiling doctor. *The New York Times Magazine.* May 5, 2002.
2. Exner DV, Dries DL, Domanski MJ, et al. Lesser response to angiostentin-converting enzyme inhibitor therapy in black as compared to white patients with left-ventricular dysfunction. *N Engl J Med* 2001; 344:1351–1357.
3. Yancy CW, Fowler MB, Colucci WS, et al. Race and the response to adrenergic blockade with carvedilol in patients with chronic heart failure. *N Engl J Med* 2001; 344:3558–3565.

Understanding the Reading

1. Why do some doctors think medical racial profiling is scientifically dangerous?

2. What is the difference between a person's race and a person's genetic makeup?
3. Why can geographic information about a person's ancestors be important when identifying and treating an illness?

Suggestions for Responding

1. Have a debate on the dangers or benefits of medical racial profiling, using this article and the preceding one, by Satel.
2. Research your family's medical history; find out whether certain illnesses are more common in the part of the world from which your family came. ✦

10

El Hilo Que Nos Une/ *The Thread That Binds Us: Becoming a Puerto Rican Woman*

CELIA ALVAREZ

My mother migrated to New York in the early 1950s during the period of rapid urbanization and industrialization concomitant with Operation Bootstrap[1] on the Island. She was also a seamstress. She married soon after her arrival and subsequently had the three of us, one right after the other.

Raised in the projects of downtown Brooklyn near the Brooklyn Navy Yard I often wondered: What were we doing here? How did we get here? And why? Nobody said too much, however; no one wanted to talk about the poverty and pain, the family truces and secrets which clouded the tremendous upheaval from Ponce[2] to San Juan to New York.

I grew up speaking Spanish, dancing *la pachanga, merengue,* and *mambo,* eating *arroz con habichuelas* and drinking *malta y café.* I was smart, and learned to play the chords of the bureaucratic machinery of housing, education, and welfare very well at a very young age. I translated for everyone—my mother, her friends, our neighbors, as well as my teachers. My parents kept us close to home and it was my responsibility to keep my brother and sister in tow.

It was hard to understand it all, to try to make sense of who I was as a Puerto Rican in New York, so I read everything I could get my hands on; watched the games the government would play between Afro-Americans and Puerto Ricans with social service monies; heard the poverty pimps tell their lies; watched the kids die of dope or heard about them getting killed down elevator chutes in the middle of a burglary; noted the high over-priced tags on old food being sold in the only supermarket in the neighborhood; knew of kids being raped and thrown off the roof. And I asked, "Why?"

The socially active local parish church became my refuge. It was there that I began to make connections with the poor whites, Afro-Americans, and Asians in my community, and said there had to be a better way for us all. I participated in a variety of activities including youth programs, the local food coop, and newsletter, which basically involved me in community organizing, although I didn't know you called it grassroots work then. I got swept up by the energy of the civil rights movement and wanted to go to the march on Washington[3] but my mother said, "No!" She worried about me—didn't like me wearing my Martin Luther King button or getting involved in politics. She was afraid I would get hurt. I always liked being out on the street talking to people, however, and she knew from way back that I was not destined to stay inside.

Tensions flourished when I turned fourteen and told my parents I was going out with a Puerto Rican boy in the neighborhood. Unfortunately, "boyfriend" in America and *novio* in Puerto Rico did not translate to mean the same thing. In 1968 I was chaperoned and followed by my father wherever I went because of that grave mistake. Their biggest fear? That I would get pregnant. They even threatened to send me to Puerto Rico. I had it all planned out that I would run away and stay with my cousin. She was the first to move out and get her own place. At least we could keep each other company. It never happened but we've been close ever since.

During this same period I started high school in a predominantly white school in the heart of Flatbush.[4] I found myself desegregating the Catholic school system, one of five or six *latinas* and Afro-Americans in my class. I was known as one of the girls from the ghetto downtown and was constantly called upon to defend my race. One day it went too far. Someone said my father didn't work and that their parents supported my coming to their school. I "went off"! You just didn't talk about my family!

I never told my parents about the racist slurs—never had the heart. They were breaking their backs to send me to school; my father kept his job at a city hospital for thirty years and took on a second job at the docks. We would all go to help him clean offices at night and on weekends after our day outings together. My mother went back to work in a paper factory down the street. Prior to that, she had taken care of the children of women in the neighborhood who worked. I've also worked since about the time I was fourteen.

Anyway, I graduated high school with honors. I had every intention of going to college—I thought it would give me the credentials to be in a position to act on the miseducation that I saw we were getting. Of course I needed money to go, so I went to talk to my guidance counselor. She always prided herself in being able to say a few words in Spanish . . . her way of "relating." I inquired about government grants programs as well as anything else that she could tell me about. All she could say to me was, "Well, you're not the only one who needs money to go to school, dear."

No thanks to her, I managed to get to college with the help of ASPIRA.[5] I marched over to their office on 14th Street—we didn't have a club in our school, there were too few of us—and presented myself to one of the counselors there. I'll always be grateful that he took me under his wing despite the fact he had an overbooked case load. I applied to about ten schools, got into most of them and decided to go to a new institution in New England that broke away from the traditional, predetermined academic program and was primarily based on a mentoring system between student and teacher.

So I left home and landed in a progressive liberal arts college which looked more like a country club than anything else. It was so quiet I had to study with my radio blasting to concentrate. Ironically, it was there that I found my first Afro-American and Puerto Rican teachers. I was relieved to know someone who understood the reference points in my life without my having to

explain. After pursuing some studies on Puerto Rico and the Caribbean—for the only formal mention of Puerto Rico in all my schooling up to that point had been in a geography class in which we had discussed its mineral resources—I studied questions of language planning, bilingualism and education, language, culture, and identity. I thought that knowledge of these areas would be useful to the Puerto Rican community. I always made it a point to keep my foot in both the community and academe. I have struggled to stay integrated as a human being despite the efforts of academic institutions to make me over or deny my existence.

To make a long story short, I went on to graduate school where I fought to keep my sanity and sense of self-worth in the midst of the racist sentiment that permeated my department, telling me in a variety of ways that I should not be there, let alone survive my course of study. If one were to look at their track record with regard to women of color one would see how they manage to justify their own position; for to survive requires that we deny who we are, from where we come, and where we are going as a people. I was told that because I had "made it" to such an elitist institution, I obviously was no longer a member of my community. I was admonished not to study the reality of Puerto Ricans because somehow I would be "getting over" and not doing valid research. Ironically, given my gender, class background, nationality, and race, I was as marginalized as ever in that setting.

Which brings me back to our oral history project. Listening to these women's stories has served as a tremendous source of inspiration and validation of my own experience as a Puerto Rican woman. They captured and brought back to life the struggles of my own socialization during the 1960s. Though born in New York, I grappled with many of the same social issues and problems as Flor, Lucila, and Eulalia. However, it was within the context of the educational opportunities historically afforded me through the civil rights movement, in conjunction with my own parents' determination, that I was able to actualize myself in higher education and be in a position to help define this project. This oral history project enabled me to integrate all the different parts of myself—my skills as an intellectual, organizer, and nurturer, as well as my experience as a working-class Puerto Rican woman.

Through the public events linked to our research, I have been able to bring this experience back home: *to my own neighborhood* in Brooklyn, which I came to find out was one of the earlier Puerto Rican settlements in New York; and *to my mother* who came to our event on Puerto Rican garment workers and finally understood what it was I did at the university and how it was not a rejection but a continuation of her legacy to me. Our relationship qualitatively changed after that event: there was more honesty between us; we spoke woman to woman. And it is because of this convergence of historical and personal circumstances that I am sharing this collective experience with you, the reader.

Beyond its impact on me individually, I believe the oral history process in which we have been engaged has provided a space for the collective experience and voice of Puerto Rican working women to be heard. For this oral history project was a process of "coming out"—not just for women of our mothers' or grandmothers' generations but for ourselves as well. For how do we see ourselves if we are invisible, if our most courageous acts as a people go unrecognized? In order to create an authentic connection with others we must first deal with the sources of our own oppression; we must break the silence of our invisibility; but we must speak in our own voice, first to ourselves and then to each other. For in moving beyond our own individual lives we can come to appreciate the connections between us, the continuity and the change, and dispel the fears which keep us apart.

This is from where we come. We respect the dignity of our people despite the devastation of economic deprivation, racial hostility, and sexual repression. We respect the struggles of the women who have preceded us for they set the groundwork upon which we will define our own destinies, for ourselves, on our own terms, in our collective struggle to be free from economic, racial and national oppression.   [1988]

Terms

1. OPERATION BOOTSTRAP: A program of tax credits and other incentives designed to encourage Puerto Rican economic development.

2. PONCE: A city in Puerto Rico; San Juan is the capital of Puerto Rico.
3. MARCH ON WASHINGTON: A 1963 civil rights demonstration in Washington, DC.
4. FLATBUSH: A neighborhood in Brooklyn.
5. ASPIRA: An organization that encourages and helps minority students obtain a college education.

Understanding the Reading

1. What difficulties did Alvarez have fitting into college?
2. What benefits did she get from her college studies?
3. What does Alvarez mean when she says that "to survive requires that we deny who we are"? Why is it required?
4. How does she feel she was "marginalized"?
5. What does she bring together as a result of her graduate work?

Suggestions for Responding

1. What have you done, or what would you like to do, to come to a fuller understanding and appreciation of one of your parents? What difference did it or would it make in your relationship?
2. Alvarez is trying to answer the question, "How do we see ourselves if we are invisible?" What might or should be done to eliminate this sense of invisibility experienced by members of some groups, or is it a societal problem at all? ✦

11

In Search of Bruce Lee's Grave

SHANLON WU

It's Saturday morning in Seattle, and I am driving to visit Bruce Lee's grave.[1] I have been in the city for only a couple of weeks and so drive two blocks past the cemetery before realizing that I've passed it. I double back and turn through the large wrought-iron gate, past a sign that reads: "Open to 9 P.M. or dusk, whichever comes first."

It's a sprawling cemetery, with winding roads leading in all directions. I feel silly trying to find his grave with no guidance. I think that my search for his grave is similar to my search for Asian heroes in America.

I was born in 1959, an Asian-American in Westchester County, N.Y. During my childhood there were no Asian sports stars. On television, I can recall only that most pathetic of Asian characters, Hop Sing, the Cartwright family houseboy on "Bonanza."[2] But in my adolescence there was Bruce.

I was 14 years old when I first saw "Enter the Dragon," the granddaddy of martial-arts movies. Bruce had died suddenly at the age of 32 of cerebral edema, an excess of fluid in the brain, just weeks before the release of the film. Between the ages of 14 and 17, I saw "Enter the Dragon" 22 times before I stopped counting. During those years I collected Bruce Lee posters, putting them up at all angles in my bedroom. I took up Chinese martial arts and spent hours comparing my physique with his.

I learned all I could about Bruce: that he had married a Caucasian, Linda; that he had sparred with Kareem Abdul-Jabbar;[3] that he was a buddy of Steve McQueen and James Coburn, both of whom were his pallbearers.

My parents, who immigrated to America and had become professors at Hunter College, tolerated my behavior, but seemed puzzled at my admiration of an "entertainer." My father jokingly tried to compare my obsession with Bruce to his boyhood worship of Chinese folk-tale heroes.

"I read them just like you read American comic books," he said.

But my father's heroes could not be mine; they came from an ancient literary tradition, not comic books. He and my mother had grown up in a land where they belonged to the majority. I could not adopt their childhood and they were wise enough not to impose it upon me.

Although I never again experienced the kind of blind hero worship I felt for Bruce, my need to find heroes remained strong.

In college, I discovered the men of the 442d Regimental Combat Team, a United States Army all-Japanese unit in World War II. Allowed to fight only against Europeans, they suffered heavy casualties while their families were put in internment camps. Their motto was "Go for Broke."

I saw them as Asians in a Homeric epic, the protagonists of a Shakespearean tragedy; I knew no Eastern myths to infuse them with. They embodied my own need to prove myself in the Caucasian world. I imagined how their American-born flesh and muscle must have resembled mine: epicanthic folds[4] set in strong faces nourished on milk and beef. I thought how much they had proved where there was so little to prove.

After college, I competed as an amateur boxer in an attempt to find my self-image in the ring. It didn't work. My fighting was only an attempt to copy Bruce's movies. What I needed was instruction on how to live. I quit boxing after a year and went to law school.

I was an anomaly there: a would-be Asian litigator. I had always liked to argue and found I liked doing it in front of people even more. When I won the first-year moot court competition in law school, I asked an Asian classmate if he thought I was the first Asian to win. He laughed and told me I was probably the only Asian to even compete.

The law-firm interviewers always seemed surprised that I wanted to litigate.

"Aren't you interested in Pacific Rim trade?" they asked.

"My Chinese isn't good enough," I quipped.

My pat response seemed to please them. It certainly pleased me. I thought I'd found a place of my own—a place where the law would insulate me from the pressure of defining my Asian maleness. I sensed the possibility of merely being myself.

But the pressure reasserted itself. One morning, the year after graduating from law school, I read the obituary of Gen. Minoru Genda—the man who planned the Pearl Harbor attack. I'd never heard of him and had assumed that whoever did that planning was long since dead. But the general had been alive all those years—rising at 4 every morning to do his exercises and retiring every night by 8. An advocate of animal rights, the obituary said.

I found myself drawn to the general's life despite his association with the Axis powers. He seemed a forthright, graceful man who died unhumbled. The same paper carried a front-page story about Congress's failure to pay the Japanese-American internees their promised reparation[5] money. The general, at least, had not died waiting for reparations.

I was surprised and frightened by my admiration for General Genda, by my still-strong hunger for images of powerful Asian men. That hunger was my vulnerability manifested, a reminder of my lack of place.

The hunger is eased this gray morning in Seattle. After asking directions from a policeman—Japanese—I easily locate Bruce's grave. The headstone is red granite with a small picture etched into it. The picture is very Hollywood—Bruce wears dark glasses—and I think the calligraphy looks a bit sloppy. Two tourists stop but leave quickly after glancing at me.

I realize I am crying. Bruce's grave seems very small in comparison to his place in my boyhood. So small in comparison to my need for heroes. Seeing his grave, I understand how large the hole in my life has been, and how desperately I'd sought to fill it.

I had sought an Asian hero to emulate. But none of my choices quite fit me. Their lives were defined through heroic tasks—they had villains to defeat and wars to fight—while my life seemed merely a struggle to define myself.

But now I see how that very struggle has defined me. I must be my own hero even as I learn to treasure those who have gone before.

I have had my powerful Asian male images: Bruce, the men of the 442d and General Genda; I may yet discover others. Their lives beckon like fireflies on a moonless night, and I know that they—like me—may have been flawed by foolhardiness and even cruelty. Still, their lives were real. They were not houseboys on "Bonanza."

[1990]

Terms

1. BRUCE LEE: A Chinese American movie star skilled in the martial arts.
2. *BONANZA*: A television series about a family of ranchers.
3. KAREEM ABDUL-JABBAR: A professional basketball star; Steve McQueen and James Coburn were white movie stars who played very physical roles.
4. EPICANTHIC FOLD: A fold of skin on the upper eyelid that tends to cover the inner corner of the eye.

5. REPARATION: Payment to Japanese Americans to compensate them for internment during World War II.

Understanding the Reading

1. Why couldn't Wu identify with his father's heroes?
2. What did the heroes Wu identified with have in common?
3. What does Wu mean when he says that the struggle for heroes "defined me"?

Suggestions for Responding

1. What "heroes" did you identify with as you grew up? Did they in any way influence your sense of your ethnic identity? If so, how? If not, why not?
2. Both Wu and Alvarez come to grips with their identity. Explain the similarities and differences in their experiences. ◆

12

Remembering My Grandmother, Remembering Lebanon

THERESE SALIBA

My grandmother's passport is written in French. When she took to traveling, she was 24, and Lebanon and Syria were under French mandate. The year was *il neuf cent vingt et un,* 1921. This document, issued by the Haut Commissariat de la République Française in Beirut, grants Mlle. Victoria Brahim Simon, born in Douma, Lebanon (*Liban*), in 1897, permission to go to Los Angeles, California, U.S.A. It describes the details of her anatomy: "age—24, size—160 cm, health—good, hair—chestnut, eyebrows—chestnut, eyes—green, forehead—ordinary, complexion—white."

But her 1929 U.S. naturalization papers state that she is 30 years old, two years younger than she would be according to her passport. The documents say that her complexion, hair, and eyes are now brown, dark brown even. Maybe, I think, this is part of the process of naturalization: the loss of years, the gaining in darkness, the irony of a procedure that as it naturalizes an alien, making her "as if a native," defines her as darker, as Other. The loss of years may have been an act of self-invention, a little lie on my grandmother's part, but the supposed darkness of her complexion can only be attributed to the monochromatic vision of an immigration clerk. As long as I knew my grandmother, her skin was fair and her eyes were green, though in later years they were clouded by age.

She came from the Old Country, a place, I imagined, where everything was dusty and worn, so she was old to me, and her ancient air was enchanting. Hers were an enduring people from a nomadic tribe who some generations ago had settled on fertile hillsides in the mountains north of Beirut. It was a comfortable place in peacetime, I was told, but the city had known little peace for longer than my grandmother could remember. Between the two great wars, fleeing famine and plague, she and her brothers ventured to the New World.

My grandmother spoke little of her old way of life, but it bled through into everything she did. Her speech was thick and heavy, scattered with unfamiliar words; her food, seasoned with foreign flavors. Her cooking was a source of her pride and was revealed in the dimensions of her round body. Her full face rested atop her shoulders, her jowls jiggling with delight as she uttered her favorite words, "*Suhtein! Suhtein!*" ("Eat! Eat!"). Her nose was large and bulbous, spreading from cheek to cheek with a slight indentation at the tip. In keeping with Arabic tradition, I called her "*Sittee,*" thinking it was her name, but I later learned that it meant "grandmother" in that foreign tongue she so often spoke.

"Sittee, I hope my nose isn't as big as yours when I get old," I giggled.

"Hmph! Well, when you stop growing, your nose doesn't, and when you've lived as long as I have, you end up with this." She chuckled, touching the tip of her nose with her red-painted fingernail.

Sittee had spent most of her life eluding years and the fragmented history of her homeland. She took from time freely, handfuls of years she felt had been stolen from her. She disguised her age as best she could, dyeing her hair rusty red, painting her lips with ruby gloss. In my eyes, she was as ancient as the land of her birth.

On weekdays I lived in an American world. But on weekends, I lived in a world of foreign foods, strange language, incense, ritual—the bazaar and the bizarre. Sittee embodied this difference. She was a widow, a bitter woman who maintained notions of her nobility from her Lebanese village even as she rolled grape leaves in the tiny kitchen of her Hollywood apartment. When she came to visit, she came bearing *fistu* (pistachio nuts), pomegranates, *kibbee* (pressed lamb), Syrian bread, and holy bread. There was something sacred and human in this culture that let you take holy bread home, bread that was thick and full, unlike the stale wafers of the Roman Catholic church where my mother often took us on Sunday mornings. I looked forward to the monthly bazaars at the Orthodox church where I could wander from table to table, tasting honeyed pastries and trying on bracelets and bangles, tightly holding my grandmother's hand. "*Ya 'albee inte,*" she would say to me, as she spread her fingers across my chest. "You are my heart."

If a woman could be a land, then Sittee was Lebanon to me. If a person could be colonized as a country, then Sittee still bore the scars of French colonization. Once while just learning to read, I explored the relics in her apartment— pointed gold slippers with braided straps, chiseled brass plates, pastel-colored glass trays holding *fistu*—and found a stash of letters scrawled with words I couldn't recognize. I pressed the thin paper to my nose. Everything, when held close, smelled of lemon jasmine and Jean Naté. Sittee saw me, pried the letters from my hands, and began reading aloud in a strange, melodic sound that I knew was not Arabic. I stood staring up at her mouth, the ruby lipstick faded from the edges of her lips, which formed round "o"s and purring "r"s. She looked down at me and drew me to her. "French," she said. "Isn't it a beauuuu-ti-ful language?" I nodded. "I learned it in school," she said, "and when you are old enough, you must study French, too." Eventually, I did. And though she never told me to learn Arabic, I studied that as well, but I never learned to speak it as fluently.

Years later at a bookstore, I heard Lebanese writer Etel Adnan explain how the nuns at the

French colonial schools told the students that they must not speak Arabic, that it was an irrational, illogical language, and that French alone was the language of rational thought. I'm not sure if Sittee believed this. But like so many of the Lebanese who chose to think of themselves as more European than Arab, tracing their descendants to the ancient Phoenicians and the wonders of the conqueror rather than the conquered, Sittee seemed to relish excessively the French language and Jean Naté perfume.

The perfume was from France, the lemon jasmine was from Lebanon, and as Sittee stood over me in the kitchen while I washed the green beans, her fragrance swam around me in the steam from the chicken boiling on the stove. The loose skin on her upper arms jiggled as she kneaded dough, and then rolled it out before my sister and me. We stood with glasses in hand arguing over who would get to cut the round forms for the meat pies, and who would fill the forms with lamb and pine nuts, then fold the edges up and press them into perfect triangles. As I was ten and my sister only eight, I would have won, had Sittee not insisted that we share the tasks. And while the meat pies baked, Sittee stuffed *koosah* (zucchini) with lamb and rice while my sister cut tomatoes for tabbouleh, and I chewed on the pine nuts spilled across the kitchen counter. Sittee never told me I would ruin my appetite—this was all part of the process of tasting and testing. In Arabic tradition, it is said that you eat as much as you love the cook. Every seed, every appetizer, counted as part of this love, and we always ate well.

As we stood in the kitchen, I asked Sittee, "Was Lebanon beautiful?"

"*Yeeee!*" she said, lapsing into memories and ramblings in Arabic, the only language that could express her country's beauty. Every time I wanted to experience Lebanon, she lapsed into sounds I could not decipher, as if a country cannot be expressed in any other language but the one that is native to it. It didn't seem to matter to Sittee that I missed the details of her yearnings, but I did understand that this country was beautiful—not in the way the French language was beautiful, but in the way a lone cedar growing out of jagged rock is beautiful. Sittee's clouded eyes watered as she spoke of Lebanon. Something awful, some great apocalypse had destroyed her country. But the way she described the cedars and their dark branches in the evening breeze from the veranda of her mountain villa, I thought surely our family was among the ancient Egyptian pharaohs. We had lost much in coming to this country, but I imagined that Cedars Sinai hospital, which stood in the heart of Los Angeles, was a modest commemoration of my family and the cedar trees that brought Sittee to tears.

When Sittee's sister Geneviève came to visit, her burnt leather face told once again how Lebanon made everything old. I had never before seen a face so creviced and dried to that prune-like quality of things left too long in the sun. Geneviève, though several years younger than Sittee, looked like her mother; it was clear that they inhabited vastly different worlds. Geneviève still lived in Douma, but moved between Lebanon and Paris when the civil war got troublesome. She had ten children, and when one of her grown sons in Beirut was shot in the head and killed while crossing the street to buy some milk, she came to visit her sister in Los Angeles. But she would return again to Douma. The root of "Douma" in Arabic means persistence, continuity, perseverance. They were the three best words I could find to define the women in our family, as Sittee and Geneviève sat on the couch in the evenings, telling stories in Arabic and running green thread through their leathered fingers, around crochet hooks, the half-made blankets falling over their knees.

Saliba, my grandfather's name, comes from the Orthodox tradition and means "bearers of the cross," a distinctly Christian name. My grandfather was from Bhetgreen, a not so-distant mountain village to the south of Douma, and I imagine my grandparents looked on similar cedar trees in the dry evenings, rustling with cicadas' wings. They met in the U.S., after an exchange of photos. Sittee was almost 40 by the time she married.

I knew my grandfather only in pictures that Sittee kept by her bedside or stored away in old shoe boxes. But by the way Sittee spoke of him, with a mixture of adoration and loss, I knew she resented the loneliness his early death had brought her. Sittee said she had never remarried because she did not want to give up the Saliba name. When she said this, she pressed her folded hands to her heart and wove long stories about my great-grandfather Saliba who was mayor of the village. During the plague, he went about burying the dead, until he too caught the disease and died. Another Saliba had been an archbishop; another had been a famous doctor who invented a cure for a disease I couldn't pronounce. These tales are all written in a book of family history; its introduction says, "History is only biography on a larger and more exhaustive scale." After tracing the Saliba name all the way from the fifth century B.C.E., the book ends: "Samuel, the fifth son of Moses, begat Ronald [my father] and Gilbert. The said Samuel died in California in 1949." The story tells only the history of men.

I knew Sittee's history only in the confused and convoluted ways of a child. By the time I was old enough to decipher the language of her movements—when I couldn't understand her speech—I was a teenager. By that time, I had learned from television that Arab men were either greedy sheikhs or terrorists, and the women were all veiled and silent. I wanted to forget my Arabness and to be like everyone else, so I didn't have much time for Sittee anymore. Besides, we had moved to Seattle, and our Saturday afternoons together diminished to brief visits in summertime.

Sittee died when I was 20. I was at college when I heard she was sick, and I drove 1,000 miles to see her. Her air of antiquity had decayed. Her gray skin hung loosely. The red dye gone, her white wisps of hair faded into the colorless sheets. I sat beside her for hours, clinging to her withered hand as she moved between wakefulness and sleep, between Los Angeles and Lebanon, and I spun remembrances of Saturday afternoons with her, as if my talk could keep her with me. And as if in the kitchen ten years earlier, I asked, "What was Lebanon like?"

But even Sittee's Arabic lay silent within her as some memory floated by her clouded vision. I wondered what she saw in her faraway thoughts—the cedar branches in the evening wind, her mother kneading dough in the kitchen, mountains rising up out of the Mediterranean on summer days at the beach.

At last she spoke. "Your life isn't worth anything," she confessed to me. "Life isn't worth a thing."

Although I tell this story over and over again, I still don't fully understand Sittee's last words to me. When I told my brother, he was sure she was referring to our worth as women, because Arab culture rides the value of masculinity with reckless bravado, and he thought that even Sittee had bought into it. (He should know, since he was the sole male grandchild and the recipient of all these benefits—as a boy, coffee cans full of pistachio nuts, boxes of color-coated almonds, and in later years, thousands of dollars.) But I find his interpretation too simple, because Sittee was a strong woman and not likely to be beaten down because of her gender, no matter what tradition said. Because Arab culture is deeply rooted in the family and grows with the sustenance of our grandmothers, I knew my life intertwined with Sittee's in ways I was just beginning to understand. Still, I think for her, her final words convey the history of her slow accumulation of loss—of homeland, of husband, of heart.

Sittee trusted in the promise of America. She believed what she read in the morning paper as she ate sour yogurt. She evoked the nobility of her lineage to ease her sense of displacement. Yet, as I later came to understand, it was not her Arabness that gave her pride. To her, French was beautiful and red hair and white skin were beautiful; she always told me to stay out of the sun because my olive skin had grown as dark as a coffee bean. The Palestinians, she said, had destroyed her homeland.

As a child, I believed all her stories. But as an adult, I learned that the situation was far more complicated. I read that Britain and France had taken control of and carved up the Middle East, then exploited Lebanon's religious and class divisions. Sittee herself belonged to the Christian elite who aligned themselves with the West against the Arab Muslims. She blamed the Palestinians, who had been driven from their homeland by Israel. And those Western countries Sittee trusted so much, including the U.S., had a powerful hand in the civil war that ripped her country into shredded memories.

When I got my first job teaching high school in the inner city, I went shopping for several new outfits to wear. When I returned home, I spread them out before my father. He looked up at me over the top of his wire-rimmed glasses and said, "You're young. What do you want to wear all these dark clothes for? You'll look like those old ladies from the Old Country."

I gathered up the clothes and stood before my father, thinking of my aunts and great-aunts who sat in Sittee's kitchen, rolling grape leaves as their Arabic bounced across the table, their fingers as busy as their mouths. Their dark clothes had not struck me then, but now I think perhaps I inherited a history of mourning.

But I have also inherited a history of strength and perseverance. For in ironic ways, Sittee passed on to me a lasting pride in the same Arab heritage she herself had often tried to deny.

Sittee appears to me in dreams now, standing beneath a lamppost at night, her shadow spreading up the stairs of my apartment building. I walk down toward her, calling her name. She motions me to follow, and together we glide along the sidewalk, my fingers reaching for the fringes of her crocheted shawl fluttering in the night wind. She is taking me somewhere, I don't know where. As we wind our way through the deserted alleyways of the bazaar, past tables of jewelry, perfume, and ceramics, past shops without vendors, I reach for her hand and we stand together beneath the domed archway of the night, speaking Arabic, her language I have come to know.   [1994]

Understanding the Reading

1. Why do you think the descriptions on Sittee's passport and her naturalization papers differed?
2. What Lebanese cultural features does Saliba emphasize, and why do you think she highlights them?
3. Why do you think Sittee lapses into Arabic when she describes Lebanon?
4. What do you think Sittee's last words, "Life isn't worth a thing," mean?
5. What do you learn about the complexities of Lebanese history in this selection?

Suggestions for Responding

1. If you have a family member (or family friend) who grew up in a different culture, write a remembrance of that person and the unique cultural features that you are particularly fond of.
2. What does this selection reveal about Lebanese culture that especially interests you? Explain why. ✦

13

American Dreamer

BHARATI MUKHERJEE

The United States exists as a sovereign nation; "America," in contrast, exists as a myth of democracy and equal opportunity to live by, or as an ideal goal to reach.

I am a naturalized U.S. citizen, which means that, unlike native-born citizens, I had to prove to the U.S. government that I merited citizenship. What I didn't have to disclose was that I desired "America," which to me is the stage for the drama of self-transformation.

I was born in Calcutta and first came to the United States—to Iowa City, to be precise—on a summer evening in 1961. I flew into a small airport surrounded by cornfields and pastures, ready to carry out the two commands my father had written out for me the night before I left Calcutta: Spend two years studying creative writing at the Iowa Writers' Workshop, then come back home and marry the bridegroom he selected for me from our caste and class.

In traditional Hindu families like ours, men provided and women were provided for. My father was a patriarch and I a pliant daughter. The neighborhood I'd grown up in was homogeneously Hindu, Bengali-speaking, and middle-class. I didn't expect myself to ever disobey or disappoint my father by setting my own goals and taking charge of my future.

When I landed in Iowa 35 years ago, I found myself in a society in which almost everyone was Christian, white, and moderately well-off. In the women's dormitory I lived in my first year, apart from six international graduate students (all of us were from Asia and considered "exotic"), the only non-Christian was Jewish, and the only nonwhite an African-American from Georgia. I didn't anticipate then, that over the next 35 years, the Iowa population would become so diverse that it would have 6,931 children from non-English-speaking homes registered as students in its schools, nor that Iowans would be in the grip of a cultural crisis in which resentment against immigrants, particularly refugees from Vietnam, Sudan, and Bosnia, as well as unskilled Spanish-speaking workers, would become politicized enough to cause the Immigration and Naturalization Service to open an "enforcement" office in Cedar Rapids in October for the tracking and deporting of undocumented aliens.

In Calcutta in the '50s, I heard no talk of "identity crisis"—communal or individual. The concept itself—of a person not knowing who he or she is—was unimaginable in our hierarchical, classification-obsessed society. One's identity was fixed, derived from religion, caste, patrimony, and mother tongue. A Hindu Indian's last name announced his or her forefathers' caste and place of origin. A Mukherjee could *only* be a Brahmin from Bengal. Hindu tradition forbade intercaste, interlanguage, interethnic marriages. Bengali tradition even discouraged emigration: To remove oneself from Bengal was to dilute true culture.

Until the age of 8, I lived in a house crowded with 40 or 50 relatives. My identity was viscerally connected with ancestral soil and genealogy. I was who I was because I was Dr. Sudhir Lal Mukherjee's daughter, because I was a Hindu Brahmin, because I was Bengali-speaking, and because my *desh*—the Bengali word for homeland—was an East Bengal village called Faridpur.

The University of Iowa classroom was my first experience of coeducation. And after not too long, I fell in love with a fellow student named Clark Blaise, an American of Canadian origin, and impulsively married him during a lunch break in a lawyer's office above a coffee shop.

That act cut me off forever from the rules and ways of upper-middle-class life in Bengal, and hurled me into a New World life of scary improvisations and heady explorations. Until my lunch-break wedding, I had seen myself as an Indian foreign student who intended to return to India to live. The five-minute ceremony in the lawyer's office suddenly changed me into a transient with conflicting loyalties to two very different cultures.

The first 10 years into marriage, years spent mostly in my husband's native Canada, I thought of myself as an expatriate Bengali permanently stranded in North America because of destiny or desire. My first novel, *The Tiger's Daughter,* embodies the loneliness I felt but could not acknowledge, even to myself, as I negotiated the no-man's land between the country of my past

and the continent of my present. Shaped by memory, textured with nostalgia for a class and culture I had abandoned, this novel quite naturally became an expression of the expatriate consciousness.

It took me a decade of painful introspection to put nostalgia in perspective and to make the transition from expatriate to immigrant. After a 14-year stay in Canada, I forced my husband and our two sons to relocate to the United States. But the transition from foreign student to U.S. citizen, from detached onlooker to committed immigrant, has not been easy.

The years in Canada were particularly harsh. Canada is a country that officially, and proudly, resists cultural fusion. For all its rhetoric about a cultural "mosaic," Canada refuses to renovate its national self-image to include its changing complexion. It is a New World country with Old World concepts of a fixed, exclusivist national identity. Canadian official rhetoric designated me as one of the "visible minority" who, even though I spoke the Canadian languages of English and French, was straining "the absorptive capacity" of Canada. Canadians of color were routinely treated as "not real" Canadians. One example: In 1985 a terrorist bomb, planted in an Air-India jet on Canadian soil, blew up after leaving Montreal, killing 329 passengers, most of whom were Canadians of Indian origin. The prime minister of Canada at the time, Brian Mulroney, phoned the prime minister of India to offer Canada's condolences for India's loss.

Those years of race-related harassments in Canada politicized me and deepened my love of the ideals embedded in the American Bill of Rights. I don't forget that the architects of the Constitution and the Bill of Rights were white males and slaveholders. But through their declaration, they provided us with the enthusiasm for human rights, and the initial framework from which other empowerments could be conceived and enfranchised communities expanded.

I am a naturalized U.S. citizen and I take my American citizenship very seriously. I am not an economic refugee, nor am I a seeker of political asylum. I am a voluntary immigrant. I became a citizen by choice, not by simple accident of birth.

Yet these days, questions such as who is an American and what is American culture are being posed with belligerence, and being answered with violence. Scapegoating of immigrants has once again become the politicians' easy remedy for all that ails the nation. Hate speeches fill auditoriums for demagogues willing to profit from stirring up racial animosity. An April Gallup poll indicated that half of Americans would like to bar almost all legal immigration for the next five years.

The United States, like every sovereign nation, has a right to formulate its immigration policies. But in this decade of continual, large-scale diasporas,[1] it is imperative that we come to some agreement about who "we" are, and what our goals are for the nation, now that our community includes people of many races, ethnicities, languages, and religions.

The debate about American culture and American identity has to date been monopolized largely by Eurocentrists and ethnocentrists whose rhetoric has been flamboyantly divisive, pitting a phantom "us" against a demonized "them."

All countries view themselves by their ideals. Indians idealize the cultural continuum, the inherent value system of India, and are properly incensed when foreigners see nothing but poverty, intolerance, strife, and injustice. Americans see themselves as the embodiments of liberty, openness, and individualism, even as the world judges them for drugs, crime, violence, bigotry, militarism, and homelessness. I was in Singapore in 1994 when the American teenager Michael Fay was sentenced to caning for having spraypainted some cars. While I saw Fay's actions as those of an individual, and his sentence as too harsh, the overwhelming local sentiment was that vandalism was an "American" crime, and that flogging Fay would deter Singapore youths from becoming "Americanized."

Conversely, in 1994, in Tavares, Florida, the Lake County School Board announced its policy (since overturned) requiring middle school teachers to instruct their students that American culture, by which the board meant European-American culture, is inherently "superior to other foreign or historic cultures." The policy's misguided implication was that culture in the United States has not been affected by the American Indian, African-American, Latin-American, and Asian-American segments of the population. The sinister implication was that our national identity is so fragile that it can absorb diverse and immigrant cultures only by recontextualizing them as deficient.

Our nation is unique in human history in that the founding idea of "America" was in opposition to the tenet that a nation is a collection of like-looking, like-speaking, like-worshiping people. The primary criterion for nationhood in Europe is homogeneity of culture, race, and religion—which has contributed to blood-soaked balkanization in the former Yugoslavia and the former Soviet Union.

America's pioneering European ancestors gave us the easy homogeneity of their native countries for a new version of utopia. Now, in the 1990s, we have the exciting chance to follow that tradition and assist in the making of a new American culture that differs from both the enforced assimilation of a "melting pot" and the Canadian model of a multicultural "mosaic."

The multicultural mosaic implies a contiguity of fixed, self-sufficient, utterly distinct cultures. Multiculturalism, as it has been practiced in the United States in the past 10 years, implies the existence of a central culture, ringed by peripheral cultures. The fallout of official multiculturalism is the establishment of one culture as the norm and the rest as aberrations. At the same time, the multiculturalist emphasis on race- and ethnicity-based group identity leads to a lack of respect for individual differences within each group, and to vilification of those individuals who place the good of the nation above the interests of their particular racial or ethnic communities.

We must be alert to the dangers of an "us" vs. "them" mentality. In California, this mentality is manifesting itself as increased violence between minority, ethnic communities. The attack on Korean-American merchants in South Central Los Angeles in the wake of the Rodney King beating trial is only one recent example of the tragic side effects of this mentality. On the national level, the politicization of ethnic identities has encouraged the scapegoating of legal immigrants, who are blamed for economic and social problems brought about by flawed domestic and foreign policies.

We need to discourage the retention of cultural memory if the aim of that retention is cultural balkanization. We must think of American culture and nationhood as a constantly reforming, transmogrifying "we."

In this age of diasporas, one's biological identity may not be one's only identity. Erosions and accretions come with the act of emigration. The experience of cutting myself off from a biological homeland and settling in an adopted homeland that is not always welcoming to its dark-complexioned citizens has tested me as a person, and made me the writer I am today.

I choose to describe myself on my own terms, as an American rather than as an Asian-American. Why is it that hyphenation is imposed only on nonwhite Americans? Rejecting hyphenation is my refusal to categorize the cultural landscape into a center and its peripheries; it is to demand that the American nation deliver the promises of its dream and its Constitution to all its citizens equally.

My rejection of hyphenation has been misrepresented as race treachery by some India-born academics on U.S. campuses who have appointed themselves guardians of the "purity" of ethnic cultures. Many of them, though they reside permanently in the United States and participate in its economy, consistently denounce American ideals and institutions. They direct their rage at me because, by becoming a U.S. citizen and exercising my voting rights, I have invested in the present and not the past; because I have committed myself to help shape the future of my adopted homeland; and because I celebrate racial and cultural mongrelization.

What excites me is that as a nation we have not only the chance to retain those values we treasure from our original cultures but also the chance to acknowledge that the outer forms of those values are likely to change. Among Indian immigrants, I see a great deal of guilt about the inability to hang on to what they commonly term "pure culture." Parents express rage or despair at their U.S.-born children's forgetting of, or indifference to, some aspects of Indian culture. Of those parents I would ask: What is it we have lost if our children are acculturating into the culture in which we are living? Is it so terrible that our children are discovering or are inventing homelands for themselves?

Some first-generation Indo-Americans, embittered by racism and by unofficial "glass ceilings," construct a phantom identity, more-Indian-than-Indians-in-India, as a defense against marginalization. I ask: Why don't you get actively involved in fighting discrimination? Make your voice heard. Choose the forum most appropriate for you. If you are a citizen, let your vote count. Reinvest your energy and resources into revitalizing your city's disadvantaged residents and neighborhoods. Know your constitutional rights, and when they are violated, use the agencies of redress the Constitution makes available to you. Expect change, and when it comes, deal with it!

As a writer, my literary agenda begins by acknowledging that America has transformed me. It does not end until I show that I (along with the hundreds of thousands of immigrants like me) am minute by minute transforming America. The transformation is a two-way process: It affects both the individual and the national-cultural identity.

Others who write stories of migration often talk of arrival at a new place as a loss, the loss of communal memory and the erosion of an original culture. I want to talk of arrival as gain.

[1997]

Terms

1. DIASPORA: The geographical disbursement of a cultural people.

Understanding the Reading

1. What distinction does Mukherjee make between her American experience and "America"?
2. Compare and contrast Mukherjee's Indian background and her American experience.
3. What is the Canadian attitude toward people of color?
4. How do Indians and Americans see themselves, and how do foreigners see them?
5. How is America different from traditional nations?
6. What is Mukherjee's advice to immigrants to America?

Suggestions for Responding

1. Talk to an older family member about how his or her culture of origin has transformed Amer-

ican culture and how American culture has transformed him or her. Take good notes for use when you write your "identity" report. ✦

14

On the Other Side of the War: A Story

Elizabeth Gordon

I. The Way We Came to America

The way we came to America was this: My father, who was in the Army, made an overseas call to his mom and dad in West Virginia.

"Listen," he said, "I've decided to adopt this poor little Vietnamese baby and bring her to America. What do you think?"

Now, both Grandma and Grandpa were true hillbillies in their lineage, habits, and mental faculties—which means they were as broke, as stubborn, and as sharp as folks can be. Not that my father's story required much genius to be seen right through. A twenty-four-year-old enlisted man wanting to bring home some mysterious oriental infant? They hadn't brought him up *that* good.

"It's all right, Skip," they told him. "You can get married, if you love her, and bring 'em both. Bring 'em both on home."

II. No One Had Expected

No one had expected anything like that to happen, least of all the people it happened to.

My father had been quite prepared to meet and marry a sweet girl with a name like Layuna or Ginny Lee. A girl who hailed from one of the good neighboring towns of Beckley or Rainelle. A girl with a daddy, like his, who liked to work on cars, who'd every once in a while hit the booze and start cursing about black lung. There'd been no Nguyen Ngoc Huong from Saigon in *his* crystal ball.

And my mother never dreamed she'd live in an aluminum house on wheels, or see shaved ice swirling down from the sky. Her kitchen window looked out onto a pasture of cows, who stood utterly still with the weather piling up around their legs. It was a difficult thing for her to understand.

So while my father was out climbing telephone poles for Ma Bell, my mother was in the trailer with me, crying and crying for the cows who had not a plank against the cold.

III. Things Got Mixed Up

Things got mixed up sometimes between them. Though it was my father's unshakable belief that Common Sense prevailed in all circumstances, he seemed to forget that Common Sense is commonly rendered senseless whenever it crosses a few time zones.

For example, my mother would constantly confuse "hamburger" with "pancake," presumably because both were round, flat, and fried in a pan. So my father, after asking for his favorite breakfast, would soon smell the juicy aroma of sizzling ground beef coming from the kitchen. Other times, he'd find a stack of well-buttered flapjacks, along with a cold bottle of Coca-Cola, waiting for him at the dinner table.

One morning, before my father left for work, he asked my mother to make corn bread and pinto beans for supper. The result of this request was that my mother spent the remainder of the day peeling, one by one, an entire pound of pinto beans. How could she have known any better?

When my father returned home that night, he found her with ten sore fingers and a pot full of mush. He didn't know whether to laugh or cry, but he kissed her because there was nothing he could say.

IV. The Photograph

The photograph, circa 1965, is somewhat unusual. In the background there is a row of neat, nearly identical frame houses. The street in front of the houses is spacious and clean, as wholesome and as decent as sunshine.

Up a little closer, there is a car. It's a two-tone Chevy with curvaceous fenders, gleaming as though it's just been washed and waxed by hand. The weather looks like Sunday.

In the foreground not unexpectedly, a woman with a small child. The woman is a wife because she wears a gold ring. She is also a mother because of the way she holds her child.

The woman has a slim, dainty figure. Her smile is wide and loose, as though she is close to laughter. Maybe her husband, who is taking her picture, is telling a joke or making a silly face. It seems quite natural that the photographer is the husband. Who else would it be?

But something in the photograph seems not quite right. Strangers often tilt their heads when looking at it, as if it is uncomfortable to view straight up and down. Possibly, it's the incomparable blackness of the woman's hair, or the way it seems forced into a wave it can barely hold. Or maybe it has something to do with the baby's eyes which, though blue, are shaped exactly like the woman's: round at the center, narrow at the corners, and heavy-lidded.

What are eyes like that doing among frame houses and a shiny Chevrolet? It seems a reasonable thing to ask.

V. When I Started School

When I started school there were numerous forms to be filled out. Some of the questions were so simple, I could have answered them myself.

The task belonged to my mother, though. She handled most of the questions with ease, and I liked to watch the way she filled all those boxes and blanks with her pretty handwriting.

There was one question, however, that gave my mother a lot of trouble. Even though it was multiple choice, none of the answers seemed to fit. She decided to ask my father what to do.

He didn't have an answer right away, and for some reason that made him angry. The problem was, I was supposed to be in a race, but he couldn't figure out which one.

Finally, he told my mother to put an "H" in that blank. "For *human* race," he said.

I didn't understand what that meant, back then. But it sounded like a good race to me.

[1989]

Understanding the Reading

1. Why do you think Skip initially announces that his plan was to adopt a Vietnamese baby? Were you surprised by his parents' response?
2. What do Gordon's mother's cooking errors illustrate about Americans' assumptions about our food?
3. Explain what Gordon is trying to show in her description of the photograph.
4. How do you think Gordon's parents should have filled out the school form?

Suggestions for Responding

1. If you have an old family photo that especially intrigues you, write a description of it and try to explain what it means to you.
2. If you have had occasion to eat the food of another culture, try to describe it and your reaction to it. ✦

15

Medicalization of Racial Features: Asian American Women and Cosmetic Surgery

Eugenia Kaw

Throughout history and across cultures, humans have decorated, manipulated, and mutilated their bodies for religious reasons, for social prestige, and for beauty (Brain 1979). In the United States, within the last decade, permanent alteration of the body for aesthetic reasons has become increasingly common. By 1988, 2 million Americans, 87% of them female, had undergone cosmetic surgery, a figure that had tripled in two years (Wolf 1991:218). The cosmetic surgery industry, a $300 million per year industry, has been able to meet an increasingly wide variety of consumer demands. Now men, too, receive services ranging from the enlargement of calves and chests to the liposuction of cheeks and necks (Rosenthal 1991a). Most noticeably, the ethnic

Reproduced by permission of the American Anthropological Association from Medical Anthropology Quarterly. 7(1):74–89. Not for sale or further reproduction.

composition of consumers has changed so that in recent years there are more racial and ethnic minorities. In 1990, 20% of cosmetic surgery patients were Latinos, African Americans, and Asian Americans (Rosenthal 1991b). Not surprisingly, within every racial group, women still constitute the overwhelming majority of cosmetic surgery patients, an indication that women are still expected to identify with their bodies in U.S. society today, just as they have across cultures throughout much of human history (Turner 1987:85).[1]

The types of cosmetic surgery sought by women in the United States are racially specific. Like most white women, Asian American women who undergo cosmetic surgery are motivated by the need to look their best as women. White women, however, usually opt for liposuction, breast augmentation, or wrinkle removal procedures, whereas Asian American women most often request "double-eyelid" surgery, whereby folds of skin are excised from across their upper eyelids to create a crease above each eye that makes the eyes look wider. Also frequently requested is surgical sculpting of the nose tip to create a more chiseled appearance, or the implantation of a silicone or cartilage bridge in the nose for a more prominent appearance. In 1990, national averages compiled by the American Society of Plastic and Reconstructive Surgeons show that liposuction, breast augmentation, and collagen injection were the most common surgical procedures among cosmetic patients, 80% of whom are white. Although national statistics on the types of cosmetic surgery most requested by Asian Americans specifically are not available, data from two of the doctors' offices in my study show that in 1990 eyelid surgery was the most common procedure undergone by Asian American patients (40% of all procedures on Asian Americans at one doctor's office, 46% at another), followed by nasal implants and nasal tip refinement procedures (15% at the first doctor's office, 23% at the second).[2] While the features that white women primarily seek to alter through cosmetic surgery (i.e., the breasts, fatty areas of the body, and facial wrinkles) do not correspond to conventional markers of racial identity, those features that Asian American women primarily seek to alter (i.e., "small, narrow" eyes and a "flat" nose) do correspond to such markers.[3]

My research focuses on the cultural and institutional forces that motivate Asian American women to alter surgically the shape of their eyes and noses. I argue that Asian American women's decision to undergo cosmetic surgery is an attempt to escape persisting racial prejudice that correlates their stereotyped genetic physical features ("small, slanty" eyes and a "flat" nose) with negative behavioral characteristics, such as passivity, dullness, and a lack of sociability. With the authority of scientific rationality and technological efficiency, medicine is effective in perpetuating these racist notions. The medical system bolsters and benefits from the larger consumer-oriented society not only by maintaining the idea that beauty should be every woman's goal but also by promoting a beauty standard that requires that certain racial features of Asian American women be modified. Through the subtle and often unconscious manipulation of racial and gender ideologies, medicine, as a producer of norms, and the larger consumer society of which it is a part encourage Asian American women to mutilate their bodies to conform to an ethnocentric norm.

Social scientific analyses of ethnic relations should include a study of the body. As evident in my research, racial minorities may internalize a body image produced by the dominant culture's racial ideology and, because of it, begin to loathe, mutilate, and revise parts of their bodies. Bodily mutilation and adornment are symbolic mediums most directly and concretely concerned with the construction of the individual as social actor or cultural subject (Turner 1980). Yet social scientists have only recently focused on the body as a central component of social self-identity (Blacking 1977; Brain 1979; Daly 1978; Lock and Scheper-Hughes 1990; O'Neill 1985; Turner 1987). Moreover, social scientists, and sociocultural anthropologists in particular, have not yet explored the ways in which the body is central to the everyday experience of racial identity.

METHOD AND DESCRIPTION OF SUBJECTS

In this article I present findings of an ongoing ethnographic research project in the San Francisco Bay begun in April 1991. I draw on data from structured interviews with physicians and patients, medical literature and newspaper articles, and basic medical statistics. The sample of informants for this research is not random in the strictly statistical sense since informants were difficult to locate. In the United States, both clients and their medical practitioners treat the decision to undergo cosmetic surgery as highly confidential, and practitioners do not reveal the names of patients without their consent. In an effort to generate a sample of Asian American woman informants, I posted fliers and placed advertisements in various local newspapers for a period of at least three months, but I received only one reply. I also asked doctors who had agreed to participate in my study to ask their Asian American patients if they would agree to be interviewed. The doctors reported that most of the patients preferred not to talk about their operations or about motivations leading up to the operation. Ultimately, I was able to conduct structured, open-ended interviews with eleven Asian American women, four of whom were referred to me by doctors in the study, six by mutual acquaintances, and one through an advertisement in a local newspaper. Nine have had cosmetic surgery of the eye or the nose; one recently considered a double-eyelid operation; one is considering a double-eyelid operation in the next few years. Nine of the women in the study live in the San Francisco Bay Area, and two in the Los Angeles area. Five had their operations from the doctors in my study, while four had theirs in Asia—two in Seoul, Korea, one in Beijing, China, and one in Taipei, Taiwan. Of the eleven women in the study, only two, who received their operations in China and in Taiwan, had not lived in the United States prior to their operations. The two who had surgery in Korea for their surgeries because the operations were cheaper there than in the United States and because they felt doctors in Korea are more "experienced" since these types of surgery are more common in Korea than in the United States.[4] The ages of the women in the study range from 18 to 71; one woman was only 15 at the time of her operation.

In addition to interviewing Asian American women, I conducted structured, open-ended interviews with five plastic surgeons, all of whom practice in the Bay Area. Of the eleven doctors I randomly selected from the phone book, five agreed to be interviewed.

Since the physicians in my study may not be representative of plastic surgeons, I reviewed the plastic surgery literature. To examine more carefully the medical discourse on the nose and eyelid surgeries of Asian American women, I examined several medical books and plastic surgery journals dating from the 1950s to 1990. I also reviewed several news releases and informational packets distributed by such national organizations as the American Society of Plastic and Reconstructive Surgeons, an organization that represents 97% of all physicians certified by the American Board of Plastic Surgery.

To examine popular notions of cosmetic surgery and, in particular, of how the phenomenon of Asian American women receiving double-eyelid and nose-bridge operations is viewed by the public and the media, I referenced relevant newspaper and magazine articles.

For statistical information, I obtained national data on cosmetic surgery from various societies for cosmetic surgeons, including the American Society of Plastic and Reconstructive Surgeons. Data on the specific types of surgery sought by different ethnic groups in the United States, including Asian Americans, are missing from the national statistics. At least one public relations coordinator told me that such data are quite unimportant to plastic surgeons. To compensate for this, I requested doctors in my study to provide me with data from their clinics. One doctor allowed me to review his patient files for basic statistical information. Another doctor allowed his office assistant to give me such information, provided that I paid his assistant for the time she had to work outside of normal work hours reviewing his patient files. Since cosmetic surgery is generally not covered by medical insurance, doctors often do not record their patients' medical information in their computers; therefore, most doctors told me that they have very little data on their cosmetic patients readily available.

MUTILATION OR A CELEBRATION OF THE BODY?

The decoration, ornamentation, and scarification of the body can be viewed from two perspectives. On the one hand, such practices can be seen as celebrations of the social and individual bodies, as expressions of belonging in society and an affirmation of oneness with the body (Brain 1979; Scheper-Hughes and Lock 1991; Turner 1980). On the other hand, they can be viewed as acts of mutilation, that is, as expressions of alienation in society and a negation of the body induced by unequal power relationships (Bordo 1990; Daly 1978; O'Neill 1985).

Although it is at least possible to imagine race-modification surgery as a *rite de passage* or a bid for incorporation into the body and race norms of the "dominant" culture, my research findings lead me to reject this as a tenable hypothesis. Here I argue that the surgical alternation by many Asian American women of the shape of their eyes and nose is a potent form of self, body, and society alienation. Mutilation, according to *Webster's*, is the act of maiming, crippling, cutting up, or altering radically so as to damage seriously essential parts of the body. Although the women in my study do not view their cosmetic surgeries as acts of mutilation, an examination of the cultural and institutional forces that influence them to modify their bodies so radically reveals a rejection of their "given" bodies and feelings of marginality. On the one hand, they feel they are exercising their Americanness in their use of the freedom of individual choice. Some deny that they are conforming to any standard—feminine, Western, or otherwise—and others express the idea that they are, in fact, molding their own standards of beauty. Most agreed, however, that their decision to alter their features was primarily a result of their awareness that as women they are expected to look their best and that this meant, in a certain sense, less stereotypically Asian. Even those who stated that their decision to alter their features was personal, based on individual aesthetic preference, also expressed hope that their new appearance would help them in such matters as getting a date, securing a mate, or getting a better job.

For the women in my study, the decision to undergo cosmetic surgery was never purely or mainly for aesthetic purposes, but almost always for improving their social status as women who are racial minorities. Cosmetic surgery is a means by which they hope to acquire "symbolic capital" (Bourdieu 1984 [1979]) in the form of a look that holds more prestige. For example, "Jane," who under-went double-eyelid and nose-bridge procedures at the ages of 16 and 17, said that she thought she should get her surgeries "out of the way" at an early age since as a college student she has to think about careers ahead:

> Especially if you go into business, whatever, you kind of have to have a Western facial type and you have to have like their features and stature— you know, be tall and stuff. In a way you can see it is an investment in your future.

Such a quest for empowerment does not confront the cultural and institutional structures that are the real cause of the women's feelings of distress. Instead, this form of "body praxis" (Scheper-Hughes and Lock 1991) helps to entrench these structures by further confirming the undesirability of "stereotypical" Asian features. Therefore, the alteration by many Asian American women of their features is a "disciplinary" practice in the Foucauldian sense; it does not so much benignly transform them as it "normalizes" (i.e., qualifies, classifies, judges, and enforces complicity in) the subject (Foucault 1977). The normalization is a double encounter, conforming to patriarchal definitions of femininity and to Caucasian standards of beauty (Bordo 1990).

Gramsci anticipated Foucault in considering subjected peoples' complicity and participation in, as well as reproduction of their own domination in everyday practice. In examining such phenomena as Asian American women undergoing cosmetic surgery in the late 20th-century United States, however, one must emphasize, as Foucault does, how mechanisms of domination have become much more insidious, overlapping, and pervasive in everyday life as various forms of "expert" knowledge such as plastic surgery and surgeons have increasingly come to play the role of "traditional" intellectuals (Gramsci 1971) or direct agents of the bourgeois state (Scheper-Hughes 1992:171) in defining commonsense reality.

Particularly in Western, late capitalist societies (where the decoration, ornamentation, and scarification of the body have lost much meaning for the individual in the existential sense of "Which people do I belong to? What is the meaning of my life?" and have instead become commoditized by the media, corporations, and even medicine in the name of fashion), the normalizing elements of such practices as cosmetic surgery can become obscured. Rather than celebrations of the body, they are mutilations of the body, resulting from a devaluation of the self and induced by historically determined relationships among social groups and between the individual and society.

INTERNALIZATION OF RACIAL AND GENDER STEREOTYPES

The Asian American women in my study are influenced by a gender ideology that states that beauty should be a primary goal of women. They are conscious that because they are women, they must conform to certain standards of beauty. "Elena," a 20-year-old Korean American said, "People in society, if they are attractive, are rewarded for their efforts . . . especially girls. If they look pretty and neat, they are paid more attention to. You can't deny that." "Annie," another Korean American who is 18 years old, remarked that as a young woman, her motivation to have cosmetic surgery was "to look better" and "not different from why [other women] put on makeup." In fact, all expressed the idea that cosmetic surgery was a means by which they could escape the task of having to put makeup on every day. As "Jo," a 28-year-old Japanese American who is thinking of enlarging the natural fold above her eyes, said, "I am still self-conscious about leaving the house without any makeup on, because I feel just really ugly without it. I feel like it's the mask that enables me to go outside." Beauty, more than character and intelligence, often signifies social and economic success for them as for other women in U.S. society (Lakoff and Scherr 1984; Wolf 1991).

The need to look their best as women motivates the Asian American women in my study to undergo cosmetic surgery, but the standard of beauty they try to achieve through surgery is motivated by a racial ideology that infers negative behavioral or intellectual characteristics from a group's genetic physical features. All of the women said that they are "proud to be Asian American" and that they "do not want to look white." But the standard of beauty they admire and strive for is a face with larger eyes and a more prominent nose. They all stated that an eyelid without a crease and a nose that does not project indicate a certain "sleepiness," "dullness," and "passivity" in a person's character.

"Nellee," a 21-year-old Chinese American, said she seriously considered surgery for double eyelids in high school so that she could "avoid the stereotype of the 'Oriental bookworm'" who is "*dull* and doesn't know how to have fun." Elena, who had double-eyelid surgery two years ago from a doctor in my study, said, "When I look at Asians who have no folds and their eyes are slanted and closed, I think of how they would look better more *awake*." "Carol," a 37-year-old Chinese American who had double-eyelid surgery seven years ago and "Ellen," a 40-year-old Chinese American who had double-eyelid surgery 20 years ago, both said that they wanted to give their eyes a "more spirited" look. "The drawback of Asian features is the puffy eyes," Ellen said. "Pam," a Chinese American aged 44, who had had double-eyelid surgery from another doctor in my study two months earlier, stated, "Yes. Of course. Bigger eyes look prettier. . . . Lots of Asians' eyes are so small they become little lines when the person laughs, making the person look *sleepy*." Likewise, Annie, who had an implant placed on her nasal dorsum to build up her nose bridge at age 15, said:

> I guess I always wanted that *sharp* look—a look like you are smart. If you have a roundish kind of nose, it's like you don't know what's going on. If you have that sharp look, you know, with black eyebrows, a pointy nose, you look more *alert*. I always thought that was cool. [emphasis added]

Clearly, the Asian American women in my study seek cosmetic surgery for double eyelids and nose bridges because they associate the features considered characteristic of their race with negative traits.

These associations that Asian American women make between their features and personality characteristics stem directly from stereotypes created by the dominant culture in the United States and by Western culture in general, which historically has wielded the most power and hegemonic influence over the world. Asians are rarely portrayed in the U.S. popular media and then only in such roles as Charlie Chan, Suzie Wong, and "Lotus Blossom Babies" (a.k.a. China Doll, Geisha Girl, and shy Polynesian beauty). They are depicted as stereotypes with dull, passive, and nonsociable personalities (Kim 1986; Tajima 1989). Subtle depictions by the media of individuals' minutest gestures in everyday social situations can socialize viewers to confirm certain hypotheses about their own natures (Goffman 1979). At present, the stereotypes of Asians as a "model minority" serve a similar purpose. In the model minority stereotype, the concepts of dullness, passivity, and stoicism are elaborated to refer to a person who is hard-working and technically skilled but desperately lacking in creativity and sociability (Takaki 1989:477).

Similar stereotypes of the stoic Asian also exist in East and Southeast Asia, and since many Asian Americans are immigrants or children of recent immigrants from Asia, they are likely to be influenced by these stereotypes as well. U.S. magazines and films have been increasingly available in many parts of Asia since World War II. Also, multinational corporations in Southeast Asian countries consider their work force of Asian women to be biologically suited for the most monotonous industrial labor because the "Oriental girl" is "diligent" and has "nimble fingers" and a "slow wit" (Ong 1987:151). Racial stereotypes of Asians as docile, passive, slow witted, and unemotional are internalized by many Asian American women, causing them to consider the facial features associated with these negative traits as defiling.

Undergoing cosmetic surgery, then, becomes a means by which the women can attempt to permanently acquire not only a feminine look considered more attractive by society, but also a certain set of racial features considered more prestigious. For them, the daily task of beautification entails creating the illusion of features they, as members of a racial minority, do not have. Nellee, who has not yet undergone double-eyelid surgery, said that at present she has to apply makeup every day "to give my eyes an illusion of a crease. When I don't wear makeup I feel my eyes are small." Likewise, Elena said that before her double-eyelid surgery she checked almost every morning in the mirror when she woke up to see if a fold had formed above her right eye to match the more prominent fold above her left eye: "[on certain mornings] it was like any other day when you wake up and don't feel so hot, you know. My eye had no definite folds, because when Asians sleep their folds change in and out—it's not definite." The enor-

mous constraints the women in my study feel with regard to their Asian features are apparent in the meticulous detail with which they describe their discontent, as apparent in a quote from Jo who already has natural folds but wants to enlarge them: "I want to make an even bigger eyelid [fold] so that it doesn't look slanted. I think in Asian eyes this inside corner of the fold [she was drawing on my notebook] goes down too much."

The women expressed hope that the results of cosmetic surgery would win them better acceptance by society. Ellen said that she does not think her double-eyelid surgery "makes me look too different," but she nonetheless expressed the feeling that now her features will "make a better impression on people because I got rid of that sleepy look." She says that she will encourage her daughter, who is only 12 years old, to have double-eyelid surgery as she did, because "I think having less sleepy-looking eyes would help her in the future with getting jobs." The aesthetic results of surgery are not an end in themselves but rather a means for these women as racial minorities to attain better socioeconomic status. Clearly, their decisions to undergo cosmetic surgery do not stem from a celebration of their bodies.

MEDICALIZATION OF RACIAL FEATURES

Having already been influenced by the larger society's negative valuation of their natural, "given" features, Asian American women go to see plastic surgeons in half-hour consultation sessions. Once inside the clinic, they do not have to have the doctor's social and medical views "thrust" on them, since to a great extent, they, like their doctors, have already entered into a more general social consensus (Scheper-Hughes 1992:199). Nonetheless, the Western medical system is a most effective promoter of the racial stereotypes that influence Asian American women, since medical knowledge is legitimized by scientific rationality and technical efficiency, both of which hold prestige in the West and increasingly all over the world. Access to a scientific body of knowledge has given Western medicine considerable social power in defining reality (Turner 1987:11). According to my Asian American informants who had undergone cosmetic surgery, their plastic surgeons used several medical terms to problematize the shape of their eyes so as to define it as a medical condition. For instance, many patients were told that they had "excess fat" on their eyelids and that it was "normal" for them to feel dissatisfied with the way they looked. "Lots of Asians have the same puffiness over their eyelid, and they often feel better about themselves after the operation," the doctors would assure their Asian American patients.

The doctors whom I interviewed shared a similar opinion of Asian facial features with many of the doctors of the patients in my study. Their descriptions of Asian features verged on ideological racism, as clearly seen in the following quote from "Dr. Smith."

> The social reasons [for Asian Americans to want double eyelids and nose bridges] are undoubtedly continued exposure to Western culture and the realization that the upper eyelid *without* a fold tends to give a *sleepy* appearance, and therefore a more *dull* look to the patient. Likewise, the *flat* nasal bridge and *lack of* nasal projection can signify *weakness* in one's personality and by *lack of* extension, a *lack of force* in one's character. [emphasis added]

By using words like "without," "lack of," "flat," "dull," and "sleepy" in his description of Asian features, Dr. Smith perpetuates the notion that Asian features are inadequate. Likewise, "Dr. Khoo" said that many Asians should have surgery for double eyelids since "the eye is the window to your soul and having a more open appearance makes you look a bit brighter, more inviting." "Dr. Gee" agreed:

> I would say 90% of people look better with double eyelids. It makes the eye look more spiritually alive. . . . With a single eyelid frequently they would have a little fat pad underneath [which] can half bury the eye and so the eye looks small and unenergetic.

Such powerful associations of Asian features with negative personality traits by physicians during consultations can become a medical affirmation of Asian American women's sense of disdain toward their own features.

Medical books and journals as early as the 1950s and as recent as 1990 abound with similar metaphors of abnormality in describing Asian features. The texts that were published before 1970 contain more explicit associations of Asian features with dullness and passivity. In an article published in 1954 in the *American Journal of Ophthalmology,* the author, a doctor in the Philippines armed forces, wrote the following about a Chinese man on whom he performed double-eyelid surgery:

> [He] was born with mere slits for his eyes. Everyone teased him about his eyes with the comment that as he looked constantly sleepy, so his business too was just as sleepy. For this reason, he underwent the plastic operation and, now that his eyes are wider, he has lost that sleepy look. His business, too, has, picked up. [Sayoc 1954:556]

The doctor clearly saw a causal link between the shape of his patient's eyes and his patient's intellectual and behavioral capacity to succeed in life. In 1964 a white American military surgeon who performed double-eyelid surgeries on Koreans in Korea during the American military occupation of that country wrote in the same journal: "The absence of the palpebral fold produces a passive expression which seems to epitomize the stoical and unemotional manner of the Oriental" (Millard 1964:647). Medical texts published after 1970 are more careful about associating Asian features with negative behavioral or intellectual characteristics, but they still describe Asian features with metaphors of inadequacy or excess. For instance, in the introductory chapter to a 1990 book devoted solely to medical techniques for cosmetic surgery of the Asian face, a white American plastic surgeon begins by cautioning his audience not to stereotype the physical traits of Asians.

> Westerners tend to have a stereotyped conception of the physical traits of Asians: yellow skin pigmentation . . . a flat face with high cheek bones; a broad, flat nose; and narrow slit-like eyes showing characteristic epicanthal folds. While this stereotype may loosely apply to the central Asian groups (i.e., Chinese, Koreans, and Japanese), the facial plastic surgeon should appreciate that considerable variation exists in all of these physical traits. [McCurdy 1990:1]

Yet, on the same page, he writes that the medicalization of Asian features is valid because

Asians usually have eyes that are too narrow and a nose that is too flat.

> However, given an appreciation of the physical diversity of the Asian population, certain facial features do form a distinct basis for surgical intervention. . . . These facial features typically include the upper eyelid, characterized by an absent or poorly defined superior palpebral fold . . . and a small flattened nose with poor lobular definition. [McCurdy 1990:1]

Thus, in published texts, doctors write about Asians' eyes and noses as abnormal even when they are careful not to associate negative personality traits with these features. In the privacy of their clinics, they freely incorporate both metaphors of abnormality and the association of Asian features with negative characteristics into medical discourse, which has an enormous impact on the Asian American patients being served.

The doctors' scientific discourse is made more convincing by the seemingly objective manner in which they behave and present themselves in front of their patients in the clinical setting. They examine their patients as a technician diagnosing ways to improve a mechanical object. With a cotton swab, they help their patients to stretch and measure how high they might want their eyelids to be and show them in a mirror what could be done surgically to reduce the puffy look above their eyes. The doctors in my study also use slides and Polaroid pictures to come to an agreement with their patients on what the technical goals of the operation should be. The sterile appearance of their clinics, with white walls and plenty of medical instruments, as well as the symbolism of the doctor's white coat with its many positive connotations (e.g., purity, life, unaroused sexuality, superhuman power, and candor) reinforce in the patient the doctor's role as technician and thus his sense of objectivity (Blumhagen 1979). One of my informants, Elena, said that, sitting in front of her doctor in his office, she felt sure that she needed eyelid surgery: "[Dr. Smith] made quite an impression on me. I thought he was more than qualified—that he knew what he was talking about."

With its authority of scientific rationality and technical efficiency, medicine effectively "normalizes" not only the negative feelings of Asian American women about their features but also their ultimate decision to undergo cosmetic surgery. For example, "Dr. Jones" does not want to make her patients feel "strange" or "abnormal" for wanting cosmetic surgery. All the doctors in my study agreed that their role as doctor is to provide the best technical skills possible for whatever service their patients demand, not to question the motivation of their patients. Her goal, Dr. Jones said, is "like that of a psychiatrist in that I try to make patients feel better about themselves." She feels that surgeons have an advantage over psychiatrists in treating cosmetic surgery patients because "we . . . help someone to change the way they look . . . psychiatrists are always trying to figure out why a person wants to do what they want to do." By changing the patients' bodies the way they would like them, she feels she provides them with an immediate and concrete solution to their feelings of inadequacy.

Dr. Jones and the other doctors say that they only turn patients away when patients expect results that are technically impossible, given such factors as the thickness of the patient's skin and the bone structure. "I turn very few patients away," said Dr. Khoo. And "Dr. Kwan" notes

> I saw a young girl [a while back] whose eyes were beautiful but she wanted a crease. . . . She was gorgeous! Wonderful! But somehow she didn't see it that way. But you know, I'm not going to tell a patient every standard I have of what's beautiful. If they want certain things and it's doable, and if it is consistent with a reasonable look in the end, then I don't stop them. I don't really discuss it with them.

Like the other doctors in my study, Dr. Kwan sees himself primarily as a technician whose main role is to correct his patient's features in a way that he thinks would best contribute to the patient's satisfaction. It does not bother him that he must expose an individual, whom he already sees as pretty and not in need of surgery, to an operation that is at least an hour long, entails the administering of local anesthesia with sedation, and involves the following risks: "bleeding," "hematoma," "hemorrhage," formation of a "gaping would," "discoloration," scarring, and "asymmetry in lid folds" (Sayoc 1974:162–166). He finds no need to try to change his patients' minds. Likewise, Dr. Smith said of Asian American women who used to come to him to receive really large double eyelids: "I respect their ethnic background. I don't want to change them drastically." Yet he would not refuse them the surgery "as long as it was something I can accomplish. Provided I make them aware of what the appearance might be with the changes."

Though most of my Asian American woman informants who underwent cosmetic surgery recovered fully within six months to a year, with only a few minor scars from their surgery, they nonetheless affirmed that the psychologically traumatic aspect of the operation was something their doctors did not stress during consultation. Elena said of her double-eyelid surgery: "I thought it was a simple procedure. He [the doctor] should have known better. It took at least an hour and a half. . . . And no matter how minor the surgery was, I bruised! I was swollen." Likewise, Annie could remember well her fear during nose surgery. Under local anesthesia, she said that she was able to witness and hear some of the procedures.

> I closed my eyes. I didn't want to look. I didn't want to see like the knives or anything. I could hear the snapping of scissors and I was aware when they were putting that thing [implant] up my nose. I was kind of grossed out.

By focusing on technique and subordinating human emotions and motivations to technical ends, medicine is capable of normalizing Asian American women's decision to undergo cosmetic surgery.

MUTUAL REINFORCEMENT: MEDICINE AND THE CONSUMER-ORIENTED SOCIETY

The medical system bolsters and benefits from the larger consumer-oriented society by perpetuating the idea that beauty is central to women's sense of self and also by promoting a beauty standard for Asian American women that requires the alternation of features specific to Asian American racial identity. All of the doctors in my study stated that a "practical" benefit for Asian American women undergoing surgery to create or enlarge their eyelid folds is that they can put eye makeup on more appropriately.

Dr. Gee said that after double-eyelid surgery it is "easier" for Asian American women to put makeup on because "they now have two instead of just one plane on which to apply makeup." Dr. Jones agreed that after eyelid surgery Asian American women "can do more dramatic things with eye makeup." The doctors imply that Asian American women cannot usually put on makeup adequately, and thus, they have not been able to look as beautiful as they can be with makeup. By promoting the idea that a beautiful woman is one who can put makeup on adequately, they further the idea that a woman's identity should be closely connected with her body and, particularly, with the representational problems of the self. By reinforcing the makeup industry, they buttress the cosmetic surgery industry of which they are a part. A double-eyelid surgery costs patients $1,000 to $3,000.

The medical system also bolsters and benefits from the larger consumer society by appealing to the values of American individualism and by individualizing the social problems of racial inequality. Dr. Smith remarked that so many Asian American women are now opting for cosmetic surgery procedures largely because of their newly gained rights as women and as racial minorities:

> Asians are more affluent than they were 15 years ago. They are more knowledgeable and Americanized, and their women are more liberated. I think in the past many Asian women were like Arab women. The men had their foot on top of them. Now Asian women do pretty much what they want to do. So if they want to do a surgery, they do it.

Such comments by doctors encourage Asian American women to believe that undergoing cosmetic surgery is merely a way of beautifying themselves and that it signifies their ability to exercise individual freedom.

Ignoring the fact that the Asian American women's decision to undergo cosmetic surgery has anything to do with the larger society's racial prejudice, the doctors state that their Asian American women patients come to cosmetic surgeons to mold their own standards of beauty. The doctors point out that the specific width and shape the women want their creases to be or the specific shape of nose bridges they want are a matter of personal style and individual choices. Dr. Smith explains:

> We would like to individualize every procedure. There is no standard nose we stamp on everybody so that each patient's need is addressed individually. My goal is to make that individual very happy and very satisfied.

Dr. Kwan also remarked, "I think people recognize what's beautiful in their own way." In fact, the doctors point out that both they and their Asian American patients are increasingly getting more sophisticated about what the patients want. As evidence, they point to the fact that as early as a decade ago, doctors used to provide very wide creases to every Asian American patient who came for double eyelids, not knowing that not every Asian wanted to look exactly Caucasian. The doctors point out that today many Asian American cosmetic surgery patients explicitly request that their noses and eyelids not be made to look too Caucasian.

Recent plastic surgery literature echoes these doctors' observations. A 1991 press release from the American Academy of Cosmetic Surgery quotes a prominent member as saying, "The procedures they [minorities, including Asian Americans] seek are not so much to look 'western' but to refine their features to attain facial harmony." The double-eyelid surgery, he says, is to give Asian eyes "a more open appearance," not a Western look. Likewise, McCurdy points out in his book that double-eyelid procedures should vary in accordance with whether or not the patient actually requests a Western eyelid.

> In patients who desire a small "double eyelid," the incision is placed 6–7mm above the ciliary margin; in those patients desiring a medium-sized lid, the incision is placed 8mm above the ciliary margin; in patients who request westernization of the eyelid, the incision is placed 9–10mm above the ciliary margin. [McCurdy 1990:8]

Fifty percent of all Asians in the world do have a natural crease on their eyelids, and thus it can be argued that those Asians who undergo surgery for double eyelids are aiming for Asian looks, that they are not necessarily conforming to a Western standard. Yet, by focusing on technique, that is, by focusing on how many millimeters above the eyes their Asian American pa-

tients want their fold to be or how long across the eyelid they want their fold to be drawn, the doctors do not fully recognize that the trend in Asian American cosmetic surgery is still toward larger eyes and a more prominent nose. They ignore the fact that the very valuation attached to eyes with "a more open appearance" may be a consequence of society's racial prejudice. If the types of cosmetic surgery Asian Americans opt for are truly individual choices, one would expect to see a number of Asians who admire and desire eyes without a crease or a nose without a bridge. Yet the doctors can refer to no cases involving Asian Americans who wanted to get rid of their creases or who wanted to flatten their noses. Moreover, there are numerous cases of Asian Americans, such as many Southeast Asians, who already have a natural eyelid crease but feel the need to widen it even more for a less puffy appearance.[5] Clearly, there is a pattern in the requests of Asian American cosmetic surgery patients.

In saying that their Asian American women patients are merely exercising their freedom to choose a personal style or look, the doctors promote the idea that human beings have an infinite variety of needs that technology can endlessly fulfill, an idea at the heart of today's U.S. capitalism. As Susan Bordo explains, the United States has increasingly become a "plastic" culture, characterized by a "disdain for material limits, and intoxication with freedom, change, and self-determination" (Bordo 1990:654). She points out that many consumer products that could be considered derogatory to women and racial minorities are thought by the vast majority of Americans to be only some in an array of consumer choices to which every individual has a right. She explains:

> Any different self would do, it is implied. Closely connected to this is the construction of all cosmetic changes as the same: perms for white women, corn rows on Bo Derek, tanning, makeup, changing hair styles, blue contacts for black women. [Bordo 1990:659]

CONCLUSION

Cosmetic surgery on Asian American women for nose bridges and double eyelids is very much influenced by gender and racial ideologies. My research has shown that by the conscious or unconscious manipulation of gender and racial stereotypes, the American medical system, along with the larger consumer-oriented society of which it is a part, influences Asian American women to alter their features through surgery. With the authority of scientific rationality and technological efficiency, medicine is effectively able to maintain a gender ideology that validates women's monetary and time investment in beauty even if this means making their bodies vulnerable to harmful and risky procedures such as plastic surgery. Medicine is also able to perpetuate a racial ideology that states that Asian features signify "dullness," "passivity," and "lack of emotions" in the Asian person. The medicalization of racial features, which reinforces and normalizes Asian American women's feelings of inadequacy, as well as their decision to undergo cosmetic surgery, helps to bolster the consumer-oriented society of which medicine is a part and from which medicine benefits.

Given the authority with which fields of "expert" knowledge such as bio-medicine have come to define commonsense reality today, racism and sexism no longer need to rely primarily on physical coercion to legal authority. Racial stereotypes influence Asian American women to seek cosmetic surgery. Yet, through its highly specialized and validating forms of discourse and practices, medicine, along with a culture based on endless self-fashioning, is able to motivate women to view their feelings of inadequacy as individually motivated, as opposed to socially induced, phenomena, thereby effectively convincing them to participate in the production and reproduction of the larger structural inequalities that continue to oppress them.

[1993]

Notes

Acknowledgments. I would like to thank Nancy Scheper-Hughes, Aihwa Ong, and Cecilia de Mello for their help, insight, and inspiration from the inception of this research project.

This research was funded by the Edward H. Heller Endowment and a President's Undergraduate Fellowship, University of California, Berkeley.

Correspondence may be addressed to the author at 2226 Durant Avenue #302, Berkeley, CA 94704.

Reproduced by permission of the American Anthropological Association From Medical Anthropology Quarterly. 7(1): 74–89. Not for sale or further reproduction.

[1]In a 1989 study of 80 men and women, men reported many more positive thoughts about their bodies than did women (Goleman 1991).

According to the American Society of Plastic Surgeons, 87% of all cosmetic surgery patients in 1990 were women. In my study, in one of the two doctors' offices from which I received statistical data on Asian American patients, 65% of Asian American cosmetic surgery patients in 1990 were women; in the other, 62%.

[2]At the first doctor's office, the doctor's assistant examined every file from 1990. In all, 121 cosmetic procedures were performed, 81 on white patients, 20 on Asian American patients. Closely following national data, the most common procedure among white patients was liposuction (58% of all cosmetic surgeries performed on white patients).

The second doctor allowed me to survey his patient files. I examined the 1990 files for all patients with last names beginning with the letters A through L. Of these files, all the cosmetic patients were Asian American. Thus, I do not have data on white patients from this office.

It is important to note that at the first doctor's office, where data on white cosmetic surgery patients were available, the patients were older on average than the Asian American cosmetic surgery patients at the same clinic. Of the Asian American patients, 65% were in the age range of 19 to 34 years, compared with only 14.8% of whites. Only 20% of Asian American cosmetic surgery patients were in the age group of 35 to 64 years, however, compared with 80.2% of white cosmetic patients. All the other doctors in my study confirmed a similar trend in their practices. They stated that this trend results from the tendency of whites to seek cosmetic procedures to remove fat and sagging skin that results from aging, in contrast to Asian Americans, who usually are not concerned with "correcting" signs of aging.

[3]The shapes of eyes and noses of Asians are not meant in this article to be interpreted as categories that define an objective category of people called Asians. Categories of racial groups are arbitrarily defined by society. Likewise, the physical traits by which people are recognized as belonging to a racial group have been determined to be arbitrary (see Molnar 1983).

Also, I use the term "Asian American" to collectively name the women in this study who have undergone or are thinking about undergoing cosmetic surgery. Although I realize their ethnic diversity, people of Asian ancestry in the United States share similar experiences in that they are subject to many of the same racial stereotypes (see Takaki 1989).

[4]Cosmetic surgery for double eyelids, nasal-tip refinement, and nose bridges is not limited to Asians in the United States. Asians in East and Southeast Asia have requested such surgeries since the early 1950s, when U.S. military forces began long-term occupations of such countries as Korea and the Philippines. (See Harahap 1982; Millard 1964; Sayoc 1954; and Kristof 1991.)

I do not mean to imply, however, that the situation within which Asian women develop a perspective on the value and meaning of their facial features is identical in Asia and the United States, where Asian women belong to a minority group. The situation in Asia would require further studies. My observations are limited to the United States.

[5]Dr. Smith informed me that numerous Vietnamese, Thai, and Indonesian women come to him to widen their eyelid creases. I was allowed to see their before-and-after surgery photographs.

References

Blacking, John
1977 The Anthropology of the Body. London: Academic Press.
Blumhagen, Dan
1979 The Doctor's White Coat: The Image of the Physician in Modern America. Annals of Internal Medicine 91:111–116.
Bordo, Susan
1990 Material Girl: The Effacements of Postmodern Culture. Michigan Quarterly Review 29:635–676.
Bourdieu, Pierre
1984[1979] Distinction: A Social Critique of the Judgment of Taste. R. Nice, trans. Cambridge, MA: Harvard University Press.
Brain, Robert
1979 The Decorated Body. New York: Harper and Row.
Daly, Mary
1978 Gyn/ecology: The Metaethics of Radical Feminism. Boston: Beacon Press.
Foucault, Michel
1977[1975] Discipline and Punish: The Birth of the Prison. A. Sheridan, trans. New York: Vintage Books. (Original: Surveiller et punir: naissance de la prison.)
Goffman, Erving
1979 Gender Advertisement. Cambridge, MA: Harvard University Press.
Goleman, Daniel
1991 When Ugliness Is Only in the Patient's Eye, Body Image Can Reflect a Mental Disorder. New York Times 2 October:B9.
Gramsci, Antonio
1971 Selections from the Prison Notebooks of Antonio Gramsci. Q. Hoare and G. N. Smith, eds. New York: International.
Harahap, Marwali
1982 Oriental Cosmetic Blepharoplasty. In Cosmetic Surgery for Non-White Patients. Harold Pierce, ed. Pp. 79–97. New York: Grune and Stratton.
Kim, Elaine
1986 Asian Americans and American Popular Culture. In Dictionary of Asian American History. Hyung-Chan Kim, ed. Pp. 99–114. New York: Greenwood Press.
Kristof, Nicholas
1991 More Chinese Look "West." San Francisco Chronicle. 7 July: Sunday Punch 6.
Lakoff, Robin Tolmach, and Raquel L. Scherr
1984 Face Value: The Politics of Beauty. Boston, MA: Routledge and Kegan Paul.
Lock, Margaret, and Nancy Scheper-Hughes
1990 A Critical-Interpretive Approach in Medical Anthropology: Rituals and Routines of Discipline and Dissent. In Medical Anthropology: Contemporary Theory and Method.

Thomas M. Johnson and Carolyn F. Sargent, eds. Pp. 47–72. New York: Praeger.

McCurdy, John A.
1990 Cosmetic Surgery of the Asian Face. New York: Thieme Medical Publications.

Millard, Ralph, Jr.
1964 The Oriental Eyelid and Its Surgical Revision. American Journal of Ophthalmology 57:646–649.

Molnar, Stephen
1983 Human Variation: Races, Types, and Ethnic Groups. Englewood Cliffs, NJ: Prentice-Hall.

O'Neill, John
1985 Five Bodies. Ithaca, NY: Cornell University Press.

Ong, Aihwa
1987 Spirits of Resistance and Capitalist Discipline: Factory Women in Malaysia. Albany: State University of New York Press.

Rosenthal, Elisabeth
1991a Cosmetic Surgeons Seek New Frontiers. New York Times 24 September:B5–B6
1991b Ethnic Ideals: Rethinking Plastic Surgery. New York Times 25 September:B7.

Sayoc, B. T.
1954 Plastic Construction of the Superior Palpebral Fold. American Journal of Ophthalmology 38:556–559.
1974 Surgery of the Oriental Eyelid. Clinics in Plastic Surgery 1(1):157–171.

Scheper-Hughes, Nancy
1992 Death without Weeping. Berkeley: University of California Press.

Scheper-Hughes, Nancy, and Margaret M. Lock
1991 The Message in the Bottle: Illness and the Micropolitics of Resistance. Journal of Psychohistory 18:409–432.

Tajima, Renee E.
1989 Lotus Blossoms Don't Bleed: Images of Asian Women. *In* Making Waves: An Anthology of Writings by and about Asian American Women. Diane Yeh-Mei Wong, ed. Pp. 308–317. Boston, MA: Beacon Press.

Takaki, Ronald
1989 Strangers from a Different Shore. Boston, MA: Little Brown.

Turner, Bryan
1987 Medical Knowledge and Social Power. London: Sage.

Turner, Terence
1980 The Social Skin. *In* Not Work Alone.

J. Cherfas and R. Lewin, eds. Pp. 112–140. London: Temple Smith.

Wolf, Naomi
1991 The Beauty Myth: How Images of Beauty Are Used against Women. New York: William Morrow.

Understanding the Reading

1. What is the difference between the cosmetic surgery of these Asian American women and of Caucasian women?
2. Why does the author object to it?
3. What are the reasons these Asian American women give for getting cosmetic surgery?
4. What are the influences that encourage these women to undergo surgery?
5. What are the character traits they associate with their physical features?

Suggestions for Responding

1. Debate whether this is a mutilation or a celebration of the body and whether this is an "individual" choice or a socially pressured decision.
2. Discuss stereotypes of Asian males and females in the United States and whether these have changed lately, perhaps as a result of Hollywood.
3. Research and discuss male cosmetic surgery in the United States. ✦

16

Before the Great Gorge

CARLOS CUMPIÁN

She raised the oven's temperature,
he unpeeled the plump poultry
from its factory plastic wrap,
they chopped onion, garlic, celery,
poured teaspoons of salt and sage,
stirred together ground black pepper
green parsley, a moon of dry bread to expand
beneath steaming giblet broth, as the round
dining table sprouted silver knives, forks and spoons.

Back during Squanto's time, wild bird meat simmered
    with acorn stuffing
and hot honey pumpkin
    joined sweet yams in bright buttery optimism,
releasing great appetites among Pilgrims
    in the new Massachusetts' air.

No parade of football mascots' sportsbabble
had spread like unbelted American waistlines.
But even then, bald babies and tipsy husbands
took satisfied afternoon naps,
while tired women did all the work.

Squanto's great, great, great, great grandchildren
take Thanksgiving in stride, drink cokes, coffee or beer
after finishing tonight's meal made from reservation
    deer,
someone offers fat and meat scraps to backyard dogs,
    another clears
the table as three sisters talk about finding work
    before Christmas,
cars fill up to drive mothers, uncles, aunties and
    cousins home,
teenagers smoke cigarettes, their words cloud around
    school,
past due assignments, and basketball,
no one speaks of the dark Dutch
or English sailing ships that landed
on these shores long ago or pale-eyed captains
    conquering
a "savage-continent" for pagan crown and Christ.

What was Squanto's peoples' reward
    after more sullen travelers survived?
Warrior-proud Wampanogs or Algonquins
    did not serve them like some
brown-skinned waiters and waitresses,
    happy in Pocahontas feathers
with hands eager for jive-glass bead wampum tips,
or acting Tonto phonies, "You smart, Kemo sabe,"
after sharing a thousand-year-old tradition, then to
    be told,
"Thanks for the popcorn chief, now head West!"
                          [1996]

From Carlos Cumpián, Armadillo Charm. C. 1996 by Carlos Cumpián. Reprinted by permission of the author.

Understanding the Reading

1. Why does the poet describe the food of a modern Thanksgiving, followed by that of the seventeenth century?

2. What is different and what is similar between the celebrations?
3. Do the Indians of today celebrate Thanksgiving in this poem?
4. What is the poet's view of this day?
5. What does the last paragraph mean?

Suggestions for Responding

1. Read about early Colonial history and relationships with northeastern Indian nations.
2. Research the contemporary legal battle between the Oneida Nation and New York State.
3. Research how much land owned by Indian nations has been contaminated, used as a toxic waste dump by large commercial concerns. ✦

17

Beyond the Melting Pot

WILLIAM A. HENRY III

Someday soon, surely much sooner than most people who filled out their Census forms last week realize, white Americans will become a minority group. Long before that day arrives, the presumption that the "typical" U.S. citizen is someone who traces his or her descent in a direct line to Europe will be part of the past. By the time . . . elementary students . . . reach midlife, their diverse ethnic experience in the classroom will be echoed in neighborhoods and workplaces throughout the U.S.

Already 1 American in 4 defines himself or herself as Hispanic or nonwhite. If current trends in immigration and birth rates persist, the Hispanic population will have further increased an estimated 21%, the Asian presence about 22%, blacks almost 12% and whites a little more than 2% when the 20th century ends. By 2020, a date no further into the future than John F. Kennedy's election is in the past, the number of U.S. residents who are Hispanic or nonwhite will have more than doubled, to nearly 115 million, while the white population will not be increasing at all. By 2056, when someone born today will be 66 years old, the "average" U.S. resident, as defined by Census statistics, will trace his or her descent to Africa, Asia, the Hispanic world, the Pacific Islands, Arabia—almost anywhere but white Europe.

While there may remain towns or outposts where even a black family will be something of an oddity, where English and Irish and German surnames will predominate, where a traditional (some will wistfully say "real") America will still be seen on almost every street corner, they will be only the vestiges of an earlier nation. The former majority will learn, as a normal part of everyday life, the meaning of the Latin slogan engraved on U.S. coins—E PLURIBUS UNUM, one formed from many.

Among the younger populations that go to school and provide new entrants to the work force, the change will happen sooner. In some places an America beyond the melting pot has already arrived. In New York State some 40% of elementary- and secondary-school children belong to an ethnic minority. Within a decade, the proportion is expected to approach 50%. In California white pupils are already a minority. Hispanics (who, regardless of their complexion, generally distinguish themselves from both blacks and whites) account for 31.4% of public school enrollment, blacks add 8.9%, and Asians and others amount to 11%—for a nonwhite total of 51.3%. This finding is not only a reflection of white flight from desegregated public schools. Whites of all ages account for just 58% of California's population. In San Jose bearers of the Vietnamese surname Nguyen outnumber the Joneses in the telephone directory 14 columns to eight.

Nor is the change confined to the coasts. Some 12,000 Hmong refugees from Laos have settled in St. Paul. At some Atlanta low-rent apartment complexes that used to be virtually all black, social workers today need to speak Spanish. At the Sesame Hut restaurant in Houston, a Korean immigrant owner trains Hispanic immigrant workers to prepare Chinese-style food for a largely black clientele. The Detroit area has 200,000 people of Middle Eastern descent; some 1,500 small grocery and convenience stores in the vicinity are owned by a whole subculture of Chaldean Christians with roots in Iraq. "Once America was a microcosm of European nationalities," says Molefi Asante, chairman of the department of African-American studies at Temple University in Philadelphia. "Today America is a microcosm of the world."

History suggests that sustaining a truly multiracial society is difficult, or at least unusual. Only a handful of great powers of the distant past—Pharaonic Egypt and Imperial Rome, most notably—managed to maintain a distinct national identity while embracing, and being ruled by, an ethnic mélange. The most ethnically diverse contemporary power, the Soviet Union,[1] is beset with secessionist demands and near tribal conflicts. But such comparisons are flawed, because those empires were launched by conquest and maintained through an aggressive military presence. The U.S. was created, and continues to be redefined, primarily by voluntary immigration. This process has been one of the country's great strengths, infusing it with talent and energy. The "browning of America" offers tremendous opportunity for capitalizing anew on the merits of many peoples from many lands. Yet this fundamental change in the ethnic makeup of the U.S. also poses risks. The American character is resilient and thrives on change. But past periods of rapid evolution have also, alas, brought out deeper, more fearful aspects of the national soul.

POLITICS: NEW AND SHIFTING ALLIANCES

A truly multiracial society will undoubtedly prove much harder to govern. Even seemingly race-free conflicts will be increasingly complicated by an overlay of ethnic tension. For example, the expected showdown in the early 21st century between the rising number of retirees and the dwindling number of workers who must be taxed to pay for the elders' Social Security benefits will probably be compounded by the fact that a large majority of recipients will be white, whereas a majority of workers paying for them will be nonwhite.

While prior generations of immigrants believed they had to learn English quickly to survive, many Hispanics now maintain that the Spanish language is inseparable from their ethnic and cultural identity, and seek to remain bilingual, if not primarily Spanish-speaking, for life. They see legislative drives to make English the sole official language, which have prevailed in some fashion in at least 16 states, as a political backlash. Says Arturo Vargas of the Mexican American Legal Defense and Educational Fund: "That's what English-only has been all about—a reaction to the growing population and influence of Hispanics. It's human nature to be uncomfortable with change. That's what the Census is all about, documenting changes and making sure the country keeps up."

Racial and ethnic conflict remains an ugly fact of American life everywhere, from working-class ghettos to college campuses, and those who do not raise their fists often raise their voices over affirmative action and other power sharing. When Florida Atlantic University, a state-funded institution under pressure to increase its low black enrollment, offered last month to give free tuition to every qualified black freshman who enrolled, the school was flooded with calls of complaint, some protesting that nothing was being done for "real" Americans. As the numbers of minorities increase, their demands for a share of the national bounty are bound to intensify, while whites are certain to feel ever more embattled. Businesses often feel whipsawed between immigration laws that punish them for hiring illegal aliens and anti-discrimination laws that penalize them for demanding excessive documentation from foreign-seeming job applicants. Even companies that consistently seek to do the right thing may be overwhelmed by the problems of diversifying a primarily white managerial corps fast enough to direct a work force that will be increasingly nonwhite and, potentially, resentful.

Nor will tensions be limited to the polar simplicity of white vs. nonwhite. For all Jesse Jackson's rallying cries about shared goals, minority groups often feel keenly competitive. Chicago's Hispanic leaders have leapfrogged between white and black factions, offering support wherever there seemed to be the most to gain for their own community. Says Dan Solis of the Hispanic-oriented United Neighborhood Organiza-

tion: "If you're thinking power, you don't put your eggs in one basket."

Blacks, who feel they waited longest and endured most in the fight for equal opportunity, are uneasy about being supplanted by Hispanics or, in some areas, by Asians as the numerically largest and most influential minority—and even more, about being outstripped in wealth and status by these newer groups. Because Hispanics are so numerous and Asians such a fast-growing group, they have become the "hot" minorities, and blacks feel their needs are getting lower priority. As affirmative action has broadened to include other groups—and to benefit white women perhaps most of all—blacks perceive it as having waned in value for them.

THE CLASSROOM: WHOSE HISTORY COUNTS?

Political pressure has already brought about sweeping change in public school textbooks over the past couple of decades and has begun to affect the core humanities curriculum at such élite universities as Stanford. At stake at the college level is whether the traditional "canon" of Greek, Latin and West European humanities study should be expanded to reflect the cultures of Africa, Asia and other parts of the world. Many books treasured as classics by prior generations are now seen as tools of cultural imperialism. In the extreme form, this thinking rises to a value-deprived neutralism that views all cultures, regardless of the grandeur or paucity of their attainments, as essentially equal.

Even more troubling is a revisionist approach to history in which groups that have gained power in the present turn to remaking the past in the image of their desires. If 18th, 19th and earlier 20th century society should not have been so dominated by white Christian men of West European ancestry, they reason, then that past society should be reinvented as pluralist and democratic. Alternatively, the racism and sexism of the past are treated as inextricable from—and therefore irremediably tainting—traditional learning and values.

While debates over college curriculum get the most attention, professors generally can resist or subvert the most wrong-headed changes and students generally have mature enough judgment to sort out the arguments. Elementary- and secondary-school curriculums reach a far broader segment at a far more impressionable age, and political expediency more often wins over intellectual honesty. Exchanges have been vituperative in New York, where a state task force concluded that "African-Americans, Asian-Americans, Puerto Ricans and Native Americans have all been victims of an intellectual and educational oppression. . . . Negative characterizations, or the absence of positive references, have had a terribly damaging effect on the psyche of young people." In urging a revised syllabus, the task force argued, "Children from European culture will have a less arrogant perspective of being part of a group that has 'done it all.'" Many intellectuals are outraged. Political scientist Andrew Hacker of Queens College lambastes a task-force suggestion that children be taught how "Native Americans were here to welcome new settlers from Holland, Senegal, England, Indonesia, France, the Congo, Italy, China, Iberia." Asks Hacker: "Did the Indians really welcome all those groups? Were they at Ellis Island when the Italians started to arrive? This is not history but a myth intended to bolster the self-esteem of certain children and, just possibly, a platform for advocates of various ethnic interests."

VALUES: SOMETHING IN COMMON

Economic and political issues, however much emotion they arouse, are fundamentally open to practical solution. The deeper significance of America's becoming a majority nonwhite society is what it means to the national psyche, to individuals' sense of themselves and their nation— their idea of what it is to be American. People of color have often felt that whites treated equality as a benevolence granted to minorities rather than as an inherent natural right. Surely that condescension will wither.

Rather than accepting U.S. history and its meaning as settled, citizens will feel ever more free to debate where the nation's successes sprang from and what its unalterable beliefs are. They will clash over which myths and icons to invoke in education, in popular culture, in ceremonial speechmaking from political campaigns to the State of the Union address. Which is the more admirable heroism: the courageous holdout by a few conquest-minded whites over Hispanics at the Alamo, or the anonymous expression of hope by millions who fled through Ellis Island? Was the subduing of the West a daring feat of bravery and ingenuity, or a wretched example of white imperialism? Symbols deeply meaningful to one group can be a matter of indifference to another. Says University of Wisconsin chancellor Donna Shalala: "My grandparents came from Lebanon. I don't identify with the Pilgrims on a personal level." Christopher Jencks, professor of sociology at Northwestern, asks: "Is anything more basic about turkeys and Pilgrims than about Martin Luther King and Selma? To me, it's six of one and half a dozen of the other, if children understand what it's like to be a dissident minority. Because the civil rights struggle is closer chronologically, it's likelier to be taught by someone who really cares."

Traditionalists increasingly distinguish between a "multiracial" society, which they say would be fine, and a "multicultural" society, which they deplore. They argue that every society needs a universally accepted set of values and that new arrivals should therefore be pressured to conform to the mentality on which U.S. prosperity and freedom were built. Says Allan Bloom, author of the best-selling *The Closing of the American Mind:* "Obviously, the future of America can't be sustained if people keep only to their own ways and remain perpetual outsiders. The society has got to turn them into Americans. There are natural fears that today's immigrants may be too much of a cultural stretch for a nation based on Western values."

The counterargument, made by such scholars as historian Thomas Bender of New York University, is that if the center cannot hold, then one must redefine the center. It should be, he says, "the ever changing outcome of a continuing contest among social groups and ideas for the power to define public culture." Besides, he adds, many immigrants arrive committed to U.S. values; that is part of what attracted them. Says Julian Simon, professor of business administration at the University of Maryland: "The life and institutions here shape immigrants and not vice versa. This business about immigrants changing our institutions and our basic ways of life is hogwash. It's nativist[2] scare talk."

CITIZENSHIP: FORGING A NEW IDENTITY

Historians note that Americans have felt before that their historical culture was being over-whelmed by immigrants, but conflicts between earlier-arriving English, Germans and Irish and later-arriving Italians and Jews did not have the obvious and enduring element of racial skin color. And there was never a time when the non-mainstream elements could claim, through sheer numbers, the potential to unite and exert political dominance. Says Bender: "The real question is whether or not our notion of diversity can successfully negotiate the color line."

For whites, especially those who trace their ancestry back to the early years of the Republic, the American heritage is a source of pride. For people of color, it is more likely to evoke anger and sometimes shame. The place where hope is shared is in the future. Demographer Ben Wattenberg, formerly perceived as a resister to social change, says, "There's a nice chance that the American myth in the 1990s and beyond is going to ratchet another step toward this idea that we are the universal nation. That rings the bell of manifest destiny.[3] We're a people with a mission and a sense of purpose, and we believe we have something to offer the world."

Not every erstwhile alarmist can bring himself to such optimism. Says Norman Podhoretz, editor of *Commentary*: "A lot of people are trying to undermine the foundations of the American experience and are pushing toward a more Balkanized[4] society. I think that would be a disaster, not only because it would destroy a precious social inheritance but also because it would lead to enormous unrest, even violence."

While know-nothingism[5] is generally confined to the more dismal corners of the American psyche, it seems all too predictable that during the next decades many more mainstream white Americans will begin to speak openly about the nation they feel they are losing. There are not, after all, many nonwhite faces depicted in Norman Rockwell's paintings. White Americans are accustomed to thinking of themselves as the very picture of their nation. Inspiring as it

may be to the U.S. role in global politics, world trade and the pursuit of peace, becoming a conspicuously multiracial society is bound to be a somewhat bumpy experience for many ordinary citizens. For older Americans, raised in a world where the numbers of whites were greater and the visibility of nonwhites was carefully restrained, the new world will seem even stranger. But as the children . . . in classrooms across the nation are coming to realize, the new world is here. It is now. And it is irreversibly the America to come.   [1990]

Terms

1. SOVIET UNION: The former European Asian nation, which included Russia, that dissolved in 1991; many of its republics now form the Commonwealth of Independent States.
2. NATIVIST: A policy of favoring native inhabitants over immigrants.
3. MANIFEST DESTINY: A nineteenth-century belief that White people had the duty and right to control and develop the entire North American continent.
4. BALKANIZED: Divided into small, hostile groups; the term derives from the division of the Balkan Peninsula into many nations.
5. KNOW-NOTHINGISM: A reference to a mid-nineteenth-century political movement that was hostile to immigrants and Catholics.

Understanding the Reading

1. What problems does Henry see that make it difficult to sustain "a truly multiracial society"?
2. What does *cultural imperialism* mean?
3. According to Henry, what is wrong with "a revisionist approach to history"? Why do some people advocate it?
4. What distinction do traditionalists make between a "multiracial" society and a "multicultural" one?

Suggestions for Responding

1. Do you think that, as Professor Bender asks, "our notion of diversity can successfully negotiate the color line"?

2. What does Wattenberg mean when he suggests that America is "the universal nation"? What does Podhoretz mean when he warns against America becoming "a more Balka-nized society"? Which view do you support? Why?

3. What will living in a "conspicuously multiracial society" mean to your personal future? ✦

SUGGESTIONS FOR RESPONDING TO PART I

1. Write a paper analyzing the racial and ethnic features of your identity. Consider your ancestral origins and how your heritage has influenced who you are today. Reflect on such factors as physical characteristics, language, religion, and family customs and traditions. Also, think about such expressive behaviors as dress, music, dance, family stories, holidays, and celebrations. These all may be markers of your ethnic heritage.

   If you think you have nothing to write about, remember that in the United States everyone has a racial and ethnic heritage. Whereas it is central to some people's identity, others may not be conscious of it at all. This is often because they are members of the dominant racial and ethnic culture, which assumes its values and traditions are "universal" or at least most significant or appropriate. If you belong to this group, look at yourself from the outside, from the perspective of another cultural system, several of which have been represented in these readings.

2. In response to the Gwaltney selection, you wrote questions you would ask if you were conducting an oral history interview. Singly or as a member of a group, evaluate those questions again. Then use them to interview an older person in your family or community.

   Many people find it helpful to write the questions on file cards, so they can be reorganized to adjust to the direction the interview takes. You may find some questions no longer relevant once the interview is underway; also, more important questions may occur to you on the spot. A tape recorder is useful, especially if you plan to prepare a word-for-word transcript, but always ask your informant for permission before you switch it on. Either with or without a recorder, it is important to take written notes (unless it makes your informant uncomfortable); in this way, you can highlight key pieces of information.

   Your final report could resemble Gwaltney's selection (a verbatim transcription of the words of your informant), or it may be more interpretive. In either case, listen to the tape and reread your notes *several* times before you begin to write, and refer to them after you have completed your report to confirm its accuracy.

3. Your instructor may want you to make an oral presentation of your ethnicity analysis or your oral history. In this case, prepare *brief* notes, again on file cards. Try to talk naturally and not read word for word. Rehearse your presentation several times to be sure you stay within the required time limit. You will feel more comfortable in front of your class if you have rehearsed at least once before an audience (a friend or roommate, for example). If this isn't possible, try speaking to a wall mirror. Above all, relax. Try to look at your audience, even if it seems difficult, because their reactions will be encouraging. Remember, you are talking to friends.

4. After completing Part I, how would you answer the questions "Who is an American?" and "Is there an American culture?" Support your responses with evidence from the readings.

II
Gender Identity

"IS IT A GIRL OR A BOY?" THIS IS INEVITABLY THE FIRST question asked about a new baby. As we grow older, we identify ourselves and each other as boys or girls, as women or men. In American culture, gender is the most salient feature of one's identity. It shapes our attitudes, our behavior, our experiences, our beliefs about ourselves and about others. Gender is so central to our perception of social reality that we often are not even conscious of how it shapes our behavior and our social interactions.

We all know the traditional definitions of masculinity and femininity. A "real man" should be **masculine**—that is, he should be strong and mechanically oriented, ambitious and assertive, in control of his emotions, knowledgeable about the world, a good provider. A "real woman," in turn, should be **feminine**—that is, passive and domestic, nurturing and dependent, emotional, preoccupied with her appearance, and maternal. These gender-appropriate characteristics and behaviors affect many areas of our lives: physical and psychological aspects, occupational choices, interpersonal relations, and so on.

The basis for gender distinctions is not wholly clear as of now, and the "nature/nurture" debate—whether or to what degree gendered behavior is controlled by biology or by socialization—continues. Scientists are investigating the roles that hormones, genes, chromosomes, and other physical features play in women's and men's psychological development, but these issues are complex and beyond the scope of this book.

We will concentrate on the view of many social scientists who study the diversity of appropriate or "natural" male and female behaviors in different cultures and other times. They see in this diversity strong evidence of the central role that culture plays in creating gender roles. As a result, they distinguish between **sex,** the biological "fact" of one's physiological and hormonal characteristics, and **gender,** the social categories that ascribe roles, appropriate behaviors, and personality traits to women and men. In this sense, male and female **sex roles** are differences in reproductive traits. The masculine and feminine behaviors are features of **gender roles.**

Social scientists believe that we learn our appropriate gender roles by a process called **socialization.** Gender roles are only one kind of role we learn. A **role** is any socially or culturally defined behavioral expectation that is presumed to apply to all individuals in the category. Socialization includes the many pressures, rewards, and punishments that compel us to conform to social expectations. These are deeply embedded in every aspect of our culture. Our treatment of infants and children, language, education, mass media, religion, laws, medical institutions and mental health systems, occupational environments, intimate relationships—all teach and reinforce appropriate gender behaviors.

The first three readings look at how we are taught gender beliefs and behaviors. In the first selection, Angela Phillips describes how parents and others begin to mold children into "appropriate" gender roles from birth—even when parents intend to raise them **androgynously,** having both female and male gender characteristics; she also considers the internal psychological factors that may influence gender learning. Ellen J. Reifler writes about how adults (and children) make assumptions about gender in children and reinforce traditional expectations, even when the parents themselves may be trying to raise their children in a nonsexist way. Next, Janet Shibley Hyde examines what we all learn about women from the very language we speak—about how it reinforces male superiority and female inferiority. Included in her report is a description of two studies that demonstrate how the use of gendered language, such as *he, she,* or *they,* affect the way both college students and elementary school children interpret the meaning of a sentence.

In the United States, White, middle-class values are too often received as the "norm." The next reading challenges that assumption. Janet Shibley Hyde discusses how American Indian culture, African American historical experiences, assumptions of Asian American culture, and Hispanic values lead to gender role expectations and experiences that differ from one another, as well as from those of the dominant culture.

The next reading, Rebecca Fiske's "August Genesis," brings us into a dreamlike creation story, as a woman goes about creating a man, using coral for his bones, blue chicory flowers and dung for his flesh, and her own hair for his spirit. She fills him with her own memories. Then Paula Gunn Allen speaks from her own experience about the value most Indian peoples attribute to women, despite distortions presented by the White mainstream.

The following three selections consider male gender roles. Doug Cooper Thompson describes the male stereotype and analyzes what it costs men to conform to those expectations. Leonard Kriegel relates his efforts to "beat" polio and prove himself a real American man. Carl Ryan looks at the stereotypical taboo against men's crying in public, even though a number of public figures have done so.

Male and female gender roles often lead to differences in the behaviors of women and men. Deborah Tannen considers differences in the ways that men and women interact with society and with one another, including reasons for dissimilarities in their attitudes about asking for and providing help.

The readings in this part should help us assess our own gender identity and give us fuller insight into the experiences of the opposite sex. A clearer sense of some of the consequences of traditional gender roles and gender expectations may encourage us to question just how "natural" traditional gender roles are. It will also help us consider whether or not we want to see changes in gender roles and sexual relationships and how to act on our decisions.

18

In the Beginning There Are Babies

ANGELA PHILLIPS

The making of a man starts from the moment of birth, or even before then, when the eye of the ultrasound scanner picks up the shadow that marks out a boy baby and Granny starts knitting in blue instead of pink. In many cultures the birth of a boy is overtly celebrated as a matter of more significance than that of a girl. A Pakistani friend told me that her husband had been considered very odd when he chose to celebrate the birth of a girl with the same show as he had the birth of his son.

Fathers in less traditional societies may not be able to make an overt display of their pleasure when they father a son, but surveys of fathers' behavior show that they still tend to take more interest in their male babies than in their female babies. They stay longer in the delivery room, handle them more, ask more questions about them, and stimulate them more. Girl babies are cuddled; boy babies are stimulated.

The research doesn't show nearly as much difference in the way mothers handle their different sex children as in the way fathers do after the first few weeks. To begin with, mothers tend to touch their daughters more than their sons—though they take care not to do so in the presence of their husbands—and they are also more likely to stimulate their daughters and to cuddle their sons, but after this early period the major difference lies in the fact that boys tend to be breast-fed for longer.

The similarity in the mothers' handling of boys and girls may lie in the fact that the physical demands of a small baby take up most of a mother's time. She doesn't differentiate her behavior because it is the baby who sets the pace of her care. A crying baby needs to be soothed no matter what its sex. Someone who only plays with a baby when it is clean, fed, and happy is more likely to initiate communication rather than simply responding to needs.

Nevertheless, while mothers may handle their small babies the same way, many express a very early sense of their sons as "different" and their daughters as extensions of themselves. One mother said to me: "I never expected to be the mother of sons. I don't know anything about boys." Another said: "My first sight of him was as very separate. My first thought was that he was very self-confident." I was reminded of my own first thoughts about my son that it wasn't me who knew how to feed him. He knew and showed me himself.

A newborn baby has no way of knowing that it is a separate being. As far as it is concerned, the body of its mother is an extension of its own body. When the baby cries this body is there. It is the difference between the person who mainly cares for the baby and other adults who come and go that helps the baby to understand both that people are separate creatures with their own boundaries and that people can leave—and come back.

The process of learning their separateness takes place between the ages of six months and eighteen months. At the same time the baby is also absorbing information about its gender. Indeed, some studies suggest that children as young as twelve months old can tell whether a strange child is male or female and will favor the child of the same sex. Most parents will testify that, once words come, they will very soon be used to divide and codify the world: big, little; boy, girl; man, woman.

For a girl, the road at first seems simple and straight. She realizes very early on that she is to become a woman. A woman is what her mother is. She is going to become a mother just like her own. She will be powerful, loving, and wise. Later she may come to understand that her father has a greater power, out in the world; but in these first few years identification with the mother means that she is firmly rooted. She has already identified her future—she simply has to grow into it.

For a boy, the way ahead is not so simple. He learns that the person who leaves (if he has a resident father at all) is the person he is going to be like. He is not going to grow up to be like Mommy. For the girl, the moment of recognition is also a moment of power. For the boy, it is a moment of uncertainty. Even in families in which both parents go out to work, the mother is, almost always, the biggest and most important person in his universe, but he will never be like her. His destiny is to be different. He is going to grow up to be a man, and from the moment he discovers this difference the search is on to discover the elements of masculinity.

If his father is accessible he will provide him with a sense of what it is to be male. He will play rougher games, talk to him differently, offer him "appropriate" toys. However, in most families the father is rarely available, and in an increasing number of families he is not available at all. So the things that the father does are distant, remote, difficult. While a girl finds, in these early years, an easily available model of what it is to be female, her brother is floundering. In the first two years he is much the same as the girls he sees, but in order to be a boy he must define his difference from them. He starts looking for clues.

Research indicates that, even in the very first year of life, boys tend to be more exploratory, whereas girls are more "person-oriented." Yet these little explorers are also more anxious and more easily upset when the object of their exploration proves frustrating. Perhaps this little boy is searching for himself, for the person he is going to be, whereas the little girl stays close to Mother (or a female caregiver), the living model of her future. Indeed, it is the inherent difficulty of this search for masculinity that, according to psychoanalyst Robert Stoller, is the reason why there are so many more men than women who grow up biologically normal and yet feel themselves to belong to the opposite sex (transsexuals).

The first clues are the easy ones. He finds that he has a little thing at the front that makes him different from girls. Depending on the culture he comes from, quite a lot of fuss may be made of this little thing. It will be given a name, it may be played with while his diaper is being changed. It may be the object of interested comment. It is outside his body, easy to see, and, what is more, feels interesting.

Soon he will start picking up other clues. If there is a man around his house he will gravitate toward him. Fathers tend to play more with their sons than with their daughters and, when they do play, tend to play more physical rough-and-tumble games. For most boys the intervention of the father is an event. Most of the time he is not there. In his absence, his mother and the other women who care for him have to provide verbal evidence of what a man is. Marianne

Grabrucker, in her diary of her daughter's first three years, noticed that mothers of boys were constantly referring to their "manliness":

> Whenever Martin has managed a little crap in the loo, it's praised as being just like a man's; if Martin has hurt himself and bleeds a little, it's described as being real man's blood; at mealtimes he's told to eat his food, just like a man, just like Daddy. . . . No one has ever told Aneli that she should eat up her food like a real woman.

Grabrucker sees this as part of the way in which a boy learns that men are more powerful. However, it could also be seen as one of the only ways in which mothers can present an image of the male to a boy who rarely sees his father. It isn't necessary to tell Aneli that she will grow up to be a real woman. Mommy is there and she can see her. A boy has to do much of his learning about men through what his mother says about them. His mother's view of men will become part of his own view—for good or ill.

When a female child is cared for wholly by a father rather than a mother, she too is likely to feel unsure of her gender role and need to be reminded that she will grow up to be a woman, "like Mommy." The few girls I know who have been brought up mainly by their fathers displayed very little interest in the homemaking games that occupy so much time for most other girls. Without the model of a mother to follow, housework games had little appeal. That is not what, in their eyes, Mommies do.

In families where both parents are equally involved in child care, gender difference in the behavior of children may still be quite marked, not because of what the parent is deliberately feeding in but because of what the child is looking for and adding to the sum of his or her own identity.

This father of two has a firm commitment to bringing up his children as equals. He works from home and has a high level of involvement with their day-to-day care. I asked him what games he plays with his children. He told me: "Football, Frisbee, kite flying, swimming, board and card games. Different only due to their ages." He then added: "But my daughter likes to play with the Playmobile [a construction set with people in it], while my son likes to construct complicated things with rope, wood and engines [real or imagined]. He liked cars best; she played with dolls from an early age."

Already these children seem to be selecting the characteristics that apply particularly to their same-gendered parents and practicing those with more diligence than the others. Of course, they are helped with their selecting by clues from elsewhere. Both these children have been cared for while their parents work. The alternative caregivers are female. Most of the other adults encountered during the first two years will have been female. The other male adults will have been, on the whole, fairly remote.

As soon as they start mixing regularly with other children, they will start picking up new clues. This same father says: "I remember my son playing with the toy stove and other home-making things and being chased out by a girl who said boys weren't allowed in there. He was clearly shocked." A mother of three sons, who have mainly been cared for by their father, reported a similar experience:

> Claudio had two friends home from nursery and they played in my old doll's house. Claudio put the father doll in the kitchen and said, "Daddy's making dinner." His two male friends giggled and said, "Daddies don't make dinner." Claudio said, "Mine does," but he never played with the doll's house again.

In fact, boys have very little idea of what fathers actually do. Boys in a London primary school were asked: "What do fathers do which is different from mothers?" They answered: "Sit down a lot; laze about; smoke a pipe." Asked what fathers in the olden days might have done, one said: "They might have been challenging each other with duels and swords and stuff." Another suggested, "Pirates." When asked what fathers were for, two said: "To look after us." Another suggested: "To be sensible and don't rob banks and that." A third: "Helping you to live because they buy your clothes."

They were then asked what it would be like if the men had babies. One child said: "Maybe they might decide to give the women more difficult complicateder jobs, where you get more money and more sort of dangerous jobs like being a diver, which I don't think women are allowed to do." Another added, "Also being a police officer or a fire officer."

When my daughter and her friends play with boys, they always insist that the boys play "Daddies," which in this context always means getting bossed around or being sent out to "work"— whatever that means. Given their understanding of what their own fathers do, it isn't surprising that the boys quickly tire of such a role and ask to play the baby instead, where at least they can clown around.

So while most girls are industriously home-building with whatever they can lay their hands on, boys have no simple role to inhabit. Even those boys with no men in their lives will have picked up pretty early on the fact that men drive cars, trains, buses—and they will drive them too. Those with the coordination to do so may start making things (though boys often lag behind in the fine motor skills that would allow them to paint, draw, and color). Given encouragement, they will also dress up—though they soon work out that most dressing up includes dresses, which are intended for girls; men in our culture don't dress up, and boys have to make do with firemen's helmets while girls are swathing themselves in lace.

So just how can a three-year-old boy play out the fantasy of being a man? Is it any wonder that many of them are running around being loud and silly, trying to find a role to inhabit? In any given situation, small girls are more likely to be quietly getting on with something, learning to do something that their mother can do, while their male peers are still running around like mad things, as if trying to divine from the air a sense of what it is they would like to be getting on with. Perhaps this is one of the reasons why boys from as young as a year old appear to be naughtier than girls and are more often reprimanded.

However vague and imprecise the information about masculinity, there is no more dedicated detective than a small child in search of knowledge. Superheroes provide the most obvious and overt messages, just as folk and fairy tales have done in the past. If your son is behaving like Hulk Hogan, Superman, or Captain Planet, it is hardly surprising. These figures are very clearly identified as male. They are mostly involved in fighting and protecting other, more fragile (often female) people and they are also, clearly and unambiguously, *good*. . . .

LEARNING NOT TO BE GENTLE

What of the many boys who are not anxious, aggressive, and excitable? While most surveys confirm that boys are more likely than girls to be naughty and aggressive, they also show that the gender difference is not universal. In any group there are likely to be more aggressive boys than aggressive girls, but there will also be almost as many unaggressive boys as there are unaggressive girls. Gentleness is almost as often a male attribute as it is a female one, but it is not *labeled* as masculine behavior and it is not counted in surveys.

Between the ages of eighteen months and three years it is very common for both boys and girls to go through a phase in which they push, grab, and defend what they see as their own territory from others. Some children may take longer than others to learn how to control what is theirs and work out how to allow another child to "borrow" something without fearing that they will lose it forever. This behavior may be described as aggressive. Other children are so fearful that they never really manage to work out how they can hang on to what is theirs, nor do they learn how to lend. They feel perpetually at the mercy of more powerful forces.

Girls and boys may belong to either category. This is how one father described his son and daughter: "My son has been more dependent, more easily frightened and hurt, less communicative emotionally, and more likely to brood." A mother talked about her son's experience of starting nursery school: "He was desperately unhappy and I was desperately worried about him. He couldn't cope with the number of people and the range of options. He spent much of the time hiding under the table." A third parent said: "I stopped going to my NCT [National Childbirth Trust mothers' group] after my second child because his brother, at three, was being victimized by the other boys."

These parents worry about their children's lack of assertiveness, and they may not be aware that many of the boys who spend their time running around and shouting, or losing their tempers and screaming, may also be demonstrating their anxiety. When John started nursery school at two and a half, he went into a small group of five children with one staff member. The day

was well organized and he clearly felt safe and happy. After a few weeks, the staff decided that, since he was physically bigger than the other children and seemed more advanced in his play, he should join the older group of three- to five-year-olds. His behavior immediately deteriorated. He reacted to the bigger space, larger numbers, and less structured activity not by withdrawing but by running wildly around the room.

A child who is running wild and apparently out of control is far more likely to hurt someone else than a child who is sitting quietly building with Lego. This doesn't necessarily mean that he is aggressive, but it may well be seen that way. John, "promoted" because of his maturity, was now in danger of being labeled as a problem. In the preschool years boys are persistently scored as more aggressive than girls by researchers. The difference is more marked than at any other life stage.

The fact is that there is no socially sanctioned way in which boys can show their anxiety and ask for help. If they are rough and anxious they are seen as aggressive, but they are given precious little encouragement to show weakness. While girls are encouraged to seek help from adults, boys are expected to learn to cope. This encouragement may, again, not be explicit, but it is worth noting that girls and boys get different responses both to aggressive behavior and to defensive behavior.

Little girls quickly learn that by crying they will enlist adult help on their side. Crying is therefore a more effective defense than hitting back. It might be in the interests of boys to learn the same strategy, but too often crying in boys will elicit a very different and far less positive response.

In a study on the effects of divorce, researchers discovered that in all the family groups they studied: "Crying and distress in boys received less frequent and shorter periods of comforting and more ambivalent comforting than did distress signals from girls." By *ambivalent* the researchers meant responses such as "a hug, combined with: 'There, there! Boys don't cry.' Girls were far more likely to be given unqualified reassurance."

Because there are no models of gentle boys, these children may find that they also receive confusing messages about the way they should behave. Says Clarissa:

> At four, Justin seems to get on better with girls. He loves singing and dancing and playing musical instruments and he also likes imaginary play, which is as much to do with things like going on holiday, going to a restaurant, or being Peter Pan and sprinkling people with pixie dust as it is with playing monsters.
>
> I really do love him just as he is, but sometimes I feel slightly anxious. Are we making him too gentle, in a way which might open him to bullying later on? Are we overly soppy and affectionate with him, and might that make him different from the other boys? Should we toughen him up a bit? And that's really the dilemma. I am an avowed feminist. I want him to grow up to be gentle and kind. I want him to respect women as equals. But I also want him to hold his own in a world of men, and I don't want anyone, male or female, to regard him as a wimp. I keep thinking it's something of a battleground out there. But then I think, Would I even be asking these questions if Justin were a girl? I think not.   [1994]

Understanding the Reading

1. How do fathers and mothers tend to handle boy babies and girl babies differently?
2. What are the differences between girl infants and boy infants?
3. Infant boys are described as being more "exploratory" than infant girls are. What may be the cause?
4. How does being cared for by a father affect a female child?
5. What else, besides parents, influences gender behavior in small children?
6. How are boys affected by the relative unavailability of adult males in their lives?
7. What causes preschool boys to run wild and appear to be out of control?

Suggestions for Responding

1. If you know someone who has an infant, or if you can get permission to observe at a day-care center, watch the behaviors of a care-giver with girl infants and/or boy infants. Report on whether your observations conform with Phillips' analysis.

2. Watch parents of small children in some public place, like a park or mall, and note the differences between the males and females in their interactions with the little ones. ✦

19

Time Warp in the Toy Store

ELLEN J. REIFLER

Last week Linda went to the drive-up window at McDonald's and ordered a kid's meal for her daughter. "Is this for a boy or a girl?" asked the clerk. Annoyed, Linda turned to Shaina and translated.

"Do you want the Hot Wheels or the Barbie?"

"I want the car, Mommy."

How can this conversation be possible in 1994? Our children's world is littered with the sex role stereotypes we adults have tossed in the garbage.

It is 25 years since newspapers stopped categorizing their help-wanted sections by male and female. It is illegal to deny a job to someone on the basis of gender. But despite the resolve of many parents of the '70s, in the '90s there is still a firmly-entrenched time warp in the toy store. Girls play with dolls, tot-sized housewares, and make-up, reflecting the holy trinity of childcare, housework, and seduction. Boys play with cars, construction sets, and superheroes; that is, they operate vehicles, erect buildings, and rescue people.

OBSESSED BY GENDER

The rigid role-typing starts at birth. Try dressing a child in a gender-neutral way and see what happens. People are mortified when they guess the wrong sex. Once when I was out with my four-week-old son, who was dressed in yellow, an admiring grandma commented, "What a pretty girl." "Thanks, but he's a boy," I responded. Visibly embarrassed, she quickly countered, "What a big boy!"

Something similar happened after I gave birth to my daughter. Like all newborns, she bore a remarkable resemblance to Winston Churchill. However, the nurse felt socially obligated to comment on her girlish features. "Only little girls have such feminine eyebrows," I was told. In fact, she does have beautiful brows, which angle sharply down, just like her father's.

Beyond Pink and Blue

Studies show that girls are handled, cuddled, and spoken to more than boys, and we have all observed that parents bounce and roughhouse more with their sons than with their daughters. By kindergarten, children have received thousands of hours of gender conditioning.

We also interpret their individual characteristics according to our preconceived notions, disregarding what doesn't fit. Watch a child playing quietly, building something in a sand box. Do you see a good girl playing quietly or a boy who is a budding engineer? Same sand box, only now the child has lost interest and is throwing sand. Is she manipulating for attention or is he acting out his natural aggressive instincts?

Culture Cops

Why? Why is a tantrum-throwing girl labeled manipulative and a tantrum-throwing boy called aggressive? Why is a clinging girl, who cries when Mommy leaves, seen as timid, while the same behavior in a boy is labeled oedipal? (Or, as one parent put it, "Little boys just have a thing about their mommies!")

Children can even become their own gender police. After all, one of the jobs of childhood is trying to figure out what it means to be a girl or a boy. My five-year-old daughter was told by another little girl, "You shouldn't watch Power Rangers, that's a boy's show." Clearly, my child could skip this show without missing out on a culturally enriching experience. But it does make me angry that someone is trying to stop her from identifying with superheroes. (Anyway, at least two of the five "Power Rangers" are women.)

What's going on here? It seems so easy for parents to accept, and even encourage, this sex-typing. And so hard to accept the obvious truth that children's personality traits and interests are not gender-based.

One reason may be a deeply-ingrained desire to perpetuate the family line. Parents may want their son to grow up to be the kind of father who willingly shares the childcare, but they fear that if he's too "sensitive" there may be no grandchildren at all.

But parental fears probably go deeper than this. Most of us didn't have kids to create a grandchildren factory. Besides, we're all aware of gay men and lesbians who joyfully had babies or adopted them and who are wonderful parents.

I believe that the real answer lies in our deeply rooted homophobia, grafted onto our cultural conditioning. Some of our best friends may be gay but most parents are dead set against such a fate for their own children. Partly, they fear the social stigma. Parents are not lulled by the veneer of acceptance found on TV talk shows. They know the world is harsher and harder on those who are different, and they want to protect their children from that reality. Add to this the fear of AIDS and you have a potent brew of paranoia. And parents' fears are not only for their children, but for themselves, too. What would it say about them if their children turned out to be gay? Deep-seated fears like these explain why so many people who believe in equal opportunity still want to preserve the illusion that boys and girls are intrinsically different. Unfortunately, the result is that these fears, unconscious or deliberate, limit their children's world.

A Modest Proposal

What do I suggest? Since I don't advocate censorship or toy burning, I don't want to ban "Barbie" or "GI Joe." What I would like to do is get rid of the artificial categories. When I walk into a toy store, I want the clerk to ask, "Do you want construction toys or dolls?" instead of "Is this for a boy or a girl?" Furthermore, if I were in charge, I would put the action figures on the same shelf as the Barbies. Yes, it will be a hundred years, if ever, before boys buy baby dolls in the same proportion as girls. So what? My point is, let's open up their universe and not limit it. Give girls more chances to build and to rescue and give boys more dolls to love.

I have seen one of my own children, at age four, play happily with a doll house and then

20 minutes later, stage a fight with toy soldiers. I can remember watching my son, at age six, play fight games with his favorite action figure (actually a boy doll but never described as such in TV ads) in the afternoon. At night, he made a bed out of a shoebox and lovingly tucked his action figure into it. Despite all the messages my six-year-old had been exposed to, he remained open to the whole range of "Let's pretend." Shouldn't we help that process? Life will place limits on our children all too soon. It's our responsibility to expand their world and let them find their own individual place in it.   [1994]

Understanding the Reading

1. What role do adults play in teaching children gender-appropriate behavior?
2. How is such behavior influenced by other children?
3. How does homophobia affect sex-typing?
4. What does Reifler recommend that we do to reduce or eliminate sex-typing?

Suggestions for Responding

1. Visit a toy store and observe how gender stereotypes affect its layout. Write a letter to the store manager, commenting on your observations and making any suggestions you feel might be appropriate.
2. Ask several people what they think about a preschool boy playing dress-up in female clothes and about a rough-and-tumble preschool girl. Report on their responses, especially on how their attitudes differ toward the boy and the girl. ✦

20

How Women Are Treated in Language

Janet Shibley Hyde

Feminists have sensitized the public to the peculiar properties of terms like *man* used to refer to the entire species. Here we shall discuss patterns that emerge in the way the English language treats women and concepts of gender.

Male as Normative

One of the clearest patterns in our language is the normativeness of the male. The male is regarded as the normative (standard) member of the species, and this is expressed in many ways in language. These ways include the use of *man* to refer to all human beings, and the use of *he* for a neutral pronoun (as in the sentence "The infant typically begins to sit up around six months of age; he may begin crawling at about the same time"). The male-as-normative principle in language can lead to some absolutely absurd statements. For example, there is a state law that reads, "No person may require another person to perform, participate in, or undergo an abortion of pregnancy against his will."

Sometimes students in their essays mistakenly use the phrase "the male species" (the expression they really mean to use is "the male of the species"). But in a way they are expressing the principle well—the male is the species.

At the very least, the male-as-normative usage introduces ambiguity into our language. When someone uses the word *men,* does *he* mean males, or does he mean people in general? When Dr. Karl Menninger writes a book entitled *Man Against Himself,* is it a book about people generally, or is it a book about the tensions experienced by males?

Some people excuse such usage by saying that terms like *man* are generic. Such an explanation, however, is not adequate. To illustrate how weak the "generic" logic is, consider the objections raised by some men who have recently joined the League of Women Voters. They have complained that the name of the organization should be changed, for it no longer adequately describes its members, some of whom are now men. Suppose in response to their objection they were told that by *woman* is meant "generic woman," which of course includes men. Do you think they would feel satisfied?

The male-as-normative principle is also reflected in the *female-as-the-exception* or *female as other* phenomenon. A newspaper reported the results of the Bowling Green State University women's swimming team and men's swimming team in two articles close to each other. The headline reporting the men's results was "BG Swimmers Defeated." The one for the women was "BG Women Swimmers Win." As another example, when the University of Wisconsin recently picked a new chancellor, the headline read, "UW Picks Woman Chancellor." It is hard to believe that had a man been chosen, the headline would have been "UW Picks Man Chancellor." His maleness would not have been considered newsworthy. The point is that we consider athletes and prestigious professionals to be normatively male. In cases where they are female it seems important to note this fact as an exception.

PARALLEL WORDS

Another interesting phenomenon in our language is how parallel words for males and females often have quite different connotations. For example, consider the following list of parallel male and female words:

MALE	FEMALE
bachelor	spinster
dog	bitch
master	mistress

Note that the female forms of the words generally have negative connotations; a bachelor is viewed as a carefree, happy person, while a spinster is the object of pity. Also note that the negative connotation to the female words is often sexual in nature. For example, a man who is a master is good at what he does or is powerful, but a woman who is a mistress is someone who is financially supported in return for her sexual services.

Of course, many of these parallel words originally had equivalent meanings for male and female. An example is *master* and *mistress,* terms originally used to refer to the male and female heads of the household. Over time, however, the female term took on negative connotations, a process known as *pejoration.* Linguist Muriel Schulz has argued that this process is caused simply by prejudice. That is, terms applied to women take on negative meanings because of prejudice against women.

EUPHEMISMS

Generally when there are many euphemisms for a word, it is a reflection of the fact that people find the word and what it stands for to be distasteful or stressful. For example, consider all the various terms we use instead of *bathroom* or *toilet.* And then there is the great variety of terms such as *pass away* that we substitute for *die.*

Feminist linguists have argued that we similarly have a strong tendency to use euphemisms for the word *woman.* That is, people have a tendency to avoid using the word *woman,* and instead substitute a variety of terms that seem more "polite" or less threatening, the most common euphemisms being *lady* and *girl.* In contrast to the word *man,* which is used quite frequently and comfortably, *woman* is used less frequently and apparently causes some discomfort or we wouldn't use euphemisms for it.

INFANTILIZING

A 25-year-old man wrote to an advice columnist, depressed because he wanted to get married but had never had a date. Part of the columnist's response was

> Just scan the society pages and look at the people who are getting married every day. Are the men all handsome? Are the girls all beautiful?

This is an illustration of the way in which people, rather than using *woman* as the parallel to *man,* substitute *girl* instead. As noted in the previous section, this in part reflects the use of a euphemism. But it is also true that *boy* refers to young males, *man* to adult males. Somehow *girl,* which in a strict sense should refer only to young females, is used for adult women as well. Women are called by a term that seems to make them less mature than they are; women are thus *infantilized* in language. Just as the term *boy* became very offensive to Black activists, so *girl* has become offensive to feminists.

There are many other illustrations of this infantilizing theme. When a ship sinks, it's "Women and children first," putting women and children in the same category. Other examples in language are expressions for women such as *baby, babe,* and *chick.* The problem with these terms is that they carry a meaning of immaturity and perhaps irresponsibility.

HOW IMPORTANT IS ALL THIS?

Although many of the tenets of the women's movement—such as equal pay for equal work—have gained widespread acceptance, the importance of changing our language to eliminate sexism has not. Many people regard these issues as silly or trivial. Just how important is the issue of sexism in language?

It is true that language reflects thought processes. This being the case, sexism in language may be the symptom, not the disease. That is, things like the generic use of *man* and *he* may simply reflect the fact that we do think of the male as the norm for the species. The practical conclusion from this is that what needs to be changed is our thought processes, and once they change, language will change with them.

On the other hand, one of the classic theories of psycholinguistics, the Whorfian hypothesis, states that the specific language we learn influences our mental processes. If that is true, then things like the generic use of *man* make us think that the male is normative. This process might start with very young children when they are just beginning to learn the language. If such processes do occur, then social reformers need to pay careful attention to eliminate sexism in language because of its effect on our thought processes.

An important study demonstrated that even when *he* and *his* are used in explicitly gender-neutral contexts, people tend to think of males. College students were asked to make up stories creating a fictional character who would fit the theme of a stimulus sentence. The students were divided into six groups, for three of the groups, the stimulus sentence was as follows:

> In a large coeducational institution the average student will feel isolated in ——— introductory courses.

One of the groups received *his* in the blank space, another received *their,* and the third received *his or her.* The other three groups received one of those alternative pronouns in this stimulus sentence:

> Most people are concerned with appearance. Each person knows when ——— appearance is unattractive.

Averaging the responses of all groups, when the pronoun was *his,* only 35 percent of the stories were about females; for *their,* 46 percent were about females; and for *his or her,* 56 percent were about females. Females were chosen as characters more often for the second stimulus sentence (concerned about appearance) than for the first. But the important point is that even though a sentence referred to "the average student," when *his* was used most people thought of males. Though a linguist may say that *he* and *his* are gender-neutral, they are certainly not gender-neutral in a psychological sense.

It seems likely that both processes—thought influencing language and language influencing thought—occur to some extent. Insofar as language does have the potential for influencing our thinking, sexism in language becomes a critical issue.

I became interested in a related question raised earlier—namely, the effect of sexist language on children—and so I began a series of studies to investigate the question. First, I generated an age-appropriate sentence like the one used by Moulton and her colleagues and asked first-, third-, and fifth-grade children to tell stories in response to it:

> When a kid goes to school, ——— often feels excited on the first day.

As in the study by Moulton and her colleagues, one-third of the children received *he* for the blank, one third received *they,* and one-third received *he or she.* The results were even more dramatic than those of Moulton and her colleagues with college students. When the pronoun was *he,* only 12 percent of the stories were about females. In fact, when the pronoun was *he,* not a single elementary school boy told a story about a girl. It is clear, then, that when children hear *he* in a gender-neutral context, they think of a male. I also asked the children some questions to see if they understood the grammatical rule that *he* in certain contexts refers to everyone, both males and females. Few understood the rule; for example, only 28 percent of the first-graders gave answers showing that they knew the rule.

I also had the children fill in the blanks in some sentences such as the following:

If a kid likes candy, ——— might eat too much.

The children overwhelmingly supplied *he* for the blank; even 72 percent of the first-graders did so.

Therefore, this research shows two things. First, the majority of elementary school children have learned to supply *he* in gender-neutral contexts (as evidenced by the fill-in task). Second, the majority of elementary school children do not know the rule that *he* in gender-neutral contexts refers to both males and females and have a strong tendency to think of males in creating stories from neutral *he* cues. For them, then, the chain of concepts is as follows: (1) The typical person is a "he." (2) *He* refers only to males. Logically, then, might they not conclude that (3) the typical person is a male?   [1995]

Understanding the Reading

1. What does the concept "male as normative" mean, and how does our language reinforce it?
2. Why are the female terms in parallel words more pejorative than the male ones?
3. Why do we tend to use more euphemisms for *woman* than for *man?*
4. How does our language infantilize women?
5. How important is sexism in the English language?
6. Hyde reports on two studies about the influence of pronoun usage. What did these studies reveal?

Suggestions for Responding

1. In a small group, expand on Hyde's list of parallel male and female words and analyze the connotations in each pair. Try to identify some parallels in which the female term has a more positive connotation than the male one.
2. In a small group, develop a list of slang terms for women and another list for men. Discuss what this exercise demonstrates about social attitudes regarding women and men. ✦

21

Gender Roles and Ethnicity

JANET SHIBLEY HYDE

Against [the] background of the cultural heritages of women of color in the United States, let us consider the gender roles that have evolved in these various ethnic communities. A basic tenet of feminist theory is that gender and ethnicity interact as social norms are formed and as they affect behavior. Thus gender roles are defined in the cultural context of a particular ethnic group, and it is not surprising that there are variations in gender roles from one ethnic group to another.

GENDER ROLES AMONG AMERICAN INDIANS

It is clear today that the early work of anthropologists misrepresented women's roles in Indian culture. The tale is an interesting one of how sex bias and race bias can easily pervade research in the social sciences. The researchers were male and non-Indian. As such, they focused on male activities and had greater access to male informants. A stereotyped dichotomy of Indian woman as either princess or squaw emerged, much like the saint/slut dichotomy that was drawn for Victorian white women. Furthermore, because the anthropologists were non-Indians and therefore outsiders, they were able to observe only public behaviors and how Indians interacted with outsiders, thereby missing private interactions. In some tribes, dealing with outsiders was an activity assigned to men. Therefore, researchers over estimated male power within the tribe because they did not observe Indian women's powerful roles within the private sphere. In some tribes, for example, there was a matrilineal system of inheritance, meaning that women could own property and that property passed from mother to daughter. Indian women, doubtless wary after the legacy of white violence against Indians, were unlikely to share their intimate rituals or feelings with these outsiders.

As an example of the problems with this early research, scholars claimed that there was a pattern of isolating menstruating women from the tribe and its activities, keeping them in a secluded menstrual hut, based on the Indian view that women were contaminated at this time. Firsthand accounts from Indian writers, however, provide a different interpretation. Menstruating women were not shunned as unclean, but rather were considered extremely powerful, with tremendous capacities for destruction. Women's spiritual forces were thought to be especially strong during menstruation, and women were generally thought to possess powers so great that they could counteract or weaken men's powers. The interpretation makes all the difference—shifting from a view of a shunned, powerless woman to that of a too-powerful woman.

A woman's identity and gender roles in traditional Indian culture were rooted in her spirituality, extended family, and tribe. The emphasis was on the collective and on harmony with the spiritual world, the world of one's family and tribe, and the natural world.

The evidence shows that some North American Indian tribes had a system of egalitarian gender roles, in which separate but equally valued tasks were assigned to males and females. It is important to remember tribal variations, for not all tribes had such egalitarian patterns, but certainly some—for example, the Klamath—did.

There is also evidence that some tribes—such as the Canadian Blackfeet—had institutionalized alternative female roles. There was the role of the "manly hearted woman," a role that a woman who was exceptionally independent and aggressive could take on. There was a "warrior woman" role among the Apache, Crow, Cheyenne, Blackfoot, and Pawnee tribes. In both cases, women could express "masculine" traits or participate in male-stereotyped activities while continuing to live and dress as a woman.

The *berdache* is another interesting variation in gender roles for women. A custom found among at least 33 tribes, it involved a woman's complete shift to the male role, including dressing as a man and performing male-stereotyped work. Although early anthropologists viewed this practice through the lenses of their own norms and were horrified, the most recent scholarship indicates that female *berdaches* had excellent reputations and were highly valued members of the tribe.

GENDER ROLES AMONG AFRICAN AMERICAN WOMEN

A methodological point must be recognized, one that is apparent in research on African Americans but is a problem with research on other ethnic groups as well. The problem in much of the research to be cited is the *confounding of race and social class*. Because Blacks tend to be overrepresented in the lower class and whites in the middle class, it is generally not clear whether differences between Blacks and whites should be attributed to race or to social class. Research techniques generally have not been powerful enough to conquer this ambiguity. As you read this material on gender and ethnicity, you should keep in mind that much of what seem to be race differences may actually be due to social-class differences.

Multiple gender roles—mother, worker, head of household, wife—have been a reality for African American women for generations, in contrast to the situation for white middle-class American women, for whom these multiple roles are more recent. Reflecting on the absurdity of defining women's role on the pedestal in white middle-class Victorian terms, the Black abolitionist Sojourner Truth commented at a women's rights convention in the 1800s:

> That man over there says that women need to be helped into carriages, and lifted over ditches, and to have the best place everywhere. Nobody ever helps me into carriages, or over mud puddles, or gives me any best places. . . . And ain't I a woman? Look at me! Look at my arm! . . . I have plowed and planted, and gathered into barns, and no man could head me—and ain't I a woman? I could work as much and eat as much as a man (when I could get it), and bear the lash as well—and ain't I a woman? I have borne thirteen children and seen most of them sold off into slavery, and when I cried out with a woman's grief, none but Jesus heard—and ain't I a woman?

African American women have had to define their identity in terms of roles other than exclusively housewife-mother. Although motherhood is still a prime gender-role definer, African American women have taken on additional roles, such as worker and head of household. Black women generally expect that they must hold paying jobs as adults, and this expectation has important consequences for their educational and occupational attainments, as we shall see later.

The role of the African American woman as head of household has received a great deal of publicity under the term *Black matriarchy,* suggesting that the Black woman has greater power than the man does in the Black family and culture. The high frequency with which Black households, as compared with white households, are headed by women is usually given as evidence for this phenomenon. In 1987, 43 percent of Black families were headed by women, as were 23 percent of Hispanic families and 13 percent of white families. Three factors contribute to the greater rates of female-headed households among African Americans: (1) the obstacles African American men have encountered in seeking and maintaining jobs necessary to support their families; (2) the rules of the welfare system, which make it financially desirable for the man to live separately from his family; and (3) the greatly disproportionate gender ratio (number of males to number of females) among Blacks. Among those aged 25 to 44, there are 99.6 men for every 100 women among whites, but only 85.7 men for every 100 women among Blacks; thus (in the context of social norms that discourage interracial marriage) there are just not enough men to go around. On the other hand, the emphasis on the matriarchal domination of African American families ignores the fact that if 43 percent of Black households are headed by women, then 57 percent must be headed by men or by men and women jointly. Thus, the female-headed household, while more common among Blacks than whites, is not typical, since the majority of Black households are not female-headed. Furthermore, there is a clear trend toward an increase in the number of female-headed households among whites.

Other studies have not looked at the simple notion of head of household, but rather have tried to assess more subtle patterns of *spouse dominance* by examining the ways in which couples solve problems such as childcare and purchasing. The conclusions from this research are that there are no race differences in patterns of spouse domination; the egalitarian pattern is by far the most common for both Blacks and whites. There are also regional variations: in the South, lower-class, intact Black families are more frequently patriarchal than white ones are, while in the North, the reverse pattern seems to hold.

Indeed, some scholars argue that the extent of Black matriarchy, with attending psychological castration of the Black man, has been magnified out of all proportion in the writings of white social scientists. The strengths of African American women, standing in sharp contrast to the passivity of the female role among whites, have been misinterpreted as being dominance. In addition, the importance to the Black woman of the emotional and financial support of male partners has generally been ignored. Certainly problems arise in research in this area as a result of evaluating Black behavior by white standards. At the very least, the term *Black matriarchy* oversimplifies the complex relationships between Black men and women.

Among the elderly, the role of Black women also differs from that of white women. The feelings of uselessness and the lack of roles experienced by white women in their youth-oriented culture are not so common among African Americans. The extended-family structure among Blacks provides a secure position and role for the elderly. The "granny" role—helping to care for young grandchildren, giving advice based on experience—is a meaningful and valued role for the elderly Black woman. Elderly Black women seem to have a more purposeful and respected role than elderly white women do. This pattern of seeing elderly women as wise and respected is also found among American Indians.

GENDER ROLES AMONG ASIAN AMERICAN WOMEN

It is popular in the 1990s to think of Asian Americans as the "model minority." According to the 1980 census, for example, the median earning of Asian Americans was $23,600, higher than the median of $20,800 for whites. Currently, 42 percent of Asian Americans graduate from college—a rate double that of whites. Nonetheless, feminist Asian Americans believe that Asian American women are victims of both racism and sexism. For example, the higher wages of Asian Americans disguise the fact that they are underpaid relative to their educational attainments. And distorted stereotypes remain in the mass media.

The expectations from traditional culture—for family interdependence, preservation of group harmony, and stoicism—are expected of Asian American women specifically. Asian American women, as part of a bicultural existence, experience gender-role conflict, the gender roles expected in traditional culture being considerably different from those expected in modern Anglo culture, which increasingly prizes independence and assertiveness for women. Another conflict involves the Anglo emphasis on equality in male-female relationships, an emphasis that is at odds with the traditional Asian focus on female subservience.

GENDER ROLES AMONG HISPANICS

In traditional Latin American cultures, gender roles are rigidly defined. Such roles are emphasized early in the socialization process for children. Boys are given greater freedom, are encouraged in sexual exploits, and are not expected to share in household work. Girls are expected to be passive, obedient, and weak, and to stay in the home.

These rigid roles are epitomized in the concepts of machismo and marianismo. The term *machismo,* or *macho,* has come to be used rather loosely in American culture today. Literally, *machismo* means "maleness" or "virility." The cultural code of machismo among Latin Americans mandates that the male must be the provider and the one responsible for the well-being and honor of his family. Males hold a privileged position and are to be treated as authority figures. In extreme forms, machismo can include tolerance for men's sexual infidelities and physical domination of women.

Marianismo is the female counterpart of machismo. The term derives from the Catholic worship of Mother Mary, who is both virgin and madonna. According to the ideal of marianismo, women, like Mary, are spiritually superior and therefore capable of enduring the suffering inflicted by men. Latin American culture attributes high status to motherhood. The woman is expected to be self-sacrificing in relation to her children and the rest of her family, but Hispanic culture at the same time holds mothers in high esteem. Although superficially these roles may seem to endorse male domination and female submissiveness, the true situation is complex. Women who do exceptionally well in the marianista role come to be revered as they grow older and their children feel strong alliances with them, so that they wield considerable power within the family.

Most Latin American cultures assign the healing role to women. Most *espiritistas* (spiritual healers) are female. According to research on Hispanic female healers in the United States, the role is associated with power and status.

Thus, although the traditional role for Latinas involves passivity and subservience, this generalization masks the powerful roles that these women play within the family, and that they may gain in certain specialized roles, such as that of *espiritista.*   [1995]

Understanding the Reading

1. What influences a woman's identity and gender roles in traditional Indian culture?
2. What alternative gender roles were available to women in some tribes?
3. How do African American women's traditional roles differ from those of White, middle-class American women?
4. What factors contribute to the number of African American households headed by women?
5. How does the role of the elderly differ between White and African American women?
6. How do racism and sexism affect Asian American women?
7. Explain *machismo* and *marianismo.*

Suggestions for Responding

1. Explain how your ethnicity, even if it is European American, has influenced your beliefs and attitudes about your gender role.

2. Discuss gender roles with someone from an ethnic group that differs from yours. Report on the differences you discover. ✦

22

August Genesis

Rebecca Fiske

First Day: August 17

I lie on my belly in a late summer's field of red clover, timothy weed and rye grass. Why can the sun's rays beat into me and mock my loneliness? Sweat forms behind my knees, trickles from my armpits, beads above my lips. I want to make a man, and I have gathered the ingredients: coral washed in brine, fresh blue chicory flowers, rich, black angus dung, and my own hair. The coral will be his bones, the chicory and dung his flesh, my hair his spirit. I will tell him stories as I create him and fill him with rushing, bitter time and pools of memory. He must know me. When I have formed him in every detail, I will breathe life-breath into his mouth. He will be my only lover; together, we will people our world with fat, warm babies. This man will have the power to claim me as his own.

In the distance a chain saw sings. I think of my father, whom I saw naked only once, in the middle of the night, when he was older, perhaps seventy. He walked down the hall, past my open bedroom door, toward the bathroom. I saw his thin, long body, but when he realized I was watching him, he cupped his penis with his hands and hurried past me. His back was muscular, his ass round, his legs sinewy and long. Only his face and forearms were tanned. The rest was white. I thought of him as a curious sort of man, more greyhound than human somehow, nervous, racing.

So, I should start with the tailbone, the small of the back, the rounded part just a little above the crack in the butt, a bit askew, a bit not quite right. I want my man to be healthy, but I want him to be human. He must feel the spinous process ache, the coccygeal nerve burn, the sacrum crack as he is born out of the brine.

My mother loved sea horses, and we had them mailed to us a few times from Sea Shell City, in Brandon, Vermont, about thirty miles north of us. Even then I knew there was no sea around, only trout streams, Otter Creek, and peeper marshes. Still, my mother had seen the ocean—Old Orchard Beach. She knew about sea horses. They came by UPS, delivered in sturdy cardboard boxes. Inside the boxes were thick plastic bags, kept tightly closed with rubber bands. Each bag held one brown adult male, and inside the male were the foals. Somehow, my mother explained, the male sea horses gave birth while the females were not around. We had a ten gallon fish tank which we decorated with bits of pink, pet shop coral. The expectant fathers swam quite freely in their labor. Once born, the babies took on the color of whatever came their way, and our sea foals slowly turned pink. Perhaps they thought we could not see them and that they were safe, in the West Indian waters.

This coral I have now is the deep red secretion of sea-fans: gorgonia with spiky, winged skeletons. I bought six large pieces in the gift shop at the Middlebury College Museum, though I wonder if their sale is legal, coral being so precious. Still, for my purposes sea-fans are the best creatures to rob. Their trunks and heads are armored, their colonies secure. The plastic stuff of childhood play will not do, and while I am a thief, my sea hoard will serve me well. The largest I broke in two, and the other five I fractured in many bits. Then I put them all in brine to soak. Each calcareous coral piece must fit together to form my man's frame. The small of his back will be smooth. Here is a piece for his iliac crest, and another for his coccyx. These will do for vertebrae. I will follow the subtle curves of his spine, trace his ways, attach ribs that curve like fingers, until I reach his cervical plexus. There I'll need these beauties for his first and second cervical vertebrae, the axis and atlas: they must be strong because they'll touch the base of his skull. I have a jagged one for his jaw and a large coral chunk for his cranium.

What seems suitable for his limbs? Sea-fans secrete nothing worthy of the femur shaft or the humerus, so I have no choice but puzzle-piece the shoulders, arms, wrists, hands, fingers, hips, thighs, knees, tibiae, fibulae, ankles, feet and toes. This work will take hours, and I'll need the aid of dung and chicory as well for binding. The dung I bought from a neighbor four years ago. He trucked it in and dumped it just south of my vegetable garden so that I could use it as fertilizer each spring when I planted. Weeds have covered it over; no one would know that rich earthy gold hides just beneath the green. I shoveled some into a wheelbarrow and have it here beside me. The chicory flowers have just bloomed: that is why it is time to make my man, why I have waited until today when I could pick the sweetest ones and work them into the manure. I am the mason now, laying coral into chicory dung, fitting femur to trochanter, piecing metacarpals.

This dung is sweet and generous, and when it feels too dry, I add a little salt water from my coral pail so that it keeps its pasty texture. Its odor brings me home to Quaker Village, Vermont (near Middlebury and Rutland). It brings me closer, closer to my grandfather's corn fields, and then beyond: to trillium, adder-tongues, lilies of the valley, peonies, daddy longlegs, great blue heron, gray squirrel, hayloft, sugar house, sap buckets, rock maple, walnut, teats, milkers, hayloft, chores. (I mustn't forget my chores). I am making a man. His name will be Aaron.

Aaron, did you know that before a calf is born the mother lows for hours, calling her cowherd for help? She stands and waits, her neck stuck hard between the milker bars. The calf's front legs come first, and then the farmer ties some sturdy rope around them and begins to pull gently as the mother lows and lows. It takes time, perhaps a half hour or more until the newborn slides into the air and falls, crashing to the bloody hay. All slick and matted, the thing doesn't move for minutes, doesn't seem to breathe. The mother delivers the big bloody balled placenta, and then the calf stirs. Sometimes, the mother turns and watches her calf. Sometimes she just blinks her cow eyes. In a day or two, the calf will take your whole hand into his toothless mouth and suck the salt from your sweaty fingers. The first time a calf sucked my hand, I thought I was done for: I thought the thing would suck every bit of life from me, leave me white as ash. Perhaps I was seven, perhaps six, and my Uncle George said "Look, Becky, just let her lick your fingers and see." This particular calf was days old, tethered tight to the side of a stall, near the bull, in the second barn where no

milking happens and the grain bin sits. I swear I was so very brave. I offered her my hand. She licked it once, and her tongue was very, very rough, nothing like I had expected. I let her lick again. She opened her little toothless mouth and began to low until I let her take my fingers and then my whole hand into her. It did not hurt at all; indeed, it felt a bit wet, a bit sticky, a bit like I was helping this poor thing get along.

There now. Aaron is formed. Coral and chicory dung have become bones and flesh. I use my fingers to pinch out his penis and to smooth his muddy face, make eyes and nose, cheeks and chin, ears. I sprinkle snips of my hair on his head, under his arms, between his legs. I press my lips to him and open his mouth with my tongue. The sun begins to set, and the sky is heavy with lemon and blood.

I am shivering. My man must sleep now, must forget he is part father, part sea treasure. He must forget he has a small of the back and that he has been in my mind in the August sun. He must not know I am here.

Once, in a dream, I saw an old woman in her house. She came to the front door, pushed open the screen, walked down her steps, wiped her hands on her apron, and pointed her finger at a wild rose bush. The great bush was blooming. Aaron, sleep now. Don't worry. This next part is just another dream, just a silly woman's dream. I give it to you so that you'll not feel alone, so that the night urges will stir in you. In the morning, I will return.

SECOND DAY: AUGUST 18

I failed. Aaron will not wake, and now I must try to make another man. His bones will still be made of this coral. But first, I will carry Aaron to the bank of the pond down the road. Then, I will use the brine in my pail to wash the hair and chicory dung from him and from my hands and my mouth. The failed one's flesh will melt and soak into the ground. And I will dip my empty pail in the pond, wash off the salt, fill it with fresh water and then the coral pieces, and return home.

I will begin again. I've dumped the coral on an old bath towel and reassembled the pieces just as they were with Aaron. See, this pelvic surface is my concern. The sacral hiatus must point down, down to the tail tip. The pelvic and dorsal surfaces should be porous and yellow-brown, not pink or red. I'll tangle my hair around these coral bits, rope them together with spirit, not chicory dung, because inside these fragments of coral is the sacral canal, and there flows love. My man will have a sacral canal which carries the bitterness from me. Listen, my man. Listen to your first memories:

I remember before my mother died she said we would go on a trip to Lake Champlain, take a ferry to New York, stay in a hotel with real white linen for our beds at night and fresh cream for our cereal in the morning. This strand of hair, this white one, is for the linen and the cream.

I remember a spot beside a pond, where an old love died. I am sure, even now silver beech leaves scatter in the wind. Canadian geese glide across the sky. Will you go there with me? Come with me now, in summer, before the snow says to forget my foolish, woman hopes, all heat and sweat and desire. Will you come with me before the bitter ice says to forget my longing for the taste of him? I want to remember his eyes watching me wanting more and more. Will you come with me down the dirt road, past the mailbox, to the place beside the pond where he died, and will you do it quickly, before it is too late? My man, when we are together, we will dream. This tiny blond braid is for August dreams. We will dream that he is beneath us, warm, brown, breathing in and out, thinking of the West Indies and stolen gold. He is laughing loss, laughing salty tears. He is whispering secrets. He is just a dream. Don't think of it.

You sing lilac water, rhubarb, lemon grass. You sing Atlantic salmon, silver coins, bitter hoar leaves, crushed violet, cybernetics. When you sing to me, I listen so long until the music touches first my lips, then my tongue, in a tangle of hair and skin and soft, soft belly.

Is it too late now? Is it too late to build a fire, pile high some hard-tack brush and set it blazing in the night? As we sit together, feeding the fire, I will tell you all the stories, all the memories except one. I wish that one were a lie, or even a dream. I wish it were a drunken, bottle-smashing lie. I wish it were about how maple leaves rot sweetly into humus and bucks butt off their antlers in the spring. I wish it were about the coy dogs and the Green Mountains, about sap icicles and the coal bins. This is true: once

I saw a Chinese man's black ponytail sticking out of the compost pile behind my house, and I grabbed a shovel from my mother's garden so I could dig him free. Another time I found a robin's egg (gentle, milky blue) sunk to the brook's pebbled bottom. My man, do you hear me? These strands of hair are for protection, for warmth; I'll coat your vertebral body from coccyx to atlas with ash-blond ligaments and spinal nerves.

I'm cold. One winter my father cut cedar fence posts in Chittenden Swamp. He'd wear layers: long johns, red plaid work shirt, khaki pants, three, four pair wool socks, good green Packs tied nice and tight. He would leave before light and come home late, full of stories. Wild dogs had howled. Lug headed young tree-choppers had bragged. Chain saws had flown back on him. A broom waited on the front porch to sweep the snow off before he came inside, and a bench and a wrought iron boot jack stayed in the hallway to help with the pulling off of his boots. You had to keep the winter outside.

Inside, my mother stood, looking into the bathroom mirror. She patted her face with pressed powder from her plastic compact, lined her lips red, looked down at me and touched my face.

In the cellar, right next to the furnace and the coal bin, underneath the stairs, my father kept his army rifle. It had a long barrel and a walnut butt-end. Every November he took it out for deer hunting. He'd tell the familiar stories about Parris Island and Japan: having to stand at attention (not so much as a blink) for hours on the beach while the sand fleas crawled into his eyes; trading cartons of rationed cigarettes for a silk kimono and a strand of pearls; feeling the earth quake on Okinawa. It seemed to me then that my father knew the secrets of the exotic. He knew about war and pain and boot camp. He knew that pearls and silk were worth more than cigarettes, even after a bombing. He knew how to swear like a marine "God damn son of a bitch of a God damn" and how to say "Good morning. How are you?" in Japanese. Sometimes, he would sing truths, starting gently, softly, his throat vibrating, humming. He told us that angels flew over prison walls. He taught that the dawn comes up like thunder. He reminded us that the round-up days were over, and that there were pastures full of clover.

My father knew things Vermont men were supposed to know, and before he knew those things, he did what boys were supposed to do. He could hitch harnesses to horses; chase his brothers with pitchforks; gather blackberries from the back fields and skim cream from the milk pails for Sunday ice cream. He could find the heron's nest amid the cattails on Lemon Fair, a muddy branch of Otter Creek. But he couldn't sit still in school or in church. The world was too big, and the seats were too hard. He needed action.

"If you can't do, then teach. If you can't teach, then write," Dad would say. He tried to teach Trinity Church Sunday School, fifth grade, to help handle the boys, but he got tired of it and went back to the choir, bass section. He also kept a notebook and a pencil on his night stand. I often saw him writing his thoughts. Mostly, his writing was political: trailers should be allowed in Bridgeport, and the land in Middlebury should be re-zoned. Sometimes, he sent letters to the editor of the local paper. He was a Republican. He believed the poor Vermonter should be able to have a house, and the rich New Yorker should not be able to buy up farm land. He never wrote about blackberries or wild dogs or silk kimonos. Of course, if he knew that I was trying to make a man, he would shake his head and remind me that I was "book-smart, only book-smart." He would not have been angry or even worried. Rather, he would have looked at me and not known what to do. What was in my mind was a mystery to him.

"You can't make a silk purse out of a sow's ear." He would always laugh whenever he thought about his inadequacy in the face of cultured, womanly things, creations of all sorts: music, art, poetry, babies. Mabel Ryder, his mother, an Addison County school teacher, wrote her memoirs and gave them to him, wrapped in brown paper. He kept them in the top left drawer of his desk, along with his reading glasses. But even Mabel would have raised an eyebrow at you.

Now I have a decision to make. The two large chunks, jaw and cranium, are before me. What hair belongs to them? What spirit should fill the skull of the man I will love? It is not mine to choose. I'll let the water and the wind decide. I know that this is crazy, but I will walk again down the dirt road, and again I will go to Aaron's spot. Then, I will strip: it is fine. No one will drive past. The water will be cold, and there will be muck in the bottom as I wade in and find the drop off place. I'll let myself fall into the deepest water, close my eyes, hold my breath. Then, when I can't stay submerged any longer, I'll float up, break surface, and breathe in the dusky air. The frogs won't croak. The heron won't watch. I'll take my fingers and run them through my hair until I've harvested a handful. But it will need to dry, so that will be enough work for this day.

THIRD DAY: AUGUST 19

I am troubled. It is not my right to take this man, my creation, as a husband. How can I be his maker and have him stir life into my belly? Would our babies be monsters, somehow defiled? Have I forgotten the taboo?

His skeletal form is nearly complete, but he is not alive. I can tell because he does not dream or quiver or reach toward me in any way. It must be the dung and chicory which signal consciousness, and I have kept them far from him. Here, beside me, is the hair from yesterday's swim. It is in a tangle and fits in my palm, like a hummingbird's nest. I put my two hands together, cup my hair and smell. It lacks the familiar scent of shampoo and seems more akin to clover and rye and Vermont evening air, likely because it has been out all night, anchored down by the jaw chunk, drying. Here is my man's secret thoughts, his private spirit, his mysteries. I breathe my breath into my hands, and I make this wish. May he live a life without me. Let there be another's lips to kiss, belly to stir, fat babies to make. May I die never knowing his fate. May he be my gift.

Then, I squeeze my hands together tightly, compress the nest, and begin to twist and twist until I form a dread. I use the dread to hitch my man's jaw to his cranium, and I set the head carefully on the atlas and axis. It is time for the dung, but I am afraid. Again, I must let what is outside of me do the work. I know that I can't see the finished product. I can't know the shape of his face or the texture of his skin. I can't even taste his bittersweet mouth. So I take the four corners of the towel beneath him and wrap him in it, swaddle him carefully. Next, I carry him to my manure pile, where I've dug a deep trench right down the middle. This dung will form him slowly, over the years. The earth worms and beetles will smooth his features. The roots of the green weeds will reach down and comfort him. Some morning, when I am gone, he will wake. I'm shaking.

As I lower him into his bed, I can't stop crying. I want to sing sweet songs or murmur rhymes, but I can not. Instead, once he is settled, I scatter the rest of the chicory flowers on top of him and sprinkle the pond water, then some dung, then some pond water, then some dung, until he is completely covered, resting, waiting.

[2003]

Understanding the Reading

1. Why does the woman want to create a man?
2. What are her hopes?
3. What are the materials she uses to create the man?
4. Why is she thinking about the birth of a calf as she forms Aaron?
5. What happens on the second day?
6. How are her memories being made a part of the man?
7. Why does she decide not to take him as her lover?

Suggestions for Responding

1. Read creation myths of different cultures and compare the themes you find in each myth with this creation story. ✦

23

Where I Come From Is Like This

PAULA GUNN ALLEN

I

Modern American Indian women, like their non-Indian sisters, are deeply engaged in the struggle to redefine themselves. In their struggle they must reconcile traditional tribal definitions of women with industrial and postindustrial non-Indian definitions. Yet while these definitions seem to be more or less mutually exclusive, Indian women must somehow harmonize and integrate both in their own lives.

An American Indian woman is primarily defined by her tribal identity. In her eyes, her destiny is necessarily that of her people, and her sense of herself as a woman is first and foremost prescribed by her tribe. The definitions of woman's roles are as diverse as tribal cultures in the Americas. In some she is devalued, in others she wields considerable power. In some she is a familial/clan adjunct, in some she is as close to autonomous as her economic circumstances and psychological traits permit. But in no tribal definitions is she perceived in the same way as are women in western industrial and postindustrial cultures.

In the west, few images of women form part of the cultural mythos, and these are largely sexually charged. Among Christians, the madonna is the female prototype, and she is portrayed as essentially passive: her contribution is simply that of birthing. Little else is attributed to her and she certainly possesses few of the characteristics that are attributed to mythic figures among Indian tribes. This image is countered (rather than balanced) by the witch-goddess/whore characteristics designed to reinforce cultural beliefs about women, as well as western adversarial and dualistic perceptions of reality.

The tribes see women variously, but they do not question the power of femininity. Sometimes they see women as fearful, sometimes peaceful, sometimes omnipotent and omniscient, but they never portray women as mindless, helpless, simple, or oppressed. And while the women in a given tribe, clan, or band may be all these things, the individual woman is provided with a variety of images of women from the interconnected supernatural, natural, and social worlds she lives in.

As a half-breed American Indian woman, I cast about in my mind for negative images of Indian women, and I find none that are directed to Indian women alone. The negative images I do have are of Indians in general and in fact are more often of males than of females. All these images come to me from non-Indian sources, and they are always balanced by a positive image. My ideas of womanhood, passed on largely by my mother and grandmothers, Laguna Pueblo women, are about practicality, strength, reasonableness, intelligence, wit, and competence. I also remember vividly the women who came to my father's store, the women who held me and sang to me, the women at Feast Day, at Grab Days, the women in the kitchen of my Cubero home, the women I grew up with; none of them appeared weak or helpless, none of them presented herself tentatively. I remember a certain reserve on those lovely brown faces; I remember the direct gaze of eyes framed by bright-colored shawls draped over their heads and cascading down their backs. I remember the clean cotton dresses and carefully pressed hand-embroidered aprons they always wore; I remember laughter and good food, especially the sweet bread and the oven bread they gave us. Nowhere in my mind is there a foolish woman, a dumb woman, a vain woman, or a plastic woman, though the Indian women I have known have shown a wide range of personal style and demeanor.

My memory includes the Navajo woman who was badly beaten by her Sioux husband; but I also remember that my grandmother abandoned her Sioux husband long ago. I recall the stories about the Laguna woman beaten regularly by her husband in the presence of her children so that the children would not believe in the strength and power of femininity. And I remember the women who drank, who got into fights with other women and with the men, and who often won those battles. I have memories of tired women, partying women, stubborn women, sullen women, amicable women, selfish women, shy women, and aggressive women. Most of all I remember the women who laugh and scold and sit uncomplaining in the long sun on feast days and who cook wonderful food on wood stoves, in beehive mud ovens, and over open fires outdoors.

Among the images of women that come to me from various tribes as well as my own are White Buffalo Woman, who came to the Lakota long ago and brought them the religion of the Sacred Pipe which they still practice; Tinotzin the goddess who came to Juan Diego to remind him that she still walked the hills of her people and sent him with her message, her demand and her proof to the Catholic bishop in the city

nearby. And from Laguna I take the images of Yellow Woman, Coyote Woman, Grandmother Spider (Spider Old Woman), who brought the light, who gave us weaving and medicine, who gave us life. Among the Keres she is known as Thought Woman who created us all and who keeps us in creation even now. I remember Iyatiku, Earth Woman, Corn Woman, who guides and counsels the people to peace and who welcomes us home when we cast off this coil of flesh as huskers cast off the leaves that wrap the corn. I remember Iyatiku's sister, Sun Woman, who held metals and cattle, pigs and sheep, highways and engines and so many things in her bundle, who went away to the east saying that one day she would return.

II

Since the coming of the Anglo-Europeans beginning in the fifteenth century, the fragile web of identity that long held tribal people secure has gradually been weakened and torn. But the oral tradition has prevented the complete destruction of the web, the ultimate disruption of tribal ways. The oral tradition is vital; it heals itself and the tribal web by adapting to the flow of the present while never relinquishing its connection to the past. Its adaptability has always been required, as many generations have experienced. Certainly the modern American Indian woman bears slight resemblance to her forebears—at least on superficial examination—but she is still a tribal woman in her deepest being. Her tribal sense of relationship to all that is continues to flourish. And though she is at times beset by her knowledge of the enormous gap between the life she lives and the life she was raised to live, and while she adapts her mind and being to the circumstances of her present life, she does so in tribal ways, mending the tears in the web of being from which she takes her existence as she goes.

My mother told me stories all the time, though I often did not recognize them as that. My mother told me stories about cooking and childbearing; she told me stories about menstruation and pregnancy; she told me stories about gods and heroes, about fairies and elves, about goddesses and spirits; she told me stories about the land and the sky, about cats and dogs, about snakes and spiders; she told me stories about climbing trees and exploring the mesas; she told me stories about going to dances and getting married; she told me stories about dressing and undressing, about sleeping and waking; she told me stories about herself, about her mother, about her grandmother. She told me stories about grieving and laughing, about thinking and doing; she told me stories about school and about people; about darning and mending; she told me stories about turquoise and about gold; she told me European stories and Laguna stories; she told me Catholic stories and Presbyterian stories; she told me city stories and country stories; she told me political stories and religious stories. She told me stories about living and stories about dying. And in all of those stories she told me who I was, who I was supposed to be, whom I came from, and who would follow me. In this way she taught me the meaning of the words she said, that all life is a circle and everything has a place within it. That's what she said and what she showed me in the things she did and the way she lives.

Of course, through my formal, white, Christian education, I discovered that other people had stories of their own—about women, about Indians, about fact, about reality—and I was amazed by a number of startling suppositions that others made about tribal customs and beliefs. According to the un-Indian, non-Indian view, for instance, Indians barred menstruating women from ceremonies and indeed segregated them from the rest of the people, consigning them to some space specially designed for them. This showed that Indians considered menstruating women unclean and not fit to enjoy the company of decent (nonmenstruating) people, that is, men. I was surprised and confused to hear this because my mother had taught me that white people had strange attitudes toward menstruation: they thought something was bad about it, that it meant you were sick, cursed, sinful, and weak and that you had to be very careful during that time. She taught me that menstruation was a normal occurrence, that I could go swimming or hiking or whatever else I wanted to do during my period. She actively scorned women who took to their beds, who were incapacitated by cramps, who "got the blues."

As I struggled to reconcile these very contradictory interpretations of American Indians' traditional beliefs concerning menstruation, I realized that the menstrual taboos were about power, not about sin or filth. My conclusion was later borne out by some tribes' own explanations, which, as you may well imagine, came as quite a relief to me.

The truth of the matter as many Indians see it is that women who are at the peak of their fecundity are believed to possess power that throws male power totally out of kilter. They emit such force that, in their presence, any male-owned or -dominated ritual or sacred object cannot do its usual task. For instance, the Lakota say that a menstruating woman anywhere near a yuwipi man, who is a special sort of psychic, spirit-empowered healer, for a day or so before he is to do his ceremony will effectively disempower him. Conversely, among many, if not most, tribes, important ceremonies cannot be held without the presence of women. Sometimes the ritual woman who empowers the ceremony must be unmarried and virginal so that the power she channels is unalloyed, unweakened by sexual arousal and penetration by a male. Other ceremonies require tumescent women, others the presence of mature women who have borne children, and still others depend for empowerment on postmenopausal women. Women may be segregated from the company of the whole band or village on certain occasions, but on certain occasions men are also segregated. In short, each ritual depends on a certain balance of power, and the positions of women within the phases of womanhood are used by tribal people to empower certain rites. This does not derive from a male-dominant view; it is not a ritual observance imposed on women by men. It derives from a tribal view of reality that distinguishes tribal people from feudal and industrial people.

Among the tribes, the occult power of women, inextricably bound to our hormonal life, is thought to be very great; many hold that we possess innately the blood-given power to kill—with a glance, with a step, or with a judicious mixing of menstrual blood into somebody's soup. Medicine women among the Pomo of California cannot practice until they are sufficiently mature; when they are immature, their power is diffuse and is likely to interfere with their practice until time and experience have it under control. So women of the tribes are not especially inclined to see themselves as poor helpless victims of male domination. Even in those tribes where something akin to male domination was present, women are perceived as powerful, socially, physically, and metaphysically. In times past, as in times present, women carried enormous burdens with aplomb. We were far indeed from the "weaker sex," the designation that white aristocratic sisters unhappily earned for us all.

I remember my mother moving furniture all over the house when she wanted it changed. She didn't wait for my father to come home and help—she just went ahead and moved the piano, a huge upright from the old days, the couch, the refrigerator. Nobody had told her she was too weak to do such things. In imitation of her, I would delight in loading trucks at my father's store with cases of pop or fifty-pound sacks of flour. Even when I was quite small I could do it, and it gave me a belief in my own physical strength that advancing middle age can't quite erase. My mother used to tell me about the Acoma Pueblo women she had seen as a child carrying huge ollas (water pots) on their heads as they wound their way up the tortuous stairwell carved into the face of the "Sky City" mesa, a feat I tried to imitate with books and tin buckets. ("Sky City" is the term used by the Chamber of Commerce for the mother village of Acoma, which is situated atop a high sandstone table mountain.) I was never very successful, but even the attempt reminded me that I was supposed to be strong and balanced to be a proper girl.

Of course, my mother's Laguna people are Keres Indian, reputed to be the last extreme mother-right people on earth. So it is no wonder that I got notably nonwhite notions about the natural strength and prowess of women. Indeed, it is only when I am trying to get non-Indian approval, recognition, or acknowledgment that my "weak sister" emotional and intellectual ploys get the better of my tribal woman's good sense. At such times I forget that I just moved the piano or just wrote a competent paper or just completed a financial transaction satisfactorily or have supported myself and my children for most of my adult life.

Nor is my contradictory behavior atypical. Most Indian women I know are in the same bicultural bind: we vacillate between being dependent and strong, self-reliant and powerless, strongly motivated and hopelessly insecure. We resolve the dilemma in various ways: some of us party all the time; some of us drink to excess; some of us travel and move around a lot; some of us land good jobs and then quit them; some of us engage in violent exchanges; some of us blow our brains out. We act in these destructive ways because we suffer from the societal conflicts caused by having to identify with two hopelessly opposed cultural definitions of women. Through this destructive dissonance we are unhappy prey to the self-disparagement common to, indeed demanded of, Indians living in the United States today. Our situation is caused by the exigencies of a history of invasion, conquest, and colonization whose searing marks are probably ineradicable. A popular bumper sticker on many Indian cars proclaims: "If You're Indian You're In," to which I always find myself adding under my breath, "Trouble."

III

No Indian can grow to any age without being informed that her people were "savages" who interfered with the march of progress pursued by respectable, loving, civilized white people. We are the villains of the scenario when we are mentioned at all. We are absent from much of white history except when we are calmly, rationally, succinctly, and systematically dehumanized. On the few occasions we are noticed in any way other than as howling, bloodthirsty beings, we are acclaimed for our noble quaintness. In this definition, we are exotic curios. Our ancient arts and customs are used to draw tourist money to state coffers, into the pocketbooks and bank accounts of scholars, and into support of the American-in-Disneyland promoters' dream.

As a Roman Catholic child I was treated to bloody tales of how the savage Indians martyred the hapless priests and missionaries who went among them in an attempt to lead them to the one true path. By the time I was through high school I had the idea that Indians were people who had benefited mightily from the advanced knowledge and superior morality of the Anglo-Europeans. At least I had, perforce, that idea to lay beside the other one that derived from my daily experience of Indian life, an idea less dehumanizing and more accurate because it came from my mother and the other Indian people who raised me. That idea was that Indians are a people who don't tell lies, who care for their children and their old people. You never see an Indian orphan, they said. You always know when you're old that someone will take care of you—one of your children will. Then they'd list the old folks who were being taken care of by this child or that. No child is ever considered illegitimate among the Indians, they said. If a girl gets pregnant, the baby is still part of the family, and the mother is too. That's what they said, and they showed me real people who lived according to those principles.

Of course the ravages of colonization have taken their toll; there are orphans in Indian country now, and abandoned, brutalized old folks; there are even illegitimate children, though the very concept still strikes me as absurd. There are battered children and neglected children, and there are battered wives and women who have been raped by Indian men. Proximity to the "civilizing" effects of white Christians has not improved the moral quality of life in Indian country, though each group, Indian and white, explains the situation differently. Nor is there much yet in the oral tradition that can enable us to adapt to these inhuman changes. But a force is growing in that direction, and it is helping Indian women reclaim their lives. Their power, their sense of direction and of self will soon be visible. It is the force of the women who speak and work and write, and it is formidable.

Through all the centuries of war and death and cultural and psychic destruction have endured the women who raise the children and tend the fires, who pass along the tales and the traditions, who weep and bury the dead, who are the dead, and who never forget. There are always the women, who make pots and weave baskets, who fashion clothes and cheer their children on at powwow, who make fry bread and piki bread, and corn soup and chili stew, who dance and sing and remember and hold within their hearts the dream of their ancient peoples—that one day the woman who thinks will speak to us again, and everywhere there will be peace.

Meanwhile we tell the stories and write the books and trade tales of anger and woe and stories of fun and scandal and laugh over all manner of things that happen every day. We watch and we wait.

My great-grandmother told my mother: Never forget you are Indian. And my mother told me the same thing. This, then, is how I have gone about remembering, so that my children will remember too.   [1986, 1992]

Understanding the Reading

1. How do American Indian beliefs about womanhood differ from Western images?
2. What did Allen learn about being a woman from her mother, grandmother, and other women she grew up with?
3. How are women portrayed in tribal legends?
4. What did Allen learn from the stories she heard growing up?
5. How did White society distort tribal customs relating to women?
6. How do Indian women respond to living in a bicultural world?
7. How does the White society's representation of Indians differ from the Indian culture Allen knows?
8. What changes in Indian society has the dominant White society created?

Suggestions for Responding

1. Research and report on one or more Native American legends about women.
2. Allen says her mother told her stories that taught her who she is. Describe some of the stories you heard in your childhood that told you who you are. ✦

24

The Male Role Stereotype

DOUG COOPER THOMPSON

When you first consider that many men now feel that they are victims of sex role stereotyping, your natural response might be: "Are you kidding? Why should men feel discriminated against? Men have the best jobs; they are the corporation presidents and the political leaders. Everyone says, 'It's a man's world.' What do men have to be concerned about? What are their problems?"

It is obvious that men hold most of the influential and important positions in society, and it does seem that many men "have it made." The problem is that men pay a high cost for the ways they have been stereotyped and for the roles that they play.

To understand why many men and women are concerned, we need to take a look at the male role stereotype. Here is what men who conform to the stereotype must do.

CODE OF CONDUCT: THE MALE ROLE STEREOTYPE

1. Act "Tough"
   Acting tough is a key element of the male role stereotype. Many boys and men feel that they have to show that they are strong and tough, that they can "take it" and "dish it out" as well. You've probably run into some boys and men who like to push people around, use their strength, and act tough. In a conflict, these males would never consider giving in, even when surrender or compromise would be the smartest or most compassionate course of action.

2. Hide Emotions
   This aspect of the male role stereotype teaches males to suppress their emotions and to hide feelings of fear or sorrow or tenderness. Even as small children, they are warned not to be "crybabies." As grown men they show that they have learned this lesson well, and they become very efficient at holding back tears and keeping a "stiff upper lip."

3. Earn "Big Bucks"
   Men are trained to be the primary source of income for the family. So men try to choose occupations that pay well, and then they stick with those jobs, even when they might prefer to try something else. Boys and men are taught that earning a good living is important. In fact, men are often evaluated not on how kind or compassionate or thoughtful they are, but rather on how much money they make.

4. Get the "Right" Kind of Job
   If a boy decides to become a pilot, he will receive society's stamp of approval, for that is the right kind of a job for a man. But if a boy decides to become an airline steward, many people would think that quite strange. Boys can decide to be doctors, mechanics, or business executives, but if a boy wants to become a nurse, secretary, librarian, ballet dancer, or kindergarten teacher, he will have a tough time. His friends and relatives will probably try to talk him out of his decision, because it's just not part of the male role stereotype.

5. Compete—Intensely
   Another aspect of the male role stereotype is to be super-competitive. This competitive drive is seen not only on athletic fields, but in school and later at work. This commitment to competition leads to still another part of the male stereotype: getting ahead of other people to become a winner.

6. Win—At Almost Any Cost
   From the Little League baseball field to getting jobs that pay the most money, boys and men are taught to win at whatever they may try to do. They must work and strive and compete so that they can get ahead of other people, no matter how many personal, and even moral, sacrifices are made along the way to the winner's circle.

Those are some of the major features of the male stereotype. And certainly, some of them may not appear to be harmful. Yet when we look more closely, we find that many males who do "buy" the message of the male role stereotype end up paying a very high price for their conformity.

THE COST OF THE CODE: WHAT MEN GIVE UP

1. Men who become highly involved in competition and winning can lose their perspective and good judgment. Competition by itself is not necessarily bad, and we've all enjoyed some competitive activities. But when a man tries to fulfill the male stereotype, and compete and win at any cost, he runs into problems. You've probably seen sore losers (and

even sore winners)—sure signs of over-commitment to competition. Real competitors have trouble making friends because they're always trying to go "one-up" on their friends. And when cooperation is needed, true-blue competitors have a difficult time cooperating.

The next time you see hockey players hitting each other with their hockey sticks or politicians or businessmen willing to do almost anything for a Senate seat or a big deal, you know that you are seeing some of the problems of the male sex role stereotype: an overcommitment to competition and the need to win at any cost.

2. Hiding emotions can hurt. For one thing, hiding emotions confuses people as to what someone's real feelings are. Men who hide their emotions can be misunderstood by others who might see them as uncaring and insensitive. And men who are always suppressing their feelings may put themselves under heavy psychological stress. This pressure can be physically unhealthy as well.

3. The heavy emphasis that the male stereotype puts on earning big money also creates problems. Some men choose careers they really do not like, just because the job pays well. Others choose a job which at first they like, only later to find out that they would rather do something else. But they stay with their jobs anyway, because they can't afford to earn less money.

In trying to earn as much as possible, many men work long hours and weekends. Some even take second jobs. When men do this, they begin to lead one-track lives—the track that leads to the office or business door. They drop outside interests and hobbies. They have less and less time to spend with their families. That's one reason why some fathers never really get to know their own children, even though they may love them very much.

4. Many men who are absorbed by competition, winning, and earning big bucks pay a terrible price in terms of their physical health. With the continual pressure to compete, be tough, earn money, with little time left for recreation and other interests, men find themselves much more likely than women to fall victim to serious disease. In fact, on the average, men die 8 years sooner than women. Loss of life is a high cost to pay for following the code of the male role stereotype.

5. Those boys and men who do not follow the male code of conduct may also find their lives more difficult because of this stereotype. For example, some boys choose to become nurses rather than doctors, kindergarten teachers rather than lawyers, artists rather than electricians. Social pressure can make it terribly difficult for males who enter these nonstereotyped careers. Other boys and men feel very uncomfortable with the continual pressure to compete and win.

And some boys do not want to hide their feelings in order to project an image of being strong and tough. These males may be gentle, compassionate, sensitive human beings who are puzzled with and troubled by the male role stereotype. When society stereotypes any group—by race, religion, or sex—it becomes difficult for individuals to break out of the stereotype and be themselves.   [1985]

Understanding the Reading

1. How are the six characteristics of the male role stereotype connected?
2. What characteristics does Cooper Thompson omit, and how do they relate to his six?
3. Explain the costs to men of conforming to this stereotype.
4. What other costs might Cooper Thompson have included?

Suggestions for Responding

1. Have masculine and/or feminine stereotypes undergone changes in recent years? If you think so, describe those changes and explain what has caused them. If not, explain why you think they have not changed.
2. Using Cooper Thompson's analysis as a model, analyze the "Code of Conduct" and the "Cost of the Code" of the female role stereotype. ✦

25

Taking It

Leonard Kriegel

In 1944, at the age of eleven, I had polio. I spent the next two years of my life in an orthopedic hospital, appropriately called a reconstruction home. By 1946, when I returned to my native Bronx, polio had reconstructed me to the point that I walked very haltingly on steel braces and crutches.

But polio also taught me that, if I were to survive, I would have to become a man—and become a man quickly. "Be a man!" my immigrant father urged, by which he meant "become an American." For, in 1946, this country had very specific expectations about how a man faced adversity. Endurance, courage, determination, stoicism—these might right the balance with fate.

"I couldn't take it, and I took it," says the wheelchair-doomed poolroom entrepreneur William Einhorn in Saul Bellow's *The Adventures of Augie March*. "And I *can't* take it, yet I do take it." In 1953, when I first read these words, I knew that Einhorn spoke for me—as he spoke for scores of other men who had confronted the legacy of a maiming disease by risking whatever they possessed of substance in a country that believed that such risks were a man's wagers against his fate.

How one faced adversity was, like most of American life, in part a question of gender. Simply put, a woman endured, but a man fought back. You were better off struggling against the effects of polio as a man than as a woman, for polio was a disease that one confronted by being tough, aggressive, decisive, by assuming that all limitations could be overcome, beaten, conquered. In short, by being "a man." Even the vocabulary of rehabilitation was masculine. One "beat" polio by outmuscling the disease. At the age of eighteen, I felt that I was "a better man" than my friends because I had "overcome a handicap." And I had, in the process, showed that I could "take it." In the world of American men, to take it was a sign that you were among the elect.

An assumption my "normal" friends shared. "You're lucky," my closest friend said to me during an intensely painful crisis in his own life. "You had polio." He meant it. We both believed it.

Obviously, I wasn't lucky. By nineteen, I was already beginning to understand—slowly, painfully, but inexorably—that disease is never "conquered" or "overcome." Still, I looked upon resistance to polio as the essence of my manhood. As an American, I was self-reliant. I could create my own possibilities from life. And so I walked mile after mile on braces and crutches. I did hundreds of push-ups every day to build my arms, chest, and shoulders. I lifted weights to the point that I would collapse, exhausted but strengthened, on the floor. And through it all, my desire to create a "normal" life for myself was transformed into a desire to become the man my disease had decreed I should be.

I took my heroes where I found them—a strange, disparate company of men: Hemingway, whom I would write of years later as "my nurse"; Peter Reiser, whom I dreamed of replacing in Ebbets Field's pastures and whose penchant for crashing into outfield walls fused in my mind with my own war against the virus; Franklin Delano Roosevelt, who had scornfully faced polio with aristocratic disdain and patrician distance (a historian acquaintance recently disabused me of that myth, a myth perpetrated, let me add, by almost all of Roosevelt's biographers); Henry Fonda and Gary Cooper, in whose resolute Anglo-Saxon faces Hollywood blended the simplicity, strength and courage a man needed if he was going to survive as a man; any number of boxers in whom heart, discipline and training combined to stave off defeats the boy's limitations made inevitable. These were the "manly" images I conjured up as I walked those miles of Bronx streets, as I did those relentless push-ups, as I moved up and down one subway staircase after another by turning each concrete step into a personal insult. And they were still the images when, fifteen years later, married, the father of two sons of my own, a Fulbright professor in the Netherlands, I would grab hold of vertical poles in a train in The Hague and swing my brace-bound body across the dead space between platform and carriage, filled with self-congratulatory vanity as amazement spread over the features of the Dutch conductor.

It is easy to dismiss such images as adolescent. Undoubtedly they were. But they helped remind me, time and time again, of how men handled their diseases and their pain. Of course, I realized even then that it was not the idea of manhood alone that had helped me fashion a life out of polio. I might write of Hemingway as "my nurse," but it was an immigrant Jewish mother—already transformed into a cliché by scores of male Jewish writers—who serviced my crippled body's needs and who fed me love, patience and care even as I fed her the rhetoric of my rage.

But it was the need to prove myself an American man—tough, resilient, independent, able to take it—that pulled me through the war with the virus. I have, of course, been reminded again and again of the price extracted for such ideas about manhood. And I am willing to admit that my sons may be better off in a country in which "manhood" will mean little more than, say, the name for an after-shave lotion. It is forty years since my war with the virus began. At fifty-one, even an American man knows that mortality is the only legacy and defeat the only guarantee. At fifty-one, my legs still encased in braces and crutches still beneath my shoulders, my elbows are increasingly arthritic from all those streets walked and weights lifted and stairs climbed. At fifty-one, my shoulders burn with pain from all those push-ups done so relentlessly. And at fifty-one, pain merely bores—and hurts.

Still, I remain an American man. If I know where I'm going, I know, too, where I have been. Best of all, I know the price I have paid. A man endures his diseases until he recognizes in them his vanity. He can't take it, but he takes it. Once, I relished my ability to take it. Now I find myself wishing that taking it were easier. In such quiet surrenders do we American men call it quits with our diseases.   [1997]

Understanding the Reading

1. Explain what Kriegel's father meant when he told his son to "be a man!"
2. What distinction does Kriegel make between male and female polio victims?
3. Who were Kriegel's heroes, and why did he admire each?

Suggestions for Responding

1. Write about a condition you faced that limited your ability to live up to the cultural ideal for your gender. ✦

26

Tears Still Taboo for Average Guy

CARL RYAN

Thad Jones well remembers his reaction when a colleague dropped dead at work a few months ago, only inches away from him, of a heart attack.

He cried.

"We were seated at a table looking toward the front of the room," he recalls. "I was not looking right at him at the time, but he was just off my right shoulder. Everyone heard what sounded like a snore. I turned around and his face was on the table. Then the second snore came. I wondered how he could fall asleep. But the snore was a death rattle."

As tears poured from his eyes, Jones knew what he was doing is taboo for men. But the Ohio department of transportation traffic analyst couldn't help himself.

"I completely lost it," he says. "Here I am, a guy who is 52 years old. The ego says you don't cry in public. We were friends. I can't say good friends. But his death was so sudden, and he was sitting so close. This on top of my work pressures was just too much."

Bawling, blubbering, sobbing, wailing, weeping, whimpering, whining, sniveling—no matter what term you use, crying is crying, and it's off limits for men. Women can get away with tears, but not men. In them, this is considered weak and emotional behavior.

Nevertheless, men cry publicly all the time.

Remember Edmund Muskie, the then-senator from Maine who wanted to run for president in 1972? Disparaging remarks about his wife in the Manchester Union Leader so upset him that he broke down in tears at an outdoor press conference during the New Hampshire primary.

As snow fell, cameras whirred, and spectators gawked, Muskie's floundering campaign for the Democratic nomination suffered fatal damage, all because of a crying jag.

Other well-known public criers come to mind, although their tears didn't have the same calamitous career results: former president George Bush and fallen evangelists Jim Bakker and Jimmy Swaggart. Soon-to-be Senate majority leader Robert Dole, a hard-edged guy if ever there was one, broke into sobs during an interview on "60 Minutes."

Public crying even occurs among the macho men of sports: Lou Piniella, manager of the Seattle Mariners, shed tears after the White Sox clinched the American League West by beating his team during the '93 season. Marty Schottenheimer, coach of the Kansas City Chiefs and a frequent crier, choked back (or up) tears when his team suffered a 17–16 playoff loss to the Miami Dolphins. . . . And Duke basketball coach Mike Krzyzewski had wet eyes after his team lost in the '93 NCAA regionals and he realized he would never again coach Bobby Hurley and Thomas Hill.

Magic Johnson cried during a ceremony to retire his Los Angeles Lakers jersey and after he broke the record for NBA career assists.

But don't believe that all this boohooing by men in the public eye means the cultural prohibition has weakened much. At least, that's the perception.

"Men aren't supposed to cry. That's as much the case now as it's ever been," says Jones, who is thankful his male co-workers didn't give him a hard time. "You don't cry, and you definitely don't cry in front of someone else. I felt like an ass."

Consulting psychologist Eric Summons says, "Generally it's not acceptable for a man to cry at work. But it is acceptable for women to cry at work. This is simply a cultural distinction. I think that as a male I could understand a man crying in the workplace, but I wouldn't expect it."

Outside the workplace there is perhaps some latitude, Dr. Summons believes. "Men in groups in a non-work setting will accept men crying, but it makes them uncomfortable. This is from personal experience, not professional."

Even as an abstract conversational topic, men have a hard time dealing with other men's crying. He adds, "This is a subject that men are often not comfortable discussing."

In "Gone with the Wind," Clark Gable cried to Olivia de Havilland, but not without misgivings, according to Jack Nachbar, professor of popular culture at Bowling Green State University. The star, considered the quintessence of manliness, didn't want to do the scene for fear of appearing weak. He had to be talked into it.

During World War II, the movies even discouraged crying in women at a time when the nation's focus was on resoluteness in defeating its enemies. In the 1943 film "Tender Comrade," Ginger Rogers gets a telegram informing her that her soldier-husband has been killed.

"But she refuses to let herself cry because it would be unpatriotic," says Nachbar. "It was a sign of toughness and of keeping with the stiff-upper-lip mentality not to cry."

Research shows that men cry less than women, but whether this is due more to biology or to acculturation isn't clear. So says Dr. William Frey II, a biochemist and research director of the Ramsey Dry Eye and Tear Research Center in Saint Paul.

"We do know that women cry about four times as often as men," says Frey. His research found that women average 5.3 crying episodes a month, and men 1.4. "There are some basic biological differences that contribute to this."

And crying styles are different in men and women, he continues. In men, tears tend to accumulate around the eyes; in women, they course down the face. Crying, then, is harder to spot in men.

The lacrimal glands, which produce tears and are situated above and behind the eyeballs, are anatomically different in men and women. Frey believes that the hormone prolactin, which stimulates the production of milk and occurs in higher levels in women, may also stimulate greater tear production in them.

"We know that boys and girls under the age of 12 cry the same amount," Frey explains. "But by the time they are 18, there is this difference. We suspect the change occurs in large part because of hormonal changes." Testosterone, the male hormone, may also play a role.

He cautions that the effects of societal conditioning should not be underemphasized. "We give the message that crying is a sign of weakness and loss of control," he says.

There are women who don't cry at all or very rarely, and there are men who cry as frequently as women. Among his research subjects, 6 percent of women failed to cry during the month they were tracked; for men, the figure was 50 percent.

Men and women cry most often between 7 and 10 P.M. "We think that's because people are with their significant others, and most crying is related to interpersonal things. And that's the end of the day. People have a decreased threshold for crying when they are fatigued."

For men, the crying-avoidance impulse may be behind their much-lamented (by women) insensitivity, Frey continues.

"It's much easier to avoid crying by not getting upset in the first place. Trying to tune out or disengage is a coping mechanism that many males develop to keep from crying. You hide your feelings from others and from yourself. But it's very important for men to know their feelings if they are going to communicate well and have good relationships."

So, men, loosen up.

Don't be afraid to show your vulnerability by crying. That's the advice of clinical psychologist Ruth Ann Roehrig, who acknowledges there are certain women who would consider a crying man to be a wimp. But what she calls "the healthy majority" of women would not.

"As a rule, women see men as being very guarded," she says. "So when men cry in front of them, it increases the sense of intimacy. It's hard to feel intimate with someone who only shows a portion of himself. Showing this more vulnerable side would allow a woman to feel more connected, more a part of, more trusted."

There is no consensus on the salutary effects of crying for either gender, or even if they exist. Frey says his research shows that 85 percent of women and 73 percent of men reported feeling better after crying.

Tears shed for emotional reasons are chemically different from tears caused by eye irritation, according to Frey, who believes that crying may remove chemicals accumulating in the body from stress. "That's a theory. It's not proven."

Psychologist Christopher Layne rejects this.

"Crying isn't beneficial," he says flatly. "There's a myth that says you should cry it out; that you should have a catharsis. Everyone seems to think that expression of emotion leads to dissipation of emotion, but the exact opposite is true.

"Look at how you can make anger grow by behaving angrily. Crying may seem to help indirectly for the short term, because while you're crying, time is passing. But you would have felt just as good if you'd run around the block."

[1995]

Understanding the Reading

1. If crying in public is taboo for men, why have so many public men done so?
2. What causes women to cry more and differently than men?
3. What influences the time when people cry?
4. What effects does the taboo on male crying have on male-female relationships?
5. According to psychologists, why is crying beneficial or not beneficial?

Suggestions for Responding

1. Do you think it is still taboo for men to cry in public? Why or why not?
2. Think of a behavior that is taboo for women to perform in public. Describe and analyze it as Ryan does for male crying. ✦

27

Asymmetries in Communication

Deborah Tannen

"Don't Ask"

Talking about troubles is just one of many conversational tasks that women and men view differently, and that consequently cause trouble in talk between them. Another is asking for information. And this difference too is traceable to the asymmetries of status and connection.

A man and a woman were standing beside the information booth at the Washington Folk Life Festival, a sprawling complex of booths and displays. "You ask," the man was saying to the woman. "I don't ask."

Sitting in the front seat of the car beside Harold, Sybil is fuming. They have been driving around for half an hour looking for a street he is sure is close by. Sybil is angry not because Harold does not know the way, but because he insists on trying to find it himself rather than stopping and asking someone. Her anger stems from viewing his behavior through the lens of her own: If she were driving, she would have asked directions as soon as she realized she didn't know which way to go, and they'd now be comfortably ensconced in their friends' living room instead of driving in circles, as the hour gets later and later. Since asking directions does not make Sybil uncomfortable, refusing to ask makes no sense to her. But in Harold's world, driving around until he finds his way is the reasonable thing to do, since asking for help makes him uncomfortable. He's avoiding that discomfort and trying to maintain his sense of himself as a self-sufficient person.

Why do many men resist asking for directions and other kinds of information? And, it is just as reasonable to ask, why is it that many women don't? By the paradox of independence and intimacy, there are two simultaneous and different metamessages implied in asking for and giving information. Many men tend to focus on one, many women on the other.

When you offer information, the information itself is the message. But the fact that you have the information, and the person you are speaking to doesn't, also sends a metamessage of superiority. If relations are inherently hierarchical, then the one who has more information is framed as higher up on the ladder, by virtue of being more knowledgeable and competent. From this perspective, finding one's own way is an essential part of the independence that men perceive to be a prerequisite for self-respect. If self-respect is bought at the cost of a few extra minutes of travel time, it is well worth the price.

Because they are implicit, metamessages are hard to talk about. When Sybil begs to know why Harold won't just ask someone for direc-

tions, he answers in terms of the message, the information: He says there's no point in asking, because anyone he asks may not know and may give him wrong directions. This is theoretically reasonable. There are many countries, such as, for example, Mexico, where it is standard procedure for people to make up directions rather than refuse to give requested information. But this explanation frustrates Sybil, because it doesn't make sense to her. Although she realizes that someone might give faulty directions, she believes this is relatively unlikely, and surely it cannot happen every time. Even if it did happen, they would be in no worse shape than they are in now anyway.

Part of the reason for their different approaches is that Sybil believes that a person who doesn't know the answer will say so, because it is easy to say, "I don't know." But Harold believes that saying "I don't know" is humiliating, so people might well take a wild guess. Because of their different assumptions, and the invisibility of framing, Harold and Sybil can never get to the bottom of this difference; they can only get more frustrated with each other. Keeping talk on the message level is common, because it is the level we are most clearly aware of. But it is unlikely to resolve confusion since our true motivations lie elsewhere.

To the extent that giving information, directions, or help is of use to another, it reinforces bonds between people. But to the extent that it is asymmetrical, it creates hierarchy: Insofar as giving information frames one as the expert, superior in knowledge, and the other as uninformed, inferior in knowledge, it is a move in the negotiation of status.

It is easy to see that there are many situations where those who give information are higher in status. For example, parents explain things to children and answer their questions, just as teachers give information to students. An awareness of this dynamic underlies one requirement for proper behavior at Japanese dinner entertainment, according to anthropologist Harumi Befu. In order to help the highest-status member of the party to dominate the conversation, others at the dinner are expected to ask him questions that they know he can answer with authority.

Because of this potential for asymmetry, some men resist receiving information from others, especially women, and some women are cautious about stating information that they know, especially to men. For example, a man with whom I discussed these dynamics later told me that my perspective clarified a comment made by his wife. They had gotten into their car and were about to go to a destination that she knew well but he did not know at all. Consciously resisting an impulse to just drive off and find his own way, he began asking his wife if she had any advice about the best way to get there. She told him the way, then added, "But I don't know. That's how I would go, but there might be a better way." Her comment was a move to redress the imbalance of power created by her knowing something he didn't know. She was also saving face in advance, in case he decided not to take her advice. Furthermore, she was reframing her directions as "just a suggestion" rather than "giving instructions."

"I'll Fix It If It Kills Me"

The asymmetry implied in having and giving information is also found in having and demonstrating the skill to fix things. . . . To further explore the framing involved in fixing things, I will present a small encounter of my own.

Unable to remove the tiny lid that covers the battery compartment for the light meter on my camera, I took the camera to a photography store and asked for help. The camera salesman tried to unscrew the lid, first with a dime and then with a special instrument. When this failed, he declared the lid hopelessly stuck. He explained the reason (it was screwed in with the threads out of alignment) and then explained in detail how I could take pictures without a light meter by matching the light conditions to shutter settings in accordance with the chart included in rolls of film. Even though I knew there wasn't a chance in the world I would adopt his system, I listened politely, feigning interest, and assiduously wrote down his examples, based on an ASA of 100, since he got confused trying to give examples based on an ASA of 64. He further explained that this method was actually superior to using a light meter. In this way, he minimized

the significance of not being able to help by freeing the battery lid; he framed himself as possessing useful knowledge and having solved my problem even though he couldn't fix my camera. This man wanted to help me—which I sincerely appreciated—but he also wanted to demonstrate that he had the information and skill required to help, even though he didn't.

There is a kind of social contract operating here. Many women not only feel comfortable seeking help, but feel honor-bound to seek it, accept it, and display gratitude in exchange. For their part, many men feel honor-bound to fulfill the request for help whether or not it is convenient for them to do so. A man told me about a time when a neighbor asked him if he could fix her car, which was intermittently stalling out. He spent more time than he could spare looking at her car, and concluded that he did not have the equipment needed to do the repair. He felt bad about not having succeeded in solving her problem. As if sensing this, she told him the next day, and the next, that her car was much better now, even though he knew he had done nothing to improve its performance. There is a balance between seeking help and showing appreciation. Women and men seem equally bound by the requirements of this arrangement: She was bound to show appreciation even though he hadn't helped, and he was bound to invest time and effort that he really couldn't spare, in trying to help.

Another example of the social contract of asking for help and showing appreciation occurred on a street corner in New York City. A woman emerged from the subway at Twenty-third Street and Park Avenue South, and was temporarily confused about which direction to walk in to reach Madison Avenue. She knew that Madison was west of Park, so with a little effort she could have figured out which way to go. But without planning or thinking, she asked the first person to appear before her. He replied that Madison did not come down that far south. Now, she knew this to be false. Furthermore, by this time she had oriented herself. But instead of saying, "Yes, it does," or "Never mind, I don't need your help," she found a way to play out the scene as one in which he helped her. She asked, "Which way is west?" and, on being told, replied, "Thank you. I'll just walk west."

From the point of view of getting directions, this encounter was absurd from start to finish. The woman didn't really need help, and the man wasn't in a position to give it. But getting directions really wasn't the main point. She had used the commonplace ritual of asking directions of a stranger not only—and not mostly—to find her way on emerging from the subway, but to reinforce her connection to the mass of people in the big city by making fleeting contact with one of them. Asking for help was simply an automatic way for her to do this.

"I'll Help You
If It Kills You"

Martha bought a computer and needed to learn to use it. After studying the manual and making some progress, she still had many questions, so she went to the store where she bought it and asked for help. The man assigned to help her made her feel like the stupidest person in the world. He used technical language in explaining things, and each time she had to ask what a word meant she felt more incompetent, an impression reinforced by the tone of voice he used in his answer, a tone that sent the metamessage "This is obvious; everyone knows this." He explained things so quickly, she couldn't possibly remember them. When she went home, she discovered she couldn't recall what he had demonstrated, even in cases where she had followed his explanation at the time.

Still confused and dreading the interaction, Martha returned to the store a week later, determined to stay until she got the information she needed. But this time a woman was assigned to help her. And the experience of getting help was utterly transformed. The woman avoided using technical terms for the most part, and if she did use one, she asked whether Martha knew what it meant and explained simply and clearly if she didn't. When the woman answered questions, her tone never implied that everyone should know this. And when showing how to do something, she had Martha do it, rather than demonstrating while Martha watched. The different style of this "teacher" made Martha feel like a different "student": a competent rather than stupid one, not humiliated by her ignorance.

Surely not all men give information in a way that confuses and humiliates their students. There are many gifted teachers who also happen to be men. And not all women give information in a way that makes it easy for students to understand. But many women report experiences similar to Martha's, especially in dealing with computers, automobiles, and other mechanical equipment; they claim that they feel more comfortable having women explain things to them. The different meanings that giving help entails may explain why. If women are focusing on connections, they will be motivated to minimize the difference in expertise and to be as comprehensible as possible. Since their goal is to maintain the appearance of similarity and equal status, sharing knowledge helps even the score. Their tone of voice sends metamessages of support rather than disdain, although "support" itself can be experienced as condescension.

If a man focuses on the negotiation of status and feels someone must have the upper hand, he may feel more comfortable when he has it. His attunement to the fact that having more information, knowledge, or skill puts him in a one-up position comes through in his way of talking. And if sometimes men seem intentionally to explain in a way that makes what they are explaining difficult to understand, it may be because their pleasant feeling of knowing more is reinforced when the student *does not* understand. The comfortable margin of superiority diminishes with every bit of knowledge the student gains. Or it may simply be that they are more concerned with displaying their superior knowledge and skill than with making sure that the knowledge is shared.

A colleague familiar with my ideas remarked that he'd seen evidence of this difference at an academic conference. A woman delivering a paper kept stopping and asking the audience, "Are you with me so far?" My colleague surmised that her main concern seemed to be that the audience understand what she was saying. When he gave his paper, his main concern was that he not be put down by members of the audience—and as far as he could tell, a similar preoccupation was motivating the other men presenting papers as well. From this point of view, if covering one's tracks to avoid attack entails obscuring one's point, it is a price worth paying.

This is not to say that women have no desire to feel knowledgeable or powerful. Indeed, the act of asking others whether they are able to follow your argument can be seen to frame you as superior. But it seems that having information, expertise, or skill at manipulating objects is not the primary measure of power for most women. Rather, they feel their power enhanced if they can be of help. Even more, if they are focusing on connection rather than independence and self-reliance, they feel stronger when the community is strong.

"TRUST ME"

A woman told me that she was incredulous when her husband dredged up an offense from years before. She had been unable to get their VCR to record movies aired on HBO. Her husband had looked at the VCR and declared it incapable of performing this function. Rather than accepting his judgment, she asked their neighbor, Harry, to take a look at it, since he had once fixed her VCR in the past. Harry's conclusion was the same as that of her husband, who was, however, incensed that his wife had not trusted his expertise. When he brought it up years later, the wife exclaimed in disbelief, "You still remember that? Harry is dead!" The incident, though insignificant to the wife, cut to the core of the husband's self-respect, because it called into question his knowledge and skill at managing the mechanical world.

Trust in a man's skill is also at issue between Felicia and Stan, another couple. Stan is angered when Felicia gasps in fear while he is driving. "I've never had an accident!" he protests. "Why can't you trust my driving?" Felicia cannot get him to see her point of view—that she does not distrust *his* driving in particular but is frightened of driving in general. Most of all, she cannot understand why the small matter of involuntarily sucking in her breath should spark such a strong reaction.

"BE NICE"

Having expertise and skill can reinforce both women's and men's sense of themselves. But the stance of expert is more fundamental to our notion of masculinity than to our concept of femininity. Women, according to convention, are more inclined to be givers of praise than givers of information. That women are expected to praise is reflected in a poster that was displayed in every United States post office branch inviting customers to send criticism, suggestions, questions, and compliments. Three of these four linguistic acts were represented by sketches of men; only compliments were represented by a sketch of a woman with a big smile on her face, a gesture of approval on her fingers, and a halo around her head. The halo is especially interesting. It shows that the act of complimenting frames the speaker as "nice."

Giving praise, like giving information, is also inherently asymmetrical. It too frames the speaker as one-up, in a position to judge someone else's performance. Women can also be framed as one-up by their classic helping activities as mothers, social workers, nurses, counselors, and psychologists. But in many of these roles—especially mothers and nurses—they may also be seen as doing others' bidding.

OVERLAPPING MOTIVATIONS

When acting as helpers, women and men typically perform different kinds of tasks. But even the same task can be approached with eyes on different goals, and this difference is likely to result in misjudgments of others' intentions. The end of my camera story underlines this. At a family gathering, I brought the camera to my brother-in-law, who has a reputation in the family for mechanical ability. He took it to his workshop and returned an hour and a half later, having fixed it. Delighted and grateful, I commented to his daughter, "I knew he would enjoy the challenge." "Especially," she pointed out, "when it involves helping someone." I felt then that I had mistaken his displayed concern with the mechanics of the recalcitrant battery cover as reflecting his ultimate concern. But fixing the camera was a way of showing concern for me, of helping me with his effort. If women directly offer help, my brother-in-law was indirectly offering help, through the mediation of my camera.

A colleague who heard my analysis of this experience thought I had missed an aspect of my broken-camera episode. He pointed out that many men get a sense of pleasure from fixing things because it reinforces their feeling of being in control, self-sufficient, and able to dominate the world of objects. (This is the essence of Evelyn Fox Keller's thesis that the conception of science as dominating and controlling nature is essentially masculine in spirit.) He told me of an incident in which a toy plastic merry-go-round, ordered for his little boy, arrived in pieces, having come apart during shipping. His wife gave the toy to her uncle, renowned in the family as a fixer and helper. Her uncle worked for several hours and repaired the toy—even though it was probably not worth more than a few dollars. The uncle brought this up again the next time he saw them, and said he would have stayed up all night rather than admit he couldn't put it together. My colleague was convinced that the motivation to gain dominion over the plastic object had been stronger than the motivation to help his sister and nephew, though both had been present.

Furthermore, this man pointed out that he, and many other men, take special pleasure in showing their strength over the world of objects for the benefit of attractive women, because the thanks and admiration they receive is an added source of pleasure and satisfaction. His interpretation of my revised analysis was that my niece and I, both women, would be inclined to see the helping aspect of an act as the "real" or main motive, whereas he still was inclined to see the pleasure of demonstrating skill, succeeding where the camera expert had failed, and whacking the recalcitrant battery lid into line as the main ones.

The element of negotiating status that characterizes many men's desire to show they are knowledgeable and skillful does not negate the connection implied in helping. These elements coexist and feed each other. But women's and men's tendencies to place different relative weights on status versus connection result in asymmetrical roles. Attuned to the metamessage of connection, many women are comfortable both receiving help and giving it, though surely there are many women who are comfortable only in the role of giver of help and support. Many men, sensitive to the dynamic of status, the need to help women, and the need to be self-reliant, are comfortable in the role of giving information and help but not in receiving it.

[1990]

Understanding the Reading

1. According to Tannen, why do men and women tend to have different attitudes about asking for information?
2. Why does Tannen think men feel compelled to "fix things"?
3. What differences does Tannen describe in the way men and women ask for and provide help?
4. Why do women and men differ in giving praise?

Suggestions for Responding

1. Poll some of your female and male friends about what they would do if they couldn't find an address. Report on whether your findings support Tannen's contentions or not.
2. Write an essay, using examples from your experience, agreeing or disagreeing with Tannen's analysis.

SUGGESTIONS FOR RESPONDING TO PART II

1. The readings in this part have examined both traditional and changing gender roles in our society. As the introduction suggested, our socialization into gender-appropriate behavior is complex and both subtle and overt.

Consider how you learned to behave appropriately in terms of your gender. Think back to your earliest memories. When were you first aware of being male or female? How did your placement in your family (first-born, only child, etc.) affect your family's expectations about you as a girl or a boy? If you have siblings of the other sex, were they treated differently than you or held to different standards of behavior? At various points in your life, you were probably quite self-consciously masculine or feminine. Can you explain those moments? Also, your attitudes toward your femininity or masculinity have probably undergone changes; record these changes and try to figure out what triggered them. After you have reflected on these matters, write an autobiography of your gender development.

2. The importance of gender in our society can scarcely be overstated. Whether we accept or reject all the social mandates of our assigned gender role, we cannot escape its influence. However, try to imagine that you were born the other sex. How would your life have been different, and what would you be like today? Think about specific moments in your life when the switch would have been especially important—from your earliest childhood through adolescence into adulthood. Consider how it would influence and alter your expectations for your own future. Write an autobiography of this imaginary you.

3. Describe your versions of the female stereotype and of the male stereotype. Then describe your ideal woman and your ideal man. Analyze the differences between the two pairs and explain what this reveals about stereotypes and reality.

4. Many of the selections in Part II focus on the difficulties of traditional femininity or masculinity, yet most of us are quite content to be who we are. Write an essay about why you like being the sex you are. You probably want to look at both its advantages and rewards and the disadvantages and difficulties of the opposite sex.

III
Sexual Identity

THIS PART SHEDS LIGHT ON THE DISTINCT AREAS THAT affect our sexual orientations. As the first author, Jessica R. Stearns, writes: "first there is the anatomical sex of a person (M/F), second, the gender (M/F), then, third, sexual orientation (Hetero/Homosexual)." Although most people have all three segments the same and are heterosexual, there can be any combination. Most of us have been brought up to think only in terms of male and female. These five authors help us relearn this important piece of being human. Jessica R. Stearns, in "A Transsexual's Story," writes of her life, which began in 1940 as John Robert Stearns in rural Alabama. From her earliest memories, she remembers having the feeling of being a girl, but in the 1940s and 1950s there was very little known about transgendered people in this country. She joined the Air Force, became a pilot, and flew missions into Berlin and Vietnam. She eventually had very high security clearance but said, "If they had ever known!" Under great pressure from the military to conform to a particular masculine image, she married, became a father, and eventually flew for Continental Airlines. When she decided to go for the sex reassignment operation (strongly supported by her family and doctors), Continental Airlines fired her. Jessica sued and won. She made national headlines, was featured on the *Sally Jesse Raphael* show, and here writes her story for the first time.

The second reading, by Anne Fausto-Sterling, "Two Sexes Are Not Enough," confronts us first with the information that the Western world has invested a great deal in the idea that there are only two sexes and, so, denies what biology does not: that intersexuals (those with a combination of male and female sexual organs) have always been around. Second, she asks us to question the ethics of "assigning" a sex by surgically altering a newborn. Fausto-Sterling suggests, instead, that we consider acknowledging what is already in nature: a five-sex system.

The following three articles place us squarely in perhaps the most divisive topic in which the United States has been engaged in this millennium. Elisabeth Bumiller discusses what unnerves Americans who approve of civil unions but oppose gay marriage. Ann Marie Nicolosi, in "When the Political Is Personal," describes her coming out as a lesbian to her university students, and why. Finally, Mildred L. Rice Jordan gives her account of visits from a gay family to her race, class, gender, and ethnicity course and of the students' reactions, in "Putting a Face on Difference: A Gay Family Visits the College Classroom."

From this part, students and professors can discuss, debate, and pursue the implications of all the information within each essay. For example, when is sexual assignment surgery ethical, if ever? Do you think gay marriage will become a national right, as it has in other countries? Why or why not? Should gay couples adopt? Would you prefer to know if your professor were gay or lesbian, or should the professor maintain that distance? Are there differing circumstances? What sorts of public policies would change if we acknowledged the existence of five sexes? Would an intersexed person be allowed to marry, and would it be to a man or to a woman? How would we organize the separation of sexes in prisons? Would they be eligible for a military draft?

Because of the complexity of sexuality, where external organs, internal organs, and our endocrine system all help sort out who we are and what makes us happy, there is a constant tension in our society when the jigsaw pieces do not fit the way we have been told they should. On June 26, 2003, the Supreme Court overruled a Texas sodomy law legalizing gay sexual conduct. In dissent, Justice Antonin Scalia declared it a cultural war. On August 5, 2003, the Episcopal Church's first openly gay bishop was approved, the Reverend Gene Robinson of New Hampshire, and on November 18, 2003, Massachusetts' highest court ruled that gay couples have the right to marry. In contrast, in December the *Washington Post* reported that the Department of Defense is discharging linguists, including Arabic speakers, because they are homosexual. (Ten thousand have been discharged in the past decade because of sexual orientation.) In a time when national security is supposed to be top priority, and Arabic linguists are badly needed in Iraq, sexual orientation trumps the war on terrorism. There is a great deal of politics surrounding our sexuality these days, and the geographical fault lines show fairly clearly that the United States is split on subjects dealing with sexual identity.

28

A Transsexual's Story

JESSICA R. STEARNS

What is a transsexual? For a great part of my life the term was little known. It was not even included in the dictionary. During the 1960's I could find no reference to the term in any dictionary or in any reference book in the public library. It was not until the late 1970's that Webster's included a definition. It was: *Transsexual:* 1. One predisposed to become a member of the opposite sex. 2. One whose sex has been changed externally by surgery and by hormone injections.

By the 1990's the term transsexual was becoming replaced by the more inclusive term Transgendered. This new term was meant to reduce the harsh narrow term of transsexual, and to include a broader group of people who may identify as transsexual but do not have the desire or means to undergo sex reassignment surgery, and may include cross dressers, transvestites and others who did not fit more restricted categories. The term continues to change with medical research, legal advances, and societal factors.

Though the term was first used by Dr. Harry Benjamin, author of the book "Transsexual Phenomenon," and came to public attention by the sex change of Christine Jorgenson in 1952, it seemed that it was such a provocative term that it was talked around, not used. I was 12 years old at the time of Christine's surgery. The impact on me was very powerful, it scared me. How could I be such a person, what would become of me if I was such a person? I was very troubled by this news. Some 51 years later I can remember the four photos published and most of the text of that Sunday Parade Magazine article. To even use the "T" word is difficult at best for a true transsexual.

What is a true transsexual? Dr. Benjamin developed a sexual orientation scale, one to six. On a scale of five a person was defined as wanting to be a member of the opposite sex, but not desiring to undergo surgery. A person rated as a six was a true transsexual who had to have sur-

gery in order to have a chance of happiness and even survive. At first it was considered a mental disease thought curable by psychiatric treatment. One of the theories was that as a person got older the urge to change their sex would decrease. Perhaps the rate of suicide for older transsexuals helped discredit this theory.

Only in the past 15 years has the subject of transsexuality/transgender become a topic talked about through TV talk shows, news media, and progress has been made to legally protect the Transgender. Steps to protect the Transgender through the courts have met with great resistance. Only with great persistence, struggle, and dedicated legal help has any progress been made. The Gay/Lesbian community has had more success at getting anti-discrimination laws passed. The average attorney not only lacks training in handling a transgender case, but is unwilling for fear of being adversely labeled.

One more thing about sex/sexual orientation; first there is the anatomical sex of a person (M/F), second, the gender (M/F), then, third, sexual orientation (Hetero/Homosexual). These are distinct areas of a person's make-up. Of course they can occur in combinations with many variances. For most of the human population these three factors are the same, so that an individual only thinks in terms of male/female with no thoughts given to other factors. At a very early age, most say from their early memories, transsexuals identified with the opposite sex. However, the socialization process governs the process of growing up. A child rapidly learns to adapt to expectations of the sexual role in which they are born. The inner conflict of feeling that they were born in the wrong body is there from the start. It will never go away.

The desire to change sex is a matter of identity. Who am I? What am I? I feel like a girl, but I have a male body. The conflict is intense. This occurs at an age when the child can't understand why those feelings exist. Parents only desire a normal child. Even when they perceive that the behavior patterns are somewhat different, they will strive to reinforce what they perceive as normal behavior. This of course will only lead to greater conflict.

My story began on August 3rd, 1940. Born as John Robert Stearns in Birmingham, Alabama, I was the first grandchild to a family of farmers in

Blount Co. My father, at the time, a traveling salesman from New York City, had been married to my mother only a year. My mother was 16 when married and had never been off the farm. I can't even recall if she finished high school. I know that we moved several times because I have photos of me as an infant in Jacksonville, FL. My sister was born in New Orleans, LA (no photos). My brother was born in Kansas City, MO. I do remember some events from when we lived in Little Rock, Arkansas. I also remember my father's brutality to my mother. I am the only one of the three of us to have any childhood memories of their being together. They were divorced when I was 3½. My mother moved to Birmingham to find work. Most of the time that was at being a waitress. My grandparents had had six children; the first died in infancy, two had their own families, one was engaged to be married, the youngest was in high school and served as an older sibling, and my mother, who was struggling in Birmingham. Having to raise three more children was now a burden for my grandparents.

In 1946 my mother married a taxi driver who lived in Birmingham. Not only did he refuse to permit us to live with them, but also he was an alcoholic who was verbally and physically abusive to my mother. The task of our rearing fell upon my grandparents. We got to visit with our mother on rare occasions. Our grandparents were to become our sole caregivers for the next few years.

I can remember identifying with the female members of our family before I was four. I wanted to help my grandmother in the kitchen and about the house rather than be with the male members in the barns or fields. Our farm was typical of the time and area. Electricity had not been routed to our farm and the roads were unpaved. Mules were used to work the fields. Grandfather did have a 1935 Chevy truck; I still remember the WWII lead lease symbol on the doors. Everyone was expected to do all sorts of farm work. The day started by 5:00 AM and didn't stop until after dark. Almost every thing we ate was grown on our farm and processed by us. Work was long, hard and never ending. Still, the lessons I learned have always been of benefit. Just because a task was difficult, it had to be done and there was a certain satisfaction of doing it well. I learned to see a correlation between effort expended and rewards reaped.

Though I preferred helping my grandmother, all of us had assigned chores to accomplish day or night, every day, and without fail. Shirking was not tolerated and failure was severely punished. On the morning of my sixth birthday my grandfather called me into the living room. He told me that since I was getting to be a pretty big boy, he would only tell me to do something once. Then he gave me a small penknife, and wished me a happy birthday. I can still remember the few times he told me twice. Each time I wasn't able to sit for several hours. Grandfather was a stern disciplinarian and did not tolerate noncompliance. Still, I learned a lot from him that would help me cope with future trials.

During the summer my two female first cousins would travel by train to spend the summer with us. My oldest cousin Gail was only three months younger than me and very much a tomboy. We enjoyed playing with each other more than with the others. Many hours were spent exploring the wooded hollows on the farm and playing in the three streams that flowed through the farm. We climbed trees, built hay forts in the barn mow, picked blackberries, ate wild strawberries and persimmons that grew on the farm, and sometimes snitched a watermelon from a neighboring farm, though there were acres of them on our farm. My grandmother had stored boxes of her old clothes in one of the sheds on the farm. One day Kate and I found them, called the other children to join us and spent the afternoon dressing up. I not only found it fun, but suddenly felt that this was the proper clothing for me. When grandmother found out about this, she scolded us and told us not to do it any more. However, I would play dress up when I could do so without the fear of being caught. When I was seven, my grandmother actually punished me by making me wear one of my sister's dresses. I would hide behind the wood-burning stove in the kitchen, out of sight from prying eyes, and contentedly stay until called out and told to change into my boy clothing. No one knew that my punishment was actually very pleasing. I did not know why, except that somehow I really felt that I wanted to be a girl.

My early years were a mixture of very mixed feelings about myself. As a boy, my grandparents expected me to adhere to the male path. However, from the time that I was five until I was about 14 years old, my health was marginal. I easily caught colds, caught the whooping cough frequently, suffered from bronchitis, and other respiratory related ailments. My tonsils were removed at age six, but that didn't help much. The doctor at the country clinic told my grandparents that I'd probably not survive my childhood. To assist my health I was often restricted indoors. This I really didn't mind as I liked to help my grandmother and enjoyed being able to read any newspaper, magazine or book that I could get my hands on. Whenever I found an article about aviation I would read it over and over. On my very first day in school, my first grade teacher, Miss Haynes, asked us all to stand in turn and state what we wanted to be when we grew up. I was next to last and announced in a determined voice that I would grow up to be an airplane pilot. The spring before starting school I had seen two yellow Army Air Corps trainers fly low over the field we were working in, and knew at that instant what I wanted to be when I grew up; if I did.

I repeated 4th grade because of being very ill. I think that this prompted my grandparents into insisting that my father come for a visit from Brooklyn, NY to assess my health during the summer of 1950, as well as get to know his three children whom he hadn't seen in over six years. The visit was short but the financial help improved. New store-bought clothes were a treat to wear versus the home-made ones usually made from chicken feed sacks. Though we didn't have much, our status was the same as all the other farm families around us, so we didn't know different and accepted life as we knew it.

A decision was made to send my brother and me to visit my father in Brooklyn, NY during the summer of '51. Grandmother packed our cardboard suitcases, a box of food to last the 24-hour train trip from Birmingham to NYC. The conductors had been instructed to look after us. Our faces were glued to the windows viewing the changing countryside as the train rolled north. We arrived in NYC's Grand Central Station about 5:00 PM the next day, totally lost and not know-

ing where to look for our dad. The size of the station and throng of people was overwhelming. It seemed like an eternity before he found us, scared and close to tears. For us it was like arriving in a foreign country. We could hardly understand the language and our senses were on overload from the hustle and bustle of the big city. Occasional trips to Birmingham had not prepared us for this.

Dad worked in a hotel at Gramercy Park. My brother and I were left on our own at the apartment to read, play games and try to amuse ourselves. There was no TV or radio. We were top floor of a 5th floor walk up. The roof was used to hang laundry and it afforded us a bird's eye view of Brooklyn Heights. We started exploring the area using some of the high buildings as reference marks, just as I had learned to use tall trees or hills on the farm. Off we went to find and play in small city parks, or wander along the palisade overlooking the East River and docks. Within two weeks we wandered too far and became lost. Since I was the oldest the responsibility was mine and I knew that if we didn't get home before dad arrived, I would really be in trouble. At last I spotted a tall building that I recognized. It was a long walk home. Dad had called the police, but he saw us first, and had to call the police to say that we'd returned. I didn't sit down for a few hours.

Dad decided to keep us with him in Brooklyn. After finding a suitable apartment, we were enrolled in school. Me in the 5th grade and my brother in the 4th. Because of our very southern accent and lack of city smarts, we were the targets of neighborhood bullies. We learned to take a different route each time we went to school or any other destination. A classmate introduced me to his friends at a local church that had an after school program. Soon my brother and I were able to play in the gym. I became a member of the boy's choir when I found out that I'd be paid 15 cents for practice and 25 cents for Sunday service. That winter the church put on the play "Show Boat" and each of us had several parts. The cast was short of girls and I was talked into playing two scenes as a girl. I was embarrassed because of the teasing of the boys, but decided that I was brave enough to do it. Strangely, once I was dressed and made up, I secretly enjoyed it.

I still have a photo taken of us girls and years later when a flight attendant friend saw it she couldn't pick me out from the other girls.

After a year in Brooklyn, my dad decided that we needed to move from the big city, but where? During the summer of '52 we visited all the towns and cities between NYC and Boston. He could not find work, so we backtracked and by late August found ourselves in Philadelphia. He was able to find work at a small hotel and a 5th floor-walkup apartment a few blocks away. This would be our home for the next few years. It was during the fall of '52 that the newspapers carried the sensational story of Christine Jorgenson. Its impact on me was profound. I felt scared. I didn't want to be like this person, but somehow I knew that I was. I couldn't tell anyone. There was no one to tell. If I told my dad, I was terribly afraid of his reaction. I had to keep my feelings a secret, no matter what. Besides, it would ruin my chances of becoming a pilot. It would ruin my life.

My sister joined us a year later. The apartment was just too small for four of us. Dad refused to get a larger one. During this time my sister and I became quite close, often playing together, or going to pretend shop for clothes, as we did not have money to buy any. I started running errands, bagging groceries, selling flowers for a street vendor, or anything I could do to earn money. I soon found that half of what I earned had to go to the household, then I could buy clothes for the three of us. As the oldest, I had to cook, clean house, shop for food, do laundry, and supervise my brother and sister.

The family situation began to deteriorate. Three of us were too much for my dad. My sister was literally shipped off to my grandparents, who by this time had sold the farm in Alabama and moved to Logansport, IN to be near their oldest son and his family, plus some cousins. I deeply missed my sister and being able to interact with her on a daily basis. For the rest of my teen years I would only see her for brief visits in Logansport.

It was becoming very clear to me that if I were to escape a life of hardships, then doing my best in school was imperative. I did well in the 6th grade, but upon entry to Jr. HS I still had a very heavy southern accent and was assigned to a remedial grade section. The first report period I received all A's, but I was made to wait to the next semester to be placed in the advanced section. I threw myself into my schoolwork. I avoided the rough and tumble activities of the boys while getting the two really smart girls to help me with English or any other area of study that I was weak in.

In 1953 I joined the Boy Scouts. I enjoyed outdoor activities because I had enjoyed the outdoors of the farm. Most of what was taught, I already knew. It was also a way for me to get out of the apartment one or two nights a week. The scoutmaster raised funds by collecting newspapers to sell at 2 cents per pound. Once a month three of us would make the rounds in his 1930's LaSalle, pack it full of newspapers, deliver them to the scrap dealer, and have enough to pay for a troop outing. He was everything my father wasn't, and I learned a lot from him.

Throughout my teen years I did very well in school, but was never comfortable socializing with boys. I did so at a level that helped me fit in so that I would not be harassed. In Jr. High I felt an attraction to some of the girls in my class but was too shy to get to know them well. Puberty had commenced and I felt uncomfortable with the male changes taking place. I did not look forward to shaving. It seemed that I wanted to live in a world that I could not enter. On weekends I went to the main library of Philadelphia to get any book that I could find on aviation and space. I also spent hours thumbing through books in the psychology section, but in those days there was nothing to explain what I felt I was going through. I needed knowledge, but it was not there.

One of my disappointments was not getting into Central HS for Boys. I needed to score 110 on the entrance exam. I scored 109.5. The school principal just told me that I didn't measure up. I desperately wanted to get into a four year high school and going to So. Philly HS where gangs were rampant was not in my plans. Fortunately, a friend told me of a small selective HS in the northwest section of the city that had both academics and agricultural tracks. The schedule called for doing three weeks of academics in two weeks, then spending a week learning agricultural subjects. Although it meant riding the bus for over two hours a day, I talked my father into letting me interview for a slot. The principal asked me to describe milking a cow. Well I knew, but my graphic description embarrassed his secretary, who was taking notes. I was admitted with no further questions.

The summer of '55 was spent at the school farm working in the barn, in the fields, and maintaining the school grounds. It was like being on the farm, but in the city at the same time. The school also provided contacts to local residents for students to mow grass and maintain yard work. A nearby family hired me to take care of their place. The dollar an hour would be used (after a 50% contribution to the household) to build up my bank account for future flying lessons. At the time I didn't know that this relationship would someday be my salvation. My routine was study, work and more work. Scouting and an occasional movie were my only recreation.

My relationship with my father was on the down slope. He could not be pleased. I determined to do the best that I could, as I now knew that my future depended solely on my efforts. I began to pay my brother to do some of my chores so that I would have more time for work and he would have his own money to spend. Dad was always bringing boxes of used clothing home for me to make repairs on; then he'd resell them. It was in this way that I accumulated a few female articles and wore them in secret. It was my only moments of being in tune with my identity. I was never sure if my brother ever found me out. He never said so.

For a couple of years I had been building model airplanes and rockets. Some flew and some didn't. When dad would get angry with me, he'd smash some of them. One day after he'd done just that, I told him that I would never build another model and that I would start taking flying lessons in a real airplane. I was almost 16 and had saved about $500.00 toward that goal. The weekend after my birthday I showed up at a flight school at the Philadelphia International Airport for my first lesson. When asked if my parents approved, I said that they didn't, but I had the money and knew what I wanted. On August 27th I came back and told them that I wasn't leaving until I had received a flight lesson. I'll never forget that 30-minute flight. I was at home in the air and now knew that my future would be in aviation. After each flight lesson, I would go over to the airport weather room, control tower and radar room. The men took me under their wings and taught me many valuable things about aviation. I became their mascot, and their knowledge filled me as water fills a sponge. On my sister's birthday, Oct. 27th, 1957, I passed my Private Pilot's flight test. However, storm clouds were on the horizon. I had also joined the Civil Air Patrol and loved every aspect of the program. I was the only cadet actually flying.

In the winter of '57, my father suddenly bought a farm in New Portland, Maine. It was a very small town, isolated, and 20 miles from the nearest high school located in another county. The four-room school that my brother and I were to attend was not even accredited and dad wouldn't pay for us to go to the school in Farmington. I could see that this was not going to work. In addition, dad had become very temperamental and physically abusive to us. He had a Jekyll & Hyde personality that was impossible to live with. One summer day, as I had just finished roofing the house, he started beating my brother. I came down from the roof to stop him. When he raised his fists at me, I blocked the blows and told him that he'd no longer hit us. He blew up, ordering us out of the house. We each packed a suitcase and walked a mile to our only friends' house. The couple agreed to let us stay in one of their three hunter's cabins. For two weeks I tried to find a way for us to get home to our grandparents. Living with mother was out of the question. I had fifteen dollars to my name. The local Red Cross refused to help. After two weeks, the couple took us to Portland, Maine. I bought bus tickets to Boston. We arrived there on a Monday evening just before the Traveler's Aid Society office closed. I had 50 cents left in my pocket.

The caseworker was in a state of disbelief after I told him our story. After he called my friends in New Portland he took us to a rooming house, gave us five dollars, and told us to be at his bus station office at 9:00 AM. We were assigned a new caseworker. For the next week, we lived on five dollars a day while it was determined who would take us and when we would leave. Finally, a week later we were given bus tickets to Birmingham and forty dollars for expenses. I did not really want to return to what I knew would be a life of hardship. We had to change buses in NYC so when we reached there I put my brother on the bus to Birmingham, gave him twenty dollars, and I took the one to Philadelphia. I had twenty dollars, enough money to last me two or three days. My goal was to find a job, a place to live, and finish my last year of school.

As I spent the day downtown looking for work, not having any luck, I was walking along Broad St. when I heard my name called. It was my old boss who owned a Center City newsstand. After a brief talk, he agreed to sublease his news stand to me. That would provide the money to live on. Next I went to my school to see about enrolling. They were very happy to see me and agreed that if I could find a sponsor, there would be no tuition. As I walked back to the bus stop, I saw the people whose yard I had maintained for three years. After hearing my story, they gave me a room to live in and at the end of the first week invited me to stay with them on a permanent basis. I was to work off my room and board by doing chores and maintaining the yard. They arranged with my mother to have guardianship. Their three children had completed college, moved on, and were raising families of their own. Robert and Anne F . . . were the first people to treat me as a son, and take a real interest in my life, and goals. I thrived in this atmosphere. For a while I was able to sublimate all feminine desires.

It was during this year that I had to register for the draft. I knew that upon graduation from high school I would be called up unless I was accepted to college or was rated Four F, not fit. My final year of school went very well. Once again, I was flying, earning a good living, and competing for scholarships. In '59, scholarships were few and no college would let me work part time and go to school part time. I had scored very high on the Air Force Officer Qualifying Tests but was only selected for an alternate slot for the academy. The principle candidate decided to go to the Air Force Academy, so I lost out. Sure enough, I received my draft notice. I went to the AF Recruiter and was selected for pilot training as a cadet. While awaiting orders I managed a small farm until my assignment came. That was not to be. The USAF decided that they had too many pilots, so the class was cancelled and the program shut down. I had to get into flying. I went back to the recruiter and was told that the Aviation Cadet Navigator program was still open. I signed up.

On June 20th, 1960 I reported to start training; little did I know of the challenges facing me. The month I started training the AF decided that they had too many navigators. The wash out rate was about 66% for my class. Bust one exam or flight check and you were done for. I learned to live one half day at a time. Somehow I got through the next ten months, and graduated as a Transport Navigator and was commissioned a Second Lieutenant. I was not an AF pilot, but at least I was flying, and becoming a pilot was very much a possibility. My first operational assignment was to Dover AFB, DE. Over the next five years I would see a great deal of the world.

The pay of a 2nd Lt. was just enough to survive on. Still, I was close enough to drive to Philadelphia and visit with my foster family and friends. I still had my old room. During this period I met a young lady and we began to date. I had dated occasionally but never cemented a relationship. Over the next four years we dated to the point that when I was 24 we actually thought of marriage. During this period, I gave her many gifts that I'd bought around the world, many of them of an intimate nature. I was also in a very confused state of mind about my own sexuality. I knew that I was not homosexual, but could not determine the source of my feelings. In private, I had acquired a limited female wardrobe. Dressed in these garments in private, I felt a sense of relief but also felt that I was committing a sin of sorts. I did not like the feeling. I often drove through Wilmington on the way to Philadelphia. I looked up a psychiatrist to try to find out what was going on with me. After three visits, he asked if I had ever had sex. Finding that I was still a virgin, he told me to go have sex and that after a dozen or so times, I'd give up my foolish notions when I found how good it was. I left there even more confused. I tried but it didn't work. My thoughts kept drifting back to the Christine Jorgenson case. I was scared and had no one to turn to.

When a transsexual gets up each morning and looks in the mirror, he/she sees a picture that doesn't match the mental image of who they want to be. As I grew older the disparity between mirror image and who I felt I was began to diverge. All around me I saw my friends getting married and fitting the societal image that I knew would probably not be mine. The current image of a military officer was a married one. My superiors would ask me about my prospects at least once a month. I had to develop a fantasy life to keep their curiosity at bay. All I wanted to do was fly and be left alone. Besides, if any of them suspected anything my career would be over in 24 hours. When I was not on a trip, I tried to get away from the base. In those days the world seemed to be in constant conflict and we pulled a lot of alert duty. Being in close contact with five other crewmembers for days at a time could lead to some very prying questions. I became very adept at revealing little and what I did say protected me.

I was in the Philippines when I received my promotion to Captain and orders to pilot training. My engagement had ended and I felt free to concentrate on my dream of becoming a jet pilot. I reported to Graig AFB in Selma, Al. to start class in June of 1966. By now, I was a seasoned officer and knew what to concentrate on so that I'd graduate in the top 10 and get a choice assignment. By now I had 3300 hours of navigator flight time and 300 hours as a civilian pilot. During the first week I took the final exams for most of the academic courses. Since I was a Captain I assisted with the administration of my classmates and did a lot of tutoring. Most of the students were 2nd Lieutenants and needed close supervision. Some would not survive the rigors of flight training. For me it was a time to excel, and I did.

As a single officer I was required to live on base, but I found a nice apartment in Selma and gave the phone number to my training officer. It rang at both locations so most never knew where I really lived. The privacy was essential at this time. I was cross-dressing frequently when in my apartment. I felt so relaxed and my concentration for study was much better. On non-flying weekends I would go visit relatives in north Alabama, take in a play in Birmingham, or drive down to the gulf coast for a weekend on the beach. Life was good. By now I had given up the thought of marriage, though the official pressure was still there. About six weeks into training a classmate talked me into going to a mixer dance in Montgomery. He was not familiar with the area and I was.

Little did I know that I would meet my future wife that evening. When we met it was the meeting of two lost souls who had been searching for each other for a long time, and had finally arrived at the same time in space. Still, I was un-

certain about having a relationship that may lead to places in life I was afraid to go to. I had already faced serious danger in flight, had dealt with it, and survived. It was the emotional part of life that I was ill prepared for. To date, I had found very little information about the subject of transsexuality. I couldn't define it, let alone understand how and if it related to me, or how it would impact marriage.

As our relationship grew more intimate, I really began to feel that marriage was the solution. I purged my closet of all female things and with her on my arm at base social functions, basked in the warmth of having finally arrived. In five months my life consisted of flying and building a life with Beth. The way my superiors treated me now that I had a beautiful woman in my life gave me confidence that it would work. Little did I realize the deceptions that lay ahead. By January we made the decision to get married before I graduated. We were married at the base chapel with a few family members, friends, and some classmates present. To get a weekend off, I had flown two training flights daily for two weeks. We moved into a duplex near the base and set up housekeeping. While I was flying, she was getting to know the other wives and learn about AF life. We were only married ten days when a mid-air collision with a hawk almost did me in. Upon arriving home I stripped off a rather foul smelling flight suit, stuffed it into a trash bag, and went inside for a good stiff drink. It was her introduction to: flying can be dangerous. There would be many more close calls in the future.

Graduation day finally came. We said our goodbyes and headed off to my first operational assignment as a USAF pilot. I'd got my pick and chose to fly a C-141 Starlifter at Warner Robbins AFB, GA. Flying a heavy jet was a good way to move ahead in my career. We bought a small house in a nice neighborhood and got busy becoming part of the community. In 1967 the war in Viet Nam was really heating up. My turn to fly combat came sooner than I expected. Already, most of my flying in the C-141 was to Viet Nam, hauling in supplies and often flying the wounded and bodies out. No one talked on the body bag flights. They still haunt me.

I started my training as a Forward Air Controller in late '68. FAC's flew light unarmed aircraft and controlled the air strikes by directing fighter aircraft to enemy targets. That's a nice way of saying that I killed people by telling the fighters where to drop the bombs. I arrived in Viet Nam in April of '69. What I didn't know was whether I could keep the bomb from going off inside me. I flew up to two times a day; three times when a battle was raging. The disparity of who I was and who I felt I should be was also raging. I even rationalized that it would be better to die a war hero, rather than live with the internal conflicts that raged within me. I guess that I did have a desire to live as I returned to base each day unscathed, though the army ground commanders were sure that my aircraft had taken hits.

At the nine-month point Beth and I met in Hawaii for a five day R & R. It was tough getting reacquainted but we did have a good visit. I made sure that she departed on her flight before I left on mine. I shall never forget the look of sorrow on her face at that time. Six weeks later I received a tape telling me that we were now expectant parents. This news encouraged me to be a little more cautious in my flying. After a year in the hell of Viet Nam and 381 combat missions, I got on the "Freedom Bird" and 18 hours later found myself in NJ exposed to an ungrateful nation.

For the next six years McGuire AFB would be our home. The flying continued to be a joy, but I knew that it would just be a matter of months before I would be tapped for a staff assignment. Our daughter was born in October and I was assigned to the training division at the same time. This permitted me to control my schedule to be able to be home most nights to help with the care of our little girl. Life seemed to be on track, except for . . .

The internal pressure continued to grow. Beth had suspected something was wrong after my return from Viet Nam. I finally screwed up the courage to tell her about how I felt. We came close to separating, but I promised to seek help so we decided not to do anything until we knew more. Besides we did have a very good life together and our love was sound. Our daughter was two and I really loved her. It took months of searching to find a doctor in Philadelphia who was experienced with transsexuals. What a disappointment! On the second visit he gave me an injection of testosterone saying: if this doesn't cure you in six months, then we'll reverse the hormones. On the drive home I felt so distraught that he might as well have injected me with arsenic. That night I walked the base golf course crying and screaming, "God—why me?"

I called every hospital and was told that the Pennsylvania Hospital had a doctor with the expertise that I needed. I made an appointment with him immediately. He gave me every test that was known, and after six sessions made his pronouncement. He said that I was a true transsexual but since I had been able to cope with military life for thirteen years, he believed as I got older the urge would decrease and therefore he would not recommend surgery. He referred me to a psychologist for group therapy. At the time this seemed a better course of action to me. Upon examination by the new doctor, group therapy was ruled out. Instead, he put me on a very low dose of hormone treatment to help me cope with the stress and inner conflicts. The new course of treatment enabled me to cope with the stress and help me delay decision time until I had more information. Simply stopping the hormones would reverse the treatment.

My spouse and I talked over the situation. We decided to remain together and live life as normally as possible. I made a promise to complete my AF career so that we would always have a modicum of income. I would also not do anything until our daughter had completed high school. We both began to get counseling so that we could keep open communications and cope with the high level of stress caused by my problem. From all outward appearances we were the model of a very normal military family.

In the spring of 1976, I obtained my last staff assignment. I was to be a liaison and training officer. My new assignment took us to the Sacramento area of California. Though stationed at Mather AFB, I worked over the six western states of our region. Once again I purged myself of my feminine wardrobe and tried to be a normal straight guy. Within a year I had failed. The hunt for a new doctor began. Finally I found one nearby who was experienced. He felt that he should work with both of us to fully understand how we had coped and stayed together for so long. Once again I was put on a low dose of hormones, but not enough to cause any outward changes. I still had to pass my annual AF flight physicals.

My last four years passed quickly as I enjoyed my work, the flying, and our life in CA. I was retired from active duty at the end of June, 1980. Now I had to find a new career. Flying jobs were scarce. The airlines were not hiring and related fields were stagnant. I had taken the management exam for the major Bell Company and was hired to supervise an installation and repair crew of ten technicians. I mastered the technical aspects of the job in short order, but the other managers resented an outsider. It took three months for them to come around. During my three years with the company, I had three management jobs. However, I was hired just as deregulation had been ordained. The company went through several rounds of reorganization and lay offs. Two weeks shy of three years and tenure, my pink slip arrived. I decided that it was time to get back into the flying business.

Though I had flown four engine heavy jets in the Air Force, I did not have the required Airline Transport Pilot rating or Flight Engineer rating required for an interview. I went back to giving flight instruction and flying charter to hone my skills. One job I had was to deliver bank checks in the wee hours of the morning, bad weather or not. Many a young pilot has bought the farm doing this type of flying. As soon as I had the written exams and ATP flight check passed, my resumes went to all the airlines. In the spring of '84 I interviewed with People Express Airlines at Newark, NJ. Fortune was with me and I was to start training in August. The move back to NJ was a tough one. We managed to get almost everything into a large rental truck and the overflow into a trailer. We found a rental house near Princeton and settled in for the next phase of our lives.

While making the move, I decided to purge once more. Besides, I had left my doctor in CA and felt that for my and my family's sake I should try once again to be a real man. Getting the household set up, getting settled in the community, and getting checked out as a Boeing 727 Flight Engineer kept me so busy that I didn't have time to think about gender problems. No matter how I tried to sublimate my feelings, like a cancer, they came back with a vengeance. By the spring of '85 I knew that I needed help. Again, the lack of information made it extremely difficult to find help. The doctor that I had gone to in Philadelphia had moved on. Through a medical listing I started blanket calling psychiatrists on the list, finally finding one in north NJ. My telephone interview with him was very unsatisfactory. It seemed that he was more interested in the weekly fee, which was very steep, than my well-being. The needle in the haystack search began once more. I went to the NYC Public Library to start the search. There I found an article written by Dr. Leo Wollman, who had been an associate of Dr. Harry Benjamin. A check of the telephone directories was next. No listing under medical, physicians, or doctors could be found. I checked the residential listings next. To my amazement his name and number was there, moreso when I nervously dialed the number and he answered. My heart raced as I told him how I felt. Suddenly, he simply said: "Come to my office on Coney Island next week, we need to talk." Oh, how I looked forward to that.

It was a cold, rainy day as I drove to the office located in a nondescript building on Mermaid Avenue in the Coney Island section of Brooklyn. I had remembered it as a bustling place with a grand boardwalk, the Cyclone and Parachute Jump from '51. Now it was run down, bleak as the weather that day and I feared for my safety. Arriving at the office I signed in and took a seat among the very poor of the neighborhood. I really felt out of place, but I was as desperate as those around me. I was scheduled as the last patient, and as Dr. Wollman called me in, he told his nurse that she could go home. Just the two of us to deal with my future. Dr. Wollman pointed to a chair at the side of his desk for me to sit in. He then pulled his chair to a position directly in front of me with little distance between us. I briefly told him of my life and occupation. He cut me off and asked a question: "Tell me, who are you?" I tried to answer in an indirect manner but once again he asked: "Who are you?" He looked me in the eyes. I knew that I had to answer directly. Finally, I stammered, I am a woman. He leaned back and then said: "And what are you going to do about that?" I stated that I was here to begin the process and needed his help. He said okay, but it's going to be very difficult and that he would make sure that I knew what faced me, and that there would be many tests.

I suddenly felt very much better and asked him what his medical training consisted of. He told me that he'd started as a general practitioner, and then became a gynecologist, then a surgeon, then an endocrinologist, and finally a psychiatrist, and had worked with many transsexual patients before retiring. He explained that he became bored, so he set up a community clinic for the poor, started treating transsexuals, and volunteered at a nearby military hospital. He called a local pharmacy to confirm that they had female hormones, wrote out a prescription and since my flying schedule changed each month, told me to call him for an appointment. It was snowing as I left, but to me it seemed like the spring of my life.

Throughout the next four years I would meet once a month on a Saturday at his home with a group of other trans-gendered people. One was post op, a couple were well along and no longer resembled their former selves, and the few others had been in the program a year or so. They immediately made me feel welcome and comfortable. Still, there was a lot that I didn't understand but my education had begun.

As I took the hormones, my body slowly began to change. One day I asked Dr. Wollman about it and he asked if I had experienced a short or long puberty. I said long. He then told me that as I changed, the male hormones would fight back and that I'd experience a long puberty once again. There was a war going on in my body. After an injection I would be nauseous and even have morning sickness for a while. So this is what women go through, I thought. It would take two to three years before my physical changes would become noticeable, and I didn't want to call undue notice to myself. By '88 my family doctor had picked up on my changed appearance during an annual physical and told me that he was requesting a mammogram. I told him what was going on and he said that that was my business, but it was his business to keep me healthy. The radiologist was taken aback, but I took the position that they only needed to know enough to accomplish what my doctor had ordered. It worked. Each year I also had to get a flight physical from an FAA Aero medical doctor. The medical certificate is necessary to exercise pilot privileges. Again, the doctor was surprised but wished me the best and issued the medical certificate. Both doctors demonstrated a compassion for my well being that I would find lacking in most of society.

Throughout the period from '85, when I started taking hormones, to my decision point, the matter of my transsexuality weighed more heavily on the lives of my wife and daughter. Beth and I still enjoyed closeness, were affectionate and intimate, and really tried to effect, at least from outward appearances, a normal relationship. It was difficult for her to see that she was slowly losing her husband. We discussed how it would affect our relationship, the difficulties of my transition, legal and financial matters. It seemed that no matter how logically and methodically I continued, a disaster was in the making. In the AF, I had learned how to write operations plans. I did so now. My plan had sections for medical, legal, financial, logistics, etc. We would go over it from time to time and she asked a lot of "what if" questions. The unknown had to be thought of and dealt with. The plan was revised many times.

One of the most critical aspects facing me was that of money. I had monthly retirement income from the military, Beth worked full time, I made a good salary as an airline pilot, and I would have to—as I had done so far—pay the full expense of the surgery. Transsexual surgery is an elective procedure according to insurance companies. They won't pay for it. They ignore the suicide rate for TS victims. Though the FAA was the agency that finds a pilot fit and capable of flying, I anticipated that my company would probably fire me for some business or medical reason. The future was very uncertain. Flying was the one place I truly felt at home and I would have to fight to stay there. At the same time I also knew that if I didn't achieve a union of body and psyche, I had no future. I squirreled away money as I could to fund the plan.

We had rented a house since we'd moved to NJ. We had to leave California at a time when the interest rates were 18% and we were forced to sell for the amount of the loans. All equity was lost. We started off in NJ at a time of rapidly increasing housing costs. My salary in the first four years was not enough to purchase a home, so we rented. By the spring of '89, our daughter was working and living with friends so we started house hunting. We found a nice townhouse nearby and bought it using my VA loan entitlement. Now we had the advantages of home ownership at a cost much less than renting. In the event I was fired, the mortgage was affordable.

During my daughter's last three years of high school, she became much more aware of my problem. Though she didn't talk directly to me about it, I knew that she had read my books on the subject that I had placed in the bookcases. She did start to ask her mom what was going on. I was in counseling when my wife sought counseling at our church. One of the priests, a woman, felt that something deeply troubled us. She made herself available and we both went to talk with her, singly and together. She also helped us find a psychologist for our daughter to talk to. At last we were able to express our innermost fears, concerns, and feelings with each other through the priest and doctor, and at times directly. In one session when my daughter was asked how she felt about my impending change, she replied, "I don't want to lose my father figure, but he's not happy and he deserves happiness, so I guess that I'll learn to accept him." Having her say this in front of me in the presence of her mother and the doctor brought tears to my eyes. Much debate had gone on between Beth and I about my future name. That was solved one day when my daughter arrived home from school. I was "dressed at the time" and didn't expect her home for another hour. She called up to the second floor where I was working on administrative matters in the office and announced that when she finished her snack, that she wanted to talk with me. Surprised, I told her to wait until I changed clothes. She said, don't bother—it doesn't matter. A short time later she came into the office and pulled up a chair. I asked what she wanted to talk about, but was not prepared for what was to follow.

When she was born we had a difficult time deciding on her first name. Two names were finalized but we couldn't seem to agree on which one. On the ninth day the head nurse gave us an ultimatum, decide today or it will be "Baby Girl." With that prompt, my choice won out. My daughter knew this so she said, "Since you got to name me I think it's only right for me to name you." I sat there stunned, then looked at her and

said, "OK, what's it going to be?" "Jessica Page," she said. I had not tried Jessica and suddenly it seemed to fit. I told her that I liked the first name, but wanted to keep my initials of JRS. She told me that was okay and that we'd think of something. As she left, she turned and said: "Nice pumps—why don't I have some like that?" I told her to buy some if she wanted. Two weeks later she was wearing her pair. Though I knew that our troubles were far from over, this had given me hope that our relationship would survive. I am proud to have been named by my daughter.

The decision to undergo sex reassignment surgery must never be taken lightly and without thorough preparation. Once done, there is no going back. I did not know when I would arrive at my decision point. It happened the second Sunday of September '89. As my wife and I knelt in church to recite the Lord's prayer and as I said "thy will be done," I felt seized by only what I can say was the Holy Spirit, and instantly knew what had to be done. As we left the church, she suddenly turned to me and spoke: "You've made your decision." It was not a question, but a statement of fact. In reply, I simply said yes to her statement. We then went for brunch and only discussed the subject when we returned home.

The FAA had just completed the evaluations of the many exams required of me, and informed me by letter that I was cleared to proceed. Upon completion of surgery, I was to send the documents needed to obtain new pilot and medical certificates. I knew it would be different with the airline. I wrote a detailed letter explaining my situation, enclosed a copy of the FAA letter, and waited for the fireworks. I went to fly one early morning in November and as I tried to pull up the trip schedule in the computer, could not find it. When my Assistant Chief Pilot showed up two hours later he told me that I had been administratively grounded and he didn't know why. We stepped into his office, closed the door, and I told him why. We'd known each other in the AF and he told me that he'd always thought the best of my flying and staff work. He promised to do what he could do to help me but thought that the decision made at the highest level, by one of the most despised airline CEO's, would be impossible to overcome. Fortunately, we had a pilots' union and contract, but that would only enable me to go through the prescribed grievance process.

The company said that I was psychologically unsound, not fit to fly, would be a hazard in the cockpit, and passengers would not fly with me. The VP for Flight Operations ordered me to see the company drug abuse specialist and psychologist in LA. In early December my wife and I flew out to see Dr. GB. The company didn't know that he'd already helped several people like me and knew what was going on. He strongly recommended that I be returned to flying and be permitted to fly as a woman. The company rejected that idea, but I was returned to duty for a short time. In February of '90, the second letter came. I was fired. My fight had begun in earnest. Before I went to Viet Nam as a Forward Air Controller, I was fighter qualified. When a flight of fighters arrives over the target they set up a wheel formation so that when they roll off their high altitude perch, they can be most effective at striking from any direction. I now put myself in this mental mode of striking back. I needed help though; a tough, go-for-the-throat attorney who would not be afraid to take on a large corporation, and who would be understanding of my finances. I had read of a local attorney who liked to take on tough, unusual, and challenging cases. He had just beaten a large university in two cases. He sounded like the man for me. When I explained why I needed him, he was in a state of disbelief. He finally said okay, then looked at me and said that I would have to educate him. I paid his retainer and told him that on the next visit he would be seeing Jessica.

I had filed a discrimination complaint with the state and was quickly scheduled for a hearing. At the time my attorney was a little uncomfortable with me as a female, so for the hearing he asked that I appear in men's clothing. Mentally, I had made the switch to female and having to appear dressed as a man was very distressing to me. Of course the airline attorney and chief pilot jumped on that and tried to discredit me. He realized his mistake and quickly told them in very stern terms that it was he who was uncomfortable and that from then on he would treat me properly, as a woman. He apologized and the hearing was completed. As we walked from the room he put his arms around me, apologized again, and told me that the airline was going to be in for one hell of a fight. A couple of months later I was notified that the Division on Civil Rights had found for me, but that didn't mean that I could readily get my job back.

My date for surgery was set for August 28th, 1990 in Trinidad, Colorado. My sister, who was still uncertain about my decision, told me that she would be going with me. The hospital stay was scheduled for ten days and travel afterwards was going to be difficult and painful. Her car was a Lincoln Town car. The ride would prove to be very beneficial for me on the journey home. Her daughter lived in Topeka, Kansas, which was about halfway between Indianapolis and Trinidad, so we stopped there both ways. During '89 I had made the rounds of relatives and close friends to inform them of my plans. This came as a shock to most, but after the news sank in and they began to understand my feelings, most reacted with feelings of love and support. I don't recommend this as a way to find out who your real friends are, or who truly loves you, but you'll soon know. The level of love and support surprised me, and that helped to sustain me during some very dark hours. My sister and I spent a weekend at Colorado Springs. We felt like two sisters on vacation. The weather was perfect as we took the cog rail train to the top of Pikes Peak, walked about the Garden of the Gods, shopped and dined in quaint restaurants.

About an hour from Trinidad my sister told me that it was OK with her if I changed my mind, that she'd love me just as much if I said no. My life was ahead, and as a woman. In my mind, there was no going back. Dr. Biber gave me my final exam on a Monday morning and I was admitted to the hospital that afternoon. Final checks were made, paperwork completed, and fees paid. I met all the staff involved and was given every chance to change my mind. For the first time in my life I felt totally at ease. All that I despised would soon be removed.

I was awakened at 6:30 AM Tuesday morning, rechecked and given a last chance to say no. By 7:00 I was in the operating room. Within seconds of being given a sedative I was asleep. I was told that the surgery took over four hours.

When I awoke, numb as a log, the wall clock said 2:10 PM; Dr. Biber and the O.R. nurses were standing at the foot of my bed, with my blood on their scrubs, and smiling. Dr. Biber said to me: "Welcome to the world, Sleeping Beauty." Those words I'll never forget. I was truly born again. It would be a week before I was allowed out of bed. The pain was intense. I endured it, as I knew it would recede as my body healed. My sister came each morning and spent a lot of time with me and the other four new girls in our special section of the ward. Liz, Margaret and I bonded and to this day we consider ourselves sisters. My strength gradually returned, and on day eleven I was released into the world.

My sister did most of the driving on the return trip. The back seat of the town car was my bed. We spent two nights in Topeka with her daughter, and then drove on to Indianapolis. For two days I rested there before heading back to NJ in my car. I could go about one and a half hours between stops for rest and a change of bandages. When I arrived back in Princeton I truly felt that I had started over. Now I could focus on the legal fight ahead. Though my funds were low, I was getting unemployment, and earning some money from photography. In a short time I would find some part time work to pay for rent and living expenses. For now, I needed to concentrate on learning in months, what the normal female has years to learn. Fortunately, I had a lot of help from friends and family. Never once during my transition had I been challenged about who I was. That had given me a lot of confidence.

As the legal battle began, my airline filed for bankruptcy. Now I had to petition Federal Bankruptcy Court in Delaware in order to sue for reinstatement. More expense but I prevailed. After a lot of legal jousting, my case was taken by the Federal District Court in Trenton, NJ. No argument that the airline presented impressed the court. My case was put on a fast track, and we were kept busy with research, presentations, and legal arguments. At each hearing, the results favored me. Just before a trial was set to start, a summary court hearing was conducted. During the hearing, the judge suddenly ordered the airline attorney and mine to his chambers. He told the company that they would want to settle with me as they were going to lose. They were given thirty days to come to terms. I wrote out the terms and though they tried to weasel, I said to them: "Agree or I'll see you at trial." They gave in.

Almost two and a half years had passed since I'd been fired. I was excited about returning to the profession that I loved. I had made the national news twice and a level of public support had begun which gave me confidence that I could win. I had been on several TV and radio talk shows that helped me deal with public perception and questions about functioning and fitting in with society. Still, I knew that there would be many who didn't want me there, let alone fly with me. During a special interview with the company VP of Flight Operations, I told him that I was back to fly and do my job as a professional, not because they wanted me, but because a federal court had ordered it. If any pilot had a problem with who I was, it was their problem, not mine. Many of the pilots actively supported me, others had a wait-and-see attitude, while some tried to make my life miserable. On July 21st, 1992 I reported to training for requalification. It was good to be home.

Because I had beaten the company, stood up for my rights, and went after any pilot that harassed me, the flight attendants and gate agents were open about how they felt. I'd become a folk hero of sorts. They warmly greeted me for each flight, made sure I had a bottle of water, made fresh coffee for me, and saved first class meals when possible. Many of the employees would let me know about the plots of those who wanted to embarrass or cause me problems. It took a while to get used to being stared at by pilots in the crew room. I knew that it would take some time to be accepted, but I earned it by conducting myself in a professional and friendly manner at all times. Those who crossed me learned that I knew how to use published pilot policies to stop harassment immediately. One of my captain friends told me one day that the word was "Don't mess with Jess."

Of over five thousand pilots, my company only had sixty-three female pilots in '93. It was rare to fly with another female, but a treat when it happened. I had upgraded to Captain before having an entire female crew. We had a lot of fun and it was amusing to see some of the passengers' expressions and hear their comments when they found out that the whole crew was female. When I flew to Mexico or South America airport employees, mostly male, reacted with surprise and amazement upon seeing a female Captain, especially one who wore a skirt instead of slacks. Some even whistled at me.

After I healed from surgery and had resumed as normal a life as I could, I started to become more social. I had to find out how I felt about men in a more intimate way. I was attractive enough that as I went about my daily routine I became aware of how others were looking at me. When I went to a dance it was as if I could read the minds of the men in the room. I knew exactly what they wanted. The question was, do I or how far do I let them go? I considered myself heterosexual before surgery, now how would I feel in the intimate company of men? I needed to find out. I had met a scientist at a church singles group and he always arranged to have me in the discussion group that he led and at the monthly dance would dance with me often. One Sunday he told me that he wanted to get to know me better. I invited him to dinner one cold winter evening when I had the house to myself. I discovered after dinner that his interests were more physical than intellectual. Now I'd been there in the past, but was I going to let him do to me what I knew he wanted? It was the situation every female finds herself in and has to decide—do I, or don't I? Well, I did and thus began my journey into the intimacy of being female. In a year I knew that I enjoyed being the object of men's desires.

How do men react when they find out that the woman they are attracted to turns out to have had that very different past? Those who are confident of their own sexuality have told me that since they only knew me as Jessica, it didn't matter. Others run immediately, while others become fearful of what their peers will think. I found that some men are very intimidated by a woman who has advanced education, highly developed technical skills, has coped with extreme danger, and has not had to ask a man to do it for her. My lady friends have done a reasonable job of teaching me, so that I don't scare off the prospective suitor. Of course, I could now write volumes about how women are treated at the local garage, hardware store, car dealership, etc. I won't, but I use that knowledge to my advantage.

In summary, I like to stress that no human chooses to be a transsexual. I feel that half of my life's energy was spent in coping with this. Statistics available in 1990 indicated that the population of transsexual people, both male and female, was about .0004%. Of that number only ten percent will achieve the goal of surgery. In a nation concerned about human health and well-being, we are left to fend for ourselves with little help. The situation has got somewhat better because some of us have been willing to educate, speak out, go to court (I was the first to win in a federal court), and insist that we deserve and have the right to happiness promised to all. Today one needs only to go to the World Wide Web to find support groups and resources for the transgendered. In the past few years, many local and state governments have passed anti-discrimination laws to help protect gays, lesbians, and transgendered people. Many companies have been in the lead as they value the employee and realize that disharmony in the work place affects profits.

When asked if I am happy. I can say without a doubt that I am. I have no regrets about having lived my life as I did. There's no going back, only forward with the total continuity of "freedom of identity."   [2003]

Understanding the Reading

1. What is a transsexual?
2. Do you think Jessica was born this way, or is it because of something in her background?
3. Describe her personality, as you see her.
4. In what different ways did she attempt to deal with her transsexuality throughout her life?
5. After her surgery, how did her employer react?
6. What was the legal outcome?

Suggestions for Responding

1. Research laws concerning transsexuality and report on them.
2. Find out what the U.S. Armed Forces' policy is toward transsexuals. What would have happened to her career had they known about her transsexuality?

3. Have a class discussion on why you think Jessica sought a career in flying, as traditionally it has been a very masculine arena. ✦

29

Two Sexes Are Not Enough

ANNE FAUSTO-STERLING

In 1843 Levi Suydam, a 23-year-old resident of Salisbury, Connecticut, asked the town's board of selectmen to allow him to vote as a Whig in a hotly contested local election. The request raised a flurry of objections from the opposition party, for a reason that must be rare in the annals of American democracy: It was said that Suydam was "more female than male," and thus (since only men had the right to vote) should not be allowed to cast a ballot. The selectmen brought in a physician, one Dr. William Barry, to examine Suydam and settle the matter. Presumably, upon encountering a phallus and testicles, the good doctor declared the prospective voter male. With Suydam safely in their column, the Whigs won the election by a majority of one.

A few days later, however, Barry discovered that Suydam menstruated regularly and had a vaginal opening. Suydam had the narrow shoulders and broad hips characteristic of a female build, but occasionally "he" felt physical attractions to the "opposite" sex (by which "he" meant women). Furthermore, "his feminine propensities, such as fondness for gay colors, for pieces of calico, comparing and placing them together, and an aversion for bodily labor and an inability to perform the same, were remarked by many." (Note that this 19th-century doctor did not distinguish between "sex" and "gender." Thus he considered a fondness for piecing together swatches of calico just as telling as anatomy and physiology.) No one has yet discovered whether Suydam lost the right to vote. Whatever the outcome, the story conveys both the political weight our culture places on ascertaining a person's correct "sex" and the deep confusion that arises when it can't be easily determined.

European and American culture is deeply devoted to the idea that there are only two sexes. Even our language refuses other possibilities; thus to write about Levi Suydam I have had to invent conventions—s/he and h/er to denote individuals who are clearly neither/both male and female or who are, perhaps, both at once. Nor is the linguistic convenience an idle fancy. Whether one falls into the category of man or woman matters in concrete ways. For Suydam—and still today for women in some parts of the world—it meant the right to vote. It might mean being subject to the military draft and to various laws concerning the family and marriage. In many parts of the United States, for example, two individuals legally registered as men cannot have sexual relations without breaking anti-sodomy laws.[1]

But if the state and legal system has an interest in maintaining only two sexes, our collective biological bodies do not. While male and female stand on the extreme ends of a biological continuum, there are many other bodies, bodies such as Suydam's, that evidently mix together anatomical components conventionally attributed to both males and females. The implications of my argument for a sexual continuum are profound. If nature really offers us more than two sexes, then it follows that our current notions of masculinity and femininity are cultural conceits. Reconceptualizing the category of "sex" challenges cherished aspects of European and American social organization.

Indeed, we have begun to insist on the male-female dichotomy at increasingly early stages, making the two-sex system more deeply a part of how we imagine human life and giving it the appearance of being both inborn and natural. Nowadays, months before the child leaves the comfort of the womb, amniocentesis and ultrasound identify a fetus's sex. Parents can decorate the baby's room in gender-appropriate style, sports wallpaper—in blue—for the little boy, flowered designs—in pink—for the little girl. Researchers have nearly completed development of technology that can choose the sex of a child at the moment of fertilization. Moreover, modern surgical techniques help maintain the two-sex system. Today children who are born "either/or—neither/both"—a fairly common phenomenon—usually disappear from view because doctors "correct" them right away with surgery. In the past, however, intersexuals (or hermaphrodites, as they were called until recently), were culturally acknowledged.

Hermaphroditic Heresies

In 1993 I published a modest proposal suggesting that we replace our two-sex system with a five-sex one. In addition to males and females, I argued, we should also accept the categories herms (named after "true" hermaphrodites), merms (named after male "pseudohermaphrodites"), and ferms (named after female "pseudohermaphrodites"). [*Editor's note:* A "true" hermaphrodite bears an ovary and a testis, or a combined gonad called an ovo-testis. A "pseudohermaphrodite" has either an ovary or a testis, along with genitals from the "opposite" sex.] I'd intended to be provocative, but I had also been writing tongue in cheek and so was surprised by the extent of the controversy the article unleashed. Right-wing Christians somehow connected my idea of five sexes to the United Nations–sponsored Fourth World Conference on Women, to be held in Beijing two years later, apparently seeing some sort of global conspiracy at work. "It is maddening," says the text of a *New York Times* advertisement paid for by the Catholic League for Religious and Civil Rights, "to listen to discussions of 'five genders' when every sane person knows there are but two sexes, both of which are rooted in nature."

[Sexologist] John Money was also horrified by my article, although for different reasons. In a new edition of his guide for those who counsel intersexual children and their families, he wrote: "In the 1970's nurturists . . . became . . . 'social constructionists.' They align themselves against biology and medicine . . . They consider all sex differences as artifacts of social construction. In cases of birth defects of the sex organs, they attack all medical and surgical interventions as unjustified meddling designed to force babies into fixed social molds of male and female . . . One writer has gone even to the extreme of proposing that there are five sexes . . . " (Fausto-Sterling).

Meanwhile, those battling against the constraints of our sex/gender system were delighted by the article. The science fiction writer Melissa Scott wrote a novel entitled *Shadow Man,* which includes nine types of sexual preference and several genders, including fems (people with testes, XY chromosomes, and some aspects of female genitalia), herms (people with ovaries and testes), and mems (people with XX chromosomes and some aspects of male genitalia). Others used the idea of five sexes as a starting point for their own multi-gendered theories.

Clearly I had struck a nerve. The fact that so many people could get riled up by my proposal to revamp our sex/gender system suggested that change (and resistance to it) might be in the offing. Indeed, a lot *has* changed since 1993, and I like to think that my article was one important stimulus. Intersexuals have materialized before our very eyes, like beings beamed up onto the Starship Enterprise. They have become political organizers lobbying physicians and politicians to change treatment practices. More generally, the debate over our cultural conceptions of gender has escalated, and the boundaries separating masculine and feminine seem harder than ever to define. Some find the changes under way deeply disturbing; others find them liberating.

I, of course, am committed to challenging ideas about the male/female divide. In chorus with a growing organization of adult intersexuals, a small group of scholars, and a small but growing cadre of medical practitioners, I argue that medical management of intersexual births needs to change. *First,* let there be no unnecessary infant surgery (by *necessary* I mean to save the infant's life or significantly improve h/er physical well-being). *Second,* let physicians assign a provisional sex (male or female) to the infant (based on existing knowledge of the probability of a particular gender identity formation—penis size be damned!). *Third,* let the medical care team provide full information and long-term counseling to the parents and to the child. However well-intentioned, the methods for managing intersexuality, so entrenched since the 1950s, have done serious harm.   [1999]

Notes

1. The antisodomy laws were overturned by the U.S. Supereme Court in June, 2003.

Understanding the Reading

1. Why was there a question as to whether Levi Suydam should be allowed to vote?
2. What does the author mean when she says that biology has no interest in maintaining only two sexes?
3. What is "corrective" surgery for intersexuals and when is it done?
4. Do you think "corrective" surgery is ethical? If not, what is the alternative?
5. Why does the author suggest we change to a five-sex system?

Suggestions for Responding

1. What are the implications of changing to a five-sex system? Spend ten minutes outlining what would change, on a public policy level, interpersonal level, and psychological level.
2. Debate the ethics of assigning a sex through surgery, delaying surgery until after puberty, or not doing surgery at all. ◆

30

Cold Feet: Why America Has Gay Marriage Jitters

ELISABETH BUMILLER

CRAWFORD, Tex.—The cultural change has been swift, radical and seemingly irreversible. Gay characters star in prime-time television shows like "Will & Grace," and real gays appear in reality programming like "Queer Eye for the Straight Guy." Most Americans say they know someone who is gay, and a vast majority support equal rights for gays in the workplace. One of Vice President Cheney's daughters is openly gay; so is a daughter of a Democratic presidential candidate, Representative Richard A. Gephardt.

Americans have even become less censorious about gay sex itself. In 1991, 71 percent said gay sex was always wrong, according to the General Social Survey, a leading cultural barometer. By 2002, that number had fallen to 53 per-

cent, and another 32 percent said that gay sex was not wrong at all.

But something extraordinary occurred last month: an important statistic that measures the acceptance of gays abruptly reversed. A Gallup poll released in late July, after the Supreme Court struck down a Texas sodomy law, found that 57 percent opposed gay civil unions. In May, a similar Gallup poll found that only 49 percent were opposed.

What happened? Pollsters, sociologists and gay rights leaders say the answer lies in large part in the culturally explosive word "marriage," which entered the debate after the Supreme Court ruling in June. The word came first from Justice Antonin Scalia, who in a sharp dissent to the sodomy decision accused the court of having "largely signed on to the so-called homosexual agenda." He predicted that same-sex marriage would be the logical next step.

Social conservatives quickly took up the warning that traditional marriage as Americans knew it was gravely endangered. President Bush was pressured by his conservative supporters to oppose gay marriage publicly, which he did last month in the Rose Garden—when he used a question about homosexuality to talk specifically about gay marriage. This declaration put him in agreement with 70 percent of Republican voters.

But most of the Democratic presidential candidates oppose gay marriage, too, as do 50 percent of Democratic voters. All the candidates support extending legal rights to gay partners, and some explicitly support same-sex unions. The key to getting legal rights for gay partners, these candidates argue, is to banish the word "marriage" from the public debate, because it most often triggers a deep emotional and negative response.

"I've been writing for a long time about how tolerant Americans are, and how the culture has changed, yet gay marriage is the line," said Alan Wolfe, a Boston College professor of political science and an authority on cultural and religious issues in American politics. "Marriage is the one institution that touches on everything that Americans really care deeply about."

Pollsters say most Americans consider marriage essentially a religious institution intended explicitly for a man and a woman. A vast majority of Americans are, after all, married in a religious ceremony—86 percent, according to a poll last month by Peter D. Hart Research Associates. "People who would never step inside a church for religious reasons will get married in one," Mr. Wolfe said. "That's what churches are for many people these days."

Americans marry in civil ceremonies at City Hall, too, but pollsters say that for most people, marriage is still something that happens at the altar. Most religious denominations in the United States do not approve of gay unions—even Episcopal Church leaders rejected a proposal for the blessing of same-sex unions a day after approving the election of the church's first openly gay bishop. So the term "gay marriage" is particularly threatening in the most religious industrialized society in the world.

"I know a lot of people who want to give all the rights and privileges to gay couples that married people have, but they don't want to change the traditional meaning of the term marriage," said Norval D. Glenn, a professor of sociology at the University of Texas who specializes in the demography of the family. "We're more traditional in how we define marriage in this country than is the case in most of the Western world."

So far only the Netherlands and Belgium allow gay marriage, but the Canadian cabinet approved a new national policy in June to pave the way for same-sex unions.[1] A week before, Ontario's highest court had ruled that the nation's federal marriage laws were discriminatory and therefore unconstitutional, and opinion polls showed that a majority of Canadians agreed. "You have to look at history as an evolution of society," Prime Minister Jean Chrétien said.

Gay rights leaders in the United States say that bringing God into the debate misses the point, and that the religious aspect of marriage has been played up by American conservatives fomenting a backlash.

"In a secular democracy, this is a legal question, not a religious question," said Tony Kushner, the playwright, who won a Pulitzer Prize for "Angels in America." "The debate over gay marriage should not be on religious grounds."

For that reason, gay rights leaders say their most immediate goal is to try to convince the public that they want gay civil unions, and that they are not seeking to knock down the doors of the nation's religious institutions.

"No church is going to be forced to recognize gay marriage," said David M. Smith, a senior strategist and spokesman for the Human Rights Campaign, the nation's largest gay advocacy organization.

Instead, Mr. Smith said, gay leaders are emphasizing that marriage is also a legal matter between two people and the state, and that civil unions are a way to confer rights on the domestic partners of gays.

As of now, Vermont is the only state that gives gay couples the rights that all married couples enjoy, but the Defense of Marriage Act, signed by President Clinton in 1996, still prohibits them from enjoying hundreds of federal rights, like Social Security benefits paid to a surviving partner.

"Gay people pay into Social Security all of their lives, but if something happens, gay partners aren't covered," Mr. Smith said. "When you talk about things like that, people support those rights in large numbers. They get uncomfortable when it's packaged in the notion of marriage because of the religious sanction that people perceive marriage to be."

Other analysts say American opposition to gay marriage is more about threatened sexuality than religion.

"I think the average American disapproves of homosexual sex, but tolerates it, much as they respect rights of privacy and self-expression," said Andrew J. Cherlin, a professor of public policy at Johns Hopkins University who specializes in the sociology of the family. "For the average American, civil unions sound like tolerance, but marriage sounds like approval."

Paul Rudnick, a playwright and screenwriter, agreed. "I guess on a certain level it's the difference between sympathy and equality," he said. "When people can view gay people as somehow underprivileged, woeful and in need of social work, it's just easier to feel a kind of regal sympathy for them. But when you're actually dealing with the two guys or the women next door planning a wedding just like your daughter, and expecting gifts, that's another matter entirely."

Peter Wolson, a Beverly Hills psychoanalyst and the past president of the Los Angeles Institute and Society for Psychoanalytic Studies, said the prospect of gay marriage threatens people with a government stamp of approval on homosexuality.

"If that's the case, it's a normal form of sexuality, and that threatens people with their own fear of homosexual impulses in themselves," Dr. Wolson said.

The prospect of gay marriage, Dr. Wolson added, also strikes at the traditional nuclear anchor of American life and powerful childhood forces. "It challenges the basic black and white stereotypes we grow up with," he said. "And once that black and white is challenged, it brings us all into this crazy zone of existential uncertainty."

Or as William Schneider, a CNN commentator and a longtime public opinion analyst, put it: "Look, if you don't call it marriage, you'll get more support."   [2003]

Notes

1. As of December, 2003, many same-sex marriages have been performed in British Columbia and Ontario provinces, and the Massachusetts Supreme Court has said that gay couples have the right to marry under the state constitution.

Understanding the Reading

1. What has changed from 1991 to 2002 regarding Americans' attitude toward homosexuality?
2. What happened in public opinion after the Supreme Court overturned a Texas sodomy law?
3. Why might someone favor extending civil rights to gays but oppose gay marriage?

Suggestions for Responding

1. Invite members of Friends of Lesbians and Gays to your classroom; discuss, among other things, the idea of gay marriage.
2. Research laws and attitudes concerning homosexuals in China, the Netherlands, Brazil, and Nigeria.
3. Debate whether same-sex marriage should become a federal right in the United States.
4. Make a list of countries and states that are considering legalizing same-sex marriage. ✦

31
When the Political Is Personal

ANN MARIE NICOLOSI

Like many other colleges and universities across the nation, The College of New Jersey (TCNJ) has grappled with issues of diversity, tolerance, and, in the case of its GLBT [gay, lesbian, bisexual, transgendered] student body, staff and faculty, increased visibility. This essay is a narrative of personal conflict, and how a public exhibition of hate can stir up the most private inner struggles that are part of the GLBT experience and identity. . . .

Although I never hid the fact that I am a lesbian, I never publicly announced it in front of students either. I'm sure that some students knew, given the nature of campus grapevines, but most did not. When the decision was made to become more visible to the campus community, I had to take stock of my own unresolved feelings of shame, fear, and self-hate which I thought I had conquered years before. Suddenly, the memories and pictures of a lesbian teenager in the late 1970s who hid in the shadows surfaced. The name calling, sexual harassment, parental loathing, and physical violence of those years came to consciousness again. Would I return to my office one day to find "lezzie" spray-painted or chalked on my door as I had found on the door to my apartment when I was nineteen years old? Would some of my older colleagues look at me with the same disgust I had seen in my mother's eyes? Would I lose my credibility as a teacher if students only saw "the dyke from Women's and Gender Studies," which would provide further ammunition for those who deride the discipline, and perhaps deter budding feminist heterosexual women from joining our program for fear that someone might question their sexuality? And, what bothered me most was the possibility that I was afraid to give up the

Excerpted from "A Community's Response to Hate: Reactions of a College Campus to Expressions of Homophobia and Heterosexism." *Transformations*, vol. XIII, No. 2, Fall 2002. Reprinted by permission of the New Jersey Project C-2002.

heterosexual privilege I enjoyed because of my ability to "pass" as a straight woman, and to experience what my butch sisters face everyday.

Yet, how could I not openly proclaim my lesbianism when my students were standing in front of their peers and teachers and doing so? How could I call myself an advisor or mentor to GUTS and to the students, GLBT and straight, of the College if I were afraid to do what they were so bravely doing?

I decided I would start by coming out to my Gender and Popular Culture class. By a stroke of luck, we were in the midst of a section on GLBT representation in the media, and I had scheduled to show the film *The Celluloid Closet* for this class. I was quite nervous and felt my heart race and my palms sweat. I opened with a general discussion about what was happening on the campus with [some anti-gay] hate messages and the College's plans to respond to them. I told them that one of the ways to combat homophobia is with increased visibility, and that GLBT teachers were being encouraged to come out. "So, it starts here. Some of you might know this, most probably do not, but I suspect by this afternoon the entire school will know that I am a lesbian. I have never said this in a public forum, and I am quite nervous. But please feel free to ask me any questions—within reason—about what it's like to be gay in our society."

Well, I can honestly say that I never had their undivided attention as I did that morning. And being an opportunistic teacher, I seized the moment as an opening to discuss heterosexual privilege and homophobia and to speak to them openly as a person who lives as a homosexual in a heterosexual world. As we began our discussion, I noticed one of my lesbian students sitting quietly in the back of the room in tears. I saw in her eyes admiration and pride, and she gave me exactly what I needed to bolster my courage that rainy morning in March.

We began to discuss the concept of heterosexual privilege. My students had already read Peggy Macintosh's "Unpacking the Knapsack of White Privilege" so they were familiar with the concept of the systemic privilege of race as well as gender. But the privilege of sexuality is a bit more obscure; they needed to see how that privilege works. I used my partner, Marisa, and my-

self as an example. And as I did so, I realized what a relief it was to speak about my partner as my colleagues spoke of their husbands and wives.

I created a scenario in which I was at a social function or cocktail party. Invariably, someone will ask me if I am married or have a boyfriend. If I had heterosexual privilege, my answer would be automatic, said without thinking. But because I do not have that privilege, I must assess the situation in about ten seconds and make a decision how to handle the situation. I must determine if I am safe or not. If I feel safe, I can then say I'm not married, I'm gay and I have a partner. If not, I can either play the pronoun game, or I can deny the existence of the woman with whom I've chosen to share my life. I then asked the students to imagine if their parents (if they are still together and if they are heterosexual) had to deny the existence of one another, would they be able to do it? How would it change their lives if they had to? Would it put a strain on the relationship if they had to hide it?

It ended up being the most productive class I have ever taught. I think that my willingness to be vulnerable enabled the students to open up to each other about their own homophobia. The result was an honest dialogue among students who were grappling with the complex ways in which our world uses not only gender but also sexuality to organize and maintain privilege and hierarchical structures.

Having the ability to speak freely in front of my students was a liberating experience. Yes, I am sure that there are those who refer to me as "the dyke from Women's and Gender Studies," but my misgivings about being totally out and public were ill-founded. My trepidation has now been replaced with a sense that I can give my GLBT students something I never had: a positive, out and proud—and public—role model.

But I am also under no delusions. Despite the success of the teach-in and all the other activities that took place in response to the hate that plagued our community, I know that momentum fades and there is a tendency to backslide into complacency. It is easy and it is comfortable. There needs to be a sustained effort on the part of administration, faculty, and staff to make sure that issues of racism, sexism, heterosexism, and homophobia have a prominent place in the curriculum and in the mission of the institution. On our campus, as I'm sure on many others, Women's Studies and Gender Studies programs, along with African American and Ethnic Studies programs, lead the way in keeping these topics in the forefront of academic inquiry. We must also have visible support for our GLBT students. As those of us who are queer know, the coming out process can be frightening, painful, and risky. It is essential that we provide, as Edward Stiles' group did, a haven for students struggling with their identity and coming to terms with their sexuality.

The phrase "silence equals death," which became popular during the early years of the AIDS crisis, is as applicable in the academy as it is in the streets and the halls of Congress. Certainly there remains the threat of physical violence against GLBT communities in our institutions, but a more pervasive threat is the emotional death and damage to the psyche that homophobia causes. Being closeted, no matter how comfortable or personally advantageous, assists in upholding the systemic oppression that queer people across the world live under. How can we expect our GLBT children to have the emotional and psychological health necessary to face their lives under this system if we ourselves are afraid to provide the role models they need to do so? How can we instill in them the courage of their convictions if we ourselves lack the courage of our own?   [2002]

References

Agostini, A. (2001, April 10). College should pander to majority [Letter to the editor]. *The Signal,* p. 9.

Burtnik, M & D'Agnolo, M. (2001, September 11). Alleged victim arrested after deluding campus. *The Signal,* p. 3.

Houston, B. (2001, April 17). Do days off matter? [Letter to the editor]. *The Signal,* p. 9.

McIntosh, P. (2001) Unpacking the invisible knapsack. In P. Rothenberg (Ed.), *Race, Class and Gender in the United States* (pp. 143–152). New York: Worth Publishers.

Pharr, S. (2001). Homophobia as a weapon of sexism. In P. Rothenberg (Ed.), *Race, Class and Gender in the United States* (pp. 143–152). New York: Worth Publishers.

Rogers, M. (2001, April 3). Chalking was pointless [Letter to the editor]. *The Signal,* p. 9.

Sullivan, K. (2001, April 10). Anti-chalking letter misdirected [Letter to the editor]. *The Signal,* p. 9.

Understanding the Reading

1. What does GLBT mean?
2. What moved the author to tell her students that she is a lesbian?
3. Why was she so afraid?
4. What actually happened in the class once she had revealed her secret?
5. Why does Nicolosi consider being "closeted" an extreme threat against GLBT communities?

Suggestions for Responding

1. Compare U.S. attitudes toward lesbians as opposed to those toward homosexuals. Watch the media and talk with family and friends.
2. If you know someone who is homophobic, strategically plan to challenge his or her fears, perhaps moving your friend toward change. (This is sometimes done by bringing people together, friends who have you in common but who have never met each other.) ◆

32

Putting a Face on Difference: A Gay Family Visits the College Classroom

MILDRED L. RICE JORDAN

Dave and Bob generally begin their presentation to my classes by introducing themselves, giving extensive background on their education, employment, how they met, and how Elizabeth was

Transformations, vol. XIII, No. 2, Fall 2002. Reprinted by permission of the New Jersey Project c. 2002

adopted. Both men are intelligent and well educated. Bob has a B.S. in Communications and majored in Radio, Television, and Film. He is a multimedia editor for a financial news service. Dave has a B.A. in Psychology, a certificate in Elementary Education, and a M.A. in Christian Education. He works for a religious institution where he is an administrator. The family is religious, attends church regularly, and participates actively in many church-related activities.

After sharing their backgrounds with students, Dave begins to talk about the adoption process. Although he and Bob had lived together before the adoption, they separated because of it. Dave had a strong desire to become a parent, but Bob did not. In studies comparing lesbian and gay men to heterosexual single parents, homosexuality was not found to be incompatible with fatherhood or motherhood (Sears, 1995).

Bob says that for him the separation was very painful. Yet, he felt that his reason was a valid one: "I just could not see bringing a child into this kind of relationship. It's hard enough for an adult." Dave, on the other hand, was determined to be a father. After the two separated, he went ahead with his plans to adopt a child. He learned of Elizabeth's birth about a month before she was born. He picked her up from the hospital when she was only five days old. The adoption agency did not ask Dave about his sexual orientation. However, he strongly suspects that they already knew. He says that there were no complications with the adoption process.

The two men resumed their relationship when Bob saw the baby and found her irresistible. They bought a house together and began life as a gay family. Then six months after the adoption Dave began to wonder what would happen to Elizabeth if he were not there to care for her. Unlike heterosexual marriages, his relationship with Bob was not a legal one. In such cases, the next of kin of the adoptive parent would be able to get custody of the minor. Seeking legal advice from ACLU [American Civil Liberties Union] lawyers, Dave was told that a second-parent adoption would be the solution to this problem.

The second-parent adoption was also a relatively smooth process. However, the biggest challenge came when both men wanted their names on Elizabeth's birth certificate. What do you put on a birth certificate that says mother and father when both parents are of the same sex? None of the social service agencies knew how to approach this problem. Finally, it was decided that a new birth certificate should be issued. Dave and Bob made history for being the first parents in the state of New Jersey to have a birth record that reads "Parent and Parent."

THE MOST FREQUENTLY ASKED QUESTIONS

My students write anonymous questions on cards. . . . Over the years, the same questions have repeatedly emerged. I have chosen five of these to address here. . . .

Elizabeth is now fourteen years old. I have witnessed her develop greater self-confidence in the college classroom as she has matured.

Question One: What do your neighbors and other people think of your lifestyle?

The family lives in a home on a quiet suburban street in Lawrenceville, New Jersey. Their single, split-level house is typical of suburban homes in many upper-middle class communities. At the beginning of the interview, I asked how Dave and Bob felt about the refusal of the majority of my students—even the most culturally sensitive ones—to believe they have a normal life. Dave shared with me his feelings about the students' anticipation that everyone would object to (or even be revolted by) their family. He states, "I think that there is a lot of stereotyping in the students' heads over this. Particularly the way they throw around the word lifestyle." Dave describes for me the same experiences that he has always shared with my students. Their lifestyle is just that of parents and a child—a family. The fact that they are gay makes hardly any difference between the way they live and the way the people next door live. He sees himself and Bob as being just two working parents, no different from many of their neighbors.

According to the family, during the ten years that they have lived in their suburban community, they have never experienced any overt acts, words, or reactions of a negative nature from their neighbors. They are even invited to all of the neighborhood social functions.

Despite the family's insistence that their life is *normal,* many students still question how this can be possible. . . . Responses to Question One (What do your neighbors and other people think of your lifestyle?) demonstrate how resistant students can be:

> Because I was brought up knowing a family is made up of a mother, father and children, it is hard for me to come to terms with two males representing what a 'traditional family' should be. I would feel uncomfortable with them living next to me if I had kids.

> One view I did not agree with is that they said that their family is just like any heterosexual family. This cannot be true because their life-style is not the normal function of our society.

There are some students who express very strong religious beliefs:

> They seem like good-hearted people but I don't understand how they can call themselves a Christian. In the Bible, it clearly states that homosexuality is not normal and cannot be looked upon as being like everybody else. I would not like them living next door to me. . .

> . . . it troubled my heart to hear a man that has studied the Word of God be carrying out homosexual acts with another person. Almost all fundamental faiths teach that homosexuality is a sin against God. . . . it is a demonic spirit that possesses the person to do these activities.

The student could not believe that none of the gay family's neighbors objected to having them live in their community. It was as if the family's portrayal of an idyllic life was a way of concealing their real problems. One student wrote:

> I felt like their story was sugar coated. They didn't share any negative stories. And I don't think their lives are as perfect as they made it sound. I wanted to know the hardships they have gone through by being the parents of Elizabeth. I am sure there were a lot.

Question Two: What about school? Don't the kids make fun of you?

Elizabeth responds that her family is no different from any other. Some kids have a mother and a grandmother they live with. Other kids live with a father and an uncle, says Elizabeth. "There's nothing that is different about my family. Besides, having two dads is fun because not many children have a family like mine."

Elizabeth denies having had *any* (my emphasis) problems in or out of school at any time about having two parents of the same sex. She insists that people like and accept her for herself. According to her, the sexual preferences of her parents have absolutely nothing to do with her social life either in or out of school. Besides, she firmly emphasizes, if people do object to her family, then she does not wish to have them as friends or associates.

Dave, who is a former elementary school teacher, has a keen understanding of schooling and knows how to negotiate with school personnel. He and Bob began exploring the atmosphere for family diversity with top-level administrators in their school district. . . . From nursery school through middle school (which she is now attending), they have visited Elizabeth's schools together and met with teachers and school administrators to make them aware of their family structure. Additionally, they have advocated that the district adopt an inclusive curriculum and institute anti-discrimination policies. They have always had the complete cooperation of her teachers and school administrators. Recently, they had a social event at their home and invited school personnel. They were surprised that all of Elizabeth's teachers came.

Question Three: How do you plan to prepare her for high school?

Several current research studies suggest adolescence is a time when children of gay and lesbian families are most likely to experience harassment from their peers. Their parents' sexual identity will subject these children to rejection by peers, teasing, and other homophobic types of behavior. . . .

Concerned about Elizabeth's high school experiences, my students predict that she will face some challenges in the future. One student writes:

> I think she will find it very difficult adjusting to the high school life. Although she has been growing up with these people all her life, they are going to realize that she is one of the few members in their community with homosexual parents. This is unfair . . . because she didn't choose the sexual preference of her parents when they adopted her.

> In high school everyone gets made fun of; any little thing wrong with a person someone will notice and make a point to humiliate them about it. If their daughter continues to think that all people are going to judge her for who she is then she has something else coming to her . . . from my experiences in high school only a few judge you for who you really are.

Elizabeth's parents are not naïve in thinking that because things have gone relatively well there is no need for concern. Dave teaches Sunday School at a Presbyterian Church. His sixth graders think it is the "in thing" to talk about "fags." What he would like to see is a school curriculum that teaches respect for gays—one that would discourage this kind of behavior. Currently, however, they are preparing Elizabeth for the possibility of these probable experiences instilling in her a high level of self-esteem. . . .

Question Four: Will your sexual orientation influence Elizabeth to become gay?

These fathers, like many heterosexual fathers, want their daughter to be happy, well adjusted, and healthy. Although they have never questioned her about her sexuality, they believe from her behavior that she is heterosexual.

When I asked about the possibility of Elizabeth ever becoming gay, Dave said, "No. I have talked to other gay parents about this. We were all raised by straight parents. It has nothing to do with it. Studies are showing there is not much difference, but they are still ongoing." Dave and Bob feel that they must be vigilant about looking for any indications in Elizabeth that she is confused about her sexuality. As for now, they are just permitting her to be herself.

Elizabeth has human sexuality classes in her middle school and at church. Whenever Dave mentions anything about sexuality to her, however, she comments, "Oh Daddy, I don't need to hear from you about this." Bob feels that she is embarrassed to discuss these personal matters with males. He bought her a video about everything there is for kids to know about sex, and she refused to watch it.

Question Five: How do you plan to teach Elizabeth about the role of a female?

My students' commentaries on this question reveal further resistance to the idea of diverse models of family structure. Some believe it unfair for Elizabeth to be brought into an environment deplete of female role models, and their responses have argued this point.

> . . . another point I would like to address is that she has no female in the home. Girls have certain concerns and problems that a father cannot take care of. Not only do they offer a certain type of emotional support, but they also can help out with female matters. The two dads will be scratching their heads and on the phone the first time she has a matter that she needs help with. I think that if the couple had adopted a boy it would have been better since all their sexes would be the same. A man has an easier time raising a boy than a girl. But then having two gay dads, you wonder if he too will turn out gay somehow. Overall, I question a gay couple having kids. I don't think it is a natural and comfortable environment to bring a child in the world to.

> . . . it is possible for the girl to be confused with her sexuality. As much as her fathers tell her how things are normally with heterosexuals, she is constantly in the presence of her two gay individuals. Furthermore, she is missing a motherly figure in her every day life. The family mentions of a lady who supposedly handles these responsibilities but is this the same as a mother? The lady is not around constantly as they implied, and she lacks the special bond that a child and a mother have. I believe that they are not realistic in this aspect.

Some of these reactions were written before Elizabeth reached puberty. She has now successfully passed through major developmental milestones such as her menses and her first bra. In fact, she was helped through these by females. Her adopted grandmother has been a supportive female figure in her life. She takes Elizabeth out frequently. Other females in her life such as her girl friends and a sister that she recently discovered all provide her with gender role models. Still, now that she has reached puberty her fathers are deeply concerned about preparing her for other gender specific issues that might be imposed upon her by a predominantly heterosexual society.

Although this information is presented to my students, they continue to be concerned about Elizabeth being raised by two males. As one student states, "I think personally that I wouldn't be able to live without a mother. . . ."

STUDENTS' TRANSFORMATIONS

Although being exposed to a gay family through an interactive format can have a powerful impact, we must question whether students experience an immediate transformation.

We can each make our own decisions about whether the following reactions from my students reflect true transformations:

After the discussion we had in class with the gay couple and their daughter, I gained a whole new respect for homosexuals. I realized more that they are people just like us . . .

Before I met the gay family . . . I was completely against gay adoption. I felt that it was a completely unnatural environment to grow up in and that the child may not really be sure what is considered normal. . . the child would suffer through a lot of ridicule by his or her classmates and in turn suffer from any emotional problems. The speakers really made me think a lot about the views I had previously held. My feelings changed when I saw the love and affection the two fathers gave to the child.

The class period when these people came in was almost opposite what I thought it would be. I thought I would feel uncomfortable and disgusted, but I was not. I do not totally agree with homosexuality, but because of that class session I've been able to come to grips with it. They were

normal people who lived a normal life. The only thing is when I think about two men together, it makes me feel a little uncomfortable. I am very content knowing that I learned more about an area of life that I normally wouldn't find out about in every day life. This was something I have never been faced with, and I am glad that I was forced to deal with it. I am also glad that I got all the stereotypes cleared up. If you were to ask me my opinion of a gay relationship with the adoption of a daughter I would have had many negative things to say. I'm glad I cleared all of this up.

CONCLUSIONS

In the words of one student:

Having a gay family in to talk to us as a class was one of the most interesting things I have ever encountered as a college student. I hope you continue doing this for every Race, Class, and Gender class that you teach.

Visitors can help us to share the burden of convincing our students that there are diverse perspectives of race, class, and gender that have legitimacy. . . . In essence, what we accomplish for students and ourselves is the invaluable gift of *putting a face on difference*.   [2002]

References

Adams, M. Bell, L.A., & Griffin, P. (1997). *Teaching for Diversity and Social Justice: A Sourcebook.* New York: Routledge.

Boyd, B. (1999). Should gay and lesbian issues be discussed in elementary school? *Childhood Education, 76*(1), 40–41.

Cyrus, V. (2000). *Experiencing Race, Class, and Gender in the United States,* 3rd Ed., California: Mayfield Publishing Company.

Educational Advocacy Committee of the Family Pride Coalition (1999). *Opening Doors: Lesbian and Gay Parents and Schools.*

Ettelbrick, P. (1998). Confronting Obstacles to Lesbian and Gay Equality. In Rothenberg, P. (Ed.), *Race, Class, and Gender in the United States: An Integrated Study,* 4th Ed. (pp 437–447). New York: St. Martin's Press, Inc.

Flannery, B. & Vanterpool, M. (1990) A model for infusing cultural diversity concepts across

the curriculum. *To Improve the Academy. 9,*
159–175,

Grossman, H. (1995). *Teaching in a Diverse Society.* Boston: Allyn and Bacon.

Lipkin, A. (1999), *Understanding Homosexuality,
Changing Schools.* Boulder, Colorado: Westview Press.

Wickens, E. (1991). Penny's Question: "Will I
Have a Child in My Class with Two Mothers?
What Do you Know About This?" *Young Chil-
dren,* 25–28.

Understanding the Reading

1. How did these three people become a family?
2. Why did Bob and Dave separate?
3. Why did they reconcile?

4. Why did Dave go to the ACLU?
5. What are the most frequently asked questions by students who meet Dave, Bob, and
   Elizabeth in a college classroom?

Suggestions for Responding

1. Discuss whether gays should adopt children;
   be familiar with your state's laws and practices regarding adoption by gays or lesbians,
   as well as child custody laws in regard to gay
   or lesbian parents.
2. Research what the attitudes of indigenous
   peoples of the United States (i.e. American
   Indian nations, Alaskan and Hawaiian Natives) have been toward gays, lesbians, and
   gay families.

IV
Economics and the American Dream

THE AMERICAN DREAM! WE ALL KNOW WHAT THAT means—a good job with plenty of opportunity for advancement, a good family, a nice house with at least one car (probably two) in the driveway, plenty of good food and frequent dining out with enough money left over for the kids' education at good schools, a few luxuries, and an annual vacation. Each of us can add specific details—appliances, electronic games, and so on—but we would probably agree on the general features of the dream.

This dream arrived on our shores with the early Puritans, who held to the doctrine that God rewarded virtue with earthly wealth; to them, economic success was a way to glorify God. Thus, the **Protestant work ethic** became a core principle of American culture. This ethic is the belief in the importance of hard work and productivity and the corresponding faith that this behavior will be rewarded appropriately. In the eighteenth century, national icon Benjamin Franklin and his "Poor Richard's" maxims advocating frugality, initiative, industry, diligence, honesty, and prudence secularized and popularized the doctrine. Franklin personified the ethic, both for his contemporaries and for succeeding generations, right up to today.

Franklin also represents another facet of the American dream: the ideal of the **self-made man** (who, of course, adheres to the Protestant work ethic). The self-made man has appeared throughout this country's history. In the nineteenth century, Horatio Alger made a fortune with his popular fictional heroes who rose "from rags to riches" by "luck and pluck and hard work." One of the most admired American presidents is the log-cabin-born, rail-splitting Abraham Lincoln, another self-made man. Recent presidents also tend to flaunt their humble beginnings, from grocer's son Richard Nixon to peanut farmer Jimmy Carter to alcoholic's son Ronald Reagan. George Bush Sr. prefers to be seen as an oil-field wildcatter rather than as a privileged Yale graduate, and Bill Clinton plays up the single-parent family of his early childhood. George W. Bush, despite his family wealth, places himself as an anti-elitist, with a folksy way of speaking, shown frequently on his Texas ranch, doing manual labor. One might say that in America if you are self-made, you have "made it."

The myth of the American dream, based as it is on the assumption that opportunities are boundless and that success depends solely on one's character, has a flip side that makes the dream more like a nightmare for many Americans. If individuals are responsible for their own success, they must also be responsible for their own failure and, therefore, deserving of their fate. Even in the beginning of the twenty-first century, we still hold to these myths, which conceal the realities of class distinctions. We like to think of the United States as a **classless society;**

we don't even like to talk about class, except to claim that we all belong to the middle class. This thinking makes it possible for us to ignore the problems created by inequitable economic distribution.

The disparity between the wealthiest and the poorest members of society is, in fact, extensive; while 20 percent of U.S. children live in poverty according to the U.S. Census Bureau in 2003, congressional figures indicate that the richest 5 percent of the American population own up to 83 percent of the wealth of the country. This disparity increases as the rich get richer and the poor get poorer. According to the U.S. Census Bureau, the percentage share of aggregate U.S. income received by the poorest 20 percent of families fell from 5.4 percent in 1970 to 4.2 percent in 1996. In the same period, percentage of income of the richest 5 percent rose from 15.6 percent to over 20 percent, yet there is resistance to changing the system because we have faith in **upward mobility,** the possibility that we will some day strike it rich ourselves— the good old American dream. Yet the median hourly wage of a former welfare recipient is $6.61, and the number of Americans living in poverty increased by 1.7 million in 2002.

Sherman Alexie, a best-selling author from Spokane, Washington, opens Part IV with "This Is What It Means to Say Phoenix, Arizona." Soon after losing his job, Victor, a Spokane Indian, finds that his father has died in Phoenix, and it is his job to collect his father's ashes. However, he has no car and no money to make the trip from the Spokane Indian Reservation. The Tribal Council can afford to give him only $100.

Janet Zandy's essay is an analysis of what class is—more than the amount of money one has, class is also defined by economic privilege and power and access to resources. Zandy suggests five ways we can use to see and understand class and our own class positions. She also points out how the dominant class controls knowledge, especially historical knowledge, and has distorted our understanding of our national past. She closes with student responses to her argument when she presented it as a lecture. The next selection speaks to the issue of upward mobility. Gary Soto recalls being aware, even as a child, of the disparity between his impoverished barrio life and the televised portrayal of the

upper-middle-class world—one to which he already aspired. Nonetheless, his faith in the American dream leads him to decide "to become wealthy, and right away!" In contrast to Soto's enthusiastic embrace of life, Sallie Bingham describes the disadvantages of being a woman in a very wealthy family. She argues that such women are suppressed and controlled to serve the interests of the family wealth, to which they have only indirect access. Next, Jody Kolodzey debunks rich and famous women's claim to the label "working mother" in the sense the term is applied to ordinary working-class women.

Upward mobility may create its own difficulties. Bebe Moore Campbell's story of Leanita McClain, a highly successful Black woman reporter, reveals the dark side to this aspect of the American dream. Torn between the demands of the middle-class world in which she works and the impossibility of forgetting where she came from, she is propelled into ultimate despair and suicide. On the other hand, some people learn to cope with the stresses. Author bell hooks attended and now teaches at "elite" universities, embracing a lifestyle that differs from the one she experienced growing up as part of a poor, rural, Black family. Although her decision to be part of a different world caused tension between her and her mother, she has managed to turn her "outsider" status in her professional life into an asset.

The next three selections examine what it means to grow up very poor. Bernice Mennis recalls her childhood as the daughter of working-class immigrants and explains how this shaped her values and personality. Caffilene Allen relates how the attitudes of teachers in her town school alienated her from her impoverished, rural Tennessee family, especially her mother. Growing up in poverty that he hated, Randall Williams was ashamed to take friends to his house.

It is difficult to think about socioeconomic class without addressing the issue of welfare, the theme of the next two readings. Colin Greer reports on children so poor that they do not get enough to eat. Ariel Gore, who was an unwed teenage mother, describes the stigma society attaches to welfare and food stamp recipients.

Finally, Part IV ends with three descriptions of the homeless experience. Peter Swet's interview with Gerald Winterlin helps us see that homeless people are hardworking Americans who just happen to fall between the cracks and that they want to pull themselves back up. Jackie Spinks describes his experiences as he lived in his old van and ate junk food and in a mission soup kitchen; he details the psychological and physical impact of this lifestyle. In Marge Piercy's short story, we watch as one woman's life spirals downward from the upper-middle-class suburbs to the streets, shelters, and soup kitchens.

Although the myth of a classless, middle-class America is an appealing concept, the readings in Part IV reveal that it is a myth and not an accurate description of our nation. It masks many cruel realities that are embedded in our economic system. In addition, our faith in the American dream and its underlying principles of hard work and self-reliance allow us to ignore the problems of those who are ill-served by the system and even to *blame those victims* for their plight. On the other hand, upward mobility, while possible, exacts a considerable toll on those who are forced to choose between the behavior patterns, beliefs, values, and even family and friends of their original world and the chance to "move up," to enter a culture that is both alien and alienating. Thus, in many senses, class in our "classless" society is problematic.

33

This Is What It Means to Say Phoenix, Arizona

SHERMAN ALEXIE

Just after Victor lost his job at the BIA, he also found out that his father had died of a heart attack in Phoenix, Arizona. Victor hadn't seen his father in a few years, only talked to him on the telephone once or twice, but there still was a genetic pain, which was soon to be pain as real and immediate as a broken bone.

Victor didn't have any money. Who does have money on a reservation, except the cigarette and fireworks salespeople? His father had a savings account waiting to be claimed, but Victor needed to find a way to get to Phoenix. Victor's mother was just as poor as he was, and the rest of his family didn't have any use at all for him. So Victor called the Tribal Council.

"Listen," Victor said. "My father just died. I need some money to get to Phoenix to make arrangements."

"Now, Victor," the council said. "You know we're having a difficult time financially."

"But I thought the council had special funds set aside for stuff like this."

"Now, Victor, we do have some money available for the proper return of tribal members' bodies. But I don't think we have enough to bring your father all the way back from Phoenix."

"Well," Victor said. "It ain't going to cost all that much. He had to be cremated. Things were kind of ugly. He died of a heart attack in his trailer and nobody found him for a week. It was really hot, too. You get the picture."

"Now, Victor, we're sorry for your loss and the circumstances. But we can really only afford to give you one hundred dollars."

"That's not even enough for a plane ticket."

"Well, you might consider driving down to Phoenix."

"I don't have a car. Besides, I was going to drive my father's pickup back up here."

"Now, Victor," the council said. "We're sure there is somebody who could drive you to Phoenix. Or is there somebody who could lend you the rest of the money?"

"You know there ain't nobody around with that kind of money."

"Well, we're sorry, Victor, but that's the best we can do."

Victor accepted the Tribal Council's offer. What else could he do? So he signed the proper papers, picked up his check, and walked over to the Trading Post to cash it.

While Victor stood in line, he watched Thomas Builds-the-Fire standing near the magazine rack, talking to himself. Like he always did. Thomas was a storyteller that nobody wanted to listen to. That's like being a dentist in a town where everybody has false teeth.

Victor and Thomas Builds-the-Fire were the same age, had grown up and played in the dirt together. Ever since Victor could remember, it was Thomas who always had something to say.

Once, when they were seven years old, when Victor's father still lived with the family, Thomas closed his eyes and told Victor this story: "Your father's heart is weak. He is afraid of his own family. He is afraid of you. Late at night he sits in the dark. Watches the television until there's nothing but that white noise. Sometimes he feels like he wants to buy a motorcycle and ride away. He wants to run and hide. He doesn't want to be found."

Thomas Builds-the-Fire had known that Victor's father was going to leave, knew it before anyone. Now Victor stood in the Trading Post with a one-hundred-dollar check in his hand, wondering if Thomas knew that Victor's father was dead, if he knew what was going to happen next.

Just then Thomas looked at Victor, smiled, and walked over to him.

"Victor, I'm sorry about your father," Thomas said.

"How did you know about it?" Victor asked.

"I heard it on the wind. I heard it from the birds. I felt it in the sunlight. Also, your mother was just in here crying."

"Oh," Victor said and looked around the Trading Post. All the other Indians stared, surprised that Victor was even talking to Thomas. Nobody talked to Thomas anymore because he told the same damn stories over and over again. Victor was embarrassed, but he thought that

From Sherman Alexie, *The Lone Ranger and Tonto Fistfight in Heaven*, c. 1993 Reprinted by permission of Grove/Atlantic.

Thomas might be able to help him. Victor felt a sudden need for tradition.

"I can lend you the money you need," Thomas said suddenly. "But you have to take me with you."

"I can't take your money," Victor said. "I mean, I haven't hardly talked to you in years. We're not really friends anymore."

"I didn't say we were friends. I said you had to take me with you."

"Let me think about it."

Victor went home with his one hundred dollars and sat at the kitchen table. He held his head in his hands and thought about Thomas Builds-the-Fire, remembered little details, tears and scars, the bicycle they shared for a summer, so many stories.

Thomas Builds-the-Fire sat on the bicycle, waited in Victor's yard. He was ten years old and skinny. His hair was dirty because it was the Fourth of July.

"Victor," Thomas yelled. "Hurry up. We're going to miss the fireworks."

After a few minutes, Victor ran out of his house, jumped the porch railing, and landed gracefully on the sidewalk.

"And the judges award him a 9.95, the highest score of the summer," Thomas said, clapped, laughed.

"That was perfect, cousin," Victor said. "And it's my turn to ride the bike."

Thomas gave up the bike and they headed for the fair-grounds. It was nearly dark and the fireworks were about to start.

"You know," Thomas said. "It's strange how us Indians celebrate the Fourth of July. It ain't like it was *our* independence everybody was fighting for."

"You think about things too much," Victor said. "It's just supposed to be fun. Maybe Junior will be there."

"Which Junior? Everybody on this reservation is named Junior."

And they both laughed.

The fireworks were small, hardly more than a few bottle rockets and a fountain. But it was enough for two Indian boys. Years later, they would need much more.

Afterwards, sitting in the dark, fighting off mosquitoes, Victor turned to Thomas Builds-the-Fire.

"Hey," Victor said. "Tell me a story."

Thomas closed his eyes and told this story: "There were these two Indian boys who wanted to be warriors. But it was too late to be warriors in the old way. All the horses were gone. So the two Indian boys stole a car and drove to the city. They parked the stolen car in front of the police station and then hitchhiked back home to the reservation. When they got back, all their friends cheered and their parents' eyes shone with pride. *You were very brave,* everybody said to the two Indian boys. *Very brave.*"

"Ya-hey," Victor said. "That's a good one. I wish I could be a warrior."

"Me, too," Thomas said.

They went home together in the dark, Thomas on the bike now, Victor on foot. They walked through shadows and light from streetlamps.

"We've come a long ways," Thomas said. "We have outdoor lighting."

"All I need is the stars," Victor said. "And besides, you still think about things too much."

They separated then, each headed for home, both laughing all the way.

Victor sat at his kitchen table. He counted his one hundred dollars again and again. He knew he needed more to make it to Phoenix and back. He knew he needed Thomas Builds-the-Fire. So he put his money in his wallet and opened the front door to find Thomas on the porch.

"Ya-hey, Victor," Thomas said. "I knew you'd call me."

Thomas walked into the living room and sat down on Victor's favorite chair.

"I've got some money saved up," Thomas said. "It's enough to get us down there, but you have to get us back."

"I've got this hundred dollars," Victor said. "And my dad had a savings account I'm going to claim."

"How much in your dad's account?"

"Enough. A few hundred."

"Sounds good. When we leaving?"

• • •

When they were fifteen and had long since stopped being friends, Victor and Thomas got into a fistfight. That is, Victor was really drunk and beat Thomas up for no reason at all. All the other Indian boys stood around and watched it happen. Junior was there and so were Lester, Seymour, and a lot of others. The beating might have gone on until Thomas was dead if Norma Many Horses hadn't come along and stopped it.

"Hey, you boys," Norma yelled and jumped out of her car. "Leave him alone."

If it had been someone else, even another man, the Indian boys would've just ignored the warnings. But Norma was a warrior. She was powerful. She could have picked up any two of the boys and smashed their skulls together. But worse than that, she would have dragged them all over to some tipi and made them listen to some elder tell a dusty old story.

The Indian boys scattered, and Norma walked over to Thomas and picked him up.

"Hey, little man, are you okay?" she asked.

Thomas gave her a thumbs up.

"Why they always picking on you?"

Thomas shook his head, closed his eyes, but no stories came to him, no words or music. He just wanted to go home, to lie in his bed and let his dreams tell his stories for him.

Thomas Builds-the-Fire and Victor sat next to each other in the airplane, coach section. A tiny white woman had the window seat. She was busy twisting her body into pretzels. She was flexible.

"I have to ask," Thomas said, and Victor closed his eyes in embarrassment.

"Don't," Victor said.

"Excuse me, miss," Thomas asked. "Are you a gymnast or something?"

"There's no something about it," she said. "I was first alternate on the 1980 Olympic team."

"Really?" Thomas asked.

"Really."

"I mean, you used to be a world-class athlete?" Thomas asked.

"My husband still thinks I am."

Thomas Builds-the-Fire smiled. She was a mental gymnast, too. She pulled her leg straight up against her body so that she could've kissed her kneecap.

"I wish I could do that," Thomas said.

Victor was ready to jump out of the plane. Thomas, that crazy Indian storyteller with ratty old braids and broken teeth, was flirting with a beautiful Olympic gymnast. Nobody back home on the reservation would ever believe it.

"Well," the gymnast said. "It's easy. Try it."

Thomas grabbed at his leg and tried to pull it up into the same position as the gymnast. He couldn't even come close, which made Victor and the gymnast laugh.

"Hey," she asked. "You two are Indian, right?"

"Full-blood," Victor said.

"Not me," Thomas said. "I'm half magician on my mother's side and half clown on my father's."

They all laughed.

"What are your names?" she asked.

"Victor and Thomas."

"Mine is Cathy. Pleased to meet you all."

The three of them talked for the duration of the flight. Cathy the gymnast complained about the government, how they screwed the 1980 Olympic team by boycotting.

"Sounds like you all got a lot in common with Indians," Thomas said.

Nobody laughed.

After the plane landed in Phoenix and they had all found their way to the terminal, Cathy the gymnast smiled and waved good-bye.

"She was really nice," Thomas said.

"Yeah, but everybody talks to everybody on airplanes," Victor said. "It's too bad we can't always be that way."

"You always used to tell me I think too much," Thomas said. "Now it sounds like you do."

"Maybe I caught it from you."

"Yeah."

Thomas and Victor rode in a taxi to the trailer where Victor's father died.

"Listen," Victor said as they stopped in front of the trailer. "I never told you I was sorry for beating you up that time."

"Oh, it was nothing. We were just kids and you were drunk."

"Yeah, but I'm still sorry."

"That's all right."

Victor paid for the taxi and the two of them stood in the hot Phoenix summer. They could smell the trailer.

"This ain't going to be nice," Victor said. "You don't have to go in."

"You're going to need help."

Victor walked to the front door and opened it. The stink rolled out and made them both gag. Victor's father had lain in that trailer for a week in hundred-degree temperatures before anyone found him. And the only reason anyone found him was because of the smell. They needed dental records to identify him. That's exactly what the coroner said. They needed dental records.

"Oh, man," Victor said. "I don't know if I can do this."

"Well, then don't."

"But there might be something valuable in there."

"I thought his money was in the bank."

"It is. I was talking about pictures and letters and stuff like that."

"Oh," Thomas said as he held his breath and followed Victor into the trailer.

When Victor was twelve, he stepped into an underground wasp nest. His foot was caught in the hole, and no matter how hard he struggled, Victor couldn't pull free. He might have died there, stung a thousand times, if Thomas Builds-the-Fire had not come by.

"Run," Thomas yelled and pulled Victor's foot from the hole. They ran then, hard as they ever had, faster than Billy Mills, faster than Jim Thorpe, faster than the wasps could fly.

Victor and Thomas ran until they couldn't breathe, ran until it was cold and dark outside, ran until they were lost and it took hours to find their way home. All the way back, Victor counted his stings.

"Seven," Victor said. "My lucky number."

• • •

Victor didn't find much to keep in the trailer. Only a photo album and a stereo. Everything else had that smell stuck in it or was useless anyway.

"I guess this is all," Victor said. "It ain't much."

"Better than nothing," Thomas said.

"Yeah, and I do have the pickup."

"Yeah," Thomas said. "It's in good shape."

"Dad was good about that stuff."

"Yeah, I remember your dad."

"Really?" Victor asked. "What do you remember?"

Thomas Builds-the-Fire closed his eyes and told this story: "I remember when I had this dream that told me to go to Spokane, to stand by the Falls in the middle of the city and wait for a sign. I knew I had to go there but I didn't have a

car. Didn't have a license. I was only thirteen. So I walked all the way, took me all day, and I finally made it to the Falls. I stood there for an hour waiting. Then your dad came walking up. *What the hell are you doing here?* he asked me. I said, *Waiting for a vision.* Then your father said, *All you're going to get here is mugged.* So he drove me over to Denny's, bought me dinner, and then drove me home to the reservation. For a long time I was mad because I thought my dreams had lied to me. But they didn't. Your dad was my vision. *Take care of each other* is what my dreams were saying. *Take care of each other.*"

Victor was quiet for a long time. He searched his mind for memories of his father, found the good ones, found a few bad ones, added it all up, and smiled.

"My father never told me about finding you in Spokane," Victor said.

"He said he wouldn't tell anybody. Didn't want me to get in trouble. But he said I had to watch out for you as part of the deal."

"Really?"

"Really. Your father said you would need the help. He was right."

"That's why you came down here with me, isn't it?" Victor asked.

"I came because of your father."

Victor and Thomas climbed into the pickup, drove over to the bank, and claimed the three hundred dollars in the savings account.

Thomas Builds-the-Fire could fly.

Once, he jumped off the roof of the tribal school and flapped his arms like a crazy eagle. And he flew. For a second, he hovered, suspended above all the other Indian boys who were too smart or too scared to jump.

"He's flying," Junior yelled, and Seymour was busy looking for the trick wires or mirrors. But it was real. As real as the dirt when Thomas lost altitude and crashed to the ground.

He broke his arm in two places.

"He broke his wing," Victor chanted, and the other Indian boys joined in, made it a tribal song.

"He broke his wing, he broke his wing, he broke his wing," all the Indian boys chanted as they ran off, flapping their wings, wishing they could fly, too. They hated Thomas for his courage, his brief moment as a bird. Everybody has dreams about flying. Thomas flew.

One of his dreams came true for just a second, just enough to make it real.

Victor's father, his ashes, fit in one wooden box with enough left over to fill a cardboard box.

"He always was a big man," Thomas said.

Victor carried part of his father and Thomas carried the rest out to the pickup. They set him down carefully behind the seats, put a cowboy hat on the wooden box and a Dodgers cap on the cardboard box. That's the way it was supposed to be.

"Ready to head back home," Victor asked.

"It's going to be a long drive."

"Yeah, take a couple days, maybe."

"We can take turns," Thomas said.

"Okay," Victor said, but they didn't take turns. Victor drove for sixteen hours straight north, made it halfway up Nevada toward home before he finally pulled over.

"Hey, Thomas," Victor said. "You got to drive for a while."

"Okay."

Thomas Builds-the-Fire slid behind the wheel and started off down the road. All through Nevada, Thomas and Victor had been amazed at the lack of animal life, at the absence of water, of movement.

"Where is everything?" Victor had asked more than once.

Now when Thomas was finally driving they saw the first animal, maybe the only animal in Nevada. It was a long-eared jackrabbit.

"Look," Victor yelled. "It's alive."

Thomas and Victor were busy congratulating themselves on their discovery when the jackrabbit darted out into the road and under the wheels of the pickup.

"Stop the goddamn car," Victor yelled, and Thomas did stop, backed the pickup to the dead jackrabbit.

"Oh, man, he's dead," Victor said as he looked at the squashed animal.

"Really dead."

"The only thing alive in this whole state and we just killed it."

"I don't know," Thomas said. "I think it was suicide."

Victor looked around the desert, sniffed the air, felt the emptiness and loneliness, and nodded his head.

"Yeah," Victor said. "It had to be suicide."

"I can't believe this," Thomas said. "You drive for a thousand miles and there ain't even any bugs smashed on the windshield. I drive for ten seconds and kill the only living thing in Nevada."

"Yeah," Victor said. "Maybe I should drive."

"Maybe you should."

Thomas Builds-the-Fire walked through the corridors of the tribal school by himself. Nobody wanted to be anywhere near him because of all those stories. Story after story.

Thomas closed his eyes and this story came to him: "We are all given one thing by which our lives are measured, one determination. Mine are the stories which can change or not change the world. It doesn't matter which as long as I continue to tell the stories. My father, he died on Okinawa in World War II, died fighting for this country, which had tried to kill him for years. My mother, she died giving birth to me, died while I was still inside her. She pushed me out into the world with her last breath. I have no brothers or sisters. I have only my stories which came to me before I even had the words to speak. I learned a thousand stories before I took my first thousand steps. They are all I have. It's all I can do."

Thomas Builds-the-Fire told his stories to all those who would stop and listen. He kept telling them long after people had stopped listening.

Victor and Thomas made it back to the reservation just as the sun was rising. It was the beginning of a new day on earth, but the same old shit on the reservation.

"Good morning," Thomas said.

"Good morning."

The tribe was waking up, ready for work, eating breakfast, reading the newspaper, just like everybody else does. Willene LeBret was out in her garden wearing a bathrobe. She waved when Thomas and Victor drove by.

"Crazy Indians made it," she said to herself and went back to her roses.

Victor stopped the pickup in front of Thomas Builds-the-Fire's HUD* house. They both yawned, stretched a little, shook dust from their bodies.

*Affordable housing built by the U.S. government's department of Housing and Urban Development.

"I'm tired," Victor said.

"Of everything," Thomas added.

They both searched for words to end the journey. Victor needed to thank Thomas for his help, for the money, and make the promise to pay it all back.

"Don't worry about the money," Thomas said. "It don't make any difference anyhow."

"Probably not, enit?"

"Nope."

Victor knew that Thomas would remain the crazy story-teller who talked to dogs and cars, who listened to the wind and pine trees. Victor knew that he couldn't really be friends with Thomas, even after all that had happened. It was cruel but it was real. As real as the ashes, as Victor's father, sitting behind the seats.

"I know how it is," Thomas said. "I know you ain't going to treat me any better than you did before. I know your friends would give you too much shit about it."

Victor was ashamed of himself. Whatever happened to the tribal ties, the sense of community? The only real thing he shared with anybody was a bottle and broken dreams. He owed Thomas something, anything.

"Listen," Victor said and handed Thomas the cardboard box which contained half of his father. "I want you to have this."

Thomas took the ashes and smiled, closed his eyes, and told this story: "I'm going to travel to Spokane Falls one last time and toss these ashes into the water. And your father will rise like a salmon, leap over the bridge, over me, and find his way home. It will be beautiful. His teeth will shine like silver, like a rainbow. He will rise, Victor, he will rise."

Victor smiled.

"I was planning on doing the same thing with my half," Victor said. "But I didn't imagine my father looking anything like a salmon. I thought it'd be like cleaning the attic or something. Like letting things go after they've stopped having any use."

"Nothing stops, cousin," Thomas said. "Nothing stops."

Thomas Builds-the-Fire got out of the pickup and walked up his driveway. Victor started the pickup and began the drive home.

"Wait," Thomas yelled suddenly from his porch. "I just got to ask one favor."

Victor stopped the pickup, leaned out the window, and shouted back. "What do you want?"

"Just one time when I'm telling a story somewhere, why don't you stop and listen?" Thomas asked.

"Just one?"

"Just once."

Victor waved his arms to let Thomas know that the deal was good. It was a fair trade, and that was all Victor had ever wanted from his whole life. So Victor drove his father's pickup toward home while Thomas went into his house, closed the door behind him, and heard a new story come to him in the silence afterwards.

[1993]

Understanding the Reading

1. Why did Victor need to go to Phoenix?
2. What are the conditions under which Thomas Builds-the-Fire will help him?
3. Describe Thomas and his relationship with Victor.
4. Give some examples of how Victor and his peers feel about tradition, the reservation, and the U.S. government.
5. What is the "fair trade" that Victor and Thomas make at the end of the story? Explain why it is a fair trade.

Suggestions for Responding

1. Learn about traditional story-tellers in American Indian cultures. In what ways have they been valued?
2. Research the Spokane Indian Reservation in Spokane, Washington.
3. Discuss Sherman Alexie's humor in this essay and in the following statement made by him: "The two funniest tribes I've ever been around are Indians and Jews, so I guess that says something about the inherent humor of genocide" ("What You Pawn, I Will Redeem" in *Ten Little Indians*). ◆

34

Decloaking Class: Why Class Identity and Consciousness Count

Janet Zandy

To be sure, class is one of those "where do you begin?" subjects. It is a kind of ghost issue, there but not there. Often it is named as part of a cluster of multicultural concerns, but then it seems to disappear, eclipsed by other identities. This is understandable because class is so complex and so mystified, especially in a country as large and diverse as the United States. I use the word "decloaking" in my title not only because I love Star Trek, but because the term fits the process of revealing what is clearly there, but cloaked and hidden. To reveal class involves crossing several time zones, of simultaneously having a sense of the past, the present, and the future.

Also, it involves seeing class as both personal and public, a kind of inheritance we carry with us as individuals and as a country. In other words, class is too important to ignore. I wish I could offer you a neat package of class information that would be psychologically comforting and intellectually satisfying. But, frankly, that would be about as real as a hologram on a holodeck. Instead, I want to speak out of my own experience, and to leave you with more questions than answers.

Class Identity

How many of you are first generation college students or college graduates? How many of you have grandparents who do not have college degrees? How many think that working class and middle class are essentially the same thing? How many of you are uncomfortable with these questions?

Questions about class identity seem to evoke feelings and responses that are different from questions about other identities. If I asked, how many of you are from Italian or Irish ancestry, Caribbean, or Asian, there would probably be little hesitation in your response. But class iden-

tity is not so evident. Students may be from significantly different economic circumstances—in terms of whether you need to work to stay in school or whether you have significant loans to repay after graduation or whether someone else is paying your tuition—but those differences are not apparent. And except for the styles of dress of different majors, you can't tell class difference by appearance.

Even bringing up the issue of class seems vaguely impolite, even un-American. People respond by saying: "I don't care about class identity; I treat everyone the same. What does it matter what class you come from, we are all equal."

The truth is class does count. It shapes our lives and intersects with race, ethnicity, gender, and geography in profound ways. What is class? I offer this as a working definition: Class is an experience of shared economic circumstances and shared social and cultural practices in relation to positions of power. Unlike caste (slavery), there is some mobility between classes. That is, it is possible to be born poor and acquire great wealth. (But, not likely.) Conversely, it is possible to keep a sense of one's original class identity as one moves into different economic circumstances. What needs to be understood is that although class identity is shaped by income and wealth, money is only a part of the story. It is what economic privilege can purchase in terms of access and power that really marks class difference.

Each of us is born into a family with a particular class identity and class history—sometimes it is a mixed or hybrid identity—but almost always it is part of a network of other relationships—to other families in a community, to work and jobs, and to institutions. For example, if you are born into a family that owns lands and buildings, a family that has access to the best lawyers and doctors, and has sent generations of sons (and more recently daughters) to boarding schools and then on to Yale or Dartmouth or Harvard then you have a different class history than someone whose parents may own one small house, whose grandparents had to drop out of school to go to work, who does not have easy access to lawyers and doctors, not to mention judges and lobbyists, and whose parents work long hours at a job site they do not own or control, performing labor that may be physically exhausting and even dangerous. It is conceivable that the sons and daughters from both families might even call themselves "middle class," but in terms of power, autonomy, and opportunity, they clearly are not the same.

How do we measure class? Well, it is the academic way to begin with data, definitions, and statistics. To be sure, we have plenty of statistics—most of which [come] from government sources. Even a cursory look at wealth distribution reveals the reality of the economic landscape. At the top, is a tiny, tiny percent of people who control and own an enormous amount of wealth. (And that wealth has increased dramatically in the last 15 years.) At the bottom, are the official poor (whose numbers are growing, about 32 million—about 60 percent of those people are working poor—that is, that have jobs but don't make enough to support their families). And between the rich and the growing number of poor are the middle and working classes. This is where the classification gets blurred. Although there are about twice as many working class people as middle class (about 50 percent to 20 percent), there is a media and political tendency to avoid the term working class and to lump anyone who isn't either very rich or very poor into the amorphous middle (sometimes called "working middle"). I think it is important to unpack the differences between the working class and middle class. To perceive these differences you need to go beyond definitions of a middle salary and look at the nature of work: the degree of autonomy a job has, who is managed, who is the manager; the physicality of work, working-class jobs tend to be harder on the human body, are sometimes even dangerous; the degree of control or ownership one has over one's own labor; and differences of status, options, expectations, language, education, and culture.

Both the middle class and the working class have experienced change: there are fewer well paying, blue-collar jobs, more low-paying white and pink collar jobs. There are fewer independent middle class storekeepers and farmers and more professionals and managers. What both the middle class and the working class have in common is a downward economic pull. The middle class is losing autonomy and security, and the working class is getting poorer as union jobs decline. Both groups are experiencing the economic frustration of being on a no-fat economic diet of little or no income gain in the last decade. On the other hand, the number of people reporting incomes of more than a half million increased in the same decade 985 percent. When class resentments surface, those in positions of power encourage a criticism aimed downward—at the poor—increasingly the scapegoats for people's economic frustrations—and not upward at the rich. This is perhaps a truer reflection of who owns and controls the media than it is of which class is really oppressing another.

But numbers and definitions are not sufficient to decloak class. We need to understand better the everyday class experiences of ordinary people and we need to ask what is missing or distorted in our own notions about class. I'd like to suggest some ways to break down and think about this large concept:

First, think across generations. Consider how class identity changes or stays the same from one generation to the next. For example, your class experience may be different from your parents and significantly different from your grandparents, but, on the other hand, there may be common values, attitudes, ways of using language that continue from generation to generation. That is the cultural aspect of class. Also, if you look across generations, you can see how tools and technology may have changed—bank clerks use computers instead of adding machines—but the structure of power relationships remains fairly consistent.

Second, consider the concept of relationship as a key to understanding class. That is, class is most visible in juxtaposition or in relationship to something else. You begin to know your class identity when you cross class borders and see your own circumstances through someone else's eyes. For some of you these insights come through community service. For others, class difference was evident when you left home or on your first day in college when you notice what kind of stuff students bring with them. But tangible material differences are only a part of class relationships. There are other relational questions—especially in discerning differences between the middle and working class: For example, in order to advance in the world (and what that means is not always clear), do you need to leave your home and community or can you develop within it? What are the expectations of your family? Are you encouraged to get a secure job with a future and a pension, or are you encouraged to experiment, take a year off, and find yourself? When you went to school as a child, was the language that the school teachers used in first grade familiar to you? Or was it different from the language that you heard at home? And I am referring to the dialects of spoken English, not just other languages. The middle class child does not have to switch language patterns at home and at school; the working class child often does. Also, class difference can be seen in the relationship one has to community. Do you feel alone or do you feel that you are part of a network of people and traditions? These are questions that pull us closer to understanding class as a lived experience and not just an academic category.

Third, consider the intersections between class identity and other identities, especially race and ethnicity. I think that the issue of multiculturalism would be complicated in a positive way if class is factored in. That is, it would be a very healthy thing for working-class people of all different backgrounds to know each other's work history. This would mean also that this huge category of whiteness would have to be broken down and understood in relation to issues of power. This does not mean that there is no such thing as white skin privilege; rather, it means that all whites do not have the same degree of privilege. And, of course, in terms of gender issues, all men do not have the same degree of power.

Fourth, if you want to understand class look at how work is constructed. There are careers, there is work, and there are jobs. Each nuanced differently. Most of us are so busy either preparing for future work or struggling to sustain what we have, that there isn't much time to step back and look at how our work is managed or how it fits into a larger social context. Also, how often do we see the working conditions of other people? How aware are we of the production process behind the goods we consume? It is a fact that most people on this planet do not own or control their own labor, but must sell it in order to survive. And few of them can afford to give their own children the toys and clothes they are assembling for other markets. How

work is shaped, who controls and defines it, whether it is scarce or plentiful are all class relational questions.

Fifth, consider the meaning of class consciousness. Consciousness is an awareness, an opening. Class consciousness is an awareness of mutual interests and desires. We are all bombarded with messages coaxing us to identify our interests with those at the economic top. The usual model for this kind of consciousness is the ladder—climbing in an individualistic and competitive way, higher and higher rung by rung. But there are other models. Another is the web; that is, we see ourselves as having a place in a complex network of mutually interrelated positions, and that our individual well being depends on the well being of the group—including the least privileged. This is closer to a model that you find among native peoples and it is closer to the model of a working-class consciousness. It is a sense that survival depends on helping each other out, on a sense of mutuality, not exclusion. Success—if the word is used at all—lies with collective well being not merely with individual achievement—a sense of pushing everything up with us as we rise.

How Class Is Cloaked

Let me begin with a small incident that happened several years ago at an academic conference I attended. These conferences are usually in big hotels in big cities. The usual routine is to get up early and begin attending sessions on different topics in hot crowded hotel rooms. On this occasion, I am standing in the hotel lobby and another English professor makes small talk with me. He asks, "What is your field?" I answer, "American working-class literature." After a significant pause, he replies, "Oh, I didn't know there was a working class anymore." I suggest to him that there still is a working class as I glance around the hotel lobby to see people clearing tables, carrying food, cleaning ashtrays, washing windows, setting up chairs, etc. The room hummed with human activity, but it wasn't visible. These individual workers blurred into the deep background of academic humanism.

It seems to me that this small event is telling of a larger pattern in American culture. It is a problem of seeing—an "unequal distribution of visibility." It works on two levels: people are literally invisible to each other, but also their intelligence and experience are devalued. Sometimes the working class—the class that holds everything up—has to literally punch through in order to be seen.

Part of the problem of visibility is a problem of knowledge—how knowledge is constructed, layer after layer, generation after generation. Working-class people have not had much say about how school knowledge is constructed. Textbooks, curricula, course design were developed by other class interests—initially by an elite intelligentsia or more recently driven by business and corporate needs. The formation of knowledge has not included the subjectivities and experiences and histories of working people in any significant way.

Why is this omission important to understand? It means that the point of view of the majority of people—living today and in the history of the country has not been included in the big history story—the story that gets delivered to school kids at a very young age. Perhaps it has changed since I was a student or since my children were young, but I noticed that what is taught—who won what battle and who was President at the time—doesn't seem to have a lot of connection or relevance to the lives of ordinary people. What seems to be remembered, is not a rich and dense, conflicted and complex U.S. history, but a kind of Disney-like nostalgic history. Youngsters learn about someone called Betsy Ross sweetly sewing the American flag, but nothing about the noisy, sweaty history of textile work. Or they learn about George Washington chopping down the cherry tree and not telling a lie, but not about the unsafe history of the logging industry or how many lies were told to acquire Indian land. These simplistic little stories have amazing endurance in people's memories and reference points. Indeed, children seem to be protected from serious American history.

And serious American history is violent. It is not safe; it makes people uncomfortable. Class difference and class struggle were from the very beginning—part of the story. Recent labor and social historians often use words like "hidden" "forgotten" "untold" to tell this other story. Some

of this untold story is now part of the history curriculum—but it wasn't when I was a student. I had to learn for myself how to see the point of view in the historical story, how to adjust my angle of vision to look from the bottom up instead of the top down. This adjustment in perspective makes relationships more visible: for instance, in a world of finite resources, if a small group of people own and control vast amounts, it is likely that a large group of people will have very little—no matter how hard they work. And it makes it easier to see how this imbalance is maintained by coaxing people to identify with the very forces that oppress their own kin.

When it comes to the history of class disparity there is a great deal to uncover. At the very beginning of the new nation, Alexander Hamilton advised George Washington to give to the "rich and well born . . . a distinct permanent share in the government." And he did. The very first Congress provided money for bankers to set up a national bank and manufacturers were subsidized in the form of tariffs. In the 1850s state governments gave railroad speculators 25 million acres of public land, free of charge! The first transcontinental railroad was built with government land and money.

When the story is told from the top down, we learn about the feat of building the railroad, how it opened new frontiers and provided jobs. We may not hear that 10,000 Chinese and 3,000 Irish got the opportunity to earn about $1 a day; and die by the hundreds building those *railroads*. And how those very same Chinese workers were hounded and driven out after the job was done. And how none of the workers who built the railroad could claim ownership or even a free ride.

Today, information highways have replaced railroads, but government benefits for businesses and corporations continue. And I am speaking of huge corporate entities, not small businesses or middle class family owned companies. One reason the national debt is so enormous is because of the shifting of the tax burden from corporations to individuals. In the 1950s, corporate share of federal income tax collected was 39 percent, in the 1980s it was 17 percent. By 1991 it was down to 9.2 percent, while the corporate share of state and local taxes stayed about what it was in 1965. This is trickle down economics. But I haven't seen any new cars or fur coats trickle down lately; have you?

But this is only one side of the story. What role did ordinary working people play in shaping their own economic lives? This history, what some historians call "the other civil war," is a record of resistance and endurance in the face of great odds. It seems unfair to the majority of Americans not to know it. To know, for instance, that people fought back. From time to time ordinary citizens—because of unsafe working conditions, long hours, and unlivable wages—would spontaneously refuse to work. The railroad strike of 1877, sometimes called the "great uprising of 1877," was the first national strike in United States history. Within two weeks the strike which began among the railroad workers in Martinsburg, West Virginia (triggered because of five years of wage cuts for workers on the Baltimore & Ohio line) spread through four states—Pennsylvania, Ohio, Indiana and Missouri. It was a general, national strike that included mill workers, miners, laborers, and steel workers; 100,000 workers were on strike at the same time. But they were defeated when federal troops were sent in and, at the end, 100 people were dead. This was neither the first nor the last general strike: between the years 1881–1885 there were 500 strikes a year. In 1886 there were 1,400 strikes, involving 500,000 workers. In 1934 there was a general strike in San Francisco and 130,000 workers went out. That same year, 325,000 textile workers in the South struck.

What is troubling to learn is that so many strikes were lost because the National Guard or the army were employed by business and government against working people. Workers were literally outgunned in battles with soldiers who came from the same working class backgrounds. One brief example. In 1913 in Ludlow, Colorado miners went on strike because of low wages and dangerous working conditions against the Rockefeller owned Colorado Fuel & Iron Corporation. The miners were evicted from their company-owned shacks and set up tents near the coal fields during the cold winter of 1913–14. The National Guard was called; the miners and their families, waving American flags, thought the soldiers were there to protect them. They didn't know that the Rockefellers were paying the salaries of the soldiers. On April 20, 1914 the National Guard began a machine gun attack on the tents. Women and children dug pits beneath the tents to escape the gunfire. The Guard then set fire to the tents. The next day the charred bodies of eleven children and two women were found. That became known as the Ludlow Massacre. One miner said, "Well, they value their mules more."

Seeing history from the bottom up illuminates other issues in American culture, some surprisingly current. For example, when you look at differences within the working class as a whole, you see a pattern on the part of the owners to pit one ethnic or racial group or gender against another in competition for scarce jobs. It is a strategy of divide and conquer—of terracing skills—so that one race or ethnic group comes to understand that they cannot advance beyond a certain level because they are Hispanic or Hungarian or Italian or women. But even deeper than this, and crucial to our coping with racial tensions today, is how the category of "whiteness" is used to block class awareness. What happens is that the white working class comes to think of its interests in terms of race difference rather than class oppositions. The insecurities that white workers feel about their own status—and the tensions between the ideology of equality and the reality of economic inequality—is displaced by a psychological wage of whiteness, a wage of false superiority because they are white. And so they would compensate for their feelings of class alienation by defining themselves against blackness.

This is just a sliver of American history told from the perspective of working people. It is not history as a sporting event—who won and who lost. I like to imagine what it would mean if this workers history were embedded in people's consciousness today. What if labor history were half as well known as entertainment trivia? What if the Ludlow massacre were as familiar to school children as sightings of Elvis?

But generally I suspect that most people don't know this history or understand these power relationships. The media does not focus on ordinary people pooling their resources and overcoming differences of language and culture to engage in common struggle. Instead, we have distractions—sports, sensational murder stories (sometimes sports and murder are combined), race and gender antagonisms, and false promises. Instead of examples of how collective effort can change conditions, we have an almost religious reverence for a single leader. Instead of narratives of worker consciousness we have narratives of minuscule possibility—stories of winning, stardom, and lucky breaks. Practice every day, wear these sneakers, and you will make it to the NBA. Right. Play LOTTO and you'll make it big. Hey, you never know. Indeed, you never know. There's a lot of talk about "empowerment" these days, but it doesn't appear to me that ordinary people feel particularly powerful.

TODAY'S VIRTUAL WORK REALITY

Now why should people who are just beginning their careers pay any attention to this history? What are the connections, if any, between individual achievement and communal well being? I want to share with you a bit of student writing that caused me to think about these questions. This was something a student of mine wrote in her journal in December 1988. You may remember that this particular December a bomb exploded on Pam Am Flight 103 over Lockerbie, Scotland. Two hundred and seventy people were killed, including a number of upstate New York students who were on the way home for the holidays after a semester abroad. In response to this event, this RIT student wrote, "From 31,000 feet they had no chance to save themselves. Thirty-eight students, thirty-eight fewer people competing for jobs."

I have to ask myself why this student reacted to the explosion of a packed airplane in terms of job competition. I wonder whether she was completely unique in her reaction or she voiced something that others think, but may not write down. I don't know. I wonder, though, if she reflects the experience of growing up with a different set of historical circumstances and more rigid economic opportunities. Has she gotten the message that life is a game based on scarcity, and the rules say that if someone else loses, I may win.

In a number of ways the rules have changed. Middle class families are getting new and disturbing labels—they are being called the fear of falling class or the anxious class. Part of it is un-certainty about the future. There are no guarantees—no one can say what tomorrow's cutting edge will be or where the jobs will be in ten even five years from now, or whether there will be any employment continuity in a project-driven work environment. It may be hard to believe that your parents' generation was once on the cutting edge too but now many of them are being downsized (I understand the current term is "rightsized") out. The cutting up of the work force is a class issue. What are the implications for family or community if workers are disposed of like so many Bic razors? This uncertainty is coupled with the reality of enormous college debt faced by graduating college students and their families. My generation—the 60s generation—were in some ways luckier. We had greater access to grants and scholarships rather than loans and second mortgages. And so there were many working-class kids like myself who had full scholarships to get educations their parents could never afford to give them. Also, twenty years earlier, over two million service men and women of the generation of the 1940s were able to take advantage of Public Law 346, commonly known as the G.I. Bill. Free education and a subsistence allowance to any eligible veteran. It was an enormous leap, a great opportunity to become engineers, educators, judges, lawyers and get degrees from Princeton, Yale, and Stanford via the G.I. Bill.

Today we have what some are calling job virtual reality (now the job exists, now it doesn't). We have a lot of interesting technology. And a great deal of pressure to be technically prepared to face this changing world. But, there doesn't seem to be a lot of time—unless students do it for themselves—to consider how the pleasures of engineering or the writing of an elegant computer program or the crafting of a beautiful table—how the work we enjoy doing—relates to a larger community of people. We don't have time to ask how technology conforms to existing power relationships. The computer scientist Richard Stallman asserts that "the greatest scarcity in the United States is not technical innovation, but rather the willingness to work together for the public good. It makes no sense [he says] to encourage the former at the expense of the latter."

By speaking about history tonight I was reminding myself and others whose shoulders we stand on as we climb. The theologian Dorothee Soelle says we need alternative visions to see what she describes as "work [that] is communal, not only in the space of a given community but also in time, as the shared memory of what we have received from the past that accompanies us into the future."

I realize that we academics in liberal arts tend to frustrate students by delivering a lot of critical information but not offering any solutions. But of course you know that the solutions are not simple because the issues are so complex. Frankly, I would be skeptical of anyone who offers simplistic answers to complex questions. Maybe the better way to go—if we are going to salvage a sense of community—is to figure out the right questions, especially in relation to issues of power and class.

USING CLASS DIFFERENCE PERSONALLY AND COLLECTIVELY

Since I was the first woman in my family to earn a college degree, I was driven to take in knowledge as hard and fast as I could, but not to think very critically about it. Along the way, I sensed a distance, sometimes even a rupture, between the lived experience of my working-class family and what I learned in school. In myriad subtle and not so subtle ways, I was taught in school not to value nor to see the dignity and worth of my own heritage. The message that I received as a young woman wanting to be an educated person was my working class identity had to be discarded—like a dark and heavy coat—at the university door. Getting clear about that identity was a long and complicated process. Claiming that identity as crucial to who I am and the work that I want to do in the world was at once liberating and reconciling. My work is sustained because of a sense of kinship and responsibility to my beginnings—not despite them. This is not about survivor's guilt, nor is it about romanticizing economic hardship; there's nothing romantic about not having enough money. Rather, it is trusting what you know even if it is not part of officially sanctioned knowledge. I realized that I could write, research, and act out of my own sense of class difference. And that what I needed to do was to use my resources and privileges to

provide a space for some of this history and culture that was so frequently ignored or even despised. And the work had to be collective, not just my own story.

In *Calling Home* I wanted to create a book that would prove that working-class women have created their own written literary culture, that an aesthetic sense is shaped by class but does not belong to one class. I also wanted to show that the experiences of working class women were not the same as those of working class men or of middle class women. Without any lofty expectations of what might happen, I began collecting writing by working class women and putting it into shoe boxes and then bigger boxes, and finally filing two file drawers. I shaped the material around the interplay of different and linked voices—I, we, and they. And finally—ten years later—I mustered the courage to send it out. No one was more surprised than I was when two prestigious university presses competed for this book. To produce it, I used the tools that I learned in the academy, but the writing itself is grounded outside the academy in the work lives of people like my parents.

In this second book, *Liberating Memory: Our Work and Our Working-Class Consciousness,* I wanted to show how this effort of linking working-class lived experience to cultural work was not unique to me. I wanted to make visible how other working class people like myself managed to use their class experiences in culturally productive ways. I asked for memory, not nostalgia. That is, not a sugar-coated celebration of the past, a self-congratulating, "look how far I've come," but rather a painful reconstruction of class experiences and loss, a way of using grief to tell a larger story. These essays written by photographers and painters and academics and secretaries and musicians and social activists all begin with a biographical record: I was born at this time and in this place and this is the work that my parents and my grandparents did. All of the writers grew up with the uncertain economic rhythms of working class life. Their parents' work included: seamstress, short order cook, chemical factory worker, auto line worker, welder, rubber plant worker, bookkeeper, tenant farmer, truck driver, riveter, millwright, domestic, and housewife. All the writers bring the knowledge of physical labor either personally or through the lives of their parents into the current work that they do. This is a knowledge of the body that is not easily articulated and not often part of bourgeois intellectual circles. All of the contributors oppose the dehumanization of workers—of turning human beings who do not own and control their own labor into things. They all see risk taking as necessary for their cultural work—not because they are more heroic than anyone else—but because it is strategically necessary in order to accomplish democratic change. All of the contributors know what it feels like to be cut out of the action, even though they are of the majority class, the working class. And they all love learning and books.

I'll finish with this short excerpt from the introduction to *Liberating Memory* that describes an episode of class consciousness among working people. It takes place on April 28, Workers Memorial Day.

For the last five years, hundreds of communities across the country have held memorial services on this day to remember dead and injured workers. In Rochester we meet late in the afternoon on a windy knoll in Highland Park. The setting is landscaped with junipers and white and yellow daffodils. Nested in the grass is a small memorial plaque inscribed with Mother Jones' feisty injunction to "Pray for the dead, but fight like hell for the living."

The event is organized by the local labor council. Dignitaries, public officials, politicians, and the media often show up—though how many depends on whether or not it is an election year. The crowd is mostly a mixture of activists, union leaders, and working people. Some are retired; some were able to get off early from work. We do not necessarily know each other, but faces are familiar and recognizable year after year. We hold red carnations and carry names of fallen workers. We are working class people who have come to honor our own.

The ceremony begins. After the speeches, the display of public language, comes the remembrance. One by one we walk to the podium and read the name of a worker who has died or been injured in the Rochester area, and we place a carnation on the memorial. Sometimes people use this moment at the podium to remember special friends, co-workers, heroes of the labor move-

ment. This year Cesar Chavez was remembered along with the three women social service workers who were gunned down in their offices. One by one, the names are read, and the blood-red carnations accumulate on the memorial.

The reading of the names opens us to each other. Not just the names, but the experience of unsafe work behind the names. A shift occurs. We are no longer an assemblage of strangers, but a community who share a special knowledge about work and struggle. Two local men died this year. In accidents that didn't have to happen. One was digging a tunnel, laying the foundation for a new Taco Bell. Perhaps because of the heavy spring rains, or because of inadequate shoring, the earth gave way, and he was buried alive. The other was a young carpenter. He was injured on the job and died within a week. There were many blue carpenter's union caps this year, the man's family was there, his wife and two young sons. The look on the wife's face was familiar—the flat stare of shock. It is the body's way of absorbing the knowledge of loss. Then shock wears off and grief permeates the body.

Grief is physical. On this chilly April afternoon we share communal grief. It is a particular kind of knowledge—of the body at risk because of the conditions of work, of swift and sudden economic uncertainty. How to live with this knowledge is a personal question. How to put this knowledge to good use is a public and cultural question. That is the question I want to leave with you.

William: I actually took the opportunity to watch the video of this lecture twice, taking several days to think about the topic between viewing. I enjoyed the lecture very much. I could quickly identify with the awareness that I do not come from the same class background as many of my friends or even my peers in the workplaces. I come from a working class family and am experiencing many changes as I prepare to graduate. It's a sobering feeling to realize that in a few weeks I will begin the first job of my career with a starting salary higher than my father ever made in his life, working overtime and supporting a family of four. Class does matter. It affects who I believe I am and what I believe I'm capable of.

While there were many provocative points to the lecture, I really felt strongly about the teachings of other class perspectives in the class-room. As I recall the history lessons I was taught in both elementary and high school, I remember covering essentially the same material year after year. "The Great Roman Empire fell when . . . The Renaissance started in this country . . . The cause of World War was . . . " The stories were lifeless and had nothing to do with me. . . . I liked very much hearing the quote about having a sense of community in time, and I think that's a very important issue that is not being ad-dressed in our educational system.

Gaetana: I understood what you meant by hav-ing to work even harder in school because you were the first to attend college . . . with my fam-ily it is the same. I was the first to go to school and I had so much pressure on me it seemed all the time to do well and not smear the family name. I wonder how many students could actu-ally relate to that? My parents were not educated. I even was almost held back from first grade be-cause I could not speak English well just Italian. So I have had to work at everything 100 percent all alone since I could not lean on my parents to help me with my academic career. Even today my dad makes me laugh because he insists on weekends I have to come home since I don't have school . . . he thinks that on weekends, breaks, or even after school you have no home-work to do.

Charles: The central theme of Decloaking Class was the problems faced by people in this world against the stigma of class and the struggles to not only recognize it but to see class for what it is. . . . Being a 29 year old full-time student and worker, class identification is more notice-able to me now than ever before. I see it every-where I go, in school, at work, and even places I go to eat. . . . The sad fact is that I've experi-enced it firsthand, I lived in the inner-city grow-ing up and when friends of mine learned that, it was enlightening how their attitudes toward me changed. The one incident that Professor Zandy referenced which was especially poi-gnant to me was the Ludlow incident of April 20, 1914. I have taken many history classes during school and I never recall hearing of this before this lecture. To me this is a perfect example of class invisibility.

Michael: Professor Zandy's examples of the working class being erased, distorted and omit-ted from history stand out the most to me. For me, and most every one else attending the lec-ture, it was the first time I had ever heard about the Ludlow Massacre, the National Strikes other-wise known as the Great Uprising of 1877, or the treatment of the Chinese who built the railroad. I think that many of my high school history teachers were good at what they did, but now when I look back on it I realize they often spent a lot of time on the important characters in his-tory such as George Washington and Abe Lin-coln. They often spent little time, if any, on the working class. I can remember learning all about the wealthy Rockefeller, Morgan, and Carnegie families, but very little about the workers they used to gain their wealth.

Jennifer: Being a college student, you get used to everyone being pretty much like yourself—poor. You usually don't have much spending money to speak of, chances are you live in a hole in the wall, whether it's on or off campus, and it's expected that you'll be especially broke around the first of the month. For us, there is very little class distinction. But growing up, I felt that my family was definitely part of the lower-working class. All you had to do was walk by our house to see that. It never occurred to me that my parents might be ashamed of the way we lived. I just figured, one day I'll get out of this. No big deal. I never thought about my parents never getting out of it, never being able to keep the Joneses in sight, let alone keep up with them. I didn't think about the fact that while I'll probably eventually have a better life than them, they'll die that way. I don't want them to die ashamed. I'm scared that my Dad al-ready has.

Your lecture was the first time I had ever heard of Workers Memorial Day or the Ludlow massacre. It's very frightening to think that huge numbers of Americans will go through life totally ignorant of what goes on in our society, of how small a percentage of people control such enor-mous amounts of power and wealth. The major-ity of us fall into the category of working and lower classes. Do the majority of us feel desolate and ashamed? Your point about invisibility is something I see every day here at school. I was so glad to hear it mentioned. Maybe that is the first step. Maybe decloaking class and teaching people that because they are struggling doesn't mean they have to be ashamed is possible. My father said he wanted me to have a better life than he did. I now wish I had told him that I hoped I was half as good a person as he was, instead of telling him that someday I'd buy him the Cadillac he always wanted.

Mike: Professor Zandy, in your lecture "Decloaking Class: Why Class Identity and Consciousness Count" you have raised very important, but not easy to talk about issues. I would like to talk about wealth distribution. In three months I will be graduating from RIT as a Financial Manager and I am worried. My professors gave me knowledge and ability to comprehend complex economic and financial problems. I excelled at it, and I have my grades and letters of recommendation to show my future employers. I, probably, should be happy, go out, get a job, make a pot of money and live happily ever after. However, I am worried. I will always remember what [my professor] said in his Corporate Finance course. He said that our knowledge is a very powerful "sword," and our decisions will affect other people's lives, and that we need to be careful in how we make our decisions. That's why I am worried.

Before coming to the United States, I thought that there are no classes. Six years taught me a lot. In my opinion, people are judged by who they are more often than not. If you are born to a wealthy family your chances of becoming poor are almost nil, but if you are born in a ghetto your chances of becoming rich are almost nil. We always hear that if you work hard you will eventually succeed. I find it difficult to believe.

Distribution of wealth in the society plays an important role in how we live our lives, what values we value, how we communicate with each other. How could the richest country in the world have so many poor and homeless people? Believe me, being born in the former Soviet Union, I am not a socialist. However, I am for social justice.

United States remains a land of opportunity, although I wish this opportunity was available for everyone.   [1996]

Understanding the Reading

1. What does Zandy mean when she calls class a "ghost issue"?
2. How does Zandy define class?
3. What are the differences between the working class and the middle class?
4. How does power factor into our understanding of class?
5. What impact does class have on the construction of knowledge?
6. Explain the role of government in the strikes of the late nineteenth and early twentieth centuries.
7. In what ways have the rules changed today since earlier generations (the 1960s and the 1940s)?
8. What did Zandy want her books to accomplish?
9. Explain the purpose and impact of the Workers Memorial Day ceremony.

Suggestions for Responding

1. Write a paper responding to Zandy's questions in the first paragraph of the "Class Identity" section.
2. Research and report on one of the labor strikes Zandy mentions.
3. Write your response to the Zandy selection—what you learned and how you now feel about the working class. ✦

35

Looking for Work

Gary Soto

One July, while killing ants on the kitchen sink with a rolled newspaper, I had a nine-year-old's vision of wealth that would save us from ourselves. For weeks I had drunk Kool-Aid and watched morning reruns of *Father Knows Best*, whose family was so uncomplicated in its routine that I very much wanted to imitate it. The first step was to get my brother and sister to wear shoes at dinner.

"Come on, Rick—come on, Deb," I whined. But Rick mimicked me and the same day that I asked him to wear shoes he came to the dinner table in only his swim trunks. My mother didn't notice, nor did my sister, as we sat to eat our beans and tortillas in the stifling heat of our kitchen. We all gleamed like cellophane, wiping the sweat from our brows with the backs of our hands as we talked about the day: Frankie our neighbor was beat up by Faustino; the swimming pool at the playground would be closed for a day because the pump was broken.

Such was our life. So that morning, while doing-in the train of ants which arrived each day, I decided to become wealthy, and right away! After downing a bowl of cereal, I took a rake from the garage and started up the block to look for work.

We lived on an ordinary block of mostly working class people: warehousemen, egg candlers,[1] welders, mechanics, and a union plumber. And there were many retired people who kept their lawns green and the gutters uncluttered of the chewing gum wrappers we dropped as we rode by on our bikes. They bent down to gather our litter, muttering at our evilness.

At the corner house I rapped the screen door and a very large woman in a muu-muu[2] answered. She sized me up and then asked what I could do.

"Rake leaves," I answered, smiling.

"It's summer, and there ain't no leaves," she countered. Her face was pinched with lines; fat jiggled under her chin. She pointed to the lawn, then the flower bed, and said: "You see any leaves there—or there?" I followed her pointing arm, stupidly. But she had a job for me and that was to get her a Coke at the liquor store. She gave me twenty cents, and after ditching my rake in a bush, off I ran. I returned with an unbagged Pepsi, for which she thanked me and gave me a nickel from her apron.

I skipped off her porch, fetched my rake, and crossed the street to the next block where Mrs. Moore, mother of Earl the retarded man, let me weed a flower bed. She handed me a trowel and for a good part of the morning my fingers dipped into the moist dirt, ripping up runners of Bermuda grass. Worms surfaced in my search for deep roots, and I cut them in halves, tossing them to Mrs. Moore's cat who pawed them playfully as they dried in the sun. I made out Earl whose face was pressed to the back window of the house, and although he was calling to me I couldn't understand what he was trying to say. Embarrassed, I worked without looking up, but I imagined his contorted mouth and the ring of keys attached to his belt—keys that jingled with each palsied step. He scared me and I worked quickly to finish the flower bed. When I did finish Mrs. Moore gave me a quarter and two peaches from her tree, which I washed there but ate in the alley behind my house.

I was sucking on the second one, a bit of juice staining the front of my T-shirt, when Little John, my best friend, came walking down the alley with a baseball bat over his shoulder, knocking over trash cans as he made his way toward me.

Little John and I went to St. John's Catholic School, where we sat among the "stupids." Miss Marino, our teacher, alternated the rows of good students with the bad, hoping that by sitting side-by-side with the bright students the stupids might become more intelligent, as though intelligence were contagious. But we didn't progress as she had hoped. She grew frustrated when one day, while dismissing class for recess, Little John couldn't get up because his arms were stuck in the slats of the chair's backrest. She scolded us with a shaking finger when we knocked over the globe, denting the already troubled Africa. She muttered curses when Leroy White, a real stupid but a great softball player with the gift to hit to all fields, openly chewed his host when he made his First Communion; his hands swung at his sides as he returned to the pew looking around with a big smile.

Little John asked what I was doing, and I told him that I was taking a break from work, as I sat comfortably among high weeds. He wanted to join me, but I reminded him that the last time he'd gone door-to-door asking for work his mother had whipped him. I was with him when his mother, a New Jersey Italian who could rise up in anger one moment and love the next, told me in a polite but matter-of-fact voice that I had to leave because she was going to beat her son. She gave me a homemade popsicle, ushered me to the door, and said that I could see Little John the next day. But it was sooner than that. I went around to his bedroom window to suck my popsicle and watch Little John dodge his mother's blows, a few hitting their mark but many whirring air.

It was midday when Little John and I converged in the alley, the sun blazing in the high nineties, and he suggested that we go to Roosevelt High School to swim. He needed five cents to make fifteen, the cost of admission, and I lent him a nickel. We ran home for my bike and when my sister found out that we were going swimming, she started to cry because she didn't have the fifteen cents but only an empty Coke bottle. I waved for her to come and three of us mounted the bike—Debra on the cross bar, Little John on the handle bars and holding the Coke bottle which we would cash for a nickel and make up the difference that would allow all of us to get in, and me pumping up the crooked streets, dodging cars and pot holes. We spent the day swimming under the afternoon sun, so that when we got home our mom asked us what was darker, the floor or us? She feigned a stern posture, her hands on her hips and her mouth puckered. We played along. Looking down, Debbie and I said in unison, "Us."

That evening at dinner we all sat down in our bathing suits to eat our beans, laughing and chewing loudly. Our mom was in a good mood, so I took a risk and asked her if sometime we could have turtle soup. A few days before I had watched a television program in which a Polynesian tribe killed a large turtle, gutted it, and then stewed it over an open fire. The turtle, basted in a sugary sauce, looked delicious as I ate an afternoon bowl of cereal, but my sister, who was watching the program with a glass of Kool-Aid between her knees, said, "Caca."

My mother looked at me in bewilderment. "Boy, are you a crazy Mexican. Where did you get the idea that people eat turtles?"

"On television," I said, explaining the program. Then I took it a step further. "Mom, do you think we could get dressed up for dinner one of these days? David King does."

"*Ay, Dios,*" my mother laughed. She started collecting the dinner plates, but my brother wouldn't let go of his. He was still drawing a picture in the bean sauce. Giggling, he said it was me, but I didn't want to listen because I wanted an answer from Mom. This was the summer when I spent the mornings in front of the television that showed the comfortable lives of white kids. There were no beatings, no rifts in the family. They wore bright clothes; toys tumbled from their closets. They hopped into bed with kisses and woke to glasses of fresh orange juice, and to a father sitting before his morning coffee while the mother buttered his toast. They hurried through the day making friends and gobs of money, returning home to a warmly lit living room, and then dinner. *Leave It To Beaver* was the program I replayed in my mind:

"May I have the mashed potatoes?" asks Beaver with a smile.

"Sure, Beav," replies Wally as he taps the corners of his mouth with a starched napkin.

The father looks on in his suit. The mother, decked out in earrings and a pearl necklace, cuts into her steak and blushes. Their conversation is politely clipped.

"Swell," says Beaver, his cheeks puffed with food.

Our own talk at dinner was loud with belly laughs and marked by our pointing forks at one another. The subjects were commonplace.

"Gary, let's go to the ditch tomorrow," my brother suggests. He explains that he has made a life preserver out of four empty detergent bottles strung together with twine and that he will make me one if I can find more bottles. "No way are we going to drown."

"Yeah, then we could have a dirt clod fight," I reply, so happy to be alive.

Whereas the Beaver's family enjoyed dessert in dishes at the table, our mom sent us outside, and more often than not I went into the alley to peek over the neighbor's fences and spy out fruit, apricots or peaches.

I had asked my mom and again she laughed that I was a crazy *chavalo*[3] as she stood in front of the sink, her arms rising and falling with suds, face glistening from the heat. She sent me outside where my brother and sister were sitting in the shade that the fence threw out like a blanket. They were talking about me when I plopped down next to them. They looked at one another and then Debbie, my eight-year-old sister, started in.

"What's this crap about getting dressed up?"

She had entered her profanity stage. A year later she would give up such words and slip into her Catholic uniform, and into squealing on my brother and me when we "cussed this" and "cussed that."

I tried to convince them that if we improved the way we looked we might get along better in life. White people would like us more. They might invite us to places, like their homes or front yards. They might not hate us so much.

My sister called me a "craphead," and got up to leave with a stalk of grass dangling from her mouth. "They'll never like us."

My brother's mood lightened as he talked about the ditch—the white water, the broken pieces of glass, and the rusted car fenders that awaited our knees. There would be toads, and rocks to smash them.

David King, the only person we knew who resembled the middle class, called from over the fence. David was Catholic, of Armenian and French descent, and his closet was filled with toys. A bear-shaped cookie jar, like the ones on television, sat on the kitchen counter. His mother was remarkably kind while she put up with the racket we made on the street. Evenings, she often watered the front yard and it must have upset her to see us—my brother and I and others—jump from trees laughing, the unkillable kids of the very poor, who got up unshaken, brushed off, and climbed into another one to try again.

David called again. Rick got up and slapped grass from his pants. When I asked if I could come along he said no. David said no. They were two years older so their affairs were different from mine. They greeted one another with foul names and took off down the alley to look for trouble.

I went inside the house, turned on the television, and was about to sit down with a glass of Kool-Aid when Mom shooed me outside.

"It's still light," she said. "Later you'll bug me to let you stay out longer. So go on."

I downed my Kool-Aid and went outside to the front yard. No one was around. The day had cooled and a breeze rushed the trees. Mr. Jackson, the plumber, was watering his lawn and when he saw me he turned away to wash off his front steps. There was more than an hour of light left, so I took advantage of it and decided to look for work. I felt suddenly alive as I skipped down the block in search of an overgrown flower bed and the dime that would end the day right.   [1985]

Terms

1. EGG CANDLERS: Workers who examine eggs for freshness in front of a light.
2. MUU-MUU: A long, loose dress that hangs from the shoulders.
3. *CHAVALO:* Young man.

Understanding the Reading

1. List the details that illustrate the socio-economic class of Soto's family.
2. In what ways does the boy illustrate the Protestant work ethic?
3. What is wrong with the school Soto attends?
4. What are the strengths of the Soto family's lifestyle?
5. Why does young Soto want to behave more like the families he sees on television?
6. Why are these children thought of as "unkillable kids"?

Suggestions for Responding

1. Compare the reality of your childhood with the portrayals of the families you saw on television as you were growing up. ◆

36
The Truth About Growing Up Rich

SALLIE BINGHAM

Very few people think of rich women as being "highly vulnerable." We are usually portrayed as grasping and powerful, like Joan Collins's character in the television miniseries "Sins." Yet in reality, most rich women are invisible; we are the faces that appear behind well-known men, floating up to the surface infrequently, palely; the big contributors, often anonymous, to approved charities, or the organizers of fund-raising events. Rich women have been so well rewarded by an unjust system that we have lost our voices; we are captives, as poor women are captives, of a system that deprives us of our identities.

Growing up a daughter in a very rich family placed me in this special position. It was important to avoid all displays of pride; what made me unusual, after all, was not really my own. I hadn't earned it. It had been given to me, willy-nilly, along with a set of commandments, largely unspoken, that enforced my solitariness:

- Always set a good example.
- Do not condescend to those who have less.
- Never ask the price of anything.
- Avoid being conspicuous in any way.

These commandments were backed by fear. Rich women are always vulnerable to criticism; we do not share the justifications of the men who actually made the money. We neither toil, nor do we spin, yet we have access to a wide range of material comforts. But here there is a delicate line. The jewels must not be too big, nor the furs too obvious.

Often in a rich family the jewels are inherited, obscuring, with their flash and dazzle, the ambivalent feelings of the women who first wore them. In my family, attention was focused on a pair of engagement rings, one made of diamonds, the other of sapphires, which had belonged to our grandmothers. When the time came to divide the rings, my two older brothers, then adolescents, were allowed to choose. Knowing nothing about the value of jewels, but liking the color of the sapphires, the eldest chose it for his eventual bride; the younger brother took possession, by default, of the much more valuable diamonds.

Both those rings were conspicuous, which broke a cardinal tenet of my childhood. It was a rule I had broken before. All bright children are naturally conspicuous; they talk in loud voices and move about in unhampered ways. But when the whole world is watching for a mistake, this natural exuberance must be curbed. And when the child in question is a girl, the curbing is especially intense: as a sexual object, she represents the family's peculiar vulnerability to outsiders, predators—husbands. The little rich girl must learn to sit with her legs firmly crossed and her skirt prudently down at the same time she is learning to modulate both the tone of her voice and the color of her opinions. The result is paleness.

Her models are pale as well. The hard-driving ancestor who made the fortune is not a good choice for his retiring granddaughter. Yet her female relatives, because of their learned conformity, offer little color or originality to the small girl; their rebellions are invisible, their opinions matched to the opinions of their male counterparts. The most sympathetic woman may be a maid or nurse, but her educational and social limitations restrict her effectiveness as a model. This, in turn, can lead to a split between love and admiration: the cozy, uneducated nurse is loved; the remote, perfect mother is admired. How can one satisfactory role be forged out of two contradictions?

The little rich girl realizes, with a chill, that she must treat the women around her differently. When I was a very small child, I kissed my nurse and the servants when I felt like it; as I grew older, I realized that such displays embarrassed them. As a very small child, I pitied my nurse because she had to work so hard, tending five children; a little later, I realized that such pity was inappropriate. The love doesn't change, but the little girl must look elsewhere for someone to imitate.

Obeying all the rules can never be enough, however. No amount of proper behavior can place a rich woman on comfortable terms with a world where there is so much poverty and suffering. She will always be suspect in a democracy, either as a decoration for a tyrant or a parasite with little feeling for women struggling to survive.

Another obligation is added to the role of the third- or fourth-generation heiress, whose male relatives have led lives nearly as protected as her own. From private boarding school and Ivy League college, these men return to the family fold and a lifetime career managing assets or running the family business. The harsh bustle and hard knocks of independent life have been avoided, at some cost. Yet since these sheltered individuals are men, they are expected to play roles of some importance in society, as executives or politicians, donors or secret political kingmakers. Unused to stress and criticism, they must be protected if they are to survive; here, the rich woman's role as peacemaker becomes crucial.

Most women are expected to balance demands for equity with a special sensitivity to human needs. We are asked to value compassion more than fairness, understanding more than critical judgment. Since family fortunes and family businesses usually descend to male heirs, this protective duty becomes essential to the maintenance of the whole structure. If the inheriting males are revealed as vulnerable and uncertain, the whole enterprise is likely to fall. And so the role of rich women becomes, essentially, that of buttressing rich men.

From this buttressing and sheltering springs an intolerance for conflict, for the harsh give-and-take that characterizes most families. A silken silence prevails, a nearly superhuman attempt to agree on every issue. This is the example provided for the children, who are at the same time secretly or openly competing for affection and favor. Emotional inhibition does not really quell raging emotional needs, which are seldom satisfied in families that value appearances highly. And since there can be no open conflict, no channels are carved out for carrying off animosity. Everything must go underground. This is a recipe for an explosion.

Explosions don't wreck most families. At worst, they cause hurt feelings and temporary alienation. But where there are no channels for the resolution of conflict, an explosion leaves nothing but desolation behind it. No one knows how to proceed.

In addition, explosions in rich families may cause a widespread tremor. Employees may be laid off, elaborate households may be dismembered because of a purely personal falling-out. The rich family supports a large number of dependents: domestics, poor relations, down-at-heel friends, the managers of charitable foundations and their grantees, enormous business ventures with their scaled layers of managers and employees, and a huge retinue of legal and financial advisers. All these people tremble when the family that supports them disagrees. This is a strong inducement to contrived peace.

But to preserve a contrived peace, some people will be permanently silenced. And since the point of view of women is generally less acceptable than the point of view of men, it will be women, in rich families, who are silenced for the sake of peace.

This leads to a good deal of distance between the women in such families. Young girls, like young boys, usually express some degree of rebellion. However, there is no way to express such a rebellion inside such a family without causing the tinkling of crystal chandeliers, which sounds too much like tears. And so the rebellious girl will never find an ally to moderate or encourage her in mother, sister, grandmother, or aunt. They have subscribed to a system that supports them in comfort, and so the system cannot be questioned. The rebel must learn silence or leave.

Rich families shed, in each generation, their most passionate and outspoken members. In the shedding, the family loses the possibility of renewal, of change. Safety is gained, but a safety that is rigid and judgmental. And the price, for the mothers, is terrible: to sacrifice their brightest, most articulate children to the dynasty.

So around the main fire of the wealthy family one usually sees the little winking campfires of the cast-out relatives. Lacking in skills, these relatives may spend their lives on the fringes of poverty, dependent on an occasional check from home. Often they retain emotional ties with the main fire, strengthened by unresolved conflicts; but they will never thrive either within its glow or in outer darkness. Some of these cast-out souls are women.

For no matter how well paid we are for our compliance, in the end, we do not inherit equally. Most rich families work on the English system and favor male heirs. There's an assumption that the women will marry well and be taken care of for life; there's an assumption that the men will do the work of the world, or of the family, and should be adequately compensated for it. When the will is read, the women inherit houses, furniture, and jewels; the men inherit cash, stocks, and securities. Yet the same commandments that rule out conspicuous behavior prevent rich women from fighting for their inheritance. Instead, we learn early to accept, to be grateful for what we are given. The slave mentality abounds in the palaces of the rich, even when the slave is decked in precious attire. We are dependent, after all, on the fickle goodwill of those who will never proclaim us their heirs.

What a fruitless arrangement this is for families, as well as for the society as a whole, may be seen in the absence of wealthy women from positions of power and influence. Without strong women models and allies, we sink into silence. Bribed by material comfort, stifled by guilt, we are not strong leaders, strong mothers, or strong friends. We are alone. And often, we are lost.

For what personal ethic can transcend, or transform, the ethic of the men in our lives? What sense of self-justification can grow out of a sheltered, private, silenced life?

A fine sense of decorum often prevents us from cherishing friendships with women, friendships that are often untidy, provocative, and intimate. The same sense of decorum makes us hesitate to join groups that may also contain unruly elements. Our good looks and fine clothes are separating devices as well; our smooth, sophisticated deportment doesn't encourage intimacies. And so the most envied women in this country today are probably the loneliest, the least effective, the most angry and forlorn. Yet we have everything. How do we dare to complain?

"Everything" is largely material. It's the charge cards, the jewelry, the clothes. We are not taught skills, self-discipline, or self-nurturing; we are left, by and large, to fend for ourselves inside prohibitions that discourage us from experimenting. And if we are unable to persuade or force our daughters to follow our example, we will lose them, in the end. And in the end, we may find ourselves totally dependent on our male relatives, for friendship, status, affection, a role in life—and financial support. Such total dependence breeds self-distrust, bitterness, and fear.

It doesn't have to be this way. But in order to change, the women in a rich family must realize that its covenants are simply self-perpetuating prejudices: a prejudging of events and individuals so that no untoward thought or action will upset the family's ethic, which is, first and foremost, to preserve the status quo.

Young girls growing up isolated by wealth must find their allies, whether inside or outside the family. They must get themselves educated and prepared for careers, not at the Eastern establishments that are geared to perpetuating male leadership, but at schools and colleges that are sympathetic to the special fears and vulnerabilities of women. And they must rid themselves of their guilt and their compulsion to smooth the way for the heirs.

This is a large bill. But the releasing of energy and hope, for this small group of wealthy women, would have results, in the country at large, far out of proportion to our numbers. What a difference it would make, for example, if rich women contributed their wealth to the causes that benefit poor women rather than to the sanitized, elitist cultural organizations favored by their fathers, brothers, and financial advisers.

What a difference it would make to women running for political office if they could draw on the massive resources of rich women, as men political candidates have drawn on the rich for generations.

What a difference it would make if wealthy women, who hire so many professionals, made sure those professionals were women lawyers, doctors, bankers, and advisers.

What a difference it would make to women as a whole if we, who are so misperceived, became visible, actively involved in working out our destiny.

Wealthy men have always influenced the course of this nation's history. Wealthy women have, at best, worked behind the scenes. We share our loneliness, our sense of helplessness, and our alienation from the male establishment with all our sisters. Out of our loneliness and alienation, we can learn to transform the world around us, with a passion for equality that we learned, at close hand, from observing the passionate inequalities practiced by wealthy families.   [1986]

Understanding the Reading

1. What does Bingham mean when she says rich women are captives?
2. What is the responsibility of a rich woman to her family, especially to its males?
3. Why is conflict especially difficult in rich families?
4. Why are rich women "silenced" and lonely?
5. What effects would changing the lives of rich women have on society?

Suggestions for Responding

1. Most of us dream that being rich would make us happy; however, as Bingham points out,

wealth has disadvantages. What drawbacks, beyond those she describes, do you think you might face if you were a female or a male member of a very wealthy family?

2. What advantages does Soto's working-class life have over Bingham's upper-class life? ✦

37

The Working Mother as Fashion Victim

JODY KOLODZEY

New York fashion designer Eileen Fisher, whose $80 turtlenecks and $170 wraparound skirts have given her a net worth of more than $50 million, describes her morning routine to two writers from a business magazine:

> "Every morning, I have breakfast with my kids (Sasha, three, and Zachary, six)," she says. "Then I drop my son off at school and get to the office by nine a.m."

"It's a routine familiar to many women," the writers observe.

Yeah, but . . .

Two paragraphs later, we learn that Fisher has two full-time domestic servants.

"I don't cook, I don't shop," she tells the magazine, and the writers sympathize:

> The reason is universal, she says: "I like to be with my kids as much as I can so when I'm home, instead of cooking or cleaning, I like to be there for them with my full attention."

What mother wouldn't? But how many can afford to?

Among the rich and famous, the label "working mother" has become a fad, and those who wear it have deluded themselves into believing they are connecting with the masses. But as usually happens when something becomes fashionable, it gets priced out of the range of ordinary people. A woman may have kids and a job, but in order to fit the current media image of a "working mom," she needs a lot more than that.

Fisher has a doppelganger of sorts in makeup artist Bobbi Brown, who started out painting faces for New York fashion shows and now has her own line of cosmetics ($18 for a lipgloss at Nieman Marcus, as compared to $5 for Revlon at the Rite Aid). In an interview with Brown last year, *New York Times* reporter Carol Lawson played up the "working mom" angle:

> In a high gloss business, she resembles nothing so much as a harried working mother. And that may be part of her appeal: juggling work and family as the mother of two young sons, she connects with customers who are, like her, too busy to fuss with makeup.
>
> "Many women come up to me and say, 'I'm a working mom too,'" Ms. Brown said.

Brown doesn't have it quite as together as Fisher in the morning. (Then again, her company is worth only $30 million.) Lawson writes:

> Her day typically begins with taking one of her children to school (no time to take both) in a chauffeur-driven car before heading into Manhattan. She puts on her makeup in the back-seat.

Gee, that must be rough, all those sharp instruments near your eye in traffic and all. But I'm really wondering about that other kid. Does he ever make it to school? Will he grow up scarred from the experience of being left behind? Will he resent his brother, lamenting like Tommy Smothers that "Mom always liked you best"?

The article closes with Brown saying, "My idea of a good time is being home in my kitchen in big socks and making soup."

For most working parents, preparing meals isn't a luxury, it's reality.

I remember my own mother on weekday mornings, standing at the hall mirror with a mascara wand in one hand and a coffee cup in the other, periodically calling up the stairs to make sure we kids had roused ourselves; she had a job that started before school opened, so there was no diurnal bonding ritual around the breakfast table in our house. And nobody drove her to work or us to school; we walked or took the bus.

The point is that the rich are different.

Last month, the *New York Times* devoted an entire issue of its *Sunday Magazine* to "the joy and guilt of modern motherhood." In it, there were a full-page ad for—yes!—Eileen Fisher clothes and an article on how to "baby yourself" after delivery by wearing—yes again!—Bobbi Brown cosmetics. Brown's prescription, according to fashion writer Mary Tannen, is to "take two minutes first thing in the morning to put makeup on. The weeks after birth can be an emotional time, and it always helps to look as good as possible." Brown also advised the new mother to "enlist any help she could get."

Ah, the help she could get . . .

The most disturbing item in the issue was Lucinda Frank's article on the relationship between a white psychotherapist and her black nanny, an immigrant from an unnamed Caribbean island. The psychotherapist was the one depicted as the "working mother." This even though the nanny has three children of her own—two of whom are still living with relatives in the Caribbean because after working here for nine years, the nanny still can't afford to bring them to New York. Meanwhile, the psychotherapist and her financial-consultant husband have a second home in the Hamptons. But they are good to her, the nanny believes: They helped her get a green card and taught her to drive.

The true nature of the relationship surfaced when the nanny realized she was pregnant with her third child. She recalled her thought process:

> "What was I going to do? Send another child away? But how could I raise it in this country? And then I remembered it wasn't my decision alone."

It sounds as if she's referring to the baby's father. She's not. She means her employers.

When she told them, the financial consultant was morally outraged and wondered "what kind of message" her being "pregnant and not married" would send to his own children. It wasn't her lack of resources that bothered him; it was "bringing up a child without a father." When the nanny told him she could take care of the baby herself, he retorted: "You can't. And I'm not going to."

I guess that's one way to assuage your guilt about not paying your employees enough: Shift the emphasis from your business ethics to their personal morality. Then the problem isn't that

they can't afford to have families; the problem is that it's shameful for them to want to have families.

This sort of insensitivity to non-middle-class culture and values is one big reason working-class women never fully embraced feminism. Gender identity and gender roles are not constant across economic and social lines.

Poor women don't hire domestic workers, poor women *are* domestic workers.

Frank Lentricchia, a Duke University literary theorist, grew up in Utica, N.Y., where his mother labored on a General Electric assembly line, then came home and did the dishes. He once complained that "many American literary feminists can't tell the difference between Nancy Reagan and my mother: the difference between a woman of privilege, a 'lady,' and a working woman."

The new editor of *Cosmopolitan* can't tell the difference either. "I probably resemble [my readers] in most ways," Bonnie Fuller told the *New York Times* when she took over the reins from Helen Gurley Brown last year. Except that Fuller's salary is at least six digits, while the average *Cosmo* reader's income is around $40,000.

After Fuller's last pregnancy, it was "not practical" for her to take maternity leave, *Times* reporter Janny Scott informs us. "So, she took a couple of days off, then started working from home" (with the help of a household staff that includes a nanny, a uniformed baby nurse, and an editorial assistant). During Scott's interview, she sat at her kitchen table, nursing her baby while "wearing slim black pants [and] two-inch heels," and waxed philosophical about "working mother guilt."

Yes, despite their glamorous jobs, lofty incomes, and retinues of servants to do the child-rearing, these women still find time to complain about how hard they have it. And to expect empathy. In a cover story last year on the actresses and supermodels who comprise "The New Sexy Moms," *People Magazine* said:

> . . . every Hollywood mom finds that the toughest task of all is fitting the role of nurturing mother into a helter-skelter life of auditions, 14-hour days, long absences on far-flung locations and, when possible, a night on the town for old times' sake.

I keep wanting to yell, "What do they know about it?"

Well, I suppose they feel they have to identify themselves as working mothers because if they looked for sisterhood (or customers) simply by proclaiming themselves "working women," bona fide working-class women wouldn't buy it.

But just because they both have kids doesn't suddenly create parity between a privileged woman and a wage slave. Their jobs and their lifestyles, their concerns and the things they take for granted, remain forever outside one another's ken.

With Mother's Day upon us, I realize that my mother, Elizabeth Kolodzey, and Lentricchia's aren't whom Americans like to picture when they hear the words "working mom." They prefer Eileen Fisher and Bobbi Brown and Niki Taylor on the cover of *People*.

Sure, it's just the latest fashion.

Too bad it isn't one-size-fits-all.   [1998]

Understanding the Reading

1. Why does Kolodzey think Eileen Fisher is not a representative working mother?
2. Answer the same question for Bobbi Brown.
3. Describe the relationship between Lucinda Frank and her Black nanny.
4. What was Bonnie Fuller's experience with pregnancy?
5. What is Kolodzey's attitude toward the glamorous mothers she describes?

Suggestions for Responding

1. All of us have had cross-class experiences: Your family has had a cleaning lady or was one for a well-to-do household, for instance, or you have a friend from a different socioeconomic class. Write an essay considering such an experience and reflect on the impact of class difference in the encounter(s). ✦

38

To Be Black, Gifted, and Alone

BEBE MOORE CAMPBELL

By the time Leanita McClain was 32, the black journalist had won the Peter Lisagor Award from the Headline Club (the Chicago Chapter of Sigma Delta Chi, the national journalism honorary fraternity); the 1983 Kizzy Award for outstanding black women role models; and top honors from the Chicago Association of Black Journalists for commentary. She was also the first black to become a member of the *Chicago Tribune*'s editorial board in that newspaper's 137-year history: a prestigious position that carried with it a salary of approximately $50,000 and the opportunity to influence the attitudes of millions of people. In March 1984, McClain was selected by *Glamour* magazine as one of the ten most outstanding working women in America.

Two months later, on the evening of May 29, 1984—Memorial Day—McClain killed herself.

To many observers, McClain's accomplishments seemed even more astounding because she had grown up in a housing project in Chicago's predominantly black south side, an area known for gang warfare, poverty, and despair. Her success had netted her a posh address in the city's predominantly white, gentrified north side, but McClain wasn't entirely comfortable in her new setting. In October 1980, in *Newsweek*'s "My Turn" column, she wrote, "It is impossible for me to forget where I came from as long as I am prey to the jive hustler who does not hesitate to exploit my childhood friendship. I am reminded, too, when I go back to the old neighborhood in fear—and have my purse snatched—and when I sit down to a business lunch and have an old classmate wait on my table. I recall the girl I played dolls with who now rears five children on welfare, the boy from church who is in prison for murder, the pal found dead of a drug overdose in the alley where we once played tag. . . . Sometimes when I wait at the bus stop with my attaché case, I meet my aunt getting off the bus with other cleaning ladies on their way to do my neighbors' floors."

McClain realized that she couldn't go home again. Yet, despite her fair skin and sandy hair, despite her credentials and awards, she didn't have full access to her new world either. "I . . . have fulfilled the entry requirements of the American middle class, yet I am left, at times, feeling unwelcomed and stereotyped," she wrote.

She confided to a friend that she feared being a token on her job, and she worked at a frenzied pace to prove her competence.

Her dress-for-success uniform belied the fact that her emotional underpinnings had been created on the other side of town. "She got thrown into a white world and was expected to act the part," says a friend. "She was often fighting and grappling with her real self. She couldn't even write what she wanted. She had to bottle up her rage."

While McClain the journalist scaled corporate heights, her private life was conflicted, and her personal problems were exacerbated by her rapid professional rise. "She was sort of guilty about her success," says Monroe Anderson, a columnist and reporter for the *Chicago Tribune* and a close friend of McClain's. "Her parents still lived in the ghetto. Their problems were her problems."

But she had problems of her own as well. Her eight-year marriage to Clarence Page ended in 1982. Page, a journalist who has since been named to replace McClain on the *Tribune*'s editorial board, says the divorce was McClain's idea. "She began to express dissatisfaction with the marriage; she wanted love to come and hit her out of the blue. I told her, 'You're looking for something that's not there.'"

McClain found that her success could be intimidating. Her new-world expectations demanded that a mate match or better her salary and status. She dated a younger man, Keenan Michael Coleman, a computer salesman; their affair was stormy, yet McClain, desiring marriage, held on. She purchased an expensive house in Chicago's Hyde Park section, only to put it back on the market 24 hours later when her relationship dissolved.

As her personal desires eluded her and the values of her old and new worlds collided, close friends witnessed spells of hysterical crying, brooding silence, and mounting depression. She began stockpiling the potent antidepressant amitriptyline prescribed by her physician. For all of her accoutrements of professional success, McClain was as full of despair as any ghetto dweller.

On the night of what would have been her tenth wedding anniversary, McClain swallowed a huge overdose of amitriptyline and left both worlds behind.

It is rare for a black woman to ascend to the professional heights that McClain attained. Black women in corporate America are still scarce: According to the Bureau of Labor Statistics report for 1984, among the classification "executive, administrative, managerial, and professional specialty," there were only 1,474,000 black women, 5.9 percent of the total, as opposed to 22,250,000 white women, 91 percent of the total number of working women in this category. Understandably, then, the loss of McClain's influence, power, and her ability to be a role model is perceived by some blacks as a group loss. "It hurt me to see a black woman who's achieved so much take it all away from us," says Paulette, a 38-year-old television producer in Los Angeles. Paulette is one of a small random sampling of black female executives—most working in upper middle management positions for large corporations and earning between $40,000 and $80,000 annually—who agreed to talk to SAVVY under a cloak of anonymity. These women admit that a black woman's climb to corporate power is at least as arduous as survival in the ghetto: They see a part of themselves in Leanita McClain's life, if not in her death.

Stress is the common experience these women all share. Not the Alka Seltzer stress of fighting deadlines and office politics while maintaining homes and families, this stress is from the oppressive combination of racism, sexism, and professional competition that separates black women not only from their white colleagues, but also insidiously pits them against their black male professional counterparts. The overload on black executive women often results in their pulling away from a cultural identity that includes family and old friends. Corporate racism, they expected. What was unexpected was the various degrees of culture shock, isolation, and alienation that black women experience as they attempt to acclimate professionally and to assimilate their culturally distinct selves into organizations that reward uniformity.

"I met Leanita a month or so before she died," says the director of a large, midwestern state agency. "We were both receiving the same award. When she sat down, I took one look at her and said to myself, 'The sister has problems.' I noticed it because I've been there before. . . . It was hard for me to believe that she committed suicide just because of job stress. When you're down there competing with white folks, you go through any number of changes. We've been brought up to expect that."

No one ever imagined the time when blacks would be insiders. Although Martin Luther King dreamed aloud of that day and Malcolm X railed against it, and thousands of blacks and whites marched, fought, and died to prevent or bring the moment closer, no one fully understood what overcoming the barriers of discrimination would mean for people who had been outsiders for centuries. Freedom, yes. But freedom to do what? To be whom?

When Leanita McClain began working for the *Chicago Tribune* in 1973, she was part of the first generation of corporate blacks that affirmative action[1] helped to create. Although it may have appeared that McClain easily glided from one world into another, her transition, like that of other black female executives, was far from smooth.

"I was very uneasy around whites when I first entered the corporation," says Yolanda, 35, a human resource manager for a large hair-care firm in New York City. "I come from a middle-class family. My father is a lawyer, and my mother is a teacher. My grandparents went to college. We were far from poor, yet I still grew up in a black world. My childhood was spent in a middle-class section of Los Angeles. I went to all-black schools from elementary school through college."

In 1970, Yolanda began her career as one of two blacks out of 40 people in a Sears management training program in Los Angeles. "Coming into big business, I had culture shock, but I didn't know it," Yolanda explains. "The sixties had just ended," she recalls, "and I was wearing my hair in a six-inch Afro. My consciousness was as high as my hair. One evening, my manager, a white man, took me aside and told me to wear jeans and a T-shirt to work the next day, because I'd be on the loading docks. Now I realize that working there was standard procedure, but I can remember wondering then if he was going to give me menial work to do because I'm black."

What some people would term Yolanda's "hypersensitivity" is a cultural orientation that most American blacks share and find difficult to shed: a tendency to be preoccupied with race and racism.

"Preoccupation with race can be very debilitating," says Ron Brown, Ph.D., a psychologist whose firm, Banks and Brown, counsels white and black managers from Fortune 500 companies on racial attitudes. "Back in the late sixties, it was obvious that black managers were having difficulty adjusting to the cues and norms of the corporate environment. Some of them were starting from ground zero. Blacks are trying to learn an ingrown system without coaching and mentoring. They can do it, but it takes longer. And some are paying a heavy price in stress."

Even after ten successful years in the corporate world, Yolanda still struggles with some degree of cultural unease. "I'm still uncomfortable around whites in social situations," she says. "If I have to go to cocktail parties with whites, I don't feel completely at ease. We're all uncomfortable. When we're away from the job, the differences between us appear greater."

Many black executive women claim that in addition to the usual conformity that is required of all corporate professionals, if they want to succeed, they must make the whites around them feel comfortable, a difficult feat. Black women consciously choose their speech, their laughter, their walk, their mode of dress and car. They trim and straighten their hair, lest kinky curls or corn-rows set them apart. At work, they try not to congregate in groups of more than two, so that white colleagues will not suspect a "plot."

McClain, fair and freckled as she was, couldn't blend in with her white co-workers even by changing her style. In *Newsweek* she declared, "I am painfully aware, that even with my off-white trappings, I am prejudged by my color. . . ." Although white women may chafe under corporate dress codes, behavioral constraints, and sexism, they don't have the additional burden of compromising their cultural selves. If black women, however, truly relinquish their cultural selves, they are unable to function in the old world that still claims them. They learn to wear a mask.

"Each day, when I get into my car, I always begin the ride to work by turning on a black radio station so that it blares," says Karen, 35, a Harvard MBA who works for an Atlanta-based telecommunications corporation. "I boogey all the way down the highway. A few blocks from my job, I turn the music down and stop shaking my shoulders. When my building comes into view, I turn the music off, because I know the curtain is about to go up."

"I try hard not to be what they expect," says Estelle, 31, a fair-skinned black woman who is the vice president of the business division of a large bank in Los Angeles. "I don't misconjugate verbs. I don't wear a natural. . . . It probably helps that I'm not real dark-skinned. That's sad, but I know that kind of thing influences them."

Regardless of how black executive women may want to express themselves—and not all feel a conflict—they are pragmatic. Karen concludes, "The choice to enter the corporation is a choice to conform. Loudness, street talking, afros, flashy cars—that's not what white folks buy into. I've given up some self-expression. That trade-off for the salary is to play by the rules."

McClain knew the rules well. She came to work dressed for success and she wore her light brown hair in a straightened style. She lunched with white co-workers. She was articulate and pleasant. "Most whites thought Leanita was wonderful," says Monroe Anderson. "She was an actress around them."

As black executive women move up, they become isolated from those in their old world. McClain's parents and her two sisters were unaware of the pressures she was under. "Her sisters had no idea what bad shape she was in," one co-worker said. "She wasn't confiding in them." Many black executive women have few people to confide in. As they move up the corporate ladder they also become isolated from other blacks who work in lower positions in the same company.

"Not long ago, my division laid off several hundred people," says the 36-year-old director

of career development for minorities at a New York television network. "Two of my closest friends were let go. There was nothing that I could have done to prevent it. I was hurting with them. Once they left, they told the other blacks in the company not to talk to me because I was management. I was very, very hurt. Blacks began to stay away from me. What could I do? I couldn't go to my boss about it. I felt as though I'd been ripped apart."

Some accept the isolation as par for the course. "The higher up you move, the more you'll be isolated," says the Los Angeles banker matter-of-factly. "I have less in common with those people who used to be my friends. I have more in common with those of the same class or income, be they black or white."

If some black women are pragmatic about assimilation, many are pained by the thought of "losing their blackness" and strive to maintain cultural ties. For Linda, a human resources manager for a fast-food chain headquartered outside of Chicago, the decision to remain in the black south side brings turmoil. "I firmly believe, although it's being chipped away, that if blacks don't live in the black community, there will be no role models for inner-city kids."

But Linda's voice is weary as she talks about the disadvantages. "I have a 35-mile one-way commute. Obviously, property values are much lower. And two company cars have been stolen from in front of my house. One was right in the driveway.

"I've been to the homes of whites I work with who live in the suburbs; I haven't invited them to mine."

Leanita McClain had felt guilty about moving away from her old friends; she felt awkward about fitting the militant blacks' stereotype of a "sell out." "I am not comfortably middle class," she wrote. "I am uncomfortably middle class."

Not assimilating into the corporate mold, which includes an acceptable lifestyle away from the job, isn't overlooked by companies. "Eventually, when upper management considers someone who maintains a visibly black lifestyle for increased responsibility, she might be ruled out as not being a 'good fit,'" says Ron Brown.

If being alienated from blacks brings stress, at the same time there are new pressures from those in the old world who view the executive woman as having made it. Black organizations demand time and money, as do friends and family. Some black executives find themselves alternately being used and abused as they are made to pay for their success. "I am a member of the black middle class who has had it with being patted on the head by white hands and slapped in the face by black hands," wrote McClain.

Isolated from blacks, black executive women often are alienated from the whites with whom they are supposed to assimilate. "When I was placed in a fast-track development program, I was really estranged from my white co-workers," says Cora, 33, who manages 105 people in a Chicago communications company. "I felt that they were all watching me. They had all worked their way up to management. I came in off the street into a management position. They knew I'd been tapped to move up. They were waiting for me to fall on my face. They resented me because I was black, female, young, and headed to be a company executive."

"I have to interpret what my white managers are saying two and a half times," says Yolanda, the hair-care manager. "They filter out information because I'm a black woman."

McClain clearly questioned the ties that bound her to some of her white peers. She wrote, "Some of my 'liberal' white acquaintances hint that I am a freak, that my success is less a matter of talent than of luck and affirmative action. I may live among them, but it is difficult to live with them."

For some blacks, the mask they wear begins to crack under the pressure as their rage bubbles to the surface. When Chicago Mayor Harold Washington, a black man, was running for office, Chicago became a hate-filled city. In a series of columns, McClain vented her feelings of anger and disillusionment, but it was in *The Washington Post* that her article, "How Chicago Taught Me to Hate Whites," potently articulated the rage that she felt as the mayoral campaign progressed to what she called "a race war." Her anger was directed toward whites who spoke disparagingly of "the blacks." "'The blacks,'" McClain wrote. "It would make me feel like machine-gunning every white face on the bus."

McClain could powerfully externalize her fury, but most black women lack that access to public confrontation. They turn their rage inward. Nearly all of the women interviewed by SAVVY show a series of disturbing symptoms: hair loss, nervous exhaustion, chronic stomach pains, insomnia, and depression. "I thought I had high blood pressure," says the Los Angeles television producer. "My heart was beating fast and I had shortness of breath. I had migraines. The physician couldn't find anything wrong. Finally I went to a therapist and we discussed my negative feelings about my job and career. That gave me some relief."

"I see a high rate of alcoholism and cocaine and marijuana abuse. Lots of tranquilizers," says Audrey B. Chapman, a therapist and human relations trainer in Washington, D.C., who specializes in stress management seminars for female professionals. "The women exhibit a lot of psychosomatic pain in their backs and necks. They have severe menstrual cramps. The pain isn't so much physical as it is mental," says Chapman. "The stress leads to the real killers of black women—hypertension, diabetes, and strokes."

As prevalent as racism is, many black executive women declare that, at times, they are aware of discrimination because of gender even more than of race.

According to findings from Black Values in the American Workplace, a conference held in March 1984, funded by the Xerox Corporation and organized by John L. Jones, that company's director of affirmative action, sexism is a major problem for black executive women.

"I was in the hall talking with one of the big bosses, an older white guy," says the Los Angeles television producer. "As I turned to leave, he swatted me on my behind with a rolled-up newspaper. I was in a state of shock. If anybody ever does that to me again, I swear, I'll grab him by his collar and throw him up against a wall."

Although white males see them as fair game, black women complain that black males are most often the perpetrators of sexist behavior. "Most of my trouble came from black men," says the agency head from Illinois. "They had problems because I was a firm manager. I fired all of them eventually because they did a poor job. One of the men I let go came to me and said, 'Your problem is that you're just evil.' I told him,

'Evil is what your girlfriend or woman may be. I'm efficient. And your ass is gone.' He couldn't believe that a woman would let him go."

If a black woman's managerial status is threatening to the black men with whom she works, so it is that her success may inhibit or spoil her personal relationships. No other group is as likely to be divorced: In 1983, according to the Census Bureau's report of marital status and living arrangements, 297 black women were divorced per 1,000 marriages—over twice the rate as for white women. The divorce rate for black women is 10 percent higher for those with college degrees, 15 percent higher with one year of graduate school, and 19 percent higher for those with two years of graduate school.

Among the never-married, the search for a "suitable" mate is frustrating. According to the 1980 Census figures, there are nearly 1.5 million more black females than males: the largest difference in male/female ratio of any racial group in the country. And, for many years, there have been more college-educated black females than males. According to Joyce Payne, director, Office for the Advancement of Public Black Colleges, between 1976 and 1981, the number of black women awarded professional degrees increased by 71 percent; there was a 12 percent decline for black males. The single women interviewed all told stories of failed relationships with professional black males. These women claim that the male/female ratio allows men to "romp"; they add that black professional men are intimidated by the success of the women.

"I've had long-term relationships that have ended, and the next thing I knew, my ex-boyfriend was dating a secretary," says the midwestern agency director. "I think that black professional women must be too honest. I was going with a man who headed a local agency and who was trying to go into business for himself. He had some good ideas, but he had some dumb ones, too. Maybe I should have just pretended that everything he said was wonderful. Also, he had this irritating habit. Whenever he'd come to my office, he'd close the door, sit in my chair, put his feet up on my desk, and say, 'Now, if I were the boss, this is how I'd run this agency.'"

"In the old days, black women who were professionals married pullman porters and postal workers, the only jobs most black men could get," says Chapman. "What today's women expect is less available." Still the hunt for the elusive black male professional continues.

Toward the end of her life, Leanita McClain's loneliness was perhaps a heavier burden than her professional struggles. The combination was, for her, unbearable.

"It wasn't a question of either her professional problems or her personal ones causing her the most difficulty," says Monroe Anderson, the *Tribune* reporter. "Her focus was on her personal life. What happened was that with her rapid success and her still not being happy, the personal came into focus. It's difficult for a black woman to make it without a personal relationship. Black women have to battle racism and sexism and then come home to loneliness, or again do battle. For the majority of professional black women, it's not good."

Yet, most black executive women admit that their brothers' quest for professional ascendancy is far more frustrating than their own. "Black men have a harder time," says one executive black woman, echoing most others, "because white males are intimidated by them."

The progress of black men is tied to the progress of black women. Black women cannot contribute the best of their talents to the corporation if they are placed in the position of being an affirmative action buffer zone, fulfilling federal government standards at the expense of professional opportunity for black men. Until black women develop strategies to overcome many of their own self-inflicted problems, they will be ensnared by their own success, forging ahead while straining under a staggering emotional load.

Leanita McClain finally laid her burden down and escaped the narrow alley located between pain and desire to another place. Her unanswered question continues to haunt her sisters.

"I have made it, but where?"   [1984]

Terms

1. AFFIRMATIVE ACTION: A federal program requiring businesses to seek out qualified employees from traditionally excluded and underrepresented groups.

Understanding the Reading

1. What does Campbell mean when she says, "McClain realized that she couldn't go home again"?
2. What causes stress for McClain and other Black women executives?
3. Why would differences between Blacks and Whites appear greater away from the job?
4. According to the article, what is the cultural self that Black corporate women must relinquish? What does losing their Blackness mean?
5. Why are relationships between successful Black women and Black men so problematic?

Suggestion for Responding

1. Describe how some facet of your heritage (in the broadest sense) put you into a double bind because of the expectations of two different groups. How did the tension make you feel, and how did you respond? ✦

39

Keeping Close to Home: Class and Education

BELL HOOKS

We are both awake in the almost dark of 5 A.M. Everyone else is sound asleep. Mama asks the usual questions. Telling me to look around, make sure I have everything, scolding me because I am uncertain about the actual time the bus arrives. By 5:30 we are waiting outside the closed station. Alone together, we have a chance to really talk. Mama begins. Angry with her children, especially the ones who whisper behind her back, she says bitterly, "Your childhood could not have been that bad. You were fed and clothed. You did not have to do without—that's more than a lot of folks have and I just can't stand the way y'all go on." The hurt in her voice saddens me. I have always wanted to protect mama from hurt, to ease her burdens. Now I am

part of what troubles. Confronting me, she says accusingly, "It's not just the other children. You talk too much about the past. You don't just listen." And I do talk. Worse, I write about it.

Mama has always come to each of her children seeking different responses. With me she expresses the disappointment, hurt, and anger of betrayal: anger that her children are so critical, that we can't even have the sense to like the presents she sends. She says, "From now on there will be no presents. I'll just stick some money in a little envelope the way the rest of you do. Nobody wants criticism. Everybody can criticize me but I am supposed to say nothing." When I try to talk, my voice sounds like a twelve year old. When I try to talk, she speaks louder, interrupting me, even though she has said repeatedly, "Explain it to me, this talk about the past." I struggle to return to my thirty-five year old self so that she will know by the sound of my voice that we are two women talking together. It is only when I state firmly in my very adult voice, "Mama, you are not listening," that she becomes quiet. She waits. Now that I have her attention, I fear that my explanations will be lame, inadequate. "Mama," I begin, "people usually go to therapy because they feel hurt inside, because they have pain that will not stop, like a wound that continually breaks open, that does not heal. And often these hurts, that pain has to do with things that have happened in the past, sometimes in childhood, often in childhood, or things that we believe happened." She wants to know, "What hurts, what hurts are you talking about?" "Mom, I can't answer that. I can't speak for all of us, the hurts are different for everybody. But the point is you try to make the hurt better, to heal it, by understanding how it came to be. And I know you feel mad when we say something happened or hurt that you don't remember being that way, but the past isn't like that, we don't have the same memory of it. We remember things differently. You know that. And sometimes folk feel hurt about stuff and you just don't know or didn't realize it, and they need to talk about it. Surely you understand the need to talk about it."

Our conversation is interrupted by the sight of my uncle walking across the park toward us. We stop to watch him. He is on his way to work dressed in a familiar blue suit. They look alike, these two who rarely discuss the past. This interruption makes me think about life in a small town. You always see someone you know. Interruptions, intrusions are part of daily life. Privacy is difficult to maintain. We leave our private space in the car to greet him. After the hug and kiss he has given me every year since I was born, they talk about the day's funerals. In the distance the bus approaches. He walks away knowing that they will see each other later. Just before I board the bus I turn, staring into my mother's face. I am momentarily back in time, seeing myself eighteen years ago, at this same bus s   ce, continually tu   returned to col   ok me away h   g was as painf   ment away make   n intensifies dista   onal.

To a southern black   class background who had neve   bus, who had never stepped on an   who had never travelled by plane, leaving u   om-fortable confines of a small town Kentucky life to attend Stanford University was not just frightening, it was utterly painful. My parents had not been delighted that I had been accepted and adamantly opposed my going so far from home. At the time, I did not see their opposition as an expression of their fear that they would lose me forever. Like many working-class folks, they feared what college education might do to their children's minds even as they unenthusiastically acknowledged its importance. They did not understand why I could not attend a college nearby, an all-black college. To them, any college would do. I would graduate, become a school teacher, make a decent living and a good marriage. And even though they reluctantly and skeptically supported my educational endeavors, they also subjected them to constant harsh and bitter critique. It is difficult for me to talk about my parents and their impact on me because they have always felt wary, ambivalent, mistrusting of my intellectual aspirations even as they have been caring and supportive. I want to speak about these contradictions because sorting through them, seeking resolution and reconciliation has been important to me both as it affects my development as a writer, my effort to be fully self-realized, and my longing to remain close to the family and community that provided the groundwork for much of my thinking, writing, and being.

Studying at Stanford, I began to think seriously about class differences. To be materially underprivileged at a university where most folks (with the exception of workers) are materially privileged provokes such thought. Class differences were boundaries no one wanted to face or talk about. It was easier to downplay them, to act as though we were all from privileged backgrounds, to work around them, to confront them privately in the solitude of one's room, or to pretend that just being chosen to study at such an institution meant that those of us who did not come from privilege were already in transition toward privilege. To not long for such transition marked one as rebellious, as unlikely to succeed. It was a kind of treason not to believe that it was better to be identified with the world of material privilege than with the world of the working class, the poor. No wonder our working-class parents from poor backgrounds feared our entry into such a world, intuiting perhaps that we might learn to be ashamed of where we had come from, that we might never return home, or come back only to lord it over them.

Though I hung with students who were supposedly radical and chic, we did not discuss class. I talked to no one about the sources of my shame, how it hurt me to witness the contempt shown the brown-skinned Filipina maids who cleaned our rooms, or later my concern about the $100 a month I paid for a room off-campus which was more than half of what my parents paid for rent. I talked to no one about my efforts to save money, to send a little something home. Yet these class realities separated me from fellow students. We were moving in different directions. I did not intend to forget my class background or alter my class allegiance. And even though I received an education designed to provide me with a bourgeois sensibility, passive acquiescence was not my only option. I knew that I could resist. I could rebel. I could shape the direction and focus of the various forms of knowledge available to me. Even though I sometimes envied and longed for greater material advantages (particularly at vacation times when I would be one of few if any students remaining in the dormitory because there was no money for travel), I did not share the sensibility and values of my peers. That was important—class was not just about money; it was about values which showed and determined behavior. While I often needed more money, I never needed a new set of beliefs and values. For example, I was profoundly shocked and disturbed when peers would talk about their parents without respect, or would even say that they hated their parents. This was especially troubling to me when it seemed that these parents were caring and concerned. It was often explained to me that such hatred was "healthy and normal." To my white, middle-class California roommate, I explained the way we were taught to value our parents and their care, to understand that they were not obligated to give us care. She would always shake her head, laughing all the while, and say, "Missy, you will learn that it's different here, that we think differently." She was right. Soon, I lived alone, like the one Mormon student who kept to himself as he made a concentrated effort to remain true to his religious beliefs and values. Later in graduate school I found that classmates believed "lower class" people had no beliefs and values. I was silent in such discussions, disgusted by their ignorance.

Carol Stack's anthropological study, *All Our Kin,* was one of the first books I read which confirmed my experiential understanding that within black culture (especially among the working class and poor, particularly in southern states), a value system emerged that was counter-hegemonic, that challenged notions of individualism and private property so important to the maintenance of white-supremacist, capitalist patriarchy. Black folk created in marginal spaces a world of community and collectivity where resources were shared. In the preface to *Feminist Theory: from margin to center,* I talked about how the point of difference, this marginality can be the space for the formation of an oppositional world view. That world view must be articulated, named if it is to provide a sustained blueprint for change. Unfortunately, there has existed no consistent framework for such naming. Consequently both the experience of this difference and documentation of it (when it occurs) gradually lose presence and meaning.

Much of what Stack documented about the "culture of poverty," for example, would not describe interactions among most black poor today irrespective of geographical setting. Since the black people she described did not acknowledge (if they recognized it in theoretical terms) the oppositional value of their world view, apparently seeing it more as a survival strategy determined less by conscious efforts to oppose oppressive race and class biases than by circumstance, they did not attempt to establish a framework to transmit their beliefs and values from generation to generation. When circumstances changed, values altered. Efforts to assimilate the values and beliefs of privileged white people, presented through media like television, undermine and destroy potential structures of opposition.

Increasingly, young black people are encouraged by the dominant culture (and by those black people who internalize the values of this hegemony) to believe that assimilation is the only possible way to survive, to succeed. Without the framework of an organized civil rights or black resistance struggle, individual and collective efforts at black liberation that focus on the primacy of self-definition and self-determination often go unrecognized. It is crucial that those among us who resist and rebel, who survive and succeed, speak openly and honestly about our lives and the nature of our personal struggles, the means by which we resolve and reconcile contradictions. This is no easy task. Within the educational institutions where we learn to develop and strengthen our writing and analytical skills, we also learn to think, write, and talk in a manner that shifts attention away from personal experience. Yet if we are to reach our people and all people, if we are to remain connected (especially those of us whose familial backgrounds are poor and working-class), we must understand that the telling of one's personal story provides a meaningful example, a way for folks to identify and connect.

Combining personal with critical analysis and theoretical perspectives can engage listeners who might otherwise feel estranged, alienated. To speak simply with language that is accessible to as many folks as possible is also important. Speaking about one's personal experience or speaking with simple language is often considered by academics and/or intellectuals (irrespective of their political inclinations) to be a sign of intellectual weakness or even anti-intellectualism. Lately, when I speak, I do not stand in place—reading my paper, making little or no eye contact with audiences—but instead make eye contact, talk extemporaneously, digress, and address the audience directly. I have been told that people assume I am not prepared, that I am anti-intellectual, unprofessional (a concept that has everything to do with class as it determines actions and behavior), or that I am reinforcing the stereotype of black people as non-theoretical and gutsy.

Such criticism was raised recently by fellow feminist scholars after a talk I gave at Northwestern University at a conference on "Gender, Culture, Politics" to an audience that was mainly students and academics. I deliberately chose to speak in a very basic way, thinking especially about the few community folks who had come to hear me. Weeks later, Kum-Kum Sangari, a fellow participant who had shared with me what was said when I was no longer present, and I engaged in quite rigorous critical dialogue about the way my presentation had been perceived primarily by privileged white female academics. She was concerned that I not mask my knowledge of theory, that I not appear anti-intellectual. Her critique compelled me to articulate concerns that I am often silent about with colleagues. I spoke about class allegiance and revolutionary commitments, explaining that it was disturbing to me that intellectual radicals who speak about transforming society, ending the domination of race, sex, class, cannot break with behavior patterns that reinforce and perpetuate domination, or continue to use as their sole reference point how we might be or are perceived by those who dominate, whether or not we gain their acceptance and approval.

This is a primary contradiction which raises the issue of whether or not the academic setting is a place where one can be truly radical or subversive. Concurrently, the use of a language and style of presentation that alienates most folks who are not also academically trained reinforces the notion that the academic world is separate from real life, that everyday world where we constantly adjust our language and behavior to meet diverse needs. The academic setting is separate only when we work to make it so. It is a false dichotomy which suggests that academics and/or intellectuals can only speak to one another, that we cannot hope to speak with the masses. What is true is that we make choices, that we choose our audiences, that we choose voices to hear and voices to silence. If I do not speak in a language that can be understood, then there is little chance for dialogue. This issue of language and behavior is a central contradiction all radical intellectuals, particularly those who are members of oppressed groups, must continually confront and work to resolve. One of the clear and present dangers that exist when we move outside our class of origin, our collective ethnic experience, and enter hierarchical institutions which daily reinforce domination by race, sex, and class, is that we gradually assume a mindset similar to those who dominate and oppress, that we lose critical consciousness because it is not reinforced or affirmed by the environment. We must be ever vigilant. It is important that we know who we are speaking to, who we most want to hear us, who we most long to move, motivate, and touch with our words.

When I first came to New Haven to teach at Yale, I was truly surprised by the marked class divisions between black folks—students and professors—who identify with Yale and those black folks who work at Yale or in surrounding communities. Style of dress and self-presentation are most often the central markers of one's position. I soon learned that the black folks who spoke on the street were likely to be part of the black community and those who carefully shifted their glance were likely to be associated with Yale. Walking with a black female colleague one day, I spoke to practically every black person in sight (a gesture which reflects my upbringing), an action which disturbed my companion. Since I addressed black folk who were clearly not associated with Yale, she wanted to know whether or not I knew them. That was funny to me. "Of course not," I answered. Yet when I thought about it seriously, I realized that in a deep way, *I* knew them for they, and not my companion or most of my colleagues at Yale, resemble my family. Later that year, in a black women's support group I started for undergraduates, students from poor backgrounds spoke about the shame they sometimes feel when faced with the reality of their connection to working-class and poor black people. One student confessed that her father is a street person, addicted to drugs, someone who begs from passersby. She, like other Yale students, turns away from street people often, sometimes showing anger or contempt; she hasn't wanted anyone to know that she was related to this kind of person. She struggles with this, wanting to find a way to acknowledge and affirm this reality, to claim this connection. The group asked me and one another what we do to remain connected, to honor the bonds we have with working-class and poor people even as our class experience alters.

Maintaining connections with family and community across class boundaries demands more than just summary recall of where one's roots are, where one comes from. It requires knowing, naming, and being ever-mindful of those aspects of one's past that have enabled and do enable one's self-development in the present, that sustain and support, that enrich. One must also honestly confront barriers that do exist, aspects of that past that do diminish. My parents' ambivalence about my love for reading led to intense conflict. They (especially my mother) would work to ensure that I had access to books, but would threaten to burn the books or throw them away if I did not conform to other expectations. Or they would insist that reading too much would drive me insane. Their ambivalence nurtured in me a like uncertainty about the value and significance of intellectual endeavor which took years for me to unlearn. While this aspect of our class reality was one that wounded and diminished, their vigilant insistence that being smart did not make me a "better" or "superior" person (which often got on my nerves because I think I wanted to have that sense that it did indeed set me apart, make me better) made a profound impression. From them I learned to value and respect various skills and talents folk might have, not just to value people who read books and talk about ideas. They and my grandparents might say about somebody, "Now he don't read nor write a lick, but he can tell a story," or as my grandmother would say, "call out the hell in words."

Empty romanticization of poor or working-class backgrounds undermines the possibility of true connection. Such connection is based on understanding difference in experience and perspective and working to mediate and negotiate these terrains. Language is a crucial issue for folk whose movement outside the boundaries of poor and working-class backgrounds changes the nature and direction of their speech. Coming to Stanford with my own version of a Kentucky accent, which I think of always as a strong sound quite different from Tennessee or Georgia speech, I learned to speak differently while maintaining the speech of my region, the sound of my family and community. This was of course much easier to keep up when I returned home to stay often. In recent years, I have endeavored to use various speaking styles in the classroom as a teacher and find it disconcerts those who feel that the use of a particular patois excludes them as listeners, even if there is translation into the usual, acceptable mode of speech. Learning to listen to different voices, hearing different speech challenges the notion that we must all assimilate—share a single, similar talk—in educational institutions. Language reflects the culture from which we emerge. To deny ourselves daily use of speech patterns that are common and familiar, that embody the unique and distinctive aspect of our self is one of the ways we become estranged and alienated from our past. It is important for us to have as many languages on hand as we can know or learn. It is important for those of us who are black, who speak in particular patois as well as standard English to express ourselves in both ways.

Often I tell students from poor and working-class backgrounds that if you believe what you have learned and are learning in schools and universities separates you from your past, this is precisely what will happen. It is important to stand firm in the conviction that nothing can truly separate us from our pasts when we nurture and cherish that connection. An important strategy for maintaining contact is ongoing acknowledgement of the primacy of one's past, of one's background, affirming the reality that such bonds are not severed automatically solely because one enters a new environment or moves toward a different class experience.

Again, I do not wish to romanticize this effort, to dismiss the reality of conflict and contradiction. During my time at Stanford, I did go through a period of more than a year when I did not return home. That period was one where I felt that it was simply too difficult to mesh my profoundly disparate realities. Critical reflection about the choice I was making, particularly about why I felt a choice had to be made, pulled me through this difficult time. Luckily I recognized that the insistence on choosing between the world of family and community and the new world of privileged white people and privileged ways of knowing was imposed upon me by the outside. It is as though a mythical contract had been signed somewhere which demanded of us black folks that once we entered these spheres we would immediately give up all vestiges of our underprivileged past. It was my responsibility to formulate a way of being that would allow me to participate fully in my new environment while integrating and maintaining aspects of the old.

One of the most tragic manifestations of the pressure black people feel to assimilate is expressed in the internalization of racist perspectives. I was shocked and saddened when I first heard black professors at Stanford downgrade and express contempt for black students, expecting us to do poorly, refusing to establish nurturing bonds. At every university I have attended as a student or worked at as a teacher, I have heard similar attitudes expressed with little or no understanding of factors that might prevent brilliant black students from performing to their full capability. Within universities, there are few educational and social spaces where students who wish to affirm positive ties to ethnicity—to blackness, to working-class backgrounds—can receive affirmation and support. Ideologically, the message is clear—assimilation is the way to gain acceptance and approval from those in power.

Many white people enthusiastically supported Richard Rodriguez's vehement contention in his autobiography, *Hunger of Memory,* that attempts to maintain ties with his Chicano background impeded his progress, that he had to sever ties with community and kin to succeed at Stanford and in the larger world, that family language, in his case Spanish, had to be made secondary or discarded. If the terms of success as defined by the standards of ruling groups within white-supremacist, capitalist patriarchy are the only standards that exist, then assimilation is indeed necessary. But they are not. Even in the face of powerful structures of domination, it remains possible for each of us, especially those of us who are members of oppressed and/or

exploited groups as well as those radical visionaries who may have race, class, and sex privilege, to define and determine alternative standards, to decide on the nature and extent of compromise. Standards by which one's success is measured, whether student or professor, are quite different for those of us who wish to resist reinforcing the domination of race, sex, and class, who work to maintain and strengthen our ties with the oppressed, with those who lack material privilege, with our families who are poor and working-class.

When I wrote my first book, *Ain't I A Woman: black women and feminism,* the issue of class and its relationship to who one's reading audience might be came up for me around my decision not to use footnotes, for which I have been sharply criticized. I told people that my concern was that footnotes set class boundaries for readers, determining who a book is for. I was shocked that many academic folks scoffed at this idea. I shared that I went into working-class black communities as well as talked with family and friends to survey whether or not they ever read books with footnotes and found that they did not. A few did not know what they were, but most folks saw them as indicating that a book was for college-educated people. These responses influenced my decision. When some of my more radical, college-educated friends freaked out about the absence of footnotes, I seriously questioned how we could ever imagine revolutionary transformation of society if such a small shift in direction could be viewed as threatening. Of course, many folks warned that the absence of footnotes would make the work less credible in academic circles. This information also highlighted the way in which class informs our choices. Certainly I did feel that choosing to use simple language, absence of footnotes, etc. would mean I was jeopardizing the possibility of being taken seriously in academic circles but then this was a political matter and a political decision. It utterly delights me that this has proven not to be the case and that the book is read by many academics as well as by people who are not college-educated.

Always our first response when we are motivated to conform or compromise within structures that reinforce domination must be to engage in critical reflection. Only by challenging ourselves to push against oppressive boundaries do we make the radical alternative possible, expanding the realm and scope of critical inquiry. Unless we share radical strategies, ways of rethinking and revisioning with students, with kin and community, with a larger audience, we risk perpetuating the stereotype that we succeed because we are the exception, different from the rest of our people. Since I left home and entered college, I am often asked, usually by white people, if my sisters and brothers are also high achievers. At the root of this question is the longing for reinforcement of the belief in "the exception" which enables race, sex, and class biases to remain intact. I am careful to separate what it means to be exceptional from a notion of "the exception."

Frequently I hear smart black folks, from poor and working-class backgrounds, stressing their frustration that at times family and community do not recognize that they are exceptional. Absence of positive affirmation clearly diminishes the longing to excel in academic endeavors. Yet it is important to distinguish between the absence of basic positive affirmation and the longing for continued reinforcement that we are special. Usually liberal white folks will willingly offer continual reinforcement of us as exceptions—as special. This can be both patronizing and very seductive. Since we often work in situations where we are isolated from other black folks, we can easily begin to feel that encouragement from white people is the primary or only source of support and recognition. Given the internalization of racism, it is easy to view this support as more validating and legitimizing than similar support from black people. Still, nothing takes the place of being valued and appreciated by one's own, by one's family and community. We share a mutual and reciprocal responsibility for affirming one another's successes. Sometimes we have to talk to our folks about the fact that we need their ongoing support and affirmation, that it is unique and special to us. In some cases we may never receive desired recognition and acknowledgement of specific achievements from kin. Rather than seeing this as a basis for estrangement, for severing connection, it is useful to explore other sources of nourishment and support.

I do not know that my mother's mother ever acknowledged my college education except to ask me once, "How can you live so far away from your people?" Yet she gave me sources of affirmation and nourishment, sharing the legacy of her quilt-making, of family history, of her incredible way with words. Recently, when our father retired after more than thirty years of work as a janitor, I wanted to pay tribute to this experience, to identify links between his work and my own as writer and teacher. Reflecting on our family past, I recalled ways he had been an impressive example of diligence and hard work, approaching tasks with a seriousness of concentration I work to mirror and develop, with a discipline I struggle to maintain. Sharing these thoughts with him keeps us connected, nurtures our respect for each other, maintaining a space, however large or small, where we can talk.

Open, honest communication is the most important way we maintain relationships with kin and community as our class experience and backgrounds change. It is as vital as the sharing of resources. Often financial assistance is given in circumstances where there is no meaningful contact. However helpful, this can also be an expression of estrangement and alienation. Communication between black folks from various experiences of material privilege was much easier when we were all in segregated communities sharing common experiences in relation to social institutions. Without this grounding, we must work to maintain ties, connection. We must assume greater responsibility for making and maintaining contact, connections that can shape our intellectual visions and inform our radical commitments.

The most powerful resource any of us can have as we study and teach in university settings is full understanding and appreciation of the richness, beauty, and primacy of our familial and community backgrounds. Maintaining awareness of class differences, nurturing ties with the poor and working-class people who are our most intimate kin, our comrades in struggle, transforms and enriches our intellectual experience. Education as the practice of freedom becomes not a force which fragments or separates, but one that brings us closer, expanding our definitions of home and community.   [1989]

Understanding the Reading

1. Explain the conflict between hooks and her mother.
2. In what ways did hooks' working-class realities separate her from her fellow students at Stanford?
3. As a member of the Black working class, what cultural values are important to hooks?
4. Why is hooks perceived to be anti-intellectual?
5. Why were hooks' parents ambivalent about her reading?
6. Explain hooks' attitude about language and academic practices (like footnotes).
7. Why does hooks believe it is important to retain the values of the class she was born into?

Suggestions for Responding

1. Do you agree with hooks that it is important to retain the values of one's origins? Why or why not?
2. Why do you think hooks was able to survive and thrive by her move into the middle class, whereas Leanita McClain was destroyed by her move? ✦

40

Jewish and Working Class

BERNICE MENNIS

When I was called to speak at this conference about working-class experience, my immediate reaction was: "No, get someone else." One voice said: "I have nothing worthwhile to say." A second voice said: "I was not born poor. I always ate well. I never felt deprived. I have not suffered enough to be on this panel." Both voices silenced me. The first came from my class background—a diminished sense of competence, ability, control, power. ("Who are you anyway? You have nothing to say. No one cares or will listen.") The second, the guilt voice, comes from a strange combination of my Jewishness, my fear of anti-Semitism, my own psychological reaction to my own deprivations: a denial of my own pain if someone else seems to suffer more.

Economic class has been a matter of both shame and pride for me, depending on the value judgments of the community with which I identified. The economic class reality has always remained the same: My father had a very small outdoor tomato and banana stand and a small cellar for ripening the fruit. Until he was 68, he worked twelve hours a day, six days a week, with one week vacation. Although he worked hard and supported our family well, my father did not feel proud of his work, did not affirm his strength. Instead, he was ashamed to have me visit his fruit stand; he saw his work as dirty, himself as an "ignorant greenhorn." The legacy of class.

And I accepted and echoed back his shame. In elementary school, when we had to go around and say what work our parents did, I repeated my father's euphemistic words: "My father sells wholesale and retail fruits and vegetables." It's interesting that later, when I was involved in political actions, my shame turned to pride of that same class background. The poorer one was born, the better, the more credit.

Both reactions—shame and pride—are based on a false assumption that one has control and responsibility for what one is born into. (Society—those in power, institutions—is responsible for people being born into conditions of economic limitation and suffering, for racism and classism. But as individuals we do not choose our birth.) That blame/credit often prevents us from seeing clearly the actual effects of growing up in a certain class: what it allows, what it inhibits, blocks, destroys. Also, if we take credit for what is out of our control, we sometimes do not take sufficient credit and responsibility for what is in our control: our consciousness, our actions, how we shape our lives.

What becomes difficult immediately in trying to understand class background is how it becomes hopelessly entangled with other issues: the fact that my father was an immigrant who spoke with a strong accent, never felt competent to write in English, always felt a great sense of self-shame that he projected onto his children; that my father had witnessed pogroms[1] and daily anti-Semitism in his tiny *shtetl*[2] in Russia, that we were Jewish, that the Holocaust occurred; that neither of my parents went to school beyond junior high school; that I was the younger daughter, the "good" child who accepted almost everything without complaining or acknowledging pain; that my sister and I experienced our worlds very differently and responded in almost opposite ways. It's difficult to sort out class, to see clearly. . . .

Feelings of poverty or wealth are based on one's experiences and where one falls on the economic spectrum. The economic class and the conditions we grow up under are very real, objective, but how we label and see those circumstances is relative, shaped by what we see outside ourselves. Growing up in the Pelham Parkway–Lydig Avenue area of the Bronx, I heard my circumstances echoed everywhere: Everyone's parents spoke Yiddish and had accents; they all spoke loudly and with their hands; few were educated beyond junior high school; no one dressed stylishly or went to restaurants (except for special occasions) or had fancy cars or dishwashers or clothes washers. (Our apartment building had, and still has, only one washing machine for 48 apartments. The lineup of baskets began early in the morning. My mother and I hung the clothes on the roof.) We ate good kosher food and fresh fruits and vegetables (from my [father's] stand). My mother sewed our clothes or we would shop in Alexander's and look for bargains (clothes with the manufacturers' tags removed). Clothes were passed between sisters, cousins, neighbors. I never felt poor or deprived. I had no other perspective, no other reality from which to judge our life.

When I went to the World's Fair and watched the G.E. exhibit of "Our Changing World," I remember being surprised that what I believed was a modern-day kitchen—an exact duplicate of our kitchen at home—was the kitchen of the '40s. When I received a fellowship for graduate school, I was surprised to discover I was eligible for the maximum grant because my parents' income fell in the lowest income category. I was surprised when I met friends whose parents talked about books and psychology and art, when I met people who noticed labels and brand names and talked about clothes and cars (but never mentioned costs and money).

What I also didn't see or appreciate was all the work and struggle of my parents to maintain and nourish us, work done silently and without any credit for many years. A few years ago I wrote a poem called "The Miracle" about my mother and her skilled unacknowledged work.

Clearly our assumptions, expectations, and hopes are unconsciously shaped by our class backgrounds. At a very young age I learned to want only what my parents could afford. It was a good survival mechanism that allowed me never to feel deprived or denied. At a later age, when I would read in natural history books about the "immortal species," the lesson was reaffirmed: The key to survival was always to become smaller, to minimize needs. Those species that had become dependent on more luxuriant conditions perished during hard times. Those used to less survived.

There is something powerful about surviving by adapting to little. The power comes from an independence of need, an instinct that allows us to get by. But it is a defense, and, like any defense, its main fault was that it never allowed me to feel the edge of my own desires, pains, deprivations. I defined my needs by what was available. Even now I tend to minimize my needs, to never feel deprived—a legacy of my class background.

Class background reveals itself in little ways. Around food, for example. My family would sip their soup loudly, putting mouth close to bowl. We would put containers directly on the table and never use a butter dish. We would suck bone marrow with gusto, pick up chicken bones with our hands, crunch them with our teeth, and leave little slivers on our otherwise empty plates. We would talk loudly and argue politics over supper. Only later did I become conscious of the judgment of others about certain behavior, ways of eating, talking, walking, dressing, being. Polite etiquette struck me as a bit absurd, as if hunger were uncivilized: the delicate portions, the morsels left on the plate, the proper use of knife and fork, the spoon seeming to go in the opposite direction of the mouth. The more remote one was from basic needs, the higher one's class status. I usually was unconscious of the "proper behavior": I did not notice. But if I ever felt the eye of judgment, my first tendency would be to exaggerate my "grossness" in order to show the absurdity of others' snobbish judgments. I would deny that that judgment had any effect other than anger. But I now realize that all judgment has effect. Some of my negative self-image as *klutz, nebbish,* ugly, unsophisticated is a direct result of the reflection I saw in the judging, sophisticated eye of the upper class.

Lack of education and lack of money made for an insecurity and fear of doing almost anything, a fear tremendously compounded by anti-Semitism and World War II. My parents were afraid to take any risks—from both a conviction of their own incompetence and a fear that doing anything big, having any visibility, would place them in danger. From them I inherited a fear that if I touched something, did anything, I would make matters worse. There was an incredible nervousness in my home around fixing anything, buying anything big, filling out any forms. My mother still calls me to complete forms for her. When my father was sick, my parents needed me to translate everything the doctor said, not because they did not understand him, but because their fear stopped them from listening when anyone very educated or in authority spoke.

I did not inherit the fear of those in authority. In fact, my observation of people's condescension, use of authority, and misuse of power helped shape my politics at a young age. I identified with the underdog, was angry at the bully, fought against the misuse of power. But I did inherit their fear of taking risks, of doing anything big, of trying anything new. I have trouble with paper forms; I've never been able to write a grant proposal; I have no credit cards. I sometimes seek invisibility as a form of safety.

For poorer people, for people who experience prejudice, there is a strong feeling that one has no power, no ability to affect or control one's environment. For nine years my family and I lived in a very small three-room apartment; my sister and I had no bedroom of our own. When we moved from the fifth floor to the sixth, we got a tiny room just big enough for two beds and a cabinet. I never thought to put up a picture, to choose a room color or a bedspread. I had no notion of control over private space, of shaping my environment.

That feeling of lack of control over one's environment, of no right to one's own space, was psychologically intensified by my parents' experiences of anti-Semitism and by the Holocaust. These fostered a deep sense of powerlessness

and vulnerability and, on an even more basic level, a doubt whether we really had a right to exist on this earth.

In college I took a modern dance class. A group of us began "dancing" by caving in on ourselves, slinking around the side walls of the gym. I remember the teacher saying that to dance one needed to be able to open one's arms and declare the beauty of one's being, to take up one's space on the dance floor: to say "I am here." For many women who experience poverty and prejudice this kind of self-assertion feels foreign, impossible, dangerous. One of the unconscious effects of being born wealthy is a natural sense of one's right to be here on this earth, an essential grace that comes from the feeling of belonging. (The danger, of course, is that wealthier people often take up too much space. They do not see the others crushed under their wide flinging steps.) Where the poorer person's danger is the self-consciousness that shrinks us into invisibility, the wealthier one's is the unconscious arrogance that inflates.

But what happens when one feels self-conscious and small and is seen as large, wealthy, powerful, controlling? At a young age, I knew the anti-Semitic portrait of the wealthy, exploitative Jew. I also knew that I did not feel powerful or controlling. My parents and I felt powerless, fearful, vulnerable. We owned nothing. All my parents saved, after working fifty years, would not equal the cost of one year of college today. What does it mean to have others' definition of one's reality so vastly different from one's experience of it? The effects are confusion, anger, entrapment. I lost touch with what was real, what my own experiences really were.

As a political person I felt particularly vulnerable to the hated image of "the Jew." I knew it was a stereotype and not my experience or the experience of the Jews I grew up with—but it still made me feel guilt, not pride, for any success I did have, for any rise in status. If the stereotype said "Jews have everything," the only way I could avoid that stereotype would be to have nothing. If you are poor, you are not a Jew. If you are successful, you are a bad Jew. The trap.

The economic and professional success of many second-generation Jews became tinged for me, as if we had done something wrong. To feel bad about achievement, to hold back one's power, is very destructive. My aunts and uncles, my parents, my friends' parents all had little education and little money. Yet we—my cousins, my sister, my friends—not only went to college, but even to graduate school and law school. I was speaking the other day with my aunt, who was saying what a miracle it was that her four children were all professionals and she was poor and uneducated. But the miracle was not really a miracle at all. It was the result of parents who saw education as very, very important—as a way out of the entrapment of class and prejudice. It was the result of parents who worked desperately hard so that their children could have that way out. It was a City College system in New York City that provided completely free education while we worked and lived at home.

In one generation we created an incredible economic, class, professional, and educational distance between ourselves and our parents. The danger of this success is that we forget the material soil that nourished us, the hard work that propped us up; that we lose our consciousness of the harm and evil of condescension, exploitation, oppression, the pain of being made to feel inferior and invisible. Anzia Yezierska, a Jewish immigrant writer, says "Education without a heart is a curse." But to keep that consciousness and that heart and to be able to step onto the dance floor of life and say "I am here," reflecting back to our parents the beauty and strength we inherited from them, that would be a very real "miracle" indeed.   [1987]

Terms

1. POGROMS: Organized and often politically encouraged massacres or persecutions of minority groups, especially ones conducted against Jews.
2. *SHTETL:* A ghettoized Jewish village in Eastern Europe.

Understanding the Reading

1. Why does Mennis think she should be neither shamed nor proud of her impoverished background?
2. What other issues complicate Mennis' understanding of her class status?

3. As Mennis matures, what experiences make her aware of her class status?
4. How was Mennis shaped by her childhood background?
5. How does Mennis feel about the success of the second generation?

Suggestions for Responding

1. How do you feel about personal space—the room your body takes up, your sleeping area, your home, and so on? Do you take possession of such spaces or, like Mennis, do you minimize your impact on them? Write a short paper explaining how you feel about space and what you think may have influenced those feelings.
2. Mennis says that both she and her father were shamed by his vocation. Write a short reflection on how you feel (and felt as a child) about your parents' vocations.
3. Compare and contrast hooks' and Mennis' experiences of and attitudes about upward mobility. ✦

41

First They Changed My Name . . .

CAFFILENE ALLEN

Although I was born in 1951, I grew up speaking the English of an earlier century—a fact I was reminded of one Sunday afternoon at my mother's rest home. A nurse drew me aside and, blushing a little, said uncertainly, "Your mother says Esther has been 'progging' again."

Quickly, I put her mind at ease. How well I knew what progging meant. It had been the cause of all my spankings as a young child. Progging was the act of going through belongings that were not yours, digging into clothes drawers, purses, anything that contained intriguing items in its mysterious depths.

Though words like "progging" seemed strange to the nurse, the rest home was not more than 12 miles from Tumbling Creek, Tennessee, the town where I grew up. What we called "old"

English was the only language that I knew until I was six years old, when I was dragged, wailing and sobbing, onto the school bus. In school, I soon discovered that the lack of communication links from Tumbling Creek to the outside world, as well as the clannish nature of the people who lived there, had allowed two separate cultures, divided by centuries, to exist within miles of each other. At the school, I heard such unfamiliar words as "church," "couch," "living room," "Christ," and "isn't." At home, we used "meetinghouse," "divanette," "front room," "the Good Man," and "ain't." I had vague memories of some of those strange words being spoken occasionally, but whoever had used them had been immediately accused of trying to be like the "towndoogers" (town dwellers). That these were the terms my teachers wanted me to use was incomprehensible.

Perhaps my confusion helps explain why I was surprisingly meek when my teachers took it upon themselves to change my name, thinking that I had misspelled it. They were probably not too far from the truth. Coming from English, Scottish, Irish, and German stock that never left the Tennessee hill area, I inherited a linguistic pattern that was mostly oral and did not include the "th" sound. My mother was most likely trying to give me the good Irish name of Kathleen, but pronounced the "th" with an "f" sound and then spelled it phonetically for the nurse. All went well until I got to the first grade, where my teacher first decided that my name must be Caffie Lene but then settled on Kathleen. She told me I had to start writing it that way. My mother had no objection: whatever the God-Teacher said must be done—even if it meant changing my name.

In the second grade, my teacher told me that it was a law that everyone had to have a middle name, and that I should choose one for myself, so she could put it on my permanent record. I was delighted. Here was my chance to be Barbara Allen, the focus of an English ballad in which the heroine rejects "sweet William," supposedly causing his death. When they both eventually die of broken hearts, a rose grows from William's grave and a briar from Barbara Allen's. Why I wished to become the namesake of such a person is something that I have never wanted to examine too closely, but I was abso-

lutely thrilled when my teacher wrote Kathleen Barbara Allen on my permanent record.

If I had known how much frustration would result from these changes, I would have been less thrilled. I soon discovered that Kathleen was one of the most common names in school, and that I was doomed to almost always have a number added after my name to distinguish me from the others with the same name. By the sixth grade I had developed a somewhat oversensitive approach to life, and began to notice that I was never Kathy #1 but always Kathy #2 or #3. I still had enough of my mother's awe for teachers that I was never able to express my displeasure to them.

I was given the chance to reclaim my name when, as a senior in high school, I was required to produce a birth certificate in order to graduate. By that time, I had almost forgotten about Caffilene, so I was very surprised to see the name on my birth certificate. My teachers were even more surprised, since the ones who had changed my name were long gone. A new problem loomed: I was one name on the school records and another on my birth certificate—therefore, I couldn't graduate. It took several teachers and a great deal of trouble to convince the bureaucracy I should be allowed to graduate.

Changing my name had a profound effect on my sense of identity, but my teachers had an equally long-lasting impact on my relationship with my mother, who believed that if the teacher said it was right, it was so. Having only a third-grade education obtained in a one-room country schoolhouse, she had the same reverence for schoolteachers as she had for the mysterious government, which kept her and her five children alive by sending a monthly Social Security check after my father was killed in the copper mines when I was 16 months old. To her, the government and the teachers were the keepers of some noble and powerful system upon which our survival and well-being depended, and we would be nothing less than ungrateful fools if we questioned their sterling wisdom. My four older brothers and sisters seemed to catch on sooner than I did: if my mother ever found out that the teachers she revered had a low opinion of her way of speech and life, she would be deeply hurt. For her peace of mind, my siblings learned to behave and speak one way at school and another way at home, whereas I would bound home, armed with linguistic rules that created a lifelong conflict between my mother and me. My first demand was that she allow me to call her Mommy rather than Miney (actually, her name was de Sara de Mina de Magdalene Pless Allen, but we couldn't get all of that out).

"What for?" was her reply. None of her ancestors had ever done such a thing.

"Because the teacher said I wasn't showing proper respect."

She became even more puzzled. "What does that mean?"

I had to admit that I didn't know. "But she said I was supposed to call you Mommy, and so I'm going to."

Well, the God-Teacher had said it, so it had to be.

She had an easier time with my second question. After I learned to read about Dick and Jane, I soon realized that everyone—even Jane—was sometimes referred to as "he." Having a strictly literal approach to life, I couldn't understand. When I asked my teachers why only the male pronoun was used, they laughed at me, so I took my question home to my mother. Readily, she replied with the only answer that a good Baptist could give, and one which she sincerely believed: "Because men are better than women." I soon learned to stop asking my mother questions.

By the fourth grade I had become increasingly ashamed of my mother and almost came to despise her for her manner and speech. One evening at the supper table when she was speaking improper English, chewing with her mouth open, and propping her elbows on the table, I found myself staring in open disgust. Suddenly, she stopped speaking in mid-sentence and glared at me, her face turning purple. By now, I was familiar enough with this scene to know what was going to happen next. Sure enough, I escaped from my seat just in time to miss being hit by the fork that she threw at my eyes. "Stop looking at me like I was a freak!" she screamed. Later, after the dishes were washed and put away, I went into the kitchen to get a glass of water. Through the screen door, I saw my mother sitting on the back steps, watching the sun go down behind the Blue Ridge Mountains. Her shoulders were shaking with silent sobs. For the first time, I sensed the depth of her isolation and despair; I also got my first inkling that she was not the one who was in the wrong. An intelligent, beautiful woman raised in a fundamentalist culture that assured her that she was nothing simply because she was a woman, she now was confronted with the scorn, brought home to her by her daughter, of those whom she had once revered as her benevolent protectors. Now she was sure that she was truly worthless.

Even though that moment gave me some understanding of my mother, it did not give me enough to change my ways totally. I continued to try to convince her that she needed to speak and act more like the people in town. I didn't have much success by myself, but I eventually got help from a rather surprising source. My mother had adamantly refused to get a telephone or a car, which were becoming more and more common in Tumbling Creek by the mid-1960s, so it was an incredible surprise to me when, one day when I was in the seventh grade, she brought home a television. Never in my life, not before or since, have I felt such a sense of wonder as when the television was first turned on in our house and people showed up on the screen in my living room who were fun to watch and listen to. Suddenly, the mountains seemed a little less lonely and my mother a little less mean.

By this time, I was pretty much considered an oddity by everyone who knew me. Since I always ate first, with the men rather than with the women, who had to wait until the men were finished before they could even sit down at the table, I became a third sex; people would say, "the men, the women, and Kathy." My love for books and writing seemed especially odd and somewhat slothlike to those working in the fields and the house morning, noon, and night in order to survive (which seemed to include everyone except me). And more than once, students in my class had been sent to the principal's office for calling me a nigger-lover. (No one in Tumbling Creek or Copperhill had ever met a person of color, but racism existed there, and my support of the civil rights movement increased my isolation.) But there, on the television, were people who gave me some inkling of another world out there where I might find others with ideas like mine. Peter, Paul, and Mary showed up singing "Blowing in the Wind" at a civil rights march.

One afternoon, while my mother and I were watching *Who Do You Trust?*, newscasters interrupted to report a confrontation between Governor George Wallace and a black student trying to enter the University of Alabama. My spirits rose. Although at first they all seemed to be losing, at least there were people out there fighting for the same things that I thought were right.

I picked up "correct" pronunciation and grammar from TV, as well as an accent that gradually replaced my east Tennessee twang. My mother, on the other hand, changed the words to suit her own style of speech. Once, she told me that her favorite TV show was "Feenanzie." When I told her there was no such show, she retorted that there certainly was: "It's the one that has Hoss Cartwright and Little Joe and advertises Chevrolets."

Nevertheless, my mother did let television temper her cultural approach to life. She stopped trying to compliment my friends by telling them they were "just as fat as a little pig." She learned to stop asking the kids I brought home if they wanted a "dope," which meant a soft drink in Tumbling Creek. Most important, through TV, she learned to understand me and the ways that I had already adopted, and so television made life a little easier for both of us.

Many years have gone by. I grew up and left Tumbling Creek, as my teachers and my mother always knew I would. But even now, thinking back on those times and conflicts, I find my emotions toward my mother and my teachers still bound up in the same love-hate web most of us reserve for our families only. In a way, my teachers were my family. They were the first to encourage my love for learning, to find scholarships for me, to bring me books to read during the long, lonely summer months, to encourage my writing, to express their belief that I could even make a living as a writer. But at the same time, they taught me to hate my culture, to despise people who had a different linguistic approach to life, even if one of those people was my mother. After many long years, I have managed finally to reconcile to some extent my world with my mother's. Regaining a sense of pride in my Appalachian heritage and an appreciation for who my mother was as a person was one of the hardest and most valuable tasks of my adult life.   [1994]

Understanding the Reading

1. Describe the differences between Tumbling Creek and the town where Allen goes to school.
2. Explain why Allen's birth name was troublesome for her.
3. What were the conflicts between Allen's home life and her school life?
4. How did television alter the Allens' way of life?

Suggestions for Responding

1. Write a brief commentary on words and other language usages that were unique to your family or community. Reflect on how these made you feel when you interacted with broader society.
2. Discuss how you feel about each of your names and all of them together. ◆

42

Daddy Tucked the Blanket

RANDALL WILLIAMS

About the time I turned 16, my folks began to wonder why I didn't stay home anymore. I always had an excuse for them, but what I didn't say was that I had found my freedom and I was getting out.

I went through four years of high school in semirural Alabama and became active in clubs and sports; I made a lot of friends and became a regular guy, if you know what I mean. But one thing was irregular about me: I managed those four years without ever having a friend visit at my house.

I was ashamed of where I lived. I had been ashamed for as long as I had been conscious of class.

We had a big family. There were several of us sleeping in one room, but that's not so bad if you get along, and we always did. As you get older, though, it gets worse.

Being poor is a humiliating experience for a young person trying hard to be accepted. Even now—several years removed—it is hard to talk about. And I resent the weakness of these words to make you feel what it was really like.

We lived in a lot of old houses. We moved a lot because we were always looking for something just a little better than what we had. You have to understand that my folks worked harder than most people. My mother was always at home, but for her that was a full-time job—and no fun, either. But my father worked his head off from the time I can remember in construction and shops. It was hard, physical work.

I tell you this to show that we weren't shiftless. No matter how much money Daddy made, we never made much progress up the social ladder. I got out thanks to a college scholarship and because I was a little more articulate than the average.

I have seen my Daddy wrap copper wire through the soles of his boots to keep them together in the wintertime. He couldn't buy new boots because he had used the money for food and shoes for us. We lived like hell, but we went to school well-clothed and with a full stomach.

It really is hell to live in a house that was in bad shape 10 years before you moved in. And a big family puts a lot of wear and tear on a new house, too, so you can imagine how one goes downhill if it is teetering when you move in. But we lived in houses that were sweltering in summer and freezing in winter. I woke up every morning for a year and a half with plaster on my face where it had fallen out of the ceiling during the night.

This wasn't during the Depression; this was in the late 60's and early 70's.

When we boys got old enough to learn trades in school, we would try to fix up the old houses we lived in. But have you ever tried to paint a wall that crumbled when the roller went across it? And bright paint emphasized the holes in the wall. You end up more frustrated than when you began, especially when you know that at best you might come up with only enough money to improve one of the six rooms in the house. And we might move out soon after, anyway.

The same goes for keeping a house like that clean. If you have a house full of kids and the house is deteriorating, you'll never keep it clean.

Daddy used to yell at Mama about that, but she couldn't do anything. I think Daddy knew it inside, but he had to have an outlet for his rage somewhere, and at least yelling isn't as bad as hitting, which they never did to each other.

But you have a kitchen which has no counter space and no hot water, and you will have dirty dishes stacked up. That sounds like an excuse, but try it. You'll go mad from the sheer sense of futility. It's the same thing in a house with no closets. You can't keep clothes clean and rooms in order if they have to be stacked up with things.

Living in a bad house is generally worse on girls. For one thing, they traditionally help their mother with the housework. We boys could get outside and work in the field or cut wood or even play ball and forget about living conditions. The sky was still pretty.

But the girls got the pressure, and as they got older it became worse. Would they accept dates knowing they had to "receive" the young man in a dirty hallway with broken windows, peeling wallpaper and a cracked ceiling? You have to live it to understand it, but it creates a shame which drives the soul of a young person inward.

I'm thankful none of us ever blamed our parents for this, because it would have crippled our relationships. As it worked out, only the relationship between our parents was damaged. And I think the harshness which they expressed to each other was just an outlet to get rid of their anger at the trap their lives were in. It ruined their marriage because they had no one to yell at but each other. I knew other families where the kids got the abuse, but we were too much loved for that.

Once I was about 16 and Mama and Daddy had had a particularly violent argument about the washing machine, which had broken down. Daddy was on the back porch—that's where the only water faucet was—trying to fix it and Mama had a washtub out there washing school clothes for the next day and they were screaming at each other.

Later that night everyone was in bed and I heard Daddy get up from the couch where he was reading. I looked out from my bed across the hall into their room. He was standing right over Mama and she was already asleep. He pulled the blanket up and tucked it around her shoulders and just stood there and tears were dropping off his cheeks and I thought I could faintly hear them splashing against the linoleum rug.

Now they're divorced.

I had courses in college where housing was discussed, but the sociologists never put enough emphasis on the impact living in substandard housing has on a person's psyche. Especially children's.

Small children have a hard time understanding poverty. They want the same things children from more affluent families have. They want the same things they see advertised on television, and they don't understand why they can't have them.

Other children can be incredibly cruel. I was in elementary school in Georgia—and this is interesting because it is the only thing I remember about that particular school—when I was about eight or nine.

After Christmas vacation had ended, my teacher made each student describe all his or her Christmas presents. I became more and more uncomfortable as the privilege passed around the room toward me. Other children were reciting the names of the dolls they had been given, the kinds of bicycles and the grandeur of their games and toys. Some had lists which seemed to go on and on for hours.

It took me only a few seconds to tell the class that I had gotten for Christmas a belt and a pair of gloves. And then I was laughed at—because I cried—by a roomful of children and a teacher. I never forgave them, and that night I made my mother cry when I told her about it.

In retrospect, I am grateful for that moment, but I remember wanting to die at the time.

[1975]

Understanding the Reading

1. How did Williams feel about his life as a child? Why?
2. Why did Williams' parents fight?
3. How did Williams' parents really feel about each other?
4. What impact do peers and the media have on impoverished children?

Suggestions for Responding

1. Write a short essay describing why you think Williams' parents finally divorced.
2. Research how problems of poverty and homelessness are solved in other modern industrial nations. How do their rates of poverty compare to ours? ◆

43

Something Is Robbing Our Children of Their Future

COLIN GREER

"Sometimes I don't have enough to feed the whole family," said Sandra, 43, of McClellanville, S.C. "I feed my three children first, and then I'll go without a meal." Sandra has completed two years of college and now works full-time for a social-services agency for about $12,000 a year. "We're hungry," she said, "but we're not starving. It's a real battle."

When Americans think of starving people, they think of Third World countries. But what many people don't realize, says Robert Fersh, president of the Food Research and Action Center (FRAC), a nonprofit organization working to alleviate hunger, is that millions of people endure hunger right here at home. Parents are going to bed without food so they can feed their children. Baby formula is mixed with water to make it last longer. People are eating rice and beans, because there isn't enough money for groceries at the end of the month.

Over the next few months, the question of hunger will dominate the welfare-reform debate, as Congressional committees hear testimony on hunger and federal food-assistance programs.

The Action Center reports that more than 5 million children under 12 go hungry each month. . . . The U.S. Census Bureau acknowledged that 39.3 million Americans, or about 15 percent of our population, lived in poverty in 1993.

The federal government considers a family of four to be in poverty if its total annual income is

$14,800 or less. If the same family earns $27,380, it is considered low-income. The government uses these definitions to determine the level of assistance a family receives in various welfare and food programs. (Almost 90 percent of families on welfare also receive food stamps.) Nearly 42 percent of American children grow up in low-income families, and about 23 percent—almost one child in four—grow up in poverty. This is double the child-poverty rate of any other industrialized country.

Not surprisingly, the strongest predictor of hunger is poverty.

The Food Research and Action Center is a legal advocacy group created in 1970 to represent the concerns of classes of citizens who could not defend their own interests (another example is the Children's Defense Fund). Originally financed by the federal government, it is now supported by such foundations as Ford and Prudential. FRAC regularly reviews upcoming legislation that affects the hungry. "An important part of the Action Center's work," says Robert Fersh, a lawyer who previously was the staff director of a House Subcommittee on Nutrition that was chaired by Leon Panetta, "is to discover the extent of hunger in America, to educate Americans about what we find and to coordinate an effective response to eradicate hunger and malnutrition. Policy-makers need to know the extent of hunger in America."

In 1984, the Action Center convened a group of scientists who developed the Community Childhood Hunger Identification Project, or CCHIP (pronounced "chip"), to scientifically document hunger in America. Seven sites were included in the initial study: Alabama, California, Connecticut, Florida, Michigan, Minnesota and New York.

The Hunger Project's second study [included] eleven more sites in nine states—Indiana, Maine, New York, Pennsylvania, Utah, Kansas, Ohio, South Carolina and Texas—and Washington, D.C. . . .

"We took great care in designing our survey and carrying it out," said Cheryl Wehler, the project's director, who received her Ph.D. in nutritional biochemistry from M.I.T. "We hired the same consultant to design our survey who works on surveys for the Department of Health and Human Services and the National Census Bureau.

We interviewed more than 8000 low-income families in communities from every region of the U.S. (Most national polls interview far fewer people. For instance, the Gallup Organization, one of the leading national polling services, uses a basic sample of about 1000 people.) We chose sites that represent the national variation of population size, proportion of population living in urban and rural areas, and different racial and ethnic groups.

"We wanted to know not only what hunger looks like in America but also how it looks in a region and in a specific community," added Wehler. "This type of specificity takes a lot of legwork."

That legwork was done by people already working to combat poverty in community-based groups—many of them in or close to poverty themselves. Cheryl Wehler and her assistant taught these individuals interview techniques to implement the extensive, 165-question survey. "The response rate has been phenomenal!— 80 percent," said Wehler. "The people interviewed really wanted to help others understand what it is like to be hungry and what they have to go through daily."

To qualify for the study, a household had to be considered low-income and include at least one child under age 12. A computer program was used to randomly select qualifying households. A family was defined as hungry if it experienced at least five of eight indicators of hunger in the [preceding] 12 months. They included:

- Does your household ever run out of money to buy food to make a meal?
- Do you ever cut the size of meals or skip meals because there is not enough money for food?
- Do you ever rely on a limited number of foods to feed your children because you are running out of money to buy food for a meal?
- Do any of your children ever go to bed hungry because there is not enough money to buy food?

"The last week of the month is a real juggling act," says George Garrett of Mulberry, Kan. He is the father of George Jr., 5, and Kayla, 6. His family lives in the same three-bedroom house in which George grew up. "We eat a lot of beans, and sometimes there's no fresh bread or milk for our kids," he said.

George, 50, worked for 25 years as an auto mechanic before he had two heart attacks in the last three years. His wife, Kelly, 28, is in a job-training program. "I want my children to eat well," he said. "We get scared wondering where the next dollar will come from."

For three years, the Garrett family has received Aid to Families With Dependent Children—what most people mean when they talk about welfare—and food stamps. They now get $454 in aid and $311 in food stamps each month. (Federal statistics show that two-thirds of welfare recipients in 1993 were children—9.5 million out of 14.1 million people.)

"On TV and around, you hear people making fun of people on welfare and getting so mad about it," George said. "It's like racism—judging people by the surface. Maybe people get sick, lose their job, lose their house—they can't afford to buy food, and their kids suffer. It's what happened to me."

The U.S. Census Bureau reports that more than one million Americans fell into poverty in 1993. Since 1990, more than 7 million people have been added to the food-stamp program. One in 10 Americans now receives food stamps—with more than half of the food stamps going to feed children.

"Sometimes it's just noodles and bouillon," says Kathleen Krausmann, 41, of McKeesport, Pa. "I always worry that the kids aren't getting enough protein and fresh vegetables." Her husband, Gary, 40, works at a video store for $5.50 an hour while Kathleen cares for three young sons, including an 11-year-old at home with cerebral palsy, and a niece. "We get about $175 a month in food stamps," she said, "and I don't know how we'd get by without them. We've needed local programs for food—maybe a turkey and fixings for a holiday—and that really helps. It's nice to know there are people who care."

Like George Garrett, Kathleen is sensitive to the stigma that comes from receiving welfare assistance. "I know that it's easier to think people getting assistance are just lazy," she said, "but we're a working family trying to get by. We just can't make it with all the bills and the cost of food. It just shows you that even if you're working, you may not really be making a living."

In fact, the 1991 Hunger Project study indicates that 46 percent of hungry households have at least one wage-earner. Households like Kathleen's spend an average of 54 percent of their gross income on shelter costs, compared to the typical American family, which spends 20 percent. The average hungry household is only able to spend 68 cents per person per meal, which turns out to be nearly a third of their gross monthly income.

Susanna, 36, of Garland, Tex., had to feed her 9-year-old son and 4-year-old daughter on her husband's $20,000-a-year salary. "My son has asthma and, even with insurance, the co-payments and transportation to and from doctors cost a lot of money," she said. "Then there are the rent, utility bills and on and on. For two years, the four of us got by on $100 a month for food. You have to be creative to feed a family for that little. I can make a little bit of hamburger go a long way."

Susanna finally landed a job at a nursing home but still worries about those hard times. "I wonder if my kids were getting the vitamins they needed," she said.

Her fears are not unfounded. Hunger and undernutrition rob children of their potential, a 1993 Tufts University study concluded, resulting in lost knowledge, brainpower and productivity. Hungry children are more than four times as likely as other children to suffer from fatigue and twice as likely to suffer from frequent colds, ear infections and headaches. Hungry children miss school because of sickness more often and, as the Hunger Project found, they go to the doctor almost twice as often.

Monica, 25, from Washington, D.C., received assistance from the Women, Infants and Children program when she was pregnant with her third child. This program provides nutritious foods, nutrition education and access to health care to low-income women who are pregnant or caring for an infant.

"I don't know how I would have been able to eat properly without it," Monica said. She now works part-time as a cashier and has completed two years of college. "I've been getting help," she said, "but I'm looking forward to getting a degree and having a better life for my three kids and me too."

Poor diet is closely related to low birth-weight, which is a factor in the deaths of infants during their first 12 months. Twenty-three other developed nations have lower infant-mortality rates than the United States.

Robert Fersh noted that a Department of Agriculture study found that for every $1 spent on a pregnant woman in its Women, Infants and Children program, $1.77 to $3.13 is saved in Medicaid costs during her child's first 60 days of life.

"If children don't get the nutrition necessary for concentration and learning," Fersh stressed, "America won't get the educated workforce and high productivity it needs.

"The Hunger Project study is a warning."

[1995]

Understanding the Reading

1. Why are American children hungry?
2. How did CCHIP conduct its survey and for what reason?
3. Why do people receive food stamps?
4. What are the effects of hunger on children?

Suggestions for Responding

1. If you went to bed hungry as a child, describe how you felt. If you never did, imagine how hunger might have made you feel, and write about it.
2. If you have seen or known people who shop with food stamps, describe what you thought about them and what assumptions you made about their character. ✦

44

Mother Courage

ARIEL GORE

A young woman with a sticky baby in a stroller stands ahead of me in line at the check-cashing place on Broadway. It is the ninth of the month so the wait to pick up our food stamps is short.

Her turn comes and she pushes the stroller to the counter. She slips her state ID card under the bullet-proof glass and watches the woman who picks it up.

"Sixty-four," the woman says, and passes a pink card to the young mother to sign.

"I'm supposed to get a hundred, not sixty-four," she snaps.

"I don't know, I just give out the food stamps," the woman behind the glass says meekly.

I'm sure the flurry of profanities that escape from the young mother's mouth can be heard from the street. By the time she quiets, the woman behind the glass is holding the food stamps to her chest. "I'm not going to give them to you," she says matter-of-factly.

The mother suddenly assumes a diplomatic tone. "I'm sorry," she says. "I know it's not your fault. Can I please have my food stamps so my baby can eat?"

The woman behind the counter gives in to the plea, but as soon as the mother wraps her pale fingers around the small pile of bills and pulls them safely away from the glass, she starts in again.

I sign for my own food stamps quickly, and rush out into the brisk morning. As the glass door shuts behind me I can hear the mother screaming. "You think I'm going to kiss your ass . . ."

The mood in the food stamp line this month is more strained than usual. By now everyone has heard something of Washington's plans for "welfare reform," and we know the complaints aren't with the welfare system itself, but with us.

Even I, who have never made any secret about being on welfare and never apologized for procreating before my 20th birthday, have begun glancing over my shoulder when I am in line at the grocery store waiting to pay with brightly colored government coupons. At the bank, I now hesitate before taking my AFDC check out of the county envelope it arrived in and placing it on the counter in front of a mani-cured teller. And from long talks and brief encounters with other women on government aid, I know I am not alone.

At our most panicked we envision a social worker hammering on the door and hauling our children off to an orphanage. On calmer days we simply try to make ends meet, acutely aware that the climate has shifted, that our families have been judged, and that the verdict is guilty.

The "welfare debate" has been going on for a long time, longer than the four years I have been on the rolls. The politicians' wranglings always revolve around how severely to cut our checks this year. The personal attacks I have encountered in my day-to-day life range from grocery baggers' snide comments to a neighbor who pounded on the glass panes of my front door periodically, demanding to know "whose responsibility is it to raise your damn kid anyway?"

Young motherhood quickly taught me never to question that child rearing was a mother's responsibility alone, and to be eternally grateful for whatever help I received to keep my baby from starving. When I got pregnant at 18, I could have had an abortion. I had the political and personal freedom to terminate the pregnancy. I had a choice. And I decided to have a baby. Like studying English instead of medicine, I knew motherhood was a bad economic decision. I didn't calculate my finances—there weren't any. So just as I was toting up the resources I could gather to pay for college, I also had to think about how I would take care of my child: there was marriage, private charities, or AFDC. Mercifully, I had the support to get out of an abusive relationship shortly after my daughter was born, so wedding plans—shotgun or otherwise—were out of the question. Private charities proved to be helpful but underfunded at best, paternalistic and underfunded at worst.

So when my daughter was six months old and I was about to start college, I got on the welfare rolls. I used what I still consider to be sound logic, but in the afternoon it took to fill out the welfare forms I had become a part of what conventional wisdom now refers to as a "social pathology." I might add that although I have received significantly more government assistance to pay skyrocketing university tuition than to feed my baby, I have never been pathologized for pursuing an education I couldn't afford.

Now the powers that be, from Newt Gingrich to Bill Clinton, are calling for an intensification of stigmas against teenage pregnancy, and out-of-wedlock births. Erstwhile political opponents have come together to declare open season on any mom who dares procreate without a husband and a stable income. Linking teen motherhood to gun violence "and other social pathologies" lends urgency to their arguments. As Jonathan Alter put it in a . . . column in *Newsweek,* "every threat to the fabric of this country—from poverty to crime to homelessness—is connected to out-of-wedlock teen pregnancy."

I realize that I might be called a radical when I suggest that these stigmas should really be applied to lawmakers who cut welfare benefits without serious plans to end poverty. I might even be crossing the line when I suggest that they should be branded on batterers whose violence is responsible for displacing 50 percent of the homeless women and children in this country. The vast majority of young mothers I have come into contact with over the years are good mothers. But disrespect, shame and schemes to cut off the few available resources a woman has do not bolster good parenting. These assaults merely drain our spirits and shorten our fuses. And we all know that after food, clothing and shelter, what a mother needs most is patience and spirit.

When I tell people how I wound up on the welfare rolls, my story is often met with nods of understanding and a reminder that I am an exception, that I am different from other teen parents. For a time I believed the assertion that somewhere out there lived the stereotypical teen moms who had children for money and did not deserve the few hundred dollars a month they received from the state. But the more young mothers I meet in the welfare office, in college classrooms and in high school continuation programs, the more I find there is a world of exceptions, a world of human beings each with their own stories of understandable life choices.

Because I have been somewhat outspoken in my belief that young women have the same right to parent as older adults, a lot of folks, including one local TV reporter and several radio-show hosts, have asked whether I am not encouraging teen pregnancy. Had any of them given me more than 30 seconds to respond I would have told them what I tell pregnant teens who ask for my advice: Countless women and men have fought for our reproductive freedom. Countless women and men have fought for our right not to have to marry, whether we choose to remain single because of violence or simple lack of chemistry (assuming, of course, that dad left a forwarding address). But *you* will have to fight for your own right to parent. Family, neighbors and society at large will make it extremely difficult for you. But if, given all that you know about this country, you choose to take on parenting before "conventional wisdom" says you may, I have faith that you can succeed.

You are not wrong. You have not sinned. You have burned no bridges, though you may have to pay a heavier toll to cross over again. Your nights will be sleepless and your days filled with diaper changing and impossible budgeting, but you are not alone. Afford your children all the respect few will afford you.

It is possible that life had discouraged the red-haired woman at the check-cashing place long before she became a mother, or maybe her mood this morning had more to do with sleep deprivation than with Newt Gingrich. I don't know. But I am willing to bet my welfare check what she needs isn't shame and stigma. The $36 worth of food stamps in question isn't likely to do the trick either, but they might feed her family [for a week], and that will be something.

[1995]

Understanding the Reading

1. Explain the attitudes of the young woman with the stroller and the woman at the counter.
2. How does Gore feel about her own welfare assistance?
3. When she got pregnant, what options did Gore think she had?
4. Explain the irony in Gore's receiving federally assisted child support and a federally assisted scholarship.
5. What does Gore think about current political attitudes toward single mothers?
6. How do people feel about Gore's personal experience and decisions as an unmarried mother?
7. What advice does Gore give pregnant teens and why?

Suggestions for Responding

1. Explain why you agree or disagree with Gore's advice to unwed teen mothers. ✦

45

"We're Not Bums"

PETER SWET

For more than three years, Gerald Winterlin, now in his 40s, was one of the estimated 3 million homeless Americans. Forced by joblessness to live in his car or abandoned buildings, he had to cope with a sense of hopelessness and despair that could, and occasionally did, destroy others like himself.

Now he lives in a warm, modest apartment near the University of Iowa, where he's a scholarship student working on his degree in accounting and maintaining a 3.9 average. I traveled to Iowa to speak with him, hoping to understand how this bright, well-spoken, typical-seeming American could ever have hit such a deep low in his life. Just as important, I wanted to know how he fought his way back.

On the first of two long nights we would spend talking together, the burly Winterlin sat at his kitchen table and recalled an incident that still haunts him.

"I was on the cashier's line at a supermarket," he began, "behind this young, healthy-looking black woman. When her groceries were rung up, she pulled out a bunch of food stamps. I said, 'Hey, get a job. I'm tired of having money taken from my paycheck for people like you!' I expected a sharp answer, but instead she looked embarrassed and said, 'There's nothing I'd like better than a job, but nobody will give me one.' 'Bull,' I shot back, then turned away. Twenty years later, I'd love to find that lady and tell her I'm sorry. Little did I realize that what happened to her could happen to anyone. It happened to me."

Winterlin was born in an area known as the Quad Cities, encompassing Davenport and Bettendorf on the Iowa side of the Mississippi River, with Rock Island and Moline on the Illinois side. One of four children of a tool-and-die man, he graduated from Bettendorf High and eventually began work at the International Harvester plant. "I worked there about eight years," he said, "till '82, after the farm recession hit. Quad Cities is a world center for manufacturing farm equipment, and over 18,000 people, including me, were laid off."

"At first we figured the government would help," he said, adjusting his large framed glasses. "Hell, they bailed out Chrysler, right? But, instead, weeks turned into months with no work. With only two or three weeks of unemployment left, my demands dropped real fast, from $15 an hour to begging to sweep floors—anything. One day I just picked up the phone book and started with the A's. I made a list of every company I applied to. The final number was 380, and I remember realizing that what few jobs there were went to younger people. Still, I'd go out all day looking."

Winterlin heaved a deep sigh and glanced out the window at the cold Iowa night. "I kept thinking there'd be a tomorrow. Late one night, I finally said, 'Well, Gerry, this is it. No tomorrow.' I packed what I hadn't already sold or pawned and walked out. I never planned on living in my car for long," he added, "but then, no one *plans* to be homeless."

What about his family—couldn't they help? "They'd have probably taken me in," he said, "but people who ask that don't understand how impossible it is to say, 'Hey, folks, here I am in my late 30s, such a pathetic loser I can't even take care of myself.' Besides, my old man had lost his own job after 25 years, just six months shy of a full pension."

I asked about welfare, and Winterlin laughed. "Don't get me started on that," he said. "Welfare is the fast route to nowhere. They give you everything except what you need—a job. Some people have no option, like women with kids, but guys like me who want just enough to get started again would rather freeze than fall into a system that gives you a roof but robs you of hope. You trade your individualism and spirit for survival, and for some of us that's not a fair trade. Homeless people are proud people too."

For months, Winterlin lived in his '60 Mercury with rags stuck in the rust holes. Finally, the car died, and he was forced to find shelter wherever he could. "Somehow I made it from day to day," he said. "I tried to look as good as I could, to keep clean. Sometimes I did odd jobs, but never enough to put a roof over my head. I kept trying, but before I knew it, three years of my life were gone."

"Unless you've been there, you can't understand the loneliness, the misery, the humiliation, the self-disgust at what you've been reduced to," Winterlin continued. "I knew guys who just couldn't take it anymore and did themselves in. We're talking big, proud men, not junkies or drunks. They killed themselves, but I say they died of broken hearts because they couldn't handle the way people look at you, the loss of self-respect."

We both fell silent for a moment, then I asked how he had managed to persevere. "When times got darkest," Winterlin answered, "when thoughts of death and feelings of hatred began to overwhelm me, I thought of the people in my life who have known how to give, not just take. One of them was Linda, the girl I should have married. I wish I could name all the others, but the good people know who they are. It's for them that I wanted to succeed."

"Anyway," he added, "I read about something called the Dislocated Workers Program, which was designed to help people from old, dying industries become trained in new technologies. They put me into Scott Community College in the Quad Cities. I got straight A's. Everything looked great, then the program was cut back after six months. I almost fell apart, but because my grades were so good a woman named Mary Teague took the time to care, to help me piece together enough funding to keep going."

I noted the framed scholarship certificates displayed proudly on the wall, and Winterlin smiled, putting a hand up to conceal the spaces where he'd once been forced to pull his own teeth. "No big secret to that," he laughed. "Just plain hard work." He studies 50 hours a week, besides attending classes and working 20 hours at a part-time job. He has no friends, he admitted, and spends weekends alone. "I know it wasn't my fault, but when you're homeless you lose so much self-respect, you stay away from people." I asked if he felt his fellow Americans understood the homeless problem.

"The thing most people *don't* understand," he replied, "is that most of the folks you see huddled in doorways in Eastern cities or living in parks in Santa Monica or begging for a roof right here in America's Heartland aren't there by *choice*. I didn't ask to lose my job. None of us did. We're not bums," he said pointedly, his voice rising. "We're good, hardworking Americans who happened to fall between the cracks."

How does he see his future? He hopes that, after receiving his degree, "at least one person out there will say, 'Hey, I hire a person by what he's got, not by his age or where he has been.'" He added, "I've got to prove I can be part of society again, that Gerald Winterlin and the millions of other homeless out there really do count. There are just five words I'm determined to leave behind me—words that no one can ever, ever take away from me. The words are 'Gerald Winterlin, summa cum laude.'"   [1990]

Understanding the Reading

1. What beliefs underlie Winterlin's confrontation with the woman in the supermarket?
2. How did Winterlin initially respond to unemployment?
3. Why didn't he turn to his family for help or go on welfare?
4. Why do some homeless men commit suicide?
5. Why may Winterlin escape his homelessness permanently? What obstacles does he face?

Suggestions for Responding

1. Winterlin says that the welfare system "robs you of hope." In what ways does Gore's story illustrate this point?
2. Imagine that you, like Winterlin, were suddenly made homeless due to unemployment. Describe the difficulties you would face, especially the obstacles to pulling yourself out of it on your own. ✦

46

Poverty or at Home in a Car

JACKIE SPINKS

For seven months, my home has been my 1973 Dodge van. Life in a car is similar to life in a garbage can: trash filled, cramped, and with a smell to die from. Before that, I lived in a shed. I live here because I was kicked out of the shed.

Guys, suited in black worsted, the authority clothes of caliphs-in-waiting, circle around me; avoiding eye contact.

Sometimes I wonder what's going through their minds when they see me? Do they ever wonder what's going through mine? Or do they give a damn? Or maybe they assume I don't have a mind? Or are they thinking, "Bum! Loser! What's the matter with you? There's work out there. It isn't a recession. You corks think you're too good to work. So okay, be a stiff, but why do I have to support you, and why do you dirty up nice streets? Where's your pride? Where's your work ethic?"

Yeah, I pretty much know them. But they don't know me from marmalade. So here's to making my acquaintance.

I'm one of those seedy guys at the bottom of America's class system, who knows that he's going to stay there. I'm not taken in by that "rags to riches" hooey our teachers, parents, media, in fact, the whole culture, fed us. I am 40-years old, and have not earned more than $20,000 in my entire life, which means I've lived on less than $100 a month, for the past 20 years. So I know, after all this time, I'm not going anywhere.

Before I go on I'd better forewarn you: I'm not a curator of America's art of scrimping, a chronicler of poverty's abasements, or a bemoaner of its inequality. I'm just a down-and-outer trying to puzzle out my life, figure out how guys like me get where they are, especially when they don't have the excuse of alcohol or dope for their downward spiral.

I sold my Yamaha for $100 and bought this beater I'm living in for $75. Pretty lucky break. I got it for $75 because the interior was gutted, the windows broken, the roof rusted through. It was ready for the compactor, so nobody bid on it at the city auction. Thus, I have a home—my first in a long time.

I tinkered with it and got it moving. The reverse gear needs money to fix, so I can only go forward. The back brakes are bad (more money) and I worry driving, because of the brakes. So I don't drive it far. Besides, I have to hang onto my space, where my car's parked. But every once in a while I take a spin around the block just to keep my beater alive, as who knows when the local Praetorians will hustle me off. They'll give me a ticket for something, probably driving without registration. The constabulary knows and hates me. Not only am I an outcast, but being only five and a half feet tall, I'm an easy nab.

Mostly I stay where I am. What's important is keeping my corner. Three other guys have found my spot and are now parked near me. If I move my car, they'll grab it, as it is the best space, so I protect my claim. It's particularly valuable to me, as it's the only place where I can move forward and don't need to go into reverse.

It's a challenge, living in a crouched position in my van: minus toilet, water, telephone, electricity, and privacy. But the toughest part is the temperature: 95 degrees in the summer and freezing in winter.

I eat at the mission. Before I forced myself to check out the place (I was afraid of it), I lived on stuff like vanilla wafers, nachos, half-eaten pizzas, or sandwiches I found lying around.

Why the mission spooked me was, first, it was strange; and second, a lot of beefy guys with nothing to lose hung around the entrance. I had no weapon, no back-up, and there's always some guy hankering to beat up a little guy. On the one hand, poverty makes brutes, but on the other hand, people are poor because they're basically passive. Telling myself they all just want to be somebody and have you recognize it, I stiffened my mettle.

Nevertheless, just to avoid trouble, I smiled. I'm the kind of guy who smiles a lot, tells jokes, shows he's a regular guy. But I confess the adrenaline was pumping, and a rigid smile was shellacked on my face when I ambled cool, but not cocky, into the mission. It smelled like fat frying, a good smell, and the eating space was big—a high-ceilinged room with about 80 guys and 2 women sitting at long tables.

A lot of the guys were Mexican farmworkers, all talking in Spanish. They had serious faces. A couple years back, I climbed on a field bus and for about two weeks, picked strawberries. Those people were fast, about four times as fast as me. A little girl about 10 picked faster than I ever could—if I lived to be 100. I watched her to figure out her method. She'd kind of hold the bush and pull three or four berries at one reach. And did it with miniature fingers, that didn't crush the berries—such ingenuity wasted on a berry bush. She said she wanted a house and three kids when she grew up.

The food at the mission will never disturb McDonald's, but it fills me up and that's what counts. For instance, on my first day, they gave us two choices: bean soup or venison soup. We have a lot of deer hunters in this part of the country and most of them dislike venison, so the mission gets a lot of venison.

Most of the guys chose venison soup, but I chose bean soup. I'm a vegetarian, more by necessity than by conviction, but I think going without meat is a good idea. Besides, I have a soft spot for deer.

The mission, also, gets a lot of good pastries, the kind you buy at a bakery, usually about a week old. I eat a lot of doughnuts. You can take them with you when you leave. Sometimes we have ripe bananas. Sometimes we even have salad.

Often the food at the mission is spoiled, but nobody reports it, as it's better to be sick than risk closure. The bathroom, which is next to the kitchen, has been without toilet paper or paper towels for months. Four of the six toilets don't flush and nobody mops or uses cleanser, so you can figure it's a shopping mall of microbes, but nobody expects Trump Towers. Often I puke. Once, I did it for two days, but as one guy said, "How do you know it was the food at the mission. It could have been the flu."

Illness is for the rich. The poor that try to join that club, get two minutes and a swift heave-ho. It's been 20 years since I've been to a doctor. A few weeks back, I drove a guy with a severed finger to emergency, and sat with some mothers, who said they'd been waiting three hours. The mothers held their sick kids and scolded the others.

Many of the guys at the mission are here illegally. Nervous. Worried about trouble, too. Like me. And they're dirty. Like me. I can't speak Spanish, maybe a few words like "por favor, como esta, adios, and gracias." Wish I knew more. A big regret—flunking Spanish in high school. Their English is better than my Spanish, but still hard to understand. So mostly we just smile at one another.

My little forays into conversation with mission Saxons usually consist of mutual brag-a-thons. You'd think we'd all just dumped our portfolios with our brokers and decided to do a little slumming. And, if not that, we all have ships that will be tooting in, around the bend, any minute.

According to all of us displaced whites (I gas along with the best), we just need a little capital to get started. Some of the guys have pretty good ideas. One guy, a wood carver, thought he'd make Sasquash dolls and sell them at local fairs and bazaars. Another guy built a toilet for car dwellers, but fearing theft of his idea, was cagey in explaining how it operated. I listened up on that one. Then his paranoia took over, and he clammed up. Another had an idea for paper blankets.

It's all just talk. Nobody will ever do anything. To build up our self-esteem, we peg ourselves as 20th century pariahs, like frontier sheep farmers. We perceive ourselves as urban pioneers staking our claims, front runners of things to come. We carve out places, on the street, protect our turf, think of ourselves as prototypes of those guys who straggled over the Cascades without a penny to their names: sometimes desperate, often lonely, frequently surviving by their wits. They were giants. Stoics. Squatters like us. Our heroes. Deep in all of us, we mourn not having been born in the 18th century. Because we believe (probably incorrectly), that then poverty was a clean and honorable estate, not just wacko actions and fantasizing, like it is today.

How does a homeless, jobless, middle-aged man occupy his day? Well, first off, I sleep. Besides sleeping I post myself in the library. I arrive at opening time, ten in the morning, and stay most of the day. It's cool in there. Air conditioned. But temperature is only a minor reason I like the library. The main reason is the people. The people are quiet. No one bothers me or tells me to move on.

I read everything: religion, carpentry, mechanics, electrical, police training, political, biographies, nutrition, baseball novels, and a lot of gun, boat, news, and alternate press magazines. Sometimes I walk along the docks, examine the boats, imagine stowing away on a Russian cargo ship.

I scrutinize, with the eye of a tourist: buildings, factories, guys working—and I especially like to study bees. When I've exhausted looking, I sit in my car and read.

How do I live? Well, I use a can for my bowels and dump my loo near some pole beans and tomatoes in a garden nearby. I expected big beans and red, ripe tomatoes in that spot, but to my surprise they're limping along. One of my fellow car-dwelling aficionados said, "Living on the streets, you probably got toxic crap." I do my "miss congeniality" smile, but don't think it's funny. I don't think he meant it to be funny. I used recycled newspaper for toilet paper.

I mosey up to the college about once a month and sneak a shower in the college gym. I'm careful to use it when it's empty, shower as quickly as possible, just in case I get caught.

Probably the biggest problem for guys like me is water. I'm always looking for water. Every chance I get, I fill up a jug I carry everywhere in my backpack and haul it back to my Dodge. And that's strictly for drinking—not to wash hands, face, dishes, or clothes.

Apart from begging, the thing about poor people that riles rich people the most is our grime. Cleanliness is identified with goodness in America. It's next to Godliness. Dirt is evil. I think we're supposed to clean up and pretend we're real. I don't oppose cleanliness. It's that cleanliness for someone living in a car is a labyrinthine ordeal.

First, to wash and dry two loads of clothes— it costs about $5.00 total. Plus, you need a way to get to the laundry; plus, you need soap; plus, you need something to wear while you're washing the clothes.

But now and then a car-dwelling paisano does spiff up. Once cleaned up, he isn't too bad. I wonder why I've been going on ad nauseam about cleanliness and appearance? I just have some insecurity there. But then, so when aren't we insecure?

As for work, in my 20s when hope bloomed, I choo-chooed along, the little engine that could—but not anymore. Now, it's "tote that barge, lift that bail, wish to hell I could land in jail." I've worked for bosses that were drill sergeants with little concern about their oxen's safety, who expected it to plow away at minimum pay. I got chemical burns on my hands that ate away chunks of the flesh, burns that still eat my fingers ten years later. I have no hope for anything better than a grinding $4.60 an hour.

A guy at the mission said, "I'd rather be poor than work. Why should I help make the rich richer?"

I'm anxious all the time. Until I found the mission, I worried constantly about where my next meal was coming from; I was anxious about my future; anxious about people. But mostly I was anxious that if—by some remote possibility I landed a decent job—that after so many years of non-work, with its absence of punctuality, drive, and concentration, I would fail again.

Hey, I sound like the mother of all belly-achers, bitching about contaminated food, cleanliness, jobs, pisspots, anxiety. I forget the other class has troubles, too; that they whip themselves, unmercifully, if some friend gains on them. That if their cash flow falls from ten million to two million, they worry they're finished and stumble home, get swacked, and feel like they'll never be a real player.

I heard some social worker-type talk about homelessness being a new deviant career. Sure am glad I have a career at last. Deviant or otherwise. Is homelessness better than being male, white, 40, and working at McDonalds? Yeah, I guess so, but then, Hell, McDonalds wouldn't hire a bum like me—even if he did have nice teeth.

The inner awareness I live with and fight every day is that I'm nothing. To get rid of this feeling, I'd like to try Prozac. But two bucks for a pill, without a buzz. Then again, maybe I'm lucky. At some later date, they'd probably discover Prozac caused some kink, like edema of the brain, or elephantiasis, or more likely, an old stand-by like high blood pressure or cancer. They always find some pea to stick in our comfort zone. So I sleep Prozacless.

Because I sleep a lot, the books I've read label me depressed. I question that, as I've never contemplated suicide; but maybe I am depressed and don't know it. Or maybe I sleep because I'm bored. About the only truism about poverty in America in the 1990s is that it's one giant yawn.

Maybe that's what depression is—nothing to do. Rutsville. And doing the rut alone, at ebb tide, and feeling it's all your fault. That everything's your fault. Feeling something's wrong with you because you would rather be poor than be under the foot of a master. So who wants to think. Better to sleep.

About our depression, whenever you channel onto a poor person's wave, male or female, what you discover is that—underneath the defenses, they're thinking, "There's something haywire with me. I'm worse than second-rate, I'm

rotten. I can't do anything right. Nobody will ever hire a creep like me for any job that has a future. I'll never do anything that's even slightly smart."

To illustrate, a guy at the mission, came out from lunch and found the side of his Kawasaki dented. A few minutes before he'd been chair of the brag-a-thon. Now, you'd expect the guy to say, "I'm gonna kill the bastard who did this." But no, all this poor jerk could do was stare and mutter, "It's all my fault. I can't do anything right."

We all walked away, but it hit close. We understood.

In contrast to Americans, who place so much emphasis on individualism, people from other countries don't blame themselves. A Hindu cab driver, so black that he felt forced to reiterate three times, to our inquiring minds, that he was Caucasian, told us about an experience he had here. He was sitting in a park and noticed several Americans going over to a marble protrusion, bending over it, and when water gushed out, drinking. Being thirsty, he went over to the protrusion, bent over it, but no water came out. He bent over it several times, still no water. Finally, he walked away, telling himself even the water over here in America is prejudiced.

Now that's what we considered an intelligent response, the kind we wish we could make.

It's like the world has a negative image of us, so we absorb that image, make it ours, and agree with the world, that, yes, because we aren't successes, we're slime.

Yeah, we're lazy. The dictionary definition of lazy is slow moving, resistant to exertion, slothful. And gadzooks, the perfect definition of depression.

Those active, employed people, who run around doing this and that, who talk briskly, walk with that high-stepping gait, who complain about having too much on their calendar, who, after a quick handshake, dash off to another appointment, are as strange to us as a bidet. We watch, and wonder, and shuffle off, when we're around them. I guess they don't understand us either; the passive, the depressed, the underclass. Yet, we all share the same boat and it's gaining water. And maybe we know it better than they do.

Whatever. So, I sleep about 11 or 12 hours a day. Wish it were the sleep of the frazzled or anesthetized, but it's a half awake sleep. When awake I contemplate ways to make our world better. On good days, I dream of a revolution in concept. On bad days I decide, "Blow 'er up. Start over."

As I lie here, watching the rain drip alongside the car window, I forage around for something positive to say about poverty. What I come up with is freedom. Yeah, I have freedom—no worry about stocks or kids or lovers. I click around the idea of freedom for a while and finally decide, next to a high IQ, freedom is the most over-rated quality any sociologist ever extolled.   [1996]

Understanding the Reading

1. Describe Spinks' life in his van.
2. What does he think about eating at the mission?
3. How do Saxons at the mission talk? Why?
4. How does Spinks occupy his day? Why?
5. How does he take care of his sanitary needs?
6. How do poor people respond to negative occurrences in their lives?

Suggestions for Responding

1. Write a paper explaining why you do or do not believe in the "rags to riches" proposition.
2. Imagine you were homeless and describe how you would cope with that situation. ✦

47

The Fall

MARGE PIERCY

With so many of her people gone, Mary had little cleaning work. However, she had places to stay, surreptitiously. She would be owed money from dog walking and pet feeding when her clients returned. She figured that going in and out of the Anzio house much was asking for trouble. She was content to lie low and watch TV. She even made a pot of soup, something she hardly ever got to do. She drank hot tea all day long. She took two long warm baths a day, soaking her weary achy body until it shone. She tried a little of each bubble bath, gel, and oil. Damask rose was her favorite. She washed her hair, laundered her clothes, polished her shoes, and cleaned her galoshes. In damp cold weather, everything got wet and never dried out, till she smelled like a garage floor.

By Friday morning, she was fit again. It was those church basements that got her, and hanging around the streets till she could sneak in someplace. Summers had their own problems—she couldn't close up the houses as tight so that the light wouldn't show—although in her observation, most people left lights on nowadays, and the sun set so late that she had to wait till eight thirty to slip into her chosen shelter. But if she got caught short, she could sleep in a garage for a night. It was dirty and it didn't feel safe, but it was better than the streets. Twice she spent the night in a gazebo of a fancy house on Brattle Street.

Winter was a different story. Night came down early, but sleeping outside could kill her. Hadn't she almost died, back when she was new to life on the streets? It was always dangerous from the weather and from the men who would hurt any woman they could.

After every meal, she put her garbage neatly into a plastic bag in her shopping bag. She was always prepared. She carried her own knife, fork, spoon, and plastic bowl; anything of theirs she used, she washed at once: compulsive, but part of her daily discipline. She had always been a mad housekeeper who never left dishes in the sink or beds unmade or dust under the couch. Besides, she owed it to the people whose houses she borrowed to return them at least as clean as she found them. Third, she had a policy, leave no traces.

The Anzios were in Florida over Christmas, to visit his parents who'd retired to Sanibel Island. About thirty years ago, her husband, her children, and she spent ten days there. She remembered her two-piece turquoise bathing suit Jim was crazy about. It was a color they used a lot then, in architecture, in furnishings, in clothing. He couldn't keep his hands off her when she wore that suit. She was fair and she had to be careful in the sun. Nobody had heard of sunscreen in those days so she just burned. Sea shells. Conch shells. On the terrace was an outdoor shower behind a screen. Once, feeling daring, they had made love in it while the children were at the beach. When a man was so crazy about you, it was hard to imagine that a time would come when he just wanted you out of his way, when he treated you like a piece of cheese that had turned bad. Her sin was to get middle-aged. Time nibbled away at her looks.

It happened so gradually that she simply didn't realize she wasn't a pretty girl any longer. Mary never got fat. Oh, she put on some weight—not as much as he did, but some. She thickened around the middle, in the ankles and upper arms. Since she was a baby she had always been pretty, so she took it for granted. Maybe she should have dyed her hair, but when she asked Jim, he pooh-poohed it, saying he liked her the way she was, he liked her natural. All her ladies dyed their hair. She should have had sense enough just to do it and keep her mouth shut.

Mary had thought she was exempt from the adultery she knew had rotted many suburban marriages around them. Those scandals were the problems of other women, who had failed in their marriages. She thought because she knew how to shop and how to run a house and how to make conversation with a judge or an undersecretary's wife or a urologist, that she knew all about life. She imagined because her husband wanted her passionately into her thirties, that he would always want her.

A housewife didn't give much weight to boredom, because whether she was waiting for a husband to come home or a baby to be born or a load of clothes to dry or a roast to cook, she spent a lot of time exercising her patience. From one little crisis to the next pressing job, the days unwound. She was worrying about Jaime's grades in algebra or whether Cindy was going to fit into her prom dress, and she was thinking about how they said a new diet would take off weight or help the heart, and whether she could get her family to eat that way. She was thinking that Jaime didn't want to go to the Maryland shore this year and where should they take a vacation that would satisfy everybody—not including herself, because she took for granted that if they were satisfied, so was she. She was

thinking about, the driveway cement is cracking and the dog has to go to the vet for his shots and is it Ed Vickers or Ed Simmons that Dr. Caldwell can't stand at the dinner table with him? Yes, she had been swimming in a big pink aquarium, and she never thought that somebody would come along with a hammer and break it until she was gasping for her life and everything she had taken for granted, for permanent, was gone.

At times she let herself pretend she lived in the Anzio house. She was always amazed how much changed in this home, how often Mrs. Anzio got rid of a couch or ordered new draperies. Suddenly a painting disappeared or half the furniture was moved around. Vases, bric-a-brac came and went. Nobody understood how precious were the things they were used to, until they lost them. If she had a little cot of her own, she would love it like a pet. The day after Christmas, the Anzios were due back, but the Baers were leaving. She would clean up carefully early tomorrow morning and decamp. The malls would be mobbed, and she could hang out.

Today, Christmas, she must see Beverly. Beverly had been a bag lady operating nearby, whom Mary had greeted when she went to clean in that neighborhood every Wednesday and Friday. After Beverly had been attacked and left for dead in a Dumpster, Mary had begun visiting her in the hospital. Beverly was the only person in the world Mary could talk to honestly, the only person who knew she was homeless too.

She had bought Beverly wool pants at Goodwill. The lining was torn, but Mary had spent the evening mending it. She had fixed the pockets too, so they would hold a lot. The pants were dark red and really warm. She would also bring Beverly a couple of chocolates from a party at the Millers'. She had discreetly hidden treats as she was cleaning up, including most of a plate of only slightly stale tiny sandwiches—canapés such as she had put out in her days as a Bethesda hostess. That had been her supper, although the pâté had given her indigestion. Her stomach must be more delicate these days, from not eating much. When she was younger, she could eat anything, no matter how fiery or spicy, and not even belch. Her ex-husband Jim used to say, Mary has an asbestos tummy.

Catering must be a nice business. All that food to snack on. Marry a professional man, they told her when she was growing up; they should have said, be a caterer, buy a property and pay it off fast. Never mind the rest. Get a job around food and a roof over your head that belongs to you and you alone. Now that was advice no romantic young girl would ever heed.

The nurse's station had been perfunctorily decorated, a plate of Christmas cookies set out on the counter. Beverly sat up in the half empty room. Two of the patients had been released in time for the holiday. None of the original women with whom Beverly had shared the ward were still there. The others had been discharged; different women had come in their place and left again. Beverly's injuries had been serious, her condition bad, but they were also keeping her rather than discharge her to the street. Someone had taken an interest. A program had been found to cover her, but she was going to have to leave soon.

Beverly was fiddling with her ragged gray hair, growing back where they had shaved her head. "They're going to discharge her to Rosie's Place."

Mary nodded. She was used to the way Beverly spoke of herself in the third person. Living on the streets made a woman a little weird. "You can't go on the streets the way you are. Better to stay in a shelter till the weather warms up. As long as they let you stay."

"She always managed. She's tough. But she hates the noise and the prying. She remembers the Pine Street shelter in the old days. They took your stuff away at night. It was all the time waiting in line. They took your soul away."

"I didn't like shelters, either," Mary said. "But if I was injured, I'd do it till I was strong again. The winter's so hard."

Beverly loved the pants. Why could she do the right thing for her friend, but never for her daughter or her grandchildren? That night, lying on the Anzios' couch, she kept thinking about Beverly leaving the hospital. It was one of the worst days of her life when she had to leave her little apartment. Not that it was so wonderful— she had been ashamed of it, not understanding how lucky she was to have a so-called studio apartment, not matter how noisy and dilapidated and scurrying with mice that fouled her food. B.U. had bought the building to turn into student housing.

Her apartment and her job vanished together. She worked in a stationer's shop in the same block, and the renovation threw the store out a couple of months before she was evicted. Teodoro's Stationers could not find rent low enough so the marginal business could thrive. Mr. Teodoro was soon working at Stop & Shop, and she was running through her money in bottom-drawer motels.

Before she had been evicted, it had become evident she could afford nothing that existed, and the wait for public housing was forever and a day. Finally they had thrown her few things on the sidewalk in a pitiful pile she had to walk away from, carrying her two suitcases and her raincoat and winter coat, her quilt. She was too stunned, too numb to cry. She kept looking back at her table, her chair, her bed, her pots and dishes. What would become of her?

There had always been neighborhoods of cheap rooming houses when she was growing up. When had they disappeared? Where did poor people live now? Everything she could find was beyond her income. She wrote to Cindy and she wrote to Jaime. Cindy sent her a letter full of advice on budgeting her income, a check for two hundred dollars, and a long complaint about the cost of raising children in the Washington area. Two of her kids were in private schools. She simply did not have any discretionary income. What had happened to the settlement Daddy had given her?

Given me, Mary thought. I earned every penny, and he never gave me a cent more than the nasty judge made him part with. Where did it go? To relocate here. To pay bills. To buy medical insurance, now lapsed because she could not make the payments. To buy a winter coat. To put down as a deposit on phone, electricity, rent. To fix her car, while she had been able to keep it running.

Jaime put a twenty in an envelope and said he would send money whenever he could. The next month he sent another twenty. Nothing the next month. Then again. Once in a while he sent a twenty, always folded up neatly in a card with a joke on it. She forgave his failure to help her. Over the years he had probably given her more in his impulsive and disjointed way than Cindy with her lists and her excuses. And he had far less money to start with. Cindy made some money from her silly boutique, and her husband minted it.

Every day for the next two months, Mary looked for a job, but jobs were like ex-husbands: they wanted someone young and slender. She had had friends in the building, but they were scattered. Several had gone back where they came from, moving in with relatives in Tennessee or Kansas. Three women had moved together into a winter rental on Revere Beach, where they let her use their phone. She got into the Y for three weeks, then her money ran out. She could not find a job, and soon she was down to her last ten dollars. She was frankly terrified.

She had sold off her microwave, her jewelry, her good watch, her clock radio, and most of her wardrobe. She had to winnow the artifacts of her life, the photos, the letters, the mementos. She threw away her old report cards and honors and diplomas. She tossed her wedding and divorce papers. Most of the mementos of her children she sent to Cindy and Jaime, keeping only a couple of photos. To Jaime she sent most of the photos of her parents, her grand-parents, baby pictures, the record of her life. The letters she simply tore up.

She ended up with what would fit on her back, into a small suitcase, and into a large fabric carryall she had used to take to the beach all her kids' paraphernalia. On April 7 she walked out of the Y she had been calling home and into the city, with no idea what was going to become of her.

She was on the streets and terrified. She had no idea what to do with herself, where to go, how to manage. In six months she had gone from being a woman with a job and a little apartment and all the normal wardrobe and items— clock radio, electric toothbrush, microwave— that she had taken for granted as props of any normal life, to being a woman with a small suitcase she lugged about with her and a large fabric carryall. She did not know where to go to the bathroom. During the daytime hours, she used the public library bathroom or the bathrooms in the department stores.

The first night she tried to sleep in a doorway, the suitcase was stolen. That simplified everything. It was the other street people who told her what to do. They thought she was funny, trying to sleep on the street in a peach-colored satin down quilt she still had from her old life, carrying around a little pillow for her head.

The first days on the street, she kept bursting into tears. She could not believe this was happening. She was becoming dirty. She smelled bad. Her clothes were beginning to fray, stiff with dirt and wrinkled from being slept in. She was Mary Ferguson Burke. She had gone to college. She had raised two children. She had entertained the assistant undersecretary of commerce. She had belonged to a country club. She had had an all-electric kitchen. She had been photographed with Cindy both astride bays for an article in a local paper on summer activities. She had owned forty pairs of shoes and eight coats and a dozen cocktail dresses. Now she was sleeping in a cardboard box in an alley, wearing filthy rags and smelling like garbage.

People would look at her and look away, they would stare through her. They would give her glances of disgust. She was a pile of dog shit on the pavement. She should be scraped off and put in a Dumpster. A younger black woman named Samantha took her in tow. She had been hit by a car in an alley and walked stiff-legged, favoring her right side. She had lost half her teeth, but she still had a smile that made Mary feel warmed. Mary learned to stay away from her when she had not had a drink yet and again when she had too much, but in between, Samantha was kind and wanted to help. She decided Mary should try shelters. Samantha preferred life on the streets because she was crazy in love with an alkie they called Sly. She took Mary to Morgan Memorial, showed her the shelters, soup kitchens, and where to get off the streets to keep warm, where to get water, how to pee in alleys without being seen. "Remember, honey, everything you got to do is wrong. It's against the law to sleep, to wash yourself, to pee, to take a shit. Everything you got to do, you can't do it if the law see you. Now, I can't pass no more. They know me. But you, you can still walk through a crowd, but you can't go along shuffling. You got to pick up your head and look like one them tight white women. Then you can pass and hang out without them hassling you all the time. They like to beat on us. I can't get by no more, but you can. You just got to try."

Samantha, dead of hypothermia three Januaries before. She had seen it on the evening news while camping in one of her clients' houses. Samantha was the first black friend she had ever had. Without her, she would not have made it.

Even now the smells overwhelmed her: sweat, vomit, urine, dust, disinfectant, the smells from the big kitchen. Always twenty people were coughing every moment. Stand in line to get in the door. Stand in the ugly lobby waiting to get inside. Get in line for your foam cup, your paper plate, your utensils, your starchy supper. Get in line for your towel. Line up for a shower. Line up to get your bed for the night. Line up if you want a locker, but there's a four-month waiting list. Get in line for your meds if they gave you tranks. Lots of the women were on Thorazine or something equally numbing or destructive. Stand in line to get clothes from the room, get a clean nightie.

The beds were a foot apart and she slept on her purse and wallet. She could hear this one muttering, that one in some kind of withdrawal, the other just crying. She could hear and smell them all and she could guess what she must seem like to others.

She could not let herself be pushed down into the faceless mass of "guests." She was not an alcoholic, she did not use drugs, she had not been abused beyond the ability to function. She began to volunteer. She wanted to distinguish herself in the eyes of the staff from the helpless hopeless women around her. But it was hard. It was hard to remember that she had ever had a real life. At five A.M. they had to be up and by eight, they were out on the street again to pass the day until late afternoon.

She had felt like a baggy body for which there was no room but this large storage bin. Many women were sick. Some were severely malnourished. Many had ulcerating sores on their legs or feet, sores that stank. It was not avoidable when a woman walked all day long on pavement in ill-fitting shoes and worse-fitting socks with holes in them.

There was no privacy, no silence, no place she could call her own. Every night that she managed to get into the shelter, never certain because beds for women were limited, she never knew where she would sleep. Nothing belonged to her. No space was her own. She was called a "guest" but she was on sufferance. Act up and you were excluded. The staff had changing blacklists of women who were no longer allowed inside. Life and death in the winter and sometimes in warmer weather. Life on the streets killed you slow, but sometimes people or the weather saw that it happened a lot faster.

She volunteered, she made herself useful, and the staff liked that. Soon she no longer smelled. She showered, she washed her hair. She began trying to get work again, but putting down the address of the shelter was iffy. Still, it was better than no address. She had been a secretary, she had sold in stores, she had been a cashier. She could find nothing. She looked far older than she had six months before. Her hair was scraggly and iron gray with an odd stain that had got into it one night when she slept on a grate.

She took pains with her appearance, but it was difficult. There were only three little mirrors over the three washbasins for the whole facility. The light was dim. Still she put on makeup Saturday and went to see her old friends in Revere Beach. They were scared too. They had to be out of their rental by the end of May, and they had no idea where they were going. They asked her where she was living, and she said, with a friend. I just sleep on her couch—it's temporary. They apologized and said they couldn't offer her their couch as Gigi was sleeping on it. But Gigi cut her hair and gave her a home perm. It felt wonderful to be with people who remembered her, who did not know she was no longer a person but a statistic, one of the despised who were thrust from the table and the room.

The shelter was a holding area to keep the women alive one more night. When she finally got a job with a cleaning service, she decided that she was rejoining the ranks of the living, however much stealth and subterfuge that took. She would hide like a mouse in the walls of the middle class. And she had.   [1994]

Understanding the Reading

1. After the first three or four paragraphs, what did you think Mary's lifestyle was?
2. What caused the marital problems between Mary and her husband, Jim?

3. Describe their lifestyle while they were married.
4. Who is Beverly, and why does Mary visit her in the hospital?
5. Why did Mary lose her apartment?
6. What help did Mary get from her children?
7. How does Mary feel that other people perceive her?
8. What did Mary learn from Samantha?
9. What is life in the shelters like?

Suggestions for Responding

1. Write a letter to Mary, advising her on how she should have dealt with the changes in her life.
2. Compare and contrast Winterlin's and Spinks' experiences of homelessness with that of Mary in Piercy's short story. Does their gender make a difference?
3. Write a poem to your mother, who has just become homeless. ◆

SUGGESTIONS FOR RESPONDING TO PART IV

1. Most of the writers in Part IV discuss in one way or another how family values and attitudes, language, leisure activities, manners, dress, possessions, and education influence and reflect socioeconomic class. Describe how your socioeconomic class was reflected in such features during your own childhood and youth. Since socioeconomic class is strongly influenced by race and ethnicity, some of your considerations may overlap with those you discussed in your ethnic heritage report for Part I. Careful thinking should help you sort out the economic factors and come to a fuller understanding of another of the complex factors that shape your identity.

2. If you no longer live in the socioeconomic class into which you were born, consider how and why the change took place. In what ways have you retained the influences of your earlier class experience? What charac-

teristics, behaviors, and values of that class have you rejected, either consciously or unconsciously? Evaluate the strengths of both classes.

3. In recent years, homelessness has become a severe problem throughout the country. Research the manifestations of homelessness in your region. What are the estimated number and proportion of homeless people? What demographic categories—such as gender, age, racial and ethnic groupings—do they represent? To what causes can your local homelessness problem be attributed? What programs, both governmental and private-sector ones, exist to assist the homeless? What additional services are needed?

4. Your instructor may want you to make an oral presentation of your report. In preparation, review the suggestions about oral reports given at the end of Part I.

SUGGESTIONS FOR RESPONDING TO IDENTITY

Apply the concepts you have explored in "Identity" to write an autobiographical report about how your present identity has been shaped by your race and ethnicity, your gender, and your economic class.

Power in its simplest sense means the ability to do, act, think, and behave as we like, to have control over our own lives. Because we are members of society as well as individuals, however, there are substantial restrictions on our ability to exercise this kind of personal power. Society influences who we are, what we can do, how we act, what we believe or think about, and—central to our purposes here—how we interact with others.

Most interpersonal relationships reflect the relative power of the individuals involved, and the individual with the greater power can exercise greater control. We derive power from our capacity to distribute rewards or punishment, from being liked or admired, or from our position of authority or expertise. If, for example, John is more in love with Shelby than she with him, she can exercise power over him, deciding where they go for dinner or how often they go out. She can reward him with her company or punish him by refusing to see him. Similarly, you may proofread a paper more carefully for a professor

Power

you like than for one whose lectures you find boring. Physicians and plumbers have power over their clients who need their expert services. However, not all social power differentials are determined by or are under the control of the individual.

Our society is organized **hierarchically;** that is, it is structured according to rank and authority, and power is distributed unevenly within this hierarchy. Moreover, membership in a particular group, in and of itself, tends either to enhance or to reduce one's power because some groups of people have more power and others have less. Access to power and our place in the social hierarchy both depend on a number of variable factors, including gender, race, sexual orientation, socioeconomic class, age, and religion.

In our society, men generally have more power than women, White people more power than people of color, heterosexuals more than homosexuals, wealthy people more than workers, and so on. The intersection of these hierarchies confers the greatest social power on the group at the "top" of each scale: White heterosexual men *as a group*. Their power relative to other groups both rests on and reflects their greater wealth, more prestigious positions, and greater access to information and education. Thus, even though individual men may be relatively powerless (a gardener employed by a wealthy widow, for instance), *as a group* White, heterosexual men are better able to control their own lives, to influence and control others, and to act in their own interests.

People who have established power under any social system find it beneficial to retain that system and maintain the status quo. The interests and needs of members of less powerful social groups are not relevant to their goals. In fact, within any social system, mechanisms operate to **marginalize,** confine to the edges of society, and subordinate its less powerful members. This is often accomplished by projecting stereotypes onto others.

A **stereotype** is a set of assumptions and beliefs about the physical, behavioral, and psychological characteristics assigned to a particular group or class of people. If we know that someone belongs to a given group, we make other suppositions about that person by attributing to him or her those qualities and characteristics we associate with that group. Stereotypes exist for every class of people imaginable; they can be based on such identifiers as age, education, profession, regional origin, economic status, family role, interests, sexual orientation, and disability. Stereotypes assigned by gender, race and ethnicity, and socioeconomic class, however, are the ones most deeply embedded in our culture, and the ones that we examine in the "Power" division.

Even though we may not like to admit that we stereotype people, we all do it. Stereotyping makes it easier to function in a world filled with unknowns. We use the oversimplified and exaggerated generalizations of stereotypes to filter and interpret the complexities of reality. They provide us with an easy way to both respond to and interact with this often confusing world; they also provide a simplified way to structure our social relationships.

The trouble with stereotypes, however, is that the filter also blocks our perceptions. If we see people in terms of the standardized pictures we project onto a group to which they belong, we don't see or interact with them as individuals. Worse still, we usually block and deny any characteristics that don't fit our preconceived ideas. The word *stereotype* originally referred to the solid metal plate of type used in printing. This origin reveals the truth about stereotypes: Not only are they rigid and inflexible, but they also perpetuate unchanging images.

Although some stereotypes may seem harmless enough, in general, stereotyping is hardly a benign process. This is made clear by the fact that none of us likes to be pigeonholed. We actively resist seeing ourselves and those with whom we are intimate in stereotypic ways; we insist on our individuality. We apply stereotypes only to others—to those who are unknown to us or who are different from us. And herein lies the rub.

Because difference often makes us uneasy and because we tend to fear the unknown, our collective characterizations of "others" incorporate many undesirable or less valued traits or behaviors. This provides the basis for prejudice against members of those groups. Without knowledge of specific individuals or examination of how they present themselves, we make adverse judgments about them.

We come to believe in their inferiority based solely on such traits as race, ethnicity, sex, class, age, disability, or sexual orientation.

In "Power," we look at what happens when these **prejudices,** belief in the inferiority of people because of their membership in a certain group, are acted on. **Discrimination** is behavior that disadvantages one group in relation to another group and maintains and perpetuates conditions of inequality. In our culture, it is practiced most often against women, minority men, lesbians and gay men, and poor people. Both individuals and organizations can discriminate, either consciously or unconsciously, and discrimination can be **institutionalized,** built into the system. **Institutionalized discrimination** includes those policies, procedures, decisions, habits, and acts that overlook, ignore, or subjugate members of certain groups or that maintain control by one group of people over another group— lighter-skinned people over darker-skinned individuals or groups, men over women, heterosexuals over homosexuals, rich over poor. Such discrimination creates obstacles and barriers for its targets and provides unfair privileges for its beneficiaries.

In Part V, "Power and Racism," we examine the experience of racism, discrimination against and subordination of a person or group because of color. Part VI, "Power and Sexism," takes a comparable look at discrimination against and subjugation of women simply because of their sex and the corollary mistreatment of lesbians and gays. We also focus on the power of the federal government, when research scientists are warned that their work on HIV/AIDS may be "politically controversial." In Part VII, "Power and Classism," we consider the impact of socioeconomic class in the United States, focusing on the forces that cause economic inequities and poverty.

We like to think of America as a place of liberty, equality, and justice for all, but, as the readings in "Power" document, this ideal has yet to be realized. Racism, sexism, and classism, as we will see, are intertwined and augment and reinforce one another. Moreover, they are not simply problems for minorities, women, and the poor; they are, as a bumper sticker declares, "a social disease." The more fully each of us understands these problems, the closer we all will be to finding a cure.

Power and Racism

RACISM IS NOT SIMPLY A BLACK AND WHITE ISSUE; IT is the subordination of any person or group because of skin color or other distinctive physical characteristics. As discussed in the introduction to Part I, racial identity is not as fixed and immutable as we think. It is a **social construct**—a classification based on social values—that could be said to exist only in the eye of the beholder. At one point or another, many different peoples have been considered to be racial groups—Jews, Irish, Italians, Poles, Latinas, Latinos, Native Americans, Asian Americans, and African Americans—and have been subjected to racist treatment.

With few exceptions, Americans agree that racism is a bad thing, but there is less consensus about precisely what racism is or how it actually operates. The U.S. Commission on Civil Rights identifies two levels of racism. The first, **overt racism,** is the use of color and other visible characteristics related to color as subordinating factors. The roots of overt racism lie in our national history: the institution of slavery, the belief in the "manifest destiny" of European Americans to rule the entire North American continent, and the sense of America as a Christian nation, to name just three.

These beliefs provided the basis for and justification of racially discriminatory laws, social institutions, behavior patterns, language, cultural viewpoints, and thought patterns. Even after the Civil War and the abolition of slavery, new segregationist laws and practices, known as **Jim Crow,** extended overt racism against African Americans into the middle of the twentieth century. Shifting federal policies—such as removals, termination of tribal status, Indian boarding schools—greatly harmed much of the Native American culture and population. Exclusionary immigration laws and **restrictive covenants,** excluding members of certain groups from living in specified areas, limited the opportunities of Jews and Asian Americans.

The civil rights movement of the 1950s and 1960s awakened most White Americans to the evils of overt racism. However, this change of attitude by itself has been inadequate to address the residual racial inequities that survive in the second level of racism, indirect institutional subordination. More subtle, often invisible, **institutionalized racism** does not explicitly use color as the subordinating mechanism. Instead, decisions are based on such other factors as skill level, residential location, income, and education—factors that appear to be racially neutral and reasonably related to the activities and privileges concerned.

In reality, however, such practices continue to produce racist inequities because they fail to take into account the problems created by a 300-year history of overt racist practices. For example, having a parent with insufficient job training is likely to mean that a child will grow up poor and attend poor schools, without access to sufficient job training, leading to another generation of deprivation and poverty. In this way, no matter how unintentionally, a wide variety of policies, procedures, decisions, habits, attitudes, actions, and institutional structures perpetuate racism—the subordination and subjugation of people of color.

Part V examines the behavioral extension of racial prejudice: racial discrimination. One can be **prejudiced,** believing in the inferiority of certain kinds of individuals based on their membership in a certain group, but not **discriminate,** not act on those beliefs. As stated earlier, discrimination is individual, organizational, or structural behavior that disadvantages one group in relation to another group and that maintains and perpetuates conditions of inequality for members of the disadvantaged group.

The first three selections in Part V take a broad look at the manifestations of racism that have plagued our country since it was formed. Evelyn Hu-DeHart challenges the dominant version of U.S. history and demonstrates how different the record is when viewed through the experience of non-European Americans. The U.S. Commission on Civil Rights reports on immigration policies, codified in a series of racial exclusion orders beginning with the 1882 Chinese Exclusion Act, which was extended to 1924 to Japanese, Koreans, Burmese, Malayans, Polynesians, Tahitians, and New Zealanders. Unfortunately, as the report makes clear, these were not the only immigration laws enacted for racist purposes. Immigration discrimination continues. In this decade, hostility toward immigrants by White supremacists has increased as the Southern Poverty Law Center has documented; the center also suggests ways that law enforcement can help counteract this phenomenon.

Next, Reshma Baig brings us into the world of a second grader, recently immigrated, and attending school in Queens, New York. More currently, Gloria Yamato writes of the various expressions of racism she has had to endure, but she also provides some concrete suggestions for steps that individuals, both Whites who want to be allies of people of color and people of color who are working through internalized racism,

can take to combat racism. Then, Peggy McIntosh looks at the other side of the coin as she examines the invisible privileges that light-skinned people enjoy simply because of their skin color, and she recommends the extension of those positive advantages to all people.

The next four selections consider racist treatment to which Native Americans have been and continue to be subjected. As Michael Dorris reports, the federal government has consistently initiated policies that regulate and restrict Native Americans, despite legal treaties between the Indian nations and the U.S. government. Even today, Native Americans face continued encroachments on their rights. In "Urban Indians," by Roberta Fiske-Rusciano, we learn of the history of the U.S. government's attempt to speed up the process of assimilation of American Indians, by enticing them to leave their communities and relocate to large U.S. cities. Although relocation of the 1950s was a failure, Indians from many tribal nations have found a place, permanently or seasonally, in America's largest cities, often forming large communities of kin.

Carol Lee Sanchez shows how, over the past 150 years, novels, movies, and even children's games have negated the humanity of American Indians. She also offers five actions non-Indians can take to counteract the stereotypes—to everyone's benefit. On a subtler level, as Ward Churchill argues, the exploitation of Indian names, images, and symbols by mainstream society is racist and degrading and should be eliminated.

It may surprise some of us to learn that there have been groups that we today consider to be White who faced racial discrimination, but as Italian American Daniela Gioseffi reports, her forebears also experienced racist treatment, including lynching, despite their European roots. Also, Robert Cherry reviews the various theories that historians have offered to explain one manifestation of religion based racism: the widespread anti-Semitism of the late nineteenth and early twentieth centuries.

Next, Elizabeth Martinez passionately argues for our country to acknowledge that many groups besides African Americans are subjected to overt racism, especially, she says, Latinos. Since the population will be 32 percent Latino, Asian/Pacific American, and Native American by the year 2050, we need greater knowledge of, understanding of, and openness to learning about all ethnic groups if we are to work together as a society and live in harmony. Latina writer Judith Ortiz Cofer reports how insensitive strangers treat her as no more than a servant or sexual object, a not-so-subtle racist act.

Most of us know the shameful episode in our national history when 40,000 Japanese aliens and 70,000 Japanese American citizens were evacuated from the entire West Coast to inland relocation camps during World War II. John Hersey's detailed narrative makes clear the racism implicit in that policy. Anti-Asian racism did not end with the war, though. Susan Shimizu Taira, in "A Personal Narrative," gives us her and her family's experience with being incarcerated in Japanese American internment camps. When her father protested that his civil rights were being violated, he was deported to Japan.

As Asian Americans understand, even being assigned a positive stereotype is damaging; Robert Daseler demonstrates how the 30-year-old claim that they are the "model minority" is destructive to Asian Americans, as well as to other minority groups, which are compared with them. This is evident in Michael Laslett's report describing how new racial immigrants—in particular, Southeast Asian refugees—find themselves facing violent racial discrimination as they try to establish new lives. Laslett feels that ignorance about cultural differences, aggravated by the poverty of the African American and Latino communities, leads to resentment and violent actions against the new outsiders.

The following selection, by Benjamin Quarles, considers anti-Black racism in the latter part of the nineteenth century. After the Civil War, the abolition of slavery, and the enfranchisement of African American males, the dominant segment of society used a variety of tactics to continue the oppression of the former slaves. Well into the twentieth century, African Americans were subjected to random acts of violence intended to intimidate them and to enforce their "Jim Crow" inferiority.

Next, Greg Palast and Martin Luther King III, in "Jim Crow Revived in Cyberspace," discuss the computerized purges of voter rolls as a threat to minority voters. Earl Ofari Hutchinson reviews how sociologists, theologians, journalists, and other intellectual leaders purportedly "proved" the inferiority of the Negro race, especially its males.

Teenager Emmett Till was one of more than 40 people murdered between 1955 and 1968 in Mississippi and Alabama by White terrorists who wanted to "set an example" to Blacks and civil rights workers. As the Southern Poverty Law Center reports, Till was murdered and mutilated because he "thought he was as good as any White man." Unfortunately, such racist violence is not only a thing of the past; Kyle Johnson reports on the brutal racist murder of James Byrd in Jasper, Texas, in 1998.

Unfortunately, not all racist violence receives the kind of media coverage the Jasper case got. The Klanwatch Project of the Southern Poverty Law Center documents the more common violence perpetrated to resist integration of neighborhoods; this takes the form of cross burnings, vandalism, arson, threats, and assaults, all to maintain segregated housing.

Salim Muwakkil criticizes the media, especially television news, for their reliance on stereotypes of Blacks, Whites, and criminal behavior, and he discusses the detrimental effect this practice has on society. Today, overt racism may be generally unacceptable, but David K. Shipler describes how echoes of racist beliefs remain current in our society and result in the subtle racism that continues to disadvantage Black citizens. Robert Anthony Watts describes similar experiences that Blacks are perpetually subjected to, regardless of their achievements.

Racism continues to exist in our society because the subordination of people of color benefits those who do the subordinating. These psychological, economic, and political benefits will be reduced if racism is eliminated. However, the social costs of excluding a substantial proportion of our population from full participation in society—contributing to as well as benefiting from its bounty—are immense. Hearing the voices of those subjected to racism gives us fuller and more sympathetic insight into the problem. Even those of us who personally reject overt racism still need to work to loosen its less visible institutionalized tentacles.

48

Rethinking America

Evelyn Hu-DeHart

- Neoconservative columnist George Will wishes to "affirm this fact: America is predominantly a product of the Western tradition and predominantly good because that tradition is good."
- Neoconservative writer and editor Charles Krauthammer, in discussing the triumphalist march of Euroamericans in the "opening of the American West," otherwise known as Manifest Destiny,[1] rationalized the genocide of millions of Native Americans and the forcing of survivors into "homelands" this way: "The real question is, What eventually grew on this bloodied soil? . . . The great modern civilizations of the Americas—a new world of individual rights, an ever-expanding circle of liberty, and twice in this century, a savior of the world from total barbarism."
- Liberal historian of Camelot[2] fame Arthur Schlesinger asserts: "The U.S. escaped the divisiveness of a multiethnic society by a brilliant solution: the creation of a brand new identity. The point of America was not to preserve old cultures but to forge a new, American culture. 'By an intermixture with our people,' President George Washington told V.P. John Adams, 'immigrants will get assimilated to our customs, measures and laws: in a word, soon become one people.'" What these "immigrants" have in common, he continues, is "the Western tradition [which] is the source of the ideas of individual freedom and political democracy."
- Yale historian and undergraduate dean Donald Kagan lectured to a recent incoming freshman class: "Except for the slaves brought from Africa, most came voluntarily, as families and individuals, usually eager to satisfy desires that could not be met in their former homelands. They swiftly became citizens and, within a generation or so, Americans. In our own time finally . . . African-Americans also have achieved freedom, equality before the law, and full citizenship. . . . What they

have in common and what brings them together is a system of laws and beliefs that shaped the establishment of the country, a system developed within the context of Western Civilization."

For many Americans educated and socialized in this dominant version of history, which is also the official view, the kind usually taught in our schools and universities, there may seem nothing wrong with the above statements. Indeed, for those Americans from European immigrant backgrounds, they probably ring true as accurate renditions of their shared historical experience in America's great melting pot. And they can justifiably take pride in having defined "our national identity" and "our national culture."

But there is also a problem with this version of national history for Americans of non-European heritage, some of whom have been here since the beginning. The fact of the matter is, the "our" in "our national identity" and "our national culture," and the "we" in "we the people" have also been historically exclusive. Bluntly put, there is another history that these "other" Americans have lived through. For one truth that is omitted in all these declarations of Western triumphalism is that, in thinking of the people who built America and benefitted from it, the images are overwhelmingly and almost exclusively those of European immigrants and their descendents.

African Americans, as even Donald Kagan had to concede, were not voluntary immigrants and not part of the national process in its formation. Indeed, in order to sidestep the obvious contradiction between slavery and "All Men are Created Equal," the Founding Fathers—all white male property owners—defined blacks and slaves as less than full human beings. And even if Kagan wishes to suggest that equality before the law has brought them nominal freedom and full citizenship, the reality is fraught with contradictions, as the Los Angeles uprising of May 1992 demonstrated all too clearly. The lingering and still institutionalized legacies of slavery, Jim Crow[3] and legal apartheid which endure to this day, and which have left most African Americans still largely excluded or alienated from national life, cannot be blithely brushed aside, as triumphalists like Kagan would wish.

The Federal Government did not extend universal citizenship to Native Americans, the original inhabitants of this land, until 1924, shamed into doing so only after many had served and died in defense of this country during WWI. By then, most Native American peoples had lost their land and waters; many more had been destroyed by war and disease; still others [had been] removed and relocated far from their original homelands. Those not wantonly thrown into the streets of the inner cities to sink or swim on their own are still confined to reservations on desolate land in remote places, unemployed and unable to even scratch out a decent living, out of sight and therefore out of our conscience and consciousness. Is it any wonder that so many Native Americans actively protested Columbus Quincentenary celebrations, which to them appeared to be celebrating a history of genocide? As peoples whose relationships with the U.S. government were founded on treaty rights— a Western concept, after all—signed over the course of three centuries, and of which hundreds still remain on the books, they continue to insist on the sovereignty which signing treaties explicitly recognized. Why is it that triumphalists seldom speak of the sovereignty rights of Indian peoples in America, not to mention physical and cultural genocide committed against them in the name of Western democracy and freedom?

During the mid-19th century, America won by force, or bought at bargain basement prices vast chunks of land from Mexico, amounting to half of her national territory, and incorporated wholesale the vast, settled population of mainly Spanish-speaking mestizos (mixed Spanish-Indian heritage). Although, according to the Treaty of Guadalupe Hidalgo[4] of 1848, they were promised citizenship and the right to retain their languages and cultures, these commitments have been honored mainly in the breach. Hardly voluntary immigrants to begin with, later arrivals from Mexico have more often been branded wetbacks and illegal aliens, seldom welcomed as legitimate immigrants. These brown-skinned Mexicans became a disenfranchised, disadvantaged minority group whose ranks would later be swelled by other forcefully incorporated, dark complexioned Spanish-speakers on American soil, such as Puerto Ricans, and [who would be] collectively known by the government-imposed term "Hispanics." Their distant connection with Catholic Spain and more recent connection with backwards, chaotic, Spanish-speaking Latin America (notably Mexico, Central America and parts of the Caribbean) render them problematic for purposes of racial classification. Are Hispanics white and European, or are most of them "different" by virtue of their religion (Catholicism), their language (Spanish), and their openly acknowledged legacy of miscegenation with Indians and blacks?

In this brief and admittedly oversimplified summary of the history of non-European peoples in the U.S., Asian/Pacific Americans remain to be considered. They indeed did migrate to America, but usually not so voluntarily, at least not in the 19th century when they first came as cheap laborers, lonely men for the most part unaccompanied by families and kin. If European immigrants to America were regarded as potential citizens, that unfortunately did not apply to Asians, for it was decided even before their arrival that they would have no access to citizenship. The U.S. Naturalization Law enacted in 1790, which remained in effect until 1952, specifically barred non-white immigrants from citizenship. Thus, when tens of thousands of Asian workers were brought to the American West during the 19th century to build the railroads, work the mines, clear virgin land for agriculture, they found themselves denied full political participation and social integration into this society. From 1882 to WWII, the Chinese also became the only people in American history singled out as an undesirable "race" that must be barred from further immigration to this country. During WWII, thousands of Japanese alien residents on the West Coast, [who] like the Chinese [were] ineligible for citizenship at the time, and their American born children were interned in camps behind barbed wire fences, even when not a single one of them had committed any act of disloyalty or sedition against their adopted country. The recent (since the late 1970s) elevation of Asian Americans to the status of "model minority," deemed superior to other minorities because of their apparent greater ability to assimilate white middle class virtues, cannot erase this long history of exclusion and unequal treatment.

In summary, from the vantage points of Native Americans, African Americans, Mexican

Americans and Asian Americans, there is an underside of Western triumphalism in America that has not been acknowledged, recorded and told. The history of individual choice and freedom, and of democracy, described so eloquently and defended so passionately by Will, Krauthammer, Schlesinger, Kagan and many others, unfortunately does not speak to the truth as most of them and their predecessors in America have experienced it. These fundamental contradictions, between America's multiracial origins and growing multiracial reality on the one hand, and its still dominant self image as white and European on the other, between stated ideals of freedom and democracy for all, alongside a racialist social order that had historically relegated peoples of color to an inferior status as cheap labor, at best, and extraneous population at worst, but in any case not equal citizens, are what multicultural scholars have identified and attempt to resolve.

The noted historian Alexander Saxton, who happens to be white and male, says it well in his recent book, *The Rise and Fall of the White Republic:* "America's supposed openness to newcomers throughout most of its history has been racially selective. By the time of Jefferson and Jackson the nation had already assumed the form of a *racially exclusive democracy*—democratic in the sense that it sought to provide equal opportunities for the pursuit of happiness by its white citizens through the enslavement of African Americans, extermination of the Indians and further expansion at the expense of Indians and Mexicans. If there was an 'American orientation' to newcomers, it was not toward giving equal opportunity to all but toward inviting entry by white Europeans and excluding others. It is true that the United States absorbed a variety of cultural patterns among European immigrants at the same time that it was erecting a *white supremacist social structure. Moderately tolerant of European ethnic diversity, the nation remained adamantly intolerant of racial diversity. It is this crucial difference that has been permitted to drop from sight*" (emphasis added). Ethnic Studies and other scholars committed to the multicultural project are determined to bring this "crucial difference" back into focus. For contrary to the Western triumphalists, multicultural scholars assert that there was no national identity or national culture that embraced all Americans, thus no actual consensus or unity ever existed to be ripped apart by the newborn attention to the histories of the excluded groups. Rather, an official history has been shoved down the throats of those unable to speak for themselves until recently.

If triumphalists insist there is really only one viewpoint in history, or at least one true or "best" viewpoint, multiculturalists acknowledge multiple perspectives, depending on one's status and station in society that is determined in turn by race, class, gender, and other factors. The supportives, no one of which speaks the whole truth, can be in sharp conflict, may or may not be ultimately resolved, but in any case, together form a more complete picture of our national history, our national identity, our national culture. Accordingly, the New York State Dept. of Education Curriculum Task Force calls for a "new conceptualization of history, one that recogized multiplicity and contradiction instead of homogeneity and consensus as the basis of our national community." In short, multiculturalists would only concede that, once the triumphalists confront the past honestly, then acknowledge it openly, once those excluded Americans can come forth freely to reclaim their histories, and once institutional barriers to equal opportunity for all Americans have been removed, only then can we speak of seeking common ground, of forging unity and consensus. Until then, liberals like Schlesinger will plead for unity in vain, while rap singers speak greater truths to young blacks in the "hood" and Latinos in the barrio.   [1993]

Terms

1. MANIFEST DESTINY: A nineteenth-century belief that White people had the duty and right to control and develop the entire North American continent.
2. CAMELOT: The idealized image of John F. Kennedy's presidential administration as being enlightened, cultured, worldly, and progressive.
3. JIM CROW: Segregationist laws and practices, such as racially separate drinking fountains, railroad cars, and schools.
4. TREATY OF GUADALUPE HIDALGO: The treaty ending the Mexican-American War, ceding the lands that are now Texas, California, Ne-

vada, and Utah; most of Arizona, New Mexico, and Colorado; and part of Wyoming to the United States.

Understanding the Reading

1. What is the common theme of the four opening quotations?
2. What has been the "American experience" of African Americans? Of Native Americans? Of Hispanic Americans? Of Asian Americans?
3. What does Hu-DeHart mean by "a racialist social order"?
4. What are the goals of multicultural education?

Suggestions for Responding

1. Write a short essay agreeing or disagreeing with Hu-DeHart.
2. Describe your own personal "American experience." ✦

49

Historical Discrimination in the Immigration Laws

U.S. COMMISSION ON CIVIL RIGHTS

THE EARLY YEARS

During the formative years of this country's growth, immigration was encouraged with little restraint. Any restrictions on immigration in the 1700s were the result of selection standards established by each colonial settlement. The only Federal regulation of immigration in this period lasted only 2 years and came from the Alien Act of 1798, which gave the President the authority to expel aliens who posed a threat to national security.

Immigrants from northern and western Europe began to trickle into the country as a result of the faltering economic conditions within their own countries. In Germany, unfavorable economic prospects in industry and trade, combined with political unrest, drove many of its nationals to seek opportunities to ply their trades here. In Ireland, the problems of the economy, compounded by several successive potato crop failures in the 1840s, sent thousands of Irish to seaports where ships bound for the United States were docked. For other European nationals, the emigration from their native countries received impetus not only from adverse economic conditions at home but also from favorable stories of free land and good wages in America.

THE NATIVIST MOVEMENTS

As a result of the large numbers of Catholics who emigrated from Europe, a nativist movement began in the 1830s. It advocated immigration restriction to prevent further arrivals of Catholics into this country. Anti-Catholicism was a very popular theme, and many Catholics and Catholic institutions suffered violent attacks from nativist sympathizers. The movement, however, did not gain great political strength and its goal of curbing immigration did not materialize.

Immigrants in the mid-19th century did not come only from northern and western Europe. In China, political unrest and the decline in agricultural productivity spawned the immigration of Chinese to American shores. The numbers of Chinese immigrants steadily increased after the so-called Opium War, due not only to the Chinese economy, but also to the widespread stories of available employment, good wages, and the discovery of gold at Sutter's Mill,[1] which filtered in through arrivals from the Western nations.

The nativist movement of the 1830s resurfaced in the late 1840s and developed into a political party, the Know-Nothing Party.[2] Its western adherents added an anti-Chinese theme to the eastern anti-Catholic sentiment. But once again, the nativist movement, while acquiring local political strength, failed in its attempts to enact legislation curbing immigration. On the local level, however, the cry of "America for Americans" often led to discriminatory state statutes that penalized certain racially identifiable groups. As an example, California adopted licensing statutes for foreign miners and fishermen, which were almost exclusively enforced against Chinese.

In the mid-1850s, the Know-Nothing Party lost steam as a result of a division over the question of slavery, the most important issue of that time. The nativist movement and antiforeign sentiment receded because of the slavery issue and the Civil War. It maintained this secondary role until the Panic of 1873 struck.

CHINESE EXCLUSION

The depression economy of the 1870s was blamed on aliens who were accused of driving wages to a substandard level as well as taking away jobs that "belonged" to white Americans. While the economic charges were not totally without basis, reality shows that most aliens did not compete with white labor for "desirable" white jobs. Instead, aliens usually were relegated to the most menial employment.

The primary target was the Chinese, whose high racial visibility, coupled with cultural dissimilarity and lack of political power, made them more than an adequate scapegoat for the economic problems of the 1870s. Newspapers adopted the exhortations of labor leaders, blaming the Chinese for the economic plight of the working class. Workers released their frustrations and anger on the Chinese, particularly in the West. Finally, politicians succumbed to the growing cry for exclusion of Chinese.

Congress responded by passing the Chinese Exclusion Act of 1882. That act suspended immigration of Chinese laborers for 10 years, except for those who were in the country on November 17, 1880. Those who were not lawfully entitled to reside in the United States were subject to deportation. Chinese immigrants were also prohibited from obtaining United States citizenship after the effective date of the act.

The 1882 act was amended in 1884 to cover all subjects of China and Chinese who resided in any other foreign country. Then in 1888, another act was enacted that extended the suspension of immigration for all Chinese except Chinese officials, merchants, students, teachers, and travelers for pleasure. Supplemental legislation to that act also prohibited Chinese laborers from reentering the country, as provided for in the 1882 act, unless they reentered prior to the effective date of the legislation.

Senator Matthew C. Butler of South Carolina summed up the congressional efforts to exclude Chinese by stating:

> [I]t seems to me that this whole Chinese business has been a matter of political advantage, and we have not been governed by that deliberation which it would seem to me the gravity of the question requires. In other words, there is a very important Presidential election pending. One House of Congress passes an act driving these poor devils into the Pacific Ocean, and the other House comes up and says, "Yes, we will drive them further into the Pacific Ocean, notwithstanding the treaties between the two governments."

Nevertheless, the Chinese exclusion law was extended in 1892 and 1902, and in 1904 it was extended indefinitely.

Although challenged by American residents of Chinese ancestry, the provisions of these exclusion acts were usually upheld by judicial decisions. For example, the 1892 act mandated that Chinese laborers obtain certificates of residency within 1 year after the passage of the act or face deportation. In order to obtain the certificate the testimony of one credible white witness was required to establish that the Chinese laborer was an American resident prior to the passage of the act. That requirement was upheld by the United States Supreme Court in *Fong Yue Ting v. United States*.

LITERACY TESTS AND THE ASIATIC BARRED ZONE

The racial nature of immigration laws clearly manifested itself in further restrictions on prospective immigrants who were either from Asian countries or of Asian descent. In addition to extending the statutory life of the Chinese exclusion law, the 1902 act also applied that law to American territorial possessions, thereby prohibiting not only the immigration of noncitizen Chinese laborers from "such island territory to the mainland territory," but also "from one portion of the island territory of the United States to another portion of said island territory." Soon after, Japanese were restricted from free immigration to the United States by the "Gentleman's Agreement"[3] negotiated between the respective governments in 1907. Additional evidence would be provided by the prohibition of immigration from countries in the Asia-Pacific Triangle as established by the Immigration Act of 1917.

During this period, congressional attempts were also made to prevent blacks from immigrating to this country. In 1915 an amendment to exclude "all members of the African or black race" from admission to the United States was introduced in the Senate during its deliberations on a proposed immigration bill. The Senate approved the amendment on a 29 to 25 vote, but it was later defeated in the House by a 253 to 74 vote, after intensive lobbying by the NAACP.[4]

In 1917 Congress codified existing immigration laws in the Immigration Act of that year. That act retained all the prior grounds for inadmissibility and added illiterates to the list of those ineligible to immigrate, as a response to the influx of immigrants from southern and eastern Europe. Because of a fear that American standards would be lowered by these new immigrants who were believed to be racially "unassimilable" and illiterate, any alien who was over 16 and could not read was excluded. The other important feature of this statute was the creation of the Asia-Pacific Triangle, an Asiatic barred zone, designed to exclude Asians completely from immigration to the United States. The only exemptions from the zone were from an area that included Persia and parts of Afghanistan and Russia.

The 1917 immigration law reflected the movement of American immigration policy toward the curbing of free immigration. Free immigration, particularly from nations that were culturally dissimilar to the northern and western European background of most Americans, was popularly believed to be the root of both the economic problems and the social problems confronting this country.

THE NATIONAL ORIGINS QUOTA SYSTEM

Four years later, Congress created a temporary quota law that limited the number of aliens of any nationality who could immigrate to 3 percent of the United States residents of that nationality living in the country in 1910. The total annual immigration allowable in any one year was set at 350,000. Western Hemisphere aliens were exempt from the quota if their country of origin was an independent nation and the alien had resided there at least 1 year.

The clear intent of the 1921 quota law was to confine immigration as much as possible to western and northern European stock. As the minority report noted:

> The obvious purpose of this discrimination is the adoption of an unfounded anthropological theory that the nations which are favored are the progeny of fictitious and hitherto unsuspected Nordic ancestors, while those discriminated against are not classified as belonging to that mythical ancestral stock. No scientific evidence worthy of consideration was introduced to substantiate this pseudoscientific proposition. It is pure fiction and the creation of a journalistic imagination. . . .
>
> The majority report insinuates that some of those who have come from foreign countries are nonassimilable or slow of assimilation. No facts are offered in support of such a statement. The preponderance of testimony adduced before the committee is to the contrary.

Notwithstanding these objections, Congress made the temporary quota a permanent one with the enactment of the 1924 National Origins Act. A ceiling of 150,000 immigrants per year was imposed. Quotas for each nationality group were 2 percent of the total members of that nationality residing in the United States according to the 1890 census. Again, Western Hemisphere aliens were exempt from the quotas (thus, classified as "nonquota" immigrants). Any prospective immigrant was required to obtain a sponsor in this country and to obtain a visa from an American consulate office abroad. Entering the country without a visa and in violation of the law subjected the entrant to deportation without regard to the time of entry (no statute of limitation). Another provision, prohibiting the immigration of aliens ineligible for citizenship, completely closed the door on Japanese immigration, since the Supreme Court had ruled that Japanese were ineligible to become naturalized citizens. Prior to the 1924 act, Japanese immigration had been subjected to "voluntary" restraint by the Gentleman's Agreement negotiated between the Japanese Government and President Theodore Roosevelt.

In addition to its expressed discriminatory provisions, the 1924 law was also criticized as discriminatory against blacks in general and against black West Indians in particular.

THE MEXICAN "REPATRIATION" CAMPAIGN

Although Mexican Americans have a long history of residence within present United States territory, Mexican immigration to this country is of relatively recent vintage. Mexican citizens began immigrating to this country in significant numbers after 1909 because of economic conditions as well as the violence and political upheaval of the Mexican Revolution. These refugees were welcomed by Americans, for they helped to alleviate the labor shortage caused by the First World War. The spirit of acceptance lasted only a short time, however.

Spurred by the economic distress of the Great Depression, federal immigration officials expelled hundreds of thousands of persons of Mexican descent from this country through increased Border Patrol raids and other immigration law enforcement techniques. To mollify public objection to the mass expulsions, this program was called the "repatriation" campaign. Approximately 500,000 persons were "repatriated" to Mexico, with more than half of them being United States citizens.

EROSION OF CERTAIN DISCRIMINATORY BARRIERS

Prior to the next recodification of the immigration laws, there were several congressional enactments that cut away at the discriminatory barriers established by the national origins system. In 1943 the Chinese Exclusion Act was repealed, allowing a quota of 105 Chinese to immigrate annually to this country and declaring Chinese eligible for naturalization. The War Brides Act of 1945 permitted the immigration of 118,000 spouses and children of military servicemen. In 1946 Congress enacted legislation granting eligibility for naturalization to Filipinos and to races indigenous to India. A Presidential proclamation in that same year increased the Filipino quota from 50 to 100. In 1948 the Displaced Persons Act provided for the entry of approximately 400,000 refugees from Germany, Italy, and Austria (an additional 214,000 refugees were later admitted to the United States).

THE McCARRAN-WALTER ACT OF 1952

The McCarran-Walter Act of 1952, the basic law in effect today, codified the immigration laws under a single statute. It established three principles for immigration policy:

1. the reunification of families,
2. the protection of the domestic labor force, and
3. the immigration of persons with needed skills.

However, it retained the concept of the national origins system, as well as unrestricted immigration from the Western Hemisphere. An important provision of the statute removed the bar to immigration and citizenship for races that had been denied those privileges prior to that time. Asian countries, nevertheless, were still discriminated against, for prospective immigrants whose ancestry was one-half of any Far Eastern race were chargeable to minimal quotas for that nation, regardless of the birthplace of the immigrant.

"OPERATION WETBACK"

Soon after the repatriation campaign of the 1930s, the United States entered the Second World War. Mobilization for the war effort produced a labor shortage that resulted in a shift in American attitudes toward immigration from Mexico. Once again Mexican nationals were welcomed with open arms. However, this "open arms" policy was just as short lived as before.

In the 1950s many Americans were alarmed by the number of immigrants from Mexico. As a result, then United States Attorney General Herbert Brownell, Jr., launched "Operation Wetback," to expel Mexicans from this country. Among those caught up in the expulsion campaign were American citizens of Mexican descent who were forced to leave the country of their birth. To ensure the effectiveness of the expulsion process, many of those apprehended were denied a hearing to assert their constitutional rights and to present evidence that would have prevented their deportation. More than

1 million persons of Mexican descent were expelled from this country in 1954 at the height of "Operation Wetback."

THE 1965 AMENDMENTS

The national origins immigration quota system generated opposition from the time of its inception, condemned for its attempts to maintain the existing racial composition of the United States. Finally, in 1965, amendments to the McCarran-Walter Act abolished the national origins system as well as the Asiatic barred zone. Nevertheless, numerical restrictions were still imposed to limit annual immigration. The Eastern Hemisphere was subject to an overall limitation of 170,000 and a limit of 20,000 per country. Further, colonial territories were limited to 1 percent of the total available to the mother country (later raised to 3 percent or 600 immigrants in the 1976 amendments). The Western Hemisphere, for the first time, was subject to an overall limitation of 120,000 annually, although no individual per-country limits were imposed. In place of the national origins system, Congress created a seven category preference system giving immigration priority to relatives of United States residents and immigrants with needed talents or skills. The 20,000 limitation per country and the colonial limitations, as well as the preference for relatives of Americans preferred under the former selections process, have been referred to by critics as "the last vestiges of the national origins system" because they perpetuate the racial discrimination produced by the national origins system.

RESTRICTING MEXICAN IMMIGRATION

After 1965 the economic conditions in the United States changed. With the economic crunch felt by many Americans, the cry for more restrictive immigration laws resurfaced. The difference from the 19th century situation is that the brunt of the attacks is now focused on Mexicans, not Chinese. High "guesstimates" of the number of undocumented Mexican aliens entering the United States, many of which originated from Immigration and Naturalization Service sources, have been the subject of press coverage.

As a partial response to the demand for "stemming the tide" of Mexican immigration,

Congress amended the Immigration and Nationality Act in 1976, imposing the seven category preference system and the 20,000 numerical limitation per country on Western Hemisphere nations. Legal immigration from Mexico, which had been more than 40,000 people per year, with a waiting list 2 years long, was thus cut by over 50 percent.

RECENT REVISIONS OF THE IMMIGRANT QUOTA SYSTEM*

Although the annual per-country limitations have remained intact, Congress did amend the Immigration and Nationality Act in 1978 to eliminate the hemispheric quotas of 170,000 for Eastern Hemisphere countries and 120,000 for Western Hemisphere countries. Those hemispheric ceilings were replaced with an overall annual worldwide ceiling of 290,000.

In 1980 the immigrant quota system was further revised by the enactment of the Refugee Act. In addition to broadening the definition of refugee, that statute eliminated the seventh preference[5] visa category by establishing a separate worldwide ceiling for refugee admissions to this country. It also reduced the annual worldwide ceiling for the remaining six preference categories to 270,000 visas, and it increased the number of visas allocated to the second preference[6] to 26 percent.   [1980]

Terms

1. SUTTER'S MILL: The site where gold was discovered in 1848, precipitating the California gold rush.
2. KNOW-NOTHING PARTY: A political movement in the mid-19th century that was antagonistic to Catholics and immigrants.
3. GENTLEMAN'S AGREEMENT: The 1908 treaty between Japan and the United States to restrict, but not eliminate altogether, the issuance of

---

*After the terrorist attacks on 9/11/01, the Immigration and Naturalization Service was folded into the Department of Homeland Security, whose main priority is to protect the country against attacks and to gather intelligence. The broad liberties given to the federal government by the Patriot Act have frightened many immigrants, who are afraid of being targeted, and have slowed down all immigration procedures.

passports allowing Japanese immigration to the United States, except that wives could enter, including "picture brides," who were married by proxy.

4. NAACP: National Association for the Advancement of Colored People.
5. SEVENTH PREFERENCE: Refugee status.
6. SECOND PREFERENCE: Spouses and unmarried children of U.S. citizens.

Understanding the Reading

1. What were the nativist movement and the Know-Nothing Party?
2. Explain the Chinese Exclusion laws.
3. Explain the National Origins quota system.
4. What was Operation Wetback?
5. How do the 1965 amendments perpetuate racial discrimination?

Suggestions for Responding

1. Explain what current immigration policy is and why you think it is good and/or bad.
2. Research and report on one law or policy that was mentioned in the article. ✦

50

Anti-Immigrant Violence

SOUTHERN POVERTY LAW CENTER

Hostility toward immigrants and efforts by white supremacists to exploit fears about immigration are at their highest levels in 70 years, causing a rash of violent bias crimes against anyone who is perceived as "foreign."

"The brutal violence and hysteria surrounding the immigration issue are almost identical to the 1920s when the Ku Klux Klan became its most formidable," says Klanwatch Director Danny Welch.

"Anti-immigrant violence is an enormous problem that is causing widespread and complex societal problems, and there is not enough attention given to the matter," says hate crime expert Jack McDevitt, associate director of the

Center for Applied Research at Northeastern University.

Typical examples include:

- A 19-year-old Vietnamese American pre-med student in Coral Springs, Fla., was beaten to death in August 1992 by a mob of white youths who called him "chink" and "Vietcong."
- Two Hispanic day laborers were shot in a drive-by attack in Vista, Calif., in 1992.
- A Hispanic man in Alpine, Calif., was beaten with baseball bats in October 1992 by six white men at a camp for homeless migrant workers. The assailants later reportedly bragged about "kicking Mexican ass."
- A Hispanic immigrant activist in Davis, Calif., was assaulted twice in April 1993 by white men who wrote "wetback" on her body.
- A 21-year-old Cambodian immigrant in Falls River, Mass., died in August 1993 after being kicked in the head and taunted with racial slurs by a dozen white men.
- An Indian immigrant in New York City was beaten and burned with a cigarette by three teenagers who reportedly told him they did not like Indians.

Despite its prevalence, there are no precise statistics available on the number of anti-immigrant hate crimes. The incidents are usually attributed by police to prejudice based on ethnicity so the problem becomes obscured by other types of hate crime.

McDevitt says the raging anti-immigrant sentiment and violence are partially the fault of political rhetoric that blames newcomers for the nation's economic problems.

"The rhetoric sends a message to the hater that no one will care if they go out and bash those people," he said.

Some political candidates claim that [problems such as] budget deficits, unemployment, higher taxes, rising crime and overwhelmed public facilities such as schools and hospitals could be solved by enacting stricter immigration laws. Other officials blame immigrants for overcrowded and deteriorating roadways, saying the numbers of new vehicles have overburdened their areas.

Polls show a majority of Americans agree with politicians who contend that the country can no longer afford to welcome impoverished immigrants.

Sixty percent of the participants in recent major media surveys were opposed to continuing current immigration policy that in the next decade is expected to attract an unprecedented number of newcomers—most of them Hispanic, Asian and black.

Klanwatch's Welch says that intelligent debate about immigration is necessary, but the issue should not be exploited by politicians to get votes.

"Demagoguery can easily lead to scapegoating and violence," Welch says.

Recognizing that economic problems make white Americans more sympathetic to their message, many hate group leaders are exploiting anti-immigrant fears to attract mainstream followers.

At their public rallies and through their literature, telephone recordings and radio and television programs, hate leaders spread fear that immigrants are overrunning and ruining the country.

White Aryan Resistance [WAR] leader Tom Metzger of Fallbrook, Calif., publishes cartoons about "dirty Mexicans" and the "Asian Invasion," along with scathing editorials that accuse Jews of plotting to establish an international government by bankrupting the country with a flood of immigrants.

Thomas Robb, national director of the Knights of the Ku Klux Klan, urges sending U.S. troops to the Mexican border to repel illegal immigrants.

Young white supremacists—the group most likely to act out violently on prejudices—are particularly susceptible to the anti-immigrant message of hate group leaders, Klanwatch's Welch says.

Hate crimes against immigrants have been linked to white supremacist rhetoric.

A group of Skinheads organized by an agent of WAR's Metzger beat an Ethiopian immigrant to death with a baseball bat in Portland, Ore., in 1990.

A Sacramento teenager who in 1993 firebombed the home of an Asian American city official and several agencies that work with immigrants told authorities that he read white supremacist literature and listened to hate group telephone recordings.

The white supremacist group American Spring, of Orange County, Calif., is organized solely on the anti-immigration issue. The group stages annual protests in San Ysidro against illegal immigration and calls for a military closure of the border. At American Spring's June 1992 protest, a supporter was arrested after he drove a truck through a mostly Hispanic crowd of counterprotesters.

Anti-immigrant sentiment and violence are most pervasive among whites, but the problem crosses all racial and social lines.

Economic fears and resentments inflamed by political rhetoric are turning ethnic minorities against each other. A prime example occurred during the recent Los Angeles riots when businesses owned by Asian Americans were targeted, despite the fact that Asian Americans had no role in the Rodney King case.

Some native-born Hispanics, Asians and blacks also object to immigrants of their own races.

"They want to pull up the ladder," Northeastern's McDevitt says. "They fear that if too many people come up it behind them, they will lose."

Klanwatch's Welch says the growing number of immigrants and a slow economy pit ethnic groups against each other.

"The anti-Semitic and racist rhetoric of people like Louis Farrakhan of the Nation of Islam just adds fuel to the fire," Welch says.

Attitudes toward immigrants today are frighteningly similar to those of the mid-1920s when the United States passed restrictive laws to halt massive immigration from southern Europe. Klan violence against Catholics, Jews and blacks was rampant during that era, McDevitt notes.

During the 1920s, the Klan grew to its greatest strength with 5 million members, including politicians and other influential government officials who helped get the restrictive immigration legislation passed. The Klan spread from the south for the first time during this period amid widespread fears that millions of European immigrants would take jobs away from native white Americans.

Improved economic conditions and the civil rights movement in the 1960s led to a rebirth of tolerance toward newcomers and a wave of immigration through the passage of a relaxed immigration law.

The hospitality was short-lived, and renewed anti-immigrant sentiment in the 1970s saw the Klan patrolling the U.S. and Mexican borders and organizing attacks on Vietnamese immigrants to drive them away from the Texas shrimping industry.

The Immigration and Naturalization Service [INS] reports that 8.9 million newcomers have arrived in the last decade, mostly from Latin America, Asia and the Caribbean. Another 3 million have entered the United States illegally.

Illegal immigrants are the scapegoats in the immigration policy controversy. The flashpoint is California, where it is estimated that 200,000 illegal immigrants, representing 9 percent of the total population, live in San Diego County alone.

Critics of current immigration policy claim that there are more illegal immigrants living in California than there are legal residents in 18 other states.

Legal immigrants have also flocked to California. More than a third of all legal immigrants, mostly Hispanic and Asian, have settled there. Within a decade whites will probably be a minority in California.

Anti-immigration hysteria fueled by politicians' rhetoric has created a crisis on the border, says Roberto Martinez, of the American Friends Service Committee of San Diego which monitors the violence. Brutal acts against illegal immigrants and other Hispanics by area residents and INS border patrol guards are widespread and frequent, he says.

"It is an explosive situation," Martinez says. "We attribute the violence directly to all of the talk against immigrants—it encourages hate crimes."

A new report by the group details 55 incidents of alleged brutality and other misconduct by INS border guards in 1993 alone, including the death of a Mexican who was chased by border patrol guards and several serious injuries. Ten of the complainants were U.S. citizens, 27 were legal residents or visitors and 18 were undocumented, according to the report.

INS officials say they investigate all complaints and fire guards or take other disciplinary action when there is evidence of physical or verbal abuse. Officials also contend that the complaints are minor in view of the number of people the border patrol apprehends—as many as 1,400 in one night in the San Diego sector alone, they add.

LAW ENFORCEMENT SUPPORT NEEDED

Among the most troubling aspects of anti-immigration sentiment are the reports of brutality by authorities and the indifference of some law enforcement officers to the plight of immigrants targeted by hate crime, Klanwatch's Welch says.

"Law enforcement officers have a sworn obligation to put their personal feelings aside and protect all people," Welch says. "Immigrants are often terrified and afraid to report the crimes."

Because every area of the nation is becoming more diverse as a result of escalating immigration, all law enforcement agencies should conduct training courses to make officers more sensitive to people of other cultures, Welch says.

Boston is one of many cities that have taken comprehensive steps to meet the challenge of rapidly diversifying ethnic populations.

Deputy Supt. Bill Johnston of the Boston Police Department says city officials recognize the enormity of anti-immigrant violence.

As an example, although Vietnamese make up only 1 percent of the population in Boston, they represent 15 percent of the victims in reported hate crimes in the city, Johnston says. Anti-immigration sentiment is suspected to be the primary motivation in hate crimes against Vietnamese, he says.

To help protect immigrants, Boston is reaching out to immigrant populations through the school system. Police officers regularly visit schools to establish relationships with immigrant children and help their families.

The Boston Police Department has also conducted training courses to teach officers about different cultures, hired interpreters, taught officers simple foreign language skills and published field guides to help officers interact with immigrants.

Police should establish liaisons with the immigrant communities, network with cultural and advocacy groups and publicize their willingness to protect the victims of anti-immigrant violence, says hate crime expert Brian Levin, a Newport Beach, Calif., attorney and former policeman. Information about immigrant communities is available through universities, national cultural advocacy groups, U.S. government publications and census reports.

Even if new laws are passed to restrict immigration, the nation will continue to become more diverse as the large number of immigrants already here relocate from ports of entry such as California, Florida and Texas, Klanwatch's Welch says. Today, at least 19 million foreign-born people live in the United States, more than in any other country.

"It is essential that community and government leaders and law enforcement authorities speak out against anti-immigrant violence to counteract the dangerous messages of white supremacists and some politicians," Welch says. "People need to recognize that hatred and violence are wrong, and they must resist the impulse to make scapegoats of other people."

[1994]

Understanding the Reading

1. Describe anti-immigrant hate crimes.
2. Why is anti-immigrant sentiment growing?
3. How are hate groups exploiting the growth of anti-immigrant feelings?
4. How are ethnic minorities responding to anti-immigrant feelings?
5. What is the immigrant situation in California?
6. How have law enforcement officers reacted to immigrants?
7. What is Boston doing to protect immigrants?

Suggestions for Responding

1. Research and report on the immigrant population in your area.
2. Write a letter to the editor of your local newspaper, expressing your thoughts on immigrants and immigration policies. ◆

51

2-205

RESHMA BAIG

Mrs. Silverstein was my second grade teacher. She was the blue haired queen of the second floor. The green eyeshadowed matron of innocent six-year-olds poised on the precipice of a new world. Every night of my second grade life hinged on the fear that I would have to take my seat in row 2 seat 2 and watch the frosted pink lips of my large hipped teacher mouth out phrases, words, numbers and dates in scary slow motion so that those new to "*our* country" could understand.

For a child who had recently immigrated from a country where primary schools were *always* built on ground level, a child who hadn't had enough time to learn to trust her environment, life was scary enough without having to trudge back to a room guarded by the gaze of a woman who announced freely that doom resided in the dense blood of her red marker pen.

Every morning, I faced the prospect of returning to a room full of felt numbers, flag pledging and bathroom visits in pairs.

The maze of hallways on the second floor of PS 20 were purely frightening. At any turn, you could find yourself face to face with another pair of disoriented second graders who, like you and your "bathroom buddy," had found themselves lost while using the pass. If you were truly unlucky, you would find yourself at the mercy of tall third or fourth graders who called you a "baby bumper" before they knocked you into a wall. If there existed the fate of something worse, it could probably have been traced back to the confines of room 2-205. This was the place where the fears of my six-year-old mind began *and* ended.

Every night after I finished my homework, when the reality of returning to room 2-205 crept up in my mind, the fear would start again. That was one thing I had no control over.

From Reshma Baig, *The Memory of Hands,* c. 1998 by Reshma Baig. Reprinted by permission of author.

The things that I did have control over were sheets of crisp, lined paper, sharpened pencils and tightly-bound black and white notebooks. All these things brought me joy, and when I found a pink eraser on my father's desk one day, it just made everything magical. If I made a mistake, it rubbed clean off. Just blow on the paper a little and everything could be scrubbed brand new. Then the paper was clean and ready. With the pink eraser, there was always a second chance for straight etched *T's,* swirling *S's* and rapid *O's.*

After the last page of homework, just after Mary and Dick took the last skip around their yard, the fear planted itself in my head. I was knotted in sweaty sleep until the morning. I smelled the classroom in my dreams and felt the swift pummel of Mrs. Silverstein's fist on my desk if any spelling errors should arise.

In the morning I washed my face with hard splashes of cold water. Like a soldier, I thought. I would freeze the skin on my face and deal with the agony of the day.

Mum'i would always be smiling and issuing advice for the day as I wiped the sleep from my eyes at 7:15 a.m. She sweetly hollered as she peeked at me from the kitchen, "Zafran, fix that collar and put some socks on! Come here so I can pin the hair away from your face. Zafran! Remember to say Bismillah before you eat."

While I ate my corn flakes, she came over to kiss the side of my head, say three prayers and then blow softly on my face. The wooly nubs of her cardigan brushed my cheek, embracing me in the scent of sandalwood: the perfume of safety and strong women who promised to raise even stronger daughters.

My mother was the sixth child in a family of seven. She was named after a constellation of seven stars, moved with my father to three countries and spoke five languages. While cooking four dishes at a time, she could still find the time to comb my hair, slide in two hair pins and find the missing plastic sheep from the Fisher-Price Farm Family.

She was all these things as well as a woman of beauty and kindness who always packed the tomatoes separately, so the bread would not get mushy. She was the doctor of lunch distress who cured the morning blahs by wrapping toffee and cake in floral paper napkins. They would be waiting in the corner of my lunch box providing five minutes of sweet relief in a lunchroom sagging from the misery and stench of cold bologna and spilt milk.

After leaving my mother's gentle hands, I had to find the strength to battle the Dragon Lady of room 2-205. Mum'i didn't know that dragons awaited me in PS 20. I never told her.

"School is good for little girls. You both should be thankful that you have a school to go to," was what Mum'i said in her melodious voice before she kissed Sugrah and [me] . . . good-bye at All Grades morning line-up in the school yard.

Morning line-up was first call to the lunch-box army. The portly assistant principal, Mr. Kaufman, blew his whistle to signal ranks of three and a half foot soldiers, outfitted in Garanimals and Health-Tex separates, to march slowly, methodically to their designated rooms. Each infantry followed a bouffant haired drill sergeant armed with a pocket book and silver necklace of twenty-nine keys. Clanging keys dangled over hearts pierced like a sieve to mark thirty-four long years with short people of many requests.

After following Mrs. Silverstein's double-knit hem to the confines of room 2-205, there would be another line-up to deposit lunch box, coat and school-bag inside the closet. The closet was opened by a willowy sixth grade monitor, named Lisa, who was assigned to Mrs. Silverstein for the year. Among her other duties were to get a "sugar no [cream]" coffee for our teacher from the teachers' lounge and bring us down to lunch.

Lisa always did the same thing after lunch. She led our class into the middle of the school yard and separated us into dodgeball teams. Even if we didn't want to play dodgeball, we were forced to comply. Lisa was taller than any of us, and she was **the monitor.** She even had a green and yellow badge that said Service Squad. What Lisa wanted, Lisa got. As she swung her waist-length blond hair to the side, and adjusted the cuffs on her hip-hugging bell-bottoms, she stuck a wad of gum on the back of her hand and pointed to the yellow line on the ground. That meant we had to line up while she separated us into specific teams. If there was a protester or two, a couple of kids who questioned their team assignment, they were immediately served a red demerit card and forced to stand with their faces against the chain-link fence until the end of recess.

Lisa, with her polished skills of sorting (probably acquired by way of South Africa or Mississippi), always divided the two teams according to the Lisa Principle. According to this principle, all the cutesy boys and pretty girls were placed on Team A. And all the non-white and recently immigrated children were placed on Team B. If anyone on Team B touched Lisa at any point during the game, she would squeal "Yuck, foreigner cooties." This would incite Team A members to follow her lead in stereo.

Lisa made sure there was no horsing around while we hung our coats on metal hooks which protruded like gunmetal question marks from the recesses of the closet. Mrs. Silverstein put her in charge while she went to her personal closet at the back of the room to change her shoes. This happened every day like clockwork. Third graders who had her last year told stories about her closet at lunch time. Mrs. Silverstein's closet became the last frontier, a place of mystery and unmentionable amazement, a Pandora's box of secrets which entranced the observer with a sharp whiff of Ben-Gay ointment.

The students who were on the back of the closet hang-up line always peered inside Mrs. Silverstein's closet to see which shoes would be stalking up the aisles for the day. Inside her closet lay a neat shelf of shoes, a mirror and a large photograph of her with . . . three happy looking kids who looked just like her.

As she locked her closet with one of the twenty-nine keys around her neck, Mrs. Silverstein placed the day's pair next to her neat desk by the window. She carefully sat down, adjusted the pleats of her skirt, briskly reprimanded her aching knees and then slipped off the rubber soled shoes to reveal stubby, soft pink toes that looked like a family of hard boiled eggs.

For an old lady who spent most of her time with those who hadn't even mastered the skill of fine motor coordination, Mrs. Silverstein was still very particular with the shape, style and color of her shoes. There were always little bows or large rhinestones on the back of brightly colored, well polished pumps.

The shoes designated the day's turn of events. Open toes meant art in the afternoon. Double straps meant some sorry child would be called to the board for a math problem which would inevitably result in the wrong answer. Stacked black heels always meant a child would vomit after a spelling test; but red high heels were a flag in the wind. Red heels were cause for celebration. They signaled that at the end of the day one lucky row would get to pick prizes from the Scholastic Books grab bag.

There was no need for fortunes resting on the tiny faces of tea leaves. We, the crayon bearing masses of 2-205, always received the daily horoscope, squished and screaming, from inside Mrs. Silverstein's pumps.

After gongs signaling the end of first hour, the class was led down to the music room for recorder lessons. Recorders, fake plastic flutes for the safety-scissors population, were dependable, easy and generous with immediate gratification. They gave us meaning even though we were pinched if we played the wrong note.

Going down to the music room always meant being greeted by a bob-haired teacher named Mrs. Heleno. A woman who never seemed to blink and perpetually picked lint off her clingy Quiana wrap-dresses. She was the type of teacher whose sharply outlined lips gave credence to the rumor that there were people on this planet who actually did eat children for breakfast.

The rumors were there, but the worst we were forced to endure was maybe a nasty pinch or two if we were off key for "Three Blind Mice."

Mrs. Heleno was a woman for whom music was something pathological. It was a thing that consumed oneself—a thing to suffer for and make others suffer for as well. Before each lesson, she would clear her throat and with an air of pride deliver Words Of Meaning in her lilting First Lady of MGM via the Sorbonne accent.

"I used to play weez zah London Symphony and seeng weez zah Paris Opera. But ven I came to zees country, I decided I vaz going to help leetle cheeldren. You too can become great person of museek like your teejher."

We couldn't disappoint a woman of such experience and passion. We were going to play those saliva sprayed recorders, and we were going to play them well.

"Cheeldren, if you punish the museek, then you, too, must be punished."

If we played incorrectly, we were pinched. Some of us wore our tiny black and blues like battle scars. We had suffered for the music, and for Mrs. Heleno, that was noble suffering, indeed.

The end of recorder lessons would be followed with American Folk Songs Unit Four. We had graduated from "She'll Be Coming Around The Mountain" to the epic "This Land is Your Land."

It was only during the squeaky voiced singing of these songs that America would come alive. It was only during these songs that my classmates and I actually sang at the top of our lungs. The fear of the day would somehow dissolve for a three minute reverie of redwood forests, purple mountains and darling Clementine.

We looked at one another, backs straight, hands locked at our waists and smiled. We looked at Mrs. Heleno's bob swaying, her fingers pounding with furious intensity at her Board of Education piano and felt that things were not all that bad after all. Our voices, within the wood floored music room of a public elementary school in Queens, sang high. For that moment, our lungs were strengthened with something small and mighty that mattered.

It was usually at this point that Mrs. Silverstein showed up. Her shoes announced her arrival. She stood nodding her head and smiling. Smiling? Smiling at us with a face glowing under a fresh dusting of powder. She stood, feet firmly stationed nine inches apart, batting ancient eyelashes covered in the tar of mascara petrified since 1953. The weight on her lids alone could have most certainly caused blindness. Yet, she saw us clear enough to put a smile on her face. She looked at us with surprised doe eyes full of hope and expectation. As though she had accidentally come upon twenty-four of her best friends while purchasing discounted nylons in the hosiery section of Gertz department store on Roosevelt Avenue.

When we finished our song, Mrs. Silverstein clapped along with all of us. She even joined Mrs. Heleno in a flurry of "Bravos."

As she walked to the front of the room, she tapped me and each person in row five on the shoulder. "Very nice, children. Very nice."

She smelled like Ponds cold cream and when she came closer, I saw that her hands and arms were covered with light brown spots. Spots which moved with the sudden shift of the fragile skeleton they clung to. Spots just like my Nan'na's.

She could be somebody's grandma I thought. And if she could be somebody's grandma, she most certainly was somebody's mother. I pictured her powdered face next to her grandchild's. I pictured her putting a warm plate of eggs and toast in front of her children.

A six year old philosophized about teachers actually being people and having real families. That a teacher could have a life outside of class 2-205 and sit with an actual family outside the red brick walls of PS 20 was something truly bizarre.

Second graders should be the nation's philosopher laureates. Their experience in the world at the bright old age of six or seven proves that even the most primitive of philosophies arises from the Original Truth. Namely, that human suffering always occurs as a result of mean teachers and cheap parents. And if a teacher could actually be nice, then there was always room to celebrate and abrogate the Original Truth—even it was only half-way.

While Mrs. Silverstein and Mrs. Heleno exchanged gossip and class behavior notes before the twin gongs signaling third hour, I thought about my Nan'na who always took her chai in a garden of wild grass and jasmine three oceans away. A Nan'na whose name meant leader of women. An aging spirit who rose before dawn for her morning prayers and counted tasbee beads with fingers embroidered in black henna.

With all her fiery breath, expert frigidity and favoritism, Mrs. Silverstein was only human after all. Had I been born in Queens to an American family named Silverstein, I could very well be calling her grandma and speaking with a weird American accent to some cousin named David.

Although the thought had a frightening ring to it, it actually comforted me in a way. I still hated her for making me feel the seizing fear each night but now she was no longer a dragon lady. She was different. She was human and had spots on her hands just like my Nan'na.   [1998]

Understanding the Reading

1. What was so frightening about Zafran's second-grade teacher?
2. Compare her mother with her teacher.

3. What is the Lisa Principle?
4. Why do the children notice Mrs. Silverstein's shoes?
5. Describe Mrs. Heleno's method of teaching music.
6. What made Zafran realize that her teacher was "only human after all"?

Suggestions for Responding

1. Find out something about the author's native country—Tanzania, East Africa.
2. Zafran drew strength from her knowledge and memories of her mother and grandmother, who helped her understand her world. Do you have one person from whom you draw strength? ✦

52

Something About the Subject Makes It Hard to Name

Gloria Yamato

Racism—simple enough in structure, yet difficult to eliminate. Racism—pervasive in the U.S. culture to the point that it deeply affects all the local town folk and spills over, negatively influencing the fortunes of folk around the world. Racism is pervasive to the point that we take many of its manifestations for granted, believing "that's life." Many believe that racism can be dealt with effectively in one hellifying workshop, or one hour-long heated discussion. Many actually believe this monster, racism, that has had at least a few hundred years to take root, grow, invade our space and develop subtle variations . . . this mind-funk that distorts thought and action, can be merely wished away. I've run into folks who really think that we can beat this devil, kick this habit, be healed of this disease in a snap. In a sincere blink of a well-intentioned eye, presto— poof—racism disappears. "I've dealt with my racism . . . (envision a laying on of hands) . . . Hallelujah! Now I can go to the beach." Well, fine. Go to the beach. In fact, why don't we all go to the beach and continue to work on the sucker over there? Cuz you can't even shave a little piece off this thing called racism in a day, or a weekend, or a workshop.

When I speak of *oppression,* I'm talking about the systematic, institutionalized mistreatment of one group of people by another for whatever reason. The oppressors are purported to have an innate ability to access economic resources, information, respect, etc., while the oppressed are believed to have a corresponding negative innate ability. The flip side of oppression is *internalized oppression.* Members of the target group are emotionally, physically, and spiritually battered to the point that they begin to actually believe that their oppression is deserved, is their lot in life, is natural and right, and that it doesn't even exist. The oppression begins to feel comfortable, familiar enough that when mean ol' Massa lay down de whip, we got's to pick up and whack ourselves and each other. Like a virus, it's hard to beat racism, because by the time you come up with a cure, it's mutated to a "new cure-resistant" form. One shot just won't get it. Racism must be attacked from many angles.

The forms of racism that I pick up on these days are (1) aware/blatant racism, (2) aware/covert racism, (3) unaware/unintentional racism, and (4) unaware/self-righteous racism. I can't say that I prefer any one form of racism over the others, because they all look like an itch needing a scratch. I've heard it said (and understandably so) that the aware/blatant form of racism is preferable if one must suffer it. Outright racists will, without apology or confusion, tell us that because of our color we don't appeal to them. If we so choose, we can attempt to get the hell out of their way before we get the sweat knocked out of us. Growing up, aware/covert racism is what I heard many of my elders bemoaning "up north," after having escaped the overt racism "down south." Apartments were suddenly no longer vacant or rents were outrageously high, when black, brown, red, or yellow persons went to inquire about them. Job vacancies were suddenly filled, or we were fired for very vague reasons. It still happens, though the perpetrators really take care to cover their tracks these days. They don't want to get gummed to death or slobbered on by the toothless laws that supposedly protect us from such inequities.

Unaware/unintentional racism drives usually tranquil white liberals wild when they get called on it, and confirms the suspicions of many people of color who feel that white folks are just plain crazy. It has led white people to believe that it's just fine to ask if they can touch my hair (while reaching). They then exclaim over how soft it is, how it does not scratch their hand. It has led whites to assume that bending over backwards and speaking to me in high-pitched (terrified), condescending tones would make up for all the racist wrongs that distort our lives. This type of racism had led whites right to my doorstep, talking 'bout, "We're sorry/we love you and want to make things right," which is fine, and further, "We're gonna give you the opportunity to fix it while we sleep. Just tell us what you need. 'Bye!!"—which *ain't* fine. With the best of intentions, the best of educations, and the greatest generosity of heart, whites, operating on the misinformation fed to them from day one, will behave in ways that are racist, will perpetuate racism by being "nice" the way we're taught to be nice. You can just "nice" somebody to death with naïveté and lack of awareness of privilege. Then there's guilt and the desire to end racism and how the two get all tangled up to the point that people, morbidly fascinated with their guilt, are immobilized. Rather than deal with ending racism, they sit and ponder their guilt and hope nobody notices how awful they are. Meanwhile, racism picks up momentum and keeps on keepin' on.

Now, the newest form of racism that I'm hip to is unaware/self-righteous racism. The "good wife" racist attempts to shame Blacks into being blacker, scorns Japanese-Americans who don't speak Japanese, and knows more about the Chicano/a community than the folks who make up the community. They assign themselves as the "good whites," as opposed to the "bad whites," and are often so busy telling people of color what the issues in the Black, Asian, Indian, Latino/a communities should be that they don't have time to deal with their errant sisters and brothers in the white community. Which means that people of color are still left to deal with what the "good whites" don't want to . . . racism.

Internalized racism is what really gets in my way as a Black woman. It influences the way I see or don't see myself, limits what I expect of myself or others like me. It results in my acceptance of mistreatment, leads me to believe that

being treated with less than absolute respect, at least this once, is to be expected because I am Black, because I am not white. Because I am (*you fill in the color*), you think, "Life is going to be hard." The fact is life may be hard, but the color of your skin is not the cause of the hardship. The color of your skin may be used as an excuse to mistreat you, but there is no reason or logic involved in the mistreatment. If it seems that your color is the reason; if it seems that your ethnic heritage is the cause of the woe, it's because you've been deliberately beaten down by agents of a greedy system until you swallowed the garbage. That is the internalization of racism.

Racism is the systematic, institutionalized mistreatment of one group of people by another based on racial heritage. Like every other oppression, racism can be internalized. People of color come to believe misinformation about their particular ethnic group and thus believe that their mistreatment is justified. With that basic vocabulary, let's take a look at how the whole thing works together. Meet "the Ism Family," racism, classism, ageism, adultism, elitism, sexism, heterosexism, physicalism, etc. All these ism's are systematic, that is, not only are these parasites feeding off our lives, they are also dependent on one another for foundation. Racism is supported and reinforced by classism, which is given a foothold and a boost by adultism, which also feeds sexism, which is validated by heterosexism, and so it goes on. You cannot have the "ism" functioning without first effectively installing its flip-side, the internalized version of the ism. Like twins, as one particular form of the ism grows in potency, there is a corresponding increasing in its internalized form within the population. Before oppression becomes a specific ism like racism, usually all hell breaks loose. War. People fight attempts to enslave them, or to subvert their will, or to take what they consider theirs, whether that is territory or dignity. It's true that the various elements of racism, while repugnant, would not be able to do very much damage, but for one generally overlooked key piece: power/privilege.

While in one sense we all have power we have to look at the fact that, in our society, people are stratified into various classes and some of these classes have more privilege than others. The owning class has enough power and privilege to not have to give a good whinney what the rest of the folks have on their minds. The power and privilege of the owning class provides the ability to pay off enough of the working class and offer that paid-off group, the middle class, just enough privilege to make it agreeable to do various and sundry oppressive things to other working-class and outright disenfranchised folk, keeping the lid on explosive inequities, at least for a minute. If you're at the bottom of this heap, and you believe the line that says you're there because that's all you're worth, it is at least some small solace to believe that there are others more worthless than you, because of their gender, race, sexual preference . . . whatever. The specific form of power that runs the show here is the power to intimidate. The power to take away the most lives the quickest, and back it up with legal and "divine" sanction, is the very bottom line. It makes the difference between who's holding the racism end of the stick and who's getting beat with it (or beating others as vulnerable as they are) on the internalized racism end of the stick. What I am saying is, while people of color are welcome to tear up their own neighborhoods and each other, everybody knows that you cannot do that to white folks without hell to pay. People of color can be prejudiced against one another and whites, but do not have an ice-cube's chance in hell of passing laws that will get whites sent to relocation camps "for their own protection and the security of the nation." People who have not thought about or refuse to acknowledge this imbalance of power/privilege often want to talk about the racism of people of color. But then that is one of the ways racism is able to continue to function. You look for someone to blame and you blame the victim, who will nine times out of ten accept the blame out of habit.

So, what can we do? Acknowledge racism for a start, even though and especially when we've struggled to be kind and fair, or struggled to rise above it all. It is hard to acknowledge the fact that racism circumscribes and pervades our lives. Racism must be dealt with on two levels, personal and societal, emotional and institutional. It is possible—and most effective—to do both at the same time. We must reclaim whatever delight we have lost in our own ethnic heritage or heritages. This so-called melting pot has only succeeded in turning us into fast food-gobbling "generics" (as in generic "white folks" who were once Irish, Polish, Russian, English, etc. and "black folks," who were once Ashanti, Bambara, Baule, Yoruba, etc.). Find or create safe places to actually *feel* what we've been forced to repress each time we were a victim of, witness to or perpetrator of racism, so that we do not continue, like puppets, to act out the past in the present and future. Challenge oppression. Take a stand against it. When you are aware of something oppressive going down, stop the show. At least call it. We become so numbed to racism that we don't even think twice about it, unless it's immediately life-threatening.

Whites who want to be allies to people of color: You can educate yourselves via research and observation rather than rigidly, arrogantly relying solely on interrogating people of color. Do not expect that people of color should teach you how to behave non-oppressively. Do not give in to the pull to be lazy. Think, hard. Do not blame people of color for your frustration about racism, but do appreciate the fact that people of color will often help you get in touch with that frustration. Assume that your effort to be a good friend is appreciated, but don't expect or accept gratitude from people of color. Work on racism for your sake, not "their" sake. Assume that you are needed and capable of being a good ally. Know that you'll make mistakes and commit yourself to correcting them and continuing on as an ally, no matter what. Don't give up.

People of color, working through internalized racism: Remember always that you and others like you are completely worthy of respect, completely capable of achieving whatever you take a notion to do. Remember that the term "people of color" refers to a variety of ethnic and cultural backgrounds. These various groups have been oppressed in a variety of ways. Educate yourself about the ways different peoples have been oppressed and how they've resisted that oppression. Expect and insist that whites are capable of being good allies against racism. Don't give up. Resist the pull to give out the "people of color seal of approval" to aspiring white allies. A moment of appreciation is fine, but more than that tends to be less than helpful. Celebrate yourself. Celebrate yourself. Celebrate the inevitable end of racism.   [1988]

Understanding the Reading

1. Explain oppression and internalized oppression.
2. Explain the four forms of racism Yamato describes.
3. How does internalized racism work?
4. How do power and privilege reinforce "the Ism Family"?
5. What steps does Yamato suggest need to be taken to combat racism?

Suggestions for Responding

1. Describe an incident when you were a victim of, witness to, or perpetrator of racism; then, analyze what feelings you were forced to repress.
2. What power and privileges do you enjoy as a result of your race, class, age, gender, sexual orientation, and so forth? ✦

53

White Privilege: Unpacking the Invisible Knapsack

PEGGY MCINTOSH

Through work to bring materials from Women's Studies into the rest of the curriculum, I have often noticed men's unwillingness to grant that they are over-privileged, even though they may grant that women are disadvantaged. They may say they will work to improve women's status, in the society, the university, or the curriculum, but they can't or won't support the idea of lessening men's. Denials which amount to taboos surround the subject of advantages which men gain from women's disadvantages. These denials protect male privilege from being fully acknowledged, lessened or ended.

Thinking through unacknowledged male privilege as a phenomenon, I realized that since

hierarchies in our society are interlocking, there was most likely a phenomenon of white privilege which was similarly denied and protected. As a white person, I realized I had been taught about racism as something which puts others at a disadvantage, but had been taught not to see one of its corollary aspects, white privilege, which puts me at an advantage.

I think whites are carefully taught not to recognize white privilege, as males are taught not to recognize male privilege. So I have begun in an untutored way to ask what it is like to have white privilege. I have come to see white privilege as an invisible package of unearned assets which I can count on cashing in each day, but about which I was "meant" to remain oblivious. White privilege is like an invisible weightless knapsack of special provisions, maps, passports, codebooks, visas, clothes, tools and blank checks.

Describing white privilege makes one newly accountable. As we in Women's Studies work to reveal male privilege and ask men to give up some of their power, so one who writes about having white privilege must ask, "Having described it, what will I do to lessen or end it?"

After I realized the extent to which men work from a base of unacknowledged privilege, I understood that much of their oppressiveness was unconscious. Then I remembered the frequent charges from women of color that white women whom they encounter are oppressive. I began to understand why we are justly seen as oppressive, even when we don't see ourselves that way. I began to count the ways in which I enjoy unearned skin privilege and have been conditioned into oblivion about its existence.

My schooling gave me no training in seeing myself as an oppressor, as an unfairly advantaged person, or as a participant in a damaged culture. I was taught to see myself as an individual whose moral state depended on her individual moral will. My schooling followed the pattern my colleague Elizabeth Minnich has pointed out: whites are taught to think of their lives as morally neutral, normative, and average, and also ideal, so that when we work to benefit others, this is seen as work which will allow "them" to be more like "us."

I decided to try to work on myself at least by identifying some of the daily effects of white privilege in my life. I have chosen those conditions which I think in my case *attach some-*

what more to skin-color privilege than to class, religion, ethnic status, or geographical location, though of course all these other factors are intricately intertwined. As far as I can see, my African American co-workers, friends and acquaintances with whom I come into daily or frequent contact in this particular time, place, and line of work cannot count on most of these conditions.

1. I can if I wish arrange to be in the company of people of my race most of the time.
2. If I should need to move, I can be pretty sure of renting or purchasing housing in an area which I can afford and in which I would want to live.
3. I can be pretty sure that my neighbors in such a location will be neutral or pleasant to me.
4. I can go shopping alone most of the time, pretty well assured that I will not be followed or harassed.
5. I can turn on the television or open to the front page of the paper and see people of my race widely represented.
6. When I am told about our national heritage or about "civilization," I am shown that people of my color made it what it is.
7. I can be sure that my children will be given curricular materials that testify to the existence of their race.
8. If I want to, I can be pretty sure of finding a publisher for this piece on white privilege.
9. I can go into a music shop and count on finding the music of my race represented, into a supermarket and find the staple foods which fit with my cultural traditions, into a hairdresser's shop and find someone who can cut my hair.
10. Whether I use checks, credit cards, or cash, I can count on my skin color not to work against the appearance of financial reliability.
11. I can arrange to protect my children most of the time from people who might not like them.
12. I can swear, or dress in second hand clothes, or not answer letters, without having people attribute these choices to the bad morals, the poverty, or the illiteracy of my race.
13. I can speak in public to a powerful male group without putting my race on trial.
14. I can do well in a challenging situation without being called a credit to my race.

15. I am never asked to speak for all the people of my racial group.
16. I can remain oblivious of the language and customs of persons of color who constitute the world's majority without feeling in my culture any penalty for such oblivion.
17. I can criticize our government and talk about how much I fear its policies and behavior without being seen as a cultural outsider.
18. I can be pretty sure that if I ask to talk to "the person in charge," I will be facing a person of my race.
19. If a traffic cop pulls me over or if the IRS audits my tax return, I can be sure I haven't been singled out because of my race.
20. I can easily buy posters, postcards, picture books, greeting cards, dolls, toys, and children's magazines featuring people of my race.
21. I can go home from most meetings of organizations I belong to feeling somewhat tied in, rather than isolated, out-of-place, outnumbered, unheard, held at a distance, or feared.
22. I can take a job with an affirmative action employer without having co-workers on the job suspect that I got it because of race.
23. I can choose public accommodation without fearing that people of my race cannot get in or will be mistreated in the places I have chosen.
24. I can be sure that if I need legal or medical help, my race will not work against me.
25. If my day, week, or year is going badly, I need not ask of each negative episode or situation whether it has racial overtones.
26. I can choose blemish cover or bandages in "flesh" color and have them more or less match my skin.

I repeatedly forgot each of the realizations on this list until I wrote it down. For me white privilege has turned out to be an elusive and fugitive subject. The pressure to avoid it is great, for in facing it I must give up the myth of meritocracy. If these things are true, this is not such a free country; one's life is not what one makes it; many doors open for certain people through no virtues of their own.

In unpacking this invisible knapsack of white privilege, I have listed conditions of daily experience which I once took for granted. Nor did I think of any of these perquisites as bad for the holder. I now think that we need a more finely differentiated taxonomy of privilege, for some of these varieties are only what one would want for everyone in a just society, and others give licence to be ignorant, oblivious, arrogant and destructive.

I see a pattern running through the matrix of white privilege, a pattern of assumptions which were passed on to me as a white person. There was one main piece of cultural turf; it was my own turf, and I was among those who could control the turf. *My skin color was an asset for any move I was educated to want to make.* I could think of myself as belonging in major ways, and of making social systems work for me. I could freely disparage, fear, neglect, or be oblivious to anything outside of the dominant cultural forms. Being of the main culture, I could also criticize it fairly freely.

In proportion as my racial group was being made confident, comfortable, and oblivious, other groups were likely being made inconfident, uncomfortable, and alienated. Whiteness protected me from many kinds of hostility, distress, and violence, which I was being subtly trained to visit in turn upon people of color.

For this reason, the word "privilege" now seems to me misleading. We usually think of privilege as being a favored state, whether earned or conferred by birth or luck. Yet some of the conditions I have described here work to systematically overempower certain groups. Such privilege simply *confers dominance* because of one's race or sex.

I want, then, to distinguish between earned strength and unearned power conferred systematically. Power from unearned privilege can look like strength when it is in fact permission to escape or to dominate. But not all of the privileges on my list are inevitably damaging. Some, like the expectation that neighbors will be decent to you, or that your race will not count against you in court, should be the norm in a just society. Others, like the privilege to ignore less powerful people, distort the humanity of the holders as well as the ignored groups.

We might at least start by distinguishing between positive advantages which we can work to spread, and negative types of advantages which unless rejected will always reinforce our present hierarchies. For example, the feeling that one belongs within the human circle, as Native Americans say, should not be seen as privilege for a few. Ideally it is an *unearned entitlement*. At present, since only a few have it, it is an *unearned advantage* for them. This paper results from a process of coming to see that some of the power which I originally saw as attendant on being a human being in the U.S. consisted [of] *unearned advantage* and *conferred dominance*.

I have met very few men who are truly distressed about systemic, unearned male advantage and conferred dominance. And so one question for me and others like me is whether we will be like them, or whether we will get truly distressed, even outraged, about unearned race advantage and conferred dominance and if so, what we will do to lessen them. In any case, we need to do more work in identifying how they actually affect our daily lives. Many, perhaps most, of our white students in the U.S. think that racism doesn't affect them because they are not people of color; they do not see "whiteness" as a racial identity. In addition, since race and sex are not the only advantaging systems at work, we need similarly to examine the daily experience of having age advantage, or ethnic advantage, or physical ability, or advantage related to nationality, religion, or sexual orientation.

Difficulties and dangers surrounding the task of finding parallels are many. Since racism, sexism, and heterosexism are not the same, the advantaging associated with them should not be seen as the same. In addition, it is hard to disentangle aspects of unearned advantage which rest more on social class, economic class, race, religion, sex and ethnic identity than on other factors. Still, all of the oppressions are interlocking, as the Combahee River Collective[1] Statement of 1977 continues to remind us eloquently.

One factor seems clear about all of the interlocking oppressions. They take both active forms which we can see and embedded forms which as a member of the dominant group one is taught not to see. In my class and place, I did not see myself as a racist because I was taught to recognize racism only in individual acts of meanness by members of my group, never in invisible systems conferring unsought racial dominance on my group from birth.

Disapproving of the systems won't be enough to change them. I was taught to think that racism could end if white individuals changed their attitudes. [But] a "white" skin in the United States opens many doors for whites whether or not we approve of the way dominance has been conferred on us. Individual acts can palliate, but cannot end, these problems.

To redesign social systems we need first to acknowledge their colossal unseen dimensions. The silences and denials surrounding privilege are the key political tool here. They keep the thinking about equality or equity incomplete, protecting unearned advantage and conferred dominance by making these taboo subjects. Most talk by whites about equal opportunity seems to me now to be about equal opportunity to try to get into a position of dominance while denying that *systems* of dominance exist.

It seems to me that obliviousness about white advantage, like obliviousness about male advantage, is kept strongly inculturated in the United States so as to maintain the myth of meritocracy, the myth that democratic choice is equally available to all. Keeping most people unaware that freedom of confident action is there for just a small number of people props up those in power, and serves to keep power in the hands of the same groups that have most of it already.

Though systemic change takes many decades, there are pressing questions for me and I imagine for some others like me if we raise our daily consciousness on the perquisites of being light-skinned. What will we do with such knowledge? As we know from watching men, it is an open question whether we will choose to use unearned advantage to weaken hidden systems of advantage, and whether we will use any of our arbitrarily-awarded power to try to reconstruct power systems on a broader base.

[1989]

Terms

1. COMBAHEE RIVER COLLECTIVE: A group of Black feminist women in Boston from 1974 to 1980.

Understanding the Reading

1. Why is it important to consider the concept of being overprivileged as well as the concept of being disadvantaged?

2. Explain what each of the conditions that arise from White privilege reveals about our cultural values.
3. Why are these privileges important?
4. What does McIntosh mean when she says she must give up the "myth of meritocracy"?
5. Which White privileges "give licence to be ignorant, oblivious, arrogant and destructive"?
6. What assumptions underlie White privilege?
7. What connections does McIntosh make among privilege, power, and dominance?
8. How is Whiteness a racial identity?

Suggestions for Responding

1. What did you learn from McIntosh's analysis of racism and White privilege, and what did you begin to think about after reading it? What additional privileges can you add to McIntosh's list? What will you do with such knowledge? ✦

54

Native Americans v. the U.S. Government

MICHAEL DORRIS

The turn of the twentieth century was an unhappy time for the Native people of America. Their total population was at its lowest ebb, the vast majority of their land had been taken away, their religions were outlawed, their children removed from home and incarcerated in hostile institutions where it was deemed a crime to so much as speak in one's own language. In 1900 few Native Americans were citizens and as a group they constituted the poorest, unhealthiest, and least likely to survive—much less succeed—population in all of the United States. And yet they not only survived, but they survived as a culturally intact group of peoples; against all odds, tribes maintained their languages and wisdom, guarded their art and music and literature, and for the most part, chose to continue to be Indians rather than assimilate and disappear.

The United States government, however, continued to advocate a melting-pot policy, and in

1924 Congress passed the Curtis Act, which conferred American citizenship on all native-born Indians. In many areas, such a change in status did not mean automatic access to the ballot box, however, and Native "citizens" remained disenfranchised "persons under guardianship" in Arizona and New Mexico until 1948.

Nevertheless, citizenship did, in the minds of some congressmen and others, abrogate the rights to special status which were guaranteed through treaty. Questions like "How can we have treaties with our own citizens?" (with its correlative answer: "We can't, therefore throw out the treaties and open up the land!!") should have been asked and answered before any such act was passed. *If* it had been made clear that United States citizenship meant abandonment of Native American identity, and *if* the opinion of Native American people had been solicited, it is improbable that even a significant minority of Indian people would have opted for it in 1924.

In effect, the Curtis Act was tantamount to the American government deciding to celebrate the Bicentennial in 1976 by unilaterally declaring all inhabitants of the Western Hemisphere "American citizens" and then immediately forcing any (former) Brazilian, Canadian, or Venezuelan engaging in international trade to comply with United States tariff restrictions and oil prices. Such an expanded Monroe Doctrine precludes all argument. The American experiment with instant naturalization is not unique: The Portuguese tried it in Angola, the Belgians in Zaire, and the French in Algeria—but somehow most Africans apparently never *felt* like Europeans. Most Native Americans didn't either, but by the twentieth century they lacked the population or resources to successfully dispute the denial of their sovereignty.

Four years later, a blue-ribbon congressional committee chaired by Lewis Meriam issued a report on conditions in Indian country. Its aim was to assess the effects of the Dawes[1] and Curtis acts and to inform the government of the progress these pieces of legislation had made possible for Native American people. The situation on reservations in 1928, however, yielded little in the way of optimistic forecast. Since 1887 conditions had universally worsened: The educational level was in most cases lower, the poverty greater, the death rate higher (and for younger people) than at any time previous to the enactment of the "benevolent" policies. Federal enforcement of the misguided and totally unjust severalty laws[2] was, in effect, cultural genocide.

In 1934 President Roosevelt appointed the anthropologist John Collier as Commissioner of Indian Affairs. Unlike too many of his predecessors in office, Collier actually knew something of at least one Native society (Pueblo) and had long opposed the Allotment policy[3] both for its inhumanity and its naiveté. His major achievement was to assist in the development and passage of the Indian Reorganization Act (the Wheeler-Howard Act), a policy which sought to undo most of the provisions of the Dawes Act and begin to remedy the disasters recounted in the Meriam Report of 1928.

Almost half a century, however, was a long time, and it was beyond realistic possibility that either the land base or the cultural, educational, and economic health of Native American societies could be restored as they were in 1880.

The Wheeler-Howard Act aimed to revive the traditional "bilateral, contractual relationship between the government and the tribes." Commissioner Collier emphasized the Native American right to a kind of self-determination and banned any further allotment of tribal land. The Indian Reorganization Act further authorized severely limited appropriations to purchase new holdings and reclaim certain lost property; it also established a federal loan policy for Native groups and reaffirmed the concept of self-government on reservations.

Many tribes opposed this legislation, however, on the basis of the restrictions and regulations it placed on the participating tribes. The act, for instance, prohibited any individual transfer of tribal land without governmental approval, and it required that all tribal governments conform to a single political system based on majority rule. No tribe was eligible for a single benefit of the act unless it agreed to it *in toto,* and therefore its acceptance necessarily became widespread.

The period following the Collier administration and extending into the early 1950's was one in which many Americans seemed to forget about Indians and assumed that *at last* "they" had finally vanished as predicted. The national interest was focused on World War II and the Korean War, and domestic treaties seemed a thing of the far-distant past.

After one of these "dormant cycles," the public and its government usually seem particularly piqued and frustrated to discover that Native Americans are still very much alive and intact. Once again in the 1950's, as in the 1880's, the presumptuous and thoroughly invalid assumption was made that if Indians had not chosen to disappear into the melting pot, something sinister was to blame. It seems never to have occurred to those in power that Crows or Yakimas, for instance, simply preferred being Crows or Yakimas!

As usual, the federal government, liberal "friends of the Indian," and rural land developers concluded that special status, and the reservation system in particular, were somehow retarding Native assimilation, and therefore it was decided, once again, to breach all legal precepts of international and United States law and unilaterally break treaty agreements. It was further concluded that if some Native Americans insisted that they didn't want to change their relationship with the government, they simply didn't know what was good for them. The rivers were still running, the grass was still growing, but the promises made by the American government and written to apply in perpetuity could not exist for even a century without twice being violated.

A committee was therefore appointed to divide, like Gaul,[4] all reservations into three parts: the "prosperous," the "marginal," and the "poor." Even with this license, only a handful of tribes could be found to fit, by any stretch of the imagination, into the first category, and these were marked for quick termination. The implications of this policy are clear: Apparently Congress regarded reservations as transitionary steps between "primitive" and "modern" society. As soon as a group achieved a margin of success (according to the ethnocentric standards of American culture), a reservation ceased to have a rationale for existence. This self-serving attitude totally ignores both the political circumstances which brought about the reservation system in the first place (e.g., aboriginal right of title), and the legal treaties and sanctions which supposedly protected it.

Two of the most economically self-sustaining tribes, the Klamath in Oregon and the Menominee in Wisconsin, were located in timberland areas and operated logging industries. The government exerted tremendous pressure, employ-ing levers of doubtful legal and ethical practice, and the manipulation of misunderstanding, to force these tribes to submit to termination. Whether this consent was ever actually granted in either case is a debatable point, but it is clear that neither group, had it sufficiently understood the policy, would have agreed.

Termination meant the absolute cessation, in exchange for a monetary settlement, of any special treaty arrangements or status which existed between the tribe and its members and the United States government. Upon termination, the Menominees would be expected, in legal effect, to cease being Indians and to somehow turn themselves into Wisconsonians overnight. On a date set by the government, the dependent, sovereign Menominee Nation, hundreds of years old, would become simply another county within the state.

Historical retrospect clearly shows that in all cases the termination policy was even more ill-conceived and socially disruptive than the Allotment policy had been before it—and just as illegal. The net effects of termination were the loss of large amounts of valuable land by the tribes involved, plus an enormous psychological blow to thousands of Indian people. The fallacy of the policy was patently obvious so quickly that it was suspended shortly after implementation, sparing other tribes similar losses. To date, one of the victimized tribes, the Menominee, has, through persistent and valiant efforts of a group of its members, managed to be reestablished as a reservation in 1973. But as a direct result of termination, the new Menominee lands were much smaller and poorer than the reservation had been before 1953.

Subsequent government policies aimed at assimilating the Native American were more subtle. Among these were the urban relocation programs, often hastily conceived and poorly managed attempts to induce Native Americans to migrate to cities. A substantial percentage of the participants in these programs eventually returned, frustrated and cynical, to their reservations. [1975]

Terms

1. DAWES ACT: The federal law that abolished tribal organizations and allotted 160 acres to the head of each family.

2. SEVERALTY LAWS: Laws mandating that land must be held by individuals rather than in common by the whole group.
3. ALLOTMENT POLICY: The distribution of reservation land under the Dawes Act and the opening of undistributed land to Whites.
4. GAUL: An ancient name for what are now France and Belgium. Julius Caesar opened his history with the statement "All Gaul is divided into three parts."

Understanding the Reading

1. What effect did the Curtis Act have on Native Americans?
2. What were conditions like on reservations in 1928?
3. What were the benefits and restrictions of the Indian Reorganization Act?
4. What was "termination," and what were its effects?

Suggestions for Responding

1. Dorris presents the analogy of the U.S. government unilaterally declaring all inhabitants of the Western Hemisphere to be American citizens. Suppose this actually happened and write about how you would respond personally if you were a citizen of one of the annexed countries.
2. Research one of the governmental policies Dorris mentions; explain what it was supposed to do and what it actually did. ✦

55

Urban Indians

ROBERTA FISKE-RUSCIANO

The term "urban Indians" is problematic for most non-Native Americans. Whether thinking of Native Americans brings forth positive, negative, or neutral images, most non-natives do not imagine natives as members of an urban, technological

"Urban Indians" reprinted by permission of the publisher, Salem Press, Inc. c. 1995 by Salem Press. Inc.

society, and this lack of urban image has led to a blindness regarding the presence and needs of Native Americans in the cities. Identification of the urban Native American has therefore been one of the central problems surrounding government policy-making regarding American Indians since the early 1960's.

RELOCATION AND MIGRATION

All members of a federally recognized tribe in the United States, according to the U.S. Constitution, are due certain benefits and services, by right of their heritage. This unique legal relationship with the U.S. government was never meant to end once an individual moved to a metropolitan area, but in effect that is what has happened. In the mid-1950's, the Bureau of Indian Affairs (BIA), in accord with Congress, began the Voluntary Relocation Program. BIA officers on each reservation were instructed to "sell" the idea of city living to likely candidates. Individuals, and sometimes families, were given a one-way ticket to the chosen city, where housing and employment awaited, all arranged by the BIA. Subsistence money was guaranteed for six weeks, after which these newest immigrants were on their own. It was informally known as a "sink-or-swim policy." As anthropologist Sol Tax noted twenty years after relocation, however, "Indians don't sink or swim, they float."

Most Indians who arrived in the city under the relocation program left as soon as they got a good look at their new way of life. Many of the jobs were unskilled, and Native Americans found they were able to afford only the worst housing available in the city. Under these conditions, transition to city dwelling was, for many, impossible. Yet the BIA did not recognize the shortcomings of its multimillion-dollar program and continued to relocate as many Native Americans as possible. Noticing that many of their clients were returning to their reservations, the BIA began relocating people as far away from their reservations as could be managed, to make it as difficult as possible to return. Part of the plan was to terminate the reservations eventually. Authors Watt Spade and Willard Walker illustrate one Indian view of this phase of the relocation program. They wrote of overhearing two Indian men humorously discussing the government's wanting to land a man on the moon. It could be done, one man said, but nobody knew how to get the man home again after he landed on the moon. All the government had to do, he said, was put an Indian in the rocket ship and tell him he was being relocated: "Then, after he got to the moon, that Indian would find his own way home again and the government wouldn't have to figure that part out at all." The Voluntary Relocation Program was a failure according to its own goals. This program was based on the prejudiced notion that Native American culture and life-ways will, and should, disappear. The BIA and the U.S. Congress of the 1950's counted on America's cities to speed that process.

Most Native Americans presently living in urban areas did not arrive through the relocation program but migrated independently, usually looking for employment, and settled near relatives or friends from their reservation or hometown. Many are permanent residents, but an approximately equal number are transient—relocating within the city, going from city to city, or spending part of the year in the city and part on the reservation. There is no known "typical" pattern of migration; tribal nations, families, and individuals differ according to their needs. A family may live in the city during the winter so the children can stay in school, then leave for the reservation in the summer. Construction workers are often busy in the cities during the warm months and leave in the winter. The powwow season and harvests also draw many urban Native Americans back to the reservations. Jeanne Guillemin points out in *Urban Renegades* (1975) that the young Micmac women of Boston often prefer to return to their kin in the Canadian Maritime Provinces when it is time to give birth. There they receive the physical, emotional, and spiritual support they need and avoid the frightening aspects of the city, such as its clinics and hospitals. The frequent moving to and from the reservation and within the city is one factor in the urban Native American's invisibility or elusiveness.

URBAN INDIAN IDENTITY

Another factor until recently has been their reluctance to identify themselves as Native Americans to non-Native Americans in the city. In 1976 the director of the American Indian Health Ser-

METROPOLITAN STATISTICAL AREAS WITH LARGEST NATIVE AMERICAN POPULATIONS, 1990	
Metropolitan Statistical Area	Population
*Los Angeles-Anaheim-Riverside, CA	85,004
Tulsa, OK	48,116
Oklahoma City, OK	45,623
*New York-Northern New Jersey-Long Island, NY-NJ-CT	44,437
*San Francisco-Oakland-San Jose, CA	39,255
Phoenix, AZ	37,708
*Seattle-Tacoma, WA	29,643
Minneapolis-St. Paul, MN-WI	23,621
Tucson, AZ	20,231
San Diego, CA	19,564
*Dallas-Fort Worth, TX	18,608
*Detroit-Ann Arbor, MI	17,731
Sacramento, CA	16,650
Albuquerque, NM	16,201
*Chicago-Gary-Lake County, IL-IN-WI	15,098
*Denver-Boulder, CO	13,600
*Portland-Vancouver, OR-WA	13,034
*Philadelphia-Wilmington-Trenton, PA-NJ-DE-MD	10,962
Washington, DC-MD-VA	10,685
*Houston-Galveston-Brazoria, TX	10,677

Source: U.S. Bureau of the Census, *Census of Population and Housing, 1990. Summary Tape on CD-ROM.* Washington, D.C.: U.S. Government Printing Office, 1991.
*Indicates a combined metropolitan statistical area (CMSA).

vice in Chicago illustrated this problem with an anecdote. A young man had been playing baseball and had been hit hard by the bat. When he was taken to the emergency room, he removed all his turquoise beads, giving them to a friend to keep for him, and stuffed his long braids inside his baseball cap; he said, "Now the receptionist will think I'm a Mexican." His friend said they frequently try to pass as Mexicans in order to be treated better. The urban Native Americans' attempts to remain unidentified, coupled with the tremendous mobility of individuals and families, has made it impossible in past years for the U.S. Census to come close to an accurate count in the cities. In the 1990 U.S. Census, however, there was a huge increase in people identifying themselves as Native Americans, Eskimos, and Aleuts. As the increase cannot be completely explained by actual population growth, there is much speculation regarding what has made so many more Native Americans willing to be identified. Some cynical observers insist that the motive must be monetary: to obtain funds and services that are due Native Americans under the law. One thing that scholars studying Native American culture have learned over the decades, however, is that Native Americans usually cannot be coaxed to take a particular course of action because of the promise of money. Most Native Americans living in cities do not receive federal funds or services of any kind, because of distrust of Indian or non-Indian agencies and a preference for finding survival strategies among one another.

In the past, most sociological studies have focused on the atypical urban Native American—the one most visible, "lying in the gutter," cut off from kin. It is important to learn how most urban Native Americans (neither the upper middle-class professionals nor the indigent) have found their way in this foreign environment, maintaining strong kin relationships and networks and not necessarily assimilating. Native Americans have arrived in cities all over the United States for many reasons; work opportunities and education are the most commonly cited. Guillemin states another very important reason in her chapter "The City as Adventure." For the Micmac of Canada, she points out, going to Boston is seen as extending one's tribal boundaries. While trying to survive in this environment, the young Micmac learn much about coping with conditions as they meet them in the South End, a settling ground for immigrants from all over the world. Their risk-taking and networking are important parts of a young urban Native American's education. Flexibility is seen as one key to their tribal nation's survival. While it is often assumed that cities temper and neutralize (if not actually melt) the unique cultures of their residents, in this case a native people is claiming the city as their own and using it for their own purposes—to strengthen themselves as members of an Indian nation as well as to survive and enjoy themselves. Some cities, such as Chicago, operate high-quality schools for Native American children as further insurance against their losing precious traditions and ways of thinking.

GAMBLING AS URBAN LEGACY

One clear consequence of Native Americans learning to deal with the bureaucratic state has been the success stories of Indian nations using the existing laws to repair damages done to their nations, such as bringing an economic base to their reservation. One example comes from the small Pequot Nation in Ledyard, Connecticut. In response to a 1988 ruling holding that federal law allows recognized Indian tribes to have gambling on reservations if the state in which they live allows some sort of gambling off the reservation, the Pequots set up a large gambling center, the Foxwoods Resort and Casino. The gambling question affects reservations all over the country; from California to New Jersey, Native Americans are debating the serious question of what effects the presence of casinos would have on their reservations. Many are now in operation. Although most reservation casinos are not located in large metropolitan areas, the situation clearly involves the bringing of some aspects of the city (in concentrated doses) to the reservation. Although various forms of gambling have existed traditionally among many Native American nations, the dangers and problems that seem to surround non-Native American casino centers worry many people. It has been predicted that the Pequots will become millionaires, for example; whether this will help the Pequots to strengthen their nation or will pull it apart at the seams is an unanswered question. Many of the same questions that have concerned native peoples for generations—about the quality of life left for their people—continue to worry them, whether they be on an impoverished reservation, in a large city, or on a reservation that has made casino gambling the economic base of its people's lives. Certainly the revenues are benefiting many people now, Indian and non-Indian alike.

It is impossible to predict accurately what the long-term effects of such changes will be, but it is likely that current and future generations of Native Americans will be able to draw upon the resilience typical of Indian peoples. They will remain strong and independent as a group while balancing the need to protect their traditions with the need to accept, even embrace, change.   [1995]

References

Fiske, Roberta. "Native American Artists in Chicago." In *A Report on the Chicago Ethnic Arts Project.* Washington, D.C.: Library of Congress, American Folklife Center, 1978.

Guillemin, Jeanne, *Urban Renegades.* New York: Columbia University Press, 1975.

Johnson, Kirk. "Seeking Lost Culture at a Pow-wow: Pequots Draw Ritual Dancers Across U.S. with Rich Prizes." *The New York Times,* September 19, 1993, 52.

Kaufman, Michael T. "A James Bond with $100 Tries out a Tribal Casino." *The New York Times,* March 18, 1994, C1.

Lurie, Nancy. "The Contemporary American Indian Scene." In *North American Indians in Historical Perspective,* edited by Eleanor Burke Leacock and Nancy Lurie. New York: Random House, 1971.

Spade, Watt, and Willard Walker. "Relocation." In *The Way: An Anthology of American Indian Life,* edited by Shirley Hill Witt and Stan Steiner. New York: Alfred A. Knopf, 1972.

Understanding the Reading

1. What was the purpose of the Voluntary Relocation Program?
2. Why was it a failure?
3. Why do Native Americans go to cities to live?
4. Why have they been reluctant, until recently, to be identified as Indians in urban areas?
5. What is one survival strategy they have learned, as a result of dealing with the bureaucratic state?

Suggestions for Responding

1. Research which American Indians live nearest to you. How do they make a living?
2. Look for data on the general health and other socioeconomic markers of Indians in any U.S. urban area. ✦

56

Sex, Class, and Race Intersections: Visions of Women of Color

CAROL LEE SANCHEZ

"As I understand it," said the American Indian [to one of the Puritan fathers], "you propose to civilize me."
"Exactly."
"You want to get me out of the habit of idleness and teach me to work."
"That is the idea."
"And then lead me to simplify my methods and invent things to make my work lighter."
"Yes."
"And after that I'll become ambitious to get rich so that I won't have to work at all."
"Naturally."
"Well what's the use of taking such a roundabout way of getting just where I started from? I don't have to work now."
—[American jokelore]

To identify Indian is to identify with an invisible or vanished people; it is to identify with a set of basic assumptions and beliefs held by *all* who are not Indian about the indigenous peoples of the Americas. Even among the Spanish speaking Mestizos or mezclados,[1] there is a strong preference to "disappear" their Indian blood, to disassociate from their Indian beginnings. To be Indian is to be considered "colorful," spiritual, connected to the earth, simplistic, and disappointing if not dressed in buckskin and feathers; shocking if a city-dweller and even more shocking if an educator or other type of professional. That's the positive side.

On the negative side, to be Indian is to be thought of as primitive, alcoholic, ignorant (as in "Dumb Indian"), better off dead (as in "the only good Indian is a dead Indian" or "I didn't know there was any of you folks still left"), unskilled, non-competitive, immoral, pagan or heathen, untrustworthy (as in "Indian-giver") and frightening. To be Indian is to be the primary model that is used to promote racism in this country.

How can that happen, you ask? Bad press. One hundred and fifty years of the most consistently vicious press imaginable. Newspapers, dime novels, textbooks and fifty years of visual media have portrayed and continue to portray Indians as savage, blood-thirsty, immoral, inhuman people. When there's a touch of social consciousness attached, you will find the once "blood-thirsty," "white-killer savage" portrayed as a pitiful drunk, a loser, an outcast or a mix-blood not welcomed by, or trusted by, either race. For fifty years, children in this country have been raised to kill Indians mentally, subconsciously through the visual media, until it is an automatic reflex. That shocks you? Then I have made my point.

Let me quote from Helen Hunt Jackson's book, *A Century of Dishonor,* from the introduction written by Bishop H. B. Whipple of Minnesota, who charged that

> the American people have accepted as truth the teachings that the Indians were a degraded, brutal race of savages, who it was the will of God should perish at the approach of civilization. If they do not say with our Puritan fathers that these are the Hittites[2] who are to be driven out before the saints of the Lord, they do accept the teaching that manifest destiny[3] will drive the Indians from the earth. The inexorable has no tears or pity at the cries of anguish of the doomed race.

This race still struggles to stay alive. Tribe by Tribe, pockets of Indian people here and there. One million two hundred thousand people who identify as Indians—raised and socialized as Indian—as of the 1980 census, yet Cowboys and Indians is still played every day by children all over America of every creed, color, and nationality. Well—it's harmless, isn't it? Just kids playing kill Indians. It's all history. But it's still happening every day, and costumes are sold and the cheap western is still rolling out of Hollywood, the old shoot-'em-up westerns playing on afternoon kid shows, late night T.V. Would you allow your children to play Nazis and Jews? Blacks and KKKs? Complete with costume? Yes! It is a horrifying thought, but in thinking about it you can see how easy it is to dismiss an entire race of people as barbaric and savage, and how almost impossible it is, after this has been inculcated in you, to relate to an Indian or a group of Indians today. For example, how many famous Indians do you know offhand? Certainly the great warrior chiefs come to mind first, and of course the three most famous Indian "Princesses"—Pocahontas, Sacajawea and La Malinche. Did you get past ten? Can you name at least five Indian women you know personally or have heard about? That's just counting on one hand, folks.

As Indians, we have endured. We are still here. We have survived everything that European "civilization" has imposed on us. There are approximately 130 different Indian languages still spoken in North America of the some 300 spoken at contact; 180 different Tribes incorporated and recognized by the Federal Government of the approximately 280 that once existed, with an additional 15 to 25 unrecognized Tribes that are lumped together on a reservation with other Tribes. We still have Women's Societies and there are at least 30 active women-centered Mother-Rite Cultures[4] existing and practicing their everyday life in that manner, on this continent.

We have been displaced, relocated, removed, terminated, educated, acculturated and in our hearts and minds we will always "go back to the blanket"[5] as long as we are still connected to our families, our Tribes and our land.

The Indian Way is a different way. It is a respectful way. The basic teachings in every Tribe that exists today as a Tribe in the western hemisphere are based on respect for all the things our Mother gave us. If we neglect her or anger her, she will make our lives very difficult and we always know that we have a hardship on ourselves and on our children. We are raised to be cautious and concerned for the *future* of our people, and that is how we raise our children—because *they* are *our* future. Your "civilization" has made all of us very sick and has made our mother earth sick and out of balance. Your kind of thinking and education has brought the whole world to the brink of total disaster, whereas the thinking and education among my people forbids the practice of almost everything Euro-Americans, in particular, value.

Those of you who are socialists and marxists have an ideology, but where in this country do you live communally on a common land base from generation to generation? Indians, who have a way of life instead of an ideology, do live on communal lands and don't accumulate anything—for the sake of accumulation.

Radicals look at reservation Indians and get very upset about their poverty conditions. But poverty to us is not the same thing as poverty is to you. Our poverty is that we can't be who we are. We can't hunt or fish or grow our food because our basic resources and the right to use them in traditional ways are denied us. In order to live well, we must be able to provide for ourselves in such a way that we can continue living as we always have. We still don't believe in being slaves to the "domineering" culture systems. Consequently, we are accused of many things based on those standards and values that make no sense to us.

You want us to act like you, to be like you so that we will be more acceptable, more likeable. You should try to be more like us regarding communal co-existence; respect and care for all living things and for the earth, the waters, and the atmosphere; respect for human dignity and the right to be who they are.

During the 1930s, '40s and '50s, relocation programs caused many Indians to become lost in the big cities of the United States and there were many casualties from alcoholism, vagrancy and petty crime. Most Indians were/are jailed for assault and battery in barroom brawls because the spiritual and psychological violation of Indian people trying to live in the dominant (domineering) culture generally forces us to numb ourselves as frequently as possible. That is difficult, if not impossible, for you to understand. White science studies dead things and creates poisonous substances to kill and maim the creatures as well as the humans. You call that progress. Indians call it insanity. Our science studies living things; how they interact and how they maintain a balanced existence. Your science disregards—even denies—the spirit world: ours believes in it and remains connected to it. We fast, pray to our ancestors, call on them when we dance and it rains—at Laguna, at Acoma, at Hopi—still, today. We fight among ourselves, we have border disputes, we struggle to exist in a modern context with our lands full of timber, uranium, coal, oil, gasoline, precious metals and semi-precious stones; full—because we are taught to take only what we need and not because we are too ignorant to know what to do with all those resources. We are caught in the bind between private corporations and the government—"our guardian"—because they/you want all those resources. "Indians certainly don't need them"—and your people will do *anything* to get their hands on our mineral-rich lands. They will legis-late, stir up internal conflicts, cause inter-Tribal conflicts, dangle huge amounts of monies as compensation for perpetual contracts and promise lifetime economic security. If we object, or sue to protect our lands, these suits will be held in litigation for fifteen to twenty years with "white" interests benefiting in the interim. Some of us give up and sell out, but there are many of us learning to hold out and many many more of us going back to the old ways of thinking, because we see that our ancestors were right and that the old ways were better ways. So, more Indians are going "back to the blanket," back to "Indian time," with less stress, fewer dominant (domineering) culture activities and occupations. Modern Indians are recreating Indian ways once again. All this leads to my vision as an Indian woman. It is my hope:

1. that you—all you non-Indians—study and learn about our systems of thought and internal social and scientific practices, leaving your Patriarchal Anthropology and History textbooks, academic training and methodologies at home or in the closet on a dusty shelf.
2. that your faculties, conference organizers, community organizers stop giving lip service to including a "Native American" for this or that with the appended phrase: "if we only knew one!" Go find one. There are hundreds of resource lists or Indian-run agencies, hundreds of Indian women in organizations all over the country—active and available with valuable contributions to make.
3. that you will strongly discourage or STOP the publication of any and all articles *about* Indians *written by non-Indians,* and publish work written by Indians about ourselves—whether you agree with us, approve of us or not.
4. that you will *stop colonizing us* and reinterpreting *our* experience.
5. that you will *listen* to us and *learn* from us. We carry ancient traditions that are thousands of years old. We are modern and wear clothes like yours and handle all the trappings of your "civilization" as well as ours; maintain your Christianity as well as our ancient religions, and we are still connected to our ancestors, and our land base. You are the foreigners as long as you continue to believe in the progress that destroys our Mother.

You are not taught to respect our perfected cultures or our scientific achievements which have just recently been re-evaluated by your social scientists and "deemed worthy" of respect. Again, let me re-state that 150 years of bad press will certainly make it extremely difficult for most white people to accept these "primitive" achievements without immediately attempting to connect them to aliens from outer space, Egyptians, Vikings, Asians and whatever sophisticated "others" you have been educated to acknowledge as those who showed the "New World" peoples "The Way." Interestingly, the only continents that were ever "discovered" (historically) where people already lived are North and South America. Who discovered Europe? Who discovered Africa? Who discovered Asia? Trade routes, yes—continents, no. Manifest Destiny will continue to reign as long as we teach our children that Columbus "discovered" America. Even this "fact" is untrue. He actually discovered an island in the Caribbean and *failed* to discover Cathay!

When we consistently make ourselves aware of these "historical facts" that are presented by the Conqueror—the White Man—only then can all of us benefit from cultural traditions that are ten to thirty thousand years old. It is time for us to *share* the best of all our traditions and cultures, all over the world; and it is our duty and responsibility as the women of the world to make this positive contribution in any and every way we can, or we will ultimately become losers, as the Native Race of this hemisphere lost some four hundred years ago.   [1988]

Terms

1. MESTIZOS OR MEZCLADOS: The Latin-American name for the offspring of a Native American and a Spaniard.
2. HITTITES: Ancient non-Black peoples of Asia Minor and Syria.
3. MANIFEST DESTINY: A nineteenth-century belief that White people had the duty and right to control and develop the entire North American continent.
4. MOTHER-RITE CULTURES: Societies in which motherhood is the central kinship bond and women are highly valued and have considerable influence.

5. "GO BACK TO THE BLANKET": A phrase used by missionaries and White educators referring to "educated" Indian children who rejected White "civilized" values and returned to their native culture.

Understanding the Reading

1. What are the positive and negative stereotypes of Indians?
2. What does Sanchez mean when she says, "Children of this country have been raised to kill Indians"?
3. How does Sanchez characterize the Indian way?
4. Why do you think Sanchez objects to "articles about Indians written by non-Indians"?
5. What point is Sanchez making by her list of hopes?

Suggestions for Responding

1. Name and identify all the Native Americans you can think of. What does your list show you?
2. Write a summary of what you learned and thought about Indians when you were a child. Analyze how this correlates with Sanchez's assertions about cultural stereotypes of Indians. ✦

57

Crimes Against Humanity

WARD CHURCHILL

During the past couple of seasons, there has been an increasing wave of controversy regarding the names of professional sports teams like the Atlanta "Braves," Cleveland "Indians," Washington "Redskins," and Kansas City "Chiefs." The issue extends to the names of college teams like Florida State University "Seminoles," University of Illinois "Fighting Illini," and so on, right on down to high school outfits like the Lamar (Colorado) "Savages." Also involved have been team adoption of "mascots," replete with feathers, buckskins, beads, spears and "warpaint" (some fans have opted to adorn themselves in the same fashion), and nifty little "pep" gestures like the "Indian Chant" and "Tomahawk Chop."

A substantial number of American Indians have protested that use of native names, images and symbols as sports team mascots and the like is, by definition, a virulently racist practice. Given the historical relationship between Indians and non-Indians during what has been called the "Conquest of America," American Indian Movement leader (and American Indian Anti-Defamation Council founder) Russell Means has compared the practice to contemporary Germans naming their soccer teams the "Jews," "Hebrews," and "Yids," while adorning their uniforms with grotesque caricatures of Jewish faces taken from the Nazis' anti-Semitic propaganda of the 1930s. Numerous demonstrations have occurred in conjunction with games—most notably during the November 15, 1992 match-up between the Chiefs and Redskins in Kansas City—by angry Indians and their supporters.

In response, a number of players—especially African Americans and other minority athletes—have been trotted out by professional team owners like Ted Turner, as well as university and public school officials, to announce that they mean not to insult but to honor native people. They have been joined by the television networks and most major newspapers, all of which have editorialized that Indian discomfort with the situation is "no big deal," insisting that the whole thing is just "good, clean fun." The country needs more such fun, they've argued, and "a few disgruntled Native Americans" have no right to undermine the nation's enjoyment of its leisure time by complaining. This is especially the case, some have argued, "in hard times like these." It has even been contended that Indian outrage at being systematically degraded—rather than the degradation itself—creates "a serious barrier to the sort of intergroup communication so necessary in a multicultural society such as ours."

Okay, let's communicate. We are frankly dubious that those advancing such positions really believe their own rhetoric, but, just for the sake of argument, let's accept the premise that they are sincere. If what they say is true, then isn't it time we spread such "inoffensiveness" and

"good cheer" around among *all* groups so that *everybody* can participate *equally* in fostering the round of national laughs they call for? Sure it is—the country can't have too much fun or "intergroup involvement"—so the more, the merrier. Simple consistency demands that anyone who thinks the Tomahawk Chop is a swell pastime must be just as hearty in their endorsement of the following ideas—by the logic used to defend the defamation of American Indians—[to] help us all really start yukking it up.

First, as a counterpart to the Redskins, we need an NFL team called "Niggers" to honor Afro-Americans. Half-time festivities for fans might include a simulated stewing of the opposing coach in a large pot while players and cheerleaders dance around it, garbed in leopard skins and wearing fake bones in their noses. This concept obviously goes along with the kind of gaiety attending the Chop, but also with the actions of the Kansas City Chiefs, whose team members—prominently including black team members—lately appeared on a poster looking "fierce" and "savage" by way of wearing Indian regalia. Just a bit of harmless "morale boosting," says the Chiefs' front office. You bet.

So that the newly-formed Niggers sports club won't end up too out of sync while expressing the "spirit" and "identity" of Afro-Americans in the above fashion, a baseball franchise—let's call this one the "Sambos"—should be formed. How about a basketball team called the "Spearchuckers"? A hockey team called the "Jungle Bunnies"? Maybe the "essence" of these teams could be depicted by images of tiny black faces adorned with huge pairs of lips. The players could appear on TV every week or so gnawing on chicken legs and spitting watermelon seeds at one another. Catchy, eh? Well, there's "nothing to be upset about," according to those who love wearing "war bonnets" to the Super Bowl or having "Chief Illiniwik" dance around the sports arenas of Urbana, Illinois.

And why stop there? There are plenty of other groups to include. "Hispanics"? They can be "represented" by the Galveston "Greasers" and San Diego "Spics," at least until the Wisconsin "Wetbacks" and Baltimore "Beaners" get off the ground. Asian Americans? How about the "Slopes," "Dinks," "Gooks," and "Zipperheads"? Owners of the latter teams might get their logo ideas from editorial page cartoons printed in the nation's newspapers during World War II: slant-eyes, buck teeth, big glasses, but nothing racially insulting or derogatory, according to the editors and artists involved at the time. Indeed, this Second World War–vintage stuff can be seen as just another barrel of laughs, at least by what current editors say are their "local standards" concerning American Indians.

Let's see. Who's been left out? Teams like the Kansas City "Kikes," Hanover "Honkies," San Leandro "Shylocks," Daytona "Dagos," and Pittsburgh "Polacks" will fill a certain social void among white folk. Have a religious belief? Let's all go for the gusto and gear up the Milwaukee "Mackerel Snappers" and Hollywood "Holy Rollers." The Fighting Irish of Notre Dame can be rechristened the "Drunken Irish" or "Papist Pigs." Issues of gender and sexual preference can be addressed through creation of teams like the St. Louis "Sluts," Boston "Bimbos," Detroit "Dykes," and the Fresno "Fags." How about the Gainesville "Gimps" and Richmond "Retards," so the physically and mentally impaired won't be excluded from our fun and games?

Now, don't go getting "overly sensitive" out there. None of this is demeaning or insulting, at least not when it's being done to Indians. Just ask the folks who are doing it, or their apologists like Andy Rooney in the national media. They'll tell you—as in fact they *have* been telling you—that there's been no harm done, regardless of what their victims think, feel, or say. The situation is exactly the same as when those with precisely the same mentality used to insist that Step 'n' Fetchit was okay, or Rochester on the Jack Benny Show, or Amos and Andy, Charlie Chan, the Frito Bandito, or any of the other cutesy symbols making up the lexicon of American racism. Have we communicated yet?

Let's get just a little bit real here. The notion of "fun" embodied in rituals like the Tomahawk Chop must be understood for what it is. There's not a single non-Indian example used above which can be considered socially acceptable in even the most marginal sense. The reasons are obvious enough. So why is it different where American Indians are concerned? One can only conclude that, in contrast to the other groups at issue, Indians are (falsely) perceived as being too few, and therefore too weak, to defend themselves effectively against racist and otherwise offensive behavior.

Fortunately, there are some glimmers of hope. A few teams and their fans have gotten the message and have responded appropriately. Stanford University, which opted to drop the name "Indians" from Stanford, has experienced no resulting dropoff in attendance. Meanwhile, the local newspaper in Portland, Oregon, recently decided its long-standing editorial policy prohibiting use of racial epithets should include derogatory team names. The Redskins, for instance, are now referred to as "the Washington team," and will continue to be described in this way until the franchise adopts an inoffensive moniker (newspaper sales in Portland have suffered no decline as a result).

Such examples are to be applauded and encouraged. They stand as figurative beacons in the night, proving beyond all doubt that it is quite possible to indulge in the pleasure of athletics without accepting blatant racism into the bargain.

On October 16, 1946, a man named Julius Streicher mounted the steps of a gallows. Moments later he was dead, the sentence of an international tribunal composed of representatives of the United States, France, Great Britain, and the Soviet Union having been imposed. Streicher's body was then cremated, and—so horrendous were his crimes thought to have been—his ashes dumped into an unspecified German river so that "no one should ever know a particular place to go for reasons of mourning his memory."

Julius Streicher had been convicted at Nuremberg, Germany, of what were termed "Crimes Against Humanity." The lead prosecutor in his case—Justice Robert Jackson of the United States Supreme Court—had not argued that the defendant had killed anyone, nor that he had personally committed any especially violent act. Nor was it contended that Streicher had held any particularly important position in the German government during the period in which the so-called Third Reich had exterminated some 6,000,000 Jews, as well as several million Gypsies, Poles, Slavs, homosexuals, and other unter-menschen (subhumans).

The sole offense for which the accused was ordered put to death was in having served as publisher/editor of a Bavarian tabloid entitled *Der Stürmer* during the early-to-mid 1930s, years before the Nazi genocide actually began. In this capacity, he had penned a long series of virulently anti-Semitic editorials and "news" stories, usually accompanied by cartoons and other images graphically depicting Jews in extraordinarily derogatory fashion. This, the prosecution asserted, had done much to "dehumanize" the targets of his distortion in the mind of the German public. In turn, such dehumanization had made it possible—or at least easier—for average Germans to later indulge in the outright liquidation of Jewish "vermin." The tribunal agreed, holding that Streicher was therefore complicit in genocide and deserving of death by hanging.

During his remarks to the Nuremberg tribunal, Justice Jackson observed that, in implementing its sentences, the participating powers were morally and legally binding themselves to adhere forever after to the same standards of conduct that were being applied to Streicher and the other Nazi leaders. In the alternative, he said, the victorious allies would have committed "pure murder" at Nuremberg—no different in substance from that carried out by those they presumed to judge—rather than establishing the "permanent benchmark for justice" which was intended.

Yet in the United States of Robert Jackson, the indigenous American Indian population had already been reduced, in a process which is ongoing to this day, from perhaps 12.5 million in the year 1500 to fewer than 250,000 by the beginning of the 20th century. This was accomplished, according to official sources, "largely through the cruelty of [Euro-American] settlers," and an informal but clear governmental policy which had made it an articulated goal to "exterminate these red vermin," or at least whole segments of them.

Bounties had been placed on the scalps of Indians—any Indians—in places as diverse as Georgia, Kentucky, Texas, the Dakotas, Oregon, and California, and had been maintained until resident Indian populations were decimated or disappeared altogether. Entire peoples such as the Cherokee had been reduced to half their size

through a policy of forced removal from their homelands east of the Mississippi River to what were then considered less preferable areas in the West.

Others, such as the Navajo, suffered the same fate while under military guard for years on end. The United States Army had also perpetrated a long series of wholesale massacres of Indians at places like Horsehoe Bend, Bear River, Sand Creek, the Washita River, the Marias River, Camp Robinson, and Wounded Knee.

Through it all, hundreds of popular novels—each competing with the next to make Indians appear more grotesque, menacing, and inhuman—were sold in the tens of millions of copies in the U.S. Plainly, the Euro-American public was being conditioned to see Indians in such a way as to allow their eradication to continue. And continue it did until the Manifest Destiny[1] of the U.S.—a direct precursor to what Hitler would subsequently call Lebensraumpolitik (the politics of living space)—was consummated.

By 1900, the national project of "clearing" Native Americans from their land and replacing them with "superior" Anglo-American settlers was complete; the indigenous population had been reduced by as much as 98 percent while approximately 97.5 percent of their original territory had "passed" to the invaders. The survivors had been concentrated, out of sight and mind of the public, on scattered "reservations," all of them under the self-assigned "plenary" (full) power of the federal government. There was, of course, no Nuremberg-style tribunal passing judgment on those who had fostered such circumstances in North America. No U.S. official or private citizen was ever imprisoned—never mind hanged—for implementing or propagandizing what had been done. Nor had the process of genocide afflicting Indians been completed. Instead, it merely changed form.

Between the 1880s and the 1980s, nearly half of all Native American children were coercively transferred from their own families, communities, and cultures to those of the conquering society. This was done through compulsory attendance at remote boarding schools, often hundreds of miles from their homes, where native children were kept for years on end while being systematically "deculturated" (indoctrinated to think and act in the manner of Euro Americans rather than as Indians). It was also accomplished through a pervasive foster home and adoption program—including "blind" adoptions, where children would be permanently denied information as to who they were/are and where they'd come from—placing native youths in non-Indian homes.

The express purpose of all this was to facilitate a U.S. governmental policy to bring about the "assimilation" (dissolution) of indigenous societies. In other words, Indian cultures as such were to be caused to disappear. Such policy objectives are directly contrary to the United Nations 1948 Convention on Punishment and Prevention of the Crime of Genocide, an element of international law arising from the Nuremberg proceedings. The forced "transfer of the children" of a targeted "racial, ethnical, or religious group" is explicitly prohibited as a genocidal activity under the Convention's second article.

Article II of the Genocide Convention also expressly prohibits involuntary sterilization as a means of "preventing births among" a targeted population. Yet, in 1975, it was conceded by the U.S. government that its Indian Health Service (IHS), then a subpart of the Bureau of Indian Affairs (BIA), was even then conducting a secret program of involuntary sterilization that had affected approximately 40 percent of all Indian women. The program was allegedly discontinued, and the IHS was transferred to the Public Health Service, but no one was punished. In 1990, it came out that the IHS was inoculating Inuit children in Alaska with Hepatitis-B vaccine. The vaccine had already been banned by the World Health Organization as having a demonstrated correlation with the HIV-Syndrome which is itself correlated to AIDS. As this is written, a "field test" of Hepatitis-A vaccine, also HIV-correlated, is being conducted on Indian reservations in the northern plains region.

The Genocide Convention makes it a "crime against humanity" to create conditions leading to the destruction of an identifiable human group, as such. Yet the BIA has utilized the government's plenary prerogatives to negotiate mineral leases "on behalf of" Indian peoples, paying a fraction of standard royalty rates. The result has been "super profits" for a number of preferred U.S. corporations. Meanwhile, Indians, whose reservations ironically turned out to be in some of the most mineral-rich areas of North America, which makes us, the nominally wealthiest segment of the continent's population, live in dire poverty.

By the government's own data in the mid-1980s, Indians received the lowest annual and lifetime per capita incomes of any aggregate population group in the United States. Concomitantly, we suffer the highest rate of infant mortality, death by exposure and malnutrition, disease, and the like. Under such circumstances, alcoholism and other escapist forms of substance abuse are endemic in the Indian community, a situation which leads both to a general physical debilitation of the population and a catastrophic accident rate. Teen suicide among Indians is several times the national average.

The average life expectancy of a reservation-based Native American man is barely 45 years; women can expect to live less than three years longer.

Such itemizations could be continued at great length, including matters like the radioactive contamination of large portions of contemporary Indian Country, the forced relocation of traditional Navajos, and so on. But the point should be made: Genocide, as defined in international law, is a continuing fact of day-to-day life (and death) for North America's native peoples. Yet there has been—and is—only the barest flicker of public concern about, or even consciousness of, this reality. Absent any serious expression of public outrage, no one is punished and the process continues.

A salient reason for public acquiescence before the ongoing holocaust in Native North America has been a continuation of the popular legacy, often through more effective media. Since 1925, Hollywood has released more than 2,000 films, many of them rerun frequently on television, portraying Indians as strange, perverted, ridiculous, and often dangerous things of the past. Moreover, we are habitually presented to mass audiences one-dimensionally, devoid of recognizable human motivations and emotions; Indians thus serve as props, little more. We have thus been thoroughly and systematically dehumanized.

Nor is this the extent of it. Everywhere, we are used as logos, as mascots, as jokes: "Big Chief" writing tablets, "Red Man" chewing tobacco, "Winnebago" campers, "Navajo" and "Cherokee" and "Pontiac" and "Cadillac" pickups and automobiles. There are the Cleveland "Indians," the Kansas City "Chiefs," the Atlanta "Braves," and the Washington "Redskins" professional sports teams—not to mention those in thousands of colleges, high schools, and elementary schools across the country—each with their own degrading caricatures and parodies of Indians and/or things Indian. Pop fiction continues in the same vein, including an unending stream of New Age manuals purporting to expose the inner works of indigenous spirituality in everything from pseudo-philosophical to do-it-yourself styles. Blond yuppies from Beverly Hills amble about the country claiming to be reincarnated 17th century Cheyenne Ushamans ready to perform previously secret ceremonies.

In effect, a concerted, sustained, and in some ways accelerating effort has gone into making Indians unreal. It is thus of obvious importance that the American public begin to think about the implications of such things the next time they witness a gaggle of face-painted and war-bonneted buffoons doing the "Tomahawk Chop" at a baseball or football game. It is necessary that they think about the implications of the grade-school teacher adorning their child in turkey feathers to commemorate Thanksgiving. Think about the significance of John Wayne or Charlton Heston killing a dozen "savages" with a single bullet the next time a western comes on TV. Think about why Land-o-Lakes finds it appropriate to market its butter with the stereotyped image of an "Indian princess" on the wrapper. Think about what it means when non-Indian academics profess—as they often do—to "know more about Indians than Indians do themselves." Think about the significance of charlatans like Carlos Castaneda and Jamake Highwater and Mary Summer Rain and Lynn Andrews churning out "Indian" best-sellers, one after the other, while Indians typically can't get into print.

Think about the real situation of American Indians. Think about Julius Streicher. Remember Justice Jackson's admonition. Understand that the treatment of Indians in American popular culture is not "cute" or "amusing" or just "good, clean fun."

Know that it causes real pain and real suffering to real people. Know that it threatens our very survival. And know that this is just as much a crime against humanity as anything the Nazis ever did. It is likely that the indigenous people of the United States will never demand that those guilty of such criminal activity be punished for their deeds. But the least we have the right to expect—indeed, to demand—is that such practices finally be brought to a halt.   [1993]

Terms

1. MANIFEST DESTINY: A nineteenth-century belief that White people had the duty and right to control and develop the entire North American continent.

Understanding the Reading

1. Why do American Indians object to the use of Indian names, images, and symbols?
2. How has such usage been justified by non-Indians?
3. How does Churchill expose the racism and degradation of this practice?
4. How is this practice beginning to change?
5. Why was Julius Streicher executed after World War II?
6. What caused the dramatic decline in the Native American population?
7. What happened to Native American children between the 1880s and the 1980s?
8. What is the U.N. Genocide Convention, and how has it been violated in the United States?
9. What are the conditions of life in the Indian community?
10. How have Indians been portrayed in the mass media?

Suggestions for Responding

1. Write a short essay explaining why you think American Indians have been singled out by the sports industry.
2. Write a letter to the editor of your local newspaper stating your position on the exploitation of Native American images. ◆

58

Beyond Stereotyping

DANIELA GIOSEFFI

My internship at WSLA-TV in Selma, Alabama, came to a climax when the Ku Klux Klan burned a cross on the lawn of the studio, in 1961; this was after I'd appeared, a white spokesperson, enlisting Freedom Riders on an all-black gospel show.

The town was racially tense with sit-ins at lunch counters and with freedom rides. Following Rosa Parks's[1] example, black and white students from the Student Nonviolent Coordinating Committee (SNCC) rode one morning on a bus seething with heat and emotion. It was the first such ride for me. Afterward, with other integrated demonstrators, I'd drunk from a water fountain marked "Colored."

Demonstrators on our ride were immediately arrested. They assumed that I wasn't booked and jailed because I was blond, blue-eyed, and young, but my arrest came later in the evening, when I tried to enter my boarding house on a deserted street. A deputy sheriff, with his pistol drawn, whisked me away in his squad car, warning me to shut up or he'd shoot me for resisting arrest: "No one'll be the wiser if I do. Ain't none of your big-shot niggers or northern lawyers around to protect you!" He laughed as he cuffed my wrists behind my back. We were alone in his unmarked police car on the way to the jail. He reached over and squeezed my left breast hard. "You're nice-lookin' for such a piece of nervy northern guinea trash. Your papa must be the dumbest guinea goin' to let you come down here all alone. Your folks is probably Commies like them Jew lawyers who come down here tellin' us what to do."

I spoke quietly, remembering the nonviolent tactics I'd learned: "People are people. We all have feelings."

"Niggers ain't people, our preacher said. The Holy Bible says so! Neither is guinea nigger lovers. We've lynched Jews and guineas here, too, ya know."

Later, in the jailhouse, my head hit the brick wall of the cell as he pushed me to the cot. "You piece of guinea trash!" He stood over me in the dingy cell as he unzipped his pants.

I understood that I wasn't to be a Rosa Luxemburg,[2] but an unknown casualty.

Now, at age 51, when I hear a recorded speech by Martin Luther King, Jr., telling of nonviolent resistance and equality for all, I ruminate, watery-eyed, over those years of hope when we believed and sang "We Shall Overcome." It wasn't that I was brave, just naive. I'd grown up in Newark, New Jersey, attending an integrated public school. There was plenty of racism in Newark, but it didn't seem unusual to me to live and work among black people. I'd been called a "nigger lover" in third grade, for befriending a "colored girl," Silvy Jackson. I remember having bonded with her because we were the only kids in our class who didn't have the 35 cents a week that other students brought for milk money.

Now, with menopausal hot flashes, I'm a graying blond who rides the New York subways at night with looks of hatred coming at me from tired nightshift workers who think I'm the enemy—who don't stop to realize that we all suffer from hate and stereotyping, the whole earth bleeding now like a Selma mimosa blossom.

Over 30 years since that horrible night in Selma, with a quarter-century's activism for peace and social justice, and six published books to my name, I'm still not sure I exist as an American—because a name like "Daniela Gioseffi" has too many vowels or syllables for most citizens to roll trippingly from their tongues. Yet I'm grouped together with "white Europeans" as a privileged class. There's little acknowledgment of the subtle form of prejudice that still plagues U.S. citizens with my kind of ethnic name.

"The Island of Tears" (*Isola delle lacrime*) was what Italian immigrants called Ellis Island, and it proved for my father a prophetic name when he arrived from Puglia in 1913. He had plenty of stories to tell of the epithets that came his way: "dumb guinea, greaseball, dago, wop, spaghetti bender." He never knew a member of the Mafia, but had to hear joke after Hollywood smear about his ethnicity. (Remember how Geraldine Ferraro, in her run for the vice presidency, was unjustly connected with the Mafia, as Mario Cuomo has been—with not a jot of evidence? Many readers might still find it difficult to disconnect an Italian politician from this cruel stereotype.)

In my case, as a second generation Italian American woman writer, there were no critically acclaimed role models in U.S. literature to aspire to in a "new girl" network. Writing for me, as for people of color, has been a continuing fight for cultural identity. I look at the roster of the PEN American center and recognize five or six Italian female names (and not many more male ones) among the thousands. Frances Winwar, who was forced to change her name from "Francesca Vinciguerra" in order to publish her biographical novels, is as much forgotten as Grazia Deledda, the second female writer to win the Nobel Prize for Literature, in 1926. Accomplished Italian American women writers like Maria Mazziotti-Gillan, Diane Di Prima, Helen Barolini, Sandra Mortola-Gilbert, Phyllis Capello, Laura Stortoni, Lucia Maria Perillo, Patricia Storace, and Dorothy Barresi are fairly invisible on the literary scene. Few people seem to know of Vittoria Colonna, of Marino (1492–1547), the first European woman to publish a collection of poetry that was widely read.

Women don't need to hear how important role models are to one's aspirations, yet when I've tried to broach this subject, it's usually been pooh-poohed by generally enlightened feminists, let alone establishment males. Most intelligent, educated, sensitive people (to say nothing of equal-opportunity-grant applications) don't realize I'm of a minority that was lynched by the Ku Klux Klan, along with African Americans and Jewish Americans, all through the earlier part of this century. Hardly anyone remembers the murders and lynching of Italians that took place in New Orleans in 1891 and continued as far west as Colorado well on through the 1920s, or the execution of Sacco and Vanzetti,[3] sentenced by the bigoted Judge Thayer of Massachusetts, who dubbed the labor activists "dagos."

Few are aware—and perhaps Italian Americans are ashamed to remember— that in certain southern states, Italians were segregated in schools and it was as unacceptable to intermarry with a "guinea, wop, or dago," as with a Jew or "Negro." Such facts are hard to remember amidst horrors like the wholesale slaughter of Native Americans, or black slavery, or the Holocaust, and the continued suffering of so many other groups, like Latinos or Asian Americans—all the ongoing prejudice against and between ethnic groups.

For that matter, most are unaware that the machismo "Black Hand" or "Mafia" (a word now used generically for all syndicated crime) began in southern Italy as an indigenous peoples' movement to protect the women and land from rape and pillaging during many foreign invasions. Few realize what a mixture of cultures the Italian peninsula encompasses—with invasions by the French, German, Spanish, and Phoenician armies. Teutonic Lombards and Gaelic tribes and northern Africans mixed together with Albanians and Slavs. All cultures are inextricably mixed when you study them, which is why prejudice is so insane.

Meanwhile sociopolitics continues on the same course: divide and conquer, while the powerful thugs laugh all the way to the S & L scandalized bank.

I even puzzle over putting the whole rap on Cristoforo Colombo as if he were a Mafioso who ran the world, especially since he sailed for Spanish kings who were Hapsburg Teutons. Why pin *all* the rancor on Columbus for starting the demise of multiculturalism? He died a pauper in prison for his pains.

If Italian Americans are sometimes stereotypically *Moonstruck*, portrayed as families screaming over spaghetti dinners, they are more often portrayed as syndicated gangsters, as in *Prizzi's Honor*. Even a progressive satirist like Woody Allen felt fine stereotyping Italians as Sicilian Mafiosi, in another Academy Award winning film of the 1980s, *Broadway Danny Rose*.

Not only are all Sicilians not in the Mafia, but not all Italian Americans are Sicilian—no more than all Africans are Zulu; all Irish, Catholics; all Jews, Israelis; or all Asians, Chinese. We Italian women don't all have hair on our upper lips and stir spaghetti sauce as our main occupation. Neither are we all passive girlfriends or wives of mobsters. And neither are we the only prejudiced folks in town, as media sensationalizing of many bias crimes would lead us to believe.

Media coverage of the 1986 Howard Beach racial attack left the misconception that the chief perpetrators of the biased murder crime were

Italian youths of an Italian neighborhood. But it was an Englishman by the name of Jon Lester who was the main assailant convicted of manslaughter in the death of the black teen Michael Griffith, along with Scott Kern and Jason Ladone of the mixed neighborhood. Nevertheless, stereotypically, "pizza boycotts" were instituted. Few recall that an Italian woman, Marie Toscano, gave testimony that helped *convict* those teenagers who were found guilty. For that matter, it seems nearly no one remembers Elizabeth Galarza, an Italian woman who ran from her apartment into a street where gunfire was heard, and tried to offer comfort and hands-on assistance to Yusuf Hawkins—in the infamous Bensonhurst incident.[4]

Once the media circus arrived in Bensonhurst, hundreds of peaceful neighborhood citizens who held a prayer vigil on the site of Hawkins' murder were ignored. One can't easily find a media reference to the six Italian neighborhood women who visited the Stewart/Hawkins home to offer sorrow and empathy: Nancy Sottile, Edie Bonavita, Teodolinda Mellace, Rita Schettini, Rosa De Guida, and Rosalie Campione.

Rosalie Campione, a college student from Bensonhurst, feels wounded by the media portrayal of her home turf as a place of unalloyed bigotry. Rosalie helps to run a Bensonhurst Tenant Association Displaced Homemakers Program—for women who have lost a job or a mate through widowhood or divorce, or who simply wish to improve their job skills and self-image. The program, though run by the Federation of Italian American Organizations of Brooklyn, deliberately accommodates women of *every* ethnic background.

Michael McQuillan, adviser to the Brooklyn Borough President's Office for Racial and Ethnic Affairs, offered his observation: "In my experience, as I work in the neighborhoods, women are often more willing to speak frankly about ethnicity. They reach out with a spontaneous sense of empathy for the suffering of other people, perhaps because the reality of the experience of sexism in a male-dominated society contributes to their empathy for the plight of, for example, people of color in a white-dominated society."

For myself, I think about the 15-year-old Italian American girl who was raped on January 14, 1992, in the Flatbush-Flatlands area of Brooklyn. She was on her way to school when she was accosted and forced into a car, raped, sodomized, and then dumped by two men (both of them African American) who used racial epithets. Since she was a minor, her name was withheld by the press. She was classified as white, so no one made a big deal about this Italian American child.

I think of how no Italians will march on a black neighborhood to protest her rape. I think of all the racial crime taking place between this and that group around the nation and the world, and I get very depressed.

It's crucial to acknowledge that African Americans and Jewish Americans and indigenous peoples have had the worst of it in recent history. But we Italian Americans have suffered and are suffering, too. And the civil rights I got bashed for trying to help institute are being eroded along with the rights I thought I gained over my female body, let alone my Italian name.

We don't marvel enough at the peace and decency that we *are* capable of, the little acts of heroism performed by an Elizabeth Galarza, for example. Such people, especially women, are forgotten. History is such a bloodbath of hatreds fueled by warlords and weapons manufacturers that we become cynical about the capacities of our species. But deep down, I believe that we *shall* overcome. And I am glad that I stood up for what was decent in Selma long ago.

I'm sorry that the lessons of the past have to be constantly relearned. The rise of neo-Nazism, the KKK gaining "respectability," is the saddest phenomenon today. It's happening just when we all need to pull together to deinvest in the war machine, and to save Mother Earth—the only teardrop of love and laughter we know of afloat in cold unillumined space.   [1992]

Terms

1. ROSA PARKS: The civil rights activist who refused to give up her seat on the bus to a White man, precipitating the Montgomery, Alabama bus boycott.
2. ROSA LUXEMBURG: A German socialist, whose murder made her a martyr.
3. SACCO AND VANZETTI: Italian-born American anarchists who were executed in 1927 despite widespread protests.

4. Yusuf Hawkins and the Bensonhurst incident: A young Jewish boy was murdered in the Bensonhurst neighborhood of New York City.

Understanding the Reading

1. What were Gioseffi's Alabama experiences?
2. Why is Gioseffi uncertain about her Americanness?
3. In what ways was Gioseffi's father discriminated against?
4. How have Italian writers been treated?
5. Historically, how were Italian Americans treated?
6. What stereotypes are applied to Italian Americans?
7. How were the Howard Beach and Bensonhurst racial incidents distorted in the media?
8. How does Gioseffi feel about her life?

Suggestions for Responding

1. Research one of the Italian American writers Gioseffi mentions and describe whether and how your effort was successful.
2. Write a short essay describing your ethnic heritage or a portion of it that has been stereotyped. ◆

59

Anti-Semitism in the United States

Robert Cherry

From most accounts, it appears that anti-Semitism was most intense during the period 1877 to 1927, from the time Joseph Seligman was refused admittance to the Grand Hotel in Saratoga, New York, until Henry Ford publicly apologized for anti-Semitic articles in his Dearborn Press.[1] Prior to this period, there were examples of anti-Semitism, beginning with the reluctance of Peter Stuyvesant to allow the first group of Jews to enter New York in 1654. Anti-Semitism also was part of the Know Nothing party's[2] anti-immigration campaign in the 1850s and General Grant's policies during the Civil War. However, anti-Semitism became widespread only during the latter part of the nineteenth century.

Oscar Handlin and Richard Hofstadter identify anti-Semitism with the short-lived agrarian Populist movement[3] of the 1890s. They contend that the Populists associated traditional Jewish stereotypes with the evils faced by the yeomanry. Increasingly forced into debt peonage, the yeomanry demanded elimination of the gold standard. However, President Cleveland pursued a scheme with the Rothschild banking empire[4] to protect the gold standard. This led many Populists to attack Jews for what they perceived as Jewish control of world finance. Also, the yeomanry often divided society into those who engaged in productive labor and those who did not. Typically, Jews in rural areas were identified with nonproductive labor—that is, they were commercial and financial middlemen who gained income from the work of others.

Other historians claim that early twentieth century anti-Semitism was associated with xenophobic fears fueled by mass immigration. Later Jewish immigrants tended to be poorer, less skilled, and less urbanized than the Jews who had emigrated from Germany during the 1850s. They were considered a dangerous criminal element. In 1908 New York City's police commissioner Theodore Bingham suggested that half of all criminals were Jews. The 1910 report of the Dillingham commission claimed that large numbers of Jews scattered throughout the United States seduced and kept girls in prostitution and that many were petty thieves, pickpockets, and gamblers. The report stated, "Jews comprise the largest proportion of alien prisoners under sentence for offenses against chastity."

During this era, Jews were not pictured simply as petty criminals. The stereotypic Jewish businessman was one who manipulated laws and engaged in white-collar crimes, especially insurance fraud. [Michael N.] Dobkowski gives numerous examples of how these stereotypes became part of the popular culture. In describing a Jewish businessman, *Puck,* a popular New York City humor magazine, noted that "despite hard times, he has had two failures and three fires." It claimed, "There is only one thing [their] race hates more than pork—asbestos." So pervasive were these images that the Anti-Defamation

League (ADL)[5] in 1913 noted, "Whenever a theatre producer wishes to depict a betrayer of the public trust, a white slaver or other criminal, the actor is directed to present himself as a Jew." Indeed, for more than fifty years, *Roget's Thesaurus* included the word *Jew* as a synonym for usurer, cheat, extortioner, and schemer.

Some historians, including John Higham, believe that anti-Semitism was more significant among the elite than among either the rural yeomanry or middle-class xenophobic nativists. Higham notes that the patrician class, typified by Henry and Brooks Adams, realized that the industrialization process was transforming the United States into a materialistic, pragmatic society that had less concern for tradition and culture than previously. This transformation, which meant the end of patrician hegemony over political and economic affairs, was thought to be the result of Jewish influence.

According to Higham, the patrician class believed that Jewish commercial values undermined basic American traditions. While most became defeatist, some, including Henry Cabot Lodge and John J. Chapman, attempted to reduce Jewish influence. In 1896 Lodge proposed legislation requiring immigrants to be literate in the language of their country of origin rather than in another language. Since most Polish and Russian Jews were literate in Yiddish but not in Polish or Russian, this would have made them ineligible for immigration. Lodge's legislative proposal was defeated, and Jewish immigration continued. Chapman was an active urban reformer who did not have anti-Semitic values until the time of World War I. Dobkowski contends that his inability to reform urban society led him to agree with Henry Adams that the reason for urban decay was growing Jewish influence.

Dobkowski documents how progressive muckrakers,[6] including George Kibbe Turner, Jacob Riis, and Emily Balch, echoed many of the charges against Jews made by the patrician class. Lamenting the decay of cities, Turner considered Jewish immigrants to be at the "core of this festering human cancer." Riis believed that the lack of social values among Jewish immigrants was overwhelming urban society. He thought that recent Jewish immigrants believed that "money is God. Life itself is of little value compared with even the leanest bank account." Even Balch, a leading defender of social welfare reforms, accepted negative Jewish stereotypes.

Liberal sociologist E. A. Ross believed that Jewish immigrants were cunning in their ability to use their wit to undermine business ethics and to commercialize professions and journalism. He claimed that attempts to exclude Jews from professional associations and social clubs had nothing to do with discrimination; instead they reflected a strong desire not to associate with individuals from an immoral culture. Tom Watson, a former Populist and later KKK leader, used Ross's writings to justify his organization's anti-Semitism.

These examples of anti-Semitic views sometimes provide the basis for contentions that Jews faced discrimination similar to that of other groups. Thomas Sowell implies this when he states, "Anti-Semitism in the United States assumed growing and unprecedented proportions in the last quarter of the nineteenth century with the mass arrival of eastern European Jews. . . . [H]elp wanted ads began to specify 'Christian,' as they had once specified 'Protestant' to exclude the Irish."

This is an incorrect assessment. During the last quarter of the nineteenth century, the United States adopted a reservation program for American Indians, an exclusionary policy for Orientals, Jim Crow laws for blacks, and an anti-immigration movement to harass Italian and Polish newcomers. In contrast, before World War I, Jewish immigrants faced few anti-Semitic barriers to their advancement. For example, in 1910 it was estimated that only 0.3 percent of employment advertisements specified Christians and no colleges had adopted restrictive entrance policies.

Only after World War I and the Bolshevik Revolution when xenophobic fears peaked did anti-Semitic restrictions become significant. Zosa Szakowski documents the vigorous attack on Jews during the anti-immigrant Palmer raids[7] in 1919. In 1920, 10 percent of employment ads specified Christians, rising to 13.3 percent by 1926. [Stephen] Steinberg summarizes the restrictive entrance policies many prestigious universities, including Columbia and Harvard, adopted at that time to reduce Jewish enrollment.

At about this time, Henry Ford began publishing anti-Semitic tracts in his Dearborn Press.

Like Ross, Ford was a Progressive. He supported Wilson,[8] social legislation, antilynching laws, and urban reforms. Unlike Ross, Ford had nothing but praise for the ordinary Jewish businessman, and he could count Jews among his personal friends. However, Ford thought that industrialists were at the mercy of financial institutions controlled by international Jewry.

Adopting a similar perspective, Robert La Follette introduced a petition to Congress in 1923 assigning responsibility for World War I to Jewish international bankers. This petition also asserted that Wilson, Lloyd George, Clemenceau, and Orlando[9]—the officials in charge of negotiating the peace treaty at Versailles—were surrounded by Jewish advisors.

World's Work and other liberal publications also complained that Jews were not 100 percent American. They not only identified Jews with draft dodgers and war profiteers, but also complained that Jews, though taking advantage of the opportunities given by democracy, had not taken "the one essential act of a democratic society. . . . They are not willing to lose their identity." By the end of the decade, however, after immigration restrictions laws had been passed and the anticommunist hysteria had subsided, anti-Semitism again subsided to a minimum level.   [1989]

Terms

1. DEARBORN PRESS. The publisher of the very conservative, anti-Semitic magazine, the *Dearborn Independent*.
2. KNOW NOTHING PARTY: A political movement in the mid-nineteenth century that was antagonistic to Catholics and immigrants.
3. POPULIST MOVEMENT: A political movement advocating the rights of the common people.
4. ROTHSCHILD BANKING EMPIRE: An international financial empire created by a Jewish banking dynasty during the first half of the nineteenth century.
5. ANTI-DEFAMATION LEAGUE (ADL): A Jewish civil rights organization.
6. MUCKRAKERS: Investigative reporters who focused on corruption.
7. PALMER RAIDS: Raids authorized by Attorney General A. Mitchell Palmer, who zealously enforced the Espionage Act of 1917 to suppress antiwar and socialist publications.

8. WILSON: Woodrow Wilson, Democratic president of the United States, 1913–1921.
9. LLOYD GEORGE, CLEMENCEAU, AND ORLANDO: David Lloyd George, British prime minister, 1916–1922; Georges Clemenceau, French premier, 1906–1909, 1917; Vittorio Emanuele Orlando, Italian prime minister, 1917–1919.

Understanding the Reading

1. Explain why the Populists attacked Jews.
2. What stereotypes were assigned to Jews in the early part of the twentieth century?
3. Why were the elites anti-Semitic?
4. What other justifications have been given to rationalize anti-Semitism?

Suggestions for Responding

1. Describe the Jewish stereotype that underlies the various beliefs Cherry discusses, and explain its inconsistencies.
2. Do you agree with the claim by *World's Work* that losing one's identity is "the one essential act of a democratic society"? Why or why not? ◆

60

Seeing More Than Black and White

ELIZABETH MARTINEZ

A certain relish seems irresistible to this Latina as the mass media [have] been compelled to sit up, look south of the border, and take notice. Probably the Chiapas[1] uprising and Mexico's recent political turmoil have won us no more than a brief day in the sun. Or even less: liberal Ted Koppel still hadn't noticed the historic assassination of presidential candidate Colosio three days afterward. But it's been sweet, anyway.

When Kissinger[2] said years ago "nothing important ever happens in the south," he articulated a contemptuous indifference toward Latin America, its people and their culture which has long dominated U.S. institutions and attitudes. Mexico may be great for a vacation and some people like burritos but the usual image of Latin America combines incompetence with absurdity in loud colors. My parents, both Spanish teachers, endured decades of being told kids were better off learning French.

U.S. political culture is not only Anglo-dominated but also embraces an exceptionally stubborn national self-centeredness, with no global vision other than relations of domination. The U.S. refuses to see itself as one nation sitting on a continent with 20 others all speaking languages other than English and having the right not to be dominated.

Such arrogant indifference extends to Latinos within the U.S. The mass media complain, "people can't relate to Hispanics"—or Asians, they say. Such arrogant indifference has played an important role in invisibilizing La Raza[3] (except where we become a serious nuisance or a handy scapegoat). It is one reason the U.S. harbors an exclusively white-on-Black concept of racism. It is one barrier to new thinking about racism which is crucial today. There are others.

In a society as thoroughly and violently racialized as the United States, white-Black relations have defined racism for centuries. Today the composition and culture of the U.S. are changing rapidly. We need to consider seriously whether we can afford to maintain an exclusively white/Black model of racism when the population will be 32 percent Latino, Asian/Pacific American and Native American—in short, neither Black nor white—by the year 2050. We are challenged to recognize that multi-colored racism is mushrooming, and then strategize how to resist it. We are challenged to move beyond a dualism comprised of two white supremacist inventions: Blackness and Whiteness.

At stake in those challenges is building a united anti-racist force strong enough to resist contemporary racist strategies of divide-and-conquer. Strong enough, in the long run, to help defeat racism itself. Doesn't an exclusively Black/white model of racism discourage the perception of common interests among people of color and thus impede a solidarity that can challenge white supremacy? Doesn't it encourage the isolation of African Americans from potential allies? Doesn't it advise all people of color to spend too much energy understanding our lives in relation to Whiteness, and thus freeze us in a defensive, often self-destructive mode?

For a Latina to talk about recognizing the multi-colored varieties of racism is not, and should not be, yet another round in the Oppression Olympics. We don't need more competition among different social groupings for that "Most Oppressed" gold. We don't need more comparisons of suffering between women and Blacks, the disabled and the gay, Latino teenagers and white seniors, or whatever. We don't need more surveys like the recent much publicized Harris Poll showing that different peoples of color are prejudiced toward each other—a poll patently designed to demonstrate that us coloreds are no better than white folk. (The survey never asked people about positive attitudes.)

Rather, we need greater knowledge, understanding, and openness to learning about each other's histories and present needs as a basis for working together. Nothing could seem more urgent in an era when increasing impoverishment encourages a self-imposed separatism among people of color as a desperate attempt at community survival. Nothing could seem more important as we search for new social change strategies in a time of ideological confusion.

My call to rethink concepts of racism in the U.S. today is being sounded elsewhere. Among academics, liberal foundation administrators, and activist-intellectuals, you can hear talk of the need for a new "racial paradigm" or model. But new thinking seems to proceed in fits and starts, as if dogged by a fear of stepping on toes, of feeling threatened, or of losing one's base. With a few notable exceptions, even our progressive scholars of color do not make the leap from perfunctorily saluting a vague multi-culturalism to serious analysis. We seem to have made little progress, if any, since Bob Blauner's 1972 book *Racial Oppression in America.* Recognizing the limits of the white-Black axis, Blauner critiqued White America's ignorance of and indifference to the Chicano/a's experience with racism.

Real opposition to new paradigms also exists. There are academics scrambling for one flavor of ethnic studies funds versus another. There are politicians who cultivate distrust of others to keep their own communities loyal. When we hear, for example, of Black/Latino friction, dismay should be quickly followed by investigation. In cities like Los Angeles and New York, it may turn out that political figures scrapping for patronage and payola have played a narrow nationalist game, whipping up economic anxiety and generating resentment that sets communities against each other.

So the goal here, in speaking about moving beyond a bi-polar concept of racism, is to build stronger unity against white supremacy. The goal is to see our similarities of experience and needs. If that goal sounds naive, think about the hundreds of organizations formed by grassroots women of different colors coming together in recent years. Their growth is one of today's most energetic motions and it spans all ages. Think about the multicultural environmental justice movement. Think about the coalitions to save schools. Small rainbows of our own making are there, to brighten a long road through hellish times.

It is in such practice, through daily struggle together, that we are most likely to find the road to greater solidarity against a common enemy. But we also need a will to find it and ideas about where, including some new theory.

Until very recently, Latino invisibility—like that of Native Americans and Asian/Pacific Americans—has been close to absolute in U.S. seats of power, major institutions, and the non-Latino public mind. Having lived on both the East and West Coasts for long periods, I feel qualified to pronounce: an especially myopic view of Latinos prevails in the East. This, despite such data as a 24.4 percent Latino population of New York City alone in 1991, or the fact that in 1990 more Puerto Ricans were killed by New York police under suspicious circumstances than any other ethnic group. Latino populations are growing rapidly in many eastern cities and the rural South, yet remain invisible or stigmatized—usually both.

Eastern blinders persist. I've even heard that the need for a new racial paradigm is dismissed in New York as a California hangup. A black Puerto Rican friend in New York, when we talked about experiences of racism common to Black and brown, said, "People here don't see Border Patrol brutality against Mexicans as a form of police repression," despite the fact that

the Border Patrol is the largest and most uncontrolled police force in the U.S. It would seem that an old ignorance has combined with new immigrant bashing to sustain divisions today.

While the East (and most of the Midwest) usually remains myopic, the West Coast has barely begun to move away from its own denial. Less than two years ago in San Francisco, a city almost half Latino or Asian/Pacific American, a leading daily newspaper could publish a major series on contemporary racial issues and follow the exclusively Black-white paradigm. Although millions of TV viewers saw massive Latino participation in the April 1992 Los Angeles uprising, which included 18 out of 50 deaths and the majority of arrests, the mass media and most people labeled that event "a Black riot."

If the West Coast has more recognition of those who are neither Black nor white, it is mostly out of fear about the proximate demise of its white majority. A second, closely related reason is the relentless campaign by California Gov. Pete Wilson to scapegoat immigrants for economic problems and pass racist, unconstitutional laws attacking their health, education, and children's future. Wilson has almost single-handedly made the word "immigrant" mean Mexican or other Latino (and sometimes Asian). Who thinks of all the people coming from the former Soviet Union and other countries? The absolute racism of this has too often been successfully masked by reactionary anti-immigrant groups like FAIR blaming immigrants for the staggering African-American unemployment rate.

Wilson's immigrant bashing is likely to provide a model for other parts of the country. The five states with the highest immigration rates—California, Florida, New York, Illinois and Texas—all have a Governor up for re-election in 1994. Wilson tactics won't appear in every campaign but some of the five states will surely see intensified awareness and stigmatization of Latinos as well as Asian/Pacific Islanders.

As this suggests, what has been a regional issue mostly limited to western states is becoming a national issue. If you thought Latinos were just Messicans down at the border, wake up—they are all over North Carolina, Pennsylvania and 8th Avenue Manhattan now. A qualitative change is taking place. With the broader geographic spread of Latinos and Asian/Pacific Islanders has come a nationalization of racist practices and attitudes that were once regional. The west goes east, we could say.

Like the monster Hydra, racism is growing some ugly new heads. We will have to look at them closely.

A bi-polar model of racism—racism as white on Black—has never really been accurate. Looking for the roots of racism in the U.S. we can begin with the genocide against American Indians which made possible the U.S. land base, crucial to white settlement and early capitalist growth. Soon came the massive enslavement of African people which facilitated that growth. As slave labor became economically critical, "blackness" became ideologically critical; it provided the very source of "whiteness" and the heart of racism. Franz Fanon would write, "colour is the most outward manifestation of race."

If Native Americans had been a crucial labor force during those same centuries, living and working in the white man's sphere, our racist ideology might have evolved differently. "The tawny," as Ben Franklin dubbed them, might have defined the opposite of what he called "the lovely white." But with Indians decimated and survivors moved to distant concentration camps, they became unlikely candidates for this function. Similarly, Mexicans were concentrated in the distant West; elsewhere Anglo fear of them or need for control was rare. They also did not provide the foundation for a definition of whiteness.

Some anti-racist left activists have put forth the idea that only African Americans experience racism as such and that the suffering of other people of color results from national minority rather than racial oppression. From this viewpoint, the exclusively white/Black model for racism is correct. Latinos, then, experience exploitation and repression for reasons of culture and nationality—not for their "race." (It should go without saying in Z^4 that while racism is an all-too-real social fact, race has no scientific basis.)

Does the distinction hold? This and other theoretical questions call for more analysis and more expertise than one article can offer. In the meantime, let's try out the idea that Latinos do suffer for their nationality and culture, especially language. They became part of the U.S. through the 1846–48 war on Mexico and thus a foreign population to be colonized. But as they were reduced to cheap or semi-slave labor, they quickly came to suffer for their "race"—meaning, as non-whites. In the Southwest of a super-racialized nation, the broad parallelism of race and class embraced Mexicans ferociously.

The bridge here might be a definition of racism as "the reduction of the cultural to the biological," in the words of French scholar Christian Delacampagne now working in Egypt. Or: "racism exists wherever it is claimed that a given social status is explained by a given natural characteristic." We know that line: Mexicans are just naturally lazy and have too many children, so they're poor and exploited.

The discrimination, oppression and hatred experienced by Native Americans, Mexicans, Asian/Pacific Islanders, and Arab Americans are forms of racism. Speaking only of Latinos, we have seen in California and the Southwest, especially along the border, almost 150 years of relentless repression which today includes Central Americans among its targets. That history reveals hundreds of lynchings between 1847 and 1935, the use of counter-insurgency armed forces beginning with the Texas Rangers, random torture and murder by Anglo ranchers, forced labor, rape by border lawmen, and the prevailing Anglo belief that a Mexican life doesn't equal a dog's in value.

But wait. If color is so key to racial definition, as Fanon and others say, perhaps people of Mexican background experience racism less than national minority oppression because they are not dark enough as a group. For White America, shades of skin color are crucial to defining worth. The influence of those shades has also been internalized by communities of color. Many Latinos can and often want to pass for whites; therefore White America may see them as less threatening than darker sisters and brothers.

Here we confront more of the complexity around us today, with questions like: What about the usually poor, very dark Mexican or Central American of strong Indian or African heritage? (Yes, folks, 200–300,000 Africans were brought to Mexico as slaves, which is far, far more than the Spaniards who came.) And what about the effects of accented speech or foreign name, characteristics that may instantly subvert "passing"?

What about those cases where a Mexican-American is never accepted, no matter how light-skinned, well-dressed or well-spoken? A Chicano lawyer friend coming home from a professional conference in suit, tie and briefcase found himself on a bus near San Diego that was suddenly stopped by the Border Patrol. An agent came on board and made a beeline through the all-white rows of passengers direct to my friend. "Your papers." The agent didn't believe Jose was coming from a U.S. conference and took him off the bus to await proof. Jose was lucky; too many Chicanos and Mexicans end up killed.

In a land where the national identity is white, having the "wrong" nationality becomes grounds for racist abuse. Who would draw a sharp line between today's national minority oppression in the form of immigrant-bashing and racism?

None of this aims to equate the African American and Latino experiences; that isn't necessary even if it were accurate. Many reasons exist for the persistence of the white/Black paradigm of racism; they include numbers, history, and the psychology of whiteness. In particular they include centuries of slave revolts, a Civil War, and an ongoing resistance to racism that cracked this society wide open while the world watched. Nor has the misery imposed on Black people lessened in recent years. New thinking about racism can and should keep this experience at the center.

The exclusively white/Black concept of race and racism in the U.S. rests on a western, Protestant form of dualism woven into both race and gender relations from earliest times. In the dualist universe there is only black and white. A disdain, indeed fear, of mixture haunts the Yankee soul; there is no room for any kind of multifaceted identity, any hybridism.

As a people, La Raza combines three sets of roots—indigenous, European and African—all in widely varying degrees. In short we represent a profoundly un-American concept: *mestizaje* (pronounced mess-tee-zah-hey), the mixing of peoples and emergence of new peoples. A highly racialized society like this one cannot deal with or allow room for *mestizaje*. It has never learned to do much more than hiss "miscegenation!" Or, like that Alabama high school principal

who recently denied the right of a mixed-blood pupil to attend the prom to say: "your parents made a mistake." Apparently we, all the millions of La Raza, are just that—a mistake.

Mexicans in the U.S. also defy the either-or, dualistic mind in that, on the one hand, we are a colonized people displaced from the ancestral homeland with roots in the present-day U.S. that go back centuries. Those ancestors didn't cross the border; the border crossed them. At the same time many of us have come to the U.S. more recently as "immigrants" seeking work. The complexity of Raza baffles and frustrates most Anglos; they want to put one neat label on us. It baffles many Latinos too, who often end up categorizing themselves racially as "Other" for lack of anything better. For that matter, the term "Latino" which I use here is a monumental simplification; it refers to 20-plus nationalities and a wide range of classes.

But we need to grapple with the complexity, for there is more to come. If anything, this nation will see more *mestizaje* in the future, embracing innumerable ethnic combinations. What will be its effects? Only one thing seems certain: "white" shall cease to be the national identity.

A glimpse at the next century tells us how much we need to look beyond the white/Black model of race relations and racism. White/Black are real poles, central to the history of U.S. racism. We can neither ignore them nor stop there. But our effectiveness in fighting racism depends on seeing the changes taking place, trying to perceive the contours of the future. From the time of the Greeks to the present, racism around the world has had certain commonalities but no permanently fixed character. It is evolving again today, and we'd best labor to read the new faces of this Hydra-headed monster. Remember, for every head that Hydra lost it grew two more.

Sometimes the problem seems so clear. Last year I showed slides of Chicano history to an Oakland high school class with 47 African Americans and three Latino students. The images included lynchings and police beatings of Mexicans and other Latinos, and many years of resistance. At the end one Black student asked, "Seems like we have had a lot of experiences in common—so why can't Blacks and Mexicans get along better?" No answers, but there was the first step: asking the question.   [1994]

Terms

1. CHIAPAS: A southeastern Mexican state where peasant uprisings have occurred.
2. KISSINGER: Former U.S. Secretary of State Henry Kissinger.
3. LA RAZA: Spanish for "the people."
4. *Z:* The magazine where this article originally appeared.

Understanding the Reading

1. How is political culture in the United States self-centered?
2. Why do we need to see that racism is not simply a Black-White matter?
3. What opposition is there to the growing new paradigms of racism?
4. What examples of coalition building does Martinez identify?
5. How do attitudes toward Latinos and Asian/ Pacific Islanders differ on the East Coast and the West Coast and why?
6. According to Martinez, how do Latinos suffer from racism?
7. Why, according to Martinez, is it difficult for Americans to see beyond dualistic thinking and to accept multifaceted complexity?

Suggestions for Responding

1. Write a short paper agreeing or disagreeing with Martinez's thesis that racism is not just a Black and White issue. ✦

61

The Myth of the Latin Woman: I Just Met a Girl Named Maria

JUDITH ORTIZ COFER

On a bus trip to London from Oxford University where I was earning some graduate credits one summer, a young man, obviously fresh from a pub, spotted me and as if struck by inspiration went down on his knees in the aisle. With both hands over his heart he broke into an Irish tenor's rendition of "Maria" from *West Side Story*. My politely amused fellow passengers gave his lovely voice the round of gentle applause it deserved. Though I was not quite as amused, I managed my version of an English smile: no show of teeth, no extreme contortions of the facial muscles—I was at this time of my life practicing reserve and cool. Oh, that British control, how I coveted it. But Maria had followed me to London, reminding me of a prime fact of my life: you can leave the Island, master the English language, and travel as far as you can, but if you are a Latina, especially one like me who so obviously belongs to Rita Moreno's gene pool, the Island travels with you.

This is sometimes a very good thing—it may win you that extra minute of someone's attention. But with some people, the same things can make *you* an island—not so much a tropical paradise as an Alcatraz, a place nobody wants to visit. As a Puerto Rican girl growing up in the United States and wanting like most children to "belong," I resented the stereotype that my Hispanic appearance called forth from many people I met. . . .

It is surprising to some of my professional friends that some people, including those who should know better, still put others "in their place." Though rarer, these incidents are still commonplace in my life. It happened to me most recently during a stay at a very classy metropolitan hotel favored by young professional couples for their weddings. Late one evening after the theater, as I walked toward my room with my new colleague (a woman with whom I was coordinating an arts program), a middle-aged man in a tuxedo, a young girl in satin and lace on his arm, stepped directly into our path. With his champagne glass extended toward me, he exclaimed "Evita!"

Our way blocked, my companion and I listened as the man half-recited, half-bellowed "Don't Cry for Me, Argentina." When he finished, the young girl said: "How about a round of applause for my daddy?" We complied, hoping this would bring the silly spectacle to a close. I was becoming aware that our little group was attracting the attention of the other guests.

"Daddy" must have perceived this too, and he once more barred the way as we tried to walk past him. He began to shout-sing a ditty to the tune of "La Bamba"—except that the lyrics were about a girl named Maria whose exploits all rhymed with her name and gonorrhea. The girl kept saying "Oh, Daddy" and looking at me with pleading eyes. She wanted me to laugh along with the others. My companion and I stood silently waiting for the man to end his offensive song. When he finished, I looked not at him but at his daughter. I advised her calmly never to ask her father what he had done in the army. Then I walked between them and to my room. My friend complimented me on my cool handling of the situation. I confessed to her that I really had wanted to push the jerk into the swimming pool. I knew that this same man—probably a corporate executive, well educated, even worldly by most standards—would not have been likely to regale a white woman with a dirty song in public. He would perhaps have checked his impulse by assuming that she could be somebody's wife or mother, or at least *somebody* who might take offense. But to him, I was just an Evita or a Maria: merely a character in his cartoon-populated universe.

Because of my education and my proficiency with the English language, I have acquired many mechanisms for dealing with the anger I experience. This was not true for my parents, nor is it true for the many Latin women working at menial jobs who must put up with stereotypes about our ethnic group such as: "They make good domestics." This is another fact of the myth of the Latin woman in the United States. Its origin is simple to deduce. Work as domestics, waitressing, and factory jobs are all that's available to women with little English and few skills. The myth of the Hispanic menial has been sustained by the same media phenomenon that made "Mammy" from *Gone With the Wind* America's ideal of the black woman for generations; Maria, the housemaid or counter girl, is now indelibly etched into the national psyche. The big and the little screens have presented us with the picture of the funny Hispanic maid, mispronouncing words and cooking up a spicy storm in a shiny California kitchen.

This media-engendered image of the Latina in the United States has been documented by feminist Hispanic scholars, who claim that such portrayals are partially responsible for the denial of opportunities for upward mobility among Latinas in the professions. I have a Chicana friend working on a Ph.D. in philosophy at a major university. She says her doctor still shakes his head in puzzled amazement at all the "big words" she uses. Since I do not wear my diplomas around my neck for all to see, I too have on occasion been sent to that "kitchen," where some think I obviously belong.

One such incident that has stayed with me, though I recognize it as a minor offense, happened on the day of my first public poetry reading. It took place in Miami in a boat-restaurant where we were having lunch before the event. I was nervous and excited as I walked in with my notebook in my hand. An older woman motioned me to her table. Thinking (foolish me) that she wanted me to autograph a copy of my brand new slender volume of verse, I went over. She ordered a cup of coffee from me, assuming that I was the waitress. Easy enough to mistake my poems for menus, I suppose. I know that it wasn't an intentional act of cruelty, yet of all the good things that happened that day, I remember that scene most clearly, because it reminded me of what I had to overcome before anyone would take me seriously. In retrospect I understand that my anger gave my reading fire, that I have almost always taken doubts in my abilities as a challenge—and that the result is, most times, a feeling of satisfaction at having won a convert when I see the cold, appraising eyes warm to my words, the body language change, the smile that indicates that I have opened some avenue for communication. That day I read to that woman and her lowered eyes told me that she was embarrassed at her little faux pas, and when I willed her to look up at me, it was my victory, and she graciously allowed me to punish her with my full attention. We shook hands at the end of the reading, and I never saw her again. She has probably forgotten the whole thing, but maybe not.

Yet I am one of the lucky ones. My parents made it possible for me to acquire a stronger footing in the mainstream culture by giving me the chance at an education. And books and art have saved me from the harsher forms of ethnic and racial prejudice that many of my Hispanic *compañeras* have had to endure. I travel a lot around the United States, reading from my books of poetry and my novel, and the reception

I most often receive is one of positive interest by people who want to know more about my culture.

There are, however, thousands of Latinas without the privilege of an education or the entrée into society that I have. For them life is a struggle against the misconceptions perpetuated by the myth of the Latina as whore, domestic, or criminal. We cannot change this by legislating the way people look at us. The transformation, as I see it, has to occur at a much more individual level.

My personal goal in my public life is to try to replace the old pervasive stereotypes and myths about Latinas with a much more interesting set of realities. Every time I give a reading, I hope the stories I tell, the dreams and fears I examine in my work, can achieve some universal truth which will get my audience past the particulars of my skin color, my accent, or my clothes.

I once wrote a poem in which I called us Latinas "God's brown daughters." This poem is really a prayer of sorts, offered upward, but also, through the human-to-human channel of art, outward. It is a prayer for communication, and for respect. In it, Latin women pray "in Spanish to an Anglo God / with a Jewish heritage," and they are "fervently hoping / that if not omnipotent, / at least He be bilingual."   [1993]

Understanding the Reading

1. What happened to Cofer in London?
2. What happened to her in the hotel corridor?
3. Why can Cofer deal with such incidents better than many other Latin women?
4. Explain what happened to Cofer at the poetry reading.
5. What is the Latina stereotype?

Suggestions for Responding

1. If you have ever been treated as if you fit a stereotype, describe the incident and your reactions to the experience.
2. Describe how you would have responded to one of the experiences Cofer recounts. ✦

62

Behind Barbed Wire

JOHN HERSEY

On March 31, 1942, there appeared on notice boards in certain communities on the Western Seaboard of the United States a number of broadsides bearing the ominous title, "Civilian Exclusion Orders." These bulletins warned all residents of Japanese descent that they were going to have to move out of their homes. No mention was made of where they would have to go. One member of each family was directed to report for instructions at neighboring control stations.

The Japanese attack on Pearl Harbor had taken place a little less than four months earlier. These Exclusion Orders cast a wide net. There were about 125,000 persons of Japanese ancestry scattered along the coastal tier of states then, and 7 out of 10 of them, having been born there, were full-fledged citizens of the United States; yet no distinction between alien and native was made among those summoned to control stations. The United States had declared war on Germany and Italy, as well as Japan, but no German or Italian enemy aliens, to say nothing of German-Americans or Italian-Americans, were subjected to these blanket Exclusion Orders. Only "Japanese aliens and non-aliens," as the official euphemism put it.

Each person who responded to the summons had to register the names of all family members and was told to show up at a certain time and place, a few days later, with all of them, bringing along only such baggage as they could carry by hand—for a trip to a destination unknown. Names had become numbers.

"Henry went to the control station to register the family," wrote a Japanese-American woman years later. "He came home with 20 tags, all numbered 10710, tags to be attached to each piece of baggage, and one to hang from our coat lapels. From then on, we were known as Family No. 10710." "I lost my identity," another woman would assert, describing the replacement of her name by a number. "I lost my privacy and dignity."

There followed a period of devastating uncertainty and anxiety. "We were given eight days to liquidate our possessions," one of the evacuees testified at an investigation by the Department of Justice many years later. The time allowed varied from place to place. "We had about two weeks," another recalled, "to do something. Either lease the property or sell everything." Another: "While in Modesto, the final notice for evacuation came with a four-day notice." Under the circumstances, the evacuees had to dispose of their businesses, their homes and their personal possessions at panic prices to hostile buyers.

"It is difficult," one man would later testify, "to describe the feeling of despair and humiliation experienced by all of us as we watched the Caucasians coming to look over our possessions and offering such nominal amounts, knowing we had no recourse but to accept whatever they were offering because we did not know what the future held for us." One woman sold a 37-room hotel for $300. A man who owned a pickup truck, and had just bought a set of new tires and a new battery for $125, asked only that amount of a prospective buyer. "The man 'bought' our pickup for $25." One homeowner, in despair, wanted to burn his house down. "I went to the storage shed to get the gasoline tank and pour the gasoline on my house, but my wife . . . said don't do it, maybe somebody can use this house; we are civilized people, not savages."

By far the greatest number of Nisei—the term for first-generation Japanese-Americans that came to be used as the generic word for all ethnic Japanese living in America—were in agriculture, growing fruit, vegetables, nursery plants and specialty crops. They had worked wonders in the soil. They owned about one-fiftieth of the arable land in the three Pacific Coast states, and what they had made of their farms is suggested by the fact that the average value per acre of all farms in the three states in 1940 was roughly $38, while an acre on a Nisei farm was worth, on average, $280.

But now the farmers had to clear out in a matter of days. The Mother's Day crop of flowers, the richest harvest of the year, was about to be gathered; it had to be abandoned. An owner of one of the largest nurseries in southern California, unable to dispose of his stock, gave it all to the Veterans Hospital adjoining his land. A strawberry grower asked for a deferral of his evacuation summons for a few days, so he could harvest his crop. Denied the permission, he bitterly plowed the berries under. The next day, the Federal Bureau of Investigation charged him with an act of sabotage and put him in jail.

Assured by authorities that they could store property and reclaim it after the war, many put their chattels in impromptu warehouses—homes and garages and outbuildings—only to have the stored goods, before long, vandalized or stolen. Some leased their property but never received rents. Some were cheated by their tenants, who sold the property as if it were their own.

On the day of departure, evacuees found themselves herded into groups of about 500, mostly at railroad and bus stations. They wore their numbered tags and carried hand-baggage containing possessions that they had packed in fear and perplexity, not knowing where they were going. They embarked on buses and trains. Some trains had blacked-out windows. Uniformed guards carrying weapons patrolled the cars. "To this day," one woman recalled long afterward, "I can remember vividly the plight of the elderly, some on stretchers, orphans herded onto the train by caretakers, and especially a young couple with four preschool children.

"The mother had two frightened toddlers hanging on to her coat. In her arms, she carried two crying babies. The father had diapers and other baby paraphernalia strapped to his back. In his hands he struggled with duffel bag and suitcase."

Each group was unloaded, after its trip, at one of 16 assembly centers, most of which were located at fairgrounds and racetracks. There seeing barbed wire and searchlights, and under the guard of guns, these "aliens and non-aliens" were forced to realize that all among them—even those who had sons or brothers in the United States Army—were considered to be dangerous people. At the entrance to the Tanforan Assembly Center, one man later remembered, "stood two lines of troops with rifles and fixed bayonets pointed at the evacuees as they walked between the soldiers to the prison compound. Overwhelmed with bitterness and blind with rage, I screamed every obscenity I knew at the armed guards, daring them to shoot me." Most evacuees were silent, dazed. Many wept.

A typical assembly center was at the Santa Anita race track. Each family was allotted a space in the horse stalls of about 200 square feet, furnished with cots, blankets and pillows; the evacuees had to make their own pallets, filling mattress shells with straw. There were three large mess halls, in which 2,000 people at a time stood in line with tin plates and cups, to be served mass-cooked food that cost an average of 39 cents per person per day—rough fare, usually overcooked, such as brined liver, which, one testified, "would bounce if dropped."

"We lined up," another later wrote, "for mail, for checks, for meals, for showers, for washrooms, for laundry tubs, for toilets. . . ." Medical care, under jurisdiction of the Public Health Service, was provided by evacuee doctors and nurses who were recruited to serve their fellow inmates in an improvised clinic, supplied at first with nothing more than mineral oil, iodine, aspirin, sulfa ointment, Kaopectate and alcohol. Toilets were communal, without compartments. The evacuees bathed in what had been horse showers, with a partition between the men's and the women's section. When the women complained that men were climbing the partition and looking at them, a camp official responded, "Are you sure you women are not climbing the walls to look at the men?"

Toward the end of May 1942, evacuees began to be transferred from these temporary assembly centers to 13 permanent concentration camps—generally called by the more decorous name of "relocation centers"—where they would be held prisoner until several months before the end of the war. By Nov. 1, some 106,770 internees had been put behind barbed wire in six western states and Arkansas.

Thus began the bitterest national shame of the Second World War for the sweet land of liberty: the mass incarceration, on racial grounds alone, on false evidence of military necessity, and in contempt of their supposedly inalienable rights, of an entire class of American citizens— along with others who were not citizens in the country of their choice only because that country had long denied people of their race the right to naturalize. (A 1924 federal law had cut off all Japanese immigration and naturalization; it was not rescinded until 1952.)

"My mother, two sisters, niece, nephew, and I left" by train, one recalled in later years. "Father joined us later. Brother left earlier by bus. We took whatever we could carry. So much we left behind, but the most valuable thing I lost was my freedom."

The Manzanar camp was quickly built in the desert country of east-central California. Its second director, a humane and farsighted man named Ralph Merritt, realized that history ought to have some testimony of what its victims had managed to salvage from an unprecedented American social crime. He had seen the consummate artistry of photographs taken in nearby Yosemite National Park by a friend of his, Ansel Adams, and he invited the great photographer to come to the camp to capture its woes and its marvels on film.

"Moved," Adams would later write, "by the human story unfolding in the encirclement of desert and mountains, and by the wish to identify my photography . . . with the tragic momentum of the times, I came to Manzanar with my cameras in the fall of 1943."

Adams' photographs restore energy to the sorry record—and remind us that this very word "record" in its ancient origins meant "to bring back the heart."

But first it seems appropriate to re-engage the mind, for the stories of Manzanar and the other camps raise grave questions for the American polity: Could such a thing occur again? How did this slippage in the most precious traditions of a free country come about?

The Japanese attack on Pearl Harbor on Dec. 7, 1941, threw the American psyche into a state of shock. Despite four years' demonstration of the skill and dispatch—and cruelty—of the Japanese invasion of China, American military commanders in the Philippines and elsewhere had issued boastful statements, over and over again, about how quickly the "Japs," as they were scornfully called, would be wiped out if they dared attack American installations.

Then suddenly, within hours, the United States Pacific Fleet was crippled at anchor. Most of the United States air arm in the Philippines was wrecked on the ground. American pride dissolved overnight into American rage and hysteria—and nowhere so disastrously as on the country's Western shores.

President Franklin D. Roosevelt promptly proclaimed, and Congress voted, a state of war against Japan, and within days the other Axis powers, Germany and Italy, also became belligerents. The President issued orders that classified nationals of those countries as enemy aliens. These orders gave responsibility for carrying out certain restrictions against enemy aliens of all three countries to Attorney General Francis Biddle and the Department of Justice. Biddle was given authority to establish prohibited zones, from which enemy aliens could be moved at will; to seize as contraband any weapons and other articles as required for national security; to freeze enemy aliens' funds, and to intern any of them who might be deemed dangerous. These were perfectly normal wartime precautions against enemy aliens only, for which there had been statutory precedent under President Woodrow Wilson in the First World War.

With great speed and efficiency, beginning on the very night of the attack, the Justice Department arrested certain marked enemy aliens of all three belligerent nations. Within three days, 857 Germans, 147 Italians and 1,291 Japanese (367 of them on the Hawaiian Islands, 924 on the continent) had been rounded up.

On the night of Dec. 8, when Pearl Harbor jitters were at their highest pitch, San Francisco suffered a false alarm of an air incursion. Military and/or naval radio trackers reported that enemy aircraft were soaring in over the Bay Area and later that they had turned back to sea without attacking. Planes of the Second Interceptor Command took off from Portland, Ore., and searched as far as 600 miles offshore for a nonexistent Japanese aircraft carrier, from which the enemy planes were assumed to have been launched. At the first alarm, sirens sounded a warning, and San Francisco was supposed to be blacked out at once. But skyscrapers blazed, neon lights winked at hundreds of night spots, and Alcatraz was like a heap of sparkling diamonds in the bay.

Enter, the next morning, to center stage, a military figure in a high state of excitation. As commanding officer of the Fourth Army and Western Defense Command, Lieut. Gen. John L. DeWitt was charged with making sure that there would be no Pearl Harbors on the West Coast. That morning, a meeting at City Hall was called with Mayor Angelo Rossi and 200 of the city's civic leaders, and as *Life* magazine would put it, DeWitt "almost split with rage."

"You people," he said to them, "do not seem to realize we are at war. So get this: Last night there were planes over this community. They were enemy planes. I mean Japanese planes. And they were tracked out to sea. You think it was a hoax? It is damned nonsense for sensible people to think that the Army and Navy would practice such a hoax on San Francisco."

He shouted that it might have been "a good thing" if some bombs *had* been dropped. "It might have awakened some of the fools in this community who refuse to realize that this is a war."

On the night of this "air attack," one of De Witt's subordinates, Maj. Gen. Joseph W. Stilwell, later to be the famous "Vinegar Joe" of the doomed campaigns in Burma and China, wrote in pencil in a dime-store notebook that he used as a diary, "Fourth Army"—obviously meaning its headquarters—"kind of jittery." Two nights later, DeWitt and his staff, hearing that there was to be an armed uprising of 20,000 Nisei in the San Francisco area, whipped up a plan to put all of them in military custody. The plan fortunately was aborted by the local F.B.I.[1] chief of station, Nat Pieper, who told the Army that the "reliable source" for their news of the uprising was a flake whom Pieper had once employed and had had to dismiss because of his "wild imaginings."

Next, on Dec. 13, came "reliable information" that an enemy attack on Los Angeles was imminent, and DeWitt's staff drafted a general alarm that would have advised all civilians to leave the city. Fortunately, it was never broadcast. That night, General Stilwell wrote in his notebook that General DeWitt was a "jackass."

The first week of the war brought news of one setback after another. The Japanese struck at Midway, Wake, the Philippines, Hong Kong, the Malay Peninsula and Thailand. On Dec. 13, they captured Guam. The American dream of invulnerability had suddenly been replaced by a feeling that the Japanese could do just about anything they wanted to do—including landing at any point along DeWitt's vast coastal command.

Two days after Pearl Harbor, Navy Secretary Frank Knox went to Hawaii to try to find out what had gone wrong there. On Dec. 15, he returned to the mainland from his scouting trip and called a press conference at which he said, "I think the most effective fifth-column work[2] of the entire war was done in Hawaii, with the possible exception of Norway." He carried back to Washington this report of treachery by resident Japanese, "both from the shores and from the sampans," and his absurdly impracticable recommendation that all those with Japanese blood be evacuated from Oahu.

His charges were quickly denied, in confidential reports, by J. Edgar Hoover of the F.B.I.; by John Franklin Carter, a journalist whom Roosevelt had enlisted to give him intelligence reports; and, after a few days, by Lieut. Gen. Delos C. Emmons, the newly appointed commanding officer in the Hawaiian Islands. But Frank Knox's statement was never denied by the Government—which, from Pearl Harbor to V-J Day, would record not a single case of sabotage by a Japanese alien or a Japanese-American worse than the plowing under of strawberries.

In 1943, when General DeWitt would submit to the Secretary of War his "Final Report" on the removal of the Japanese from the West Coast, one of its first assertions would be: "The evacuation was impelled by military necessity." DeWitt wrote, "There were hundreds of reports nightly of signal lights visible from the coast, and of intercepts of unidentified radio transmissions."

Hoover scornfully ridiculed the "hysteria and lack of judgment" of DeWitt's Military Intelligence Division. An official of the Federal Communications Commission reported on the question of radio intercepts: "I have never seen an organization that was so hopeless to cope with radio intelligence requirements. . . . The personnel is unskilled and untrained. . . . As a matter of fact, the Army air stations have been reported by the Signal Corps station as Jap enemy stations."

DeWitt urged random spot raids on homes of ethnic Japanese to seize "subversive" weapons and cameras. Attorney General Biddle stipulated that raiders should follow the constitutional requirement of finding probable cause for arrest, but DeWitt argued that being of Japanese descent was in itself probable cause. He insisted on searches without warrants, even of the homes of citizens. Yet the Justice Department concluded from F.B.I. reports: "We have not found a single machine gun, nor have we found any gun in any circumstances indicating that it was to be used in a manner helpful to our enemies. We have not found a camera which we have reason to believe was for use in espionage."

When it came right down to it, the mere fact of having Japanese blood and skin was, to DeWitt, enough basis for suspicion. When he wrote in his "Final Report" of the way the ethnic Japanese population was scattered through his Defense Command, he used the military term "deployed"—"in excess of 115,000 persons deployed along the Pacific Coast"—as if these people, these farmers and merchants and house servants, had been posted by plan, poised for attack.

Testifying before a Congressional subcommittee, DeWitt would say, as if this alone proved the military necessity he was trying to assert, "A Jap is a Jap."

The news from the Pacific after the first shock of Pearl Harbor grew worse and worse, and nerves in the Presidio[3] tightened. On Dec. 24 and 25, 1941, the Japanese took Wake Island and Hong Kong. On Dec. 27, Manila fell, and United States forces retreated to the Bataan Peninsula.

On Dec. 19, DeWitt urged on the War Department "that action be initiated at the earliest practicable date to collect all alien subjects 14 years of age and over, of enemy nations and remove them" to inland places, where they should be kept "under restraint after removal." This recommendation covered only aliens—Germans and Italians as well as Japanese.

Toward the end of the month, according to Roger Daniels, who has written two authoritative books on the evacuation, DeWitt began talking by phone—outside the normal chain of command, without telling his superiors—with an officer he knew in Washington, Maj. Gen. Allen W. Gullion. Gullion was Provost Marshal General, the Army's top law enforcement officer. Since the fall of France in June 1940, he had been concerning himself with the question of how the military could acquire legal control over civilians in wartime—in case there should be a domestic fifth column—and DeWitt, evidently stung by the ridicule of his alarms by civilian agencies like the F.B.I. and the F.C.C.,[4] was much attracted by Gullion's views.

Gullion had the chief of his Aliens Division, Major Karl R. Bendetsen, draft a memorandum proposing that the President "place in the hands of the Secretary of War the right to take over aliens when he thought it was necessary."

In one of their turn-of-the-year conferences, Bendetsen outlined to DeWitt plans for surveillance and control of West Coast Nisei; if the Justice Department wouldn't do the job, Bendetsen told DeWitt, then it would be up to the Army— really, to the two of them—to do it. According to notes taken at the session, DeWitt went along with Bendetsen, saying that he had "little confidence that the enemy aliens are law-abiding or loyal in any sense of the word. Some of them, yes; many, no. Particularly the Japanese. I have no confidence in their loyalty whatsoever."

In organizations like the Native Sons of the Golden West and the American Legion, clamor for the incarceration of all Nisei was growing. Congressman Leland Ford of Los Angeles argued for their removal with a most peculiar logic. On Jan. 16, he wrote to Secretary of War Henry L. Stimson a formal recommendation "that all Japanese, whether citizens or not, be placed in inland concentration camps. As justification for this, I submit that if an American-born Japanese, who is a citizen, is really patriotic and wishes to make his contribution to the safety and welfare of this country, right here is his opportunity to do so. . . . Millions of other native-born citizens are willing to lay down their lives, which is a far greater sacrifice, of course, than being placed in a concentration camp."

There were, in fact, lots of patriotic Nisei. Many of them were fiercely and showily patriotic precisely because so many "real Americans" doubted their fidelity. Some had joined together in the Japanese-American Citizens League, which did all it could to flaunt its members' loyalty. Their idealistic creed, adopted before Pearl Harbor, said, "Although some individuals may discriminate against me, I shall never become

bitter or lose faith, for I know that such persons are not representative of the majority of American people."

Nisei in many cities and towns helped with civil defense. Furthermore, many young Nisei volunteered for the Army. (In Italy and France, the Japanese-American 442d Combat Regimental Team would turn out to be one of the most decorated units in the entire United States Army— with seven Presidential Distinguished Unit Citations, one Congressional Medal of Honor, 47 Distinguished Service Crosses, 350 Silver Stars, 810 Bronze Stars and more than 3,600 Purple Hearts. President Truman, attaching a Presidential Distinguished Unit Citation to the regimental colors, would say, "You fought not only the enemy, but you fought prejudice. . . .")

DeWitt's anxieties, however, flowered more and more, and they soon bore fruit. On Jan. 21, 1942, he recommended to Secretary Stimson the establishment of 86 "prohibited zones" in California, from which all "enemy" aliens would be removed, as well as a handful of larger "restricted zones," where they would be kept under close surveillance.

On Jan. 25, persuaded by DeWitt's reports of danger, Stimson recommended to Biddle that these zones be established. Since this request touched only enemy aliens, and meant moving them in most cases for very short distances, Biddle acceded.

At the beginning of February, voices raised on the West Coast against Japanese-Americans became more and more shrill. The Los Angeles Times took up the cry that Japanese citizens were just as much enemies as Japanese aliens: "A viper is nonetheless a viper wherever the egg is hatched—so a Japanese-American, born of Japanese parents, grows up to be a Japanese, not an American." California's liberal Governor, Culbert L. Olson, who had earlier taken the position that Japanese-Americans should continue in wartime to enjoy their constitutional rights, reversed himself in a radio address. Evidently on information from DeWitt, he said: "It is known that there are Japanese residents of California who have sought to aid the Japanese enemy by way of communicating information, or have shown indications of preparation for fifth-column activities." He hinted that there might have to be large-scale removals.

Biddle wanted to issue a press release jointly with the Army, designed to calm public fears on the West Coast about sabotage and espionage, and on Feb. 4, he, Assistant Attorney General James Rowe Jr., J. Edgar Hoover, Stimson, Mc-Cloy, Gullion and Bendetsen met to discuss it. Gullion later described this encounter:

"[The Justice officials] said there is too much hysteria about this thing; said these Western Congressmen are just nuts about it and the people getting hysterical and there is no evidence whatsoever of any reason for disturbing citizens, and the Department of Justice—Rowe started it and Biddle finished it—the Department of Justice will [have] nothing whatsoever to do with any interference with citizens, whether they are Japanese or not. They made me a little sore, and I said, well listen, Mr. Biddle, do you mean to tell me that if the Army, the men on the ground, determine it is a military necessity to move citizens, Jap citizens, that you won't help me? He didn't give a direct answer, he said the Department of Justice would be through if we interfered with citizens and writ of habeas corpus,[5] etc."

When DeWitt, on Feb. 9, asked for the establishment of much larger prohibited zones in Washington, Oregon and Arizona, Biddle refused to go along. "Your [recommendations] of prohibited areas . . . include the cities of Portland, Seattle, and Tacoma," he wrote, "and therefore contemplate a mass evacuation of many thousands. . . . No reasons were given for this mass evacuation. . . . The Department of Justice is not physically equipped to carry out any mass evacuation."

If there were to be any question of evacuating citizens, the Attorney General wanted no part of it—yet in washing his hands of this eventuality, he now conceded that the Army might justify doing this as a "military necessity. . . . Such action, therefore, should in my opinion, be taken by the War Department and not by the Department of Justice."

Two days later, Stimson went over Biddle's head to Roosevelt. Unable to fit an appointment into a busy day, the President talked with Stimson on the phone. The Secretary told Roosevelt that the Justice Department was dragging its feet and asked if he would authorize the Army to move American citizens of Japanese ancestry as well as aliens away from sensitive areas. Further, he asked whether the President would favor evacuating more than 100,000 from the entire West Coast; 70,000 living in major urban areas; or small numbers living around critical zones, such as aircraft factories, "even though that would be more complicated and tension-producing than total evacuation."

Right after Stimson hung up, Assistant Secretary John J. McCloy jubilantly called Bendetsen in San Francisco to say that the President had declined to make a specific decision about numbers himself but had decided to cut out the Justice Department and had given the Army "*carte blanche*[6] to do what we want to." Roosevelt's only urging was to "be reasonable as you can."

The very next day—so promptly as to suggest that there had been some orchestration—the most influential newspaper pundit in the country, Walter Lippmann, in a column entitled "The Fifth Column on the Coast," [laid] out the basis for advocating the removal of citizens as well as aliens. "The Pacific Coast," he wrote, "is in imminent danger of a combined attack from within and without. . . . It is a fact that the Japanese Navy has been reconnoitering the coast more or less continuously. . . . There is an assumption [in Washington] that a citizen may not be interfered with unless he has committed an overt act. . . . The Pacific Coast is officially a combat zone. Some part of it may at any moment be a battlefield. And nobody ought to be on a battlefield who has no good reason for being there. There is plenty of room elsewhere for him to exercise his rights."

The day after the Lippmann article, the entire Pacific Coast Congressional delegation signed and delivered to Roosevelt a resolution urging "the immediate evacuation of all persons of Japanese lineage and all others, aliens and citizens alike, whose presence shall be deemed dangerous or inimical to the defense of the United States from . . . the entire strategic areas of the states of California, Oregon, and Washington, and the Territory of Alaska."

On Feb. 14, freed by Roosevelt's green light to the Army, doubtless encouraged by Lippmann and by the vociferousness of the West Coast press and West Coast Congressmen, DeWitt finally submitted to Stimson his recommendation for "Evacuation of Japanese and Other Subversive Persons From the Pacific Coast," to be carried out by his command. In justifying the "military necessity" of such an action, DeWitt wrote that ". . . along the vital Pacific Coast over 112,000 potential enemies, of Japanese extraction, are at large today. There are indications that these are organized and ready for concerted action at a favorable opportunity. The very fact that no sabotage has taken place to date is a disturbing and confirming indication that such action will be taken."

Here was logic worthy of "Animal Farm":[7] Proof that all ethnic Japanese were "ready for concerted action" lay in their not having taken it yet.

On Feb. 17, Biddle, in a letter to the President, made a last-ditch protest. "My last advice from the War Department," he wrote, "is that there is no evidence of imminent attack and from the F.B.I. that there is no evidence of planned sabotage."

The protest came too late. By this time, the Attorney General—whose voice had been absolutely solo in reminding those in power of central values in the Bill of Rights—was not only ignored; he was brutally vilified. Congressman Leland Ford told later of a call to Biddle:

"I gave them 24 hours' notice that unless they would issue a mass evacuation notice I would drag the whole matter out on the floor of the House and of the Senate and give the bastards everything we could with both barrels. I told them they had given us the runaround long enough . . . and that if they would not take immediate action, we would clear the goddamned office out in one sweep. . . ."

On the day Biddle transmitted his final protest to Roosevelt, Stimson convened a meeting with War Department aides to plan a Presidential order enabling a mass evacuation under Army supervision. Gullion was sent off to draft it.

That evening, McCloy, Gullion and Bendetsen went to Biddle's house, and Gullion read his draft aloud to the Attorney General. The order was to be sweeping and open-ended. Basing the President's right as Commander in Chief to issue it on a war powers act that dated back to the First World War, it authorized "the Secretary of War, and the military commanders whom he may from time to time designate . . . to prescribe military areas . . . from which any or all persons

may be excluded, and with respect to which, the right of any person to enter, remain in, or leave shall be subject to whatever restriction the Secretary of War or the appropriate military commander may impose in his discretion."

On Feb. 19, 1942, Roosevelt set his signature to Executive Order No. 9066, "Authorizing the Secretary of War to Prescribe Military Areas."

The next day, Secretary Stimson formally appointed DeWitt "the military commander to carry out the duties and responsibilities" under Executive Order 9066. He specified that DeWitt should not bother to remove persons of Italian descent. There was widespread affection for Italian-Americans. The Mayor of San Francisco was one, and the baseball stars Joe and Dom DiMaggio, whose parents were aliens, were among the most popular idols in the country. "I don't care so much about the Italians," Biddle later quoted Roosevelt as having said in his cavalier way. "They are a lot of opera singers. . . ."

Stimson took a slightly harder line on German aliens, though he never authorized evacuating German-Americans. Instructions to DeWitt were that German aliens who were "bona fide refugees" should be given "special consideration." In any case, the F.B.I. had long since taken into custody German aliens who had been marked as potentially subversive.

As to ethnic Japanese, the message was clear. Classes 1 and 2 of those who were to be moved out were "Japanese Aliens" and "American Citizens of Japanese Lineage." A sharp racist line had been drawn.

Congress had set up a Select Committee to investigate the need for what it euphemistically called "National Defense Migration." Testifying in San Francisco on Feb. 21, Earl Warren, then Attorney General of California, echoed DeWitt's amazing "proof" of trouble to come. "Unfortunately [many] are of the opinion that because we have had no sabotage and no fifth column activities in this State . . . that none have been planned for us," Warren said. "But I take the view that this is the most ominous sign in our whole situation. It convinces me more than perhaps any other factor that the sabotage we are to get, the fifth column activities we are to get, are timed just like Pearl Harbor was timed and just like the invasion of France, and of Denmark, and of Norway, and all of those other countries."

Two evenings later, almost as if designed to make irrational fears like these seem plausible, a Japanese submarine, the I-17, having recently returned to the coastal waters, fired about 25 five-and-a-half-inch shells at some oil storage tanks on an otherwise empty hillside west of Santa Barbara. There were no casualties. But was this a prelude to an invasion?

The next night, the Army detected nonexistent enemy airplanes over Los Angeles, and at 2:25 A.M., an antiaircraft battery opened fire. Other gun crews, hearing the explosions, began firing, and within a couple of hours, 1,430 three-inch shells had gone off above the city. Their fragments rained down, causing a fair amount of damage to automobiles. It took quite a while before this happening could be given the joking title it came finally to bear: "The Battle of Los Angeles." At the time, it reinforced the public's panic.

On Feb. 27, the Cabinet in Washington met to discuss how the evacuations should be carried out. Bendetsen had been arguing that the Army should not bear the burden of administering the removals because, as he said in a phone call to the State Department, the Army's job was "to kill Japanese, not to save Japanese." And indeed, the Cabinet did decide that day that the "resettlement" should be handled by a new civilian agency, which would eventually be called the War Relocation Authority. Milton S. Eisenhower, an official of the Department of Agriculture, brother of the popular general who would one day be elected President, was put in charge of it. The Army would round up the evacuees and move them to temporary collection centers, and then the civilian W.R.A. would settle and hold them for the duration of the war in permanent camps.

On March 2, DeWitt established as Military Area No. 1—the field of hottest imaginary danger—the entire western halves of Washington, Oregon and California, and the southern half of Arizona. Presumably somewhat cooler was Military Area No. 2, comprising the remainder of the four states.

DeWitt did not yet, however, issue any orders for actual removals, because in Washington, Gullion had realized that there was no law on the books that made a civilian's disobedience of a military command a crime, so there was no way for DeWitt to force anyone to move. Gullion's office therefore went to work drawing up a statute—something absolutely new in American legal history—that would invent such a crime. DeWitt urged that imprisonment be mandatory, and that the crime be classified as a felony because, he argued, "you have a greater liberty to enforce a felony than you have to enforce a misdemeanor, *viz,* You can shoot a man to prevent the commission of a felony."

On March 9, Stimson submitted to Congress the proposed legislation, which would subject any civilian who flouted a military order in a military area to a year in jail and a fine of $5,000. Only one person in either House rose in debate to challenge the measure: the archconservative Senator Robert A. Taft of Ohio, who would be known in later years as "Mr. Republican." This bill, he said, was "the 'sloppiest' criminal law I have ever read or seen anywhere."

When it came to a vote, not a single member of either House voted against the bill, which was signed into law by Roosevelt on March 21. The way was cleared. On March 31, 1942, with the posting of Civilian Exclusion Orders, the cruel capture of the ethnic Japanese was set in motion.

By early 1943, McCloy and others in the War Department and Army had clearly seen that "military necessity" could no longer, by the wildest imagining, justify keeping loyal American citizens of Japanese ancestry—or loyal aliens—away from the West Coast in "pens." DeWitt was horrified, but the War Department had had enough of his obsessive fears and complaints. He was relieved of his Western Defense Command that fall.

In the spring of 1944, the War Department finally urged the President to dissolve the camps. Others, however, urged caution. "The question appears to be largely a political one," wrote Under Secretary of State Edward Stettinius Jr., in a memo to the President. Roosevelt would be running for a fourth term in November. The evacuees would have to wait.

At the first Cabinet meeting after Roosevelt's re-election, it was decided that all evacuees who passed loyalty reviews could, at last, go home.

They went home to a bitter freedom. It took more than a year to empty all the camps. Given train fare and $25, the evacuees returned to the coast, many to learn that their goods had been stolen or sold; their land had been seized for unpaid taxes; strangers had taken possession of their homes. Jobs were plentiful, but not for the returning detainees, who met with notices: "No Japs Wanted." Housing was hard to find; whole families moved into single rooms.

One man, who had a brother still overseas with the 442d Regimental Combat Team, would testify that his mother "finally had enough money for a down payment on a house. We purchased the house in 1946 and tried to move in, only to find two Caucasian men sitting on the front steps with a court injunction prohibiting us from moving in because of a restrictive covenant.[8] If we moved in, we would be subject to a $1,000 fine and/or one year in the County Jail."

One ordeal had ended; another had begun.
[1988]

Terms

1. F.B.I.: Federal Bureau of Investigation.
2. FIFTH-COLUMN WORK: Secret subversive activities aiding an invading enemy.
3. THE PRESIDIO: The U.S. Army base in San Francisco that served as DeWitt's headquarters.
4. F.C.C.: Federal Communications Commission.
5. WRIT OF HABEAS CORPUS: An order to release or bring a prisoner before a court.
6. *CARTE BLANCHE:* Full discretionary power.
7. "ANIMAL FARM": A satirical novel by George Orwell with the climactic slogan "All animals are equal, but some animals are more equal than others."
8. RESTRICTIVE COVENANT: A law prohibiting certain ethnic groups from residing in a given area.

Understanding the Reading

1. What were the Civilian Exclusion Orders?
2. What was the economic impact of the orders?
3. In what ways were the Japanese Americans treated like criminals?
4. What were conditions like at the Assembly Centers?
5. What was Lieutenant General DeWitt's response to the supposed San Francisco flyover by Japanese planes?
6. What was the single case of sabotage by a Japanese American?

7. What were some of the problems with the Military Intelligence Division?
8. What were some of the most bizarre justifications offered in support of the evacuation?
9. What was the 442d Combat Regimental Team, and what was its service record like?
10. What triggered the "Battle of Los Angeles"?
11. Why did evacuation have to wait for Congress to act?
12. What problems did Japanese Americans face after they left the camps?

Suggestions for Responding

1. Hersey raises the question of whether such an incident as the relocation program could occur again. How would you answer him?
2. Imagine you were a Japanese American attending a West Coast university at the time of the evacuation order. How would you have reacted?
3. Explain DeWitt's role in the evacuation. ◆

63

A Personal Narrative

SUSAN SHIMIZU TAIRA

Three days before I was born, Japan bombed Pearl Harbor, and war was declared by the United States. Although we were Japanese Americans with no reason to be suspected as spies, we were forcibly removed from our home and incarcerated behind barbed wire and armed guards. The racist decision to incarcerate us, people who were visually identifiable and the victims of slanderous press and racism since our arrival on these shores, differed from the decisions made about European Americans whose countries were also at war with the United States.

In the early months of our incarceration, my father's actions of protest against this violation of our human and civil rights resulted in our removal to Tule Lake, the camp for those who

Excerped from Susan Shimizu Taira, "The American Behavioral Scientist," vol. 45, issue 8, pp. 1265–1266, c. Apr 2002 by Sage Publications, Inc. Reprinted by Permission of Sage Publications.

would not sign the loyalty oath. This hard-working man of tremendous integrity and uncrushable will was subsequently identified as a significant threat and secretly removed to the New Mexico desert where he was placed under the authority of the Department of Justice. During this time, my mother spent anguishing months not knowing the whereabouts of my father. Later, my father was labeled as an "undesirable alien" by the U.S. government and deported to Japan.

Having lost our father, my biggest fear was losing my mother. A vivid recollection is a fire that broke out in our camp while my mother had gone to the mess hall to get our food. The fire separated us. The fear and panic enveloped me long after my mother reunited with us. For a long time, I could feel physical anxiety whenever I remembered the fire. In fact, it took many years to be able to convert the power of the fire into my own inner strength.

My mother, older brother, older sister, and I were able to return to Los Angeles in 1946 with nothing more than my mother's courageous determination to make a life for us. Upon our return, in every phase of our lives we encountered racism—in school as non-English speakers, in seeking housing, in our neighborhood, in job opportunities, and in retail establishments. I remember the exciting prospect of finally eating lunch in a coffee shop, only to be ignored by the staff and later forced to walk out ashamed that we couldn't be served. These were frightening experiences and made me wonder what horrible ailment we had that caused people to treat us as if we were less than human. We survived because my mother wouldn't give in or give up.

The act of incarceration by the U.S. government burdened us with a label of "suspected enemy," which was totally unwarranted and undeserved. But reason alone couldn't explain the acts of violence perpetrated on us or the resulting public sentiment of hatefulness. The pernicious wartime experiences and the acts of prejudice we encountered afterward had begun to seep into our unconscious and psyche—no amount of washing or purging could eradicate or cleanse us. It persuaded us to doubt our worth and our goodness. It informed us of our limited value as people and pulled out from under us our sense of belonging. In a strange way, we became less certain of our own innocence. For many years, there seemed to be less distinction

between the U.S. story and our story. Truly, the process of internalized oppression is powerful.

For my mother, survival was setting aside our Japanese cultural heritage and proving over and over again that we were loyal Americans. Remember, maintaining purity and innocence in the face of the government takes extraordinary strength, which we weren't ready to exert. Our mother quietly encouraged us to make the transition to speaking English and put aside our knowledge of Japanese as a language and as an identity.

Partly because of her quest to be accepted as American, she was born here, and partly because of the shame she bore because her husband had been deported, my mother did not choose to live too close to the Japanese American community. I tried to imagine my mother's pain at being abandoned by the U.S. government as a citizen and being ostracized by some in her community because her husband was identified as an undesirable alien by the government. To complicate her identity crisis, she had given up her U.S. citizenship as her act of defiance and support for her husband during the war. Although she was able to receive her citizenship after the war, these series of critical incidents must have fed her quiet determination.

It was not until many years later when she chose to spend her last days in a Japanese American convalescent home did I understand that she had taken off the garb of defendant. When I took my mother to the Keiro Nursing Home, staff members rushed up to greet her in Japanese. My mother smiled; she allowed herself to go home. She was weary of bearing the personal and social costs of her victimization. She came full circle.

My mother died the evening the senior Japanese Americans received the president's apologies for the incarceration. One sleepless night during my mourning, I wrote the following tribute to her:

My Mother's Love Was a Brave Love

> *In 1947, she went to court to reclaim her
>   citizenship.
> A proud first step to proving her loyalty
> Her right to be an American, to be good
>   enough*

For a country that had stripped her of her
   home and husband.
My father was allowed to return to the States
   in 1954.
Now teenagers, the three of us sat silently
   wondered
About a father we hadn't seen in twelve years.
Who was unjustly taken from us.
My mother's love drew us together.
Years later I met courageous Appalachian
   activists
Fighting for their right to unpolluted water.
My mother's image appeared and I knew to
   go to her
With tears, I thanked my mother for being
   brave for us.
She wept, "No one ever told me I was brave."
On October 9, 1990, the overdue ceremony
   in D.C.
To issue reparations to the community elders.
America publicly acknowledged its grievous
   crime.
My mother died in her sleep that night in Los
   Angeles.
Mutsu Shimizu was set free and left us a
   legacy of courage.   [2002]

Understanding the Reading

1. Why were Taira and her family taken from their home and incarcerated?
2. Why was her father deported?
3. What was life like for them after the war?
4. What effect did this have on Taira's mother? What were her strategies for coping?

Suggestions for Responding

1. Discuss whether such a thing could ever happen again; compare it with prisoners being held by the United States in Guantánamo Bay, Cuba. Is it the same national response as sixty years ago, or not?
2. Speak to Arab Americans about their treatment since 9/11. ✦

64

Asian Americans Battle "Model Minority" Stereotype

ROBERT DASELER

For decades, Asian Americans have borne the peculiar burden of being the "model minority." Their signal success, especially in technical and scientific fields, has resulted in their being viewed more favorably than other American minorities, who supposedly lack their initiative.

The idea that Asians can serve as a model for other minorities seems to have originated in the 1960s, during the heyday of the civil rights movement. In a 1966 *New York Times Magazine* article, Berkeley sociologist William Petersen wrote: "By any criterion of good citizenship that we choose, the Japanese Americans are better than any other group in our society, including native-born whites. They have established this remarkable record, moreover, by their own almost totally unaided effort."

Later in the article, Petersen, having further elaborated the accomplishments of Japanese Americans, made the invidious comparison to other minorities: "This is not true (or, at best, less true) of such 'non-whites' as Negroes, Indians, Mexicans, Chinese, and Filipinos."

Despite the fact that Petersen included Chinese and Filipinos on his list of less successful minorities, the idea spread that Asians generally work hard, send their children to college, rise rapidly in American society, and are "by any criterion of good citizenship that we choose" better than, for example, African Americans, Latinos, and Native Americans.

Although Petersen did not explicitly state that other minorities ought to emulate Japanese Americans or other Asian Americans, the notion of Asians as a model minority acquired a certain popular acceptance in the 1970s and 1980s.

According to . . . Ruth Gim, a Pomona College psychologist whose family emigrated to this country from Korea in 1970, the "model minority" tag stereotypes Asians, denying their many social, psychological, and financial difficulties and falsifying the actual record of their assimilation into American culture.

In Gim's view, the model minority image is dangerous to Asian Americans because it results in the denial of their actual needs, it imposes a set of expectations for Asian Americans that they do not create for themselves ("Someone else is prescribing to us what we should be"), and it biases their relations with other minorities.

Gim also believes that there was an implicit message behind the development of the myth of the model minority: "It was sending a message to the other minorities, saying, 'Why can't you be like them?' It was trying to use one minority group to send a message to another minority group." Many Asian Americans came quite naturally to resent the dubious distinction of being hailed as models for other minorities.

A study, released by UCLA in May, pointed out that Asian Americans are just as likely to be impoverished and disadvantaged as they are to be economically successful. According to Paul Ong, editor of the report, "It's been an uphill battle to get decision-makers and the population overall to realize that the Asian Pacific American population is a diverse one." The UCLA study paints a picture of a rapidly growing population (the 1990 Census said the nation's Asian and Pacific Islander population totaled 7,273,662, more than double the 1980 total) whose veneer of success camouflages some disturbing struggles.

At a series of luncheons sponsored by Pomona's Asian American Resource Center during the spring semester, Gim, who directs the center, and other speakers examined the myth, trying to understand its origins, the reasons for its widespread acceptance (even among many Asian Americans), and its dangers.

PROMOTING SUPER-ACHIEVERS

Gim, who teaches courses in Asian American studies and psychology at Pomona, was the lead-off speaker in the series. Promoting Asians as super-achievers was, in effect, a tactic that conservatives could use to undercut criticism of mainstream culture by dissidents within the minority communities, Gim said.

In fact, Petersen, in his 1966 piece, emphasized the point that discrimination against Japanese Americans had been, if anything, more virulent than discrimination against other minorities. The implication of the Petersen article was clear: if other minorities did not prosper, it was because they were not as industrious or as determined as the Japanese.

By holding up Asian Americans as a model for other minorities, mainstream culture could, in effect, deny that racial prejudice was to blame for unemployment and poverty among African Americans, Latinos, and others. Drawing attention to the success of thousands of Asian Americans was, in other words, an indirect way of placing the blame for racial inequality upon the minorities themselves, rather than the dominant culture.

Gim believes that embedded in the model minority myth was an assumption of cultural determinism: that Asian cultures are superior to other cultures, and for that reason, Asians tend to rise to the top of whatever culture they enter. She asserts that this presumption of Asian superiority is actually harmful for Asian Americans, especially those who are not academic superstars.

Gim also notes, ironically, that the model minority portrayal of Asian Americans is in stark contrast to the "Yellow Peril" image of them promulgated earlier in the century.

In the years prior to World War II, the prevailing view of Asians was represented by the figure of Charlie Chan, the movie detective who outwitted (usually Irish) policemen to solve crimes. Chan was an icon of the "inscrutable" Oriental: astute, mysterious, and ultimately risible. (Although he possessed a good vocabulary, his grammar was defective.)

Gim points out that many Asian Americans have internalized the "model minority" image, resulting in a narrowing of their social horizons. They know they are expected to enter technical and scientific fields—mathematics, engineering, medicine, economics—but not the humanities. Asian American students who do *not* do well in math or technical subjects often feel that they have not lived up to the expectations they have inherited. Asian American students do not have the freedom to be mediocre.

Furthermore, those who want to study history, sociology, or art often feel they are stepping over an invisible line between what is and is not an appropriate career path.

Contrary to the myth of invulnerability, Asian American students have a significantly higher rate of major depression and diagnosed schizophrenia than European Americans. "The superficial view seems to support the model minority image," Gim says, "but when you dig deeper, you find that cultural factors influence the underutilization of psychological services by Asian American students."

Moreover, the severity of psychiatric problems reported by Asian American students belies the image of them as programmed automatons.

The pressure on these students is coming not only from the culture, of course, but primarily from their families, who often steer the students into traditional and lucrative professions.

The concluding speaker in the series, Linus Yamane, as assistant professor of economics at Pitzer College, further debunked the myth by noting that, while the average family income of Asian Americans, $42,250, is higher than that for European Americans, $36,920, the proportion of Asian Americans living below the poverty line is much higher than for European Americans.

Yamane also pointed out that Asian American families tend to be larger than families of European Americans, somewhat vitiating their higher average income.

Yamane drew a complex picture of Asians in the United States, saying that poverty rates for Chinese, Japanese, and Korean families are lower than for European Americans, while poverty rates for Filipino and Native American families are higher.

Yamane also argued that discrimination against Asians in the work force varies with their ethnic background. Japanese and Korean males are found to do as well as European American males with comparable education, but Chinese and Filipino males do less well, and Native American men earn about 30 percent less, on the average, than European American males with comparable education.

Management Glass Ceiling

Yamane believes that there is a "glass ceiling" for Asian Americans in management. Studies appear to show that, while Asian Americans rise rapidly in the lower ranks of organizations, they are excluded from higher managerial positions.

Between Gim and Yamane came three other speakers. One of these was David Yoo, a historian at Claremont McKenna College, whose specialty is ethnicity, immigration, and race. Yoo characterized the model minority view of Asian Americans as just the latest wrinkle in the evolution of the stereotype of Asians in America.

Proclaiming Asian Americans to be a model minority "works against the true notion of a multicultural America," Yoo says. "It reinforces a racial hierarchy, which is kept intact if you can pit one minority against another."

Yoo believes that embracing Asians as exemplary gives people an excuse not to ask more fundamental questions about race and inequality.

While debunking the model-minority image as a myth, Gim, Yamane, and Yoo agree that there is some truth to the characterization of Asian Americans as high achievers. The proportion of Asian American students at highly selective colleges and universities is itself an indicator that at least a few ethnic groups within the Asian American community place high status on education, discipline, and intellectual distinction.

In March, homosexuality in the Asian Pacific Islander communities was discussed by Eric Reyes, a member of the Asian Pacific AIDS Intervention Team in Los Angeles, and Alice Y. Hom, a doctoral candidate in history at The Claremont Graduate School; and Jack Ling, a psychologist and environmental consultant, spoke on the subject of Asian American gangs. Reyes, Hom, and Ling highlighted aspects of the Asian American experience that conflict with the model-minority stereotype.

The number of Asian American students at The Claremont Colleges and in the University of California system does not signify that the story of Asian Americans is one of unalloyed success and social advance. Stereotyping, a pervasive sense of being suspended between two strong cultures, high stress levels, and a concern about loss of identity also are elements in the story.

Asian American students tend, for the most part, to associate with one another, and sometimes this leads to resentment by European American students, who view the Asians as cliquish and unfriendly.

A Pomona sophomore, who asked that his name not be mentioned, is a good example of the Asian American student who has taken the traditional path toward a career. With a double major in chemistry and Chinese, he is conforming, at least for the moment, to his father's expectation that he should become a doctor.

"He has one thing in mind," this young man says of his father, who was raised in Taiwan. "He thinks medicine is the best way to go."

A graduate of a prep school at which there was "a substantial" number of Asian students, the young man associated primarily with other Asian students in high school. At Pomona College, too, he associates with other Asians more than with Caucasian students. "Just for some reason, a lot of the people I know happen to be Asian," he says. He thinks that Koreans tend to be more cliquish than other Asians, though.

This sophomore learned about the model minority myth when he took Ruth Gim's "Asian American Perspectives" class as a freshman.

"You can apply it to some people," he says, "but I don't think you can apply it to Asians as a whole. Asians do work hard and try to do well in school. I think the model-minority myth could be applied to a lot of my friends, but a lot of my Caucasian friends would fit the myth, too, if they were Asians."

A recent graduate, who also asked for anonymity, chose a nontraditional major for a student whose parents were born, as the sophomore's were, in Taiwan. She majored in sociology and Women's Studies, and in her senior thesis, she compared the cultural sensitivity of two centers for battered women: one mainstream, the other for Pacific Islanders and Asians.

Except for her social sciences major, she believes that "I do fall into what people would call a model-minority category." That is, she works hard, attends a prestigious college, and will pursue graduate studies. She also acknowledges the generational linguistic and class privileges that have allowed her to achieve these goals.

She is troubled by the stereotype, however, "I think it's very dangerous," she says. "It creates suspicion between groups, and it prevents us from forming coalitions in our similar struggle."

She says that majoring in sociology and Women's Studies wasn't something she planned. "I could barely do the natural sciences," she admits. So she switched into a field in which she had an interest . . . and could excel.

She graduated from a high school in Cerritos, California, in which the Asian Pacific Islander enrollment was 75 percent.

"It was the most comfortable social environment I was ever in or that I expect I ever will be in," she says. "It was difficult adjusting to Pomona, where suddenly I was the minority. I was not a part of the dominant culture."

Although being in the majority was pleasant, she now believes that "she would have benefited more from high school if there had been a greater diversity of students, particularly more African American and Latino students."

She took a course from Gim, who helped her put the Asian American experience in perspective. "It really allowed me to see the Asian American contributions to American history," she says.

Growing up in Riverside and Orange counties, Gim found that there were two ways for her to compensate for being a minority: "I made sure I did better academically [than other students]. I don't think I really was smarter than other kids, but I made sure I worked harder. The other defense mechanism was that I dressed well."

Gim hopes that the increasing number of Asian American courses will help Asian American students find their own identity in a dominantly European American culture, without having to rely upon stereotypes imposed either by that culture or by their own minority culture.

"I am more American than most Americans walking around," Gim asserts. "I really believe that. I don't think most people realize what it is to be an American. I believe I have a better understanding and appreciation of what it means to be an American because of my bicultural background."   [1994]

Understanding the Reading

1. What led to the development of the myth that Asian Americans are a "model minority"?
2. Why is this image dangerous for Asian Americans?
3. What is the reality of life in the United States for Asian/Pacific Americans?
4. What impact has the model-minority image of Asian Americans had on other minorities?
5. How has it affected Asian Americans themselves?
6. How are Asian Americans affected by the "glass ceiling"?
7. How do Asian American students tend to behave in college?
8. How do college classes in Asian American studies affect Asian American students?

Suggestions for Responding

1. Think about Hersey's description of Japanese Americans during World War II and write an explanation of why you think their image has changed so much in the past sixty years.
2. Write a short essay explaining how your life has been affected by a stereotype that others have applied to you. ✦

65

Inter-Racial Violence: Conflicts of Class and Culture

MICHAEL LASLETT

On March 14, 1987, a Black assailant shot and killed Mo Yi, a Korean merchant who owned a corner store in Anacostia, Maryland, a predominantly Black suburb of Washington, DC. The attacker also shot Yi's wife in the arm, shattering her elbow, and shot Yi's 20-year-old daughter in the shoulder. The gunman and his accomplice returned later that evening and emptied the cash register and took food and cigarettes. Yi was one of three Korean merchants killed in Washington since October, 1986. In 1986, at least 11 Korean-owned businesses were firebombed in Anacostia.

Over the past two years in Tacoma, Washington, Black youth have beaten several Southeast Asian students and an elderly Cambodian man, and the tires of Southeast Asian–owned cars are slashed on a regular basis. Tom Dixon, president of the Tacoma Urban League, says that this type of conflict is common among poor people. Referring to the growing poverty in the United States and the slashing of social services by the Reagan administration, Dixon remarks: "When poor people have less they strike out at each other. It's happening all over the city, all over America. The priorities of the country are upside down, and things are going to get worse before they get better."

These outbreaks of violence are not isolated incidents. The past five years have seen a sharp rise in the number of conflicts between recent Asian immigrants and refugees and the Black, Latino and other poor communities they move into. For example:

- On November 4, 1986, 30 to 40 Black youth assaulted seven Cambodian high school students as they walked home from school through Olney, a predominantly Black neighborhood in Philadelphia.
- In the fall of 1986, two incidents of interracial violence occurred in East Dallas, Texas: in the first, three Latino men dragged a Cambodian man from his car, beat him and took his money; in the second, a group of Latinos fired, unprovoked, into a crowd of Cambodians standing on the street.
- In the western section of Oakland, California, conflict between the Black and Southeast Asian Refugee populations has led to the deaths of two Blacks and one Southeast Asian.

In spite of the growing pattern of Black and Latino violence against Asians, many minority community leaders and activists insist that the problem not be viewed simply as one of racial antagonism. Black and Latino aggression against newly-arrived Asians is far more complex: it is the consequence of differences in economic class, of language barriers and cultural misunderstandings, and of the government's inadequate preparation of low-income residents for the sudden influx of Asian immigrants and refugees into their communities.

IMMIGRANTS AND REFUGEES: TWO DISTINCT GROUPS

The complexity of this issue deepens when one takes into account the diversity of the Asian population and their relationships to other racial groups in the U.S. Contrary to popular belief, the Asian community is neither homogeneous nor monolithic. Some Asians enter the United States as immigrants with education, financial resources and skills. The majority, however, are impoverished refugees fleeing war and repression. When these diverse populations arrive, they occupy different positions in the communities they live in and enter into different economic and social relationships with the long-term residents they encounter. Given this diversity, it follows that the motivations behind an attack on Korean or Chinese merchants in the Black community are not identical with those behind a physical assault on Southeast Asian refugees in the schools or on the streets.

One factor which differentiates segments of the Asian population in the U.S. is when they arrived. The Asian population in the United States more than doubled between 1970 and 1980. In 1970 nearly 90 percent of Asian Americans were of Japanese, Chinese, or Filipino descent. By 1980, census reports listed 19 distinct Asian and Pacific Island populations, with the three largest groups comprising only 62 percent of the total.

The first wave of Southeast Asians arrived in the U.S. in 1975 following the U.S. defeat in Vietnam. In that year 133,633 Indochinese were admitted into the U.S. Between 1976 and 1978 the numbers dropped considerably, followed by an increase to 80,700 in 1979, to 166,700 in 1980 and to more than 200,000 between 1981 and 1982. Although the majority of Southeast Asians are from Vietnam, the proportion of Cambodians and Laotians has increased in recent years, particularly since 1980.

In contrast to the Indochinese refugees, Asian immigrants such as the ethnic Chinese from Vietnam, China, Hong Kong and Singapore, as well as many recently-arrived Koreans, come from relatively privileged backgrounds in their own countries. It is largely by virtue of this fact that they are able to afford the cost and negotiate the paperwork necessary to come to the U.S. in the first place. The Chinese and Koreans also have pre-existing communities and support systems in the United States. Many do not have to be able to speak English to get a job because they can work within the Korean or Chinese communities.

Since many of these immigrants were merchants and shopowners in their home countries, this background, coupled with fear of discrimination in the American job market, makes it logical for them to work as small entrepreneurs. By pooling their financial resources extended family networks are able to gather the initial start-up capital needed to open a business.

Communal traditions help these families to reduce costs. Asian immigrants will often reduce living expenses by eating inexpensively and by crowding several families into one house or apartment. Likewise, Asian merchants often reduce labor costs by employing family members. The free labor supplied by their large families also allows Asian immigrants to maintain very long hours. These factors are crucial to their businesses' viability. The low rents and abandoned storefronts available in poor minority communities make these areas a logical choice for Asian merchants to locate their businesses.

Southeast Asian refugees follow a very different path into minority communities. Most of them spend years in refugee camps in Southeast Asia waiting for their turn to move to the United States. When they arrive they are distributed around the country by the federal government. The only assistance they receive is provided by the Refugee Act of 1978. Under the Act, the State Department allocates $565 per refugee, distributed through local agencies. Local agencies are then obligated to help the refugees obtain food, housing, transportation and other living expenses for their [first] 30 days in the U.S. After that period, if they have not found work, the refugees are placed in the general category of welfare recipients with no special assistance or privileges.

Most Southeast Asian refugees, unlike the Asian immigrants, are not urban people. They are peasants with no formal education and little previous contact with Western culture and customs. Unlike the Chinese and Koreans, Southeast Asian refugees have no pre-established communities to join. They enter the U.S. on the lowest rung of American society and move into poor and minority neighborhoods and housing projects.

POVERTY + SUSPICION = TENSION

When refugees arrive they often enter a minority community which has been homogeneous for many years. The residents, who are generally given no warning or preparation for the influx of a population so completely different from any group they have known, view the newcomers with suspicion.

Wayne Luk of the Southeast Asian Refugee Center in San Francisco tells of a typical scenario of escalating Black-Asian tension in a poor Black community. In 1981 several Southeast Asian families were moved into a housing project in Hunter's Point, a predominantly Black area of San Francisco. Part of the housing project had been closed for renovations and several Black families were forced to move out. When it re-opened and Southeast Asians moved in, it appeared to the Blacks that the Asians had received preferential treatment. What they did not know was that the refugees had waited three years, just like everyone else, to get into the project. The lack of preparation necessary to adjust both the Asian and the Black communities to living with each other, coupled with the resentment Blacks felt toward the perceived preferential treatment of the Asians, led to several incidents of Black-on-Asian violence at Hunter's Point.

Many poor minority communities view the Asian refugees as competitors for already scarce resources. "They're taking over," says one Black man in Tacoma, Washington. "They're getting our housing, they're taking our jobs." While any addition to a poor community stretches resources a little thinner, there is debate over whether the refugees take jobs that would otherwise go to long-time community residents. As Booker Neal, a member of the Eastbay Violence Against Asians Taskforce and a community conciliation worker with the Justice Department, points out, many refugees will accept wages, hours and working conditions that a Black community member would refuse: "A job here at $3.50 an hour is a step up the ladder from a war-torn country and refugee camps. But to a black in that neighborhood that job is the same old poverty—probably the last step on the ladder."

Sam Cacas, a Filipino community activist in Oakland, California, and former director of the Community Violence Prevention Project, claims that most American citizens feel that they have the first right to jobs and services over immigrants, and that Asians are seen as foreigners no matter how long they have lived in the U.S. Recent immigrants have always been pitted against other low-income groups by having to compete with each other at the bottom of American society, Cacas argues. In the case of Asians, the friction is made worse by a long tradition of anti-Asian racism, a tradition in which Blacks, as well as whites, participate.

Although there are isolated incidents of refugees getting help from their sponsors, most receive little additional assistance after their first month in the U.S. However, these isolated incidents fuel the perception among poor minorities that refugees get preferential treatment and generate resentment in poor neighborhoods. For example, when an arson fire destroyed the home of four Cambodian families and one Black family in Tacoma, Washington, the Asians found temporary shelter with their sponsors, who also helped them find new housing. The Black family had to rely on the Red Cross, which provided a motel room for months while the family looked for a permanent place to live.

In East Dallas, Blacks and Latinos have witnessed a predominantly Anglo church, which sponsors Southeast Asian refugees, bring the refugees food and clothing, take them to the clinic and help them find jobs.

Long-time residents are also angered by the perception that Asian newcomers succeed soon after they arrive in a community, while Blacks continue to struggle. As Booker Neal explains, the community watches as the Asians move in and within a year have a job and after two years have a new car. What the community does not see, however, is that often ten families contribute to buy the car. The new car masks the daily sacrifices made to buy it: the long working hours, the mostly-rice diet and the cramped living quarters.

The hope and enthusiasm of upward mobility in the "land of opportunity" motivates newly-arrived refugees to strive in neighborhoods where, according to Booker Neal, Blacks experience only frustration. This frustration is most acute among teenagers, who suffer the highest levels of unemployment—nearly 40 percent. It is not surprising, says Neal, that the majority of attacks on Asian refugees within the Black community are committed by teenagers. "In an area of unemployment, drugs, crime, and poverty, you're not going to have some sixteen-year-old trying to learn about the culture, problems, and history of Laotian immigrants," Neal points out.

Many Southeast Asian refugees become victims because they are seen as passive and unwilling to fight back, behavior which is in part integral to their cultures, and in part a survival skill learned while living under repressive regimes in

Southeast Asia. Many are unwilling to call the police because of the violent nature of police in their home countries.

Mary Cousar, a Black woman who is chairperson of the Logan Multi-Cultural Task Force in Philadelphia, also points out that the Southeast Asians are targets because they have darker skin than the Chinese and Koreans. "I've heard little black children refer to Cambodians as 'nigger Chinese,'" she says.

General disorientation in a new culture also makes the refugees targets for harassment. Yang Sam, the executive director of the Philadelphia Southeast Asian Mutual Aid Assistance Association Coalition, argues that "the way [Asian refugees] walk in the street" reflects their "insecurity and makes them easy targets of crime. [They] are not really comfortable, not confident yet in themselves" in the United States.

Sam Cacas argues that the current resurgence of anti-Asian sentiment is also reinforced by general ignorance, among all sectors of the American population, of the history of Asians in the United States. Most people are unaware of anti-Asian laws such as the Chinese Exclusion Act[1] or the internment of Japanese-Americans during World War II, and that most people think of racism as purely a Black/white problem, Cacas argues. He compares the unequal media coverage of the Howard Beach attack[2] and the killing of Vincent Chin[3] as evidence of this perception.

Cacas also points out that both the Black and Asian communities absorb the racist beliefs prevalent in society at large. While Blacks accept the model minority myth,[4] many Asians generalize from their experience in Black neighborhoods, as well as from images of Blacks in the media that all Blacks are prone to crime and violence. Many Asians are also unaware of the history of oppression that Blacks have suffered in the United States. Wayne Luk points out that before coming to the U.S., many Asian refugees and immigrants were unaware of the racial diversity in the United States, and have a distrust of Blacks.

ASIAN MERCHANTS: A CONFLICT OF CLASS

The tension between low-income minorities and the Chinese and Korean merchants who operate small businesses in their communities is in some respects similar to the conflicts between Blacks and Southeast Asian refugees. There are the same misunderstandings, cultural ignorance on both sides, and the vulnerability of the Asian shop-owners as newcomers. But there are also significant differences.

According to Professor Edna Bonacich, a sociologist at the University of California at Riverside who has studied the growing phenomenon of Asian merchants, the Asian shopowners have entered into a fundamentally antagonistic economic relationship with the community. That antagonism, she says, is due primarily to class, not race or culture.

By definition, argues Bonacich, merchants of any race make their living by making a profit from their customers, in this case poor minorities. Since the merchants do not live in the community, no portion of their profits is reinvested into the community. Because the stores are family-run operations, they also provide no employment to the community. In addition, Asian merchants often operate businesses which are antithetical to the community's general welfare. Bonacich cites the example of Korean merchants opening numerous liquor stores in Watts, Los Angeles, despite the complaints of community leaders. "The Korean storeowners don't have to live with the increased amount of alcohol circulating in the community" says Bonacich. "They are willing to open any store that makes money."

Asian merchants, however, play a role that Bonacich describes as "middleman minority." These merchants are "middlemen," Bonacich argues, because while they are exploiting the community, they are also being exploited by the large, corporate manufacturers. Since large department stores and supermarket chains have evacuated poor and minority areas for more profitable, less turbulent neighborhoods, small minority-owned businesses have become the sole outlets for the products of manufacturing corporations in minority communities, which represent an important consumer market. The corporations also benefit from the free labor provided by Asian extended families, which allows the stores to stay open longer, Bonacich points out. In a paper on immigrant entrepreneurship Bonacich writes: "Their long hours mean that even the dribble-in trade will be picked up. . . . More of the producers' goods are sold, and thus more profits are made from the immigrants' activities."

As middlemen, it is the Asian merchants, not the corporate manufacturers, who must endure personal attacks and absorb the costs of operating a business in a crime-filled area. Small business also lends itself to self-exploitation, says Bonacich. Families have to devote their entire lives to keeping the business afloat. Often the entire first generation of an Asian immigrant family is sacrificed to allow the children to go to college and move up the economic ladder.

Although they make a profit from the community, most Asian merchants are far from rich. Some of their profit is taken by corporate manufacturers, as Bonacich points out. Michael Perez of the Minority Business Development Agency, an arm of the U.S. Commerce Department, explains that close to 35 percent of Asian-owned businesses earn less than $5,000 a year.

However, Asian merchants are the "frontline" representatives of large corporate business in minority communities and therefore face the anger of a poor population. When minority communities respond, it is sometimes with political organizing. For example, the Black community in Harlem called a boycott of Asian stores in part because Black community members accused the merchants of taking dollars out of their community. However, the firebombings and beatings of Asian merchants in Philadelphia and Washington, DC, are examples of another, more common expression of anger and frustration.

IS RECONCILIATION POSSIBLE?

Sam Cacas has worked closely with several efforts to address the problems of Black/Asian tension. As director of the Community Violence Prevention Project, Cacas participated in a successful campaign to make emergency assistance more accessible to recent immigrants and refugees. In response to this community pressure the Alameda County Board of Supervisors approved a translation service for the 911 emergency assistance number in late 1986. The service includes more than 80 languages, which Cacas hopes will particularly help recently-arrived Asians who are the victims of intimidation or attack.

To resolve conflicts between the Asian and Black communities, Cacas advocates legislation requiring the police to keep statistics on racially-motivated crimes so that evidence of such attacks is easier to accumulate. He also argues for effective human relations commissions to mediate community conflicts and for increasing "sensitivity training" for service providers who handle racial conflict.

Educational projects in schools stressing ethnic studies and interracial relationships are also necessary, says Cacas. Often aggressors are ignorant about who their victims are, what their problems are, and how they share common interests.

Asian merchants and Blacks are peacefully coexisting in one Black neighborhood in Philadelphia. There, Korean business-owners are participating in efforts to improve the community. Says Jewel Williams, president of the Susquehanna Neighborhood Advisory Council: "Ever since 1980, we have been trying to assist people who are needy, and the Koreans have been helping. Susquehanna Avenue has been a blighted area since the 1960's, since the riots in 1964. We've asked business people to come in here and make Susquehanna live again. The Koreans are the only ones who came. They've come in and done a good job. If they weren't here, it would be blighted again."

An innovative program at Fremont High School in East Oakland, California, has successfully begun to address the specific problem of tension between Blacks and Southeast Asian refugees. The project, jointly conceived by Asian Community Mental Health Service (ACMHS) and Conciliation Forums of Oakland (CFO), trains students to mediate the conflicts of other students. The mediators, who take a 26-hour preparation course, learn what CFO project coordinator Millie Cleveland calls "active listening." They validate and empathize with both sides of the conflict and they summarize what was said back to the hostile parties.

For every complaint or report of a conflict, a panel of trained student mediators is established. Each panel is chosen to insure that both people in conflict feel confident that their point of view will be fairly heard. For many students, says Cleveland, this is the first time they have been able to tell their side to a sympathetic ear. They express anger and other feelings about the conflict, and in the course of talking the disputants begin to communicate with each other.

According to Cleveland, this process enables both sides to see each other as individuals, to see the other person's point of view, and to psychologically prepare themselves for compromise. Cleveland explains how the hostile parties began to express regret for the conflict and talk about "how they would act next time" in a similar situation. The parties then sign a contract, drawn from the comments of the disputants, which formalizes their agreement to use communication and compromise to resolve conflicts. Often, says Cleveland, it becomes clear that the conflict is between two individuals rather than between representatives of different ethnicities or nationalities.

Since the implementation of the Fremont High project, there have been no reoccurrences of conflict between students who took their problem to a panel, says Cleveland. "All the disputants agreed that it was worth coming, and that in absence of the panel something worse would have happened," she says.   [1987]

Terms

1. CHINESE EXCLUSION ACT: A law that prohibited Chinese from immigrating to the United States.
2. HOWARD BEACH ATTACK: Three young African Americans were attacked and beaten at a pizza parlor in the White community of Howard Beach, New York; one was killed by a car when he ran onto a highway to escape.
3. VINCENT CHIN: A Chinese American mistaken for a Japanese, who was clubbed to death by White autoworkers in Detroit.
4. MODEL MINORITY MYTH: The stereotype that all Asian Americans are both academically and financially successful.

Understanding the Reading

1. What relationship does Tom Dixon see between poverty and racial conflict?
2. What are the differences between Asian immigrants and Asian refugees?
3. How do existing minority communities respond to newcomers from Southeast Asia?
4. Do Asian refugees take jobs away from other minority people?

5. Why are Asian newcomers likely to seem prosperous to Blacks and Latinos?
6. Why are Asian refugees easy targets of violence and harassment?
7. Why are Asian shopkeepers especially resented by the minority community?
8. What can be done to reduce interracial violence?

Suggestions for Responding

1. Explain the complex web of causes of bias against Asians and Asian Americans within the minority communities.
2. How is anti-Asian violence similar to and different from White violence against African Americans? ◆

66

"Jim Crow" Law

BENJAMIN QUARLES

If the Conservatives in the South were aided by the do-nothing policy of the Republican party, they were abetted in a more positive way by the Supreme Court. This high tribunal consistently interpreted the Fourteenth and Fifteenth Amendments[1] in such a way as to weaken their protection of the Negro.

A variety of considerations moved the Court in its handling of the war amendments and the acts of Congress relating to the Negro. Rightly concerned with maintaining a proper balance between the power of the national government and those of the states, the Court tended to restrict federal powers which it felt were excessive. Moreover, the Courts of the nineteenth century did not regard the purely human factor as crucial as the assumed first principles of the law: the letter of the law took precedence over its spirit. And, finally, the men of the Supreme Court could not escape the influence of public opinion on matters of race and color; for all their apparent Olympian aloofness, the justices were subject to the all-pervasive temper of the times.

In a series of cases, the Court set up four basic principles that worked in the interests of the southern whites. To begin with, it decreed that the war amendments applied only to actions taken by states or their agents, and not to private parties. Hence if a private individual or group kept a Negro from voting, the latter had no recourse in the federal courts. Another principle related to the emphasis on appearance rather than reality: if a state law were not plainly discriminatory, the Court would not attempt to ascertain whether it was being applied alike to black and white. A third principle was that of holding the state's police power paramount and therefore more important than the rights given to the individual under the Fourteenth Amendment. The state's police power—its inherent right to protect the public health, safety, or morals—of necessity had to be broad. At any rate, the Court obligingly found that state "Jim Crow" laws were a valid exercise of this power. Finally, the Court favored the white southerner in its ruling that there was a substantial difference between "race discrimination" and "race distinction," the latter not being contrary to the Constitution.

The two most publicized of the Court's decisions affecting Negroes were the Civil Rights Cases of 1883 and *Plessy v. Ferguson,* thirteen years later. The former related to the Civil Rights Act of 1875, a measure which sought to secure equal rights for all citizens at hotels, theaters, and other places of public amusement. It also stipulated that no person should be disqualified to sit on juries because of race. This bill had been strongly supported by Negroes, James T. Rapier of Alabama, in a speech in Congress, having called attention to the fact that there was "not an inn between Washington and Montgomery, a distance of more than a thousand miles, that will accommodate me to a bed or meal."

The Civil Rights Act remained on the books for only eight years before the Court struck it down. Negroes were up in arms, holding a series of indignation meetings, heaping ridicule and invective on the Court, and offering it les-

sons in constitutional law. Anxious to soften the blow to its colored population, many nonsouthern states, numbering eighteen by 1900, passed state civil rights bills. But the national legislature was not destined to pass another such measure until seventy-five years after the Court's adverse ruling in 1883.

After the Court's action in the Civil Rights Cases, no one should have been unprepared for the *Plessy* decision. The high-water mark of the constitutional sanction of state "Jim Crow" laws, this decision in 1896 upheld a Louisiana law calling for separate railroad accommodations for white and colored passengers. Revealing something of the popular belief in white superiority, the Court ruled that laws were "powerless to eradicate racial instincts or to abolish distinctions based upon physical differences." In his dissenting opinion, Justice John Marshall Harlan pointed out that the "Constitution is color-blind, and neither knows nor tolerates classes among citizens." He ventured the opinion that "the judgment this day rendered will, in time, prove to be quite as pernicious as the decision made by this tribunal in the *Dred Scott Case.*"[2] Prophetic words, but in 1896, Justice Harlan's was a lone voice. "*Plessy* was bad law: it was not supported by precedent," writes Barton J. Bernstein. But it remained the law of the land for over half a century.

The Court's rulings encouraged the white South to launch a final bloodless offensive to relegate the Negro to his proper political and social sphere. Regarding voting, the white South felt that the time was ripe to exclude the Negro legally, that it could adopt better and more permanent techniques of disfranchisement than those of intimidation and violence.

Mississippi was the first state to employ the new devices. In 1890 her constitution established three conditions for voting: a residence requirement, the payment of a poll tax, and the ability to read or to interpret a section of the state constitution. Five years later South Carolina adopted these same requirements, adding to them a list of crimes—such as larceny, which had a high incidence among Negroes—which disfranchised the offender. Another requirement southern states found useful was the good-character test: an applicant seeking to become a voter had to produce a responsible witness to vouch for his worth and standing. In many states, tricky registration procedures were legalized, giving local registers broad powers to thwart the Negro applicant. "White primary" laws were passed, asserting that the Democratic party was a voluntary association of citizens and could therefore limit voting as it pleased in party elections.

So sweeping and effective were these measures to disfranchise the Negro that they caught in their dragnet a number of whites, particularly the poor and illiterate. Hence some southern states hastened to pass "grandfather clauses," bestowing the franchise upon those whose grandfathers had voted. This measure added to the total number of voters, but all the persons on whom it bestowed the vote were white, since no Negro's grandfather had voted or been eligible to vote. (Such measures were declared unconstitutional in 1915.)

The white South's grim determination to keep the Negro voteless was strengthened by a half-hearted, unsuccessful attempt by Congress in 1890 to pass a "Force Bill," which would enforce the section of the Fourteenth Amendment stipulating that if a state denied the suffrage to its adult population, its representation in the House would be proportionately reduced. The South was more angered than alarmed by the "Force Bill," but it aroused her spirit of defiance and thus fanned her zeal for Negro disfranchisement.

More than any other factor, the white South's determination to totally separate the Negro from the ballot stemmed from the Populist revolt. Populism was the outgrowth of an effort by the American farmer to improve his lot. Believing that both major political parties were the creatures of business interests in the North, the aroused farmers formed a People's Party.

In the South the leaders of the agrarian crusade—Tom Watson, for example—sought Negro support, holding that the poor white man and the poor colored man were in the same economic strait jacket. Seeking cooperation across the color line, many southern Populists appealed to the remaining Negroes who could vote and tried to obtain the vote for those Negroes from whom it had been wrested. Taking alarm, many of the businessmen and planters decided to fight fire with fire. They, too, sought the Negro vote, opening their pursestrings for barbecues and entertainment, and for the services of Negro spellbinders. Where Populism was suc-

cessful at the polls, as in North Carolina, Negroes were placed in such offices as alderman, magistrate, deputy sheriff, and collector of the port. But this reemergence of the Negro voter and officeholder as a power to be reckoned with during the mid-nineties was shortlived.

Reviving the cry of "Negro domination," defeated or ambitious politicians charged that the Populists were taking the South back to the days of the carpetbagger. The Populists were stigmatized as the lineal descendants of the Loyal Leaguers. Such charges spelled doom, for in the South no political accusation was more fatal than that of being the party of the Negro. Although the reform measures championed by the Populists were directly aimed to benefit the poor white farmer, he tended to forget everything else whenever someone shouted Negro, and the white South closed ranks, determined to eliminate the agrarians. Populism's failure in the South stemmed in large measure from its attempt to bridge the color line.

To Negroes the aftermath of the Populist revolt was particularly galling. Seeking a scapegoat, many of the party's former leaders turned on the Negro, blaming him for its downfall. Moreover, the growing political influence of the poor whites and their pronounced anti-Negro bias led to the widespread adoption of "Jim Crow" legislation. To bolster their own self-esteem, the lower-class whites insisted on their social superiority to the Negro, and even such titles as "Hon." or "Mr." for the exceptional Negro were abandoned. In most southern states this sentiment received more formal expression in the laws requiring that Negroes be segregated at inns, hotels, restaurants, theaters, and on public carriers. And, as was to be expected, those who advocated "Jim Crow" measures had no trouble in convincing themselves that segregation was in the Negro's own best interests—indeed, that it upheld a status that he himself wanted.   [1969]

Terms

1. FOURTEENTH AND FIFTEENTH AMENDMENTS: Post–Civil War constitutional amendments; the Fourteenth guaranteed due process and equal protection, and the Fifteenth granted Negro male suffrage.
2. DRED SCOTT CASE: The Supreme Court ruled in 1857 that the federal government was ob-

ligated to protect the ownership rights of slaveholders, even in the "free" states, thus effectively legalizing slavery throughout the country, even though many states had banned it.

Understanding the Reading

1. Why did the Supreme Court's decisions weaken the protection of Blacks guaranteed by the Fourteenth and Fifteenth Amendments?
2. Explain the four basic principles the Supreme Court established that favored the interests of southern Whites.
3. What was the Civil Rights Act of 1875?
4. Explain the *Plessy v. Ferguson* decision.
5. How did southern states stop Blacks from voting?
6. Why did the Populists court the Black vote, and why did they then turn against Blacks?

Suggestions for Responding

1. Why do you think the Supreme Court didn't protect the rights of African Americans at the end of the nineteenth and beginning of the twentieth centuries?
2. Research the *Plessy v. Ferguson* decision and explain its impact on African Americans for the subsequent sixty years. ✦

67

Jim Crow Revived in Cyberspace

GREG PALAST AND MARTIN LUTHER KING III

Birmingham, Ala.—Astonishingly, and sadly, four decades after the Rev. Martin Luther King Jr. marched in Birmingham, we must ask again, "Do African-Americans have the unimpeded right to vote in the United States?"

In 1963, Dr. King's determined and courageous band faced water hoses and police attack dogs to call attention to the thicket of Jim Crow

laws—including poll taxes and so-called "literacy" tests—that stood in the way of black Americans' right to have their ballots cast and counted.

Today, there is a new and real threat to minority voters, this time from cyberspace: computerized purges of voter rolls.

The menace first appeared in Florida in the November 2000 presidential election. While the media chased butterfly ballots and hanging chads, a much more sinister and devastating attack on voting rights went almost undetected.

In the two years before the elections, the Florida secretary of state's office quietly ordered the removal of 94,000 voters from the registries. Supposedly, these were convicted felons who may not vote in Florida. Instead, the overwhelming majority were innocent of any crime—and just over half were black or Hispanic.

We are not guessing about the race of the disenfranchised: A voter's color is listed next to his or her name in most Southern states. (Ironically, this racial ID is required by the Voting Rights Act of 1965, a King legacy.)

How did mass expulsion of legal voters occur?

At the heart of the ethnic purge of voting rights was the creation of a central voter file for Florida placed in the hands of an elected, and therefore partisan, official. Computerization and a 1998 "reform" law meant to prevent voter fraud allowed for a politically and racially biased purge of thousands of registered voters on the flimsiest of grounds.

Voters whose name, birth date and gender loosely matched that of a felon anywhere in America were targeted for removal. And so one Thomas Butler (of several in Florida) was tagged because a "Thomas Butler Cooper Jr." of Ohio was convicted of a crime. The legacy of slavery—commonality of black names—aided the racial bias of the "scrub list."

Florida was the first state to create, computerize and purge lists of allegedly "ineligible" voters. Meant as a reform, in the hands of partisan officials it became a weapon of mass voting rights destruction. (The fact that Mr. Cooper's conviction date is shown on state files as "1/30/2007" underscores other dangers of computerizing our democracy.)

You'd think that Congress and President Bush would run from imitating Florida's disastrous system. Astonishingly, Congress adopted the absurdly named "Help America Vote Act," which requires every state to replicate Florida's system of centralized, computerized voter files before the 2004 election.

The controls on the 50 secretaries of state are few—and the temptation to purge voters of the opposition party enormous. African-Americans, whose vote concentrates in one party, are an easy and obvious target.

The act also lays a minefield of other impediments to black voters: an effective rollback of the easy voter registration methods of the Motor Voter Act; new identification requirements at polling stations; and perilous incentives for fault-prone and fraud-susceptible touch-screen voting machines.

No, we are not rehashing the who-really-won fight from the 2000 presidential election. But we have no intention of "getting over it." We are moving on, but on to a new nationwide call and petition drive to restore and protect the rights of all Americans and monitor the implementation of frighteningly ill-conceived new state and federal voting "reform" laws.

Four decades ago, the opposition to the civil right to vote was easy to identify: night riders wearing white sheets and burning crosses. Today, the threat comes from partisan politicians wearing pinstripe suits and clutching laptops.

Jim Crow has moved into cyberspace—harder to detect, craftier in operation, shifting shape into the electronic guardian of a new electoral segregation.   [2003]

Understanding the Reading

1. What does the title "Jim Crow Revived in Cyberspace" mean?
2. How exactly were minority voters targeted in this example?
3. How has Congress reacted to this allegation, since the 2000 election?

Suggestions for Responding

1. Make a list of ways minorities have been nonviolently disenfranchised in the United States throughout history.
2. Have a class discussion on how the possibility of computer fraud and improprieties could be eliminated from future U.S. elections. ✦

68

The Negro a Beast . . . or in the Image of God

EARL OFARI HUTCHINSON

I wish Rodney King[1] would read Charles Carroll's *The Negro a Beast or in the Image of God*. He might understand why many white folks said rotten things about him. This is what I mean. In November 1992, King spoke to about seventy-five students at Tustin High School in the mostly white southern California suburban bedroom community of Orange County. This was King's first major public appearance in nearly a year. King, being a modest unassuming man, had purposely kept a low profile.

It didn't help. People still bad-mouthed him. They called him a doper, an alcoholic and a violence-prone ex-convict. Many openly grumbled that King himself had provoked the cops. Some even smirked and whispered that he deserved the ass-whipping. In the Simi Valley trial of the four LAPD[2] cops who beat King, defense attorneys in a bravura performance used this sneaky racism to their advantage and got them off. One unnamed juror said of King, "He was obviously a dangerous person, massive size and threatening actions."

King and his attorney Milton Grimes were fed up with this kind of talk. They figured that high school students would be sympathetic. King, himself a high school dropout, would benignly tell the kids to stay in school. They hoped this would improve his image.

It didn't. The following day, angry readers deluged the *Los Angeles Times* with calls objecting to school officials letting "a dangerous parolee" on a high school campus. The Tustin High School principal felt the heat, back-pedaled fast and claimed it was all a mistake. Sounding properly indignant, he agreed that King was not a suitable "role model."

II

He was "dangerous," of "massive size," "threatening," and "a poor role model." Remember those words as I turn back the pages of history a century and more. Carroll said that and much more about black men in his grotesque little book published in 1900. Reading the passages of his book even without the filter of America's hideous racial past, one might have reason to laugh.

Carroll, however, was dead serious. His book was not published by the Ku Klux Klan in rural Mississippi or Alabama, but by the American Book and Bible House in St. Louis. The book was a brisk seller. Carroll argued that the black man was left out of human creation and was a subspecies of the animal world.

Carroll was not a quack. He did not make any of this up. He considered himself a man of pure science. He based his "theory" on the meticulous research of Alexander Winchell, a distinguished professor of geology and paleontology at the University of Michigan. When the evidence got a little skimpy in some places, Carroll retreated into scripture. He swore that God warned that since creation the world's troubles began when human beings let the Negro "beast" mingle among them.

Carroll had his critics. Georgia theologian W. S. Armstead was indignant that he would dare bring the word of God into this. By calling black men beasts, he felt Carroll was letting them off the hook. Armstead said the black man was a cunning, calculating degenerate who followed his "murderous heart" and brutally "waylaid" white women.

Armstead didn't have much chance against learned men like Carroll and Winchell. They were Northerners and for nearly a half century they had beaten the South to the punch every time when it came to propagating myths about black bestiality.

George Fitzhugh, a Virginia newspaperman, sometime planter and always articulate defender of slavery, was delighted to find that his Northern brethren were very receptive to his views. In 1854, Fitzhugh, in *Sociology for the South,* wrote that "slavery rescued blacks from idolatry and cannibalism, and every brutal vice and crime that can disgrace humanity."

Fitzhugh took his act on the road and headed North. He quickly discovered that many influential power brokers thought that his *Sociology for the South* should be the sociology for the North. Many leading newspapermen quoted him. Businessmen wined and dined him. Some Northern congressman snipped quotes from his writings and placed them into the *Congressional Globe* (later *Record*).

During the Civil War, dozens of Northern newspaper editors and politicians were livid because Old Abe and his Republican political cronies had the audacity to shed white blood to free black savages. At every turn, they raised the bloody flag and tried to sabotage the war effort.

III

The Civil War ended legal slavery, but it did not put the old planters entirely out of business. They still had one big trump card to play: The Black Scare. They played it hard by convincing whites, North and South, that blacks were out to get land, power and white women. Soon men in white sheets silhouetted the night sky with their fiery crosses. Their terror campaign to whip the black beasts back in line was a smashing success.

Reconstruction[3] was dead. The abolitionists who had pricked the conscience of the nation were too old and tired to care anymore. The ranks of the Radicals in Congress were thinning by the hour. And, Northern whites were dead set against risking their necks to fight for the rights of men who they didn't really believe were men.

Meantime, the learned men of the North like Carroll were busy mangling science to shape the image of the black man as criminal, sex crazed, violent and degenerate. Dr. Frank Hoffman, in 1896, backed Carroll to the hilt. Hoffman like Carroll was not a Southerner. In fact, he was not a Northerner. In fact, he was not even an American. Hoffman, writing from Germany, declared that there was such an "immense amount of immorality and crime" among black men it had to be part of their "race traits and tendencies."

The message to worried whites: sit back, relax and let nature take its course. All those decadent black men would soon die out from their own "inferior organs and constitutional weaknesses." Hoffman's wise words were rushed into print by the prestigious American Economic Association (AEA).

Another learned Northerner, Walter F. Wilcox, chief statistician for the U.S. Census Bureau, thought the good doctor had the right

ZEITGEIST. Three years later with the blessing of the American Social Science Association, Wilcox pinned up his charts, juggled figures and solemnly predicted that blacks were "several times" more likely to commit crime than whites. He wasn't finished. The next year he told the social scientists that Hoffman was right. Blacks were doomed to go the way of the Dodo Bird and Dinosaur because of "disease, vice and profound discouragement."

The American Economic Association was on a fast track to get the official words of its scholars out to the public. They rushed Historian Paul Tillinghast's paper on "The Negro in Africa and America" into print. Tillinghast agreed with the other scholars. He cautioned them not to forget that blacks were "seriously handicapped by the inherited conditions" they brought with them from savage Africa.

Around the same time, Dr. G. Stanley Hall was determined not to be outdone by the AEA. The president of the American Psychological Association and founder of the *American Journal of Psychology* thought his fellow academics were putting too much emphasis on "race traits." As a clinician, he believed there were murky forces at work in the black psyche. According to his diagnosis, the black man's "disthesis, both psychic and physical is erethic, volatile, changeable, prone to transcoidal, intensely emotional and even epileptoid states." Buried somewhere between the "erethic" and "transcoidal" gibberish was a hopeless dimwit. The public should be on the alert.

A soon to be president didn't dispute this. In 1901, [Princeton] University Professor Woodrow Wilson in the *Atlantic Monthly* asked what could one really expect of individuals who were really little more than a "host of dusky children," "insolent and aggressive, sick of work, covetous of pleasure."

The line-up of highbrow intellectual magazines that endorsed this gobbledygook read like a roll call of academia. They included *Popular Science Monthly, The Annals of the American Academy of Political and Social Science, Medicine* and the *North American Review*. They all chimed in with volumes of heady research papers, articles and scholarly opinions that "proved" blacks were hopelessly inferior, crime- and violence-prone defectives from which society had to be protected.

IV

Since art does imitate life, it was only a matter of time before this pap crept into the literature. At first, Northern and Southern novelists did not lay it on too thick. The blacks in their stories were mostly grinning, buck-dancing, lazy, slightly larcenous darkies. As the scientists kept up their drumbeat warnings about the black menace, the novelists soon turned vicious. Upton Sinclair had impeccable credentials as a Socialist crusader. Still, in his popular muckraking novel, *The Jungle,* published in 1905, Sinclair was appalled that white girls working in Chicago's hellish stockyards rubbed shoulders "with big black buck Negroes with daggers in their boots."

This was too tame for Thomas Nelson Page. He wasn't a man of subtlety when it came to racial matters. But, first, he had to lay the proper groundwork. In an essay, *The Negro: The Southerner's Problem,* he warned that the old time darkies were dying off and that the "new issue" was "lazy, thriftless, intemperate, insolent, dishonest and without the most rudimentary elements of morality." In his novel, *Red Rock,* he continued to warn of the dangers of the black peril.

Thomas Dixon, Jr., wasn't satisfied with this. Page only talked about the "new issue" Negro. Dixon set out to vanquish him. In his big, sprawling novel, *The Clansman,* published in 1905, Dixon described him as "half child, half animal, the sport of impulse, whim and conceit . . . a being who left to his will, roams at night and sleeps in the day, whose speech knows no word of love, whose passions once aroused, are as the fury of the tiger." It sent collective chills up the spines of much of white America. Bolt the doors. Turn out the lights. Praise the Lord and pass the ammunition. The black beast was coming. In *The Clansman,* Dixon had the right men to defend society and (white womanhood) from this creature, the Ku Klux Klan.

Dixon knew he was on to something big. When *The Clansman* was adapted for the stage, it brought down theater houses everywhere. Audiences were delirious. They had to see the KKK destroy the black beasts. Soon Broadway's great white way picked up on Dixon and made him the toast of New York. *Theater IV,* the trendy magazine of the *haute art* crowd, gave him a free platform to explain "Why I Wrote *The Clansman.*" Dixon swore that he wasn't a bigot

[and] that it was based on "historical authenticity." *The New York Evening Post* was impressed. It praised him for tackling "a question of tremendously vital importance."

Filmmaker D. W. Griffith wanted Americans to know just how important it was. A decade later, he turned *The Clansman* into *Birth of a Nation*. He brushed off vehement protests from the NAACP[4] and black leaders that it was all a lie. He could afford to. By then cash registers were jingling everywhere as the film smashed house records nationally. When the film hit the White House, an ecstatic Woodrow Wilson exclaimed, "It's like writing history with lightning." Griffith wasn't the only filmmaker who sniffed dollars and glory in foisting the black brute's criminal image on the public. Between 1910–1911, these gems graced the screen, *Rastus in Zululand, Rastus and Chicken, Pickaninnies and Watermelon* and *Chicken Thief.*

NOTE: *I always thought it appropriate that these parts were played by white actors in messy cream black face. I knew then who the real toms, coons, mulattos, mammies and bucks were.*

By then, there were many whites who didn't need to read Dixon's novel, or see Griffith's film to know what to do with the "half child, half animal." The year *The Clansman* was published, more than one black person was lynched, burned, shot or mutilated every week in America. The year Griffith's film debuted the weekly lynch toll was still the same.

The NAACP's W. E. B. DuBois bitterly called lynching America's "exciting form of sport." Page was undaunted. He chalked lynching up to the "determination to put an end to the ravishing of their women by an inferior race."

NOTE: *Many people still think that black men were lynched because they committed rape. They weren't. In most cases, they weren't even accused of rape. Even then, the apologists for "the sport" knew this. . . .*

V

Politicians, being politicians, seemed to feel that if the public believed that black men were inherent rapists, then why spoil it with the truth. So, when Teddy Roosevelt rose to address Congress in 1906, lynching was very much on his mind. He sternly lectured that "The greatest existing cause of lynching is the perpetration, especially by black men, of the hideous crime of rape."

The old Rough Rider didn't want anyone to get the idea that he was condoning lynching, [for] after all, it would look a little odd for the man sworn to uphold the law to applaud those who broke it. He obligingly denounced the "lawbreakers." But Teddy had made his point. The *Cincinnati Inquirer* in 1911 railed against black men for committing the "unspeakable crime" and bragged that "the mob is the highest testimony to the civilization and enlightenment and moral character of the people."

The *Inquirer* was not a lone voice. The press, always on the lookout for a sensational story, read the public mood. In the crimson days before the doughboys of World War I marched off to save the world for democracy, the press milked the black beast angle for all it was worth. The *New York Times, Chicago Tribune, Boston Evening Transcript, San Francisco Examiner, Atlantic Monthly* and *Harpers* heisted the lingo from the academics and had great fun ridiculing, lampooning, butchering and assailing black men in articles and cartoons. They were "brutes," "savages," "imbeciles," "moral degenerates," and always "lazy, lazy, lazy." *Century Magazine* claimed it overheard this exchange between two blacks:

Uncle Rastus: "Now dat you daddy too ole to work, why don yah get a job?
Young Rastus: "No! indeed ain't going to have folks say everybody works but father 'bout mah family."

Remember Uncle Rastus was a good ole darkie. The young one, well . . .

The San Francisco Examiner had a word about him and his ilk. In a cartoon a menacing-looking darkie shouts: "Don't be bumping into me, white man. I'se tough, Remembah the Civil War is over I'se tough."

Between World Wars I and II, a few liberals and radicals hoped that the press and the public would knock off the crude stuff and start down the path of racial enlightenment. Black editors knew better. They were still fighting tough battles to get the white press to stop stereotyping black men. Whenever a crime was committed, if a black was involved or suspected, newspapers almost always mentioned it. In case some were slow to make the connection, they would plaster a black face across the page.

NOTE: Black folks, as always, tried to find some humor in the situation. They joked that if a black ever wanted to get the white press to write about them, commit a crime and make sure the victim was white.

The defeat of Hitler and America's ascension to superpowerdom ushered in the American Century. This was supposed to be the era [when] American military might and economic muscle would bring permanent prosperity and freedom to the world. It would be an era when the winds of racial change would end segregation and race hate forever.

For a short while it seemed that blacks might get a little breathing space. The civil rights movement pricked the consciences of many whites. Congress, the White House and the Courts, with varying degrees of enthusiasm, finally relented and eliminated legal segregation. But, with the death of Martin Luther King, Jr., and Malcolm X, the collapse of the civil rights movement, political repression and the self-destruction of black power radicalism, young blacks were organizationally adrift.

Recession and economic shrinkage began to wreak havoc on the black poor. Many whites once again began to use terms about black men that sounded faintly reminiscent of the by-gone days, "law and order," "welfare cheats," "crime in the streets," "subculture of violence," "subculture of poverty," "culturally deprived" and "lack of family values."

By the end of the Reagan years, the language got rougher. The press now routinely tossed around terms like "crime prone," "war zone," "gang infested," "crack plagued," "drug turfs," "drug zombies," "violence scarred," "ghetto outcasts" and "ghetto poverty syndrome." Some, in the press, let it all hang out and called black criminals "scum," "leeches" and "losers." Their pictures routinely began to appear on the front pages, and for some strange reason they were all mostly black males.

NOTE: Why drag up what happened a century ago? Americans don't believe any of this any-

more. On October 31, 1993, two students at Yosemite High School in Oakhurst, a community just south of San Francisco, showed up at the school's Halloween party in Ku Klux Klan costumes. A third student wore black face.

The two students proceeded to stage a mock lynching of the "black." The three self-appointed white Knights may not have known any better. But what about school officials, parents and the other students? The three won prizes for their costumes. Students said it was "cool, like original." The principal took no disciplinary action against them. That's why! [1994]

Terms

1. RODNEY KING: A Black man whose beating by Los Angeles police officers was caught on videotape.
2. LAPD: Los Angeles Police Department.
3. RECONSTRUCTION: The period after the Civil War (1865–1877) during which the states of the Southern Confederacy were controlled by the federal government and forced to reorganize their political and social institutions as a prerequisite to full readmission to the Union.
4. NAACP: National Association for the Advancement of Colored People, a civil rights organization.

Understanding the Reading

1. Explain the purpose of and reaction to Rodney King's appearance at a mostly White high school.
2. What was Charles Carroll's theory about race?
3. Why did W. S. Armstead object to Carroll's book?
4. What was the response to George Fitzhugh's book?
5. What was "The Black Scare"?
6. What arguments were put forward to show that African Americans were doomed?
7. What was *The Clansman* about, and what impact did it have?
8. How did the press of the late nineteenth century treat Black men?
9. Why is late-nineteenth-century racism relevant today?

Suggestions for Responding

1. Try to view the film *Birth of a Nation* and describe your reactions to it.
2. Write a short essay responding to Hutchinson's closing anecdote about the Oakhurst high school Halloween party. ✦

69

Emmett Louis Till, 1941–1955

SOUTHERN POVERTY LAW CENTER

Mamie Till was a devoted, well-educated mother who taught her son that a person's worth did not depend on the color of his or her skin. Nevertheless, when she put 14-year-old Emmett on a train bound for Mississippi in the summer of 1955, she warned him: "If you have to get down on your knees and bow when a white person goes past, do it willingly."

It was not in Emmett Till to bow down. Raised in a working-class section of Chicago, he was bold and self-assured. He didn't understand the timid attitude of his Southern cousins toward whites. He even tried to impress them by showing them a photo of some white Chicago youths, claiming the girl in the picture was his girlfriend.

One day he took the photo out of his wallet and showed it to a group of boys standing outside a country store in Money, Mississippi. The boys dared him to speak to a white woman in the store. Emmett walked in confidently, bought some candy from Carolyn Bryant, the wife of the store owner, and said "Bye baby" on his way out.

Within hours, nearly everyone in town had heard at least one version of the incident. Some said Emmett had asked Mrs. Bryant for a date; others said he whistled at her. Whatever the details were, Roy Bryant was outraged that a black youth had been disrespectful to his wife. That weekend, Bryant and his half-brother J. W. Milam went looking for Till. They came to the cotton field shack that belonged to Mose Wright, a 64-year-old farmer and grandfather of Emmett Till's cousin. Bryant demanded to see "the boy that did the talking." Wright reluctantly got Till

out of bed. As the white men took Emmett Till away, they told Wright not to cause any trouble or he'd "never live to be 65."

A magazine writer later paid Milam to describe what happened that night. Milam said he and Bryant beat Emmett Till, shot him in the head, wired a 75-pound cotton gin fan to his neck and dumped his body in the Tallahatchie River.

When asked why he did it, Milam responded: "Well, what else could I do? He thought he was as good as any white man."

SO THE WORLD COULD SEE

Till's body was found three days later—a bullet in the skull, one eye gouged out and the head crushed in on one side. The face was unrecognizable. Mose Wright knew it was Till only because of a signet ring that remained on one finger. The ring had belonged to Emmett's father Louis, who had died ten years earlier, and bore his initials L.T.

Mamie Till demanded the body of her son be sent back to Chicago. Then she ordered an open-casket funeral so the world could see what had been done to Emmett. *Jet* magazine published a picture of the horribly disfigured corpse. Thousands viewed the body and attended the funeral.

All over the country, blacks and sympathetic whites were horrified by the killing. Thousands of people sent money to the NAACP[1] to support its legal efforts on behalf of black victims.

In the meantime, J. W. Milam and Roy Bryant faced murder charges. They admitted they kidnapped and beat Emmett Till, but claimed they left him alive. Ignoring nationwide criticism, white Mississippians raised $10,000 to pay the legal expenses for Milam and Bryant. Five white local lawyers volunteered to represent them at the murder trial.

Mose Wright risked his life to testify against the men. In a courtroom filled with reporters and white spectators, the frail black farmer stood and identified Bryant and Milam as the men who took Emmett away.

Wright's act of courage didn't convince the all-white jury. After deliberating just over an hour, the jury returned a verdict of not guilty.

The murder of Emmett Till was the spark that set the civil rights movement on fire. For those who would become leaders of that movement, the martyred 14-year-old was a symbol of the struggle for equality.

"The Emmett Till case shook the foundations of Mississippi," said Myrlie Evers, widow of civil rights leader Medgar Evers, ". . . because it said even a child was not safe from racism and bigotry and death."

NAACP Executive Director Roy Wilkins said white Mississippians "had to prove they were superior . . . by taking away a 14-year-old boy."

Fred Shuttlesworth, who eight years later would lead the fight for integration in Birmingham, said, "The fact that Emmett Till, a young black man, could be found floating down the river in Mississippi just set in concrete the determination of the people to move forward . . . only God can know how many Negroes have come up missing, dead and killed under this system with which we live."   [1989]

Terms

1. NAACP: National Association for the Advancement of Colored People.

Understanding the Reading

1. What did Emmett Till do to provoke the White Southerners?
2. What did Bryant and Milam do to Till?
3. What were the charges and the verdict against Bryant and Milam?
4. Nationally, what effect did Till's death produce, and why?

Suggestions for Responding

1. Write a short essay explaining why an incident like this could or could not happen today; support your position with some specific examples. ✦

70

As Media Furor Subsides, Jasper Sorts Out Its Future

KYLE JOHNSON

The politicians and the special-interest groups are moving on now. The TV crews and the newspaper reporters from around the country are packing up their gear as Jasper, Texas, searches for solace and healing, resisting the efforts of others to make it a symbol of skirmishing ground for America's debate over race relations.

Last week's killing of James Byrd, a black man, allegedly by three white men with ties to racist groups, has been called America's most brutal hate crime since the 1955 lynching of black teenager Emmett Till.

The crime, as well as Mr. Byrd's funeral and other events surrounding it, has drawn armed militants from the New Black Panther Party, prompted efforts by the Ku Klux Klan to march, and brought a crush of politicians and civil rights leaders.

Jesse Jackson called for "redemption over retaliation" and urged those here to "turn a crucifixion into a resurrection."

No one in the shell-shocked community of 8,000 believes life can simply go on as usual in the wake of the tragedy. But the healing of Jasper is foremost viewed as Jasper's job to do.

Or, as the Rev. Bobby Hudson put it, "People from outside can come in and stir things up, but when the glare of the media is gone, they'll be gone with it. We still have to figure out how to live here." Mr. Hudson is the minister at the First Baptist Church in nearby Pinewood.

OUTSIDERS' INFLUENCE

Nowhere was the influence of the outside world more acutely expressed than last Thursday at the Greater New Bethel church during the first communitywide prayer vigil for the family.

More than 300 residents wedged into the hall, ablaze with flashbulbs and tangled in electrical wires leading to 12 TV news vans outside. As the Rev. Kenneth Lyons called for a prayer of unity, the hall's public-address system was co-opted by a wireless microphone in the parking lot. For half a minute the prayer was drowned out by a live news report on the district attorney's progress in building a death-penalty case.

The Rev. Mr. Jackson was soon calling for the town to host a national forum as part of President Clinton's race initiative—an offer which was speedily rejected by Hudson (who is black), president of the Jasper County League of Ministers. Jasper's own efforts at healing starts in earnest tonight with a community memorial service. Prayers will be offered and hymns sung. But there'll be no speeches, no platform for special interests.

It will be a moment, hopes Mr. Lyons, when people here can "start getting our city back together." Lyons is pastor of the Greater New Bethel Baptist Church and minister for the Byrd family.

Other steps are being taken. Civic, religious, and business leaders here—black and white—have formed their own 25-member ad hoc task force to discuss ways to begin the healing.

Race relations have historically been strong in Jasper, a town with a 45 percent African American population, where the mayor and two of the five city council members are black.

But the Byrd tragedy points to a responsibility to delve beneath the surface of the issue, said Lyons, who is a member of the city's newly formed task force.

Since the timber industry disappeared three years ago, unemployment has reached 12 percent in Jasper, Lyons said. Whites received a disproportionate share of the jobs that are left, he adds, leaving primarily low-paying, service industry jobs for African-Americans. "If this task force is going to do anything about race, we need to bring new industry in this town. Our educated black men have no future here."

COMPASSION IN JASPER

But those are longer-range considerations, and for the moment it is individual expressions of concern and compassion that count. The father of one of the alleged attackers publicly expressed remorse for what happened. Many whites have reached out to the Byrd family.

"We are Christian, and this community grieves about this," says David Woodall, who owns a dry cleaner's here. "But we need to work together to move forward. All the attention focuses on the tragedy, but we need to move forward to overcome it."

Still, there is recognition that Jasper's story is—and must continue to be—a national story.

"We know coming here that you've wanted to be left alone," said US Transportation Secretary Rodney Slater, who is black. "But we need to be here for ourselves . . . because we can ill afford to have what has happened here happen anywhere else across this land."   [1998]

Understanding the Reading

1. How did our nation respond to the murder of James Byrd?
2. How is the town of Jasper responding to this event?

Suggestions for Responding

1. If you were a resident of Jasper, Texas, what do you think the community should do in the wake of the killing of James Byrd?
2. What should the country do to respond to James Byrd's death? ✦

71

Terror in Our Neighborhoods

THE KLANWATCH PROJECT
OF THE SOUTHERN POVERTY LAW CENTER

Imagine. It's your first night in your new home, on a quiet street where no one knows your name. Every sound seems strange; everything looks and feels different. You think about the children as you try to sleep. Will they like their new school? Will they find new friends?

And then it happens. The sound of a gasoline explosion, the blinding light of flames. You look outside your window and see a cross on fire.

Shock turns to fear, and finally, when the flames have died, to overwhelming sadness. How will you explain this to the children?

You can't believe it still happens.

But it does. It happened to a Chinese-American family in California last year, and a Jewish family in Connecticut. It happened to a 67-year-old black woman in Virginia who lived alone, and to a white woman in New Jersey whose children happen to have a black friend. And it happens to black families and interracial families all over the country.

Not only cross burnings, but vandalism, arsons, threats, and assaults greet minorities who choose to live in mostly white neighborhoods.

"Of all the incidents of hate violence which occur in this country, the terrorism of minorities in white neighborhoods is probably the most common, and the most devastating," said Pat Clark, Director of the Klanwatch Project of the Southern Poverty Law Center. "It destroys the security of families and breeds an environment of mistrust and resentment where there should be community."

Last year, Klanwatch documented a significant increase in the incidence of housing violence—attacks by neighbors upon neighbors because of race, color, religion, or ethnic background. Most of these attacks were directed at minorities who had recently moved into predominantly white neighborhoods. Others were aimed at people who had been living quietly in the neighborhood for years. And a significant number were only the latest in a long series of harassment against the same victims.

"Throughout the 1980s, about a third of the racial violence incidents we tracked were housing-related," said Clark. "Then in 1989, we saw a tremendous increase in neighborhood attacks. By the end of the year, incidents of housing violence accounted for roughly half of all the racial violence incidents we reported. This was particularly alarming because 1989 was also the year we saw a surge in hate violence of all types."

Of 289 hate crimes documented by Klanwatch, 130 were housing-related. "What we have to remember, though," said Clark, "is that the reports we receive are only a sampling of the overall problem. Since there is no national data collection on hate crime, our figures are necessarily incomplete, so we are probably looking at only a fraction of the violence that actually occurred."

The lack of reliable data on hate crimes has always hampered efforts to understand and address the problem of housing violence, but a new law will soon require police agencies to keep track of all bias-motivated crimes. Once the new monitoring procedures are in place, experts believe, the number of documented hate crimes will skyrocket.

The U.S. Department of Justice, the agency charged with implementing the Hate Crimes Statistics Act, has already witnessed a dramatic rise in hate crime cases in its jurisdiction. While all racial violence cases prosecuted by the Justice Department have gone up in recent years, cases involving housing violence have increased at a much higher rate. Statistics for combined fiscal years 1988 and 1989 show that housing violence cases comprised 75 percent of all federally-prosecuted racial violence cases.

HOUSING DISCRIMINATION PERSISTS

The rise in housing violence is clearly related to a hard-core resistance to integrated neighborhoods that has persisted in this country despite decades of racial progress in other areas.

While they may sit beside blacks at work, in schools and in restaurants, many whites still believe they have a right to keep their own neighborhoods segregated. And anyone who attempts to change that pattern of segregation is taking a risk.

The evidence of residential segregation has been substantiated across the country:

- A nationwide *Washington Post* survey conducted in 1989 showed that a third of white respondents believed they should have the right to refuse to sell their homes to blacks, despite federal housing laws that prohibit housing discrimination.
- A 1984 study by the U.S. Department of Housing and Urban Development, based on national and regional audits conducted in 1979, showed that blacks had a 27 percent chance of encountering discrimination in rental housing, and a 15 percent overall

chance of discrimination in real estate sales. (The 15 percent figure does not include instances of "steering," the illegal practice of leading minority buyers or renters away from property in white neighborhoods.) A report scheduled for release by HUD this fall will update the 1979 data.

- A statistical analysis of metropolitan housing patterns conducted by University of Pennsylvania researchers in 1987 showed that between 1970 and 1980, blacks and whites made almost no progress toward integrated living. "Blacks may have won political freedom, and may have made substantial progress in attaining their economic goals, but they have not yet achieved the freedom to live wherever they want."

TERROR AT HOME

The greatest obstacle to that freedom is fear—the terror that comes from being victimized, often many times over, by your own neighbors.

That terror comes in many forms—"KKK" scrawled on the sidewalk, garbage thrown in the front yard, shouts from passing cars, anonymous harassing phone calls, doors painted with swastikas, windows broken.

Sometimes the incidents seem "minor" to an outsider, said Sgt. Bill Johnston, head of the Boston Police Department Bias Investigation Unit. "The mistake I first made, and a lot of people make, is you look at the crime, and you say 'it's only a broken window.'

"But I remember talking to one father of a family that had numerous broken windows. He had bought a house that was going to be his dream house, and during the course of the years it turned into a nightmare. Vandals were trying to force him out. He had already had more than a dozen incidents there, and then one night in February, it happened again. He had one child in the bathroom calling for him, another watching TV, and his wife was in the kitchen preparing dinner. And 18 windows in his house go out at once. His children and his wife started screaming for him, and he didn't know who to run to first. He was just paralyzed."

When Johnston arrived on the scene, he said, the man had tears in his eyes. He asked Johnston to talk to his wife, because his wife was frantically asking him to do something. "Will you explain to her," the man asked Johnston, "that if I go outside that door, I am going to kill somebody or somebody is going to kill me?"

"Until we put our heads inside the broken windows we have no idea how traumatic these incidents are," said Johnston.

SHOCK IS THE FIRST RESPONSE

The first time a family is victimized, their reaction is "almost always extreme surprise," said Patrick Kelly of the Neighbors Network, a volunteer organization that works with housing violence victims in Georgia. "For the most part, victims are hardworking people that think because they are hardworking people that no one would mind where they lived. Often they say, 'we didn't even look to see if all our neighbors were white.'"

Richard Nichols and his wife lived in their Olathe, Mo., home for two years without any trouble. Then someone painted "KKK" on their garage door last Halloween. "It's kind of shocking," said Nichols. "It's something we've seen happen to other people and heard about, but when it happens to you, you feel violated and hurt. It makes you wonder who's out to get you."

A white woman who shared a house with a black coworker in Jacksonville, Fla., said, after a series of vandalisms and a cross-burning, "It's like being raped. I feel just as black as she does."

After her car was doused with paint thinner in a Los Angeles suburb, a black mother of three said, "It makes you paranoid. If I see someone on the street, I don't know if I want to talk to them. It makes me less open."

In families with small children, one of the first concerns of victims is to help their children understand what happened to them and why. Sometimes they understand it all too well. It means they are not wanted.

When racial slurs and threats were painted on the door of Mr. and Mrs. William Cromer's new home on Staten Island, Mrs. Cromer said, "It didn't really get to me but it got to my daughter. Now she is scared to go outside; she said 'you see, there's nobody else here like us.'"

About two-thirds of families who are victimized move, said Kelly. They see initial acts of harassment as warnings of trouble to come, and they are not willing to risk their family's safety.

Former U.S. Marine George Lewis wanted to move his family back to his home of Jackson, Miss., from Florida. He got a job in Jackson and found a brick house big enough for his wife and three children. Then one day, before the family had moved in, Lewis went to check on the house. "When I went to the back, I saw some writing on the outside in some kind of black ink. 'Nigger Go Home.' I couldn't believe it." Lewis quit his job and returned to Florida.

A 32-year-old Portsmouth, Va., man who found his car covered with racial slurs decided to move out of the mostly white neighborhood he was living in. "If somebody is bold enough to come up into my front yard and destroy my car, then the next move is to burglarize my house," said E. Brian Ashton.

Others "feel they have to stay," said Kelly, often as a way of showing their children how to stand up for their rights despite the risks involved.

"It's not something you'd expect in a million years," said another black woman who had a cross burned on her lawn in Modesto, Calif. "I thought Modesto was quiet. But they can come back—we're not leaving." When her home was burned down by arsonists, Audrey Goodwin of Rantoul, Ill., said, "I'm not gonna budge from this spot," and made plans to rebuild the house that she had lived in for 11 years.

ENFORCING THE LAW

Most acts of neighborhood terrorism are covered by a variety of state and federal laws. In addition to the standard criminal charges available for assault, arson, threats and vandalism, the federal Fair Housing Act gives broad protection to minorities who are victims of neighborhood attacks.

The Fair Housing Act, amended last year, outlaws any act designed to intimidate or frighten someone away from a neighborhood because of their race, color, religion, sex, handicap, familial status, or national origin. Violators can be fined up to $1,000 or sentenced to a year in prison, or both; and if bodily injury results the

maximum fine increases to $10,000 and the maximum prison term to ten years. In addition, individual victims may bring civil action under the provision of the federal law.

Despite the laws, many acts of neighborhood terrorism go unprosecuted. Victims often do not report initial incidents, and sometimes simply move away rather than take their battle to court. Others in the neighborhood may be reluctant to provide information on the perpetrators for fear of being the next victim. Police in some areas do not pursue neighborhood terrorism as aggressively as other crimes.

One repeated victim of housing violence in Temperance, Mich., had little help from his local police. Charles Wilder not only had a cross burned at his house last March, but he was also allegedly beaten by police officers. His problems finally got the attention of U.S. Rep. John Conyers, who called for a federal investigation into the case.

Sometimes, the victims themselves are not aware of their housing rights.

"For many recent arrivals to this country," said Boston Police Sgt. Bill Johnston, "civil rights laws aren't even in their vocabulary, and the police don't even find out about the problem until after the second, third or fourth incidents."

MAKING A DIFFERENCE

Better law enforcement, Johnston and others believe, begins with education—not only for communities, but for police as well. A program begun this year by the Boston Police Department sends officers into schools to show videotapes of actual bias crimes and teach children about civil rights laws. So far, 2,000 students in kindergarten through high school have heard the message that bias crimes in Boston will be punished.

In addition, Johnston and Northeastern University sociologist Jack McDevitt conduct training for police around the country in bias crime investigation, and will be advising the U.S. Justice Department in its efforts to establish a national monitoring system.

"No amount of education will stop people from committing hate crimes, as long as there are people who believe the rights they have should not be available to others," said Klanwatch Director Pat Clark. "But better data on the problem, heightened law enforcement attention to housing violations, and community support networks can make a big difference in terms of opening up our neighborhoods to people of all colors, religions and nationalities."

"There's two places you should be able to shut the door and feel secure," said Johnston. "One is your place of worship and the other is your home. No matter how bad the world is out there, you should be able to close your door and say I'm home."   [n.d.]

Understanding the Reading

1. What is the cause of rising housing violence?
2. Why has there been little progress in integrating housing?
3. Why is "minor" damage actually very serious?
4. How do Blacks respond to this harassment?
5. Explain the federal Fair Housing Act.
6. Why is its protection ineffective?
7. What can be done to stop neighborhood harassment and violence?

Suggestions for Responding

1. If a hate crime were committed against your neighbor, how would you respond? If you knew the perpetrator was "an all-right guy" except when he's had a "little too much to drink," what would you do?
2. Compare the kind of incidents discussed here with the experience of the Blacks described by Robert Anthony Watts in Part V. ◆

72

Real Minority, Media Majority

SALIM MUWAKKIL

Chicago cops have just finished a big drug bust on the city's South Side. Local television crews are on hand, taping young black men, their heads bowed and hands cuffed, as they file into the police wagon. Later in the evening, those images will be shown on all the major television stations, filling up TV screens across the Chicago metropolitan area with the sight of young, black offenders.

Such scenes are par for the course on television news programs in major urban areas. But do these images accurately reflect the problems of race and crime in American cities? A number of recent studies show that the media— especially television—often present commonly held stereotypes about blacks, whites and criminal behavior, rather than the more complicated realities. They do so to the great detriment of the black community—and to race relations in general.

African-American men comprise about 6 percent of the U.S. population, yet they represent 51 percent of the prison population, according to the Sentencing Project. Nearly one-third of all black men in their 20s are under the control of the criminal justice system. Black Americans are eight times as likely to be incarcerated as are whites. And in 12 states and the District of Columbia, that ratio is more than 10-to-1. Most are in prison for drug possession or other drug-related crimes.

This difference in incarceration rates is no secret. Most Americans are aware of the disparity, and attribute it to black people being more involved in the drug trade than white people. Thus, most Americans would probably be stumped by this question: What percentage of America's drug users are black? According to a 1996 study by the Justice Department's Bureau of Justice Statistics, 12 percent are black and 70 percent are white—roughly the same as in the population at large.

One reason for this disparate treatment, a number of academics argue, is negative stereotypes projected through the media. William Drummond, a professor of journalism at the University of California-Berkeley, studies how blacks are depicted on television. "News media have taken the lead in equating young African-American males with aggressiveness, lawlessness and violence," he says. "And entertainment media have eagerly taken their cue from journalists." The most common stereotype, says Drummond, "is that African-American men engage in drug abuse in disproportionate numbers."

In a recent article, Drummond cites data from the 1996 Bureau of Justice Statistics survey showing that only 6 percent of African-Americans have used cocaine even once in their lives, and that the great majority of those—65.5 percent—have tried it 10 times or less. Among white respondents, 10.6 percent had used cocaine. "This is not the impression one gets from watching the evening news or even an episode of a television program like *Cops,*" says Drummond.

Why does the media seem to reflect a different notion of reality? For years, television stations have insisted that they are rooting out bias. But old stereotypes die hard, especially those that are useful to reporters as cultural shorthand. When a newscaster described a community as "gang-ravaged," he or she imparts crucial information without having to bother with details or context. "I'll never forget the time a news director sent a camera crew out to tape some welfare mothers in public housing, and one of our more rebellious black cameramen chose to tape white mothers at one of the city's few integrated public housing projects," recalls Monroe Anderson, community affairs director at WBBM-TV, Chicago's CBS affiliate. "He came back with some shots of white welfare mothers and the news director exploded in anger. He didn't want images of white welfare mothers. He wanted footage that was authenticated by traditional stereotypes."

Of course, racial stereotyping of African-Americans has a long history in the United States, going all the way back to the slave codes. But the association of blackness with crime became most prevalent during and immediately after Reconstruction, when whites re-enslaved blacks under the ruthless system of Jim Crow. The legal system was a crucial component of this process. For example, vagrancy laws in many states allowed blacks to be arrested for the "crime" of being unemployed. "After the Civil War, the crime problem in the South became equated with the 'Negro Problem' as black prisoners began to outnumber white prisoners in all southern prisons," writes sociologist Shirley Vinning-Brown. "The terms 'slave,' 'Negro' and 'convict' were interchangeable."

By the late 1880s, when the influence of newspapers began to explode, most of the country's prestigious publications routinely projected vile stereotypes of blacks. When historian Rayford Logan surveyed the popular media from 1901 to 1912, he found that many described African-Americans with words like "brutes," "savages," "imbeciles" and "moral degenerates." Even after Jim Crow laws were firmly in place, the media set out on a mission to protect white Americans from what a February 1905 *Boston Evening Transcript* editorial called the "scourge of black crime." Popular entertainment was no less racist. Thomas Dixon's popular 1905 novel, *Clansman,* glorified the Ku Klux Klan and demonized former slaves. A few years later, D. W. Griffith transformed it into a groundbreaking and immensely popular movie, *Birth of a Nation.*

Although such crude expressions of bias are no longer routine fare, seemingly neutral code words have come to embody many of the same racist assumptions. Terms like "gang-related," "drug turf," "crack plague," "crack babies," "welfare queens" and "inner-city pathologies" impart the same biased message as did the indelicate phrases of the openly racist past. The power of institutional racism lies in its familiarity, normality and indirectness. By popularizing familiar, negative stereotypes, the media become one of the institutions that reinforces racism.

Take, for example, the findings of Children Now, an Oakland, Calif., children's rights organization. Children most often associate positive qualities—financial and academic success, leadership, intelligence—with whites, and associate negative qualities—lawbreaking, financial hardship, laziness, goofy behavior—with minorities, particularly blacks. Children of all races say the news media tend to portray blacks and Latinos more negatively than whites and Asians, particularly when reporting about young people. "You always see black people doing drugs and carrying around drugs, shooting people and stealing things," one white girl told the Children Now researchers.

Amy Jordan, who directs children's television research at the University of Pennsylvania's Annenberg Public Policy Center, says that those results are consistent with other research on minorities and television. Minorities, she argues, are also underrepresented in entertainment television, where they are also more likely to be cast as criminals or buffoons, or as having low-class jobs. Television recycles successful formulas, which often are "rooted in stereotypes," Jordan says.

Fortunately, several organizations are working to change U.S. media coverage. San Francisco State University's Center for Integration and Improvement of Journalism has compiled a list of recommendations. The center argues that news shows should cover a variety of stories about minorities, not just those related to race, and that they should find out how issues affect different segments of society. Reporters and editors should become more familiar with the communities they cover, expand their Rolodexes to include minorities who can provide authoritative opinions on a variety of subjects, and keep an informal checklist of every story's cultural implications. Meanwhile, newsroom management ought to redefine and expand its concept of what constitutes "news," so that they don't only assign negative stories about minorities.

Most experts on the issue agree that the most important factor is to include more African-Americans and other minorities as editors and other decision-makers. Unfortunately, to that end, the American Society of Newspaper Editors (ASNE) recently rescinded its goal of achieving parity between the newsrooms and the African-American population by 2000. Although there has been some progress since ASNE made its commitment, a spokesman for the group conceded that the problem is more difficult than it originally anticipated.

The public representation of "blackness" is a distorted one. African-Americans are routinely portrayed as marginal, deviant members of society. The exceptions to these portrayals—and there have been some—have been insufficient to alter the public's perceptions. Our public language on the problems of race and crime makes it difficult to redress these habits of media stereotyping. But if we don't attend to the issue, those problems will just get worse.   [1998]

Understanding the Reading

1. Why does Muwakkil object to news coverage of crime in American cities?

2. What percentage of drug users in the United States are Black and what percentage are White?
3. What percentage of Blacks have ever used cocaine and what percentage of Whites have?
4. What racial stereotypes did the Children Now study reveal?

Suggestions for Responding

1. Watch local television news for a week and tabulate the proportion of Black law violators to White and/or other ethnic groups.
2. Similarly tabulate the proportion of positive and negative news stories about minorities.
   ✦

73

Subtle vs. Overt Racism

David K. Shipler

In Washington recently, after a panel discussion on race, a black attorney approached me with the following story. He had just headed a project for a federal agency. Midway through the work, one of his subordinates, a white woman, had confided to several other whites that she could not bear to take orders from a black person.

The whites, one of whom had been regarded by the black attorney as a friend, said nothing to him about her remark. Not until months later, toward the end of the project, did the friend finally inform him of the white woman's bias, and he then realized that the woman had been quietly sabotaging the work. The Federal agency dismissed her.

Incidents like this pockmark the surface of America, but they're rarely visible. Usually, whites camouflage their prejudices more deftly and are seldom fired for them. Here, however, the contradictory contours of the country's racial landscape were in plain view. On the one hand, a black man had risen to be the boss, and the white woman lost her job for acting out her bigotry—testimony to the anti-racism that has evolved since the civil rights movement.

But hidden roots of racial prejudice and tension were revealed: The white woman said what many whites feel but do not say—that blacks in authority make them uncomfortable. And many whites, like the black attorney's friend, are paralyzed into silence by others' expressions of racism. Where was the white friend's loyalty to the black boss? Had the friendship survived? I asked the black man. "We're working on it," he said.

COMPLICATIONS

The United States now finds itself in an era of race relations more complex than in the days of legal segregation. Bigotry then was blatant, so entrenched that it could be shattered ultimately only by the conscience of the country and the hammer of the law. Today, when explicit discrimination is prohibited and blatant racism is no longer fashionable in most circles, much prejudice has gone underground. It may have diminished in some quarters, but it is far from extinct. Like a virus searching for a congenial host, it mutates until it finds expression in a belief, a statement, or a form of behavior that seems acceptable.

The camouflage around such racism does not make it benign. It can still damage life opportunities. Take the durable, potent stereotype of blacks as unintelligent and lazy.

In 1990, when the National Opinion Research Center at the University of Chicago asked a representative sample of Americans to evaluate various racial and ethnic groups, blacks ended up at the bottom. Most of those surveyed across the country labeled blacks as less intelligent than whites (53 percent); lazier than whites (62 percent); and more likely than whites to prefer being on welfare than being self-supporting (78 percent).

Much of this prejudice is no more than a thought, of course. To inhibit the translation of biased thoughts into discriminatory actions, American society has built a superstructure of laws, regulations, ethics and programs that include affirmative action and diversity training. Still, images manage to contaminate behavior, often subtly and ambiguously.

It happens in the Air Force, explained Edward Rice, a black B-52 pilot who was a lieutenant colonel and a White House Fellow when I met him several years ago. I asked him why, despite the military's exemplary record of opening doors to minorities, only about 300 of nearly 15,000 pilots in the Air Force were black. This shapes careers, since key commands are barred to Air Force officers who are not pilots. Why do many blacks wash out of flight school?

Rice offered a theory. In the cockpit with a black trainee, a white flight instructor must make split-second decisions about when to take control of the aircraft. If he thinks the trainee is flying dangerously, he will grab the stick. If in the back of the instructor's mind there lurks that age-old, widely held suspicion that blacks are less intelligent and less capable, perhaps he will move just a little more quickly to take control from a black trainee than from a white. And if he does that repeatedly, Rice noted, the black will not advance to the next level of training.

Consider another example. A white couple in northern California adopted a biracial girl as an infant. Their two biological children, both boys, were close in age, so all three youngsters attended the same high school at around the same time. When the white boys fell behind in class, notes and calls came home from teachers. But when the biracial girl had academic problems, there were no notes or calls. She looked black and hung out with black friends, and her parents concluded that the teachers had written her off.

Those teachers did not wear white hoods and stand in the schoolhouse door. They came from the mainstream of white America, where the images of blacks as less capable run strongly just beneath the surface of polite behavior. Even in the finest integrated schools across the country, I found black youngsters, pushed hard by their parents, who complained that white teachers made insufficient demands on them, assumed that they would be satisfied with less than A's, and discouraged them from taking honors courses or applying to top colleges.

ECHOES OF THE PAST

Decoding such encrypted racism is an uncertain art that requires a sense of history—the history of racial stereotyping in America—and a capacity to listen and observe how frequently the present echoes the past.

Many institutions that look integrated, for example, are often segregated within, for integration has largely meant the mere physical mixing of people of various races, not the sharing of power and the blending into an integral whole. Therefore, blacks who enter mostly white institutions often feel like invited guests—and not always very welcome guests—who are there at the pleasure of the whites. Rarely do the blacks attain ownership, authority, or the standing to set agendas. They are confronted by glass walls that whites often do not see.

A black man worked for IBM for three years before learning that every evening a happy hour was taking place in a nearby bar. Only white men from the office were involved—no women, no minorities. Had it been strictly social it would have been merely offensive. But it was also professionally damaging, for business was being done over drinks, plans were being designed, connections made. Excluded from that network, the black man was excluded from opportunity for advancement, and he left the job.

This is a common experience among blacks and women who have integrated the workplace, and it raises questions about possible remedies. Two come to mind: affirmative action and diversity training.

Assume that the white men at the happy hour are not extreme racists, do not decide deliberately to exclude blacks and don't think about the implications of their gatherings at the bar. They go to the bar with people with whom they are most comfortable, and the most comfortable are people like themselves.

If an affirmative action plan were in place, promotions into management would be monitored by race and gender, and the marginalization of minorities and women—whether intentional or not—would become a matter of concern.

Just calling attention to the problem could be enough to make the white men conscious of the need to consider the black man for promotion. They might even reflect on how to bring him into the loop. Beyond that, diversity workshops, where office dynamics are discussed and minority employees can be heard, would highlight the happy hour as a tool of exclusion.

The difficulty is that one has to perceive the problem to embrace the solutions. If you think that racism isn't harmful unless it wears sheets or burns crosses or bars blacks from motels and restaurants, you will support only the crudest anti-discrimination laws and not the more refined methods of affirmative action and diversity training. If you recognize how subtle racism can be, the subtler tools seem appropriate.

One of the great divides in the country is between those Americans who see only blatant racism and those who see the subtle forms as well. It is such a fundamental disagreement that it has shaped much of the current debate over affirmative action.

Opponents of affirmative action believe that prejudice and discrimination have diminished enough to have leveled the playing field for non-whites. The argument holds that affirmative action introduces unfairness and demeans non-whites by suggesting that they could not succeed without it.

FEELING BRANDED

Every solution, however, creates at least one new problem, and affirmative action is no exception. It is designed in principle to require that the best candidates be recruited from groups that have suffered discrimination. Nothing in the concept calls for the acceptance of unqualified people. Yet some managers have been so skittish about lawsuits or so eager to prove themselves non-racist that they have pushed certain black employees into jobs where they have foundered. That has played to the age-old stereotype of blacks as less competent than whites.

Many blacks complain about being branded with an assumption that without affirmative action they would not be in this college or on that construction crew or in that corporate office. Occasionally that reinforces self-doubt. A few black students at Princeton told me that when papers came due and exam time approached, they wondered if they really belonged at such a demanding school.

But it is wise to remember that these doubts—and even blacks' self-doubts—have existed for generations, since long before desegregation and affirmative action. The assumption that blacks were less able was a major reason that affirmative action was needed to overcome the obstacles to admitting, hiring and promoting them.

The old stereotype of blacks as unintelligent and lazy remains a constant as the remedy changes, and the constant hangs itself on whatever hook happens to be available. Before, it was said that blacks were unqualified and therefore weren't hired. Now, the argument goes, blacks are unqualified but are hired because they're black—same belief, different outcome.

If we have to choose—and apparently we do—it is the outcome that matters more than the belief. Would the black student rather be at Princeton and be thought less competent, or be thought less competent and *not* be at Princeton? Before affirmative action, Princeton and other top colleges admitted precious few blacks.

Another key criticism of affirmative action holds that it works against more qualified whites. Here again, the assumption is that whites are more qualified than blacks. Polls and focus groups have found that while most whites think that under affirmative action less qualified blacks are hired and promoted over more qualified whites, most blacks think that *without* affirmative action, less qualified *whites* are hired and promoted over more qualified *blacks*. Both sides want fairness, but each has a different notion of how to achieve it.

Surveys show that few whites can cite personal experience to justify their fears. With the total black population at just 13 percent, and a smaller percentage of blacks in a position to compete for jobs covered by affirmative action, the chance of edging out a more qualified white is slim. Moreover, even when a white person thinks he has been passed over for a less qualified black, he may be wrong. Some supervisors admit that they have told whites whom they didn't want to hire or promote, "I'd love to take you, but I've got to take a black—you know how it is." It's easier than telling the applicant that he doesn't measure up.

THE BOTTOM LINE

Paradoxically, just as affirmative action is being chipped away by the courts, legislators, and by voters in referendums, it is putting down deeper roots in colleges, corporations and government

agencies. In many places, institutional ethics have evolved to the point where an all-white workforce or management team is automatically seen as inadequate and a diverse staff is seen as beneficial. The rationale has shifted from altruism to pragmatism, from high-minded compassion to bottom-line competition.

Business, for example, looks at the demographics of its potential employees and of its customers and reasons that it must diversify racially to profit. Colleges look at the world for which they're preparing students and conclude that a homogeneously white setting does not provide the best education. It may be sad, but morality is less potent than self-interest.

For the last 20 years, the military has managed race relations by emphasizing behavior, not beliefs. "You can think anything you want—that's your business," the military says to its members. "But what you do is our business. If you act in ways that deny opportunity on the basis of race, you interfere with the cohesiveness of the unit, and it becomes the concern of the service."

As practical as this is, it is a bit of a false dichotomy. Thoughts and actions interact with each other, cause each other, reinforce each other. And to assess behavior across racial lines, you have to keep coming back to beliefs as a reference point. It is not an institution's role to enforce certain beliefs on its students or employees, but in addressing racial dynamics the entrenched stereotypes need to be kept in mind. They illuminate and explain the actions.

Getting at the stereotypes requires some acknowledgement that whites benefit from racial prejudice, even as society suffers as a whole. Few white Americans reflect on the unseen privileges they possess or the greater sense of worth they acquire from their white skin. In addition to creating the traditional alignments of power in America, negative beliefs about blacks tend to enhance whites' self-esteem.

If blacks are less intelligent, in whites' belief, then it follows that whites are more intelligent. If blacks are lazier, whites are harder working. If blacks would prefer to live on welfare, then whites would prefer to be self-supporting. If blacks are more violent, whites are less violent—and the source of violence can be kept at a safe distance.

Many conservatives these days urge us to make an "optimistic" assessment of the racial situation. At the same time, they refuse to see the pernicious racism that persists. That blindness does not justify optimism. Legitimate optimism comes from facing the problems squarely and working to overcome the insidious subtleties of bigotry that still abide in the land.   [1998]

Understanding the Reading

1. What is the point of the Black attorney's story about the White woman employee?
2. Why didn't the Black attorney's White friend tell him about the woman's bias?
3. Why does Edward Rice think so few Air Force pilots are Black?
4. Why is it significant that the Black IBM male employee wasn't included in the happy hour?
5. How does Shipler evaluate affirmative action programs and why?
6. Why do many colleges, businesses, and government agencies apply affirmative action even when they are not legally bound to?

Suggestions for Responding

1. Write a letter to Shipler, adding support for or arguing against his thesis about racism.
2. Do you think affirmative action is a good or bad policy? Why? Be specific. ✦

74

Blacks Feel Indignities

ROBERT ANTHONY WATTS

Joe Reed grew up in the birthplace of the civil rights movement, hearing haunting stories from his relatives about the horrors of segregation.

But when Reed considers the impact of racism on his life, his mind moves north from Montgomery, Ala., to the corridors of power of Congress, where he began working as a legislative aide this year.

Reed repeatedly was stopped by lobbyists sponsoring receptions and asked to produce identification, while white aides walked in without question. Sometimes, he was turned away, told the gatherings were restricted to members of Congress, then learned later that was a lie.

"It makes you angry," says Reed, who is 23. "It makes you feel second class. No matter how far you go, no matter how well-dressed you are, you're still black."

For many black Americans, these kinds of snubs and slights are common experiences in restaurants, stores and social settings.

Usually subtle and almost never involving slurs, the incidents are far less obvious than Jim Crow laws that prevailed in the South three decades ago.

But still, many blacks say, such behavior is jarring, leads to simmering anger and widens the racial divide in America. They say they rarely share the slights with white friends and co-workers, fearing they'll be considered overly sensitive.

• • •

In one of the most notable examples, some blacks contend they were given poor or no service at restaurants run by the Denny's chain and asked to pre-pay for their meals.

Six black Secret Service agents filed suit against the chain in May, alleging that they were waited on, then ignored and not served, while white agents sitting nearby in the Annapolis, Md., outlet received prompt service.

The agents' lawsuit came on the heels of a similar suit filed by 32 blacks in California against Denny's, which has signed a non-discrimination settlement in which it admitted no wrongdoing. The chain did, however, say it would stop certain practices, such as asking customers in some restaurants to pre-pay.

Dr. Carl Bell, a Chicago psychiatrist known for his work on racism, says such behavior is called "micro-insults" or "micro-aggressions." The experiences can be particularly frustrating for blacks, he says, because they are so personal and subjective.

"How do you prove that someone jumped in line in front of you?" Bell said. "You go into a store and look at a suit, the guy takes you to the cheapest suits in the store. How can you prove racial bias in that? It's not hard evidence. . . .

White people can blow you off and say, 'No, you're just touchy.' And you walk away feeling, maybe I was."

But in Reed's case, one of his white colleagues, Ken Mullinax, also noticed the difference in treatment on Capitol Hill. Both men worked for U.S. Rep. Earl Hilliard, an Alabama Democract, before Reed left to start law school at the University of Pittsburgh.

"It's weird," said Mullinax, who often was the lone white among Hilliard aides attending the receptions. "We all go together, and every time, they let me walk right in."

But black aides "are always stopped and questioned," he said. "It has happened so many times now, I can't think it's anything else but a black-white issue.

Reed said snubs continued in the receptions, where lobbyists seemed reluctant to shake his hand, uninterested in what he has to say and more attentive to white aides.

"Sometimes you almost want to cry, but you start to believe it sometimes," he said. "You start to feel like, 'Is there really something wrong with me?'"

• • •

Many blacks—especially those who grew up under segregation—say such modern-day insults, even subtle ones, are jolting because they occur at moments when they feel they have escaped the burden of race.

"As bad as segregation is, the rules are clear," said Melvin Sikes, a retired black psychologist in Austin, Texas, who still is angry over an experience three years ago with a cab driver. "If you are prepared to be hit—even if you are hit—you know how to absorb it. This, you don't know how to deal with."

Sikes and his wife, Zeta, say their 1990 anniversary weekend was ruined when a cab driver bypassed them and picked up a white couple.

After returning from a wonderful celebration aboard a dinner train in nearby San Antonio, the couple had walked to the street to hail a cab. A white couple came up behind them, Sikes said, and agreed to wait for a second cab.

But when the first cab arrived and Sikes reached to open the door for his wife, the cab rolled past, he said, pulling up to the white couple, who, after a short exchange with the driver, climbed inside.

"Had it been 20 years ago, it wouldn't have bothered me, because that was the story of my life," said Mrs. Sikes, 75, who grew up at a time when blacks couldn't vote in Texas. "But in 1990, I certainly didn't expect that."

Unable to forget the experience, the couple cut short a planned stay out of town and returned home.

• • •

Michael Thurmond, a lawyer and former chairman of the Black Caucus in the Georgia Legislature, remembers the sting of leaving an elegant reception for lawmakers at the Ritz-Carlton hotel in Atlanta last year and being asked by an elderly white woman, and then her husband, to retrieve their car.

Thurmond, dressed in a $250 tailor-made blazer, white shirt and silk tie, was standing by the hotel door waiting for his car when the wife approached him. Thurmond says he politely told her he was not an employee.

But when her husband asked moments later, Thurmond angrily snapped at the man, who stammered an apology and nervously walked away.

"I was really ticked," Thurmond said. "Here I am being entertained upstairs as chairman of the black caucus with all these business people trying to shake your hand, and you come downstairs and get mistaken for a parking attendant."

[1993]

Understanding the Reading

1. How was legislative aide John Reed treated in Congress?
2. How did Denny's treat six Black Secret Service agents?
3. What is a "micro-insult" or "micro-aggression"?
4. How did Ken Mullinax react to the treatment of his Black colleague?
5. What indignity did Melvin Sikes experience?
6. Describe Michael Thurmond's experience at an Atlanta hotel.

Suggestions for Responding

1. How do you think Blacks should respond to "micro-insults"?

2. Compare and contrast the incidents described here with those Cofer describes in "The Myth of the Latin Woman: I Just Met a Girl Named Maria." ✦

SUGGESTIONS FOR RESPONDING TO PART V

1. Research and report on a specific example of racism in American history, such as the Cherokee removal and the Trail of Tears, anti-Semitic quotas in admission to colleges such as Harvard in the 1920s, restrictive covenants, the "scientific" studies that "proved" racial inferiority on the basis of such characteristics as brain size and physique, or the treatment of Mexican citizens under the treaty of Guadalupe-Hidalgo.

2. Investigate a minority "first," such as baseball player Jackie Robinson; athlete James Thorpe; Harriet Tubman, the "Moses" of the Underground Railroad; Virginia governor Eugene Wilder; Arctic explorer Matthew Henson; Rosa Parks, the woman whose arrest prompted the Montgomery Bus Boycott; Olympic athlete Jesse Owens; Olympic gold medalist Kristi Yamaguchi; Supreme Court Justice Thurgood Marshall; tennis champion Arthur Ashe; heavyweight boxing champion Joe Lewis; poet Phillis Wheatley; Jean Baptiste Point du Sable, founder of Chicago; Nobel Peace Prize winner Ralph Bunche; congressional representatives Hiram Fong and Daniel Inouye; Academy Award winner Sidney Poitier; Springfield, Ohio, mayor Robert C. Henry; Senator Edward Brooke; Dr. Daniel Hale Williams, the physician who performed the first open-heart surgery; or any of the many others. Report on their achievements, and focus on the racial barriers they faced and overcame.

3. Imagine you are a member of a different race, and write an autobiography in which you analyze the impact that your new race has on your opportunities and accomplishments.

4. Research how the stereotype of one racial or ethnic group in America evolved—for example, the image of Native Americans as noble savages evolving into the drunken Indian or the inscrutable Chinese into the model minority. Analyze how historical contexts influenced the various characterizations and how each variation benefited the dominant culture.

5. In American society, it is almost impossible not to be affected in some way by racism. Write a critical analysis of a manifestation of your own racism.

VI

Power and Sexism

SCARCELY MORE THAN A GENERATION AGO, TRADI-tional gender roles were accepted as natural, normal, even inevitable. Men were expected to be strong, unemotional, aggressive, competitive, and devoted to concerns of the outside world; women were to be gentle, emotional, passive, nurturing, and devoted to home and family. Those who violated these norms were labeled deviant. A man whose eyes appeared to moisten in public was immediately perceived as less than fully qualified to be U.S. president. An ambitious middle-class woman who wanted more than a domestic role was declared by psychiatrists to be suffering from a psychological personality disorder.

The word *sexism* did not exist until forty years ago. In the early 1960s, everyone assumed that women had the same rights and opportunities that men had and that they were content with their domestic role, caring for their homes and families. Magazines, movies, television, school textbooks, church leaders, politicians—every-one, everywhere, including most women—extolled the virtues of the traditional division of labor: man the breadwinner and woman the homemaker.

However, economic reality was already mak-ing this ideal more and more difficult for White, middle-class women to maintain. Increasingly, they had to work outside the home, but working women were also expected to continue to serve as wife and mother. In the workplace, however, they were restricted in the kinds of jobs they could get. Newspapers printed ads under sepa-rate "Help Wanted—Male" and "Help Wanted—Female" listings, shunting even women with col-lege degrees, for example, into secretarial rather than professional positions. Paying less for women's work was considered natural because men were regarded as the family breadwinners.

In 1963, Betty Freidan published *The Femi-nine Mystique,* in which she investigated the unhappiness and malaise that haunted the well-educated suburban homemaker. Suddenly, everybody began talking about the "woman problem." Women organized **consciousness raising groups,** where they shared their ex-periences as women. Simple as this sounds, this sharing almost immediately altered the way people saw the gendered social system. Prob-lems previously regarded as personal were re-vealed to be part of a larger web of social limi-tations that society imposed on women simply because of their sex.

The value of women and a women-centered perspective and the advocacy of social, political, and economic equality for both women and men became the widely accepted and widely debated platform of modern **feminism.** Scruti-nizing every facet of society through a feminist lens revealed that fundamental gender inequal-ity was (and still is) embedded in the entire social system. The system was exposed as **patriarchal,** meaning that it is hierarchical and that its structures of power, value, and culture are **androcentric;** that is, they are male-centered and male-dominated. Every aspect of society—employment, education, religion, media, law, economic arrangements, and even the family—reinforced and maintained men's social superiority and women's social inferiority and subordination.

As soon as feminist analysis exposed the inherent inequities of this system, women organized to change it. Equating the position of all women with that of Blacks, they coined the term *sexism* to emphasize the correspondence between racism and the discriminatory treatment to which women were subjected. **Sexism** is the subordination of an individual woman or a group of women and the assumption of the superiority of an individual man or a group of men, based solely on sex. Like racism, sexism is reflected in both individual and institutional acts, decisions, habits, procedures, and policies that neglect, overlook, exploit, subjugate, or maintain the subordination of an individual woman or all women.

Feminist activism throughout the past forty years has changed society dramatically. Textbooks from basal readers to medical volumes are scrupulously edited to eliminate blatant sexism and gender stereotyping. Women today have access to higher education and professional training, and they are represented in nearly every occupation from carpentry and mining to the clergy and the securities market. Men are more likely to share housework and child-care responsibilities. Advertisements present women taking business trips (other than to the supermarket) and climbing telephone poles.

These changes have led many of us to believe that women in the United States have come closer to achieving equality with men than most other women in the world. In fact, however, when it comes to women's nonagricultural wage as a percentage of men's, the United States ranks behind thirty other countries—including Hungary, Tanzania, Vietnam, Jordan, Zambia, and most of western Europe. In 1995, American women earned 75 percent of what men earned, even when the comparisons were adjusted for education and experience. Moreover, the current

ratio of male corporate executive officers (CEOs) to female CEOs in the 1,000 largest U.S. companies is 997 to 3. Thus, despite the progress that has been made, sexism continues to exist in many forms, as the readings in Part VI reveal.

Because our culture tends to view the world in dualistic terms—that is, in an either-or framework—we hold to the belief that everyone is either male or female. Moreover, because White, middle-class, heterosexual men are dominant and the traditional norms of society are based on their lives, experiences, and values, members of other social categories are judged by male standards, and individuals having different characteristics are devalued. In the first reading of Part VI, Jackson Katz and Sut Jhally explain that professional wrestling's greatest threat is not that it teaches violence but that it presents a "multiplexed model for success." Andrew Sullivan argues "The Conservative Case for Gay Marriage" as gay marriage arrives in the Western Hemisphere—Canada and Massachusetts. He points out that this change in law is promoting exclusive love of two people, responsible families, and a greater personal investment of gay individuals in U.S. society. As Martha Burk and Kirsten Shaw show, movies, advertising, television, and music all exploit and degrade women, making gender-specific violence seem acceptable.

In "Gender Warriors Fight the Wrong Battle," Laura Sessions Stepp brings us into the arguments of education and public policy leaders about which sex is getting shortchanged in higher education. Does the fact that there are more women than men on U.S. college campuses mean that women have advanced at the expense of men, or are there increasing opportunities for everyone? As the gay marriage debate gets louder, Andrew Sullivan, a gay Catholic, writes in "Losing a Church, Keeping the Faith" about his reaction when a gay couple, who have sung in the choir for twenty-five and thirty-two years, are told they may no longer be part of the choir. Students can decide whether this is a decision made according to theological doctrine or is a political one.

The next three readings elaborate on the thesis that sexism is intricately woven into our society. Kathleen Sharp describes the illegal inequities between women's and men's school sports programs, despite Title IX of the Education

Amendments, which requires equity. Then, Susana McCollom argues that current self-help books and antidepressants exploit the negative stereotype that there is something inherently wrong with women. Katrine Ames describes how women's health issues have been ignored and how the claim that female hormones complicate research projects is used to justify this exclusion, a striking example of the principle of male-as-norm.

One of the most serious problems women face in the workplace is **sexual harassment,** which is unwanted, unsolicited, and nonreciprocated sexual behavior or attention. The testimony by Anita Hill before the Senate Judiciary Committee finally brought this issue fully into the public awareness. She contested the qualifications of Clarence Thomas to serve on the United States Supreme Court, charging that he had sexually harassed her when she worked for him at the Equal Employment Opportunity Commission. In her article, she shares her understanding of the impact such harassment has had on the women who responded to her presentation.

Sexist attitudes and beliefs and homophobia continue to be challenged on many fronts. Barbara Trees describes how women trying to break into the building trades still have to endure extreme sexual harassment and humiliation simply to keep their jobs.

Sexism is prevalent beyond the workplace and affects even our most intimate relationships. Because aggressiveness and control are the central features of the traditional male gender role and passivity and weakness are the central features of the traditional female role, the potential for aggression and violence against women is built into traditional male-female relationships. **Violence** is the use of physical force to control the behavior of another person, to compel him or her to follow a certain course of action or enforced inaction, to coerce him or her into acting or thinking in whatever way the person with power dictates, and to leave the victim with no alternative except compliance. In other words, violence—physical, verbal, emotional, and sexual—is used to enforce the dominance of the perpetrator and the subordination of the victim.

The following two selections address the issues of battery, what is often referred to as *domestic violence* or *spousal abuse* but which is more accurately labeled *wife beating.* Wife beating is the most common and least reported crime in this country, afflicting women of all races and classes. According to FBI statistics, a woman is beaten by her husband or partner every eighteen seconds. As Mariah Burton Nelson reports, wife beating seems almost built-in to sports culture, which uses the degradation of women to affirm the masculinity of its participants. Furthermore, battery is not confined to marital relationships. Nancy Worcester reports on violence against adolescent women and its effects on the victims, particularly on their self-esteem; Worcester insists that society must recognize this problem and work to rectify it.

In "Why Doesn't She Just Leave?" Clarethia Ellerbe brings us face-to-face with specific methods of controlling a woman in an intimate relationship, with and without the threat of physical violence. The author first interviews an aunt, who had been in a physically violent marriage for almost forty years. Next, she interviews a man who straightforwardly explains his methods of being a "controller": "I start by building her ego. . . send her flowers. . . . She now opens up. . . . I listen to every word she has to say. . . . This is my opportunity to find out which of her girlfriends or family members has the strongest influence on her. . . . I start planning how to eliminate that person from her circle. . . ." It is an unforgettable window into the insidiousness of emotional and psychological abuse.

Violence and fear of violence control all women's behavior. The threat of **rape,** of being forced to have sex without consent, keeps every woman from moving freely wherever she wants and from dressing however she likes. A woman learns to be cautious about every man she encounters, even if she already knows him. The threat is real. A woman is raped every six minutes, and one out of every three women will be raped in her lifetime. Studies of college-age men have revealed that up to half of them thought they might commit a rape if they could be sure of getting away with it. Notwithstanding the frequency with which this crime occurs, rape victims are still treated with skepticism, even by friends and family. If a rape survivor decides to press charges against her attacker and the case goes to trial, the defense may try to introduce her behavior into the proceedings and may well claim that she enticed her assailant or that she wanted or enjoyed it.

The next four selections address this issue. One of the most important points James A. Doyle makes is that rape is an act of dominance, not sex; he explains why, despite general recognition of this fact, society tends to **blame the victim,** accusing her of being somehow responsible for what was done to her. Doyle also examines how **pornography,** which links violence against women with sexuality, contributes to the degradation of women. In the next reading, Kathleen Hirsch analyzes fraternity gang rape; she sees it as the effort of young men to establish their heterosexual identity and to create male bonds at the expense of women. She also contends that the tendency of universities to protect the perpetrators more than the victim silences women—the victim herself *and* all women on campus. On a lighter note, the anonymous sketch "'The Rape' of Mr. Smith" tellingly exposes the injustice of our societal attitudes toward and treatment of rape victims. Next, Anne Finger discusses the mistreatment of people with disabilities, from sexual assault and rape to legal and psycho-sexual assault and denial.

Erica Goode then alerts us to the fact that the federal government is threatening not to fund scientific research grants that contain certain words, such as *homosexuality*. Here, the politics of sexuality (as seen by the U.S. government) has extended into epidemiology, threatening to set scientific research agendas.

The final two readings in Part VI examine the issue of **sexual orientation,** an individual's physical and/or emotional attraction to members of the same sex **(homosexuality)** or both sexes **(bisexuality),** as well as the other sex **(heterosexuality). Heterosexism** is the cultural assumption that heterosexuality is the only natural and proper sexual behavior. In our society, homosexuality and bisexuality present a challenge to gender identity, one's personal sense of maleness or femaleness. That identity rests on the acceptance and internalization of appropriate and stereotypic gender behavior. Homosexuals are thought of as violating these stereotypes: The lesbian stereotype emphasizes a woman's presumed mannishness, whereas the stereotype of the gay man represents him as effeminate and womanish.

The hostility created by the perceived homosexual threat to the "normal" heterosexual order is generally referred to as **homophobia,** fear of being labeled homosexual and hatred of homosexuals.

On somewhat more optimistic notes, Lindsy Van Gelder shares her experiences as a lesbian mother and how she and her partner dealt with their neighbors and their children's school and friends. Randy Shilts looks at another kind of discrimination, the military's anti-gay regulations, and his report makes clear just how arbitrarily they are enforced for the sake of expedience. As mentioned in Part III, in the past decade, 10,000 homosexuals have been discharged from military service in the United States for being gay. In 2003, in the middle of a war with Iraq, thirty-seven linguists were discharged for the same reason, including the much-needed Arabic linguists.

Today, it is not fashionable to express racist and, to a lesser extent, sexist attitudes. Although racism and sexism may have become less visible recently, both remain well entrenched in our culture and within ourselves. They continue to distort our perceptions of one another and to impair our interpersonal behavior. They constrict the educational, economic, social, and cultural opportunities of people of color, women, and gay men and lesbians. Bad as this situation is, even worse is the use of law and violence to oppress some groups and to serve the interests of others.

75

Manhood on the Mat

JACKSON KATZ AND SUT JHALLY

As professional wrestling explodes in popularity, cultural analysts are struggling to catch up to its significance for society. The traditional ways of seeing it—for example, as a morality play of good vs. evil—have been transcended, as wrestling has morphed into perhaps the ultimate expression of the entertainment industry's new, multiplexed model for success.

Vince McMahon, head of the World Wrestling Federation, describes it as "contemporary sports entertainment which treats 'professional wrestling' as an action/adventure soap opera. With the sexuality of '90210,' the subject matter of 'NYPD Blue,' the athleticism of the Olympics, combined with reality-based story lines, the WWF presents a hybrid of almost all forms of entertainment and sports combined in one show." Add to that the fertile brew of traditional advertising, product merchandising, and frequent pay-per-view special events and the result is revenue in the tens of millions of dollars, not to mention a forceful new strain of sports entertainment.

But understanding pro wrestling's immense popularity, especially with (white) men and boys, requires viewing it in the broader context of shifting gender relations.

The accomplishments of social movements such as feminism, as well as the shift to a postindustrial, high-tech era of automated production and e-commerce, have challenged the culture to construct new definitions of masculinity. In the new social, cultural, and employment context, there is less emphasis on characteristics such as strength and physicality that, in an earlier age, not only clearly defined men and women in very different ways, but made masculinity dominant.

In threatened response, many men have retreated into the safe and cartoonish masculinity of a more primal gender order, a world typified by the wildly popular program "WWF Smackdown!" where size, strength, and brutality are rewarded. In wrestling's contemporary incarnation, it's not who wins and loses that matters, but how the game is played. And the way the game is played in the WWF and its companion league, World Championship Wrestling, or WCW, reinforces the prime directive—might makes right, with extreme violence defining how power is exercised.

In the past, discussions about wrestling's effects on "real world" violence have typically centered on the behavioral effects of exposure to it. Does it cause imitative violence?

But that misses the point. For the question is not, "Are children imitating the violence they see?" but "Are children learning that taunting, ridiculing, and bullying define masculinity?"

We know from decades of research that depictions of violence in the entertainment media create a cultural climate in which such behavior is accepted as a normal, even appropriate, response to various problems.

We can see this process of normalization clearly in pro wrestling, where intimidation, humiliation, control, and verbal aggression (toward men as well as women) is the way that "real men" prevail. Manhood is equated explicitly with the ability to settle scores, defend one's honor, and win respect and compliance through force of conquest.

Already, this definition of manhood is at the root of much interpersonal violence in our society. For example, abusive men use force (or the threat of it) in an attempt to exercise power and control in their relationships with women. While there is no causal relationship between pro wrestling and male violence, it is clear that the wrestling subculture contributes to a larger cultural environment that teaches boys and men that manhood is about achieving power and control.

Real (or simulated) physical violence actually comprises a small percentage of the length of a pro wrestling telecast. Most of the time is devoted to setting up the narratives, and to verbal confrontation and bullying. In wrestling video games, each combatant not only has signature moves, but also verbal taunts that can be directed against either an opponent or the crowd. The object of the game is to see who can be the most effective bully.

It is a lesson that resonates all too clearly in our schools: A recent survey of 6,000 children in grades 4 to 6 found that about 1 in 10 said they were bullied one or more times a week, and 1 in 5 admitted to being bullies themselves. And we know from the 1990s' series of school shootings that, all too often, guns become the great equalizer for boys who have been bullied, ridiculed, and verbally taunted.

The hyper-masculine wrestling subculture is also deeply infused with homophobic anxiety. Macho posturing and insults ("wimps," and other worse epithets) can barely mask the fear of feminization that is always present in the homoerotic entanglement of male bodies. (The most popular of the trademark taunts by the wrestler X-Pac involves a thrusting of the crotch, accompanied by a sexual vulgarity, and his signature move of humiliation is to back his opponent into a corner and "ride" his face.)

As the enactment of gender has moved to center stage in wrestling narratives, so have women become much more central to the plot lines. In the days of Hulk Hogan and the Macho

Man, women were essentially restricted to a couple of sexualized figures. But now, there are many stereotypically hyper-sexualized female characters, especially in the WWF.

More frequently male wrestlers have "girlfriends" who accompany them to the ring. And every week, in one of the most overtly racist and sexist characterizations on contemporary television, the Godfather, an over-the-top stereotype of a hustling pimp (and one of the few important black figures in the WWF) leads out his "ho train" of scantily-clad white women to the leering and jeering crowds.

As female sexuality is increasingly used in the scripts, the line between the bimbo/prostitute sidekick and the female wrestlers is eroding. A recent WWF women's champion is Miss Kitty, a former hyper-sexualized sidekick, who during one pay-per-view event removed her top. And the big contests for female wrestlers often involve mud or chocolate baths, or the "evening dress" contest (where you lose by having your dress ripped from your body).

The few exceptions, such as Chyna, a wrestler in her own right (who, with The Rock, graced last week's Newsweek magazine cover) emerge from another place in heterosexual male fantasy, the Amazon warrior—tall, muscular, lithe, and buxom.

While ambiguity about proper gender assignments may be the contemporary norm, in the mock-violent world of professional wrestling, masculinity and femininity are clearly defined. And while pro wrestling shares many of the values sometimes associated with elements of the political far right (among them patriarchy, opposition to homosexuality, and respect for hierarchy), many conservatives have condemned its vulgarity and sexuality.

This criticism (much of it egged on by master promoters like McMahon) fuels the erroneous belief of some youngsters that somehow the WWF and WCW are alternative and rebellious. However, one of the great insights of cultural studies is that adherence to a conservative and repressive gender order can appear powerful and liberating—or rebellious—even as it assigns greater suffering to those deemed less powerful in the social order.

Some people will argue that analyzing the social impact of wrestling is a useless exercise because, after all, it's only play acting, right? But

to those who still believe that there is no connection between popular culture and broader social and political issues, that an analysis of wrestling has nothing to teach us about where our culture is heading, we have two words of caution: Jesse Ventura.   [2000]

Understanding the Reading

1. If teaching violence isn't the main problem with professional wrestling, then what is, according to the authors?
2. Why do men, especially, like this kind of entertainment, according to the authors?
3. How is masculinity defined within the world of professional wrestling?
4. How might the lessons of bullying be threatening to us as a society?

Suggestions for Responding

1. Watch a tape of WWF or WCW as a class; debate its messages vs. its entertainment value.
2. Research the political views of Jesse Ventura—professional wrestler and former governor of Minnesota. ◆

76

The Conservative Case for Gay Marriage

ANDREW SULLIVAN

A long time ago, the New Republic ran a contest to discover the most boring headline ever written. Entrants had to beat the following snoozer, which had inspired the event: WORTHWHILE CANADIAN INITIATIVE. Little did the contest organizers realize that one day such a headline would be far from boring and, in its own small way, a social watershed.

Canada's federal government decided last week not to contest the rulings of three provincial courts that had all come to the conclusion that denying homosexuals the right to marry violated Canada's constitutional commitment to civic equality. What that means is that gay marriage has now arrived in the western hemisphere. And this isn't some euphemism. It isn't the quasi-marriage now celebrated in Vermont, whose "civil unions" approximate marriage but don't go by that name. It's just marriage—for all. Canada now follows the Netherlands and Belgium with full-fledged marital rights for gays and lesbians.

Could it happen in the U.S.? The next few weeks will give us many clues. The U.S. Supreme Court is due to rule any day now on whether it's legal for Texas and other states to prosecute sodomy among gays but not straights. More critical, Massachusetts' highest court is due to rule very soon on whether the denial of marriage to gays is illicit discrimination against a minority. If Massachusetts rules that it is,[1] then gay couples across America will be able to marry not only in Canada (where there are no residency or nationality requirements for marriage) but also in a bona fide American state. There will be a long process of litigation as various married couples try hard to keep their marriages legally intact from one state to another.

This move seems an eminently conservative one—in fact, almost an emblem of "compassionate conservatism." Conservatives have long rightly argued for the vital importance of the institution of marriage for fostering responsibility, commitment and the domestication of unruly men. Bringing gay men and women into this institution will surely change the gay subculture in subtle but profoundly conservative ways. When I grew up and realized I was gay, I had no concept of what my own future could be like. Like most other homosexuals, I grew up in a heterosexual family and tried to imagine how I too could one day be a full part of the family I loved. But I figured then that I had no such future. I could never have a marriage, never have a family, never be a full and equal part of the weddings and relationships and holidays that give families structure and meaning. When I looked forward, I saw nothing but emptiness and loneliness. No wonder it was hard to connect sex with love and commitment. No wonder it was hard to feel at home in what was, in fact, my home.

For today's generation of gay kids, all that changes. From the beginning, they will be able to see their future as part of family life—not in conflict with it. Their "coming out" will also al-low them a "coming home." And as they date in adolescence and early adulthood, there will be some future anchor in their mind-set, some ultimate structure with which to give their relationships stability and social support. Many heterosexuals, I suspect, simply don't realize how big a deal this is. They have never doubted that one day they could marry the person they love. So they find it hard to conceive how deep a psychic and social wound the exclusion from marriage and family can be. But the polls suggest this is changing fast: the majority of people 30 and younger see gay marriage as inevitable and understandable. Many young straight couples simply don't see married gay peers next door as some sort of threat to their own lives. They can get along in peace.

As for religious objections, it's important to remember that the issue here is not religious. It's civil. Various religious groups can choose to endorse same-sex marriage or not as they see fit. Their freedom of conscience is as vital as gays' freedom to be treated equally under the civil law. And there's no real reason that the two cannot coexist. The Roman Catholic Church, for example, opposes remarriage after divorce. But it doesn't seek to make civil divorce and remarriage illegal for everyone. Similarly, churches can well decide this matter in their own time and on their own terms while allowing the government to be neutral between competing visions of the good life. We can live and let live.

And after all, isn't that what this really is about? We needn't all agree on the issue of homosexuality to believe that the government should treat every citizen alike. If that means living next door to someone of whom we disapprove, so be it. But disapproval needn't mean disrespect. And if the love of two people, committing themselves to each other exclusively for the rest of their lives, is not worthy of respect, then what is?   [2003]

Notes

1. Massachusetts ruled in favor of gay marriages.

Understanding the Reading

1. What was the "worthwhile Canadian initiative"?

2. Why did Canada decide to extend the right of marriage to gays?
3. How does the author argue that this is actually in line with conservatives' values?
4. Why is having the choice to marry or not important to gays and lesbians?

Suggestions for Responding

1. Since we are a nation of laws, get a copy of your state's constitution, study it, and discuss whether your state is in compliance with its written commitment on the matter of gay marriage or, in fact, is illegally discriminating. ✦

77

How the Entertainment Industry Degrades Women

MARTHA BURK AND KIRSTEN SHAW

When 1992 draws to a close, how will media watchers remember it? As the year TV gave us a single mother who became the target of a phony "family values" crusade by the Republican party? Or the year when police and the "decent people" recruited by politicians shook their fists at the Time-Warner Corporation to get the anti-police song "Cop Killer" taken off the market?

Presumably few will notice that 1992 was the year in which neither politicians nor the public raised so much as an eyebrow about a song on the same album, entitled "KKK Bitch," that described the sodomizing of a Klansman's daughter. Nor did many protest the thousands of images of violence against women in movies, on TV, in advertising, and in music. 1992 will pass without remark as yet another year in which women were demeaned, degraded, and abused in the mass media.

The very survival of American women is being threatened by an epidemic of gender-specific violence that is legitimized and glamorized every day in the media while politicians and the public sit back and enjoy, even pay to see it. Battery is now the single largest cause of injury to women in America—more common than auto accidents, muggings, and rapes combined. You wouldn't know it from the media images pushed on society and the silent acceptance coming back in answer.

A woman is more likely to be killed by her husband or boyfriend than by anyone else. A woman is raped every five minutes. Yet popular movies such as *Basic Instinct*, opening with a gratuitous date-rape; *Batman Returns*, a "children's" movie depicting a woman thrown from a skyscraper by her boss; or *Unforgiven*, where a woman is knifed repeatedly in the face, trade on images of women as the passive victims of rape, murder, and abuse.

This epidemic of violence against women has evoked only complacency that is shored up by the background noise of media images telling us it is acceptable.

"Gangster rap" has been roundly criticized for its promotion of violence against the police. Yet "bitches" and "ho's" are the only female characters it portrays. Women are objectified as sex objects and scorned as manipulators who must be controlled with a fist or a weapon: "If I have to go get a gun you girls will learn." N.W.A.'s recently released Niggaz4life album includes graphic lyrics boasting about the abuse, rape, and murder of women.

Opponents of Ice-T's "Cop Killer" worried that its malicious anti-police message demoralized officers working in an already hostile environment. Women live every day in a hostile world, though there has been no demonstration of concern about the malice continually expressed against them.

Gangster rap, of course, is only guilty of graphically depicting the messages that more mainstream media send out regularly—that women must be kept in their place through violence, and that they deserve and even enjoy being abused.

"Her body's beautiful so I'm thinkin' rape / Shouldn't have had her curtains open so that's her fate." Such a rhyme is not really shocking in the context of an industry where one of every eight Hollywood movies depicts a rape theme. And it's not a modern phenomenon—in the classic *Gone with the Wind* Scarlett O'Hara is all smiles the morning after she is raped by her own husband.

Slasher movies, popular with teenagers, rely almost exclusively on the torture and murder of women for their plots. The same basic theme is churned out every year in sequels of *Halloween, Friday the 13th,* and *Nightmare on Elm Street:* young women are slaughtered one by one by an anonymous killer (typically cheered by the audience) who in the end escapes or is reborn. The murder and mutilation is broken only with a smattering of scenes of women undressing and engaging in sexual activity. The viewer is led to believe they got what they deserved.

Directors like Brian DePalma and David Lynch, hailed as artistic geniuses, derive an "aesthetic effect" from graphic images of torture, mutilation, and murder of females. Lynch's television series "Twin Peaks" featured abuse of most of its women characters, and a glamorous rape scene embellished his movie *Wild at Heart.*

Television embraces its share of violent themes as well, with women in "jep" (jeopardy) a common element. Sex and violence are the core of MTV fare, with 18 instances of aggression each hour and women's bodies the most common decorative element. Rivaling in frequency the image of woman as victim is that of woman as sex object. Popular series like "Married . . . with Children" get their laughs from the die-hard portrait of woman as empty-headed sex fiend. The devaluation of women through this kind of objectification lays the necessary groundwork for their exploitation and abuse.

Madison Avenue capitalizes on degrading images of women to sell everything from beer to blue jeans. Advertisements featuring sex, implied domination, and sometimes explicit bondage appear as often in women's magazines as those aimed at men. From roadside billboards to prime time television, gratuitous bikini-clad beauties ornamenting product slogans sustain society's perception of women as secondary, decorative, and expendable. The September issue of *Vogue* featured a full color picture of a woman with a bare, bruised back dressed in a red formal gown against the backdrop of a dungeon complete with chains.

The connection between viewing an act of violence and committing one has been dismissed as ludicrous by supporters of unregulated corporate free speech. While there is more to violence than mere imitation, psychologists have demonstrated an association time and time again. When a person continually sees dehumanization and physical abuse glamorized and legitimized through television, movies, music, and magazines, it is hard to imagine how that message could fail to be internalized and sometimes acted on.

Studies on children have shown that aggressive behavior increases after viewing aggression on television, even in cartoons. This violence, combined with the ever-present images of the victimization of women, is also sending powerful messages about inappropriate sex role behavior.

Adults are prone to the influence of media violence and victimization as well. Studies show that men watching movies depicting violence against women become progressively more callous toward the humanity of the victims and the reality of their suffering. Other research has shown that after viewing these films men are more inclined to believe that women want to be raped and actually enjoy the pain.

Trainers in the armed forces harden men for combat by desensitizing them to the sounds of screaming and the humanity of their enemies. In the same way, the profusion of images of violence and degradation of women make men (and even young boys) more callous toward women and more insensitive to their humanity.

And women are not immune to the messages. While men are learning to regard women with contempt and use force to deal with them, women are learning to expect and accept the abuse as their due.

Assumptions about women are formed at an early age. A now famous survey of Rhode Island youngsters found that at least half the boys and almost as many girls thought it was okay for a man to force a woman to kiss him if he had spent at least $15 on her. Rap fans in D.C. schools interviewed by the *Washington Post* this year expressed similar opinions. "Women get what they deserve," one eleven-year-old commented.

Last summer politicians were stumbling all over each other to express their concern that children were being harmed by the images and language of "cop killer" music, since kids are unable to see it as metaphor and are likely to take it at face value. They should be equally concerned by the portrayals of women that the majority of children see daily in the mass media.

If politicians wish to concern themselves with whether "cop killer" music is offensive and soapbox on "family values," they need to look at what those values are. Are females valued equally?

Women must hold media corporations accountable. Women are 52% of the population, and despite our low pay compared to men, we have considerable economic clout. If a few picketing police officers could force Time-Warner to stop selling violence against the police, imagine what a few million women could do if we decided to fight back with economic boycotts of companies that debase us for the bottom line.

Women did not let the openly misogynist treatment of Anita Hill[1] or the anti-feminist rhetoric of the Republican convention pass without comment. Neither should we ignore the daily barrage of anti-woman images that are pushed as entertainment. [These are] images that influence both adults and children, male and female. These are the more subtle tools of indoctrination, and ultimately the more devastating. [1992]

Terms

1. ANITA HILL. Hill testified before the Senate Judiciary Committee against the nomination of Clarence Thomas for the Supreme Court.

Understanding the Reading

1. What is the impact of the images of violence against women in the mass media?
2. How are women portrayed in "gangster rap," and how does that image compare with portrayals in the mainstream media and slasher movies?
3. Is there a connection between violent images and behavior?

Suggestions for Responding

1. Explain why you think politicians are concerned about "cop killer" music but are silent about the portrayal of women in popular media.
2. "Family values" is a popular political theme these days. What do you think this term means? Do you think it should be a political concern? Why or why not? ◆

78

Gender Warriors Fight the Wrong Battle

LAURA SESSIONS STEPP

Ten years ago we were reading that girls were being shortchanged in grades K through 12. Then we were told, no, it's boys who are in real trouble.

This year, the battlefield has moved to college campuses. Step onto one and you'll notice more women than men. The gender soldiers have noticed, too.

One of the warriors is Tom Mortenson, a higher education consultant from Iowa. He lectures around the country on the subject, often asking the question, "What's wrong with the guys?" One of his points: The majority of associate and bachelor degrees are now awarded to women. "Girls have earned what they've achieved," he says. "But some of their progress has come at the expense of men."

Some higher education consultants and commentators are calling this a crisis. They haul out the numbers as further evidence that schooling at all levels has become increasingly unfriendly to males. The media have jumped on the story.

They all need to take a deep breath. There is no general educational crisis among men. Let's look at the government's data, analyzed by Jacqueline King, director of policy analysis for the American Council on Education, a think tank on higher education.

The proportion of young men enrolled in two- or four-year colleges immediately after high school has gradually risen since 1980 to about 60 percent, and the proportion of young men who received a bachelor's degree has hovered at about 25 percent.

Over this same period, young women have entered college in higher proportions. Twenty years ago, about 50 percent of them entered college; today's figure is slightly less than 70 percent. Four-year degree-holders have increased from 21 percent of young women to 29 percent.

So it's not that fewer boys are going to college; it's that more girls are. If education is simply one pie, then boys are getting a smaller share. But they aren't being shut out. Universities and colleges have expanded the number of students they admit, so we're talking about more opportunities for everybody.

One male subgroup, however, does deserve closer attention, and amid all the hype, it isn't getting enough of it: men from lower-income families.

Middle- and upper-income parents send their sons and daughters to college in almost equal proportions (with the exception of well-off African American families, whose sons still lag considerably behind in the number of years of schooling completed). But that gender balance disappears as family income declines: Men become far less likely than women to go to college, or to stay in school once they get there.

This appears to be true especially for low-income white men, who enter college at even lower rates than low-income blacks or Hispanics.

"The story is about income and race, not gender," says Susan Choy, a consultant to the Department of Education on post-secondary schooling.

Why? Because a young man from a poor family sees less financial advantage than his female counterpart in continuing his schooling, educational authorities say. As soon as he graduates from high school, he can go into a field such as auto repair or construction, which pays, on average, about $33,000 a year—$10,000 more than the retail or service jobs that most young women can find, according to King.

"He still thinks of good jobs as being the old kind, like truck driving," says Harry Holzer, professor of public policy at Georgetown. If Dad or Granddad ran a rig, maybe it's good enough for him, too.

When that same man considers the debt he'll incur should he continue his education, and the years he'll be out of full-time work, "it's not entirely clear that college is the meal ticket," says Carol Tavris, a social psychologist in California.

He is less likely than other, more affluent men to have the skills that make him attractive to college recruiters. He has fewer resources, social as well as financial, to support a college search. For reasons that baffle educators, he also is less likely than a young woman living in similar circumstances to show the determination he needs to move out of his situation and the discipline to carry through his plans.

Patricia Gandara, a professor of education at the University of California, Davis, says she has noticed "amazingly low aspirations" among Latino high school boys in the low-income and working-class neighborhoods she studies. They say things like "College is not important to me" and "I don't do homework," and say they'd rather be viewed by their classmates as "popular" or "good-looking" than "a good student." Latina girls, by contrast, put being "a good student" at the top.

Such negative attitudes about learning extend to men in other ethnic groups, as well: According to data collected by Mortenson, high school senior boys of all races and ethnic groups report they spend most of their time outside of school exercising, watching television and playing video games. Girls are more likely to say they do homework or take part in extracurricular activities. One unfortunate result is this: Federally funded organizations that give out higher education grants to needy students say two-thirds of their clients are female. No matter what they do, the young men just don't show up.

Words such as motivation and persistence bring up another question: Whether boys, especially lower-income boys, aren't inspired to go to college because they're turned off years earlier by teachers and curricula that either don't hold their interest or make them feel dumb.

According to Mortenson, boys in grades K through 12 are about three times more likely than girls to be diagnosed as having serious emotional problems or learning disabilities. If not enrolled in higher-level academic classes by eighth grade—and many of these labeled boys are not—they are unlikely to make it to college or to stay if they get there.

Christina Hoff Sommers, a fellow at the American Enterprise Institute, argues that curricula and teaching styles have changed to better fit the way girls learn. Strategies to capture boys' imagination and energy, such as competitive games and war stories, have been replaced by lessons in cooperation and family life. Schools, she says, are "increasingly hostile to boys."

Are college admissions offices hostile as well? Nothing indicates that boys are applying to college in fewer numbers, according to Joyce

Smith, executive director of the National Association for College Admission Counseling. So if women outnumber men on certain campuses, it must have something to do with the admissions process, and indeed, a number of colleges and universities are looking at their own procedures.

There is a danger in engaging in any gender talk about college, however. It reinforces the assumption that every young person should go there—a notion that people such as Samuel Halperin characterize as dangerous class snobbery. Halperin, founder of the American Youth Policy Forum, is a political scientist who has spent much of his career working to increase job opportunities and job training for young people who do not intend to go to college. He has not seen much progress.

College advocates talk a lot about the salary differences over a lifetime for the college graduate versus the non-college graduate. But their figures are misleading, Halperin says, because they include "ministers and teachers and lawyers. If you broke out the figures by occupation, you'd find that while you do make more going to college, you don't make a whole lot more. I'm not sure college is as big a deal as the culture has decided."

Colleges and universities "will keep singing the song about college" because they need larger enrollments to keep up with rising costs, Halperin says. But they and other institutions need to think harder about how to recruit and train young men—and young women—for the critical jobs that don't require a bachelor's degree but keep the country's infrastructure together.

"Of course we're going to need brilliant scientists and computer engineers," he says. "But where is our greater need, for them or for airport security checkers and Metrobus drivers? The kids paying $40,000 a year to go to college are going to make out all right. It's the others I'm worried about."

Halperin is worrying about something real. The gender watchers would serve their cause better if they followed suit.   [2002]

Understanding the Reading

1. According to the author, is there an educational crisis among men, since females out-

number males in U.S. colleges? Why or why not?
2. Which group of males is definitely being shut out of universities?
3. Why would a low-income male be less likely to attend college than a low-income female?

Suggestions for Responding

1. The tradition of American public education has been that everyone has the right to a free, classical education, as opposed to a vocational one. Debate this policy, versus the European tradition of strong vocational education after approximately the age of 13 for those not going on to a university. ✦

79

Losing a Church, Keeping the Faith

ANDREW SULLIVAN

Last week, something quite banal happened at St. Benedict's Church in the Bronx. A gay couple were told they could no longer sing in the choir. Their sin was to have gotten a civil marriage license in Canada. One man had sung in the choir for 32 years; the other had joined the church 25 years ago. Both had received certificates from the church commending them for "noteworthy participation." But their marriage had gained publicity; it was even announced in The New York Times. This "scandal" led to their expulsion. The archbishop's spokesman explained that the priest had "an obligation" to exclude them.

In the grand scheme of things, this is a very small event. But it is a vivid example of why this last year has made the once difficult lives of gay Catholics close to impossible. The church has gone beyond its doctrinal opposition to emotional or sexual relationships between gay men and lesbians to an outspoken and increasingly shrill campaign against them. Gay relationships were described by the Vatican earlier this year as "evil." Gay couples who bring up children were described as committing the equivalent of "violence" against their own offspring. Gay men are being deterred from applying to seminaries and may soon be declared unfit for the priesthood, even though they commit to celibacy. The American Catholic church has endorsed a constitutional amendment that would strip gay couples of any civil benefits of any kind in the United States.

For the first time in my own life, I find myself unable to go to Mass. During the most heated bouts of rhetoric coming from the Vatican this summer, I felt tears of grief and anger welling up where once I had been able to contain them. Faith beyond resentment began to seem unreachable.

For some, the answer is as easy as it always has been. Leave, they say. The gay world looks at gay Catholics with a mixture of contempt and pity. The Catholic world looks at us as if we want to destroy an institution we simply want to belong to. So why not leave? In some ways, I suppose, I have. What was for almost 40 years a weekly church habit dried up this past year to close to nothing. Every time I walked into a church or close to one, the anger and hurt overwhelmed me. It was as if a dam of intellectual resistance to emotional distress finally burst.

But there was no comfort in this, no relief, no resolution. There is no ultimate meaning for me outside the Gospels, however hard I try to imagine it; no true solace but the Eucharist; no divine love outside of Christ and the church he guides. In that sense, I have not left the church because I cannot leave the church, no more than I can leave my family. Like many other gay Catholics, I love this church; for me, there is and never will be any other. But I realize I cannot participate in it any longer either. It would be an act of dishonesty to enable an institution that is now a major force for the obliteration of gay lives and loves; that covered up for so long the sexual abuse of children but uses the word "evil" for two gay people wanting to commit to each other for life.

I know what I am inside. I do not believe that my orientation is on a par with others' lapses into lust when they also have an option for sexual and emotional life that is blessed and celebrated by the church. I do not believe I am intrinsically sick or disordered, as the hierarchy teaches, although I am a sinner in many, many ways. I do not believe that the gift of human sexuality is always and everywhere evil outside of procreation. (Many heterosexual Catholics, of course, agree with me, but they can hide and pass in ways that gay Catholics cannot.) I believe that denying gay people any outlet for their deepest emotional needs is wrong. I think it slowly destroys people, hollows them out, alienates them finally from their very selves.

But I must also finally concede that this will not change as a matter of doctrine. That doctrine—never elaborated by Jesus—was constructed when gay people as we understand them today were not known to exist; but its authority will not change just because gay people now have the courage to explain who they are and how they feel. In fact, it seems as if the emergence of gay people into the light of the world has only intensified the church's resistance. That shift in the last few years from passive silence to active hostility is what makes the Vatican's current stance so distressing. Terrified of their own knowledge of the wide presence of closeted gay men in the priesthood, concerned that the sexual doctrines required of heterosexuals are under threat, the hierarchy has decided to draw the line at homosexuals. We have become the unwilling instruments of their need to reassert control.

In an appeal to the growing fundamentalism of the developing world, this is a shrewd strategy. In the global context, gays are easily expendable. But it is also a strikingly inhumane one. The current pope is obviously a deep and holy man; but that makes his hostility even more painful. He will send emissaries to terrorists, he will meet with a man who tried to assassinate him. But he has not and will not meet with openly gay Catholics. They are, to him, beneath dialogue. His message is unmistakable. Gay people are the last of the untouchables. We can exist in the church only by silence, by bearing false witness to who we are.

I was once more hopeful. I saw within the church's doctrines room for a humane view of homosexuality, a genuinely Catholic approach to including all nonprocreative people—the old, the infertile, the gay—in God's church. But I can see now that the dialogue is finally shutting down.

Perhaps a new pope will change things. But the odds are that hostility will get even worse. I revere those who can keep up the struggle within the channels of the church. I respect those who have left. But I am somewhere in between now.

There are moments in a spiritual life when the heart simply breaks. Some time in the last year, mine did. I can only pray that in some distant future, some other gay people not yet born will be able to come back to the church, to sing in the choir, and know that the only true scandal in the world is the scandal of God's love for his creation, all of it, all of us, in a church that may one day, finally, become home to us all.

[2003]

Understanding the Reading

1. Why was the gay couple expelled from the church choir, after so many decades of service?
2. What kind of a change in response does this signal for the Catholic Church?
3. What was the reaction of the author?
4. Why can he not leave the Church?
5. What is the one way, according to the author, a gay Catholic can exist in the Church?

Suggestions for Responding

1. If you belong to a faith, what is your religion's official stance toward homosexuality? How does that translate into practice? What do you believe? Are there any elements of your faith with which you disagree?
2. Many churches and synagogues within the United States are dividing over the issue of homosexuality. Research these discussions, find out which churches and synagogues are involved, and determine whether they have resolved anything.
3. Research Islam's and Hinduism's stances toward homosexuality. ✦

80
Foul Play

Kathleen Sharp

The game is tied and Cori Close dribbles the ball, racing for the basket while searching for an open teammate. Her players close in instinctively, but each is covered by defense. Then, like a lazy eye, teammate Sasha Scardino wanders to the side. Without a glance, Close passes to Scardino, who sinks a three-pointer.

When the buzzer signals the game's end, the small rabid crowd goes bonkers. Close, Scardino, and the women's team at the University of California, Santa Barbara, have won yet another game, despite a skeleton staff, a sliver of a budget, and a low profile. Although the men's Gaucho team is richer, and more visible, the "Lady" Gauchos rely on an uncanny, extrasensory style.

"With us, it's not about how much one person can score," said Close. "It's about working together. The more we rely on all parts of our bodies—our legs, our eyes, our hearts—the better we get."

Last season, the team was among the best in the West. In four years, it climbed from the bottom of the league to the top, winning the prestigious Big West tournament in 1992 and 1993. In the last two years, it has gone on to win the first round of the National Collegiate Athletics Association (NCAA) Tournament—the nation's top play-offs.

Off the court, the team's challenges are more daunting. The women ride buses to most games—some of which are 12 hours away. On one grueling weekend during final exams, as the women traveled 350 miles to play the first of three games, their bus broke down on a snowy mountain pass. By contrast, the male Gauchos, who have never won the Big West championship and haven't made the NCAA play-offs for three years, fly to many of their games and stay comfortably in hotels.

The women's coach, Mark French, is paid about $33,000—less than half the salary of Jerry

Pimm, the head coach of the male Gauchos. French's full-time assistant works additional jobs to eke out a living. The men's team is coddled by five well-paid staff members.

Glaring inequities between women's and men's school sports are common—and illegal. Two decades after Title IX of the Education Amendments was passed to eliminate sex discrimination, the women's field is riddled with potholes. In the last three years, a growing corps of women have complained to deans, filed formal complaints with the Office of Civil Rights, and exhausted all "proper" channels to uphold the law. Now, these women are suing Ivy League schools, big college football powers, and respected state universities. In almost every case women are winning. Said Judy Sweet, former NCAA president: "Women are getting fed up."

Title IX prohibits schools that receive federal funds from discriminating against students on the basis of gender. Under the law, female athletes are required to receive the same opportunities extended to men. That means if female students make up 50 percent of the student body, they must make up 50 percent of varsity slots, or the school must demonstrate that it is meeting the level of interest of women athletes or has a history of expanding women's programs.

The nation's schools had six years to comply with the new standards. At first, the number of women's teams exploded, so that by 1978 women accounted for 33 percent of the nation's college athletes. "Unfortunately, that's where we've remained for the last fifteen years," said Donna Lopiano, executive director of the Women's Sports Foundation (WSF). Although 53 percent of college students today are female, they occupy only 34 percent of athletic slots. When Lopiano testified before Congress last winter, she didn't mince words: "Intercollegiate athletics in our nation's universities are openly discriminating against women."

In fact, from kindergarten to college most schools are currently in violation of Title IX. "You pick a school and I'll bet it's in violation," said Kathryn Reith, WSF assistant director. But school administrators tend to resist addressing their Title IX problems. "There's a lot of fear out there, especially in athletic departments where men's sports are sacrosanct," said Diane Henson, a law-

yer who litigates sex discrimination cases. Added Ellen Vargyas, senior counsel of the National Women's Law Center: "There's a firm conviction that women's sports are not as good, lucrative, or important as men's. Somehow, men's teams are more valuable, financially and cosmically."

Female athletes have long understood this reality. But it wasn't until 1992, when the NCAA released its benchmark study of gender equity, that the rest of us started to understand the extent of the problems. The survey found that:

- Men make up nearly 70 percent of students who play in top-level college sports.
- Female athletes receive less than a third of all college scholarships.
- Women's teams receive only 23 percent of school athletic budgets.
- Men's teams receive five times more money to recruit new members.
- Coaches of men's teams are paid 81 percent more than coaches of women's teams.

With fewer resources and opportunities, it's more difficult for women to succeed in college sports, said Vargyas. Male sports directors argue that the numbers are imbalanced because few women want to play college sports. According to Vargyas: "That's like a Southerner in the 1950s saying African Americans don't like to ride in the front of the bus."

Indeed, the resistance to Title IX goes to the heart of our cultural stereotypes regarding the proper roles of women and men. Nowhere is this concept more entrenched than at schools with large football programs. Take the University of Texas, where women make up 47 percent of students but only 23 percent of the athletes. "And this is for a school that's known for its top women's varsity teams," said Henson, who represented female plaintiffs at Texas.

In July 1992, athletes on the Texas women's crew, gymnastics, softball, and soccer clubs sued the school and asked it to upgrade their teams to varsity level. The school objected, claiming that it was meeting women's interest in sports and that female athletes were underrepresented because the men's football program is so big and popular. By law, that excuse is no defense. Yet it underscores one of the great myths in the Title

IX debate. "Men like to claim that football makes money, so they can't possibly cut those programs," said Henson. "But more often than not, football loses money." Still, nostalgic alumni tend to treat college pigskin programs like a golden goose, when it's more of a white elephant.

Texas' football program makes money, although it depends heavily on university funds and alumni donations. "These guys spend money like there's no tomorrow," said Henson. Country club dues, cars, and other perks are given to the football team's staff. The men's athletic department spent $167,000 on mahogany office furniture and redecorating. That money probably didn't contribute much to athletic performance and it could have funded a women's soccer team, said Henson. The men's athletic department also has a $5 million "rainy day" account. "I told them their rainy day was about to arrive," she said. Henson won a settlement that will double women's sports participation over the next three years.

Most of the Title IX cases involve women's club teams simply seeking varsity team status, which would mean the school would devote substantial resources to their teams. Last year, however, the Supreme Court ruled that women can also sue for monetary damages as part of their Title IX rights. In June, a Washington, D.C., jury awarded Howard University basketball coach Sonya Tyler $2.4 million (later reduced by a judge to $1.1 million) in her sex discrimination suit against the school. Now, the specter of large financial penalties hangs over offending institutions, many of which are already strapped for cash. Still, based on pending Title IX litigation, it appears most schools would rather fight than comply:

- In April 1990, female hockey players sued Colgate University because it had repeatedly denied the club team varsity status. Women paid for their own gear, uniforms, and transportation—unlike the varsity men. In September 1992, U.S. magistrate David N. Hurd ordered Colgate to elevate the women's team to varsity status. "The men's hockey players are treated as princes while the women are treated as chimney sweeps," he said. Colgate appealed. This spring, the appeals court de-

clared the case moot because all the female plaintiffs were about to graduate.

- In June 1992, Colorado State University cut its NCAA Division I women's varsity softball team, along with men's baseball. The women sued, claiming that Colorado didn't give women equal opportunities. In February 1993, the court ordered Colorado to reinstate the women's team, a decision that was upheld on appeal.

- After Brown University cut its women's gymnastics and volleyball teams, players sued to restore their teams to varsity status. In December 1992, the court ordered the Ivy League school to reinstate the teams. Brown got a temporary stay, which delayed implementation of the court's order. Brown then appealed. In April 1993, the appeals court upheld the stay and remanded the case to lower court for trial.

- At Auburn University, the women's soccer club has for years requested varsity status. The women must practice on a half-sized, poorly kept field they share with a rugby team. "Two players have already suffered injuries because of holes in the field," said plaintiffs' attorney Nancy Ryan. Auburn, located in rural Alabama, has plenty of fields for men's baseball and football, but the school won't let the women play on them, added Ryan.

In October 1992, one of the women filed a complaint with the Office of Civil Rights, which found Auburn in noncompliance after a lengthy investigation. In April the club filed a class action suit, which was settled the following month when the university agreed to institute a varsity soccer program this fall.

These legal cases reflect poorly on educators and officials, who waste thousands of dollars to thwart the legal rights of young female athletes, say Title IX advocates. "These 18-year-old women are not only attending school and succeeding in sports, they're taking on the most powerful institutions in their lives," said Patricia Flannery, an attorney who has worked on Title IX cases. Added Ryan, "Enforcing the law is falling on the shoulders of these young women."

The Auburn women have enjoyed widespread campus support, but that's not the case on all campuses. For example, after publicly voicing her concerns about Title IX problems, Harvard lacrosse coach Carole Kleinfelder found her car tires slashed. At California State University (CSU) at Fullerton, women's volleyball coach Jim Huffman lost his job after he successfully sued to reinstate his varsity team. At CSU's San Diego campus, women's volleyball coach Rudy Suwara was fired when he lobbied for more money for all school women's programs. His wrongful termination suit seeks $1 million in damages.

Perhaps Title IX problems wouldn't be so rampant if more women headed big athletic departments. Yet, of the 107 schools in the NCAA's top division, only two employ a female athletic director who oversees both men's and women's athletics. Employment discrimination in college athletics is strong but subtle, said Lopiano. "Single women are assumed to be lesbians or women with children are thought to have too many responsibilities."

Lately, Title IX has reverberated beyond the university walls. This February, the California chapter of the National Organization for Women sued the entire CSU system, claiming that the system has "actually regressed from gender equity since 1978." But for every suit filed by women, there are legions of girls fighting for the chance to play on a team. In small grammar and high schools, few students even know about Title IX, let alone understand their rights.

One exception is Misty Allen of Alabama. She attended a rural, predominantly black high school in Talladega County that funded boys' football, track, basketball, and baseball teams but nothing for girls. On her own, Allen formed a girls' basketball team, which was funded and coached by volunteers and parents. After its first season, the principal, John Stamps, cut the team, complaining he had to pay for referees.

Through Allen, the WSF explained the law to Stamps. In short order, he reinstated the team, which eventually placed in a regional tournament. However, weeks before the play-off, he gave the wrong game date to the coach, which caused the team to forfeit its game and lose the championship, said WSF's Reith. On top of that, Stamps made the girls pay the $500 forfeiture fine. Who can explain such meanness to girls who fought for a chance to learn a game their brothers take for granted?

Despite their geographic distances, the girls in Alabama share much with the women in Texas, New York, and California. They are being squashed by mostly male teachers and administrators who don't seem to understand what it really means to be a sport: to value honor, fairness, and graceful acceptance of results—win, lose, or draw. "It benefits all of society to teach both men *and women* about teamwork, competition, and cooperation," said basketball player Cori Close. "That's the only way to play." To instill that lesson in only half of our society is to hobble us from participating fully in life's larger contests. And that way, we all lose.   [1993]

Understanding the Reading

1. Describe the inequalities between the University of California, Santa Barbara, women's team and men's team.
2. What is the purpose of Title IX of the Education Amendments, and how effective has it been?
3. In what ways have schools resisted compliance with Title IX?

Suggestions for Responding

1. Investigate and report on gender equality in the athletic program at your school.
2. Talk to students about their feelings about the Women's National Basketball Association and its impact on collegiate programs for women. ✦

81

Reincarnating Freud

Susana McCollom

Freud is not likely to be a name found on a woman's list of heroes. While he is recognized as the pioneer of psychotherapy, Freud cemented historical labels of women as "hysterical" and "neurotic," and recommended years of psychoanalysis to cure these ailments. It was Freud who asked "what does a woman want?"

Lucky for Freud that he was around in the 1890s and not today. Women of the 1990s would never tolerate such putdowns, right? Wrong. The Freudian phenomenon is happening right under our noses. It is a more subtle version of Freud's gender labeling which leads us back to the same "hysterical" women whose only hope for curing their natural frailties is years of counseling, anti-depressants, or a steady diet of self-help publications.

Freud's contemporary followers have one advantage. The capacity for selling these images of women has skyrocketed as a result of technological innovations and mass media. The subtlety of these images and their messages is continuously overlooked as women's educational, political, and financial strides convince many that gender equality is becoming a reality. The professional heirs of Freud are joined by marketing wizards (including women) in helping self-help book authors and publishers, women's magazines, and pharmaceutical companies to promote the notion that women need help. And women are buying it.

THE PACKAGING OF NEUROSIS

"When a man goes into his cave, it is important for a woman to do something enjoyable. Read a book, do some gardening, take a bath, go for a walk, go shopping or call a girl friend for a good chat."

No, this is not a quote from Freud. This advice comes from the contemporary relationship expert, Dr. John Gray, author of *Men Are From Mars, Women Are From Venus*. Gray asserts that men and women are from different planets, resulting in communication problems which can only be solved by accepting our gender differences. What are these differences? Chapter Seven, "Women Are Like Waves," is a prime example. He claims "a woman's self-esteem rises and falls like a wave. When she hits bottom it is time for an emotional housecleaning."

According to Gray, women exhibit "warning signs" which should alert a man that his spouse or girlfriend is entering her "well." The warning signs vary according to a woman's mood. She may feel insecure, resentful, confused, passive, controlling or demanding. But fortunately for men, there are 101 ways to "score points" with women (as opposed to 26 ways to score points with men).

The theme is very straightforward: men must learn to appease women's natural tendency to chatter or cry at the drop of a pin. A man should "compliment her on how she looks," "give her four hugs a day," or "pay more attention to her than to others in public." Women, on the other hand, need to resist the urge to constantly nag their mates. They "score big with men," if "he makes a mistake and she doesn't say I told you so," "if he disappoints her and she doesn't punish him," or if "she really enjoys having sex with him."

Like women in the 1800s, today's women are characterized as neurotic and lacking any sex drive. Yet since it was first published in 1992, *Men Are From Mars, Women Are From Venus* has remained a bestseller in the United States. Gray has since published additional versions of his planetary discoveries, further advising men and women on relationship skills both in and out of bed.

However, while Gray's appeal to (mostly) women has made him a relationship guru, his advice singles out married and committed couples. For the single, presumably miserable women who have failed in their attempts to capture a husband, help has arrived. In *The Rules: Time-tested Secrets for Capturing the Heart of Mr. Right*, Ellen Fein and Sherrie Schneider guide the single woman in search of the man of their dreams—or any man, really. Unlike Gray's book, many women and men alike scoff at *The Rules* and its "outdated" advice.

What are some of these rules? First, women must "look the part" by wearing lipstick while they jog or by getting a nose job if it means a man will find them more attractive. But equally important is acting the part. Fein and Schneider advise, "Be feminine . . . don't be a loud, knee-slapping, hysterically funny girl . . . when you're with a man you like, be quiet and mysterious, act ladylike, cross your legs and smile . . . You may feel that you won't be able to be yourself, but men will love it."

The authors acknowledge the differential responses to their "timeless" advice and respond to skeptics such as the cynical career woman. "A relationship with a man is different from a job" claim the authors, ". . . the man must take charge. He must propose. We are not making this up—biologically, he's the aggressor." Fein and Schneider's message is basically that women must play hard to get. Really hard to get. Even if it means they have to set a timer to ten minutes to get off the phone first. The authors claim that "when you do *The Rules,* he somehow thinks you're the sexiest woman alive! . . . you don't have to worry about being abandoned, neglected, or ignored!" Fein and Schneider promote and encourage behavior which polarizes men and women. Essentially, the authors attempt to reinstate the "say no but mean yes" mentality that oppressed women for years and which only recently, through advocacy, education, and policy changes, has begun to subside. So much for the vindication of women's rights. According to these authors, women are too stupid to know they have any. While seemingly ridiculous, *The Rules* remains a bestseller and provides the authors with a string of public appearances.

Women as the Target

The irony in today's self-help mania is that neither Fein, Schneider, nor most men are responsible for placing this book on the bestseller list. Nor are they the ones raving about gender planetary differences. On the contrary, women are the die-hard supporters of the self-help book market.

Recent research suggests that anxiety, the nation's leading psychological problem, strikes twice as many women as men. Psychologists, women's magazines, and the general media have seized this finding as they eagerly promote self-help books, articles, and anti-depressants to women. Through their advertising they reinforce the concept that women are inherently neurotic—ringing the 1890's bell louder than ever.

The pharmaceutical industry also contributes to the perpetuation of this neurotic image. Historically, "female" diseases were treated through physiological methods including hysterectomies, a recommended cure for hysteria. Freud's predecessors also suggested hours of bathing to treat hysteria, often resulting in life-threatening dehydration. While these remedies are likely to be perceived as inhumane today, anti-depressants

have become the contemporary physiological remedy for "female" anxiety. By targeting women in college, at work, and at home, drug companies join the self-help industry in selling and profiting from the image of the neurotic female.

Although the media and self-help industry produce and perpetuate negative female stereotypes, apparently much of our society remains willing to accept them. Women—many of whom are encouraged to undergo years of counseling and physiological treatment as they did during Freud's era—are the most likely to accept and perpetuate such stereotypes by succumbing to the means through which they are marketed, purchasing self-help books and magazines as fast as they are published.

Self-empowerment, through means including education, sports, and community involvement, is less interesting to the profit-oriented media. Such pursuits may enhance women's self-esteem, but they don't sell as many books. Even exercise [and] a healthy diet are not sold to women as ways to relieve stress, but rather as methods to lose pounds. The ultimate message is that there is something wrong with women, either socially, mentally or physically.

It is unfortunate that negative female stereotypes are continuously accepted in our society. More tragic, however, is that so many women acquiesce to the subtle but massive marketing of Freud's depiction of them. His labels are bought again and again, in printed or bottled versions of products that cause too many women to accept their own worst self-perceptions and make many men perceive them as the basket cases they were—and still are—advertised to be. Research may show that women are twice as likely to suffer from anxiety as men, but if this finding is accepted at face value and is mass marketed, it not only implies that psychological problems plague a huge number of women—it indicates that we have a serious social problem and a potential self-fulfilling prophecy.   [1997]

Understanding the Reading

1. Briefly explain Freud's description of women's ailments and how his theories influence current attitudes toward women's mental health.

2. What does John Gray mean when he says that women and men are from different planets?

3. Summarize the advice John Gray and Ellen Fein and Sherrie Schneider give women.

4. On what negative stereotypes of women do psychologists, the media, and the drug companies rely?

Suggestions for Responding

1. Read and review John Gray's *Men Are from Mars, Women Are from Venus* or Ellen Fein and Sherrie Schneider's *The Rules: Time-Tested Secrets for Capturing the Heart of Mr. Right.* ✦

82

Our Bodies, Their Selves

KATRINE AMES

Heart disease kills women and men in almost equal numbers: it has no gender bias. Medical researchers have. In clinical trials for any number of health problems, including heart disease, they usually employ only male subjects—whether humans or rodents. In 1988, research on 22,071 male doctors revealed that aspirin reduces the risk of heart attacks. The benefit for women? Who knows? A study published this fall indicated that heavy coffee intake did not increase the incidence of heart attacks or strokes. The 45,589 subjects, aged 40 to 75, were men.

Such studies are firing up women's health activists and raising the profile of women's health issues. As women become more aware of inequities in medical research, they're mobilizing to put on the pressure. More women are entering the male-dominated research field, and publicly funded research is becoming more responsive to taxpayers' concerns. The sure way to build government support for women's health, says Rep. Patricia Schroeder, is to make it a political issue: "Women pay half the taxes. If they don't get a fair share of research, they ought to go after the guys who don't allow it to happen."

Congress, led by the Caucus for Women's Issues, is getting involved. Concerned that the National Institutes of Health had not monitored a 1986 policy that urged researchers to include women in their studies, the 150-member group—founded in 1977 and cochaired by Schroeder—requested that the General Accounting Office investigate. The result: a report on the NIH's insensitivity to women's concerns. Last September the NIH—which may soon have its first woman director, Dr. Bernadine Healy, former president of the American Heart Association—opened an office on women's health in Bethesda, Md.

Ignoring women's health issues, Schroeder says, is "a nonfeasance issue, not a malfeasance issue. In politics, folks fund what they fear, so almost anything dealing with women doesn't get funded." But politics—specifically, pressure from the right—may be what stymies some research. Government-funded fertility research is virtually nonexistent; there's no ob/gyn research program at NIH. Anti-choice activists helped derail fetal-tissue research in Parkinson's disease this year, after allegations that it would lead to abortions performed to obtain fetal tissue.

Many organizations and individuals are attempting to circumvent the politics. Last year Lilly Tartikoff, an adviser to Max Factor (a Revlon subsidiary) and the wife of NBC executive Brandon Tartikoff, secured a $2.4 million grant from Revlon to establish the Revlon/UCLA Women's Cancer Research Program. She told Revlon chairman Ronald O. Perelman, "We've been buying your products at the local drugstore since we were 10 or 12, and I feel it's your responsibility to give back to the women who have been supporting your company."

"Blatant sexism": Researchers' justification for omitting women is that female hormonal changes "complicate" work and that there may be fetal risk if a participant is pregnant and doesn't know it. The explanation, which some women consider shaky at best, can be outright absurd—as when a major NIH study on aging initially excluded females, despite the fact that postmenopausal women vastly outnumber their male contemporaries. As Rep. Henry Waxman, chairman of a House subcommittee on health and the environment, says, "It's not discrimination by intent, but it certainly is by result."

Diane Curtis, a founding member of New York City-based Women's Health Action and Mobilization (WHAM), puts it more bluntly: "Saying that women's bodies are complicated is saying that there is a norm out there and that norm is the male body. It's such blatant sexism." The results of such sexism, accidental or not, can be devastating. Treatments developed to alleviate a host of problems are tested on men, but they're used by women. And in matters of health, what's good for the gander can be harmful, even fatal, for the goose.

Many women are focusing attention on breast cancer, but there are several other issues that could benefit from a shot of activism. Osteoporosis-related problems kill as many women every year as breast cancer does, yet the debilitating disease gets less than half the government funds allocated for breast cancer and scientists still know little about it. Menopause is a vast unstudied area. Chlamydia, a frequently asymptomatic sexually transmitted disease, leaves thousands of women sterile every year, yet remains a virtual unknown. AIDS is a growing concern for women. The World Health Organization predicts that within 10 years as much as 80 percent of all AIDS cases will be transmitted heterosexually—and a healthy woman who has sex with an infected man is 14 times more likely to contract the AIDS virus than a healthy man who sleeps with an infected woman. According to Dr. Patricia Kloser of University Hospital in Newark, N.J., laboratory studies of AZT, the only AIDS drug approved by the federal government, revealed a terrible side effect in female mice: vaginal cancer.

Scientists, women's groups and others are beginning to work together on agendas, but much remains to be done. Washington-based consultant Joanne Howes wants to bring drug companies and medical groups into the discussion. "The challenge is to continue to build knowledge and to identify the issues," she says. "Otherwise [all this activity] will just be a blip on the screen."   [1990]

Understanding the Reading

1. How do medical researchers show an insensitivity to women's health problems?

2. How are women responding to this sexist bias?
3. Why do researchers discriminate against women?

Suggestions for Responding

1. Research the incidence (the proportion of people with the disease) and mortality rates for women and for men of the diseases Ames mentions. Analyze what this comparison reveals. ✦

83

The Nature of the Beast

ANITA HILL

The response to my Senate Judiciary Committee testimony[1] has been at once heartwarming and heart-wrenching. In learning that I am not alone in experiencing harassment, I am also learning that there are far too many women who have experienced a range of inexcusable and illegal activities—from sexist jokes to sexual assault—on the job.

My reaction has been to try to learn more. As an educator, I always begin to study an issue by examining the scientific data—the articles, the books, the studies. Perhaps the most compelling lesson is in the stories told by the women who have written to me. I have learned much; I am continuing to learn; I have yet ten times as much to explore. I want to share some of this with you.

"The Nature of the Beast" describes the existence of sexual harassment, which is alive and well. [It is] a harmful, dangerous thing that can confront a woman at any time.

What we know about harassment, sizing up the beast:

Sexual harassment is pervasive . . .

1. It occurs today at an alarming rate. Statistics show that anywhere from 42 to 90 percent of women will experience some form of harassment during their employed lives. At

least one percent experience sexual assault. But the statistics do not fully tell the story of the anguish of women who have been told in various ways on the first day of a job that sexual favors are expected. [Nor do they tell] the story of women who were sexually assaulted by men with whom they continued to work.

2. It has been occurring for years. In letters to me, women tell of incidents that occurred 50 years ago when they were first entering the workplace, incidents they have been unable to speak of for that entire period.

3. Harassment crosses lines of race and class. In some ways, it is a creature that practices "equal opportunity" where women are concerned. In other ways it exhibits predictable prejudices and reflects stereotypical myths held by our society.

We know that harassment all too often goes unreported for a variety of reasons . . .

1. Unwillingness (for good reason) to deal with the expected consequences;
2. Self-blame;
3. Threats of blackmail by coworkers or employers;
4. What it boils down to in many cases is a sense of powerlessness that we experience in the workplace, and our acceptance of a certain level of inability to control our careers and professional destinies. This sense of powerlessness is particularly troubling when one observes the research that says individuals with graduate education experience more harassment than do persons with less than a high school diploma. The message: when you try to obtain power through education, the beast harassment responds by striking more often and more vehemently.

That harassment is treated like a woman's "dirty secret" is well known. We also know what happens when we "tell." We know that when harassment is reported the common reaction is disbelief or worse . . .

1. Women who "tell" lose their jobs. A typical response told of in the letters to me was: I not only lost my job for reporting harass-

ment, but I was accused of stealing and charges were brought against me.

2. Women who "tell" become emotionally wasted. One writer noted that "it was fully eight months after the suit was conducted that I began to see myself as alive again."

3. Women who "tell" are not always supported by other women. Perhaps the most disheartening stories I have received are of mothers not believing daughters. In my kindest moments I believe that this reaction only represents attempts to distance ourselves from the pain of the harassment experience. The internal response is: "It didn't happen to me. This couldn't happen to me. In order to believe that I am protected, I must believe that it didn't happen to her." The external response is: "What did you do to provoke that kind of behavior?" Yet at the same time that I have been advised of hurtful and unproductive reactions, I have also heard stories of mothers and daughters sharing their experiences. In some cases the sharing allows for a closer bonding. In others a slight but cognizable mending of a previously damaged relationship occurs.

What we are learning about harassment requires recognizing this beast when we encounter it, and more. It requires looking the beast in the eye.

We are learning painfully that simply having laws against harassment on the books is not enough. The law, as it was conceived, was to provide a shield of protection for us. Yet that shield is failing us: many fear reporting, others feel it would do no good. The result is that less than 5 percent of women victims file claims of harassment. Moreover, the law focuses on quid pro quo,[2] but a recent New York *Times* article quoting psychologist Dr. Louise Fitzgerald says that this makes up considerably less than 5 percent of the cases. The law needs to be more responsive to the reality of our experiences.

As we are learning, enforcing the law alone won't terminate the problem. What we are seeking is equality of treatment in the workplace. Equality requires an expansion of our attitudes toward workers. Sexual harassment denies our treatment as equals and replaces it with treatment of women as objects of ego or power gratification. Dr. John Gottman, a psychologist at the University of Washington, notes that sexual harassment is more about fear than about sex.

Yet research suggests two troublesome responses exhibited by workers and by courts. Both respond by . . .

1. Downplaying the seriousness of the behavior (seeing it as normal sexual attraction between people) or commenting on the sensitivity of the victim.
2. Exaggerating the ease with which victims are expected to handle the behavior. But my letters tell me that unwanted advances do not cease—and that the message was power, not genuine interest.

We are learning that many women are angry. The reasons for the anger are various and perhaps all too obvious . . .

1. We are angry because this awful thing called harassment exists in terribly harsh, ugly, demeaning, and even debilitating ways. Many believe it is criminal and should be punished as such. It is a form of violence against women as well as a form of economic coercion, and our experiences suggest that it won't just go away.
2. We are angry because for a brief moment we believed that if the law allowed for women to be hired in the workplace, and if we worked hard for our educations and on the job, equality would be achieved. We believed we would be respected as equals. Now we are realizing this is not true. We have been betrayed. The reality is that this powerful beast is used to perpetuate a sense of inequality, to keep women in their place notwithstanding our increasing presence in the workplace.

What we have yet to explore about harassment is vast. It is what will enable us to slay the beast.

Research is helpful, appreciated, and I hope will be required reading for all legislators. Yet research has what I see as one shortcoming: it focuses on our reaction to harassment, not on the harasser. How we enlighten men who are cur-

rently in the workplace about behavior that is beneath our (and their) dignity is the challenge of the future. Research shows that men tend to have a narrower definition of what constitutes harassment than do women. How do we expand their body of knowledge? How do we raise a generation of men who won't need to be reeducated as adults? We must explore these issues, and research efforts can assist us.

What are the broader effects of harassment on women and the world? Has sexual harassment left us unempowered? Has our potential in the workplace been greatly damaged by this beast? Has this form of economic coercion worked? If so, how do we begin to reverse its effects? We must begin to use what we know to move to the next step: what we will do about it.

How do we capture our rage and turn it into positive energy? Through the power of women working together, whether it be in the political arena, or in the context of a lawsuit, or in community service. This issue goes well beyond partisan politics. Making the workplace a safer, more productive place for ourselves and our daughters should be on the agenda for each of us. It is something we can do for ourselves. It is a tribute, as well, to our mothers—and indeed a contribution we can make to the entire population.

I wish that I could take each of you on the journey that I've been on during all these weeks since the hearing. I wish that every one of you could experience the heartache and the triumphs of each of those who have shared with me their experiences. I leave you with but a brief glimpse of what I've seen. I hope it is enough to encourage you to begin—or continue and persist with—your own exploration. And thank you.
[1992]

Terms

1. SENATE JUDICIARY COMMITTEE TESTIMONY: Anita Hill testified against the nomination of Clarence Thomas to the Supreme Court on the grounds that he sexually harassed her when she worked for him at the Equal Employment Opportunity Commission.
2. QUID PRO QUO: The demand for sexual favors in exchange for employment, job retention, promotion, a salary increase, and so on.

Understanding the Reading

1. How pervasive is sexual harassment?
2. Why don't women report sexual harassment?
3. What are the frequent responses to reported harassment?
4. Why are women angry about harassment?
5. What is the drawback to research on harassment?
6. What are the broader effects of harassment?

Suggestions for Responding

1. Hill asks what we will do about sexual harassment. How would you answer her question?
2. Have you, or has someone you know, experienced or been witness to sexual harassment? Describe the incident, including the victim's response and what you now think the response should have been.
3. Investigate and report on the anti-harassment policies and procedures on your campus. ◆

84

Like a Smack in the Face: Pornography in the Trades

Barbara Trees

I want to tell you a bit about myself and construction work because most people who don't work in construction have no idea what it's like. I am a carpenter in New York City. I applied to the Carpenters' Union in 1978 and began my four-year apprenticeship in 1980. I am college educated and was thirty years old at the time. There were maybe ten women—tops—and 20,000 men in the union at the time.

I wanted to be a carpenter because it was daring, well paid, and out of the mainstream. I thought women merely had to prove we could do the work and then many more women would join us.

It made perfect sense to see the building trades as a great opportunity for women to achieve equality with men. Jobs were available, and the apprenticeships were open to people with limited educations. But, in spite of the possibilities, this field has not really opened up for women. And the mistreatment of women in construction is a horror story which has not been adequately told.

A woman who is sent to a job at a construction site can usually expect to be the only one on a crew of hundreds of men. For the first five or six years I went through the motions of fitting in. I guess we all did, we "first women." It was so very important to get along. The job sites were dirty and dangerous and the work was hard; we all got the difficult jobs, not the "tit" jobs, as easy work is called. The men we were supposed to learn the trade from usually had no intention of teaching us. They thought it was the most preposterous thing that women actually wanted to do this work.

These men found ways to push us out, and they were *not* nice about it. They were scary and belligerent and did not want "girls" around (the lone woman on a job or crew is always called "the girl"). The atmosphere was and is horrible. There is filthy language. There is total contempt for women and wives. The men piss and shit out in the open and on the floor instead of in toilets. Women are given the worst jobs to do, made to work alone at a job two or three men would do, and laid off first without cause. There are no changing facilities or bathrooms with locks for women. The men use binoculars to look for women in nearby buildings, and when they spot one in a bathroom or undressed, they yell, "There's one, there's one!" In addition to all this harassment, physical violence is common. I know of several women who were hit or punched by fellow construction workers, and nothing was done about it.

Pornography is commonplace on construction jobs. You see it in the locker rooms; on drinking fountains, on and inside lunch boxes, on and inside toolboxes, on tools, on walls in management, union, and other offices. It is often posted on job sites or on half-constructed buildings. I found it humiliating. I began to avoid areas where I found it and tore it down when I saw it. After that, it had a funny way of showing up where I was working or walking—just one little dirty picture, like a smack in the face—and nobody around to take the credit. The men feel they have an absolute right to display these pictures. It is very risky to complain about pornography in the construction industry. You can get harassed. You can get hurt. You can get fired, and once fired, you have no recourse. The contractor does not have to say why you were fired. The union stewards don't want to hear about it. There is no grievance procedure. I was fired from a job after politely asking a foreman to remove a beaver shot from our shanty, but only found out a year later that that was why I was fired. But losing your job is not the only threat. The mafia, some of whom deal in prostitution and pornography, lurk everywhere. Most of us who are activists have nightmares about construction workers chopping our doors down to get into our homes. We fear for our lives.

Many women in the trades try to ignore the pornography, but I could not do that and survive. I had listened to filthy woman-hating "jokes," had coworkers "accidentally" touch my breasts or ass, and put up with the idea of women as funny—the mere mention of breasts or anything about women's bodies bringing smirks. I just couldn't take it anymore.

So I got sick, quite seriously sick, and stayed out of work for two years. For women, this is not an uncommon reaction to these pressures in the nontraditional work world. But during the time I was ill, I thought about the situation, and when I went back I vowed that I would practice pro-woman self-defense. It worked. It gave me a sense of entitlement—to dignity, to the job, to fight for the women in my union as if we are the most important people on earth. It meant that I refused to listen to men bad-mouthing women, that I took these "jokes" and remarks for the insults they were, and that I responded accordingly.

In 1989, I founded New York Tradeswomen, a support group for women in the building trades. We formed a Women Carpenters Committee in the New York City District Council. I was appointed a shop steward in my local union in 1990, the first woman in my 2,000-member local to hold this position. As a steward, the union representative for the carpenters on a particular job site, I've battled pornography for the last three years. The union office gave me the pro-

tection to fight it and not be fired. But I still have problems. I've had long pornographic phone messages placed on my answering machine from men who boasted of being in my local. I've had a contractor tell me to go fuck myself when I asked him to remove the pornography from the trailer where, as a steward, I had to go to call my union. I told a teamster that I wouldn't hang a door in his shanty until he removed a nude picture. Later he chases me around waving a nude picture, yelling, "This is beautiful, this is good!" Once a pornographic picture showed up on the cooler. I saw it and took off my hard hat and bashed the closest guy to me over the head with it and said, "Is that yours?!" He may not even have put it there, but I didn't care, I was so mad. When I asked a tin knocker to simply turn his large toolbox, which was covered with beaver shots, away from the door so that I wouldn't have to see them, he accused me of being ridiculous and said that I should know better, that these pictures are everywhere, that this is the way it is in the construction industry, that I had to fit in, and that I would be to blame if he got fired over something so "minor." After I complained to union officials, this same guy followed me, glaring, to the subway.

I thought that women could change these job sites, but so far we haven't. There aren't enough of us, and the men are picking us off, one by one, both the weak and the strong. Using pornography and other forms of sexual harassment, men have successfully kept women out of construction in any significant numbers. Now that the recession has hit, we are devastated.

[1994]

Understanding the Reading

1. Why did Trees want to become a carpenter?
2. How are women in construction mistreated?
3. What was Trees' response to the harassment she endured?

Suggestions for Responding

1. Interview a woman you know who works in a traditionally male field about her experience of sexual harassment and pornography on the job. ✦

85

Bad Sports

Mariah Burton Nelson

O.J. Simpson is not alone.

The baseball star Darryl Strawberry has admitted beating his wife and pointing a gun in her face.

John Daly, the golfer, was arrested at his home after allegedly hurling his wife against a wall, pulling her hair and trashing the house. He pleaded guilty to a misdemeanor harassment charge and was placed on two years' probation with the stipulation that he complete a domestic violence treatment program.

The basketball star Moses Malone was accused by his wife of physical and verbal brutality, including death threats. He insisted he never hit her or threatened to kill her but admitted having "moved her out of the way."

Wimp Sanderson resigned as the men's basketball coach at the University of Alabama in 1992 after his secretary, Nancy Watts, filed a sex discrimination complaint against him. Ms. Watts, with whom he had had a longtime affair, alleged that he hit her as part of a continuing pattern of physical and sexual abuse, and was awarded $275,000 in a settlement. Mr. Sanderson claimed in court documents that Ms. Watts got her black eye by colliding with his outstretched hand.

Juanita Leonard testified in divorce court in 1991 that her husband, Sugar Ray Leonard, often punched her, threw her around and harassed her "physically and mentally in front of the children." He threatened to kill himself with a gun, she said. He threw lamps and broke mirrors.

The boxer denied none of this. At a press conference, he admitted having struck his wife with his fists. Yet he justified the behavior by saying that he and Juanita "fought, argued" and "grabbed each other," but that it "was in our house, between us."

Spectators also get into the spirit of things. Boston Celtics fans have hung banners saying they like to beat rival teams almost as much as they like to "beat our wives."

"I'm going to go home and beat my wife," Coach Joe Paterno of Penn State once said at a press conference after his football team lost to the University of Texas. Later he defended the statement as "just part of the sports culture, locker room talk, harmless, a joke that did not mean anything."

What is this "harmless" sports culture?

Whether hockey fights, football tackles or baseball brawls, intentionally hurtful acts are portrayed as natural—for men. Society's concept of violence is inextricably interwoven with its concept of expected, condoned male behavior. Boys are given boxing gloves as toys; girls and women who try to join wrestling or football teams are often ridiculed, sexually harassed or simply barred from taking part.

Most of the women whom male players see are not coaches or other athletes. They are the short-skirted cheerleaders and the university "hostesses" who escort them around campus during the recruiting process. The locker room is not a place to brag about your wife's or girlfriend's accomplishments. It is a place where men discuss women's bodies in graphic sexual terms, where they boast about "scoring" and joke about beating women.

In *The Hundred Yard Lie*, Rick Telander, a reporter for *Sports Illustrated,* writes that he has heard so much degrading talk of women in the locker room he's sure that "the macho attitudes promoted by coaches contribute (perhaps unwittingly) to the athlete's problems in relating to women."

Sexist comments can get men fired in some circles. But in sports, a world where sexism is a badge of honor, it is a common ground, a familiar language.

Timothy Jon Curry, an Ohio State sociologist who employed researchers to record locker-room conversations over several months, found that talk of women as objects took the form of loud performances for other men. Talk about ongoing relationships with women, on the other hand, took place only in hushed tones, often behind rows of lockers, and was subject to ridicule. "This ridicule tells the athlete that he is getting too close to femaleness, because he is taking relatedness seriously," he writes. "'Real men' do not do that."

A former college football star who spoke to me only on the condition that he not be named said of Mr. Curry's research: "That's right on target. We never talked about respecting women." This man, who later signed with the Philadelphia Eagles, recalls college teammates making crude boasts about sexual conquests. His college teammates hosted "pig parties." The man who brought the ugliest date would win a trophy. This football star says he learned to respect women from his mother and three athletic sisters, and did not attend the parties. But he would laugh at his teammates' jokes, which he now regrets.

"I remember the first time they showed the trophy, in the locker room," he says. "I was a 17-year-old freshman in a room full of upperclassmen. It was boisterous, raunchy, there was screaming and yelling. I laughed along. Men are extremely cliquish. I didn't want to be left out."

When quarterback Timm Rosenbach of the Phoenix Cardinals quit pro football after the 1992 season, he told Ira Berkow of *The New York Times:* "I thought I was turning into some kind of animal. You go through a week getting yourself up for a game by hating the other team, the other players. You're so mean and hateful, you want to kill somebody. Football's so aggressive. Things get done by force. And then you come home, you're supposed to turn it off? 'Oh, here's your lovin' daddy.' It's not that easy. It was like I was an idiot. I felt programmed. I had become a machine."

O. J. Simpson, who pleaded not guilty to charges of murdering his former wife and her friend, was programmed. He was, like all of us, a product of a culture that allows more than two million women each year to be beaten by husbands or boyfriends. About 1,400 women a year die at the hands of these "lovers." He was also part of a football culture that taught him to equate masculinity with violence.

Our society reveres athletes regardless of their behavior off the field. Even after he pleaded no contest to beating his wife on New Year's Day 1989, Mr. Simpson continued to work for Hertz and NBC, and to be described by fans and in the media as a "great guy" and an "American hero." When he was chased by police cars along the Los Angeles freeways, commuters stopped their cars to wave to him and chant, "Go, O. J., go!" They acted as if nothing—not wife-beating, not alleged murder—mattered, as if star athletes should be able to do exactly as they please.

Which is what they will continue to do until we stop glorifying them and stop training them to hate women.   [1994]

Understanding the Reading

1. How do the sports figures mentioned here rationalize their violence against the women in their lives?
2. What factors lead to and reinforce such male violence?
3. What did Timothy Jon Curry's research show?

Suggestions for Responding

1. Why do you think so many professional sports figures are involved in domestic violence?
2. Imagine that your favorite sports figure has just been convicted of sexual violence. Write him or her a letter expressing your feelings about the conviction. ✦

86

A More Hidden Crime: Adolescent Battered Women

NANCY WORCESTER

Domestic violence has often been referred to as our nation's most hidden crime. However, after 15 years of activism and the establishment of more than 1000 battered women's shelter programs around the country, the battered women's movement has made many people and community services aware of the fact that huge numbers of women are entrapped in relationships of ongoing abuse of power, control, and physical coercion. The FBI estimates that a woman is battered every 15–18 seconds in this country and that approximately one of every three women experiences some physical violence in her long-term relationship(s). The pervasiveness of the violence may be best represented by the statement that one of every five women probably experiences five or more serious battering incidents each year.

Just as there is finally a public consciousness of the magnitude of the problem of women being battered, we are discovering an even more hidden, perhaps even more prevalent crime—violence against adolescent women. It turns out that most of the understanding of the dynamics of power and control in intimate relationships gained from the battered women's movement applies as much to adolescent women in dating relationships as it does to adult women. Tragically, the ramifications of violence for younger women are often exaggerated by a number of factors, but there are far fewer resources and options available to adolescent than adult women who are trying to end the violence in their lives.

Working to prevent violence in young people's lives must be a high priority for any of us committed to creating a better world for the next generation and to helping young women maximize on their full potential. The isolation and lowered self-esteem which are so often a *consequence* of violence will have exaggerated ramifications for a young woman if they cause her to limit or eliminate skill-building, career options, or educational opportunities which could affect the rest of her life. (It is important to emphasize that the isolation, lowered self-esteem, and unhealthy coping mechanisms which are often observed in abused women are predictable *consequences* of violence and are not the *cause* of the violence. Confusing a consequence of violence with a cause can lead to dangerous, victim-blaming misunderstandings of the violence.)

If a woman is experiencing violence in her dating relationship(s), it will almost certainly be related to many other issues in her life. Anyone working with adolescents will benefit from seeing the connections between violence and the issues they already address. Why she is not always able to show up for study group, why she "had to go" to a concert instead of studying the night before an important exam, why she is no longer best friends with "the nice girl who seemed to have such a positive influence on her," or why she "suddenly" started dressing in a way which always *or* never shows off her figure may be explained by knowing that a young woman is in a relationship where someone else

is taking control over almost all aspects of her life. Health educators need to recognize that many women are beaten up if they try to insist that male partners wear a condom or abstain from sexual activity. Because battering so often starts or accelerates during pregnancy and because sexual assault and other forms of violence are so intimately connected, anyone who works with adolescent pregnancy or sexual assault issues needs to be aware of the connections.

Ironically, many women learn about motherhood and battering at exactly the same time. Retrospective studies show that 25% of battered women experienced their first physical abuse during a pregnancy and that 40–60% of battered women were abused during a pregnancy or during pregnancies. The consequences are a much higher rate of miscarriage, stillbirth, premature delivery, and low birth weight infants in battered than non-battered women. The problem may be even more exaggerated in pregnant teens. A study looking specifically at physical abuse during teen pregnancy found that 26% of pregnant teens reported they were involved with a man who physically hurt them and 40–60% said that the battering had begun or escalated since their boyfriends knew they were pregnant. This study also provides an urgent reminder that services are not addressing the issue of violence for adolescent women: 65% of pregnant teens had not talked to *anyone* about the abuse.

Looking at the continuum of violence issues (The Power and Control and Equity Wheels by the Duluth Domestic Abuse Intervention Project and the Continuum of Family Violence Chart from Village to Village, by the Alaska Dept. of Public Safety are particularly useful), it becomes apparent how a range of forms of violence—physical, verbal, emotional, and sexual—are used by abusers to dominate their partners. The more subtle forms of sexual violence (unwanted touching, sexual name calling, unfaithfulness or threat of unfaithfulness, saying "no one else will ever love you," false accusations) are clearly emotionally as well as sexually controlling. These need to be identified as "violence issues" which are related to, and can escalate into, unwanted sex, unprotected sex, hurtful sex, and other forms of sexual assault. Sexual violence is often the expression of violence which is the most painful for a woman to discuss. Emotional abuse is almost always present if there are other forms of abuse in a relationship but a clever abuser may achieve sufficient control by emotional abuse without ever resorting to other forms. Women consistently say that emotional abuse is the hardest form to identify (Is this really happening? Is this abuse? Am I making too much of this?) but recognize it as the form of abuse which has the most impact on their lives and their view of themselves. Many women who have been in life-threatening situations say, "The physical battering was nothing compared to the daily emotional abuse." Helping young women see the interconnectedness of verbal, emotional, physical, and sexual power and control issues may be the most useful information in empowering them to end *all* forms of violence in their lives.

By the time adolescents start experimenting with their own dating relationships, they have been bombarded with messages that violence against women is tolerated and even encouraged and that dominance, aggression, and abuse of power and control are appropriate masculine behaviors which are rewarded by society. Today's young people have been exposed to a tolerance and perpetuation of male violence which is unique to this generation. They grew up in the era when the average child was watching 24 hours of television a week with children's programming averaging 15.5 violent acts per hour. By the time they reach 18, the average US adolescent has witnessed approximately 26,000 murders, in their own homes, via the TV screen.

The role of television in sex-role socialization and the perpetuation of male violence has been grossly exaggerated for today's young people because changes in federal regulations, in the early 1980s, allowed the sale of toys directly connected to TV shows, removed regulations limiting the amount of advertising allowed on children's programming, and ruled that product-based shows were legal. The result was a totally new integration of the TV and toy industries. By 1986 all of the ten best selling toys had shows connected with them and by 1988, 80% of children's TV programming was produced by toy companies. Parallel marketing promoted definitions of masculinity and femininity as clearly defined as the distinct lines of boys' toys vs. girls' toys. Because of the new integration of TV and toys, today's young people did not learn to ex-

plore their own creativity or imagination in healthy ways but instead learned to "act out their scripts" as dominant and competitive or caring, helpless, and concentrating on appearance, either as GI Joe or Ghostbusters vs. Barbie or My Little Pony.

With electronic video games, an even newer and unstudied phenomenon, young people get to act out and be rewarded for playing their violent roles. The direct participation in "performing" the violence of video games is predicted to magnify whatever effect more passive TV viewing has on one's acceptance or perpetuation of violence. In a violence promoting and accepting culture, it is not surprising to find that most video games are very violent (a sampling of 120 machines in three arcades in Madison, Wisconsin, found that more than 70 involved either hand-to-hand combat or shooting to kill enemies) and that the most popular games in an arcade are the most violent.

Consequently, *unlearning* the tolerance of violence and *learning* how to achieve violence-free, equal relationships are skills which are now as crucial to *teach* young people as reading, writing, math, and the use of computers. The way people learn, in their earliest experimentation, to be in intimate relationships can set the pattern for what they expect in future relationships. It is a time when the highest standards should be set! Adolescents need to see models of healthy, equal, violence-free relationships, in order to aim for that in their own lives, and *to be able to model that for their peers*.

At this stage, many teens do not have the knowledge or skills to prevent or react against violence in their own lives or in their friends' lives. In fact, exactly the opposite is much more likely. Many young women have said that even when they have told friends they were being hurt by their boyfriends, the response was that they were lucky to have boyfriends. There is enormous peer pressure not to break up. Many teens regard violence as a normal part of dating and have no idea they deserve better. Extreme possessiveness, jealousy, dominance, and not being "allowed" to break up get wrongly identified as desirable, positive signs of caring, love, and commitment, rather than strong warning signs that they are in an unhealthy, potentially dangerous relationship.

Figuring out what to expect in relationships may be particularly confusing for anyone who grew up in a home where there was violence. Many young men only see abusing males (in reality *and* in the media) as role models. Many young women who told their mothers about being hurt by their boyfriends have heard, "you have to learn to take the bad and the good in a relationship to make it work."

Many teens who have grown up in violent homes face the difficulty of trying to figure out how they want to be in their own young adult relationships while they are still learning (or not learning) to cope with being affected by the violence with which they grew up. The battered women's movement has very effectively identified that when a woman is battered, her children are almost always affected by the violence. Seventy-five percent of women who are battered in this country have children living at home. Children in homes where domestic violence occurs are physically abused or seriously neglected at a rate 1500% higher than the national average in the general population. Even witnessing domestic violence can have a tremendous impact on young people and may result in symptoms very similar to those seen in people who have been abused. Helping these young people learn healthy relationship skills can be particularly challenging as many teens do not recognize the impact the violence in their homes has had on them and many teens do not want to talk about witnessing or experiencing abuse.

Particularly crucial to how we help young people learn relationship skills *and* acknowledge that violence in their lives may have already influenced their attitudes and behaviors is how we address the impact of the "intergenerational transmission of violence." There is a confusing body of work which examines how the cycle of violence can be passed on through the generations. We now know the old "dad beats mom, mom beats the children, and the children beat the pets" picture was much too simplistic and inaccurate. Increasingly, it is being shown that the person beating mom may also be the one beating the children and protecting the mother is often the best way to protect the children. Although research is inconsistent in documenting the rates of intergenerational transmission of violence, there is a consistent trend

which shows that boys who witness domestic violence as children are more likely to batter their female partners as adults than are men from non-violent homes.

How we use this information can be a key factor in determining whether we help break the intergenerational transmission of violence or actually contribute to its perpetuation. Too much of the literature deals with this pattern as if it were inevitable. Central to breaking the pattern is addressing and researching a different set of questions. If 30% of boys who witness violence become abusers, the question must be asked, "What can we learn from the 70% who witness violence but do not become abusers?" What factors help young people who have witnessed violence learn to resist violent behavior? Young people from violent homes who have experienced the ugliness of violence and have learned to value non-violent relationships can be exactly the people most committed to breaking the cycle of violence and can be incredibly effective peer leaders.

Most important, young people must *never* learn that violence is inevitable. Many dating violence resources (including some of the materials I highly recommend on other aspects) include information on the intergenerational transmission of violence without making it clear that the cycle can be broken. Information on warning signs of potential abusers almost always includes "boys who grew up in violent homes." What does it feel like to see that information if you are a young man who witnessed violence at home? We must make certain that none of our materials or our messages ever contribute towards a young man feeling that he is destined to be violent.

Studies on dating violence consistently show that many teens in violent relationships have not talked to *any* adults about the violence in their lives. We need to start identifying the barriers which have made us so ineffective on this issue and acknowledge that we are only starting to have the language and tools for opening a dialogue on dating violence.

The good news is that a wide range of excellent resources, curricula, and videos have been produced on dating violence issues and violence-free relationships in recent years. It's a very exciting stage to be working on this issue because no one needs to "start from scratch." However, work needs to be done to make the excellent resources and services available to, and appropriate for, many more teens. Few of the resources address the issue in a way that has any meaning for lesbian, gay, or bisexual teens or for young people of color. Many of the materials seem to have the underlying assumption that children grow up in homes where there is one male and one female adult. Special issues for teens with disabilities need to be addressed because of both the high rate of sexual assault of people with disabilities and the complexities of dating which arise from the myth that people with disabilities are "asexual." The obsession with body image and a very narrow definition of attractiveness can also be particularly cruel and abusive in adolescence.

"You deserve to be treated with respect."

"You are not alone if someone is hurting you. There are excellent resources to help you end the violence in your life."

These messages which we have been giving adult battered women for the last 15 years are now the same messages we have to give to much younger women.   [1993]

Understanding the Reading

1. Describe the magnitude of battery against women.
2. How do young women react to violence in their dating relationships?
3. What is the relationship between pregnancy and battering, especially for adolescent women?
4. What forms does this violence take?
5. What makes emotional abuse difficult to deal with?
6. What is the influence of television on sex role behaviors and violence in relationships?
7. Why may video games increase violent relationships?
8. Why is it important for young people to learn to have violence-free, equal relationships?
9. What impact does growing up in a violent home have on children?
10. What have studies shown about the intergenerational transmission of violence?
11. What can be done to reduce or eliminate dating violence?

12. In addition to young people from traditional, middle-class families, what other groups of adolescents need to be addressed?

Suggestions for Responding

1. What factors do you think may help young people who have witnessed violence learn to resist becoming violent themselves?
2. After watching Saturday morning television, write a description of the violent episodes you witnessed, and try to analyze what effect viewing this violence would have on young children. ✦

87

Why Doesn't She Just Leave?

CLARETHIA ELLERBE

On the first night of a university course I was taking, "Gender, War and Peace", the class viewed a film called "Speak Truth to Power." Rita Moreno was one of the actors reading the testimony of a Russian woman who had created a hotline for abused women. After the film, the class discussed the film's contents, but spoke very little on the subject of domestic violence. This made me wonder whether the topic was taboo, or just something that people do not feel comfortable discussing. Or, is it something that society is not aware of, or feels that it only happens in a certain part of society?

Before viewing this film I had never really given domestic violence much consideration. As I sat there listening to Rita Moreno, a celebrity reading the words of a woman fighting domestic violence, it made me want to do some research on how deeply it cuts. From my research, I learned that when people hear the words "domestic violence", they often think of the physical aspect of it, such as pushing, shoving, hitting,

Excerpted from Clarethia Ellerbe, "Why Doesn't She Just Leave?" Reprinted by permission of the author.

twisting arms, punching, choking and slapping. While the abuser and the victim are in the relationship, they are not willing to admit to themselves or anyone else that they are in an abusive relationship. A co-worker once told me that her husband could beat her the night before and she could wear a one-piece bathing suit the next day, and you, as the observer, could not detect her bruises. I asked her how he was able to accomplish this. She had no answer, but her statement did make me wonder about the abuser's view of domestic violence. Observing relationships of some of my family and friends, I decided to ask the ones that appeared to be in abusive relationships, or have been in the past.

INTERVIEW I

The following story is told me by my aunt, who was in an abusive marriage for almost forty years. "At the age of 16, I met my husband, and I enjoyed a wonderful, romantic courtship with him. Then people began to make comments, like: 'Why would a pretty girl like you get married to an ugly duckling'; that is when my problems started. The comments led him to thoughts of jealousy, verbal and mental abuse, and eventually physical abuse."

"It got to the point where he painted our windows black and did not allow me and the children to visit with relatives or friends. I had choke marks on my neck, and wore these bruises as if they were some kind of trophy. Along with my bruises, I received cuts, wounds and black eyes. My head was banged against the walls, doors, the floor, and the refrigerator, and during all this time I thought he loved me. When people used to ask me about the beatings I was taking from my husband, I would say: 'If a man doesn't beat you every now and then, he doesn't love you.' I strongly believed that all his hitting was about him loving me, and teaching me the right way to go in life. It makes me laugh when I tell someone that my husband was going to teach me the right things to do. I have asked myself a thousand times, 'What could my husband have taught me, as dumb as he was?' I'm glad that my husband didn't love me to death! But it would be nice if one day he came to me and asked me to forgive him."

INTERVIEW II

Joe is a friend of the family, and we grew up in the same town. He likes to call himself a controller. This is his story about his method for control. Joe says: "When I first meet someone who I want to be in my life, I start by building her ego, you know, like telling her things I know women like to hear. I tell her how beautiful she is, and I might add something like how lucky I am to have found her. Women love it when a man talks like that to them, especially when the guy tells them that they are a cut above all the common Janes."

"After the first few dates I send her flowers or some other token gift. You know, not an expensive gift, but just something to make her feel good about herself. By now, she is thanking her lucky stars that she finally met the man of her dreams. I know how women like to brag to their girlfriends about meeting the man of their dreams. Soon I have her all happy and excited about the start of her ideal relationship with her ideal man. She now opens up and begins to talk freely about what she wants. I listen to every word she has to say. She talks about her girlfriends, as well as her family, at this stage of the game. This is my opportunity to find out which of her girlfriends or family members has the strongest influence in her life."

"After I learn the name of the strongest person in her life, I start planning how to eliminate that person from her circle of friends. Because I know that this person is strong, I know that this person will not let me treat her friend in an unkind way. I know that she will come between me and my woman, once she sees me trying to mistreat her friend. Women have something called 'sisterhood', and once they get this sisterhood working there is nothing in the world that a man can do to break this bond. I am not strong enough to break that bond; it is a bond that will take me out of life so fast I wouldn't know what hit me. We men are afraid of the sisterhood bond; women don't really know how powerful that sisterhood is. We men keep you women fighting amongst yourselves, so you guys cannot form that strong bond."

"But once I eliminate her strongest friend, it is easy to keep her away from her other friends, co-workers, as well as interfering family members. I am now in control. My strategy is to control her completely and make her totally dependent on me, to the point where she cannot make her own decisions without first asking me, which also includes when and where to go to the bathroom. Feeling powerful and feeling the need for more control, I begin to downplay all her achievements she made before she met me. It doesn't matter if she had a better job than me, or if she owns her own home, or has a car and I don't. I am constantly telling her that if it weren't for me she would have nothing. I am the one who makes her look good in the eyes of her friends, her co-workers, and family. I make her look respectable in the neighborhood, as well as to her female friends and family. I make her feel like all of her friends are jealous of her good man."

While doing this research I learned that an abused person's perceptions are altered by the abuse, and that domestic violence has nothing to do with conflict resolution. It has a purpose of its own. That purpose is to establish a relationship of power over and control of the partner.

[2003]

References

Domestic Violence Statistical Summary (www.fultonpd.com/stats.htm)

www.dasi.org

MSN Learning and Research—Domestic Violence http://encarta.msn.com/encnet/refpages/RefArticle.aspx?refid=762529482

Dr. Susan Forward and Joan Torres (1987). *Men Who Hate Women & the Women Who Love Them*

Aunt "Jane," personal communication, 2003.

"Joe," personal communication, 2003.

Understanding the Reading

1. What kinds of abuse are featured in this essay?
2. Why did the author's aunt stay with her husband for so long?
3. How does Joe control women?
4. Why does Joe control women?
5. What is his greatest obstacle?

Suggestions for Responding

1. Interview someone who was in an abusive relationship (without asking why he or she stood for it).
2. Share stories in the class of people you have known who were in abusive relationships.
3. Invite a representative from a women's shelter to speak to the class. ✦

88

Rape and Sexual Assault

JAMES A. DOYLE

Few words strike as much terror in a person's heart as rape. Few human acts are so fraught with misinformation and misconception as rape. Few other acts so degrade a human being as rape. And few other acts show the imbalance of power between men and women and men's quest for domination over women as rape does.

Rape is first and foremost an act of *violence*, an attempted or completed sexual assault instigated by one or more persons against another human being. The historical roots of rape run deep in the patriarchal tradition of male violence toward women. Rape, to be understood, must not be seen as simply a violent sexual act of a few lunatics or pathologically disordered persons, but rather a violent sexual act performed by many and reinforced by the dominant patriarchal values coming to the fore in their most twisted and disturbing forms in our culture. A few cultures may be less prone to violent sexual acts between males and females, but ours and most others are definitely "rape-prone" cultures. No discussion of power and its imbalance between women and men would be complete without a discussion of rape.

. . . We will first take up the issue of rape as an act of dominance (not sex) and of power (not pathology) that is ingrained in the very fiber of the male's gender role. Next we will attempt to put the statistics of rape in perspective by trying to give some scope to the enormity of the act of rape in the everyday lives of many women and some men. And then, we will note the rising concern and some of the actions taken among feminists and nonfeminists alike over the issue of rape as a social phenomenon of epidemic proportions and not merely an isolated criminal act affecting a few.

RAPE AND POWER

Throughout most of this century those who influenced what others thought about rape saw it as a "victim-precipitated phenomenon." Sigmund Freud, in his study of the female personality, theorized that the female was more "masochistic" than the male and that rape—either in fantasy or in fact—was the one sexual act wherein the female acted out her masochism to the utmost. However, such nonsense was soon dismissed by the psychiatric and psychological communities who began to speculate that rape was the result of a disordered or aberrant sexual impulse within a certain small group of men. Today, however, rape—whether the victim is female or male—is seen as an act of power or dominance of one person over another. Recently, some social scientists have noted that rape is one of the most terrifying means used by men to dominate other men inside and outside of prison. To focus on rape as a power or dominance act we need only analyze how rape is used in prison:

> Rape in prison is rarely a sexual act, but one of violence, politics and an acting out of power roles. "Most of your homosexual rapes [are] a macho thing," says Col. Walter Pence, the Chief of Security here at the Louisiana State Penitentiary at Angola. "It's basically one guy saying to another: 'I'm a better man than you and I'm gonna turn you out ["turn you out" is prison slang for rape] to prove it.' I've investigated about a hundred cases personally, and I've not seen one that's just an act of passion. It's definitely a macho/power thing among the inmates."

A prime ingredient in rape is the element of aggression that is so deeply embedded in the male's gender role. For many men, aggression is one of the major ways of proving their masculinity and manhood, especially among those men who feel some sense of powerlessness in their lives. The male-as-dominant or male-as-aggressor is a theme so central to many men's self-concept that it literally carries over into their sexual lives. Sex, in fact, may be the one area where the average man can still prove his masculinity when few other areas can be found for him to prove himself manly or in control, or the dominant one in a relationship. Diana Russell addresses this issue when she declares that rape is not the act of a disturbed male, but rather an act of an overconforming male. She writes:

> Rape is not so much a deviant act as an overconforming act. Rape may be understood as an extreme acting-out of qualities that are regarded as super masculine in this and many other societies: aggression, force, power, strength, toughness, dominance, competitiveness. To win, to be superior, to be successful, to conquer—all demonstrate masculinity to those who subscribe to common cultural notions of masculinity, i.e., the *masculine mystique*. And it would be surprising if these notions of masculinity did not find expression in men's sexual behavior. Indeed, sex may be the arena where these notions of masculinity are most intensely played out, particularly by men who feel powerless in the rest of their lives, and hence, whose masculinity is threatened by this sense of powerlessness.

The fusion of aggression and sexuality for many men can be seen when we examine the area of sexual arousal as stimulated by graphic scenes of rape. Initially, researchers found that convicted rapists were more sexually aroused by depictions of violent sexuality than were men who had not raped. Thus it was thought that rapists must have a very low threshold for sexual arousal, and that the least little provocation would set off a male rapist (e.g., a woman who would assertively say "no" to sexual advances or even put up a fight was enough to trigger off a rapist, or so it was thought). In more recent studies, however, when men who had never raped were exposed to depictions of sexual assault, they reported a heightened sexual arousal from such scenes and an increase in their rape fantasies. Another disquieting note is that when nonrapist males were shown depictions of sexual assault, they reported the possibility that they would even consider using force themselves in their sexual relations. The research appears to suggest that most men (i.e., rapists and non-rapists) find violence a stimulant to heighten or arouse their sexual feelings. There is evidence that seems to indicate that males in general find sexuality related at some level to an expression of aggression, and in turn aggression heightens their sexual fantasies or actual sexual behaviors.

In summary, we can say that sexual assault or rape is first and foremost an act of sexual violence that to some degree draws upon the sexual fantasies of the rapist; it is linked to the rapist's need to show superiority and dominance over another.

The Problem of Numbers

Rape is one of the most underreported of all serious crimes in the United States and in other countries as well. When we try to get a true picture of the enormity of its incidence, we find the issue complicated by the lack of reliable rape statistics. The crime of rape presents some uniquely confounding problems.

One problem we encounter is the simple fact that many, if not most, rape victims simply refuse to come forward and report to the authorities incidents of sexual violence. For many rape victims, a sense of shame or guilt or self-blame about their role in the rape assaults may be enough to prevent them from coming forward and pressing charges. Those who do press charges, however, are apt to meet with questions, accusations, and other degrading and humiliating experiences by the very authorities that are sworn to uphold the laws of society that make the rape of a person a serious felony.

Another problem is that when rape victims do press charges against their assailants, their life histories, especially sexual activities, are dragged before the public. In many instances, the public seems willing to blame the victim for the assault rather than the rapist. The reason for such an attribution of guilt to the victim rather than to the assailant seems to lie in the fact that many people have a tendency to blame others for their misfortunes, as if the world we live in

was and is a "just world" where bad things happen only to those who somehow bring on or somehow deserve the consequences of their acts. Consequently, a likely result of such a "just world" orientation is that more often than not, the defenders of rapists will try to show that the rape victims acted in such a manner as to infer their complicity in the sexual assaults or that they "had it coming" because of their actions. We find such a courtroom tactic used by many defense attorneys, and it was one that apparently did not work in the much publicized 1984 New Bedford, Massachusetts, gang-rape case. There the rape-victim's motives for stopping at a bar were questioned and inferences were made impugning her behavior while in the bar. For example, during the trial, it was pointed out that the rape victim had talked with several of the accused rapists before the gang rape occurred. (If the mere act of talking is sufficient cause in some people's minds for a group of men to rape a woman, then we indeed have a twisted view of the causes of rape.) Thus, with all the barriers preventing the victims of sexual assault from coming forward, it is no wonder that rape continues to be one of the most underreported crimes. Even so, the Federal Bureau of Investigation reported that in the decade between 1967 and 1977 the number of reported rapes doubled in the United States. [I have] noted that:

> During 1977 alone, over 63,000 cases of rape were reported by the FBI. The most shocking feature of these statistics is that rape is considered by many experts in crime statistics to be one of the *least* reported violent crimes. The best available estimates suggest that for every one reported rape case there are anywhere from three to ten unreported cases. The conservative estimate of three means that over a quarter of a million women were forcibly raped in the United States in 1977!

While we have no absolute statistics for the total number of completed or attempted rapes committed annually in North America, we can estimate the probability of a woman being the victim of sexual assault during her lifetime. Allan Johnson estimated that "Nationally, a *conservative* estimate is that, under current conditions, 20–30 percent of girls now twelve years old will suffer a violent sexual attack during the remainder of their lives." Even with this estimate, however, we should keep in mind that this percentage excludes females under twelve, married women, and male rape victims. The enormity of the incidence of rape becomes even more staggering when we note that untold numbers of children under twelve are often the victims of sexual assault, as well as the many cases of male rape both inside and outside of prison.

RAPE AS A SOCIAL CONCERN

Due to the mounting concern over women's rights heralded by the reemergent women's movement, sexual assaults and their debilitating consequences for the victims have become one of the more pressing central issues of the 1970s and 1980s. Consequently, many social scientists have turned their attention toward understanding the dynamics of rapists and their motives, the institutional and cultural factors promoting rape, and of course, the various factors affecting the assault on rape victims and their reactions.

To combat the growing number of rapes, more and more people are beginning to think in terms of prevention and not only of ways to deal with the debilitating aftermath of sexual assault. Many different ways have been suggested to stop the growing wave of sexual assaults in our society.

Two such preventive approaches commonly thought of are, first, a "restrictive approach" that focuses on women changing their life-styles (e.g., not going out alone or not talking to strangers), and second, an "assertive approach" that suggests that women learn martial arts in order to fight back if assaulted. Both of these approaches have, however, some drawbacks. The restrictive approach, asking women to change their pattern of living, is an affront to women. Do we ask merchants to stop keeping money in their cash registers to prevent robberies? Why then should women change, for example, their dress or their social habits? The assertive approach has one possible value: the demise of the myth of the "defenseless woman." However, one problem with this approach is that many times in order to coerce a victim a rapist uses a deadly weapon, which totally nullifies any preventive

action or force a victim may take to ward off an assailant.

Along with teaching young children and women to skillfully defend themselves, it seems that a broader based attack against sexual assaults should be taken against the social and institutional factors that promote sexual violence in our society. Two additional areas should be addressed if we are to see a reduction and, hopefully, an elimination in sexual assaults in our society. First, we need to examine the male's gender role with its prescriptive aggressive element, especially aggression against women. Aggression and violence are still seen by many as an integral part of the male's gender role. One way to reduce sexual assault in our society would be to redefine the male gender role, incorporating nonaggressive or nonviolent elements rather than aggressiveness. Of course, many people would object to such a major change in the male role, fearing that our country would fall prey to its national enemies who may wish to attack a nation of nonaggressive men.

Another controversial change that would reduce the number of sexual assaults is an open attack on hard-core and violence-oriented pornography and the multi-million dollar business that supports it. First of all, we should dismiss the notion that only males find sexually explicit materials arousing. Research has found that men *as well as* women find various kinds of erotic material sexually stimulating. However, the pornography industry has mainly directed its sales to a male audience. Although some erotic material does not focus on violent sexual aggression, a large proportion of the male-oriented pornography that is sold in stores across our country portrays the female as the victim of physical and sexual assault.

Researchers Neil Malamuth and Edward Donnerstein have found that exposure to violent pornography generally increases sexual arousal as well as negative attitudes toward women and favorable attitudes toward sexual assault. Thus one possible way to reduce the sexual violence in our society against women would be to eliminate such material. However, those who oppose such a plan immediately bring up the issue of a person's First Amendment rights, which guarantee freedom of speech; such opposition, however, misinterprets the Constitution and its intent.

Would society be as accepting if various media presented graphic anti-Semitic portrayals of Jews being shoved into gas chambers or American Indians being shot for sport for their land? And yet many people support the multi-million dollar industry that shows women assaulted and maimed for the sake of sexual stimulation.

If our society is to rectify the age-old problem of unequal power between females and males, we need to challenge many of our behaviors, our attitudes, and our social institutions that continue to cast women in an inferior role. Until that day, the problem of inequality between the genders is everyone's concern.   [1985]

Understanding the Reading

1. How does rape reflect patriarchal values?
2. How have theories about rape changed during the past 100 years, and how is it viewed today?
3. How is rape an act of an overconforming male?
4. How are aggression and sexuality related for most men?
5. Why is it difficult to know accurately the incidence of rape?
6. Why do people tend to "blame the victim" of sexual assault?
7. Explain the difference between the "restrictive approach" and the "assertive approach" to rape prevention and what is wrong with each.
8. What social and institutional factors promote sexual violence?

Suggestions for Responding

1. Doyle proposes that the male role be changed to eliminate its emphasis on aggression. Do you think this is desirable or not? Why? How might we go about making such a change?
2. Doyle also proposes that eliminating violent pornography is one way to reduce violence against women, and he dismisses the claim that this would be an infringement of First Amendment rights. Do you agree or disagree with his position? Why? ✦

89

Fraternities of Fear

KATHLEEN HIRSCH

Some scenes from the ivory tower: Five lacrosse team buddies and another student at St. John's University in Queens, New York, allegedly invited friends in to watch, last March, while they brutally sodomized a female student. A full month went by before the police were notified by university officials, who claimed to be protecting the victim's privacy. Because of the charges, all six men were suspended for the duration of the academic year. The woman has withdrawn from school.

At Colgate University, in Hamilton, New York, two women reported that a student sexually harassed two women, then raped a third, during the course of one evening last February. A doctor presented physical evidence to the university's judicial board of the rape victim's condition, which was said to include severe bruising and a ripped vagina. The student was found "guilty." His punishment, suspension in abeyance, was changed following campus protest to suspension for two semesters. The public authorities were never contacted.

In 1987, two fraternity sophomores at the University of New Hampshire, in Durham, were accused of sexually assaulting a woman student in a dormitory. A university disciplinary board, comprised of students, faculty, and staff, found the men "not guilty" of sexual assault but suspended the men for a semester, because of disrespect to others. The lack of sterner sanctions led students to a sit-in protest at the dean of students' office; 11 activists were eventually arrested. In a criminal hearing, the accused men, pleading guilty to misdemeanor charges, were sentenced to what amounted to 90 days in jail. The woman withdrew from school; the men eventually graduated, their degrees safely in hand.

The bad news this fall is that college campuses are unsafe for women. This is not because violent crimes occur more frequently there than anywhere else—actually, in the case of sex crimes, the rate runs about the same as the general population. Rather, it is because colleges do almost nothing about their student aggressors. In case after case of campus rape, university officers rely on administrative judicial boards that mete out absurdly lenient punishments; they fail to file criminal complaints in an effort to ward off bad publicity; and they largely succeed in creating the impression that crimes against women are aberrations in otherwise civilized communities devoted to the refinement of the mind.

Here are the facts. One out of four women will be sexually assaulted on a college campus. At the very most, only one in ten of those will report it. Their attackers will be fellow students 80 percent of the time, and the most likely location of the attack will be a dormitory room or a fraternity house.

Fraternities in particular seem to be breeding grounds for campus sexual aggression, from jeering verbal abuse to acquaintance rape. A 1969 study by the dean's office at the University of Illinois at Urbana-Champaign found that frat men, a quarter of its male student population, perpetrated 63 percent of student sexual assault at the institution. From such studies it is also becoming clear that fraternities promote the most heinous form of sexual assault, the gang rape. Unlike widely publicized gang rapes that conform to class and racial stereotypes, this crime, if committed behind a fraternity's doors, becomes a boy's prank—or even a sanctioned rite of passage into the grown-up world of male dominance, privilege, and power.

The fraternity gang rape almost always conforms to script. New, naive students, or women from a nearby college, are invited to their first frat party, usually early in the fall term (although gang rapes take place at *any* time of the year, with women of *any* age). Alcohol is plentiful. In some cases, drinking is a prerequisite to entering the actual party, either by consuming a few cocktails in an upstairs room or having successive ones in several rooms. The point is for women to become as inebriated as possible—without suspecting negative consequences.

The victim is selected, either before the party or soon after she arrives, by a frat brother, and is "worked over," in a perverse parody of seduction, relying on a variety of ruses from flattery to subtle threats. The woman may actually believe that the student is seriously interested in

her, "unaware that the 'friendly' persuasion of the [brother] is actually a planned pursuit of easy prey," wrote Julie K. Ehrhart and Bernice R. Sandler, in the paper "Campus Gang Rape: Party Games?"

The woman is led to one of the frat rooms, under the impression that she'll be with one man, or left alone to "sleep off" the alcohol. She is assaulted as soon as she enters his room, where other brothers are waiting for her. Or, more frequently, she regains consciousness while she is being raped by several men.

It is not enough, sensitive observers say, to recognize the pattern of a gang rape in order to protect oneself or reduce its occurrence. Gang rape—like pornography—is pervasive, because it is a key feature of male bonding rituals within patriarchal societies.

Peggy Reeves Sanday, an anthropology professor at the University of Pennsylvania and the author of *Fraternity Gang Rape: Sex, Brotherhood, and Privilege on Campus* (New York University Press), found that fraternities attract a certain type of male, more insecure than average; men whose psychological and social bonds to parents, especially their mothers, have not yet been broken.

The security delivered by the fraternity "alter ego" is a powerful allure for these young men. They voluntarily endure humiliating and often physically painful initiations designed to break family allegiances. Forcibly torn from one set of norms, they are inducted into new ones that promise self-assurance—provided that they comply with the brotherhood's tightly enforced conformity.

These new norms have been described as "highly masculinist" by two Florida State University sociologists, Patricia Yancey Martin and Robert A. Hummer, writing in *Gender and Society*. The world of fraternities is characterized chiefly by "concern with a narrow, stereotypical conception of masculinity and heterosexuality; a preoccupation with loyalty . . . and an obsession with competition, superiority, and dominance."

"Almost always, male bonding turns against women," Sanday said. "It's a matter of degree, not kind. The way in which men extract loyalty from one another almost always means that they elevate male bonding by making women the despised other, and the scapegoat."

During Sanday's interviews, men degraded the women they slept with, "using such terms as gash, horsebags, heifers, scum, scum bags, queen, swanks, scum buckets, scum doggies, wench, life-support systems, beasts, bitch, swatches, and cracks." Laura McLaughlin, a resident adviser at Colgate, says it isn't unusual for women visiting with friends to be greeted at a fraternity house with comments like "Who's the chick? Who'd you bring us?"

Degrading women unites men in a culture that requires them to compete intensely. But, more important, at an age when their sexual identity is still fluid and a source of profound anxiety, frat men alleviate any insecurities about homoerotic attachments—and satisfy them—by having sex in front of each other, by abusing and dehumanizing women. In short, through gang rape.

Incredible amounts of time and energy go into planning, executing, documenting (in frat logs), and recollecting these bonding rituals. An entire underground lexicon of these practices exists: "rude-hoggering" (bedding the "ugliest" woman at a party), "landsharking" (kneeling on the floor behind a woman and biting her buttocks), and "baggings" (a group of men cornering a woman, dropping their trousers, wriggling their penises, and offering to gang rape her).

"Men rape for other men," contends Claire Walsh, director of Sexual Assault Recovery Services at the University of Florida. "It's a way of maintaining the myth of macho masculinity; a way to confirm their feelings of sexual adequacy. If a man in the room didn't participate, his sexual capacity could be called into question."

Kristen Buxton's assault at Colgate University in 1987 was horribly typical. Although Buxton, entering her junior year, was no newcomer to the university's social scene, she accepted an invitation to Sigma Chi's end-of-summer party because she was at emotional loose ends: her grandmother had just died, and she just had ended a serious relationship that had enabled her to avoid the more raucous "singles" side of Colgate life.

As nightfall approached, the weather in Hamilton, New York, that Saturday in late August was "great," Kristen remembers. In the company of old friends, she was glad to be at the party.

Twelve hours later she sat in her mother's living room north of Boston, unable to speak.

"Her face was all swollen from crying," Marah Buxton says. "I assumed she was upset over my mother. She wasn't able to get any words out of her mouth. I looked at Andrew [the friend who'd driven her home], and I said, 'I'm frightened. Give me a clue.'"

He answered, "This is going to take a while."

According to Kristen, shortly before midnight she was shown to a second-floor bedroom of Sigma Chi where the party was taking place, and went to sleep. She was awakened when two freshman athlete recruits gang raped her. Her screams, loud enough to break through the party noise below, brought friends to her aid.

If Buxton's experience was typical, her response, however, was not. For one thing, she was clear about what happened and decided, from the beginning, to prosecute. In part because she had the good fortune to be taken to a hospital emergency room near her hometown, she was immediately put in touch with police officers who pursued the criminal case.

The vast majority of sexual assault survivors on campuses keep it to themselves—blaming themselves, either because they were drinking or because they were "stupid enough" to have been in the wrong place at the wrong time. Women also believe, erroneously, that because the man was a friend, it couldn't have been rape.

Survivors' silence plays directly into the self-protective impulses of university officials. The morning after her daughter's rape, Marah Buxton phoned the school to inform them of the crime. In the three traumatic years that have passed since then, she says, "only one dean called. They distanced themselves completely."

Traumatized and often physically injured victims who deal directly with college clinics and officials may discover impassive bureaucracies instead of supportive advocates. "It's a syndrome," says Jeffrey Newman, Kristen Buxton's attorney and an expert on campus sexual assault. "We hear this over and again. The clinic head usually sends them to the school administration. The administration usually meets with the parents, probably with the attorney from the school present, to explain the benefits of undergoing the judicial process within the school, as opposed to the outside."

"What they're trying to do," says Newman's associate, Rosanne Zuffante, "is intimidate the young woman into backing off. And they succeed most of the time."

University tactics can violate a woman's due process, says Howard Clery, of Security on Campus, Inc., who insists that "a university cannot adjudicate a felony." But, typically, colleges attempt to do just this. Once a victim is persuaded to keep her accusations within the university, a judicial board hears testimony from all involved. The boards, normally composed of several faculty members, were originally established to review plagiarism cases and honor code violations. Now they determine the "innocence" or "guilt" of accused rapists, and dole out any punishments they deem fit.

On many campuses, the penalty for rape is identical to, or less severe than, the sanctions for plagiarism—one year's suspension. Frequently, confessed rapists are not even removed from campus. They are placed on "probation." (In Buxton's case, the athletes accused of rape withdrew from Colgate.)

Brave women who, like Buxton, press charges with the local authorities face several hurdles. Advocates say that district attorneys are reluctant to handle campus rape cases, and it's not only because they are difficult to win.

"It's a political game," says Newman. "Usually there are strong connections between the D.A.'s office and the higher-ups in the university. Most of the time you find the D.A.'s drop the case or they never take it. They say, look, there's just not enough evidence."

Buxton says she came under severe pressure from her D.A. to agree to a plea bargain that resulted in misdemeanor convictions, probation punishments, and, worst of all, no trace of the crime on her assailants' records.

Even more pressure is applied by peers. Buxton sometimes thought she was in hell after she returned to campus that fall—reading news accounts of the incident, feeling as if everyone was looking at her differently—but never more so than when she was finally persuaded by friends to join them at a downtown Hamilton pub.

"A bunch of fraternity members surrounded my table and just kind of stood there," she recounts. "Another time, I was standing in the middle of the room and a couple of them came over and were joking: 'Oh, look who's out.' They tried to intimidate me a lot."

This isn't uncommon. "Most women feel that if they make a public statement they have to leave," admits Ann Lane, founder of Colgate's women's studies program. "They receive threats from frat brothers, obscene phone calls. One woman [at Colgate] got a rock thrown through her window."

It is the rare victim who is offered adequate counseling. At best, institutions run a support group moderated by a faculty adviser or a clinic staffer.

"There was never any support," Buxton says of her own case. "Just kind of a blank stare."

It is the female students who pay the price for institutional passivity. Victims drop out of the classes they share with their assailants. Their grades go down. They experience chronic depression and have trouble concentrating. Eventually, many women, like Buxton, leave school for a period of time, or drop out altogether.

The code of silence exerts a ripple effect, observers say, through the entire female student population. It diminishes everything from classroom assertiveness and performance to confidence levels. Overall, says Professor Sanday, it suppresses a woman's initiative.

"There's a lot of anxiety," says Colgate resident adviser McLaughlin. "Almost every woman you talk to has a story."

And, interviews reveal, many have stories about a botched university clinic "rape kit" (the semen, blood, and other physical evidence of the assault) or a member of the judicial board unversed in the legal definition of rape. The unofficial negligence of universities reveals itself on many, mutually reinforcing levels.

By ignoring rape victims and their needs, universities succeed in minimizing adverse press. Sex crimes, characterized as "isolated incidents," keep consumers (students and their parents) and donors (alumni) ignorant and happy. The boat doesn't get rocked, and another generation learns the dynamics of domestic violence.

According to Sanday, what's at stake is "Brotherhood. That's older males protecting younger males, protecting their lost youth, and protecting their actual fraternity brothers. Protecting the American dream. The dream in which the young man goes out with his buddies, works his way up, becomes head of everything, and makes a fortune. Along the way, if he has to rape a few people—competitors, women—that's sort of what we expect. The American dream is very misogynistic."

But victims, feminists, and advocates on campus are fighting back. Victims are suing universities in civil court—successfully claiming, in many cases, that the institution is liable for security breaches or rule infractions that contributed directly to the rape. Colgate is currently defending itself in a $10 million civil damage suit filed by Buxton, who charges that the school should have forbidden the Sigma Chi party, because the fraternity had already been sanctioned for serving alcohol to minors. (Despite several requests, university officials were unavailable for comment.)

After lawsuits, the most sweeping effort to make universities responsible for campus criminal activity has been legislative. In June, the House of Representatives passed the "Student Right To Know and Campus Security Act"—despite keen back-room opposition from organized education lobbyists. If it becomes law, the act will require all institutions receiving federal aid to release their yearly crime statistics. It will also allow victims the right to know what happens to the perpetrators of crimes against them.

Howard and Connie Clery, whose own daughter was raped and murdered by a fellow student, urge any victim of campus rape to contact the police and the local district attorney's office. If possible, hire a lawyer. Security on Campus, their two-year-old organization in Gulph Mills, Pennsylvania, will provide the names of attorneys and other information needed to pursue a legal case.

Finally, protests, vigils, and marches by campus feminists have pushed administrators to take a more active stand against the abuse of women and overt institutional sexism. Thanks to them, and to a growing number of enlightened deans and college presidents, there is room for cautious optimism.

For example, at the University of Pennsylvania (the site of several highly publicized rapes) an ongoing rape education program, including films, regular discussions, and lectures, has increased the number of women reporting and asking for help.

After the 1987 protests at the University of New Hampshire, the institution developed the Sexual Harassment and Rape Prevention Program, geared toward averting sexual violence. The University of Illinois at Urbana-Champaign investigates every case of sexual assault and battery, whether the attack occurs on or off campus. The institution hired a victims' advocate, and requires all perpetrators found guilty of sexual assault to participate in counseling. It also is developing an educational program for men with a family history of domestic violence.

Inevitably, there is the question of the fraternities themselves. It would seem that women's obvious recourse is to avoid, even boycott, fraternity social events and seek entertainment elsewhere. But it isn't that simple. Most campuses with fraternities have virtually abdicated responsibility for social life to "the houses," which are among the few places where minors can find easy access to alcohol.

Instead of abolishing the system, some colleges have forced fraternities to grow up. At Bowdoin and Trinity colleges, coed frats have appeared. Colby College voted to abolish its eight fraternities and two sororities in 1984, and the University of Illinois has banned alcohol at after-hours frat parties, and a brother in most houses is trained to counsel and intervene when a potentially violent situation develops.

At Colgate, where fraternities have been an issue for the last ten years, more than 500 students and staff staged a protest last year against them; the faculty subsequently voted to abolish the system. "It's detrimental to humane learning in a very broad sense," says Colgate's Lane, who lobbied for change. "It's anti-intellectual in its core. Fraternities foster values that are in opposition to values we all uphold and respect."

In response, Colgate's board of trustees established a subcommittee to investigate the houses. Its report, with recommended solutions, should be delivered this fall.

One hopes that the board considers the many women who silently share Kristen Buxton's story. These are not alums who will remember their alma maters at giving time. Buxton graduated. . . a year behind the classmates with whom she entered. As she tries to assess her four years of college, she only begins to suggest the legacy of male aggression in America—even to society's most privileged and educated women:

"I'm a lot more hesitant about things, more cautious. I'm much more comfortable with things I'm used to. I think I'm probably more scared. Like, I'm much more comfortable just being home."   [1990]

Understanding the Reading

1. How do colleges and universities generally respond to rape and sexual assault? Why?
2. What is the "script" for a fraternity gang rape?
3. How are fraternity members characterized in this article?
4. How do fraternity members degrade women, and why?
5. Why are most campus rapes not prosecuted?
6. What effect does campus rape have on the victim and other women on campus?
7. Why don't universities play a more active role in fighting campus rape?
8. What steps have been taken to stop campus rape?

Suggestions for Responding

1. Why do colleges and universities treat rape differently than the law does? Should they?
2. Investigate and report on the procedures followed in sexual assault cases on your campus. ✦

90

"The Rape" of Mr. Smith

UNKNOWN

The law discriminates against rape victims in a manner which would not be tolerated by victims of any other crime. In the following example, a holdup victim is asked questions similar in form to those usually asked a victim of rape.

"Mr. Smith, you were held up at gunpoint on the corner of 16th & Locust?"

"Yes."

"Did you struggle with the robber?"

"No."

"Why not?"

"He was armed."

"Then you made a conscious decision to comply with his demands rather than to resist?"

"Yes."

"Did you scream? Cry out?"

"No. I was afraid."

"I see. Have you ever been held up before?"

"No."

"Have you ever given money away?"

"Yes, of course—"

"And did you do so willingly?"

"What are you getting at?"

"Well, let's put it like this, Mr. Smith. You've given away money in the past—in fact, you have quite a reputation for philanthropy. How can we be sure that you weren't *contriving* to have your money taken from you by force?"

"Listen, if I wanted—"

"Never mind. What time did this holdup take place, Mr. Smith?"

"About 11 P.M."

"You were out on the streets at 11 P.M.? Doing what?"

"Just walking."

"Just walking? You know that it's dangerous being out on the street that late at night. Weren't you aware that you could have been held up?"

"I hadn't thought about it."

"What were you wearing at the time, Mr. Smith?"

"Let's see. A suit. Yes, a suit."

"An *expensive* suit?"

"Well—yes."

"In other words, Mr. Smith, you were walking around the streets late at night in a suit that practically *advertised* the fact that you might be a good target for some easy money, isn't that so? I mean, if we didn't know better, Mr. Smith, we might even think you were *asking* for this to happen, mightn't we?"

"Look, can't we talk about the past history of the guy who *did* this to me?"

"I'm afraid not, Mr. Smith. I don't think you would want to violate his rights, now, would you?"

Naturally, the line of questioning, the innuendo, is ludicrous—as well as inadmissible as any sort of cross-examination—unless we are talking about parallel questions in a rape case. The time of night, the victim's previous history of "giving away" that which was taken by force, the clothing—all of these are held against the victim. Society's posture on rape, and the manifestation of that posture in the courts, help account for the fact that so few rapes are reported.   [n.d.]

Suggestions for Responding

1. Why do you think rape victims are treated so differently than victims of other crimes? ✦

91

Forbidden Fruit

Anne Finger

Before she became a paraplegic, Los Angeles resident DeVonna Cervantes liked to dye her pubic hair "fun colours"—turquoise, purple, jet black. After DeVonna became disabled, a beautician friend of hers came to the rehabilitation unit and, as a Christmas present, dyed DeVonna's pubic hair a hot pink.

But there's no such thing as "private parts" in a rehab hospital. Soon the staff, who'd seen her dye job when they were catheterizing her, sent the staff psychiatrist around to see her. Cervantes says that he told her: "I know it is very hard to accept that you have lost your sexuality but you don't need to draw attention to it this way." Cervantes spent the remainder of the 50-minute session arguing with him, and, in perhaps the only true medical miracle I've ever heard of, convinced him that he was wrong—that this was normal behaviour for her.

Cervantes' story not only illustrates woeful ignorance on the part of a "medical expert"; equating genital sensation with sexuality. But it shows clearly a disabled woman's determination to define her own sexuality.

Sadly, it's not just medical experts who are guilty of ignoring the reproductive and sexual rights and needs of people with disabilities. The movements for sexual and reproductive freedom have paid little attention to disability issues. And the abortion rights movement has sometimes crudely exploited fears about "defective fetuses" as a reason to keep abortion legal.

Because the initial focus of the women's movement was set by women who were overwhelmingly non-disabled (as well as young, white, and middle-class), the agenda of reproductive rights has tended to focus on the right to abortion as the central issue. Yet for disabled women, the right to bear and rear children is more at risk. Zoe Washburn, in her poem "Hannah," grieves the child she wanted to have and the abortion she was coerced into: " . . . so she went to the doctor, and let him suck Hannah out with a vacuum cleaner. . . . The family stroked her hair when she cried and cried because her belly was empty and Hannah was not only dead, but never born. They looked at her strange crippled-up body and thought to themselves, thank God that's over."

Yet the disability rights movement has certainly not put sexual rights at the forefront of its agenda. Sexuality is often the source of our deepest oppression; it is also often the source of our deepest pain. It's easier for us to talk about—and formulate strategies for changing—discrimination in employment, education, and housing than to talk about our exclusion from sexuality and reproduction. Also, although it is changing, the disability rights movement in the U.S. has tended to focus its energies on lobbying legislators and creating an image of "the able disabled."

Barbara Waxman and I once published an article in *Disability Rag* about the U.S. Supreme Court's decision that states could outlaw "unnatural" sex acts, pointing out the effect it could have on disabled people—especially those who were unable to have "standard" intercourse. The *Rag* then received a letter asking how "the handicapped" could ever be expected to be accepted as "normal" when we espoused such disgusting ideas.

Because reproduction is seen as a "women's issue," it is often relegated to the back burner. Yet it is crucial that the disability-rights movement starts to deal with it. Perhaps the most chilling situation exists in China where a number of provinces ban marriages between people with developmental and other disabilities unless the parties have been sterilized. In Gansu Province more than 5,000 people have been sterilized since 1988. Officials in Szechuan province stated: "Couples who have serious hereditary diseases including psychosis, mental deficiency and deformity must not be allowed to bear children." When disabled women are found to be pregnant, they are sometimes subjected to forced abortions. But despite widespread criticism of China's population policies, there was almost no public outcry following these revelations.

Even in the absence of outright bans on reproduction, the attitude that disabled people should not have children is common. Disabled women and men are still sometimes subject to forced and coerced sterilizations—including hysterectomies performed without medical justification but to prevent the "bother" of menstruation. Los Angeles newscaster Bree Walker has a genetically transmitted disability, ectrodactyly, which results in fused bones in her hands and feet. Pregnant with her second child, last year, she found her pregnancy the subject of a call-in radio show. Broadcaster Jane Norris informed listeners in a shocked and mournful tone of voice that Bree's child had a 50-percent chance of being born with the same disability: "Is it fair to bring a child into the world knowing there's two strikes against it at birth. . . . ? Is it socially responsible?" When a caller objected that it was no one else's business, Norris argued, "It's everybody's business." And many callers agreed with Norris's viewpoint. One horrified caller said, "It's not just her hands—it's her feet, too. She has to [dramatic pause] wear orthopaedic shoes."

The attitude that disabled people should not have children is certainly linked with the notion that we should not even be sexual. Yet, as with society's silence about the sexuality of children, this attitude exists alongside widespread sexual abuse. Some authorities estimate that people with disabilities are twice as likely to be victims of rape and other forms of sexual abuse as the general population. While the story of rape and sexual abuse of disabled people must be told and while we must find ways to end it, the current focus on sexual exploitation of disabled people can itself become oppressive.

As Barbara Faye Waxman, the former Disability Project Director for Los Angeles Planned Parenthood states, "The message for disabled kids is that their sexuality will be realized through their sexual victimization. . . . I don't see an idea that good things can happen, like pleasure, intimacy, like a greater understanding of ourselves, a love of our bodies." Waxman sees a "double whammy" effect for disabled people, for whom there are few, if any, positive models of sexuality, and virtually no social expectation that they will become sexual beings.

The attitude that we are and should be asexual seems to exist across a broad range of cultures. Ralf Hotchkiss, famous for developing wheelchairs in Third World countries, has travelled widely in Latin America and Asia. He says that while attitudes vary "from culture to culture, from subculture to subculture," he sees nearly everywhere he travels, "extreme irritation [on the part of disabled people] at the stereotypical assumptions that people . . . make about their sexuality, their lack of it." He also noted: "In Latin American countries once they hear I'm married, the next question is always, 'How old are your kids?'"

Some of these prejudices are enshrined in law. In the U.S., "marital disincentives" remain a significant barrier. To explain this Byzantine system briefly: benefits (including government-funded health care) are greatly reduced and sometimes even eliminated when a disabled person marries. Tom Fambro writes of his own difficulties with the system: "I am a 46-year-old black man with cerebral palsy. A number of years ago I met a young lady who was sexually attracted to me (a real miracle)." Fambro learned, however, that he would lose his income support and, most crucially, his medical benefits, if he married. "People told us that we should just live together . . . but because both of us were born-again Christians that was unthinkable. . . . The Social Security Administration has the idea that disabled people are not to fall in love, get married, have sex or have a life of our own. Instead, we are to be sexual eunuchs. They are full of shit."

Institutions—whether traditional hospital or euphemistically named "homes," "schools," or newer community-care facilities—often out-and-out forbid sexual contact for their residents.

Or they may outlaw gay and lesbian relationships, while allowing heterosexual ones. Disabled lesbians and gays may also find that their sexual orientation is presumed to occur by default. Restriction of access to sexual information occurs on both a legal and a social plane. The U.S. Library of Congress, a primary source of material for blind and other print-handicapped people, was instructed by Congress in 1985 to no longer make *Playboy* available in braille or on tape. And relay services, which provide telecommunication between deaf and hearing people, have sometimes refused to translate sexually explicit speech. In her poem "Seeing," blind poet Mary McGinnis writes of a woman being watched by sighted men while bathing nude:

> . . . *the guys sitting at the edge of the pond*
> *looked at her, but she couldn't see them . . .*
> *and whose skin, hair, shirts and belts*
> *would remain unknown to her*
> *because she couldn't go up to them and*
> *say, now fair is fair, let me touch the places*
> *on your bodies you try to hide,*
> *it's my turn—don't draw back or sit on*
> *your hands, let me count your rings, your*
> *   scars,*
> *the hairs coming from your nose. . . .*

I have quoted poets several times in this piece; many disability-rights activists now see that while we need changes in laws and policies, the formation of culture is a key part of winning our freedom. Disabled writers and artists are shaping work that is often powerful in both its rage and its affirmation. In Cheryl Marie Wade's "side and belly," she writes:

> *He is wilty muscle sack and sharp bones*
> *   fitting my gnarlypaws.*
> *I am soft cellulite and green eyes of middle-*
> *   age memory. We are*
> *side and belly trading dreams and fantasies*
> *   of able-bodied*
> *former and not real selves: high-heel booted*
> *   dancers making love*
> *from black rooftops and naked dim*
> *   doorways. . . .*
> *. . . Contradictions in the starry night of wars*
> *   within and being*

> *not quite whole together and whole. Together*
> *   in sighs we say yes*
> *broken and fire and yes singing.*   [1997]

Understanding the Reading

1. How did the psychiatrist respond to Cervantes' dyed pubic hair, and why?
2. Explain the complexity of the relationship between the reproductive rights movement and disability issues.
3. What does Barbara Faye Waxman see as a "double whammy" effect for disabled people?
4. How do U.S. law and institutional policies disadvantage disabled people?

Suggestions for Responding

1. Write your reflections on the sexuality of the disabled—for your eyes only—and think about what assumptions underlie your beliefs.
2. Write a letter to newscaster Bree Walker, telling her your opinion about her pregnancy, which could result in a disabled child. ✦

92

Certain Words Can Trip Up AIDS Grants, Scientists Say

ERICA GOODE

Scientists who study AIDS and other sexually transmitted diseases say they have been warned by federal health officials that their research may come under unusual scrutiny by the Department of Health and Human Services or by members of Congress, because the topics are politically controversial.

The scientists, who spoke on condition they not be identified, say they have been advised they can avoid unfavorable attention by keeping certain "key words" out of their applications for grants from the National Institutes of Health [N.I.H.] or the Centers for Disease Control and Prevention. Those words include "sex workers," "men who sleep with men," "anal sex" and "needle exchange," the scientists said.

Bill Pierce, a spokesman for the health and human services department, said the department does not screen grant applications for politically delicate content. He said that when the department singles out grants it is usually to send out a news release about them. But an official at the National Institutes of Health, who spoke on condition of anonymity, said project officers at the agency, the people who deal with grant applicants and recipients, were telling researchers at meetings and in telephone conversations to avoid so-called sensitive language. But the official added, "You won't find any paper or anything that advises people to do this."

The official said researchers had long been advised to avoid phrases that might mark their work as controversial. But the degree of scrutiny under the Bush administration was "much worse and more intense," the official said.

Dr. Alfred Sommer, the dean of the Bloomberg School of Public Health at Johns Hopkins University, said a researcher at his institution had been advised by a project officer at N.I.H. to change the term "sex worker" to something more euphemistic in a grant proposal for a study of H.I.V. prevention among prostitutes. He said the idea that grants might be subject to political surveillance was creating a "pernicious sense of insecurity" among researchers.

Dr. Sommer said that if researchers feared that federal support for their work might be affected by politics, whether it was true or untrue, it could take a toll. "If people feel intimidated and start clouding the language they use, then your mind starts to get cloudy and the science gets cloudy," he said, adding that the federal financing of medical research had traditionally been free from political influence.

At the National Institutes of Health, for example, grant applications are evaluated and rated by a panel of independent reviewers. The grant application is then given a score.

In another example of the scrutiny the scientists described, a researcher at the University of California said he had been advised by an N.I.H. project officer that the abstract of a grant application he was submitting "should be 'cleansed' and should not contain any contentious wording like 'gay' or 'homosexual' or 'transgender.'"

The researcher said the project officer told him that grants that included those words were "being screened out and targeted for more intense scrutiny."

He said he was now struggling with how to write the grant proposal, which dealt with a study of gay men and H.I.V. testing. When the subjects were gay men, he said, "It's hard not to mention them in your abstract."

The titles and abstracts of federally financed grants are available to the public on a computer database maintained by the national institutes. The database, called CRISP, is also frequently read by Congressional staff members on the lookout for research on topics that are of concern to the politicians they work for. Over the years, studies on cloning, abortion, animal rights, needle-exchange programs and various types of AIDS research have been criticized by members of Congress.

But researchers said they feared that the concerns of individual members of Congress were now being taken more seriously by the health and human services department.

John Burklow, a spokesman for the N.I.H., said project directors at the agency were responsible for "providing advice and guidance on myriad issues related to grant applications," but he did not confirm or deny that the project officers were cautioning researchers about the language they used.

He said that the health and human services department "from a management perspective has a right to oversee N.I.H. affairs" but that department officials "have not interfered with the awarding or renewing of any N.I.H. grant."

[2003]

Understanding the Reading

1. Why have certain scientists been warned by federal health officials about their research?
2. What key words must be kept out of their grant applications?
3. How are the researchers reacting?
4. What is "cleansing" a grant application?

Suggestions for Responding

1. This topic directly involves most American research universities. Research this to see which grants have been turned down.
2. Discuss the far-reaching consequences of federal interference with scientific research, especially concerning HIV/AIDS.
3. Write to your members of Congress, if this alarms you. ✦

93

Mothers of Convention

Lindsy Van Gelder

My daughters were four and seven when Pamela moved in. There was never any question about lying to them about the nature of our relationship, on both ethical and practical grounds. The year before, when Pam and I first became good friends—back when I had a boyfriend and she had another girlfriend—I had made it a point to tell the kids that some people had lovers of the same gender (and that other people might not like such arrangements: dopey bigots of the same sort that might not like someone because of their religion or color). They got it.

That was 14 years ago, when lesbian mothers' foremost fear was losing their kids altogether. Custody is still a concern for many women who conceived within heterosexual marriages (rather than by alternative insemination), especially outside the bicoastal urban areas. But the battleground for a lot of us has now shifted to the culture beyond the courtroom, where the very concept of a "lesbian mother" still computes about as well as "ice-pick-wielding First Lady" or "Mother Teresa centerfold." In liberal, sophisticated New York City, where I live, a school board recently banned all references to gay parents from the curriculum on the grounds that such things are "not appropriate" for children.

To the extent that we're visible at all, it's often assumed that lesbian moms are probably screwing up our kids, since, if we loved them, why would we be "putting them through this"? Our lesbianism is also the "explanation" for anything at all that goes wrong. Last year, I set up a folder on Compuserve so that every time the word "lesbian" is mentioned on a major news service, the story falls into a file that I can retrieve by modem. The only two stories with references to lesbians as mothers have been about people who had murdered their children. (Can you imagine a headline that blared HETEROSEXUALS CHARGED WITH KILLING THEIR 18-MONTH-OLD?) My own kids are almost tediously high-achieving, preppie-dressing, non-substance-abusing types, but when one was having a conflict with a male teacher, it was none-too-delicately suggested to both of us (and in the face of contrary evidence in her dealings with other teachers) that she must have a "problem" with men in general.

In fact, we mothers have problems, large and small, for which we get no feedback in the typical women's magazines or the standard child-rearing texts. My friend Sue is the coparent of her lover's two-year-old foster daughter (although she has no legal standing since gays in most states still can't foster-parent as a couple; in New Hampshire, it's illegal for gays to foster-parent at all). Sue and her lover are out to their social workers, but the lover runs a children's summer camp and is certain she would be fired if she came out at work.

"The thing that disturbs me the most these days is the double standard that we'll have to ask Kerry to live," says Sue. "While we spend years showing her that our relationship is O.K., we then will have to say that she cannot go around randomly telling people that Mommy and Sue sleep together and are very much in love. I hate the thought of teaching kids about hate and fear."

"I have sort of an ongoing war story about coming out to other parents," says my friend Val, the mother of two preteen boys. "I feel like it's important that I come out to the parents of kids who come over here often, and that it's clear this is just business as usual, *not* a problem. The thing is, if someone's going to do a major freak-out over gayness, I'd rather they go ahead and do it before kids get attached to each other, or before there's some question about corrupting children. But it's a chore."

"Not a single person around school has ever reacted badly—at least not to my face," she adds. "Of course, I used to say the same about the previous school, but I have since found out that my best friend there, another mom, spent a ridiculous amount of time telling other moms that it was not O.K. to bad-mouth me to her, that she was happy to have her girls over at my house anytime."

Val and her lover broke up several months ago. They had made it a matter of honor to appear as a couple at school gatherings for years, and to exact the same respect for the lover that any stepparent would automatically be entitled to. On top of the normal grief of the breakup, Val had the extra burden of worrying that all the straight parents were now concluding that gay relationships are transitory and doomed to fall into the Well of Loneliness.

Despite her convictions about coming out, when one of Val's sons was tested for learning disabilities, she deliberately didn't mention her orientation to the tester. "I was worried that it would skew her recommendations. I felt guilty about doing that, but I could not see how 'mom's queer' has anything to do with his writing letters backward, and I was worried that if she had that red herring to distract her, we might never find out why he was having trouble. Maybe I sold her short, but I felt like it was important that he not get pigeonholed."

Then there's my friend Frances, whose children are now college age. "It's been very hard to tell which stuff was about [being a lesbian] and which was because there was No Father in the Home," she recalls. "For women, it seems to me that the line between homophobia and sexism is wavy. When you add the fact that you're out not only as a woman and a dyke, but also as a feminist, then you know it's your fault your son sews his own buttons on, but you don't know which of your defects caused it."

She also remembers the custody anxieties of a decade ago. "Even though my lawyer looked out for me on that one, I still feared it—and not just from my ex. The state is often willing to 'rescue' kids in queer homes—or in those days I felt it was. I was afraid of the authorities accusing me of neglect for having a messy house." She was also afraid to leave the kids alone with her lover—ironically, their former baby-sitter—because she might be vulnerable to the nasty stereotype of gays as sexual abusers. (If lesbian mothers suffer from bad P.R., their lovers have an even worse image. The partner is perceived as the "true lesbian" dragon lady who seduced the hetero-salvageable biological mother and/or she's discounted as a coparent, no matter how much time she's logged packing lunches and helping with homework. More than once, I've had to correct someone who has referred to me as a "single parent.")

"Fortunately, I knew a closeted dyke who was a social worker in the school system and gave me lots of clues about helping the kids survive," says Frances. "She tipped me off about who was homophobic, and about the deal on the 'permanent record' on a kid. I can't tell you how important it felt to have a spy. If I had it to do over, I would start a gay parents' group not just for mutual support, but also to be right there in the face of the school system. So they couldn't keep us all fearing for our kids, each alone."

I was a lesbian mother for years before I met other women who were out to their kids, much less to the universe. Although there are lesbian mother groups in most cities, Sue, Val, Frances, several other parents, and I originally met on a computer bulletin board and we now rely on each other for our context. We're there to commiserate on those occasions when our kids are embarrassed by us, but also to remind each other that if we had a disability or were married to someone of a different race, no one would suggest that we were wicked, selfish mothers. My friends gave advice and hugs in the 1980s when my kids briefly moved in with their father after a fight about inviting Pamela to a school function. They were also there to cheer when one of my kids wrote her college essay on the appreciation of diversity she learned from growing up in a lesbian home, and the other helped arrange for Pam and me to give a speech to the campus gay group (which she and her boyfriend attended).

What makes the need for our support group especially odd, however, is that study after study has shown that kids of gay parents are pretty much like other kids. The only way that lesbian parents are different, according to a 1989 study at Fairleigh Dickinson University in New Jersey, is that we believe in "using less physical punishment and more reasoning," and we're less interested than straight parents in presenting ourselves "in a socially desirable light." Most of the time, we're just Moms.

There is something very strange about having the most boringly normal, workaday, doing-the-laundry parts of your life seen as the flowers of evil. If my family and my values are an affront to "family values," where does that leave me?

[1992]

Understanding the Reading

1. What attitudes does society have about lesbian mothers?
2. What problems do lesbian mothers of school-age children face?
3. What problems do the partners of lesbian mothers face?
4. How can lesbian mothers get support?
5. What have studies shown about children of homosexual parents?

Suggestions for Responding

1. Do you think lesbians and gay men should be allowed to raise children or be teachers? Why or why not?
2. Imagine that you were a parent in a heterosexual relationship who discovered that you actually were homosexual. What would your response be?
3. Imagine that, when you were a child, your parents announced that one of them was homosexual and was moving out. How would that have made you feel? Would it have been different if they had "merely" gone through a divorce? ✦

94

What's Fair in Love and War

RANDY SHILTS

On the first night of the Scud missile attacks on American troops in the Persian Gulf, an army specialist fourth class with the 27th Field Artillery found himself cramped in a foxhole with three other men. Like many young enlisted men, the specialist (who asked that his name not be used) had previously confided to the other men, his friends, that he was gay.

During that night in the foxhole, they huddled together in their suffocating suits meant to protect them from chemical and biological warfare agents. They could not see one another, but to reassure themselves that they were still there, still alive, each man kept one hand on the other. Nobody seemed to mind that one reassuring hand belonged to a homosexual, the soldier recalls—there were more important things to think about.

Defense Department policy contends that the purpose of excluding gays from the armed forces is to preserve the "good order, discipline and morale" of the military, because no heterosexual soldier would want to serve with, take orders from or share a foxhole with a homosexual. America's experience in its past three wars suggests otherwise. The behavior of military officials in accepting gays during these wars also suggests that the generals themselves know their arguments are fallacious. At no time is good order, discipline and morale more crucial for a fighting unit than in time of combat; at no time have the military's regulations against gays been more roundly ignored than in periods when troops were sent out to fight.

President Clinton's intention of integrating acknowledged lesbians and gay men into the armed forces has raised a great cry from opponents of reform, most of whom question how soldiers will respond to sharing a foxhole with a gay soldier. These arguments belie the fact that gay soldiers have served in U.S. military foxholes since the days of Valley Forge, some openly.

From the first days of the Defense Department's anti-gay regulations in the early 1940s, the government was willing to waive the for-heterosexuals-only requirement for military service if barring gays interfered with manpower exigencies. In 1945, just two years after the regulation was adopted, and during the height of the final European offensive against the Third Reich, Secretary of War Henry Stimson ordered a review of all gay discharges in the previous two years, with an eye toward reinducting gay men who had not committed any in-service homosexual acts. At the same time, orders went out to "salvage" homosexuals for the service whenever possible.

The Korean War saw a dramatic plunge in gay-related discharges. In the late 1940s, the navy meted out 1,100 undesirable discharges a year to gay sailors. In 1950, at the height of the Korean War, that number was down to 483. But in 1953, when the armistice was signed at Panmunjom, the navy cracked down again with vigor, distributing 1,353 gay-related undesirable discharges in that year alone.

The Vietnam War provides some of the most striking examples of the military's tacit acceptance of homosexuality in times of war. When Air Force Sgt. Roberto Reyes-Colon was seen leaving his base near the demilitarized zone with his Marine Corps boyfriend, military police brought him before his commanding officer the next day. The commander listened to the MPs complain that they had seen Reyes-Colon kiss the Marine, but once they left the room, the commanding officer ripped up the report they had written on the incident. Reyes-Colon's defense was that "there's a war going on," and the officer agreed.

Marine Corps Lt. Ben Dillingham, assigned to lead a reconnaissance platoon in Vietnam in 1970, was surprised to discover that two of his enlisted men were lovers, inseparable, patrolling together, even sleeping together under the same blanket. All the other soldiers in the tightly knit platoon were aware of the relationship, and no one cared. It seemed to Dillingham that with a war going on, and everyone's life depending on the others, no one had time to quibble about gay soldiers.

Discharges for homosexuality still occurred, but Pentagon statistics themselves bear out that the armed forces became strangely uninterested in enforcing their regulations against homosexuals during this period. Between 1963 and 1966, the navy, which at the time was the only branch of the military to keep detailed statistics of gay discharges, "separated" between 1,600 and 1,700 enlisted members a year for homosexuality. From 1966 to 1967, as the Vietnam buildup began in earnest, the number of gay discharges dropped from 1,708 to 1,094. In 1969, at the peak of the escalation, gay discharges dropped to 643. A year later, only 461 sailors were relieved of duty for being gay.

These dramatic reductions occurred during a period of some of the service's highest membership since World War II. It was not that there were any fewer gays in the navy; by all appearances there were many more. But the navy had effectively stopped enforcing regulations against homosexuality. Draftees who announced themselves to be homosexual at their induction centers frequently were told by army doctors that they were welcome in the army just the same. In at least three circumstances in the early 1970s, gay activists had to go to federal court to force the government to observe its own policies regarding the exclusion of gays.

History repeated itself . . . during Operation Desert Storm when numerous military personnel, most serving in the reserves, tried to escape mobilization by telling their reserve commanders they were gay—and many reserve commanders responded that gay soldiers could serve anyway. When a lesbian officer in a Western medical-support group told her commander that she was a lesbian, he replied, "That's all right. We wouldn't have a medical service without gays." When army reservist Donna Lynn Jackson told her commander she was a lesbian, she says he told her bluntly that she would go to Saudi Arabia, and be discharged for homosexuality at the end of the war. Jackson went to the newspapers, and an embarrassed Pentagon discharged her quickly, insisting that such cases were aberrations and that the Defense Department had an ironclad ban on gays in the military.

Despite the public pronouncements, military commanders made it as difficult as possible to separate gay personnel for the duration of the conflict. Decade-old Defense Department regulations demanded that anyone who even intimated that he or she was gay—or had the "intent" to commit gay sexual acts in the future—must be discharged, with no exceptions allowed. In the days before the ground war in the gulf started, however, the staff judge advocate's office of the Marine Corps Reserve Support Center instructed a lesbian who had acknowledged her homosexuality that "claimed sexual preferences do not constitute an exemption from the mobilization process."

At the 40th Aeromedical Evacuation Squadron at McChord Air Force Base in Washington, another gay reservist seeking to avoid mobilization by announcing she was gay was told that she would not be certified as a homosexual by the air force unless she produced a marriage license listing another woman as a spouse. No jurisdiction in the United States allows gays to marry. Demanding that the woman produce a marriage license was like insisting she produce a piece of Mars.

Once stationed in the gulf, many of the gay military personnel found a remarkably accepting environment. When officers supervising a navy corpsman stationed with a Marine Corps unit on the front lines of Kuwait became concerned that his Marines all knew he was gay, the corpsman was transferred to another unit. The Marines in the new unit soon heard the rumors that he was gay, but befriended him anyway, and even jokingly nicknamed him "Precious," after the miniature poodle in the movie "The Silence of the Lambs."

The acceptance of gays in some quarters does not mean that lesbians and gay men will be easily integrated into every fighting unit. As with African-Americans and with women, the ability of the tradition-bound institution to accommodate gay members will take years, if not decades. The travails of gays in the military will not stop with a new president's executive order—they will just begin.

Still, animosity toward gays in the armed forces is not nearly so ingrained as opponents of the change would have us believe. For the past several years, some navy ship commanders have been privately candid with their crews about no longer having any intention of enforcing the ban on homosexuals. In 1990, the reluctance of ship commanders to pursue lesbians led Vice Adm. Joseph Donnell, commander of the U.S. Atlantic fleet, to order all his commanding officers to enforce regulations more aggressively against lesbians. The memorandum acknowledged why many commanders were reluctant to do this: because, Donnell wrote, "the stereotypical female homosexual" was "hardworking, career-oriented, willing to put in long hours on the job and among the command's top professionals."

Tens of thousands of gay military personnel, particularly those in the enlisted ranks, serve with some degree of openness in the military today, informing their co-workers, though not the press or their officers, that they are gay. Over the past

five years, many more officers have served openly as well, though they do not tempt fate by allowing their names to be released publicly. Typical of stories from the new military is the tale I heard of an air force major serving in Florida whose colleagues threw him a 40th birthday party, and enlisted the major's lover to organize it.

This brings us to the fundamental truth about the military's policies toward homosexuals. The point is not to eject all gays, but to allow the military to say it does not accept homosexuals. This preserves its image as the upholder of traditional notions of masculinity, the one institution in the nation that claims to take boys and turn them into men. In harsh economic times, this raises the question as to whether the taxpayers grant the Defense Department nearly $300 billion a year to provide the most cost-effective defense for the nation, or whether it is an investment in preserving a club where heterosexual men can assure themselves of their masculinity.

The argument that gays will unalterably subvert discipline and good order in the armed forces is also hard to justify within the context of the history of the U.S. military. History tells us that the man who first instilled discipline in the ragtag Continental Army at Valley Forge was the Prussian Baron Frederick William von Steuben. It was he who took what were essentially 13 different colonial militias and molded them into one army.

Von Steuben at first had declined Benjamin Franklin's offer of the job, because the Continental Congress could not pay him. But when von Steuben learned that ecclesiastical authorities were planning to try him for homosexuality, he renegotiated with Franklin and was appointed a major general to the Continental Army. When he came to Valley Forge to begin his drills, he appeared with a 17-year-old French interpreter, who must have had other talents useful to the general, because it soon became clear that he had no linguistic skills.

Nevertheless, von Steuben, the army's first inspector general, came to have an incalculable impact on the U.S. military, writing the drill books that would be used for the next 35 years by the fledgling U.S. Army. His plans for a military academy became embodied in West Point. Some military historians have judged von Steuben as one of only two men whose contributions were "indispensable" toward winning the Revolutionary War; the other was George Washington.

It is a crowning irony that anti-gay policies are defended in the name of preserving the good order and discipline of the U.S. military, when that very order and discipline was the creation of a gay man.   [1993]

Understanding the Reading

1. What arguments does the military use to support the exclusion of homosexuals?
2. What reveals the hypocrisy of that position?
3. How were homosexuals who were open about their sexual orientation treated during Operation Desert Storm?
4. Why doesn't the military, discharge homosexuals during periods of conflict?
5. Why are many naval commanders reluctant to enforce regulations against lesbianism?
6. Why does the military not eject gays but still claim not to accept homosexuals?

7. What is ironic about the Revolutionary War service of Baron von Steuben?

Suggestions for Responding

1. Both racial and sexual integration were resisted by the military using arguments similar to those now used against integrating lesbians and gay men. How do you account for this similarity?
2. President Clinton accepted a "don't ask, don't tell" policy for homosexuals in the military. Do you agree or disagree with this position, and why?
3. Do you think openly homosexual men and women should be allowed to serve in the military? Why or why not?
4. In 2003, thirty-seven linguists were discharged from the U.S. military for being gay, including much-needed Arabic linguists. Debate this action in terms of the military's policy toward homosexuals vs. national security and intelligence gathering.

SUGGESTIONS FOR RESPONDING TO PART VI

1. Write a research report on the male-female pay differentials in the field you have chosen as a career. If at all possible, try to control for differences in the education and experience of the two groups.
2. Investigate the federal Women's Educational Equity Agency to find out what kinds of research it conducts and the kinds of services it provides to public schools. If there is a similar agency in your state or area school district, learn about its activities and services.
3. Research the initial entry of women into higher education—in women's colleges such as Mount Holyoke in 1837 and Vassar in 1865 and at the coeducational Oberlin College in 1832. How did the educational and extracurricular experiences differ in the two kinds of

institutions? How were women treated differently than men at Oberlin?
4. If you are heterosexual, attend a meeting of the gay and/or lesbian group or center on your campus. Find out what its priorities are, and explore ways that you could help reduce the prejudice and discrimination it faces.
5. Title IX of the Education Amendments of 1972 prohibits sex discrimination in all federally funded educational programs. Its intent is to encourage equity in athletic programs, requiring colleges and universities to provide and equally support comparable sports offerings for women and men. See if your school is in compliance. How many sports are offered for women and for men? How many women and men participate? Are

budgets for the two overall programs equitable? Are scheduling and access to facilities fair to both women and men? Do the number and rank of the coaches reflect appropriate gender balance?

6. Investigate and report on a governmental or volunteer organization formed to protect rape victims or victims of domestic violence to learn what support is available to women in your area.

7. The Cleary Act demands that colleges disclose and *give full access to* rape statistics on campus. Is your college in compliance with the Cleary Act? If you have never seen these statistics, take action by inviting the appropriate administrators to your classroom. Make demands and write letters to your school newspaper.

VII
Power and Classism

MOST AMERICANS LIKE TO THINK OF OURS AS A CLASS-less society, and thus we tend to ignore class as an aspect of our lives. If we do think of class, most of us tend to identify ourselves as middle-class. Historically, the sense of a classless nation arose because most early European immigrants were neither nobility nor serfs but, rather, generally were "commoners"—farmers, craftsmen, small tradesmen, and such. Due to the abundance of land on this continent, these early immigrants could also become property owners and enjoy a substantial degree of autonomy. From the beginning, of course, this view of a middle-class nation was inaccurate because, among other things, it ignored slaves, indentured servants, Native Americans, and others whose reality did not meet this idyll. Additionally, in the colonial era, White land-owning males only constituted about 7 percent of the population.

Socioeconomic inequities became more generalized and pronounced with the nineteenth-century onset of the **industrial revolution,** the transformation of methods of production, transportation, and communication through the substitution of machines for hand labor. This mechanization of production systems brought about massive social and economic changes, and America began developing an identifiable class structure. More and more people moved from being self-sufficient and independent to being wage earners working for and dependent on factory and business owners.

This shift signaled the growth of **capitalism,** an economic system characterized by private (or corporate) ownership of capital assets and by free-market determination of prices, production, and distribution of goods. The capitalist system was reinforced by a belief in **free enterprise,** the freedom of private businesses to operate competitively for profit with minimal government regulation.

Satisfaction of capitalist interests inevitably resulted in an inequitable distribution of power, resources, and property. To realize maximum profits, it was in the employers' interest to pay the lowest possible wages to the workers and to require the highest possible production from them, an arrangement that seriously disadvantaged the workers. This inequality led wage earners, during the latter decades of the nineteenth century and the first half of the twentieth, to respond by organizing and forming **unions** to advance their interests, to collectively improve wages and working conditions, and to enhance job security. Union successes, however, were uneven as the owners often had the law (and private police forces) enforcing their interests.

Capitalism also created a number of "panics" and **depressions,** periods of drastic decline in the national economy characterized by decreasing business, falling prices, and rising un-employment. Although both owners and work-ers suffered from these economic declines, hard times fell most heavily on the latter, especially during the Great Depression of the 1930s, which led to the social reforms of President Franklin D. Roosevelt's New Deal.

New Deal social policies included farm sup-ports; federal reforms of the financial system; na-tional control of the stock market, banking, and public utilities; the development of public works projects and housing programs; relief for the un-employed; minimum wage standards; and the Social Security system. Some people bitterly complained that these policies conflicted with the values of capitalism and free enterprise and that they moved this country toward socialism. They were not wholly misguided: **Socialism** is an economic system in which the producers (workers) possess both political power and the means of producing and distributing goods and in which government provides for human wel-fare needs, including health care, education, economic security, and so on.

Nonetheless, New Deal social programs and post–World War II economic prosperity led to the growth of a broad middle class during the 1950s and 1960s. But since then, wage growth for full-time wage and salary workers has been stagnant, with average weekly earnings of pro-duction falling from $450 in 1967 to $424 in 1997. (Economic data in this introduction are based on the U.S. Census Bureau, Official Statistics, as re-ported in *Statistical Abstracts of the United States,* October 1998.)

It is important to distinguish between *income* and wealth. Income is what one earns, whereas *wealth,* or *net worth,* is the total value of what one has. Recently, there has been apparent growth in the median (middle) household income in the United States. The median household income had regained its 1989 level by 1997. But this came about because the median family in 1997 worked more hours, equivalent to about six full-time weeks per year. According to the U.S. Cen-sus Bureau, the percentage share of aggregate income received by the poorest 20 percent of families fell from 5.4 percent in 1970 to 4.2 per-cent in 1996. By way of contrast, that received by the richest 5 percent rose from 5.6 percent in 1970 to over 20 percent in 1996.

By another measure of prosperity, **national wealth**—all of America's cash, real estate, stocks, bonds, factories, art, personal property, and anything else of financial value—the wealthiest have fared even better. In 1976, the wealthiest 1 percent of America's families owned 19.2 percent of the total of our national wealth. By 1983, those at this 1 percent tip of our econ-omy owned 34.3 percent of our wealth and, by 1997, this top 1 percent controlled about 40 per-cent of the nation's wealth and possessed more wealth than the bottom 90 percent.

The 1993 share of national income going to the richest fifth of households (48.2 percent) was the highest ever recorded. At the same time, the shares of income going to the middle class and the poorest fifth dropped to the lowest levels on record, with the bottom fifth receiving only 3.6 percent of the national income. Tellingly, to-day the income of corporate executive officers (CEOs) of the Fortune 500 is 150 times the wages of the average worker.

Most Americans are more conscious of the problems and impediments caused by race, gen-der, and sexual orientation than we are of those based on socioeconomic class. Class in America is difficult to define because we are reluctant to talk about it and because the boundaries be-tween classes are blurred. **Class** is related to rel-ative wealth, but socioeconomic culture is also a component, as is relative access to power. Roughly, we tend to speak of the upper class, upper middle class, middle class, working class, poor, and underclass, but these categories are fluid and dependent on context.

Despite definitional difficulties, class is a re-ality in the United States, as are the related stereotypes, prejudices, and discrimination that provide the basis for our classism. Because of **classism,** the wealthy and the financially better off are privileged and assigned high status, whereas poor and working-class people and their cultures are stigmatized and disadvantaged simply because of their relative wealth. It should come as no surprise to anyone that those at the top of the economic hierarchy benefit most from classist values and those at the bottom suffer the most from classism.

Race has a substantial impact on economic prosperity. More specifically, the median **net worth** of White households in 2000 was $81,700, but it was only $10,000 for Black households. Thus, the median net worth of White households is now roughly eight times that of Black households.

The official federal **poverty line** is based on the cost of a "Thrifty Food Plan," which is not considered nutritionally adequate for long-term use, multiplied by three to account for nonfood expenses and adjusted for family size and for changes in the consumer price index. In 1996, 7 percent of Whites and 26 percent of Blacks and Hispanics fell below the poverty line. Further, the trend is disturbing: The overall 1996 poverty rate for White children was 15.5 percent but almost 40 percent for Black children and Hispanic children.

Our social stereotype of the "lazy, freeloading poor" notwithstanding, 3.5 million people who worked full-time, year round in 1993 were below the official poverty line; over 7 million were at 150 percent of the poverty line, an alternative measure of poverty, which is still inadequate to cover such essential expenses as child care. In the 1970s, a full-time, minimum wage worker with two children lived above the poverty line; today, the same family ends up with $8,840 a year—far below the 1995 poverty line of $12,188.

In addition, the **Federal Reserve Board,** which controls the money supply, interest rates, and inflation, sets policies that keep millions of people unemployed in order to control inflation. In 1994, 8 million people were unemployed, and millions more were involuntarily working part-time as temporary and part-time jobs were substituted for full-time positions. In the same year, Black unemployment was 11.5 percent, or more than double the rate of 5.2 percent for Whites, a disparity that has existed ever since the Bureau of Labor Statistics began keeping unemployment figures.

Gender is as critical a factor in determining socioeconomic class as race is. Nearly two thirds of poor adults are women, probably for several reasons. For one thing, women today, even with similar education and employment experience, still earn less than 70 percent of what men do. Furthermore, although the official 1993 unemployment rate for women maintaining families was 7.7 percent for Whites and 13.7 percent for Blacks, the real jobless and underemployment

rates are much higher. It is also worth noting that women's standard of living drops 33 percent after divorce, whereas men's rises 10 to 15 percent; more than 60 percent of the fathers pay no child support after five years. Additionally, the number of households headed by women has more than doubled since 1970: in 1992, women maintained 12 million families on their own.

Contrary to common knowledge, single-mother families, both Black and White, increased at a higher rate in the 1970s than in the 1980s or 1990s. Unfortunately, in 1996 men had a median income of over $26,000, whereas women earned almost half that ($13,500). The typical woman behind the rise in never-married mothers in the 1980s, according to the U.S. General Accounting Office, was not an unemployed teenage dropout but, rather, a working woman between the ages of twenty-five and forty-four who had completed high school. Also contrary to image, the proportion of Black children born to unmarried mothers—most of them not teenagers —has grown mainly because the birthrates for married Black women have fallen dramatically.

Poverty does disproportionately affect women of color. Blacks are 38 percent of those on welfare, a percentage that has been going down since 1969, when it was 45 percent. Even though disproportionately more people of color are poor, unemployed and underemployed, they have disproportionately less access to government income support programs, such as unemployment insurance, workers' compensation, and Social Security.

A number of misconceptions about welfare are accepted as truths by American society. In contrast to our assumptions, about 72 percent of families on welfare have only one or two children; families with four or more children are just 10 percent of the total, and that number keeps going down. Equally inaccurate is the stereotype that the welfare mother is a fifteen-year-old with a new baby. In reality, 0.1 percent of mothers receiving Aid to Families with Dependent Children (AFDC) are fifteen or younger, less than 4 percent are eighteen or younger, and only 8 percent are under twenty years old. About 39 percent of families now receiving AFDC are White, 38 percent African American, 18 percent Latino, 3 percent Asian, and 1 percent Native American. Moreover, the average monthly welfare payment to most families (food stamps and AFDC combined) is $645, or $7,740 a year, well below the 1995 poverty line of $12,188.

Despite the "welfare-as-a-way-of-life" stereotype, the typical recipient is a short-term user of AFDC. Most families receiving AFDC are enrolled for less than two years, if single spells are considered, and cumulatively less than four years total, if multiple spells over time are considered. Long-term recipients usually face serious obstacles to getting off welfare: They may lack prior work experience, a high school degree, or child care; suffer from poor health or a disability; or need to care for a child with a disability.

The economic realities have substantial adverse effects on our nation's children. Today, more than 40 percent of our poor are children: Of White children under age eighteen, 16.9 percent now live in poverty, as do 46.6 percent of Black children. In 1991, 21 percent of all children lived below the poverty line; of them, 16 percent were White, 45 percent Black, and 39 percent Latino. Further, the number of AFDC child recipients as a percentage of children living below the official poverty line fell from a high of 81 percent in 1973 to 63 percent in 1992. In other words, fewer poor children now receive welfare assistance. According to the Children's Defense Fund, poor children are twice as likely as other children to die from birth defects; three times as likely to die from all causes; four times as likely to die from fires; and five times as likely to suffer from infectious diseases and parasites. It seems clear that children are the greatest victims of poverty.

To most of us, classism tends to be less visible than racism or sexism. Moreover, we also believe that we live in a **meritocracy,** in which advancement is based on ability or achievement. Thus, we hold to the myth that, although people cannot determine their race or sex, individuals can control their economic well-being and are responsible for their economic success or failure. As a result, we tend to blame the poor for their poverty. The readings in Part VII show that such beliefs and stereotypes misrepresent reality.

Part VII opens with several analyses of the current economic conditions in our society. First, Holly Sklar describes the socioeconomic realities of the United States that contradict our national self-image, our ideals, and our proclaimed values. Next, Jeffrey H. Reiman analyses the popular concept of what crime is and who a criminal is. He then explains why poor people are much more likely than the wealthy to be charged with criminal behavior, arrested, tried, convicted, and sentenced more harshly than wealthy or middle-class people. David Moberg asks why Americans tolerate such extreme economic disparities in income, and especially in wealth, that characterize the country today, and he reports on the negative effects this inequality has on our nation.

Christopher D. Cook explores the concerns of the growing number of **contingent workers,** temporary, leased, and "contract" workers who are not covered by U.S. labor laws and are frequently paid less than their full-time colleagues and denied benefits.

The next reading details the social impact of our current economic system. Celine-Marie Pascale reports on the unemployment, income distribution, personal debt, and poverty that now characterize our national fiscal and social health.

Many of our social assumptions and practices contribute to class distinctions and classism and reinforce discrimination, which can be unconscious and unintentional. Robert Cherry, for example, examines how discrimination is **institutionalized**—that is, how the various parts of our social system work together to create a self-perpetuating cycle of discrimination and economic disadvantage. For instance, people with lower educational levels have limited access to good jobs with good pay, whereas affordable housing is available only in neighborhoods with poor schools, which means the next generation is doomed to lower educational levels and on and on.

Other economic practices intentionally discriminate against the poor. For example, "redlining," decisions by banks and insurance companies not to invest in certain areas—most often, older, inner-city, and minority neighborhoods—contributes to their increasing impoverishment and deterioration. Leslie Brown reports on the judicial ruling against National Mutual Insurance Company for this practice; the company had refused to issue policies to Black individuals or in Black communities.

The next two selections address the controversial subject of welfare. Ellen L. Bassuk, Angela Browne, and John C. Buckner report on a study of homeless and housed women and narrate a life history of a representative homeless mother. Then, they analyse the effects of welfare on the women's conditions and consider the likely effects on their well-being, as well as the likely effects the 1996 welfare reform will have on such mothers, challenging the fallacious assumptions on which the bill was based. Then, Lucky Jean comments on an unnoticed problem raised by welfare reform: the potential removal of children from homes that lack middle-class amenities.

Renu Nahata focuses on how the media inaccurately portray welfare recipients; she charges the media with the responsibility for perpetuating popular acceptance of these distorted images. Then, Rita Henley Jensen puts a human face on the welfare experience by sharing her experience as a welfare mother; her personalized account challenges many of the assumptions about this program.

Part VII closes with two articles examining the growing problem of homelessness in this country. First, Doug A. Timmer, D. Stanley Eitzen, and Kathryn D. Talley begin their analysis of this problem with an overview of the general problems caused by poverty and then focus on the homeless themselves, challenging the belief that people are homeless as a result of personal disabilities. They conclude that lack of low-cost housing is a central factor in the increased rate of homelessness, as is the low level of public assistance. Finally, Christian Parenti reports on the use of private security forces that wage antihomeless campaigns for business communities and develop quasi-governmental Business Improvement Districts. These security forces use illegal tactics—the destruction of property, beatings, and questionable "outreach" efforts. According to Parenti, this response detaches the business community from, and circumvents its involvement in, larger movements for social reform because it simply displaces the problem rather than creating alternatives.

These readings give us an unflattering image of ourselves as a society, making these class issues difficult for us to digest and making it even harder for us to do something about them. It is tempting to deny the structural and individual elements of classism and to hold onto the myths about poverty and the rewards of hard work and discipline. However, as we move into the twenty-first century, we must not comfort ourselves with a dismissive rationalization, such as "for ye have the poor always with you." Instead, we as a society must provide for the least privileged and most oppressed among us if the American community that we all value is to remain strong and a true world leader.

95

Imagine a Country

HOLLY SKLAR

Imagine a country where one out of four children is born into poverty, and wealth is being redistributed upward. Since the 1970s, the top 1 percent of families have doubled their share of the nation's wealth—while the percentage of children living in extreme poverty has also doubled.

Highlighting growing wage inequality, the nation's leading business newspaper acknowledges, "The rich really are getting richer, and the poor really are getting poorer."

Imagine a country where the top 1 percent of families have about the same amount of wealth as the bottom 95 percent. Where the poor and middle class are told to tighten their belts to balance a national budget bloated with bailouts and subsidies for the well-off.

It's not Mexico.

Imagine a country which demands that people work for a living while denying many a living wage.

Imagine a country where wages have fallen for average workers, adjusting for inflation, despite significant growth in the economy. Real per capita GDP (gross domestic product) rose 33 percent from 1973 to 1994, yet real weekly wages fell 19 percent for non-supervisory workers, the vast majority of the workforce.

It's not Chile.

Imagine a country where the stockmarket provides "payoffs for layoffs."

Imagine a country where workers are downsized while corporate profits and executive pay are up-sized. The profits of the 500 leading corporations rose a record 23 percent in 1996 and CEO compensation (including salary, bonus, and long-term compensation such as stock options) shot up 54 percent, while workers' wages and benefits barely kept pace with inflation. The average CEO of a major corporation was paid as much as 42 factory workers in 1980, 122 factory workers in 1989, and 209 factory workers in 1996.

A leading business magazine says, "People who worked hard to make their companies competitive are angry at the way the profits are distributed. They think it is unfair, and they are right."

It's not England.

Imagine a country where living standards are falling for younger generations despite the fact that many households have two wage earners, have fewer children, and are better educated than their parents. Since 1973, the share of workers without a high school degree has been cut in half. The share of workers with at least a four-year college degree has doubled.

The entry-level hourly wages of male high school graduates fell 27.3 percent between 1979 and 1995, and the entry-level wages of women high school graduates fell 18.9 percent.

A college degree is increasingly necessary, but not necessarily sufficient to earn a decent income. Between 1989 and 1995, the entry-level wages of male college graduates fell 9.5 percent, and the entry-level wages of women college graduates fell 7.7 percent.

Imagine a country where the percentage of young full-time workers (ages 18–24) earning low wages doubled from 23 percent in 1979 to 47 percent in 1992. Where families with household heads ages 25 to 34 had 1994 incomes that were $4,611 less than their 1979 counterparts.

It's not Russia.

Imagine a country where leading economists consider it "full employment" when the official unemployment rate reaches 6 percent (over 7 million people). You're not counted officially as unemployed just because—you're unemployed. To be counted in the official unemployment rate you must have searched for work in the past four weeks. The government doesn't count people as "unemployed" if they are so discouraged from long and fruitless job searches they have given up looking. It doesn't count as "unemployed" those who couldn't look for work in the past month because they had no child care, for example. If you need a full-time job, but you're working part-time—whether 1 hour or 34 hours—because that's all you can find, you're counted as employed.

A leading business magazine observes, "Increasingly the labor market is filled with surplus workers who are not being counted as unemployed."

Imagine a country where there is a shortage of jobs, not a shortage of work. Millions of people need work and urgent work needs people—from creating affordable housing, to repairing bridges and building mass transit, to cleaning up pollution and converting to renewable energy, to staffing after-school programs and community centers.

Imagine a country where for more and more people a job is not a ticket out of poverty, but into the ranks of the working poor. Between 1979 and 1992, the proportion of full-time workers paid low wages jumped from 12 percent to 18 percent—nearly one in every five full-time workers.

Imagine a country where one out of four officially poor children live in families in which one or more parents work full time, year round. The official poverty line is set well below the actual cost of minimally adequate housing, health care, food, and other necessities.

Imagine a country where more workers are going back to the future of sweatshops and day labor. Corporations are replacing full-time jobs with disposable "contingent workers." They include temporary employees, contract workers, and "leased" employees—some of them fired and then "rented" back at a large discount by the same company—and involuntary part-time workers, who want permanent full-time work.

It's not Spain.

How do workers increasingly forced to migrate from job to job, at low and variable wage rates, without health insurance or paid vacation, much less a pension, care for themselves and their families, own a home, pay for college, save for retirement, plan a future, build strong communities?

Imagine a country where after mass layoffs and union-busting, less than 15 percent of workers are unionized. One out of three workers were union members in 1955.

Imagine a country where the concerns of working people are dismissed as "special interests" and the profit-making interests of globetrotting corporations substitute for the "national interest."

Imagine a country whose government negotiates "free trade" agreements that help corporations trade freely on cheap labor at home and abroad.

One ad financed by the country's agency for international development showed a Salvadoran woman in front of a sewing machine. It told corporations, "You can hire her for 33 cents an hour. Rosa is more than just colorful. She and her co-workers are known for their industriousness, reliability and quick learning. They make El Salvador one of the best buys." The country that financed the ad intervened militarily to make sure El Salvador would stay a "best buy" for corporations.

It's not Canada.

Imagine a country where more than half of all women with children under age 6, and three-fourths of women with children ages 6–17, are in the paid workforce, but affordable child care and after-school programs are scarce. (Families with incomes below the poverty line spend nearly one-fifth of their incomes on child care.) Apparently, kids are expected to have three parents: Two parents with jobs to pay the bills, and another parent to be home in mid-afternoon when school lets out—as well as all summer.

Imagine a country where instead of rooting out discrimination, many policy makers are busily blaming women for their disproportionate poverty. Back in 1977, a labor department study found that if working women were paid what similarly qualified men earn, the number of poor families would decrease by half. A 1991 government study found that even "if all poor single mothers obtained [full-time] jobs at their potential wage rates," given their educational and employment background and prevailing wages, "the percentage not earning enough to escape from poverty would be 35 percent."

Two out of three workers who earn the miserly minimum wage are women. Full time work at minimum wage pays below the official poverty line for a family of two.

Imagine a country where discrimination against women is pervasive from the bottom to the top of the payscale, and it's not because women are on the "mommy track." In the words of a leading business magazine, "at the same level of management, the typical woman's pay is lower than her male colleague's—even when she has the exact same qualifications, works just as many years, relocates just as often, provides the main financial support for her family, takes no time off for personal reasons, and wins the same number of promotions to comparable jobs."

It's not Japan.

Imagine a country where the awful labeling of children as "illegitimate" has again been legitimized. Besides meaning born out of wedlock, illegitimate also means illegal, contrary to rules and logic, misbegotten, not genuine, wrong—to be a bastard. The word illegitimate has consequences. It helps make people more disposable. Single mothers and their children have become prime scapegoats for illegitimate economics.

Imagine a country where violence against women is so epidemic it is their leading cause of injury. So-called "domestic violence" accounts for more visits to hospital emergency departments than car crashes, muggings, and rapes combined. About a third of all murdered women are killed by husbands, boyfriends and ex-partners (less than a tenth are killed by strangers). Researchers say that "men commonly kill their female partners in response to the woman's attempt to leave an abusive relationship."

The country has no equal rights amendment. It's not Algeria.

Imagine a country where homicide is the second-largest killer of young people, ages 15–24; "accidents," many of them drunk-driving fatalities, are first. Increasingly lethal weapons designed for hunting people are produced for profit by major manufacturers and proudly defended by a politically powerful national rifle association. Half the homes in the country contain firearms, and guns in the home greatly increase the risk of murder and suicide for family members and close acquaintances.

Informational material from a national shooting sports foundation asks, "How old is old enough?" to have a gun, and advises parents:

> Age is not the major yardstick. Some youngsters are ready to start at 10, others at 14. The only real measures are those of maturity and individual responsibility. Does your youngster follow directions well? Would you leave him alone in the house for two or three hours? Is he conscientious and reliable? Would you send him to the grocery store with a list and a $20 bill? If the answer to these questions or similar ones are yes then the answer can also be yes when your child asks for his first gun.

Imagine a country where children are taught violence is the way to resolve conflict through popular wars and media "entertainment." "In the media world, brutality is portrayed as ordinary and amusing" and often merged with sex, observed a prominent public health educator. The screen "good guys" not only use violence as a first resort, but total war is the only response to the dehumanized "bad guys" who often speak with foreign accents. War cartoons and violent "superhero" shows are created expressly to sell toys to children. Video and computer games showcase increasingly graphic and participatory "virtual" violence. The strong consensus of private and government research is that on-screen violence contributes to off-screen violence.

It's not Australia.

Imagine a country whose school system is rigged in favor of the already-privileged, with lower caste children tracked by race and income into the most deficient and demoralizing schools and classrooms. Public school budgets are heavily determined by private property taxes, allowing higher income districts to spend much more than poor ones. In one large state in 1991–92, spending per pupil ranged from $2,337 in the poorest district to $56,791 in the wealthiest.

In rich districts kids take well-stocked libraries, laboratories, and state-of-the-art computers for granted. In poor schools they are rationing out-of-date textbooks and toilet paper. Rich schools often look like country clubs—with manicured sports fields and swimming pools. Poor schools often look more like jails—with concrete grounds and grated windows. College prep courses, art, music, physical education, field trips, and foreign languages are often considered necessities for the affluent, luxuries for the poor.

Wealthier citizens argue that lack of money isn't the problem in poorer schools—family values are—until proposals are made to make school spending more equitable. Then money matters greatly for those who already have more.

It's not India.

Imagine a country where Black unemployment and infant mortality is more than twice that of whites, and Black life expectancy is seven years less. The government subsidized decades of segregated suburbanization for whites while the inner cities left to people of color were treated as outsider cities—separate, unequal, and disposable. Recent studies have documented continuing discrimination in employment, banking, and housing.

Imagine a country whose constitution once defined Black slaves as worth three-fifths of whites. Today, median Black per capita income is three-fifths of whites.

It's not South Africa.

Imagine a country which pretends that anyone who needs a job can find one, while its federal reserve board enforces slow growth economic policies that keep millions of people unemployed, underemployed, and underpaid.

Imagine a country with full prisons instead of full employment. The prison population has more than doubled since 1980. The nation is Number One in the world when it comes to locking up its own people. The bureau of justice statistics reports that in 1985, 1 in every 320 of the nation's residents were incarcerated. By the end of 1995, the figure had increased to 1 in every 167.

Imagine a country where prison labor is a growth industry and so-called "corrections" spending is the fastest growing part of state budgets. Apparently, the government would rather spend $25,000 a year to keep someone in prison than on cost-effective programs of education, community development, addiction treatment, and employment to keep them out. In the words of a national center on institutions and alternatives, this nation has "replaced the social safety net with a dragnet."

Imagine a country that has been criticized by human rights organizations for expanding rather than abolishing use of the death penalty—despite documented racial bias and numerous cases of innocents being put to death.

It's not China.

Imagine a country that imprisons Black men at a rate nearly five times more than apartheid South Africa. One out of three Black men in their twenties are either in jail, on probation or on parole. Meanwhile, one out of three Black men and women ages 16–19 are officially unemployed, as are nearly one out of five ages 20–24. Remember, to be counted in the official unemployment rate you must be actively looking for a job and not finding one. "Surplus" workers are increasingly being criminalized.

A 1990 justice department report observed, "The fact that the legal order not only countenanced but sustained slavery, segregation, and discrimination for most of our Nation's history—and the fact that the police were bound to uphold that order—set a pattern for police behavior and attitudes toward minority communities that has persisted until the present day." A 1992 newspaper article is titled, "GUILTY . . . of being black: Black men say success doesn't save them from being suspected, harassed and detained."

Imagine a country waging a racially biased "War on Drugs." More than three out of four drug users are white, but Blacks and Latinos are much more likely to be arrested and convicted for drug offenses and receive much harsher sentences. Almost 90 percent of those sentenced to state prison for drug possession in 1992 were Black and Latino.

A study in a prominent medical journal found that drug and alcohol rates were slightly higher for pregnant white women than pregnant Black women, but Black women were about ten times more likely to be reported to authorities by private doctors and public health clinics—under a mandatory reporting law. Poor women were also more likely to be reported.

It is said that truth is the first casualty in war, and the "War on Drugs" is no exception. Contrary to stereotype, "The typical cocaine user is white, male, a high school graduate employed full time and living in a small metropolitan area or suburb," says the nation's former drug czar. A leading newspaper reports that law officers and judges say, "Although it is clear that whites sell most of the nation's cocaine and account for 80 percent of its consumers, it is blacks and other minorities who continue to fill up [the] courtrooms and jails, largely because, in a political climate that demands that something be done, they are the easiest people to arrest."

Imagine a country which intervenes in other nations in the name of the "War on Drugs," while it is the number one exporter of addictive, life-shortening tobacco. It is also number four in the world in alcohol consumption—the drug most associated in reality with violence and death—and number one in drunk-driving fatalities per capita. Those arrested for drunk driving are overwhelmingly white and male and typically treated much more leniently than illicit drug offenders.

It's not France.

Imagine a country where the cycle of unequal opportunity is intensifying. Its beneficiaries often slander those most systematically undervalued, underpaid, underemployed, underfinanced, underinsured, underrated, and otherwise underserved and undermined—as undeserving, "underclass," impoverished in moral and social values, and lacking the proper "work ethic." The oft-heard stereotype of deadbeat poor people masks the growing reality of dead-end jobs and disposable workers.

Imagine a country abolishing aid to families with dependent children while maintaining aid for dependent corporations.

Imagine a country slashing assistance to its poorest people, disabled children, and elderly refugees to close a budget deficit produced by excessive military spending and tax cuts for corporations and the rich. Wealthy people—whose tax rates are among the lowest in the world—not only benefited from deficit spending and tax breaks, they earn interest on the debt as government bond holders.

Imagine a country with a greed surplus and justice deficit. According to a former secretary of labor, "were the tax code as progressive as it was even as late as 1977," the top 10 percent of income earners "would have paid approximately $93 billion more in taxes" than they paid in 1989. How much is $93 billion? About the same amount as the combined 1989 government budget for all these programs for low-income persons: aid to families with dependent children, supplemental security income, general assistance, food and nutrition benefits, housing, jobs and employment training, and education aid from preschool to college loans.

Imagine a country where state and local governments are rushing to expand lotteries, video poker, and other government-promoted gambling to raise revenues, disproportionately from the poor, which they should be raising from a fair tax system.

Imagine a country whose military budget continues consuming resources at nearly average Cold War levels although the Soviet Union no longer exists. In the post–Cold War world, the "Peace Dividend" means the congress gives the military more than it asks for. This nation also leads the world in arms exports.

Imagine a country that ranks first in the world in wealth and military power, and 26th in child mortality (under five). If the government were a parent it would be guilty of child abuse. Thousands of children die preventable deaths.

Imagine a country where health care is managed for healthy profit. In many countries health care is a right, but in this one 42 million people have no health insurance and another 29 million are underinsured, according to the nation's college of physicians. Lack of health insurance is associated with a 25 percent higher risk of death.

Imagine a country where descendants of its first inhabitants live on reservations strip-mined of natural resources. Life expectancy averages in the 1940s—not the 1970s. Infant mortality is seven times higher than the national average and a higher proportion of people live in poverty than any other ethnic group. An Indian leader is the country's best known political prisoner.

Imagine a country where 500 years of plunder and lies are masked in expressions like "Indian giver." Where the military still dubs enemy territory, "Indian country."

Imagine a country which has less than 5 percent of the world's population, but uses 25 percent of the world's oil resources. Only 3 percent of the public's trips are made by public transportation. It has felled more trees since 1978 than any other country. It is the number one contributor to acid rain and global warming.

It's not Brazil.

Imagine a country where half the eligible voters don't vote. The nation's house of representatives is not representative of the nation. It is overwhelmingly male and disproportionately white. The senate is representative of millionaires.

Imagine a country where white men who are "falling down" the economic ladder are being encouraged to believe they are falling because women and people of color are climbing over them to the top or dragging them down from the bottom. That way, they will blame women and people of color rather than the system. They will buy the myth of "reverse discrimination."

Never mind that white males hold 95 percent of senior management positions (vice president and above).

Imagine a country where on top of discrimination comes insult. It's common for people of color to get none of the credit when they succeed—portrayed as undeserving beneficiaries of affirmative action and "reverse discrimination"—and all of the blame when they fail. A study of the views of 15-to-24-year-olds found that 49 percent of whites believe that it is more likely that "qualified whites lose out on scholarships, jobs, and promotions because minorities get special preferences" than "qualified minorities are denied scholarships, jobs, and promotions because of racial prejudice." Only 34 percent believed that minorities are more likely to lose out.

Imagine a country where scapegoating thrives on misinformation. The majority of whites in a national 1995 survey said that average Blacks held equal or better jobs than average whites. Survey respondents also wrongly estimated the white share of the population to be under 50 percent—rather than 74 percent.

Imagine a country where a former presidential press secretary boasted to reporters: "You can say anything you want in a debate, and 80 million people hear it. If reporters then document that a candidate spoke untruthfully, so what? Maybe 200 people read it, or 2,000 or 20,000."

Imagine a country where a far-right television commentator-turned-presidential candidate—whose heroes include U.S. Senator Joe McCarthy, Spanish dictator Franco, and Chilean dictator Pinochet—told the national convention of one of the two major parties: "There is a religious war going on in this country. It is a cultural war." Delegates waved signs saying "Gay Rights Never"—the 1990s version of segregation forever. Referring to recent rioting in a major city, following the acquittal of police officers who had severely beaten a Black man, the once and future candidate said: "I met the troopers of the 18th Cavalry, who had come to save the city . . . And as those boys took back the streets of [that city], block by block, my friends, we must take back our cities and take back our culture and take back our country."

It's not the former Yugoslavia.

Imagine a country where scapegoating fuels fear and fear fuels scapegoating. The list of scapegoats grows rapidly with homeless people, women and children receiving welfare, people of color, gays and lesbians, Jews, undocumented immigrants, long-time legal immigrants, people with disabilities. More and more children are declared illegitimate. More and more people are treated as disposable.

It's not Germany.

It's the disUnited States.

Decades ago Martin Luther King, Jr., warned, in *Where Do We Go From Here: Chaos or Community?* (Harper & Row, 1967), "History is cluttered with the wreckage of nations and individuals who pursued [the] self-defeating path of hate." King declared:

> A true revolution of values will soon cause us to question the fairness and justice of many of our past and present policies. We are called to play the good samaritan on life's roadside; but . . . one day the whole Jericho road must be transformed so that men and women will not be beaten and robbed as they make their journey through life. . . .
>
> A true revolution of values will soon look uneasily on the glaring contrast of poverty and wealth. . . . There is nothing but a lack of social vision to prevent us from paying an adequate wage to every American citizen whether he be a hospital worker, laundry worker, maid or day laborer. There is nothing except shortsightedness to prevent us from guaranteeing an annual minimum—and *livable*—income for every American family. There is nothing, except a tragic death wish, to prevent us from reordering our priorities, so that the pursuit of peace will take precedence over the pursuit of war.   [1997]

Understanding the Reading

1. Why, after each description, does Sklar choose to name a country that she is not describing?
2. Reread the selection with the knowledge that Sklar is describing the United States and reflect on what is unacceptable in a country with our ideals and values.

Suggestions for Responding

1. Write a personal essay in which you consider the impact these issues have had on you directly, either positively or negatively. ✦

96

The Rich Get Richer and the Poor Get Prison

Jeffrey H. Reiman

A Crime by Any Other Name . . .

Think of a crime, any crime. Picture the first "crime" that comes into your mind. What do you see? The odds are you are not imagining a mining company executive sitting at his desk, calculating the costs of proper safety precautions and deciding not to invest in them. Probably what you do see with your mind's eye is one person physically attacking another or robbing something from another via the threat of physical attack. Look more closely. What does the attacker look like? It's a safe bet he (and it is a *he*, of course) is not wearing a suit and tie. In fact, my hunch is that you—like me, like almost anyone else in America—picture a young, tough, lower-class male when the thought of crime first pops into your head. You (we) picture someone like the Typical Criminal described above. The crime itself is one in which the Typical Criminal sets out to attack or rob some specific person.

This last point is important. It indicates that we have a mental image not only of the Typical Criminal but also of the Typical Crime. If the Typical Criminal is a young, lower-class male, the Typical Crime is *one-on-one harm*—where harm means either physical injury or loss of something valuable or both. If you have any doubts that this is the Typical Crime, look at any random sample of police or private eye shows on television. How often do you see the cops on "NYPD Blue" investigate consumer fraud or failure to remove occupational hazards? And when Jessica Fletcher (on "Murder, She Wrote") tracks down well-

heeled criminals, it is almost always for garden-variety violent crimes like murder. A study of TV crime shows by The Media Institute in Washington, D.C., indicates that, while the fictional criminals portrayed on television are on the average both older and wealthier than the real criminals who figure in the FBI *Uniform Crime Reports,* "TV crimes are almost 12 times as likely to be violent as crimes committed in the real world." A review of several decades of research confirms that violent crimes are overrepresented on TV news and fictional crime shows, and that "young people, black people, and people of low socioeconomic status are underrepresented as offenders or victims in television programs"—exactly opposite from the real world in which nonviolent property crimes far outnumber violent crimes, and young, poor and black folks predominate as offenders and victims. As a result, TV crime shows broadcast the double-edged message that the one-on-one crimes of the poor are the typical crimes of all and thus not uniquely caused by the pressures of poverty; *and* that the criminal justice system pursues rich and poor alike—thus, when the criminal justice system happens mainly to pounce on the poor in real life, it is not out of any class bias.

In addition to the steady diet of fictionalized TV violence and crime, there has been an increase in the graphic display of crime on many TV news programs. Crimes reported on TV news are also far more frequently violent than real crimes are. An article in *The Washingtonian* says that the word around two prominent local TV news programs is, "If it bleeds, it leads." What's more, a new breed of nonfictional "tabloid" TV shows has appeared in which viewers are shown films of actual violent crimes—blood, screams, and all—or reenactments of actual violent crimes, sometimes using the actual victims playing themselves! Among these are "COPS," "Real Stories of the Highway Patrol," "America's Most Wanted," and "Unsolved Mysteries." Here, too, the focus is on crimes of one-on-one violence, rather than, say, corporate pollution. The *Wall Street Journal,* reporting on the phenomenon of tabloid TV, informs us that "television has gone tabloid. The seamy underside of life is being bared in a new rash of true-crime series and contrived-confrontation talk shows." Is there any surprise that a survey by *McCall's* indicates that its readers have grown more afraid of crime in the mid-1980s—even though victimization studies show a stable level of crime for most of this period?

It is important to identify this model of the Typical Crime because it functions like a set of blinders. It keeps us from calling a mine disaster a mass murder even if ten men are killed, even if someone is responsible for the unsafe conditions in which they worked and died. One study of newspaper reporting of a food-processing plant fire, in which 25 workers were killed and criminal charges were ultimately brought, concludes that "the newspapers showed little consciousness that corporate violence might be seen as a crime." I contend that this is due to our fixation on the model of the Typical Crime. This particular piece of mental furniture so blocks our view that it keeps us from using the criminal justice system to protect ourselves from the greatest threats to our persons and possessions.

What keeps a mine disaster from being a mass murder in our eyes is that it is not a one-on-one harm. What is important in one-on-one harm is not the numbers but the *desire of someone (or ones) to harm someone (or ones) else*. An attack by a gang on one or more persons or an attack by one individual on several fits the model of one-on-one harm; that is, for each person harmed there is at least one individual who wanted to harm that person. Once he selects his victim, the rapist, the mugger, the murderer all want this person they have selected to suffer. A mine executive, on the other hand, does not want his employees to be harmed. He would truly prefer that there be no accident, no injured or dead miners. What he does want is something legitimate. It is what he has been hired to get: maximum profits at minimum costs. If he cuts corners to save a buck, he is just doing his job. If ten men die because he cut corners on safety, we may think him crude or callous but not a murderer. He is, at most, responsible for an *indirect harm,* not a one-on-one harm. For this, he may even be criminally indictable for violating safety regulations—but not for murder. The ten men are dead as an unwanted consequence of his (perhaps overzealous or undercautious) pursuit of a legitimate goal. So, unlike the Typical Criminal, he has not committed the Typical Crime—or so we generally believe. As a result,

ten men are dead who might be alive now if cutting corners of the kind that leads to loss of life, whether suffering is specifically aimed at or not, were treated as murder.

This is my point. Because we accept the belief—encouraged by our politicians' statements about crime and by the media's portrayal of crime—that the model for crime is one person specifically trying to harm another, we accept a legal system that leaves us unprotected against much greater dangers to our lives and well-being than those threatened by the Typical Criminal. . . .

WEEDING OUT THE WEALTHY

> The offender at the end of the road in prison is likely to be a member of the lowest social and economic groups in the country.

This statement in the *Report of the President's Commission on Law Enforcement and Administration of Justice* is as true today as it was over three decades ago when it was written. Our prisons are indeed, as Ronald Goldfarb has called them, the "national poorhouse." To most citizens this comes as no surprise—recall the Typical Criminal and the Typical Crime. Dangerous crimes, they think, are mainly committed by poor people. Seeing that prison populations are made up primarily of the poor only makes them surer of this. They think, in other words, that the criminal justice system gives a true reflection of the dangers that threaten them.

In my view, it also comes as no surprise that our prisons and jails predominantly confine the poor. This is not because these are the individuals who most threaten us. It is because the criminal justice system effectively weeds out the well-to-do, so that at *the end of the road in prison,* the vast majority of those we find there come from the lower classes. This weeding out process starts before the agents of law enforcement go into action. . . . Our very definition of crime *excludes* a wide variety of actions at least as dangerous as those included and often worse. Is it any accident that the kinds of dangerous actions excluded are the kinds most likely to be performed by the affluent in America? Even before we mobilize our troops in the war on crime, we have already guaranteed that large numbers of upper-class individuals will never come within their sights.

This process does not stop at the definition of crime. It continues throughout each level of the criminal justice system. At each step, from arresting to sentencing, the likelihood of being ignored or released or lightly treated by the system is greater the better off one is economically. As the late U.S. Senator Philip Hart wrote:

> Justice has two transmission belts, one for the rich and one for the poor. The low-income transmission belt is easier to ride without falling off and it gets to prison in shorter order.
>
> The transmission belt for the affluent is a little slower and it passes innumerable stations where exits are temptingly convenient.

This means that the criminal justice system functions from start to finish in a way that makes certain that "the offender at the end of the road in prison is likely to be a member of the lowest social and economic groups in the country."

For the same criminal behavior, the poor are more likely to be arrested; if arrested, they are more likely to be charged; if charged, more likely to be convicted; if convicted, more likely to be sentenced to prison; and if sentenced, more likely to be given longer prison terms than members of the middle and upper classes. In other words, the image of the criminal population one sees in our nation's jails and prisons is distorted by the shape of the criminal justice system itself. It is the face of evil reflected in a carnival mirror, but it is no laughing matter.

The fact in the criminal justice carnival mirror is also, as we have already noted, very frequently a black face. Although blacks do not make up the majority of the inmates in our jails and prisons, they make up a proportion that far outstrips their proportion in the population. . . .

In the remainder of this chapter, I show how the criminal justice system functions to *weed out the wealthy* (meaning both middle- and upper-class offenders) at each stage of the process and thus produces a distorted image of the crime problem. . . .

Arrest and Charging

The problem with most official records of who commits crime is that they are really statistics on who gets arrested and convicted. If, as I will show, the police are more likely to arrest some people than others, these official statistics may tell us more about police than about criminals. In any event, they give us little reliable data about those who commit crime and do not get caught. . . .

A number of other studies support the conclusion that serious criminal behavior is widespread about middle- and upper-class individuals, although these individuals are rarely, if ever, arrested. Some of the studies show that there are no significant differences between economic classes in the incidence of criminal behavior. The authors of a recent review of literature on class and delinquency conclude that "research published since 1978, using both official and self-reported data, suggests . . . that there is no pervasive relationship between SES [socioeconomic status] and delinquency." . . .

Others conclude that while lower-class individuals do commit more than their share of crime, arrest records overstate their share and understate that of the middle and upper classes. Still other studies suggest that some forms of serious crime—forms usually associated with lower-class youth—show up *more frequently* among higher-class persons than among lower. For instance, Empey and Erikson interviewed 180 white males aged 15 to 17 who were drawn from different economic strata. They found that "virtually all respondents reported having committed not one but a variety of different offenses." Although youngsters from the middle classes constituted 55 percent of the group interviewed, they admitted to 67 percent of the instances of breaking and entering, 70 percent of the instances of property destruction, and an astounding 87 percent of all the armed robberies admitted to by the entire sample. . . .

Even those who conclude "that more lower status youngsters commit delinquent acts more frequently than do higher status youngsters" also recognize that lower-class youth are significantly overrepresented in official records. Gold writes that "about five times more lowest than highest status boys appear in the official records; if records were complete and unselective, we estimate that the ratio would be closer to 1.5:1." The simple fact is that for the same offense, *a poor person is more likely to be arrested and, if ar-*

rested charged, than a middle- or upper-class person.

This means, first of all, that poor people are more likely to come to the attention of the police. Furthermore, even when [people are] apprehended, the police are more likely to formally charge a poor person and release a higher-class person *for the same offense.* Gold writes that

> boys who live in poorer parts of town and are apprehended by police for delinquency are four to five times more likely to appear in some official record than boys from wealthier sections who commit the same kinds of offenses. These same data show that, at each stage in the legal process from charging a boy with an offense to some sort of disposition in court, boys from different socioeconomic backgrounds are treated differently, so that those eventually incarcerated in public institutions, that site of most of the research on delinquency, are selectively poorer boys.

From a study of self-reported delinquent behavior, Gold finds that when individuals were apprehended, "if the offender came from a higher status family, police were more likely to handle the matter themselves without referring it to the court."

Terence Thornberry reached a similar conclusion in his study of 3,475 delinquent boys in Philadelphia. Thornberry found that among boys arrested *for equally serious offenses* and who had *similar prior offense records,* police were more likely to refer the lower-class youths than the more affluent ones to juvenile court. The police were more likely to deal with the wealthier youngsters informally, for example, by holding them in the station house until their parents came rather than instituting formal procedures. Of those referred to juvenile court, Thornberry found further that for *equally serious offenses* and with *similar prior records,* the poorer youngsters were more likely to be institutionalized than were the affluent ones. The wealthier youths were more likely to receive probation than the poorer ones. . . .

Recent studies continue to show similar effects. For example, Sampson found that, for the same crimes, juveniles in lower-class neighborhoods were more likely to have some police record than those in better-off neighborhoods.

Again, for similar crimes, lower-class juveniles were more likely to be referred to court than better-off juveniles. If you think these differences are not so important because they are true only of young offenders, remember that this group accounts for much of the crime problem. Moreover, other studies not limited to the young tend to show the same economic bias. McCarthy found that, in metropolitan areas, for similar suspected crimes, unemployed people were more likely to be arrested than employed. . . .

Any number of reasons can be offered to account for the differences in police treatment of poor versus well-off citizens. Some argue that they reflect that the poor have less privacy. What others can do in their living rooms or backyards the poor do on the street. Others argue that a police officer's decision to book a poor youth and release a middle-class youth reflects either the officer's judgment that the higher-class youngster's family will be more likely and more able to discipline him or her than the lower-class youngster's, or differences in the degree to which poor and middle-class complainants demand arrest. Others argue that police training and police work condition police officers to be suspicious of certain kinds of people, such as lower-class youth, blacks, Mexicans, and so on, and thus more likely to detect their criminality. Still others hold that police mainly arrest those with the least political clout, those who are least able to focus public attention on police practices or bring political influence to bear, and these happen to be the members of the lowest social and economic classes.

Regardless of which view one takes, and probably all have some truth in them, one conclusion is inescapable: One of the reasons the offender "at the end of the road in prison is likely to be a member of the lowest social and economic groups in the country" is that the police officers who guard the access to the road to prison make sure that more poor people make the trip than well-to-do people.

Likewise for prosecutors. A recent study of prosecutors' decisions shows that lower-class individuals are more likely to have charges pressed against them than upper-class individuals. . . .

The *weeding out of the wealthy* starts at the very entrance to the criminal justice system: The decision about whom to investigate, arrest, or charge is not made simply on the basis of the offense committed or the danger posed. It is a decision distorted by a systematic economic bias that works to the disadvantage of the poor.

This economic bias is a two-edged sword. Not only are the poor arrested and charged out of proportion to their numbers for the kinds of crimes poor people generally commit—burglary, robbery, assault, and so forth—but when we reach the kinds of crimes poor people almost never have the opportunity to commit, such as antitrust violations, industrial safety violations, embezzlement, and serious tax evasion, the criminal justice system shows an increasingly benign and merciful face. The more likely that a crime is the type committed by middle- and upper-class people, the less likely that it will be treated as a criminal offense. When it comes to crime in the streets, where the perpetrator is apt to be poor, he or she is even more likely to be arrested and formally charged. When it comes to crime in the suites, where the offender is apt to be affluent, the system is most likely to deal with the crime noncriminally, that is, by civil litigation or informal settlement. . . . Not only is the main entry to the road to prison held wide open to the poor but the access routes for the wealthy are largely sealed off. Once again, we should not be surprised at whom we find in our prisons.

Many writers have commented on the extent and seriousness of "white-collar crime," so I will keep my remarks to a minimum. Nevertheless, for those of us trying to understand how the image of crime is created, four points should be noted.

1. White-collar crime is costly; it takes far more dollars from our pockets than all the FBI Index crimes combined.
2. White-collar crime is widespread, probably much more so than the crimes of the poor.
3. White-collar criminals are rarely arrested or charged; the system has developed kindlier ways of dealing with the more delicate sensibilities of its higher-class clientele.
4. When the white-collar criminals are prosecuted and convicted, their sentences are either suspended or very light when judged by the cost their crimes have imposed on society.

The first three points will be discussed here, and the fourth will be presented in the section on sentencing below.

Everyone agrees that the cost of white-collar crime is enormous. In 1985, *U.S. News and World Report* reported that "experts estimate that white-collar criminals rake in a minimum of $200 billion annually." Marshall Clinard also cites the $200 billion estimate in his recent book, *Corporate Corruption: The Abuse of Corporate Power.* Nonetheless, $200 billion probably understates the actual cost. Tax evasion alone has been estimated to cost from 5 to 7 percent of the gross national product. For 1994, that would be between $336 and $470 billion.

In some areas of the economy, white-collar crime is growing dramatically. For example, the North American Securities Administrators Association conducted a survey of state enforcement actions and found that $400 million had been lost to investors as a result of fraud and abuse in the financial planning industry during the period from 1986 to 1988. Most striking, however, was their finding that "the number of state actions against financial planners rose 155 percent and the amount of lost investor funds climbed 340 percent" since their previous survey in 1985. Then of course there is the recent news about fraud in the savings and loan industry, which we look at later in this chapter.

All we need is a rough estimate of the cost of white-collar crime so that we can compare its impact with that of the crimes reported on by the FBI. For this purpose, we can use the conservative estimates in the U.S. Chamber of Commerce's *A Handbook on White-Collar Crime.* Because the *Handbook* was issued in 1974, we will have to adjust its figures to take into account both inflation and growth in population to compare these figures with losses reported for 1994 by the FBI. (In light of the avalanche of statistics the government puts out on street crimes, it's worth wondering why the Chamber has not seen fit to revise its 23-year-old figures, and why no other private or public institution—neither the FBI nor the U.S. Department of Commerce— keeps up-to-date statistics on the overall cost of white-collar crime.) In some categories, I shall modify the Chamber's figures in light of more recent estimates. As usual, I use conservative estimates where there is a choice. The result will be a rough estimate of the costs of different categories of white-collar crime, as well as of the overall total.

First, the modifications. As might be expected, the cost of computer crime is far beyond the $0.1 billion estimated by the Chamber in 1974. Current estimates run from $3 to $6 billion annually. I will use the $3 billion estimate. Government revenue loss has also outstripped the Chamber's estimate of $12 billion annually. The IRS "estimates that tax cheaters in legitimate business skim as much as $50 billion a year from the tax collector." Since this doesn't include defense and other procurement fraud, we can take it as a conservative estimate. Credit card fraud has also exceeded the Chamber's expectations, with several sources estimating its annual cost at over $1 billion, a figure we can safely use. The cost of pilferage must be increased as well. "The Bureau of National Affairs estimates total employee theft at $15 billion to $25 billion, while the U.S. Chamber of Commerce [recently] says it may be as high as $20 billion to $40 billion. And that's not including theft by government workers, which can be significant. I'll use the low end of the range recently given by the Chamber. Insurance fraud has also gone far beyond the Chamber's 1974 estimates. The National Insurance Crime Bureau says that automobile and health care insurance fraud costs insurers $18 to $50 billion. I will use the $18 billion figure. It will also come as no surprise, after the era of Boesky and Milken, that security thefts and frauds have far outstripped the Chamber's 1974 estimate of $4 billion. The North American Securities Administration Association estimates that investors lost $40 billion in 1987. And there is now a new category, not even dreamt of by the Chamber in 1974: theft of cellular phone services, estimated to cost $1 billion a year. . . .

With upper-class lawbreakers, the authorities prefer to sue in civil court for damages or for an injunction rather than treat the wealthy as common criminals. Judges have on occasion stated in open court that they would not make criminals of reputable businessmen. One would think it would be up to the businessmen to make criminals of themselves by their actions, but alas, this privilege is reserved for the lower classes.

Examples of reluctance to use the full force of the criminal process for crimes not generally committed by the poor can be multiplied ad infinitum. We shall see later that a large number of potential criminal cases arising out of the savings and loan scandals have been dismissed by Federal law enforcement agencies because they lack the labor power to pursue them—even as we hire 100,000 new police officers to fight street crime.

Let me close with one final example that typifies this particular distortion of criminal justice policy. Embezzlement is the crime of misappropriating money or property entrusted to one's care, custody, or control. Because the poor are rarely entrusted with tempting sums of money or valuable property, this is predominantly a crime of the middle and upper classes. The U.S. Chamber of Commerce estimate of the annual economic cost of embezzlement, adjusted for inflation, is $11.28 billion—more than two-thirds the total value of all property and money stolen in all FBI Index property crimes in 1995. (Don't be fooled into thinking that this cost is imposed only on the rich or on big companies [with] lots of resources. They pass on their [losses]—and their increased insurance costs—to [consu]mers in the form of higher prices. Embez[zlers t]ake money out of the very same pockets [that mu]ggers do: yours!) Nevertheless, the FBI [reports] that in 1995, when there were 2,128,600 [arrests f]or property crimes, there were 15,200 ar[rests for] embezzlement nationwide. Although [the cos]t to society is comparable, the number [of arrest]s for property crimes was 140 *times* [greater th]an the number of arrests for embezzle[ment. Rou]ghly, this means there was one prop[erty crime] arrest for every $7,000 stolen, and one em[bezzle]ment arrest for every $742,000 "misap[propriated]": Note that even the language be[comes mo]re delicate as we deal with a "better" clas[s of cro]ok.

[The cli]entele of the criminal justice system form[s an ex]clusive club. Entry is largely a privilege of the poor. The crimes they commit are the crimes that qualify one for admission—and they are admitted in greater proportion than their share of those crimes. Curiously enough, the crimes the affluent commit are not the kind that easily qualify one for membership in the club. . . .

Conviction

Between arrest and imprisonment lies the crucial process that determines guilt or innocence. Studies of individuals accused of similar offenses and with similar prior records show that the poor defendant is more likely to be adjudicated guilty than is the wealthier defendant. In the adjudication process the only thing that *should* count is whether the accused is guilty and whether the prosecution can prove it beyond a reasonable doubt. Unfortunately, at least two other factors that are irrelevant to the question of guilt or innocence significantly affect the outcome: One is the ability of the accused to be free on bail prior to trial, and the second is access to legal counsel able to devote adequate time and energy to the case. Because both bail and high-quality legal counsel cost money, it should come as no surprise that here as elsewhere the poor do poorly.

Being released on bail is important in several respects. First and foremost is that those not released on bail are kept in jail like individuals who have been found guilty. They are thus punished while they are still legally innocent. "On June 30, 1995, an estimated 44 percent of the nation's adult jail inmates had been convicted on their current charge. An estimated 223,000 adult jail inmates were serving a sentence, awaiting sentencing, or serving time in jail for a probation or parole violation. Between 1985 and 1995 the number of convicted inmates rose by nearly 100,000—up from 123,409. During the same period, the number of unconvicted jail inmates, including those on trial or awaiting arraignment or trial, doubled (from 127,059 to an estimated 284,100)." Beyond the obvious ugliness of punishing people before they are found guilty, confined defendants suffer from other disabilities. Specifically, they cannot actively aid in their own defense by seeking out witnesses and evidence. Several studies have shown that among defendants accused of the same offenses, those who make bail are more likely to be acquitted than those who do not. In a recent study of unemployment and punishment, Chiricos and Bales found that "after the effects of other factors [seriousness of crime, prior record, etc.] were controlled, an unemployed defendant was 3.2 times more likely to be incarcerated before trial than his employed counterpart."

Furthermore, because the time spent in jail prior to adjudication of guilt may count as part of the sentence if one is found guilty, the accused are often placed in a ticklish position. Let us say the accused believes he or she is innocent, and let us say also that he or she has been in the slammer for two months awaiting trial. Along comes the prosecutor to offer a deal: If you plead guilty to such-and-such (usually a lesser offense than has been charged, say, possession of burglar's tools instead of burglary), the prosecutor promises to ask the judge to sentence you to two months. In other words, plead guilty and walk out of jail today (free, but with a criminal record that will make finding a job hard and insure a stiffer sentence next time around)—or maintain your innocence, stay in jail until trial, and then be tried for the full charge instead of the lesser offense! In fact, not only does the prosecutor threaten to prosecute for the full charge, but this is often accompanied by the implied but very real threat to press for the most severe penalty as well—for taking up the court's time.

Plea bargaining such as this is an everyday occurrence in the criminal justice system. Contrary to the Perry Mason image, the vast majority of criminal convictions in the United States are reached without a trial. It is estimated that between 70 and 95 percent of convictions are the result of a negotiated plea, that is, a bargain in which the accused agrees to plead guilty (usually to a lesser offense than he or she is charged with or to one offense out of many he or she is charged with) in return for an informal promise of leniency from the prosecutor with the tacit consent of the judge. If you were the jailed defendant offered a deal like this, how would you choose? . . .

The advantages of access to adequate legal counsel during the adjudicative process are obvious but still worthy of mention. In 1963, the U.S. Supreme Court handed down the landmark *Gideon v. Wainwright* decision, holding that the states must provide legal counsel to the indigent in all felony cases. As a result, no person accused of a serious crime need face his or her accuser without a lawyer. However, the Supreme Court has not held that the Constitution entitles individuals to lawyers able to devote equal time and resources to their cases. Even though

Gideon represents significant progress in making good on the constitutional promise of equal treatment before the law, we still are left with two transmission belts of justice: one for the poor and one for the affluent. There is an emerging body of case law on the right to effective assistance of counsel; however, this is yet to have any serious impact on the assembly-line legal aid handed out to the poor.

Indigent defendants, those who cannot afford to retain their own lawyers, will be defended either by a public defender or by a private attorney assigned by the court. Because the public defender is a salaried attorney with a case load much larger than that of a private criminal lawyer, and because court-assigned private attorneys are paid a fixed fee that is much lower than they charge their regular clients, neither is able or motivated to devote much time to the indigent defendant's defense. Both are strongly motivated to bring their cases to a close quickly by negotiating a plea of guilty. Because the public defender works in day-to-day contact with the prosecutor and the judge, the pressures on him or her to negotiate a plea as quickly as possible, instead of rocking the boat by threatening to go to trial, are even greater than those that work on court-assigned counsel. . . .

As might be expected, with less time and fewer resources to devote to the cause, public defenders and assigned lawyers cannot devote as much time and research to preparing the crucial pretrial motions that can often lead to dismissal of charges against the accused. A recent study of 28,315 felony defendants in various county and city jurisdictions in Tennessee, Virginia, and Kentucky shows that public defenders got cases dropped for 11.3 percent of their defendants, and private attorneys got dismissals for *48 percent of their defendants*. As also might be expected, the overall acquittal rate for privately retained counsel is considerably better than that for public defenders. The same study shows that public defenders achieved either dismissal of charges or a finding of not guilty in 11.4 percent of the indictments they handled, and private attorneys got their clients off the hook in *56 percent of their cases*. The superior record of private attorneys held good when comparisons were made among defendants accused of similar offenses and with similar prior records. The pic-

ture that emerges from federal courts is not much different. . . . Writes Linda Williams in the *Wall Street Journal,*

> The popular perception is that the system guarantees a condemned person a lawyer. But most states provide counsel only for the trial and the automatic review of the sentence by the state appeals court. Indigent prisoners—a description that applies to just about everybody on death row—who seek further review must rely on the charity of a few private lawyers and on cash-starved organizations like the Southern Prisoners Defense Committee.

A recent *Time* magazine article on this topic is entitled "You Don't Always Get Perry Mason." Says the author, "Because the majority of murder defendants are . . . broke . . . , many of them get court-appointed lawyers who lack the resources, experience or inclination to do their utmost. . . . Some people go to traffic court with better prepared lawyers than many murder defendants get."

Needless to say, the distinct legal advantages that money can buy become even more salient when we enter the realm of corporate and other white-collar crime. Indeed, it is often precisely the time and cost involved in bringing to court a large corporation with its army of legal eagles that is offered as an excuse for the less formal and more genteel treatment accorded to corporate crooks. This excuse is, of course, not equitably distributed to all economic classes, any more than quality legal service is. This means that regardless of actual innocence or guilt, one's chances of beating the rap increase as one's income increases. Regardless of what fraction of crimes are committed by the poor, the criminal justice system is distorted so that an even greater fraction of those convicted will be poor. And with conviction comes sentencing.

Sentencing

On June 28, 1990, the House Subcommittee on Financial Institutions Supervision, Regulation and Insurance met in the Rayburn House Office Building to hold hearings on the prosecution of savings and loan criminals. The chairman of the subcommittee, Congressman Frank Annunzio, called the meetings to order and said:

The American people are furious with the slow pace of prosecutions involving savings and loan criminals. These crooks are responsible for 1/3, 1/2, or maybe even more, of the savings and loan cost. The American taxpayer will be forced to pay $500 billion or more over the next 40 years, largely because of these crooks. For many Americans, this bill will not be paid until their grandchildren are old enough to retire.

We are here to get an answer to one question: "When are the S&L crooks going to jail?"

The answer from the administration seems to be: "probably never."

Frankly, I don't think the administration has the interest in pursuing Gucci-clad, white-collar criminals. These are hard and complicated cases, and the defendants often were rich, successful prominent members of their upper-class communities. It is far easier putting away a sneaker-clad high school dropout who tries to rob a bank of a thousand dollars with a stick-up note, than a smooth talking S&L executive who steals a million dollars with a fraudulent note.

Later in the hearing, Chairman Annunzio questioned the administration's representative:

You cited, Mr. Dennis, several examples in your testimony of successful convictions with stiff sentences, but the average sentence so far is actually about 2 years, compared to an average sentence of about 9 years for bank robbery. Why do we throw the book at people who rob a bank in broad daylight but we coddle people who . . . rob the bank secretly?

The simple fact is that the criminal justice system reserves its harshest penalties for its lower-class clients and puts on kid gloves when confronted with a better class of crook.

We will come back to the soft treatment of the S&L crooks shortly. For the moment, note that the tendency to treat higher-class criminals more leniently than the lower-class criminals has been with us for a long time. In 1972, the *New York Times* did a study on sentencing in state and federal courts. The *Times* stated that "crimes that tend to be committed by the poor get tougher sentences than those committed by the well-to-do," that federal "defendants who could not afford private counsel were sentenced nearly twice as severely as defendants with private or no counsel," and that a "study by the Vera Insti-

tute of Justice of courts in the Bronx indicates a similar pattern in the state courts."

More recently, D'Alessio and Stolzenberg studied a random sample of 2,760 offenders committed to the custody of the Florida Department of Corrections during fiscal year 1985. Although they found no greater sentence severity for poor offenders found guilty of property crimes, they found that poor offenders did receive longer sentences for violent crimes, such as manslaughter, and for moral offenses, such as narcotics possession. Nor, by the way, did sentencing guidelines reduce this disparity. . . .

Chiricos and Bales found that, for individuals guilty of similar offenses and with similar prior records, unemployed defendants were more likely to be incarcerated while awaiting trial, and for longer periods, than employed defendants. They were more than twice as likely as their employed counterparts to be incarcerated upon a finding of guilt. And defendants with public defenders experienced longer periods of jail time than those who could afford private attorneys. McCarthy noted a similar link between unemployment and greater likelihood of incarceration. In his study of 28,315 felony defendants in Tennessee, Virginia, and Kentucky, Champion also found that offenders who could afford private counsel had a greater likelihood of probation, and received shorter sentences when incarceration was imposed. A study of the effects of implementing Minnesota's determinate sentencing program shows that socioeconomic bias is "more subtle, but no less real" than before the new program.

Tillman and Pontell examined the sentences received by individuals convicted of Medicaid provider fraud in California. Because such offenders normally have no prior arrests and are charged with grand theft, their sentences were compared with the sentences of other offenders convicted of grand theft and who also had no prior records. While 37.7 percent of the Medicaid defrauders were sentenced to some jail or prison time, 79.2 percent of the others convicted of grand theft were sentenced to jail or prison. This was so even though the median dollar loss due to the Medicaid frauds was $13,000, more than ten times the median loss due to the other grand thefts ($1,149). Tillman and Pontell point out that most of the Medicaid defrauders were health professionals, while most of the others convicted of grand theft had low-level jobs or were unemployed. They conclude that "differences in the sentences imposed on the two samples are indeed the result of the different social statuses of their members." . . .

Here must be mentioned the notorious "100-to-1" disparity between sentences for possession of cocaine in powder form (popular in the affluent suburbs) and in crack form (popular in poor inner-city neighborhoods). Federal laws require a mandatory five-year sentence for crimes involving 500 grams of powder cocaine or 5 grams of crack cocaine. This yields a sentence for first-time offenders (with no aggravating factors, such as possession of a weapon) that is higher than the sentence for kidnapping, and only slightly lower than the sentence for attempted murder! About 90 percent of those convicted of Federal crack offenses are black, about 4 percent are white. "As a result, the average prison sentence served by Black federal prisoners is 40 percent longer than the average sentence for Whites." In 1995, the United States Sentencing Commission recommended ending the 100-to-1 disparity between powder and crack penalties, and, in an unusual display of bipartisanship, both the Republican Congress and the Democratic President rejected their recommendation. . . .

The federal government has introduced sentencing guidelines and minimum mandatory sentences that might be expected to eliminate discrimination, and many states have followed suit. The effect of this, however, has been not to eliminate discretion but to transfer it from those who sentence to those who decide what to charge—that is, from judges to prosecutors. Prosecutors can charge in a way that makes it likely that the offender will get less than the mandatory minimum sentence. Says U.S. District Judge J. Lawrence Irving of San Diego, "The system is run by the U.S. attorneys. When they decide how to indict, they fix the sentence." And discrimination persists. . . .

As I have already pointed out, justice is increasingly tempered with mercy as we deal with a better class of crime. The Sherman Antitrust Act is a criminal law. It was passed in recognition of the fact that one virtue of a free enterprise economy is that competition tends to drive consumer prices down, so agreements by competing firms to refrain from price competition is the equivalent of stealing money from the consumer's pocket. Nevertheless, although such conspiracies cost consumers far more than lower-class theft, price fixing was a misdemeanor until 1974. In practice, few conspirators end up in prison, and when they do, the sentence is a mere token, well below the maximum provided in the law.

In the historic *Electrical Equipment* cases in the early 1960s, executives of several major firms secretly met to fix prices on electrical equipment to a degree that is estimated to have cost the buying public well over a billion dollars. The executives involved knew they were violating the law. They used plain envelopes for their communications, called their meetings "choir practice," and referred to the list of executives in attendance as the "Christmas card list." This case is rare and famous because it was one in which the criminal sanction was actually imposed. Seven executives received and served jail sentences. In light of the amount of money they had stolen from the American public, however, their sentences were more an indictment of the government than of themselves: *thirty days in jail!*

Speaking about the record of federal antitrust prosecution, Clinard and Yeager write that

> even in the most widespread and flagrant price conspiracy cases, few corporate executives are ever imprisoned; of the total 231 cases with individual defendants from 1955 to 1975, prison sentences were given in only 19 cases. Of a total of 1,027 individual defendants, only 49 were sentenced to prison.

There is some (slight) indication of a toughening in the sentences since anti-trust violations were made a felony in 1974 and penalties were increased. "In felony cases prosecuted under the new penalties through March 1978, 15 of 21 sentenced individuals (71 percent) were given terms averaging 192 days each." Nevertheless, when the cost to society is reckoned, even such penalties as these are hardly severe.

After the "anything goes" attitude of the Reagan era, which brought us such highly publicized white-collar skulduggery as the multibillion dollar savings and loan scandal, the 1990s have seen a kind of backlash, with the government under pressure to up the penalties for corporate offenders. Here too, however, progress follows a slow and zigzagging course. . . .

Studies have shown that even though corporate and white-collar lawbreakers are being more frequently brought to justice and more frequently being sanctioned, they still receive more lenient sentences than do those who are sentenced for common property crimes. A study by Hagan and Palloni, which focuses particularly on the differences between pre- and post-Watergate treatment of white-collar offenders, concludes that likelihood of prosecution after Watergate was increased, but that the effect of this was canceled out by the leniency of the sentences meted out:

> the new incarcerated white-collar offenders received relatively light sentences that counterbalanced the increased use of imprisonment. Relative to less-educated common criminals, white-collar offenders were more likely to be imprisoned after Watergate than before, but for shorter periods.

Even after the heightened public awareness of white-collar crime that came in the wake of Watergate and the S&L scandals, it remains the case that the crimes of the poor receive stiffer sentences than the crimes of the well-to-do. . . . Keep in mind while looking at these figures that *each* of the "crimes of the affluent" costs the public more than *all* of the "crimes of the poor" put together.

I do not deny that there has been some toughening of the treatment of white-collar offenders in recent years. Nonetheless, this toughening has been relatively mild, especially when compared with the treatment dealt out to lower-class offenders. Before turning to the "great" scandal of the savings and loan industry, here are two "small" cases that illustrate the new developments.

In September 1991, a fire destroyed a chicken-processing plant in Hamlet, North Carolina. When the 100 employees in the plant tried to escape, they found that the company executives had ordered the doors locked "to keep out insects and to keep employees from going outside for coffee breaks, or stealing chickens." Twenty-five workers died in the fire, some were found burned to death at the doors they couldn't open. Another 50 people were injured. The owner of the company and two plant managers

were charged with involuntary manslaughter. The outcome: The owner pleaded guilty and was sentenced to 19 years and 6 months in prison. You may or may not think this is severe as a punishment for someone responsible for 25 very painful deaths, but note three revealing facts. First, as part of the plea agreement, the involuntary manslaughter cases against the two plant managers were dismissed, though they surely knew that the doors were locked and what the risks were. Second, the owner is eligible for parole after two and one half years. And third, the sentence is "believed to be the harshest judgment ever handed out for a workplace safety violation."

. . . In September 1989, "the worst American mining accident in nearly a decade occurred . . . at the William Station Mine near Madisonville," Kentucky. Ten workers were killed in a methane explosion. "The grand jury found that supervisors at the William Station Mine had falsified daily and weekly safety reports, including those that recorded methane levels." Other violations were cited as well, "including requiring miners to work under unsupported roofs, historically the leading causes of deaths in mines." On February 20, 1993, the company that operates the mine "pleaded guilty to a pattern of safety misconduct there and agreed to pay the Government a fine of $3.75 million," said to be "the largest criminal fine ever imposed for violations of the Mine Safety Act." Is this severe for ten deaths? Was this an accident, if it resulted from intentionally covered up safety violations? Note that there was the possibility of a prison sentence for this. "James H. Tichenor, who was acting foreman at the mine, pleaded guilty to charges of falsifying records of methane levels. . . . Prosecutors said that Mr. Tichenor [who was the only individual charged] was cooperating in the investigation and that they had agreed to recommend he receive a minimum sentence. Under Federal guidelines, the minimum sentence for his violations could be probation to six months in prison."

We turn now to [one of] the greatest examples of upper-class crime in our era, the savings and loan debacle. . . . The federally insured system of savings and loan banks (also known as "thrifts") was created in the 1930s to promote the building and sales of new homes during the

Great Depression. The system had built into it important limitations on the kinds of loans that could be made and was subject to federal supervision to prevent the bank failures that came in the wake of the depression of 1929. Starting in the 1970s and speeding up in the early 1980s, this entire system of regulation and supervision was, first, loosened, and then essentially dismantled, as part of the Reagan administration's policy of deregulation. Although S&L's could now make riskier investments, their deposits were still insured by the Federal Savings and Loan Insurance Corporation (FSLIC). Translation: The S&Ls could take risky investments shooting for windfall profits, with the taxpayers picking up the tab for losses. This combination proved to be financial dynamite. The thrifts made high-risk investments, and many failed. By 1982, the bill to the FSLIC for bailing out insolvent thrifts was over $2.4 billion. By 1986, the FSLIC was itself insolvent! In 1996, the *Wall Street Journal* announced that a Government Accounting Office report put the total cost to the American taxpayer of the S&L bailout at $480.9 billion!

Not all this loss is due to crime. Some is due to foolish but legal investments, some is due to inflation, and some is due to foot-dragging by federal agencies that allowed interest to accumulate. Nonetheless, there is evidence that fraud was a central factor in 70 to 80 percent of the S&L failures. Much of this fraud took the form of looting of bank funds for the personal gain of bank officers at the expense of the institution. The commissioner of the California Department of Savings and Loans is quoted as saying in 1987, "The best way to rob a bank is to own one." Says *Fortune* magazine, "Though yet perceived only in hazy outline, today's S&L fraud dwarfs every previous carnival of white-collar crime in America."

In response to the enormity of this scandal, American public opinion has hardened toward white-collar crime, and federal law enforcement agencies have been prosecuting, fining, and even jailing offenders at unprecedented rates. Nonetheless, considering the size of the scandal and the far-reaching damage it has done to the American economy, the treatment is still light-handed compared with that of even nonviolent "common" crime. According to a study con-

ducted at the University of California at Irvine, "The average prison term for savings and loan offenders sentenced between 1988 and 1992 was 36 months, compared to 56 months for burglars and 38 months for those convicted of motor vehicle theft." The study goes on to point out that S&L offenders were sentenced to longer than first-time property crime offenders (who received an average sentence of 26 months), but, lest we think that this shows a new severity, the study notes that the average loss in an S&L case is $500,000. The average loss per property offense in 1995 was $1,251.

Note that these sentenced S&L offenders represent just a small fraction of the crooks involved in the S&L looting. One observer points out that "from 1987 to 1992, Federal bank and thrift regulators filed a staggering 95,045 criminal referrals with the FBI. The volume was so large that more than 75 percent of these referrals have been dropped without prosecution." At the same time, the Justice Department advised against funding for 425 new agents requested by the FBI and 231 new assistant U.S. attorneys, and the administration recommended against increasing funds authorized by Congress for the S&L investigations from $50 million to $75 million. And yet we now find the president and the Congress ready to spend $23 billion on criminal justice and hire 100,000 new police officers to keep our streets safe! . . .

Of the estimated 711,643 people in state prisons in June 1991, 33 percent were not employed at all (full or part time) prior to their arrests. About half of these were looking for work and half were not. Another 12 percent had only part-time jobs before prison, making fully 45 percent who were without full-time employment prior to arrest. These statistics represent a general worsening compared with 1986, when 31 percent of state inmates had no pre-arrest employment at all, and 43 percent had no full-time pre-arrest employment. Of those 1991 state inmates who had been free at least a year before arrest, 19 percent had some pre-arrest annual income but less than $3,000; and 50 percent had some pre-arrest annual income but less than $10,000.

To get an idea of what part of society is in prison, we should compare these figures with comparable figures for the general population. Because 95 percent of state inmates are male, we can look at employment and income figures for males in the general society in 1990. Statistics on employment and income for 1990 are close to those for 1988 and 1989, and so will give us a fair sense of the general population from which the current state inmates came.

In 1990, 5.6 percent of males, 16 years old and above, in the labor force were unemployed and looking for work. This corresponds to half the state inmates who were unemployed before arrest, because the other half who were unemployed were not looking for work. Where 16 percent of state prisoners had been unemployed and still looking for work, only 5.6 percent of males in the general population were in this condition. Thus, prisoners were unemployed and looking for work at a rate three times that of males in the general population. But this doesn't give us the full picture, because it doesn't capture the unemployed prisoners who had not been seeking work. To capture that, let us assume that, as among the prisoners, the number of males in the general population who are unemployed and not looking is equal to the number in the labor force who are unemployed and looking. (Note that this assumption is high, but for present purposes conservative, as the higher it is the more it will decrease the relative difference between prisoners and general male population.) The 5.6 percent of males in the labor force represents approximately 3,799,000 persons. If we double it, we get 7,598,000 as an estimate of the total number of males in the general population who are unemployed, looking for work or not. As a percentage of the total noninstitutionalized population of males 16 and over, this is 8.5 percent. Compare this with the 33 percent of state inmates who were unemployed prior to being arrested. *Then, state prisoners were unemployed at a rate nearly four times that of males in the general population.*

Where 19 percent of prisoners with any pre-arrest income at all earned less than $3,000 a year, 6.8 percent of males in the civilian labor force in 1900 earned between $1 and $2,499 a year, and 12.3 percent earned between $1 and $10,000, while 25 percent of males in the general population earned in that range.

Our prisoners are not a cross-section of America. They are considerably poorer and con-siderably less likely to be employed than the rest of Americans. Moreover, they are also less educated, which is to say less in possession of the means to improve their sorry situations. Of all U.S. prison inmates, 47 percent did not graduate from high school, compared to 21 percent of the U.S. adult population. Sixteen percent of prisoners said they had some college, compared to 43 percent of the U.S. adult population.

The criminal justice system is sometimes thought of as a kind of sieve in which the innocent are progressively sifted out from the guilty, who end up behind bars. I have tried to show that the sieve works another way as well. It sifts the affluent out from the poor, so it is not merely the guilty who end up behind bars, but the *guilty poor.*

. . . The criminal justice system does not simply weed the peace-loving from the dangerous, the law-abiding from the criminal. At every stage, starting with the very definitions of crime and progressing through the stages of investigation, arrest, charging, conviction, and sentencing, the system *weeds out the wealthy.* It refuses to define as "crimes" or as serious crimes the dangerous and predatory acts of the well-to-do—acts that, as we have seen, result in the loss of thousands of lives and billions of dollars. Instead, the system focuses its attention on those crimes likely to be committed by members of the lower classes. Thus, it is no surprise to find that so many of the people behind bars are from the lower classes. The people we see in our jails and prisons are no doubt dangerous to society, but they are not *the danger* to society, not *the gravest danger* to society. Individuals who pose equal or greater threats to our well-being walk the streets with impunity.

. . . I have argued that the criminal justice system works to make crime appear to be the monopoly of the poor by restricting the label crime to the dangerous acts of the poor and not those of the well off . . . and by more actively pursuing and prosecuting the poor rather than the well off for the acts labeled crime. . . . *The joint effect of all these phenomena is to maintain a real threat of crime that the vast majority of Americans believes is a threat from the poor.* The criminal justice system is a carnival mirror that throws back a distorted image of the dangers that lurk in our midst—and conveys the impression that those dangers are the work of the poor. . . .   [1998]

Understanding the Reading

1. When Reiman asks you to picture a crime, what do you imagine?
2. How does television distort our sense of crime and the criminal justice system?
3. Why don't we think a preventable mine disaster is a crime?
4. Explain why, in general, those who are in prisons are likely to be poor people?
5. What do studies show about the socioeconomic class of those who commit serious crimes?
6. Why is a poor person more likely to be arrested than a middle-class or upper-class person?
7. How do the police treat poorer boys differently than they do more affluent boys for equally serious offenses?
8. Explain how the well-to-do are weeded out of the criminal justice system.
9. Explain the comparative seriousness of white-collar crime and the popular image of crime.
10. Why are convicted white-collar criminals given relatively light sentences?
11. How do FBI Index property crimes compare with embezzlement, both in economic costs and in arrests?
12. Why are poor defendants more likely to be found guilty than are more affluent defendants?
13. Explain the Supreme Court ruling in *Gideon v. Wainwright.*
14. How is our justice system doubly biased against the poor?
15. What is the evidence of racial discrimination in sentencing?

Suggestions for Responding

1. Monitor your local television news or newspaper to see the proportion of crime stories that are reported about poor people and more affluent people.
2. Similarly, monitor sentences handed down to the well-to-do and the poor, as well as to Black and to White criminals. ✦

97

The Great Divide

David Moberg

It's time for this year's Dubious Distinction Award in economics, and once again the United States is the easy winner: It has far and away the greatest inequality in both wealth and income of all major industrialized countries, according to two recent studies. And it is growing more unequal at a faster rate than virtually everyone else, as well.

Such an achievement flies in the face of the image of the United States as an egalitarian country populated by one big happy middle class. Early in this century, extremes of wealth and poverty were far more pronounced in northern European countries than in the United States. Now, inequality in the United States is so extreme that New York University professor Edward N. Wolff argues it's far outside the mainstream of the industrialized world.

But does it really matter? Apologists for the status quo argue that such inequality is necessary to generate investment and reward risk-taking, thereby creating a prosperous economy. Besides, they say, Americans aren't bothered by the presence of an unprecedented number of millionaires in their midst. Certainly U.S. citizens are far less likely than most Europeans to favor government action to equalize incomes.

Today, many liberals have simply given up on the fight for income equality, while conservatives actively promote policies that will further concentrate both wealth and income in the hands of the upper class.

But it is wrong to celebrate or even ignore inequality. It's not just a question of fairness. As much as congressional Republicans may argue otherwise, inequality is bad for society and damaging to national economic performance.

In *Top Heavy,* a new study for The Twentieth Century Fund, Wolff reports that in 1989 the top 1 percent of U.S. households controlled 39 percent of the nation's "marketable wealth" (that is, real estate, securities and so on) and 48 percent of the financial wealth. If social security and pensions are included, the share of the top 1 percent declines, but the trend remains the same.

In many ways differences in wealth are more important than differences in income. As economists define it, "wealth" includes income-generating property, such as stocks and bonds, as well as personal assets, such as homes and cars. Income, by contrast, is the money received from wages, property, pensions or government programs. Wealth—especially in stocks, bonds and business shares—is crucial because it provides both economic and political power and family financial security.

Essentially, the study shows that the rich were able to capture almost all the new wealth and much of the income generated in the '80s. From 1983 to 1989, the richest 1 percent obtained 62 percent of the increase in marketable wealth. During the same period, the bottom four-fifths of all American households captured only 1 percent of the nation's increase in wealth—and so its share of the wealth dropped by one-fifth. Looking only at financial wealth, the bottom four-fifths actually *lost* 3 percent, while the top 1 percent captured 66 percent of the increase.

In a new international comparative study on income inequality, economist Timothy Smeeding of Syracuse University reports that "America has the most inequality of any modern nation we've looked at." From 1983 to 1989, according to Wolff, the top 1 percent garnered 37 percent of the gains in real income, while the bottom 80 percent got only 24 percent. Only in Britain has the rise of inequality been greater, and there only slightly more. In the United States, Smeeding says, not only has the gap between the highest and lowest earners been greater than in any other industrial country, but welfare state policies that redistribute income have also been weakest. As a result, America's poorest are in absolute terms poorer than people in a comparable position in most European countries.

There's a link between the good fortune of the rich and the misfortune of the rest. "The rich have gotten richer because the middle class and poor have gotten poorer," Wolff explains. "Keeping wages low has caused property income and stock prices to increase, which has shown up in increased wealth and income of the rich." This was intensified in the takeover and leveraged buy-out craze, which enriched a handful of speculators while driving down wages of workers in debt-laden companies. Similarly, the boom in the stock market over the last decade and a half has served to further enrich the already rich, who tend to put their money in stocks. In contrast, the major investments of middle-class families are their homes—which have appreciated less in value than stock have.

Top Heavy relies on figures from the years before 1990. According to Wolff, inequality has increased even more rapidly since then. Since 1989, middle-class family incomes have declined in real terms. And ordinary Americans can no longer cope with the earnings squeeze by sending another family member off to work, because so many families already rely on two wage earners. Private pensions are less common, and Social Security is more insecure than ever. Republican policies, from tax breaks for the rich to cutbacks in welfare or middle-class student loan programs, will only make things worse.

What does the United States get in return for this inequality, which supposedly creates savings and rewards entrepreneurs? There is no more social mobility or economic growth in the United States than in other industrial countries. And our lower unemployment rate comes at a high price for workers: Nearly one-fourth of the workforce here now earns less in real terms than the 1968 minimum wage.

And there is a growing body of evidence that inequality, rather than promoting economic growth, actually hurts the economy. For both industrialized and developing countries, economists have found that where inequality is greatest, economic growth is slowest. For example, a recent study of 41 countries found that the countries that performed the best from 1960 to 1985 had the strongest educational systems and the lowest levels of inequality of income and wealth.

A British study of industrialized countries from 1979 to 1990 similarly showed that the strongest performers typically had the most egalitarian distribution of income.

Economists are unsure why inequality has this negative effect, but University of Massachusetts–Boston professor Arthur MacEwan suggests four possible reasons. First, he argues, high inequality leads to conflict and social disorder, which is bad for business. Second, the relatively high wages in countries with more egalitarian distributions of income tend to push employers to purchase labor-saving machinery, which increases productivity. Third, workers are more motivated to work if they feel economic rewards are fairly distributed and wages are relatively high. Fourth, greater equality leads to more spending on health and education, since people are more likely to identify their own well-being with improving the health care and schooling of the whole society.

Currently, the opposite dynamic is at work in American society. New York University associate professor Roland Benabou notes that rich Americans may flee to the suburbs to get better education for their kids, then refuse to help pay for inner-city education. But, while their children gain an advantage, society overall becomes less efficient and productive because of the ill-trained city workers, and even the suburban children may lose. Several recent studies conclude that even within the United States, the metropolitan economies with the greatest disparity between urban and suburban incomes perform the worst. The "savage inequality" of our educational system (to borrow Jonathan Kozol's term) thus perpetuates and worsens income inequality in the broader society, especially at a time when only highly educated workers can hold their own.

None of the new critics of inequality would disagree with the importance of savings and investment. But, as Benabou has argued, it's "not just how much of national income is saved and invested in human capital" that counts, but to whom it goes. "How income gets distributed matters not just for justice but also for efficiency," he argues.

In short, inequality is not only wrong; it's bad business as well.   [1995]

Understanding the Reading

1. How do supporters of the status quo justify income inequality?
2. What is the distinction between wealth and income?
3. Why is it wrong to ignore income inequality?
4. What is the relationship between the increasing wealth of the richest people and the declining wealth of the middle class and the poor?
5. Why does inequality hurt the economy?

Suggestions for Responding

1. Have you and/or your family benefited from or been hurt by the recent trend toward income inequality? Write a short paper describing how you have been affected.
2. Write a letter to Moberg agreeing or disagreeing with his analysis.
3. Investigate and report on one of the leveraged buy-outs of the past decade or so. ✦

98

Unprotected Work

CHRISTOPHER D. COOK

Workers were a hot item in 1996. Born-again populists of both parties jostled for votes from the anxious and the downsized. Labor was Big again, elevating workers' issues—at least ones that contrasted Democrats from Republicans— back onto the electoral stage. But the AFL-CIO's $35 million pro-Democrat gambit did nothing to illuminate a massive legal crisis affecting some 30 million of America's burgeoning class of contingent workers, who comprise nearly one-third of the U.S. workforce. Lacking union protection and political clout, these temporary, leased and "contract" workers are slipping through widening cracks in U.S. labor laws.

Numerous studies and court cases indicate a fundamental contradiction between contingent employment and labor rights which were scripted for full-time, permanent workers.

A groundbreaking study sponsored by the Department of Labor provides potent evidence of this disconnect—but it may never see the light of day. In an unpublished report scuttled by Congress, the National Commission on Employment Policy (NCEP) documented major failings in a wide array of labor statutes. "Frequently, Federal protections afforded full-time, permanent employees do not reach the contingent worker," the commission concluded, upon extensive analysis of federal civil rights, labor organizing, equal pay, and other laws.

From well-paid computer engineers and business consultants in contract jobs to temporary and leased workers, janitors, and taxicab drivers, contingent workers of all collars are discovering their legal rights are even less secure than their jobs. The list of exclusions encompasses nearly every aspect of U.S. labor law:

- Contingent workers—of whom two-thirds are women and minorities—get unequal protection when it comes to equal pay. Proving that contingent positions require the same skills and responsibilities, and therefore the same pay, as core staff jobs is exceedingly difficult, many legal experts say. Bureau of Labor Statistics data show temporary and part-time workers earn as much as $5.00 per hour less than full-time employees in similar jobs.
- Temporary, leased, and contract workers rarely receive workers' compensation, and most are not protected by the Occupational Safety and Health Act, which only requires companies to provide a safe workplace for their own employees.
- Millions of temporary and part-time workers do not qualify for unemployment insurance, even after a full year's work. A temporary worker earning the industry's average of $6.42 per hour for 30 hours a week would fail the minimum earnings requirement in 19 states, according to Francois Carre, an economist and labor expert with the Center for Labor Research at the University of Massachusetts. Thirty-eight states prohibit independent contractors from collecting unemployment compensation, and many others explicitly bar part-time workers from receiving benefits during a job search.

- Part-time, temporary and casual workers at small businesses have little protection against discrimination, according to NCEP's study. Companies that employ people sporadically often fall below employee numerical thresholds which determine whether an employer is liable for civil rights violations.
- Independent contractors are excluded from anti-discrimination protections covering civil rights violations and sexual harassment. They are also exempted from workers' compensation insurance. The General Accounting Office has found that 40 percent of supposed "contract workers" are actually employees who are improperly denied legal protections.

Rising from the ashes of corporate downsizing, contingent labor has arrived as a permanent fixture in corporate cost-cutting wars. A June 1996 Labor Department report boasting a 5.3 percent official unemployment rate also revealed temporary labor's increasingly central role in job growth. Far outpacing new construction and factory employment, temporary-help agencies accounted for 35,000 of the 239,000 payroll jobs created in the second quarter of 1996. While temporary labor makes up 2 percent of the overall workforce, it comprised 15 percent of the latest jobs.

A 1995 Conference Board study found that contingent employment has become a primary, if not vital, ingredient in corporate downsizing. The management research firm's survey of corporations concluded that contingent labor is "closely identified with continued downsizing, since headcount restrictions are often imposed on managers to keep the core employment down once the job cuts have been made." Eighty percent of the respondents said a just-in-time workforce "gives them the ability to add and subtract workers with little notice, a strategy that has become more urgent because of unpredictable conditions in the global marketplace." The business world aptly terms this "accordion management"—the inhaling and exhaling of workers according to peak production and marketing cycles.

One of America's hottest yet lesser-known business trends, staff leasing, is cashing in on both ends of this accordion effect. "Professional employer organizations (PEOs)," as leasing firms prefer to call themselves, are making a booming business of liability outsourcing—assuming labor law obligations for their client companies' workers. To avoid the headaches of personnel management and labor law compliance, more and more businesses are firing their staffs and renting their workers from a leasing company.

The Your Staff leasing firm, a 5,000-employee subsidiary of the Kelly Services temporary labor corporation, is one such company promising, as a promotional video puts it, to "provide your company with an extra measure of insulation against damaging litigation and inflated insurance costs . . . Your Staff becomes the employer of record for your employees, while you maintain day-to-day control over directing them."

The promotions are working. Leasing's member group and lobbying arm, the National Association of Professional Employer Organizations (NAPEO), reports a staggering industry-wide revenue growth rate of 30–40 percent per year. According to the Bankers Trust Company, an investment analysis firm in New York City, this boom is likely to continue through the next five to ten years.

In the past 12 years, leasing has exploded from 98 firms leasing 10,000 workers in 1984, to 1,700 companies which now employ 2 to 3 million workers. Gregory Hammond, the former general counsel of NAPEO's predecessor, the National Staff Leasing Association, predicts leasing's exponential growth will "culminate sometime in the next 10 or 50 years at a point when no one will ever again be employed by the people for whom they perform services."

The industry advertises this detachment of workers from employers as the most efficient way to run a business in the global economy. Retired Air Force Colonel Regis Canney, a top industry executive, calls leasing "America's secret weapon" in the global business battlefield. But leasing's primary allure is that it exploits loopholes in family leave, pension, and worker health and safety laws. In order to qualify for Family and Medical Leave Act protection, workers must log 1,250 hours in a year for a single employer. But according to Cathy Ruckelshaus, a staff attorney with the National Employment Law Project in New York City, a business can "employ a worker for eleven and a half months

and then switch over to a leasing arrangement to avoid the requirements."

Businesses also use leasing as a "secret weapon" against union organizing drives. When the Service Employees International Union attempted to organize janitors employed by Advance Building Maintenance, which cleans Toyota headquarters offices in Torrance, California, Advance opted to lease its workers. According to Jono Shaffer, organizing coordinator for the Service Employees International Union's building services division, Advance "tried to take the position that they were no longer employing the workers, that our dispute was with the leasing company." Through aggressive corporate campaigning, SEIU forced Advance to settle collective bargaining agreements and numerous wage and hour disputes.

With such tantalizing loopholes, this risky business of liability outsourcing is expanding rapidly under minimal regulatory oversight. Only 13 states require PEOs to obtain a license or register their business. Likewise, the industry's self-monitoring body, the Institute for the Accreditation of PEOs, reports that but 13 of the nation's 1,700 leasing firms have met the group's standards for ethical behavior and financial stability.

In their quest for cheap, hassle-free labor, more and more companies are finding creative—often illegal—ways to erase workers' rights. As a condition of employment, taxicab firms now require drivers to sign "lease agreements" which, on paper at last, turn employee drivers into independent contractors, thus denying them minimum wage, unemployment insurance, workers' compensation, and other protections.

Workers' compensation is routinely denied to cab drivers, who, according to a recent study by the National Institute for Occupational Safety and Health, hold the most hazardous job in America. In 1994, 86 drivers lost their lives on the job, the study found. Thousands more are badly injured, and frequently these uninsured workers must pay enormous hospital bills out of pocket.

In a profession where knifings and beatings are part of the job description, signing away your rights to workers' compensation seems suicidal. But drivers say that under the cab industry's contracts—recently ruled illegal in a class-action lawsuit—it's "economic suicide" to become an employee.

According to the industry-authored lease agreement, "lease-drivers"—those who sign as independent contractors—pay $85 to rent a cab for a 10-hour night shift, while "employee-drivers" must pay $103. For the extra $18 a night, employee drivers get workers' compensation and unemployment insurance. Over the course of a year, access to these basic employment rights costs $3,500 to $4,000 a year—forcing drivers to choose between higher incomes and employment rights.

"It's gangsterism," adds Paulsen, a driver for DeSoto Cab company since 1976. "You either drive for these guys or you don't drive at all. You have no control . . . The driver is kind of like an economic slave."

Spurred by the near-fatal, on-the-job beating of driver John Coleman, thousands of San Francisco cab drivers joined and recently won a class-action lawsuit against three major taxi firms. According to the original complaint, "Taxicab drivers who are injured in the course and scope of their service . . . are unable to obtain medical care for their injuries, lose employment, are denied unemployment insurance benefits, and in many instances are forced on welfare." If it withstands appeal, the San Francisco Superior Court ruling will force taxi companies to cover their drivers for workers' compensation, unemployment insurance, and other employee rights.

But Ruach Graffis, a long-time organizer with San Francisco's United Taxicab Workers, says major financial incentives still encourage worker misclassification. "This will keep happening forever, until we get national health care, because these companies don't want to pay workers' compensation," says Graffis.

Legal aid lawyer Christopher Ho, who represented the drivers and has handled similar cases involving strawberry pickers, agrees. "This whole independent contractor misclassification thing has really taken off. Employers are doing it with increasing frequency because it's easy for them to avoid statutory obligations . . . The fact that it's happening so far afield shows that employers are using this as a ruse to save money."

Low-wage and immigrant workers are not the only victims. Even highly paid independent contractors by choice are denied basic rights. Minnesota business consultant Caryn Wilde en-

dured sexual harassment by a county development official for more than a year before filing a restraining order. Within two weeks of her complaint, the county agency, Wilde's largest client, "voted to cease all communications" with her, Wilde testified in court. Two months later, according to Wilde, the agency terminated all its business with Wilde.

Meanwhile, Wilde's legal and medical expenses related to the case soared to more than $30,000. After losing her biggest client and tens of thousands of dollars due to her sexual harassment complaint, Wilde also lost in Federal Court. The judge ruled that since Wilde was an independent contractor, she was not protected by Title VII of the 1964 Civil Rights Act; nor was she covered by the Minnesota Human Rights Act. When Wilde appealed to a Circuit Court, the EEOC took notice and, at first, offered its support. According to Wilde, the agency soon backed out, saying that "although they were very interested in the case, they were still living under the narrow interpretation of the term 'employee' as ordered by the Reagan/Bush Administration."

The EEOC's about-face corroborates the National Commission on Employment Policy's finding that Reagan-era Federal courts have narrowed the scope of employee status, often denying workers legal protection. "The breadth of . . . the legislative language is narrowing," the report stated. "Congress may want to expand coverage by extending the definition of employee to independent contractors." To date, this has not happened.

The ultimate challenge, says Anthony Carnavale, who headed the National Commission on Employment Policy, "is how to reconcile the need to furnish contingent workers protections in the workplace similar to those afforded permanent employees while continuing to provide employers with the work force flexibility they need to be competitive in a global economy." The commission warned that expanding contingent labor without extending labor rights promises dire results: "It is incumbent upon us to decide if, in the long-term, it is economically and socially viable for this country to sustain a large portion of the American working population in such a precarious and insecure employment status."

The commission answered its own question rather boldly, which may explain why congressional Republicans and the Clinton administration agreed to eliminate the group. "Our goal should be to provide all workers with the same level of protection to reduce the incentives to create a two-tiered labor market," the report said.

But as contingent labor proliferates, policy makers are ignoring this challenge. Only two members of Congress have proposed reforms, and both (Ohio Senator Howard Metzenbaum, and Colorado Representative Patricia Schroeder) have opted for retirement—effectively removing contingent labor from the national policy making map. The two congressional attempts to extend legal protections to contingent workers languish in archival obscurity.

Senator Metzenbaum's "Contingent Workforce Equity Act," proposed in October 1994, remains by far the most comprehensive attempt to protect contingent workers. It proposed to "extend the protections of Federal labor and civil rights laws to part-time, temporary, and leased employees, independent contractors, and other contingent workers, and to ensure equitable treatment of such workers." Among other provisions, the bill would have made it illegal for companies to pay temporary and part-time workers less than regular employees doing similar jobs. The European Court of Justice has already taken a similar tack, ruling that unequal pay for part-time workers is discriminatory.

When Metzenbaum retired the measure was passed along to now-retiring Illinois Senator Paul Simon; it has since been forgotten. Nonetheless, the bill amply reflected attempts by advocacy groups and unions to write contingent workers into the law. The National Employment Law Project, a New York City–based group advocating for the unemployed and working poor, is urging the Equal Employment Opportunities Commission to include Workfare recipients and other contingent workers within its antidiscriminatory aegis. The aim, according to staff attorney Cathy Ruckelshaus, is to "make it clear in the definition of employee that they're covered."

The Law Project and many policy researchers urge a complete overhaul of U.S. labor law, arguing that single-issue reforms "simply encourage the development of new forms of contingent status," a coalition of worker advocacy groups told the Dunlop Commission on the Future of Worker-Management Relations in 1994. "Mandating fair treatment for employees . . . gives employers a reason not to directly hire 'employees,' but instead to hire 'temps,' 'lease' workers or engage 'independent contractors' for whom they have no responsibility."

Francois Carre and fellow labor experts Virginia duRivage and Chris Tilly, say the National Labor Relations Act needs to be re-framed to allow new forms of union association—enabling temps and other transient workers to join collective bargaining units based on their occupation or geographic location, rather than on the traditional NLRA model of employer-based unionism.

Proposals for reform pile up by the dozens at labor conferences and in congressional archives. What's missing is government will and interest in discouraging unprotected work and expanding labor protections. If the silent slaying of NCEP's report is any indicator, politicians of both parties would rather not even discuss it. And while some unions, most notably the Service Employees International Union and the United Food and Commercial Workers, have pressed hard to address the needs of part-time and contract workers, the labor movement has been slow to embrace contingent workers as the new frontier for organizing.

Even in seemingly labor-friendly circles, the legal problems of contingent workers are merely "a topic that merits further inquiry." Such was the conclusion of the Dunlop Commission, a Clinton Administration fact-finding panel that many saw as the best hope for progressive labor law reform. Contingent workers merited but 2 pages in the commission's 200-page report, which failed to promote any reforms. According to one labor union source close to the commission, chair John Dunlop, the U.S. Labor Secretary under President Gerald Ford, "just didn't want to talk about it. He didn't think contingent workers were an issue that needed to be addressed." [1997]

Understanding the Reading

1. Who are "contingent workers"?
2. What labor laws exclude them?
3. Explain the relationship between corporate downsizing and contingent workers.
4. Why do employers find contingent workers and independent contractors attractive?
5. What employment rights do contingent workers and independent workers lose?

6. How does the law need to be changed to protect these workers?

Suggestions for Responding

1. Write a letter to your federal senator or representative expressing your beliefs about providing contingent workers with equitable legal employment rights. ✦

99

Normalizing Poverty

CELINE-MARIE PASCALE

The United States has experienced a dramatic realignment of wealth in the recent past; even by U.S. Census accounts, the rich continue to grow richer and the poor continue to grow poorer. As the Gross National Product continues to increase, real wages are steadily declining—we are seeing higher profits not higher wages.

High paying jobs are being replaced with jobs in service industries where both wages and the chance for promotion are low. *Fortune Magazine* reported in 1992 that 78 percent of new jobs are in the service sector; most of those jobs are for janitors or maids. Not surprisingly, 25.7 percent of American workers in 1992 held low-wage jobs. The Department of Labor reports that 7 million people now need more than one job in order to survive.

While millions of middle-class Americans are working their way into poverty, income and wealth continue to accumulate among the top 20 percent of the population. Commonly accepted definitions of wealth, unemployment, poverty and income often obscure more than they clarify. For instance:

Although capital gains accounted for trillions of dollars of wealth in 1991, the U.S. Census Bureau does not include capital gains in the standard definition of income. This has far reaching consequences in the way Americans understand the distribution of resources. By refusing to acknowledge capital gains as income, the government obscures vast amounts of wealth as well as

the programs and shelters that protect it. For instance, Social Security benefits are calculated in such a way that places limits on income derived from employment; however, income from capital gains is not limited.

Executives typically are compensated generously in ways which are not counted as salary. For example, in 1992, senior managers at Time Warner were promised an annual bonus not less than 125 percent of their base salaries.

Federal definitions of unemployment exclude a growing number of Americans who are not part of the labor force. Kevin Phillips noted in his book *The Politics of Rich and Poor: Wealth and the American Electorate* that in 1988, when the government reported 5.3 percent unemployment, nationally, 34.5 percent of American workers were not accounted for in the work force. This discrepancy reflects the fact that many unemployed workers are hard for a government bureaucracy to track. Unless [workers qualify] for unemployment benefits, they are virtually impossible to identify. Even workers who once qualified for unemployment fall out of the system once their benefits end. In 1988, 1.5 million workers were laid-off; two years later, in 1990, 22 percent of those workers were still left out of the labor force but were no longer counted in the federal unemployment figures.

A comprehensive tally of distressed workers would include those who are employed well below their skill level, those who cannot find more than part-time work, people earning poverty-level wages, all workers who have been jobless for more than four weeks at a time and all those who have grown discouraged and quit looking. In 1992 distressed workers totaled 36 million, or 40 percent of the American labor force, according to the Washington-based Economic Policy Institute. During this same time period, unemployment was recorded at 7.6 percent.

A NATIONAL RIFT

The 1980s, like the 1920s, could be called "the era of the rich." Capital gains tax was cut from 49 percent to 20 percent and reductions in corporate tax rates lowered corporate income tax revenues to an all time low of 6.2 percent. The 1980s saw the number of millionaires nearly triple (1,500,000), as did the number of decamillionaires (100,000) and centimillionaires (1,200) while the number of billionaires quadrupled (51). By contrast, the roaring 1920s, famous for their prosperity, only doubled the number of millionaires and billionaires.

During 1987, while the nation experienced only 4 percent inflation, 339 of the nation's largest publicly held corporations increased their CEOs' compensation by an average of 48 percent. The typical CEO in 1987 took home $1.8 million. By 1988, their compensation increased 14 percent more and CEO earnings averaged $2.02 million. A typical CEO today earns a salary that is about 150 times that of the average worker in service industries. But that is only an average. In 1989, Steven Ross, CEO of Time Warner, saw his pay rise to more than 9,000 times the pay of average workers. (By contrast, Japanese CEOs earn no more than 20 times the salary of workers.)

During this same period, the standard of living for millions of Americans was plummeting. Between 1987 and 1989, while CEO salaries increased robustly, more than 1.5 million workers were laid-off across the country. By 1989, 23 percent of all year-round, full-time workers did not earn enough to keep a family of four out of poverty. In other words, 23 percent of full-time workers made less than $14,000 a year. One million of these workers had college degrees; 2.5 million had high school degrees.

In 1991, 42.4 percent of blacks and 32.8 percent of Hispanics had household incomes under $15,000. Two years later, in the spring of 1993 the United Nations released a report announcing that many white Americans enjoy the highest standard of living on earth, but the quality of life for black and Hispanic Americans, on average, approximates that of residents of Trinidad and Tobago. The same could be said for many women who are single heads of households. In 1991, 47.1 percent of all female-headed families with children under 18 lived below the federal poverty line.

Americans tend to believe that poverty is the plight of those who are unable or unwilling to compete—that poverty is a sign of personal failure, rather than the consequence of corporate policies. Similarly, Americans want to believe that a Horatio Alger story lurks behind every millionaire despite the fact that it is hard to find family fortunes that are not linked to labor exploitation and/or inherited wealth. With 40 percent of the nation's labor force experiencing economic distress, we continue to want to believe that, by definition, the "middle class" is protected from "real" poverty—even as they use credit cards to pay some of the monthly bills.

If poverty was once the burden of the destitute or unemployed, it no longer is. Today, an increasing number of fully employed workers and their families live in poverty—they are unable to afford the basic necessities of food, housing, clothing and medical care. The new poor include people who remain poor despite having jobs as well as those who fell into poverty when they lost their jobs.

In 1991, 39.2 percent of white American households had incomes less than $25,000. Among Hispanics, 54.4 percent of household incomes were below $25,000. For black Americans the picture was particularly bleak: 60.6 percent had household incomes less than $25,000 in 1991. For blacks and Hispanics the fastest growing category of income is that for households earning less than $10,000 a year. In 1991, 30.8 percent of the black population and 20.7 percent of the Hispanic population had annual household incomes under $10,000 according to *The Statistical Abstract of the United States*. The decline in household income was compounded by the overall increase in the cost of consumer items. *The Statistical Abstract of the United States* reveals that between 1982 and 1992, the cost of groceries increased 39 percent; the average cost of shelter rose 36 percent and medical care increased 106 percent. Millions of Americans, even though employed full-time at one or more jobs, had insufficient incomes to afford food, clothing and housing.

Not surprisingly, working- and middle-class borrowing has been steadily rising. During the early 1980s, 72.7 percent of all families fell into debt, according to *The Statistical Abstract of the United States*. Even grocery stores began to accept credit cards for food purchases. Household debt climbed to over $3 trillion and consumer installment credit more than tripled. By 1989, credit card debt claimed a greater percentage of household debt than mortgages. The government estimates that by the year 2000 credit card debt alone will be more than $432.9 billion. [Editor's Note: According to the Federal Reserve Bulletin of July, 2002, by 2002, U.S revolving debt, which is almost entirely credit card debt, reached $730 billion.]

The number of pawn shops has doubled in the past decade to an estimated 10,000. Cash America, Jack Daugherty's chain of pawn shops, is now on *INC* magazine's list of fastest growing companies. Today, its stock is traded on the New York Stock Exchange. C. Jensen and Project Censored reported on Cash America in their book, *Censored: The News That Didn't Make The News*. The average interest rate on loans at Cash America hovers at 200 percent, a common industry rate. In 1993, Cash America reported $13 million in profits on $186 million in revenues. With profits riding high, Daugherty claims to have tapped only one-sixth of the market—which he estimates to include 60 million people.

Pawn shops and check-cashing outlets serve low-income people, usually in urban ghettos, who aren't served by mainstream banks. These services, now known as "fringe banking," are becoming a standard subsidiary of major banks. Fringe banking is one of the highest profit centers in the banking industry. There's no secret to their success. Check-cashing outlets charge as much as 10 percent of the check's value for their service. This means an individual would pay $5 to cash a $50 check and $10 to cash a $100 check.

The Consumer Federation of America and the U.S. Public Interest Research Group surveyed 300 large banks and discovered that the average annual cost of a regular checking account is rising at twice the rate of inflation. From 1990 to 1993, the cost of checking accounts increased 18.5 percent to $184; consequently, the portion of American families without a bank account is also rising. In 1993, 14 percent of all families could not afford a bank account. More and more families are being forced by economic necessity to use fringe banking services. Not surprisingly, the number of high-profit, check cashing outlets jumped from 2,000 in 1987 to nearly 5,000 in 1993.

A rapid growth in debt combined with an increase in the cost of living and a decrease in wages forces a new definition of middle class. While a strict definition of "middle class" includes only salaried white-collar workers, many Americans believe that middle class means middle income, regardless of whether or not the income is hourly or salaried, blue collar or white. The dramatic trend in downward mobility for both blue and white collar workers leaves very few people earning middle incomes regardless of their class. We need a perspective for understanding what this downward mobility means.

THE BOTTOM LINE

Sixteen percent of all Americans, or 39.7 million people, live at or below the poverty line established by the federal government. The federal poverty line for a family of four is about $14,000. However, the realities of daily life clearly set a different definition of poverty. Just what does the national poverty line represent?

Formulated in the 1960s at the birth of the War on Poverty, this measure starts with the idea that poverty signifies the inability of families to afford the basic necessities. The calculation begins with the minimum amount of money needed to buy food that would meet minimum nutritional requirements. At the time that the poverty line was set, food made up one-third of a family budget; consequently, the federal poverty line was set at three times the cost of the minimum food budget. For a family of four, in 1970 it was $3,968; in 1980, it was $8,414. By the early 1980s, however, food expenses had fallen to about one-fifth of the average family budget. Correctly calculated by the original standard, the poverty line in 1980 should have been $14,000—60 percent higher than was claimed.

In 1994, the federal poverty line continues to be meaningless. The basic calculations for [the] federal poverty line have not been adjusted since it was developed 30 years ago; since then, the percentage of income spent on food has dropped to one-sixth of the total family budget. Americans earning as much as 155 percent of the official federal poverty line are not self-sufficient by the definition of poverty.

If the original principles used to develop the federal poverty line were applied today, these views would shift dramatically. Assuming that one-third of the federal poverty line ($4,667) reflects the minimum annual cost of food for a family of four and that food costs now comprise one-sixth of the total family budget, a federal poverty line of $28,000, or six times the cost of food for a family of four, would be more consistent with the original intent and methodology.

Schwarz and Volgy compiled their own low-income budget based on figures gathered from government estimates. The budget includes the costs of all necessities, not just food. The lower-income family budget they compiled was $20,658 in 1990—166 percent of the federal poverty line.

To arrive at this minimal annual income necessary for a family of four, they calculated rent, phone and utilities to total $375 a month. If this rent allocation seems unreasonable, it certainly reinforces the lack of reality inherent in the federal poverty line. Even Supplemental Security Income (SSI) which allocates funds and vouchers for low income housing allows as much as $600 per month for housing alone in California.

The monthly income detailed by this poverty-line budget is $1,722 and one could easily imagine a monthly rent of $516 (30 percent of the monthly income is the HUD rule of thumb) in addition to utility and phone expenses. To avoid homelessness and reduce expenses, many renters are doubling-up and sharing housing. *The Statistical Abstract of the United States* shows that in the years 1989–1990, 41.6 percent of renter-occupied housing units were shared with another householder, as compared with 4.2 percent before 1969.

Whether one recalculates the federal poverty line to place an annual food budget in perspective ($28,000) or uses the low-economy budget ($20,658), the number of Americans experiencing poverty is at least double the official government estimate of 39.7 million; 79.4 million, or one-third of all Americans, live in poverty. Two parents working full-time at minimum wage jobs earn only $16,320 in pre-tax income—and the Republicans are working to abolish minimum wage. Employed at the median hourly wage for production and nonsupervisory workers ($10.02/hour, or $20,841 a year), a full-time worker scarcely earns enough to reach the threshold of self-sufficiency for a family of four! Twenty-five percent of all workers currently earn $7.50 an hour ($14,400 a year) or less.

The median income for white families in 1991 was $37,783; for black families it was $21,548 and for Hispanic families, $23,895. (Median income for households was much lower.) For black and Hispanic families, median income has become synonymous with poverty. Race, like gender, is clearly a strong factor in disparate rates of pay and consequently, level of poverty. However, because they are so dominant in the work force, white males head the largest group of working poor households. Between 1989 and 1992, nearly 25 percent of the 1.7 million children who fell into poverty lived in two-parent white families.

Creating fair employment patterns with equal pay, regardless of race or gender, would go a long way toward resolving problems of poverty but not far enough to make a radical difference. Nor is education at the bottom of this problem; even if everyone's education equaled that of the upper half of the population, the problem of poverty would not be solved. Poverty cannot be eliminated completely by wage equity and increased education combined because there has been a decline in jobs. By 1993, the United States was averaging more than 2,000 job layoffs a day.

The pursuit of private wealth has not produced "the good society" as many had believed. Instead, millions of Americans have worked their way into poverty. Clearly, this is not the kind of problem that can be solved by philanthropy or "trickle-down economics." Public and corporate policies, not personal defects, are devastating the standard of living for one-third of the nation's workers—in addition to these millions of workers, there also are millions of poor and homeless people who aren't reflected in any discussion of the labor system.

Belief in the American myth that "everyone can make it" remains national identity—despite the fact that each day millions of responsible Americans are not making it. Because Americans learn to believe that hard work and intelligence will be rewarded—that we live in a meritocracy—Americans blame themselves for their failure to succeed. As a society we want to believe that the poor deserve to be poor and the rich deserve to be rich. As a consequence, only the economic hardships of the desperately poor become visible.

Almost 80 million workers struggle with daily issues of poverty, yet Republicans insist that a solution to national economic problems demands orphanages for the children of poor families, dissolution of the minimum wage and cuts in entitlements. Pervasive poverty is linked to corporate profits, not children, not immigrants, not minimum wage, and not welfare.

We've grown accustomed to homelessness, to low wages and insecure jobs, to the need for two-parent incomes. We've gotten used to a new kind of normal, making it that much harder to change. As long as we remain silent, we face the dangers of believing that the pervasive economic disaster is nothing more than our own personal problems.   [1995]

Understanding the Reading

1. What does Pascale mean when she says "millions of middle-class Americans are working their way into poverty"?
2. What is wrong with the way we define income?
3. How are the rates of unemployment misrepresentative?
4. What made the 1980s "the era of the rich"?
5. How did the 1980s affect workers, minorities, and women?
6. Describe the indicators of the growth of household debt.
7. What is wrong about the way the federal poverty line is calculated?
8. What can and cannot be done to resolve the issues of poverty?

Suggestions for Responding

1. Check the most recent *Statistical Abstract of the United States* and compare such figures as those on household income or personal debt with Pascale's earlier figures. Using that evidence, report on whether economic times are improving or declining.
2. Check your local want ads to identify what kind of housing is available for a family of four for about $300, 30 percent of the 1995 poverty line of $12,188. Report your findings and what you learn from your research. ✦

100

Institutionalized Discrimination

ROBERT CHERRY

Individuals and institutions may use decision-making procedures that inadvertently discriminate and reinforce inequalities. For example, income differentials can cause unequal access to education even though the school system does not intend to discriminate; locational decisions of firms may have the unintended impact of reducing access to jobs. Similarly, when housing is segregated by income (race), all individuals do not have equal access to job information, as higher-income (white) households will tend to have greater access to job information through personal contacts than lower-income (black) households. Thus, employers will have more higher-income white applicants than if housing was distributed without regard to race or income. Also, employers attempting to reduce their screening costs might rely on group stereotypes rather than more individualized information when deciding which applicants to interview.

In none of these instances is discrimination consciously undertaken, but disadvantaged groups, having unequal access to education, job information, and the interviewing process, are nonetheless harmed. Though unintentional, these problems reinforce the "vicious cycle" of poverty.

INCOME DIFFERENTIALS AND EDUCATIONAL ATTAINMENT

Income constraints place heavy burdens on the allocation decisions of low-income households. Often they must "choose" to do without many necessities, such as education. In addition, children from low-income households often have explicit household responsibilities that take time away from school activities. This may involve responsibility for household activities (baby-sitting, shopping, and so on) or earning income. In either case, economists would argue that on average low-income students have a greater opportunity cost[1] on their time than high-income students. Since their opportunity costs are greater, lower-income students rationally allocate less time to studying and school-related activities than equally motivated higher-income students.

At the college level, even the availability of low-cost public institutions does not necessarily equalize the economic cost of education to all students. Just as at the elementary and secondary school level, lower-income students have a greater opportunity cost on their time than comparable higher-income students. Even if family responsibilities are negligible, students still require income for their own support. This invariably requires lower-income students to work at least part-time while attending school and has often led to the sending of male but not female offspring to college.

The level of income required is influenced by whether the student can live at home while attending college. Historically, public colleges were located in rural areas. For example, none of the original campuses of the Big Ten or Big Eight colleges are located in the states' largest metropolitan areas. The original campus of the University of Illinois is not located in Chicago and the University of Missouri is not located in St. Louis or Kansas City. Thus, not only did lower-income students have to pay for room and board away from home, but it was usually difficult to find part-time employment in these rural communities. This implies that even the availability of low-cost public colleges did not necessarily place the lower-income student on an equal footing with more prosperous students.

Theoretically, low-income youths with appropriate abilities and motivation should be able to borrow money to finance their education. As long as the economic returns from schooling are greater than the interest rate, students will gain from borrowing rather than forgoing additional education. The equalizing of economic costs can occur only if all students of equal promise can borrow at the same rates. Financial institutions, however, cannot accept expectations or probabilities of future income as sufficient collateral for loans. They require bank accounts or other tradable assets, which are normally held by upper-income but not lower-income households. Thus, students from lower-income households cannot borrow readily for education without government intervention.

It also appears that schools in poorer neighborhoods tend to have larger classes and weaker teachers. John Owen found that within the same city, as the mean neighborhood income rose by 1 percent, class size decreased by 0.24 percent and the verbal ability of teachers rose by 0.11 percent. This inequality is even more glaring when comparisons are made between cities. Owen found that for each 1 percent increase in the mean income of a city, there was a rise of 0.73 percent in real expenditures per student and a 1.20 percent increase in the verbal ability of teachers. Thus, students living in poorer neighborhoods in poorer cities have a double disadvantage.

If higher opportunity costs and lower-quality education were not sufficient to discourage educational attainment, Bennett Harrison found that for black inner-city youths, incomes are hardly affected by increases in educational attainment. He notes, "[A]s their education increases, blacks move into new occupations, but their earnings are hardly affected at all by anything short of a college degree, and there is no effect whatever on their chances of finding themselves without a job over the course of the year." Thus, independent of conscious discrimination by the educational system, we should expect low income minority youths to have lower educational attainment than white youths, even when ability and motivation are held constant.

During the 1970s, a number of policies were implemented in an attempt to compensate for the influence of family income on educational attainment. First, legislatures began funding state universities in larger urban areas. Second, court rulings forced states to change funding formulas so that per capita funding from wealthy and poor communities within each state would become more equal. Third, guaranteed student loans reduced the disadvantage low-income students faced when attempting to finance their education.

DIFFERENTIAL IMPACT OF INCOMPLETE INFORMATION

In the most simplified labor models, it is assumed that workers and firms act with complete information: Workers know the jobs that are available, and firms know the productivity of job seekers. In this situation, competitive firms would hire the best applicants for the jobs available, and workers would gain the maximum wage obtainable.

Economists have recently developed models in which information has a price; it is only "purchased" up to the point at which its benefits are at least as great as its costs. Neither firms nor workers rationally attempt to gain complete information concerning the labor market opportunities available. Workers find that some additional job information is not worth its cost, while firms find that some information on the productivity of applicants is not worth the additional personnel expenses. Liberals have argued that when workers and firms rationally decide to act on the basis of optimal rather than complete information, biases are generated.

Let us begin by analyzing how firms decide the optimal productivity information they should obtain. A firm benefits from additional productivity information if it translates into hiring a more profitable work force. A firm must weigh this increased profitability against the cost involved in seeking the additional information. After some point, it is likely that the benefits from additional information are insufficient to outweigh its cost. Even though the firm realizes additional information would probably result in hiring a somewhat more productive worker than otherwise, it knows that the added screening expenses would be even greater.

When a strong profit motive and wide productivity differentials among applicants are present, extensive screening will occur. This is the case with professional sports teams, especially since television revenues have transformed ownership from a hobby to a profit-making activity. Liberals believe, however, that in the vast majority of situations, productivity differentials among applicants are quite small and benefits from extensive screening are minimal.

Liberals suggest that the initial screening of applicants is often done with very little individual productivity information available. For firms with a large number of relatively equally qualified applicants, there is no reason to spend much time determining which applicants should be interviewed. These firms simply take a few minutes (seconds) to look over applications and select a promising group to interview. The employer realizes that such a superficial procedure will undoubtedly eliminate some job applicants who are slightly more productive than those selected for interviews. Since productivity differentials are perceived to be minor, however, this loss is not sufficient to warrant a more extensive (expensive) screening procedure.

There would be no discrimination if the job applicants victimized were random, but let us see why the screening method might cause the consistent victimization of individuals from disadvantaged groups. Suppose a firm considering college graduates for trainee positions decides that it has many equally qualified candidates. Looking at résumés, the firm can quickly identify each applicant's race, sex, and college attended. If the firm has enough applicants from better colleges, it is likely to say, "All things being equal, students from these colleges are likely to be more qualified than applicants who attended weaker colleges." Thus, the firm dismisses applicants from the weaker colleges, even though it realizes that weaker schools produce some qualified applicants. The firm has nothing against qualified graduates of weaker colleges. It simply reasons that the extra effort required to identify them is not worth the expense.

However unintentional, highly qualified graduates from weaker schools are discriminated against. Discrimination occurs because this screening method determines the selection for interviews on the basis of group characteristics rather than individual information. More generally, highly qualified applicants from any group that is perceived to have below-average productivity would be discriminated against by this superficial screening method.

Suppose employers believe that black and female applicants are typically less productive than their white male counterparts. If the firm has sufficient white male applicants, it will not interview black or female applicants. The firm will decide that although there are some black and female applicants who are slightly more productive than some white male applicants, it is not worth the added expense to identify them. The process by which individuals are discriminated against when firms use group characteristics to screen individuals is usually called statistical discrimination.

Statistical discrimination can occur indirectly. A firm hiring workers for on-the-job training may be primarily interested in selecting applicants who will stay an extended period of time. The firm does not want to invest training in individuals who will leave the firm quickly. Presumably, if the firm had a sufficient number of applicants who worked more than four years with their previous employer, it would not choose to interview applicants with more unstable work experience. Again, the firm reasons that although there are likely to be some qualified applicants among those with an unstable work record, it is too costly to identify them. This method of screening is likely to discriminate because of the nature of seniority systems, which operate on a "last hired, first fired" basis. Many minorities and women have unstable work records because they are hired last and fired first. Thus, even when firms do not use racial or gender stereotypes, they discriminate, since women and minorities are more likely to come from weaker schools and have more unstable work records than equally qualified white male applicants.

FINANCIAL AND OCCUPATIONAL EFFECTS

Many economists believe the job market is divided between good (primary) and bad (secondary) jobs. Good jobs have characteristics such as on-the-job training and promotions through well-organized internal labor markets. Bad jobs have little on-the-job training and minimum chance for promotions; they are dead-end jobs. Since on-the-job training is a significant aspect of primary-sector jobs, employment stability and behavioral traits are often more important than formal education and general skills. Both conservative and liberal economists agree that workers who do not possess the proper behavioral traits, such as low absenteeism and punctuality, will not be employed in the primary sector. Most liberals believe that many women and minority workers who possess the proper behavioral traits also will not find jobs in the primary sector as a result of statistical discrimination.

Facing discrimination in the primary sector, many qualified female and minority workers shift to secondary labor markets. As a result, secondary employers have a greater supply of workers and can reduce wages and standards for working conditions. Primary employers and majority workers also benefit from statistical discrimination. Since majority workers face less competition, more of them will gain primary employment than they would in the absence of statistical discrimination.

Primary employers may have to pay somewhat higher wages and employ somewhat less productive workers as a result of statistical discrimination, but the reduced screening costs more than compensate for the higher wages and productivity losses. Moreover, many primary employers also hire secondary workers. For them, the higher cost of primary employees will be offset by the resulting reduction in wages paid to secondary workers and their somewhat higher productivity.

Since primary workers, primary employers, and secondary employers benefit from statistical discrimination, there are identifiable forces opposed to change. Thus, rather than the market disciplining decision makers, statistical discrimination creates groups having a financial stake in its perpetuation.

APPLICANTS AND THEIR SEARCH FOR JOB INFORMATION

For job seekers, the cheapest source of job information is personal contacts, including neighbors and relatives and their acquaintances. Additional information can be obtained from newspaper advertisements and government employment offices. The most costly information is obtained from private employment agencies. A significant difference in the cost of job information would occur if one individual had few personal contacts and was forced to use private employment services, while another individual had extensive personal contacts. All things being equal, the individual with the lower cost of obtaining information would be better informed and hence more likely to obtain higher earnings.

The job information minorities receive from their search effort is likely to be less valuable than the job information received by their white counterparts. The fact that an individual is recommended by a personal contact might be sufficient reason to grant the person an interview. Those who obtain information from newspaper ads or government employment services do not have this advantage. This distinction is summed up in the adage "It's not what you know but who you know that counts."

Low-income (minority) individuals tend to have fewer contacts than high-income (white) individuals of equal abilities and motivation. High-income (white) individuals tend to have many neighbors or relatives who have good jobs, own businesses, or are involved in their firm's hiring decisions. Low-income (minority) individuals, having few personal contacts, are forced to spend additional time and money to obtain job information. Even if the job information is as valuable as that obtained by their white counterparts, minorities might give up searching for employment sooner because it is more costly. They do not do so because they are less able or less motivated; they simply face greater expenses.

AFFIRMATIVE ACTION

Affirmative action legislation is the major government attempt at counteracting the discriminatory features of the hiring process. Affirmative action assumes that discrimination results from employment decisions based on incomplete information. The role of the government is simply to encourage firms to hire all qualified applicants by forcing them to gather individualized productivity information.

Guidelines stipulate that all government agencies and private firms doing business with the government must publicly announce job openings at least forty-five days prior to the termination of acceptance of applications. This provision attempts to offset the information inequality disadvantaged workers face. More importantly, these employers must interview a minimum number of applicants from groups that tend to be victims of statistical discrimination.

It is important to remember the difference between affirmative action and quotas. Under affirmative action, there is no requirement to hire; employers are required only to interview female and minority applicants and make sure they have access to job information. Quotas are more

drastic actions reserved for situations in which firms are not making good faith efforts to seek out and hire qualified female and minority applicants. For example, if a firm attempts to circumvent affirmative action guidelines by announcing job openings in papers that reach only the white community or, after interviewing applicants, uses discriminatory procedures to eliminate women from employment, the government can impose quotas. Thus, quotas are imposed only when it is demonstrated that the lack of female or minority employment reflects something more conscious than the unintentional effects of incomplete information.

Besides the government, some private groups have attempted to compensate for unequal access to information. Women's groups have attempted to set up networks to aid female job applicants for management positions. Female executives are encouraged to share as much information as possible with other women to offset the traditional networking done by men. In many areas, male networking is referred to as the old boy network, and entry into it has historically been critical to obtaining the most desirable jobs. Thus, the lack of personal contacts is at least partially offset by networks that direct job information to disadvantaged workers and provide low-cost productivity information to firms.

SKILL AND LOCATIONAL MISMATCHES

Many individuals reject the view that groups are held back due to external pressures by noting that "when we came to America, we faced discrimination but were able to overcome it." In particular, these individuals often believe that internal inadequacies are responsible for the seemingly permanent economic problems minorities face. One response is to argue that the discrimination minorities face is more severe and their economic resources fewer than those of European immigrants at the turn of the century. Another response dominated the U.S. Riot Commission's assessment of black poverty. This presidential commission, which was created to study the causes of the urban rebellions of the late 1960s, noted,

When the European immigrants were arriving in large numbers, America was becoming an urban-industrial society. To build its major cities and industries, America needed great pools of unskilled labor. Since World War II . . . America's urban-industrial society has matured: unskilled labor is far less essential than before, and blue-collar jobs of all kinds are decreasing in numbers and importance as sources of new employment. . . . The Negro, unlike the immigrant, found little opportunity in the city; he had arrived too late, and the unskilled labor he had to offer was no longer needed.

This commission, commonly known as the Kerner commission, avoided blaming either the victims (culture of poverty) or society (discrimination) for black economic problems; they were simply the result of technological change. To compensate for the higher skill levels required for entry-level positions, the Kerner commission recommended extensive job-training programs. Supposedly, once these skills were obtained, blacks would enter the employment mainstream and racial income disparities would diminish.

Job-training programs became the centerpiece of the liberal War on Poverty initiated during the Johnson administration. To an extent, these job-training programs complemented compensatory educational programs. Whereas the compensatory programs attempted to develop general skills, job-training programs attempted to develop specific job-related skills. Whereas the compensatory programs were attempts to increase white-collar skills, job-training programs were attempts to increase blue-collar skills.

The government's involvement in job-training programs was pragmatic; it sought upward mobility in ways that would not conflict with the interests of other groups. Thus, it did not aggressively institute training programs that would conflict with the objectives of many craft unions. This meant that in many of the construction trades, which had historically restricted membership, the government accepted union prerogatives. Job-training success also was impeded by the seeming irrelevance of many of the skills taught, and there were complaints that training programs did not use the latest equipment and the newest methods.

Many liberals discounted these complaints. They agreed with conservatives that the problems disadvantaged groups faced stemmed from their internal inadequacies. These liberals thought the actual technical skills developed were irrelevant; what was critical was the development of the proper behavioral traits of punctuality and low absenteeism. These liberals also recommended more restrictive programs that would train only the least deficient of the disadvantaged group. In contrast, those liberals who believed that external pressures, particularly discrimination, were dominant proposed costly training programs and a more aggressive approach to craft unions.

Job-training success also was impeded by the shifting of blue-collar jobs out of Northeastern and Midwestern urban areas. After World War II, technological changes decreased the viability of central city locations. First, trucking replaced the railroads as the major transportation mode. When firms delivered their output (and received their input) on railcars, central city locations were ideal. When trucking became dominant, traffic tie-ups made those locations too costly. Indeed, recognizing these costs, the federal government built a new interstate highway system so that travelers could bypass congested central city areas.

Second, new technologies emphasized assembly-line techniques that required one-level production. No longer could manufacturing firms use factory buildings in which they operated on a number of floors. High land costs made it too expensive to build one-level plants in urban centers, so manufacturing firms began to locate in industrial parks near the new interstate highways on the outskirts of urban areas. This intensified minority employment problems, as most minorities continued to live in the inner city.

Minorities with the proper behavioral requirements, education, and skills have difficulty obtaining employment due to these locational mismatches. Inner-city residents are likely to lack the financial ability to commute to suburban jobs. They are unlikely to own a car or to earn a sufficient income to justify the extensive commuting required, even if public transportation is available. Minorities also are less likely to have access to these jobs because they have fewer personal contacts working in suburban locations.

Liberals have offered a number of recommendations to offset locational mismatches. Some economists have favored government subsidies to transportation networks that would bring inner-city workers to suburban employment locations. These subsidies would be cost-effective if the added employment generated greater income tax revenues and government spending reductions. Other economists have favored subsidizing firms to relocate in targeted inner-city zones. This approach was even endorsed by President Reagan under the catchy name "Free Enterprise Zones."   [1989]

Terms

1. OPPORTUNITY COST: The relative proportion of time or resources that can be invested in a given activity.

Understanding the Reading

1. In what ways does having a lower income level limit one's educational attainment?
2. Explain what Cherry means by "purchasing information" and how it affects discriminatory employment practices or statistical discrimination.
3. What causes higher wages in the primary sector and lower wages in the secondary sector?
4. How are low-income people disadvantaged in their job searches?
5. Explain how affirmative action is supposed to work and how it differs from quotas.
6. What were the objectives and problems of job training as a solution to minority unemployment or underemployment?

Suggestions for Responding

1. Apply Cherry's analysis to the circumstances described in one of the selections in Part IV.
2. Write a brief essay in which you speculate on how the "cycle of poverty" that Cherry describes might be broken. ✦

101
Jury Whops Insurer

LESLIE BROWN

On October 26, the Richmond Circuit Court awarded a $100 million judgment against Nationwide Mutual Insurance Company upon finding that the company had discriminated against blacks in the city. The judgment was the largest civil rights verdict in U.S. history.

The ruling closed the first case in the nation where an insurance company was brought to trial for redlining—the illegal practice of avoiding business in minority neighborhoods. During the two-week trial, the plaintiff, Housing Opportunities Made Equal of Richmond (HOME), argued that the insurance company restricted its target market to predominately white neighborhoods, overcharged blacks for coverage and made race-based decisions in deciding whom to target for premium sales. "Nationwide was deaf and blind to its own obvious racial bigotry," says attorney Thomas Wolf, a senior member of the legal team that represented HOME. "The lesson here for large corporations is that if they don't root out their racism—conscious or subconscious—they may pay a heavy price for it."

This was not the first time Nationwide had been accused of racial discrimination. In 1992, the National Fair Housing Alliance conducted an investigation after widespread reports began surfacing that the company regularly turned down blacks for premiums. The group eventually filed a complaint with the Department of Housing and Urban Development (HUD).

In 1994, HUD began giving grants to local fair housing groups across the country to investigate racial discrimination by Nationwide and other insurance companies. HOME received three grants for $1.2 million to investigate 30 companies in the Richmond area. Eleven testers—both black and white—were trained to pose as home-buyers and seek rate quotes for home insurance.

The testing began in June 1995. During the following 15 months, HOME conducted approximately 220 tests. The probe quickly began to focus on Nationwide. "We found problems in other companies but the most egregious was with Nationwide," says Connie Chamberlin, executive director of HOME and president of the National Fair Housing Alliance.

In 15 paired tests of similar houses, black testers seeking homes in black neighborhoods received only six insurance quotes while white testers seeking homes in white neighborhoods received 12 quotes. In the nine cases in which black testers were denied quotes, Nationwide agents told them their homes were too old, did not meet minimum value standards and that there was not enough time until the closing on the house to permit the required inspection. When blacks were able to obtain coverage, they were charged as much as 15 percent more for their premiums.

HOME also discovered that Nationwide targeted zip codes in the largely white suburbs of Richmond, ignoring those with a significant black population. Additionally, the investigation uncovered that Nationwide was moving all of its agents outside of the city of Richmond—which has a predominately black population—into the white suburbs. The company justified the decision by saying they were trying to target people who were more likely to buy both homeowners and auto insurance policies.

Nationwide denies that they violated state insurance regulations or federal laws regarding racial discrimination. However, company officials were unable to answer why there was a higher rate of blacks turned down for coverage than whites. Moreover, Nationwide had admitted in marketing documents that they excluded affluent, predominately black neighborhoods, but included trailer parks that they determined were more than 90 percent white.

"The plaintiffs have not presented any factual evidence to support their claims against Nationwide," says a company statement issued after the verdict. "Instead, they swayed the jury by relying on insinuations and emotionally charged allegations which have no place in a court of law."

Nationwide spokesman Bob Sohovich says the company thought the facts were clear and convincing in the trial and maintains that the company has not violated any laws. "We are committed to marketing in all areas, including the urban market," he says. "We took this to court because we thought we had done nothing wrong."

Lawyers for Nationwide said the company will appeal the verdict to the Virginia Supreme Court.

In addition to the $100 million in punitive damages, the jury awarded HOME $500,000 in compensatory damages to reimburse the group for the cost of investigating Nationwide. "The ruling signifies a couple of things," Wolf says. "Institutional racism can be proven when it is laid out before a jury. The jury sent a strong message to corporate America that this type of corporate racism is not going to be tolerated."

[1998]

Understanding the Reading

1. What is redlining?
2. How did HOME gather evidence against Nationwide?

Suggestions for Responding

1. To combat redlining in banking, Congress passed the Community Reinvestment Act in 1977; research and report on its regulations, and try to develop a comparable plan to combat insurance redlining. ✦

102

Single Mothers and Welfare

ELLEN L. BASSUK,
ANGELA BROWNE,
AND JOHN C. BUCKNER

In 1992 the Better Homes Fund, a nonprofit organization based in Massachusetts, began a study of 216 women in low-income housing and 220 homeless women, along with 627 of their dependent children. All these women in Worcester, Mass., were raising their families single-handedly, and the majority were receiving cash assistance. Despite this aid, most of the families lived below the federal poverty level ($12,156 for a family of three in 1995). We wanted to understand what had pushed some of these families into homelessness, what their lives were like and what role welfare—in their case, Aid to Families with Dependent Children (AFDC)—played in their survival.

We found that these low-income women often faced insurmountable barriers to becoming self-supporting. Unlike popular stereotypes, most of the women who received welfare were neither teenage mothers nor the daughters of women who had been on welfare; they used welfare episodically, in times of crisis, rather than chronically. Despite limited education and the demands of child care—the average age of their children was five and a half years—approximately 70 percent of them had worked for short periods. Yet the study revealed that even full-time employment at minimum wage is not enough to enable a single mother to climb out of poverty. Many of the housed mothers lived in extremely precarious circumstances, only one crisis away from homelessness.

We also discovered that there was little significant difference in the quality of life of homeless and housed mothers. The housed mothers typically lived in dilapidated apartments, doubling or tripling up with other families to reduce the rent burden. Most of the women in both groups had histories of violent victimization that resulted in emotional and physical problems. Having had to escape repeatedly from abusive situations, many of them were bereft of social supports such as family. Indeed, we found that a major factor protecting these women and their children from becoming homeless was AFDC.

The welfare revisions passed by Congress on August 1, 1996, abolished AFDC as an entitlement, ending six decades of guaranteed federal assistance to poor parents and their children. Cash relief is now tightly tied to work, and strict time limits are set on maintaining support. In addition, the legislation severely restricts eligibility for food stamps, Medicaid and other benefits, cutting $56 billion from antipoverty programs. What remains of welfare will now be directly administered by the states through block grants. This reform, we expect, will put many of the housed families in our study on the streets. Nationwide, 12.8 million people on welfare—of whom eight million are children—are now at risk of homelessness.

Sally, a 26-year-old white woman, was born in New Hampshire. When she was five, Sally's mother left her abusive husband—and also Sally and her two older brothers. The family moved in with Sally's paternal grandmother. Sally's father was an alcoholic, always in and out of jobs—and, because he had wanted a third son and resented Sally, he often became violent with his daughter.

When Sally was 13, her father remarried. Sally's stepmother had four children and was angry when Sally was forced to move in with them. The stepmother confined Sally to her room after school; she also beat Sally with extension cords and wood boards to "discipline" her and once held her underwater, threatening her with drowning. Sally fled when she was 16, moving in with some friends in Massachusetts. She began drinking; at the same time, she worked at odd jobs and obtained her high school equivalency degree.

Sally then moved to Texas and found full-time employment. At the age of 21, she became pregnant and decided to stop drinking. After the child was born, Sally found temporary care for her and entered a detoxification program. Once her substance abuse problem was identified, however, she was declared an unfit mother, and her child was taken away.

After completing the program, Sally worked full-time for two years in a manufacturing plant for $4 an hour. At 24 years old she became pregnant again. The father of her second child was abusive during her pregnancy, threatening to kill her and punching her in the head and stomach. Sally went into labor during one of these attacks and delivered three months prematurely. The child survived but had severe developmental delays as well as attention and behavior problems. Sally briefly received AFDC in Texas, but, unable to find affordable child care and thus unable to work, she decided to return to Massachusetts.

She moved into a two-room apartment with two other women and their children but was only able to stay there for a month. There was a six-month delay in receiving benefits in Massachusetts. Having no income, Sally requested emergency shelter—where we met her.

Although Sally was diagnosed with post-traumatic stress disorder (PTSD), we found her to be hard-working and optimistic. While job hunting during her shelter stay, Sally met her current husband. Although finances are extremely tight, he is able to support the family. Sally worked briefly, but because of the high cost of child care, she now stays home with her son and stepdaughter.

The events that led Sally and her son to a shelter are unique to them but reflect larger patterns. With very limited economic resources, the demands of single parenting (especially of a disabled child) can easily become overwhelming. One more stressor may be enough to tip the balance, catapulting someone onto the streets. Sally struggled to get on her feet despite a traumatic childhood. Although she had a good work history and was able to conquer her alcohol problem, her relationship with an abusive man, child care demands and the loss of her AFDC benefits forced her to turn to a shelter for refuge. As with Sally, violence accompanies poverty in the lives of many women in our study. The interplay of violence and poverty reduces the likelihood of escaping from either.

For a poor family, welfare is often what makes the difference between having a home or not. Those who had not received assistance, we found, were more likely to be homeless: 24 percent of the homeless women had not been granted AFDC in the past year (compared with 7 percent of the housed). These women had struggled to put together meager annual incomes that averaged $7,637, largely through jobs supplemented with some assistance from family and friends. (According to the Massachusetts Department of Transitional Assistance, the rent and utility burden alone for unsubsidized housing is $7,081 per year.)

Women who had received AFDC were doing somewhat better. AFDC, created in 1935, was a joint state and federal program; states determined their own level of benefits, but all persons who met eligibility requirements were guaranteed assistance. In 1995 the annual AFDC grant for a family of three in Massachusetts was $6,984 (or $582 per month); nationally, the average payment for such a family was $4,464. The women in our study who were on AFDC also obtained other support; together these benefits may have provided the critical margin for the families to stay housed.

At the time of the interviews, the majority of the low-income mothers in our study were on AFDC for short to moderate periods, with about one third having used AFDC more than once. Although the process of cycling on and off welfare is not fully understood, a body of research indicates that women often leave or return to welfare because of work or relationship changes. The median lifetime stay for women in our study was about two years for the homeless and 3.5 years for the housed. About a third of the women had used AFDC for a total of five years or more.

Almost never was AFDC the only source of income. About 30 percent of the women on AFDC worked; others supplemented their income through housing subsidies, food stamps, WIC (a nutritional program for pregnant women and their infants) and child support.

Nationally, only 57 percent of poor mothers have court-awarded child support. In 1989 the average annual award for poor women was only $1,889, but no more than half these women received the full amount. Growing caseloads and varying procedures and laws in each state make child support difficult to enforce. The new law cuts welfare benefits to a mother by at least 25 percent if she does not identify the father of her child. Given the high rate of violence by male partners against both women and children, our study suggests that many women will continue to refuse for fear of physical retaliation.

In addition to the economic hardship and residential instability that the mothers in our study experienced, the study found that most of them had undergone severe traumas. A shocking 91.6 percent of the homeless and 81.8 percent of the housed mothers reported physical or sexual assaults at some point in their lives. Even using a conservative measure—one that excluded spanking, shoves and slaps—almost two thirds of both groups reported violence by parents or other caretakers during childhood. More than 40 percent of both groups had been sexually molested before reaching adulthood. Sixty-three percent reported assaults by intimate male partners—again based on a conservative measure that included being punched, kicked, burned, choked, beaten and threatened or attacked with a knife or gun but excluded being pushed, shoved or slapped fewer than six times. And one quarter reported physical or sexual attacks by nonintimates.

As a result, many mothers in our study were distressed. Low-income housed and homeless mothers reported suffering from at least one emotional disorder in their lifetime at roughly the same rates, 69.3 and 71.7 percent, respectively. (In contrast, 47 percent of women in the general population report at least one lifetime disorder.) The lifetime and current prevalence of major depressive disorder, PTSD and substance abuse was extremely high. But unlike women and men who are on the streets alone, homeless mothers in our sample did not suffer disproportionately from severe disabling conditions such as schizophrenia or anxiety disorder.

PTSD consists of the long-term effects of early physical or sexual abuse as well as other traumas. Its hallmarks include feelings of terror and helplessness. A person suffering from PTSD may have sleep disturbances, irritability, hypervigilance, heightened startle responses, and flashbacks of the original trauma. Periods of agitation alternate with emotional numbness. Severe depression, substance abuse and suicide attempts are frequently associated with the disorder. Indeed, 31.2 percent of the homeless and 25.6 percent of the housed mothers reported that they had attempted suicide an average of twice in their lifetime, usually in adolescence.

Together the homeless and housed mothers in our study suffered three times the prevalence of PTSD in their lifetime that women in general do. Because their intimate relationships unfolded within the context of earlier, sometimes profound, betrayal, the women's lives were often characterized by difficulty in maintaining boundaries, as well as by disconnection and distrust. Both groups had few relationships they could count on. Because of the demands of single parenting, histories of family disruption and loss, and the ever present threat of violence in their neighborhoods, many remained socially isolated.

Medically, the well-being of our subjects was greatly compromised as well. Even though most of the women were in their late twenties, a disproportionate number of them were subject to chronic medical problems, such as asthma (22.8 versus 5.4 percent in a national sample of women under age 45), anemia (17.5 versus 2.4 percent), chronic bronchitis (7.8 versus 5.8 percent) and ulcers (5.7 versus 1.4 percent).

It should be noted, however, that although many mothers in our sample suffered from PTSD and depression or substance abuse, these disorders were equally prevalent in both the homeless and the housed. Despite our initial hypothesis that violence and its aftermath would be strongly associated with homelessness, multivariate modeling of housing status did not bear out this surmise. Economic factors were most salient in predicting the onset of homelessness.

The tale of these mothers and their families is a cautionary one and not specific to Worcester. In most cities with a similarly sized population of between 100,000 and 250,000, 15 percent or so of the citizens are living below the poverty line. During the past decade, as the American economy has slowed and shifted away from manufacturing to service-sector jobs, real wages have declined. Wealth has also been drastically redistributed: in 1993 the top 20 percent of U.S. households received 48.9 percent of the total income, whereas those in the bottom 20 percent shared only 3.6 percent. Between 1991 and 1992, 1.2 million more Americans became poor, for an estimated total of 36.9 million citizens living below the federal poverty level.

At the same time, people are spending more on rent than ever before. According to the Joint Center for Housing Studies, between 1970 and 1994 the median income of renter households fell 16 percent to $15,814, whereas rents increased more than 11 percent to $403 a month. Today 83 percent of renters living below poverty level spend more than the 30 percent of their income on rent that is considered reasonable by standards of the federal housing program.

The effects of increased rents and economic shifts can be seen most dramatically in the growing numbers of homeless persons. During the mid-1980s, many of us reassured ourselves that once affordable housing was provided, homelessness would disappear. Instead it is more prevalent than ever. A 1990 telephone survey led by Bruce G. Link of Columbia University estimated that 13.5 million (or 7.4 percent of) adult

Americans have been homeless at some time. But since the early 1980s, federal construction and rehabilitation programs for low- and moderate-income housing have virtually stopped. Many cities have low vacancy rates, and waiting lists for public housing are years long.

The composition of the homeless population has also changed. Approximately 36.5 percent of the nation's homeless now consist of families with dependent children—an increase of 10 percent since 1985. Not since the Great Depression have families in such substantial numbers been among the homeless. An estimated 88 percent of these families are headed by women [see "Homeless Families," by Ellen L. Bassuk; *Scientific American,* December 1991].

According to the U.S. Conference of Mayors, increasing numbers of low-income families are at risk of becoming homeless. By 1993 nearly 40 percent of all families headed by women lived below the federal poverty level. Among blacks and Hispanics, the rates were 50.2 and 49.3 percent, respectively. Twenty-three percent of children in the U.S. live in poverty; no other industrial nation comes close to this figure. As sole providers and caretakers, women heading households must juggle child care, households and work. Despite the challenge of balancing these tasks, 39.9 percent of poor single mothers and 48.3 percent of poor married mothers do work.

Although the gap between men's and women's incomes has narrowed, women still earn less. The average man without a high school diploma earns 58 percent more than a woman with a similar education. Single mothers, especially those of color or with limited education, are more likely to be working for minimum wage or at part-time, dead-end jobs. One quarter of women workers are employed part-time; 44 percent of these women are working part-time because full-time work is unavailable to them.

For single mothers, the need to care for young children makes consistent employment difficult. In our study, 59 percent cited unavailability of affordable child care as a barrier to work. According to a 1994 General Accounting Office report, the probability of a poor mother working would increase by as much as 158 percent if adequate subsidies for child care were available. Despite the federal allocation of $2.2 billion in 1992 to

such programs, however, demand far outweighs supply. Further, programs often do not account for realities of the workplace—some, for example, impose arbitrary time limits. Recent national studies have also raised concerns about the quality of child care programs, suggesting that many threaten the safety, development and well-being of their charges.

The new legislation ends the 60-year-old federal guarantee that families and children living below subsistence levels will receive cash assistance. Through block grants, power has been transferred to the states to set eligibility requirements and benefit levels. In the context of our findings, this legislation seems certain to be devastating to the millions of children currently living in poverty, as well as to single mothers and many low-income working families. There is little doubt that many states will impose even more stringent limitations than those mandated by the new bill. It is also likely that an ensuing "race to the bottom" will occur, in order to discourage potential recipients of welfare from moving between states.

The federal welfare bill places draconian limits on eligibility for benefits—allowing a maximum of two years for adequate education or training and finding employment that will fully support a family, along with a five-year lifetime limit on welfare. The creation of a corresponding job base, however, has been completely neglected. The new law would necessitate that states quadruple the number of jobs for unskilled and semiskilled labor, a task that will be especially daunting in areas that are already impoverished or lack employment opportunities. And despite increased allocations for child care, demand will quickly outstrip supply given the new work requirement. According to data from the Congressional Budget Office, states will face shortfalls in child care funding in every year after fiscal year 1998.

Even more disturbing is that the legislation reflects a "get tough" attitude that seems to be based on four assumptions that are not supported by empirical findings. The first is that welfare perpetuates dependency rather than serving as a stopgap measure during hard times. Our data confirm other studies indicating that most poor and homeless women use welfare for relatively short periods. Also, two thirds of the mothers in our sample had not grown up in families that were receiving welfare—a fact that debunks the stereotype of intergenerational dependency.

The second fallacy is that welfare compromises the work ethic. Many low-income mothers supplemented their AFDC grants by working at low-paying jobs with no benefits. Because of limited opportunities, many were forced to work part-time. The women most able to maintain jobs had at least a high school education, access to affordable child care and a social network that had some financial resources.

The third ill-conceived argument is that teen mothers and single-parent families are responsible for the growing poverty rate in the U.S. Nationally, however, only 7.6 percent of all mothers who received welfare in 1993 were under 18 years old and unmarried. The median age of our sample was 27.4 years, with 24.5 percent under 21 years and 7.1 percent under 18 years.

And, finally, the fourth myth holds that welfare costs contributed significantly to the growing federal budget and to increased taxes. Taken together, AFDC spending, food stamp benefits and Medicaid for AFDC recipients made up less than 5 percent of all entitlement spending and not quite 3 percent of the total federal outlay. AFDC, Medicaid, Supplemental Security Income and nutrition entitlement programs since 1964 amounted to only about 6.6 percent of total federal spending over the past 30 years. Yet even at painfully low amounts, cash assistance limited the risk of homelessness for poor families.

With the passage of the new law the onus is now on the states to protect these vulnerable families. An understanding of poor women's experiences and the impact of those experiences on their present circumstances is vital in restructuring antipoverty programs and policies. An effective response should include creating more educational and job opportunities, guaranteeing that basic needs for housing, food, medical care and safety are met, and ensuring that disabled individuals and children are well cared for.

Low-income women with at least a high school diploma are more likely to find gainful employment and support their children. As the Institute for Women's Policy Research has shown, "completing high school increases the chances of

escaping poverty to 31 percent." Low-income mothers who continue their education need various kinds of support—such as transportation and child care—to enable regular attendance. To be effective, educational opportunities must also be linked to the realities of the labor market: job training must be aimed at helping these women obtain full-time work that pays a livable wage and offers essential benefits. Once these mothers begin work, health care and child care benefits should be provided for an adequate period.

At the current minimum wage, a woman working full-time generates $8,840 annually. The new minimum wage is being phased in, and the full amount of $5.15 per hour will not be attained until September 1, 1997. Basic yearly costs of $21,816 for a family of three (unlike the federal poverty level, this figure includes rent, child care, health care and transportation) inevitably force this family into debt. Health care insurance, subsidies for child care and expansion of the earned income tax credit would improve the economic status of these parents and make work a more realistic option than welfare.

Moreover, violence at the hands of male partners is a major barrier to building a successful work history for many women. Effective back-to-work policies must take into account the long-term, devastating effects of childhood and adult victimization, as well as the extremely high rates of violent assaults faced by women living in poverty. Given the pervasiveness of this violence, communities should create comprehensive services to address the emotional and behavioral effects experienced by both women and children.

If a low-income parent is faced with an economic crisis or is unable to work—for example, because of a disability—it is essential that some income guarantees exist to protect his or her well-being, and also that of the children. The new welfare bill eliminates the federal government's role in establishing a safety net. Previously, the federal government set basic eligibility criteria and ensured minimal funding levels for cash assistance to the poor. With the shift in responsibility to the states, these guarantees will be gone. Will the states continue to protect those who are disadvantaged—by poverty or disability, or both?

In a society as affluent as ours, the possibility that large numbers of families will be cast aside raises troublesome questions about our moral values. We pride ourselves on being family-oriented, particularly treasuring the future of our children. But the new legislation suggests that low-income families headed by women are expendable. Creating realistic state programs is far more cost-effective than the financial and social burden that will result if thousands of families and children are left destitute. That situation is inevitable if jobs and child care are not available by the time a woman's eligibility for assistance expires. The future of our country depends on how we usher children through critical developmental years. Without adequate support of mothers in their challenging roles, all of society will suffer.   [1996]

Understanding the Reading

1. What difference between homeless single mothers and housed single mothers did the Massachusetts study discover?
2. What are some general characteristics of homeless women?
3. How long were most of the women on welfare studied? How many go on welfare more than once?
4. How do women supplement their AFDC income?
5. How many single mothers have court-ordered child support, and why don't many identify the child's father?
6. How many single mothers have suffered abuse, what kind of abuse, and by whom?
7. What kinds of health problems do these women experience?
8. Describe the housing problems these women face.
9. Describe their employment experience, especially the problems they face at work.
10. What are the four assumptions on which welfare reform has been based?
11. What programs should states implement to get their citizens off welfare?

Suggestions for Responding

1. Volunteer at a local soup kitchen and observe how many clients are single women with children; estimate the number of children each woman has. Write an analysis of your findings, and compare them with the information provided by the article.
2. Write a letter to the editor expressing your feelings about poor and/or homeless single mothers. ✦

103

The Gestapo of Welfare Reform

Lucky Jean

There is a sinister trend emerging in the area of welfare reform that has gone largely unnoticed by non-poor people: the role of CSD (Children's Services Department).

While CSD is supposed to help children by removing them from abusive and/or neglectful parents, what they have ended up doing in many cases is to define conditions of poverty or voluntary simplicity as "neglect" and demand that parents live a middle-class American lifestyle or lose their kids.

Here in Josephine County, Oregon, several people have been threatened with the removal of their children for such parental "neglect" as having no electricity, phones, or hot running water. Many families have done without such amenities for years, especially those who have been dependent on welfare, since, as has been repeatedly pointed out, welfare checks are not really sufficient to survive on. If a family has no other source of income—help from relatives, under the table jobs, or income from illegal activities—then they're probably doing without something, like a car or a phone. They may be living in a bus or a "substandard" house.

Middle-class people who assume that a welfare check is sufficient to achieve a middle-class lifestyle (erroneous information in *Reader's Digest* and elsewhere [claims] that a family on welfare gets $30,000 a year) assume that the "extra" money must be going for booze and drugs, when, in fact, there is no extra money in the first place.

Now, of course, under welfare reform, if these families do not work a certain number of hours a week, their check will be reduced or eventually cut off. Those who are working will also probably not lift themselves out of poverty, just maintain it as before.

Now imagine the nice, middle-class CSD workers (who probably never had to survive on a welfare check) coming in to your house to inspect for child neglect.

We used to live in a school bus, until recently, and still know families who do. We were often envied by families who had to camp in their cars waiting to be able to afford a place to live, or by friends who had to shell out 99 percent of their check every month for rent, only to worry how long they would get to live in a house before being asked to leave for some arbitrary reason. We congratulated ourselves on having a shelter of our own to live in and on not being held hostage to rent or bills every month.

We have recently moved into a house (with help from relatives) and have been shocked to hear stories from our friends, who have been told by CSD to move out of their buses and rent rooms in houses. One man told us how his woman friend took their newborn baby to live with her father because the hospital wouldn't let them take the baby home to live in a bus.

I have never, however, heard of anyone in CSD protesting the enforced poverty of welfare for the sake of the children.

Demanding that a family rent a house instead of living in a bus or other shelter reveals an attitude that supposes that families are better off being one check away from homelessness than owning anything for themselves. It also assumes that the measure of one's possessions proves the effectiveness of one's parenting. (Does this mean that grandparents who live in RVs should be forbidden from seeing their grandchildren?)

These sorts of rules, insisting that parents work hard enough to achieve middle-class lifestyles (with no help from anyone, of course) amounts to outlawing high time intensity parenting for most parents. Only those two parent families with enough money from one paycheck, or single parents with generous child support checks, are "allowed," economically anyway, to have their children spend time at home with a caregiver who loves them.

This is especially hard on single mothers, who have never earned as much money as men. Mothers who are very attached to spending the day with their children will be more likely to stay with abusive partners, or take up with men they would otherwise have little to do with, for the financial support.

If the only good parents are those with phones, electricity, hot running water, and houses—does that mean that all those parents in history that didn't have those things were neglectful? (Were the Waltons a dysfunctional family?) And what about children in other countries where such things are very scarce? Should we send out a UN version of CSD to rescue every child in the world without a middle-class American lifestyle? And why not? Are they any less deserving?

The whole idea assumes that poor people are willfully poor, and that there are no conditions in America outside oneself that could contribute to poverty. I believe this has partly to do with a class blindness on the part of non-poor Americans, who do not see poor people in their daily life and certainly not on TV in any positive way. They suffer from the same delusion afflicting third world TV viewers—everyone on American TV is rich, therefore, everyone in America is rich.

What's to stop these "standard of living" requirements from being raised later? What if parents are required to update their computers for the good of their children? What if they are required to have cars that are less than ten years old? What if they are required to live in $150,000 homes?

What will happen to our children if the trend toward mass child relocation continues? A lot of CSD workers and foster parents will have "work" for which they get paid, at the expense of children and their parents, who have been doing the job of parenting for free. Will caregivers who parent for money do a better job than those who would do it for love?   [1997]

Understanding the Reading

1. What is the role of CSD (Children's Services Department) supposed to be, and how has this mission been distorted?
2. What are some economic grounds used to threaten the removal of children from their families?
3. What relative advantages does Jean see in living in a bus?

4. What arguments does Jean make objecting to a middle-class lifestyle as a standard against which to measure effective parenting?

Suggestions for Responding

1. Write a letter to the editor of your local paper expressing your feelings about the removal of children from impoverished families. ✦

104

Persistent Welfare Stereotypes

RENU NAHATA

"There is now a fairly widespread feeling, justified or not, that some welfare recipients are not doing enough to get off the dole." Thus began *ABC World News Tonight*'s "American Agenda" segment on welfare reform (4/14/92). While Peter Jennings' opening statement acknowledges that there may be disparities between public perception and reality, this segment and many others continue to rely heavily on widely held misconceptions about welfare.

With few exceptions, the mainstream media have portrayed the issue of welfare in terms and images not too far removed from Ronald Reagan's "welfare queens." Following news coverage, one might believe that most welfare recipients are black, unwed, unemployed, teenage mothers of several children, living in the inner city. She might be, as one article suggested, "a walking statistic: a single mother of five who dropped out of high school at 17, pregnant with her first child" (*Newsday,* 9/23/90). But the statistic she represents is quite small, since only two percent of all poor children live in such households (*Washington Post,* 6/3/91).

In fact, as Jack Smith acknowledged on *This Week With David Brinkley* (4/12/92), "most recipients of welfare are white, not black; most live in the suburbs, not the inner city; most want to work and stay on welfare less than two years." According to a Health and Human Services report, the average number of children in AFDC (Aid to Families with Dependent Children) families is only 1.9—well under the national average.

Whether "justified or not," several states have based their reform measures on the perception that the welfare system's failures derive from women abusing its benefits. In response, state legislatures have taken aim at those receiving assistance, while media have further fueled these concerns by offering up a parade of mothers, unwed, unrepentant and most often black.

The Wisconsin program, considered a model for other states, reduces benefits for a second child and eliminates them for a third, on the assumption that increased benefits will encourage women to have more children. However, according to the House Ways and Means Committee's 1991 Green Book, the average size of AFDC families has been decreasing steadily for 20 years. More to the point, the Center on Budget and Policy Priorities argues that there is no significant relationship between AFDC benefit levels and birth rates. Although these statistics are readily available, most news reports about such welfare "reforms" fail to use them.

ABC World News' April 14 [1992] segment on welfare relied on the "decline in values" critique made by many of welfare's detractors. Correspondent Rebecca Chase tried to demonstrate the corrosive social impact of welfare by interviewing several black mothers, most of them unwed and in their teens, one a mother of six who has been on welfare for the past 20 years. The two questions put to these women were, "How many of you are married?" and "Do you feel like you owe the taxpayers anything for them helping you support your children?"

Chase seemed to find the moral dilemma of unmarried motherhood, and the issue of gratitude for public support, far more compelling than soaring black unemployment (particularly for males), absence of affordable child care and discriminatory hiring practices. Instead of addressing these kinds of issues, poverty and welfare are studied through the narrow lens of individual responsibility and moral double standards.

The same lens is used by *U.S. News and World Report*'s David Whitman (4/20/92), who approvingly describes the latest attitude toward those on welfare as the "new paternalism," i.e., "rewarding them for doing right and fining them for doing wrong." Given these absolute terms, Whitman's conclusion is not surprising: "No federal intervention . . . is likely to prompt legions of unwed, chronic welfare mothers to marry the fathers of their children."

This Week With David Brinkley (4/12/92), in a lengthy segment on Wisconsin's reform experiment, made an effort to dispel long-standing myths. But the show managed to undermine those facts by loading both the taped segment and the discussion that followed with repeated images of and references to urban blacks. Despite one guest's effort to raise the question of incentive in the absence of employment opportunities, larger societal factors lost ground to George Will's concern over "illegitimacy in our cities."

Even while attempting to dispel "social myths" about welfare, an Ellen Goodman column (*Boston Globe,* 4/16/92) focused on poor women with a sense of "entitlement" as the main problem with welfare. "Americans instinctively believe that the welfare poor should play by the same rules as the rest of us. A family that works does not get a raise for having a child. Why then should a family that doesn't work?"

The headline chosen by the *Globe* for Goodman's column, "Welfare Mothers With an Attitude," played up the worst aspects of the piece. And the graphic that accompanied the article, while apparently intended satirically, could just as easily be read as endorsing the stereotype of the African-American welfare mother with too many kids and too much money. At some point, repetition of stereotypical imagery merely hardens perceptions, rendering corrective caveats effectively useless.

Although most polls show that Americans still support public spending on the poor, James Patterson, a historian of social policy at Brown University, points out that "people support programs when they imagine the beneficiaries look a lot like themselves" (*New York Times,* 5/17/92). As if to substantiate this premise, just one month earlier the *Times* (4/13/92) ran "From Middle Class to Jobless: A Sense of Pride Is Shattered."

The primary concern of this article was the suffering, fear and loss of pride felt by recently unemployed white-collar workers (illustrated by a photograph of a white accountant). Mounting welfare rolls in predominantly middle-class areas like Westchester, New York, inspired the writer to feel compassion. In this case, the rise in chronic unemployment, family breakdowns, vanishing spouses, substance abuse and domestic violence are seen to stem from economic circumstances rather than vaguely defined social pathologies.

However, most welfare recipients we see in the media are black. And most efforts to reform welfare are directed at inner cities. There is little room for compassion here. The panacea generally offered for inner-city poverty and family breakdowns comes most often in the form of imposing "values."

Lawrence Mead, the author of an influential new book, *The New Politics of Poverty: The Nonworking Poor in America,* demonstrates this tendency. One of the main sources in the *U.S. News* article about the "new paternalism," Mead argued in a *New York Times* op-ed (5/19/92) that "if poor adults behaved rationally, they would seldom be poor for long in the first place. Opportunity is more available than the will to seize it." Child care, he believes, can usually be found if one only looks for it, and "the ghetto mentality," more than racism or any other factor, is the main cause of unemployment. His solution to these personal failings is "a more authoritative social policy in which the needy are told how to live instead of merely being subsidized."

When President Bush can blame the L.A. uprising on Lyndon Johnson's Great Society programs, the official view is not far from Mead's. Stories like "White House Links Riots to Welfare" (*New York Times,* 5/5/92) display a certain skepticism, yet media assumptions about welfare and poverty—focusing on inner-city black women, their supposed unchecked fertility and lack of "individual responsibility"—differ little from the administration's. Despite the fact that most media outlets recognize the prevalence of stereotypes, few seem willing to give up those stereotypes as the basis for their coverage. [1992]

Understanding the Reading

1. How are welfare recipients portrayed in the media?
2. In what ways does the welfare stereotype not fit reality?
3. What does Nahata think causes welfare dependence?
4. What economic circumstances affect welfare?

Suggestions for Responding

1. Interview someone who is or has been on welfare and describe how he or she differs from the welfare stereotype.
2. Find an op-ed article about welfare and write a brief essay about its use of stereotypes and myths. ✦

105

A Way Out

RITA HENLEY JENSEN

I am a woman. A white woman, once poor but no longer. I am not lazy, never was. I am a middle-aged woman, with two grown daughters. I was a welfare mother, one of those women society considers less than nothing.

I should have applied for Aid to Families with Dependent Children when I was 18 years old, pregnant with my first child, and living with a boyfriend who slapped me around. But I didn't.

I remember talking it over at the time with a friend. I lived in the neighborhood that surrounds the vast Columbus campus of Ohio State University. Students, faculty, hangers-on, hippies, runaways, and recent émigrés from Kentucky lived side by side in the area's relatively inexpensive housing. I was a runaway.

On a particularly warm midsummer's day, I stood on High Street, directly across from the campus' main entrance, with an older, more sophisticated friend, wondering what to do with my life. With my swollen belly, all hope of my being able to cross the street and enroll in the university had evaporated. Now, I was seeking advice about how merely to survive, to escape the assaults and still be able to care for my child.

My friend knew of no place I could go, nowhere I could turn, no one else I could ask. I remember saying in a tone of resignation, "I can't apply for welfare." Instead of disagreeing with me, she nodded, acknowledging our mutual belief that taking beatings was better than taking handouts. Being "on the dole" meant you deserved only contempt.

In August 1965, I married my attacker.

Six years later, I left him and applied for assistance. My children were 18 months and five and a half years old. I had waited much too long. Within a year, I crossed High Street to go to Ohio State. I graduated in four years and moved to New York City to attend Columbia University's Graduate School of Journalism. I have worked as a journalist for 18 years now. My life on welfare was very hard—there were times when I didn't have enough food for the three of us. But I was able to get an education while on welfare. It is hardly likely that a woman on AFDC today would be allowed to do what I did, to go to school and develop the kind of skills that enabled me to make a better life for myself and my children.

This past summer, I attended a conference in Chicago on feminist legal theory. During the presentation of a paper related to gender and property rights, the speaker mentioned as an aside that when one says "welfare mother" the listener hears "black welfare mother." A discussion ensued about the underlying racism until someone declared that the solution was easy: all that had to be done was have the women in the room bring to the attention of the media the fact that white women make up the largest percentage of welfare recipients. At this point, I stood, took a deep breath, stepped out of my professional guise, and informed the crowd that I was a former welfare mother. Looking at my white hair, blue eyes, and freckled Irish skin, some laughed; others gasped—despite having just acknowledged that someone like me was, in fact, a "typical" welfare mother.

Occasionally I do this. Speak up. Identify myself as one of "them." I do so reluctantly because welfare mothers are a lightning rod for race hatred, class prejudice, and misogyny. Yet I am aware that as long as welfare is viewed as an *African American* woman's issue, instead of a *woman's* issue—whether that woman be white, African American, Asian, Latina, or Native American—those in power can continue to exploit our country's racism to weaken and even eliminate public support for the programs that help low-income mothers and their children.

I didn't have the guts to stand up during a 1974 reception for Ohio state legislators. The party's hostess was a leader of the Columbus chapter of the National Organization for Women and she had opened up her suburban home so that representatives of many of the state's progressive organizations could lobby in an informal setting for an increase in the state's welfare allotment for families. I was invited as a representative of the campus area's single mothers' support group. In the living room, I came across a state senator in a just-slightly-too-warm-and-friendly state induced by the potent combination of free booze and a crowd of women. He quickly decided I looked like a good person to amuse with one of his favorite jokes. "You want to know how a welfare mother can prevent getting pregnant?" he asked, giggling. "She can just take two aspirin—and put them between her knees," he roared, as he bent down to place his Scotch glass between his own, by way of demonstration. I drifted away.

I finally did gather up my courage to speak out. It was in a classroom during my junior year. I was enrolled in a course on the economics of public policy because I wanted to understand why the state of Ohio thought it desirable to provide me and my two kids with only $204 per month—59 percent of what even the state itself said a family of three needed to live.

For my required oral presentation, I chose "Aid to Families with Dependent Children." I cited the fact that approximately two thirds of all the poor families in the country were white; I noted that most welfare families consisted of one parent and two children. As an audiovisual aid, I brought my own two kids along. My voice quavered a bit as I delivered my intro: I stood with my arms around my children and said, "We are a typical AFDC family."

My classmates had not one question when I finished. I don't believe anyone even bothered to ask the kids' names or ages.

If I were giving this talk today, I would hold up a picture of us back then and say we still represent typical welfare recipients. The statistics I would cite to back up that statement have been refined since the 1970s and now include "Hispanic" as a category. In 1992, 38.9 percent of all welfare mothers were white, 37.2 percent were black, 17.8 percent were "Hispanic," 2.8 percent were Asian, and 1.4 percent were Native American.

My report, however, would focus on the dramatic and unrelenting reduction in resources available to low-income mothers in the last two decades.

Fact: In 1970, the average monthly benefit for a family of three was $178. Not much, but consider that as a result of inflation, that $178 would be approximately $680 today. And then consider that the average monthly payment today is only about $414. That's the way it's been for more than two decades: the cost of living goes up (by the states' own accounting, the cost of rent, food, and utilities for a family of three has doubled), but the real value of welfare payments keeps going down.

Fact: The 1968 Work Incentive Program (the government called it WIN; we called it WIP) required that all unemployed adult recipients sign up for job training or employment once their children turned six. The age has now been lowered to three, and states may go as low as age one. What that means is you won't be able to attend and finish college while on welfare. (In most states a college education isn't considered job training, even though experts claim most of us will need college degrees to compete in the workplace of the twenty-first century.)

Fact: Forty-two percent of welfare recipients will be on welfare less than two years during their entire lifetime, and an additional 33 percent will spend between two and eight years on welfare. The statistics haven't changed much over the years: women still use welfare to support their families when their children are small.

In 1974, I ended my talk with this joke: A welfare mother went into the drugstore and bought a can of deodorant. I explained that it was funny because everyone knew that welfare mothers could not afford "extras" like personal hygiene products. My joke today would be: A welfare mother believed that if elected public officials understood these facts, they would not campaign to cut her family's benefits.

The idea that government representatives care about welfare mothers is as ridiculous to me now as the idea back then that I would waste my limited funds on deodorant. It is much clearer to me today what the basic functions of welfare public policy are at this moment in U.S. history.

By making war on welfare recipients, political leaders can turn the public's attention away from the government's redistribution of wealth to the wealthy. Recent studies show that the United States has become the most economically stratified of industrial nations. In fact, Federal Reserve figures reveal that the richest 1 percent of American households—each with a minimum net worth of $2.3 million—control nearly 40 percent of the wealth, while in Britain, the richest 1 percent of the population controls about 18 percent of the wealth. In the mid-1970s, both countries were on a par: the richest 1 percent controlled 20 percent of the wealth. President Reagan was the master of this verbal shell game. He told stories of welfare queens and then presided over the looting of the nation's savings and loans by wealthy white men.

Without a doubt, the current urgency for tax cuts and spending reductions can be explained by the fact that President Clinton tried to shift the balance slightly in 1992 and the wealthy ended up paying 16 percent more in taxes the following year, by one estimate.

The purpose of this antiwelfare oratory and the campaigns against sex education, abortion rights, and aid to teenage mothers is to ensure a constant supply of young women as desperate and ashamed as I was. Young women willing to take a job at any wage rate, willing to tolerate the most abusive relationships with men, and unable to enter the gates leading to higher education.

To accomplish their goals, political leaders continually call for reforms that include demands that welfare recipients work, that teenagers don't have sex, and that welfare mothers stop giving birth (but don't have abortions). Each "reform" addresses the nation's racial and sexual stereotypes: taking care of one's own children is not work; welfare mothers are unemployed, promiscuous, and poorly motivated; and unless the government holds their feet to the fire, these women will live on welfare for years, as will their children and their children's children.

This type of demagoguery has been common throughout our history. What sets the present era apart is the nearly across-the-board cooperation of the media. The national news magazines, the most prestigious daily newspapers, the highly regarded broadcast news outlets, as well as the supermarket tabloids and talk-radio hosts, have generally abandoned the notion that one of their missions is to sometimes comfort the afflicted and afflict the comfortable. Instead, they too often reprint politicians' statements unchallenged, provide charts comparing one party's recommendations to another's without really questioning those recommendations, and illustrate story after story, newscast after newscast, with a visual of an African American woman (because we all know they're the only ones on welfare) living in an urban housing project (because that's where all welfare recipients live) who has been on welfare for years.

When *U.S. News & World Report* did a major story on welfare reform this year [1995], it featured large photographs of eight welfare recipients, seven of whom were women of color: six African Americans and one Latina or Native American (the text does not state her ethnicity). Describing the inability of welfare mothers to hold jobs (they are "hobbled not only by their lack of experience but also by their casual attitudes toward punctuality, dress, and coworkers"), the article offers the "excuse" given by one mother for not taking a 3 P.M. to 11 P.M. shift: "I wouldn't get to see my kids," she told the reporter. You can't win for losing—should she take that 3-to-11 job and her unsupervised kids get in trouble, you can be sure some conservative would happily leap on her as an example of one of those poor women who are bad mothers and whose kids should be in orphanages.

Why don't the media ever find a white woman from Ohio or Iowa or Wisconsin, a victim of domestic violence, leaving the father of her two children to make a new start? Or a Latina mother like the one living in my current neighborhood, who has one child and does not make enough as a home health care attendant to pay for her family's health insurance? Or a Native American woman living on a reservation, creating crafts for pennies that will be sold by others for dollars?

Besides reinforcing stereotypes about the personal failings of welfare recipients, when my colleagues write in-depth pieces about life on welfare, they invariably concentrate on describing welfare mothers' difficulties with the world at large: addictions, lack of transportation, dangerous neighbors, and, most recently, shiftless boyfriends who begin beating them when they do get jobs—as if this phenomenon were limited to relationships between couples with low incomes.

I wonder why no journalist I have stumbled across, no matter how well meaning, has communicated what I believe is the central reality of most women's lives on welfare: they believe all the stereotypes too and they are ashamed of being on welfare. They eat, breathe, sleep, and clothe themselves with shame.

Most reporting on welfare never penetrates the surface, and the nature of the relationship between the welfare system and the woman receiving help is never explored. Like me, many women fleeing physical abuse must make the welfare department their first stop after seeking an order of protection. Studies are scarce, but some recent ones of women in welfare-to-work programs across the U.S. estimate that anywhere from half to three fourths of participants are, or have been, in abusive relationships. And surveys of some homeless shelters indicate that half of the women living in them are on the run from a violent mate.

But if welfare is the means of escape, it is also the institutionalization of the dynamic of battering. My husband was the source of my and my children's daily bread and of daily physical and psychological attacks. On welfare, I was free of the beatings, but the assaults on my self-esteem were still frequent and powerful, mimicking the behavior of a typical batterer.

As he pounds away, threatening to kill the woman and children he claims to love, the abuser often accuses his victims of lying, laziness, and infidelity. Many times, he threatens to snatch the children away from their mother in order to protect them from her supposed incompetence, her laziness, dishonesty, and sexual escapades.

On welfare, just as with my husband, I had to prove every statement was not a lie. Everything had to be documented: how many children I had, how much I paid for rent, fuel, transportation, electricity, child care, and so forth. It went so far as to require that at every "redetermination of need" interview (every six months), I had to produce the originals of my children's birth certificates, which were duly photocopied over and over again. Since birth certificates do not change, the procedure was a subtle and con-

stant reminder that nothing I said was accepted as truth. Ever.

But this is a petty example. The more significant one was the suspicion that my attendance at Ohio State University was probably a crime. Throughout my college years, I regularly reported that I was attending OSU. Since the WIN limit at that time was age six and my youngest daughter was two when I started, I was allowed to finish my undergraduate years without having to report to some job-training program that would have prepared me for a minimum-wage job. However, my caseworker and I shared an intuitive belief that something just had to be wrong about this. How could I be living on welfare and going to college? Outrageous! Each day I awoke feeling as if I were in a race, that I had to complete my degree before I was charged with a felony.

As a matter of fact, I remember hearing, a short time after I graduated, that a group of welfare mothers attending college in Ohio were charged with food stamp fraud, apparently for not reporting their scholarships as additional income.

Batterers frequently lie to their victims—it's a power thing. Caseworkers do too. For example, when I moved to New York to attend graduate school and applied for assistance, I asked my intake worker whether I could apply for emergency food stamps. She told me there was no emergency food program. The kids and I scraped by, but that statement was false. I was unaware of it until welfare rights advocates successfully sued the agency for denying applicants emergency food assistance. In another case, when someone gave me a ten-year-old Opel so I could keep my first (very low paying) reporting job, my caseworker informed me in writing that mere possession of a car made me ineligible for welfare. (I appealed and won. The caseworker was apparently confused by the fact that although I was not allowed to have any assets, I did need the car to get to work. She also assumed a used car had to have some value. Not this one.)

Then there's the issue of sexual possessiveness: states rarely grant assistance to families with fathers still in the home. And as for feeling threatened about losing custody, throughout the time I was on welfare, I knew that if I stumbled at all, my children could be taken away from me.

It is widely understood that any neighbor can call the authorities about a welfare mother, making a charge of neglect, and that mother, since she is less than nothing, might not be able to prove her competency. I had a close call once. I had been hospitalized for ten days and a friend took care of my children. After my return home, however, I was still weak. I would doze off on the sofa while the kids were awake—one time it happened when they were outside playing on the sidewalk. A neighbor, seeing them there unattended, immediately called the child welfare agency, which sent someone out to question me and to look inside my refrigerator to see if I had any food. Luckily, that day I did.

Ultimately, leaving an abusive relationship and applying for welfare is a little like leaving solitary confinement to become part of a prison's general population. It's better, but you are still incarcerated.

None of this is ever discussed in the context of welfare reform. The idiot state legislator, the prosecutor in Ohio who brought the charges against welfare mothers years ago, Bill Clinton, and Newt Gingrich all continue to play the race and sex card by hollering for welfare reform. They continue to exploit and feed the public's ignorance about and antipathy toward welfare mothers to propel their own careers. Sadly, journalists permit them to do so, perhaps for the same reason.

Lost in all this are the lives of thousands of women impoverished by virtue of their willingness to assume the responsibility of raising their children. An ex-boyfriend used to say that observing my struggle was a little like watching someone standing in a room, with arms upraised to prevent the ceiling from pressing in on her. He wondered just how long I could prevent the collapse.

Today, welfare mothers have even less opportunity than I did. Their talent, brains, luck, and resourcefulness are ignored. Each new rule, regulation, and reform makes it even more unlikely that they can use the time they are on welfare to do as I did: cross the High Streets in their cities and towns, and realize their ambitions. Each new rule makes it more likely that they will only be able to train for a minimum-wage job that will never allow them to support their families.

So no, I don't think all we have to do is get the facts to the media. I think we have to raise hell any way we can.

Our goal is simple: never again should there be a young woman, standing in front of the gates that lead to a better future, afraid to enter because she believes she must instead choose poverty and battery.   [1995]

Understanding the Reading

1. Why did Jensen become a welfare recipient?
2. Why does Jensen think it is important that she identify herself as a former welfare recipient?
3. How have welfare benefits changed in the past twenty-five years?
4. What does Jensen think has determined government welfare policies?
5. How do the media portray welfare recipients?
6. What parallels does Jensen see between a battering spouse and welfare?

Suggestions for Responding

1. Write a letter to your state legislator sharing your opinions about welfare policy.
2. If you know someone who is or has been on welfare, interview her (or him) about the circumstances that led up to that experience and how she (he) feels or felt about the experience.
3. Describe how your life would change if you or your family faced life on welfare. ✦

106

The Root Causes of Homelessness in American Cities

DOUG A. TIMMER,
D. STANLEY EITZEN,
AND KATHRYN D. TALLEY

The facts concerning poverty in the United States are grim. Data from 1991 reveal that 14.2 percent of the population (about 35.7 million Americans) were below the official poverty line (the data in this section are taken from U.S. Bureau of the Census). Over one-fifth of all children (21.8 percent) were poor. About one-third of all African Americans (32.7 percent) and almost three out of ten Hispanics (28.7 percent) were poor.

The poor face a number of obstacles. They are rejected and despised by others. They are looked down upon as lazy, shiftless, dirty, and immoral. They often receive inferior educations because they live in economically depressed school districts. They often are exposed to toxic chemicals. Many of the poor are malnourished and have health problems. In 1991 some 35.4 million Americans had no health insurance and many were refused medical care for financial reasons. The result is that on average low-income families pay one-fifth of their incomes toward health care—twice as much as the one-tenth paid by high-income families.

Whereas misery, ill health, malnutrition, and discrimination are endemic among all the poor, the most disadvantaged among them also live in substandard housing without adequate plumbing, heat, or other facilities. The poorest of the poor are often just an illness, accident, divorce, or other personal disaster away from homelessness. During the 1980s and the early 1990s the proportion of poor people who became homeless increased dramatically. An ever-increasing number of homeless were visible on the streets as the demand on shelters far outstripped the supply. Much more than at other times in U.S. history, the homeless are experiencing a severe housing shortage, which is forcing many of them to sleep in temporary shelters or even in doorways, on heating grates, in dumpsters, in cardboard boxes, and in abandoned buildings.

Three questions are raised and answered in this section: (1) What is the extent of homelessness in America? (2) Is homelessness caused by personal disabilities? and (3) Are the "new" homeless different from the "old" homeless?

The homeless are typically defined as those who have no permanent home and who must resort to streets, shelters, or other makeshift quarters. The number of homeless is impossible to determine accurately since they may be living with relatives or friends or hidden beneath bridges, in alleys, in abandoned buildings, in shelters and are therefore difficult to find and count. The low estimate, by the U.S. Department of Housing and Urban Development (HUD) during the Reagan administration, was that between 250,000 and 350,000 Americans were homeless. Political conservatives find appeal in this low figure because it means that the problem is relatively insignificant and not in need of additional public programs and resources to ameliorate it. Estimates at the high end come from advocacy groups like the National Coalition for the Homeless, which put the figure at between 3 and 4 million. Reformers, convinced of the magnitude and seriousness of the problem, are prone to accept these higher figures.

Whatever the actual numbers of the homeless, three points must be underscored. *First,* the proportion of Americans who are homeless is the highest since the Great Depression, with a rapid rise in the past fifteen years or so and still climbing. *Second,* the numbers actually minimize the seriousness of the problem because so many of the urban poor are on the brink of homelessness and many who lack housing are hidden by doubling or tripling up with relatives or friends. Jonathan Kozol estimates that there are over 300,000 hidden homeless in New York City alone and that nationwide more than 3 million families are living doubled up. When these households are added to those poor people paying more than half of their monthly income for rent, more than 20 million families are living near the edge of homelessness in the United States. And *third,* we should not become unduly focused on the numbers because they deflect us from the problem itself and the homeless themselves.

A recurrent belief among politicians, journalists, social scientists, and the public is that homelessness is a consequence of personal disabilities. That is, homeless persons tend to suffer from chronic alcoholism or from chronic physical or mental disorders and these disabilities explain their homelessness. This is a myth with damaging consequences. Although some homeless persons suffer from alcoholism, most do not. Some suffer severe mental or emotional disturbances, but most do not.

Typically, the recent rise in homelessness is seen as a consequence of the deinstitutionalization of mental patients that began in the 1950s. The data appear to support this notion, since the average daily census of psychiatric institutions dropped from 677,000 in 1955 to 151,000 in 1984. Almost all of the reduction in mental patients had occurred by 1978, yet the homeless did not begin overflowing the streets and shelters until 1983.

Several other cautions must be raised concerning the emphasis on the homeless as mentally ill. First, most of the homeless are *not* mentally ill: there is solid research evidence to indicate that no more than 10 to 15 percent of persons living on the street are mentally impaired in some way. Researcher James Wright, using data from the national Health Care for the Homeless (HCH) program, has concluded that as many as one-third of the homeless probably are mentally ill. But more recent research has confirmed the 10 to 15 percent estimate.

A second caution concerns context. Elliot Liebow, in his description and analysis of homeless women, argues that judgments about the homeless often involve descriptions of them as deviant—mentally ill, alcoholic, drug addicted—descriptions that would receive more positive judgments if they were in another setting.

> Like you, I know people who drink, people who do drugs, and bosses who have tantrums and treat their subordinates like dirt. They all have good jobs. Were they to become homeless, some of them would surely also become "alcoholics," "addicts," or "mentally ill." Similarly, if some of the homeless women who are now so labelled were to be magically transported to a more usual and acceptable setting, some of them—not all, of course—would shed their labels and take their places with the rest of us somewhere on the spectrum of normality.

In short, there is a class bias involved here. When homeless people do have mental difficulties or problems with alcohol, these situations are identified as the cause of their homelessness. But when well-housed middle-class and upper-middle-class people are mentally ill or alcoholic it is identified as an unfortunate situation requiring attention and treatment.

A third caution has to do with cause and effect. Does mental illness cause homelessness or do the stresses induced by extreme poverty and homelessness cause mental illness? Although some argue that mental illness is a cause of homelessness, there are no data to support this

claim. The much stronger argument is that mental illness is a probable consequence of homelessness. This is based on the assumption that a stable life leads to mental stability and an unstable one to mental instability.

A fourth caution is that the emphasis on the personal sources of homelessness blames the victims for their problem and deflects attention away from its structural sources. To do so leads to faulty generalizations and public policies doomed to fail.

In this regard, sociologist Michael Sosin's recent study of homeless persons in Chicago is instructive. Comparing a sample of homeless persons to a sample of "vulnerable" persons—not homeless but impoverished and precariously close to losing their shelter—Sosin found the lack of access to various social and institutional supports and resources to be a much better predictor of homelessness than any personal disabilities or "deficits."

People are homeless not because of their individual flaws but because of structural arrangements and trends that result in extreme impoverishment and a shortage of affordable housing in U.S. cities. The extent to which the homeless population is made up of the mentally ill, the physically handicapped and disabled, alcoholics, and drug abusers and addicts results from their being more vulnerable to the kind of impoverishment that excludes them from the urban housing market. Their vulnerabilities mean that they may be the first to lose permanent shelter. But the absolute shortage of low-income, affordable housing in the United States ensures that even if no one were plagued with these personal disabilities, the size of the homeless population would be roughly the same.

The current and expanding crisis of urban homelessness results from the convergence of two contradictory and proximate forces: the rapidly dwindling supply of low-income housing and the increased economic marginality among the poor and the near poor, caused by the changing economy, changes in family structure, and shifts in government policies. These proximate causes of urban homelessness, it must be remembered, are in turn embedded in and derived from the structure of a historically changing corporate capitalist economy and society.

Our analysis of housing does not focus exclusively on the homeless. To do so risks adding to the deviant identity homeless persons have thrust upon them. Singling out homeless people exacerbates their supposedly "special" character. To do so encourages a view that they are considerably different from those who are housed. In truth, the homeless are not distinct persons, nor do they have a completely distinct problem. They happen to be at the extreme end of a shelter continuum—ranging from those who are sufficiently housed, through those who are ill-housed, to those who have no housing at all. Thus, the urban homeless problem is fundamentally a housing problem.

There is not enough low-cost housing available for the economically marginal in U.S. cities. The low-income housing supply has shrunk dramatically in recent years. The inflation of the 1980s is one source of this shrinkage: The cost of housing at all levels rose rapidly. The median price of a single-family dwelling sold in 1970, for example, was $23,000; in 1980 it was $62,200; in 1989 it was $92,900; and by 1993 it was $104,000. This varied by locality, of course, with the cost of a median house in Honolulu, San Francisco, and Anaheim well over double the median and Los Angeles, San Diego, Newark, Boston, and New York City just below double the national median.

The cost of renting followed the inflationary trend of the 1970s and 1980s; in fact, it rose faster than renters' incomes. This was partly a function of the high cost of home purchases, which floods the rental market, putting upward pressure on rents. Between 1970 and 1990, for example, rents tripled while renters' incomes only doubled. This inflation in the housing market at all levels has placed increased pressures on the poor, who simply cannot afford the increased rents or must sacrifice essentials such as food to pay the higher rents. The federal standard for affordable housing is less than 30 percent of household income for rent. A survey of forty-four cities by the Center on Budget and Policy Priorities found that 75 percent of low-income households (those earning less than $10,000 annually) paid more than 30 percent of their incomes in rent. In thirty-nine of the forty-four cities surveyed, housing costs alone normally exceeded the entire grant for a family of three receiving assistance from the Aid to Families with Dependent Children (AFDC) program. Data from 1989 indicated that nearly one-half (47 percent) of those households below the poverty line *spent more than 70 percent of their incomes for housing.* Paying such a high proportion of their low income for rent places these households on the brink of homelessness, one medical crisis, one layoff, or one pay cut away from losing their shelter.

One factor explaining the increasing lack of affordable rental housing is the "rent squeeze" caused by concentrated ownership of rental housing in U.S. cities. In both New York City and Houston, for example, 5 percent of all landlords control more than one-half of the rental housing stock. In Boston, only twenty individuals own 40 percent of the city's rental units. When rental housing is controlled by a few, rents rise.

Although the rising cost of low-income housing is an important reason for the increased rates of homelessness, other factors are also important. Foremost, there has been an absolute loss in low-income units. From 1970 to 1989 the number of rental units for the poor declined 14 percent to 5.5 million while the number of poor renters—those who made less than $10,000 in 1989 dollars—increased from 7.3 million to 9.6 million.

Conspicuous among the reasons for the decline of low-income housing has been the loss of single-room occupancy (SRO) hotels, often the housing of last resort for the economically marginal in cities. About a million SRO units have been torn down nationwide since the 1970s. In New York City, for example, the stock of SROs shrunk from 127,000 units in 1975 to 14,000 in 1985.

SROs and other low-cost rental housing have disappeared because of two related trends. One is gentrification—the process of converting low-income housing to condominiums or upscale apartments for the middle and upper-middle classes. Condominium conversion involves taking rental units and turning them into apartments for sale. This practice often replaces those who cannot afford a down payment or qualify for a home mortgage with those more affluent persons who can. Gentrification typically includes buying up older and sometimes rundown property in poor and working-class neighborhoods and rehabilitating it into middle-class condominiums, townhouses, single-family dwellings, and upscale lofts and apartments. Often, the original residents of the area are displaced because they cannot afford the increased rents, purchase prices, and insurance and property taxes associated with the neighborhood's rising property values. The poor, who once had housing, are left out. Especially harmed by this process are non-whites. Research by Phillip Clay studied fifty-seven gentrifying neighborhoods in thirty cities and found that before gentrification about half the neighborhoods were predominantly black. After gentrification, 80 percent were dominated by whites and only 2 percent were predominantly nonwhite.

Slumlords have also contributed to the inner-city housing shortage. Slumlording occurs when investors buy rental properties in poor neighborhoods and purposefully fail to maintain them. Typically, the slumlords are middle class and white, the tenants poor and black. Over time serious housing code violations develop as roofs leak, stairways deteriorate, plumbing fails, and electrical wiring becomes dangerous. Slumlords simply squeeze whatever rents they can for as long as they can. The end point of this process is when the city condemns the buildings, evicts the residents, and takes over the property for delinquent taxes and unpaid utility bills.

Another market mechanism that leads to the urban housing crisis is "warehousing." Here, real estate speculators buy property on the edges of gentrifying areas and gradually empty them of their occupants by not maintaining them or by not renting them when renters leave. The goal is selling these properties to other developers for a profit. Developers are especially attracted to "warehoused" properties since they spare them the difficulties of removing poor and working-class leaseholders who will not be able to afford the newly gentrified property.

A comparison of all blacks with all whites in U.S. society showed that blacks spend more on rent than whites do. This is because African Americans are concentrated in urban areas where rents tend to be higher and because their housing options are limited by discrimination.

Rollbacks in public housing have further reduced the supply of low-income housing in U.S. cities. Federal low-income housing programs, including government subsidies for its construction, declined dramatically during the Reagan presidency. Federal support for subsidized housing dropped from $32.2 billion in 1981 to $6 billion in 1989. The U.S. Department of Housing and Urban Development (HUD) authorized the construction of 183,000 subsidized dwellings in 1980 but only 20,000 in 1989. Ameliorating the problems of the poor and the homeless was clearly not a priority of the Reagan administration: "When Reagan came to office in 1981, the federal government spent seven dollars on defense for every dollar on housing. When he left office in 1989, the ratio was forty-six to one."

These recent cutbacks in public housing exacerbate an already meager public housing sector. When compared to the industrial democracies of Europe, for example, U.S. public housing makes up a paltry share of the total housing stock. In Europe, urban public housing often accounts for as much as 40 percent of the total housing stock, compared to only 1.3 percent in the United States. Only 6 percent of U.S. households qualifying for low-income housing assistance receive it from the government. And only one-fifth of the poor live in government-subsidized housing of any kind, whether public housing run by local housing authorities, privately owned projects subsidized by HUD, or private apartments for which tenants pay rent with government vouchers. This is the lowest rate of assistance of any industrial nation in the world.

The Department of Housing and Urban Development estimates that as many as 13 million more families qualify for housing assistance but cannot be helped because of a shortage of federal funds. Of the 13 million lacking assistance, 5.1 million are considered to have "worst-case needs" because they spend more than 50 percent of their incomes on rent or live in "severely substandard" conditions.

To summarize, the dramatic shrinkage in the supply of low-cost housing is both a problem of affordability and supply. Clearly, market forces, which, according to conservative analysts should work to solve social problems, have *not* worked to furnish an adequate supply of low-cost housing in America's cities. In reality, market forces are the source of, not the solution to, the problem. Nor did the federal government step in to meet this need. The result was a shortage of affordable housing units for the poorest of the poor. And this structural change in urban housing markets was occurring at the very time that the numbers of the very poor were increasing.

The dramatic rise in homelessness over the past decade and a half is the result of a severe contradiction unfolding in the United States: As the supply of low-income housing is being reduced, increasing numbers of Americans, especially women, children, and minorities, are becoming more and more economically marginal. Just as too much money chasing too few goods causes inflation, so, too, does too many poor and marginal people chasing too few affordable apartments cause homelessness. Or, to switch the metaphor, think of this as a game of musical chairs, in which the chairs represent apartments affordable to the poor and the players are the poor seeking permanent shelter in those apartments. As the game has been played over the past fifteen years in American cities, the number of chairs has been systematically reduced by failed government policies and private-sector investment decisions. Meanwhile, the transformation of the economy and work, changes in family structure, and cutbacks in public-sector supports for the poor continue to add players to the game. The outcome of this game is that an increasing number of players are losers; they cannot find "chairs" and become homeless.

[1994]

Understanding the Reading

1. Describe poverty in the United States.
2. How many American people are homeless, and who are the hidden homeless?
3. Do disabilities cause homelessness?
4. What are the reasons for the increase in homelessness?

Suggestions for Responding

1. Investigate public assistance payments in your area and then search the "For Rent" ads in local newspapers to see what kind of housing is available for 30 percent of this payment.
2. Write an essay speculating about why low-income assistance and supported housing

that is government-supported in the United States are so far below those of most other industrialized nations. ✦

107

Sidewalk Mercenaries vs. Homeless

CHRISTIAN PARENTI

Two people wearing jackets emblazoned, "Outreach Team—Grand Central Partnership," kick a prone and silent figure. "Come on, this is private property—you got to move!"

Standing close by are four activists from Street Watch, a group which documents abuse against homeless. Lately a new private security force, known as the Grand Central Partnership (GCP) Outreach Team has been surpassing the police as the main violators of homeless rights in midtown Manhattan. The 60 maroon-clad GCP outreach workers are themselves homeless and formerly homeless people paid only $1 an hour. Officially, the outreach workers are not employees but volunteers receiving a stipend. Legally they are not allowed to ask anyone to move or leave an area.

"You're not planning to physically remove this guy, are you?" asks Street Watch Activist Matt Snyder. "Man just get the hell out of my face and let me do my job," roars an outreach worker.

The rest may soon be legal history. This altercation is just one of many which will be mentioned in a probable class action suit, that will likely be brought by the Coalition for the Homeless against the GCP. The suit is intended to counter a brutal anti-homeless campaign waged by the midtown Manhattan business community for the last four years.

It all began with the inception of the Grand Central Partnership Business Improvement District (GCP BID). The GCP BID is a private self-taxing, quasi-governmental organization with a $41 million budget. Along with the 34th Street BID, the GCP has issued over $32 million in bonds and raised millions more through property assessment fees on local businesses. While BIDs are a nation-wide trend, New York City leads with 21 separate BIDs presiding over various 30 to 50 block plots of Manhattan.

Critics charge that these enclaves amount to an emerging archipelago of private micro-governments. Cities from San Francisco to Hartford are incorporating BIDs in an attempt to find quick private solutions to the dual problems of urban decline and clumsy municipal bureaucracies. Almost all BIDs entail beautification projects and low-budget private security forces. The GCP stated aim is "improving business conditions." In the 50 block area around New York City's Grand Central Station that means improved lighting, street cleaning, and removing the homeless from the ATM vestibules and sidewalks where they camp. In pursuit of this goal the GCP created its Outreach Team. Ostensibly, these GCP outreach workers are steering their fellow homeless towards social service programs at the Saint Agnes drop-in multi-service center, but the drop-in center is more aptly described as a social dumping ground.

Because Saint Agnes is not an official shelter with beds, over 400 regular clients sleep in chairs on any given night. From Saint Agnes newly recruited homeless people are referred to local city and private shelters or if they stick around long enough a social worker may help them get into a drug rehab such as the Manhattan Bowery Corporation or Project Return.

Saint Agnes drop-in center is run not by the GCP BID but by one of its closely associated offshoots, the Grand Central Partnership Social Service Corporation. Both are nonprofit. The GCP's current social service budget is $3.2 million, [and] 55 percent of that comes from city contracts, 7 percent from property assessments (that is, revenues from the BID's self-taxing). Another 2 percent is miscellaneous and the remaining 36 percent comes from "fee for services," that is, a fee paid by businesses wishing to have GCP outreach workers clear their premises of homeless people. Homeless activists call this free-market social hygiene, but officials at the GCP see it quite differently.

Jeff Grunberg, Executive Director of the Grand Central Partnership Social Service Corporation, says that over $1 million of the GCP's $3.5 million social service budget is given directly to homeless, or formerly homeless, who are employed as staff or trainees at Saint Agnes.

Eighty staff members, 74 percent of which the GCP says are formerly homeless, run the six story building. Another 103 homeless clients participate in Saint Agnes's "pathways to employment" program. For 12 weeks these trainees receive $40 a week working in either food services, maintenance, recycling (at the World Trade Center) or, more often than not, as outreach workers. Grunberg says that after 12 weeks of training are up, trainees are eligible for real jobs or are offered a job as a staff member at the drop-in center. According to the GCP, 256 people have been placed in jobs so far; 111 of these have been employed as staff at Saint Agnes. The 145 others have been placed in jobs such as food preparation at McDonalds, selling shoes, or laboring on construction sites. What percentage of these job placements are low-paying fast food work versus better paying employment, such as construction, is unclear. According to the GCP's Cynthia Scillag, no statistical breakdown is available.

Many homeless people charge that the "pathways to employment" program is a scam and that the stipend "training" stage of the program can go on indefinitely. One homeless former resident of Saint Agnes charged that "if you start raising a fuss about the money, they fire you and then rehire you in a week, saying that you have to go through the whole 12 weeks of training again."

Some homeless also charge that the rest of what Saint Agnes's social services offers is bogus or pans out to very little. But Grunberg dismisses these accusations as the half-baked griping of stubborn, self-destructive addicts and pathologically anti-social people.

According to Grunberg, who earns $125,000 a year, 75 percent of all people on the street could be "brought inside" if they could be coupled with the appropriate social service programs. According to Grunberg: "the business community is too often excluded from the solution process." He sees the GCP as a way of "bringing business back in," adding that a lot of executives, "are really decent people." Grunberg argues that the main thing keeping most homeless on the street is not lack of programs but lack of knowledge about existing programs. Grunberg, speaking new-age business lingo, says, "the homeless should be viewed as customers and social services as the product." He says all his group is guilty of is "a persistent sales pitch." One, he argues, that gets results. "We have housed 450 people over the last five years." Most of these people seem to have ended up in YMCAs, though many have been resettled with family or in single room occupancies. Due to privacy laws Grunberg could not provide a list of all those who had been housed.

Inside Saint Agnes the air is like any other shelter, thick with cigarette smoke and body odor. "Our bathrooms are being renovated," says Grunberg excitedly, stepping into a small tiled room. "We found that underneath the urinals there was no drain. For years this place was flushing into dirt." Not surprisingly the bathrooms were constantly flooded with sewage, just as many homeless charged.

Along with bathrooms Grunberg showed off a legal clinic, a rooftop garden, self-help center, and the offices of numerous social workers. Grunberg describes the drop-in center as "a supermarket of services." While the array of purported and real social services at Saint Agnes is impressive, not everyone is buying it.

Charges of corruption and abusive outreach workers persist. Even Grunberg admits that there is no training to insure that outreach workers handle volatile situations properly and peacefully. "They'll burn your boxes down, they throw gas on you, tear your structures down, and throw your clothes away," says James Gray, who spent two years on both sides of the midtown battle. For a year and a half Gray worked for the Grand Central Partnership, first as an outreach worker—for three months—then as a cook, at the St. Agnes drop-in center. A year ago Gray quit and returned to the streets. He soon found himself on the receiving end of the GCP's outreach efforts.

Homeless people familiar with Saint Agnes charge that the staff are corrupt, the facilities unsanitary, and that the security guards, as Mr. Gray put it, "will beat the hell out of you." This picture fits neatly with a recent study of city records which found that over 1,000 violent and sexually abusive, homeless-shelter security guards have been sacked since 1987.

Also, former Saint Agnes clients say the drop-in center is an incubator for HIV and tuberculosis. Allegedly, drug use and unsafe sex are rampant. Many homeless even charge that there have been rapes at Saint Agnes, though the police say no such incidents have been reported to them. Likewise Grunberg says he knows nothing of these allegations. "Oh, rape?! No, I've never heard of a rape charge," he says. "Occasionally a woman will complain that someone has touched, or pushed, or grabbed her in an inappropriate way—what can you do?"

Back on the streets of GCP's turf, the stubbornly immobile homeless are still abundant. The Tudor Towers, a complex of luxury apartments near the United Nations, pay the Grand Central Partnership Social Service Corporation $2,600 a month to keep their property free of street people. Despite all "outreach efforts" about 10 homeless people still camp in boxes between the river of traffic on First Avenue and the sheer back face of the Tudor City high-rises.

On this narrow esplanade sits the 32-year-old Frankie. For almost two years Frankie was part of the Saint Agnes "house gang, the family." Frankie and others say that St. Agnes, like many New York shelters, has its own version of prison culture, where gangs and petty despots call the shots.

Frankie, however, was allowed to sleep upstairs on the floor. To earn his keep he cleared other homeless people out of the Grand Central area, usually with the offer of services, but when necessary, other means were used. "I seen guys get punched in the face, kicked," says Frankie. "You know it happens. I mean what would you do if you had somebody that's drunk and you got to get them out of an ATM?" Apparently the routine—as Frankie and other outreach workers explain—is to "call for back up and get busy," using what current outreach worker Chris James called "strategic force."

In November of last year Frankie found out that, like 40 percent of New York's homeless, he has HIV. He left St. Agnes because he said they weren't helping him enough. He is now looking for housing and medical care.

As for Street Watch, the activists say that their presence in the neighborhood with video cameras has already caused the GCP outreach teams to curb their abuse. According to Lisa Daugaard, Litigation Director at the Coalition for the Homeless, both the alleged brutality and the poor wages of the Grand Central Partnership's outreach program are symptoms of a larger problem posed by business improvement districts. According to Daugaard: "The BIDs are a trap door, a way for the private sector to supplant public policy." Unfortunately, the "brutal and illusionary solutions" touted by the nation's proliferating BIDs, argues Daugaard, undermine any "long-term public solutions to homelessness."

While much of what the GCP does may look good at first and may in fact be helpful, in the larger scope of urban politics BIDs are primarily a means by which the business community can detach from, and circumvent, larger movements for social reform. Ultimately BIDs avoid the question of political accountability, which lies at the heart of democracy. BIDs displace social problems rather than create alternatives. The new business mini-governments may in fact lead to the further polarization of cities, with downtown business areas becoming semi-autonomous, semi-private zones which stand in total contrast to a city's squalid, sprawling outlying boroughs—or bantustans.

But if BIDs can fund private security, why not social services? Few if any of the nation's BIDs actually fund social services. As one San Francisco merchant and BID founder told the *SF Weekly,* "None of the business owners would approve of that [funding social services]. We can't afford it."   [1994]

Understanding the Reading

1. What is the Grand Central Partnership Outreach Team?

2. What is Street Watch?
3. What are BIDs, and what purpose do they serve?
4. Describe how Saint Agnes is funded and what programs and services it provides.
5. What problems do homeless people see in the "pathways to employment" program?
6. How does Jeff Grunberg defend GCP?
7. What are some of the abuses by outreach workers?
8. Describe Frankie's experiences and observations.
9. How does Street Watch assess the GCP outreach and BIDs?
10. Summarize the strategies of resistance to addressing the socioeconomic problems of homelessness that are described in this selection. ◆

Suggestions for Responding

1. If you were a merchant in an area where homeless people tended to gather, how would you be likely to respond? How does this response make you feel about your humanity and the humanity of our society?
2. A number of the titles of groups described in this selection seem to be euphemisms. Write a short essay exploring these titles and why the group organizers chose each label; that is, explain what each label *seems* to imply.

SUGGESTIONS FOR RESPONDING TO PART VII

1. Write an autobiographical analysis of your economic life from as far back as you can remember. Besides describing changing circumstances over time, analyze the impact economic class has had on your sense of self-worth, feelings, opportunities, and experiences—as well as the effects change has had on others' responses to you.
2. Imagine a family that has two children, ages three and one half years and nine months, and two parents. Both parents work full-time

at minimum-wage jobs. The two of them together earn $16,320 in pre-tax dollars, as Celine-Marie Pascale reports in her article.

Working with a small group, develop a yearly budget for this family. In addition to food, rent, and utilities, remember such other expenses as transportation, shoes and clothing, diapers and laundry, medical and dental expenses, and insurance.

Since Pascale also notes that a quarter of all workers currently earn $7.50 an hour

($14,400 a year), next imagine that the wife in this family gets pregnant and has to leave her job for health reasons, but the husband gets a job paying this wage. Develop another yearly budget for this family.

As you write your report, include not only the projected budgets but also comments on what you each feel life would be like in these two circumstances—in which a large number of Americans now live.

3. Alternatively, imagine a twenty-one-year-old woman, divorced and with a three-year-old child. She has graduated from high school but has not gone to college. She has not worked since her child was born. While she was in high school, she worked during the summers and sometimes after school for minimum wage in retail stores and fast-food restaurants. Her ex-husband has not paid any child support, though legally he is required to do so. Her parents are no longer living, and she has no sisters or brothers. How is she going to support herself and her three-year-old child?

Looking at the classifieds of a local newspaper, find this woman a job. Find out what her yearly salary would be, and calculate her monthly income from that projected salary. Do not forget how much she will have to pay for income taxes and FICA deductions. (Information about the percentages for these deductions should be available in your library.)

After you write your report on your findings, draw some conclusions from comparing her finances with the poverty line, which is approximately $10,000 a year for a two-person family, and with your local welfare payment for a two-person family. What do these comparisons show?

4. In 1995, federal politicians from both parties committed themselves to "ending welfare as we know it." From what you *know* (not believe) about welfare and from the readings in Part VII, try (either alone or with a small group) to create a policy that would improve our welfare system.

5. After reading Part VII, identify what you feel is the central economic problem facing our nation today. Research this problem either in the library or in your community and write a paper concretely describing the problem and what you think should be done to address it.

SUGGESTIONS FOR RESPONDING TO POWER

Research one manifestation of racism and sexism or classism that you read about in this book. As an individual, you will want to focus on what may seem to be a very small part of the problem, but a group could investigate a broader problem, breaking it into its component parts, with each group member assuming responsibility for one aspect.

As a group, you could investigate sexual harassment; as an individual, you could focus on something like sexual harassment on your campus. A group could look at housing segregation; individually, you could consider redlining (refusing credit to residents and businesses in certain locations) in your community. A group could research the issue of domestic battery, but individually you could research the cycle of violence. Or a group could examine current incidents of racial or homophobic harassment, but one person could concentrate on his or her campus or community.

Other broad areas for research include government policies affecting Native Americans; "scientific proof" of the inferiority of a racial, religious, or gender group; racist, sexist, or homophobic social policies; the race and/or gender wage gap; one facet of the history of racism or sexism in American law; organized racism, historically or at present; and a manifestation of discrimination in education or employment.

Report on both the causes and the effects of the problem. Also include information about efforts that have already been made to alleviate or at least ameliorate the problem, and discuss how effective or unsuccessful they have been and why.

If your instructor plans to have you develop a "plan for action" in response to "Change," you probably want to select a topic for this assign-ment that particularly concerns you and that you would like to see changed.

As with earlier assignments, your instruc-tor may ask you or your group to present your findings orally to your classmates. If this makes you uncomfortable, review the suggestions at the end of Part I on how to prepare for such a presentation.

Change is not only possible but is also an inevitable part of life. Seasons pass. We grow older. This kind of natural change is beyond our control. We adjust to many changes without taking much notice. On the other hand, there is **social change,** caused and controlled by people acting individually and collectively.

Most of us think of social change as resulting from mass **social movements,** coalitions of groups and individuals seeking to revise social policies and transform social institutions. We recognize the strategies and achievements of the major American social movements that have affected the groups we have been reading about: abolition and civil rights, labor unions and consumer rights, woman suffrage and women's liberation, and gay and lesbian rights. This kind of direct collective action is probably the most effective way to promote social change, but it requires the strong commitment of many people who agree and will act on common objectives. However, social change does not necessarily depend on large scale political activism. In fact, each of us in our daily life participates in the processes of social change.

You may think this does not apply to you. For example, you may never have been interested in social issues, much less consider yourself a social activist, but this does not mean you have no impact on the shape of society. You may not consider yourself prejudiced, but when a friend tells you a racial joke, you might laugh so you will not offend her. Your laughter, however, indicates your approval of the joke's racist assumptions and, without your being aware of it, you have added one more stitch to the racist fabric of our society. In contrast, had you made a quiet comment that you do not care for that kind of joke, you could have begun to unravel at least one little thread. Both what you do and what you do not do influence social values.

Many of the issues raised in the first two divisions of this book are very disturbing. Because stereotypes are arbitrary oversimplifications, they blind us to the individuality of members of stereotyped groups and the rich potential of our diverse society. Prejudice, in turn, rests on such stereotyped thinking and encourages discrimination, sexism, heterosexism, racism, and classism. These "isms" support the beliefs and behaviors that lead to the pervasive neglect, exploitation, subordination, and oppression of women, minorities, lesbians, gay men, and the poor. This is a problem not just for members of these groups but for all Americans because systemic exclusion of so many people from full participation diminishes society by depriving us of their full skills, talents, wisdom, and creativity. Moreover, prejudiced convictions, and the behaviors that grow out of them, violate the most basic tenets of American society, the principles of freedom, equality, and justice. In other words, the practice of marginalizing groups is *a way of thinking*—it is not because of the presence of that group that discrimination occurs. Without a "traditional" group to oppress, another must be found, unless this behavior is no longer tolerated.

As troubling and discouraging as an awareness of these social problems may be, we do not need to accept them as inevitable or unalterable. They can be changed, and we can be instrumental in the process of effecting such change. We already have begun that process by learning about these issues, for we cannot begin to address a problem until we see and understand it. But such knowledge is only the first step.

This division, "Change," is intended to show how to make the changes we want. Part VIII, "Taking Action," gives us an understanding of the nature and dynamics of social change. By learning the step-by-step process of creating social change, we can see how to be more effective contributors to society. Of course, not everyone desires or supports certain social changes. In fact, some people will try to obstruct our efforts; others will resort to direct action to inhibit certain changes. However, people continue to exert their energies to make things better, at least according to their values. Part IX, "Change Makers," explores how people have worked to change their own lives and the world around them. Part X, "Race, Class, and Gender After 9/11," challenges us to apply the knowledge we have gained and to articulate problems and possible solutions to the specific circumstances of the new millennium. Together these readings will increase our sense of our ability to control our own lives and to influence the society in which we live.

VIII
Taking Action

AT ONE OR TIME OR ANOTHER, WE ALL WANT TO change something—our looks, our behavior, what happens to us or to others. This is one reason you are in school: You want your life to be different than it otherwise would be. Part VIII provides information about how to make change occur—how to think about problems, how to plan what we want to do, and how to do it. When we understand the way to approach change logically, we are better able to initiate and effect change ourselves.

This part describes a six-step process to effect change. By the end of Part VIII, you will understand both how social change is created and how to make such change yourself.

The first basic step in the process is **identifying the problem.** We tend initially to see a problem in its broadest form, such as the general issue of homelessness. But that problem is so extensive that it feels overwhelming, so we are likely just to shrug our shoulders and dismiss it. After all, "what can one person do?" We *can* do something, though. First, we must learn as much as we can about the specific issues that underlie the larger problem. This information will help us identify and define a specific, concrete issue to work on. Homelessness, for example, has numerous causes for us to consider: an apartment fire, high rents and low incomes in the community, job loss, and family breakups. Another way of thinking about this issue is to think about its consequences, such as lack of economic resources, sanitary facilities, or safety.

The first selection focuses on this first step, identifying a problem thoughtfully and precisely. Orlando Patterson, in "Affirmative Action: The Sequel," has us re-examine this controversial topic. Patterson considers affirmative action from many angles and gives some specifics for its revision.

This brings us to the second step in the change process: **identifying the desired outcome**—that is, defining what specific change we would like to see. Arturo Madrid considers his personal experiences of being seen as the "other" and concludes that America and Americans must come to terms with the diversity of our society, his desired outcome. Laura Hershey would like to see cooperation between the pro-life movement and the disability movement. She suggests some steps that could be taken to realize this end. Derek Schork, as a teenager, tries (in a very dramatic way) to elicit an apology from a middle-aged man, who mistakenly concludes that he is parking in a handicapped space illegally. Eloise Salholz reports on the need for political awareness and activism in the Hispanic community. Considering the example of homelessness we discussed earlier, one potential outcome might be finding a way to help the unemployed homeless find work. This would be the goal, the desired outcome.

The third step is **developing strategies** for realizing the goal. Our first idea is probably not our best idea. We are better off considering many alternatives. Brainstorming—letting our minds wander freely—is a good approach. Take plenty of time, alone or with a group, to generate as many different ideas as possible. At this stage, do not censor yourself in any way; in fact, try to be as imaginative and creative as possible because what might at first seem an unrealistic strategy can sometimes trigger an original, workable solution. This is what Charlotte Bunch is doing as she explores ways of bringing her feminist vision to bear on the public arena. Her "anything is possible" approach results in her suggesting many inventive tactics that most of us never would have dreamed of. Similarly, Andrew Kimbrell explores ways that men can work for change in their relationships with their families, with the environment, and in the community. Try brainstorming tactics that could be used to help the homeless get jobs; see how many you can list. You might realize, for instance, that, without a home, even qualified people have nowhere to receive responses to job applications. You could help solve this problem by figuring out a way to provide them with a mailing address.

Step four is **developing a plan for action.** Select the most appropriate strategies from your brainstorming and figure how to implement them. Be realistic. Consider what resources you have access to: time, energy, people, money, materials, and so on. Think about how you can augment them. After brainstorming about everything that needs to be done, develop a time line—a schedule of what needs to be done and in what order. In "Lesbian Teen Sues District for Bias," Peter Y. Hong describes one family's last-resort decision, in order to fight for their eighth-grader's civil rights. John D'Emilio presents a plan of action, including policies and other considerations, for colleges and universities that want to ensure fair and equal treatment for gay men and lesbians on their campuses.

What could you do to help the homeless receive mail service? Probably very little by yourself, but if you interested others in working with you, you might create an effective solution. For example, you could solicit funds to pay rent on a post office box and distribute its contents at a prearranged location once a day. You could approach a church that already has a soup kitchen to feed the homeless and offer to help church members establish a mail service for homeless jobseekers at the church's address. There are many other ways to tackle this problem. Once you settle on your approach, develop your plan: the resources you need, your time frame, whom you need to work with you, and so on.

Once you have carefully mapped out your action project, your next step, the fifth, is **implementing the plan.** One major difficulty you will face at this stage is motivating people, getting them to act, to agree with you or your analysis of the problem, to support or perhaps even just to accept the desirability of the change you wish to implement. This is often the most crucial part of effecting social change. People resist change because we all tend to be more comfortable with the familiar, even when we realize that it is not perfect; we all value the security of living with what we already know. As Kathleen Ryan points out, people show resistance in a number of ways, but she also suggests ways to deal with it. Robert A. Rhoads also makes clear that we ourselves can resist the change we are working for because we may have been too influenced by societal values we have internalized.

The next two readings describe different approaches to taking action and creating social change. It is easiest, of course, if you have the power and authority to require people to change their attitude and behavior. Daniel Goleman, for example, explains how educators, without making their purpose explicit, can help students overcome racism by having them work in racially and ethnically mixed teams. This is the "top-down" model of making change. However, seemingly powerless people can also create tremendous changes by organizing and working together. For example, Cynthia Diehm and Margo Ross describe how people have identified the problem of domestic violence and taken steps to alleviate it through grass-roots activism. Throughout the country, small groups of people have worked together to set up shelters and to change laws and even the criminal justice system.

The final step in any good plan for social change is **evaluating your actions**—assessing the effectiveness of your endeavor and identifying the reasons for its successes and its disappointments. This is a very important step. Appraising the degree of your achievement can enhance your sense of a job well done, contributing to the satisfaction of everyone working with you. Identifying weaknesses in your project can help you plan better strategies to use in future actions. Evaluation is not simply a matter of determining whether or not the plan worked; it is much more a function of one's beliefs and expectations. People determine the relative success of a project based on a wide variety of standards, values, attitudes, and expectations. What one person considers a success another may perceive to be a failure.

Evaluative judgments differ when they rest on different priorities or value systems. In the last two readings, two law professors evaluate college and university policies that prohibit racist, sexist, and other types of harassing language or acts on their campuses. Gerald Gun-

ther opposes them because he believes they violate our constitutional freedom of speech. Charles R. Lawrence III supports them on the grounds that such offensive speech deprives its targets of constitutionally protected equal educational opportunities. Each presents a persuasive case for his point of view and is clearly convinced that his policy is better, based on his values.

An awareness of these six steps makes it easier for us to work for social changes that we desire. However, change is never easy. Each step requires a substantial investment of time and thought, and the more basic or extensive the desired change is, the more difficult it will be to achieve. Successful action demands thorough research, careful thought, strong motivation, extensive planning, and lots of time. If you commit yourself, however, you can do more than you probably think you can.

108

Affirmative Action: The Sequel

ORLANDO PATTERSON

No issue better reveals the American tension between principle and pragmatism than the debate over affirmative action. This week the Supreme Court is expected to enter the debate with a widely anticipated ruling on the University of Michigan's admissions policies, which favor black and other minority applicants.[1] More important than the decision the court reaches will be the reasoning it uses.

As pragmatic public policy, it is easy to show that the benefits of affirmative action far outweigh its social or individual costs. It ensures the integration of our best universities and thereby promotes (if indirectly) a heterogeneous professional elite. In conjunction with antidiscrimination laws, it has directly fostered the growth of an African-American and Latino middle class.

Corporate America has also embraced the policy, mostly by choice. As a result, minorities make up a large part of the middle and top ranks at many of the country's most recognizable firms. On Fortune magazine's latest list of the 50 best companies for minorities, for example, 24 percent of officials and managers are minorities. Affirmative action has transformed the American military, making it the most ethnically varied at all levels of its organization of all the world's great forces. And, along with changing ethnic and racial attitudes, affirmative action has helped promote a powerful global popular culture, many areas of which are dominated by minorities.

Negative achievements—that is, what affirmative action has spared us—are hard to prove. But it is surely reasonable to attribute the relative infrequency of ethnic or racial riots in America to the presence of minority leadership in many of the nation's mainstream institutions.

All these gains have been achieved at very little cost to America's economic or political efficiency: our economy dominates the world; our army is history's most awesome; our great universities have few equals; our arts, science and scholarship are the envy of the world.

There are indeed costs at the individual level, borne by those whites who may not have gained places or jobs as a result of preferences for minorities. But nearly all research indicates that these costs are minuscule. Repeated surveys indicate that no more than 7 percent of Americans of European heritage claim to have been adversely affected by affirmative action programs, and it has been shown that affirmative action reduces the chances of whites getting into top colleges by only 1.5 percentage points.

For all its achievements, however, many critics fear that affirmative action violates fundamental principles that have guided this country. It is indeed difficult to reconcile affirmative action with the nation's manifest ideals of individualism and merit-based competition. But America's history is replete with just such pragmatic fudging of these ideals.

In foreign policy the United States has defended dictators, destabilized democracies and invaded other countries in the pragmatic promotion of the national interest. Domestically, Congress regularly passes laws that favor special interests—veterans, millionaire ranchers, farmers, oil-well owners, holders of patents about to expire, people with home mortgages—many with no economic justification, all costing billions of tax dollars.

Why, then, the obsession with the principle of colorblindness, especially among right-wing activists who otherwise exhibit little enthusiasm for the equality principle enshrined in the Declaration of Independence? It is hard to resist the conclusion that principles are invoked in public life to rationalize the control of the vulnerable. In relations among equals, meanwhile, pragmatism trumps virtue.

Yet these critics miss a more compelling, and more subtle, argument against affirmative action. In spite of its benefits, there are serious problems in the long run for its beneficiaries if affirmative action is not decisively modified.

First, while diversity is a goal that deserves to be pursued in its own right, it was a major strategic error for African-American leaders to have advocated it as the main justification for affirmative action. In doing so, they greatly expanded the number of groups entitled to preferences—including millions of immigrants whose claims on the nation pale in comparison to those who have been historically discriminated against. Such a development understandably alarmed many whites who were otherwise prepared to turn a pragmatic blind eye to their principled concerns about affirmative action.

Using diversity as a rationale for affirmative action also distorts the aims of affirmative action. The original, morally incontestable goal of the policy was the integration of African-Americans in all important areas of the public and private sectors from which they had been historically excluded. But if diversity is the goal, the purpose of affirmative action shifts from improving the condition of blacks to transforming America into a multicultural society. Thus the pursuit of inclusion is replaced by the celebration of separate identities.

In a more profound sense, the diversity rationale undermines a hopeful view of America. If the purpose of affirmative action is to redress past wrongs, then it requires both the minority and the majority to do the cultural work necessary to create what Martin Luther King Jr. called the "beloved community" of an integrated nation. Instead, many of its supporters see affirmative action as an entitlement, requiring little or no effort on the part of minorities.

Another consequence of this view is that it allows no recognition of the brute historical fact that the very patterns of social, educational and cultural adjustments that ensured survival, and even conferred nobility, under the extreme conditions of racist oppression no longer apply. In fact, now they may even be dysfunctional.

The gravest danger, however, and what perhaps alarms the majority most, is the tendency to view affirmative action as a permanent program for preferred minorities and, simultaneously, the refusal even to consider it a topic for public discourse. Indeed, among the black middle class, especially on the nation's campuses, blind support for affirmative action has become an essential signal of ethnic solidarity and commitment.

The nation needs this policy, but it must be modified. For starters, it should exclude all immigrants and be confined to African-Americans, Native Americans and most Latinos. It should include an economic means test. Only those who are poor or grew up in deprived neighborhoods should benefit. At the same time, poor whites from deprived neighborhoods should be phased into the program, a development that would counter the arguments of right-wing critics.

Finally, affirmative action should be severed from the goal of diversity—which, as the legal scholar Peter Schuck has argued, is best left to the private sector. Middle-class blacks and Latinos would continue to benefit from such voluntary programs, properly understood as a sharing of diverse experiences and perspectives rather than a withdrawal into ethnic glorification. There is every reason to believe the nation's corporations and universities will continue to find such a policy to be in their own best interests, and the nation's.

Americans have always recognized that high ideals, however desirable, inevitably clash with reality, and that good public policy requires compromise. But only through the struggle of affirmative action are they coming to realize that such compromises, wisely pursued, can actually serve a higher principle: the supreme virtue of being fair to those who have been most unfairly treated.   [2003]

Notes

1. The U.S. Supreme Court ruled in favor of the University of Michigan's affirmative action policy.

Understanding the Reading

1. According to Patterson, what specifically has been accomplished with affirmative action, and what are its problems?
2. What is America's dilemma, in regard to ideals of merit-based competition?
3. Why does Patterson say it is a mistake to assign diversity as the goal of affirmative action?
4. How should affirmative action be modified?

Suggestions for Responding

1. Debate Patterson's suggested revisions for affirmative action as a public policy. ✦

109

Diversity and Its Discontents

ARTURO MADRID

My name is Arturo Madrid. I am a citizen of the United States, as are my parents and as were my grandparents and my great-grandparents. My ancestors' presence in what is now the United States antedates Plymouth Rock, even without taking into account any American Indian heritage I might have.

I do not, however, fit those mental sets that define America and Americans. My physical appearance, my speech patterns, my name, my profession (a professor of Spanish) create a text that confuses the reader. My normal experience is to be asked, "And where are *you* from?" My response depends on my mood. Passive-aggressive, I answer, "From here." Aggressive-passive, I ask, "Do you mean where I am originally from?" But ultimately my answer to those follow-up questions that will ask about origins will be that we have always been from here.

Overcoming my resentment I try to educate, knowing that nine times out of ten my words fall on inattentive ears. I have spent most of my adult life explaining who I am not. I am exotic, but—as Richard Rodriguez of *Hunger of Memory* fame so painfully found out—not exotic enough . . . not Peruvian, or Pakistani, or whatever. I am, however, very clearly the *other,* if only your everyday, garden-variety, domestic *other.* I will share with you another phenomenon that I have been a part of, that of being a missing person, and how I came late to that awareness. But I've always known that I was the *other,* even before I knew the vocabulary or understood the significance of otherness.

I grew up in an isolated and historically marginal part of the United States, a small mountain village in the state of New Mexico, the eldest child of parents native to that region, whose ancestors had always lived there. In those vast and empty spaces people who look like me, speak as I do, and have names like mine predominate. But the *americanos* lived among us: the descendants of those nineteenth-century immigrants who dispossessed us of our lands; missionaries who came to convert us and stayed to live among us; artists who became enchanted with our land and humanscape and went native; refugees from unhealthy climes, crowded spaces, unpleasant circumstances; and, of course, the inhabitants of Los Alamos,[1] whose sociocultural distance from us was accentuated by the fact that they occupied a space removed from and proscribed to us. More importantly, however, they—*los americanos*—were omnipresent (and almost exclusively so) in newspapers, newsmagazines, books, on radio, in movies, and, ultimately, on television.

Despite the operating myth of the day, school did not erase my otherness. It did try to deny it, and in doing so only accentuated it. To this day what takes place in schools is more socialization than education, but when I was in elementary school—and given where I was—socialization was everything. School was where one became an American, because there was a pervasive and systematic denial by the society that surrounded us that we were Americans. That denial was both explicit and implicit.

Quite beyond saluting the flag and pledging allegiance to it (a very intense and meaningful action, given that the United States was involved in a war and our brothers, cousins, uncles, and fathers were on the frontlines), becoming American was learning English, and its corollary: not speaking Spanish. Until very recently ours was a proscribed language, either *de jure*—by rule, by policy, by law—or *de facto*—by practice, implicitly if not explicitly, through social and political and economic pressure. I do not argue that learning English was not appropriate. On the contrary. Like it or not, and we had no basis to make any judgments on that matter, we were Americans by virtue of having been born Americans and English was the common language of Americans. And there was a myth, a pervasive myth, to the effect that if only we learned to speak English well—and particularly without an accent—we would be welcomed into the American fellowship.

Sam Hayakawa[2] and the official English movement folks notwithstanding, the true text was not our speech, but rather our names and our appearance, for we would always have an accent, however perfect our pronunciation, however excellent our enunciation, however divine our diction. That accent would be heard in our pigmentation, our physiognomy, our names. We were, in short, the *other*.

Being the *other* involves contradictory phenomena. On the one hand, being the *other* frequently means being invisible. Ralph Ellison wrote eloquently about that experience in his magisterial novel, *Invisible Man*. On the other hand, being the *other* sometimes involves sticking out like a sore thumb. What is she/he doing here?

For some of us being the *other* is only annoying; for others it is debilitating; for still others it is damning. Many try to flee otherness by taking on protective colorations that provide invisibility, whether of dress or speech or manner or name. Only a fortunate few succeed. For the majority of us otherness is permanently sealed by physical appearance. For the rest, otherness is betrayed by ways of being, speaking, or doing.

The first half of my life I spent downplaying the significance and consequences of otherness. The second half has seen me wrestling to understand its complex and deeply ingrained realities; striving to fathom why otherness denies us a voice or visibility or validity in American society and its institutions; struggling to make otherness familiar, reasonable, even normal to my fellow Americans.

I spoke earlier of another phenomenon that I am a part of: that of being a missing person. Growing up in northern New Mexico I had only a slight sense of us being missing persons. *Hispanos,* as we called (and call) ourselves in New Mexico, were very much a part of the fabric of the society, and there were *hispano* professionals everywhere about me: doctors, lawyers, schoolteachers, and administrators. My people owned businesses, ran organizations, and were both appointed and elected public officials.

My awareness of our absence from the larger institutional life of the society became sharper when I went off to college, but even then it was attenuated by the circumstances of history and geography. The demography of Albuquerque still strongly reflected its historical and cultural origins, despite the influx of Midwesterners and Easterners. Moreover, many of my classmates at the University of New Mexico were *hispanos,* and even some of my professors. I thought that

would pertain at UCLA, where I began graduate studies in 1960. Los Angeles had a very large Mexican population and that population was visible even in and around Westwood and on the campus. Many of the groundskeepers and food-service personnel at UCLA were Mexican. But Mexican-American students were few and mostly invisible, and I do not recall seeing or knowing a single Mexican-American (or, for that matter, African-American, Asian, or American Indian) professional on the staff or faculty of that institution during the five years I was there. Needless to say, people like me were not present in any capacity at Dartmouth College, the site of my first teaching appointment, and of course were not even part of the institutional or individual mind-set. I knew then that we—a we that had come to encompass American Indians, Asian-Americans, African-Americans, Puerto Ricans, and women—were truly missing persons in American institutional life.

Over the past three decades the *de jure* and *de facto* types of segregation that have historically characterized American institutions have been under assault. As a consequence, minorities and women have become part of American institutional life. Although there are still many areas where we are not to be found, the missing persons phenomenon is not as pervasive as it once was. However, the presence of the *other,* particularly minorities, in institutions and in institutional life resembles what we call in Spanish a *flor de tierra* (a surface phenomenon): we are spare plants whose roots do not go deep, vulnerable to inclemencies of an economic, or political, or social nature.

Our entrance into and our status in institutional life are not unlike a scenario set forth by my grandmother's pastor when she informed him that she and her family were leaving their mountain village to relocate to the Rio Grande Valley. When he asked her to promise that she would remain true to the faith and continue to involve herself in it, she asked why he thought she would do otherwise. "Doña Trinidad," he told her, "in the Valley there is no Spanish church. There is only an American church." "But," she protested, "I read and speak English and would be able to worship there." The pastor responded, "It is possible that they will not admit you, and even if they do, they might not accept you. And that is why I want you to promise me that you are going to go to church. Because if they don't let you in through the front door, I want you to go in through the back door. And if you can't get in through the back door, go in the side door. And if you are unable to enter through the side door I want you to go in through the window. What is important is that you enter and stay."

Some of us entered institutional life through the front door; others through the back door; and still others through side doors. Many, if not most of us, came in through windows, and continue to come in through windows. Of those who entered through the front door, some never made it past the lobby; others were ushered into corners and niches. Those who entered through back and side doors inevitably have remained in back and side rooms. And those who entered through windows found enclosures built around them. For, despite the lip service given to the goal of the integration of minorities into institutional life, what has frequently occurred instead is ghettoization, marginalization, isolation.

Not only have the entry points been limited, but in addition the dynamics have been singularly conflictive. Gaining entry and its corollary, gaining space, have frequently come as a consequence of demands made on institutions and institutional officers. Rather than entering institutions more or less passively, minorities have of necessity entered them actively, even aggressively. Rather than waiting to receive, they have demanded. Institutional relations have thus been adversarial, infused with specific and generalized tensions.

The nature of the entrance and the nature of the space occupied have greatly influenced the view and attitude of the majority population within those institutions. All of us are put into the same box; that is, no matter what the individual reality, the assessment of the individual is inevitably conditioned by a perception that is held of the class. Whatever our history, whatever our record, whatever our validations, whatever our accomplishments, by and large we are perceived unidimensionally and dealt with accordingly. I remember an experience I had in this regard, atypical only in its explicitness. A few years ago I allowed myself to be persuaded to seek the presidency of a well-known state university.

I was invited for an interview and presented myself before the selection committee, which included members of the board of trustees. The opening question of that brief but memorable interview was directed at me by a member of that august body. "Dr. Madrid," he asked, "why does a one-dimensional person like you think he can be the president of a multidimensional institution like ours?"

Over the past four decades America's demography has undergone significant changes. Since 1965 the principal demographic growth we have experienced in the United States has been of peoples whose national origins are non-European. This population growth has occurred both through birth and through immigration. A few years ago discussion of the national birthrate had a scare dimension: the high—"inordinately high"—birthrate of the Hispanic population. The popular discourse was informed by words such as "breeding." Several years later, as a consequence of careful tracking by government agencies, we now know that what has happened is that the birthrate of the majority population has decreased. When viewed historically and comparatively, the minority populations (for the most part) have also had a decline in birthrate, but not one as great as that of the majority.

There are additional demographic changes that should give us something to think about. African-Americans are now to be found in significant numbers in every major urban center in the nation. Hispanic-Americans now number over 15 million people, and although they are a regionally concentrated (and highly urbanized) population, there is a Hispanic community in almost every major urban center of the United States. American Indians, heretofore a small and rural population, are increasingly more numerous and urban. The Asian-American population, which has historically consisted of small and concentrated communities of Chinese-, Filipino, and Japanese-Americans, has doubled over the past decade, its complexion changed by the addition of Cambodians, Koreans, Hmongs, Vietnamese, et al.

Prior to the Immigration Act of 1965,[3] 69 percent of immigration was from Europe. By far the largest number of immigrants to the United States since 1965 have been from the Americas and from Asia: 34 percent are from Asia; another 34 percent are from Central and South America; 16 percent are from Europe; 10 percent are from the Caribbean; the remaining 6 percent are from other continents and Canada. As was the case with previous immigration waves, the current one consists principally of young people: 60 percent are between the ages of 16 and 44. Thus, for the next few decades, we will continue to see a growth in the percentage of non-European-origin Americans as compared to European-Americans.

To sum up, we now live in one of the most demographically diverse nations in the world, and one that is increasingly more so.

During the same period social and economic change seems to have accelerated. Who would have imagined at mid-century that the prototypical middle-class family (working husband, wife as homemaker, two children) would for all intents and purposes disappear? Who could have anticipated the rise in teenage pregnancies, children in poverty, drug use? Who among us understood the implications of an aging population?

We live in an age of continuous and intense change, a world in which what held true yesterday does not today, and certainly will not tomorrow. What change does, moreover, is bring about even more change. The only constant we have at this point in our national development is change. And change is threatening. The older we get the more likely we are to be anxious about change, and the greater our desire to maintain the status quo.

Evident in our public life is a fear of change, whether economic or moral. Some who fear change are responsive to the call of economic protectionism, others to the message of moral protectionism. Parenthetically, I have referred to the movement to require more of students without in turn giving them more as academic protectionism. And the pronouncements of E. D. Hirsch and Allan Bloom[4] are, I believe, informed by intellectual protectionism. Much more serious, however, is the dark side of the populism[5] which underlies this evergoing protectionism—the resentment of the *other*. An excellent and fascinating example of that aspect of populism is the cry for linguistic protectionism—for making English the official language of the United States.

And who among us is unaware of the tensions that underlie immigration reform, of the underside of demographic protectionism?

A matter of increasing concern is whether this new protectionism, and the mistrust of the *other* which accompanies it, is not making more significant inroads than we have supposed in higher education. Specifically, I wish to discuss the question of whether a goal (quality) and a reality (demographic diversity) have been erroneously placed in conflict, and, if so, what problems this perception of conflict might present.

As part of my scholarship I turn to dictionaries for both origins and meanings of words. Quality, according to the *Oxford English Dictionary,* has multiple meanings. One set defines quality as being an essential character, a distinctive and inherent feature. A second describes it as a degree of excellence, of conformity to standards, as superiority in kind. A third makes reference to social status, particularly to persons of high social status. A fourth talks about quality as being a special or distinguishing attribute, as being a desirable trait. Quality is highly desirable in both principle and practice. We all aspire to it in our own person, in our experiences, in our acquisitions and products, and of course we all want to be associated with people and operations of quality.

But let us move away from the various dictionary meanings of the word and to our own sense of what it represents and of how we feel about it. First of all we consider quality to be finite; that is, it is limited with respect to quantity; it has very few manifestations; it is not widely distributed. I have it and you have it, but they don't. We associate quality with homogeneity, with uniformity, with standardization, with order, regularity, neatness. All too often we equate it with smoothness, glibness, slickness, elegance. Certainly it is always expensive. We tend to identify it with those who lead, with the rich and famous. And, when you come right down to it, it's inherent. Either you've got or you ain't.

Diversity, from the Latin *divertere,* meaning to turn aside, to go different ways, to differ, is the condition of being different or having differences, is an instance of being different. Its companion word, diverse, means differing, unlike, distinct; having or capable of having various forms; composed of unlike or distinct elements. Diversity is lack of standardization, of regularity, of orderliness, homogeneity, conformity, uniformity. Diversity introduces complications, is difficult to organize, is troublesome to manage, is problematical. Diversity is irregular, disorderly, uneven, rough. The way we use the word diversity gives us away. Something is too diverse, is extremely diverse. We want a little diversity.

When we talk about diversity, we are talking about the *other,* whatever that other might be: someone of different gender, race, class, national origin; somebody at a greater or lesser distance from the norm; someone outside the set; someone who possesses a different set of characteristics, features, or attributes; someone who does not fall within the taxonomies we use daily and with which we are comfortable; someone who does not fit into the mental configurations that give our lives order and meaning.

In short, diversity is desirable only in principle, not in practice. Long live diversity . . . as long as it conforms to my standards, my mind set, my view of life, my sense of order. We desire, we like, we admire diversity, not unlike the way the French (and others) appreciate women; that is, *Vive la différence!*—as long as it stays in its place.

What I find paradoxical about and lacking in this debate is that diversity is the natural order of things. Evolution produces diversity. Margaret Visser, writing about food in her latest book, *Much Depends on Dinner,* makes an eloquent statement in this regard:

> Machines like, demand, and produce uniformity. But nature loathes it: her strength lies in multiplicity and in differences. Sameness in biology means fewer possibilities and therefore weakness.

The United States, by its very nature, by its very development, is the essence of diversity. It is diverse in its geography, population, institutions, technology; its social, cultural, and intellectual modes. It is a society that at its best does not consider quality to be monolithic in form or finite in quantity, or to be inherent in class. Quality in our society proceeds in large measure out of the stimulus of diverse modes of thinking and acting; out of the creativity made possible by the different ways in which we approach things; out of diversion from paths or modes hallowed by tradition.

One of the principal strengths of our society is its ability to address, on a continuing and substantive basis, the real economic, political, and social problems that have faced and continue to face us. What makes the United States so attractive to immigrants is the protections and opportunities it offers; what keeps our society together is tolerance for cultural, religious, social, political, and even linguistic difference; what makes us a unique, dynamic, and extraordinary nation is the power and creativity of our diversity.

The true history of the United States is one of struggle against intolerance, against oppression, against xenophobia, against those forces that have prohibited persons from participating in the larger life of the society on the basis of their race, their gender, their religion, their national origin, their linguistic and cultural background. These phenomena are not consigned to the past. They remain with us and frequently take on virulent dimensions.

If you believe, as I do, that the well-being of a society is directly related to the degree and extent to which all of its citizens participate in its institutions, then you will have to agree that we have a challenge before us. In view of the extraordinary changes that are taking place in our society we need to take up the struggle again, irritating, grating, troublesome, unfashionable, unpleasant as it is. As educated and educator members of this society we have a special responsibility for ensuring that all American institutions, not just our elementary and secondary schools, our juvenile halls, or our jails, reflect the diversity of our society. Not to do so is to risk greater alienation on the part of a growing segment of our society; is to risk increased social tension in an already conflictive world; and, ultimately, is to risk the survival of a range of institutions that, for all their defects and deficiencies, provide us the opportunity and the freedom to improve our individual and collective lot.

Let me urge you to reflect on these two words—quality and diversity—and on the mental sets and behaviors that flow out of them. And let me urge you further to struggle against the notion that quality is finite in quantity, limited in its manifestations, or is restricted by considerations of class, gender, race, or national origin; or that quality manifests itself only in leaders and not in followers, in managers and not in workers, in breeders and not in drones; or that it has to be associated with verbal agility or elegance of personal style; or that it cannot be seeded, nurtured, or developed.

Because diversity—the *other*—is among us, will define and determine our lives in ways that we still do not fully appreciate, whether that other is women (no longer bound by tradition, house, and family); or Asians, African-Americans, Indians, and Hispanics (no longer invisible, regional, or marginal); or our newest immigrants (no longer distant, exotic, alien). Given the changing profile of America, will we come to terms with diversity in our personal and professional lives? Will we begin to recognize the diverse forms that quality can take? If so, we will thus initiate the process of making quality limitless in its manifestations, infinite in quantity, unrestricted with respect to its origins, and more importantly, virulently contagious.

I hope we will. And that we will further join together to expand—not to close—the circle.

[1990]

Terms

1. LOS ALAMOS: The military installation where scientists developed the atomic bomb.
2. SAM HAYAKAWA: The former president of San Francisco State University and an outspoken opponent of bilingual education.
3. IMMIGRATION ACT OF 1965: The federal law that abolished the national-origins quota system of immigration.
4. E. D. HIRSCH AND ALLAN BLOOM: The authors, respectively, of *Cultural Illiteracy* and *The Closing of the American Mind,* both of which advocate a traditional curriculum.
5. POPULISM: A political philosophy that gives primacy to the needs of common people.

Understanding the Reading

1. Why does Madrid resent being asked where he is from?
2. What does he mean by being "other"?
3. What does he mean by referring to himself as "invisible" or a "missing person"?
4. What is the distinction between a school's erasing otherness and denying it?
5. Why did his grandmother's pastor feel that it was important for her to enter the church and stay?

6. What does Madrid mean by saying he is perceived unidimensionally?
7. Why does he find *breeding* an offensive term?
8. What point is Madrid making by giving the various dictionary meanings of *quality* and *diversity?*

Suggestions for Responding

1. Do you agree or disagree with Madrid that diversity is the basis for the "quality" of the United States? Why? ◆

110

Choosing Disability

LAURA HERSHEY

In 1983, when I was in college, local antiabortion protesters commemorated the tenth anniversary of *Roe v. Wade* with a rally. Our student feminist organization held a small counterdemonstration. Frantic in their zeal, antichoice protesters assailed us with epithets like "slut" and "bitch." But the most hostile remark was directed at me. I was confronted by an angry nun whose "Abortion Is Murder" sign hung tiredly at her side. She stopped in front of me and aimed a pugnacious finger. "You see?" she announced. "God even let you be born!"

I'm not sure the sister realized that I had been part of the pro-choice demonstration. All she saw in me was a poster child for her holy crusade. I must have seemed to her an obvious mistake of nature: a severely disabled person, who, through a combination of divine intervention and legal restrictions, had been born anyway.

That was my first inkling of how attitudes about disability function in the volatile debate over reproductive rights. I understood that the nun and her co-crusaders were no friends of mine. To her, I was a former fetus who had escaped the abortionists. No room in that view for my identity as an adult woman; no room for the choices I might make. Now, more than a decade later, antiabortion groups are courting the disability community. The approach has become less clumsy, emphasizing respect for the lives of people with disabilities, and some activists have accepted the anti-choice message because they find it consistent with the goals of the disability rights movement. As a feminist, however, I recoil at the "pro-life" movement's disregard for the lives and freedom of women.

But I cannot overlook the fact that when a prenatal test reveals the possibility of a "major defect," as the medical profession puts it, the pregnancy almost always ends in "therapeutic abortion." The prospect of bearing a child with disabilities causes such anxiety that abortion has become the accepted outcome—even among people who oppose abortion rights in general.

Indeed, fear of disability played a key role in the legalization of abortion in the United States in the 1960s. When thousands of pregnant women who had taken thalidomide (a drug used in tranquilizers) or had contracted rubella (German measles) gave birth to children with "defects," doctors called for easing abortion laws.

Today, despite three decades of activism by the disability community, and substantial disability rights legislation, avoiding disability is an important factor in the use and regulation of abortion. In a 1992 Time/CNN survey, for example, 70 percent of respondents favored abortion if a fetus was likely to be born deformed.

This is the quandary we face: the choices we all seek to defend—choices individual women make about childbirth—can conflict with efforts to promote acceptance, equality, and respect for people with disabilities. I am inseparably committed to the empowerment of both people with disabilities and women. Therefore, my pro-choice stance must lie somewhere in the common ground between feminism and disability rights. I want to analyze social and scientific trends, and to vocalize my troubled feelings about where all of this may lead. I want to defy patriarchy's attempts to control women, and also to challenge an age-old bias against people with disabilities. I want to discuss the ethics of choice—without advocating restrictions on choice. To draw a parallel, feminists have no problem attacking sex-selective abortion used to guarantee giving birth to a child of the "right" sex (most often male), but we try to educate against the practice, rather than seek legislation.

In an effort to clarify my own thinking about these complex, interlocking issues, I have been reading and listening to the words of other disabled women. Diane Coleman, a Nashville-based disability rights organizer, is deeply concerned about the number of abortions based on fetal disability: Coleman sees this as "a way that society expresses its complete rejection of people with disabilities, and the conviction that it would be better if we were dead." I find myself sharing her indignation.

Julie Reiskin, a social worker in Denver who is active in both disability rights and abortion rights, tells me, "I live with a disability, and I have a hard time saying, 'This is great.' I think that the goal should be to eliminate disabilities." It jars me to hear this, but Reiskin makes a further point that I find helpful. "Most abortions are not because there's something wrong with the fetus," she says. "Most abortions are because we don't have decent birth control." In other words, we should never have to use fetal disability as a reason to keep abortion legal: "It should be because women have the right to do what we want with our bodies, period," says Reiskin.

We are a diverse community, and it's no surprise to find divergent opinions on as difficult an issue as abortion. Our personal histories and hopes, viewed through the lens of current circumstances, shape our values and politics. Like all women I interviewed, I must be guided by my own experiences of living with disability. At two years old, I still could not walk. Once I was diagnosed—I have a rare neuromuscular condition—doctors told my parents that I would live only another year or two. Don't bother about school, they advised; just buy her a few toys and make her comfortable until the end.

My parents ignored the doctors' advice. Instead of giving up on me, they taught me to read. They made sure I had a child-size wheelchair and a tricycle. My father built a sled for me, and when the neighborhood kids went to the park to fly downhill in fresh snow, he pulled me along. My mother performed much of my physical care, but was determined not to do all of it; college students helped out in exchange for housing. She knew that her own wholeness and my future depended on being able to utilize resources outside our home.

Now my life is my own. I have a house, a career, a partner, and a community of friends with and without disabilities. I rely on a motorized wheelchair for mobility, a voice-activated computer for my writing, and the assistance of Medicaid-funded attendants for daily needs—dressing, bathing, eating, going to the bathroom. I manage it all according to my own goals and needs.

My life contradicts society's stereotypes about how people with disabilities live. Across the country, thousands of other severely disabled people are working, loving, and agitating for change. I don't mean to paint a simplistic picture. Most of us work very hard to attain independence, against real physical and/or financial obstacles. Too many people are denied the kind of daily in-home assistance that makes my life possible. Guaranteeing such services has become a top priority for the disability rights movement.

Changes like these, amounting to a small revolution, are slow to reach the public consciousness. Science, on the other hand, puts progress into practice relatively quickly. Prenatal screening seems to give pregnant women more power—but is it actually asking women to ratify social prejudices through their reproductive "choices"? I cannot help thinking that in most cases, when a woman terminates a previously wanted pregnancy expressly to avoid giving birth to a disabled child, she is buying into obsolete assumptions about that child's future. And she is making a statement about the desirability of the relative worth of such a child. Abortion based on disability results from, and in turn strengthens, certain beliefs: children with disabilities (and by implication adults with disabilities) are a burden to family and society; life with a disability is scarcely worth living; preventing the birth is an act of kindness; women who bear disabled children have failed.

Language reinforces the negativity. Terms like "fetal deformity" and "defective fetus" are deeply stigmatizing, carrying connotations of inadequacy and shame. Many of us have been called "abnormal" by medical personnel, who view us primarily as "patients," subject to the definitions and control of the medical profession. "Medical professionals often have countless incorrect assumptions about our lives," says Diane Coleman. "Maybe they see us as failures on their part." As a result, doctors who diagnose fetuses with disabilities often recommend either abortion or in-

stitutionalization. "I really haven't heard very many say, 'It's O.K. to have a disability, your family's going to be fine,'" Coleman says.

The independent living movement, which is the disabled community's civil rights movement, challenges this medical model. Instead of locating our difficulties within ourselves, we identify our oppression within a society that refuses to accommodate our disabilities. The real solution is to change society—to ensure full accessibility, equal opportunity, and a range of community support services—not to attempt to eliminate disabilities.

The idea that disability might someday be permanently eradicated—whether through prenatal screening and abortion or through medical research leading to "cures"—has strong appeal for a society wary of spending resources on human needs. Maybe there lurks, in the back of society's mind, the belief—the hope?—that one day there will be no people with disabilities. That attitude works against the goals of civil rights and independent living. We struggle for integration, access, and support services, yet our existence remains an unresolved question. Under the circumstances, we cannot expect society to guarantee and fund our full citizenship.

My life of disability has not been easy or carefree. But in measuring the quality of my life, other factors—education, friends, and meaningful work, for example—have been decisive. If I were asked for an opinion on whether to bring a child into the world, knowing she would have the same limitations and opportunities I have had, I would not hesitate to say, "Yes."

I know that many women do not have the resources my parents had. Many lack education, are poor, or are without the support of friends and family. The problems created by these circumstances are intensified with a child who is disabled. No woman should have a child she can't handle or doesn't want. Having said that, I must also say that all kinds of women raise healthy, self-respecting children with disabilities, without unduly compromising their own lives. Raising a child with disabilities is difficult, but raising any child is difficult; just as you expect any other child to enrich your life, you can expect the same from a child with disabilities. But the media often portray raising a child with disabilities as a personal martyrdom. Disabled children, disabled *people,* are viewed as misfortunes.

I believe the choice to abort a disabled fetus represents a rejection of children who have disabilities. Human beings have a deep-seated fear of confronting the physical vulnerability that is part of being human. This terror has been dubbed "disabiliphobia" by some activists. I confront disabiliphobia every day: the usher who gripes that I take up too much room in a theater lobby; the store owner who insists that a ramp is expensive and unnecessary because people in wheelchairs never come in; the talk-show host who resents the money spent to educate students with disabilities. These are the voices of an age-old belief that disability compromises our humanity and requires us to be kept apart and ignored.

Disabiliphobia affects health care reform too. In the proposed Clinton health plan only people disabled through injury or illness—not those of us with congenital disabilities—will be covered. Is this exclusion premised on the assumption that those of us born with disabilities have lesser value and that our needs are too costly?

People with severe disabilities do sometimes require additional resources for medical and support services. But disabiliphobia runs deeper than a cost-benefit analysis. Witness the ordeal of Bree Walker, a Los Angeles newscaster with a mild physical disability affecting her hands and feet. In 1990, when Walker became pregnant with her second child, she knew the fetus might inherit her condition, as had the first. She chose to continue the pregnancy, which led talk-show hosts and listeners to feel they had the right to spend hours debating whether Walker should have the child (most said no). Walker received numerous hostile letters. The callers and letter writers seemed to be questioning her right to exist, as well as her child's.

Walker's experience also pointed out how easily disabiliphobia slips from decisions about fetuses with disabilities to decisions about people with disabilities. That's why abortion is an area where we fear that the devaluation of our lives could become enshrined in public policy. Pro-choice groups must work to ensure that they do not support legislation that sets different standards based on disability.

A case in point is Utah's restrictive 1991 antiabortion law (which has since been declared unconstitutional). The law allowed abortions only in cases of rape, incest, endangerment of the woman's life, a profound health risk to the woman—or "fetal defect." According to Susanne Millsaps, director of Utah's NARAL affiliate, some disability rights activists wanted NARAL and other pro-choice groups to join in opposing the "fetal defect" exemption. The groups did not specifically take a stand on the exemption; instead they opposed the entire law. I would agree that the whole statute had to be opposed on constitutional and feminist grounds. But I would also agree that there should have been a stronger response to the fetal disability exemption.

To group "fetal defect" together with rape, incest, and life-endangering complications is to reveal deep fears about disability. As Barbara Faye Waxman, an expert on the reproductive rights of women with disabilities, says: "In this culture, disability, in and of itself, is perceived as a threat to the welfare of the mother. I find that to be troublesome and offensive."

There is more at stake here than my feelings, or anyone else's, about a woman's decision. Rapidly changing reproductive technologies, combined with socially constructed prejudices, weigh heavily on any decision affecting a fetus with possible disabilities. While some women lack basic prenatal and infant care, huge amounts of money are poured into prenatal screening and genetic research. Approximately 450 disorders can now be predicted before birth. In most cases the tests reveal only the propensity for a condition, not the condition itself. The Human Genome Project aims to complete the DNA map, and to locate hundreds more physical and developmental attributes. There is little public debate about the worth or ultimate uses of this federally funded multibillion-dollar program. But there are issues with regard to abortion that we can no longer afford to ignore:

- Does prenatal screening provide more data for women's informed choices, or does it promote the idea that no woman should risk having a disabled child?
- Who decides whether a woman should undergo prenatal screening, and what she should do with the results?
- Are expensive, government-funded genetic research projects initiated primarily for the benefit of a society unwilling to support disability-related needs?

- Is society attempting to eradicate certain disabilities? Should this ever be a goal? If so, should all women be expected to cooperate in it?

The January/February 1994 issue of *Disability Rag & Resource,* a publication of the disability rights movement, devoted several articles to genetic screening. In one, feminist lawyer Lisa Blumberg argues that women are being coerced into accepting prenatal tests, and then pressured to terminate their pregnancies when disabling conditions appear likely. "Prenatal testing has largely become the decision of the doctor," Blumberg writes, and "the social purpose of these tests is to reduce the incidence of live births of people with disabilities."

A woman faced with this choice usually feels pressure from many directions. Family, friends, doctors, and the media predict all kinds of negative results should her child be disabled. At the same time, she is unlikely to be given information about community resources; nor is she encouraged to meet individuals who have the condition her child might be born with. This lack of exposure to real-life, nonmedical facts about living with a disability should make us wonder whether women are really making "informed" choices about bearing children with disabilities.

Few outside the disability community have dealt with these issues in any depth. "We are all aware of the potential for abuses in reproductive technology and in genetic testing," says Marcy Wilder, legal director for NARAL's national office in Washington, D.C. "I don't see that there have been widespread abuses—but we're certainly concerned." That concern has not led to any coalition-building with disability rights groups, however.

Many feminist disability rights activists report chilly responses when they attempt to network with pro-choice groups. Too often, when we object to positions that implicitly doubt the humanity of children born disabled, we are accused of being anti-choice. One activist I know recently told me about her experience speaking at a meeting of a National Organization for Women chapter. She mentioned feeling discomfort about the widespread abortion of disabled fetuses—and was startled by the members' reactions. "They said, 'How could you claim to be

a feminist and pro-choice and even begin to think that there should be any limitations?' I tried to tell them I don't think there should be limitations, but that our issues need to be included."

On both sides, the fears are genuine, rational, and terrifying—if not always articulated. For the pro-choice movement, the fear is that questioning the motives and assumptions behind any reproductive decision could give ammunition to antiabortionists. Defenders of disability rights fear that the widespread use of prenatal testing and abortion for the purpose of eliminating disability could inaugurate a new eugenics movement. If we cannot unite and find ways to address issues of reproductive screening and manipulation, we all face the prospect that what is supposed to be a private decision—the termination of a pregnancy—might become the first step in a campaign to eliminate people with disabilities.

I am accusing the pro-choice movement not of spurring these trends, but of failing to address them. Most pro-choice organizations do not favor the use of abortion to eliminate disabilities, but their silence leaves a vacuum in which fear of disability flourishes.

Disabiliphobia and the "genetics enterprise," as activist Adrienne Asch calls it, have also had legal implications for the reproductive rights of all women. The tendency to blame social problems such as poverty and discrimination on individuals with disabilities and their mothers has made women vulnerable to the charge that they are undermining progress toward human "perfectibility"—because they insist on a genuine choice. Some legal and medical experts have developed a concept called "fetal rights," in which mothers can be held responsible for the condition of their unborn or newborn children. According to Lisa Blumberg, "fetal rights" could more accurately be called "fetal quality control." For women with hereditary disabilities who decide to have children this concept is nothing new. Society and medical professionals have often tried to prevent us from bearing and raising children. Disabled women know, as well as anyone, what it means to be deprived of reproductive choice. More broadly, decisions involving our health care, sexuality, and parenting have been made by others based on assumptions about our inabilities and/or our asexuality.

The right to control one's body begins with good gynecological care. Low income, and dependence on disability "systems," restrict access to that care. Like many women of disability, my health care choices are limited by the accessibility of medical facilities, and by providers' attitudes toward disability and their willingness to accept the low reimbursement of Medicaid. And Medicaid will not cover most abortions, a policy that discriminates against poor women and many women with disabilities.

Paradoxically, policy is often undermined by practice. Although public funding rarely pays for abortions, many women with disabilities are encouraged to have them—even when they would prefer to have a child. Doctors try to convince us an abortion would be best for "health reasons"—in which case, Medicaid will pay for it after all. "Abortions are easier for disabled women to get," says Nancy Moulton, a health care advocate in Atlanta, "because the medical establishment sees us as not being fit parents." Most women grow up amid strong if subtle pressures to become mothers. For those of us with disabilities, there is an equal or greater pressure to forgo motherhood. This pressure has taken the form of forced sterilization, lost custody battles, and forced abortion.

Consequently, for women with disabilities, reproductive freedom means more than being able to get an abortion. It is hard for many of us to relate to those in the reproductive rights movement whose primary concern is keeping abortions legal and available. But I believe our different perspectives on reproductive freedom are fundamentally compatible, like variations on a single theme.

Whatever the reason, feminist organizations seem inclined to overlook disability concerns. Feminist speakers might add "ableism" to their standard list of offensive "isms," but they do little to challenge it. Now more than ever, women with disabilities need the feminist movement's vigorous support. We need you to defend our rights as if they were your own—which they are. Here are a few suggestions:

- Recognize women with disabilities' equal stake in the pro-choice movement's goals. That means accepting us as women, not dismissing us as "other," or infirm, or gender-

less. Recognize us as a community of diverse individuals whose health needs, lifestyles, and choices vary.

- Defend all our reproductive rights: the right to appropriate education about sexuality and reproduction; to gynecological care, family planning services, and birth control; the right to be sexually active; to have children and to keep and raise those children, with assistance if necessary; and the right to abortion in accessible facilities, with practitioners who are sensitive to our needs.

- Remove the barriers that restrict the access of women with disabilities to services. Help to improve physical accessibility, arrange disability awareness training for staff and volunteers, and conduct outreach activities to reach women with disabilities.

- Continue struggling to build coalitions around reproductive rights and disability issues. There is plenty of common ground, although we may have to tiptoe through dangerous, mine-filled territory to get to it.

- Question the assumptions that seem to make bearing children with disabilities unacceptable.

Despite our rhetoric, abortion is not strictly a private decision. Individual choices are made in a context of social values; I want us to unearth, sort out, and appraise those values. I wouldn't deny any woman the right to choose abortion. But I would issue a challenge to all women making a decision whether to give birth to a child who may have disabilities.

The challenge is this: consider all relevant information, not just the medical facts. More important than a particular diagnosis are the conditions awaiting a child—community acceptance, access to buildings and transportation, civil rights protection, and opportunities for education and employment. Where these things are lacking or inadequate, consider joining the movement to change them. In many communities, adults with disabilities and parents of disabled children have developed powerful advocacy coalitions. I recognize that, having weighed all the factors, some women will decide they cannot give birth to a child with disabilities. It pains me, but I acknowledge their right and their choice.

Meanwhile, there is much work still to be done.   [1994]

Understanding the Reading

1. Why are anti-abortion groups appealing to the disability community?
2. Why is Diane Coleman concerned about abortions based on fetal disability?
3. What is Hershey's life like now?
4. Why does she disagree with abortion based on fetal disability?
5. What is the "independent living movement"?
6. How does Hershey evaluate her quality of life?
7. What is "disabiliphobia"?
8. What changes in social attitudes about fetal disability and disability rights would Hershey like to see?

Suggestions for Responding

1. Write a letter to Bree Walker expressing your opinion on her pregnancy.
2. Write an essay considering what you personally can do to improve the rights of people with disabilities and their quality of life. ✦

111

Breakfast at Perkins

DEREK SCHORK

Yes, stereotypes and prejudices have been a part of my thinking. I don't think anyone can honestly say that they have not had a prejudiced thought at one time or another, especially in the wake of 9/11. I'd rather not go into detail about these thoughts, as I am not particularly proud of them. However, there was one time that comes to mind when I was victimized by a stereotype. It made me very angry at the time, but now almost three years later, it's very easy for me and my friends, especially those who were there, to laugh about.

From Derek Schork, "Breakfast at Perkins." Reprinted by permission of the author.

This story takes place on an early spring morning of my senior year in high school. You must know that I have a below-the-knee amputation of my left leg. This particular morning I was wearing jeans. Keep that in mind as you read on. A group of friends and I decided to go out for breakfast, instead of going to school on time. When I pulled into the parking lot at Perkins Restaurant I saw that there weren't any available parking spots on this side of the lot. Legally I am allowed to park in a handicapped spot and I have the designation that hangs from my mirror. I was running late and all of my friends were already inside so I parked in one of the handicapped spots. As I got out of my car with my friend Jamie, an older man (mid 50's) was walking into the restaurant, when he stopped and looked at us and said, "Which one of you is handicapped? You should be ashamed of yourselves." This made me irate. Who was he to question us about where we parked? He made the stereotype of seeing two kids wearing long pants (so he couldn't see my prosthesis) and he assumed that there was no way a kid could be handicapped. Well, I started yelling at him to turn around, as I rolled up my pant leg. He wouldn't turn around, which made me even madder. At this point I think he realized that he had made a mistake, but wouldn't admit it. So I continued to try to get his attention, this time by taking off my leg and hopping after him into the restaurant. Perkins Restaurant was not prepared for this scene—evident by the stunned looks on the faces of everyone as a cursing kid hopped in with leg in hand. The hostess tried to calm me down as the man walked to his seat and I re-attached myself. My friends were having a good laugh as I went and sat down, and explained to them what happened. If the old man had asked me nicely instead of making a stupid assumption, I would have had no problem explaining to him why I parked there. This story is now legendary among my friends. At least now it's a good story to tell.   [2002]

Understanding the Reading

1. Why weren't Schork and his friends in school on this particular morning?
2. Why did the man outside Perkins Restaurant assume he was parking illegally?

3. What made Schork so angry? What did he do?
4. What could have solved this problem?

Suggestions for Responding

1. Share memories with your classmates of someone making erroneous assumptions, about you or someone else, because of a physical aspect of that person. Share your own mistaken judgments as well. ✦

112

The Push for Power

ELOISE SALHOLZ

It will be months before demographers at the Census Bureau produce their portrait of who we are in the waning years of the American Century. But when the results from the 1990 count are finally in, one statistic should come as no surprise: the number of Hispanics—the nation's fastest-growing group—could be approaching 25 million, or 10 percent of the total U.S. population. Latino leaders say the census will be their community's ticket to fuller participation in American life than ever before. It seems all the more ironic, then, that the forms arriving in mailboxes across the country recently were printed only in English—another reminder that, despite their vast legions, Hispanics remain an invisible minority.

Latinos were poised to make their mark once before. "The 1980s will be the decade of the Hispanics," declared Raúl Yzaguirre, president of the National Council of La Raza, in 1978. Pollsters predicted that Hispanics would soon become a "voting time bomb." But a dozen years later, Latinos have proved largely incapable of translating their numeric strength into political and economic clout. Today Yzaguirre says, "If anything, we retrogressed in the '80s." Reagan-era cutbacks and recession pushed many Hispanics deep into poverty, while the conservative social climate permitted passage of "English Only" laws aimed at Spanish speakers. Last week, a report from Congress's General Accounting Office confirmed what Hispanics have been saying for years: the landmark 1986 immigration law,[1] which penalized employers of illegal aliens, has produced a widespread "pattern of discrimination" against job applicants with a "foreign appearance or accent"—even citizens and green-card[2] holders.

Disappointed by their lack of progress in the last decade, Hispanics are now determined to salvage the 1990s. Activists have adopted a grass-roots strategy that has already led to successes in school reform and political redistricting. The Latino leadership is looking ahead to 1992, the 500th anniversary of Columbus's discovery of the Americas. The date holds great emotional significance for Spanish-speaking Americans, and activists hope it will lure diverse Hispanics—from cosmopolitan Miami and inner-city barrios to the planting fields of California—under a single political and cultural umbrella.

But the forces that made the "decade of the Hispanics" a nonevent continue to vex the Latino community. The first problem is one of definition. The term Hispanic is an imposed label, and remains more convenient than precise: it includes Mexicans, Cubans, Puerto Ricans and others who, apart from speaking Spanish, often have little in common. And the black-white dichotomy that characterizes American thinking on minorities leaves little room for Latino concerns.

Though Latinos have had a continuous presence in this country for centuries, they have been slow to gain recognition. "Hispanic" appeared as a census term only in 1980. Relative to their numbers, they remain seriously underrepresented—there are no Hispanic senators and only 10 congressmen. A 1989 study by the Southwest Voter Registration Education Project found that Latinos vote less, attend fewer political rallies and make fewer campaign contributions than other Americans. One reason is the extreme youth of the population. Young people generally are relatively uninvolved politically; with a median age of 25, many Hispanics are also simply too young to vote. And unlike blacks, whose churches and organizations provided an institutional base for the fight against segregation, Hispanics have lacked a political superstructure and a common enemy.

The few attempts at putting together a national platform have proved ineffective. In 1987, political and corporate leaders headed by Henry Cisneros, then the mayor of San Antonio, Texas, presented the presidential candidates with a National Hispanic Agenda. Although the document drew attention to concerns about employment, education and housing, the group proved somewhat ineffectual on account of bickering between Mexican-Americans and Puerto Ricans. Because Mexicans represent more than 60 percent of the Hispanic population, committee members felt they should have greater control over the document. In general, the nation's various Hispanic groups have complained about having to compete for attention and scarce government and philanthropic funds.

To be sure, Latinos have made some impressive strides on the local level: they have won elections in many predominantly Spanish-speaking areas and were crucial to the victory of Harold Washington in Chicago and, more recently, David Dinkins in New York. But there hasn't yet been a break-through, national leader. Latino political aspirations suffered a serious setback in the fall of 1988, when Cisneros announced he wouldn't seek re-election, then confessed to an extramarital affair with a political fund raiser (he is still married and living with his wife). Cisneros, 42, once touted as a Democratic vice presidential candidate in 1984, had been the ethnic group's great hope. As it happened, polls a month after the scandal showed only a slight drop in his popularity and he remains, says Hispanic Rep. Bill Richardson, "our most logical leader." But his temporary fall from grace was unsettling. "There is no savior that will lead the Latino community to some political, economic and social promised land," says Segundo Mercado-Llorens, a labor official in Washington. "It depends upon a community of leaders who work together."

Latino talent: From New York to California, a new generation of Latino talent has emerged. Meanwhile, local leaders have set their sights close to home. "Hispanics are going to galvanize around a set of issues more than race," says Daniel Solis, head of Chicago's United Neighborhood Organization (UNO). "And because we're made up of different nationalities and different opinions, we're being forced to do it the hard way—at the grass-roots level, with local institutions." Hispanics are being elected in

growing numbers to city councils and school boards—or, as one activist put it, the "front line of democracy."

Last year's school fight in Chicago, which is more than 20 percent Hispanic, illustrates the new grass-roots strategy. Angry over the city's appalling public education, busloads of Hispanics descended on the state capitol with a reform plan centered on greater parental control. They proceeded to win nearly 25 percent of the seats on newly created parent councils. Partly as a result of their efforts, some 50 principals lost their jobs. In a key legal victory, the Texas Supreme Court last year ordered a more equitable distribution of school funding—a decision that will be an automatic boost to Hispanics.

Latino leaders are now vesting their hopes for the future in the 1990 census. A vast increase in the population should bring Hispanics new funds and additional political representation. Because the 1980 census resulted in a large undercount of Hispanics—perhaps 10 percent—a number of activists have formed a program called Hágase Contar (Make Yourself Count) to ensure a more accurate picture. They have their work cut out for them. Spanish speakers have to call to request a form in their native tongue. That alone could discourage Hispanics from participating in the count.

Up for grabs: Time and numbers may be on the side of Latinos as they sail toward the 1992 anniversary. Voter registration climbed 21 percent from 1984 to 1988. At the same time, voter turnout has dropped slightly. Hispanic organizers attribute the decline to the difficulty of keeping up with a 25 percent increase in the voting-age population, though political consultants wonder whether they simply can't get out the vote. In the coming decade, some 5 million Hispanics will become eligible for citizenship, thanks in part to the amnesty program that granted legal residency to undocumented immigrants who had lived in the United States for five years. Both the Democrats and the GOP have strengthened their outreach programs to win Hispanic votes, which are viewed as being up for grabs.

But Hispanic leaders have failed to galvanize their armies before. The '90s will be a make-or-break test of their political maturity. "We either get this nation's attention," says Elaine Coronado, Quincentennial Commission director, "or we continue being perceived as a second-rate minority group." Says Cisneros: "We don't want to ever look at a decade again and say, 'Where did it go?'"   [1990]

Terms

1. 1986 IMMIGRATION LAW: A federal law providing residency to illegal aliens who could prove they had resided in the United States for at least five years; it also made it illegal for employers to employ undocumented workers.
2. GREEN CARD: A government permit allowing an alien to be employed.

Understanding the Reading

1. In what ways did Hispanics "retrogress in the '80s"?
2. Why has it been difficult for Latinos to organize themselves politically?
3. What actions are they taking to increase their political clout?

Suggestions for Responding

1. What can Latinos do to make themselves more central to the American political system?
2. Find the most recent demographics for Latinos in the U.S. ✦

113

Going Public with Our Vision

CHARLOTTE BUNCH

TRANSFORMATIONAL POLITICS AND PRACTICAL VISIONS

To bring the feminist vision to bear on all issues and to counter the right-wing agenda for the future, require that we engage in multiple strategies for action. We must work on many fronts at once. If a movement becomes a single issue or single strategy, it runs the danger of losing its overall vision and diminishing its support, since different classes of people feel most intensely the pressure of different issues. So while we may say at any given moment that one issue is particularly crucial, it is important that work be done on other aspects of the changes we need at the same time. The task is not finding "the right issue," but bringing clear political analysis to each issue showing how it connects to other problems and to a broad-based feminist view of change in society.

Feminist concerns are not isolated, and oppression does not happen one-by-one-by-one in separate categories. I don't experience homophobia as a separate and distinct category from economic discrimination as a woman. I don't view racism as unconnected to militarism and patriarchal domination of the world.

In order to discuss the specific strategies necessary to get through this transition and bring feminism into the public arena more forcefully, we must first be clear that feminism is a transformational politics. As such, feminism brings a perspective to *any* issue and cannot and must not be limited to a separate ghetto called "women's issues." When dealing with any issue, whether it is budgets or biogenetics or wife battering, feminism as a political perspective is about change in structures—about ending domination and resisting oppression. Feminism is not just incorporating women into existing institutions.

As a politics of transformation, feminism is also relevant to more than a constituency of women. Feminism is a vision born of women that we must offer to and demand of men. I'm tired of letting men off the hook by saying that we don't know whether they can be feminists. Of course they can struggle to be feminists, just as I can and must struggle to be antiracist. If feminism is to be a transforming perspective in the world, then men must also be challenged by it.

This does not mean that we do not also need spaces and organizations for women only. Women need and want and have the right to places where we gather strength and celebrate our culture and make plans only with women. But as a political vision, feminism addresses the future for men as well as for women, for boys as well as for girls, and we must be clear that it is a politics for the future of the world, not just for an isolated handful of the converted.

If we are clear about feminism as a transformational politics, we can develop viable public alternatives to Reaganism and all patriarchal policies. These would be policy statements of how we think the world could be organized in various areas if a feminist approach is taken.

We need feminist budgets for every town, state, and nation. For example, you could take the state budget in Montana, whatever it is, take the same amount of money and prepare a budget of how you would reorganize the use of that money if feminists had control of the state government. When you finish that one, you can do a federal budget. And when you finish that, take on the UN budget! Budgets are good indicators of priorities. If we publicized our approaches, people could see that there are alternatives, that we are talking about something different, and they would get a clearer idea of what a feminist perspective means in practical terms.

I would also like to see feminist plans for housing, transportation, criminal justice, child care, education, agriculture, and so on. We need serious discussion as feminists about how we deal with the issues of defense, not only by doing critiques of militarism, but also by deciding how to cope with the competing powers and threats in this world, as they exist right now. We're not going to solve many of the problems immediately, but we have to put forward other policies and practices, so people can see the difference. If we start with how things are now, then we can talk about how to move, step-by-step, toward policies that are based on very different assumptions and values.

To use such feminist policy statements, when we engage in electoral politics for example, would give people a clear and public statement of what it means to elect a feminist. We would also have something concrete to hold a candidate accountable to after election. To work to elect feminists with clear policy content makes a campaign focus on feminism as a transforming politics rather than just on personality or on adding women without clear political statements of what they represent. It can make electoral politics part of a strategy for change rather than isolated from the movement or a substitute for other action.

Developing such policies is particularly important now because the Reagan crowd is also about a "revolution" in social policies. We could call it reactionary, but if revolution means massive change in government policies, that is what Reagan is pulling off right now. We need a creative counter to these policy changes that is not just a return to where we were in the past. We have to put forward approaches that both deal with the problems that we had before Reagan, and reveal the antiwoman, patriarchal, racist, and sexist assumptions of the right wing.

ORGANIZING FOR ACTION

Perhaps the most important thing that we need to do which underlies everything I've said, is organize. Organize. Organize. Organize. All the great ideas in the world, even feminist budgets, will mean little if we don't also organize people to act on them. We have to organize in a variety of ways.

We need to take what has been the decentralized strength of the women's movement—a multitude of separate women's projects and individuals whose lives have been radically affected by feminism—and find lasting forms for bringing that to more political power. The feminist movement has a wonderful array of creative small groups and projects. Nevertheless, when these don't have any voice in something larger, a lot of their potential power is lost simply because what is learned and done is limited to a small circle and has no larger outlet to affect the public. I don't want to abandon the small-group approach to working, but those groups need to band together into larger units that can have a political impact beyond their numbers. This can take the form of citywide or issue based alliances, which still preserve each group's autonomy. Such feminist alliances then become the basis for coalitions—as a feminist force—with other progressive groups. If we organize ourselves to join coalitions as a community, rather than having women going into other groups one by one, we have a better chance of keeping our feminist values and perspectives in the forefront of that coalition work.

We can utilize the grass-roots decentralized nature of feminism well in organizing around policy changes today, because it is at the state and local level where most of the battles with the right wing are presently focused. But to do that effectively we have to learn how to get our supporters out—to be visible about their politics. If we are trying to influence policy, the policy-makers must know that our people are reliable; if we say that a hundred thousand women will be in Washington, D.C., or a thousand in Billings, Montana, they have to know that they will be there.

The agenda for change is often set by the kind of organizing that goes on around specific issues—particularly ones that are very visible and of considerable interest to people, such as reproductive rights or the Family Protection Act.[1] Whatever the issue, as long as it is one that affects people's lives, the task of the organizer is to show how it connects to other issues of oppression, such as racism, and also to illustrate what that issue means in terms of a vision for the future. The Family Protection Act has demonstrated well these connections as its supporters have sought to bring back the patriarchal order through policies against gays, against assistance to battered women and children, against freedom in the schools, and against the organizing of workers into unions, and so on. It provides a clear case for discussing feminist versus antifeminist perspectives on life.

Another task of organizers is to devise strategies to activate people who care, but who aren't politically active. I saw a chain letter circulating among women artists, which instead of having people send a dollar, said: "Write a letter to Senator So and So (participating in the hearings on abortion), and then send this letter to eight of your friends who want reproductive rights but who aren't doing anything about it."

One mistake we often make is to act as if there is nothing that supporters can do politically if they can't be activists twenty-four hours a day, seven days a week. We must provide channels of action for people who have ten minutes a day or an hour a week, because that very action ties them closer to caring and being willing to risk or move toward a feminist vision. We must mobilize the constituency we have of concerned individuals, recognizing that many of them are very busy just trying to survive and care for their children or parents.

One of Jerry Falwell's[2] organizations sends a little cardboard church to its local supporters, who deposit a quarter a day, and at the end of the week, they dump the money out and send it to Falwell. We can learn something from this approach, which provides a daily connection to one's supporters. When I see community resources—health clinics, women's centers, whatever—closing because they're no longer getting outside support, I worry about our connections to our supporters. This movement did not start with government money. This movement started in the streets and it started with the support of women, and it can only survive if it is supported by us.

I have no objections to feminists getting government money or applying for grants as long as we remember that when they don't give us the money, we have to figure out other ways to do what has to be done by ourselves. We have to go back to our own resources if we believe in what we're doing. If the peasants of Latin America have supported the Catholic Church over the centuries, I don't see any reason why the feminists and gay men and lesbians of North America cannot support our movements.

COALITIONS: THE BOTTOM LINE

Coalitions with other progressive groups are important, but we must be clear about what makes them viable. The basis of coalitions is integrity and respect for what each group describes as its bottom line. Now that's not always easy. But with honest struggle over what each group feels is its necessary, critical minimum demand, coalitions can work. If we are to make compromises on where we put our time and energy, it has to be within that framework. Coalitions don't succeed simply for ideological or charitable reasons. They succeed out of a sense that we need each other, and that none of our constituencies can be mobilized effectively if we abandon their bottom-line concerns. Therefore, we have to know where the critical points are for each group in a coalition.

This is a difficult process, but I saw it work in Houston at the National Women's Conference[3] in 1977. As one of the people organizing the lesbian caucus, I can tell you there were moments in that process when I was ready to scream over the homophobia we encountered.

But we knew our bottom line and were clear about what compromises we could and could not accept. If it had been an event comprised only of feminists, we would have said more about lesbianism. But as a large, diverse conference, we saw our task as coalescing a critical mass recognition and support of the issue of sexual preference through working as part of the broad-based feminist coalition there.

In order to get this recognition, we had to organize our constituency so that other groups would want our support. We were clear that we would not support a compromise that left us out—that we had to have that mutual respect to make the coalition work. But the success of lesbians was based on the fact that we had organized at the state and local level as well as nationally. Our people were there and others knew we had the numbers. Many women realized that they had a lot more to gain by mobilizing our support for the overall plan by including us, than by alienating us, and creating a very public nuisance. Coalitions are possible, but they are only effective when you have mutual respect; when you have a clearly articulated bottom line; and when you have your own group mobilized for action. If you haven't got your own group organized, your own power base, when the crunch comes, no matter how politically correct or charitable people feel, they are going to align with the groups they feel will make them stronger.

We need more feminist alliances or coalitions that do not coalesce around only one event, but that establish themselves over time as representing a variety of groups and types of action, from electoral and media work to demonstrations or public education. Such ongoing political action groups are usually multi-issue and their strength lies in bringing groups together for concerted action on a city- or statewide basis. These groups then become a reliable basis for coalitions with other progressive organizations.

GOING PUBLIC

I think that it is crucial for the feminist movement to become more public. By going public, I mean we need to move beyond the boundaries of our subculture. This does not mean giving up the women's community, which remains our strength, our base, the roots of our analysis and of our sustenance. But to go more public in actions that are visible beyond our circles, demonstrating to the world that feminists have not rolled over and played dead as the media sometimes implies.

Going public involves statements about our visions for change. This can be through vehicles such as feminist policy statements on housing or the budget, as well as by demonstrating the passion of our visions with militancy, such as the civil disobedience and fasting women did in the struggle for ratification of the ERA.[4] Such actions make our issues dramatically visible, seen as matters of life and death. These also capture the public imagination and re-create some of that spirit of discovery that accompanied the early years of women's liberation. We need more creative community or media-oriented events that bring that instant recognition of what is at stake and inspire people to talk about those issues.

One of the important things that I remember about the early days of the women's movement is that we talked about feminism incessantly. We talked in the laundromat, we talked on our jobs, we talked to everybody because we were so excited about what we were discovering. And that talk spread—it excited other women, whether they agreed with us or not. The primary method by which women have become feminists is through talk, through consciousness-raising, and through talk with other feminists. It was not through the government or even the media, but through ourselves. And they cannot take that away. They can deny us money, but they cannot take away ourselves, and the way that this movement has grown is through our "beings"—through being active in the world and being visible.

We have to go public by moving out of what may be comfortable places and engage with women who don't necessarily call themselves feminists. You can go public a hundred different ways—whether that is through media-oriented action or by talking to women on the job or at established women's places. In going public, we risk the vulnerability that goes with such interaction, but the rewards are worth it. The challenge to our ideas that comes with it enables us and our ideas to expand and be more inclusive and more powerful. The interaction that comes with seeing feminism in relation to situations that are not familiar to us, or seeing women of different class or race or geographic backgrounds taking feminism in new directions, is a very good tonic for "tired feminists."

The growth of feminism depends precisely on this interaction—of different generations of feminists and of challenges that make our ideas change and go farther than when they started. If we believe that our visions are visions for the world and not just for a cult, then we have to risk them. For if our ideas cannot survive the test of being engaged in the world more broadly, more publicly, then feminism isn't developed enough yet, and that engagement will help us to know how to remold feminism and make it more viable. For if feminism is to be a force for change in the world, it too must grow and change; if we hoard it or try to hang onto it, we will only take it to the grave with us.

Going public with our visions is ultimately the only way that feminism can become a powerful force for change. There is no way that we can get more people wanting to be feminists and supporting and expanding our visions, if they can't even see them, if they never even hear about feminism from feminists rather than the media, and if they don't sense what we care about and believe in. To be seen as an alternative vision for the world, we first have to be seen. It's that simple and it's that important.

Another part of going public is coming out as feminists—in places where we might feel more comfortable not using the word or even discussing the ideas. An academic study has shown what movement activists have said for years— that the most effective counter to homophobia is "knowing one"—that is, people's antigay ideas change most when they realize that they know and care about someone who is gay. But this change would never occur if no one came out, and therefore most people could go on not realizing that they know one of "us" and accepting society's homophobia unchallenged.

"Coming out" as feminists has a similar power. It forces people to get beyond their media stereotypes and deal concretely with a feminist person and with ideas and visions as embodied by that person. Just as coming out for lesbians and gay men has to be decided on a personal basis, so too does coming out as a

feminist. Still, it is important to recognize the political power of the personal action and to see that it is useful in advancing feminism and combating the power of the right wing, which includes the effort to intimidate us into going back into closets of fear and adopting apolitical life-styles.

Coming out and going public make it possible for us to communicate our feminist visions to people—the majority of whom I believe would welcome alternatives to the state of the world and have not necessarily accepted the right-wing's visions. They want alternatives to living behind closed doors in fear of violence on the streets and contamination in the air; they want decent work that does not destroy or demean them; they want to be able to affirm freedom and justice, but they may not believe that it is possible. We have to show them that we care about those same things and that our movement is about feminist struggles to create visions of new possibilities in the world, beginning with the struggle for possibilities for women and moving outward from there.

We need to invite people to join us in this struggle, approaching them with something to offer, rather than rejecting them as if they were enemies, or ignoring them as if they were not what we think they should be. If we invite them to join us in trying to become and create something different, we engage in politics as a process of seduction as well as of confrontation. Feminism must be a process of seeing and invoking the best in people as well as in confronting the worst. In this we may discover new ways of moving politically that will enable feminist visions to emerge and to provide the leadership so desperately needed to prevent the patriarchal militaristic destruction of the planet.

This is our challenge in the '80s. It is the particular moment that we have been given in human evolution and in the struggle between the forces of justice and domination. We are the inheritors of a proud and living tradition of creators, dreamers, resisters, and organizers who have engaged in the struggle before us, and we shall pass it on to the next generation. However long each of us lives, that's how much time we have, for this is a lifetime process and a lifetime commitment.   [1987]

Terms

1. FAMILY PROTECTION ACT: A 1981 congressional bill to repeal federal laws that promote equal rights for women, including coeducational school-related activities and protection for battered wives, and to provide tax incentives for married mothers to stay at home.
2. JERRY FALWELL: The founder of the Moral Majority, a conservative political organization.
3. NATIONAL WOMEN'S CONFERENCE: As part of the United Nations Decade for Women, each member country held a meeting to establish its national priorities for improving the status of women.
4. ERA: Equal Rights Amendment.

Understanding the Reading

1. Why does Bunch believe that feminism should not be limited to women's issues?
2. What does *'transformational politics'* mean?
3. List Bunch's strategies for achieving a feminist transformation.
4. What actions does she suggest?
5. What advantages does she see in "going public"?

Suggestions for Responding

1. Choose one strategy Bunch suggests, such as a feminist budget or coalition formation, and explore the social effects it could have. ✦

114

A Manifesto for Men

ANDREW KIMBRELL

As many of us come to mourn the lost fathers and sons of the last decades and seek to reestablish our ties to each other and to the earth, we need to find ways to change the political, social, and economic structures that have created this crisis. A "wild man" weekend in the woods, or intense man-to-man discussions, can be key experiences in self-discovery and personal empowerment. But these personal experiences are not enough to reverse the victimization of men. As the men's movement gathers strength, it is critical that this increasing sense of personal liberation be channeled into political action. Without significant changes in our society there will only be continued hopelessness and frustration for men. Moreover, a coordinated movement pressing for the liberation of men could be a key factor in ensuring that the struggle for a sustainable future for humanity and the earth succeeds.

What follows is a brief political platform for men, a short manifesto with which we can begin the process of organizing men as a positive political force working for a better future. This is the next step for the men's movement.

FATHERS AND CHILDREN

Political efforts focusing on the family must reassert men's bonds with the family and reverse the "lost father" syndrome. While any long-term plan for men's liberation requires significant changes in the very structure of our work and economic institutions, a number of intermediate steps are possible: We need to take a leadership role in supporting parental leave legislation, which gives working parents the right to take time from work to care for children or other family members. And we need to target the Bush administration for vetoing this vital legislation. Also needed is pro-child tax relief such as greatly expanding the young child tax credit, which would provide income relief and tax breaks to families at a point when children need the most parental care and when income may be the lowest.

We should also be in the forefront of the movement pushing for changes in the workplace including more flexible hours, part-time work, job sharing, and home-based employment. As economic analyst William R. Mattox Jr. notes, a simple step toward making home-based employment more viable would be to loosen restrictions on claiming home office expenses as a tax deduction for parents. Men must also work strenuously in the legal arena to promote more liberal visitation rights for non-custodial parents and to assert appropriateness of the father as a custodial parent. Non-traditional family structures should also be given more recognition in our society, with acknowledgment of men's important roles as stepfathers, foster fathers, uncles, brothers, and mentors. We must seek legislative ways to recognize many men's commitments that do not fit traditional definitions of family.

ECOLOGY AS MALE POLITICS

A sustainable environment is not merely one issue among others. It is the crux of all issues in our age, including men's politics. The ecological struggles of our time offer a unique forum in which men can express their renewed sense of the wild and their traditional roles as creators, defenders of the family, and careful stewards of the earth.

The alienation of men from their rootedness to the land has deprived us all of what John Muir[1] called the "heart of wilderness." As part of our efforts to re-experience the wild in ourselves, we should actively become involved in experiencing the wilderness first hand and organize support for the protection of nature and endangered species. Men should also become what Robert Bly[2] has called "inner warriors" for the earth, involving themselves in non-violent civil disobedience to protect wilderness areas from further destruction.

An important aspect of the masculine ethic is defense of family. Pesticides and other toxic pollutants that poison our food, homes, water, and air represent a real danger, especially to children. Men need to be adamant in their call for limitations on the use of chemicals.

Wendell Berry[3] has pointed out that the ecological crisis is also a crisis of agriculture. If men are to recapture a true sense of stewardship and husbandry and affirm the "seedbearing," creative capacity of the male, they must, to the extent possible, become involved in sustainable agriculture and organic farming and gardening. We should also initiate and support legislation that sustains our farming communities.

MEN IN THE CLASSROOMS AND COMMUNITY

In many communities, especially inner cities, men are absent not only from homes but also from the schools. Men must support the current efforts by black men's groups around the country to implement male-only early-grade classes taught by men. These programs provide role models and a surrogate paternal presence for young black males. We should also commit ourselves to having a far greater male presence in all elementary school education. Recent studies have shown that male grade school students have a higher level of achievement when they are taught by male teachers. Part-time or full-time home schooling options can also be helpful in providing men a great opportunity to be teachers—not just temperaments—to their children.

We need to revive our concern for community. Community-based boys' clubs, scout troops, sports leagues, and big brother programs have achieved significant success in helping fatherless male children find self-esteem. Men's groups must work to strengthen these organizations.

MEN'S MINDS, MEN'S BODIES, AND WORK

Men need to join together to fight threats to male health including suicide, drug and alcohol abuse, AIDS, and stress diseases. We should support active prevention and education efforts aimed at these deadly threats. Most importantly, men need to be leaders in initiating and supporting holistic and psychotherapeutic approaches that directly link many of these health threats to the coercive nature of the male mystique and the current economic system. Changes in diet, reduction of drug and alcohol use, less stressful work environments, greater nurturing of and caring for men by other men, and fighting racism, hopelessness, and homelessness are all important, interconnected aspects of any male health initiative.

MEN WITHOUT HOPE OR HOMES

Men need to support measures that promote small business and entrepreneurship, which will allow more people to engage in crafts and human-scale, community-oriented enterprises. Also important is a commitment to appropriate, human-scale technologies such as renewable energy sources. Industrial and other inappropriate technologies have led to men's dispossession, degradation—and increasingly to unemployment.

A related struggle is eliminating racism. No group of men is more dispossessed than minority men. White men should support and network with African-American and other minority men's groups. Violence and discrimination against men because of their sexual preference should also be challenged.

Men, who represent more than four-fifths of the homeless, can no longer ignore this increasing social tragedy. Men's councils should develop support groups for the homeless in their communities.

THE HOLOCAUST OF MEN

As the primary victims of mechanized war, men must oppose this continued slaughter. Men need to realize that the traditional male concepts of the noble warrior are undermined and caricatured in the technological nightmare of modern warfare. Men must together become prime movers in dismantling the military-industrial establishment and redistributing defense spending toward a sustainable environment and protection of family, school, and community.

MEN'S ACTION NETWORK

No area of the men's political agenda will be realized until men can establish a network of activists to create collective action. A first step might be to create a high-profile national coalition of the men's councils that are growing around the country. This coalition, which could be called the Men's Action Network (MAN), could call for a national conference to define a comprehensive platform of men's concerns and to provide the political muscle to implement those ideas.

A MAN COULD STAND UP

The current generation of men face a unique moment in history. Though often still trapped by economic coercion and psychological co-option, we are beginning to see that there is a profound choice ahead. Will we choose to remain subservient tools of social and environmental destruction or to fight for rediscovery of the male as a full partner and participant in family, community, and the earth? Will we remain mesmerized by the male mystique, or will we reclaim the true meaning of our masculinity?

There is a world to gain. The male mystique, in which many of today's men—especially the most politically powerful—are trapped, is threatening the family and the planet with irreversible destruction. A men's movement based on the recovery of masculinity could renew much of the world we have lost. By changing types of work and work hours, we could break our subordination to corporate managers and return much of our work and lives to the household. We could once again be teaching, nurturing presences to our children. By devoting ourselves to meaningful work with appropriate technology, we could recover independence in our work and our spirit. By caring for each other, we could recover the dignity of our gender and heal the wounds of addiction and self-destruction. By becoming husbands to the earth, we could protect the wild and recover our creative connections with the forces and rhythms of nature.

Ultimately we must help fashion a world without the daily frustration and sorrow of having to view each other as a collection of competitors instead of a community of friends. We must celebrate the essence and rituals of our masculinity. We can no longer passively submit to the destruction of the household, the demise of self-employment, the disintegration of family and community, and the desecration of our earth.

Shortly after the First World War, Ford Madox Ford, one of this century's greatest writers, depicted 20th century men as continually pinned down in their trenches, unable to stand up for fear of annihilation. As the century closes, men remain pinned down by an economic and political system that daily forces millions of us into meaningless work, powerless lives, and self-destruction. The time has come for men to stand up. [1991]

Terms

1. JOHN MUIR: An American naturalist and conservationist.
2. ROBERT BLY: The author of *Iron John* and advocate of the men's movement, which

emphasizes men's exploring their inner maleness and bonding with other men.

3. WENDELL BERRY: A contemporary American writer and university professor who has a special interest in the environment.

Understanding the Reading

1. Why does Kimbrell think men need to focus on family?
2. Why would environmental activism be especially beneficial to men?
3. What can men do to improve their communities?
4. How can men improve their health?
5. Why should men be concerned about war?
6. What does Kimbrell see as the benefits men would gain by implementing his program?

Suggestions for Responding

1. Do you agree or disagree with Kimbrell that men have been victimized by society? Why or why not? ◆

115

Lesbian Teen Sues District for Bias

PETER Y. HONG

Last March, a simple question from a classmate pushed Ashly Massey from her comfortable life as an eighth-grader in the high desert community of Banning into the midst of a civil rights battle with her school.

"Are you gay?" a friend asked curiously, without any sign of hostility, recalled Ashly, now 15. The girls were in the school locker room, changing after gym class. As she thought of how, or whether, to answer, Ashly said another student didn't wait for her answer, loudly blurting out: "She's a lesbian!"

The exchange would lead to Ashly's expulsion from gym class, and weeks of taunts and insults by classmates about her acknowledged lesbianism—actions that at least one state offi-

cial said were probably a violation of the Education Code.

Banning Unified School District Supt. Kathleen McNamara said Tuesday that she would not comment on the case, nor would officials at the school, but a district official said the school's actions were improper.

Ashly and her mother, Amelia Massey, described the teen's experience Tuesday as they announced the filing of a federal civil rights lawsuit against the Banning district, the superintendent, the principal and then-vice principal of Coombs Middle School, and Karen Gill, the physical education teacher who threw Ashly out of class.

The suit, filed in U.S. District Court in Riverside, says the district violated the equal protection clause of the Constitution. It seeks changes in school policies to handle harassment of students based on sexual orientation, as well as unspecified monetary damages.

One gay rights activist said she was not shocked by the incident, and that gyms and locker rooms are often scenes of the most difficult confrontations for gay and lesbian students.

Ashly recalled Tuesday that the exchange began almost innocently with the friend's question about her sexual orientation. But then the instructor, Gill, pulled her aside.

"She reprimanded me," Ashly recalled Tuesday in an interview at her house in neighboring Beaumont. "She said, 'It's nobody's business but yours. Keep it to yourself.'"

The next day, Ashly said Gill told her, without explanation, to go to the principal's office, where she sat until the physical education class ended. That became Ashly's routine for the next two weeks, during which, she said, no one told her why she was barred from class or whether she was being punished.

She said she soon found herself targeted by classmates who hurled insults at her. Friends drifted away, invitations to sleepovers stopped and she saw her name invoked in hateful graffiti around the campus in the working-class community on the road to Palm Springs.

Ashly, who acknowledges being gay, said she hoped her stand would inspire other youths. "I hope other kids see me standing up," she said, "and maybe they'll take a stand too. Nobody should have to hide who they are."

The Masseys said they had moved two years ago from Palm Desert, where the large gay population made the teen's sexual orientation much more acceptable. In that environment, as a 13-year-old, Ashly came out as a lesbian, her mother said.

Then they arrived in this more conservative, working-class region of new subdivisions, built atop grazing land, where her newly declared sexual orientation was not so readily acceptable.

When the taunts reached a crescendo last year, the girl said that at one point she even packed a bag and considered running away to San Francisco.

Randy Patterson, president of the Banning Unified school board, said the board regretted the incident and was sorry that a student had been treated unfairly.

"Yeah, we feel bad," Patterson said. "Nothing like this has happened before. No one should be made uncomfortable due to their orientation or religion or race, color, creed, national origin." Patterson said teachers in the 4,000-student district go through diversity training each year. He would not comment on whether any staff members were disciplined as a result of the incident involving Ashly.

Marcia Matthews, an American Civil Liberties Union lawyer representing the Masseys, said the lawsuit is one of the first cases invoking the Student Safety and Violence Prevention Act, a state law enacted in 2000 following a series of campus shootings.

Roger Wolfertz, deputy general counsel for the California Department of Education, said it appeared clear that the girl's rights were violated.

"Just because this person is a disclosed homosexual . . . it would be illegal to kick her out of the class just for that," he said.

Janeane Vigliotti, chairwoman of the Gay, Lesbian, Straight Education Network in Los Angeles, said she was not surprised by the incident.

"People get panicky whenever it has to do with sexuality and they'll do something rash," she said. "Gay children do not like going to P.E. classes, and this is one of the reasons why."

Ashly, a stocky girl who wears her short brown hair in spikes, is now in ninth grade at a high school in Beaumont. The family moved to the neighboring community this summer for reasons that had nothing to do with the school incident, they said.

Amelia Massey said Banning school district officials and the staff at Coombs Middle School did little to help her daughter as she was being taunted. The Masseys believe the initial locker room incident might have blown over if not for Gill's sharp reaction.

"I asked if there was any misconduct or anything inappropriate. The teacher said, 'No.' So I said, 'I don't know what to tell you,'" the mother said.

Massey, who is a registered nurse, said Gill then told her that other girls were simply uncomfortable having Ashly in the locker room.

"It wouldn't have been a big deal," Massey said. "They would have found something bigger and better to talk about."

Ashly said her problems only were exacerbated when other students saw her sitting in the office day after day. "I felt alienated," she said. "People would point and laugh at me."

Massey said her daughter initially did not talk to her about the incident, but she sensed that Ashly was troubled.

Soon after the incident, Ashly had to shorten her schedule because of a medical treatment and so dropped the gym class for the remainder of the year.

Ashly and her mother said that did not stop the taunts. The mother called the National Center for Lesbian Rights in San Francisco, and a lawyer there agreed to take on the case. The group joined with the ACLU of Southern California to file the lawsuit.   [2002]

Understanding the Reading

1. What began Ashly's torture at school?
2. How did the gym teacher handle it?
3. How did Ashly become a target for verbal abuse throughout the school?
4. How did the rest of the school staff respond?

Suggestions for Responding

1. Research the Equal Protection clause of the U.S. Constitution.
2. Discuss whether you believe the family will win this case and whether they should have responded in some other way. ✦

116

The Campus Environment for Gay and Lesbian Life

JOHN D'EMILIO

Just over twenty years ago, a new generation of feminists coined the phrase "the personal is political." Although the slogan has carried different meanings for those who use it, one implication has been to challenge our notions of private and public. Feminists have argued, and rightly so, that defining women's sphere and women's concerns as "private" has effectively excluded women from full and equal participation in the "public realm." As more and more women in the 1970s and 1980s fought for entry into academic life, higher education institutions increasingly have had to deal with a host of issues that were once safely tucked away in the private domain.

Colleges and universities in the pre-feminist era addressed privacy only in the breach, particularly with respect to matters of sexual identity. Consider the following examples:

- In 1959, at a small midwestern college, a student told her faculty adviser that one of her friends was a homosexual. The adviser informed a dean, who called in the student in question and pressured him into naming others. Within twenty-four hours, three students had been expelled; a week later, one of them [hanged] himself.

- About the same time, a faculty member at a Big Ten[1] school was arrested in mid-semester on a morals charge (at that time, *all* homosexual expression was subject to criminal penalties). The police alerted the administration, and the professor was summarily told to leave the campus. He never appeared before his classes again.

- At an elite college in the Northeast, male students in the 1960s were in the habit of training a telescope on the windows of the women's dormitories. In one instance, they spied two female students erotically engaged. The women—not the men—were disciplined.

- At a women's college in New England, where accusations of lesbianism were periodically leveled against roommates in the 1960s, the standard solution was to separate the accused by housing them in different dorms.

I could list many more such examples. They came to me not through research but through the gay and lesbian academic grapevine. Stories like these are the substance of an oral tradition by which gay academics who came of age before the 1970s warned one another of the dangers they faced and socialized their younger peers into necessary habits of caution and discretion.

The point, I trust, is clear. For gay men and lesbians, the past is a history of privacy invaded, of an academy that enforced, maintained, and reproduced a particular moral order—a moral order aggressively antagonistic toward homosexual expression.

Since 1969, when the Stonewall Riots[2] in New York City ushered in the gay liberation movement, activists across the country have challenged that order. We have formed organizations by the thousands, lobbied legislatures, initiated public education campaigns, engaged in civil disobedience, and promoted self-help efforts. We have attempted to emancipate gays and lesbians from the laws, policies, scientific theories, and cultural attitudes that have consigned us to an inferior position in society.

When one considers that the political climate for most of the last twenty years has been conservative, and that this new conservatism has taken shape largely through an appeal to "traditional" notions of family, sexuality, and gender roles, the successes of the gay movement appear rather impressive. Half the states have repealed their sodomy laws.[3] Many of the nation's largest cities have enacted some form of gay civil rights ordinance, and a number of states are seriously debating the issue. The American Psychiatric Association has removed homosexuality from its list of mental disorders. Several religious denominations are revising their positions on the morality of homosexual relationships. And lesbian and gay organizations around the country are better financed and more stable now than at any point in their past.

Those of us associated with institutions of higher education have contributed to this movement and have benefited from it as well. Because the birth of gay liberation was so closely tied to the social movements of the 1960s, student groups have been part of the gay political and social landscape from the beginning. Currently, more than four hundred of these groups exist, in community colleges and research universities, in public institutions and private ones. Braving the ostracism and harassment that visibility sometimes brings, these young women and men have often had to battle for recognition and funding. In the process, their struggles have created a substantial body of judicial opinion that protects gay student groups as an expression of First Amendment rights of speech and assembly.

Faculty members, too, have organized. Initially forming separate organizations, such as the Gay Academic Union, they have increasingly turned to their professional associations as venues for action. Most social science and humanities disciplines now have lesbian and gay caucuses that publish newsletters, review current literature, and sponsor well-attended sessions at annual meetings. A vibrant new scholarship has emerged in the last decade that is substantial enough to spark a movement for gay studies programs in institutions as diverse as San Francisco City College, Yale University, and the City University of New York.

If one's reference point is university life a generation ago, one can say that things *are* getting better for gay faculty, students, administrators, and staff. Grit, courage, and determination have opened up some space in which it is possible to live, breathe, and work openly. Our situation no longer appears uniformly grim.

Nevertheless, being openly gay on campus still goes against the grain. Despite the changes in American society in the last two decades, gay people are still swimming in a largely oppressive sea. Most campuses do not have gay student groups. Most gay faculty members and administrators have not come out. Even on campuses that have proven responsive to gay and lesbian concerns, progress has often come through the

work of a mere handful of individuals who have chosen to be visible. And, although I do not have statistics to measure this precisely, I know that there are still many, many campuses in the United States where no lesbian or gay man feels safe enough to come out. From a gay vantage point, something is still wrong in the academy.

Oppression in its many forms is still alive, and the university is not immune to it. Indeed, as the gay population has become a better organized and stronger force in the 1980s, we have also become easier to target. In recent years, harassment, violence, and other hate-motivated acts against lesbians and gay men have surfaced with alarming frequency on campuses across the country. Institutions such as the University of Kansas and the University of Chicago, to name just two, have witnessed campaigns of terror against their gay members. At Pennsylvania State University, a report on tolerance found that bias-motivated incidents most frequently targeted gay people.

Unlike many other groups—women and African Americans, for instance—in which one's identity is clear for the world to see, most gay men and lesbians have the option to remain invisible. I cannot fault individuals who choose that path: the costs of visibility often can be high. Yet the fear that compels most gay people to remain hidden exacts a price of its own. It leads us to doubt our own self-worth and dignity. It encourages us to remain isolated and detached from our colleagues and peers, as too much familiarity can lead to exposure. And it often results in habitual patterns of mistrust and defensiveness because anyone, potentially, may cause our downfall. Hence, speaking about gay oppression involves not only addressing injustice in the abstract but also acknowledging the emotional toll it levies on particular individuals and the institutions of which they are a part.

For reasons that I cannot quite fathom, I still expect the academy to embrace higher standards of civility, decency, and justice than the society around it. Having been granted the extraordinary privilege of thinking critically as a way of life, we should be astute enough to recognize when a group of people is being systematically mistreated. We have the intelligence to devise solutions to problems that appear in our community. I expect us also to have the courage to lead rather than follow.

Although gay oppression has deep roots in American society, the actions that would combat it effectively on campuses are not especially difficult to devise and formulate. What sort of policies would make a difference? What would a gay-positive institution look like?

One set of policies would place institutions of higher education firmly on the side of equal treatment. Gay faculty, administrators, staff, and students need to know that their school is committed to fairness, to treating us on the basis of our abilities. At a minimum that would mean:

A nondiscrimination policy, formally enacted, openly announced, and in print wherever the institution proclaims its policy with regard to race, gender, and religion. Such a policy would apply to hiring, promotion, tenure, admissions, and financial aid. Because of the history of discrimination in this country, it is not enough for an administration to claim that it subscribes to the principle of fairness for everyone. Sexual orientation, sexual preference, sexual identity, or whatever term one chooses to adopt, needs to be explicitly acknowledged.

Spousal benefits for the partners of gay men and lesbians, at every level of institutional life and for every service that is normally provided to husbands and wives. These benefits include health insurance, library privileges, access to the gym and other recreational facilities, listings in school directories if spouses are customarily listed, and access to married students' housing for gay and lesbian couples.

An approach to gay student groups that is identical to that for all other groups with regard to recognition procedures, funding, and access to facilities. Administrators who place obstructions in the way of these groups are doing a costly disservice to their institutions since courts have uniformly sustained the rights of gay students to organize.

Subscribing to the above policies would simply place lesbians and gays in a *de jure*[4] position of parity. Implementing these measures would go a long way toward alleviating the fears that we live with, integrating us fully into the life of the campus, and letting us know that we are valued and "welcomed."

The university's responsibility towards its gay members goes well beyond these elementary procedures of fairness, however. Administrators will need to take an activist stance to counteract the misinformation about gays and lesbians that many members of the university community have, the cultural prejudices that are still endemic in the United States, and the growing problem of hate-motivated incidents. The following areas need attention:

1. One of the prime locations where harassment occurs is in residence halls. Dormitory directors and their assistants need to be sensitized about gay issues and trained in how to respond quickly and firmly to instances of oppressive behavior and harassment. In an age when heterosexual undergraduates routinely hold hands, walk arm-in-arm, and engage in other simple displays of affection, lesbian and gay students need to know that they will not have their rooms ransacked, or their physical safety endangered, for doing the same. They also need reassurance that campus activism on gay issues will not come back to haunt them when they return to their dorms each night.

2. Student affairs programming is an important tool in fostering toleration, understanding, and enthusiasm for differences in culture and identity. Resources should be made available to sponsor special gay awareness week events, as well as to integrate gay films, public lectures, and other events and activities into the regular programming.

3. Late adolescence is an especially stressful time for gay men and lesbians. These may be the years when they become sexually active, form their first relationships, and grapple with issues of identity. School counseling services need personnel who are sensitive to these issues and who can foster self-acceptance and self-esteem rather than reinforce self-hatred.

4. Because the issues and situations affecting lesbians and gay men range widely across the structure of large and medium-size campuses, hiring an "ombudsperson" for gay and lesbian concerns makes good institutional sense. Someone who can think expansively about these issues, provide a resource where

needed, and intervene decisively in emergencies can move a whole campus forward.

5. When hate-motivated incidents occur—and the evidence of the last few years suggests that they happen with greater frequency than we care to admit—the *highest* officers of the university need to exercise their *full* authority in condemning the attacks and correcting the underlying problems which encourage such incidents. Bias-motivated incidents are awful, but they also offer a unique opportunity for raising consciousness and for shifting the climate of opinion on a campus.
6. An institution that prohibits discrimination against gays ought not to countenance the presence on campus of institutions and organizations that engage in such discrimination. The government intelligence agencies and the military are the most egregious perpetrators of anti-gay bias. Recent actions by the military against its gay and lesbian personnel amount to a form of terrorism. Military recruiters and ROTC programs ought to be banned from American campuses until the armed forces change their policies.
7. Last, but not least, is the issue of research. The 1980s have witnessed an efflorescence of scholarship on gay and lesbian issues in several disciplines. Yet many topics go begging for researchers because faculty members know that prejudiced department heads and tenure committees will label such work trivial and insignificant. Gay scholarship, opening as it does a new window on human experience, must be encouraged.

On sunny mornings, I am optimistic that the 1990s will see a dramatic improvement in the quality of life for gay men and lesbians in higher education: the body of scholarship is growing and pressure for gay studies programs will mount; academics in many disciplines have created stable and permanent caucuses which will strengthen our networks; regional associations of gay student groups are forming to reinforce those groups already established on individual campuses. In addition, the National Gay and Lesbian Task Force in Washington, D.C., recently initiated a campus-organizing project so that gay men and lesbians on each campus no longer have to reinvent the wheel.

Of equal importance, perhaps, some administrators are moving beyond the most elementary issues of visibility and recognition. They are addressing the key areas of equal treatment and deep-rooted prejudice. Such a stance—on every campus—is long overdue.   [1990]

Terms

1. BIG TEN: The major midwestern universities.
2. STONEWALL RIOTS: After a raid on a gay bar in New York City called the Stonewall, gays rioted in protest against police brutality.
3. SODOMY LAWS: Laws criminalizing anal and oral intercourse.
4. *DE JURE*: According to law.

Understanding the Reading

1. Explain the distinctions between private and public.
2. What strategies has the gay liberation movement employed?
3. What effects has gay liberation had on academic institutions?
4. What problems do gay men and lesbians face on college campuses?
5. Explain D'Emilio's plan for combatting gay and lesbian oppression on college campuses.

Suggestions for Responding

1. Argue for or against one of the policies or practices D'Emilio recommends.
2. Develop a plan for action to implement one strategy or a group of strategies you identified in response to the Kimbrell reading. ◆

117

Resistance to Change

KATHLEEN RYAN

Resisting change is a very natural behavior; it is neither "good" nor "bad." Everyone does it from time to time. In many ways, resisting change is like driving in fog. When drivers enter a patch of fog, they should slow down, get a feel for the conditions, and then proceed at an appropriate pace. People making their way through the ambiguity and disorder of change have similar reactions. Their attitude is affected by their past experiences, their confidence in their skills, and by whether they interpreted the situation as an adventure or a problem. Their pace is influenced by how much they can learn about the change, their freedom to make decisions, and their ability to take action. In an ideal situation, past and present circumstances combine to give individuals the necessary confidence, freedom, and skills to move successfully and comfortably through a time of change. Unfortunately, few of us operate within ideal situations; we are often slowed down and encumbered by a variety of unanswered questions and unsettled concerns.

Handling resistance effectively is the unspoken challenge faced by anyone who wants to do things differently. Never knowing when it might actually surface, the change agent nevertheless needs to be ready for resistance. He or she needs to be able to:

1. Recognize resistance when it occurs;
2. Respond to the resistant person(s) in ways that identify the reasons behind the resistance;
3. Work, to whatever degree possible, with the resistant person(s) to answer the questions and ease the concerns which form the source of the resistance.

RECOGNIZING RESISTANCE

To recognize resistance when it occurs, one needs to have a sense of how resistance looks, feels, and sounds. Language and behavior are two of the primary means for identifying the source of resistance. At times the clues they give are very visible, allowing the underlying issue to be recognized easily. At other times, the source of the resistance is essentially hidden, hard to identify or connect to an event or situation.

To better understand *visible resistance,* imagine a discussion of the way the advertising media influence current images of men and women. As the conversation becomes increasingly animated, one person becomes quite hos-

tile in [her] comments. Finally, in a burst of frustration, she suddenly stands and shouts, "This is the most ridiculous discussion I've ever been in!" She leaves the room and slams the door on her way out. The exclamation of frustration, the departure, and the slamming of the door are all rather dramatic signs of resistance to a particular point or issue being discussed: They are *visible* signs of resistance.

The less obvious, *hidden resistance* is of course more difficult to identify. Consider the hypothetical case of a supervisor and a male employee. Because of a recent decision to rotate jobs temporarily, the male employee will be assigned to an all-female work crew for three months. After announcing the decision, the supervisor notices that the employee's participation in staff meetings is less enthusiastic. Even though the employee has sometimes spoken positively about the change, his general attitude on the job is less pleasant, he is less patient, and he does not seem to produce the usual amount or quality of work. In this case, the employee's small changes in attitude and behavior—extended over a period of time—can be interpreted as signs of resistance to the new job assignment. Until the supervisor confronts the employee, however, he or she has no way of knowing whether the resistance actually exists, and if so, what its cause might be.

The more skilled you become at listening and watching for signs of resistance to change, the better you will be at managing change. Simply put, if you are unable to recognize resistance when it occurs, it will be very difficult for you to take action to overcome it.

REASONS AND CLUES

People resist change for a variety of reasons. The first clues about resistance are usually found in the words people speak and in their behavior. While behavioral signs of resistance are more general, language often gives very direct clues to the reasons for resistance. The material presented in this section is designed to expand your awareness of how people's language and behavior can be tied to very specific reasons for resisting change. As you read through the following lists, think of those with whom you live and work. Think of yourself as well. Note any familiar linguistic or behavioral clues to resistance to change.

REASONS FOR RESISTANCE

1. Information. People don't have enough or accurate information about the change.

WORDS OF RESISTANCE

"I've never heard of a man who's been very successful in that kind of role."

"Well, I'm sorry, but I won't go along with this until somebody can show me an example of where she's been successful with this idea before."

2. Influence. People have a strong desire to influence what happens to them in their work and their environment. If they cannot influence these decisions, they may resist because they feel left out.

"Nobody consulted me before bringing these women down here in the shop."

"I'll never understand why they don't talk to the people who are really doing the work before they make their decisions."

3. Feelings. People have emotional reactions to change. For example, they may become angry, frustrated, or scared by something new. These feelings often remain unspoken and trigger resistance.

"I'm worried about how those guys are going to react to me. I frankly don't know if it's worth the effort or not."

"My child is not going through any program like that. I'll take him out of school before I let them teach him about *those* kinds of things."

4. Control. People have a need to control information, decisions, or other people. If they cannot do so, they may resist.

"How do you expect me to do my part when I don't have access to the information I need?"

"I haven't had enough time to coach her on the budgeting issues. I don't think she's ready for the promotion just yet."

5. Benefits. People don't see any advantage to changing.

"I wish someone would tell me what they think is so great about this new plan."

"Why in the world do you want to go back to school? You're already overqualified for half the jobs you apply for!"

REASONS FOR RESISTANCE

6. Stress. People feel overloaded; they don't want the added stress of another change.

WORDS OF RESISTANCE

"If you tell the line managers that they've got to be responsible for this EEO[1] training, you'll have a revolt on your hands. They've already got too much to handle."

"You want me to be the first woman to go out on the line? Forget it. I don't need that kind of hassle."

7. Desire to be right. People think that if they change, all their previous effort will be "wrong." They have a strong desire to be "right" in their thinking and behavior.

"I told you all along, women don't want this 'sensitive male' stuff. They want a man who can tell them what to do."

"I don't know exactly what to do. I'd hate to take a position that really upsets the way things are done around here."

8. Ability. People are not confident about their ability to handle new responsibilities or perform new tasks required by a change.

"Oh, I could never do that!"

"Nobody told me that when I volunteered for this position I'd have to play nursemaid to a bunch of prima donnas. I just want to get the job done. They keep slowing things down with all their new ideas. I don't know how to handle them."

9. Routine. People don't want to alter their living or working conditions or routine.

"You mean to tell me we may have to talk different around here?"

"There's something you need to know if you're going to fit in here. There are certain things that have always been done certain ways."

10. Status. People don't want to lose their status, authority, or power.

"What do you mean they want a female engineer out there in the field? Don't you know what they will do to morale?"

"Why do we need all these experts to tell us what to do? We're doing just fine."

REASONS FOR RESISTANCE	WORDS OF RESISTANCE	VISIBLE RESISTANCE	HIDDEN RESISTANCE
11. Structure. People have a need for structure. Change can create confusion about roles, responsibilities, and procedures.	"The new policy is clear on this issue. You can't expect me to ignore it." "Was this your father's idea?"	• constant excuses for poor performance • deliberately distorting information • cynical expression and tone • complaining to others	• forgetting • procrastination • appearing agreeable, but taking no action • signs of depression or sadness • unusual swearing • negative facial expressions • spreading gossip
12. Values. People disagree with the basic values or concepts behind the change. They may think that the change violates a basic belief about people or work, or that the change will have an undesirable effect.	"But what about the person who'll use this law to damage someone's career? If we tell our employees about this, all we're going to be doing is investigating complaints." "Schools should not have anything to do with teaching children about sexuality and family decision-making. That's the parents' job."		

While words are an important part of anyone's communication, they are not the only way we communicate. Behavior—nonverbal communication—can be just as important as words in identifying the source of resistance to change. Behavioral signs of resistance, especially when unaccompanied by words, are often very difficult to tie to resistance. Because of this, it is wise to become familiar with some of the behavioral clues to visible and hidden resistance. Some of those clues are listed here:

Behavioral Clues to Resistance to Change

VISIBLE RESISTANCE
- name-calling
- loud sighing
- unusual non-participation
- unexpected cool, aloof manner
- argumentative behavior
- obvious avoidance
- walking away
- walking out
- deliberately changing the subject
- missing appointments
- no follow-through on specific commitments
- sullen posture
- critical jokes
- quitting
- angry outbursts
- telling others it won't work
- poor attendance

HIDDEN RESISTANCE
- increased illnesses
- acting "dumb"
- blasé, disinterested attitude
- delaying tactics
- losing things
- pretending to lack information
- not passing along information
- work slow-down
- indirect communication (innuendo)
- not returning phone calls
- being placed last on a busy agenda
- unnecessarily referring a question to someone else
- consistent day-dreaming
- lack of thorough preparation
- tardiness

If we were physicians, we would look for the symptoms of a disease or illness. We would observe those symptoms carefully and use them as a basis for our diagnosis. We would not treat the disease without first considering its underlying cause. The words and behaviors listed above should be regarded in the same manner—as symptoms of resistance and clues to its cause, clues that must be considered in context of the situation in which they appear.

The most direct way to understand why a person is resisting a change is to ask the person. For example:

> You are a mid-level manager working in a large organization which has become increasingly public about its commitment to equal opportunity for women and minorities. You have been asked to join a task force which will investigate possible pay discrepancies between job classifications—including those which have been traditionally held by female employees. You become aware that your task force meetings seem to get bogged down with reports and discussions of procedures, rather than with defining critical problems and addressing questions that need attention. The task force chair-person is a colleague of yours and is known for her skillful facilitation of meetings, and it is more and more difficult to find a time when everyone can meet. You decide, because of her behavior, that the task force chairperson is somehow resisting the potential changes involved in this work. You decide to investigate further, to see if you are right.

In such a case, you might say:

> "Jane, I get the feeling you're not very comfortable with your role on this task force. You don't seem to be approaching the facilitation with your usual flair."

Or:

"Tell me what you think about where all this work will lead."

Or:

"I'll bet you're feeling some extra pressure because of chairing this task force, Jane. Do you have the kind of clerical support to be able to handle this and your regular work too?"

In cases such as these, you want to create an opportunity for the person who you think is resisting to talk. If this person trusts and respects you, you have a relatively good chance to discover whether your suspicions about the resistance are correct or not. Once you confirm that resistance exists, you should identify the reason for it. This information is critical for any action you subsequently take to overcome the resistance. In this case, Jane may be resisting because of:

Values. She believes the organization could work on other issues which would better, and more immediately, promote equal opportunity.

Benefits. Because of previous experiences with other task forces, Jane believes that in the end, no one will benefit from all this work, and no substantial changes will really take place.

Stress. She has too many other responsibilities to give this project the attention it needs.

Because you are not Jane's superior, your role in helping her to overcome her resistance is somewhat limited. There are some very positive things you could do, however.

Values. If you believe the work of this task force *is* critical for developing equal opportunity, say so. Present your reasons, along with information about studies in other organizations which have increased wage equity and reduced the risk of a disruptive, painful strike for recognition of comparable worth.

Benefits. Talk with Jane to find out her past experiences. If you agree that there's a good chance nothing will come of your current work, raise that issue with the entire task force. With Jane, or in the task force, brainstorm strategies for overcoming that likelihood. Play an active part, behind the scenes or visibly, to act on those strategies.

Stress. Work with Jane to identify the time and resource problems that are increasing her stress. Once again, develop strategies to overcome the

problems, including a proposal to Jane's boss which outlines the problems and asks for additional resources. Offer to do what you can to ease the burden of her responsibilities. Follow through on those commitments.   [1985]

Terms

1. EEO: Employment Opportunity.

Understanding the Reading

1. Explain the difference between visible resistance and hidden resistance.
2. Explain the twelve reasons for resistance.
3. How do information, feelings, and influence affect resistance?

Suggestions for Responding

1. Describe a time when someone tried to impose a change on you that you did not like. In what ways did you resist? How was the conflict finally resolved?
2. Explain what kinds of resistance to your plan of action you anticipate and how you plan to handle them. ✦

118

The Campus Climate for Gay Students

ROBERT A. RHOADS

Coming out is ultimately liberating for gays, but the process is exhausting and fraught with many fears and doubts—even at a college or university. Diversity is often celebrated rhetorically on college campuses, but they can be uncomprehending, intolerant, even hostile places for lesbian, gay, and bisexual students.

I have some idea of how difficult and significant it is for gay students to come out in college, because I have spent two years researching the subject. I have read all the literature that I can find, and I have interviewed gay students, attended meetings of gay-rights groups, participated in political protests and marches sponsored by gay organizations, and hung out with gay students at bars, clubs, and college parties. Through my research and the friendships that grew out of it, I have begun to understand why coming out is so important in seeking respect for oneself and in celebrating oneself and the freedom of leaving "the closet."

But it wasn't always that way. Three years ago, I was a doctoral student in higher education, at the dissertation phase of my academic career. My thoughts about possible topics were shaped by two principal interests: student culture and social justice. As I considered possible topics, the question kept recurring: Why not study gay students and their struggles at college? It seemed an obvious choice given my interests, but I had one big obstacle to overcome: my own homophobia. As a heterosexual male, I could not understand why gays had to make such a big deal about their sexuality.

When I began research in the fall of 1991, one of my biggest fears was being mistaken for a gay man. I believed I was an accepting and a tolerant person and open to differences, but I still had to overcome my fear of homosexuality. Although I supported gay rights, I did not want anyone to think for one minute that I might be gay myself.

Despite my anxiety, I eventually became an active participant in the gay-student community at Pennsylvania State University. "Getting in," as ethnographers like to say, was a challenge. The first meeting that I attended of the Lesbian, Gay, and Bisexual Student Alliance was traumatic: I was sure that as I entered the meeting room everyone who saw me would assume that I was gay. Later on in my research, similar fears surfaced whenever I went to the local gay bar with friends I had made through the alliance or to "alternative lifestyle" night at one of the local dance clubs.

As time passed and as I made more gay friends, I became more comfortable hanging out and being seen with gay students. Thanks to the stories of my friends Patrick, Ben, Tito, and Andrew, my perception of gay men went from a media-produced, one-dimensional caricature to one based on what I knew about their actual lives. Slowly my attitudes toward lesbian, gay, and bisexual people, and toward homosexuality, were changing; and, with the change, my fear of being mistaken for a gay man slowly faded. I attributed this to my realization that same-sex attraction is a fundamental aspect of who my friends are and is something to be celebrated, not feared.

Hearing their stories of pain and discrimination increased my support for their struggles. Patrick recalled being asked by his parents when he was 12 years old if he was gay or not. Before he answered, his parents told him they would have to send him away if he was, so that he would not "infect" his brother or sister. Patrick lied to his parents then and on many subsequent occasions. He struggles to this day to establish any kind of intimacy with his college friends.

Ben has a scar beneath his eye from the time he was beaten up at a party merely because he commented on the attractiveness of another man. Tito was harassed continually by fellow students in his residence hall. And Andrew was assaulted by several fraternity members. In fact, each of the 40 gay students I interviewed reported constant fear. One student said, "It's just something you learn to live with."

For the students in my study, coming out was a way of letting the straight world know that lesbian, gay, and bisexual people existed. Coming out is a continuing process, though, because we live in a society where nearly everyone assumes everyone else to be heterosexual. As one student explained: "Being out has created an awareness within me that everything I do is open to scrutiny by the rest of the world. . . . I just get so tired of being questioned about why I am gay and what it's like."

Over the past several years I have thought about what campuses can do to challenge homophobia and the cultural bias in favor of heterosexuals. Based upon my research, I offer the following suggestions:

- Provide training for faculty and staff members that addresses homophobia and cultural bias. It ought to include discussions of the environment that gay students face both in and out of class. Such training could take place during regular staff and department meetings or during "brown bag" lunches.

- Increase students' awareness [of] and sensitivity to differences in sexual preferences. Discussions of lesbian, gay, and bisexual issues could be introduced into orientation programs for entering students and into instruction for resident assistants.
- Insure that staff members who supervise sports teams and fraternities and sororities develop and implement educational programs about issues of sexual orientation. Research consistently shows high degrees of homophobia in these areas of student life.
- Provide stable resources and staff assistance to groups of lesbian, gay, and bisexual students. Such groups offer a vital network of support. Institutions should provide assistance similar to that provided for other student organizations—for example, funds to organize speakers' series or office space so the groups can plan their activities. Creating specific spaces where students can gather, such as a lounge or resource center in the student union, is also helpful.
- Eliminate discriminatory policies and practices. Campuses that have not established rules protecting the rights of lesbian, gay, and bisexual people must do so. Insurance plans and other benefits that cover domestic partners should cover all couples, regardless of sexual orientation.
- Make it clear that harassment and bias directed at lesbian, gay, and bisexual people are no more tolerable than racist or other sexist behavior and will be subject to the same procedures and penalties. Students should know exactly what office to go to when they have complaints. A gay hot line should be established to receive complaints and provide information.
- Encourage leaders of the faculty and administrative staffs to offer visible support to lesbian, gay, and bisexual students by attending their cultural activities. Programs such as lectures on gay or lesbian identity are intended not only for members of the gay community but for heterosexuals as well.
- Encourage faculty members to conduct research on gay issues, such as the psychological consequences of hiding one's sexual orientation and the intersections between race, gender, and sexual identity. A small grant

program might be established to support such efforts. Research and teaching are interactive processes: What is researched gets taught and vice versa.

Creating change is difficult; it takes hard work and risk taking by many people. We must constantly challenge ourselves and those around us to practice what we have learned about cultural bias if we are to create communities in which cultural differences are tolerated and even welcomed. I know, because despite my research, my new friends, and my participation in large rallies supporting gay rights, I still have some of my own homophobia to overcome.

At one meeting of the Lesbian, Gay, and Bisexual Student Alliance at Penn State, I volunteered to post flyers in the university library advertising events planned for Gay Pride Week. I had not realized that posting the flyers would be so upsetting. When I walked through the rotating doors of the library, my "I don't give a damn" attitude slowly faded, and dread and apprehension arose in its place. What will students who see me think? Will they harass me? Or, worse yet, will they just give me knowing, condescending looks? I made sure that the coast was clear before I pulled the flyers out of my book bag.

Posting the flyers brought back feelings I had had as a child when my mother used food stamps at the local grocery store. At the checkout line, my sister, Kim, and I would slowly drift away from her, disown her, so that we did not have to face "those looks"—wrinkled brows, tightened lips, upturned noses. Their looks conveyed the idea that my mother was, that we were, somehow less human than everyone else.

On many occasions since I began my research I have been assumed to be gay. Sometimes it was damaging professionally, like the time I applied for a faculty position at a university and did not get serious consideration because the chair of the search committee believed me to be gay. Or the time I taught an introductory-level sociology course and, because of my discussion of gay issues, was accused by some students in the class of "indoctrinating students to be gay." Other times the hurt was personal, such as when several young men made derogatory remarks to my friend Tito and me when we entered a local night club.

Despite the cases of mistaken sexual identity, I could always fall back on my knowledge that I actually was heterosexual, that I really belonged to the privileged, not the denigrated, group in society. But the students who consented to participate in my study did not have such a sanctuary. For me, marginality was a temporary experience from which to learn: for them, it is a fact of everyday life.   [1995]

Understanding the Reading

1. What has made Rhoads aware of the problems of coming out at college?
2. What obstacles did he face in his research?
3. What changed his attitudes toward gay, lesbian, and bisexual people?
4. What problems did his gay friends experience?
5. What suggestions does Rhoads make to challenge homophobia on campus?
6. What impact has Rhoads' research had on him?

Suggestions for Responding

1. As you go through a typical day, make note of the many manifestations of heterosexual bias, the assumption that heterosexuality is the norm, that you encounter. Write a brief report on what insights this exercise showed you.
2. Write an analysis of your own homophobia.
   ✦

119

Psychologists Find Ways to Break Racism's Hold

DANIEL GOLEMAN

As racial violence continues to roil communities like Bensonhurst and more subtle prejudice permeates many American institutions, psychologists are refining their understanding of how bigotry develops and devising new ways to fight and prevent it.

Some of the most promising techniques are aimed at grade-school children, whose biases have not had time to harden. But research has also led to a range of principles that can be used by any organization, whether university or corporation or city government or armed service, to change the atmosphere that leads to racial incidents.

"There is no single cure for racism," said Dr. Robert Slavin, a psychologist at Johns Hopkins University. But he and other psychologists have used data from experiments to identify techniques and principles for reducing the hold of racism.

INTERRACIAL LEARNING TEAMS

One of the most successful methods is dividing students into interracial learning teams, which, like sports teams, knit members together in common purpose that can lead to friendship.

Such learning groups are widespread in the United States, especially in school districts with potential or actual racial problems. In Israel, they have been used to defuse tensions between Jewish students of Middle Eastern and European descent; in Canada between Canadians and immigrants; and in California between Hispanic and non-Hispanic students.

Such cooperative groups reduce prejudice by undercutting the categories that lead to stereotyped thinking, according to research published in the August issue of *The Journal of Personality and Social Psychology*.

"Once you categorize people into groups in any way, you tend to like people in your own group more than those in others," said Dr. Samuel Gaertner, a psychologist at the University of Delaware who conducted the research.

"It happens in many situations apart from race relations," he added. "You see it often, for instance, in a corporate merger, when people in the acquiring company continue to stereotype people from the acquired company with disdain, and those from the acquired company resent what they see as a favored status for those with the acquiring firm."

In Dr. Gaertner's experiment, volunteers were formed into arbitrary groups to work on a hypothetical problem about surviving after a crash landing. Once they had become a unified group, they began to like each other more than they liked people who were put in other groups, a simulation of the process that can lead to prejudice in other circumstances.

When the working groups were then mixed with others into a single unified group to work on another problem, their preferences shifted again.

"Cooperation widens your sense of who's in your group," Dr. Gaertner said. "It changes your thinking from 'us and them' to 'we.' People you once saw as part of some other group now are part of your own. That's why team learning groups can reduce bias."

The need for such efforts is as great as ever, psychologists say. Incidents like the killing of Yusuf K. Hawkins, the black teen-ager shot during an attack by whites in the Bensonhurst section of Brooklyn on Aug. 23, are only the most visible and public reminders.

SUBTLE PREJUDICE PERSISTS

Although surveys show a decline over the last 40 years in the number of people who openly express bigotry, prejudice persists in more subtle forms. Dr. Howard Gadlin, a psychologist at the University of Massachusetts in Amherst, says the behavior of college students is a telling indication of racial attitudes. Campuses were in the forefront of the civil rights movement in the 1960's; yet in the past two years, he notes, "racial incidents have been on the rise on campuses across the country."

In devising ways to combat racism, psychologists can turn to a strong body of research into the mental processes that lead to bigotry. Dr. Janet Schofield, a psychologist at the University of Pittsburgh, has demonstrated ways in which social barriers between racial groups can create suspicion and mistrust.

In one junior high school she observed, the students were split into hostile racial cliques. "A socially active black kid was more likely to be seen as aggressive than was a white kid doing exactly the same thing," Dr. Schofield said. "For instance, if he asked someone in the cafeteria,

'Can I have your cake?' or even if he happened to bump someone in the hall, that was interpreted as an aggressive act if it was done by a black kid, but not by a white."

That perception was part of a cycle in which the social distance between blacks and whites fostered stereotypes that could not be broken down even by positive experiences.

"Whites and blacks avoided each other," Dr. Schofield said. "Because the whites were prone to interpret even normal social activity by blacks as hostile and aggressive, they felt afraid of social contact. That made the blacks see the whites as stuck-up, which tended to actually make them hostile in response."

PIGEONHOLES OF THE MIND

The most widely used technique for promoting racial harmony, mixing racial or ethnic groups into teams where they cooperate for a common goal, is intended to break down just such barriers to understanding.

The growing consensus from psychological experiments is that racial and ethnic prejudices are an unfortunate byproduct of the way the mind categorizes all experience. Essentially, the mind seeks to simplify the chaos of the world by fitting all perceptions into categories. Thus it fits different kinds of people into pigeonholes, just as it does with restaurants or television programs.

That is where the problem begins, psychologists say. Too often people see the category and not the individual. Once these categories are formed, the beliefs and assumptions that underlie them are confirmed at every possible opportunity, even at the cost of disregarding evidence to the contrary.

David Hamilton, a psychologist at the University of California at Santa Barbara, has found in [a] series of experiments that people tend to forget facts that would change their assumptions about categories, while seeking and remembering information that would confirm those assumptions. When they meet someone who does not fit the stereotype, they tell themselves the individual is an exception.

The strength of stereotypes—both innocent and hostile—is attributed to the mind's natural bent to seek to confirm its beliefs. While several experiences to the contrary can challenge those beliefs, an isolated experience is unlikely to do so.

THE POWER OF TEAMWORK

Such self-confirmation of stereotypes is especially likely when members of different groups have little contact with each other. Merely integrating a school, business or neighborhood may fail to change old stereotypes if the groups keep to themselves.

The learning-team approach was based on pioneering work on intergroup harmony in the 1950's by psychologists like Dr. Gordon Allport and Dr. Muzafer Sherif. It was given added scientific impetus by research on prejudice among high school students in the 1970's. That work, by Dr. Slavin and others, found that in mixed-race schools, students with the least prejudice and most friends from other races were members of sports teams or bands in which they had to work together.

The most widespread approach puts students together in four- or five-member "learning teams." The racial or ethnic makeup of each team reflects the overall makeup of the school. While members study together and are encouraged to teach each other, they are tested individually. But the team gets a score or other recognition of its work as a unit. Teams work together for about six weeks, and then students are reassigned to a new team to promote as many contacts as possible among students.

"No point is made of the fact that these are mixed racial groups," Dr. Slavin said. "The kids see nothing unusual; it seems random. The effects are very positive, especially in junior and senior high school, where the problem is greatest."

After the students work together in teams, Dr. Slavin and other researchers have found a significant increase in the number who say their friends are from other races or ethnic groups.

"ZERO TOLERANCE" FOR BIAS

"Even in cooperative groups, students may still carry biases into the sessions," Dr. Schofield said. "Blacks may expect that the whites will dominate, for instance. Sometimes you can combat these attitudes by giving minority kids a head start on a lesson, and having them teach it to the white kids."

Apart from engineering mixed-race working groups, psychologists say the overall social climate is also important in fighting racism. They say those in charge can establish a clear norm that racism will not be tolerated.

"Administrators and managers can show that they have zero tolerance for racial putdowns," Dr. Slavin said.

The psychologists say a sense of fairness is also important. If one group is perceived to be treated better or to have higher status than another, the situation is ripe for tensions. For that reason, psychologists stress the importance of openly acknowledging differences in the ways groups are treated.

"My research shows that when people try to act colorblind, as though there were no racial or ethnic differences, it backfires," Dr. Schofield said.

Dr. Slavin says school officials need to recognize and address such differrences.

"If 90 percent of the kids suspended are black or Hispanic, or all the kids on the student council are Oriental or white, you need to bring that fact into the open before you can deal with it," he said. "The worst thing is for members of some group to feel, 'People like me have no chance here.'

"You need to pay careful attention to issues of equity. If it's a school, for instance, you need to be sure the cheerleading squad and student council are racially mixed in a way that represents the student body, even if that means a certain proportion are appointed."

Many universities are now appointing ombudsmen to deal impartially with complaints of racial, ethnic or sexual bias, among other grievances.

"It may seem obvious, but it's often overlooked," said Dr. Gadlin, who is the ombudsman at the University of Massachusetts. "You must have a system in place where those who feel racially harassed can lodge a complaint that will be acted on, not covered up.

"We need ways of dealing openly with the fears and resentments that breed racial tensions," he added. "We have no forums where you can do much more than talk around the problems in ways that are proper and polite but avoid the real issues. If you have to pretend that racial problems don't exist, the tensions will escalate until they explode."   [1989]

Understanding the Reading

1. Explain why interracial learning teams reduce prejudice.
2. What are the effects of social distance between racial groups?
3. Why do people categorize others, and what effect does such categorization have?
4. Why don't people change their assumptions about people when experience contradicts the stereotype?
5. What can administrators and managers do to combat racism?

Suggestions for Responding

1. Describe a different strategy to combat racism in schoolchildren, and explain why it might be effective. ✦

120

Battered Women

CYNTHIA DIEHM AND MARGO ROSS

Any examination of the status of American women cannot ignore the plight of the estimated three to four million or more women who are beaten by their intimate partners each year. The home, once seen as a sanctuary for women, is increasingly being recognized as a place where females may be at risk of psychological and physical abuse.

Abusive and violent behavior among people who are married, living together, or have an ongoing or prior intimate relationship is referred to as spouse abuse, battering, or domestic violence. It occurs among people of all races, age groups, religions, lifestyles, and income and educational levels. Approximately 95 percent of the victims of such violence are women.

A battering incident is rarely an isolated occurrence. It usually recurs frequently and esca-

lates in severity over time. It can involve threats, pushing, slapping, punching, choking, sexual assault, and assault with weapons. Each year, more than one million women seek medical assistance for injuries caused by battering. Battering may result in more injuries that require medical treatment than rape, auto accidents, and muggings combined.

A typical response to domestic violence is to question why women remain in abusive relationships. Actually, many women do leave their abusers. In one study of 205 battered women, 53 percent had left the relationship. Moreover, there is no way to know how many women have chosen not to identify abuse as the reason they ended their marriages.

Divorce proceedings can be particularly difficult for battered women, especially when child custody litigation is involved. If a battered woman has left the home without her children, she may lose custody of them because her action may be perceived as desertion. If the batterer is established in the community, the court may see him as a better custodial parent, regardless of his wife's accusations of violence, because she may appear to be in transition and unstable. If the woman is granted custody, the abuser usually is given child visitation rights—a situation that continually places the woman at risk of abuse. Some states have passed legislation that mandates consideration of spouse abuse as evidence in custody litigation.

Battered women, in general, do not passively endure physical abuse, but actively seek assistance in ending the violence from a variety of sources, including police, lawyers, family members, and the clergy. Frequently, it is the failure of these individuals and systems to provide adequate support that traps women in violent relationships. A study of more than 6,000 battered women in Texas found that, on average, the women had contacted five different sources of help prior to leaving the home and becoming residents of battered women's shelters.

Certainly, many battered women suffer in silence. These women endure physical abuse for a variety of reasons:

- A woman may feel that it is her duty to keep the marriage together at all costs because of religious, cultural, or socially learned beliefs.

- A woman may endure physical and emotional abuse to keep the family together for the children's sake.
- A woman may be financially dependent on her husband and thus would probably face severe economic hardship if she chose to support herself and her children on her own.
- A battered woman frequently faces the most physical danger when she attempts to leave. She may be threatened with violence or attacked if she tries to flee. She fears for her safety, her children's safety, and the safety of those who help her.

THE LEGACY OF INDIFFERENCE

Despite the severity of domestic violence, it is a problem that, until quite recently, has been cloaked in secrecy. Up to the early 1970s, battered women had few options but to suffer in silence or to attempt single-handedly to leave controlling and violent men. To understand why society is just beginning to confront domestic violence, it is essential to view the problem within its historical context.

Domestic violence is not a new phenomenon; historically, husbands had the legal right to chastise their wives to maintain authority. In the United States, wife beating was legal until the end of the nineteenth century. Alabama and Massachusetts were on record as rescinding the "ancient privilege" of wife beating in 1871, but most states merely ignored old laws.

While battering was no longer legally sanctioned by the early part of the twentieth century, the spirit of the law remained and abuse was still common. Social and justice systems have viewed domestic violence as a private family matter and have been reluctant to intervene.

CHANGE THROUGH GRASSROOTS ACTIVISM

The legacy of society's indifference to violence in the home fueled a grassroots "battered women's movement," which gained nationwide momentum in the mid-1970s. Inspired by the feminist anti-rape movement's analysis of male violence against women as a social and political issue, battered women began to speak out about the physical abuse they were suffering in their marriages and intimate relationships.

At first, battered women helped one another individually by setting up informal safe homes and apartments. In such an environment—free from intimidation by their abusers—battered women could speak openly and thus soon discovered the commonality of their experiences. As the issue was publicized, women of all races, cultures, ages, abilities, and walks of life began to expose the violence they suffered. It quickly became clear that woman battering was a pervasive problem, and a nationwide movement started to take shape.

The early experience of the movement revealed the acute need of safe shelter for battered women and their children. Unless a woman could feel truly safe, she could not effectively evaluate her situation and make clear decisions about her future. Operating on shoestring budgets, battered women's advocates began to establish formal programs around the country. Only a handful of such programs existed in the mid-1970s; today, there are more than 1,200 shelters, hot-lines, and safe-home networks nationwide. Grassroots lobbying efforts at the federal level led to congressional passage of the 1984 Family Violence Prevention and Services Act, which earmarked federal funding for programs serving victims of domestic violence.

Creating and expanding a network of shelters and services for battered women and their children, while essential, was not the only goal of the grassroots movement. Equally important was the task of promoting changes in the criminal justice system that would hold abusers accountable for their violence and uphold the rights of battered women.

In 1984, the report of the Attorney General's Task Force on Family Violence reaffirmed the need for an improved criminal justice response to domestic violence, stating: "The legal response to family violence must be guided primarily by the nature of the abusive act, not the relationship between the victim and the abuser." The report focused on the role of the criminal justice system and recommended actions for each of its components that would increase the effectiveness of its response and better ensure the victim's safety. Across the country advocates continue to work with law enforcement personnel, prosecutors, judges, and legislators to implement new policies and enact legislation.

THE CRIMINAL JUSTICE RESPONSE

Domestic violence is now a crime in all 50 states and the District of Columbia, either under existing assault and battery laws or under special legislation. However, the true extent of crimes involving domestic violence remains largely unknown, since no accurate statistics on the number of battered women exist. Neither of the two sources of national crime statistics—the Federal Bureau of Investigation's Uniform Crime Report (UCR) and the federal Bureau of Justice Statistics' National Crime Survey (NCS)—is specifically designed to measure the incidence of crime in the domestic setting.

The UCR, which is based on police department reports, only collects information on the victim-offender relationship in the homicide category. Despite the UCR's limitations, it does provide a chilling picture of the potential lethality of domestic violence. According to the latest report, 30 percent of female homicide victims were killed by their husbands or boyfriends.

To supplement the UCR, the Bureau of Justice Statistics conducts an ongoing national telephone survey of some 60,000 American households to glean information on crimes not reported to police. Originally designed to collect data on such crimes as burglary and aggravated assault, the NCS also asks respondents about their relationships to offenders and thus inadvertently obtains information on domestic violence. Results of the 1978–82 NCS led analysts to estimate that 2.1 million women were victims of domestic violence at least once during an average 12-month period. This estimate is not intended to portray the true extent of the problem; rather, it is an indication of the number of women who believed domestic violence to be criminal and who felt free to disclose such information over the telephone to an unknown interviewer.

National crime statistics are based primarily on local police department reports, which traditionally have not included a discrete category for domestic violence. Police departments in a number of jurisdictions are just beginning to develop methods to report domestic violence crimes separately. It will be many years before this practice becomes universal and a more accurate picture of the nature and incidence of domestic crimes is available.

Law enforcement has traditionally operated from a philosophy of nonintervention in cases of domestic violence. Unless severe injury or death was involved, police rarely arrested offenders. Expert police opinion was that there was little law enforcement could do to prevent such crimes. Moreover, it was believed that even if an offender were arrested, cases would never go to trial because of the victim's fear of testifying against her abuser.

The police response to domestic violence has been altered significantly in the last few years. In 1982, a study in Minneapolis found that arrest was more effective than two nonarrest alternatives in reducing the likelihood of repeat violence over a six-month follow-up period. Interestingly, only two percent of abusers who were arrested in the study went before a judge to receive court punishment. Thus, the Minneapolis study showed that arrest appears to reduce recidivism, even if it does not lead to conviction. The results of the study were widely publicized and have contributed to a more aggressive law enforcement response to domestic violence.

Research results, however, have been only partially responsible for changes in police policies. Class action lawsuits brought by victims against police departments for lack of protection also have effected policy change. In 1985, for example, a battered woman in Torrington, Connecticut, won a multimillion dollar settlement from the city for the failure of the police department to protect her from her husband's violence. *Thurman v. Torrington* was a catalyst for the state's passage of the 1986 Family Violence and Response Act, which mandates arrest in domestic violence cases when probable cause exists.

For the past several years, the Crime Control Institute has conducted a telephone survey of police departments serving jurisdictions with populations of 100,000 or more. In 1986, 46 percent of these departments indicated they had a proarrest policy in cases of domestic violence, as compared with 31 percent in 1985 and 10 percent in 1984. In addition, the percent of urban police departments reporting more actual domestic violence arrests appears to have risen from 24 percent in 1984 to 47 percent in 1986.

Other components of the criminal justice system have also begun to take a tougher stance on domestic violence. Many district attorneys' offices have established separate domestic violence units to encourage more vigorous prosecution of offenders. Judicial training on domestic violence has been promoted so that stronger court sanctions are imposed against abusive men.

The changes in the criminal justice system's response to domestic violence are quite new, however, and have not occurred universally. Although states have enacted various types of statutes to promote more aggressive treatment of domestic violence as a crime, whether this approach is upheld by individual actors within the system varies from jurisdiction to jurisdiction.

In many jurisdictions, courts can order batterers to attend special counseling programs either before the case is adjudicated or as a condition of probation. Frequently, criminal charges are dismissed if the defendant "successfully" completes the program. Unfortunately, the effectiveness of special programs for abusive men is hard to measure, and little information exists on the effectiveness of intervention.

Legal Protection for the Victim

In the early 1970s, few legal remedies existed for the battered woman seeking protection from abuse. If married, she could file for divorce, separation, or custody, and in some states obtain an injunction ordering her husband not to abuse her while domestic relations proceedings were pending.

Since that time, 47 states and the District of Columbia have enacted legislation allowing battered women to obtain civil protection or restraining orders. Depending on the state, through such legislation the court can order the abuser to move out of the residence, refrain from abuse of or contact with the victim, enter a batterers' treatment program, or pay support, restitution, or attorney's fees. However, "a protection or restraining order is meaningful only if violation of the order constitutes a crime and police are able to verify the existence of an order when a violation is alleged."

The ability of such orders to protect all domestic violence victims is inconsistent across jurisdictions. Some areas require the victim to be married to and currently cohabitating with the abuser. Abuse may be narrowly defined as an attempt or infliction of bodily injury or serious bodily injury, providing no protection from threats of violence or destruction of property. The duration of protection orders can range from 15 days to no more than one year, thereby forcing many women to relocate to avoid abuse. Moreover, it is believed that protection orders are poorly implemented and enforced. It may be quite difficult for low-income women, women of color, and women who have defended themselves against physical abuse to obtain this type of protection. The use and enforcement of civil protection orders is now under study through funding from the Justice Department.

The Importance of Prevention

Clearly, just responding to domestic violence is not sufficient. An improved criminal justice response and the development of court-ordered programs for abusive men are not panaceas for the problem. Battered women's advocates believe that to bring an end to domestic violence, it is necessary to examine how the culture teaches young men and women to play roles that lead to such violent behavior, and how restricted access to economic resources can trap women in the potentially lethal cycle of violence.

If the cycle of violence is to be broken, advocates on behalf of battered women stress that young women must be encouraged to go beyond traditionally passive, dependent roles, while young men must be taught that abusive, violent, and controlling behavior is never acceptable. To this end, battered women's advocates have established children's programs in many shelters, as well as curricula on domestic violence for use in elementary, middle, and high schools.

Finally, equal access to employment, housing, and economic resources must be available to all women. This situation is particularly acute for battered women, who frequently remain in abusive relationships simply because of economics. Thus, a critical determinant of whether a battered woman will live without violence or be forced to return to an abusive partner often is the availability of decent affordable housing, adequate pay, and other forms of economic assistance.

Violence in the home is a problem with serious repercussions for the battered woman, her children, and the entire community. Breaking the cycle of violence requires financial support for services to battered women, a strong criminal justice response that holds abusive men accountable for their violence, and, most important, ongoing social activism that focuses on improving the status of all women.   [1988]

Understanding the Reading

1. Why do women stay in abusive relationships?
2. What actions have battered women undertaken to combat domestic violence?
3. What legal action has been taken to respond to the problem of domestic violence?
4. What can be dome to *prevent* domestic violence?

Suggestions for Responding

1. How would you respond to someone you know who is in an abusive relationship? Be sure you take into account the resistance that the person may express. ✦

121

Freedom for the Thought We Hate

Gerald Gunther

I am deeply troubled by current efforts—however well-intentioned—to place new limits on freedom of expression at this and other campuses. Such limits are not only incompatible with the mission and meaning of university; they also send exactly the wrong message from academia to society as a whole. University campuses should exhibit greater, not less, freedom of expression than prevails in society at large.

Proponents of new limits argue that historic First Amendment rights must be balanced against the university's commitment to the diversity of ideas and persons. Clearly, there is ample room and need for vigorous university action to combat racial and other discrimination. But curbing freedom of speech is the wrong way to do so. The proper answer to bad speech is usually more and better speech—not new laws, litigation, and repression.

Lest it be thought that I am insensitive to the pain imposed by expressions of racial or religious hatred, let me say that I have suffered that pain and empathize with others under similar verbal assault. My deep belief in the principles of the First Amendment arises in part from my own experiences. I received my elementary education in a public school in a very small town in Nazi Germany. There I was subjected to vehement anti-Semitic remarks from my teacher, classmates, and others— "Judensau" (Jew pig) was far from the harshest. I can assure you that they hurt.

More generally, I lived in a country where ideological orthodoxy reigned and where the opportunity for dissent was severely limited.

The lesson I have drawn from my childhood in Nazi Germany and my happier adult life in this country is the need to walk the sometimes difficult path of denouncing the bigots' hateful ideas with all my power, yet at the same time challenging any community's attempt to suppress hateful ideas by force of law.

Obviously, given my own experience, I do *not* quarrel with the claim that *words* can do harm. But I firmly deny that a showing of harm suffices to deny First Amendment protection, and I insist on the elementary First Amendment principle that our Constitution usually protects even offensive, harmful expression.

That is why—at the risk of being thought callous or doctrinaire—I recently opposed attempts by some members of my university community to enlarge the area of forbidden speech to prohibit not only "personal abuse" but also "defamation of groups"—expression "that by accepted community standards . . . pejoratively characterizes persons or groups on the basis of personal or cultural differences." Such proposals, in my view, seriously undervalue the First Amendment and far too readily endanger its precious content. Limitations on free expression beyond those established by law should be eschewed in an institution committed to diversity and the First Amendment.

In explaining my position, I will avoid extensive legal arguments. Instead, I want to speak from the heart, on the basis of my own background and of my understanding of First Amendment principles—principles supported by an ever larger number of scholars and Supreme Court justices, especially since the days of the Warren Court.[1]

Among the core principles is that any official effort to suppress expression must be viewed with the greatest skepticism and suspicion. Only in very narrow, urgent circumstances should government or similar institutions be permitted to inhibit speech. True, there are certain categories of speech that may be prohibited; but the number and scope of these categories has steadily shrunk over the last fifty years. Face-to-face insults are one such category; incitement to immediate illegal action is another. But opinions expressed in debates and arguments about a wide range of political and social issues should not be suppressed simply because of disagreement with those views, with the content of the expression.

Similarly, speech should not and cannot be banned simply because it is "offensive" to substantial parts of a majority of the community. The refusal to suppress offensive speech is one of the most difficult obligations the free speech principle imposes upon all of us; yet it is also one of the First Amendment's greatest glories—indeed it is a central test of a community's commitment to free speech.

The Supreme Court's 1989 decision to allow flag-burning as a form of political protest, in *Texas v. Johnson,* warrants careful pondering by all those who continue to advocate campus restraints on "racist speech." As Justice Brennan's majority opinion in *Johnson* reminded, "If there is a bedrock principle underlying the First Amendment, it is that the Government may not prohibit the expression of an idea itself offensive or disagreeable." In refusing to place flag-burning outside the First Amendment, moreover, the *Johnson* majority insisted (in words especially apt for the "racist speech" debate): "The First Amendment does not guarantee that other concepts virtually sacred to our Nation as a whole—*such as the principle that discrimination on the basis of race is odious and destructive*—will go unquestioned in the marketplace of ideas. We decline, therefore, to create for the flag an exception to the joust of principles protected by the First Amendment." (Italics added.)

Campus proponents of restricting offensive speech are currently relying for justification on the Supreme Court's allegedly repeated reiteration that "fighting words" constitute an exception to the First Amendment. Such an exception has indeed been recognized in a number of lower court cases. However, there has only been *one* case in the history of the Supreme Court in which a majority of the justices has ever found a statement to be a punishable resort to "fighting words." That was *Chaplinsky v. New Hampshire,* a nearly fifty-year-old case involving words which would very likely not be found punishable today.

More significant is what has happened in the nearly half-century since. Despite repeated appeals to the Supreme Court to recognize the applicability of the "fighting words" exception by affirming challenged convictions, the court has in every instance refused. One must wonder about the strength of an exception that, while theoretically recognized, has for so long not been found apt in practice.

The phenomenon of racist and other offensive speech is not a new one in the history of the First Amendment. In recent decades, for example, well-meaning (but in my view misguided) majorities have sought to suppress not only racist speech but also anti-war and anti-draft speech, civil rights demonstrators, the Nazis and Ku Klux Klan, and left-wing groups.

Typically, it is people on the extremes of the political spectrum (including those who advocate overthrow of our constitutional system and those who would not protect their opponents' right to dissent were they the majority) who feel the brunt of repression and have found protection in the First Amendment; typically, it is well-meaning people in the majority who believe their sensibilities, their sense of outrage, justify restraints.

Those in power in a community recurrently seek to repress speech they find abhorrent, and their efforts are understandable human impulses. Yet freedom of expression—and especially the protection of dissident speech, the most important function of the First Amendment—is an anti-majoritarian principle. Is it too much to hope that, especially on a university campus, a majority can be persuaded of the value of freedom of expression and of the resultant need to curb our impulses to repress dissident views?

The principles to which I appeal are not new. They have been expressed, for example, by the most distinguished Supreme Court justices ever since the beginning of the court's confrontations with First Amendment issues nearly seventy years ago. These principles are reflected in the words of so imperfect a First Amendment defender as Justice Oliver Wendell Holmes: "If there is any principle of the Constitution that more imperatively calls for attachment than any other it is the principle of free thought—not free thought for those who agree with us but freedom for the thought that we hate." This is the principle most elaborately and eloquently addressed by Justice Louis D. Brandeis, who reminded us that the First Amendment rests on a belief "in the power of reason as applied through public discussion" and therefore bars "silence coerced by law—the argument of force in its worst form."

This theme, first articulated in dissents, has repeatedly been voiced in majority opinions in more recent decades. It underlies Justice Douglas's remark in striking down a conviction under a law banning speech that "stirs the public to anger": "A function of free speech [is] to invite dispute. . . . Speech is often provocative and challenging. That is why freedom of speech [is ordinarily] protected against censorship or punishment."

It also underlies Justice William J. Brennan's comment about our "profound national commitment to the principle that debate on public issues should be uninhibited, robust and wide-open, and that it may well include vehement, caustic and sometimes unpleasantly sharp attacks"—a comment he followed with a reminder that constitutional protection "does not turn upon the truth, popularity or social utility of the ideas and beliefs which are offered."

These principles underlie as well the repeated insistence by Justice John Marshall Harlan, again in majority opinions, that the mere "in-utility or immorality" of a message cannot justify its repression, and that the state may not punish because of "the underlying content of the message." Moreover, Justice Harlan, in one of the finest First Amendment opinions on the books, noted, in words that we would ignore at peril at this time:

"The constitutional right of free expression is powerful medicine in a society as diverse and populous as ours. . . . To many, the immediate consequence of this freedom may often appear to be only verbal tumult, discord and even offensive utterance. These are, however, within established limits, in truth necessary side effects of the broader enduring values which the process of open debate permits us to achieve. That the air may at times seem filled with verbal cacophony is, in this sense, not a sign of weakness but of strength."

In this same passage, Justice Harlan warned that a power to ban speech merely because it is offensive is an "inherently boundless" notion, and added that "we think it is largely because governmental officials cannot make principled distinctions in this area that the Constitution leaves matters of taste and style so largely to the individual." (The Justice made these comments while overturning the conviction of an antiwar protestor for "offensive conduct." The defendant had worn, in a courthouse corridor, a jacket bearing the words "Fuck the draft.")

I restate these principles and repeat these words for reasons going far beyond the fact that they are familiar to me as a First Amendment scholar. I believe—in my heart as well as my mind—that these principles and ideals are not only established but right. I hope that the entire academic community will seriously reflect upon the risks to free expression, lest we weaken hard-won liberties at our universities and, by example, in this nation.   [1990]

Terms

1. WARREN COURT: The Supreme Court under Chief Justice Earl Warren, which passed down such decisions as the prohibition of school segregation.

Understanding the Reading

1. Why does Gunther describe his childhood in Germany?
2. Why does he argue that speech "should not . . . be banned simply because it is 'offensive'"?

3. What connection does Gunther make between flag-burning and racist speech?
4. Why does he object to the use of the concept of "fighting words" to prohibit racist speech?
5. Explain each of the quotations of the five Supreme Court justices.

Suggestions for Responding

1. Gunther presents a persuasive advocacy of freedom of speech. Develop an argument in favor of some restrictions. ✦

122

Acknowledging the Victims' Cry

CHARLES R. LAWRENCE III

I have spent the better part of my life as a dissenter. As a high-school student, I was threatened with suspension for my refusal to participate in a civil-defense drill, and I have been a conspicuous consumer of my First Amendment liberties[1] ever since. There are very strong reasons for protecting even speech that is racist. Perhaps the most important is that such protection reinforces our society's commitment to tolerance as a value. By protecting bad speech from government regulation, we will be forced to combat it as a community.

I have, however, a deeply felt apprehension about the resurgence of racial violence and the corresponding increase in the incidence of verbal and symbolic assault and harassment to which African-Americans and other traditionally excluded groups are subjected. I am troubled by the way the debate has been framed in response to the recent surge of racist incidents on college and university campuses and in response to some universities' attempts to regulate harassing speech. The problem has been framed as one in which the liberty of free speech is in conflict with the elimination of racism. I believe this has placed the bigot on the moral high ground and fanned the rising flames of racism.

Above all, I am troubled that we have not listened to the real victims—that we have shown so little understanding of their injury, and that we have abandoned those whose race, gender, or sexual orientation continues to make them second-class citizens. It seems to me a very sad irony that the first instinct of civil libertarians has been to challenge even the smallest, most narrowly framed efforts by universities to provide African-Americans and other minority students with the protection the Constitution, in my opinion, guarantees them.

The landmark case of *Brown v. Board of Education*[2] is not a case that we normally think of as a case about speech. But *Brown* can be broadly read as articulating the principle of equal citizenship. *Brown* held that segregated schools were inherently unequal because of the message that segregation conveyed: that African-American children were an untouchable caste, unfit to go to school with white children. If we understand the necessity of eliminating the system of signs and symbols that signal the inferiority of African-Americans, then we should hesitate before proclaiming that all racist speech that stops short of physical violence must be defended.

University officials who have formulated policies to respond to incidents of racial harassment have been characterized in the press as "thought police," even though such policies generally do nothing more than impose sanctions against intentional face-to-face insults. Racist speech that takes the form of face-to-face insults, catcalls, or other assaultive speech aimed at an individual or small group of persons falls directly within the "fighting words" exception to First Amendment protection. The Supreme Court has held in *Chaplinsky v. New Hampshire* that words which "by their very utterance inflict injury or tend to incite an immediate breach of the peace" are not protected by the First Amendment.

If the purpose of the First Amendment is to foster the greatest amount of speech, racial insults disserve that purpose. Assaultive racist speech functions as a preemptive strike. The invective is experienced as a blow, not as a proffered idea. And once the blow is struck, a dialogue is unlikely to follow. Racial insults are particularly undeserving of First Amendment protection, because the perpetrator's intention is not to discover truth or initiate dialogue but to injure the victim. In most situations, members of minority groups realize that they are likely to lose if they fight back, and are forced to remain silent and submissive.

Courts have held that offensive speech may not be regulated in public forums (such as streets, where the listener may avoid the speech by moving on). But the regulation of otherwise protected speech has been permitted when the speech invades the privacy of the unwilling listener's home, or when the unwilling listener is a "captive audience" and cannot avoid the speech. Racist posters, flyers, and graffiti in dormitories, bathrooms, and other common living spaces would seem to fall within the reasoning of these cases. Minority students should not be required to remain in their rooms in order to avoid racial insult. Minimally, they should find a safe haven in their dorms and in all other common rooms that are a part of their daily routine.

I would also argue that the university's responsibility for ensuring that these students receive an equal educational opportunity provides a compelling justification for regulations that ensure them safe passage in all common areas. A minority student should not have to risk becoming the target of racially assaulting speech every time he or she chooses to walk across campus. Regulating vilifying speech that cannot be anticipated or avoided need not preclude announced speeches and rallies—situations that would give minority-group members and their allies the opportunity to organize counterdemonstrations or avoid the speech altogether.

The most commonly advanced argument against the regulation of racist speech proceeds something like this: We recognize that minority groups suffer pain and injury as the result of racist speech, but we must allow this hate-mongering for the benefit of society as a whole. Freedom of speech is the lifeblood of our democratic system. It is especially important for minorities, because often it is their only vehicle for rallying support for the redress of their grievances. It will be impossible to formulate a prohibition so precise that it will prevent the racist speech you want to suppress without catching in the same net all kinds of speech that it would be unconscionable for a democratic society to suppress.

Such arguments seek to strike a balance between our concern, on the one hand, for the continued free flow of ideas and the democratic process dependent on that flow, and, on the other, our desire to further the cause of equality. There can, however, be no meaningful discussion of how we should reconcile our commitment to equality with our commitment to free speech until it is acknowledged that racist speech inflicts real harm, and that this harm is far from trivial.

To engage in a debate about the First Amendment and racist speech without a full understanding of the nature and extent of that harm is to risk making the First Amendment an instrument of domination rather [than] a vehicle of liberation. We have not all known the experience of victimization by racist, misogynist, and homophobic speech, nor do we equally share the burden of the harm it inflicts. We are often quick to say that we have heard the cry of the victims when we have not.

The *Brown* case is again instructive, because it speaks directly to the psychic injury inflicted by racist speech by noting that the symbolic message of segregation affected "the hearts and minds" of African-American children "in a way unlikely ever to be undone." Racial epithets and harassment often cause deep emotional scarring and feelings of anxiety and fear that pervade every aspect of a victim's life.

Brown also recognized that African-American children did not have an equal opportunity to learn and participate in the school's community when they bore the additional burden of being subjected to the humiliation and psychic assault contained in the message of segregation. University students bear an analogous burden when they are forced to live and work in an environment where at any moment they may be subject to denigrating verbal harassment and assault. The same injury was addressed by the Supreme Court when it held that, under Title VII of the Civil Rights Act of 1964, sexual harassment which creates a hostile or abusive work environment violates the ban on sex discrimination in employment.

Carefully drafted university regulations could bar the use of words as assault weapons while at the same time leaving unregulated even the most heinous of ideas provided those ideas are presented at times and places and in manners that provide an opportunity for reasoned rebuttal or escape from immediate insult. The history of the development of the right to free speech has been one of carefully evaluating the importance of free expression and its effects on other important societal interests. We have drawn the line between protected and unprotected speech before without dire results. (Courts have, for example, exempted from the protection of the First Amendment obscene speech and speech that disseminates official secrets, defames or libels another person, or is used to form a conspiracy or monopoly.)

African-Americans and other people of color are skeptical about the argument that even the most injurious speech must remain unregulated because, in an unregulated marketplace of ideas, the best ones will rise to the top and gain acceptance. Experience tells quite the opposite. People of color have seen too many demagogues elected by appealing to Americans' racism, and too many sympathetic politicians shy away from issues that might brand them as being too closely allied with disparaged groups.

Whenever we decide that racist speech must be tolerated because of the importance of maintaining societal tolerance for all unpopular speech, we are asking African-Americans and other subordinated groups to bear the burden for the good of all. We must be careful that the ease with which we strike the balance against the regulation of racist speech is in no way influenced by the fact that the cost will be borne by others. We must be certain that those who will pay that price are fairly represented in our deliberations and that they are heard.

At the core of the argument that we should resist all government regulation of speech is the idea that the best cure for bad speech is good—that ideas that affirm equality and the worth of all individuals will ultimately prevail. This is an empty ideal unless those of us who would fight racism are vigilant and unequivocal in that fight. We must look for ways to offer assistance and support to students whose speech and political participation are chilled in a climate of racial harassment.

Civil rights lawyers might consider suing on behalf of African-Americans whose right to an equal education is denied by a university's failure to ensure a nondiscriminatory education climate or conditions of employment. We must embark upon the development of a First Amendment jurisprudence grounded in the reality of our history and our contemporary experience. We must think hard about how best to launch legal attacks against the most indefensible forms of hate speech. Good lawyers can create exceptions and narrow interpretations that limit the harm of hate speech without opening the floodgates of censorship.

Everyone concerned with these issues must find ways to engage actively in actions that resist and counter the racist ideas that we would have the First Amendment protect. If we fail in this, the victims of hate speech must rightly assume that we are on the bigot's side.   [1990]

Terms

1. FIRST AMENDMENT LIBERTIES: Freedom of worship, speech, press, and assembly.
2. *BROWN V. BOARD OF EDUCATION*: A case in which the U.S. Supreme Court declared segregated schools unconstitutional.

Understanding the Reading

1. What are "fighting words"?
2. Why does Lawrence feel that universities should regulate racist speech?
3. How does he answer opponents of regulation?
4. What connection does he see between *Brown v. Board of Education* and current policies on racist speech?

Suggestions for Responding

1. Lawrence presents a persuasive advocacy of some restrictions on "racist speech." Develop an argument against such restrictions.
2. Explain how you will evaluate your plan of action after you have implemented it. If you already have undertaken the action, write an evaluation of it. ✦

SUGGESTIONS FOR RESPONDING TO PART VIII

ACTION PROJECT FOR SOCIAL CHANGE

The readings in Part VIII have tried to show that you can actually do something to effect social change. Now it is time to put what you have learned into practice. Simply follow the steps described in the introduction to Part VIII, commit yourself, and take action.

First, identify something as a problem, such as becoming aware of sexism on MTV. You then have to have a desire to do something about the problem, and you need to figure out specifically what it is that you find offensive and what you want to achieve. Then, alone or together with whoever else is going to join you in your action, brainstorm about possible actions you could realistically take. With the MTV example, you could write to the producers of the videos or to the network; you could try to organize a boycott; you could undertake other, different actions. Then, plan your action project, considering what you will do, when you will do it, and how you will evaluate the success of your project. Then, do it and become a change maker yourself.

IX
Change Makers

WE USUALLY THINK OF CHANGE MAKERS AS THE movers and shakers of the world, those larger-than-life people who "really make a difference." On everyone's list would be major figures such as George Washington, Abraham Lincoln, Dwight Eisenhower, Andrew Carnegie, Henry Ford, Martin Luther King, and just maybe social worker Jane Addams. Part IX is not about people of such heroic proportions, however. Instead, it is about people like ourselves, not necessarily wealthy, privileged, or from influential families. This is not to imply that all those previously listed had these advantages; it is simply that their achievements are so embedded in our understanding of American history that they no longer seem to be "real" people like us.

The people we will read about here are young and old. Mother Jones was a fifty-year-old widow when she first became a union organizer of coal miners, whereas César Chávez, founder of the United Farm Workers Union, was a young man when he began work as a labor organizer. A third union organizer, Carmen Domingues, only recently began to organize garment workers in El Paso, Texas. Louise Palmer tells how Domingues' group, *La Mujer Obrera,* has moved beyond the workplace to address other problems of women workers and of the community.

The following three selections give some insight into the civil rights movement, possibly the most enveloping and dynamic social movement

of the past century, one that has transformed American society. A century ago, Ida B. Wells-Barnett, who was orphaned at age fourteen and who took responsibility for her younger siblings, challenged the practice of White lynching of Blacks; she earned an international reputation and eventually became a co-founder of the National Association for the Advancement of Colored People. The ultimate successes of the civil rights movement depended on similar dedication and commitment of many people whose names are not widely known today. For example, the report by the Southern Poverty Law Center summarizes the decades-long struggle of hundreds of individuals, taking stands by themselves, but more often cooperating in groups, to demonstrate the unfair policies and practices that kept Blacks subordinate in most areas of society.

Anne Moody, a college student from an impoverished southern Black family, was willing to face violence from White high school students—taking beatings, being sprayed with paint and condiments—to stand up for the right of Blacks to eat at a public lunch counter. Similarly, college student Muriel Tillinghast risked rape and other violence to assert Blacks' rights during the Freedom Summer activism.

The next three pieces introduce change makers from the most impoverished group in the United States, Native American women. Despite their lack of resources, they are improving life on their reservations. Michael Ryan tells how, despite obstructive government regulations and lack of funds, three women created on their Yakima, Washington, reservation a college that in eight years graduated over 400 students. As Valerie Taliman reports, JoAnn Tall, a mother of eight who lives on the Pine Ridge Indian Reservation in South Dakota, has spent much of her life organizing against environmental destruction on Indian reservations simply because she has reverence for "Grandmother Earth." Next, Ann Davis introduces us to the indefatigable Cecilia Fire Thunder, who has organized her tribal sisters to transform life and politics on their Lakota reservation.

Middle-class people are also effective change makers. Renée La Couture Tulloch waged a single-handed battle to get passage and gubernatorial approval of a sexual battery bill in California. Standing up for the civil rights of another oppressed group is Frank Kameny; Deb Price reports on how he fought back against governmental policy that fired workers, regardless of their competence, simply because they were homosexual.

College students also commit themselves to improving their campuses. Bonnie Pfister investigates the recent sexual codes that are becoming widespread on American college campuses.

The last two selections address an often overlooked concern that especially affects women: size discrimination. In the first, Dawn Atkins, the daughter of a fat woman, tells how she became a fat activist. Then, Mary E. Atkins, her mother, tells about her daughter's support and protests on behalf of her (and of all fat people).

All of us can learn important lessons from the change makers who speak in these pages. They show that everyday people who are committed to fighting social injustice can make a difference. Following their examples, any of us can do the same if we just care enough and make the effort to leave the world a better place for our having been here.

123

Victory at Arnot

Mary Harris "Mother" Jones[1]

Before 1899 the coal fields of Pennsylvania were not organized. Immigrants poured into the country and they worked cheap. There was always a surplus of immigrant labor, solicited in Europe by the coal companies, so as to keep wages down to barest living. Hours of work down under ground were cruelly long. Fourteen hours a day was not uncommon, thirteen, twelve. The life or limb of the miner was unprotected by any laws. Families lived in company owned shacks that were not fit for their pigs. Children died by the hundreds due to the ignorance and poverty of their parents.

Often I have helped lay out for burial the babies of the miners, and the mothers could scarce conceal their relief at the little ones' deaths. Another was already on its way, destined, if a boy, for the breakers; if a girl, for the silk mills where the other brothers and sisters already worked.

The United Mine Workers decided to organize these fields and work for human conditions for human beings. Organizers were put to work. Whenever the spirit of the men in the mines grew strong enough a strike was called.

In Arnot, Pennsylvania, a strike had been going on four or five months. The men were becoming discouraged. The coal company sent the doctors, the school teachers, the preachers and their wives to the homes of the miners to get them to sign a document that they would go back to work.

The president of the district, Mr. Wilson, and an organizer, Tom Haggerty, got despondent. The signatures were overwhelmingly in favor of returning on Monday.

Haggerty suggested that they send for me. Saturday morning they telephoned to Barnesboro, where I was organizing, for me to come at once or they would lose the strike.

"Oh Mother," Haggerty said, "Come over quick and help us! The boys are that despondent! They are going back Monday."

I told him that I was holding a meeting that night but that I would leave early Sunday morning.

I started at daybreak. At Roaring Branch, the nearest train connection with Arnot, the secretary of the Arnot Union, a young boy, William Bouncer, met me with a horse and buggy. We drove sixteen miles over rough mountain roads. It was biting cold. We got into Arnot Sunday noon and I was placed in the coal company's hotel, the only hotel in town. I made some objections but Bouncer said, "Mother, we have engaged this room for you and if it is not occupied, they will never rent us another."

Sunday afternoon I held a meeting. It was not as large a gathering as those we had later but I stirred up the poor wretches that did come.

"You've got to take the pledge," I said. "Rise and pledge to stick to your brothers and the union till the strike's won!"

The men shuffled their feet but the women rose, their babies in their arms, and pledged themselves to see that no one went to work in the morning.

"The meeting stands adjourned till ten o'clock tomorrow morning," I said. "Everyone come and see that the slaves that think to go back to their masters come along with you."

I returned to my room at the hotel. I wasn't called down to supper but after the general manager of the mines and all of the other guests had gone to church, the housekeeper stole up to my room and asked me to come down and get a cup of tea.

At eleven o'clock that night the housekeeper again knocked at my door and told me that I had to give up my room; that she was told it belonged to a teacher. "It's a shame, mother," she whispered, as she helped me into my coat.

I found little Bouncer sitting on guard down in the lobby. He took me up the mountain to a miner's house. A cold wind almost blew the bonnet from my head. At the miner's shack I knocked.

A man's voice shouted, "Who is there?"

"Mother Jones," said I.

A light came in the tiny window. The door opened.

"And did they put you out, Mother?"

"They did that."

"I told Mary they might do that," said the miner. He held the oil lamp with the thumb and his little finger and I could see that the others were off. His face was young but his body was bent over.

He insisted on my sleeping in the only bed, with his wife. He slept with his head on his arms on the kitchen table. Early in the morning his wife rose to keep the children quiet, so that I might sleep a little later as I was very tired.

At eight o'clock she came into my room, crying.

"Mother, are you awake?"

"Yes, I am awake."

"Well, you must get up. The sheriff is here to put us out for keeping you. This house belongs to the Company."

The family gathered up all their earthly belongings, which weren't much, took down all the holy pictures, and put them in a wagon, and they with all their neighbors went to the meeting. The sight of that wagon with the sticks of furniture and the holy pictures and the children, with the father and mother and myself walking along through the streets turned the tide. It made the men so angry that they decided not to go back that morning to the mines. Instead they came to the meeting where they determined not to give up the strike until they had won the victory.

Then the company tried to bring in scabs.[2] I told the men to stay home with the children for a change and let the women attend to the scabs. I organized an army of women housekeepers. On a given day they were to bring their mops and brooms and "the army" would charge the scabs up at the mines. The general manager, the sheriff and the corporation hirelings heard of our plans and were on hand. The day came and the women came with the mops and brooms and pails of water.

I decided not to go up to the Drip Mouth myself, for I knew they would arrest me and that might rout the army. I selected as leader an Irish woman who had a most picturesque appearance. She had slept late and her husband had told her to hurry up and get into the army. She had grabbed a red petticoat and slipped it over a thick cotton night gown. She wore a black stocking and a white one. She had tied a little red fringed shawl over her wild red hair. Her face was red and her eyes were mad. I looked at her and felt that she could raise a rumpus.

I said, "You lead the army up to the Drip Mouth. Take that tin dishpan you have with you and your hammer, and when the scabs and the mules come up, begin to hammer and howl.

Then all of you hammer and howl and be ready to chase the scabs with your mops and brooms. Don't be afraid of anyone."

Up the mountain side, yelling and hollering, she led the women, and when the mules came up with the scabs and the coal, she began beating on the dishpan and hollering and all the army joined in with her. The sheriff tapped her on the shoulder.

"My dear lady," said he, "remember the mules. Don't frighten them."

She took the old tin pan and she hit him with it and she hollered, "To hell with you and the mules!"

He fell over and dropped into the creek. Then the mules began to rebel against scabbing. They bucked and kicked the scab drivers and started off for the barn. The scabs started running down hill, followed by the army of women with their mops and pails and brooms.

A poll parrot in a near by shack screamed at the superintendent, "Got hell, did you? Got hell?"

There was a great big doctor in the crowd, a company lap dog. He had a little satchel in his hand and he said to me, impudent like, "Mrs. Jones, I have a warrant for you."

"All right," said I. "Keep it in your pill bag until I come for it. I am going to hold a meeting now."

From that day on the women kept continual watch of the mines to see that the company did not bring in scabs. Every day women with brooms or mops in one hand and babies in the other arm wrapped in little blankets, went to the mines and watched that no one went in. And all night long they kept watch. They were heroic women. In the long years to come the nation will pay them high tribute for they were fighting for the advancement of a great country.

I held meetings throughout the surrounding country. The company was spending money among the farmers, urging them not to do anything for the miners. I went out with an old wagon and a union mule that had gone on strike, and a miner's little boy for a driver. I held meetings among the farmers and won them to the side of the strikers.

Sometimes it was twelve or one o'clock in the morning when I would get home, the little boy asleep on my arm and I driving the mule. Sometimes it was several degrees below zero. The winds whistled down the mountains and drove the snow and sleet in our faces. My hands and feet were often numb. We were all living on dry bread and black coffee. I slept in a room that never had a fire in it, and I often woke up in the morning to find snow covering the outside covers of the bed.

There was a place near Arnot called Sweedy Town, and the company's agents went there to get the Swedes to break the strike. I was holding a meeting among the farmers when I heard of the company's efforts. I got the young farmers to get on their horses and go over to Sweedy Town and see that no Swede left town. They took clotheslines for lassos and any Swede seen moving in the direction of Arnot was brought back quick enough.

After months of terrible hardships the strike was about won. The mines were not working. The spirit of the men was splendid. President Wilson had come home from the western part of the state. I was staying at his home. The family had gone to bed. We sat up late talking over matters when there came a knock at the door. A very cautious knock.

"Come in," said Mr. Wilson.

Three men entered. They looked at me uneasily and Mr. Wilson asked me to step in an adjoining room. They talked the strike over and called President Wilson's attention to the fact that there were mortgages on his little home, held by the bank which was owned by the coal company, and they said, "We will take the mortgage off your home and give you $25,000 in cash if you will just leave and let the strike die out."

I shall never forget his reply:

"Gentlemen, if you come to visit my family, the hospitality of the whole house is yours. But if you come to bribe me with dollars to betray my manhood and my brothers who trust me, I want you to leave this door and never come here again."

The strike lasted a few weeks longer. Meantime President Wilson, when strikers were evicted, cleaned out his barn and took care of the evicted miners until homes could be provided. One by one he killed his chickens and his hogs. Everything that he had he shared. He ate dry bread and drank chicory. He knew every hardship that the rank and file of the organization knew. We do not have such leaders now.

The last of February the company put up a notice that all demands were conceded.

"Did you get the use of the hall for us to hold meetings?" said the women.

"No, we didn't ask for that."

"Then the strike is on again," said they.

They got the hall, and when the President, Mr. Wilson, returned from the convention in Cincinnati he shed tears of joy and gratitude.

I was going to leave for the central fields, and before I left, the union held a victory meeting in Bloosburg. The women came for miles in a raging snow storm for that meeting, little children trailing on their skirts, and babies under their shawls. Many of the miners had walked miles. It was one night of real joy and a great celebration. I bade them all good bye. A little boy called out, "Don't leave us, Mother. Don't leave us!" The dear little children kissed my hands. We spent the whole night in Bloosburg rejoicing. The men opened a few of the freight cars out on a siding and helped themselves to boxes of beer. Old and young talked and sang all night long and to the credit of the company no one was interfered with.

Those were the days before the extensive use of gun men, of military, of jails, of police clubs. There had been no bloodshed. There had been no riots. And the victory was due to the army of women with their mops and brooms.

A year afterward they celebrated the anniversary of the victory. They presented me with a gold watch but I declined to accept it, for I felt it was the price of the bread of the little children. I have not been in Arnot since but in my travels over the country I often meet the men and boys who carried through the strike so heroically.   [1925]

Terms

1. MARY HARRIS "MOTHER" JONES: After the loss of her four children and her husband in a yellow fever epidemic and the destruction of her dressmaking shop in the Chicago fire of 1871, "Mother" Jones became a legendary labor union organizer.
2. SCABS: Strike breakers.

Understanding the Reading

1. What were the miners' lives like?
2. Why was Mother Jones not called down to supper, and what was the real reason that she had to give up her room at the hotel?

3. What was the effect of the sheriff's putting the family who sheltered her out of their house?
4. Why did Mother Jones organize an "army of women" rather than men to face the scabs?
5. Why did the miners finally win the strike?

Suggestions for Responding

1. Describe a time when you joined with others to organize for change. ◆

124

The Organizer's Tale

CÉSAR CHÁVEZ

It really started for me 16 years ago in San Jose, California, when I was working on an apricot farm. We figured he was just another social worker doing a study of farm conditions, and I kept refusing to meet with him. But he was persistent. Finally, I got together some of the rough element in San Jose. We were going to have a little reception for him to teach the *gringo*[1] a little bit of how we felt. There were about 30 of us in the house, young guys mostly. I was supposed to give them a signal—change my cigarette from my right hand to my left, and then we were going to give him a lot of hell. But he started talking and the more he talked, the more wide-eyed I became and the less inclined I was to give the signal. A couple of guys who were pretty drunk at the time still wanted to give the *gringo* the business, but we got rid of them. This fellow was making a lot of sense, and I wanted to hear what he had to say.

His name was Fred Ross, and he was an organizer for the Community Service Organization (CSO) which was working with Mexican-Americans in the cities. I became immediately really involved. Before long I was heading a voter registration drive. All the time I was observing the things Fred did, secretly, because I wanted to learn how to organize, to see how it was done. I was impressed with his patience and understanding of people. I thought this was a tool, one of the greatest things he had.

It was pretty rough for me at first. I was changing and had to take a lot of ridicule from the kids my age, the rough characters I worked with in the fields. They would say, "Hey big shot. Now that you're a *politico,* why are you working here for 65 cents an hour?" I might add that our neighborhood had the highest percentage of San Quentin graduates. It was a game among the *pachucos*[2] in the sense that we defended ourselves from outsiders, although inside the neighborhood there was not a lot of fighting.

After six months of working every night in San Jose, Fred assigned me to take over the CSO chapter in Decoto. It was a tough spot to fill. I would suggest something, and people would say, "No, let's wait till Fred gets back," or "Fred wouldn't do it that way." This is pretty much a pattern with people, I discovered, whether I was put in Fred's position, or later, when someone else was put in my position. After the Decoto assignment I was sent to start a new chapter in Oakland. Before I left, Fred came to a place in San Jose called the Hole-in-the-Wall and we talked for half an hour over coffee. He was in a rush to leave, but I wanted to keep him talking; I was scared of my assignment.

There were hard times in Oakland. First of all, it was a big city and I'd get lost every time I went anywhere. Then I arranged a series of house meetings. I would get to the meeting early and drive back and forth past the house, too nervous to go in and face the people. Finally I would force myself to go inside and sit in a corner. I was quite thin then, and young, and most of the people were middle-aged. Someone would say, "Where's the organizer?" And I would pipe up, "Here I am." Then they would say in Spanish—these were very poor people and we hardly spoke anything but Spanish—"Ha! This *kid?*" Most of them said they were interested, but the hardest part was to get them to start pushing themselves, on their own initiative.

The idea was to set up a meeting and then get each attending person to call his own house meeting, inviting new people—a sort of chain letter effect. After a house meeting, I would lie awake going over the whole thing, playing the tape back, trying to see why people laughed at one point, or why they were for one thing and against another. I was also learning to read and write, those late evenings. I had left school in the

7th grade after attending 67 different schools, and my reading wasn't the best.

At our first organizing meeting we had 368 people: I'll never forget it because it was very important to me. You eat your heart out; the meeting is called for 7 o'clock and you start to worry about 4. You wait. Will they show up? Then the first one arrives. By 7 there are only 20 people, you have everything in order, you have to look calm. But little by little they filter in and at a certain point you know it will be a success.

After four months in Oakland, I was transferred. The chapter was beginning to move on its own, so Fred assigned me to organize the San Joaquin Valley. Over the months I developed what I used to call schemes or tricks—now I call them techniques—of making initial contacts. The main thing in convincing someone is to spend time with him. It doesn't matter if he can read, write or even speak well. What is important is that he is a man and second, that he has shown some initial interest. One good way to develop leadership is to take a man with you in your car. And it works a lot better if you're doing the driving; that way you are in charge. You drive, he sits there, and you talk. These little things were very important to me; I was caught in a big game by then, figuring out what makes people work. I found that if you work hard enough you can usually shake people into working too, those who are concerned. You work harder and they work harder still, up to a point and then they pass you. Then, of course, they're on their own.

I also learned to keep away from the established groups and so-called leaders, and to guard against philosophizing. Working with low-income people is very different from working with the professionals who like to sit around talking about how to play politics. When you're trying to recruit a farmworker, you have to paint a little picture, and then you have to color the picture in. We found out that the harder a guy is to convince, the better leader or member he becomes. When you exert yourself to convince him, you have his confidence and he has good motivation. A lot of people who say OK right away wind up hanging around the office, taking up the workers' time.

During the McCarthy era[3] in one Valley town, I was subjected to a lot of redbaiting.[4] We had been recruiting people for citizenship classes at the high school when we got into a quarrel with the naturalization examiner. He was rejecting people on the grounds that they were just parroting what they learned in citizenship class. One day we had a meeting about it in Fresno, and I took along some of the leaders of our local chapter. Some redbaiting official gave us a hard time, and the people got scared and took his side. They did it because it seemed easy at the moment, even though they knew that sticking with me was the right thing to do. It was disgusting. When we left the building they walked by themselves ahead of me as if I had some kind of communicable disease. I had been working with these people for three months and I was very sad to see that. It taught me a great lesson.

That night I learned that the chapter officers were holding a meeting to review my letters and printed materials to see if I really was a Communist. So I drove out there and walked right in on their meeting. I said, "I hear you've been discussing me, and I thought it would be nice if I was here to defend myself. Not that it matters that much to you or even to me, because as far as I'm concerned you are a bunch of cowards." At that they began to apologize. "Let's forget it," they said. "You're a nice guy." But I didn't want apologies. I wanted a full discussion. I told them I didn't give a damn, but that they had to learn to distinguish fact from what appeared to be a fact because of fear. I kept them there till two in the morning. Some of the women cried. I don't know if they investigated me any further, but I stayed on another few months and things worked out.

This was not an isolated case. Often when we'd leave people to themselves they would get frightened and draw back into their shells where they had been all the years. And I learned quickly that there is no real appreciation. Whatever you do, and no matter what reasons you may give to others, you do it because you want to see it done, or maybe because you want power. And there shouldn't be any appreciation, understandably. I know good organizers who were destroyed, washed out, because they expected people to appreciate what they'd done. Anyone who comes in with the idea that farmworkers are free of sin and that the growers are all bastards, either has never dealt with the situation or is an idealist of the first order. Things don't work that way.   [1966]

Terms

1. GRINGO: A disparaging term used in Mexico and elsewhere in Latin America for North Americans.
2. PACHUCOS: A nickname for Mexican American youth, especially delinquents and gang members.
3. McCARTHY ERA: In the 1950s, Senator Joseph McCarthy used his office to crusade against internal subversion and to charge high governmental and military officials, including several presidents, with being Communists or "fellow travelers" of Communism.
4. REDBAITING: The act of attacking or persecuting someone, accusing them of being Communist or communistic.

Understanding the Reading

1. What made Chávez interested in organizing the Mexican Americans?
2. What steps did he take to organize the new CSO chapter in Oakland?
3. What techniques did he use to make initial contacts?
4. What tactics were used to discredit Chávez?

Suggestions for Responding

1. What leadership qualities does Chávez display? ✦

125

Workers Demand Rights

LOUISE PALMER

On a hot, dusty afternoon last August [1990], someone turned out the lights in the El Paso CMT[1] garment factory. With eight years experience in the industry behind her, Carmen Domingues saw the potential for protest in the darkness of the warehouse building. Angry workers earlier had abandoned the production lines when their demands for promised Labor Day pay fell on deaf ears. So Domingues led them, one hundred weary immigrant women, out the door.

The next day the garment workers returned to CMT with the media, a lawyer, and members of the labor rights group La Mujer Obrera (Working Woman). The walk-out worked: the owner agreed to some concessions, including holiday pay. Although the concessions were hardly groundbreaking, the incident spurred on Mujer Obrera's high-profile crusade to improve working conditions in El Paso's hundred-plus garment factories. For a poor grassroots organization with 700 members, the results have been remarkable. By picketing, marching, and hunger striking, Mujer Obrera has demanded—and received—the attention of city, state, and federal officials.

The group's ability to organize is all the more notable in an industry that has historically relied upon an immigrant workforce cowed into submission by the fear of job loss. Most El Paso garment workers are recent female immigrants from Mexico who speak no English, have few skills and little education. For many, sewing or cutting cloth for $3.80 an hour is the only job they know, a job that may be the lifeline for a family of four, five, or six.

As members of the underclass, they have long been forced to withstand slavish conditions, working in dilapidated buildings with broken toilets and no toilet paper, no heating or ventilation systems, and little or no light. Many clock long hours on dangerous, out-dated machinery without worker's compensation, benefits or vacation time. Worse still are those employers who, on occasion, simply do not pay their workers.

For more than a decade, Mujer Obrera waged a low-key battle with local authorities, who all but ignored these sweat shops. With little to show for their efforts, Obrera opted for a more dramatic approach in June when Diana Fashions shut down, owing its workers weeks of pay. As a last-ditch effort to retrieve their wages, six women, including Mujer Obrera's executive director Cecilia Rodriguez, chained themselves to sewing machines located in a new factory—opened by the former owner of Diana's.

"We were desperate because we had bills to pay," said Felipa Perez, a mother of four who was dragged from the factory site by the police. "We thought it would help to go directly to him (the owner). But the only reaction we got was his silent stare and the cops, who came to throw us in jail."

Although the workers spent three nights in jail and never received their wages, the incident captured the attention of the Department of Labor [DOL], who ordered a strike force after meeting with Mujer Obrera. The inspection of fewer than half of El Paso's small factories revealed that more than 300 workers were owed $87,000 in back pay.

Such egregious violations, says DOL regional director Bill Belt, are perpetrated by unscrupulous, fly-by-night operators who exploit the weak enforcement of laws that are, in any case, filled with loopholes. Belt says government agencies do not have the power to shut down these shops or arrest their owners who owe both workers and the IRS[2] money.

"Because only a small amount of capital is needed to go into business in the garment industry," explains Belt, "you have these marginal operators who keep closing down and opening up under new names, with different partners and different capital in another part of town. Some of these people haven't paid taxes in years. Often, you can't trace the original owner back to an operation once it has closed." For a worker, that can mean writing off hundreds of desperately needed dollars.

"These conditions amount to slavery," says Mujer Obrera's development specialist, Cindy Arnold. "This lawlessness exists because these workers are women and they are immigrants." While the DOL points a finger at factory operators, Arnold and Democratic Congressman Ronald Coleman blame government agencies—including the DOL—that have not vigorously enforced the law. They say violations have mushroomed during the eighties precisely because there was no commitment to protecting worker rights in the Reagan/Bush Administration. Although the DOL and the Occupational Safety and Health Agency deny these allegations, Arnold says the agencies committed strike forces into El Paso's garment factories only when Mujer Obrera garnered the media's attention.

While six women fasted under the shade of a tent set up in the middle of a downtown El Paso park, Mujer Obrera galvanized the support of labor, Hispanic and feminist organizations through activities emphasizing worker solidarity.

The strike was a radical call to action, aimed at educating the entire community about the oppression damaging the lives of women workers in the garment industry. But it also provided an opportunity for women to exercise their leadership qualities, an essential activity for Mujer Obrera members. The organization's education, social and economic programs—food and bread cooperatives, classes, youth outreach—emphasize building self-confidence, developing individual capabilities, and promoting self-sufficiency. "The women begin to see value in themselves, and not just as objects," says Carmen Domingues, an eight year veteran of garment factories who participated in the strike. "They see that we have our rights and our struggles and they carry that attitude home, where they have been told, 'you're dumb.'"

DYING A SLOW DEATH

The odds of winning this fight are not good for Mujer Obrera. Deteriorating conditions in the factories are inextricably linked to a force beyond the group's control: the creeping paralysis in the garment industry. Over the last decade, El Paso lost almost five thousand jobs. Across the nation, the figure reads half a million. Big employers—corporate manufacturers such as Billy the Kid and Farah Inc.—moved their El Paso factories off-shore to Mexico or the Caribbean where labor is even more pliant. Industry experts view the offshore trend as yet another example of this nation's collapsing industrial base, its inability to persevere in the face of a low-rent Third World labor force.

Because cheap sewing machines are always available, shops run by subcontractors pop up overnight, existing month-to-month depending on the availability of contracts. Unlike the large manufacturing corporations, these undercapitalized shops have no money for investments in technology and upgrading, says Trish Winstead, director of El Paso Manufacturer's Association. This means that some shops are not capable of satisfying the demands of manufacturers. As a result, clothing orders are returned without pay, leaving the subcontractor—and the workers—out of pocket.

"I just had a batch of jeans come back last week," says Alejandro Ruiz, operator of Christian

Fashions. "But I've also had checks from manufacturers bounce repeatedly. When something like that happens, it creates cash flow problems for subcontractors. Some can't pay their workers because they don't have the money."

Mujer Obrera maintains that the manufacturers should shoulder at least partial responsibility for wage theft and working conditions in subcontractor shops because they benefit most. "The industry is structured so that five or six levels of people are taking cuts of profit from a single garment, with the manufacturer at the top of the pile," explains Arnold. "That dictates the kind of exploitation and enslavement that exists at the subcontractor level. Everyone wants to maintain their level of profit regardless of how much costs rise. So the lower levels of this structure are squeezed to keep prices down.

The drive to lower production costs has intensified as manufacturers move south, leaving shop operators to compete for a shrinking pool of contracts, and workers to fight for fewer and fewer jobs. Subcontractors may be struggling, but ultimately it is the workers, clinging to the lowest rung on the ladder, who bear the brunt of cost-cutting measures in the workplace.

Ironically, Mujer Obrera's efforts to secure pay and better working conditions may speed the departure of manufacturers from El Paso—and this country. Apparel manufacturers like Mark Mainwaring, Vice President of El Paso's OMSA,[3] believe Mujer Obrera may cause irreparable damage to factories in the area. "Although Mujer Obrera is obtaining short term goals, the long term effect will be to cast aspersions on the whole industry and prevent people from sending work to El Paso. They may decide it's not worth it and just move their operation across the border." For Mujer Obrera, it's a risk worth taking, says executive director Cecilia Rodriguez. "To the industry we say, 'If it's going to come down to a choice between exploiting us or leaving, we say go.'"

But Rodriguez is hopeful that El Paso's garment industry can be revived with some innovative thinking.

Through the commission, Mujer Obrera hopes to encourage manufacturers to reinvest in and upgrade shops they buy from. Mujer Obrera believes this can happen if the city commits resources to promoting and nurturing the garment industry. They say the Chamber of Commerce, for example, should lobby to attract manufacturers by advertising the advantages the city offers: skilled workers in shops that work small orders with quick turn-around time. Manufacturers can avoid red tape, quotas, delays and freight costs if the work is done in the U.S.

Mujer Obrera knows it's a long shot. But they also know the survival of the industry is not a measure of their success. Mujer Obrera has already created a dynamic group of leaders, who are prompting members of this community to reconsider their position in the ongoing struggle for equal rights in the workplace. "Our protests are meant to force you to take a moral stance," said Mujer Obrera's executive director, Cecilia Rodriguez, exhorting a crowd gathered for the hunger strike vigil. "Is this indeed what women deserve?" [1991]

Terms

1. CMT: Cut, make, and trim. CMT work is a widespread practice in the garment industry, wherever there is cheap labor available, especially in third world countries. The fabric belongs to the buyer, and the firm is paid a processing fee.
2. IRS: Internal Revenue Service.
3. OMSA: Overseas Manufacturing Systems of America.

Understanding the Reading

1. What tactics did Carmen Domingues and *La Mujer Obrera* employ to improve their working conditions?
2. What obstacles did they face?
3. Why are the garment factories in El Paso able to operate under these conditions?
4. How has *La Mujer Obrera* become more than simply a labor union?
5. What future problems does the El Paso garment industry face?
6. What response does *La Mujer Obrera* propose to them?

Suggestions for Responding

1. Write a letter to your congressperson telling him or her what you think could and should be done about the practices of the textile industry described in this article.

2. If you know someone who has belonged to a labor union, interview him or her and report on any benefits and drawbacks to membership that he or she believes there are. ◆

126

Free at Last

SOUTHERN POVERTY LAW CENTER

By 1910, blacks were caught in a degrading system of total segregation throughout the South. Through "Jim Crow" laws (named after a black minstrel in a popular song), blacks were ordered to use separate restrooms, water fountains, restaurants, waiting rooms, swimming pools, libraries, and bus seats.

The United States Supreme Court gave its approval to Jim Crow segregation in the 1896 case of *Plessy v. Ferguson.* The Court said separate facilities were legal as long as they were equal. In practice, Southern states never provided equal facilities to black people—only separate ones.

Frederick Douglass[1] tried to expose the inherent contradictions in the law of the land: "So far as the colored people of the country are concerned," he said, "the Constitution is but a stupendous sham . . . fair without and foul within, keeping the promise to the eye and breaking it to the heart."

Despite Douglass' eloquent arguments, it would be generations before the nation lived up to its promises.

FIGHTING JIM CROW

Just as slaves had revolted against being someone else's property, the newly freed blacks revolted peacefully against the forces of racism. Ida B. Wells began a crusade against lynching at age 19 that inspired a national gathering of black leaders in 1893 to call for an anti-lynch law.

George Henry White, the only black U.S. congressman at the turn of the century, was a bold spokesman for equal rights. The former slave from North Carolina sponsored the first anti-lynching bill and insisted that the federal government enforce the constitutional amend-

ments. In a speech to his fellow congressmen, White asked, "How long will you sit in your seats and hear and see the principles that underlie the foundations of this government sapped away little by little?"

One of the strongest critiques of American racism was offered by W. E. B. DuBois, a Harvard-educated sociologist. In *The Souls of Black Folk,* DuBois said American society had to be transformed if blacks were to achieve full equality.

DuBois, along with other black and white leaders, established the National Association for the Advancement of Colored People [NAACP] in 1910. The NAACP launched a legal campaign against racial injustice, began documenting racist violence, and published a magazine called *Crisis.* By 1940, NAACP membership reached 50,000.

As blacks were organizing for reform, white supremacists were organizing to stop them. By the time the NAACP was 10 years old, two million whites belonged to the Ku Klux Klan. During the 1920s, Klansmen held high positions in government throughout the country.

In the South, Klan violence surged. Blacks moved North in record numbers, hoping to escape racial terrorism and to find better jobs. Although they faced poverty, unequal education, and discrimination in the North as well, racial restrictions there were less harsh. Blacks could even vote in Northern states. Indeed, by 1944, the black vote was a significant factor in 16 states outside the South.

BRINGING DEMOCRACY HOME

With the election of President Franklin Delano Roosevelt, black Americans finally had an ally in the White House. Black leaders were included among the president's advisers. Roosevelt's New Deal made welfare and jobs available to blacks as well as whites. A more liberal Supreme Court issued rulings against bus segregation and all-white political primaries. Black labor leader A. Philip Randolph scored a major victory when he convinced President Roosevelt to issue an Executive Order banning racial discrimination in all defense industries.

The demand for equal rights surged after World War II, when black soldiers returned from battling the racist horrors of Nazi Germany only to find they remained victims of racism at home.

Determined to bring democracy to America, blacks sought new strategies. Seeing Mahatma Gandhi[2] lead the Indian masses in peaceful demonstrations for independence, the Congress of Racial Equality [CORE] decided to put the philosophy of nonviolence to work in America.

After much training and discussion, black and white members of CORE entered segregated restaurants, quietly sat down, and refused to leave until they were served. They did not raise their voices in anger or strike back if attacked. In a few Northern cities, their persistent demonstrations succeeded in integrating some restaurants.

After the Supreme Court outlawed segregation on interstate buses in 1946, CORE members set out on a "Journey of Reconciliation" to test whether the laws were being obeyed. Blacks and whites rode together on buses through the South and endured harassment without retaliating.

While the sit-ins and freedom rides of the 1940s served as models for the next generation of civil rights activists, they did not capture the broad support that was necessary to overturn segregation. The CORE victories were quiet ones, representing the determination of relatively few people.

The major battles against segregation were being fought in courtrooms and legislatures. Growing pressure from black leaders after World War II forced President Harry Truman to integrate the armed forces and to establish a civil rights commission. In 1947, that commission issued a report called *To Secure These Rights* that exposed racial injustices and called for the elimination of segregation in America.

By that time, half a million blacks belonged to the NAACP. Lawsuits brought by the NAACP had forced many school districts to improve black schools. Then, in 1950, NAACP lawyers began building the case that would force the Supreme Court to outlaw segregated schools and mark the beginning of the modern civil rights movement.

A MOVEMENT OF THE PEOPLE

Linda Brown's parents could not understand why their 7-year-old daughter should have to ride long distances each day to a rundown black school when there was a much better white school in their own neighborhood of Topeka, Kansas. Harry Briggs of Clarendon, South Carolina, was outraged that his five children had to attend schools which operated on one-fourth the amount of money given to white schools. Ethel Belton took her complaints to the Delaware Board of Education when her children were forced to ride a bus for nearly two hours each day instead of walking to their neighborhood high school in Claymont. In Farmville, Virginia, 16-year-old Barbara Johns led her fellow high school students on a strike for a better school.

All over the country, black students and parents were angered over the conditions of their schools. NAACP lawyers studied their grievances and decided that it was not enough to keep fighting for equal facilities. They wanted all schools integrated.

A team of NAACP lawyers used the Topeka, Clarendon, Claymont and Farmville examples to argue that segregation itself was unconstitutional. They lost in the lower courts, but when they took their cause to the Supreme Court, the justices ruled they were right.

On May 17, 1954, the Supreme Court unanimously ruled that segregated schools "are inherently unequal." The Court explained that even if separate schools for blacks and whites had the same physical facilities, there could be no true equality as long as segregation itself existed. To separate black children "solely because of their race," the Court wrote, "generates a feeling of inferiority as to their status in the community that may affect their hearts and minds in a way very unlikely ever to be undone."

The *Brown v. Board of Education* ruling enraged many Southern whites who did not believe blacks deserved the same education as whites and didn't want their children attending schools with black children. Southern governors announced they would not abide by the Court's ruling, and White Citizens' Councils were organized to oppose school integration. Mississippi legislators passed a law abolishing compulsory school attendance. A declaration called the Southern Manifesto was issued by 96 Southern congressmen, demanding that the Court reverse the *Brown* decision.

Despite the opposition by many whites, the *Brown* decision gave great hope to blacks. Even when the Supreme Court refused to order immediate integration (calling instead for schools to act "with all deliberate speed"), black Americans knew that times were changing. And they were eager for expanded rights in other areas as well.

WALKING FOR JUSTICE

Four days after the Supreme Court handed down the *Brown* ruling, Jo Ann Robinson wrote a letter as president of the Women's Political Council to the mayor of Montgomery, Alabama. She represented a large group of black women, she said, and was asking for fair treatment on city buses.

Blacks, who made up 75 percent of Montgomery's bus riders, were forced to enter the buses in front, pay the driver, and re-enter the bus from the rear, where they could only sit in designated "colored" seats. If all the "white" seats were full, blacks had to give up their seats.

Women and children had been arrested for refusing to give up their seats. Others who challenged the bus drivers were slapped or beaten. Hilliard Brooks, 22, was shot dead by police in 1952 after an argument with a bus driver.

Every day, black housekeepers rode all the way home after work, jammed together in the aisles, while 10 rows of "white" seats remained empty.

Blacks could shut down the city's bus system if they wanted to, Jo Ann Robinson told the mayor. "More and more of our people are already arranging with neighbors and friends to ride to keep from being insulted and humiliated by bus drivers."

The mayor said segregation was the law and he could not change it.

On December 1, 1955, Rosa Parks was riding home from her job as a department store seamstress. The bus was full when a white man boarded. The driver stopped the bus and ordered Mrs. Parks along with three other blacks to vacate a row so the white man could sit down. Three of the blacks stood up. Rosa Parks kept her seat and was arrested.

Jo Ann Robinson and the Women's Political Council immediately began to organize a bus boycott with the support of NAACP leader E. D.

Nixon. Prominent blacks hurriedly formed the Montgomery Improvement Association and selected a newcomer in town, Dr. Martin Luther King Jr., to be their leader.

On the night of December 5, a crowd of 15,000 gathered at Holt Street Church to hear the young preacher speak. "There comes a time that people get tired," King told the crowd. "We are here this evening to say to those who have mistreated us so long that we are tired—tired of being segregated and humiliated; tired of being kicked about by the brutal feet of oppression. . . . We have no alternative but to protest.

"And we are not wrong in what we are doing," he said. "If we are wrong, the Supreme Court of this nation is wrong. If we are wrong, God Almighty is wrong!"

If the bus boycott was peaceful and guided by love, King said, justice would be won. Historians in future generations, King predicted, "will have to pause and say, 'There lived a great people—a black people—who injected new meaning and dignity into the veins of civilization.'"

For 381 days, black people did not ride the buses in Montgomery. They organized car pools and walked long distances, remaining nonviolent even when harassed and beaten by angry whites. When Dr. King's home was bombed, they only became more determined. City officials tried to outlaw the boycott, but still the buses traveled empty.

On December 21, 1956, blacks returned to the buses in triumph. The U.S. Supreme Court had outlawed bus segregation in Montgomery in response to a lawsuit brought by the boycotters with the help of the NAACP. The boycotters' victory showed the entire white South that all blacks, not just civil rights leaders, were opposed to segregation. It demonstrated that poor and middle class blacks could unite to launch a successful protest movement, overcoming both official counterattacks and racist terror. And it showed the world that nonviolent resistance could work—even in Montgomery, the capital of the Confederate States during the Civil War.

King went on to establish an organization of black clergy, called the Southern Christian Leadership Conference, that raised funds for integration campaigns throughout the South. Black Southern ministers, following the example of King in Montgomery, became the spiritual force behind the nonviolent movement. Using the lessons of Montgomery, blacks challenged bus segregation in Tallahassee and Atlanta.

But when they tried to integrate schools and other public facilities, blacks discovered the lengths to which whites would go to preserve white supremacy. A black student admitted to the University of Alabama by federal court order was promptly expelled. The State of Virginia closed all public schools in Prince Edward County to avoid integration. Some communities filled in their public swimming pools and closed their tennis courts, and others removed library seats, rather than let blacks and whites share the facilities.

Blacks who challenged segregation received little help from the federal government. President Eisenhower had no enthusiasm for the *Brown* decision, and he desperately wanted to avoid segregation disputes.

Finally, in 1957, a crisis in Little Rock, Arkansas, forced Eisenhower to act.

NINE PIONEERS IN LITTLE ROCK

On September 4, 1957, Governor Orval Faubus ordered troops to surround Central High School in Little Rock, to keep nine black teenagers from entering. Despite the *Brown* ruling which said black students had a right to attend integrated schools, Governor Faubus was determined to keep the schools segregated.

That afternoon, a federal judge ordered Faubus to let the black students attend the white school. The next day, when 15-year-old Elizabeth Eckford set out for class, she was mobbed, spit upon and cursed by angry whites. When she finally made her way to the front steps of Central High, National Guard soldiers turned her away.

An outraged federal judge again ordered the governor to let the children go to school. Faubus removed the troops but gave the black children no protection. The nine black children made it to their first class, but had to be sent home when a violent white mob gathered outside the school. Faubus said the disturbance proved the school should not be integrated.

President Eisenhower had a choice: he could either send in federal troops to protect the children or allow a governor to defy the Constitution. Saying "our personal opinions have no bearing on the matter of enforcement," the president ordered in troops. For the rest of the school year, U.S. soldiers walked alongside the Little Rock nine as they went from class to class.

The next year, Governor Faubus shut down all the public schools rather than integrate them. A year later, the U.S. Supreme Court ruled that "evasive schemes" could not be used to avoid integration, and the Little Rock schools were finally opened to black and white students.

Although the Little Rock case did not end the long battle for school integration, it proved the federal government would not tolerate brazen defiance of federal law by state officials. It also served as an example for President John F. Kennedy who in 1962 ordered federal troops to protect James Meredith as he became the first black student to attend the University of Mississippi.   [1989]

Terms

1. FREDERICK DOUGLASS: An escaped slave, who became a leading abolitionist.
2. MAHATMA GANDHI: A Hindu nationalist and spiritual leader, who led the "passive resistance" movement to get the British out of India.

Understanding the Reading

1. What were Jim Crow laws?
2. How did the newly freed Blacks respond to them?
3. How did Franklin Roosevelt's presidency benefit Black Americans?
4. What gains did CORE achieve?
5. Explain the Supreme Court ruling in *Brown v. Board of Education*.
6. What made the Montgomery bus boycott effective?
7. What tactics did Whites use to avoid school desegregation?

Suggestions for Responding

1. Imagine that you were an African American in the South in the first half of the twentieth century. Choose one example of Jim Crow

segregation (separate schools, restrooms, waiting rooms, drinking fountains; prohibitions on voting; rules about having to ride in the back of the bus) and describe your experience. What would you realistically do in such circumstances?

2. Learn more details about one specific example of southern White resistance to school integration, and write a brief report on it. ◆

127

The Movement

ANNE MOODY

I had counted on graduating in the spring of 1963, but as it turned out, I couldn't because some of my credits still had to be cleared with Natchez College. A year before, this would have seemed like a terrible disaster, but now I hardly even felt disappointed. I had a good excuse to stay on campus for the summer and work with the Movement, and this was what I really wanted to do. I couldn't go home again anyway, and I couldn't go to New Orleans—I didn't have money enough for bus fare.

During my senior year at Tougaloo, my family hadn't sent me one penny. I had only the small amount of money I had earned at Maple Hill. I couldn't afford to eat at school or live in the dorms, so I had gotten permission to move off campus. I had to prove that I could finish school, even if I had to go hungry every day. I knew Raymond and Miss Pearl were just waiting to see me drop out. But something happened to me as I got more and more involved in the Movement. It no longer seemed important to prove anything. I had found something outside myself that gave meaning to my life.

I had become very friendly with my social science professor, John Salter, who was in charge of NAACP[1] activities on campus. All during the year, while the NAACP conducted a boycott of the downtown stores in Jackson, I had been one of Salter's most faithful canvassers and church speakers. During the last week of school, he told me that sit-in demonstrations were about to start in Jackson and that he wanted me to be the spokesman for a team that would sit-in at Woolworth's lunch counter. The two other demonstrators would be classmates of mine, Memphis and Pearlena. Pearlena was a dedicated NAACP worker, but Memphis had not been very involved in the Movement on campus. It seemed that the organization had had a rough time finding students who were in a position to go to jail. I had nothing to lose one way or the other. Around ten o'clock the morning of the demonstrations, NAACP headquarters alerted the news services. As a result, the police department was also informed, but neither the policemen nor the newsmen knew exactly where or when the demonstrations would start. They stationed themselves along Capitol Street and waited.

To divert attention from the sit-in at Woolworth's, the picketing started at J. C. Penney's a good fifteen minutes before. The pickets were allowed to walk up and down in front of the store three or four times before they were arrested. At exactly 11 A.M., Pearlena, Memphis, and I entered Woolworth's from the rear entrance. We separated as soon as we stepped into the store, and made small purchases from various counters. Pearlena had given Memphis her watch. He was to let us know when it was 11:14. At 11:14 we were to join him near the lunch counter and at exactly 11:15 we were to take seats at it.

Seconds before 11:15 we were occupying three seats at the previously segregated Woolworth's lunch counter. In the beginning the waitresses seemed to ignore us, as if they really didn't know what was going on. Our waitress walked past us a couple of times before she noticed we had started to write our own orders down and realized we wanted service. She asked us what we wanted. We began to read to her from our order slips. She told us that we would be served at the back counter, which was for Negroes.

"We would like to be served here," I said.

The waitress started to repeat what she had said, then stopped in the middle of the sentence. She turned the lights out behind the counter, and she and the other waitresses almost ran to the back of the store, deserting all their white customers. I guess they thought that violence would start immediately after the whites at the counter realized what was going on. There were five or six other people at the counter. A couple of them just got up and walked away. A girl sitting next to me finished her banana split before leaving. A middle-aged white woman who had not yet been served rose from her seat and came over to us. "I'd like to stay here with you," she said, "but my husband is waiting."

The newsmen came in just as she was leaving. They must have discovered what was going on shortly after some of the people began to leave the store. One of the newsmen ran behind the woman who spoke to us and asked her to identify herself. She refused to give her name, but said she was a native of Vicksburg and a former resident of California. When asked why she had said what she had said to us, she replied, "I am in sympathy with the Negro movement." By this time a crowd of cameramen and reporters had gathered around us taking pictures and asking questions, such as Where were we from? Why did we sit-in? What organization sponsored it? Were we students? From what school? How were we classified?

I told them that we were all students at Tougaloo College, that we were represented by no particular organization, and that we planned to stay there even after the store closed. "All we want is service," was my reply to one of them. After they had finished probing for about twenty minutes, they were almost ready to leave.

At noon, students from a nearby white high school started pouring in to Woolworth's. When they first saw us they were sort of surprised. They didn't know how to react. A few started to heckle and the newsmen became interested again. Then the white students started chanting all kinds of anti-Negro slogans. We were called a little bit of everything. The rest of the seats except the three we were occupying had been roped off to prevent others from sitting down. A couple of the boys took one end of the rope and made it into a hangman's noose. Several attempts were made to put it around our necks. The crowds grew as more students and adults came in for lunch.

We kept our eyes straight forward and did not look at the crowd except for occasional glances to see what was going on. All of a sudden I saw a face I remembered—the drunkard from the bus station sit-in. My eyes lingered on him just long enough for us to recognize each other. Today he was drunk too, so I don't think he remembered where he had seen me before. He took out a knife, opened it, put it in his pocket, and then began to pace the floor. At this point, I told Memphis and Pearlena what was going on. Memphis suggested that we pray. We bowed our heads, and all hell broke loose. A man rushed forward, threw Memphis from his seat, and slapped my face. Then another man who worked in the store threw me against an adjoining counter.

Down on my knees on the floor, I saw Memphis lying near the lunch counter with blood running out of the corners of his mouth. As he tried to protect his face, the man who'd thrown him down kept kicking him against the head. If he had worn hard-soled shoes instead of sneakers, the first kick probably would have killed Memphis. Finally a man dressed in plain clothes identified himself as a police officer and arrested Memphis and his attacker.

Pearlena had been thrown to the floor. She and I got back on our stools after Memphis was arrested. There were some white Tougaloo teachers in the crowd. They asked Pearlena and me if we wanted to leave. They said that things were getting too rough. We didn't know what to do. While we were trying to make up our minds, we were joined by Joan Trumpauer. Now there were three of us and we were integrated. The crowd began to chant, "Communists, Communists, Communists." Some old man in the crowd ordered the students to take us off the stools.

"Which one should I get first?" a big husky boy said.

"That white nigger," the old man said.

The boy lifted Joan from the counter by her waist and carried her out of the store. Simultaneously, I was snatched from my stool by two high school students. I was dragged about thirty feet toward the door by my hair when someone made them turn me loose. As I was getting up off the floor, I saw Joan coming back inside. We started back to the center of the counter to join Pearlena. Lois Chaffee, a white Tougaloo faculty member, was now sitting next to her. So Joan and I just climbed across the rope at the front end of the counter and sat down. There were now four of us, two whites and two Negroes, all women. The mob started smearing us with ketchup, mustard, sugar, pies, and everything on the counter. Soon Joan and I were joined by John Salter, but the moment he sat down he was hit on the jaw with what appeared to be brass knuckles. Blood gushed from his face and someone threw salt into the open wound. Ed King, Tougaloo's chaplain, rushed to him.

At the other end of the counter, Lois and Pearlena were joined by George Raymond, a CORE[2] field worker and a student from Jackson State College. Then a Negro high school boy sat down next to me. The mob took spray paint from the counter and sprayed it on the new demonstrators. The high school student had on a white shirt; the word "nigger" was written on his back with red spray paint.

We sat there for three hours taking a beating when the manager decided to close the store because the mob had begun to go wild with stuff from other counters. He begged and begged everyone to leave. But even after fifteen minutes of begging, no one budged. They would not leave until we did. Then Dr. Beittel, the president of Tougaloo College, came running in. He said he had just heard what was happening.

About ninety policemen were standing outside the store; they had been watching the whole thing through the windows, but had not come in to stop the mob or do anything. President Beittel went outside and asked Captain Ray to come and escort us out. The captain refused, stating the manager had to invite him in before he could enter the premises, so Dr. Beittel himself brought us out. He had told the police that they had better protect us after we were outside the store. When we got outside, the policemen formed a single line that blocked the mob from us. However, they were allowed to throw at us everything they had collected. Within ten minutes, we were picked up by Reverend King in his station wagon and taken to the NAACP headquarters on Lynch Street.

After the sit-in, all I could think of was how sick Mississippi whites were. They believed so much in the segregated Southern way of life, they would kill to preserve it. I sat there in the NAACP office and thought of how many times they had killed when this way of life was threatened. I knew that the killing had just begun.

"Many more will die before it is over with," I thought. Before the sit-in, I had always hated the whites in Mississippi. Now I knew it was impossible for me to hate sickness. The whites had a disease, an incurable disease in its final stage. What were our chances against such a disease? I thought of the students, the young Negroes who had just begun to protest, as young interns. When these young interns got older, I thought, they would be the best doctors in the world for social problems.

Before we were taken back to campus, I wanted to get my hair washed. It was stiff with dried mustard, ketchup and sugar. I stopped in at a beauty shop across the street from the NAACP office. I didn't have on any shoes because I had lost them when I was dragged across the floor at Woolworth's. My stockings were sticking to my legs from the mustard that had dried on them. The hairdresser took one look at me and said, "My land, you were in the sit-in, huh?"

"Yes," I answered. "Do you have time to wash my hair and style it?"

"Right away," she said, and she meant right away. There were three other ladies already waiting, but they seemed glad to let me go ahead of them. The hairdresser was real nice. She even took my stockings off and washed my legs while my hair was drying.

There was a mass rally that night at the Pearl Street Church in Jackson, and the place was packed. People were standing two abreast in the aisles. Before the speakers began, all the sit-inners walked out on the stage and were introduced by Medgar Evers.[3] People stood and applauded for what seemed like thirty minutes or more. Medgar told the audience that this was just the beginning of such demonstrations. He asked them to pledge themselves to unite in a massive offensive against segregation in Jackson, and throughout the state. The rally ended with "We Shall Overcome" and sent home hundreds of determined people. It seemed as though Mississippi Negroes were about to get together at last.

[1968]

Terms

1. NAACP: National Association for the Advancement of Colored People.

2. CORE: Congress of Racial Equality.
3. MEDGAR EVERS: The NAACP field secretary in Mississippi, who was assassinated a few weeks after this event.

Understanding the Reading

1. How do you account for the various reactions of the Whites at the lunch counter when the demonstrators sat down?
2. Why did the high school students respond differently than these people did?
3. Explain the reaction of the women in the beauty shop.

Suggestions for Responding

1. Explain how Moody's experience illustrates the various features of nonviolent resistance.
   ✦

128

Freedom Is a Constant Struggle

MURIEL TILLINGHAST

Three days after I graduated, I decided I was going to Mississippi. I didn't know what was going to happen after that, but I was definitely going to go. Now, it was already bad enough that I had let my hair grow natural—that eliminated about 90 percent of the discussion in my house—but when I decided to go to Mississippi, everyone got on my case. My parents, my family—people weren't *talking* to me.

We knew that something momentous was occurring down South. People were operating in very small groups, but they were operating in many different places. At that point the press had not yet decided what political perspective they were going to take on events in the South, so they were actually showing all this activity on television. This was a source of encouragement for us and helped to tie the lines of communication together. Of course, that didn't last. Later on, I'm sure the press boys sat down in a large room and said, "Enough of this, let's move on."

Now, I was basically a Northerner—folks from Washington, D.C., like to think that they're from the North. I had already had some experiences on the eastern shore of Maryland, which will let you know immediately that you're not North, but I hadn't really gotten ready for Mississippi. We all spent a week at the orientation center in Oxford, Ohio. SNCC[1] sent up its people, who told us all these tales about what folks had to go through just in terms of a normal life struggle. We knew that Mississippi was going to be a special place. And for all of us who went, we know we didn't come back the same.

HEADING SOUTH

So we went to Mississippi after spending a week getting ready for something you really couldn't get ready for. We headed in on Greyhound buses. People were singing and talking and joking around on the bus, but when we hit that Mississippi line there was silence. People got dropped off at various projects one by one in the dead of night. I was dropped off in Greenville. We made a point of distinguishing Greenville from Greenwood. Green*ville* was relatively liberal. If you were in Green*wood,* you were in deep. I still had hope.

In all honesty I spent my first two weeks in the office upstairs because I didn't know quite how I was going to be able to survive Mississippi. After a while it dawned on me that I would never get anybody to register that way, so I started coming downstairs and cautiously going out into the town. I functioned like a shadow on the wall, just getting used to walking in the streets.

Charles Cobb was my project director. About a month after I got to Mississippi, Charles looked at me and said, "You know, I want to do something else. So I'm going to leave you in charge of this project. You look like you can handle it." Right, sure thing . . .

I was in charge of three counties: Washington, Sharkey, and Issaquena. In Mississippi, you learn the county structure like the back of your hand, because the basis of power politics is the county structure. Greenville, which was the base of our operations, was the Washington County seat. It was the town in a county of hamlets.

Sharkey County was the home of the Klan in that part of Mississippi. Issaquena was a Black county, and it was sort of discounted at the time.

By and large we took our mandate from Stokely Carmichael [Kwame Toure], who was the project chief in our area. We were young, and we were just beginning to learn what politics and power were all about. We began to find out that power is monolithic, particularly in places where there is not a lot of competition.

People in Mississippi knew about us long before we had even gotten there. We didn't realize it at first, but we were under constant surveillance. For instance, a young white volunteer was doing some research at the library, which was in the same building as the police station, on the second floor. As she was coming out of the library, the police chief said to her, "Come here, I want to show you something." He took her to a room, and in that room was a file drawer, and in that file drawer were pictures of everybody in our project. We had no idea that they were watching us this closely. And they had pictures of every kind of activity, taken day and night, because they were using infrared.

Well, these pictures may not mean anything right now, but there were times when the political pressure really got to us. For example, we had some young gay men who were in our project, and I remember very tearfully putting one of them on the bus. He said, "Muriel, I can't have those pictures shown." I didn't even know that anything was going on, but the bottom line is that everybody's privacy was invaded. And that's *before* we had even registered anybody to vote.

In these little country towns, as soon as a foreign-sounding motor comes across the road in the middle of the night, people know that a stranger is there. You need never make an announcement. You can stay in the house all day—someone knows. "I heard a different motor last night. It stopped about two doors down the street." And they start making inquiries. There were instances when the police just opened the door and came through the house looking for us and never said a word to any of the people who lived there. Not that they were going to rough us up at that point, but someone knew that someone was keeping company with people who weren't local.

In order to encourage people to vote, we had to explain what was going on in the country and why they were in the situation that they were in. We tried to convince them of the importance of their participation in the voting process by showing them who was actually on the voting rolls—for instance, half the local cemetery! Sometimes we were able to register only a few people—why risk your life simply to sign a piece of paper or register at the county courthouse—but as people gradually came to trust us, they would talk to their neighbors, and the numbers swelled.

The Heart of the Black Belt

Later I moved out of Greenville and into Issaquena County. Until I got to Mississippi, I didn't know anything about Black counties. I began to find out that there were these towns like Mound Bayou outside of Holly Springs where Blacks had settled after the Emancipation Proclamation and established their own base.

Most people in the North don't understand why Blacks are so poor. They don't realize that when Black people left slavery, they left with nothing—I mean *nothing*. Whatever they were wearing, those were the clothes that they took with them into their new life. Whatever beans or seeds they could gather, that was going to be food. They didn't own the land they were standing on—they were immediately trespassing. And in Mississippi trespassing was a serious crime—as serious as selling a kilo of cocaine in New York City today. You were going to go to jail and your minimum time was going to be five years—just for standing on the land.

So the people had to move, and when they moved, they moved under pain of death, because the same people who had always kept Black people enslaved were again at work hunting down those bands of Blacks who were leaving by foot. Black people had no way of defending themselves. They had to travel by night, gathering up at certain places—word gets around on the grapevine. And they began to establish themselves in various places, even in the state of Mississippi. Issaquena was one of those places. It was sort of a long county, and very sparsely settled. Counting everybody standing up, the county seat at Mayersville had 50 people.

Some of you may be familiar with the name of Unita Blackwell. She made a name for herself over time as the mayor of Mayersville and as an activist, but when I met Unita, she was just an ordinary housewife. She and her husband, Jeremiah Blackwell, were the first ones to offer us a safe haven in Issaquena. That's really how we operated. We would be invited in by one household, and based on that household's sense of us as individuals and where we were going as an organization—because they knew that we were not alone—they would introduce us to someone else. This would be our next contact. And if this sounds like we were operating under war conditions, we were. You did not talk to *anybody* unless someone said it was okay. And it wasn't that obvious who was safe to talk to, because you never knew if you were talking to the State Sovereignty Commission.

The State Sovereignty Commission was an intelligence-gathering force. It was set up by the government of the state of Mississippi. Hundreds of thousands of dollars of state taxpayers' money—including Black taxpayers' money—was used to finance all this surveillance. It was responsible for gathering and spreading disinformation early in the game. Early on we thought it was *mis*information—that they just didn't get it straight—but it was really *dis*information that was deliberately designed to undermine public support for the activities that we were engaged in.

You had to be careful about who you spoke to because you could be trailed back to your base. Wherever you were staying, those people were as vulnerable to midnight raids as you were on the streets. So when they allowed you to sleep on their floor or in their best bed in the corner of their house, whatever the accommodations were, they were putting themselves in jeopardy. As Bob Moses used to say, "Mississippi needs no exaggeration." It was its own exaggeration.

I remember one family of cotton pickers that I stayed with—two adults and five kids. They were in Hollandale, a nasty little town on the highway between Greenville and Mayersville. This family was at the very bottom of the economic ladder. They worked by permission on someone else's land. They worked from sun up to sun down with no breaks. It was as close to slavery as I hope I ever see in life. I usually made a point of eating somewhere else, but one night they said, "No, you eat with us." I'll never forget that dinner. It was cornbread and a huge pot of water into which they cut three or four frankfurters. For them that was a *good* dinner.

FOUNDING A FREEDOM SCHOOL

We also started a Freedom School. Why? Well, out of natural curiosity schoolchildren wanted to know, "Why can't we vote?" So there was a need to put this particular situation into some sort of historical context. And as you talked about the history of Black people in this country, you began to see another kind of development taking place in the young people. Before they would let certain things in school go by unchallenged. They might not like something, but they wouldn't question it. Our presence gave them a support base, and they began to have the courage to say certain things, or not to read certain things, or to bring other materials to the classroom. This was unheard of. And it wouldn't take long before those kids would be sent home, first one kid, then another, and by the time a week had passed, there would be 20 kids who had been told by the principal, "Don't come back!"

Now the school system was segregated—these were Black kids in Black schools—so how could this be happening? To understand that you have to understand the power relations in the South. You don't get to be a Black principal in a Black school in Mississippi unless you are an acceptable political commodity—pure and simple. And you quickly become *un*acceptable when you start having alien thoughts—like why can't we register to vote and what is this Grandfather Clause anyway—just normal conversation. But that wasn't considered normal conversation, that was considered subversive, and these young people had to be plucked out before they spread the cancer to the rest of the student population. So even though most of us tried to maintain a low profile, it didn't take long for brush fires to occur.

SHERIFF DAVIS BUILDS A JAIL

Even though Issaquena was a Black county, all the people who had any power were white, including Sheriff Davis. When our paths crossed, which they did all too frequently, we would greet each other—"How ya doin',"—because Mississippi is country-like in that way. The first time I saw Sheriff Davis coming down the road he had a pickup truck. By the next week the pickup truck had a kind of metal grating on the top. One day he stopped me and said, "You like that, you like what I got? Well, that's for y'all."

And then Sheriff Davis told us that he was building a one-room jail out of cinder blocks— just for us! And did we like that? It was big enough to stand up in, you could sit down, and of course it was out there in the middle of the hot sun. When we told him he was really wasting his time, Sheriff Davis said, "Well, I know you're gonna do something. I know you are, and I'll keep up with you." Sometimes when we would go walking down the street, there was Sheriff Davis's car, coming right behind us. He'd sit in the front and wait, and sometimes we'd go past the person's house and go to somebody else's house in the back, because we didn't want to lead him directly to our next possible registrant.

I don't think we understand what people risked when they took those steps. As soon as we had made contact with people, as soon as they went to the courthouse to register, their boss would be right there. If they worked in the cotton fields, oftentimes they were dismissed immediately. Or they'd be cut off of their welfare rations. The power system was consolidated on the notion that no, you will not move up, you will not challenge us in any way.

WELCOMING THE KLAN

Then we began to look at other things that were going on. Why could some people plant cotton when others couldn't? There were these gentlemen farmers who planted nothing but made an awful lot of money, and then there were people who were planting cotton but were barely able to get it ginned. So early on, we began to deal with the cotton allotment system. Well, when we began to run people for the cotton allotment board, we hit the economic bell. And that brought out the Klan.

Sometimes the Klan seemed benign compared to some of the other rabid, racist organizations, like the Association for the Preservation of the White Race, who made no bones about the fact that if they saw you, they were going to kill you.

One time I called a meeting of tractor workers, thinking that I was going to organize *Black* tractor workers, and I walked right dead into a nest of Klansmen who had gotten the same word. I don't know who had told them, but they were there. As I approached them in my car— carefully—I was wondering who were all these white men standing at the church steps. They knew something was wrong because the place of the meeting was a Black church, and they didn't look happy. I kind of looked at them. They kind of looked at me. I said, "You here for the meetin'?" and they said, "Yeah. You called the meetin'?" I said, "No. I'm just looking for the person who called the meetin'." And I kind of backed on out and left.

All of us learned how to be patient, how to play for the occasion, because your life could turn on a dime. Later you might laugh, but at the time it wouldn't seem so funny. Like the time I ran into the police car. Now, you should have seen me jump out of my car all incensed, carrying on about this and that, with this poor white volunteer sitting next to me. He just knew we were dead. But this policeman was so disgusted with me that he just told me to get a move on.

LIFE LESSONS

One of the things I have learned about doing political work is that you may not be serious, or you may not know how serious a step you're taking, but when the opposition see anybody treading on their territory, they're *always* serious.

We had so many near misses, so many close calls, and we had nobody to depend on but ourselves. If you had a problem you sure couldn't call a cop! Which is almost the same situation [in which] the Black community finds itself in the inner cities today. If you have a problem and you call the cop, the cop is going to give you a *bigger* problem. So we learned to handle things ourselves as best we could.

Most of all we learned that people in Mississippi were a very special group of people. They were our country's peasant base. They were incredible in their wisdom, and many had extreme courage. I can remember this guy, Applewhite. Now Applewhite was a placid, nondescript kind of guy. You were never quite sure whether what you had to say registered or not. I didn't like riding with Applewhite because I felt that if I was going to get pushed into something, I was going to be on my own. One day we were riding down the road, and I said to Applewhite, "Do you have anything in this car in case we get stopped?" Well, you would never know what was going on in Applewhite's head—he had a perfect poker face. "Open up the glove compartment," he said. "Check down underneath the seat on my side. And on your side. Listen, we may not survive, but we sure could blaze a few holes." I said, "That's the way I want to go."

I learned that people aren't always what they appear. At the same time you're trying to organize them, they're trying to figure out where you are in this constellation of players. Are you going to be around when the action goes down? Am I talking to the State Sovereignty Commission? And essentially, is what you're telling me true? That's why we always encouraged people to read. We always encouraged people to discuss. Nothing that we did was cloaked in any kind of secrecy, which is the way I've continued to operate.

So that was my life for two years. It was about day-to-day survival but it was also about how you transform a community that really had not been touched in over 100 years by any outside force—how you get it to join the twentieth century and get enough players inside that loop to be able to carry it on after you leave. On the whole, I think we were very successful. We paid some very, very high prices for it, but I think most of us would have done it again.   [1994]

Terms

1. SNCC: Student Nonviolent Coordinating Committee.

Understanding the Reading

1. How were the volunteers prepared for going to Mississippi?
2. What were Tillinghast's responsibilities in Mississippi?
3. In what ways were the volunteers threatened by law enforcement?
4. How did the volunteers persuade people to register to vote?
5. Why were southern Blacks so poor?
6. What was the State Sovereignty Commission?
7. What was the Freedom School, and why was it established?

8. What tactics did Sheriff Davis use to intimidate the volunteers?
9. Why did Tillinghast feel the volunteers had to handle problems on their own?
10. How did she feel about the Mississippi Blacks?

Suggestions for Responding

1. List the various resistance tactics White Mississippians used, and rank-order them based on your sense of their effectiveness, justifying your choices.
2. Consider one of the experiences Tillinghast describes, and write a short narrative or essay describing how you think you might have reacted to it. Comment on how you wish you might have reacted instead. ✦

129

"Don't Tell Us It Can't Be Done"

MICHAEL RYAN

Martha Yallup, Sister Kathleen Ross and their colleagues made something wonderful happen on the Yakima Indian Reservation in Washington State a decade ago. In a poor area where higher education was almost inaccessible, they began to train Head Start[1] teachers from the Indian communities. It was hard work, but it was doubly rewarding. Not only did the program give adults new skills, but it also helped provide a leg up for the children born into the grueling poverty of the reservation. For Martha, the tribe's Head Start director, and Sister Kathleen, the academic vice president of Fort Wright College in Spokane, the program was a splendid example of how a private college and a community group could work together to change lives.

Then disaster struck.

"In 1980, the board of Fort Wright decided to close the college," Sister Kathleen recalls. "I had the job of coming down here and telling Martha that we were going to have to end the program because the home campus was closing. I gave her the bad news, and I remember she just looked at me and said: 'No, it's not closing.'"

Instead of sitting by and watching their dream die, Martha Yallup got together with a colleague, Violet Rau, and Sister Kathleen and decided on a plan of incredible daring: They would start a college on their own.

The idea seemed as doomed as it was courageous. The reservation was no place to raise the funds needed to start a college from scratch. And Fort Wright was in no position to help much. A small liberal-arts school run by the Catholic Sisters of the Holy Names of Jesus and Mary, it had been driven out of business by competition from larger, better-financed schools. And, although Martha and Violet were confident, virtually nobody believed in them—except Sister Kathleen. "People on the reservation said, 'You're crazy. It's going to fail,'" Martha recalls.

But Martha and Violet went to work on the reservation, lining up community leaders, public officials and business people to form a board of directors for the new college—and to start raising money for it. Back in Spokane, Sister Kathleen persuaded college officials to keep Fort Wright open through the spring of 1982. Then the hard work began.

First, the new college needed recognition from the IRS[2] so that it could accept donations. Sister Kathleen fought her way through the agency's bureaucracy and emerged with official recognition. Then the women tried to persuade the authorities to transfer Fort Wright's accreditation to their new school. "Our philosophy had always been, 'If you don't ask, you don't get,'" Martha says with a laugh. They failed, but they made a strong enough case that they were granted candidate status—the last step before full accreditation. That meant that their new school's courses could be recognized for full credit by other institutions.

But they had one more obstacle to clear: A college designed for some of the poorest people in the country would have to be able to offer financial aid. And the federal government's rule held that a school must be in business two years before its students qualify for federal loans. "We went to the top person in the Seattle office," Sister Kathleen says, "and he said, 'There's got to be a way,' so I asked him if I could see the book of regulations." She found a section that allowed the government to authorize financial aid when a school is sold to a new owner. It was clearly intended to cover vocational schools, but the rule didn't say that explicitly. "The guy looked at me like I was crazy," Sister Kathleen recalls. "Then he said, 'Why not?'" Sister Kathleen and her board of directors purchased their education program from Fort Wright for $1, and a new college was born.

The day I went to visit, Heritage College had been in business for eight years. It is a non-denominational institution—although a small group of nuns still holds key administrative positions at the school. Sister Kathleen Ross has been the president since before the college opened its doors. Martha Yallup, now the deputy director of the Yakima tribe's Department of Human Services, was the board's first chair and still serves as its secretary.

But the story that began with the determination of a handful of courageous women has become a story of courage and determination on the part of hundreds. This year, Heritage College will confer 199 degrees and certificates. The average Heritage student is 35 and, as the faculty likes to say, "place-bound"—inhibited by family and work commitments from traveling the 90 minutes it takes to get to the nearest college off the reservation. For most of the students, college is a dream which could never have come true without Heritage.

If you want to know how great the accomplishment of Sister Kathleen, Martha Yallup and the others is, meet Hipolito Mendez. He may be the typical Heritage student—an industrious, outgoing man who works part-time to pay his tuition and speaks eagerly of his planned career as a high school teacher. He is also a 47-year-old father of five. "My wife and I had a business, and it went down the tubes," he says. "We decided, 'Now's the time to go back to school and do something with our lives.' But we discovered we just couldn't afford to go to the state university. There wasn't much hope for us. Then we heard about Heritage."

Admittedly, he says, it felt strange for a man in middle age to become a college student, but Mendez found that Heritage's emphasis on personalized education eased his transition. "The first week, I was apprehensive," he says. "After that, I fit right in." Next fall, he will begin a new life as an educator—and his wife, Paula, will start teaching elementary school as well.

Or look at how Heritage has changed the life of Edith Walsey, 32. "If this college wasn't here, I wouldn't have gone to college, because of my family and my tradition and my husband," she confides. "I'm from the Warm Springs reservation in Oregon. The teachers here understand my customs. At first, it was kind of hard for me. My husband wasn't for me going to school. We have three children. Now he takes care of them while I'm in class and working part-time. I'm a junior studying computers. When I graduate, I hope to go home and work with my tribe."

In its eight years of existence, Heritage has grown from a three-room cottage to a set of buildings on the campus of a former elementary school in the reservation town of Toppenish. It now has 25 full-time faculty, an additional 70 or so part-time, and more than 400 degree-holding alumni. These are impressive statistics, but not as impressive as the testimonial one recent graduate gave Sister Kathleen last year. A native of the reservation, she had gone away to college but dropped out, feeling uncomfortable in an alien culture. Then she heard about Heritage. She enrolled and finished her degree. In one sentence, she summed up the magic of the school. As she told Sister Kathleen: "You allowed me not to be a failure."   [1991]

Terms

1. HEAD START: A federal program for disadvantaged preschoolers.
2. IRS: Internal Revenue Service.

Understanding the Reading

1. What problems did Yallup, Rau, and Sister Kathleen face in starting Heritage College?
2. How did they overcome each of them?
3. Evaluate the effectiveness of the project.

Suggestions for Responding

1. Describe a time when you faced what seemed to be impossible obstacles, and explain how you tackled them, alone or with the help of others. ✦

130

Saving Native Lands

VALERIE TALIMAN

When JoAnn Tall drives past the Wounded Knee burial site near her home on the Pine Ridge Indian Reservation in South Dakota, she remembers the more than 300 Lakota people—mainly unarmed women and children—who were gunned-down there by the U.S. military in the winter of 1890. The massacre forever changed the lives of the Lakota; not only were vast homelands stolen through subsequent broken treaties, but the slaughter marked the beginning of nearly a century of U.S. government suppression of Lakota religious and cultural practices.

This tragic legacy has fueled much of Tall's commitment to resisting the continued oppression and exploitation of her people. Tall, an Oglala Lakota mother of eight, has long been active in the struggle to sustain and nurture Native communities. Still, she was surprised last April when the San Francisco-based Goldman Environmental Foundation awarded her $60,000 as one of 1993's seven "environmental heroes" from around the world, who have, despite extreme hardships, committed themselves to grassroots activism.

Tall, 41, was chosen for her organizing efforts to stop toxic waste dumps and nuclear weapons testing on Indian lands. Her activism spans more than 20 years, much of it focused on the environment, most of it done behind the scenes without credit. She speaks modestly of her accomplishments, noting that "there are a lot of strong women doing this work that you never hear about. Every now and then we get lucky and one of us gets an award. But a lot more never get recognized, and yet they continue."

Tall says her dedication to environmental work is grounded in the Lakota's reverence for the natural world. To her people, Grandmother Earth (Unci Maka) is not owned, much less bought and sold. Generations upon generations of Lakota are buried throughout the Northern Plains, and many sacred places lie within their homelands. Unci Maka has sustained Her children throughout creation and must be granted reciprocal respect, according to the Lakota worldview.

Guided by a spiritual commitment that came to her over the years in Lakota ceremonies and in dreams, Tall has spent a lifetime grappling with conflict and poverty, confronting government, corporate, and even military forces that threaten Native lives and land. At 20, she was involved in the 1973 armed occupation of Wounded Knee, where elder Oglala women had assumed leadership of a resistance movement against U.S. domination over tribal government, lands, and rights.

"It was a war, an invasion of our homeland," Tall remembers. "Federal agents were shooting at us, even women and children, and I knew I could get killed. But I thought, 'How dare they—this is *our* land!' I learned how to deal with fear at Wounded Knee."

This resolve has served her in subsequent confrontations. For example, in 1987 the defense contractor Honeywell announced plans to conduct weapons tests in a Black Hills canyon that is an ancient burial and ceremonial site. Tall strode into a hearing where corporate officials were courting the Lakota residents with a slick public relations presentation. "I tore into the PR guy," she recalls. "I said, 'How dare you try to desecrate our church? That's what the Black Hills mean to us; they're our church.' I told him, 'We're going to win this war.'"

Tall immediately helped organize a resistance camp of about 150 people, who refused to leave the canyon for three months until Honeywell backed out. "During one of our ceremonies, I had a vision that symbolized the seven generations to come and I knew this missile testing would be the beginning of the end for us," Tall said. "With the help of our medicine people, we made a spiritual commitment to protect the canyon, and we won."

Inspired by this triumph, Tall cofounded the Native Resource Coalition, which stopped Connecticut-based O & G Industries from building a 5,000-acre landfill and incinerator on the Pine Ridge reservation. The coalition later found that more than 60 Indian communities had been targeted for toxic-waste sites within a two-year period.

The powerful waste industry had discovered that there are often fewer regulations governing toxic waste on Indian reservations than on land under state, county, and municipal jurisdictions. Attempting to exploit the sovereign status of tribal governments, many waste merchants began offering deals disguised as "economic development" to poverty-stricken tribes desperately in need of jobs. To make matters worse, the waste industry chose communities where language barriers exist. In many Native languages, there are no words for dioxins, PCBs, or other poisons, so the dangers are impossible to explain and translators' high-tech rhetoric makes the million-dollar waste deals sound safe.

Outraged by the idea that tribal lands were being targeted as dumping grounds, the Native Resource Coalition joined with other grassroots groups in 1991 to host a national environmental conference in the Black Hills. The meeting was designed to alert tribes to the environmental racism and economic blackmail directed at Native people, who retain only 4 percent of U.S. land. At this gathering, Tall helped form the Indigenous Environmental Network, which now boasts more than 50 member organizations helping to educate and protect Native people in the U.S. and Canada.

Tall is but one of many Native women who are doing this work. "Our women come from a long line of resistance," she notes. "History tells us that we are the backbone of everything that is." Indeed, in Native societies women are not only life-givers, caretakers, clan mothers, and matriarchs, but they are truly the center of Indian communities.

"Contrary to those images of meekness, docility, and subordination to males with which we women typically have been portrayed by the dominant culture's books and movies, anthropology, and political ideologues . . . it is women who have formed the very core of indigenous resistance to genocide and colonization since the first moment of conflict between Indians and invaders," says Juaneño/Yaqui scholar M. Annette Jaimes.

Protecting the environment is fundamental to the survival of Native peoples, many of whom still depend on their aboriginal rights to hunt, fish, and harvest natural foods and medicines. The identities, spiritual ways, cultures, and health of more than 500 Native nations in the U.S. hinge on their ability to live in a respectful interdependent relationship with their homelands.

Destruction of Native lands caused by government and industry includes strip-mining, coal-burning power plants, unregulated dumps, intensive logging, hydroelectric dams, uranium mining, contamination of rivers and waterways, and more than 800 nuclear bombs exploded as "tests." In every instance of activism against this destruction, Native women have been on the front lines. From the Navajo grandmothers fighting relocation at Big Mountain, Arizona, to the Dann sisters' stand to save Western Shoshone homelands in Nevada, to Onondaga clan mothers in New York fighting James Bay Hydro, they persevere in the resistance.   [1994]

Understanding the Reading

1. Why did JoAnn Tall receive an award for being an "environmental hero"?
2. Why did Tall oppose the Honeywell test plans?
3. What did the Native Resource Coalition accomplish?
4. Why has the waste industry targeted reservations?
5. What role do Native American women play in their society?
6. Why are Native Americans especially concerned about their homelands and the environment?

Suggestions for Responding

1. Research and report on the 1973 armed occupation of Wounded Knee. ✦

131

Cecilia Fire Thunder: She Inspires Her People

ANN DAVIS

Cecilia Fire Thunder hunches over a doll she's making, clamping one more silver buckle on the belt before she fastens it to a dark blue, shell-decorated dress. The kitchen table where she works is a cluttered stage of tall, elegant Plains Indian women, hands outstretched with an eagle wing fan or holding a fringed shawl close in to their waists.

Her small trailer home on the Pine Ridge reservation in South Dakota is a Frankenstein's[1] laboratory—plastic bags full of arms, legs, and torsos bulge beneath the planter, overflow behind the TV. Corpses waiting for heads line the sofa.

Fire Thunder sits back and studies the doll, reading glasses perched at the end of her nose. "Some of that old stuff is ugly," she mutters, attaching a small buckskin bag to the belt. "I like my bodies to resemble bodies—they don't have to look like stuffed tamales."

When Fire Thunder started making dolls a few years ago, her original impetus was simple: to reflect contemporary Plains Indian women, the friends she dances with at pow-wows around the Midwest. When her foot-high dolls won her awards and trips to Washington, D.C., to demonstrate dollmaking techniques at the Smithsonian, she took it in stride. Making art is part of her life, and speaking in public goes with the territory.

You might think dollmaking an utterly apolitical activity. Not for Fire Thunder. Even her dolls are lessons in history and cultural values. The cowrie shells on her traditional dolls reveal the extensive trade routes existing between tribes on the West Coast and the Great Plains. The tanned hides are a vehicle to talk about the Lakota's relation to other life forms and their philosophy of natural harmony.

When she talks to non-Indian audiences, Fire Thunder uses the dolls to clear away misconceptions about Native Americans. When she speaks in local schools, she uses her dolls to talk about traditional values and the problems of drugs and alcohol.

"I talk to high school kids, not about how it should be, but about how it is," Fire Thunder said. Instead of lecturing about the evils of substance abuse, Fire Thunder asks them point-blank how many still do drugs, even after years of being preached at in the schools. Most raise their hands. Then they tell her about growing up in alcoholic homes, about nights of no sleep, worrying whether they'll get beat up by a drunk adult.

Even though students understand that drugs and alcohol are bad for them, Fire Thunder believes they will not change their behavior until adult problem drinkers admit it and share their experiences with younger people.

Fire Thunder says that part of the reason she can reach Indian people at a gut level is because she is one of them. She can tell jokes that non-Indians could never get away with, jokes that in a humorous way reveal people's dysfunctional behavior to themselves. For instance, What is Indian love? Answer: a black eye and a hickie.

"The gift I have is my humor, my gift to communicate," Fire Thunder said. "No white person can say what I say." She believes it is up to Indian people to solve their own problems.

When asked if she ever gets overwhelmed by all the work, Fire Thunder says no. "My passion is what I do. The most important thing I have is that I know who I am," she says. "I still have a lot of quirks, but my identity is pretty strong. And I know when to play."

Out on the dance floor in the Rapid City Civic Center, Fire Thunder wears her traditional women's dress, decorated with cowrie shells and a handsome silver belt. Like the Pied Piper,[2] she breaks away from the movement of the group and leads a long snakeline of women in and out around a kaleidoscope of feathers and swirling fringe. She bends her head to hear a joke, laughs and continues her swinging walk, head tilted back elegantly, like one of her dolls. She's easy to pick out among hundreds of dancers. "If you feel good about yourself, you're just going to shine," says Cecilia Fire Thunder, and she does.

Fire Thunder goes non-stop. A dazzling public speaker, organizer in her home community of the Pine Ridge reservation, a founder of the Oglala Lakota Women's Society, registered nurse, mother, political lobbyist, pow-wow enthusiast, traditional dollmaker, KILI radio personality: you might think this enough for a lifetime or two. But this summer, Fire Thunder, who ran for tribal president—and lost—was also appointed tribal health planner for the Pine Ridge reservation and charged with building the first comprehensive plan to fight alcoholism.

Many community groups approved when Fire Thunder was appointed to the sensitive political post. "If anyone can do it, she can," was the comment heard frequently around the tribal

office, according to Taylor Little White Man, executive director of the Oglala Sioux Tribe.

Like her dolls, she is tall and captivating with deep brown eyes, a brilliant smile and abundant energy. And some internal switch seems to have locked in the "on" position when Fire Thunder was born. It's an intensity that delights some and frustrates others. Her rebelliousness infuriated the nuns at Red Cloud Indian School, a Catholic boarding school she attended until tenth grade. The nuns tried to convince the head priest not to let her come back; she was too influential with the other girls.

She rebelled most against the violence: How the religious brothers beat boys with thick beltstraps outside the girls' classroom windows. How the nuns humiliated "bad" girls by forcing them to bend over a big piano in front of the class, pulling down their panties and smacking them with rulers. How they did things so bad that Fire Thunder won't tell me about them.

"They hurt us to make us cry because once you cried, they'd defeated you," she said.

It took Fire Thunder years to undo the emotional damage caused by the boarding school, an internalized violence she feels she carried into her relationship with her children. "In order to do what I do, you have to confront your own devils, because something or someone will remind you of your past," Fire Thunder said. Fire Thunder's attempts at easing children's suffering is a constant in her work as community organizer, health planner, speaker, even dollmaker.

Inspired by her meeting with organizer Eileen Iron Cloud at a pow-wow in Colorado, and their discussions about empowering women and influencing state legislation at Pine Ridge, Fire Thunder, along with Iron Cloud, formed the Oglala Lakota Women's Society in 1987.

Fire Thunder recounts Lakota spiritual tradition, saying that thousands of years ago a woman gave her people a pipe and told them how to pray with it in ceremonies. This woman who came among the people was the inspiration for the women's society, says Fire Thunder. Through the society, women are able to air their concerns about community and tribal affairs.

Repeatedly, the number one issue on the nine reservations was alcohol. Not a surprising statistic, since some nine out of ten people on Pine Ridge are alcoholic.

"Part of community organizing is getting people to tell you what you already know," Fire Thunder said.

Now that women had identified their major focus, the group decided to take on the candidates for tribal election. Fire Thunder talked about sober leadership on her radio show; the women's society sent out 1,000 mailings urging voters to support sober leaders. At stump speeches, women badgered the candidates to state whether they still drank. "We didn't care who you were, what you did, what kind of past you had," Fire Thunder said. "If you were sober, we were gonna vote for you."

Though their criteria were crude, their results were impressive: after the smoke cleared on election night, 11 of the 16 new tribal council members were declared non-drinkers.

The domestic violence was next. Tribal law had required that women sign a complaint against abusive partners before the police would act. In 1988, the women's society lobbied for and won a mandatory arrest law for domestic violence. Since fall of last year, whenever there is probable cause of domestic abuse, the perpetrator automatically spends the night in jail. The complaint is signed by the arresting officer. At first, a lot of "men in shock" were sitting in jail cells, Fire Thunder said. The women's society was criticized as "manhaters" and the trial court briefly tried to overturn the law. But most have now come to accept mandatory arrest as reality.

Part of the women's focus was on helping abusive men to change. Through their efforts, they won a grant to provide counseling to men who batter. "We did this because we also love our men," Fire Thunder said. "We want them to understand their rage and anger."

The society's other main concern was child sexual abuse. In 1988, the group staged a candle-light march in support of National Child Abuse Prevention Month. Last year, they went one step further by letting abused children speak out about their experience. In a two-hour show broadcast live on radio station KILI, six children talked about how it felt to be beaten, raped, ridiculed and neglected. "In those two hours, we reached more people in the listening audience than with anything else we ever did," Fire Thunder said.

Such confrontational tactics have not always made her a popular figure. She and others in the women's society have been accused of butting into other people's business. Some reservation people have complained that women's groups are not "traditional."

But Fire Thunder brushes off the criticism, saying she is motivated more by the pain of children than the fear of criticism. "When oppression is so great, there's no nice way to get to the heart of the people," she said. "The only way was 'shock treatment'—hit 'em hard and shake 'em up. Now that they've accomplished an awareness of issues on Pine Ridge, their tactics can change," she said.

The fierce pace of the women's society has slowed in the past year. Iron Cloud says the group lost its focus. She has been studying organizing models and believes that [the] women's society needs to reorient itself to keep all women involved, rather than having a few do all the work.

Fire Thunder believes everyone just got worn out. "We pulled back because we had to. For three years, we gave 150 percent of everything in our lives" to the women's society, she [says]. Fire Thunder agrees the group needs to restructure itself for the next phase of work.

Some say Fire Thunder sold out when she accepted a position with the tribal government this summer. "They say, 'Oh, they're gonna shut her up,'" Fire Thunder says. "But I took the position with the understanding that I could do more."

Though Iron Cloud counseled her not to take the new job, she believes Fire Thunder has the strength to hang in there and not sell out to political interests.

Perhaps she will. Fire Thunder has already written grants for half a million dollars and taken charge of the committee overseeing a new plan to house all alcohol programs under one roof. She says the tribe has a lot of catching up to do to enable people to face the pain of their addictions.   [1991]

Terms

1. FRANKENSTEIN: A fictional scientist who created a monster that destroyed its maker.

2. PIED PIPER: A legendary piper whose music charmed first the rats and then the village children into following him out of town forever.

Understanding the Reading

1. What tactics does Fire Thunder use in her work with high school students?
2. What is the purpose of the Oglala Lakota Women's Society?
3. What tactics did Fire Thunder employ to combat alcoholism on the Lakota reservation?
4. How did she address the problem of domestic violence?
5. What did she do about the problem of child abuse?

Suggestions for Responding

1. The article reports that the Women's Society has lost its earlier momentum. Using your knowledge about the change process, what advice would you give them (or a similar group working on some community problem) about the one specific outcome that you feel is most necessary? Explain its priority and the strategies you would recommend to realize that outcome. ✦

132

How I Changed the Governor's Mind

RENÉE LA COUTURE TULLOCH

A young woman is attacked by a stranger who holds her in a viselike grip as he licks and bites her breasts through her clothes. He was caught in the act, but not sent to prison or forced to register as a sex offender. In fact, he could, if he wished, be licensed as a child care worker.

There was no law in California (or most other states) that could adequately address this insidious crime, because the victim was attacked through her clothing. Illegal touching was defined by sexual assault laws as skin-to-skin con-

tact, or through the clothing of the attacker. It did not include touching through the victim's clothing. The only charge that applied was battery, which carries a light maximum prison sentence and therefore is rarely prosecuted.

I am the young woman who was mentioned in the beginning of this article. I was the one who was attacked. The police watch commander told me that this crime is reported every day in his precinct, and many officers—including the one who investigated my case—even underline that portion of the sexual battery law in their penal code books. They do it, he said, to show victims that there is really nothing to be done.

I could not contain my outrage, and vowed the law would change. I knew I had to get the full attention of my assemblyman (now a state senator), Patrick Johnston. But I had no idea how to, until I was at a fund-raiser for the local battered women's shelter. One of the items up for auction was a private lunch and state capitol tour with him. I made the highest bid—$125—using my travel money for Christmas.

When I met with Johnston, I came prepared. I presented him with a package of information that he said looked better than those of most lobbyists. He also told me that another assemblyman, Bill Filante, had drafted a bill, AB 674, calling for a similar legal change. He said it had been voted on once before and failed.

I found out why after I talked with a staffer for another representative. He said assemblymen were afraid that young men in college would be with a date, fondle her, and then be charged with sexual battery. They felt that a boy shouldn't be put away for "miscommunication" with a date. He told me that most of the state assemblymen had been college boys once themselves.

I contacted Filante's office. As it turned out, a staffer said that the bill had the votes to pass this time. The big problem was that the governor at the time, George Deukmejian, had privately said that he'd veto it.

I asked what I could do. She said I could launch an all-out effort to change the governor's mind—if enough people got involved, maybe, just maybe, he'd sign it.

I wrote a paper explaining the loophole in sexual assault laws that hurt me and so many other women. I wrote sample letters to the governor and made copies of them for distribution. I told every friend to contact their friends. I gave out the pack to all my coworkers, and asked them to spread the word.

I spoke at the Women's Center of San Joaquin County and disclosed that I was a survivor. The speech generated tremendous support, especially at the sexual assault center. Women there contacted other centers around the state. I called the leaders of major women's organizations and racial equality groups. Calls, letters, and even telegrams poured into the governor's office calling for passage of AB 674, the "Sexual Battery" bill.

The day slated for the governor's veto came. I called his office with apprehension. His staffer told me that the bill was postponed for further consideration. I contacted everybody I could to keep up the pace for justice. Time was running out. The governor had to make the decision about this and a thousand other bills before midnight. He had three choices. He could either sign the bill, not sign it (in which case it would automatically become law), or veto it.

The waiting became its own hell. I could not sleep. I cried. I prayed. The next morning, September 30, 1989, I called the governor's office at 8 A.M. I asked the staffer for the status of AB 674. When I was on hold waiting, tears streamed down my face. Finally, this disembodied voice said, "It became law."

The man added, "The governor even chose to sign it. That shows he now supports the bill."

I found that one determined individual has the power to change an unjust system. Somebody asked me, "Does this mitigate your attack?" Absolutely not. I still have the scars. But no woman in California need ever again endure what I did. Still, I do worry about the other states that have this loophole. I want to inspire others (that means you) to change these terrible laws. I have found that when women, along with men who share our vision, band together we can make a difference. We can change the world

[1991]

Understanding the Reading

1. What steps did Tulloch take to get the law that protected her attacker changed?
2. How does she evaluate her success?

Suggestions for Responding

1. What law would you like to see changed? Why is the change needed, and how would you go about getting the change? ◆

133

Friends of Justice: Take Heart

Deb Price

Decade after decade, federal workers fired for being homosexual left quietly, without protest. That was until 1957, when Uncle Sam decided to kick out Frank Kameny, then a meek astronomer working for the Army Map Service.

"I took that as a declaration of war by my government upon me," Kameny recalls. "And I don't grant my government the right to declare war on me."

Suddenly radicalized, Kameny did the unthinkable: He fought back.

He poured all his meager financial resources into a long-shot appeal. Despite a doctorate from Harvard, he was impoverished by the federal blackball, which kept him from entering the young aerospace industry or returning to academia. For months he survived on 20 cents' worth of food a day.

Teaching himself the intricacies of law, he pursued his case in the courts, finally writing his own petition to the Supreme Court. Turned away by the "supreme injustices," as he calls them, he never was reinstated. His career as an observational astronomer was over. Yet he ultimately won what turned out to be an 18-year war.

Federal personnel officials "surrendered to me on July 3, 1975," Kameny says gleefully in his Washington, D.C. home. The Civil Service Commission announced homosexuality was no longer grounds for dismissals.

That historic change followed years of successful battles that Kameny waged for other gay workers fired from their federal jobs or denied security clearances. The nominal fees he charged his gay clients for his renowned expertise largely supported him.

"I've stabbed myself in the back," he jokes in his booming voice. "By killing the (anti-gay) issue as an activist, I have deprived myself of an income as a self-characterized paralegal."

Kameny credits his days as an Army private at World War II's front lines for his pit-bull activist style. "I dug my way across Germany . . . slit trench by slit trench," the former mortar-shell loader says.

That tenaciousness has served Kameny well in his many protracted battles to ensure gay people full equality. Now 68, the cheerfully dogged Kameny, surrounded by stacks of documents from his paper wars, ticks off his awesome victories with the pride of a four-star general.

His most recent triumph was the . . . repeal of Washington, D.C.'s sodomy law. While actual prosecutions are rare, sodomy laws are indirectly used to tar gay people and deny them jobs and even their own children in custody disputes. He began that fight 30 years ago as the first person to publicly denounce D.C.'s antiquated law in testimony before Congress.

Even in his defeats, Kameny gained gay ground by staking out new territory: In 1971, for example, he became the first openly gay person to run for public office when he competed for D.C. congressional delegate. Today, 128 openly gay people hold elective public office.

Kameny laid the groundwork for his most profound success in 1961 when he founded the D.C. branch of the Mattachine Society, an early gay rights group. The gay movement of that pre-Stonewall[1] era was "bland and apologetic and unassertive," Kameny recalls. He opted instead for "militancy and activism."

Kameny soon realized that a major stumbling block was the theory that gay people were mentally ill. Drawing on his formidable scientific skills, he dove in and found "shoddy . . . and just plain sleazy research in which moral, cultural and theological value judgments were cloaked in the language of science."

And so began his 10-year war with the American Psychiatric Association [APA]. "They surrendered about noontime on Dec. 15, 1973," Kameny notes with his characteristic precision, when APA's trustees voted that homosexuality was not an illness. "In one fell swoop, 15 million gay people were cured!"

Today, with his eyes fixed not on the stars but on the earthly territory yet to be won, the former astronomer is mapping a new strategy for his 31-year-old assault on the military's gay ban. "I tend not to lose my wars," he says confidently. Friends of justice should take heart.   [1993]

Terms

1. PRE-STONEWALL: In 1969, gays rioted in response to a police raid on a homosexual bar in New York City, initiating the gay rights movement.

Understanding the Reading

1. How did Kameny cause the federal government to change its policy on homosexuality?
2. Why did he fight Washington's sodomy law?
3. On what grounds did Kameny attack the American Psychiatric Association's labeling of homosexuality as a mental illness?

Suggestions for Responding

1. Write a short essay explaining your reaction to Kameny's accomplishment.
2. Research and report on the Stonewall riot. ✦

134

Negotiating Passion on Campus

BONNIE PFISTER

What's an activist to do when everyone from George Will to "Saturday Night Live" satirizes your work and accuses you of infantilizing women and taking the fun out of sex?

"I find it exciting," says Jodi Gold, coordinator of STAAR, Students Together Against Acquaintance Rape at the University of Pennsylvania in Philadelphia. "You don't get a backlash until you've ruffled some feathers. It means we've really pushed the envelope and things are happening."

The backlash has all but obscured the radical importance of student efforts to develop new—fairer—rules for sexual liaisons. The emerging new code includes the apparently controversial idea that potential lovers should *ask* before foisting sexual attention on their partners, and that partners should clearly *answer* "yes" or "no." In other words: people should communicate about their desires before making love, rather than waiting to be "swept away" by overwhelming passion.

While a deadpan legalistic approach to sex is easy to ridicule, Jodi Gold believes that the real reason media coverage of today's campus activism is so highly critical is that Americans are still scared silly by its sexual frankness—a frankness that today's generation of young people desperately need.

"Sexuality is perhaps the most defining issue for today's students," says Alan Guskin, president of Antioch College in Ohio for nine years, and a supporter of the often-mocked Sexual Offense Policy, the student-written rules for sexual conduct at the college, which have been in place since fall 1992.

"Men and women students come to the campus with a very different consciousness about sexuality," notes Dr. Guskin. "The women have learned they have a right to determine how their bodies are used, but many of the young men still think the central question is how to get women to do what they want." The best way to deal with the situation, says Guskin, is for women and men to learn to communicate with each other. "The policy gives no specific checklist or statements. But there is a sense of how you should behave."

The Antioch policy says verbal consent is needed before all sexual contact, and that consent is an on-going process that can be withdrawn at any time. Students who are sleeping or unconscious or incapacitated by alcohol or drugs are not considered capable of consent. The policy also defines offenses as unwanted touching, verbal harassment, and non-disclosure of sexually transmitted disease, including HIV, and defines punishments for violations of various parts of the policy. All students are required to attend an educational workshop on consent and sexual offense each academic year.

Guskin notes that the media swarming over the campus for two and a half months reporting on the controversial policy accomplished more student education on the issue than the college's past five years of effort.

The policy emerged when thirty feminists disrupted a campus government meeting in November, 1990, demanding institutional rules to deal with rape, says Bethany Saltman, Antioch '93 and member of the original group, the Womyn of Antioch. Even at this tiny (650 students last fall) alternative college, the administration seemed to prefer to keep rape reports under wraps. Faced with vehement, relentless protest and a flurry of local news attention, the administration reluctantly accepted the feminists' demand to remove any accused perpetrator from campus within twenty-four hours of a reported rape. But the rule was adopted on the condition that a committee of concerned staff and students would work to retool the policy while the administration consulted lawyers about its constitutionality. Womyn of Antioch demanded the policy out of strength, not weakness, notes Saltman. "We get to say who touches us, and where."

The policy has been criticized as a return to the 1950s that disempowers women by viewing them as damsels in distress and spells the death of *amour.*

Perhaps the critics are upset because they're embarrassed, says Elizabeth Sullivan, Antioch '93, now of Seattle. "It's still very hard for people to be explicit about sexual intimacy. The policy limits certain options, such as casual, thoughtless sex, while encouraging other options, such as accountability, sexual equality, and living in a community with a reduced fear of harassment or coerced sex."

Sullivan notes that critics act as though, without this policy, there is no social context influencing students' interactions at all. "Most of us acquire a whole set of norms and attitudes before we become sexual with other people. We learn who is an acceptable partner, we learn unspoken codes of how to proceed, and we develop a set of expectations about what sex should be," says Sullivan. In an intentional community like Antioch, people can choose to restructure that context.

Some students from other campuses who have adopted the Antioch rules as their own, don't understand what all the fuss is about. Matthew Mizel, a student at Stanford (CA), likens the current resistance to people's initial embarrassment about asking a partner to use a condom during the early years of the AIDS crisis. "Why do people feel asking is not romantic?" asks Mizel. "All it does is clarify things. For me, it's not a romantic situation until I know the woman is comfortable."

As a letter writer to *The New Yorker* noted, asking permission, as in—"may I kiss the hollow of your neck?"—does not have to be devoid of *amour*.

Students should be relieved to discard the old stereotypes that "masculine sexuality is dangerous, passionate, reckless, and that the woman is passive and just laying back there," according to Mizel.

Callie Cary, an Antioch spokeswoman, herself out of college for less than a decade, scoffs at the idea that the asking-before-you-touch policy infantilizes women. "The assumption that this policy is about women saying no to men is based on the idea that men initiate sex all the time. But I know there are men on this campus who feel the women are very aggressive."

ACTIVISM ON OTHER CAMPUSES

While Antioch's policy contains the most detailed rules for sexual correctness to date, feminist actions on a number of campuses have expanded from helping rape victims *after* the fact to including a preventive approach. These efforts by female—and male—students are cropping up at conservative, co-ed universities like Syracuse (NY) and Vanderbilt (TN), as well as traditionally liberal women's colleges, such as Barnard (NY) and Mount Holyoke (MA). Private schools such as Stanford and Duke (NC) Universities boast dynamic men's groups examining why men rape and striving to prevent it, while students at public Evergreen State (WA) and Rutgers University (NJ) are reaching out to local high school girls with educational programs.

On black college campuses the emphasis is on how the negative depiction of women in rap music discourages fair treatment in the sexual arena.

Most student organizers express some reservations over Antioch's policy: some hate it, while others herald it as swinging the pendulum dramatically to the side of open communication about sex—so far, in fact that they might not need to adopt such a radical approach at their own schools (phew!).

"I would love to address the Antioch policy, but from what I can gather from other people on our committee, it would be suicide for us to consider it here," says Melinda Lewis, a sophomore at Vanderbilt University in Nashville and president of Students For Women's Concerns. After speaking in spring 1992 with rape survivors who felt revictimized by the school's judicial system, Lewis returned in the fall to push for a new sexual assault policy. Although she is sensitive to Katie Roiphe–inspired charges of "victim feminism," she counters that the term does not accurately describe the activism—or the problems—she sees around her.

RATS IN THE IVORY TOWERS

At Lehigh University (PA), Jeanne Clery was robbed, sodomized and murdered in her dorm bed by a student she had never met. Jeanne's own actions that night—it is believed that she left her door unlocked for her roommate's convenience—made it clear that students are often shockingly oblivious to the dangers around them. At the time, in 1986, Lehigh students regularly propped open outside doors to allow friends to come and go easily. Lehigh had "studied" the security problem for eleven years but taken no action until after Jeanne's death, according to Lynda Getchis of Security on Campus, a group founded by Clery's parents.

After this incident, then-freshman Congressman Jim Ramstad (R-MN) joined forces with Clery's parents and crafted the Campus Sexual Assault Victims Bill of Rights. Signed into law in 1990, it requires that all post-secondary schools that receive federal funding publish annual reports about crime statistics on campus, institute policies to deal with sexual assault and offer rape awareness educational programs.

For 1991, the first year statistics were collected, 2,300 American campuses reported 30 murders, 1,000 rapes, and more than 1,800 robberies, according to *The Chronicle of Higher Education.* Most campus crime (78%) is student-on-student. While the crime incidence on campus is lower than that of the country as a whole, student and parent perceptions of the campus as a safe haven make the crime levels seem more shocking.

There is much controversy about just how many women experience sexual assault at college—the figures range from a scary 1 in 25 to a horrifying 1 in 4. But even the smallest estimates amount to a large threat to women's safety.

So it's no wonder that student activists are increasingly pressing their colleges to own up to the reality of crime and to codify, in writing, the kind of campus they want. The demands usually include more stringent acquaintance rape policies and mandatory peer education for students of both genders.

In the past five years, student activists have increasingly focused on university policies, notes Claire Kaplan, sexual assault education coordinator at the University of Virginia. "This strategy can be construed as students asking for protection, but it is not a throwback to *in loco parentis*.[1] The institution has a contract with the student—the same kind of contract that could result in a third party suit against employers or landlords who fail to provide adequate protection against crime on their premises."

Today's students are also coming of age in a litigious, capitalist culture and many adopt a consumerist creed: "I pay a lot of money to go to this school, I deserve to be protected from assault, and, at the very least, informed of its incidence on campus."

COMING OF AGE IN THE '90S

Today's young activists have a point of view so different from those of the 1960s and '70s, that commentators have had difficulty making the connections. In the '60s it was college men who

had their lives on the line with the threat of being drafted to serve in the unpopular war in Vietnam. But today it is the women, and threat of rape, that's the flashpoint.

And unlike the rebels of the '60s and '70s who were trying to tear down repressive rules, institutions and social establishments, the generation growing up in the no-rules '90s is striving to build up a foundation of acceptable personal conduct and institutionalized norms.

At Evergreen State College in Olympia, WA, the administration had spent two years, with no end in sight, developing an anti-rape protocol. In the spring of 1993, rage at slow adjudication of a rape charge boiled over into graffiti hits around campus. The scribblers named names and proclaimed, "Rape Me and I'll Kill You," said Nina Fischer, a member of the Rape Response Coalition. The university protocol went into effect last fall, and students plan to take their rape awareness workshops to local high schools this spring.

Radical approaches are less popular at a school like North Carolina State University [NCSU] in Raleigh, says Brian Ammons, a founder of that school's REAL-Men (Rape Education and Active Leadership). Originally active as the male-involvement voice in crafting a campus sex offense protocol, Ammons formed the group to examine male socialization and responsibility in a rape culture. In fact, at NCSU, it was REAL-Men that organized last fall's Take Back the Night march. The resident women's group, Help, Education and Activism on Rape (HEAR-Women) developed out of that.

"In some ways it was easier for a group of men to come together to offer some legitimacy on the issue," Ammons says. "Women on our campus are afraid to speak up about a lot of things. The fear of being labeled a feminist and being alienated here is very real."

WHITE WOMEN'S FEMINISM?

Melinda Lewis, an African American, is a sophomore at Vanderbilt and president of Students For Women's Concerns, a predominantly white feminist group. "People question my involvement," she says. "The rape issue is perceived as something with which only Anglo, middle-class women are concerned. But that's a misguided notion. Women of color are raped and assaulted much more frequently than Anglo women."

Jennifer Lipton, a Barnard College student involved in rewriting sexual offense policy for the Columbia-Barnard community amidst administrator recalcitrance, agrees that the perception of acquaintance rape as a "white women's issue" flies in the face of reality. At the rape crisis center at St. Luke's–Roosevelt Hospital nearby, where she is a volunteer, most of the survivors she sees are women of color, most very poor, some homeless.

"Their concerns are very different," Lipton says. "If their perpetrator is also black, they wonder if they should report it to the police. They are very aware of the racism of the judicial system, and worried about what it will do to their own community if they turn in this man. They also know that, as poor black women, society doesn't really value what they say."

However, at many African American colleges, date rape is a significantly less prominent gender concern than how women are depicted in rap music and advertising, reports Dionne Lyne, a student at the all-women Spelman College in Atlanta and member of the new campus organization SISTERS (Sisters in Solidarity to Eradicate Sexism). There's also anger at the persistent reference to certain Pan-Hellenic parties as "Greek Freaks," because of the use of "freak" as a disparaging term depicting black women as nymphomaniacs.

"There is a silence on the issue, a sense of, 'Yeah, it happens but we really don't want to know about it.' It reinforces the [idea] that these things happen to bad women, and we're just going to assume that we are all striving to be Spelman women, who are finer than that," Lyne says.

Spelman and brother school Morehouse College frequently co-sponsor educational programs about acquaintance rape, but Lyne says many women get the sense that Morehouse men are lecturing them about the issue, as if the men don't have a thing or two of their own to learn about date rape. Morehouse organizations have frequently scheduled their programs on Spelman's campus rather than their own, and fill the room with women and just one or two men.

Thomas Prince, associate director of counseling at Morehouse, counters that there are numerous anti-rape programs on the men's campus for co-ed groups, but his description of them seemed to indicate upon whom the responsibility is placed.

"We cover the FBI statistics, . . . talk about the things that might be contributing to the rise of acquaintance rapes and what to do if it happens to you. [That is] . . . what women can do if they find themselves in that situation," Prince said.

Prince states that there is no student group specifically organizing around this problem at Morehouse, and felt the Antioch policy did not encompass the way African-American men and women communicate about sex. "The language used around African American males is different," Prince said. "They have their own way of communicating verbally."

MEN AGAINST RAPE

Some male activists are just as disturbed as their female counterparts with men's penchants during educational programs for doggedly questioning the technical definition of rape or assault, rather than focusing on the nature of sexual relationships themselves.

"It's always coming up: 'What if this happens? Is this rape? How about that—is that rape?'" said James Newell, a senior at Syracuse University and president of the five-year-old co-ed student group SCARED (Students Concerned About Rape Education). "Men feel victimized by groups like ours. But we are not a group that's against sex."

Examining male expectations of sex is one tactic used at Duke University in Durham, NC, by the four-year-old student group Men Acting for Change (MAC). Pornography as sex education for men is a focal point of at least one [session] of the eight-session course on men and gender issues, a topic that precedes the class on rape, says Jason Schultz, a MAC co-founder who graduated in spring 1993.

While most of the women activists interviewed praised the men's organizations that are working against sexual violence, many expressed reservations and some suspicions about token support from other men's groups. One woman who asked not to be named criticized a men's group on her campus whose sole pro-feminist action is an annual day-long wearing of white ribbons to signify opposition to sexual assault. "Frankly I think it's a very shallow and trivial way of responding," she said.

Kelly Wall, a founder of HEAR-Women at North Carolina State, expressed irritation that the most visible anti-rape presence on campus before HEAR was comprised of men.

The REAL-Men group is aware of the apparent irony of the situation. "We're very conscious of what our place is. We don't want to take over the issue," Ammons says. Although his group does deal with "secondary survivors" (men who are grappling with their feelings about the rape of a lover, friend or relative), it is with some hesitation that they discuss the issues of male survivors of sexual offense.

Anti-rape activist Matthew Mizel at Stanford University says he sometimes feels his motivation questioned. Mizel founded Stanford Men's Collective in fall 1992 to discuss where rape comes from and how to stop it by examining men's own behavior. A talkative, outgoing senior easily recognized on campus by his long blond hair, Mizel says the praise he gets from women for his work generates curiosity and the occasional impression that he's doing it to "get laid."

"Men have asked if I'm trying to gain points with women and be some kind of super heterosexual. . . . And some women have asked if I'm gay—as if there was no chance that I'm just a regular person who cares about this issue," Mizel said.

These young men make it clear that anti-rape work is not just a woman's thing, and that the most progressive voices among college students are determined to rewrite the sexual code to fit the needs of their generation.

And they agree that a rewrite is necessary. At the University of Virginia, Claire Kaplan described a seminar in which several fraternity men asserted: "When you get to a certain point during sex you can't stop," an attitude she thought had long since fallen to the wayside. "That's why the Antioch policy was created," she notes. "There is still the attitude—don't talk, just do."   [1994]

Terms

1. IN LOCO PARENTIS: Literally "in place of the parent," the view that colleges have the responsibility to control all facets of student life.

Understanding the Reading

1. Why are students today implementing sexual codes on campuses?
2. What does the Antioch policy require students to do?
3. What initiated the Antioch policy?
4. How do students at schools where sexual codes exist feel about them?
5. What was the effect of the rape and murder of Jeanne Clery?
6. What role have men played in activism against sexual violence?
7. Why is sexual violence not just a White women's issue?
8. How do some men respond to rape education workshops?
9. What is a "secondary survivor"?

Suggestions for Responding

1. Alone or in a small group, develop a sexual conduct code for your campus.
2. Research and report on the crime statistics for your school. ♦

135

A Daughter's Story

DAWN ATKINS

I am the daughter of a fat woman, a wonderful, imaginative woman who raised four children in an often hostile world. When I was a teenager I helped her starve herself. One Mother's Day I gave her money to go to a hypnotherapist to lose weight. I did it because I loved her and wanted her to be happy. The world didn't see her as beautiful as I did, and it was the only way I knew to help her.

Today I am a well-known "fat activist." When I have spoken in public about body image, size discrimination, eating disorders, medical prejudice, the current research in weight and recovery, my audiences have listened intently—laughing, frowning, nodding, and shaking their heads. Most are average-size people obsessed with their weight and their looks. And when time comes for questions, someone always asks, "Why would you, obviously a thin woman, be concerned about discrimination against fat people?"

The reason is my mother. She and I discovered the women's movement at the same time, and I learned from her example to stand up to injustice in the world. Life should be fair, Mom taught me, even when it wasn't. Unlike so many other daughters of fat women who carry the weight of their mother's shame—no matter how fat or thin they are themselves—I chose to fight the injustice of size discrimination.

I have become a witness and a confessor. Every day another woman tells me her story of pain and prejudice. Sometimes I am the first person she has felt safe to tell it to: how her father beat her for not losing weight, how her mother died after stomach stapling. Women turn to me pleading for reassurance that there is some escape. I see the tears in their eyes.

And every day I confront the hate of bigots who put those tears there. I am the guest lecturer at the school where a 17-year-old boy tells me, "I don't judge people, but those people who are fat and lazy just disgust me." I am the witness at the public hearing on size discrimination when a man displays a blown-up sex doll wearing a padded shirt that says HIRE ME OR I'LL SUE.

I see the bodies. I count them. I read page after page of technical descriptions of how women are starved and mutilated. I hear the "mortality statistics"—estimates of women dead of eating disorders. I see their emaciated bodies piled up like cordwood.

I am the researcher who reads the studies and sees the lies. I am the one who knows which "obesity researchers" are on the take from the diet industry. I see how they manipulate the results for their own prejudice and profit. I read the diet-industry propaganda and financial reports and see how they make $33 billion a year with lies, shame, and fear.

As a child I didn't used to like my body. My younger sister called me "hippo-hips." I would never wear a sweater or shirt that didn't belt because I was afraid people would think I was fat. I was the "geek" other children picked on in school, and one of their favorite taunts was "fat pig." At times I was borderline anorexic, even though my mother encouraged me to love myself.

I never really "dieted"; I just went without food when I was unhappy. I was an outcast child, a thinker who didn't know when or how to keep her mouth shut. I felt that if you didn't speak up for what you believed, you were a traitor to yourself as well as others. This did not make me popular. I was always asking, "Why? How do you know that?" I drove adults and other children crazy with my need to understand.

When other children beat me for being different, my mother held me and told me she believed in me. She stood up to school administrators who didn't want to deal with a child who would tell them when and why she felt they were wrong.

In eighth grade, when I was 13 and dealing with puberty, a boy began following me around school calling me names like "Miss Charmin." In '70s teen lingo that meant my breasts were either (a) squeezable or (b) stuffed with tissue. He followed me at lunchtime and sat across from me in art class tormenting me every day. I tried to avoid him and I begged the teachers for help. I asked the art teacher just to move me away from him. I told the teacher that if she didn't do something, I would. My written appeal to her ended in the trash can, and she told me to sit down and shut up.

That was it. I told the boy that I was through taking it and that this was his last warning. He ignored me and continued. I remember pretending to go under the art table for a pencil, yanking the chair out from under him, then hitting him over the head with my art project (a board for string art). All my anger at the abuse and my desperation at the way I had been ignored went into that swing, one of the few acts of physical violence I have ever done. The teacher came unglued, screaming and ordering me to the principal. I uncrumpled the letter I had written to her and took it with me to the principal's office.

An hour later, the principal was turning blue trying to make me see that "little ladies don't do things like that." Frustrated with my total unrepentance, he finally threatened, "Well, I will have to call your mother." I smiled. I then got to watch him "Yes, ma'am"/"No, ma'am" my mother as she lectured him on the phone about sexual harassment and rape prevention. She told him in no uncertain terms that I was protecting myself and it was the school's tolerance of that kind of behavior that leads to boys raping girls.

When the principal got off the phone, he told me to return to class; he said he would have to think of how to punish this offense and get back to me. He never did. The teacher moved me and the boy to opposite ends of the classroom, and the boy never spoke to me again.

My mother not only taught me it was OK to speak up; she backed me when I did.

I think we learn to stand up to the injustice of the world through believing in ourselves and through the love of those who believe in us. In my research and activism about body image, I try to pass on the love and inspiration that my mother gave me: to show women that they are valuable and beautiful and deserve to be treated with love and respect.

Seven years ago I was always afraid of being fat or becoming fat. While I was researching a paper on the human body for an anthropology class, I learned that in places like Samoa and Africa fat women are regarded as beautiful. I wanted to know why. And once I put my feet on that path, my life was forever changed. I read books like *Shadow on a Tightrope* and *Such a Pretty Face* and I became angry. I learned that what my mother and I had been going through was not "natural" and was in fact linked to the oppression of women that we as feminists were fighting against.

The more I learned, the more I wanted to know. Suddenly all my papers for my classes were about weight and discrimination, and more anger built in me—righteous anger at injustice. When I began to study the diet industry and read the studies, I realized I had been lied to all my life. Finally I had to do something with my anger. I began teaching others the information I had uncovered. I found a way to make a difference.

I am now the proud witness when a fat woman who has hated her body and hidden all her life goes dancing for the first time. I am now the informed confessor the repeat dieter who has just "failed again" can go to and hear how to get off the diet cycle and find understanding, not condemnation. I now thrill to stories of triumph as women tell me the ways they have changed their lives and stood up to bullies and bigots. In 1992 I cheered with other fat activists and allies as we successfully changed the law in Santa Cruz, California, to make size discrimination illegal.

I want a world where people can be loved and respected in all their diversity. I want a world where I can find peace with my own body and where the women in my life can put their energy into changing the world, not their bodies.

I can now stand with my mother as she tells people that she will never diet again and that they should accept her as she is. I can now look at my own body with more love and understanding than ever before. [1996]

Understanding the Reading

1. What kind of responses does Atkins get to her lectures on size discrimination?
2. What was Atkins like as a child?
3. What happened when a boy kept calling her "Miss Charmin"?
4. How did her mother respond to the incident?
5. How was Atkins changed by her anthropology paper on the human body?

Suggestions for Responding

1. Write a letter to Atkins telling her your thoughts on size discrimination.
2. Write a short essay on your feelings about your own body. ◆

136

A Mother's Story

MARY E. ATKINS

I have been fat off and on, from one diet to the next, for the last 20 years. I raised four daughters, I gained weight with the birth of each, and I gained weight after every diet.

A year ago I went to the hospital very ill. I checked into the emergency room around 10:00 A.M. and was ferried for hours from one testing site to another. My youngest daughter, Angela, accompanied me.

Angela was not only young and scared but also pregnant and exhausted. She tried off and on all day to reach my eldest daughter, Dawn, who was at a workshop. That evening I remember looking up foggily from bed as Dawn arrived like a whirlwind, hugged me strongly, and cried, "Why aren't you dressed? You're so cold!"

All day long I had attempted to keep myself covered with a sheet. None of the hospital gowns fit.

"What is it, Mom, the sleeves?" Dawn got a gown from I don't know where. "OK, we'll tear out the sleeves." *Rip, rip*—and she dressed me, declaring to all medical staff within earshot, "My mother deserves to be treated with dignity!"

Much later, after surgery and intensive care, I was moved into a room. Once again there was no gown that would fit a fat woman. Dawn took two small-sized gowns, went to the charge nurse, and requested permission to take them home. "I'll sew these two gowns into one and have it back by morning for my mother," Dawn promised. She also told the charge nurse firmly that this was discrimination and that a patient would have difficulty getting out of bed and getting well if she did not have a gown to fit her.

"OK, I understand," the charge nurse said, "but that's not necessary. We do have large-size gowns. I'll have them brought up immediately." Dawn thanked her. Within a short time a stack of large-size gowns was placed in my room and I was dressed.

Each day a member of the medical staff would ask, "Where did you get that gown?" One

nurse said that not in three years had she seen large-size gowns; the physical therapist, not in five—and some of her male patients refused to leave their rooms because their gowns didn't cover their buttocks. Each time I relished telling the story of Dawn's activism.

After I was home and recovering, Dawn drove me to my first outpatient visit. Again no gown fit me. Dawn gave the nurse a mini-lecture on why they should have gowns to fit all sizes. Sometimes watching my daughter Dawn is like that old movie about Moses: She speaks and the waters part.

Even my surgeon became a convert. Each time I went for a checkup both Dawn and I worked on him. He began by calling me obese and asking me to go on a diet. But it got to the point that he thanked me for sending him brochures about fat people's rights and how fat people should be treated in the medical field. He said he now understands that being fat is a "condition," not a disease.

When Dawn was younger, she frequently got in trouble for questioning teachers' methods, especially if she saw favoritism or sexism. She took electronics in junior high—the first girl to do so in that suburban Oklahoma town. She had to threaten the school system with a lawsuit if they didn't let her (they had suggested she repeat home economics instead). The things she put up with in that class were a true horror story—from daily slut-jokes to being told she shouldn't touch the equipment because she might break it. She came in before and after school to do the experiments and received straight A's. They paired her with a D student who suddenly made C's by working with her. Dawn became the teacher's star example of what he could do with a girl! On ground she had broken, three more girls took electronics the next year.

The school is lucky they listened to Dawn, because when she fights you, she can make life very uncomfortable. Once our neighborhood was having a dispute with city hall because they were taking away the only commuter bus we had to the city. Dawn asked me if we wanted media attention, and I said sure. You should have seen the looks on the adults' faces when all the TV stations, radio stations, and newspaper reporters showed up at our small-town city hall. Dawn was only 17 but had learned the value of taking your fight public.

When I joined the National Organization for Women [NOW] in the mid-'70s, Dawn was there with me. Together we went on many marches for the Equal Rights Amendment. Dawn learned along with me how to organize and how empowering demonstrations can be.

Dawn had lived all her life with a mother who was on one diet or another and, by today's standards, was always overweight. When Dawn began researching weight-loss clinics for an investigative-journalism class in college, I remember her coming home and telling me again and again, "These people are lying—these people don't make sense and what they are doing is unfair." This only made her investigate more, and the more she found out, the more she realized the diet industry did not know what it was talking about and women's lives were being destroyed by the lies.

Dawn interviewed me over and over about how I felt and about the discrimination she had witnessed during her years of growing up with me. When she began her research she was fatphobic. By the time she graduated, she was a "fat activist." And I got to learn along with her. I read all the papers and went to her lectures.

I never would have become involved in the cause of fat acceptance in my own behalf if my own daughter Dawn had not first become so passionate about it. Never did I imagine how strengthening it would be, how much my own self-esteem and life would be enriched. I think I would have continued in my many organizations as an activist, but I would always have been on a diet, coming off a diet, or wishing I was on a diet. What a waste of energy, time, and money! Knowledge really is power. Dawn went out and got that knowledge and brought it back to me. And I have confidence that if Dawn found out tomorrow there was a safe, good way to diet, she would tell me immediately. She would tell everyone.

Eventually Dawn got involved in educating NOW on size issues. She and I went to the national NOW convention in 1990 to work on passing an anti-size-discrimination resolution. We met lots of big, beautiful women who were members of the National Association to Advance Fat Acceptance (NAAFA)—they had a booth right next to our NOW table. So we passed out little purple ribbons to people to wear if they supported the resolution. Well, Dawn got excited and off she went. She lobbied from morning till late night and personally passed out hundreds of those ribbons. Anyone not willing to support the resolution was met with a very persuasive argument. The resolution—which had failed the previous year—passed without a single vote of opposition.

Dawn came home from that experience and formed the Body Image Task Force, originally part of the local NOW chapter but today an independent organization. Dawn designed a T-shirt for the group: images of goddesses of all sizes with the words ALL WOMEN ARE BEAUTIFUL. It reminds us that women come in all shapes and sizes and have since the beginning of time.

Whenever you go out with Dawn you can expect a few uncomfortable moments. At a restaurant she'll check out the chairs and seating for large-size people. In a movie theater she'll do the same. She has been known to make a "scene" if it is for a good cause. And woe to whoever posts anti-fat notices or flyers! Dawn will protest loudly to the management and follow up with a letter stating why the poster was discriminatory and what could be done about it.

Sometimes I see and feel such anger and rage coming from people Dawn confronts that I get cold all over. But Dawn walks through it all carrying her knowledge of what she believes is right like a shield in front of her. It does make a difference, and it gives others courage.

By watching Dawn, I've also learned some of the things people who love and support activists can do for them as they fight on the front lines for people's rights. We can see that they believe in themselves—even when times are very dark. We can support their right to fight—even when we can't or don't want to. We can help keep their self-esteem high—even when many people are trying to pull them down.

And dare I say the rest?—make sure they eat and get plenty of sleep. I know, I know, I'm a mother. But sometimes my daughter the activist gets so busy and involved she forgets.   [1996]

Understanding the Reading

1. What did Dawn Atkins do when her mother was hospitalized?
2. What happened when Dawn Atkins wanted to study electronics in junior high?
3. How did Dawn Atkins help in the neighborhood struggle to keep the commuter bus?
4. How did Dawn Atkins' research and activism affect Mary Atkins?

5. What did Dawn Atkins do at the NOW convention?
6. What is it like to go places with Dawn Atkins?
7. What did Mary Atkins learn from her daughter Dawn about activism?

Suggestions for Responding

1. Write a short essay explaining how Mary Atkins' description of Dawn Atkins differs from and reinforces Dawn's self-description. ◆

SUGGESTIONS FOR RESPONDING TO PART IX

1. Write a personal essay describing yourself as a change maker. Make clear what problem you decided to work on, how you chose to attack it, what happened, and how successful (or unsuccessful) your effort was.
2. Make an oral presentation to the class about your action project, briefly covering the points raised in question 1.
3. Research a civil rights activist or organization, focusing on one particular action he, she, or they undertook. Write an essay describing and evaluating the project.
4. Investigate a group on your campus or in your community that is working to imple-

ment a change you consider desirable. Write an article for your local newspaper publicizing the group's efforts.
5. Explain how you are personally affected by our diverse, multicultural American society.
6. In the 1890s, Ida B. Wells-Barnett exposed and fought the racist use of lynching to control Black males, especially those who were perceived as economic threats to local Whites. Report on her work, including statistics on the incidence of lynching when she initiated her campaign and after it was underway.

X

Race, Class, and Gender After 9/11

MOST OF US HAVE HEARD IT SAID—"AFTER 9/11, everything changed." Certainly for the broken families who lost loved ones in the World Trade Center, the Pentagon, and all the hijacked planes that crashed, life is immeasurably changed. But the sentence implies more—it refers to how we feel about ourselves and others in the world, and from this has issued a large debate nationwide and worldwide. Whether or not "everything changed" depends on the reactions of individual citizens and of governments. As for individual behavior, after 9/11, there were basically three ways of carrying on day-to-day. One was to "cocoon"—basically, to go about one's business with very little social interaction and to stay close to home. The second way was to want revenge and, so, to direct anger toward those nearby and afar. The third way was to become very involved with some sort of community service or cause that the person highly valued. Many people wanted to do something to heal themselves and the world. As for national reactions, the global outpouring of sympathy and grief quickly changed when the United States announced that there were ties between Saddam Hussein and Al Qaeda and that Iraq had weapons of mass destruction. Ignoring the warnings from the United Nations Security Council, the United States invaded and occupied Iraq, at great loss of American and Iraqi life, based on disputed evidence of Iraqi weapons and ties to Al Qaeda.

What happened within the United States was equally upsetting and designed to quell any critics. With the passage of the Patriot Act, the federal government was given more power than any other administration to do surveillance on our own people, circumvent due process and First Amendment rights, prevent citizens from traveling, incarcerate whomever it sees fit, and demand access to student records from universities. Combine these policies of no checks and balances, with deep troubles in the United States economy, and anxiety over the safety of family members serving in Iraq and Afghanistan, and we see a movement of citizenry ready for change. The dialogues and "town meetings" going on all over America have been about revisiting our core values. Do we have a greater sense of unity as Americans now, or not? Does this sense cross racial, ethnic, and gender boundaries, or do we use these boundaries to structure how people see themselves and others in the world? Has being afraid made us **xenophobic**—highly fearful of anyone of foreign origin? Or perhaps mistrusting the dramatic, military approach to global and domestic problem solving, do we look forward to the time when we can again call on each other for resources, healing many of the rifts, especially with those living within America and with our traditional allies? As for law-abiding immigrants, who have been recently marginalized by an atmosphere of fear, we definitely look forward to the time when we will not feel *compelled* to fly or wear an American flag, as an attempt to not be targeted because of our accent, color of skin, or country of origin. This part of the text is dedicated to Americans, new and old, who are willing to help heal a wounded nation and world, by active citizenship and faith that we can learn from our history.

We begin Part X with "the Iowa State Daily," taking up the debate of how and what we will express with the proposed memorial sculpture at Ground Zero in New York City. Are we memorializing those who lost their lives and therefore wish to represent different types of Americans, or should we use the original photo as the model and sculpt three Caucasian firefighters raising the flag? There is much emotion surrounding this debate, as we discuss how to express ourselves as Americans in the 9/11 memorial. Next, Tram Nguyen takes us into a "Public's Truth" forum, one of several discussions planned throughout the United States, focusing on the effect the war on terrorism and change in domestic laws have had "on the lives of immigrants, refugees, and communities of color." The next article is by Muzaffar A. Chishti, Doris Meissner, Demetrios G. Papademetriou, Jay Peterzell, Michael J. Wishnie, and Stephen W. Yale-Loehr from the Migration Policy Institute, a nonpartisan, independent, nonprofit think tank that devotes its time to studying the common ground of national security, civil rights, and immigration policy. This article analyzes the effectiveness and impact of our war on terrorism, (which is primarily done through immigration control) and gives recommendations for sound immigration policy.

Ann Tickner gives a feminist analysis of September 11, 2001, and on the world's response. She points out the models of masculinity and femininity that are highlighted in times of war and offers alternative models that guide people's lives every day. Then, Laurie Goodstein introduces us to a class of evangelical Christians, whose purpose is to convert Muslims to Christianity, thus saving them from a fate of eternal Hell, they say. This article questions how one can convert with love, while hating the religion and culture of the potential convert.

The last two articles focus on two very vulnerable groups that have been adversely affected by the aftermath of 9/11. Donovan Slack describes the efforts of a refugee and relocation center in Trenton, New Jersey. After the terrorist attacks, no refugees were allowed to enter the United States for several months, even though they had been approved, and many were in great danger in refugee camps or in hiding. As a result, many died. Farai Chideya then asks, "Wouldn't it be great if people like [Jessica] Lynch and [Shoshana] Johnson didn't have to go to war to get a job or an education?" Both women came from towns with 20 percent and 24 percent unemployment, where the per capita incomes are between $13,000 and $14,000 a year. Chideya suggests that we could do better by investing as a nation in local service corps, where young people can give back to their country while gaining skills.

These articles challenge us all to share ideas, analyze, and make proposals for serious problem solving—much as the Migration Policy Institute does. If every classroom becomes a temporary think tank, our country will have made great strides, here and in the world.

137

Flag Raising at Ground Zero

The Iowa State Daily

A tribute is a service or object to show respect or gratitude to a person or group of people.

It is a representation.

That being said, apparently some people in New York City don't seem to understand it.

A statue, "Flag Raising at Ground Zero," has been criticized as an attempt to be politically correct instead of historical. They are upset because the photo that the statue is based on pictures three white firefighters raising a flag at the World Trade Center site.

But instead of sticking with this photo, the $180,000 sculpture, which will be erected in the spring at the Fire Department's Brooklyn headquarters, features one white, one black and one Hispanic firefighter, all raising the flag as in the photo.

The decision to represent different ethnicities was made by the Fire Department, the makers of the statue, and the property-management company that owns the department headquarters building and commissioned the work.

But family members of the firefighters in the photo have complained that the artist is trying to rewrite history. They say the photo, as it is, is reality, and any manipulation will subsequently change that moment.

The statue's artist has responded by saying the sculpture is meant to be a tribute to the 343 New York firefighters who lost their lives in the Sept. 11 terrorist attack, not a replica of the photo.

And that is a very important distinction.

In fact, the artist tried to purchase the copyright of the photo from North Jersey Media Group which owns the copyright, but was denied. So it is clear the statue is not supposed to be exactly the same as the original photo.

Opponents of the manipulation of the photo need to keep some things in mind when looking at the situation.

This tribute represents all races and all ethnicities of firefighters in New York City. It wasn't meant to honor the firefighters who are alive and pictured putting the flag at the World Trade Center site. It wasn't a memorial built for those three white firefighters, and it isn't a memorial for the beautiful photo taken on that fateful day.

This isn't about being politically correct, and those who are arguing that it is are misinterpreting the powerful meaning of the statue and what it is being built to represent.

This isn't about being historical. Sure, the photo pictured three white firefighters. But the memorial is more than a snapshot in time, more than a recreation of the photo down to the last detail.

This is about remembering the hundreds of firefighters that worked to save people in the World Trade Center and those that died doing so.

All of them.   [2002]

Understanding the Reading

1. What are the differences between the proposed sculpture of "Flag Raising at Ground Zero" and the photo taken on September 11, 2001?
2. What is the controversy?
3. Exactly to what is the sculpture meant to pay tribute?
4. Why is there so much emotion surrounding this issue?

Suggestions for Responding

1. This sculpture's creation has been delayed for about two years because of arguments about how and what it should portray. Debate this issue in class.
2. Architecture, museums, and memorials are meant to represent a community's ideals and often are an expression of grief or pride. As such, they are often a focus of public controversy. Research other communities that have had large, ongoing debates concerning the construction of a memorial or a building. (Suggestions: Fred Phelps' anti-gay statue of

Iowa State Daily at Iowa State University 2002. Permission from editor.

Matthew Shepard in Matthew's hometown; the architectural debate in Germany that has lasted for more than a decade. Notably, the re-building of Berlin since 1990 has kept alive the debate on how to acknowledge and express the Holocaust.) Identify the ideological sides and the emotions. ✦

138

Immigrant Families Condemn Racial Targeting

TRAM NGUYEN

Abdul Hatifie hosts a weekly radio show broadcast to the Afghan community in the Bay Area and Los Angeles. Along with announcements of community events and discussions of Afghan culture, the Alameda doctor tries to talk about discrimination and anti-immigrant scapegoating.

"(Listeners) hear me talk of people's stories and politics and they ask, 'Why do you say these things? Why can't you just stay quiet?'" I try to explain to them that to say the truth is not a crime, Hatifie said. "I am a person who has the right to speak, but now, in this country, we are taking out the Constitution, we are taking away our rights. The U.S. is not supposed to be like this."

Hatifie was one of 14 immigrants who shared their stories during a public hearing May 10 hosted at Buena Vista United Methodist Church, a Japanese American congregation in Alameda, California. Organized by the Applied Research Center, the testimonials were the first in a series of "Public's Truth" forums planned around the country to highlight the impact of the "war on terrorism" and national security on the lives of immigrants, refugees, and communities of color.

At least 1,200 immigrants have been secretly detained in the last two years, and the federal government still hasn't released any information

on their names and whereabouts. Thousands more [have been] deported or forced to flee "special registration" requirements, FBI interrogations, and INS raids. More than 10,000 immigrant workers have lost their jobs as a result of Operation Tarmac raids at airports, citizenship requirements for screeners, and social security "no-match letters" used to fire workers.

Despite widespread fear in their communities, participants at the forum were outspoken in condemning the policies and practices that have unjustly targeted them.

"Why is it acceptable for our government to tear families apart?" asked Theresa Allyn, a student at UC Berkeley whose mother was deported to the Philippines after 30 years in the U.S. Allyn's mother, a teacher, fell "out of status" with immigration authorities after she lost her green card during a 1999 robbery. Complications over replacing her green card status eventually led to her deportation in January 2003.

Other speakers related stories of attacks across a spectrum of ethnic communities and social sectors. Marwa Rifahie, an 18-year-old Egyptian American, described harassment at her high school from a teacher who called her a "Nazi." Former airport worker Erlinda Valencia recalled English-proficiency tests and citizenship requirements that resulted in her lay-off after 14 years as a screener at San Francisco airport. Community activists Kawal Ulanday and Rebecca Gordon described government scrutiny of their political activities—being visited by the FBI and put on a "no-fly" list for profiling at airports, respectively—that pointed to a larger "clamping down on all our freedoms."

The setting of the hearing, in a Japanese American Methodist church, held particular significance for audience members as Rev. Michael Yoshii drew parallels between the post-9/11 climate and the climate that led to World War II internment. This hearing, along with its antecedent held by the Hate Free Zone of Seattle last year, is modeled after national hearings held during the Japanese American redress movement during the 1980s.

One of the Public's Truth testimonials belonged to Alba Witkin, an 83-year-old resident of Berkeley, Calif. who worked with American Friends' Service Committee during the 1940s to help Japanese American internees eligible to leave the camps for placement at colleges and universities.

"I know that it is hard to understand why people didn't seem to react to the Japanese internment. A lot of people ask me how could average citizens sit back and let that happen," she recalled. "But a lot of people didn't know the full extent of what was happening. The press didn't report it. I think that is a commentary on the media in 1942 as well as the media today. I still don't think we're getting all the stories."

Future Public's Truth forums are planned for San Jose, Los Angeles, and other cities nationwide.

According to Rev. Yoshii, "We need to establish a public record of these egregious violations and take action to protect the civil liberties and human rights of all families, regardless of their race, religion, or country of origin."   [2003]

Understanding the Reading

1. What is the purpose of the "Public's Truth" forums?
2. Why is the U.S. government detaining immigrants?
3. Why was Theresa Allyn's mother deported after thirty years in the United States?
4. What kind of harassment are some community activists experiencing?
5. What are the parallels between the post-9/11 atmosphere and what happened to Japanese Americans during World War II?

Suggestions for Responding

1. Collect testimonials from your own community of how immigrants are being treated.
2. Research what policies the Homeland Security Department has changed that have made it especially difficult or impossible for thousands of law-abiding immigrants to stay in the United States. ✦

139

America's Challenge: Domestic Security, Civil Liberties, and National Unity After September 11

Muzaffar A. Chishti, Doris Meissner, Demetrios G. Papademetriou, Jay Peterzell, Michael J. Wishnie, and Stephen W. Yale-Loehr

Summary

The U.S. government's harsh measures against immigrants since September 11 have failed to make us safer, have violated our fundamental civil liberties, and have undermined national unity.

The devastating attacks of September 11 demanded a wide-ranging response. The United States has responded with military action, as in Afghanistan, through intelligence operations to disrupt al Qaeda and arrest its members; and by re-organizing homeland security.

But our new security measures must be effective rather than merely dramatic, and must not destroy what we are trying to defend. The government's post–September 11 immigration measures have failed these tests.

These actions have not only done great harm to the nation; they have also been largely ineffective in their stated goal of improving our domestic security. Despite the government's heavy-handed immigration tactics, many of the September 11 terrorists would probably be admitted to the United States today.

Al Qaeda's hijackers were carefully chosen to avoid detection: all but two were educated young men from middle-class families with no criminal records and no known connection to terrorism. To apprehend such individuals before they attack requires a laser-like focus on the gathering, sharing, and analysis of intelligence, working hand-in-glove with well-targeted criminal and immigration law enforcement.

Instead, the government conducted round-ups of individuals based on their national origin and religion. These roundups failed to locate terrorists, and damaged one of our great potential assets in the war on terrorism: the communities of Arab- and Muslim-Americans.

We believe it is possible both to defend our nation and to protect core American values and principles, but doing so requires a different approach. It is too easy to say that if we abandon our civil liberties the terrorists win. It is just as easy to say that without security there will be little room for liberty. What is hard is to take both arguments with equal seriousness and to integrate them within a single framework. We set out to reach that important balance in this report.

As we worked on this project we became convinced that more than security and civil liberties—that is, the rights of individuals—are at stake. There is a third element: the character of the nation. Our humblest coin, the penny, bears the words *e pluribus unum,* or "from many, one." The phrase goes to the heart of our identity as a nation and to the strength we derive from diversity. We strongly believe that fully embracing Muslim and Arab communities as part of the larger American society would not only serve this American value but help break the impasse between security and liberty, strengthening both.

HARSH MEASURES AGAINST IMMIGRANTS HAVE FAILED TO MAKE US SAFER

Our 18-month-long review of post–September 11 immigration measures determined that:

- The U.S. government overemphasized the use of the immigration system;
- As an antiterrorism measure, immigration enforcement is of limited effectiveness; and
- Arresting a large number of noncitizens on grounds not related to domestic security only gives the nation a false sense of security.

In some cases, the administration simply used immigration law as a proxy for criminal law enforcement, circumventing constitutional safeguards. In others, the government seems to have acted out of political expediency, creating a false appearance of effectiveness without regard to the cost.

Our research indicates that the government's major successes in apprehending terrorists have not come from post–September 11 immigration initiatives but from other efforts such as international intelligence activities, law enforcement cooperation, and information provided by arrests made abroad. A few noncitizens detained through these immigration initiatives have been characterized as terrorists, but the only charges brought against them were actually for routine immigration violations or ordinary crimes.

Many of the government's post–Sept. 11 immigration actions have been poorly planned and have undermined their own objectives. For example, the goals of the special call-in registration program have been contradictory: gathering information about nonimmigrants present in the United States, and deporting those with immigration violations. Many nonimmigrants have rightly feared they will be detained or deported if they attempt to comply, so they have not registered.

Our research also found serious problems at the Federal Bureau of Investigation (FBI) that are hampering our nation's counterterrorism efforts and damaging other key national interests. The State Department has tried for 10 years to get access to FBI information to add to its terrorist watchlists; those discussions are still going on. Automating this process would help to overcome long delays in visa approvals that are damaging U.S. political and economic relations abroad. It would also allow agencies to focus on a more in-depth risk assessment of visa applicants who raise legitimate security concerns.

Finally, the Justice Department's efforts to enlist state and local law enforcement agencies into enforcing federal immigration law risks making our cities and towns more dangerous while hurting the effort to fight terrorism. Such action undercuts the trust that local law enforcement agencies have built with immigrant communities, making immigrants less likely to report crimes, come forward as witnesses, or provide intelligence information, out of fear that they or their families risk detention or deportation.

GOVERNMENT IMMIGRATION ACTIONS THREATEN FUNDAMENTAL CIVIL LIBERTIES

The U.S. government has imposed some immigration measures more commonly associated with totalitarian regimes. As this report details, there have been too many instances of long-time U.S. residents deprived of their liberty without due process of law, detained by the government and held without charge, denied effective access to legal counsel, or subjected to closed hearings. These actions violate bedrock principles of U.S. law and society.

Take the experience of Tarek Mohamed Fayad, an Egyptian dentist arrested in southern California on Sept. 13, 2001, for violating his student visa. During Fayad's first 10 days of incarceration he was not allowed to make any telephone calls. Thereafter, he was allowed sporadic "legal" calls and only a single "social" call per month. The "legal" call was placed by a Bureau of Prisons counselor either to a designated law office or to one of the organizations on the INS's[1] list of organizations providing free legal services in the region. The privilege of making a call was deemed satisfied once the call was placed, regardless of whether the call was answered. Of the agencies on the list provided to Fayad, only one number was a working contact for an agency providing legal counseling to detainees and none of the organizations agreed to provide representation. In the meantime, Fayad's friends had hired an attorney for him, but the attorney was unable to determine his location for more than a month. Even after the attorney found out that Fayad was being detained at a federal facility in New York, the Bureau of Prisons continued to deny that Fayad was in custody.

Rather than relying on individualized suspicion or intelligence-driven criteria, the government has used national origin as a proxy for evidence of dangerousness. By targeting specific ethnic groups with its new measures, the government has violated another core principle of American justice: the Fifth Amendment guarantee of equal protection.

The government also conducted a determined effort to hide the identity, number and whereabouts of its detainees, violating the First Amendment's protection of the public's right to be informed about government actions. This right is at the heart of our democracy, and is crucial to maintaining government accountability to the public.

The government's post–September 11 actions follow a repeating pattern in American history of rounding up immigrant groups during national security crises, a history we review as part of this report. Like the internment of Japanese-Americans during World War II, the deportation of Eastern-European immigrants during the Red Scare of 1919–20, and the harassment and internment of German-Americans during World War I, these actions will come to be seen as a stain on America's heritage as a nation of immigrants and a land where individual rights are valued and protected.

REPORT PROFILES 406 DETAINEES, DESPITE GOVERNMENT SECRECY

More than 1,200 people—the government has refused to say exactly how many, who they are, or what has happened to all of them—were detained after September 11. Despite the government's determined efforts to shroud these actions in secrecy, as part of our research we were able to obtain information about 406 of these detainees.

- Unlike the hijackers, the majority of noncitizens detained since September 11 had significant ties to the United States and roots in their communities. Of the detainees for whom relevant information was available, over 46 percent had been in the United States at least six years. Almost half had spouses, children, or other family relationships in the United States.

- Even in an immigration system known for its systemic problems, the post–September 11 detainees suffered exceptionally harsh treatment. Many were detained for weeks or months without charge or after a judge ordered them released. Of the detainees for whom such information was available, nearly 52 percent were subject to an "FBI hold," keeping them detained after a judge released them or ordered them removed from the United States. More than 42 percent of detainees were denied the opportunity to post bond. Many of the detainees were subjected to solitary confinement, 24-hour lighting of cells, and physical abuse.

- Although detainees in theory had the legal right to secure counsel at their own expense and to contact family members and consular representatives, the government frequently denied them these rights, especially in the first weeks after September 11.
- Many of the detainees were incarcerated because of profiling by ordinary citizens, who called government agencies about neighbors, coworkers, and strangers based on their ethnicity, religion, name, or appearance. In Louisville, KY, the FBI and INS detained 27 Mauritanians after an outpouring of tips from the public; these included a tip from a suspicious neighbor, who called the FBI when a delivery service dropped off a box with Arabic writing on it.

  In New York, a man studying airplane design at the New York Institute of Technology went to a Kinko's store to make copies of airplane photos. An employee went into the wastebasket to get his information and then called the FBI; after nearly two months in detention, he accepted voluntary departure. Nearly 28 percent of the detainees were arrested because of a tip to the authorities by private citizens.

Most important, immigration arrests based upon tips, sweeps, and profiling have not resulted in any terrorism-related convictions against these detainees. Of the four detainees in our sample who had terrorism-related charges brought against them, all four were arrested based on traditional investigative techniques, not as the result of immigration enforcement initiatives. One has since been convicted and two have been acquitted; charges were dropped against the fourth individual, and he was deported.

Government Targeting of Arab- and Muslim-Americans Undermines National Unity

The government's actions against Arabs and Muslims have terrified and alienated hardworking communities across the nation.

President Bush's visit to a Washington mosque shortly after September 11 had a temporary positive impact on Arab- and Muslim-American communities. But the subsequent failure of government leaders to speak out on a sustained basis against discrimination, coupled with the Justice Department's aggressive immigration initiatives, sent a message to individuals and companies that discrimination against Arabs and Muslims was acceptable, leaders of these communities said. These views emerged in a coast-to-coast series of interviews that the Migration Policy Institute conducted to gauge the impact of the crisis on Arab- and Muslim-Americans.

"September 11 has created an atmosphere which suggests that it is okay to be biased against Arab-Americans and Muslims," said a regional director of an Arab-American civil rights organization.

The Justice Department's decision to conduct closed immigration proceedings for many of the detainees only increased suspicion that Arab- and Muslim-Americans were being treated under a different standard of due process. "The automatic association with terrorism is present in all these proceedings," said a prominent Arab-American lawyer in Michigan.

There is a strong belief among Arab- and Muslim-Americans that these measures are ineffective in responding to threats of terrorism, but are being undertaken for political expediency or public relations at a huge price to their communities. "This is political smoke to make people feel good," said the spokesman of a national Arab-American organization.

In a striking consensus, however, many leaders of the community have developed a positive reaction to law enforcement agencies since September 11, especially to local police. "The local police are our friends," said the chief imam of a New York Islamic center, citing their constant presence to protect his mosque.

Discrimination in the workplace soared after September 11. So overwhelming was the number of complaints it received that the Equal Employment Opportunity Commission (EEOC) created a new category to track acts of discrimination against Middle Eastern, Muslim and South Asian workers after September 11. In the 15 months between Sept. 11, 2001, and Dec. 11,

2002, the EEOC received 705 such complaints. Many more went unreported. And to add insult to injury, some of those who were detained after September 11 have been fired by their employers as a result.

Yet the experience of Arabs and Muslims in America post–September 11 is more than a story of fear and victimization. It is, in many ways, an impressive story of a community that at first felt intimidated but has since started to assert its place in the American body politic. Naturalization applications from Arab and Muslim immigrants have jumped and voter registration has risen since September 11.

September 11 and its aftermath have ushered in what could be called the "Muslim moment:" a period of rising Muslim self-consciousness, new alliances outside their own communities, interfaith dialogue, and generational change. The sense of siege has strengthened some Muslim- and Arab-American political organizations and has led them to a greater focus on civil rights, social services, economic development, and engagement with government agencies. The notion of a distinct "American Muslim" identity has gained new currency. It is an identity that seeks to assert its independence from forces abroad, one that combines the essential elements of Islam and the values of U.S. constitutional democracy. [2003]

Terms

1. INS: Immigration and Naturalization Service

Understanding the Reading

1. Why does the Migration Policy Institute say that the government's post–September 11 actions have failed to be effective and have been very destructive?
2. What was one of our best local assets in our war on terrorism?
3. How can we have both security and liberty?
4. Why hasn't the call-in registration program worked?
5. Why shouldn't local law enforcement enforce federal immigration law, according to this report? Do you agree or disagree?
6. How have our First Amendment rights been harmed?

7. Describe what the article calls the "Muslim moment."

Suggestions for Responding

1. Mayor Bloomberg of New York City has told local law enforcement not to enforce certain federal immigration laws. Find which other cities have responded in the same way and which make a point of enforcing federal immigration law.
2. Invite Arab Americans or Muslim Americans to your class to discuss practical ways of balancing security with liberty. ✦

140

Feminist Perspectives on 9/11

J. ANN TICKNER

In this article I offer a feminist analysis of September 11, 2001 and its aftermath. I demonstrate how gendered discourses are used in this and other conflict situations to reinforce mutual hostilities. I suggest that men's association with warfighting and national security serves to reinforce their legitimacy in world politics while it acts to create barriers for women. Using the framework of a post-9/11 world, I offer some alternative models of masculinity and some cultural representations less dependent on the subordination of women. Often in times of conflict women are seen only as victims. I outline some ways in which the women of Afghanistan are fighting against gender oppression and I conclude with some thoughts on their future prospects. . . .

Author's note: This article was originally presented at the Council on Foreign Relations, New York, March 2002. Thanks to Hayward Alker and Jennifer Whitaker for their helpful suggestions. While I use the term "9/11" in this article, I realize that the fears and hardships associated with terror and conflict were present for many people outside the United States before September 11, 2001.
© 2002 by International Studies Association. From J. Ann Tickner, "Feminist Perspectives on 9/11." Reprinted by permission of Blackwell Publishing. Published by Blackwell Publishing, 350 Main Street, Malden, MA 02148, USA, and 108 Cowley Road, Oxford OX4 1JF, UK.

"Our brothers who fought in Somalia saw wonders about the weakness, feebleness, and cowardlinesss of the U.S. soldier. . . . [W]e believe that we are men, Muslim men who must have the honour of defending [Mecca]. We do not want American women soldiers defending [it]. . . . The rulers in that region have been deprived of their manhood. . . . By God, Muslim women refuse to be defended by these American and Jewish prostitutes."

—Osama bin Laden[1]

"As women gain power in these [Western] countries, [they] should become less aggressive, adventurous, competitive, and violent."

—Francis Fukuyama[2]

"The operative word is men. Brawny, heroic, manly men."

—Patricia Leigh Brown[3]

"I don't want any women to go to my grave . . . during my funeral or any occasion thereafter."

—Mohamed Atta[4]

"War gives purpose to life. . . . Peace brings out the silliness in man; war makes him imitate the tiger."

—George S. Patton, Jr.[5]

*"My nation's wrath has empowered me
My ruined and burnt villages fill me with hatred against the enemy
Oh compatriot, no longer regard me weak and incapable,
My voice has mingled with thousands of arisen women
My fists are clenched with fists of thousands of compatriots
To break all these sufferings, all these fetters of slavery.
I'm the woman who has awoken,
I've found my path and will never return."*

—Meena[6]

GENDERED IMAGES

Gendered images are everywhere, many of them threatening. Osama bin Laden taunts the West for becoming feminized; Francis Fukuyama is concerned about it too. In a 1998 article in *Foreign Affairs,* Fukuyama, although more positive

than bin Laden about what they both see as the feminization of Western culture, pointed to similar dangers. He counseled against putting women in charge of U.S. foreign policy and the military because of their inability to stand up to unspecified dangers (perhaps more specific since 9/11) from "those [non-democratic] parts of the world run by young, ambitious, unconstrained men," (Fukuyama, 1998:36, 38). Five years earlier, Samuel Huntington (1993) warned of a "clash of civilizations," an only slightly veiled reference to a demographically exploding Islam, a "fault line" between Western Christian societies that have progressed in terms of economic development and democratization, and the Muslim world where young men's frustrations are fuelled by the failure of these same phenomena.[7]

For others the danger is closer to home; the "real" fault lines are here in the United States. In a 1994 article that lauded Huntington's clash of civilizations thesis, James Kurth focused attention on the "real clash," an internal one. Extolling the rise of Western civilization and the Enlightenment, a secular society based on individualism, liberalism, constitutionalism, human rights, the rule of law, free markets, and the separation of church and state, which came of age at the beginning of the twentieth century, Kurth saw the Enlightenment in decline at the century's end. What he termed "post-industrialism" has moved women into the labor market and out of the home with negative consequences for children, particularly those reared in split family or single-parent households. The U.S. is, according to Kurth, threatened not only by feminism, which bears the responsibility for the liberation of women, but also by multiculturalism—the presence, and recognition, of large numbers of African-Americans, Latino Americans, and Asian Americans who, unlike earlier immigrant populations, remain unassimilated in terms of Western liberal ideas (Kurth, 1994:14).[8]

The fears of these scholars, and Fukuyama's solution—to keep strong men in charge—may seem more real today than when they were first articulated. And post-9/11 discourse has produced some strange bedfellows! As bin Laden goads America for its moral decadency and lack of manliness, Jerry Falwell and Pat Robertson blamed 9/11 on the ACLU, homosexuals, and feminists because they "make God mad" (Scheer, 2001a). The terrorists are those unconstrained young men, some of whom have managed to live among us rather than "out there" beyond the fault line. So, contra bin Laden, masculinity is back in vogue in the United States. Since 9/11, "the male hero has been a predominant cultural image, presenting a beefy front of strength to a nation seeking steadiness and emotional grounding. They are the new John Waynes . . . men who charge up the stairs in a hundred pounds of gear, and tell everyone else where to go to be safe."[9] In spite of the Bush administration's appointment of the first female National Security Adviser, our TV screens after 9/11 were full of (mostly white) men in charge briefing us about "America's New War" both at home and abroad. We feel safer when "our men" are protecting us (against other men) and our way of life.

So where did all the women go? According to an analysis by the British newspaper *The Guardian,* women virtually disappeared from newspaper pages and TV screens after 9/11.[10] Carol Gilligan notes that men's rising star all but eclipsed that of the many heroic women who rose to the occasion, be they firefighters or police officers.[11] Women were also amongst our combat forces deployed against Afghanistan where male warriors waving guns and shouting death to America looked menacing and unrestrained. If we did see women they were likely to be faceless Afghan women in the now familiar blue *burqa.* Their shadowy and passive presence seemed only to reinforce these gendered images I have drawn.[12]

Yet the picture is more complicated. Bin Laden taunts the West for its feminization but he also rails against its "crusaders," an image more likely to invoke mediaeval knights on horseback than modern-day "feminized" men about whom Fukuyama, as well as bin Laden, is concerned. And the masculinity of bin Laden's own foot soldiers has also come under scrutiny. Mohamed Atta, whose last will and testament banned women from his grave lest they pollute it, was "a polite shy boy who came of age in an Egypt torn between growing Western influence and the religious fundamentalism that gathered force in reaction, . . . [he] had two sisters headed for careers as a professor and a doctor." Grumbling that his wife was raising him as a girl, his father

is reputed to have "told him [Atta] I needed to hear the word 'doctor' in front of his name. . . . We told him your sisters are doctors . . . and you are the man of the family."[13]

And, contra Fukuyama's and Kurth's fears about the feminized weakening of America, American women supported the war effort in overwhelming numbers while Afghan women beneath the burqa protested American bombing and exhorted their sisters to fight against gender oppression. World order scholar Richard Falk (2001) called the war the first just war since World War II,[14] and the U.S. Catholic bishops gave it qualified support on the same grounds (Cooperman, 2001) while realist John Mearsheimer (2001) counseled against it. Liberals, such as Laurence Tribe, condoned the use of military tribunals and the detention of more than 1,200 young men, none of whom (as of December 2001) had been charged in connection with the attacks.[15]

So, if the story is not a simple one where gender and other ideological lines are firmly drawn, what can a feminist analysis add to our understanding of 9/11 and its aftermath? The statements with which I begin this article offer support for the claim that war both reinforces gender stereotypes and shakes up gender expectations (Goldstein, 2002). The conduct of war is a largely male activity on both sides but Meena, the founder of RAWA, exhorts women to fight too. Nevertheless, gender is a powerful legitimator of war and national security; our acceptance of a "remasculinized" society during times of war and uncertainty rises considerably. And the power of gendered expectations and identifications have real consequences for women and for men, consequences that are frequently ignored by conventional accounts of war and civilizational clashes.

In this article I first examine the gendering of war and peace; I then situate the events of post-9/11 in this context, showing how gendered discourses are used on both sides to reinforce mutual hostilities and their consequences for both women and men. I discuss the much-publicized representation of Afghan women as victims as well as the less familiar ways—at least to us—in which they have been fighting back. Through this case, I suggest how feminist analysis exposes and questions these stereotypical gender representations and demonstrates their negative consequences. I conclude with four generalized lessons that I take from this feminist analysis. I begin by defining what I mean by gender.

DEFINING GENDER

A dictionary definition of gender refers to the social classifications "masculine" and "feminine" as opposed to sex, the physiological distinction between males and females. In this article, I build and expand on this definition. I define gender as a set of variable, but socially and culturally constructed relational characteristics. Those, such as power, autonomy, rationality, activity, and public are stereotypically associated with masculinity; their opposites, weakness, dependence, emotionality, passivity, and private are associated with femininity. There is evidence to suggest that both women and men assign a more positive value to the masculine characteristics which denote a culturally dominant ideal type, or "hegemonic" masculinity, to which few men actually conform; nevertheless, they do define what men ought to be.[16] It is important to note that gendered social relationships are relationships of power; it is through these hierarchical relationships that male power and female subordination are sustained, albeit in various degrees across time and place. Most feminists consider gendered relationships as social constructions because the specific content of these contrasted characteristics change over time and place; this allows for the possibility of female emancipation.

Gender distinctions can also be used to reinforce the power of dominant groups: minorities, and "outsiders," are frequently characterized by dominant groups as lacking in these hegemonic masculine characteristics. Gender is not, as is so often claimed, synonymous with women and feminine identities; it is also about men and masculine identities and, more important, about relations between men and women. Gender serves to legitimate certain activities and ways of thinking over others; it privileges certain societal tasks over others and assigns certain people, depending on their sex, to undertake them. The consequences for women (and for men) and for society more generally are significant. Nowhere are these gender lines more firmly drawn than in how societies view and conduct war.

GENDERING WAR AND PEACE

George Patton's claim—that war gives purpose to life, evident in post-9/11 political discourse—is one that has been widely shared by both women and men. Whereas wars frequently energize societies and foster a communal and self-sacrificial spirit among women and men alike, war-fighting is an activity that has been undertaken almost exclusively by men.

In his book *War and Gender,* Joshua Goldstein questions why we have not been more curious about this fact. In an exhaustive cross-cultural investigation of wars throughout history, Goldstein finds no biological evidence for why men are almost always the fighters; instead, he attributes it to cultural socialization. "Cultures mold males into warriors by attaching to 'manhood' those qualities that make good warriors" (Goldstein, 2001:252).[17] The toughening up of boys is found across cultures and many cultures use gender to motivate participation in combat (Goldstein, 2001:406). Warriors require intense socialization in order to fight effectively (Goldstein, 2001:252).

While Goldstein finds it remarkable that this association between masculinity and war has received so little attention from scholars who write about war, war as a masculine activity has been central to feminist investigations (Stiehm, 1983; Elshtain, 1987; Enloe, 1993, 2000). Generally supporting Goldstein's claims about militarized masculinity, feminists have suggested that "military manhood," or a type of heroic masculinity that goes back to ancient Greece, attracts recruits and maintains self-esteem in institutions where obedience is the norm. The term "patriot" is frequently associated with service in military combat. The National Organization for Women's (NOW) support for women entering the U.S. military was based on the argument that, if women were barred from participation in the armed forces on an equal footing with men, they would remain second-class citizens denied the unique political responsibility of risking one's life for the state (Jones, 1990). The lack of ability to serve in combat has also acted as a handicap for women running for political office in the United States.

The notion that (young) males fight wars to protect vulnerable people, such as women and children who cannot be expected to protect themselves, has also been an important motivator for the recruitment of military forces. "Protection" has been an important myth that has sustained support for war by both men and women.[18] I use the term "myth" because the large number of civilian casualties in recent wars severely strains the credibility of female protection.

If war is a phenomenon we associate with men and "hegemonic" masculinity, peace is a term we stereotypically associate with women and some of the devalued feminine characteristics I outlined earlier. As Jean Elshtain (1987:230) has suggested, we are afraid to let go of war because we fear even more the prospects of a sterile peace. Peace is frequently seen as an ideal, and even uninteresting, state with little chance of success in the "real" world. Women have been linked to anti-war sentiment throughout history and most peace movements have been disproportionately populated by women. Indeed, many of these movements have drawn inspiration from maternal imagery to craft their strategies. Yet I believe that the association of women with peace renders both women and peace as idealistic, utopian, and unrealistic; it is profoundly disempowering for both. And as long as peace remains associated with women, this may reinforce militarized masculinity (Goldstein, 2001:413).

The association of men with the "realities" of war and women with an "idealistic" notion of peace reinforces the gender hierarchies I outlined earlier. The consequences of this gender hierarchy are real in that it reinforces men's legitimacy and helps sustain their continued dominance in world politics; it also serves to perpetuate the barriers that women face in gaining legitimacy in foreign and military policymaking, particularly in times of conflict. In most societies, women's under-representation in international security matters and the military cannot be explained by legal barriers alone. I shall now suggest some consequences of these gender stereotypes for our post-9/11 world.

GENDERING 9/11

America Under Attack

"This is the warriors' time, the warriors, the martyrs—they're all men."[19] Those we fear today are angry young men wielding rifles and shouting death to America. Many of them were trained in madrassas—religious schools that teach little except an extreme version of Islam to boys and young men; many of them come from refugee camps where they live in poverty with few prospects in life. Frequently, they are also taught to hate women; in a situation where most of them feel powerless, the wielding of power over women can be a boost to self-esteem. Although Mohamed Atta's [the suspected leader of the September 11 hijackers and the pilot of the first plane to crash in the World Trade Center] middle-class background does not fit this profile, this training must have alleviated his sense of inferiority with respect to the women in his own domestic life.

According to Ian Buruma and Avishai Margalit (2002), this newest form of "Occidentalism," evident in the teaching of madrassas, comes out of a long, warlike tradition of hatred of the West, a hatred that appeals to those who feel impotent, marginalized, and denigrated. Tracing its roots back to nineteenth-century Russia and mid-twentieth-century Japan, they suggest that the objects of hate associated with Occidentalism, all of which played a significant role in the attacks of September 11, are materialism, liberalism, capitalism, rationalism, and feminism. All these phenomena are epitomized in city life with its multiculturalism, wealth, sexual license, and artistic freedom which result in decadence and moral laxity. The twin towers, as powerful symbols of urban secular wealth, were an apt target for vengeance against these evils. Gender symbolism, and gender ambivalence borne out of misogyny, abounds in this discourse; the West is described as individualist, rational, and hard but, at the same time, decadent, effete, and addicted to personal safety at the expense of valuing the heroic self-sacrifice expected of "real men." Today's Occidentalists taunt the West with accusations of moral decadence in this world, yet promise sexual rewards for their men in heaven after their sacrificial death for the cause.

For Occidentalists, it is women's emancipation that leads to decadence. "Westoxification" denotes a plague from the West. Those most vulnerable are women, particularly middle-class women with a Western education; these women must be brought under control and conform to an idealized construct of womanhood (Moghadan, 1994:13). The proper role for women is to be breeders of heroic men. For the Taliban, Occidental sinfulness was present even in Kabul with "girls in school and women with uncovered faces populating and defiling the public domain" (Buruma and Margalit, 2002:5). The ideational and material consequences of this misogynist discourse was brought home to us through the post-9/11 media focus on the plight of women in Afghanistan. But we must remember that it is not only those "out there" who engage in oppositional thinking with its negative gender stereotyping.

AMERICA STRIKES BACK

America may have surprised these warriors with the determination of its response. Belying bin Laden's taunts and Fukuyama's fear that the U.S. is becoming feminized and thus less able to defend itself, the U.S. military response was swift and strong; it received high approval ratings from men and women alike.[20] From the start, policymakers framed the attack and the U.S. response as a war between good and evil—the message to the rest of the world was that you are either for us or against us—there is no middle position. Random attacks on innocent people, identified by their attackers as Muslim, immediately following 9/11, which the Bush administration went to lengths to denounce, manifested an unpleasant form of Orientalism.

Given the massive sense of insecurity generated by the first foreign terrorist attack on American civilians at home, there is something reassuring about "our men" protecting us from "other men."[21] However, even though the war exceeded all expectations in its swift destruction of the Taliban and al Qaeda networks, and despite increased attention to homeland security, the U.S. remains uncertain about its ability to deter future terrorist attacks.

In light of these continued fears, the U.S. Congress passed the USA Patriot Act, legislation that allows the Attorney General to detain aliens on mere suspicion and without a hearing. Prior to its passage, the U.S. had already detained more than 1,200 young men without charge; Arab men have been subject to ethnic, as well as gender, profiling under the excuse that we are "at war." These measures have received strong

support from across the political spectrum. Criticism is seen as unpatriotic.[22] Equally disturbing is a political climate, typical of countries at war, that fosters intolerance of alternative points of view. Illustrations of this intolerance have been prevalent in media discussion as well as in political discourse.

In an article in the *New York Times,* Edward Rothstein (2001) articulated his hope that the attacks of September 11 might challenge the intellectual and ethical perspectives of postmodernism and postcolonialism thus leading to their rejection. Chastising adherents to these modes of thought for their extreme cultural relativism and rejection of objectivity and universalism, Rothstein expressed hope that, as it comes to be realized how closely the 9/11 attacks came to undermining the political and military authority of the U.S., these ways of thinking will come to be seen as "ethically perverse."

While the author did not mention feminism, feminists are frequently criticized on the same terms; women and feminists often get blamed in times of political, economic, and social uncertainty. Kurth's fear of feminists' destruction of the social fabric of society is one such example and the association of patriotism with "hegemonic" masculinity challenges women, minorities, and "aliens" to live up to this standard. It is the case that postcolonialists and feminists have questioned objectivity and universalism; but they do so because they claim these terms are frequently associated with ways of knowing that are not objective but based only on the lives of (usually privileged) men. Many feminists are sympathetic with postcolonialism, a body of knowledge that attempts to uncover the voices of those who have been colonized and oppressed. It is a form of knowledge-seeking that resonates with attempts to recover knowledge about women.

In a rather different piece, which acknowledged the recognition accorded to women of Afghanistan since 9/11, Sarah Wildman (2001) chastised American feminists on the grounds of irrelevance. Claiming that feminists have an unprecedented public platform because of the attention focused on women in Afghanistan, Wildman accused them of squandering their opportunity by refusing to support the war. Equating what she called "feminist dogma" with pacifism, Wildman asserted that there is no logical reason to believe that nonviolent means always promote feminist ends. Wildman has fallen into the essentialist trap of equating feminism with peace which I discussed earlier; this has allowed her to dismiss feminist voices as irrelevant and unpatriotic. The feminists she selected to quote may have voiced reservations about the war, but feminism encompasses a wide range of opinions many of which include fighting for justice, particularly gender justice. And feminist voices are not all Western as is often assumed. In Afghanistan, women have been fighting a war that began well before September 11, a war against women.

Women Under Attack

After November 17, when Laura Bush used the president's weekly radio address to urge worldwide condemnation of the treatment of women in Afghanistan, a speech that coincided with a State Department report on the Taliban's war against women, their plight has been in the headlines in the U.S. (Stout, 2001). Although the war is not new, women in Afghanistan have not always been so oppressed. Prior to the Soviet invasion in 1979, women had been gaining rights; they had served in Parliament and in the professions and even as army generals. In 1970, 50 percent of students at Kabul University, 60 percent of teachers, and 40 percent of doctors in Afghanistan were women (Prosser, 2001). Frequently, however, steps forward precipitated a backlash from traditional and rural communities (Amiri, 2002). In 1989, Arab militants, working with the Afghan resistance to the Soviet Union based in Peshawar, Pakistan, issued a *fatwa,* or religious ruling, stating that Afghan women would be killed if they worked for humanitarian organizations. Subsequently Afghan women going to work were shot at and several were murdered. Soon after, another edict forbade Afghan women to "walk with pride" or walk in the middle of the street. This was followed by an edict in 1990, consistent with Occidentalism, that decreed that women should not be educated; if they were, the Islamic movement would be tainted and thus meet with failure.

According to Human Rights Watch (2001), and supported by the Revolutionary Association of the Women of Afghanistan (RAWA), the various parties that made up the United Front or Northern Alliance amassed a deplorable record of attacks on civilians during the civil war that took place in Afghanistan between 1992 and 1996, including the widespread rape of women. The Taliban came to power in 1996 promising to restore law and order and create a pure Islamic state that would guarantee the personal security of women and preserve the dignity of families (Mertus, 2000:56). At first, the restoration of order was seen as beneficial. But soon it was evident that the Taliban sought to erase women from public life and make them invisible in the name of "cleansing" Afghan society. Women were banned from employment, from education, and from going into public places without the accompaniment of a close male relative; they were required to be covered from head to toe in the familiar blue *burka*. The Ministry for the Promotion of Virtue and the Prevention of Vice ruthlessly enforced these restrictions; in a mockery of female "protection," women were beaten publicly with leather batons containing metal studs for showing their hands or ankles, participating in home-based schooling, or violating any other of these restrictions.[23] For boys who have grown up and been socialized in the madrassas, the sight of a woman is the equivalent of seeing the foreign other, the incarnation of evil itself (Prosser, 2001:2). Given the ban on female employment, many women, particularly those without male relatives or supporters, were forced into begging and prostitution; restrictions on mobility meant that women and their children did not have access to health care.[24]

Since the war, many women and children who are family members of fleeing or killed foreign Taliban fighters have been stranded inside Afghanistan with nowhere to go to seek safety. And Afghanistan is the world's largest source of refugees; more than 2.5 million Afghans resided in Iran and Pakistan in refugee camps before the recent war began (Mertus, 2000:53). While all displaced people are vulnerable, displaced women are particularly subject to gender-based violence and abuse (Mertus, 2000:69). Evidence such as this offers a severe challenge to the myth that wars are fought for the protection of women and children.

Women Strike Back

Resistance in Afghanistan faced enormous hurdles as people struggled to meet daily needs and avoid physical harm, but it was ongoing and women were participating. The Revolutionary Association of the Women of Afghanistan (RAWA) was established in Kabul in 1977 as an independent organization of Afghan women fighting for human rights and social justice. RAWA's goal has been to increase the number of women in social and political activities and work for the establishment of a government based on democratic and secular values. After the Soviet occupation in 1979, RAWA became involved in the war of resistance. Its founding leader, Meena, who began RAWA's campaign against Soviet occupation and whose warrior words I quote at the beginning of this article, was assassinated by agents of KHAD (the Afghan branch of the KGB) in 1987.

RAWA continued to work underground in Afghanistan and in the refugee camps of Pakistan to bring education and health care to women, and to mobilize them in defense of their rights.[25] RAWA activities in refugee camps have been described as training grounds for a different kind of fighter. Girls have received an education and, from these sites, women with hidden cameras were sent on dangerous missions into Afghanistan to document abuse. Even in the camps themselves, operations have remained secret since Taliban-style fundamentalism thrives there also (Tempest, 2001). Tahmeena Faryal (an alias she uses for protection), a member of RAWA who visited the United States in November 2001, was described as a "soldier of sorts"; she has documented her secret return to Afghanistan in 1999 under the *burka* (Lopez, 2001). Faryal, with her goal of giving voice to the women and children of Afghanistan, claimed that no woman she met on her mission complained about the *burka;* rather, they described the insult of their daily lives and the theft of their identities. In a society where everyday survival became, and has continued to be, an almost insurmountable task, fighting back has been severely constrained. Nevertheless, it is crucial that we see these women as agents as well as victims if we are to get beyond the gender stereotyping that

we have witnessed since 9/11. I shall now suggest four lessons from this feminist analysis.

WHAT CAN WE LEARN FROM 9/11?

1. Biology Is Not Destiny, Even During Wars

Francis Fukuyama (1998) used his seemingly benign biological assertion that men are warlike and women peaceful to justify the need to channel men's aggression into activities in the political, economic, and military realms, thus diminishing opportunities for women. Yet Joshua Goldstein's study of gender and war suggests that biology is in fact less constraining than culture with respect to the roles men and women can play in war and peace (Goldstein, 2001:252). But if men are made not born, as Goldstein (2001:264) claims, could we envisage a new form of "hegemonic" masculinity less validated by a false biological association with war?

Since the "war against terrorism" began, our images of men and women, as warriors and victims, have become more rigid. Prior to September 11, we in the United States were becoming accustomed to less militarized models of masculinity. Heroes were men of global business conquering the world with briefcases rather than bullets: Bill Gates, a bourgeois hero who looks distinctly unwarrior-like amasses dollars not weapons.[26] Robert Connell (2000:26) has depicted this new type of "hegemonic masculinity" as embodied in business executives who operate in global markets as well as in the political and military leadership who support them.

Our new military heroes also are being defined in different ways: they come with a tough and tender image—"a new definition of manliness, forged from the depths of sorrow and loss."[27] Post-9/11 real men cried and tears were no longer a sign of weakness—"the ideal is that the warrior should be sad and tender, and because of that, the warrior can be very brave as well."[28]

Peace researcher Elise Boulding (2000) has suggested that men in the West are experiencing a great deal of pain due to the questioning of their traditional roles. In this transitional era, so worrying to Kurth and Fukuyama, women's gains are unsettling to many men and women, and men's role expectations are becoming more complicated. This pain may be one reason for the post-9/11 enthusiasm for old-fashioned masculinity and heroism. Nevertheless, as Boulding claims, men do not necessarily enjoy such assigned macho roles. She suggests that the Men's Movement is providing alternative roles for men; she hypothesizes that, with the diminishing of gender polarities, there are possibilities for a new model of partnership rather than domination.

Sympathetic with these new challenges to gender identities and assuming a strong social constructivist position, Robert Connell (2000:30) claims that the task is not to abolish gender but to reshape it—for example, to disconnect courage from violence and by making boys and men aware of the diversity of masculinities that already exist in the world. Democratic gender relations are those that move toward equality, nonviolence, and mutual respect; Connell claims that this reshaping requires constant engagement with women rather than separation which has been characteristic of contemporary men's movements.

While Connell outlines possibilities for shifting forms of masculinity freed from their association with war, Goldstein fears that rearing boys not to become warriors puts them at risk of being shamed by their peers. And Judith Stiehm (2000:224) has suggested that since women are biologically capable of doing everything men can do, masculinity is fragile and vulnerable; because men's superiority is socially rather than biologically defined, men need to assert and protect it. This makes shifting to new forms of masculinity a difficult task. And, as we know, it is generally harder for men to cross gender lines than it is for women.

Do new forms of masculinity in times of war depend on opening up spaces for new definitions of femininity? Clearly, women's increased visibility in public life, particularly in the military, is shaking up gender expectations. In the U.S. military, women are fighting and dying in the current conflict with much less attention than in the Gulf War where the presence of female soldiers in Saudi Arabia was one of the greatest provocations for bin Laden.[29] Yet feminists have been ambivalent about women as war-fighters—whether they should join men's wars in the name

of equality or resist them in the name of women's special relationship with peace.

We must also ask what the presence of women in combat ranks does to men's sense of masculinity as a motivator for their war-fighting. Judith Stiehm (2000:224) argues for ending men's monopoly on the legitimate use of force, thus breaking the link between gender identity and the use of state force. She believes this would reduce the overall use of force; she sees peacekeeping as an activity that challenges the association of masculinity with war. Suspicious of the association of women with peace and of any possibility of "remaking human nature," Jean Elshtain (1987:352–353) suggests the notion of a "chastened patriot," a model that could be adopted by both women and men and one that would shed the excesses of nationalism and remain committed to, but detached from and reflective about, patriotic ties and loyalties.

Understanding gender as a social construction and the fluidity of gender identities allows us to see the possibilities of change while acknowledging the power of gendering distinctions to legitimate war as well as other practices that result in the subordination of women. It is not only the gendering of war and peace that constrains women's opportunities, frequently, women are oppressed in the name of culture and religion, a phenomenon that the recent war brought to our attention.

2. Women Bear the Burdens of Religion and Culture

Religious fundamentalists, both Christian and Islamic, used the 9/11 crisis to criticize women's advances: this tendency reflects a much more general phenomenon. As many feminists have pointed out, all fundamentalist religions are, to various degrees, bad for women. Historically, most religions have been as male-dominated as militaries. The connection between religious fanaticism, be it Christian, Judaic, or Islamic, and the suppression of women is almost universal. The patriarchal family, with its control of women, is usually central to fundamentalist movements and often seen as the panacea for social ills (Yuval-Davis, 1997:63). A paradox of fundamentalist movements is that often women collude with and seek comfort in them; and, in spite of their subservience in religious institutions, women constitute a majority of active members of most religions (Yuval-Davis, 1997:63).

Often, in the name of religion, women bear the brunt of identity politics which is frequently expressed in terms of control over their life choices. At the 1994 United Nations Conference on Population and Development in Cairo and at the U.N. Women's Conference in Beijing in 1995, the Vatican, and other conservative Catholic groups, joined with right-wing Muslim forces in their opposition to women's human and reproductive rights. In many Muslim societies, the majority of the population is not literate so religious knowledge is controlled by the ruling class who interpret texts for their own benefit and use it to control others. According to Zeiba Shorish-Shamley (2002), the Qur'an gives equal rights to men and women and women were leaders in early Islam—modest clothing was recommended so that when men and women met in public discussion, intellectuality rather than sexuality would be emphasized.

"When radical Muslim movements are on the rise, women are canaries in the mine" (Goodwin and Neuwirth, 2001). In the name of Islamic fundamentalism, the definition of collective identity is increasingly being tied to definitions of gender. According to Women Living Under Muslim Laws (WLUML), an international network of women, construction of the "Muslim woman" is integral to the construction of "Muslimness," explaining, in part, the emphasis on controlling all aspects of women's lives (WLUML, 1997:2–3). Ironically, the weakening of the patriarchal family structure may be a contributing cause of these movements (Moghadan, 1994:15). Azza Karam (2000:69–70) sees the emergence of "neopatriarchy," a confluence of patriarchy and dependence that embodies the tension between internal patriarchal power structures and outside pressures of modernization. It is in the reinstatement of cultural values in response to pressures of globalization that women in the Arab world tend to be most affected. Defining "fundamentalism" as the use of religion to gain and mobilize political power, Women Living Under Muslim Laws argues that, with the ascendancy of identity politics, secular space shrinks with negative consequences for women (WLUML, 1997:3).[30] And, when women

fight for their rights, they are frequently accused of betraying their culture and religion.

Although not reducible to each other, religion bears a close relationship to culture. Gender relations come to be seen as constituting the "essence" of cultures (Yuval-Davis, 1997:43). Women are often required to carry the burden of cultural representation: their "proper" behavior embodies lines that signify a collectivity's boundaries. Women are transmitters of group values and traditions; as agents of socialization of the young their place is in the home. For some this is an honor rather than a burden so all fundamentalist movements have women supporters as well as opponents (Moghadan, 1994:19).

Rina Amiri (2001) has claimed that the Western world has contributed to the perception that the current conflict is a battle between East and West by centering on the place of women in its depiction of Islam as repressive and backward. She has also suggested that a Western approach could damage a long-term vision for an indigenous model of a just society because a Western model can be contextually inappropriate for Afghan women and Islam traditionalists who are sympathetic to women but who will reject what is perceived as Western (Amiri, 2002).

Conversely, WLUML (1997:6) has claimed that well-meaning people, wanting to distance themselves from Islam hatred and the colonial past, epitomized in Orientalist thought, have frequently fallen into the trap of cultural relativism. Consistent with some of Rothstein's more negative assessments of postcolonialism, but in the name of cultural sensitivity, this can lead to endorsement of the right to seclude women.

Issues of culture and religion have been difficult ones for both Western and non-Western feminists. Western feminists have walked a fine line between supporting a "global sisterhood," and thus imposing Western definitions of female emancipation on other cultures, and trying to be culturally sensitive. Third Wave feminism of the 1990s introduced issues of class, race, and cultural variability into its analyses in order to get beyond essentialist generalizations about women that stem from Western middle-class women's experiences. As an alternative to the universalism/relativism dichotomy, Nira Yuval-Davis (1997:1) suggests what she calls "transversal politics," or the politics of mutual support—

a form of coalition politics in which differences among women are recognized and given a voice.

In the Muslim world, women's struggles are frequently undermined by the idea of one homogeneous Muslim world, a deliberate myth fostered by both Occidentalism and Orientalism and promoted by interests within and outside (WLUML, 1997:1). In many cases, to be pro-women's rights means to be accused of being Western. Accusing women of being Westernized and, therefore, not representing an "authentic" women's voice allows for the dismissal of women's claims to justice. This has made it difficult for Muslim women to develop a discourse on their rights independent of a cultural debate between the Western and Muslim worlds.

Amiri urges moving beyond the stereotypical premise that Islam as a whole is anti-woman. She suggests that, while it is incumbent on the international community never to tolerate abuses against women in any part of the world, the West should ground its support in the positions of Muslim feminists. WLUML claims that women are frequently hampered by insufficient knowledge about their legal rights, their inability to distinguish between customs, law, and religion, and by their isolation. To this end, WLUML suggests that women pool information and create strategies across countries; they urge a respect for other voices while condemning bad practices.

All of these attempts to negotiate support for women—attempts that get beyond a false universalism based on Western norms and a type of cultural relativism that condones oppressive practices—depend on seeing women as agents rather than victims. "Moving toward gender equality is a political process—it requires new ways of thinking—in which the stereotyping of women and men gives way to a new philosophy that regards all people, irrespective of gender, as essential agents of change" (UNHDP, 1996:1).[31]

3. We Need Gender-Sensitive Conceptions of Development, Security, and Peace

The events of 9/11 brought the desperate circumstances of Afghanistan and its people to the world's attention. Afghanistan has been called a "failed state" harboring terrorists, a country whose infrastructure and government institu-tions have been destroyed by twenty years of war. Feminists have some important additional things to say about the kinds of underdevelopment and insecurity rife in that society today.

Jennifer Whitaker (2001) has suggested that there is a striking correlation between women's political and economic participation and more general advances in development. National standards of living improve—family income, education, nutrition, and life expectancy all rise and birthrates fall as women move toward equality. When women's influence increases, it strengthens the moderate center and increases economic stability and democratic order. In societies where women have social, political and economic power, there is a strong constituency for democracy and human rights.

These claims are supported by the United Nations Human Development Programme (UNHDP) which has developed indicators to measure gender inequality. The UNHDP asserts that countries with a low ranking in terms of its Gender Development Index (GDI) are among the poorest, with Afghanistan ranking at the bottom of countries measured (UNHDP, 1996).[32] Nevertheless, the UNHDP claims that gender equality does not depend on income level alone; it requires a firm political commitment, not enormous financial wealth (UNHDP, 1996:75–78). And changes are always evident: the report suggests that, between 1970 and 1992, the GDI values of all countries improved but at different rates. In many Arab states women's access to education and an increase in life expectancy brought up their values more than their increased access to income and employment (UNHDP, 1996: 75–81); indeed, economic power has always been the most difficult for women to achieve.

More recently, the UNHDP has published a report on development in the Arab region which highlights the poor treatment of women as one of the major reasons for the region's lack of development. The report notes that women's participation in their countries' political and economic life is the lowest in the world.[33] The lower women's economic power, the more likely they are to be oppressed physically, politically, and ideologically (Godenzi, 2000). Although, technically, Islam gives women the right to keep their own income and property, cultural tradition maintains men as heads of households who control sources of wealth (Karam, 2000:72). Historically, this has been true in the West also. For this reason, feminists have claimed that extending the benefits of a liberal society to women has been problematic. Values, such as individualism and free markets, extolled by Kurth, have historically been based on a male norm of rational atomistic individuals maximizing welfare through market exchange. This model has depended on free, usually female, labor for reproductive and caring tasks (Tickner, 1992:73). Seeking equality in this type of world—whether Western or Islamic—has been problematic for women because it involves fitting into structures that are already gendered.

Just as feminists have helped us rethink the meanings of development and security, they can help us rethink the meaning of peace. Feminist definitions of peace have generally included the reduction of all forms of violence, including structural violence and oppressive gender hierarchies, as well as physical violence. And a variety of studies have shown that, contra Huntington and Fukuyama, countries with large cohorts of young men are not automatically warlike. Violence is more likely to occur in unstable societies that are politically and economically underdeveloped. It is the degree of exclusion from economic and political participation that fuels unrest and gender stereotyping.[34] Islamic movements have emerged in the context of a profound economic crisis in the Middle East (Moghadan, 1994:11).

WLUML (1997:9) defines peace as breaking down the deep divisions that war induces and preventing the internalization of hatred of "the other" fostered by discourses associated with Orientalism and Occidentalism and often expressed in gender terms. They cite a growing sense of insecurity that results from decision-making that shifts further away from people, and deepening poverty that widens the division between the haves and the have-nots. Frequently, women's struggles for peace and justice focus on a secure environment free from violence and economic deprivation. For example, Afghan women are more likely to talk about their desire for peace, health care, education, food, and shelter than about having to wear the *burqa* (Mertus, 2000:59). Peace involves a struggle for justice, including gender justice; to be successful it must be seen as a responsibility of both women and men.

4. Women's Gains from War May Not Last

Paradoxically, it is sometimes the case that wars are good for women. European and American women first received the vote after World War I and Japanese women did so after World War II. Frequently, women are mobilized into the paid economy during war thereby gaining more economic independence. Women have also been mobilized in times of struggle for national liberation and sometimes they have fought in liberation armies. Quite often these gains evaporate once the war is over; in the West, the years after both World Wars saw a return to the cult of domesticity and motherhood—a move that had to do with the need for women to step aside and let men resume the jobs they had left to go to war. And women who have fought alongside men in wars of national liberation, and who have been promised a greater role in post-liberation society, often find that these promises evaporate once the struggle is over. Few revolutionary movements directly address women's problems or attempt to solve these problems in post-revolution political and social constitutions and institutions (Tetrault, 1992:92).

When women fight for their rights, they generally get less support than when they are perceived as victims. This is because gender justice demands profound structural changes in almost all societies, changes that would threaten existing elites along with existing political, social, and economic structures. And, frequently, both international governmental and nongovernmental organizations (NGOs) find these types of radical changes too politically risky to support. For example, RAWA receives very little financial support from international NGOs, undoubtedly because its agenda is to empower women in ways that would demand very different political and social relations in Afghanistan.[35]

And what of the women of Afghanistan? Clearly, the war has brought them benefits and freedoms. The presence of women at the 2002 Loya Jirga [a grand council or grand assembly used to resolve political conflicts or other national problems] called to pick the new government was a stark contrast with the Taliban years (Gall, 2002). But, in spite of the attention they have received, it is far from clear that women will play any significant role in the new government. Only two women were invited to the Bonn Conference and only two were given positions in the transitional government. One of the two, Sima Samar, the interim women's affairs minister, said recently that she feared for her safety. Under threat from Islamic conservatives, who do not believe that women should participate in public life, she has resigned as women's affairs minister and taken the less controversial post as head of the human rights commission (Gannon, 2002). Human Rights Watch has documented atrocities committed by members of the Northern Alliance in the early 1990s; RAWA has labeled them as misogynist and antidemocratic, yet they were our allies in the recent struggle and they have received rewards in the new government. There is concern that, without strong vigilance from the international community, Afghan women are unlikely to end up much better off than they were under the Taliban (Jefferson, 2001). Patriarchal culture does not vanish overnight and men are unlikely to give up the few privileges they may have in a difficult post-war period of reconstruction.

A spokesperson for the Feminist Majority recently suggested that never before has the women's movement had such an impact on American foreign policy as it is having today (Mc Namara, 2002). The Feminist Majority began its campaign, "Stop Gender Apartheid" in 1996, well before the plight of Afghan women was receiving much media attention: it played a key role in the Clinton administration's refusal to recognize the Taliban government. The Feminist Majority's optimism may be short-lived, however; it is unclear whether U.S. support for Afghan women will continue now the war against Afghanistan is over. Governments are generally reluctant to make women's human rights part of their foreign policies. There is less risk in portraying women as victims than in supporting their empowerment. The image of helpless victims behind the veil may be politically less risky than supporting articulate forceful advocates of women's rights. The Bush administration is quoted as having insisted that the campaign to highlight women in Afghanistan must be seen as a "justice issue" not a women's issue (Brant, 2001). And even if the Bush administration has put the plight of Afghan women on its foreign policy agenda, it has not been particularly progressive on other international women's issues. Twenty two years after President Jimmy Carter sent the Covenant on the Elimination of Discrimination Against Women (CEDAW) to the U.S. Senate for ratification, the Senate Foreign Relations Committee is holding hearings on it, but the Bush administration is reneging on its initial support, making ratification unlikely. The U.S. is one of a very small minority of countries that has not ratified CEDAW (Kristof, 2002).

CONCLUSION

The "war against terrorism" has been described by American officials as a new kind of war, a war against a terrorist network, not against another state. In conclusion, one may wonder if there are other, more gendered ways in which this war is unlike the other wars Americans fought in the twentieth century. The prevalence of gendered images taken to be threatening or used to belittle one's opponents could surely be found in other such wars. But somehow these references seem more fundamental in the present case.

As quoted above, al Qaeda leaders have made a special point of criticizing Western gender relations. Gender relationships are an important aspect of what are taken by many fundamentalists to be key religious or civilizational differences. Even more surprising are the cases of "strange bedfellows" on different sides of the war making the same kinds of gendered arguments. Do not these features of the above analysis suggest that the 9/11 crisis reflects a globalization of gender politics, a clash of gendered orders usually hidden by the normalizing practices of unequal societies?

In times of uncertainty, fear of social change rises as does fear of feminist agendas. However, feminists are not advocating a "feminized society" as some of their critics have suggested but rather a society where gender differences are less polarized and gender structures are less hierarchical. [2002]

Notes

1. December 1998, from an interview with al-Jazeera television. Quoted in Judt (2001).
2. Fukuyama (1998:27).

3. Brown (2001:5).
4. Will of Mohamed Atta found in a suitcase at Logan International Airport in Boston. Quoted in the *New York Times,* October 4, 2001, B5.
5. "A World Too Intoxicated by the Wine of War," *Los Angeles Times,* October 8, 2001.
6. Meena was the founding leader of RAWA (Revolutionary Association of the Women of Afghanistan). She was assassinated in Quetta, Pakistan, in 1987. Poem from RAWA website http://www.rawa.org.
7. For a more elaborated version of this argument see Huntington (1996:20–32).
8. It should be noted that women's equality was not even thought of at the birth of the Enlightenment. For a discussion of women's unequal incorporation into the modern Western state see Pateman (1988). Males in the workforce have never received much criticism for neglecting their children. For ideas, similar to Kurth's, about the negative effects of cultural diversity see also Huntington (1996:304) and Fukuyama (2000). See also Fukuyama (1999) which also emphasizes the negative effects of 1960s women's liberation.
9. Peggy Noonan, quoted in Brown (2001).
10. *The Guardian,* September 20, 2001. Cited from http://www.guardian.co.uk/analysis/story/0,3604,554794,00.html.
11. Quoted in Brown (2001).
12. This gendered image of Afghanistan—men fighting and women invisible—was further reinforced by a comment by U.S. Secretary of Defense Donald Rumsfeld on the PBS Lehrer Newshour on November 7, 2001, when he claimed that there were no people in Afghanistan who were not armed and fighting.
13. "A Portrait of the Terrorist: From Shy Child to Single-Minded Killer," *New York Times,* October 10, 2001, p. B9.
14. It should be noted that Falk, in an exchange with ten critics of his position, all but one of whom were men, subsequently retreated from his position saying he had been misled by the language of George Bush and Colin Powell which seemed initially to suggest a much more limited war than what actually evolved. See *The Nation,* November 26, 2001, p. 60.
15. *The Nation,* December 17, 2001, p. 4.
16. Women frequently describe themselves as possessing these masculine characteristics while still able to articulate what is stereotypically "feminine." There can be no hegemonic femininity since masculinity defines acceptable societal norms. The term "hegemonic masculinity" was first used by Connell (1987). Connell contrasts "hegemonic masculinity" with subordinated and devalued masculinities such as those associated with racial minorities and homosexuals.
17. This challenges Fukuyama's (1998) use of sociobiologically based arguments to support his claim about men's "innate" aggression. For further elaboration of sociobiological arguments of this type see Mesquida and Weiner (2001).
18. The Geneva Conventions extend special protections in wartime to women, mothers of small children, and children themselves. See Goldstein (2001:305).
19. Fouad Ajami, quoted in Croisette (2001).
20. On October 8, 2001, after the beginning of U.S. bombing, support for the war was running at 87 percent of both women and men (Goldstein, 2002).
21. To illustrate this more vividly, what would the reaction be to mostly female firefighters, police, and military personnel? Goldstein (2001) asserts that many women are biologically quite well suited to perform these protective tasks.
22. In light of my earlier discussion about patriotism, the naming of the USA Patriot Act was probably designed to forestall criticism.
23. It should be noted that men were also policed if their beards were not long enough or their dress not appropriate. However, men retained some control over their lives.
24. In 2000, life expectancy for Afghan women was 44 years and one in four children died before the age of 5 (Mertus, 2000:59). Of course, these deplorable statistics were as much due to years of warfare as to restrictions on women.
25. Information about RAWA may be found on their website at http://www.rawa.org.
26. For some recent IR feminist writings that take up the issue of masculinity see Zalewski and Parpart (1998) and Hooper (2001).

27. Robin Morgan, quoted in Brown (2001).
28. Tibetan Buddhist teacher Chogyam Trungpa, quoted in Wax (2001).
29. The *Los Angeles Times* (Perry, 2002) reported the death of seven U.S. Marines on a cargo plane in Pakistan on January 10, 2002, with only passing reference to the fact that one of them was a woman.
30. WLUML notes that the use of the term "fundamentalism" is a contested one within the organization. Some, but not all, find it the least objectionable term to name the phenomenon. RAWA also uses the term, at least when speaking to a Western audience. Writing in the context of the fate of Afghanistan, Robert Scheer (2001b) has suggested that President Bush must break with a popular American notion that religion is inherently a benign experience.
31. Although not the most recent, I cite the 1995 Annual Report because it contains the most extensive discussion of gender inequality of any of the Annual Reports.
32. *United Nations Human Development Report 1995,* the first annual report to use the GDI, ranked Afghanistan 130th out of 130 countries in terms of its GDI. In terms of its Human Development Index (HDI) Afghanistan was ranked 170th out of 174 countries. The UNHDP defines the HDI as the combination of a variety of quality-of-life indicators including life expectancy, education, and income. The GDI measures achievement in the same basic capabilities as the HDI but takes note of inequality in achievement between women and men.
33. A summary of the Arab Human Development Report 2002 may be found at http://www.economist.com /agenda / displaystory .cfm?story id=1212573.
34. Henrik Urdal, International Peace Research Institute, Oslo. Quoted in Sciolino (2001).
35. "About RAWA," http://www.rawa.org.

References

AMIRI, R. (2001) "Musilm Women as Symbols— and Pawns." *New York Times,* Nov. 27, p. A21.

AMIRI, R. (2002) "Afghanistan: Women in Government and Society." Panel discussion, U.S. Institute of Peace, Jan. 29. Cited from http://www.usip.org/oc/newsroom/es20020129.html.

BOULDING, E. (2000) *Cultures of Peace: The Hidden Side of History.* Syracuse, NY: Syracuse University Press.

BRANT, M. (2001) "The Bushies Unveil the Women's Issue." *Newsweek,* Nov. 26, p. 7.

BROWN, P. L. (2001) "Heavy Lifting Required: The Return of Manly Men." *New York Times,* Oct. 28, sec. 4, p. 5.

BURUMA, I., AND A. MARGALIT (2002) "Occidentalism." *New York Review of Books,* vol. 49, no. 1, Jan. 17, pp. 4–7.

CONNELL, R. W. (1987) *Gender and Power: Society, the Person and Sexual Identities.* Stanford, CA: Stanford University Press.

CONNELL, R. W. (2000) "Arms and the Man: Using the New Research on Masculinity to Understand Violence and Promote Peace in the Contemporary World." In *Male Roles, Masculinities and Violence: A Culture of Peace Perspective,* edited by I. Breines, R. W. Connell, and I. Eide, pp. 21–33. Paris: UNESCO.

COOPERMAN, A. (2001) "Roman Catholic Bishops Declare U.S. War Is Moral," *Washington Post,* Nov. 16, p. A37.

CROISETTE, B. (2001) "Living in a World Without Women." *New York Times,* Nov. 4, sec. 4, p. 1.

ELSHTAIN, J. B. (1987) *Women and War.* New York: Basic Books.

ENLOE, C. (1993) *The Morning After: Sexual Politics at the End of the Cold War.* Berkeley and Los Angeles: University of California Press.

ENLOE, C. (2000) *Maneuvers: The International Politics of Militarizing Women's Lives.* Berkeley and Los Angeles: University of California Press.

FALK, R. (2001) "Ends and Means: Defining a Just War." *The Nation,* Oct. 29, pp. 11–15.

FUKUYAMA, F. (1998) Women and the Evolution of World Politics. *Foreign Affairs* **77**(5): 24–40.

FUKUYAMA, F. (1999) *The Great Disruption: Human Nature and the Reconstitution of Social Order.* New York: Free Press.

FUKUYAMA, F. (2000) "What Divides America." *Wall Street Journal,* Nov. 15, p. A26.

GALL, C. (2002) "Afghan Women in Political Spotlight." *New York Times,* June 26, p. A8.

GANNON, K. (2002) "Female Minister Driven from Her Post." *Boston Globe,* June 24, p. A8.

GODENZI, A. (2000) "Determinants of Culture: Men and Economic Power." In *Male Roles, Masculinities and Violence: A Culture of Peace Perspective,* edited by I. Brienes, R. W. Connell, and I. Eide, pp. 35–51. Paris: UNESCO.

GOLDSTEIN, J. (2001) *War and Gender.* Cambridge: Cambridge University Press.

GOLDSTEIN, J. (2002) "John Wayne and GI Jane." *The Christian Science Monitor,* Jan. 10, p. 11.

GOODWIN, J., AND J. NEUWIRTH (2001) "The Rifle and the Veil." *New York Times,* Oct. 1. Cited from http://www.rawa.org.

HOOPER, C. (2001) *Manly States: Masculinities, International Relations, and Gender Politics.* New York: Columbia University Press.

HUMAN RIGHTS WATCH (2001) "Poor Rights Record of Opposition Commanders." Oct. 6. Cited from RAWA website, http://www.rawa.org.

HUNTINGTON, S. (1993) The Clash of Civilizations? *Foreign Affairs* **72**(3):22–49.

HUNTINGTON, S. (1996) *The Clash of Civilizations and the Remaking of World Order.* New York: Simon and Schuster.

JEFFERSON, L. (2001) "Out Go the Taliban, but Will Afghan Women Be Excluded Again?" *International Herald Tribune,* Nov. 16. Cited from http://www.hrw.org/editorials/2001 .afghan1116.htm.

JONES, K. (1990) "Dividing the Ranks: Women and the Draft." In *Women, Militarism, and War: Essays in History, Politics, and Social Theory,* edited by J. B. Elshtain and S. Tobias, pp. 125–136. Savage, MD: Rowman and Littlefield.

JUDT, T. (2001) "America and the War." *New York Review of Books,* vol. 48, no. 10, Nov. 15.

KARAM, A. (2000) "Democrats Without Democracy: Challenges to Women in Politics in the Arab World." In *International Perspectives on Gender and Democratization,* edited by S. Rai, pp. 64–82. New York: St. Martin's Press.

KRISTOF, N. (2002) "Why Won't America Ratify? A Treaty Defends Women Against Men." *International Herald Tribune,* June 19, p. 6.

KURTH, J. (1994) "The Real Clash." *The National Interest,* no. 37(Fall):3–15.

LOPEZ, S. (2001) "Afghan Woman's Tale Rises from Bottomless Well of Sadness." *Los Angeles Times,* Nov. 14, p. B1.

McNAMARA, M. (2002) "With Shift to L.A., Feminist Majority Builds on Momentum." *Los Angeles Times,* Jan. 16, sec. E, p. 1.

MEARSHEIMER, J. (2001) "Guns Won't Win the Afghan War." *New York Times,* Nov. 4, sec. 4, p. 13.

MERTUS, J. A. (2000) *War's Offensive on Women: The Humanitarian Challenge in Bosnia, Kosovo, and Afghanistan.* Bloomfield, CT: Kumarian Press.

MESQUIDA, C., AND N. WEINER (2001) "Young Men and War." *PECS News,* Environmental Change and Security Project, Woodrow Wilson Center, Fall, pp. 2–3.

MOGHADAN, V. (1994) "Women and Identity Politics in Theoretical and Comparative Perspective." In *Identity Politics and Women: Cultural Reassertions and Feminisms in International Perspective,* edited by V. Moghadan, pp. 3–26. Boulder, CO: Westview Press.

PATEMAN, C. (1988) *The Sexual Contract.* Stanford, CA: Stanford University Press.

PERRY, T. (2002) "Unspeakable Loss Shakes Marine Base." *Los Angeles Times,* Jan. 11, p. A16.

PROSSER, S. E. (2001) "Taliban and Women—Oil and Water." Women in International Law (WILIG), Washington Steering Committee *Newsletter* **14**(2):2–3.

ROTHSTEIN, E. (2001) "Attacks on U.S. Challenge the Perspectives of Postmodern True Believers." *New York Times,* Sept. 11, p. A17.

SCHEER, R. (2001a) "Falwell Should Have Listened to the Feminists." *Los Angeles Times,* Sept. 25, p. 20.

SCHEER, R. (2001b) "Secularism Unlocks the Door to Stability." *Los Angeles Times,* Dec. 18, p. B13.

SCIOLINO, E. (2001) "Radicalism: Is the Devil in the Demographics?" *New York Times,* Dec. 9, sec. 4, p. 1.

SHORISH-SHAMLEY, Z. (2002) "Afganistan: Women in Government and Society." Panel discussion, U.S. Institute of Peace, Jan. 29. Cited from http://www.usip.org/oc/newsroom/ es20020129.html.

STIEHM, J. H. (1983) *Women and Men's Wars.* Oxford: Pergamon Press.

STIEHM, J. H. (2000) "Neither Male nor Female: Neither Victim nor Executioner." In *Male Roles, Masculinities and Violence: A Culture of Peace*

Perspective, edited by I. Breines, R. W. Connell, and I. Eide, pp. 223–230. Paris: UNESCO.

STOUT, D. (2001) "Mrs. Bush Cites Women's Plight Under Taliban." *New York Times,* Nov. 18, p. B4.

TEMPEST, R. (2001) "Training Camp of Another Kind." *Los Angeles Times,* Oct. 15, p. A1.

TETRAULT, M. A. (1992) "Women and Revolution: A Framework for Analysis." In *Gendered States: Feminist (Re) Visions of International Relations Theory,* edited by V. S. Peterson, pp. 99–121. Boulder, CO: Lynne Rienner.

TICKNER, J. A. (1992) *Gender in International Relations: Feminist Perspectives on Achieving Global Security.* New York: Columbia University Press.

(UNHDP) UNITED NATIONS HUMAN DEVELOPMENT PROGRAMME (1996) *Human Development Report 1995.* New York: Oxford University Press.

WAX, N. (2001) "Not to Worry. Real Men Can Cry." *New York Times,* Oct. 28, sec. 4, p. 5.

WHITAKER, J. (2001) "Don't Betray the Women." *Washington Post,* Nov. 15, p. A47.

WILDMAN, S. (2001) "Arms Length: Why Don't Feminists Support the War?" *The New Republic,* Nov. 5, p. 23.

(WLUML) WOMEN LIVING UNDER MUSLIM LAWS (1997) "Plan of Action Dhaka 1997." Cited from http://www.wluml.org/english/publications/engpofa.htm.

YUVAL-DAVIS, N. (1997) *Gender and Nation.* London: Sage.

ZALEWSKI, M., AND J. PARPART, EDS. (1998) *The "Man" Question in International Relations.* Boulder, CO: Westview Press.

Understanding the Reading

1. How can war both reinforce "gender stereotypes and shake up gender expectations"?
2. What caused 9/11, according to the televangelist Jerry Falwell and Pat Robertson?
3. What has made it difficult for Muslim women to be listened to?
4. As women move toward equality, what happens to national standards of living? List the changes.
5. If increased access to income and work alone does not improve gender equality, what does?

6. What is a feminist definition of peace?
7. Give an example in the essay that would illustrate the author's idea that "patriarchal culture does not vanish overnight."

Suggestions for Responding

1. Go to the Feminist Majority's newswire at feminist.org and follow the U.S. government's attempts to form new policy regarding gender equity or inequity.
2. Research the ways in which Muslim and Christian fundamentalists criticize each other's gender relations. ◆

141

Seeing Islam as "Evil" Faith, Evangelicals Seek Converts

BY LAURIE GOODSTEIN

Grove City, Ohio—On a recent Saturday in a church fellowship hall here, evangelical Christians from several states gathered for an all-day seminar on how to woo Muslims away from Islam.

The teacher urged a kindly approach: always show Muslims love, charity and hospitality, he said, and carry copies of the New Testament to give as gifts. The students, scribbling notes, included two pastors, a school secretary and college students who said they hoped to convert Muslims in the United States, or on mission trips abroad.

But although the teacher, an evangelical preacher from Beirut, stressed the need to avoid offending Muslims, he projected a snappy PowerPoint presentation showing passages from the Koran that he said proved Islam was regressive, fraudulent and violent.

"Here in the Koran, it says slay them, slay the infidels!" said the teacher, who said he did not want to be identified because being a missionary to Muslims put his life at risk. "In the Bible there are no words from Jesus saying we should kill innocent people."

At the grass roots of evangelical Christianity, many are now absorbing the antipathy for Islam that emerged last year with the incendiary comments of ministers. The sharp language, from religious leaders like Franklin Graham, Jerry Falwell, Pat Robertson and Jerry Vines, the former president of the Southern Baptist Convention, has drawn rebukes from Muslims and Christian groups alike. Mr. Graham called Islam "a very evil and wicked religion, and Mr. Vines called Muhammad, Islam's founder and prophet, a "demon-possessed pedophile."

In evangelical churches and seminaries across the country, lectures and books criticizing Islam and promoting strategies for Muslim conversions are gaining currency. More than a dozen recently published critiques of Islam are now available in Christian bookstores.

Arab International Ministry, the Indianapolis group that led the crash course on Islam here, claims to have trained 4,500 American Christians to proselytize Muslims in the last six years, many of those since the 2001 terrorist attacks.

The oratorical tone of these authors and lecturers varies, but they share the basic presumption that the world's two largest religions are headed for a confrontation, with Christianity representing what is good, true and peaceful, and Islam what is evil, false and violent.

The criticism is coming predominantly from evangelicals, who belong to many independent churches and Christian denominations, including the Southern Baptist Convention.

Evangelicals have always believed that all other religions are wrong, but what is notable now is the vituperation.

"The Koran's good verses are like the food an assassin adds to poison to disguise a deadly taste," writes Don Richardson, a well-known missionary who worked in Muslim countries, in "Secrets of the Koran" (Regal Books, 2003). "Better to find the same food, sans poison, in the Bible." This month, he is scheduled to speak on Islam at churches in five American cities.

Most of the authors and teachers preach a corollary of the Christian dictum to "love the sinner and hate the sin." They assert that while the vast majority of Muslims are not evil, they have been deceived by a diabolical religion based on a flawed scripture that can never bring them salvation.

Akbar Ahmed, chairman of the Islamic studies department at American University, said he grew up attending Catholic and Protestant missionary schools in Pakistan, but never heard a negative word about Islam from the missionaries. Now, he said, the new hostility to Islam and, in particular, the insults to the prophet Muhammad have outraged the Muslim world.

"The whole range of Muslims, from orthodox to liberal secularists, are all lined up against these attacks coming from the American evangelists," said Mr. Ahmed, the author of a new book "Islam Under Siege: Living Dangerously in a Post-Honor World" (Polity Press). "Unwittingly, these evangelists have unleashed a consolidation of sentiments for Islam. Even the most moderate Muslims have been upset by this."

The push for conversions may backfire for the evangelists, he said, since Muslims who may have been open to the missionaries' presence feel their honor has been insulted.

In interviews, evangelical authors and lecturers said their work did not denigrate Islam as much as share the truth about Christianity.

Ergun M. Caner, raised a Muslim by his Turkish family, converted to Christianity as a teenager and wrote, with his brother Emir, "Unveiling Islam: An Insider Look at Muslim Life and Beliefs" (Kregel Publications), which has sold more than 100,000 copies.

"I am more interested in apologetics than polemics," said Mr. Caner, now a professor of theology and church history at The Criswell College. "Apologetics is defending your faith, and polemics is critiquing others. A Muslim has the right to worship Allah, and I have a right to stand in front of that mosque and tell them that Jesus saves. That's the hope for Iraq, the hope for Afghanistan."

Evangelical scholars and leaders cite several reasons for their quickening interest in Islam: the American defeat of a major Muslim nation, Iraq, which may open it to Christian missionaries, while other Muslim nations remain closed; the 2001 terrorist attacks, which led many Americans to see Islam as a global threat; the greater numbers and visibility of Muslims in the United States, and the demise of Communism, once public enemy No. 1 for many evangelical organizations.

"Evangelicals have substituted Islam for the Soviet Union," said the Rev. Richard Cizik, vice president for governmental affairs of the National Association of Evangelicals, which represents 43,000 congregations. "The Muslims have become the modern-day equivalent of the Evil Empire."

The National Association of Evangelicals called on Christian leaders this month to temper their anti-Islam oratory, saying it had been unhelpful to interfaith relations, and dangerous to Christians spreading the gospel to Muslims. While some evangelical leaders welcomed the criticism, others bristled and said that it was not the Christians but the Muslims who must stop the hate-speech.

Historians note that enmity between Christianity and Islam dates as far back as the Crusades, the fall of Byzantium and the reconquest of Spain.

"Keep in mind that Islam is the only religious tradition that has ever threatened the existence of Christianity," said Charles Kimball, chairman of the religion department at Wake Forest University in Winston-Salem, N.C., and author of the book "When Religion Becomes Evil" (Harper San Francisco, 2002). "That's deeply woven into our subconscious, into Western literature and culture, and so this image of an Islamic threat taps into a notion that's there already."

The conservative evangelical approach to Islam is in stark contrast with the "interfaith understanding" approach of many Orthodox, Roman Catholic and mainline Protestant churches like the Methodists, Episcopalians and Lutherans. Since 9/11, local churches in these denominations began inviting Muslims to explain their faith at a flurry of interfaith events and dialogue sessions.

"God calls all of us to have an open mind and an open heart," said the Rev. Robert Edgar, general secretary of the National Council of Churches, which represents many Protestant and Orthodox denominations. "And many of the people who are part of the National Council of Churches believe that if judgment is to be made it needs to be made by God and not by those of us who have divided ourselves up around a particular ideology."

These churches acknowledge theological differences between Christianity and Islam, but stress the common roots and essential compatibility. They teach that Muslims are monotheists,

"Allah" is simply Arabic for God, and both faiths share Abraham as patriarch.

But for many of the evangelical experts on Islam, these notions are simplistic whitewash to paint over a real theological divide.

At the daylong seminar in the fellowship hall of Southwest Grace Brethren Church, just outside Columbus, the teacher drew on his own life experience as evidence of Islam's evils. While President Bush and others have depicted Islam as a peaceful religion that has been "hijacked" by extremists, the teacher said he knew better than to believe that.

He spoke of a childhood friend in Beirut who joined the Hezbollah terrorist network and showed off his victims' severed ears. Another friend, he said, was threatened with death by his father when he converted to Christianity. (The teacher did not mention the Phalangist Christian militias that helped stoke Lebanon's civil war.)

He did not tell the class who he was, and his mysteriousness reinforced his message that Christian missionaries face danger in Muslim nations. At least six have been killed since Sept. 11, 2001.

"You can tell me Islam is peaceful, but I've done my homework," he said, reeling off a list of Koranic citations. "From the beginning of Islam, the sword brought results faster than words."

Some of what he taught would be accepted by most theologians: Muslims reject the Christian concept of a Trinitarian God—the Father, the Son and the Holy Ghost. Muslims respect Jesus as a prophet, but do not accept the Christian belief that he is the son of God.

But he intermingled accepted facts with negative accounts of Islamic teaching, history and traditions. The pilgrimage to Mecca, he said, is a dangerous event at which people are killed every year. Communal prayers each Friday are "a day of rage," he said.

And Muslims even pray differently than Christians, he said. "Muslims pray to get points," he said, "not to communicate with God." Group prayer on Fridays is for "extra points," he said.

Pat McEvoy, a secretary at a high school in Columbus, said she had known very little about Islam before the seminar. Her school has an influx of students from Somalia, and as she walked through the hallways she regarded these immigrants as "a virtual mission field."

She said she felt an obligation to save them from an eternity in Hell.

"If I had the answer for cancer, what sort of a human would I be not to share it?" Ms. McEvoy said.

The teacher concluded by giving the students tips on what to do and not to do to reach Muslims: Don't approach them in groups. Don't bring them to your church, because they will misunderstand the singing and clapping as a party. Do invite them home for a meal. Do bring them chocolate chip cookies. Do talk about how, in order to get saved, they must accept Jesus.

"Our job," he said, "is not to make the Muslim a Christian. Our job is to show them the love of Christ."   [2003]

Understanding the Reading

1. What is the point of teaching evangelicals that Islam is evil?
2. What do evangelicals say about the "good verses" in the Koran?
3. Have Christian missionaries always been this way about Islam?
4. Why might this attitude backfire?
5. Before the evangelicals saw Islam as the foremost global threat, what other belief system headed this list?

Suggestions for Responding

1. Debate in class whether one can successfully show the beauty and love of one religion, while believing that the other leads to an eternity in Hell.
2. Research how other missionaries historically have been successful in their ministries.
3. Research the U.S. Muslim population. How many Muslims live in the United States? Is Islam, as it is practiced in the United States, compatible with Democratic ideals? Learn about the variations found in this worldwide religion. ◆

142

"Empty Seats in the Lifeboat": 9/11 Fallout Stalls Refugees

Donovan Slack

Trenton—Elvis Gojkic looks like a typical teenager, but the Trenton High School student with the spiked brown hair and smiling brown eyes has seen much more than the average American teen.

"From my family, 17 men are dead," said the 18-year-old Bosnian refugee.

Growing up in Tuzla, Gojkic witnessed the worst of the Balkan conflict before he and his mother, Melvija, settled in Trenton 18 months ago, seeking refuge from their war torn homeland.

The Gojkics were lucky.

More than 220 refugees are "languishing" in Bosnian and West African camps, held up from joining family members in New Jersey by bureaucratic fallout from 9/11, according to local aid workers.

The displaced people were screened, rescreened and ultimately approved for transport to New Jersey, but only 14 of 225 slated arrivals have made their way to the States since September.

President Bush pledged in November to bring 70,000 refugees to the United States before September 30 this year, but as of May 31, only 13,763 have arrived, said Elizabeth Morley, Director of Immigration and Refugee services for Lutheran Social Ministries of New Jersey.

Morley joined about 40 locally settled refugees in marking World Refugee Day in June with an informal luncheon at the Lutheran Church of the Redeemer in Trenton. While many attendees expressed happiness and gratitude for their new lives—away from war and death—a gauze of sadness obscured the festive atmosphere.

"I miss my country, my people," said Elvis Gojkic, sipping cola from a plastic cup. "My home is empty, it's broken."

Broken homes worry Morley as well. The U.S. State Department has only a few more months to bring in thousands more refugees, hundreds destined to be reunited with family members in New Jersey, she said. If the government fails to transport the approved refugees before the deadline, Morley said, "they may not survive the wait."

"Every year they only set a certain number of slots," she said. "They represent lives—empty seats in the lifeboat."

Burlington City resident Fofi Baimba has been waiting since January 1999 for six family members to join him from Sierra Leone. At least one of them has already missed the boat.

Mamie Kormah Baimba, Fofi's 58-year-old mother, died in January 2001 after spending two weeks lost in the bush. She had been trying to return home from a refugee camp.

"She just couldn't take it anymore," Fofi said. "She was too tired."

A U.S. State Department official said the department has mounted a "super-human" effort to bring in as many people as possible, but enhanced security measures since 9/11 have hampered that effort.

While scores of refugees have been waiting abroad, agencies who normally help them settle in New Jersey have faced problems of their own.

"We can't do refugee resettlement when there's no refugees coming in," said Sister Janet Yurkanin, director of immigration and refugee services for the Catholic Diocese of Trenton.

Lutheran Social Ministries had to cut its case management staff in half when the flow of refugees slowed to a trickle, Morley said.

For those refugees lucky enough to be part of the trickle, life in America has presented hardships of another sort.

Elvis Gojkic and his mother have maintained grueling schedules, trying to support themselves and a handful of family members left behind in Bosnia. Until recently, Elvis worked in a sponge factory from 3:30 p.m. until midnight every weekday after attending classes from 8 a.m. to 3 p.m. at Trenton High. His mother, who named Elvis after the rock 'n' roll icon, works six days a week in a North Brunswick factory, taking on as many hours as her bosses will give her.

Their daily schedules are punctuated by reminders of the lives and people they left behind.

Tuesday marked the 10th anniversary of the bomb blast that killed Melvija's husband, Elvis' father.

"I hate to think about all the losses," said Melvija, looking over at Elvis, who was dressed like a typical American teen in baggy jeans and an over-sized Phillies jersey.

"I'm lucky I have him. I'm lucky I had the opportunity to get him out of that country."

[2002]

Understanding the Reading

1. Why did Elvis come to America with his mother?
2. Why are some approved refugees held up from immigrating?
3. Why did Fofi Baimba's fifty-eight-year-old mother die?
4. Describe the daily schedules of Elvis and his mother in the United States.

Suggestions for Responding

1. Refugee and relocation agencies, such as the Lutheran Social Ministries, enable refugees to leave their countries, usually in the midst of a war, by doing the legal work for entry; loaning money for plane tickets, rent, and food; and helping the family find work, enter school, get health insurance, and take language classes, if possible. Refugees must repay everything, enabling the next family to immigrate. Research Canada's national policies for refugees and compare its benefits with those of the United States. ◆

143

Working Class Women as War Heroes

FARAI CHIDEYA

Private Jessica Lynch is a hero, the kind who in her hopefully long life will never escape her youthful fame. The baby-faced 19-year-old fought off Iraqis in an ambush, endured broken bones, gunshot and stab wounds, and went eight days without food. This movie played in real time has all the elements that make fast-paced war flicks like "Behind Enemy Lines" box office magic. Her face, frozen with what must have been shock, pain and relief during her rescue, is already one of the most haunting images of the war.

Lynch is linked in more ways than one to Shoshana N. Johnson, a 30-year-old mother from El Paso, Texas. Johnson, who left her 2-year-old daughter with her parents when she deployed, joined the army to get training to be a chef. She ended up one of the first American prisoners of war in Iraq. Lynch—well, she wanted to be a kindergarten teacher.

How did a chef-in-training and a future teacher end up toting guns in the desert? Both of these female war heroes come from hometowns fighting their own battles, economic ones. Lynch comes from the you-can't-make-this-stuff-up town of Palestine, in Wirt County, a farm community in western West Virginia of 5,900 people, 99 percent of them white. Wirt has a 15 percent unemployment rate; 20 percent live below the poverty line; and the average income per person is $14,000.

El Paso County is huge by comparison— nearly 700,000 people—but no more prosperous. Seventy-eight percent of El Pasans are Latino, and 24 percent live below the poverty line. The border city, hit hard by the impact of NAFTA,[1] has a per capita income of just $13,000.

The folks in Wirt and El Paso are separated by half a country, but they have a lot in common. In both places, the economy has collapsed. The military is probably one of the best games in town. Jessica Lynch's family says she joined to get an education, something she probably couldn't have gotten otherwise. Now that she's a hero, a group of colleges have stepped forward to offer her a scholarship.

Wouldn't it be great if people like Lynch and Johnson didn't have to go to war to get a job or an education? At the same time that Americans are protesting against the war, thousands this week protested in favor of affirmative action, which faces its latest Supreme Court challenge. Working-class women and African-Americans like Lynch and Johnson will be among those to lose if affirmative action is ended. But affirmative action, as useful as it is, only gives a fraction of Americans the chance they deserve. Schools in working-class neighborhoods are becoming more like truly impoverished ones. In other words, they've become places where too many bright students lose hope.

Yale graduate and notably lackluster student George W. Bush got the benefits of an affirmative action program called "legacy admission," i.e., preference for the kids of alums (particularly the rich ones). For all his hawkishness, Bush went AWOL from his National Guard duty during the Vietnam War, 1972–1973. His father was a war hero. But these days rich men (and women) don't fight.

That's left to the working class. A New York Times article titled "Military Mirrors Working-Class America" notes, "With minorities over-represented and the wealthy and the underclass essentially absent, with political conservatism ascendant in the officer corps and Northeasterners fading from the ranks, America's 1.4 million-strong military seems to resemble the makeup of a two-year commuter or trade school outside Birmingham or Biloxi far more than that of a ghetto or barrio or four-year university in Boston."

Don't get me wrong—I'm not saying money's the only reason people join the military. A lot of enlistees are following their dreams of serving their country. Others, like a 27-year-old interviewed in the Times article, like to blow things up (though not necessarily people). And some, like a friend of mine who spent ages 17–20 in the military, think it's a great way to grow up and find your mission in life.

There are a few other options for young Americans seeking a way to give to their country, earn money for college and get skills; in particular, the service corps like City Year and Americorps. In these programs, young Americans the same age as Lynch can spend a year or two giving back to a local community—working on buildings, serving the elderly, even helping teach kindergarten. With school budgets being slashed, there's plenty of need and plenty of room for young recruits to lend a hand.

But these programs are still modest compared to the size and stability of the military. Before the motto an "Army of One," the Navy boasted the slogan, "It's Not Just a Job, It's an Adventure." Some people just want a job. What they get is far more uncertain.   [2003]

Terms

1. NAFTA. North American Free Trade Agreement is a trade agreement that went into effect on January 1, 1994, linking Canada, the U.S.A., and Mexico in a free trade sphere. This will eliminate all tariffs among the three nations by 2008. NAFTA is very controversial as to whether the economics of Canada, the U.S.A., and Mexico are benefiting or not.
2. AWOL Absent without leave. In military contexts it is deserting your post without permission.

Understanding the Reading

1. Why did Jessica Lynch and Shoshana Johnson join the army if they wanted to become a kindergarten teacher and a chef, respectively?

2. Why does the author say that George W. Bush got the benefits of an affirmative action program, and how does that relate to Jessica and Shoshana?
3. Which Americans fight wars now?
4. What other kind of service, other than military, could be an alternative if the government expanded these programs?

Suggestions for Responding

1. There has been much controversy surrounding the capture and rescue of Jessica Lynch. Research the BBC story that sharply conflicted with the U.S. government's story. Also contrary to the government rendition, Lynch has said that she would not be alive today had it not been for the care she received in the Iraqi hospital. Discuss why you think the government made a video of her rescue.

SUGGESTIONS FOR RESPONDING TO PART X

1. Read an American newspaper of note (e.g., *New York Times, Washington Post, L.A. Times,* or *Chicago Tribune*) at least three times a week, looking for news of world interest and opinion pieces on the OP/ED page. Also read a foreign newspaper (online-newspapers.com) and compare news coverage of the same story. Divide the class so that some are especially responsible for each continent or region of the world. Take note of which newspapers are state-controlled (*Arab News* or *China Daily* for example.) Also note that the rest of the world seems to know much more about the U.S. than we do about the rest of the world.
2. Research whether your surrounding community has received refugees from abroad. Find creative ways to discover how they are faring. Are the children happy in school? Are the parents working? Are they underemployed? Are these families considered an integral part of the community? Research how other parts of the country react towards their refugees.

3. Research two activist groups: The Feminist Majority and Women's International League for Peace and Freedom. The Feminist Majority, founded in 1987, has a very useful human rights watch newswire (feminist.org), which includes world news, as well as national news. Women's International League for Peace and Freedom is nearly one hundred years old (Jane Addams was its first president) and is an official nongovernmental organization, recognized by the United Nations. They, too, work locally, nationally, and worldwide. Invite speakers to your class representing each of these two agencies. Ask the WILPF representative about "The Raging Grannies."
4. Have a class discussion on ways of balancing national security with respect for civil rights. Compare America's ideals with what you see implemented by our different levels of government.
5. Compare the U.S. with other countries' reactions and solutions to "difference" as they struggle with their rapidly changing

population. For example, Europe has a debate about religious symbols and religious articles of clothing worn in public schools; and there are debates about female circumcision as a religious rite imported with some immigrant groups.

Suggestions for Responding to Change

Throughout history, important social and economic change has been the result of organized movements. The following assignments are intended to give you a better understanding of organized nongovernmental forces that have changed life in America.

1. Research the origins of a specific labor union, such as the American Federation of Labor; Congress of Industrial Organizations; AFL-CIO; Actors' Equity Association; Knights of Labor; National Women's Trade Union League; National Consumers League; International Workers of the World; National Education Association; Longshoremen's and Warehousemen's Union; United Farm Workers of America; 9–5; Teamsters; Association of Federal, State, County and Municipal Employees; International Ladies' Garment Workers Union; and so on. Write a report on the forces that led to the initial organizing and the obstacles the organizers faced.

2. Research and report on the strategies used by the abolition movement, and analyze their effectiveness.

3. Research and report on the strategies used by the National Woman Suffrage Association, the American Woman Suffrage Association, or the National American Woman Suffrage Association, and analyze the effectiveness of the organization.

4. In the post–Civil War years, women organized for a number of purposes. Research one of these organizations, such as the women's club movement, the temperance movement, settlement houses, or the National Consumer League, and report on their short-term and long-term achievements.

5. Write a biography of a major historical change maker, focusing on his or her contributions to the larger movement of which he or she was a part. Consider such activists as Lucretia Mott, Sarah and Angelina Grimké, William Lloyd Garrison, Frederick Douglass, Elizabeth Cady Stanton, Susan B. Anthony, Carrie Chapman Catt, Mary McLeod Bethune, Frances Willard, Mary Church Terrell, Jane Addams, Florence Kelley, Lillian Wald, Louis Brandeis, Sophie Loeb, Emma Goldman, Elizabeth Gurley Flynn, Rose Schneiderman, Mary Anderson, Abigail Scott Duniway, Thurgood Marshall, or Morris Dees.

6. Research and report on the goals and strategies used by one of the civil rights organizations of the 1950s and 1960s—for example, the Student Non-Violent Coordinating Committee, Southern Christian Leadership Conference, National Association for the Advancement of Colored People, Congress of Racial Equality, Black Panthers, American Indian Movement, La Raza Unida, National Organization for Women, National Abortion Rights Action League, or National Association for the Legalization of Marijuana.

7. Identify someone in your community who has effected a change that has had a direct impact on you, your family, or your friends or neighbors. Go to your local library or newspaper morgue and review the clipping file on this person; arrange for an interview if you can. Report on what motivated the person, what resources he or she had to make this effort effective, and what obstacles he or she had to overcome; assess the value of this person's efforts.

8. Invite one or more members of an Arab-American association or a Muslim-American community to speak to your class or university. If possible, combine this with a member of a Japanese-American community who was

imprisoned in a relocation camp during World War II or who had a family member imprisoned in the camps. Discuss the consequences to all Americans when civil liberties are suspended for any group.

9. As a class, watch at least the first twenty minutes of the film *Skokie* and discuss the following questions: a.) As a citizen (Jew or non-Jew) of the town of Skokie, Illinois, home to many Holocaust survivors and their descendants, how would you react if neo-Nazis marched down your street? b.) As the judge responsible for issuing or denying permits for public demonstrations, would you give a permit to these neo-Nazis to demonstrate in Skokie? c.) As the mayor of Skokie, how would you react? d.) As the head of the American Civil Liberties Union, would you accept the neo-Nazis' demand for protection of their First Amendment rights, even though many of your members would consequently leave, and also knowing that if the neo-Nazis ever came to power, the first thing they would do would be to suspend freedom of speech? Remember, as head of the ACLU you are dedicated to the protection of the liberties outlined in the Bill of Rights.

CREDITS

INDEX